WHAT COLLEGE REALLY COSTS

WHAT
COLLEGE
REALLY
COSTS

by the Staff of U.S.News & World Report

Margaret Mannix, Editor

Jodie T. Allen, Managing Editor

Robert Morse, Director of Data Research

SOURCEBOOKS, INC.
NAPERVILLE, ILLINOIS

Published by Sourcebooks, Inc.

P.O. Box 4410

Naperville, Illinois 60567-4410

(630) 961-3900 Fax: (630) 961-2168

www.sourcebooks.com

ISBN 1-4022-0341-1

First Edition

Printed and bound in the United States of America

VG 10 9 8 7 6 5 4 3 2 1

Table of Contents

Introduction

We've all read the headlines. College tuition is "soaring," rising "sharply," or jumping by "double digits." But there's good news, too. There are many ways—and combinations of ways—to get financial assistance for college as well as for graduate school. In fact, there's more money available today than ever before. And *U.S. News* is here to help you with hands-on advice about how to wend your way through the paying-for-college maze.

True, the cost of an education at a four-year college or university in the United States continues to climb. For the 2004–2005 academic year, tuition and fees at private colleges rose 6 percent—double the overall rate of inflation in the U.S. economy—to an average $20,082, according to the College Board. Throw in room and board, and the price tag jumps to $27,516. At some elite universities, the bill is much steeper, topping $40,000.

Tuition at public universities has been climbing even faster, given the budget crises that many states have been facing in recent years. In the 2004–2005 academic year, tuition and fees at four-year public universities rose 10.5 percent to $5,132. Combined with rising room and board costs—which are also growing at a much faster pace than the overall rate of inflation—the average annual total price tag for a four-year state school is now $11,354.

Good grief. No wonder many families—even middle-class families—feel there is no way they can cover tuition, let alone the full cost of sending a student off to college. Some students don't even try to get financial aid, judging it futile. A recent study found that 8 million students—yes, 8 million—never even bothered to fill out the government's Free Application for Federal Student Aid, otherwise known as FAFSA. That's a big mistake, as it's the starting point for receiving aid.

On the bright side, student aid coffers are more amply filled than ever before. But while much of that aid might come in the form of a loan, some colleges and universities are helping to ease the financial burden by rolling out more grant programs for families most in need.

Savvy families can up their chances of getting enough financial aid by mastering the ins and outs of the aid process. And that's where we come in: *U.S. News* talked to dozens of parents, students, college financial aid directors, and other experts to assemble the most authoritative advice on how to navigate the financial aid system and get your fair share of assistance. And we've packaged it in a way that is easy to understand.

First, we spell out the pros and cons of the various tools—such as 529 savings plans and Coverdell Education Savings Accounts—that parents of youngsters (and grandparents) can use to devise a long-term savings strategy for Junior's higher education. Then we've compiled what is perhaps the most important chapter of all: Chapter 2, Financial Aid Basics. We explain the nitty-gritty of the FAFSA and other financial aid applications and rundown how the government and colleges crunch the numbers on those forms to determine how much your family should be able to afford to pay

for college. (Yes, the government and individual colleges may assess your family's need differently.) Chapters 3, 4, and 5 explain the basic components of financial aid: student loans, scholarships and grants, and work-study. Then we help students and parents compare the financial aid award letters they receive from different colleges.

But we don't stop there. Chapter 7 lays out the myriad other ways and last-minute strategies students and parents can use to whittle down college bills. Still, as you are probably just now discovering, there's more to college costs than tuition and room and board, and Chapter 8 gives tips on how to tame ancillary expenses such as books and travel. Uncle Sam can also take some of the sting out of college costs with education tax breaks, which you'll learn all about in Chapter 9.

And if you're not the traditional student, we've assembled many tips in Chapter 10 for veterans, international students, children of divorced parents, and other students who may need some targeted help. Ditto for graduate students, whom we address in Chapter 11. Last but not least, we guide students (and parents) through the process of paying back their student loans.

Throughout each chapter, we tell the stories of real students and parents and how they managed to swing college costs, and we've sprinkled in some helpful hints from the many experts we consulted in writing this guide.

The *U.S. News* Insider's Index can help you assess how colleges stack up financially against one another. Want to know who gives out the most need-based financial aid? Our exclusive lists can tell you that and more. The last part of the book, the College Cost and Financial Aid Directory, provides key financial aid data for the more than 1,400 colleges and universities *U.S. News* surveys each year in its annual college rankings.

As you page through the directory sizing up schools on your wish list and buckle down with financial aid applications, keep in mind one thing our experts reminded us of over and over: Where there's a will, there's a way. If you have the will, we hope that this guide helps provide the way.

Chapter One

Devising a Long-Term Savings Plan

Parents saving for college today have more options—and better options—than ever before. But the creation and evolution of new savings vehicles in recent years, coupled with changes to the federal tax code, have made the array of savings plans more difficult to digest than ever before. In fact, saving for college has become a bit like participating in an Iron Chef competition. Without much prep time, a family is given a bunch of mystery ingredients with names like ESAs, IRAs, 529s, and UGMAs. And while the clock is ticking, they are somehow expected to whip up a sophisticated financial plan that keeps pace with ever-growing college costs.

Choosing the right blend is a tough call. There are newfangled 529 savings plans and Coverdell Education Savings Accounts (or ESAs), which are tax-advantaged investing plans that let parents save money for school much like they save in their 401(k). Then there are also prepaid tuition programs to consider. These plans (also referred to as 529s, as if things weren't complicated enough) let parents prepurchase tomorrow's education at today's prices. Some parents may also rely on their own individual retirement accounts, or IRAs, to set aside money for school. Moreover, there are traditional savings vehicles, like

---

"From a financial aid standpoint, anything in the child's name can be detrimental."

---

old-fashioned savings bonds and Uniform Gifts to Minors Act (UGMA) accounts, to weigh. And with the recent tax cuts on investments, saving money in an outside, taxable brokerage account can also be an attractive option for many parents.

Which of these college savings accounts is best for a family? That's the $64,000 question. Actually, for parents hoping to send their child to a top-tier private university, it's more like the $164,000 question. The right solution can depend on several factors: tax efficiency, the possibility of receiving financial aid in the future, the investment options one can choose from, and the transferability of funds.

It's important to understand that some of these vehicles don't cover all college-related expenses. As a result, parents may have to mix and match a couple of them. Further complicating the decision is the fact that the rules governing some of the plans are expected to "sunset" (that's Congress-speak for "expire") down the road. Unless Congress extends those provisions, some advantages of vehicles like 529 savings plans may cease to be advantages when parents are ready to send their sons and daughters off to college.

Like students who are falling behind in their course work, parents need to hit the books and do a little more homework. According to national surveys, the typical household saving for college has accumulated only around $10,000. Three out of five families have less than $20,000 saved, while 9 in 10 have less than $50,000 in the bank, meaning the vast major-ity of diligent college-savers are still shy of covering four years at a state university. Your task: learning the basic rules for contributing to, investing in, and withdrawing money from the various college savings plans.

529 savings plans

Since these investment plans were first created in 1996, 529s have become one of the fastest-growing tax-deferred college savings vehicles around, with more than $43 billion in total assets. One of the reasons why 529s are so popular is that parents of all income levels can utilize these accounts and stuff around $250,000 into them. That's far more than most other college piggy banks allow.

Moreover, 20 or so states offer tax deductions for residents who take advantage of their in-state 529. And money in a 529 is allowed to grow tax deferred, much like in a 401(k) and Roth IRA. Withdrawals from a 529 are tax free as long as the money is used for qualified educational expenses such as tuition, room and board, and mandatory fees at accredited institutions.

While 529s were named after the section of the federal tax code that gave birth to them, they are actually state-sponsored

Helpful Hints

:)

Can't decide between the in-state 529 savings plan and an out-of-state account? The law allows families to fund more than one 529. So, for instance, if the state plan offers a tax deduction but has mediocre investment options, consider taking full advantage of the tax deduction in the state plan. Then, with whatever money is left, the family can pick an out-of-state 529 that offers low fees and good investment choices.

vehicles. Today, virtually every state, as well as the District of Columbia, has established at least one 529 savings plan. Many offer multiple plans. Parents can invest in any state's plan, even if they're not residents and their children don't plan to go to school there. However, because of the state tax deductions, many experts suggest parents consider their in-state plan first to see if it offers tax breaks. Regardless of which plan they choose, parents should make sure that the management fees are relatively low, as these can erode the tax advantages associated with the accounts. To check on the fees that each plan assesses, parents can visit www.savingfor college.com, an educational resource that includes details on all the 529 plans.

Once inside a 529, money can be invested in a set of options that may include a few mutual funds as well as ready-made, age-based investment portfolios that gradually shift from aggressive to conservative as a child ages. This is in part what drew Cathie Marcolesco, the wife of an Air Force flight instructor in California and mother of five, to 529s. "For me, actively managing five separate accounts would be just too much work," says Marcolesco. So she opted to open 529s for each of her children, and put each child's nest egg in one of these age-based funds that rebalances to an appropriate mix of stocks and bonds automatically. If one of her children earns a scholarship and doesn't need the money, the funds can be transferred to a sibling without penalty.

Finally, there's one other reason why parents ought to consider a 529: financial aid. "From a financial aid standpoint, anything in the child's name can be detrimental," says Joseph Hurley, founder of the savingforcollege.com website. That's because the government deems up to 5.6 percent of parents' assets fair game in paying college bills. But 35 percent of a student's assets are expected to go toward the bills. Because money in a 529 is considered the asset of the parent or whoever established the account (grandparents and others can also open 529s), they are considered advantageous from a financial aid standpoint. (Chapter 2 explains the financial aid process in greater detail.)

Still, one major concern for investors is that tax-free withdrawals on 529s expire on December 31, 2010. In other words, unless Congress steps in and extends this provision, qualified withdrawals from such plans will cease to be tax free. They will go back to being taxed, though at the child's beneficial income tax rate. To be sure, most observers of Congress believe Uncle Sam will almost assuredly extend the tax-free status of 529s for fear of raising the ire of such a huge constituency. But it's still not guaranteed, and parents should be mindful of the potential rule change. To find out more about 529 plans in general, parents can visit www.college savings.org, the website of the College Savings Plans Network, an association of 529 plans, or www.savingfor college.com.

Regular brokerage accounts

Recent changes in the tax code have cost 529s some of their appeal over investing in a regular, taxable brokerage account. Not because 529s have gotten less generous, but rather because investment taxes have been coming down. For example, taxes on long-term capital gains, which used to be assessed at a maximum rate of 20 percent, are now capped at 15 percent. Taxes on stock dividends, which used to be slapped with ordinary income taxes, were also reduced to 15 percent in 2003. What's more, income tax rates have been lowered, with the top rate now down from 38.6 percent to 35 percent.

While these steps have certainly made investing in a taxable account more efficient than it used to be, 529s still tend to edge out taxable savings for many parents. "Tax free is almost always better than low taxes," says Whitney Dow, director of education savings research at Financial Research Corp. in Boston.

Consider this: T. Rowe Price, a Baltimore-based mutual fund company, studied the after-tax returns of an investment in a blue-chip fund earning 8 percent a year inside a brokerage account versus the same investment in a 529 savings plan. The firm discovered that if a parent were to invest

$5,000 a year in a brokerage account for 18 years, that money would grow to $189,869. In a 529, that same money would grow to $217,631. And if it were invested in a 529 plan that offers residents a state tax deduction, it would reach $223,086.

To be sure, this gap could be narrowed by investing in a tax-efficient manner in a regular brokerage—for instance, through

---

"Tax free is almost always better than low taxes."

---

passively managed index funds, which rarely sell their holdings, or any number of so-called tax-efficient mutual funds. While regular brokerage accounts are at a disadvantage because of their taxable status, an investor can make up some of that difference by investing well, reducing taxes, and avoiding unnecessary fees.

Investing in a regular brokerage account has some distinct advantages. For example, parents have complete control over how the money is invested and it can eventually be used for any purpose. And the fact that money invested through a regular brokerage account is held in the parent's name—and not the student's—is a plus from a financial aid standpoint.

Coverdell Education Savings Account

The Coverdell Education Savings Account (ESA), which used to be known as an Education IRA, often gets short shrift. That's in part because Coverdells have strict eligibility requirements. For example, married taxpayers with adjusted gross incomes higher than $220,000, and single taxpayers with incomes higher than $110,000, are ineligible. And even if a parent can open a Coverdell, the annual $2,000 cap per beneficiary hardly seems adequate to fund a four-year college education.

Yet Coverdells may have a place in a college savings plan. Like a 529, they are tax sheltered, and the gains withdrawn

from these accounts are tax free as long as the funds are used for qualified educational purposes. Unlike a 529, though, a Coverdell has virtually limitless investment options. For example, if parents want to use, say, a Vanguard mutual fund for this account, they simply have to open a Coverdell with Vanguard. Parents can also establish a Coverdell account at banks, brokerages, and many other financial institutions.

Moreover, money withdrawn from a Coverdell can also be used to pay for qualified expenses for K–12 education, including tuition at a private school, tutoring expenses, and required equipment such as computers. The 529 funds, on the other hand, can be used only to pay for postsecondary education.

Coverdells are also a good thing when Junior applies for financial aid, although that wasn't always the case. Up until 2004, assets held in a Coverdell were considered owned by the student, not the parent. However, the Department of Education has now ruled that assets held in these tax-sheltered accounts belong to the parents. And money withdrawn from a Coverdell or a 529 savings plan for qualified educational expenses does not count for purposes of financial aid eligibility.

529 prepaid tuition plans

While 529 savings plans and Coverdells are considered 401(k)s for college, 529 prepaid tuition plans are more like traditional pensions. About 20 states offer prepaid tuition plans, which allow parents to buy tomorrow's education at roughly today's prices. The student is guaranteed a certain number of years of education at an in-state public university (if he or she is accepted, that is) based on how many "credits" or "units" of education are purchased. In some cases, the units of education may cost more than a state-run university is currently charging. However, once purchased, that amount of education will be honored no matter what happens to tuition costs in the future.

Until recently, only states have run prepaid tuition plans. However, some 250 private colleges have now joined a consortium known as the Independent 529 Plan. Under this plan, parents can purchase future education at private schools such as Princeton University, Oberlin College, Vanderbilt University, and Stanford University. What's more, the schools have agreed to discount tuition to investors by at least one half of 1 percent per year. What happens if Junior—perish the thought—doesn't get into a school that participates in the prepaid plan? Parents can transfer the credits to another family member or roll the money into a 529 savings plan, where the money can be used to pay tuition at a greater number of schools. Or parents can simply seek a refund of their investments. Each prepaid plan has different rules on refunds.

Prepaid tuition plans do have some drawbacks. While these plans can be an effective tool to rein in educational expenses, the plans only pay for tuition and mandatory fees. Parents and students are on their own when it comes to paying for room and board and other supplemental college costs. And contributions to prepaid plans reduce financial aid eligibility dollar-for-dollar. On the other hand, prepaid plans can be attractive for parents who don't want to assume the investment risk of managing money on their own and who may want their child to go to a particular school, such as Mom and Dad's alma mater. To learn more about prepaid plans, visit www.college-savings.org, www.savingforcollege.com, and www.independent529plan.com.

Uniform Transfers to Minors Act Account

Before the creation of the 529 savings plan, traditional custodial accounts such as Uniform Gifts to Minors Act (UGMA) or Uniform Transfers to Minors Act (UTMA) accounts were among the most popular and tax-efficient ways to save for college. That's because these custodial arrangements allow money to be put into the child's name so that it will receive preferential tax treatment. In an UGMA or UTMA, the first $800 in investment income is considered tax free. The remainder is taxed at the child's rate if he or she is 14 or older. If the child is under 14, the next $800 in income is taxed at the child's rate, but anything beyond $1,600 is taxed at the parent's rate.

Again, T. Rowe Price crunched the numbers: The mutual fund company figures that $5,000 annual investments in a blue-chip growth stock fund in an UGMA, assuming an 8 percent average annual return, would grow to $207,885 in 18 years. While that's better than investing in a brokerage account, it's still $10,000 to $15,000 less than a parent would have earned in a 529 savings plan.

Moreover, there are two huge drawbacks when it comes to custodial accounts. For starters, in an UGMA or UTMA, the child takes control of the money once he or she turns 18, 21, or 25, depending on the state. At that point, the funds within the account are his or hers. Period. The child, theoretically, could decide to skip college and pocket the money upon reaching adulthood (or blow it all on a whim). In addition, because the money is in the student's name, these accounts are detrimental when it comes to qualifying for financial aid.

Still, there are a few reasons why some parents might want to use UGMAs or UTMAs. For example, custodial accounts shield

Helpful Hints

If parents are trying to choose between a 529 savings plan and a Coverdell Education Savings Account, they might want to consider putting the first $2,000 a year into a Coverdell and the rest into a 529. Doing so preserves the family's options. Not only can money in a Coverdell be used for K–12 education in addition to college, it can also be rolled over into a 529 savings account later on. Money in a 529, on the other hand, can't be transferred into a Coverdell.

break on interest earned on traditional Series EE bonds. Moreover, up to $30,000 a year in EE savings bonds can be purchased directly from the government, even online at www.treasurydirect.gov.

Of all the college savings choices, though, savings bonds are the most conservative, perhaps too conservative. "If you're saving in a bank account or in savings bonds, you're not going to keep pace with the goal you're saving for," says Bob Corcoran, vice president of college planning for the mutual fund giant Fidelity. At the start of 2005, for example, series EE savings bonds were earning only 3.25 percent a year, which is around the long-term historic rate of inflation. Even so-called I bonds, which are savings bonds whose value rises with inflation and that also give investors a tax break, were yielding only 3.67 percent. At that rate, $10,000 won't even double in 19 years.

Individual retirement account

Finally, parents should be aware that 529s and Coverdells aren't the only tax-deferred college savings options. In fact, any individual retirement account can be used to save for school.

As long as money withdrawn from these accounts is used for educational purposes, it isn't subject to the normal 10 percent penalty for early withdrawal, even if the account holder is younger than 59 1/2. However, it's important to understand that, depending on the owner's age, the type of IRA, and how long the account has been held, parents may have to pay taxes on the gains at withdrawal. For example, in a traditional deductible IRA, gains withdrawn for educational purposes will still be subject to income taxes. And earnings pulled from a Roth IRA, which is funded with after-tax dollars, may be subject to taxes if the account was opened less than five years prior to the withdrawal, and the parent is under 59 1/2.

Just like a Coverdell, an IRA can be set up at virtually any bank, brokerage, or mutual fund company, which means parents using IRAs for school purposes have total control over the

assets from would-be creditors. Parents who are, say, physicians or small business owners may want to consider them if they are seeking to safeguard holdings against potential lawsuits.

Also, UGMAs and UTMAs can be funded with appreciated stock. The 529 savings plans, on the other hand, can only be funded with cash. So if parents are sitting on appreciated stock and don't want to sell the shares and get hit with capital gains taxes, they can gift such stock to a child in an UGMA. Then they can use their cash to invest in a 529. A custodial account, like a Coverdell or an IRA, can be opened at most financial institutions, including banks, brokerages, and mutual fund companies.

Savings bonds

About a third of parents who are saving for college invest in a regular brokerage account while simultaneously using savings bonds. Perhaps the popularity of savings bonds stems from the fact that they have a built-in tax advantage: Married couples earning less than $119,750 in 2004 can get a tax

When Manuel Sousa started saving for his daughter's college education nearly two decades ago, there weren't a lot of options. The California resident wanted a savings vehicle with tax advantages that allowed him to put away large amounts of money. So Sousa began depositing around $100 a month in a Uniform Gift to Minors Act (UGMA) account for his daughter, Karina, when she was born 17 years ago. Later, Sousa, who runs his own court-reporting business, started a similar account for his son, Devon, now 12. But when he learned about 529 savings plans recently, he shifted the money in his children's UGMAs into 529 accounts for each of his children. "The tax advantage makes them a better account than what I had before," he says.

assets. Moreover, once inside an IRA, the money grows tax deferred. And an IRA, because it is held in a parent's name, will be beneficial to the qualifying process for financial aid.

But IRAs have the advantage over a Coverdell of no income restrictions. While Roth IRAs and traditional deductible IRAs have their own income limitations, traditional nondeductible IRAs can be funded by anyone. "There's an IRA for everyone," says Bruce Harrington, head of 529 savings plans for the mutual fund company MFS in Boston. However, many financial planners discourage parents from using IRAs for college purposes because they shouldn't shortchange their own retirement. While students have a number of other ways to pay for school, like loans, no one hands out loans to pay for retirement.

Rebate programs

Finally, parents should be aware of several new rebate programs that can help them save for school. The two best-known programs are Upromise and BabyMint. Both work in much the same way. Families receive rebates of varying amounts for purchases made at participating retailers around the country. Depending on the program, the rebates can be deposited into a 529 or Coverdell savings plan or sent directly to the parent.

While parents may want to consider these programs, since every little bit helps, it's important to understand that the goal here is to save more for school, not spend more.

Chapter Two

Financial Aid Basics

The road to financial aid starts with the federal government's assessment of how much a family can afford to contribute to a child's college costs. Halfway through the child's senior year in high school, the family should fill out the government's Free Application for Federal Student Aid, or FAFSA. Families supply their income, assets, and other financial information, which the government plugs into its special formula to churn out what's known as the "expected family contribution," or EFC.

The EFC is crucial. It is the amount of money the government deems a family should be able to chip in toward their child's college education. If the EFC is $10,000—an amount that would be in the ballpark for a family of four earning $50,000 a year—and the child attends a school that costs $40,000, the official "need" is $30,000.

At a school that costs $20,000, the need is $10,000. If the child attends a school that costs $10,000 or less, the family has no financial need.

Unfortunately, having a $30,000 need doesn't mean the student will be handed $30,000 to pay for college. More likely, the student will get a package that mixes grants with student loans and campus employment, also known as a work-study job. And not all colleges fill the package in the same way. At a school that has lots of money available for needy students, the student with $30,000 in need might get a dream package: $26,000 in grants, $2,500 in loans, and a $1,500 work-study job. At a less generous school, he or she might get a $5,000 grant, $7,500 in loans, and a $2,500 work-study job. That leaves a $15,000 gap. Today, many schools fill that gap by giving qualified parents a low-rate, government-backed loan.

But here's what's important to understand in the financial aid game: If you're eligible for substantial aid—meaning your EFC is pretty low—a school's sticker price is meaningless. You won't know how much any college will really cost until after you've been accepted and received a financial aid offer. Students and families who don't understand this fundamental fact about the financial aid process often don't even apply to colleges that seem too expensive. That's too bad. It's far smarter to concentrate on which colleges are the best academic, social, and extracurricular fit during the admissions process and worry about finances when the award letter arrives. That said, it's a good idea to apply to one or two affordable schools, just in case aid packages are disappointing. Call these financial safety schools.

A guide to the FAFSA

The easiest way to complete the FAFSA is to fill it out online (www.fafsa.ed.gov). You can also get a paper copy of the eight-page form from a high school guidance counselor, a college financial aid officer, or by calling the Federal Student Aid Information Center at (800) 433-3243. Because some aid is awarded on a first-come, first-served basis, the optimum time to file the form is as soon as possible after January 1 for the upcoming academic year (i.e., January 2005 for the 2005–2006 school year). January 1 is the earliest the federal government will accept the form, and many college's financial aid office deadlines are in early March.

The form asks about income and assets in copious detail, so the family should gather year-end pay stubs and account statements. Of course, the task will be easier if Mom and Dad have already completed—or have at least drafted—their tax return, due April 15. But many people use estimates when they haven't yet completed their Form 1040.

Student income. If you worked during the summer or part time during the school year, the government expects you to set aside a hefty portion of that income for college expenses. On the FAFSA, you report your adjusted gross income (or AGI) for the calendar year prior to the year for which you're applying for aid. After subtracting taxes and an allowance that shelters the first $2,440 in income, the government says the student should fork over 50 percent of his or her earnings to cover college costs.

Student assets. Any cash or savings in your name in a bank account, CD, mutual fund, investment account, or trust fund

Helpful Hints

Since parents are expected to contribute a far smaller percentage of their assets to college costs, families might want to consider making any big-ticket purchases—say, a car or a computer—with a student's savings before filing the FAFSA. This may earn more aid because it reduces the student's contribution from assets. Also, while debt does not reduce the EFC, car loan or credit card balances that are converted into home-equity debt would reduce the equity in the family home and thus the contribution from parents' assets at schools that count home equity.

should be reported as a student asset. While the formula recognizes that parents have many demands on their savings, it's the government's position that students should earmark a chunk of their savings for college. That's why each year 35 percent of your assets are considered available for college costs.

Parental income. Parents are routinely dumbfounded at the amount of income the government deems should go toward educating Junior. The formula starts with the parents' adjusted gross income. Then Uncle Sam subtracts the family's federal taxes and an allowance for state taxes that differs for each state. From that, the government deducts an amount to cover basic living expenses. It's modest, ranging from $11,490 for a single-parent family with one dependent in college to $29,430 for a family of six with one in college.

Of the remainder, the government assumes that 22 percent to 47 percent, depending on the level of income, is available to pay for college. A Massachusetts family of four with an income of $75,000, for example, might be able to exclude $14,500 for taxes and Social Security, plus $21,330 for basic living expenses (assuming one student in college). Of the remaining $39,170, they'd be expected to contribute $13,415 (or about 33 percent).

One quirky adjustment: Any contribution in the prior year to a retirement plan—such as a 401(k), IRA, Roth IRA, SEP-IRA or Simple IRA—is added back into the adjusted gross income.

Parental assets. Parents are expected to contribute up to 5.6 percent of their assets each year to college expenses, after an allowance that depends on the age of the oldest parent. If the oldest parent is 50, for instance, the family can exclude assets of $42,800. Assets include balances in checking, savings, and investment accounts and second homes or other real estate. However, parents should not include the equity in their primary home or any retirement assets. The cash value of a life insurance policy and any annuities are also excluded. Any balances in a 529 savings plan or Coverdell Education Savings Account should be reported as a parental asset, even though the student is the beneficiary.

Helpful Hints

Money withdrawn from a Coverdell Education Savings Account or a 529 savings plan last year to pay for qualified college expenses should be excluded from income. The FAFSA instructions don't address this, but the Department of Education has advised financial aid officers that withdrawals from either kind of account should not be counted as student income for aid purposes.

If your parents are divorced and the parent you live with is not remarried, then only that parent is expected to supply financial information on the FAFSA. However, if your custodial parent is remarried, it's the income and assets of that parent and your custodial stepparent that count.

As for the rest of the form, other questions concern the size of the family, the number of students in college, and whether the student can be classified as independent. In the latter case, only the income and assets of the student count in determining the EFC.

Family size. This is the total number of people in the household. Families can include a child that's expected during the coming year and any individuals who qualify as dependents for tax purposes, such as a grandparent living with the family or for whom your parents provide the primary support.

Number in college. If the family has two students in college at the same time, the total expected family contribution is divided between the two students. With two or more students in college, it's possible for a family with an income as high as $150,000 a year to receive grants from an expensive school. That's not the norm, says James Belvin, financial aid director at Duke University. But the split contribution for siblings in college at the same time does help some high-income families qualify for more than token aid.

Independent student. If you qualify as an independent student, your parents are off the hook money-wise. But very few undergraduates are deemed independent: You must be 24 years of age or older, a graduate student, married, an orphan, supporting a dependent, or a veteran of the armed forces. Occasionally, other extenuating circumstances will prompt a financial aid officer to classify a student as independent, such as when a student's parents are incarcerated or are truly estranged from the child. But these cases are rare and must be documented.

The Student Aid Report

Within a few days of completing the FAFSA online, or a few weeks if the form is sent via snail mail, you'll get what's known as a Student Aid Report (SAR). That's where you'll find the EFC. It's in the upper-right corner of the first page.

The report also lists all the data originally supplied on the FAFSA for review. This is your chance to check it for accuracy and make changes if necessary. If the family estimated any figures, such as income or taxes, the family can update the numbers on the SAR. Each school you've listed on the FAFSA also receives the EFC, the data on the SAR, and any corrections you make.

The PROFILE form

Most private colleges use the government EFC to award federal and state aid. However, they do have their own methodology to determine how their moneys are awarded. Usually, private colleges will ask you to complete an additional aid form, the PROFILE (administered by the College Scholarship Service) to gather information that the FAFSA doesn't. Based on that supplementary data, the institution's aid formula churns out another EFC. The number will not be disclosed, but it will be used to determine how much financial aid you qualify for from the school.

Helpful Hints

Capital gains from the sale of a stock or mutual fund can boost income and, in turn, the EFC. Try to avoid taking investment gains during the years that are assessed for financial aid. If you can't avoid taking capital gains, it's worth a try explaining to aid officers that the income is a one-time event and requesting an adjustment to your aid package.

What makes the EFC higher...

The EFC derived from the FAFSA and the EFC derived from the PROFILE often differ. Some variables on the PROFILE can bump up an EFC:

Home equity. This is a biggie for a lot of families. The federal formula excludes home equity as an asset while the institutional formula counts it. If the family's home has appreciated rapidly in recent years, the student may qualify for less aid at many private schools than anticipated. Generally, every $100,000 of home equity will add $5,000 to the institutional EFC.

Losses. While the federal formula uses adjusted gross income as a base to determine the parental contribution from income, the institutional methodology does not include losses from a business, farm, or investments (which would have reduced the AGI on the parents' tax forms). The College Board's philosophy: These tax losses usually don't represent reduced income to the family, but instead are just write-offs to save taxes.

Two in college. The institutional methodology is less generous than the federal formula when the family has two students in college at the same time. As we said earlier, a $12,000 EFC under the federal formula is divided equally between the two students. But under the institutional methodology, that same EFC for each student is 60 percent of the total, or $7,200 each.

Sibling assets. The federal formula does not count any assets held in a sibling's name, but the institutional formula does, adding them to the parental assets category. The impact is partially offset by calculations that shelter some college savings for younger siblings. But if your sibling has a lot of money saved in his or her name, that stockpile will hurt your aid eligibility.

...and what makes it lower

These differences in the EFC derived from the PROFILE, on the other hand, can help earn more financial aid:

Tax allowances. In most states, these are more generous under the College Board formula than under the federal formula. If you're a Florida resident, for instance, the federal formula lets you subtract 1 percent to 2 percent of income to cover state taxes, while the institutional formula lets the family deduct 5.5 percent to 9 percent, depending on income. A bigger deduction reduces the family's contribution from income.

Employment allowance. Both the federal and institutional formulas subtract a small amount from income for single-parent families or when both parents work. In the institutional formula, this allowance is a bit higher, up to $3,610 versus $3,000 in the federal formula.

Private school tuition and medical expense allowances. If the family is paying for private school for a younger child, the institutional formula subtracts up to $7,900 in tuition from family income. The formula also subtracts nonreimbursed medical expenses that exceed 3.5 percent of the parents' income. While you can ask for an adjustment for such expenses at a school that uses only the FAFSA, PROFILE schools reduce family income automatically, so long as the expenses are included on the form.

Family assets. The allowances that shelter a portion of parents' assets can be more or less generous than the federal allowances, depending on the parents' age and the number and age of any of your siblings. But on the plus side, the percentage of assets you're expected to contribute each year—after the allowances are taken into account—is lower than under the federal formula. Parents are expected to kick in up to 5 percent of assets (versus 5.6 percent under the federal formula), and students contribute 25 percent of assets per year (rather than 35 percent).

"It's getting more common for the institutional [EFC] to be lower than the federal [EFC]."

Helpful Hints

If a student or parent gets stymied when filling out the Free Application for Federal Student Aid (FAFSA), there's plenty of free assistance around. When completing the form online, for example, electronic prompts give warning if an error has been made. The Department of Education's Federal Student Aid Information Center also runs a toll-free hotline (800-433-3243) staffed with experts. Websites like www.finaid.org and www.studentaid.ed.gov also provide tips and advice.

The financial aid officer at the school the student is interested in attending, or even one at a nearby college, can also give pointers and answer questions. "Our staff looks at 50, 000 forms a year," says Natala Hart, director of student financial aid at Ohio State University. "It's hard to find someone more expert." State associations of college financial aid officers also run free workshops regularly. To find a state association, go to the website of the National Association of Student Financial Aid Administrators—www.nasfaa.org—and click on "association news/services," then scroll down to "state & regional web sites."

Other factors

Because of home equity in particular, a majority of families find that their EFC is higher at private colleges than at public ones. But "it's getting more common for the institutional [EFC] to be lower than the federal [EFC]," says Joe Paul Case, director of financial aid at Amherst College. About 25 percent of aid applicants at Amherst qualify for more aid under the institutional formula, Case says.

Individual schools have the right to tinker with your EFC to incorporate their own policies on awarding aid. A group of 28 top colleges (called the 568 Group for a section of federal law that allows them to collaborate), including Amherst, the University of Chicago, Duke, Stanford University, and Yale University, agreed to standardize many of their need-analysis policies. For example, the schools use a cost-of-living adjustment that reduces the contribution from income for families in high-cost cities like New York and San Francisco. They also place a cap on the value of home equity as an asset at 2.4 times the family's income. Generally, these adjustments will increase aid eligibility.

Putting together an aid package

The EFC is only the starting point for the college financial aid office as it puts together your aid package. Even if your EFC

Real World Stories

When Scott Isaacson brought home his first report card in high school, he told his mother he had ruined his chances at a free ride to college. The brother of three academic superstars, who parlayed good grades into college scholarships, Isaacson knew that his less-than-stellar performance wouldn't merit similar deals. With the exception of giving him a place to live, his parents would not be able to help Isaacson out on the tuition front. But racking up student loan debt was definitely not something the Michigan resident relished to cover the $7,610 annual tuition at Michigan Technological University in Houghton, Michigan. "I wanted to come out of college running," says Isaacson, a junior majoring in business administration.

Despite his so-so grades in high school, Isaacson qualified for $6,550 in scholarships his freshman year, including the Michigan Technological Alumni Legacy Award for $250 (his father is an alumnus), the Michigan Competitive Scholarship for $1,300 (granted on the basis of financial need and merit), and the $1,500 Clarence R. and Yvonne M. Fisher Scholarship (for business majors with financial need). Isaacson also received a $2,250 Pell grant and a work-study position in the university's internal audit department.

But his financial aid package didn't look so swell his sophomore year because many of his scholarships and grants were a one-time deal. The package did include federal student loans, but Isaacson nixed the borrowing route, instead tapping his modest savings

account and nabbing another work-study position on campus.

Last summer provided an extra boost to his savings. He worked part time in the registrar's office, served as a teaching assistant, and spent his weekends working at a nearby copy center. He'll add those earnings, $4,200, to the $3,000 in scholarships he snagged for the coming year, along with the $1,650 he'll receive from work-study. And to stretch his dollars further, Isaacson lives with his parents to save on housing expenses and cuts costs with frugal moves like ordering used books online. But all that penny pinching and hard work may not be enough this year. "The answer after this is student loans," he says.

is the same at two colleges, the financial aid offers may be very different. One could include mostly grants and the other mostly loans. However, most schools award federal and state grants and loans first, before dipping into any of their own money. So it's typical for a college to fill an aid package in this order:

First: Pell grants. Only the neediest students (with EFCs of $3,850 or less), qualify for this federal grant of up to $4,050. Most recipients come from families that earn $35,000 or less.

Second: State grants. Need-based state grants generally go to the same students who are also eligible for Pell grants. But some state grants and scholarships are awarded on a merit basis.

Third: Federal loans. There are several government-backed student loan programs that offer students and their parents low interest rates.

Fourth: Work-study. Students with financial need are awarded campus jobs through their schools, funded by a combination of federal and university money. A job that pays $2,000 to $3,000 a year is typical. An $8-an-hour job, for example, will usually require 10 hours to 15 hours a week during the academic year.

Fifth: Institutional grants. If there is outstanding need after all of the above has been tapped out, many schools will award grants from their own funds. At some schools, the grant will equal 100 percent of remaining need. Other schools may give out smaller grants.

Chapters 3, 4, and 5 explain the components of a financial aid package in greater detail.

A big grant...or a big gap?

How might a student with a $10,000 EFC fare at various colleges? Thanks to a nearly $9 billion endowment, Princeton University can afford to meet most of its undergraduates' financial need with grants rather than loans. So even though costs are about $44,000 a year, students can expect a generous amount of aid. A family with an EFC of around $10,000,

for instance, would likely get a package comprised of a $29,500 grant and a $2,500 work-study job. The college would, however, expect the student to chip in about $2,200 from his or her summer earnings.

Most other wealthy institutions will also meet 100 percent of need, but will probably throw in some student loans. At Duke, where costs are nearly $42,000 a year, the standard aid package includes $1,800 in work-study and $4,900 in student loans. A grant from the university's coffers fills any leftover need. A student with an EFC of $10,000, for example, would likely get a grant of $25,300. However, Duke limits loans and work-study to $3,000 for families with incomes of $40,000 or less; other schools have similar limits.

The story is different at universities that have smaller endowments. At the University of Wisconsin–Madison, for instance, institutional grants go to only about 900 "very high-need students," says Steve Van Ess, the university's director of financial aid. The other 27,000 students must rely on loans and work-study.

Stuck in the middle

While it's true that elite private colleges often award the best aid packages, some of the aid-formula eccentricities described earlier can also skew the numbers. In particular, if your family has a home that has appreciated significantly, the home equity you've accumulated may bump up your EFC quite a bit—and reduce your aid eligibility—at colleges that are otherwise the most generous with their aid. Consider this example: Your federal EFC is $10,000, but your family has $150,000 equity in a home. The federal formula ignores it, but a private college would likely add 5 percent of that equity, or $7,500, to your EFC. Your eligibility for federal and state grant and loan programs is based on the federal EFC of $10,000, but your eligibility for need-based grants and loans from the college is based on a $17,500 EFC. At an expensive college, this most likely means you'll get $7,500 less each year in grant aid.

A news and cultural affairs producer for a Buffalo public radio station by day, Joyce Kryszak freelances three nights a week for the Buffalo News to help put her daughter through college. A junior at Wells College in Aurora, New York, Faherty Nielsen has run from class to sling sandwiches at a nearby Subway and trudged around campus as a tour guide. Currently, she's holding down two work-study jobs: student assistant in the history department and teaching assistant for a statistics class.

That's just one prong of their college-funding plan. When Nielsen started at Wells two years ago, the "expected fami-ly contribution," the amount the government deemed her family should be able to pitch in, was about $6,000. Kryszak and her husband were paying off Kryszak's college loans and supporting her elderly mother, but managed to scrape up their share of the tab. Thankfully, Nielsen's financial aid package was a big help: She was awarded a $1,000 federal Pell grant and a $2,200 scholarship from the New York State Tuition Assistance Program (both are need-based). Wells College kicked in $9,000, defraying the cost of the $13,000 tuition and $6,400 room and board at the time.

But the financial aid slowly ran dry. One reason: Kryszak's husband's salary went up, increasing the expected family contribution. Aid calculations also counted the money Nielsen saved working summers in fast food and telemarketing jobs. Nielsen lost the Pell grant this year, and the institutional aid didn't keep pace with rising tuition. Nielsen borrowed $4,000, up from the $2,000 and $3,000 loans she relied on her first two years. Eventually, Nielsen wants to join the academic world and is hoping to earn a Ph.D. in history.

But don't get too excited. While you'll look less affluent at a state college that doesn't count home equity, a lower EFC may not always mean a better financial aid package. That's because public colleges are less apt to meet 100 percent of need. And if you're a state resident, total costs are much lower, so the college may deem that loans and a work-study job may fully meet your need.

How much do they want you?

Muddying the waters even further, many schools use financial aid as a recruiting tool. At schools that practice "preferential packaging," prospective students who would boost the school's average SAT or ACT scores or other academic statistics, or students who'd bring ethnic or geographic diversity to the school, might get bigger grants and smaller loans than students who just barely make the admissions cut. Many schools also hope to draw top students with merit scholarships. Often they're awarded without regard to need.

Aid-boosting strategies

Now you know how all those numbers you supply on the FAFSA and PROFILE forms transform into financial aid. How can you improve your chances of getting a fat offer?

- Include a couple of wealthy schools on your target list. Almost 40 universities and colleges have endowments that exceed $1 billion, led by Harvard University, Yale, and Princeton University. But some public university systems belong to the club, too, including the University of Texas, Texas A&M University, the University of

Michigan, and Ohio State University. The 100 richest schools have endowments of $400 million and up. Colleges also disclose what percentage of need they meet. Schools that meet 100 percent of need, obviously, are the better bets for a strong aid package. The College Cost and Financial Aid Directory on page 139 lists the percentage of need met by colleges and universities.

- Apply to at least one school where you're at the top of the applicant pool or you stand out in some way. For example, your SAT or ACT scores are in the top 25 percent at the school or you're a Texan at a school that draws mostly New Englanders. That makes you a top candidate for a merit award or preferential aid package.
- Consider applying to at least a couple of schools that are close competitors and seek to attract the same caliber of students. That may give you some leverage should your first-choice school offer a weaker aid package.
- Complete the aid forms accurately and on time. An error could cost you significantly. Also, some schools award their own aid on a first-come, first-served basis, so try to be an early bird.

A final bit of advice: Financial aid officers can fiddle with offers, especially if the family's financial situation changes. (To learn more about what makes a successful appeal, see Chapter 6.)

The second time around

Once you complete the process of filing for aid, you're not done for good. You must reapply for financial aid each year, using a "renewal" FAFSA that can be filed online. If applicable, a PROFILE form will also have to be filed annually.

Will you get the same aid package next year? It's typical for the loan component to increase after the first year because the limit on the most common type of federal student loan rises from $2,625 to $3,500 in the sophomore year, and to

Helpful Hints

Parents who are considering a financial aid consulting firm should look closely at the company's bona fides. Some provide a valuable service. But some don't. Be wary of firms that pledge, for example, to reveal secret strategies about the system and uncover hidden scholarships. One firm, for example, sent out letters inviting families of college-bound seniors to free financial aid seminars held in hotels around the country. But the seminars were little more than sales pitches for the company's services. Charging as much as $1,200, the firm claimed that it could get the families much more financial aid than they could get on their own. That wasn't true, says the Federal Trade Commission, the government watchdog that monitors and prosecutes financial aid and scholarship scams.

Many firms attract parents to the seminars by sending an official-looking invite that says their child has been specially selected for financial assistance, when in reality the letter is part of a mass mailing. At the seminar, a company representative conducts a spiffy presentation, exaggerating the complexities of the financial aid process and bragging about all the free money the firm can dig up for its clients.

To avoid getting stung, check out the backgrounds of firms with the Better Business Bureau, a state or local consumer protection office, or a college or high school counselor. The FTC has information regarding the warning signs of financial aid and scholarships scams (such as "the scholarship is guaranteed or your money back" and "you can't get this information anywhere else") on its website. Go to www.ftc.gov and click on "for consumers," then "scholarship & employment services."

$5,500 in the junior and senior years. If need is roughly the same, the need-based grant will probably go down accordingly. The same thing might happen with work-study, especially if a school limits the amount of time freshmen can work. A student might also see his or her need (and therefore any grants) shrink if, say, the family's income rises.

Rumors swirl about colleges using bait-and-switch tactics, such as awarding a generous grant the first year and not handing over the same amount in subsequent years. But colleges don't want students to drop out or transfer elsewhere because they can no longer afford tuition. If you're worried that your freshman-year aid package will evaporate later on, use your campus visit to investigate. Ask a few upperclassmen if their aid packages have been fairly consistent from year to year. And take heed if your questions open the gates to a flood of complaints.

Chapter Three

The Student Loan System

If scholarships and grants are the first things you think of when you hear the term "financial aid," think again. Nearly half of all financial aid to undergraduates is in the form of loans, not free money. That's right, loans. That have to be paid back. According to educational loan provider Nellie Mae, 2002 college seniors graduated with an average $18,900 in student loan debt.

While many students are afraid of shouldering such debt, student loans can be a practical solution to a tuition shortfall these days. In fact, with the ever-increasing cost of higher education, college just wouldn't be possible for many students without loans. "People don't think twice about going into a car dealership and taking on a loan for a car that's $20,000," says Rodney Oto, director of student financial services at Carleton College in Northfield, Minnesota. "If you leave college with $20,000 in debt, in my opinion, that's a very good investment. College is worth a lot more than a car."

Loans should be used sparingly, of course. Otherwise, graduates might find swinging their monthly payments so difficult that they change their career plans—opting for a higher-paying job in a less attractive field, for example—or nix plans for graduate school.

"If you leave college with $20,000 in debt, in my opinion, that's a very good investment."

The federal government has provided the best deal on student loans since it decided, years ago, to help make college more affordable by creating loans with special benefits for students. Indeed, the vast majority of student loans come from these federal programs. Most importantly, the government guarantees the loan, which means that if the student doesn't pay it back, the government will. As a result, lenders who wouldn't ordinarily look twice at an unemployed student with no credit history will happily lend him or her thousands of dollars. What's more, federal student loans typically boast lower interest rates than conventional loans.

When you receive the financial aid award letter from your college, it will list all the federal loans for which you qualify, based on your Free Application for Federal Student Aid, or FAFSA. These loans will either be Stafford loans—subsidized or unsubsidized, which we'll explain later—or, less commonly, Perkins loans, which are always subsidized. Parents of college students can qualify for a third type of federal loan, a PLUS loan. Each of these loans has different terms and benefits.

Stafford loans

The most common federal student loan, a Stafford, is available to students enrolled in college at least half time. The interest rate is variable and changes once a year based on the price of a government security (the 91-day treasury bill, to be precise). During the 2004–2005 school year, Stafford loan rates were at an all-time low of 2.77 percent for students still in school and 3.37 percent for graduates in repayment. (The rate increases once the student graduates and begins paying the loan back.) Even if interest rates rise in the future, Stafford rates are capped at 8.25 percent.

Dependent students can borrow up to $23,000 in Stafford loans during their college years, while independent students can borrow up to $46,000. The maximum amount a dependent student can borrow annually depends on class level. For freshman, that figure is $2,625; sophomores, $3,500; and juniors and seniors, $5,500 a year. The loan cap for independent freshmen is $6,625; sophomores, $7,500; and juniors and seniors, $10,500.

Where does the money come from? If your college participates in the William D. Ford Federal Direct Loan Program (DIRECT), the government lends the money. Your financial aid office will guide you in filling out the appropriate forms. If the school participates in the Federal Family Education Loan

Helpful Hints

Try to borrow only the amount of money you truly need. "We see a lot of students who overborrow," says Scott Dingwall, director of the Consumer Credit Counseling Service of Central New Jersey, which conducts financial literacy seminars on college campuses. "A student might only need $3,000 for college this year, but he'll take out $5,000, and use the extra to pay his sister back, fix up the car, things like that." Assuming that you'll land a six-figure job after college, or that you won't have competing bills like a car or house loan, may backfire. "You don't have a crystal ball," says Dingwall. "You don't know what your life will be like in a year or three years."

program (FFEL), the loan will come from a bank, credit union, nonprofit agency, or other lender selected by the student. In that case, the school will usually provide the student with a list of "preferred lenders" to contact. Students can choose another lender if they wish and it may pay to shop around (more on that at the end of this chapter). On the other hand, preferred lenders may work more smoothly with your college.

Regardless of who lends the money, students with financial need, as determined by the FAFSA, will likely be offered a subsidized Stafford. That means the government pays the interest on the loan while the student is in school, during the post-graduation grace period, and during any deferments. (While independent students can borrow up to $46,000, there is a cap on how much of that amount can be in subsidized loans.)

Students who are not deemed financially needy are usually offered an unsubsidized Stafford. On these loans, the student owes interest as soon as the loan is made, and he or she can either pay the interest while in school or let it accrue until graduation. In the latter case, the interest will be added to the total amount of the loan.

All Stafford loans have a six-month grace period after graduation before repayment begins. Staffords also offer generous deferment and forbearance, plus several flexible payment plans. We provide more details about these provisions in Chapter 12, Payback Time.

Perkins loans

In addition to Staffords, financially needy students may also be offered a federal Perkins loan. Under this program, the federal government provides a pool of money to a college, which then decides how to distribute the funds within certain guidelines. Schools can lend students up to $4,000 a year at a fixed interest rate of 5 percent. The financial aid office supplies the necessary forms. Perkins loans are subsidized, so the student doesn't pay any interest while in school. Perkins loans have a nine-month grace period before repayment begins. The federal government may forgive all or part of the loan if the student

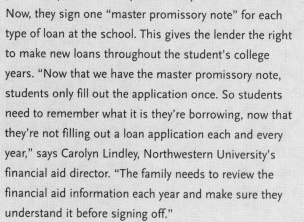

eventually enters public service or a similar profession, such as teaching, law enforcement, or health care.

Federal loans for parents

Parents can also borrow money from the federal government to help pay for their children's educations. Like Staffords, PLUS loans come from the government via the school or through third-party lenders. But PLUS loans are credit-based. Parents don't need a high credit score to qualify, but any black marks on their credit reports—like defaults or delinquent payments—can prevent them from getting a loan.

If approved, parents can borrow an amount equal to the student's cost of attendance minus the amount of financial aid awarded. For example, if the cost of attendance is $15,000 and the student receives $5,000 in financial aid, the parents can borrow up to $10,000. Interest rates change every year and are pegged at 3.1 percentage points above the 91-day treasury bill rate. But the rate is capped at 9 percent. For the 2004–2005 school year, the interest rate on a PLUS loan was 4.17 percent.

Debra Butler and her husband were shocked to learn in 2001 that the federal government thought the Washington state couple should be able to contribute $10,000 annually toward their son's college education. Though both had full-time jobs—Butler is a machine operator in a semiconductor factory while her husband works at a packaging factory—they already felt squeezed between home and car payments. "Right now we make too much to quali-fy for grants," says Butler, "but we don't make enough to have enough money."

So the Butlers, like many middle-income and working-class families today, turned to a series of loans. Tuition at Washington State University in Pullman, Washington, where son Dustin is a junior, is about $5,600 per year. With books, an off-campus apartment, and other incidentals thrown in, the total cost is much higher, at around $15,000 annually. So far, the Butlers have borrowed $33,000 under a government-backed program for parents of college students. Dustin has done his share of borrowing as well and works part time during the summer. "It sounds overwhelming," says Butler, who sells knick-knacks on eBay to help cover the monthly loan repayments. "But you have to take it month by month and break it down."

PLUS loans are not subsidized, so parents must start making payments as soon as the loan money is disbursed to the school. If the loan will be made in several payments—say, one for the fall semester, one for the spring semester—the parents begin paying on the loan after the spring semester bill is paid. But interest starts accruing immediately.

If the school participates in the DIRECT PLUS program, parents fill out an application provided by the school and borrow directly from the government. For schools that participate in the FFEL program, parents apply to lenders for the loan. The school may have a list of preferred lenders, but parents can borrow from any institution that offers such loans.

The government's *Student Guide* can provide more details on federal student loans. For a copy, visit www.studentaid.ed.gov or call the Federal Student Aid Information Center at (800) 433-3243.

State loans

Some states offer student loans or help ease the burden of federal loans. "State loans aren't always publicized very widely," says CariAnne Behr of Mapping Your Future, a nonprofit financial aid website (www.mapping-your-future.org) sponsored by 35 loan guaranty agencies. (Guaranty agencies are nonprofit or state-run organizations that promise to pay back lenders on behalf of the federal government if students default on FFEL loans.) The Minnesota Student Educational Loan Fund program, for example, offers low-interest loans to students who are residents or who attend Minnesota colleges. First and second year students can borrow up to $4,500 annually; third and fourth year students, up to $6,000 annually.

Other states offer rebates or discounts on federal loans. The Vermont Student Assistance Corp. (VSAC), for example, offers the Vermont Value program to residents and out-of-state students attending Vermont colleges. Students take out Stafford loans (or, if parents, a PLUS loan) through VSAC and receive a rebate that equals one percent of the outstanding principal balance on the loan. Students who pay their monthly loan bill via electronic transfer can get an additional 0.25 percent rebate. Over a 10-year repayment period on a $15,000 loan, those two rebates could save roughly $1,400 to $1,900.

For information on state loan programs, contact your state's higher education department. To find the agency in your home state, go to www.studentaid.ed.gov (click on the word "funding," then scroll down to "state aid") or call the Federal Student Aid Information Center at (800) 433-3243.

government and don't have the generous deferral and forbearance options that federal loans do.

"State loans aren't always publicized very widely."

Private loans

The amount a student can borrow under the Stafford loan program has topped out at $23,000 ($46,000 for independent students) since 1998. But during that time, private and public college costs have risen dramatically. As a result, many students are beginning to seek alternative or private loans issued by banks, credit unions, and other financial institutions.

Unlike federal student loans, alternative loans are not guaranteed by the government, so lenders take into account student credit history. Fortunately, the credit requirements for private student loans aren't as stringent as for other types of borrowing, such as car loans or mortgages. Interest rates on alternative loans vary according to the student's credit score. To land a lower interest rate, try asking a parent or adult with good credit to cosign the loan, promising to pay if you default. Alternative loans are not guaranteed by the federal

Shop around

Because alternative loans don't measure up to federal loans on many counts, experts recommend students look to Stafford, Perkins, or state loan programs before they consider alternative loans.

If your school provides Stafford loans directly, you can't shop around. You're stuck with the school's fees and terms. But if your school participates in the FFEL program and sends you off to find a private lender, you may be able to save a chunk of money by comparison shopping for loans. An analysis by an independent education consulting firm found that students can save up to $1,400 over 10 years of repayment by borrowing from one of several nonprofit agencies instead of the preferred lenders suggested by their schools.

To find a low-cost loan, ask potential lenders about fees as well as repayment incentives. Stafford loans carry origination

Real World Stories

As a freshman in 2003, Tristan Robinson made the 40-minute trek from his home to classes at the University of Pittsburgh several times a week. But between the commute, a part-time job, and studying, Robinson felt he was missing out on the college experience. At the start of his sophomore year, he moved on campus.

But it was a scramble to pay the bill, as housing and in-state tuition at the university run around $16,000 a year. Robinson qualified for a $2,000 Pell grant and a $3,300 state grant, and he threw in $1,000 he had saved from a summer job. A member of the cross-country team and student government, Robinson had little time for a job. So he

borrowed to pay the remainder of the tab, taking out a $3,500 subsidized Stafford student loan and a $6,300 private student loan. "It is a concern to me," says Robinson, who hopes to keep the total amount of his loans under $20,000 for all four years. "You just have to watch what you spend."

Craig Asplund, a software architect in Ohio, panicked when his oldest child got into Princeton University in 1999. The father of four hadn't saved a penny for college. And Princeton, which doesn't award merit aid, said the family didn't qualify for any need-based aid. "I thought, 'Oh, my God, I have got to do something,

time is short,'" says Asplund, who eventually scraped enough money together by taking out expensive loans. "You see one hand out there and you grab it."

But he learned his lesson. Three years later, when his daughter got into Elon University in North Carolina, he assumed he'd have to resort to pricey

borrowing again. But Elon sent him a brochure about the Missouri Higher Education Loan Authority (MOHELA), which offers low-interest government-backed loans for parents. By shifting all his borrowing to MOHELA, he has saved thousands of dollars.

---

fees of up to 4 percent of the amount borrowed (which goes to the government to help fund the loan program and to insure the loan against default). But some lenders will pay part of the fee or even the entire fee. Also, look for lenders who offer interest rate discounts, rebates, or other incentives when you start repayment. Guaranty agencies may be able to point to lenders that offer special breaks. For a list of agencies, visit www.mapping-your-future.org.

Keep the future in mind

Before you sign on the dotted line, ask your financial aid office for a ballpark estimate of how much you might owe by the end of college. Then calculate what your monthly payments will be after graduation. For example, take those 2002 graduates who owed $18,900. With an interest rate of 3.37 percent, they would be expected to pay back the loan in $186 monthly installments for 10 years. Your financial aid office and calculators at websites like www.mapping-your-future.org can also help.

The loan check

Typically, lenders send the loan money straight to the university to cover tuition and costs. When the school receives the

money, it is applied toward tuition, room and board, and fees. If there's any cash left over, the school issues you a check for the remainder. If you have an alternative loan, the loan proceeds might go to the school or to you, depending on the lender and type of loan. If you've changed your mind about taking a Stafford or Perkins loan, you can cancel all or part of it by informing your school within 14 days of notice of the loan, or by the first day of the payment period, whichever is later. Your options for cancellation or repayment of private loans vary according to the lender and the loan.

Chapter Four

Scholarships and Grants

You may have seen books by former students bragging about how they financed their way through the likes of Harvard by winning tens of thousands of dollars in scholarships. And, indeed, such free rides do exist for academic superstars. But there's also plenty of free money available for students who boast merely above average academic credentials, not to mention talented athletes, musicians, artists, public speakers, community activists, and more.

Most scholarship-seekers think first of the big, privately sponsored award competitions, some of which we describe later in this chapter. But the merit scholarships that colleges dole out to entering students are an even bigger slice of the pie. Even more free money is earmarked for students with financial need, in the form of grants from the federal government, the states, and the colleges. You apply for this largesse simply by filling out the Free Application for Federal Student Aid, or FAFSA.

From the schools

In 2002, 81 percent of students at private colleges and universities received need-based grants or merit-based scholarships from their schools, compared to 63 percent in 1990, according to the National Association of College and University Business Officers. Much of the increase comes from the growth in the number of merit scholarships. But the size of a typical scholarship or grant has grown, too, rising from 27 percent of tuition in 1990 to 39 percent of tuition in 2002.

Need-based grants

If you have a lot of financial need (in other words, your family's expected family contribution, or EFC, is low) and attend an expensive college, your financial aid package will probably include a need-based grant funded by the college (in addition to loans and work-study). Chapter 2 describes how schools determine whether a student qualifies for such a grant.

Merit-based scholarships

What many schools call a scholarship could just as easily be dubbed a "recruiting discount." Studies have shown that students are more likely to attend a school that awards them a merit scholarship than one that gives them a grant because they have financial need. That's why a growing number of schools are using merit scholarships to entice talented students.

Many schools choose scholarship recipients solely on the basis of a student's admissions application. But some universities, like Wake Forest University and the University of Richmond, require a separate application for many or all of their awards. Be sure to check with the college to find out what scholarships are available and how to qualify for them.

Lewis and Clark College, in Portland, Oregon, boasts more than 150 scholarships for its 543 entering freshmen.

Each year, the school awards up to 10 Barbara Hirschi Neely Scholarships (which cover a full year of tuition and fees) and up to 15 Trustee Scholarships (which cover one-half of tuition and fees annually) to students with top grades and test scores, with special preference given to those interested in math, science, or international studies. In addition to those plum awards, the school gives out more than 100 Dean's Scholarships, in amounts varying from $4,000 to $8,000, plus other scholarships for leadership and service, and for special talent in music or forensics.

Awards for outstanding community service and for special talents in art, music, dance, drama, writing, and other areas are common among colleges, too. Many schools offer scholarships specifically for minorities. The CIGNA Scholars Program award for African Americans at the University of Richmond, for example, covers two-thirds of the cost of a four-year education.

Some scholarships are awarded automatically. At the University of Connecticut, for example, all incoming freshmen who were high school valedictorians and salutatorians are given a Presidential Scholars award worth $3,000 to $9,300 per year, plus a one-time $2,500 research fellowship. At the website of Mary Baldwin College in Staunton, Virginia (www.mbc.edu), prospective students can enter their grade point averages and test scores into a "scholarship calculator" to see how much merit money they are likely to receive. A student with a 3.7 GPA and 1150 on the SAT, for example, is eligible for an $8,400 scholarship.

About 30 schools at the very top of the food chain—including Harvard, Princeton, and Yale universities, and the Massachusetts Institute of Technology—do not offer merit scholarships. These are the schools with so many applications for admission that they end up turning away valedictorians with perfect test scores. Students who overcome the admissions odds don't need additional inducement to enroll. Still, a few top schools do give out a handful of awards to the best of the best, including Duke University, Johns Hopkins University, the University of Chicago, and Washington

University in St. Louis. Students who have what it takes to get into the most elite schools also have what it takes to earn some serious merit money at excellent, but perhaps less prestigious, colleges. At smaller, lesser-known schools, a B average, an SAT score of 1100, and a class rank in the top third can be enough to nab a merit award.

To increase the chances of garnering a merit award, students should apply to schools where they stand out. Applicants with test scores and a class rank or GPA in the top 25 percent will often earn merit money. It can also help if the student brings ethnic or geographic diversity to the school or a special talent that's in demand. *The A's and B's of Academic Scholarships* (Octameron Associates, $10) provides a comprehensive list of merit scholarships at 1,200 colleges and universities.

What if you earn a merit scholarship and also qualify for financial aid based on need? The money should come rolling in, right? Not so fast. In the eyes of the school, you are richer than you were before; in other words, your need has shrunk. Thus the school will probably use the merit money to replace the need-based aid it would have given you otherwise. Typically, scholarships will first replace loans and work-study in your aid package. But if the award is large enough, it might also replace need-based grants.

Let's say, for instance, you earned a $10,000 merit scholarship and also qualified for $20,000 in need-based aid, which included $4,000 in loans and work-study. You wouldn't get $30,000 in aid. The $10,000 scholarship means you have $10,000 less need. The first $4,000 of your scholarship would probably replace your loans and work-study with free money, and the rest would probably replace $6,000 of your need-based grant.

Athletic scholarships

Of course, academic stars aren't the only students colleges want. If you're a standout athlete, there may be scholarship money available for you, too. Free rides are rare. They go mainly to the football and basketball players at the big-name National Collegiate Athletic Association Division I schools. In other sports, coaches have a set amount of scholarship money to allocate among all their players, and they tend to spread it around. Under NCAA rules, a Division I men's swimming coach can give the equivalent of 9.9 full-ride scholarships to his players, for instance. But the money will probably be divided among 20 or more swimmers. Some will get an award that covers tuition, others will receive the equivalent of room and board, while some students will be handed just enough money to pay for books.

Overall, only about half of the student athletes who compete at Division I or Division II schools get scholarships. Division I schools have the most money to award but are the most competitive. Division II schools generally have a smaller pool of money for scholarships, and Division III schools (along with Division I schools in the Ivy League like Harvard and Brown University) award aid based only on financial need. Smaller schools that are members of the National Association of Intercollegiate Athletics also award scholarships, but often have limited budgets. You can search for schools that field teams in your sport and look up the division at the NCAA's website, www2.ncaa.org. (Under "academics and athletes," click on "education and research," then "school-administered athletics scholarships.")

Erin Reinhardt has it good. A junior at the University of California–Berkeley, she doesn't pay a nickel of the nearly $5,000 in-state tuition (nor the more than $11,000 a year room and board). "I spend a couple hundred a semester on books," she says—and that's it. No interest-heavy loans. No dreary burger-flipping for cash. No worries.

How did Reinhardt get such a sweet deal? Because in high school, she could pull 2,000 meters on a rowing machine at a clip only a handful of girls in the nation could match. Cal noticed, espe-cially after Reinhardt earned a spot on the U.S. Junior Olympic Rowing squad, and today she rows for the Bears. "It's a really good deal," she admits with a laugh, "I mean, I would definitely have to get a job if I didn't have this scholarship."

Assuming you're not the next Michael Jordan, how do you get a coach's attention? Begin contacting coaches in your sophomore or junior year, letting them know about your interest in their program. Follow up with a résumé that sums up your athletic accomplishments, or even a video if you have some great clips of yourself in action. Make an appointment to meet the coach during your campus tour, and keep him or her updated on your senior year accomplishments. Attending summer camps run by college coaches is another good way to get noticed. Be sure to register for NCAA eligibility (www.ncaaclearinghouse.net) and pay careful attention to the recruiting rules. You wouldn't want to lose your eligibility for unknowingly breaking a rule.

As with academic scholarships, if you receive an athletic scholarship and also qualify for need-based financial aid, you won't get both. Your scholarship will likely replace any loans or work-study in your aid package, and then it might also reduce or replace the amount of any need-based grant.

From the federal government

Students from families with modest household incomes (typi-cally less than $35,000) may be awarded a federal Pell grant of up to $4,050 for each year of undergraduate study. This money, which is awarded based on the information the family provides on the FAFSA, does not have to be repaid. Because need depends on family size, the number of family members in school, and income, a large family with a higher income might qualify, for instance. The key is the EFC, which can be no high-er than $3,850 for the year.

Exceptionally needy students—typically, they can't afford any family contribution at all—may qualify for a Federal Supplemental Educational Opportunity Grant (FSEOG) in addition to a Pell grant. The amount ranges from $100 to $4,000 a year, depending on need and on the funding avail-able at the school. FSEOG grants are an example of "campus-based" federal aid, which means that colleges apply each year to the Department of Education for funding and the financial aid office determines how much each student receives.

From the states

The 50 states give out nearly $7 billion annually in financial aid, the majority of it to students with financial need. In most states, you apply by filing the FAFSA, but some states have supplemental forms or require a separate application. College financial aid officers can provide guidance on the requirements of a particular state.

One common type of award is a grant to residents that attend school in the state. North Carolina, for instance, awards an $1,800 grant to any resident who attends an in-state private college, regardless of need. Some states have reciprocal arrangements with neighboring states. A Kansas resident, for example, might qualify for a break at a participating college in Missouri. But most state grants are need-based, and often the student must have a high level of need to qualify. State grants in Wisconsin, for instance, generally go to the same students who qualify for Pell grants, says Steve Van Ess, the director of financial aid at the University of Wisconsin–Madison.

A growing number of states are giving scholarships and grants to students who meet certain academic requirements and attend an in-state college. Since 1993, the Georgia HOPE (Helping Outstanding Pupils Educationally) scholarship, the granddaddy of all the state scholarship programs, has doled out more than $2.3 billion to more than 800,000 students with B averages or better in high school. Many other states have followed suit. Florida, for instance, pays 75 percent to 100 percent of tuition and fees for residents who graduate from high school with a 3.0 or better GPA and attend college in state. South Carolina offers $5,000 to high school grads with SAT scores of 1200 or more and who rank in the top 5 percent of their class.

Some state programs combine merit and financial need. One of California's Cal Grants for the 2004–2005 school year, for instance, pays full tuition at in-state public universities or up to $9,708 toward the cost of an in-state private university if a student graduates from high school with a 3.0 GPA and the family earns no more than $60,700 to $78,100 (depending on family size). Your high school guidance counselor can tell you what kind of aid is available from your state. You can also contact your state's higher education agency, which can be found at www.studentaid.ed.gov. (Click on "funding," then scroll down to "state aid.")

From corporate and community groups

Although they amount to less than 4 percent of the grant and scholarship money awarded to undergraduates, private scholarships from civic groups like the Elks Club and corporations like Coca-Cola and Target nonetheless total more than $4 billion. Many of the biggest and most prestigious awards are thousand-to-one shots. And many other scholarships, such as those in the $500 to $1,000 range, may seem puny, but every little bit helps.

Outside scholarships are portable, which means the student can use them at the college or university of his or her choice. They're usually not based on financial need, so they're especially welcome to students who don't qualify for much need-based aid, but whose families still struggle to find cash for college. And the awards aren't just for head-of-the-class students with high SAT scores and a long list of extracurricular activities. There's also plenty of scholarship money allotted for recognizing outstanding accomplishments in arts, science, writing, community service, and other endeavors. Burger King even sponsors a scholarship that's not for the highest achievers. It's designed for students who may be sacrificing academics to work part-time out of financial need. Here's a sampling:

Academics and leadership

- *Coca-Cola Scholars* (www.coca-colascholars.org). Winners excel in academics, community service, employment, and leadership in school activities. Fifty recipients earn $20,000 scholarships, while 200 others earn $4,000.
- *Sam Walton Community Scholarship* (www.walmartfoundation.org). Wal-Mart rewards students with financial need, strong academics, community or extracurricular involvement, and work experience. There's one $25,000 award, 50 awards of $5,000, and 6,000 awards of $1,000.
- *National Merit Scholarship Awards* (www.nationalmerit.org). About 8,200 finalists are selected from top-scorers on the PSAT. All earn a $2,500 scholarship, and some are awarded additional scholarship money from their schools or from corporate foundations.

The arts and writing

- *Arts Recognition and Talent Search* (www.artsawards.org). Awards ranging from $100 to $10,000 are offered for

Now a graduate student at the University of Georgia, Mahlet Endale learned the hard way that it's important to know about any strings attached to grants and scholarships. Endale's B-plus average in high school won her a $3,000 state HOPE scholarship in 1997. And because her father, a newly minted Ph.D., hadn't yet found a job, she received lots of need-based aid from Emory University. But because calculus and chemistry proved tougher than anticipated, Endale's grades fell below HOPE's 3.0 minimum and she lost the scholarship. By that time, her dad was employed and her family's income had risen so much she wasn't eligible for much financial aid her sophomore year. Endale borrowed enough for one semester while she arranged to transfer to lower-cost University of Georgia in nearby Athens. "It was tough," says Endale. "I felt defeated." But she brought her grades back up to win the scholarship again her senior year.

excellence in dance, music, theater, visual arts, film, photography, and writing.

- *Scholastic Art and Writing Awards* (www. scholastic.com/ artandwriting). This competition leads to 900 awards of up to $10,000 in numerous art and writing categories.
- *Ayn Rand Institute Essay Competition* (www. aynrand.org/ contests). Students write an essay on Rand's *The Fountainhead*. Top prizes are $1,000 to $10,000; semifinalists and finalists earn $50 to $100.

Public speaking

- *American Legion National High School Oratorical Contest* (www.legion.org). Students deliver local speeches on topics related to the U.S. Constitution. Three national winners earn $15,500 to $19,500. Numerous state and regional winners earn smaller awards.
- *Voice of Democracy Audio Essay Contest,* sponsored by the Veterans of Foreign Wars (www.vfw.org). Students tape a short essay they've written on a patriotic topic. Sixty prizes range from $1,000 to $25,000.

Community service

- *Prudential Spirit of Community Awards* (www.prudential. com). Prudential looks for students who have performed exemplary community service. More than 100 state winners earn $1,000. Ten national winners are awarded an additional $5,000.
- *Target All-Around Scholarship Awards* (www.target. com). The retailer rewards students with a record of outstanding community service. There's one $25,000 award and 600 awards of $1,000.

Miscellaneous

- *Intel Science Talent Search* (www.sciserv.org/sts). This prestigious competition recognizes original scientific research. Top prizes are $20,000 to $100,000. The 330 semifinalists and finalists earn $1,000 to $5,000.
- *Morris K. Udall Undergraduate Scholarship* (www.udall. gov). College sophomores and juniors must have a significant record of service for environmental causes or, for Native Americans and Alaska Natives, a commitment to tribal public policy or healthcare. Scholarships of up to $5,000 go to 80 winners.
- *Discover Card Tribute Awards* (www.aasa.org). Discover recognizes students who have faced a significant roadblock or challenge in their lives. Judging is also based on community service, leadership, and special talents. There are up to nine national awards of

$25,000 and up to nine awards of $2,500 in each state.

- *Burger King Scholars Program* (www.burgerking.com/bkscholars). This scholarship is awarded to students with GPAs of 2.5 and above who must work during high school out of financial need. Candidates submit recommendations from their schools and their employers. The 1,600 winners earn $1,000 each.

The winning edge

To get a leg up on the competition, scholarship applicants should strive to become junior movers and shakers. Judges aren't expecting a long list of extracurriculars. Instead, they're looking for accomplishments that rise above the crowd: a community service project that has real impact, for instance, or participation in activities that show a true commitment to music, art, or a particular area of study.

Many competitions require an essay outlining what the student has accomplished and what it has meant to him or her. The winning compositions are typically polished and personal, with earnest detail about what it's like to, say, overcome a crisis, or what it felt like to help build a home for the less fortunate.

Helpful Hints

;)

As study abroad has grown more popular, more scholarships have popped up to help students finance their travels. In 2000, for example, Congress created the Benjamin A. Gilman International Scholarship (www.iie.org/gilman), a merit scholarship for overseas study for students who are eligible for Pell grants. Other scholarships are available from private sponsors. Chapter 8 has more tips on how to find money to study abroad.

You'll need plenty of time to work on applications and draft a compelling essay. It might help to study what prior winners have written. Scholarship sponsors sometimes post information about winners or even the entries on their websites. Or you can ask for copies of the winning essays. You may even want to ask a teacher or counselor to critique your essay. *The Scholarship Scouting Report* (Harper, $21.95) details winning entries for several dozen top competitions. Be sure to pay attention to eligibility criteria, contest rules, and deadlines. You don't want to waste your effort on an application that gets thrown out on a technicality.

The competition for the big national scholarships can be fierce. The Coca-Cola Scholars program, for instance, gets more than 91,000 applications each year for its 250 awards. The Internet is the easiest place to begin scouting for scholarships. FastWeb (www.fastweb.com) is the best-known scholarship search service, but users have to put up with lots of ads. After filling out a questionnaire, a student receives regular emails noting applicable scholarships and deadlines. Other search services include CollegeNET (www.collegenet.com) and the College Board (www.collegeboard.com/pay).

Be forewarned: The big search services probably won't include local scholarships. While the awards may be small, the competition probably won't be as stiff as the national contests because there may be only a handful of applicants. Some places to tap for local scholarship information: your high school guidance counselor, your employer or your parent's employer, professional associations in the field you plan to study, unions (if you or your parents belong to one), and community and civic groups like the Elks, Jaycees, Kiwanis, Lions, or Rotarians.

While a majority of scholarships are earmarked for entering freshmen, plenty of awards are open to upperclassmen. So once you're in college, keep in touch with your school's financial aid office and your academic department to learn about scholarships open to sophomores, juniors, and seniors.

David Whitt of Hancock, New York, remembers checking out Cornell University five years ago as he pondered his college choices. But the school lost some of its luster when he saw the $40,000 price tag. Indeed, most of the schools Whitt hoped to attend were just as expensive. His solution? Whitt applied to the Army Reserve Officer Training Corps, which trains students to be military officers while earning their degrees, and landed a four-year scholarship to Boston University. (The scholarships are highly competitive. In 2004, only 8 percent of applicants received one.) The deal-clincher for Whitt: BU covered his remaining costs. The Army ROTC also kicked in stipends for books and incidentals. "I didn't want to put my Dad through financial hardship," says Whitt.

From the armed forces

Think it's tough to get into Harvard, Yale, or Princeton? Then try West Point (www.usma.edu), the U.S. Naval Academy (www.nadn.navy.mil), and the U.S. Coast Guard Academy (www.cga.edu), which accept just 7 percent to 10 percent of their applicants. An applicant's grades, SAT or ACT scores, athletic ability, and leadership potential must be impressive enough to garner a nomination from a U.S. Senator or Representative. Students who are admitted to any of the service academies—the U.S. Air Force Academy (www.usafa.af.mil) and the U.S. Merchant Marine Academy (www.usmma.edu) are the other two—get a first-rate education along with military training. There are no tuition or room and board charges. Instead, the applicants pay for their schooling with minimum five-year service commitments.

Students might also want to consider the Reserve Officer Training Corps (ROTC) Scholarship. Applications can be found online: the U.S. Army (www.armyrotc.com), U.S. Air Force (www.afrotc.com), and U.S. Navy (www.navy.com/nrotc). Students who are selected for the scholarships typically have above-average SAT scores, rank in the top quarter of their high school class, and have been leaders in an extracurricular activity or sport. The military pays most or all of the student's tuition and also provides allowances for books, fees, and living expenses. Many colleges with ROTC programs offer additional incentives that cover any remaining tuition and/or room and board. Upon graduation, the minimum service commitment is four years full time or longer for part-time service in the Reserves or National Guard. (The College Cost and Financial Aid Directory on page 139 indicates those colleges that have ROTC programs.)

There are also ways to earn a college degree during or after a tour in the military, with Uncle Sam footing most of the bill. Chapter 10 has more details on tuition assistance for veterans.

Chapter Five

Work, Work, Work

When Corbett Cummins, a senior at California State University–Sacramento, was a freshman, he eschewed a part-time job to focus on his studies. But short on cash his junior year, Cummins started working at a coffee shop and discovered something unexpected. "When I wasn't working, my grades weren't that great," says the communications major. "Now that I have a job, I'm a straight-A student."

Cummins' experience is not unusual. Although some families worry that a job might detract from a student's college experience, research shows the opposite is true. "Students who work part time have higher retention rates, higher satisfaction with college, and higher levels of engagement in school," says Linda Sax, a professor of higher education and organizational change at the University of

California–Los Angeles. And, she adds, part-time jobs on campus make it easier for students to make friends and develop support networks. A job can also help a student learn the all-important task of time management. "If you have to work, you have to plan your time," says Cummins.

Still, working too much can interfere with studies. That's why many schools recommend that first-year students work

---

"Now that I have a job, I'm a straight-A student."

---

no more than 12 hours a week, and upperclassmen keep their work hours to 25 or less.

Work-study jobs

A job subsidized by the federal work-study program, which means the government pays up to 75 percent of your salary, is a common component of a financial aid package. If your Free Application for Federal Student Aid, or FAFSA, shows that you have financial need, you may be offered a work-study job. Some students turn up their noses at this form of "self-help," but a work-study job doesn't necessarily entail slinging hash in the campus cafeteria. Job possibilities run the gamut from working the checkout at the library to tutoring or assisting professors with research. Moreover, the pay can be competitive with off-campus employment. You'll earn at least minimum wage, but the hourly rate varies by campus. At American University in Washington, D.C., the average work-study wage is about $8.50 an hour; at the University of Iowa, it's $7.44.

Almost any job on campus can qualify as work-study. "Many schools do not classify jobs as 'this is work study, this is not,'" says Dan Madzelan, director of forecasting and policy analysis for the Office of Postsecondary Education at the Department of Education. "Basically, schools advertise jobs, and if you happen to have a work-study award, employers like to see that, because most of your wages won't be coming out of their budget." Receiving a work-study award doesn't guarantee you a job. You still have to seek out and apply for positions, which are typically posted at the school's financial aid office or career center.

Some off-campus positions might qualify as work-study, such as public service or nonprofit jobs. One important advantage of work-study jobs: The money the student makes from work-study won't be counted next year in the calculation of the expected family contribution (EFC). Ordinarily, half of the student's earnings (after taxes and an allowance for living expenses are subtracted) from employment must go toward next year's family contribution. "But if you made that $3,000 working at the bookstore in a work-study position, it won't be held against you when they calculate your financial need," says Pat Gutierrez, manager of the student employment center at the University of California–Davis.

Other jobs on campus

Even if you don't qualify for a work-study position, there are plenty of on-campus jobs. Like work-study, the types of jobs and pay vary depending on the school. Typically, the financial aid office or the college's career center maintains job listings, and many colleges now have online job boards. Professors and staff in your department may also be able to point you toward jobs related to your field of study. Science majors, for example, might find assistant positions in research labs and education students might act as tutors.

If traditional college jobs in the library or cafeteria don't sound appealing, there are a number of jobs that can give you a head start in gaining some real world experience. On many campuses, students get jobs at various student-run businesses, such as the Barnard Babysitting Service, the Princeton Bartending Agency, or Big Red Shipping and Storage at Cornell University. "I'm not investing my own money, but

A work-study job doesn't have to be on campus. Meghan Aberle, a recent graduate of American University in Washington, D.C., transformed an unpaid internship with the city's court system into a work-study position during college. "I worked at AU's child development center, and between working and my internship, I was really strapped," says Aberle, who graduated from AU's communications, legal institutions, economics, and government program. She explained the situation to her school's career center counselor, who filed the paperwork to have the job classified as work-study. Soon, Aberle was working 16 hours to 20 hours a week and earning $7.91 an hour. Today, Aberle works in the court's human resources division.

I'm experiencing what it's like to run a business," says Laura Hwang, a junior at Barnard College who, as comanager of the Barnard Babysitting Service, oversees 600 students who care for the children of Manhattanites.

If you choose to work off campus, be careful. Studies show that working a part-time job off campus tends to lower students' grades and overall satisfaction with college. What's more, an off-campus boss might not be as willing as an on-campus one to fit your work around classes and exams.

Summer jobs and internships

Summer is a prime time for college-age workers to refill their coffers or to make a little extra money to put toward next year's tuition. But many collegians will be entering the job market at the same time, so it behooves students to start looking for a summer job long before temperatures climb. "If you want to go out of town or work at summer camps, you have to start looking in January or February," says Arturo Elizondo, career counselor at the University of Texas–Arlington. "If you're more interested in local things, you can hang on a little and start your serious job search in March or April. But you want to beat the high school students," he says. Again, any income earned from a non-work-study job will be counted toward your EFC next year.

Many students work summer internships—jobs designed specifically for students to teach them about a particular industry or workplace. They range from informal jobs at small local businesses to highly structured programs at Fortune 500 companies. "With internships, there's an intentional learning component, so it's not just tasks they do on the job," says Ron Albertson, associate director of career and employment services at the University of Puget Sound in Tacoma, Washington. He notes that many employers now expect to see an internship on graduates' resumes. In fact, many of today's students complete several internships during their college careers.

Students hoping to get an internship in their field of study must be attuned to application deadlines throughout the year. "There are internship options with deadlines that come up as early as November," says Albertson. Many internships are unpaid, which often means some students find themselves juggling an unpaid internship with a paid job during the summer. "If you're not being paid, you must make sure this internship is going to be worth your while," says Jane Celwyn, director of career development at Barnard. Some campus career offices maintain a notebook of student comments about internship experiences, which can help the student decide whether the position is worthwhile.

Some universities offer grants so students can afford to take internships that would otherwise be unpaid. Amy

Stokes, a sophomore at Barnard, received a $3,000 grant from her school (slotted for internships promoting entrepreneurism). That helped Stokes complete a two-month internship in Japan, where she helped a high-end pastry company with store and product design and observed factory production.

At some schools, interns earn academic credit as well as pay. Jenny Lai, a senior at the University of Puget Sound, spent last summer at Boeing, satisfying the internship requirement for her honors program in business leadership and reaping $15.48 an hour. "It was the greatest summer of my life," she says. Assigned to the procurement department, Lai worked on an initiative to decrease the company's production costs. At the end of the summer, Boeing offered her a full-time job after graduation, and she accepted.

To receive academic credit for an internship, talk to your departmental advisor or an internship advisor in career services before you start the job. Some schools simply don't offer credit for internships, while others require you to pay summer enrollment fees, take an internship seminar, or write a paper for an academic advisor.

Many college career service offices maintain databases of internships, which help students search for, say, a job in banking or the arts. Some colleges are plugged into a wider range of internships as they share their network of such opportunities with other schools. There are also numerous websites that detail internship programs, such as www.internshipprograms.com and www.internjobs.com. Students interested in state and federal government internships can consult www.studentjobs.gov (click on "e-Scholar").

Co-op programs

Co-op programs are like internships on steroids. These highly structured programs weave together full time work experience with academic studies. Most co-op students spend a semester doing classwork on campus, then spend the next semester working full time for a company. Co-op programs typically require students to complete several semesters or quarters of work, and students often put in several stints at one company throughout the program. Students are usually given increasing amounts of responsibility with each rotation at the company, and many receive a job offer when they graduate.

Co-op positions are almost always paid, with annual incomes averaging between $2,500 (for students early in their college years or in lower-paying fields) and $14,000 (for upperclassmen in high-paying industries).

More than 400 colleges and universities around the country offer co-op programs, says Peggy Harrier, president of the Cooperative Education and Internship Association (CEIA). Originally designed for engineering students, co-op positions now exist in a variety of fields, including marketing,

Real World Stories

Ronak Davé, an operations management major at the University of Massachusetts–Amherst, is gaining some valuable work experience at the Greeno Sub Shop, a student-run campus eatery serving some 250 sandwiches nightly. "I looked at the books and noticed their prices were extremely low," says Davé, who discovered the shop was losing money on its sandwiches because prices hadn't kept pace with increasing supply costs. Davé and her fellow students at the sub shop raised prices and negotiated with vendors to lower costs. "After three semesters, we actually made money last semester," says Davé. As a "student consultant" to Greeno's, Davé earns $7.75 an hour and works 15 hours to 20 hours a week.

When Kristen Kesse graduates from the University of Cincinnati in 2007, there's an excellent chance she will have already landed a full-time job. That's because she is participating in a co-op program, a curriculum that allows students to alternate semesters of classroom study with semesters of work related to their majors. Kesse spends one term studying materials engineering, then spends the next term working at Toyota Motor Manufacturing North America in Erlanger, Kentucky. During her last co-op term, she earned $16.75 an hour in Toyota's materials quality department, researching paint defects. She'll complete six terms with the automaker before she graduates. "It helps me pay for college," says Kesse. "It's a good experience to see how my classes actually apply in the work world."

business, information technology, and health. Some schools have well-established co-op programs, such as New York City's Pace University, Northeastern University in Boston, Rochester Institute of Technology in New York, Antioch College in Yellow Springs, Ohio, and the University of Cincinnati. To find a program, students can consult the National Commission for Cooperative Education's (NCCE) *Directory of College Cooperative Education Programs*, which many high school and college guidance offices have on hand. Co-op students may qualify for additional scholarship money from NCCE (www.co-op.edu), which recently began offering $5,000 scholarships at 10 schools.

Chapter Six

Comparing Financial Aid Offers

Ah, springtime, the season of reckoning for college applicants. You find out which colleges want you, of course, but you also find out how much each of your potential alma maters will really cost. Typically, a college's financial aid award letter follows on the heels of an acceptance letter. Sometimes, it's even in the same fat envelope.

What should you do when you get the award letter? If it's offering a free ride to your dream school, just smile and sign on the dotted line. Otherwise, it's time for some serious number-crunching and maybe even some good old-fashioned negotiating.

Andrew Cole, a Bucknell University freshman from Texas, had to weigh financial aid packages from eight different schools. His expected family contribution was roughly $20,000, based on his family's income of about $100,000. But his aid offers varied dramatically. They ranged from a package consisting of a $14,000 need-based grant, a $2,625 student loan, and $900 in work-study—leaving the family an out-of-pocket bill of about $14,000—to a package with a $1,900 need-based grant, $2,625 student loan, and $1,000 in work-study. Cole's parents would have had to shell out nearly $25,000 to cover the remainder.

Bucknell University's offer fell in the middle, but the Lewisburg, Pennslyvania, school was Cole's first choice. After Bucknell awarded him a $15,000 need-based grant and a $2,625 student loan, Cole's parents were left with a $21,000 bill, which they'll cover with a government-backed loan for parents of college students. "The atmosphere of the campus struck me as somewhere I knew I could be happy, so while I got better aid packages from different schools, Bucknell was worth the extra cost," says Cole.

Deciphering a financial aid award letter

The award letter usually includes the school's official "cost of attendance," a number that is frequently misunderstood, says Bill Leith, deputy director of application processing at the Department of Education. It's not a bill. It's more like a budget, one that reflects all the various and sundry costs of attending the school. At St. Olaf College in Northfield, Minnesota, for example, the cost of attendance for the 2004–2005 school year is $32,600, while the figure is $43,185 at New York University in Manhattan.

The cost of attendance includes direct expenses, like tuition, fees, and room and board. Then schools tack on an approximate price for books, supplies, and personal expenses like laundry detergent and toothpaste. Students with frugal lifestyles, who buy used books and bypass school meal plans for ramen noodles, for instance, can probably get by on less. The flip side is also true: Students hooked on designer clothes or owning a car, with its unavoidable need for gas, repairs, and insurance, may find the allowance for supplies and personal expenses piddling. The budget for transportation and travel can vary by student. It might be meager if the student attends college close to home, or it might need to be generous enough to cover a couple of airline tickets home—when home is 3,000 miles away.

On the brighter side, the higher the estimated cost of attendance, the better the chances may be to qualify for financial aid. Let's say the cost of School A and School B is exactly the same. But School A figures a student will need $3,500 for transportation, books, supplies, and personal expenses, while School B allots the student $2,000 for the same expenses. The student's need at school A is thus greater than at School B. Need, remember, is the cost of attendance minus the expected family contribution. If both schools fully meet need, the student would get $1,500 more in aid from School A than from School B. Assuming the amount actually spent on those expenses at each school is similar, the student would come out $1,500 ahead at School A.

Things are seldom so neat and clean, of course. One school may be generous in judging costs but not fully meet need. Another might be stingier with its cost appraisal but more freehanded with grants. And a bigger travel allowance might simply reflect the fact that School A is further from your home than School B.

Figuring the real cost

The first step in determining which school offers the best deal is to identify which type of financial aid (loans, grants and scholarships, or work-study) has been offered.

While the award letter will probably tally all forms of aid together, applicants should separate the "free money" (grants and scholarships) from the "self-help" money (loans and work-study). That's not to dismiss loans and work-study. Student loans, especially if the government subsidizes them, are very inexpensive forms of borrowing. And work-study jobs often have the benefit of being flexible enough to accommodate students' schedules and their need to study at exam time, more so than a job at the local mall would. But they're nonetheless debts that have to be repaid or money that has to be earned.

With both the cost of attendance and the aid figures in hand, students and their families can compute the true out-of-pocket cost of each school by using the worksheet below.

If the school's budget for discretionary expenses doesn't seem reasonable, you will have to create your own estimate: Will you live off campus or skip the school's meal plan? Then you may be able to get by on less than the allotted amount. Will you be able to buy used textbooks or nab cheap airfares home? You may be able to shave a couple hundred dollars off the book or transportation allowance. Record any adjustments to each school's official budget.

Now add up any grants or scholarships and subtract the total from the expected cost of attendance. That's the real cost to attend the school. Compare it with the others on the list. If there's not a great deal of difference—perhaps $1,000 or $2,000 between the schools—then you can feel comfortable choosing on the merits of the school. If the difference is substantial—say, $10,000 or more—you have a tougher choice. Will it mean racking up huge student loan debt? Or do you want to start your adult life out with a degree that perhaps carries less cachet but fewer financial burdens?

Finally, tally up the loans and work-study and subtract that amount from the actual cost to determine how much money you and your parents will have to scrape up to pay for school. This number is important: Once you know exactly how much your family has to pay, it's easier to figure out whether you and your parents can swing it. That could mean withdrawing money from savings, squeezing it out of the family's regular cash flow—by sacrificing vacations, new cars, or home improvements, for instance—borrowing more money, or perhaps a combination of all three. Or it could mean your

The bottom line

	School 1	School 2	School 3
Official cost of attendance			
Adjustments			
Expected cost of attendance			
Subtract grants and scholarships			
Actual cost			
Subtract loans and work-study			
Out-of-pocket cost			

family needs to do some creative thinking, which could include some last-minute strategies like those detailed in Chapter 7.

Even with the numbers in front of you, it can be difficult to weigh one school against another. If the decision still isn't clear, there may be another lever to pull: Financial aid awards aren't always etched in stone.

Can the college do better?

A student who believes the aid package from his or her preferred school comes up short shouldn't be shy about asking the school's financial aid officer to reconsider the offer. "We get thousands of appeals," says Steve Van Ess, director of financial aid at the University of Wisconsin–Madison. At Amherst College, about 21 percent of aid applicants ask the institution to reevaluate their awards, says aid director Joe Paul Case. About 57 percent of them do get some additional aid, averaging about $3,200.

But tread gently. Financial aid officers despise the word "negotiate." They'll tell you in no uncertain terms that they don't play "let's make a deal." Instead, let the aid officer know that you'd like to "appeal" the award or ask him or her to "take another look." No doubt you'll get a friendlier reception.

Students with the best chance of upping a financial aid award typically have concrete reasons for the second look. A vague complaint that the family can't afford the price won't cut it. The formulas that determine a family's expected share of costs aren't perfect, so one way to persuade an aid officer to open the college's wallet again is to show that the formulas overestimated your family's ability to pay. Here are some arguments that aid officers say they'll seriously consider:

- *This year's income will not be as high as last year's.* College aid formulas assume that family income will be fairly steady from year to year. Any family that has experienced a job loss or a downturn in a family business, or will be receiving less overtime pay, should ask the school to rerun the numbers with a more conservative estimate for this year's income. "We will consider looking at estimated income for the coming year, especially if someone has lost their job," says Van Ess. But aim for as accurate a guess as possible. "We may review that [the estimate] after the first semester before we give them second semester aid," he adds. "If the income is higher than they estimated, we may even ask them to give back some of the first-semester money."

- *The family has extraordinary expenses.* The aid formulas allow a standard amount to cover household expenses, based on family size. But using his or her right to exercise "professional judgment," an aid officer can reduce the family contribution by counting atypical spending. "We're eager to consider nondiscretionary extenuating circumstances," says James Belvin, director of financial aid at Duke University. Those circumstances might include helping pay for a grandparent's nursing home care, graduate school for an older sibling or private school for a younger sibling, funeral expenses, or hefty legal or unreimbursed medical bills. But the family won't get much sympathy for discretionary spending like a blowout wedding or bar mitzvah, mortgage payments on a vacation home, or even sizable credit card bills. Aid officers generally view high credit card balances as reflective of debt taken on by choice, not by necessity.

- *Family finances have changed significantly because of a death, divorce, or disability.* Aid officers often boost awards in response to such family emergencies, the very situations the appeal process was designed to remedy. "We're happy to step up to the plate and consider it in detail," says Belvin.

- *The cost of attendance will be higher than budgeted.* Can you argue that the school missed the mark in deciding how much money it would take to get home for winter and summer breaks? That special equipment to accommodate a learning disability or other special need will have to be purchased? That additional travel and personal expenses will be incurred during a semester abroad? Again, asking an aid officer to increase the cost of attendance can improve aid eligibility.

> *"We will consider looking at estimated income for the coming year, especially if someone has lost their job."*

In any event, families should be prepared to document their appeal with tax forms, pay stubs, receipts, or other evidence of the new financial situation. Also, be aware that asking for special consideration may spur extra scrutiny of the original financial aid application. In other words, the family may be asked to document any previous data supplied.

Matching the competition

A student with a superior aid package from a competing school may also have a good shot at augmenting an award.

Helpful Hints

You can decline student loans or work-study jobs. Not everyone wants or needs to borrow as much as they're offered in a financial aid package. And you may prefer not to work during the academic year, or an on-campus job may not be suitable for you. But if you turn down a loan or work-study, the difference won't be made up with grants. You'll have to come up with the money from another source.

But this is another touchy subject among aid officers. It's the rare school, such as Carnegie Mellon University, that openly admits it will consider matching another school's offer. Most say they won't. But somehow, many colleges seem to have an easier time finding a financial reason to rejigger the numbers when they know another institution is dangling a more attractive offer. That's especially true if the student hasn't yet decided which school to attend.

"We're eager to consider nondiscretionary extenuating circumstances."

But again, be careful. A "top this, or else" approach may backfire. Instead, try something like this: "My second choice school sees our need differently. It gave us an extra $3,000. But you're my first choice, and some extra aid would make it possible for me to go here. Could you review our application again to see if there's an error or if anything has been overlooked?"

Of course, this strategy works best when the two schools are of equal stature in terms of admissions standards and reputation. A Duke or a Cornell University, for example, isn't going to waste time discussing an offer from Georgia's Valdosta State University. Students who are deemed a good catch for the school also have an advantage. What's a good catch? Think about what colleges want in their student bodies: brainiacs (students with grades or test scores that put them atop the applicant pool); individuals with special, in-demand talents like artistic or athletic ability; racial and geographic diversity; and a variety of majors.

Last, but not least

Okay, so you don't have any special talent, extenuating circumstances, or better aid offers. (The last will almost certainly be the case if you apply for early decision to a school and thus have only one offer to consider.) But you still believe the expected family contribution is out of line. Students can

Real World Stories

When Phil Barrett's twins were accepted to the University of Southern California last year, the news was bittersweet to the retired Air Force officer from Arizona. Barrett, who now owns an auto repair shop, and his wife, a nurse, didn't think they'd be able to swing the twins' college expenses and those of their eldest son, then a sophomore at the school. Tuition plus room and board for each child at the private university costs roughly $40,000.

Though student loans and various grants would reduce the sticker price for all three, the school expected the couple to chip in $60,000. "I was mortgaging my future," says Barrett.

So Barrett wrote to the university, declining the financial aid package and stating his intention to send all three children to a more affordable public school. He also pointed out in the letter that a $60,000 expected family contribution would leave the family

with only $18,000 to live on. Soon after, a USC financial aid officer called and offered to rework the financial aid package— and the Barretts' contribution was shaved to $40,000. With a $12,000 federally backed parent loan, the Barretts decided they could afford to send all three children to USC, at least this year. "I know in the future, I will have to go back and say, 'I can't afford this,'" he says.

Real World Stories

One college applicant for the 2004–2005 school year found that Carnegie Mellon boosted his aid award not once, but twice. An A-student and talented prospective specialty arts major, the high school senior was a "hot prospect" at both schools on his short list, Carnegie Mellon and the University of Cincinnati. (Total costs at Carnegie Mellon are about $11,000 more than at Cincinnati.) Carnegie Mellon's first offer: a $15,000 merit award, plus Stafford loans and work-study. When Cincinnati chimed in with a $6,000 departmental scholarship (in addition to a university merit award and Stafford loans), Carnegie Mellon replaced his work-study with an additional grant. Then, as the decision-making deadline neared, Cincinnati sweetened its offer with another $1,000.

Carnegie Mellon promptly matched it—which meant both schools were asking for about a $9,000 family contribution—sealing the deal for the freshman. "The appeals process became a bidding war," says the student's mom.

also ask an aid officer to simply explain how the family's need was determined. An aid officer, for instance, may have calculated a certain level of assets using the dividends and interest on the parents' tax return, or he or she may have set the value of the family home based on a national index of home appreciation. But the family may no longer own the assets that generated income in a prior year or may live in an area with below-average home appreciation rates. Asking specific questions, such as how much of the family contribution comes from parents' assets versus student assets, might bring such discrepancies to light. On the other hand, the queries might work against you and turn up an error.

Whatever the approach, be prepared to make your case in writing. These days, it's typical for the financial aid office to ask for a formal letter of appeal, which is then reviewed by a committee rather than a single aid officer. That helps to avoid uneven results based on the "individual idiosyncrasies" of aid officers, says Case.

Chapter Seven

Last-Minute and Alternative Strategies

You now know how the financial aid system can help pave the way to college. But it's not the only route. From bartering to community college to university employee discounts, there are several other tactics that can help whittle down college costs.

Low-cost schools

For many students, the single easiest way to cut the first two years of college costs is to attend a community college. Tuition and fees at two-year schools average about $2,000 a year, less than half of the tuition at a four-year public university and about 10 percent of the tuition at a private college. But it can take a lot of discipline and careful planning to make sure all your courses transfer to a four-year school. That may be one reason why half of the community college students who hope to get a bachelor's degree don't end up transferring to a four-year school.

A student should investigate transfer policies early on. Most community colleges have "articulation agreements" with nearby four-year schools, meaning credits easily transfer between the two institutions. Some of those schools even guarantee admission to local community college students who earn a certain grade point average. But at other four-year schools, only basic introductory courses can transfer.

You might also want to consider starting out at a cheaper state school and then moving on to a private institution. But some schools are even harder to get into as a transfer student than as a regular applicant. Yale University, for example, accepted only 24 transfer students in 2004 from a field of nearly 700—an even smaller percentage than its record-low admit rate of 10 percent for the 2004–2005 freshman class. However, some schools do have informal agreements with neighboring colleges that are worth exploring.

Students who plan to go to, say, medical school or law school might want to think about attending a lower-cost college as an undergraduate and splurging on graduate-level work. When job-hunting time comes, the grad school name, after all, will be more important than where the student earned his or her undergraduate degree. But it doesn't always have a happy ending. "Make sure your student will be happy at the undergraduate school," Sandy Baum, a professor of economics at Skidmore College in Saratoga Springs, New York, and a senior policy analyst for the College Board, advises parents. Despondent students are sometimes at risk of making lower grades, and a less-than-stellar transcript may close the door to that dream graduate school.

The home-state advantage

Everyone knows tuition is cheaper for residents who attend public colleges. But if you don't live in the District of Columbia—undergraduate students from the nation's capital are eligible for in-state tuition in *all* states—don't count on getting that super price away from home. In the late 1990s, most states made it increasingly difficult for carpet-bagging college students to nab in-state tuition rates. William Ehrich, an associate director of financial aid at Indiana University–Bloomington, says some of his out-of-state students are so desperate to qualify for the cheaper tuition that they take a year off after high school, move to Indiana, hold down a job, and then apply as a resident.

If that sounds a bit drastic, some states have tuition-reciprocity agreements. Students from Minnesota, for instance, can attend schools in Wisconsin, South Dakota, North Dakota, or the Canadian province of Manitoba for essentially the in-state price. Other states have similar deals for specific disciplines. Some states partner with one another to provide tuition

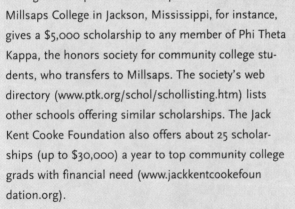

Helpful Hints

Transfer students to four-year colleges may be eligible for special scholarships.

Millsaps College in Jackson, Mississippi, for instance, gives a $5,000 scholarship to any member of Phi Theta Kappa, the honors society for community college students, who transfers to Millsaps. The society's web directory (www.ptk.org/schol/schollisting.htm) lists other schools offering similar scholarships. The Jack Kent Cooke Foundation also offers about 25 scholarships (up to $30,000) a year to top community college grads with financial need (www.jackkentcookefoundation.org).

Alex Gabrovsky thought he'd save $20,000 a year by attending community college. But he ended up saving much more than that. He did so well at Santa Monica College that the University of California–Los Angeles, which had rejected him when he applied as a freshman, gave him a full scholarship for his last two years. "Some of my teachers at Santa Monica also taught at UCLA. And we were using the same textbooks," says Gabrovsky, currently a junior. "So I really felt I was in a serious college environment. Now I'll get my degree from UCLA, and I'll have no stress about college finances."

discounts to students who want to pursue a major not available in their home state. For example, the Academic Common Market, an affiliation of 16 states, allows such students to attend public schools in the other member states for roughly 150 percent of the in-state rate. The College Board's website (www. collegeboard.com/about/association/international/residency. html) has more information about such arrangements.

University employee discounts

Many colleges and universities waive tuition for employees and their dependents. Often these schools require that an employee work for a certain period of time—it could be one, two, or five years, depending on the school—before the benefit kicks in. And part-time employees may not be eligible.

Some schools also allow dependents to get the price cut at an allied institution. Through the Tuition Exchange, a dependent of an employee of Syracuse University, for example, could use the tuition discount at more than 500 other private schools, including Regis University in Denver, Tulane University in New Orleans, and American University in Washington, D.C. The Council of Independent Colleges, a collection of approximately 330 liberal arts schools, also has reciprocal agreements, as do some groups of colleges with religious affiliations (Jesuit colleges, for example) or geographic proximity (several Texas colleges, for example).

The discount usually takes care of the tuition tab, but the family will have to cough up room and board and other expenses. And at some more expensive schools, only part of the tuition cost is covered. Also, many tuition benefits require that the student maintain a minimum grade point average.

Barter

Some colleges allow parents and students to barter for college credits, either directly or through a barter association. Green Apple Barter Services in Pittsburgh, for example, has three colleges in its network along with a number of other local technical and trade schools. Members bank credits in their accounts by providing their products and services, from copiers to dental care. In turn, members redeem their credits for products and services from their fellow barterers. Lindenwood University in St. Charles, Missouri, for example, has a special barter arrangement for kids of cash-strapped farmers. One sophomore's parent who raises cattle traded two beef steers for his daughter's tuition. The steaks and hamburgers went to the cafeteria.

Tuition-free colleges

You may have heard of so-called tuition-free colleges. They do exist, but are few and far between. And there can be a catch.

Bartering was nothing new to Al Houston. The owner of an art and frame shop in Pittsburgh, Houston had been trading his framing services for years as a member of the local Green Apple Barter Services, banking points in his account. In turn, he redeemed the points for computer equipment or advertising from his fellow barterers. Houston mostly swapped his services to nab new customers and give his business an extra boost—until he discovered that Washington and Jefferson College in Washington, Pennsylvania, participated in the network, that is. "It didn't even occur to me that you could do college on trade," says Houston.

The timing was fortuitous. Houston's son, Michael, was a high school senior contemplating premed at the college. Although Houston had set aside some money for Michael's college education, it wasn't enough. At the time, tuition at Washington and Jefferson ran around $18,300, with an additional $4,350 tab for room and board. Houston bartered the entire sum.

But during his sophomore year, Michael decided that premed and Washington and Jefferson were no longer for him.

Wanting to stick close to home, he enrolled at nearby La Roche College (tuition was then $15,220), which receives printing services and vehicles, among other things, through the barter system. The chemistry major commuted from home to help keep a lid on costs. At one point, Michael, attracted by the low interest rate, took out a $3,000 Stafford student loan, but father and son quickly decided there was no need to. "It was silly," says Houston. "We could just do full barter." Michael graduated from La Roche last year.

At Berea College in Kentucky, for instance, students work roughly 10 hours to 15 hours a week on campus or in approved jobs in the community as part of the deal. "We give students jobs related to their majors that help them really get a jump on their careers," says Jay Buckner, Berea's communications manager.

Still, at many of these schools, room and board is not included in the subsidized package. At Berea, the amount a student pays for room and board is determined by financial need. At Cooper Union in New York City, where students enjoy full-tuition scholarships, dorm living for the 2004–2005 school year is about $13,000—and only freshman can live on campus. Upperclassmen have to find housing off campus.

Head north

A Canadian college may be a bargain for some students. Canadian tuition rates for international students vary from province to province, and in some cases, depend on a student's major. For more information about study in Canada, consult the Canadian Embassy's website (www.canadian embassy.org/education). Because most Canadian colleges are accredited by the Department of Education, some forms of financial aid can be used across the Canadian border, such as Stafford and Perkins loans.

Last-minute strategies

You know, you know. Your family should have started socking away money for college years ago. But what with car payments, day care, doctor bills, and everything else, there just never seemed to be much left over. So like the vast majority of families preparing to send a member off to college, you and your parents don't have anywhere near enough saved. Don't despair. Millions of no-savings-account students have managed to earn degrees.

Apply for financial aid

We can't stress it enough. The single most important piece of advice is: Apply for financial aid. You don't get it if you don't ask.

No matter how tedious the form seems, it's worth completing. Although less than half of all those who fill out a FAFSA get a federal grant, it's the first step in qualifying for financial aid, including cheap student loans. Students have an 18-month window to apply for federal aid: For the 2004–2005 school year, for example, students can send in the form from January 1, 2004 through June 30, 2005.

Students planning to attend a private university should also complete the College Board's PROFILE form. Again, you should do it no matter how much your family makes. Don't disqualify yourself. Private schools are aware that even well-off families may have difficulty scraping up tuition money. Peter Riefler, director of financial aid at the Rhode Island School of Design (RISD), often gives aid to students from families earning as much as $145,000 a year. He once gave aid to a student whose parents earned $300,000, although in that case the parents had nine other children, five of whom were in college at the same time. The PROFILE deadlines are typically in February. But even students who miss the deadlines should fill out the forms. Many schools, such as Washington University in St. Louis, set aside a little money for laggards.

Seriously. Fill out the forms. In fact, if you haven't already filled them out, go back and reread Chapter 2, which explains the FAFSA and the financial aid process in detail.

Keep seeking scholarships and contests

It's also never too late to apply for outside aid. While most scholarship applications are due in the winter or early spring, there are several with deadlines in the late spring and summer. Students with a flair for unusual fashion can construct a prom outfit out of Duck brand duct tape to compete for a $2,500 scholarship (www.ducktapeclub.com). TextbookX.com, an online textbook seller, offers three scholarships each April and November to students who write the best essays on questions like "What is a nation?" In the spring of 2004, Anne Chmilewski of Kentucky won $1,500 toward her senior year at University of California–Berkeley by arguing that a nation is made up of people who share the same ideas. Chapter 4 can provide more tips on searching for scholarships.

Play the admissions game

These days, as we've stressed, your attractiveness to the admissions office can often determine how much financial aid you'll receive. If your test scores, grades, or talent will enhance the school's reputation, you are likely to get more scholarships and grants. At RISD, for example, aid director Riefler gets a list of all the soon-to-be-accepted students from the admissions office, ranked by how much the school wants them in its freshman class. He then gives hefty aid packages to the top candidates with financial need. Last spring, Riefler had only $1.9 million worth of grants to hand out to the 802 students admitted to the freshman class. (About half of those students chose to go to another college.) He ran out of money by the time he hit number 195. The best he could do for numbers 196 and below: student loans and work-study jobs. "We just don't have the resources to pay for everybody," says Riefler.

That's why we'll repeat this advice: Include a few "financial safety" schools (schools you can afford, in other words) in your mix. To maximize your aid options, also apply to one or two private colleges for whom you would be a real catch—schools that might need, say, a good bassoonist, or whose average grades and test scores are below yours.

Moonlighting may be harmful

Parents desperate to raise cash often consider taking a second job. But extra income now can reduce the amount of need-based financial aid in future years. Some aid counselors calculate that for every extra dollar a parent earns, taxes and the reduction in need-based aid could eat away as much as 75 cents. So an extra job is generally a good option only for parents of students who won't be getting need-based aid. Meanwhile, parents should check with their current employers about scholarship and tuition assistance programs for dependents.

High schoolers considering a part-time job to get a jumpstart on college cash should also think twice about working

> "We just don't have the resources to pay for everybody."

during the school year. For most students, a much better move is to buckle down, study, and raise grades and test scores. "If you are in your junior or senior year in high school, you are not going to make that much money in a job," says Cliff Neel, director of financial aid at Baylor University. "Higher test scores and better grades will pay off much better."

Look at Baylor's reward for hitting the books. The university awards students who score 1110 on their SATs a four-year scholarship of $6,000 (as long as the recipient maintains a 3.0 grade point average at Baylor). And those who score 1200

get $14,000. Baylor will bump up its scholarships for students who repeat the test and submit higher SAT scores even a few weeks before freshman classes start. "You won't make that kind of money at McDonald's," says Neel.

Once in college, though, working can have its rewards. Chapter 5 has details on how a part-time job can improve academic performance.

Prepay or stretch out payments

It can be very hard to come up with one big lump sum to pay for college, whether it's $10,000 or $40,000. That's why almost every college allows the bill to be paid in monthly installments. There's usually no interest, but schools typically charge a $25 to $50 fee.

Some schools make avoiding inflation painless. The Art Institute of Philadelphia and George Washington University in Washington, D.C., for example, allow students to lock in the first year's tuition rate for all four years to avoid any future price hikes.

At some schools, if you have extra cash, you are likely to save money in the long run if you can prepay future

Real World Stories

When her parents split up, Lenzy Krehbiel of Oklahoma realized she'd have to come up with most of her own cash for college. She scoured websites like FastWeb (www.fastweb.com), where she learned the details about a $2,000 scholarship for students with Cherokee heritage that she eventually won. She also checked with her high school counselor's office for local scholarships that might have

less competition. Smart move: She was the only applicant for a $1,000 scholarship from a local business group.

To save time, she drafted a couple of standard essays, including a quirky 600-or-so word piece about the black and orange stuffed clownfish she used to bring to school to cheer up her classmates and teachers. She tweaked the essays several times to meet the

rules of the different competitions. Krehbiel, a senior at Oklahoma State University, says the essays helped her win $7,500. She also told everyone she knew about her need for financial assistance and, as a result, the church that employed her part time gave her a $250 scholarship. "I've been lucky, but I did have to fill out the applications," says Krehbiel.

New Yorker Shaquieta Boyd was heart-broken in the spring of 2003 when she got her college acceptance letters. None of them offered any financial aid. Then, a recruiter for City Year, an Americorps program, told her she could earn a $4,725 tuition grant by spending a year helping her community. Boyd put off school to tutor kids in the Bronx, using the $250-a-week stipend from Americorps to cover living expenses. When she reapplied to school the next year, CUNY–Baruch College rewarded her with one of its five City Year scholarships, which covered all four years of tuition. "I applied to City Year on the rebound," she recalls. Now she encourages every high school student she meets to consider Americorps.

years' tuition. The Independent 529 Plan, offered by some 250 private schools (including Baylor University, Spelman College, and Wesleyan University), lets parents pay up to four years' of tuition at slightly less than today's rates, as long as they pay at least three years ahead of time. So even if the student is an entering freshman, the family could save about $4,000 if private school tuition keeps rising at today's 6 percent annual rate. A caveat: There's a penalty for withdrawing the money if, say, the student drops out before senior year.

Skip a class or two

Thousands of schools give credit for passing tests such as the College Level Examination Program (CLEP) or Dantes Subject Standardized Tests (DSSTs). For less than a $100 testing fee, a student can get credit for a college course without having to take it, thus saving tuition.

CLEP tests (www.collegeboard.com/clep), which are produced by the College Board, can replace 35 courses ranging from Calculus to Spanish. The tests cost $55 to $80 each, depending on location, and are accepted by 2,900 accredited colleges. The College Board sends the results to one school of the student's choice for free, but charges $20 for each extra report sent out.

DSSTs (www.getcollegecredit.com) are accepted at 1,900 schools and cost $60. That amount includes the cost of sending the score to one school; additional copies are $20 each. There are 37 different DSSTs, many of which cover introductory college courses. But some DSSTs can replace career-oriented courses such as Criminal Justice and upper-level courses such as the Rise and Fall of the Soviet Union.

It might behoove students to spring for the study guides—priced between $10 and $25—as none of the tests are complete snaps. About 75 percent of DSST test-takers pass; the College Board says that the vast majority of its takers pass the Spanish tests, but most students flunk its calculus test.

Avoid raiding the piggy bank

Often, the most tempting solution for parents is to cash out what little savings they have to pay the first year's college bills. That can be a costly mistake. Retirement savings, for example, should almost never be used, financial advisors agree. Withdrawing money from a 401(k), for example, usually triggers big financial penalties. And although parents won't pay a tax penalty now for tapping a Roth IRA, it will cost them big down the road when they don't have enough to retire on. "The worst thing that could happen is that your parents would have to call you up in 10 or 20 years and say, 'We got you through college. Now can we move in?'" says Pat Thornton, a financial planner with the Fleischer Jacobs Group in South Burlington, Vermont.

Real World Stories

When Jacob Lauser returned to the University of Arizona in 2002 after working for two years, he was dismayed to learn he would have to take a bunch of introductory courses to meet the school's new requirements. Then he remembered the College Level Examination Program, or CLEP, tests. Lauser, who has worked as a computer techie, had no problem passing the Information Systems Management test cold. But it took the Arizonian several weeks to read history books and go through the study guides before taking the English and history tests. Still, the effort was worth it. Lauser helped lower his tuition bill and plans to graduate at least a semester early by testing out of seven courses. Testing out, he says, "is the best kept secret in college."

Pinch pennies

Families willing to make some serious lifestyle sacrifices—no more cable TV, restaurant meals, fancy lattes, vacations, and the like—can typically generate several thousand dollars a year in savings, says Rick Darvis, founder of College Funding, a financial aid consulting firm in Plentywood, Montana. A less painful way to reduce monthly expenses is to consolidate car and credit card debts into a home equity line, he says. Chris Borzych, a certified financial planner for USAA in San Antonio, also recommends that parents of new college students reevaluate their life insurance policies. Now that Junior is almost grown up, parents typically need less coverage, and thus might be able to reduce monthly payments or take something out of a cash value account.

Ask Grandma

Many people find it hard to ask for money from others. But students and parents shouldn't be shy about mentioning their need for tuition assistance to relatives, friends, and neighbors. Everybody who's ever had to pay a college bill knows had hard it can be, and many are surprisingly generous. Besides, grandparents who are trying to shield their assets from estate taxes might relish a chance to hand out some largesse. They are each allowed to give up to $11,000 tax free to a child or grandchild each year. And if they haven't taken advantage of the gift exemption in the last five years, Grandma and Grandpa can front-load a 529 savings plan with up to five years' worth of gifts.

Try public service

Students who want to serve their country by joining the military can earn big tuition credits. (For more details, see Chapter 10.) Those who want to serve at home can join Americorps (www.americorps.org). Students spend one year working on projects like tutoring inner-city kids or helping with hurricane relief. They get an annual stipend (usually $10,000) to cover basic living expenses. After they finish, they receive a $4,725 grant toward tuition if they enroll in college within seven years. Many colleges, including Clark University in Worcester, Massachusetts, and Evergreen State College in Olympia, Washington, offer extras such as matching grants or course credit, which saves Americorps veterans even more time and money. While Americorps deadlines are as early as November 30 for programs that start the following August or September, some deadlines are more flexible. City Year (www.cityyear.org), an Americorps program in several major cities, for example, will take applications even in July for its mid-August sessions.

Start saving

It may not be too late to start a 529 savings plan or a Coverdell Education Savings Account. Parents of college freshmen need to think about funding the junior and senior year, as well as—don't faint—law school or other graduate study. Parents can kick start the 529 savings account by asking relatives to make donations in lieu of Christmas and birthday presents. Bruce Harrington, head of 529 savings plans for the mutual fund company MFS Investment Management in Boston, has no qualms about alerting his relatives: "I've told them. No more toys for Christmas. I'd rather have $100 in their 529 than have another toy to trip over." (Chapter 1 has details about 529s.) And the various rebate programs such as Upromise and BabyMint can help. While the rebates typically aren't bonanzas, another $100 or so a year is certainly nothing to sneeze at.

Chapter Eight

The Hidden Costs of College

You've already forked over money—lots of money—for tuition, room, and board. Isn't that enough?

Nope, sorry. You'll need a computer. And textbooks. And airline tickets home for Thanksgiving. And pocket change for the laundry machine. And a pizza every once in a while.

The cost of attending college is much more than the fixed costs charged by the school. Often it is even more than the estimated cost of attendance we explain in Chapter 6. Trouble is, it can be difficult to be precise when tabulating students' ancillary expenses.

So what kind of extra costs should college bill-payers realistically expect? And how on earth can a student live on a shoestring budget when one chemistry textbook alone costs $183? Take a deep breath, and read on.

Textbooks

Books, books, books. It's the college expense that never seems to end. According to "Rip-off 101," a report released in early 2004 by the State Public Interest Research Groups' Higher Education Project, the average student in the University of California system spends $898 on textbooks each year. And that's typical. The figure is up 40 percent from seven years ago, a jump the report attributes to the practice of bundling textbooks with CD-ROMs and workbooks that never escape their shrink-wrap. Also, new editions of old books drive up prices by making last year's version useless.

Of course, used books have always been a low-cost alternative. Instead of relying on campus bookstores, which often buy back books from students at low prices and resell them at a profit, many schools have online book exchanges that eliminate the middleman. At Brown University's bookstore last year, a new edition of *The Norton Shakespeare, Based on the Oxford Edition: Tragedies*, for example, sold for $42.60. A used version went for $31.95. The Brown Daily Jolt textbook exchange, however, hawked the book for $25.

The main problem with campus book exchanges—and relying on a campus bookstore for used tomes—is limited supply. Luckily, there are books lurking in dorm rooms in every state, so wider Internet book exchanges can be another boon for students looking for a bargain. Bigwords.com has a search engine that scours prices for used and new books all over the Web. And buyers should also peruse Half.com by eBay, where students can buy directly from a worldwide network of used booksellers.

When it proves impossible to find a used book—especially when a teacher demands a newly published title—try book behemoths like Amazon.com, Barnesandnoble.com, and Walmart.com. They can often undercut smaller bookstores as long as shipping doesn't get too expensive. And international sites (like Amazon.co.uk) usually have dramatically lower prices than their U.S. counterparts. Some websites, like Bookcentral.com, specialize in the sale of textbooks bought on the cheap from overseas vendors.

Of course, a student can always share a book with a friend or head to the library. Many schools have a few copies of all required reading material available on reserve, meaning they can be checked out for a few hours at a time. Yes, it's a hassle, but it's free.

Fees

For many colleges, tuition covers only basic lectures. Anything on top of that may cost more. Chemistry labs, for example, usually require an extra fee. Such supplemental class expenses are rising all over the country. At California State University–Long Beach, for example, the extra fees students pay for geology classes and film class screenings have been climbing in concert with tuition, says Bursar Nancy Eckhous. And, increasingly, cash-strapped colleges are socking students with a variety of a la carte fees. At Hartwick College in Oneonta, New York, for instance, one student faced a $50 fee for a pianist who spent extra time helping her rehearse for a singing recital.

Students participating in extracurricular activities should expect to pay something out of pocket these days. If you're not good enough to make the varsity soccer team at Penn State University but want to play soccer, it cost $260 last year to play with the club team. The university's spelunking club, the Nittany Grotto cavers, charges $15 a year. And you have to bring your own flashlight.

Colleges can no longer afford to indulge wasteful or tardy students. After watching its paper costs skyrocket, the University of Oregon, which has been attempting to hold the line on fees, started charging for computer lab

During the spring of 2004, Danny Yagan, then a sophomore at Harvard University, was stunned by the roughly $100 price tag on a textbook he needed for a macroeconomic theory course. Searching online, he found a European website selling the book for $40 less than the campus bookstore. "It was crazy," Yagan recalls. So Yagan and seven similarly frustrated friends created Redline Textbooks (www.redlinetextbooks.com), an online bookstore for Harvard students. The students import most of the textbooks from overseas— so far, the business is mostly limited to economic and science tomes—undercutting campus bookstore prices. "We might expand to Harvard Law School or the Medical School, or even beyond," says Yagan.

printouts in 2002. And woe to those who dillydally before deciding to drop a class. Some private schools demand that students who wait until the third week of school to drop a class forfeit 40 percent of the tuition, an average of—gulp!—$800.

Computers

Having the right computer on campus is as important as buying the right textbook. While students still use their PCs as glorified typewriters, taking notes and cranking out term papers, they also use them to sign up for classes, study course materials, email instructors, send instant messages to classmates, and play the latest movies and music. Students headed to college will most likely be buying a new computer. Some students don't have to worry because their institution provides one. All students at Stillman College in Tuscaloosa, Alabama, for example, are handed an Apple iBook on Day 1.

Before buying a computer, make sure it works well with the other computers, networks, and software on campus. For example, if the college has gone wireless, a compatible connection to take advantage of the Internet access offered in classrooms, libraries, and dorms is key. Check the college website for details. Massachusetts Institute of Technology's, for example, lists configuration recommendations plus specific computers that the university has deemed compatible.

College students can nab numerous discounts on computers, often negotiated by the school with particular manufacturers. Finding these deals may take some sleuthing. Check the school's and manufacturers' websites. The online Apple Store for Education has webpages customized for thousands of schools. School bookstores usually boast excellent deals. And in the hot summer months, many retail computer stores offer back-to-school sales.

The question of whether to buy a desktop or a laptop may have plagued previous generations of buyers, but it's a no-brainer for college students today. Laptops win hands down, as they are chock full of power and memory—and they save space in cramped dorm rooms. Wireless connectivity is a must. Most current notebook models come with built-in access to the popular Wi-Fi wireless technology. If you're buying a laptop that has Wi-Fi as an option, get it; it will be well worth it. Consider, too, the software programs that come with each machine. The computer could house an impressive library or a recording studio. If there's some wiggle room in the budget, spring for a larger display. Choosing a 14-inch screen over a 12-inch one may cost an extra couple of hundred bucks, but your eyes will thank you.

When Haley Bevers decided to attend Texas Tech University in her hometown of Lubbock in 2001, her parents bought her a new Ford Explorer. "Being local, there's an automatic assumption that travel would be cheaper for me," she says. Wrong. Bevers spends more than $1,400 a year on gas, parking permits, and maintenance for her SUV. And that's just the beginning. Over the past year, for example, Bevers flew to conferences related to her major in Dallas, Denver, and Philadelphia, drove to three sorority retreats, and vacationed with her family in Lake Tahoe.

Travel

Travel expenses can take a large bite out of a budget, even if the student lives close to school, walks everywhere, and doesn't give a hoot about spring break. Many students want to get a career edge by attending conferences in their chosen field, interviewing for jobs, or interning in far-away cities.

Because there's no one-stop-shop for cheap tickets, students who fly to and from school need to become savvy comparison shoppers. "For the most part, students have to use the same techniques that people of any age use," says Ed Perkins, author of *Business Travel When It's Your Money*. The old standby of calling travel agents and visiting the major online sites—Travelocity, Expedia, and Orbitz—to dig for deals still applies. These sites will keep students apprised of deals via email.

And don't forget low-cost airlines: Most offer low fares that are free of pesky length-of-stay restrictions. Most of the really good airfares on major airlines are for travel within a 30-day period—a difficult scenario for students considering three-month summer stays. Student travel agencies can sometimes help get around the restriction, as they negotiate special ticket arrangements with the airlines. Such agencies are often located near campuses, like STA Travel (www.statravel.com). With their flexible schedules, students can take advantage of Tuesday-through-Thursday flights and red-eye or midday flights, when fares are usually cheapest. And, of course, there are always frequent flier miles. If your home or college is a hub for one of the major airlines, you'll probably want to join its frequent flier program.

Cellphones

In this age of cellphones and high-speed Internet connections, the college student's phone bill isn't what it used to be. Many students opt to ditch their landlines in favor of cellphones. Today's national calling plans can make cellphones a money-saving choice for long-distance calls.

Parents who want their far-flung offspring to call home easily may want to consider a national service for multiple members of the family. But keep in mind that Junior won't just be calling Mom and Dad. With many plans offering unlimited "in-network" calling—customers have an infinite number of minutes to chat with people using the same service provider—it might be worth it to wait until the student's first week of school to make a decision on a phone. Certain service providers tend to be more popular on particular campuses because of stronger signals, a bevy of nearby stores, or school-sponsored discounts, especially in more rural areas. With many students living a vampire-like existence—studying and socializing into the wee hours—plans with unlimited night and weekend minutes might also be a good bet.

Parents uncomfortable giving their child carte blanche when it comes to long-distance calling may appreciate prepaid national plans. They typically charge a credit card each month for a fixed amount of minutes. If the monthly limit is met, more minutes can be added automatically or service can be cut off until the next month.

Prepaid calling cards also offer another way to avoid phone bill surprises. But take care in using them. Many prepaid calling cards impose a surcharge when used with a pay phone. And be mindful when comparing rates on the calling cards. The ones that seem to have the lowest cost may have hidden connection charges. For tips on how to choose a calling card and how to use it wisely, visit the website (www.consumer-action.org) of Consumer Action, a San Francisco–based nonprofit.

Healthcare

Picking a health insurance plan for your college years is like taking a frustrating multiple choice test: More than one answer may be correct—or none of them may be. Generally,

the easiest and perhaps best thing for most students is to continue coverage under their parents' policy. Full-time students are typically covered under most policies until the age of 23.

But be forewarned: If a parent belongs to an HMO with a local network of providers, the student may not be covered for anything outside the plan's service area except emergency care. A more open plan, like a preferred provider organiza-

"Many [health insurance] plans offered by colleges are pretty barebones."

tion, may allow students to see doctors near school, but that may rack up hefty out-of-network charges.

Most colleges offer some type of health insurance plan, with the student health center acting as the primary care provider. Many schools require enrollment if the student is not covered under any other plan. But check the plan carefully. "Many plans offered by colleges are pretty bare bones," says Mila Kofman, assistant research professor at Georgetown University's Health Policy Institute in Washington, D.C. How bare is the care? Physicals, gynecological visits, and other preventive care may not be covered. College plans also may not cover preexisting conditions, leaving you to underwrite your asthma medication or X-rays when that old knee injury flares up. Lifetime limits on coverage may be significantly lower, too.

Some students may want to consider adding the college policy to supplement Mom and Dad's plan. The college plan could pay for mental health services, for example, for much less money than the out-of-network cost under the parents' plan. But keep the parental policy for its higher lifetime limits, better drug coverage, and lack of exclusions on coverage of certain conditions. Annual premiums can range from $300 up to $3,000.

Individual insurance policies are also worth investigating. As premiums rise with age and illness, plans for the young

Helpful Hints

National cellphone plans can be a wise choice for a college student. But be sure to learn about coverage areas before choosing a provider. The more isolated campuses aren't covered by some cellphone companies, which could translate into hefty roaming charges. "On big campuses you'll usually be fine," says Sam Simon, chairman of the Telecommunications Research & Action Center, a non-profit group based in Washington, D.C. "But in more remote areas this can be a major issue."

and healthy can run as low as $30 a month, rising to $200 or $300 a month depending on the size of the deductible and whether the student suffers from a serious medical condition like diabetes. Read the fine print carefully: These policies may not cover preexisting conditions for a year and may exclude other conditions as well.

Living off campus

Many students naturally prefer apartment living to the typical stark, cramped, outdated dorm room. And for most students, the sales pitch comes junior year. They ask their parents if they can move off campus, typically with a gaggle of friends. The clincher: The move will be a major money-saver.

But will it really? Off-campus living can often be steep for students and parents who are already straining to pay tuition. According to a 2002 Washington State University study, off-campus students underestimated their expenses by 25 percent to 50 percent. That's because students forget about what comes standard with a dorm room, such as furniture and electricity.

Ditching the dorm may be more of a problem for students in large cities. At Boston University, for example, room and board on campus last year ranged from $6,000 to $8,000 per year, depending on the residence hall. By contrast, an off-campus studio apartment in Boston averaged $950 per month. Even at Auburn University in tiny Auburn, Alabama, on-campus housing cost $2,730 to $2,860 per student, a fee that includes utilities, basic cable, and telephone service. Students living in nearby shared apartments paid $300 a month—$3,600 for a 12-month lease—or $700 for a two-bedroom duplex.

At some schools, on-campus housing isn't available for upperclassmen. In those cases, some parents choose to become landlords, an attractive option considering the low mortgage rates of late. Real estate in most college towns is enjoying healthy growth, and with rising enrollments, a reversal is unlikely. Buying such places, dubbed "kiddie con-dos" by some agents, can be a lucrative investment. "If they've got the money for the down payment, without question it always makes sense to buy," says Gail Lyons, a broker-owner at Boulder Real Estate Services in Colorado.

Study abroad

More American students than ever before are hitting the road to study at higher educational institutions in other countries. Many go to perfect a foreign language or to gain new perspective on their major. And there's plenty of scholarship money to help intrepid students. In 2000, for example, Congress created the Benjamin A. Gilman Scholarship, a merit scholarship for overseas study for Pell grant students. And many international schools now offer shorter, cheaper stints overseas.

Students should start planning their trips at least a year ahead of time. Countries like the United Kingdom, Spain, and Italy still attract the most American students, but cheaper hubs like China, the Czech Republic, and Costa Rica are rising in popularity. The American Institute for Foreign Study, for example, offers a program for the 2004–2005 school year in the U.K. for $12,495 a semester, while its Czech program is $8,995. Many programs include room and board, but students who stay with a host family can save big bucks. Some costs like vaccinations and special medical insurance may up the tab a notch, but often the low general cost of living balances the scales. To find programs, visit the website of IIEPassport (www.iiepassport.org).

Heading to the study abroad office—a staple on many college campuses—is a must. Some schools allow students to transfer their financial aid to domestic universities hosting programs abroad, while others organize their own programs. The University of Minnesota has a comprehensive scholarship directory (www.umabroad.umn.edu/financial/scholarships) that lists travel grants sponsored by such groups as the Japan–America Foundation and the Rotary Club. And of course, slicing time spent overseas keeps the price in check. A four-week performing arts summer program in 2005 at Accademia dell'Arte in Tuscany costs $5,400, while a full semester is $13,400.

Credit cards

Whether parents like it or not, 4 out of 5 kids graduate from college with something more than a diploma: a wallet full of credit cards. By senior year, the average undergraduate has racked up more than $3,200 in debt, spread out over six cards. Based on a typical interest rate of 21 percent, such a debt accrues almost $700 in annual interest charges.

Yet even if students are intent on getting plastic (which they are), and even if they occasionally run up balances (which they do), there are ways to reduce some of the costs of credit. While adults have been taught to shop for credit cards based on rates, rebates, and fees, students typically aren't so choosy. They simply sign up with whichever bank sends them a preapproval letter or whichever booth on campus flags them down with a juicy enticement. "Don't automatically go to the first campus booth that's offering T-shirts or Slinkys to pick your card," says Jim Tehan, a spokesman for Myvesta.org, a credit counseling firm in Rockville, Maryland.

Parents should help their college-bound kids shop for a card with the best terms.

For a list of banks willing to extend credit to students, visit Bankrate.com. The trick is to focus on cards with the lowest rates, not rebates, since kids don't need incentives to spend. The typical student may pay a rate between 18 percent and 21 percent, but some banks charge less.

A debit card, which deducts money from a bank account, offers some of the conveniences of a credit card, and students may want to use one for smaller, frequent purchases. Of course, another alternative is to give kids an additional credit card on a parent's account—a sure-fire way to monitor spending and payments.

But there is a benefit in a student having his or her own credit card, as using it responsibly helps build the necessary credit history for postgraduation borrowing to buy cars or homes. Kids should be made aware, however, that mishandling cards can lead to black marks on credit reports, which may mean higher interest costs on those car loans and mortgages.

Many banks will bump up the interest rate because of one late payment. They'll also slap on a penalty fee, which can run as high as $49 a pop. Students should consider taking advantage of their friend, the Internet. Many card issuers offer email reminders and free online bill payment.

Real World Stories

In early 2002, Genie Lomize thought a semester studying abroad was out of the question. A University of Michigan junior at the time, Lomize was paying her tuition by working two jobs—as a house-painting supervisor and a law assistant—and there wasn't much income left over. But Lomize was able to cobble together enough scholarship money to spend a semester studying in Warsaw and a summer interning in Krakow. "I even did some souvenir shopping on the side," she says. Lomize netted $1,500 from the University of Michigan's Center for Russian and East European Studies, $1,500 from the school's study abroad office, and $5,400 from the David L. Boren scholarship, a government program for students interested in national security. (Lomize had to agree to work for a federal government agency or in higher education for a few months after graduation.) And the company overseeing the Warsaw program pitched in a $1,200 tuition waiver.

Social life

Budgeting for play is no game. Many schools seem to be Scrooges when it comes to guessing how much moola students will need for R & R. The University of Notre Dame, for example, deems $900 a year sufficient. That should cover an occasional cheese pizza, but you're on your own if you want double pepperoni, says Joseph Russo, director of Notre Dame's student financial services, jokingly.

Students in more isolated communities can generally get along on $1,000 a year or so. But Rick Darvis, founder of College Funding, a financial aid counseling firm in Plentywood, Montana, says that students near cities with temptations like nightclubs and nice restaurants might want to pencil in as much as $3,000. Even small entertainment costs can add up quickly. In many big cities, seeing half a dozen movies a semester quickly adds up to $60. Even do-gooder spring breaks aren't free. Students spending the spring holiday working for Habitat for Humanity are responsible for their own transportation. Add to that a $15 Habitat deposit, $10 a day for food, and typically $100 for accommodations and building materials.

Sororities and fraternities

Here's one thing not mentioned in flicks like *Legally Blonde* and *Animal House:* Greek life costs money. In addition to dues each semester, most fraternities and sororities charge new members an initiation fee and a national pledge fee. A new pledge to Alpha Chi Omega at the University of Wisconsin–Madison, for example, pays $925 in dues and fees the first semester and $562 for each subsequent semester.

In some cases, living in a sorority or fraternity house might be worth considering. Fraternities and sororities at Northwestern University, for example, tend to price the rent in line with dorm living, says Mark D'Arienzo, associate director of university housing administration. And at the University of North Carolina–Chapel Hill, sorority and fraternity housing is roughly equal to—and in some instances, cheaper than—off-campus digs. What's more, "our houses have furniture, high-speed Internet connections, and in-house chefs," says Jay Anhorn, director of Greek affairs at the college.

Chapter Nine

Education Tax Breaks

Anyone who has slogged through the rules regarding federal tax breaks for higher education may well feel they deserve a B.A. in tax demystification. Because of the patchwork way in which these credits and deductions became law, there are several ways to get back from Uncle Sam some of the money you've spent on educational expenses. Trouble is, each has its own complicated set of limitations and eligibility rules. "After first figuring out the breaks you qualify for, you may then have to choose among various competing ones," says former Internal Revenue Service commissioner Fred Goldberg, a partner in the law firm Skadden, Arps in Washington, D.C.

Another problem: With Congress and the White House calling the shots, the rules can change from year to year, or even expire. So you'll have to keep abreast of any program reincarnations, including changing income caps for eligibility. That's not to mention any new initiatives that might be dreamed up to make college more affordable.

But confusing or not, it can pay to get acquainted with terms such as the "Hope" and "Lifetime Learning" tax credits. And even if you rely on an accountant or other tax preparer to do the calculations, understanding the rules can help you qualify for the tax favors.

Even if they haven't saved a dime for college, the tax code can provide succor for parents feeling the sting of rising tuitions. Of course, it's always good to know about these incentives ahead of time. For example, when first starting to map out a college savings strategy. But in many cases, past financial habits do not matter when claiming them.

The tax breaks come in two forms: Some are credits, which offset taxes dollar for dollar. For example, a $1,500 credit equals a $1,500 tax savings. Others are in the form of a deduction, which reduces the amount of income on which tax is assessed. Depending on income and other circumstances, the credits and deductions can often be claimed on the tax return of the parents of a college student, a relative who provides support, or a self-supporting student. However, a family has to choose from among some of the tax benefits.

Hope credit

This credit can slice as much as $1,500 off a tax bill. But it's available only during the freshman and sophomore years of college (or qualifying vocational school) and gradually diminishes after income reaches a certain level. On returns for the 2004 tax year, the credit phases out between $85,000 and $105,000 in adjusted gross income for a couple and between $42,000 to $52,000 for a single taxpayer. Here's how it works: The first $1,000 of tuition and fees paid chop a tax bill by $1,000, then the taxpayer can claim 50 percent of the next $1,000. In other words, $2,000 in expenses can save $1,500 in tax. For parents with two kids in college at the same time, the credit can mean getting back $3,000 of tuition.

Lifetime Learning credit

This credit can also directly reduce your tax—by as much as $2,000. It's available for any year of college, including graduate school and even part-time enrollment. But there are some big catches. While parents can claim a Hope credit for each child who qualifies, they can only claim $2,000 a year in total Lifetime credits for the family, no matter how many students they support. And the Lifetime credit is calculated under a stingier formula than the Hope. Only 20 percent of

Real World Stories

When Hank and Eileen Lillis filled out their 2003 tax forms, they were disappointed to learn that their income made them ineligible to shave $2,000 off their taxes with the Lifetime Learning credit. But the New York couple was able to use the tuition deduction for their daughter Danielle's junior year at Syracuse University. "You need every break you can get," says Hank, a sales manager at a major electronics company. Their 2003 deduction saved nearly $1,000 in federal income tax and the couple will benefit from another deduction for 2004. But Hank and Eileen, a nurse, won't be off the hook. Nearing college age is their other daughter, Jennifer. "We hope a tax break will still be around," he says. "It helps."

the first $10,000 in tuition and fees may be claimed. So a $5,000 expense saves $1,000 in tax; a $10,000 or greater expense saves the maximum $2,000. Nevertheless, if tuition is high, the Lifetime credit may be better than the Hope for a freshman or sophomore. But a taxpayer will have to do the calculations to determine which of the credits is more favorable. Also, the income limits that restrict the use of the Hope credit apply to the Lifetime credit too.

The tuition deduction

The Hope and Lifetime Learning credits generally save the most tax. But some people may welcome this alternative tax deduction for 2004 and 2005, which can be claimed for as much as $4,000 of tuition and fees. For someone in the 25 percent tax bracket, a $4,000 reduction in taxable income might save $1,000 in taxes. This deduction is appealing to people whose level of income bars them from the credits or who are constrained by the Lifetime credit's family limit. But as with all these givebacks, there are income ceilings. A $4,000 deduction is allowed only if income is $130,000 or less on a joint

return or $65,000 or less on a single return. People with higher incomes, but not more than $160,000 on a joint return or $80,000 on a single return, are limited to a $2,000 deduction. And these income caps are all-or-nothing; there is no gradual phase-out. And remember: Even taxpayers who don't itemize deductions can still claim this deduction and the fixed standard deduction. However, a choice must be made among this tuition deduction and the Hope or Lifetime credits. Only one can be claimed for the same student in the same year.

Savings bonds

Now here's what might be a pleasant surprise. Interest that has accumulated on Series EE or Series I U.S. savings bonds can be tax exempt if the bonds are cashed in and the proceeds used for a dependent's tuition. School bills needn't have been the original purpose for buying the bonds. "If you happen to cash in the bonds during a year in which you are paying tuition expenses, you may be able to exclude the interest from tax," says Stephen Meyerhardt, a public affairs officer with the U.S. Treasury's Bureau of the Public Debt.

And now, those inevitable restrictions: The exemption only applies to bonds bought in 1990 or later by someone at least 24 years of age at the time of purchase. And the benefit is gradually reduced if income exceeds a certain level during the year the bonds are redeemed. The range at which the tax exemption phases out for 2004 is $89,750 to $119,750 on a joint return and $59,850 to $74,850 on a single return (including the bond interest). This exemption can be claimed along with the education credits and deductions, but a taxpayer can't double-dip by covering the same expenses.

Using that nest egg

Parents who have been diligent about saving for college should be sure to take advantage of any tax breaks on withdrawals from their stockpiles. Money in a Coverdell Education Savings Account, for example, can be tax free when used for tuition, books, room and board, and required equipment such as a computer. Income limits may be a curb when making contributions but not when the account is tapped. Money used for schooling from 529 savings plans or prepaid tuition plans is also not taxed.

Interest deduction on education loans

Uncle Sam also has a graduation present for students: Help with paying off those loans they racked up through college. Up to $2,500 a year of interest on government or private loans may be tax deductible if the borrowing paid for tuition, room and board, and other expenses—even transportation to and from school. The interest deduction is available even to people who don't itemize. Parents may be able to claim the interest deduction on education loans they incurred on behalf of a dependent.

The deductions do, however, phase out when 2004 income is between $100,000 and $130,000 on a joint return and $50,000 and $65,000 on a single return. And that $2,500 is the maximum combined deduction for a married couple, even when both spouses are paying off a student loan. Only the person legally obligated to pay back the loan can take the deduction, and the money can't be borrowed from a relative. What's more, a revolving line of credit or other similar account must be utilized exclusively for education expenses to qualify as an education loan, and adjustments may have to be made if other education tax benefits

Helpful Hints

When parental income is too high to qualify for the education tax credits or the tuition deduction, accountant and financial planner Jonathan Gassman of Gassman & Golodny in New York suggests trying a tactic that one of his clients used recently. The couple gave stock to their son, who sold the shares at a low capital gains tax rate and used the money to pay his tuition. The sale shifted enough taxable income to the son so that he could benefit from claiming a tax credit while his parents couldn't. However, under IRS rules, the student's parents had to waive a dependent exemption for him in order for him to claim the credit. But that didn't hurt because their hefty income made them ineligible to fully use the forsaken dependent exemption anyhow.

are utilized. Phew. And you thought making the dean's list was tough.

Individual schools may provide help navigating this forest, and the National Association of Student Financial Aid Administrators offers an online *Tax Benefits Guide* at www.nasfaa.org (click a link in the "shortcuts" box). The IRS has assembled information on eligibility, qualifying expenses, and the required forms to use in Publication 970, *Tax Benefits for Education*. It is available online at www.irs.gov or by calling the IRS at (800) 829-3676.

Chapter Ten

Nontraditional Students and Circumstances

What if you're not the typical college student? Lots of the advice in this book applies to you, anyway. But there are special considerations for older students, veterans, international students, children of divorced parents, and others who may find some twists and turns on the path to financial aid.

Independent students

Your parents may remember a time when it was relatively easy to qualify for lots of financial aid by becoming an "independent" student. When they were college age, their parents could stop claiming them as a dependent on tax returns, give them less than $700 or so per year, no longer house them

---

"The ones where there is a disagreement in the family are the ones we really can't help with."

---

during the summer, and bingo! Schools would then no longer count the parents' income and assets when figuring the student's financial need.

No more. In the 1990s, the federal government decided that it was giving too much aid to families that had the means to pay college expenses. So it changed the rules, making it much tougher to qualify as an independent undergraduate. Today, you're considered independent only if you:

- are age 24 or older
- are a veteran of the armed services
- are an orphan or have been a ward of the court
- are married
- have a child or other dependent
- are in graduate school

That leaves you in a tough spot if you're officially "dependent," but your parents can't or won't contribute to college expenses. Even if you live on your own, schools will expect your parents to fill out the Free Application for Federal Student Aid (FAFSA) and any other required forms and will compute your expected family contribution (EFC) based on their resources. Financial aid officers have the leeway to grant an exception, but they seldom do, unless circumstances are dire—your parents are incarcerated, missing, or severely abusive, for instance.

"For a student to be independent, there has to be irreparable damage to the family unit," says Pamela Fowler, director of the office of financial aid for the University of Michigan. And "that has to be fully documented by a third party," she adds.

If you think your own situation might warrant an exception, see a financial aid officer and be prepared to document your case with police records and/or written statements from social workers, guidance counselors, or clergy. If you do qualify as independent, only your income and assets will count toward the EFC, and you'll probably benefit from a hefty aid package.

What won't earn you independent status is a family rift over your choice of school or your boyfriend or girlfriend, or a parent's flat-out refusal to contribute. "The ones where there is a disagreement in the family are the ones we really can't help with," says Susan Little, director of the office of student financial aid at the University of Georgia.

Students who thus wind up with no aid and no parental support don't have it easy, and some do give up. But many students make it through college anyway by seeking merit-based aid, working long hours on top of class work, borrowing heavily, or choosing low-cost options, such as a community college for two years and then a state school.

Divorced or separated parents

Few things are fuzzier than financial aid for children of divorced parents. Federal rules are straightforward, but many schools (especially private schools) depart from those rules when giving out their own need-based aid. So it's not unusual for aid offers to differ dramatically from school to school, depending on whose income counts and whose doesn't.

The federal rules say that if your parents are divorced, you should report the income and assets of the parent with whom you lived more than half the time last year on the FAFSA. The family income will include any alimony or child support the custodial parent receives. But even with those additions, students who live with single parents often qualify for more aid than those whose parents are married or remarried.

If the parent you live with is remarried, you must also report your stepparent's income and assets, even if he or she won't be contributing to your college expenses. The wedding might have been last month and your stepparent might have other children to support, but the federal formulas count his or her resources regardless. That means your eligibility for Pell grants, subsidized Stafford loans, and other federal and state aid will depend on your parent's and stepparent's combined income and assets.

What complicates matters further is that many private colleges (especially the most selective colleges) also ask for financial information from your noncustodial parent and, sometimes, your noncustodial stepparent. Some schools will merely file away this information and still conform to the federal rules. Others will consider replacing the custodial stepparent's resources with the noncustodial parent's resources, especially if the remarriage was recent, when determining how much institutional aid to give. And a few have been known to increase the family contribution on the basis of the noncustodial parent's income and assets. "The methodology is all over the map," says Linda Peckham, director of communications and training in the Reston, Virginia, office of the College Board. "The College Board approach [which a majority of the most selective schools follow] is to use two parents, either the two natural parents or the two custodial parents," says Peckham. "It's up to the aid officer to decide which are the appropriate ones."

What if a parent or stepparent refuses to supply financial information? Schools are hard-nosed about this. Usually an incomplete aid application means no aid, which often puts students in the position of pleading with their parents to complete the forms. But as with independent students, aid officers will occasionally make an exception. If you can document parental abandonment, alcoholism, chemical dependency, physical abuse, or other dire circumstances, you may be able

to get a waiver that will allow you to receive aid without the parent's or stepparent's cooperation.

What if your parents are separated but not divorced? For federal aid, they'll be treated as divorced so long as you can show they live at different addresses. But for institutional aid, the school once again has discretion. "We don't accept [divorced] applications from separated parents," says the University of Michigan's Fowler. "We found they file separated and never divorce." But the University of Georgia will accommodate even newly separated parents whose most recent tax return was filed jointly. To compute family income, the school will take out the percentage of income and taxes paid that belong to the noncustodial parent, says Little.

Such varying policies can lead to vastly different aid packages from the schools you apply to. As a result, it's important to ask financial aid officers ahead of time whose income and assets will count. That will give you a good sense up front about which school is likely to offer the most generous aid. And there's always a chance that you can persuade an aid officer to, say, replace your stepfather's income with your

Helpful Hints ;)

Stepparents or noncustodial parents are sometimes reluctant to complete financial aid forms (or supply information for them) because they worry that it will commit them to contributing to college costs. It sometimes helps to tell hesitant stepparents or parents that while schools demand such information and will use it to compute your financial need, providing it does not commit them to paying the bills. Your expected family contribution may be higher based on the resources of step- and noncustodial parents, but it's up to you and your family to determine where the money comes from.

father's or vice versa, if you can make a case that such a change is appropriate.

Sometimes you can use the most favorable package to get a competing school to change its tune about whose finances count. In the end, you have to apply by the rules, be ready to appeal, and hope for the best.

Transfer students

Financial aid for transfer students is not all that different from financial aid for freshmen. Your aid package from your previous school won't transfer; you'll have to apply again at your new school. You'll fill out the same aid forms that entering freshmen do, though the deadlines will be different if you transfer in midyear. (They may even be different for fall transfers; be sure to check.)

Before awarding aid, your new school will check the National Student Loan Data System to find your "financial aid transcript," which shows how much aid you've received from other schools. That prevents a school from awarding you a loan that exceeds federal borrowing limits, for instance.

If you're transferring midyear, you may not be eligible for some grants that you might have received as a fall transfer. When grant money is limited, schools often award it on a first-come, first-served basis. By midyear, the well may be dry.

Be sure to ask or check the school's website for scholarships for which you might qualify. At some schools, you'll be a candidate for the same scholarships as freshmen; at others, there are separate scholarships for standout transfers. At Augustana College, in Rock Island, Illinois, for instance, transfer students with a GPA of 3.5 earn a $4,000 scholarship and may be eligible for an additional $2,000 for talent in music, theater, art, or debate. At Roanoke College in Virginia, a 3.5 GPA earns a $9,000 scholarship (and an additional $3,000 if you're transferring with an associate's degree from a Virginia community college).

If you know ahead of time that you'll eventually apply to transfer to another school, you can save yourself money and time by being careful to select courses that will earn you full credit at the second school. Most colleges are happy to consult with potential transfers on this; contact the office of admissions.

Older students

Financial aid isn't just for 18- to 21-year-olds. Whether you've postponed college for a few years or a few decades, most of the same financial aid resources that traditional students rely on are available to you. Assuming you're age 24 or older, you'll be considered an independent student for financial aid purposes, so only your income and assets (and your spouse's, if you're married) will count in the financial aid formulas. Your parents are out of the picture.

One sticky problem if you're quitting a job to go to school full time is that your expected family contribution will be based on last year's income, even though you won't have a steady paycheck once you start school. Thus, your initial aid offers are likely to be skimpy. Be prepared to appeal. Many financial aid officers are willing to adjust your aid award to reflect the level of income you expect once you're a full-time student.

If you continue working full time (or even part time), getting need-based aid is tougher because your stream of income will continue and the school will expect you to use a good chunk of it to cover college costs. At the least, you'll be eligible for Stafford loans. Even if they're unsubsidized, the interest rates are low. Many private lenders also offer loans, though the rates and fees will be a bit higher. Before you borrow, don't overlook your employer as a potential source of college funding. A majority of large and medium-sized companies offer tuition benefits, and the first $5,250 in benefits each year is tax free.

While many scholarships are reserved for traditional students, some are targeted to older students or have no age restrictions. So scholarship search engines such as FastWeb (www.fastweb.com) are worth a try. Some associations and foundations also have awards specifically for women training for careers. For instance, the Business and Professional Women's Foundation awards dozens of Career Advancement Scholarships (averaging $1,000) each year to women age 25 or older. And the Talbot Charitable Foundation awards scholarships of up to $10,000 to women who earned their high school diplomas or GEDs 10 or more years ago. Some schools also have their own scholarships for older students. At the University of Alabama, for instance, students over age 25 can apply for one of 18 endowed scholarships.

One more avenue: Some colleges that cater to adult students will award you credit toward your degree based on a "portfolio assessment" or "prior learning assessment" in which you demonstrate college-level knowledge of various subjects. Earning "life credits" saves you money by reducing the amount of time it takes to get your degree.

International students

It can be tough for international students, especially undergraduates, to get outside funding to go to college in the United States. More than 80 percent of international undergraduate students finance their own studies with personal or family resources, according to the Institute of International Education. Foreign students don't qualify for Pell grants, Stafford loans, and other federal and state aid, and most colleges offer little or no need-based aid for students who are not citizens of the United States, Canada, or Mexico. Before you can acquire a visa to study in the United States, you generally have to show that you can afford to pay the cost of your education and living expenses here.

One bright note, however, is that a small percentage of U.S. schools—generally the most selective ones—are devoting a portion of their financial aid budget to the cause of attracting outstanding international students. Grinnell College in Grinnell, Iowa, for instance, offers need-based financial aid, worth up to half tuition, to nearly all of its international students. In addition, exceptional students from China, Nepal, the Middle East and Asia, Africa, Latin America, and Eastern and Central Europe get merit scholarships that meet any remaining need.

Many other schools don't offer any need-based aid, but do offer merit scholarships. At Syracuse University, for instance, international students are eligible for scholarships based on academic credentials that are worth $6,000 to $12,000 a year. And most schools that award athletic scholarships make them available to students from around the world.

International students are not eligible for federal work-study jobs and, because of visa restrictions, they are usually not permitted to work off campus. But some schools do offer on-campus jobs. However, international students may not work more than 20 hours a week.

To take out a loan from a college or private lender, an international student normally must have a cosigner who is a U.S. citizen or permanent resident. One loan program that caters to international students is Citibank's CitiAssist Global Loan, with a $10,000-per-year maximum for undergraduates.

Veterans

Active-duty soldiers and veterans qualify for special tuition assistance. An armed forces recruiter can provide the details, but here are the basics:

Tuition assistance

Active-duty soldiers and some members of the Reserves can take college courses and work toward an undergraduate or graduate degree during their off-duty time. The military will pay tuition and fees up to $3,000 or $4,500, depending on the branch of service. (Under a program called "Tuition Top-Up," soldiers may also be able to tap into future GI Bill benefits to pay for more expensive coursework.) Soldiers can also qualify for a free laptop computer and Internet connection to allow them to participate in distance-learning programs.

Montgomery GI bill

To participate in the GI Bill program, you contribute $100 a month to an educational fund for a year while on active duty. After three years of service, the Veteran's Administration adds $34,848 and pays the soldier up to $1,004 a month from that fund, for 36 months, toward educational expenses. Members of the Reserves and National Guard can earn up to $22,000 in GI Bill funds and activated Reservists can earn up to $28,900. For more information, visit the GI Bill website at www.gibill.va.gov.

Chapter Eleven

Finding Money for Graduate School

With average graduate school costs for tuition and living expenses topping $26,000 a year (and costs at many law, business, and medical schools exceeding $50,000 a year), it can be tough to assemble a patchwork of loans, grants, work, and other resources to pay the bills. For students who can't pay out-of-pocket or rely on parental support, here's a laundry list of ways to scramble together the money.

Snag a fellowship or assistantship

This is where the money is for many graduate students, especially those seeking Ph.D.'s. While undergraduates generally receive grants based on need, at the graduate level such awards are usually merit-based. At wealthy institutions like Cornell and Yale universities, virtually all Ph.D. candidates

---

"The living expense choices that students make will affect how much they have to borrow."

---

are awarded a fellowship or assistantship that covers tuition and fees, pays a stipend, and provides health insurance coverage. At other schools, top students are awarded funding when admitted, but others need to apply to a departmental advisor or faculty member to line up an assistantship and may not secure a position until the second semester or second year. (Fellowships usually have no work requirement, while graduate assistants typically work up to 15 hours a week teaching, grading papers, leading discussion groups, supervising lab courses, or assisting faculty with research.)

How much fellowship and assistantship aid is available varies widely depending on the field. In engineering, computer science, and math, 82 percent of full-time Ph.D. candidates and 55 percent of master's degree students are awarded assistantships, many funded with federal and corporate dollars. Fellowships are also more plentiful in engineering and the sciences—and often more generous than in other fields. In the humanities, only about half of full-time Ph.D. students and 40 percent of full-time master's degree students have assistantships, and stipends are often lower.

Comparatively few assistantships and fellowships are available for those studying law, medicine, and business, which explains why so many professional-school students borrow heavily. Master's degree candidates in education also tend to finance their degrees with savings or loans, because a majority of them earn their degrees part-time while continu-

ing to work full time, which makes assistantships impractical (and also typically disqualifies them for subsidized student loans).

The first step toward getting a fellowship or assistantship is to indicate on your admissions application that you want to be considered for all forms of financial aid. The choicest awards are often made by departmental committees on the basis of application materials and sometimes supplemental recommendations. Many schools also have a limited number of scholarships that are awarded to help attract top students or students who would bring ethnic or geographic diversity to the campus. If they're university-wide or departmental scholarships, they'll probably be based on your application for admission—plus a bit of extra paperwork in some cases. If they're endowed scholarships, they may require a separate application.

Search for outside scholarships

To find other awards or assistantship positions, check with your school's financial aid office, graduate school office, and fellowship coordinator (if there is one), or seek out faculty members in your department who are directing research funded by outside grants. Several government agencies and private organizations also sponsor outside fellowships that students can apply for on their own. Some of the more prestigious (and competitive) programs include National Science Foundation fellowships in the sciences, mathematics, and engineering; Mellon fellowships in the humanities; Ford Foundation fellowships for minorities (African Americans, Hispanics, and American Indians); Jack Kent Cooke Foundation scholarships for new graduate students in all fields; and American Association of University Women fellowships and grants for women. Most graduate schools maintain directories of outside awards. Many schools compile listings of such awards, either on paper or online. Two good online resources are Cornell University's Graduate School

J. Briggs Cormier has financed his nine years of graduate study the way many graduate students do: with equal measures of hard work and debt. Cormier studies theater at Ohio State University–Columbus, which costs him roughly $42,000 in tuition, fees, and living expenses per year. As a master's degree student at the University of Memphis and now as a Ph.D. candidate at Ohio State, Cormier has paid for his schooling by working in a variety of graduate assistantships: He's done stints as a tour coordinator, a box office manager, a teaching assistant, a theater journal editor, and president of Ohio State's Council of Graduate Students. Each of those jobs has come with a stipend, ranging from about $900 to $1,200 a month. Nonetheless, he's had to borrow to cover living expenses. "When you add up rent, utilities, car insurance, and health insurance, you can't live on your stipend," says Cormier, who currently receives about $1,100 a month as a graduate associate in student affairs. His student loan debt, including what he borrowed as an undergraduate, is more than $100,000.

Fellowship Database (cuinfo.cornell.edu/Student/GRFN) and the listing of grants at Michigan State University's website (www.lib.msu.edu/harris23/grants/grants.htm). Also check with any civic groups, religious groups, or unions you're affiliated with, as well as honor societies, fraternities, or sororities you belonged to as an undergraduate.

Borrow wisely

While six-figure debt is more typical of law and medical school students, 54 percent of full-time graduate students and 80 percent of full-time professional-degree students find they need to borrow to cover their expenses, according to the National Center for Education Statistics. Average debt, including undergraduate loans, tops $29,000 for master's degree students and $80,000 for professional-degree students.

Federally subsidized Stafford loans are generally the cheapest way to go, as we note in Chapter 3. As a graduate student, you can borrow up to $8,500 per year ($65,500 overall). Students qualify based on financial need, so it's necessary to file federal aid forms. You can borrow an additional $10,000 a year in unsubsidized Stafford loans (and up to $138,500 in Stafford loans overall). Rates are the same as for the subsidized Stafford, and you can defer making payments, but interest begins accruing right away. If your need is high—your expected family contribution shows that the government figures that you can contribute very little or nothing to your graduate education—you may also be offered a subsidized Perkins loan of up to $6,000 per year.

For students who own a home, a home equity loan or line of credit is another attractive choice. Many banks were recently offering lines of credit at 4 percent or less, and the interest you pay is generally tax deductible. So is student loan interest for some taxpayers, depending on income.

If the federal loan limits leave you short, private lenders stand ready to lend you as much as the full cost of your education, less any financial aid. (Some schools also have their own loan programs.) Interest rates tend to be only slightly higher than the rates on Stafford loans. However, origination fees can be significantly higher—and interest begins accruing right away. To qualify for private loans, you need a clean credit history or a cosigner. (It's a good idea to check your credit report for errors before you apply.) Some popular programs include Graduate Access Loan, from Access Group (www.accessgroup.org), Signature Student Loan, from Sallie Mae (www.salliemae.com), CitiAssist Loan, from Citibank (www.studentloan.com), and Key Alternative Loan, from Key Bank (www.key.com/educate). All four lenders also offer specialized loans for business, law, and medical students.

> *"I don't need digital cable right now. I can get a roommate and live like a student."*

Find loan repayment help

Graduate students can, of course, take advantage of the flexible repayment and consolidation options described in Chapter 12. In addition, some teachers, lawyers, and doctors may be able to have their grad school debt forgiven through state and federal loan repayment assistance programs.

For teachers. Teachers who work in schools that serve low-income students for five years can have all of their Perkins loan debt forgiven; some may qualify to have portions of their Stafford loan debt forgiven. In addition, many states will repay the loans of teachers who commit to subject areas with teacher shortages, such as math, science, or foreign language; to working in special education; or to going into low-income-area schools. Under California's Assumption Program of Loans for Education, for example, teachers who serve for four years in such underserved areas in California public schools turn as much as $19,000 of their student loan debt over to the state.

For lawyers. More than 70 schools, 50 employers, and eight states offer loan repayment assistance to lawyers who practice public interest law for a nonprofit agency or who work as government prosecutors or public defenders. Among law schools, loan repayment assistance programs (LRAP) vary dramatically. Those with meager budgets may offer such programs only to a handful of students, may offer relatively small loans or grants, or may cap eligibility at salaries of $35,000 or less. Institutions with ample resources, like Harvard, Yale, Columbia, and New York universities, can afford to offer loan repayment help to more graduates, and to graduates with higher salaries (up to $82,000 at Harvard, for instance). Be aware that you may have to repay some or all of an LRAP loan if you leave your public interest job during the course of a year, and you may cease to be eligible if your income rises over a certain amount.

For doctors. Doctors who agree to practice certain kinds of medicine where there are shortages or who work in underserved areas of the country can qualify to have significant portions of their debt forgiven. Through the National Health Service Corps, for instance, doctors practicing primary care medicine in underserved areas can have up to $50,000 of debt repaid by the federal government during a two-year minimum service commitment. An additional $35,000 a year in debt repayment is available to doctors who sign up for a third or fourth year of service. Many states have similar debt repayment programs for doctors who live or are licensed in the state and who practice primary care medicine in state. A listing of state programs is available at the website of the Association of American Medical Colleges (www.aamc.org/students/financing/repayment).

Helpful Hints

;)

Don't forget Uncle Sam on another front: Graduate students can take advantage of the same tax credit available to undergrads (and their parents). Chapter 9 has details on how the various education tax breaks work.

Find work

Full-time graduate students who have financial need and who don't have an assistantship may be awarded a work-study job as part of their financial aid package. An award of $1,000 to $3,000 a year is typical, and covers the pay for 10 hours to 15 hours of work a week. Pay can range anywhere from $5.15 (the federal minimum wage) to $14.75 an hour, depending on the job and the job market where your school is located. Most jobs are on campus, although some schools place a small percentage of students with not-for-profit organizations off campus. (Full-time law and med school students are often discouraged from working in addition to their studies, but work-study jobs are available to those who feel they can handle it.) A job as a resident assistant in an undergraduate dorm is another option. The position usually includes tuition remission and a stipend.

Let your employer pick up the tab

If you're working, don't overlook your employer as a source of tuition funds. About 44 percent of employees at private firms have a benefit that helps finance job-related educational expenses, and 11 percent can tap their employer's pocket for courses that aren't job-related. The percentages are significantly higher for professional and technical employees and for employees of large and medium-sized firms. (This is an especially popular way to fund an M.B.A.: Forty-three percent of M.B.A. students receive some kind of employer aid.) At FedEx Express, for instance, about 10 percent of employees take advantage of tuition reimbursement of up to $3,500 a year for work-related courses. Thanks to a change in the tax laws in 2002, employer-provided tuition reimbursement is tax free up to $5,250 per year.

Naturally, colleges and universities tend to offer the most generous tuition benefits for employees—so much so that some prospective grad students seek out university employment to help fund their degrees. Tuition remission attracts many employees to Southern Methodist University in Dallas, says Robert Bobo, a public information officer for SMU, where full-time employees can take up to 18 hours of coursework a year in any field at no cost. Some schools restrict the benefit to job-related courses or career-related degree programs.

Go part-time

There's nothing easy about working full time and then going to class four nights a week. But part-time study allows some students to foot the bill, at least in part, from cash flow and perhaps to take advantage of employer-paid tuition. The best part-time programs are those where the same instructors teach both full-time and part-time students.

Live like a student

For those who attend school full time, graduate schools estimate the student budget for yearly housing, food, and personal expenses at an almost laughably low $15,000 or so. (Students who have dependent children can often have their living expense budgets increased to pay for child care costs, which increases the amount you can borrow.) But you can save yourself debt by taking in roommates and brown-bagging lunch. "The living expense choices that students make will affect how much they have to borrow," says Gina Soliz, director of financial aid at Syracuse University's College of Law. Students who manage to keep their debt to a minimum are the ones who say, "I don't need digital cable right now. I can get a roommate and live like a student." Even part-time students can trim their borrowing with a little belt-tightening. Every dollar you can divert to tuition from luxuries like cable TV or high-priced cafe lattes is a dollar you won't have to pay in interest down the road.

Chapter Twelve

Payback Time

Cramming is done. Graduation is over. Then comes the tricky part: paying back those loans from the government and other lenders that helped finance your higher education. Graduates must prepare for what may be their toughest assignment ever. And for those who are still in school, it wouldn't hurt to be mindful of the obligation that's coming up all too soon.

The first step toward taking control of loan payments is to attend a financial counseling session that the government requires schools to provide for graduating students with federal debts or government-guaranteed loans. Depending on the school, exit counseling may take place online (lasting about 25 minutes) or in person (workshops may run about an hour or so). The seminar will spell out your responsibilities, repayment options, what to do if you run into trouble paying the loan, and what happens if you default.

Dismiss any notion of letting a student loan linger until the lender forgets about you. They won't. Crackdowns in recent years have turned up the heat on deadbeats. "I've spoken with students who think they don't have to pay them back," says Scott Dingwall, director of the Consumer Credit Counseling Service of Central New Jersey. "But it's not so easy to get them forgiven, and unless you have a catastrophic event, you're going to have to pay the loans back."

> *"Unless you have a catastrophic event, you're going to have to pay the loans back."*

The consequences of defaulting on a student loan are severe and could haunt a borrower for years. Take a gander at what can happen:

- Your credit score can plummet, making it hard to buy a car or a house. It might also be difficult to get your first apartment or job, as some landlords and employers review applicants' credit ratings.
- Your wages can be garnished.
- Your federal and state tax refunds can be seized.
- You might be on the hook for hefty collection and late fees.
- Your professional licenses can be suspended.

The monthly obligation

How much you must pay back and how fast depends on the type of loan and who granted it. If you have a Perkins loan, the graduate makes a fixed payment of at least $40 every month until the loan is paid off. (The payment is determined by dividing the amount owed, including interest, by 120 months.)

Students with Stafford loans can choose among four repayment plans, which may vary slightly depending on the lender. Students who borrowed Stafford loans through the Federal Family Education Loan program (FFEL) can switch repayment options once a year. Those who borrowed

Staffords through the William D. Ford Federal Direct Loan program (DIRECT) can change plans virtually any time, as long as the loan is not in default. The options for graduates with Stafford loans:

- *Standard repayment.* Graduates pay a fixed amount of at least $50 a month so that the loan is paid in full within 10 years.
  - *Extended repayment.* Graduates pay at least $50 a month but can stretch out payment over a longer period (typically between 12 years and 30 years). For DIRECT Staffords, the amount of time until payoff depends on the amount owed. If less than $10,000 is owed, for example, the graduate gets 12 years to pay it off; between $10,000 and $20,000, 15 years; between $20,000 and $40,000, 20 years; and so on. This plan is available to DIRECT borrowers, and to FFEL borrowers who owe at least $30,000 and who received their first loan on or after October 7, 1998.
- *Graduated repayment.* This might be a sensible choice for graduates who believe their first incomes will be modest. The monthly payment is the greater of two numbers: the interest that accumulates every month between payments, or half of the payment under the standard repayment plan.
- *Income contingent repayment plan.* In the DIRECT version, payment is based on income, family size, interest rate, and the size of the loan. The Department of Education will verify the borrower's income with the Internal Revenue Service. The FFEL version is called "Income Sensitive Repayment" and calculates payment on income and loan amount. The lender may ask for proof of income.

With the exception of the income-contingent repayment plan, parents who borrowed under the PLUS program can choose from among the above options.

Before choosing a payback plan—especially if you intend to extend your payments over a longer period of time—consider how much the loan will cost in the long run. Think about it: If you borrowed $10,000 in unsubsidized DIRECT Stafford loans and pay it back in $123 monthly payments for 10 years, you'd pay $4,718 in interest (for a total of $14,718). But if you pay $97 a month for 15 years, you'd pay $7,464 in interest (for a total of $17,464). That's $2,746 more for the same education. Also keep in mind that the interest on student loans may be tax deductible. Chapter 9 has more details.

Consolidation

Graduates with several student loans can simplify the payment process by taking out a new consolidated loan that pays off the old debts. Why consolidate? Convenience, as there's only one monthly payment, and possibly savings, as the new loan might lock in a lower interest rate. Different types of loans can be consolidated, and you don't have to consolidate all of them.

The interest rate on the new loan will be the average of the interest rates on the loans you're consolidating, weighted for the size of each loan. You can still choose from a variety of repayment options. As of this writing, the new interest rate is fixed and will last for the rest of the loan's lifetime. However, Congress has discussed making the interest rate on consolidation loans variable. To get a glimpse of how much interest you're likely to pay if you consolidate, try the worksheet and loan calculator provided by Mapping Your Future, a nonprofit financial aid website sponsored by 35 loan guaranty agencies (www.mapping-your-future.org/features).

Consolidating isn't for everyone. Yes, you might nail down a low interest rate, a low monthly payment, deal with only one lender, and have an array of flexible payment options to choose among. It's free, and deferment is still an option. However, you can consolidate only once, so if rates go down later, you're out of luck. And if you stretch our your loan over a longer period of time, you might get stung with a higher interest tab. Depending on the loan, you may lose any forgiveness options—which we'll get to later on—and you may also wipe out other benefits. For instance, Vermont students who borrowed through the Vermont Student Assistance Corp. lose their annual loan rebate if they consolidate.

"Anything is better than going into default."

In over your head?

The federal government bends over backward to make sure you'll be able to pay off your student loans. That's one of the advantages of taking out federal loans rather than alternative loans: Private lenders don't let you defer and may be stricter when it comes to forbearance. If you're struggling with your loan payments, call your lender and look into the following options. They won't hurt your credit rating, and they could save you from destroying your financial future. "Anything is better than going into default," says Dan Madzelan, director of forecasting and policy analysis at the Office of Postsecondary Education of the Department of Education.

Helpful Hints

Never consolidate your student loans with those of your spouse. "That's always a bad idea," says CariAnne Behr of Mapping Your Future, a nonprofit financial aid website sponsored by 35 loan guaranty agencies. "If one of you dies, the loan can't be cancelled and the other spouse will have to pay it. If there's a divorce, you're both still liable for the debt."

Deferment

Generally, graduates can postpone repayment for three years if they become unemployed or experience some other economic hardship. They can defer for longer periods if they go back to college or graduate school. Graduates with Perkins loans can get a deferment if they become teachers in designated schools serving low-income families or work in nursing, law enforcement, as a medical technician, or in certain other fields.

When a subsidized Stafford or Perkins loan is deferred, the graduate stops making payments and the government pays the interest that accrues. On unsubsidized loans, the graduate must pay the interest periodically, according to the payment plan worked out with the lender, or add it to the total amount owed.

Forbearance

If you don't qualify for a deferment, forbearance is another way to suspend or reduce payment temporarily. Forbearances are granted for up to 12 months at a time. There's no limit to the number of times a lender can grant forbearance, but they won't be patient forever.

Whether your payments are reduced or suspended—it's up to you and the lender to hash out an agreement—you'll be charged interest even if your loan is subsidized. You can pay the interest during the forbearance period or add it to the total amount owed. Graduates eligible for forbearance include those who are completing medical and dental internships or residencies, whose federal student loans equal at least 20 percent of their monthly gross incomes, or who have health or personal problems. As with deferment, call your lender and explain the circumstances to see if you qualify.

Forgiveness

Depending on the type of loan, you might qualify for forgiveness, or cancellation, of your loan. In that case, you don't have to repay all or part of the loan. There are more forgiveness

Katie Rutan, who is finishing her last year at Lewis-Clark State College in Lewiston, Idaho, has two loves: She adores Idaho's Boise Valley, where she grew up, and she's passionate about sharing her knowledge of history. So applying for the Education Incentive Loan Forgiveness Program, which pays the college tuition of aspiring teachers who agree to work in Idaho, was a no-brainer. Each year, the state chooses 16 recipients by looking at grade point averages, teacher recommendations, and, in some schools, essays. Initially, Rutan was designated an alternate and resorted to student loans to pay her first-semester tab. But by the second semester, she had secured one of the coveted spots.

The state has paid Rutan's $3,126 tuition at Lewis-Clark every year (and even reimbursed her first tuition payment). In return, she must earn an undergraduate degree in teaching and work as an educator in the state for at least two years. It's a program offered in nearly every state for in-demand occupations such as teachers and nurses. Failure to fulfill the obligation means repaying the entire sum herself. "I always think it's funny they want me to be here for two years," Rutan says. "I could stay for 25."

Rutan didn't qualify for any need-based aid, but she received a $1,500 annual scholarship for good grades from her college's foundation. Her mother, a first grade reading instructor, and father, a school superintendent, give her an allowance and pay her rent in an off-campus apartment. And Rutan raises money by working 20 hours a week in the financial aid office. Even her book bill had less bite: For helping out with freshman orientation each year, Rutan garnered a $200 gift certificate to the bookstore.

provisions for Perkins loans than Stafford loans. For instance, teachers at low-income schools or who teach subjects that are experiencing teacher shortages may qualify for complete forgiveness of their Perkins loans, as well as medical technicians, nurses, and Vista or Peace Corps volunteers. With Stafford loans, up to $17,500 can be forgiven if the borrower works for five years in specific teaching positions in a school serving low-income students. Both Perkins and Stafford loans will be cancelled if the graduate dies or becomes permanently disabled.

For more information on loan repayment, deferment, and forgiveness, consult the Department of Education brochure, *Repaying Your Student Loans*. It can be found online at www.studentaid.ed.gov. (Click on "repaying" and scroll down to "paying back your loan.") If you are in default, the Department of Education's "Collections Guide to Defaulted Student Loans" website (www.ed.gov/offices/OSFAP/DCS/index.html) can explain your options.

In addition to these federal programs, some states will cancel or repay your loan for working in certain jobs. For information on state programs, contact your state's higher education agency. (Go to www.studentaid.ed.gov; click on "funding," then "state higher education agency.")

How Do Your Schools Compare?

How to Use the Insider's Index

See how your schools stack up on key measures, such as which dole out the most need-based financial aid and which turn out graduates with the most and least amounts of student loan debt. As you search for a particular college or university, you'll notice that the lists are organized by type of institution:

- National Universities, which offer a wide range of undergraduate majors as well as master's and doctoral degrees
- Liberal Arts Colleges, which emphasize undergraduate education and award at least half of their degrees in the liberal arts disciplines
- Universities–Master's, which offer a full range of undergraduate and master's programs but few, if any, doctoral programs
- Comprehensive Colleges–Bachelor's, which offer programs in the liberal arts (accounting for fewer than half of their degrees) and in professional fields such as business, nursing, and education

Schools that did not supply the necessary data do not appear in the tables. "N/A" means "not available."

Priciest private schools

The sticker price of a year at an elite private school may be a far cry from what most people actually pay, so it's a good idea not to rule out any favorites based just on price. Many high-priced institutions are generous with their financial aid. The schools are listed here by sticker price—the sum of tuition, fees, and room and board—for the 2003–2004 academic year. In addition, the table lists the average need-based financial aid package granted to undergraduates during the 2003–2004 academic year. The typical aid package has three components: need-based grants, need-based loans, and work-study. In order to qualify, students must file an annual aid application that demonstrates financial need. Expenses for 2004–2005 are provided in the directory when available.

National Universities

	Tuition, fees, room and board	Average financial aid package		Tuition, fees, room and board	Average financial aid package
New York University	$39,406	$18,686	Worcester Polytechnic Inst. (MA)	$37,404	$21,030
George Washington University (DC)	$39,110	$29,206	Univ. of Southern California	$37,324	$26,465
Columbia University (NY)	$38,590	$27,079	Tulane University (LA)	$37,288	$25,837
University of Chicago	$38,553	$25,388	Yale University (CT)	$37,000	$26,978
Brandeis University (MA)	$38,487	$22,199	Emory University (GA)	$36,872	$25,238
Georgetown University (DC)	$38,440	$22,344	Carnegie Mellon University (PA)	$36,831	$21,658
Massachusetts Inst. of Technology	$38,310	$24,875	Princeton University (NJ)	$36,649	$25,460
Washington University in St. Louis	$38,293	$24,461	University of Rochester (NY)	$36,398	$22,854
Cornell University (NY)	$38,283	$27,339	Pepperdine University (CA)	$35,790	$25,169
Tufts University (MA)	$38,270	$24,084	Northeastern University (MA)	$35,650	$15,396
Boston University	$38,194	$25,338	Stevens Institute of Technology (NJ)	$35,460	$18,336
University of Pennsylvania	$37,960	$26,029	Lehigh University (PA)	$35,310	$23,533
Brown University (RI)	$37,942	$24,402	Fordham University (NY)	$35,051	$18,363
Harvard University (MA)	$37,928	$26,939	New School University (NY)	$34,940	$12,350
Vanderbilt University (TN)	$37,897	$28,495	American University (DC)	$34,755	$24,370
Johns Hopkins University (MD)	$37,872	$26,257	Syracuse University (NY)	$34,736	$18,720
Dartmouth College (NH)	$37,770	$25,945	University of Miami (FL)	$34,608	$22,940
Boston College	$37,729	$23,215	University of Notre Dame (IN)	$34,542	$23,412
Stanford University (CA)	$37,636	$27,000	Wake Forest University (NC)	$34,090	$21,413
Rensselaer Polytechnic Inst. (NY)	$37,629	$24,842	Polytechnic University (NY)	$33,772	$20,600
Duke University (NC)	$37,555	$26,162	University of San Diego	$33,100	$21,295
Northwestern University (IL)	$37,491	$24,508			

Priciest private schools

Liberal Arts Colleges

	Tuition, fees, room and board	Average financial aid package
Sarah Lawrence College (NY)	$41,218	$25,826
Wesleyan University (CT)	$38,224	$28,950
Middlebury College (VT)	$38,100	$25,899
Harvey Mudd College (CA)	$38,080	$22,740
Trinity College (CT)	$38,040	$25,648
Skidmore College (NY)	$37,930	$24,114
Mount Holyoke College (MA)	$37,918	$25,469
Connecticut College	$37,900	$23,900
Haverford College (PA)	$37,900	$25,073
Bowdoin College (ME)	$37,790	$25,295
Swarthmore College (PA)	$37,716	$26,088
Pitzer College (CA)	$37,590	$27,950
Colby College (ME)	$37,570	$24,111
Hamilton College (NY)	$37,560	$22,980
Bates College (ME)	$37,500	$24,457
Amherst College (MA)	$37,468	$25,366
Bard College (NY)	$37,352	$22,828
Pomona College (CA)	$37,130	$26,452
Colgate University (NY)	$37,095	$25,421
Hampshire College (MA)	$37,081	$24,615
Smith College (MA)	$37,034	$27,378
Vassar College (NY)	$37,030	$24,305
Oberlin College (OH)	$36,938	$22,576
Bryn Mawr College (PA)	$36,890	$25,139
Claremont McKenna College (CA)	$36,880	$23,906
Barnard College (NY)	$36,792	$26,045
Hobart and William Smith Col. (NY)	$36,536	$22,933
Wellesley College (MA)	$36,516	$24,468
College of the Holy Cross (MA)	$36,451	$21,793
St. John's College (MD)	$36,360	N/A
Wheaton College (MA)	$36,330	$21,159
Occidental College (CA)	$36,128	$27,814
Union College (NY)	$36,005	$23,798
St. Lawrence University (NY)	$35,945	$26,013
Franklin and Marshall College (PA)	$35,930	$20,915
Bennington College (VT)	$35,910	$21,821
Dickinson College (PA)	$35,825	$22,973
Williams College (MA)	$35,750	$26,212
Lafayette College (PA)	$35,746	$22,407
Scripps College (CA)	$35,700	$24,124
Drew University (NJ)	$35,550	$21,033
Gettysburg College (PA)	$35,446	$24,317
Kenyon College (OH)	$35,370	$22,151
Bucknell University (PA)	$35,262	$19,000
Colorado College	$34,475	$23,278
Ursinus College (PA)	$34,400	$22,129
Carleton College (MN)	$34,395	$21,208
Mills College (CA)	$33,371	$20,190
Davidson College (NC)	$33,274	$17,395
Westmont College (CA)	$33,268	$16,571
Denison University (OH)	$33,050	$22,756
Hartwick College (NY)	$32,710	$22,776
Goucher College (MD)	$32,650	$18,020
Ohio Wesleyan University	$32,550	$22,149
Whitman College (WA)	$32,526	$17,750
Willamette University (OR)	$32,032	$21,027
Macalester College (MN)	$31,962	$21,386
University of Puget Sound (WA)	$31,760	$19,217
Lewis and Clark College (OR)	$31,716	$18,654
DePauw University (IN)	$31,500	$20,208
Muhlenberg College (PA)	$31,485	N/A
Wittenberg University (OH)	$31,316	$21,143
College of Wooster (OH)	$31,300	$21,812
Grinnell College (IA)	$31,060	$20,298
Whittier College (CA)	$30,966	$25,619
Sewanee–University of the South (TN)	$30,855	$19,633
Lawrence University (WI)	$30,741	$21,596
Albright College (PA)	$30,579	$16,536
Washington College (MD)	$30,540	$19,395
College of the Atlantic (ME)	$30,504	$21,823
Illinois Wesleyan University	$30,380	$17,641
Knox College (IL)	$30,294	$20,770
Allegheny College (PA)	$30,280	$19,624
St. Anselm College (NH)	$30,250	$18,380
Lake Forest College (IL)	$30,170	$19,466
Susquehanna University (PA)	$29,990	$17,158
Earlham College (IN)	$29,976	$21,215
Beloit College (WI)	$29,864	$18,635
Washington and Jefferson Col. (PA)	$29,570	$15,658
Kalamazoo College (MI)	$29,388	$19,000
Rhodes College (TN)	$29,320	$18,022
Long Island U.–Southampton Col. (NY)	$29,310	N/A
Antioch College (OH)	$29,269	$19,214
Moravian College (PA)	$29,123	$15,931
Juniata College (PA)	$29,080	$18,258
Marlboro College (VT)	$29,055	$16,791
St. John's College (NM)	$29,040	N/A
Washington and Lee University (VA)	$29,005	$20,923
Furman University (SC)	$28,976	$19,647
Eckerd College (FL)	$28,744	$18,550
Franklin Pierce College (NH)	$28,630	$16,123
St. Olaf College (MN)	$28,500	$18,172
McDaniel College (MD)	$28,440	$18,978
Randolph-Macon Woman's College (VA)	$28,430	$19,958
Hampden-Sydney College (VA)	$28,407	$15,761
Hiram College (OH)	$28,234	$21,218
Agnes Scott College (GA)	$28,230	$21,264

Universities–Master's (North)

	Tuition, fees, room and board	Average financial aid package
Fairfield University (CT)	$35,055	$17,603
Villanova University (PA)	$34,808	$18,217
Loyola College in Maryland	$34,205	$17,375
Bentley College (MA)	$33,904	$22,572
St. Joseph's University (PA)	$33,590	$13,845
Simmons College (MA)	$33,000	$15,175
Manhattanville College (NY)	$32,420	$19,872
Emerson College (MA)	$32,406	$13,083
Ithaca College (NY)	$31,730	$20,381
La Salle University (PA)	$31,160	$15,998
Quinnipiac University (CT)	$30,720	$13,160
Providence College (RI)	$30,604	$14,600
University of Scranton (PA)	$30,528	$14,666
St. Michael's College (VT)	$30,100	$17,529
Wagner College (NY)	$29,900	$14,768
Arcadia University (PA)	$29,890	$16,134
Bryant College (RI)	$29,706	$14,521
St. Joseph College (CT)	$29,685	$16,273
Suffolk University (MA)	$29,630	$12,457
Assumption College (MA)	$29,375	$14,955
University of New Haven (CT)	$29,235	$15,758
Salve Regina University (RI)	$29,210	$15,618
Alfred University (NY)	$29,206	$21,746
Sacred Heart University (CT)	$29,178	$13,393
Rider University (NJ)	$29,110	$17,733

	Tuition, fees, room and board	Average financial aid package
Regis College (MA)	$29,000	$17,940
Wheelock College (MA)	$29,000	$15,167
Fairleigh Dickinson Univ. (NJ)	$28,984	$18,183
Cabrini College (PA)	$28,970	$12,877
Lebanon Valley College (PA)	$28,870	$17,055
Rochester Inst. of Technology (NY)	$28,635	$16,300
Lesley University (MA)	$28,500	$12,015
Mount St. Mary's University (MD)	$28,400	$15,125
Long Island U.–C.W. Post Campus (NY)	$28,201	$8,791
Canisius College (NY)	$28,163	$16,917
Wilkes University (PA)	$28,060	$15,863
Iona College (NY)	$27,988	$13,144
Hood College (MD)	$27,795	$17,518
Manhattan College (NY)	$27,790	$14,185
Emmanuel College (MA)	$27,600	$16,474
Marist College (NY)	$27,473	$12,126
Marywood University (PA)	$27,434	$14,499
Philadelphia University	$27,414	$14,577
University of New England (ME)	$27,200	$17,240
Western New England College (MA)	$26,998	$12,334
King's College (PA)	$26,990	$14,394
College of Mount St. Vincent (NY)	$26,800	$15,000
St. Francis University (PA)	$26,688	$17,128
Col. of Notre Dame of Maryland	$26,675	$19,127
Chestnut Hill College (PA)	$26,450	$16,125

Universities–Master's (South)

	Tuition, fees, room and board	Average financial aid package
Rollins College (FL)	$34,300	$26,005
Lynn University (FL)	$30,750	$19,285
University of Richmond (VA)	$30,100	$19,189
Stetson University (FL)	$28,885	$19,406
Barry University (FL)	$28,750	$14,739
Loyola University New Orleans	$27,766	$16,895
Mercer University (GA)	$27,516	$21,250
Lynchburg College (VA)	$27,095	$15,969
Embry Riddle Aeronautical U. (FL)	$26,330	$12,563
Spring Hill College (AL)	$25,868	$16,836
Shenandoah University (VA)	$25,190	$12,712
Wheeling Jesuit University (WV)	$25,180	$16,062
Mary Baldwin College (VA)	$24,934	$19,276
Converse College (SC)	$24,710	$16,521
Belmont University (TN)	$24,384	$3,527

	Tuition, fees, room and board	Average financial aid package
Bellarmine University (KY)	$24,110	N/A
Jacksonville University (FL)	$24,040	$15,853
University of Tampa (FL)	$23,773	$14,162
Marymount University (VA)	$23,668	$13,276
Averett University (VA)	$23,620	$10,980
Centenary College of Louisiana	$23,100	$13,207
Meredith College (NC)	$23,065	$13,574
Christian Brothers University (TN)	$22,290	$12,767
Elon University (NC)	$22,240	$11,368
Brenau University (GA)	$21,900	$14,512
Queens University of Charlotte (NC)	$21,840	$11,243
Warren Wilson College (NC)	$21,794	$12,695
St. Thomas University (FL)	$21,400	N/A
Palm Beach Atlantic University (FL)	$20,690	$10,659

Priciest private schools

Universities–Master's (Midwest)

	Tuition, fees, room and board	Average financial aid package
Maharishi Univ. of Management (IA)	$29,230	$22,649
Butler University (IN)	$28,250	$16,000
John Carroll University (OH)	$27,658	$16,588
Rockford College (IL)	$27,270	$20,000
Xavier University (OH)	$26,850	$13,616
University of Findlay (OH)	$26,724	$11,000
Capital University (OH)	$26,550	$16,856
Creighton University (NE)	$26,332	$18,340
Carthage College (WI)	$26,220	$8,222
Valparaiso University (IN)	$26,118	$17,404
Hamline University (MN)	$25,620	$21,384
North Central College (IL)	$25,596	$18,212
University of Detroit Mercy	$25,582	$18,195
Augsburg College (MN)	$25,298	$12,966
Heidelberg College (OH)	$25,210	$16,974
University of Evansville (IN)	$25,190	$17,375
Drake University (IA)	$25,120	$16,354
College of St. Scholastica (MN)	$24,970	$15,945
Bethel University (MN)	$24,968	$14,810
Baldwin-Wallace College (OH)	$24,678	$13,257
Ashland University (OH)	$24,614	$16,446
College of St. Catherine (MN)	$24,010	$18,319

	Tuition, fees, room and board	Average financial aid package
Benedictine University (IL)	$23,700	$11,489
Dominican University (IL)	$23,610	$12,518
Concordia University–River Forest (IL)	$23,600	$11,333
Lake Erie College (OH)	$23,550	N/A
Lewis University (IL)	$23,200	$13,302
St. Xavier University (IL)	$23,134	$14,282
Rockhurst University (MO)	$23,020	$16,260
Bradley University (IL)	$22,900	$13,805
University of St. Francis (IL)	$22,870	$13,695
Ursuline College (OH)	$22,728	$15,872
College of Mount St. Joseph (OH)	$22,685	$11,400
University of Indianapolis	$22,660	$15,035
Anderson University (IN)	$22,610	$16,684
Roosevelt University (IL)	$22,580	$11,600
St. Ambrose University (IA)	$22,565	$12,467
Quincy University (IL)	$22,330	$14,835
Maryville Univ. of St. Louis (MO)	$22,090	$10,822
Columbia College (IL)	$22,020	N/A
Aquinas College (MI)	$21,894	$15,461
Webster University (MO)	$21,848	$15,845
University of Dubuque (IA)	$21,690	$15,986
Concordia University Wisconsin	$21,580	$14,124

Universities–Master's (West)

	Tuition, fees, room and board	Average financial aid package
Santa Clara University (CA)	$34,701	$17,748
Chapman University (CA)	$34,136	$18,358
University of Redlands (CA)	$34,004	$23,120
Loyola Marymount University (CA)	$33,548	$18,095
Dominican University of California (CA)	$32,430	$19,762
St. Mary's College of California	$31,210	$20,460
Notre Dame de Namur University (CA)	$29,520	$18,211
University of Portland (OR)	$28,690	$19,304
Regis University (CO)	$28,500	$20,738
Mount St. Mary's College (CA)	$28,284	N/A
Holy Names University (CA)	$27,980	$22,883
California Lutheran University	$27,600	$16,800
Woodbury University (CA)	$27,188	$15,369
Gonzaga University (WA)	$27,010	$17,077
Seattle University	$26,928	$19,380
Trinity University (TX)	$26,466	$15,486

	Tuition, fees, room and board	Average financial aid package
Whitworth College (WA)	$26,428	$17,443
George Fox University (OR)	$26,420	$14,902
Seattle Pacific University	$26,175	$16,249
Pacific Lutheran University (WA)	$25,715	$17,229
Pacific University (OR)	$25,430	$17,369
College of Santa Fe (NM)	$25,293	$18,190
Azusa Pacific University (CA)	$25,244	$12,616
Concordia University (OR)	$25,140	N/A
Point Loma Nazarene University (CA)	$25,130	$13,791
Concordia University (CA)	$24,420	$13,979
St. Martin's College (WA)	$23,245	$14,451
St. Mary's Univ. of San Antonio	$22,880	$13,454
Fresno Pacific University (CA)	$22,742	N/A
Alaska Pacific University	$22,398	$10,113
Grand Canyon University (AZ)	$22,380	N/A

Comprehensive Colleges–Bachelor's (North)

	Tuition, fees, room and board	Average financial aid package
Simon's Rock College of Bard (MA)	$36,580	N/A
Elmira College (NY)	$33,820	$20,384
Stonehill College (MA)	$30,752	$15,639
Colby-Sawyer College (NH)	$30,720	$17,721
Roger Williams University (RI)	$30,296	$14,500
Merrimack College (MA)	$29,625	$17,000
New England College (NH)	$28,860	N/A
Elizabethtown College (PA)	$28,800	$16,402
Curry College (MA)	$28,790	$14,025
Utica College (NY)	$28,190	N/A
Cedar Crest College (PA)	$28,170	$15,309
Daniel Webster College (NH)	$27,990	N/A
Marymount College–Tarrytown (NY)	$27,265	$15,968
Russell Sage College (NY)	$26,686	N/A
Delaware Valley College (PA)	$26,676	$16,030
Green Mountain College (VT)	$26,390	$11,780
Endicott College (MA)	$26,266	$12,062
Lasell College (MA)	$26,000	$15,429
Messiah College (PA)	$25,890	$12,798
Mount Ida College (MA)	$25,696	$10,749
Centenary College (NJ)	$25,370	$11,862
College of St. Elizabeth (NJ)	$25,260	$16,697
Concordia College (NY)	$25,140	N/A
Bay Path College (MA)	$24,910	$9,267
Teikyo Post University (CT)	$24,875	$8,385
Dominican College of Blauvelt (NY)	$24,810	$10,957
Becker College (MA)	$23,930	$9,298

Comprehensive Colleges–Bachelor's (South)

	Tuition, fees, room and board	Average financial aid package
Maryville College (TN)	$25,960	$19,013
Covenant College (GA)	$23,920	$16,865
University of Charleston (WV)	$23,790	N/A
Florida Southern College	$23,092	$15,001
Belmont Abbey College (NC)	$22,512	$11,294
Columbia College (SC)	$22,478	$18,516
Lenoir-Rhyne College (NC)	$22,265	$13,095
Wingate University (NC)	$22,200	$12,748
Catawba College (NC)	$22,000	$12,272
Peace College (NC)	$21,858	$12,126
Methodist College (NC)	$21,780	N/A
Alderson-Broaddus College (WV)	$21,456	$18,231
Berry College (GA)	$21,410	$13,396
Mars Hill College (NC)	$21,408	$11,609
Thomas More College (KY)	$21,400	$14,451
High Point University (NC)	$21,320	$11,400
Ferrum College (VA)	$21,265	$11,370
Coker College (SC)	$21,131	$16,531
Asbury College (KY)	$20,704	$12,170
Davis and Elkins College (WV)	$20,594	$15,769
LaGrange College (GA)	$20,500	$12,589
Virginia Intermont College	$19,800	$10,935
Barton College (NC)	$19,314	N/A
Brevard College (NC)	$19,190	$12,400
Chowan College (NC)	$19,100	$10,595
Ouachita Baptist University (AR)	$19,000	$13,022
John Brown University (AR)	$18,762	$11,400
Anderson College (SC)	$18,700	$13,694
North Carolina Wesleyan College	$18,225	N/A
Johnson C. Smith University (NC)	$18,108	$9,725
Livingstone College (NC)	$18,101	$7,270
Bryan College (TN)	$17,900	$10,117
Belhaven College (MS)	$17,800	$10,980
Midway College (KY)	$17,725	$9,028
Limestone College (SC)	$17,700	$9,350
Dillard University (LA)	$17,325	$13,443
Shorter College (GA)	$17,270	$10,051
Newberry College (SC)	$17,251	N/A
Kentucky Wesleyan College	$17,175	$11,416
Southern Adventist University (TN)	$17,080	N/A
Benedict College (SC)	$17,020	$11,000
Martin Methodist College (TN)	$17,000	N/A
Reinhardt College (GA)	$16,862	N/A
Oakwood College (AL)	$16,836	N/A
Lambuth University (TN)	$16,768	$9,704

Priciest private schools

Comprehensive Colleges–Bachelor's (Midwest)	Tuition, fees, room and board	Average financial aid package		Tuition, fees, room and board	Average financial aid package
Ohio Northern University	$30,675	$20,347	Marian College (IN)	$23,260	$13,717
Clarke College (IA)	$29,750	$14,654	Mount Union College (OH)	$23,160	$15,324
St. Mary's College (IN)	$29,263	$17,358	Northwestern College (MN)	$23,020	$13,499
Marietta College (OH)	$26,838	$17,761	Northland College (WI)	$22,750	$14,321
Otterbein College (OH)	$25,840	N/A	Carroll College (WI)	$22,740	$14,718
St. Norbert College (WI)	$25,810	$15,507	Ohio Dominican University	$22,700	N/A
Buena Vista University (IA)	$25,406	$19,049	Calvin College (MI)	$22,615	$13,270
Eureka College (IL)	$24,980	$13,978	Defiance College (OH)	$22,540	$13,493
Millikin University (IL)	$24,632	$16,233	Huntington College (IN)	$22,430	$13,794
Elmhurst College (IL)	$24,630	$15,400	Franklin College (IN)	$22,195	$13,337
Concordia University–St. Paul (MN)	$24,486	$11,339	Judson College (IL)	$22,050	$8,183
St. Joseph's College (IN)	$24,250	$13,800	Augustana College (SD)	$21,998	$14,299
Loras College (IA)	$24,233	$16,479	Briar Cliff University (IA)	$21,660	$16,995
Wilmington College (OH)	$24,172	$16,395	Morningside College (IA)	$21,610	$15,716
Concordia University (MI)	$23,995	$13,807	College of St. Mary (NE)	$21,570	$11,276
Central College (IA)	$23,898	$16,020	Mount Mercy College (IA)	$21,400	$13,649
Taylor University (IN)	$23,820	$13,351	Greenville College (IL)	$21,342	$13,704
Wartburg College (IA)	$23,730	$17,031	Trinity Christian College (IL)	$21,280	$8,469
Bluffton University (OH)	$23,690	$16,776	McKendree College (IL)	$21,120	$12,400
Simpson College (IA)	$23,658	$17,124	Waldorf College (IA)	$20,931	$15,752
Tri-State University (IN)	$23,600	$12,100	Wisconsin Lutheran College	$20,920	$13,342
Notre Dame College of Ohio	$23,502	$19,141	Midland Lutheran College (NE)	$20,730	$14,166
Manchester College (IN)	$23,390	$16,033	Dana College (NE)	$20,280	$14,623
St. Mary-of-the-Woods College (IN)	$23,290	N/A	Dordt College (IA)	$20,170	$14,665

Comprehensive Colleges–Bachelor's (West)	Tuition, fees, room and board	Average financial aid package		Tuition, fees, room and board	Average financial aid package
Menlo College (CA)	$31,010	$18,427	Concordia University–Austin (TX)	$21,705	$11,423
Linfield College (OR)	$27,110	$16,638	Carroll College (MT)	$20,476	$13,799
Sierra Nevada College (NV)	$26,106	$14,500	Texas Lutheran University	$20,370	$12,271
Master's Col. and Seminary (CA)	$23,470	$14,157	Northwest College (WA)	$19,666	$10,592
Vanguard University of Southern California	$22,278	$9,700	Rocky Mountain College (MT)	$19,015	$13,276
Pacific Union College (CA)	$22,185	$10,958	McMurry University (TX)	$17,847	$12,932
Western Baptist College (OR)	$21,798	$12,689	Bethany College (CA)	$17,800	$10,250
Northwest Christian College (OR)	$21,710	$14,157	Oklahoma Christian U.	$17,726	$11,748

Cheapest public schools

Four out of five students attend public institutions, where the costs for in-state students run far below the headline-grabbing level. The schools are listed by in-state tuition and fees for the 2003–2004 academic year. Also provided is the annual 2003–2004 charge for room and board, as well as the tuition and fees for out-of-state students. (Not all schools offer housing, so in some cases no charges appear for room and board—though you'll still have living expenses, of course.) In addition, the table lists the average need-based financial aid package granted to undergraduates during the 2003–2004 academic year. The typical aid package has three components: need-based grants, need-based loans, and work-study. In order to qualify, students must file an annual aid application that demonstrates financial need. Expenses for 2004–2005 are provided in the directory when available.

National Universities

	Tuition, fees (in-state)	Tuition, fees (out-of-state)	Room and board	Average financial aid package
University of Nevada–Las Vegas	$2,380	$8,490	$8,940	$6,911
San Diego State University	$2,488	$7,210	$8,787	$8,500
University of Louisiana–Lafayette	$2,730	$8,910	$3,126	$4,500
University of Florida	$2,780	$13,283	$5,800	$10,922
South Carolina State University	$2,785	$5,425	$3,568	N/A
University of Texas–El Paso	$2,796	$8,028	$4,255	$9,044
U. of North Carolina–Greensboro	$2,840	$15,418	$5,210	$9,269
Florida State University	$2,859	$13,887	$5,974	$5,512
University of South Alabama	$2,916	$5,672	$5,312	$2,867
University of Nevada–Reno	$2,925	$10,195	$7,275	$7,003
Florida Atlantic University	$2,943	$13,955	$5,600	$6,508
University of South Florida	$2,983	$14,011	$6,508	$8,799
Louisiana Tech University	$3,005	$6,801	$3,555	$6,233
University of Central Florida	$3,013	$14,041	$7,191	$5,397
University of New Orleans	$3,026	$10,070	$3,888	$5,605
Utah State University	$3,071	$8,946	$3,930	$4,980
N.M. Inst. of Mining and Tech.	$3,080	$9,601	$4,470	$7,641
University of Wyoming	$3,090	$8,940	$5,546	$8,944
Florida International University	$3,110	$14,138	$8,853	$6,839
East Carolina University (NC)	$3,131	$13,270	$5,540	N/A
University of Northern Colorado	$3,205	$12,331	$5,782	$7,379
University of New Mexico	$3,313	$11,954	$5,450	$7,829
University of Idaho	$3,348	$10,740	$4,868	N/A
New Mexico State University	$3,372	$11,250	$4,560	$8,292
Idaho State University	$3,448	$10,048	$4,680	N/A
University of Hawaii–Manoa	$3,465	$9,945	$5,675	$5,846
Wichita State University (KS)	$3,502	$10,744	$4,620	$5,702
West Virginia University	$3,548	$10,768	$5,822	$8,015
University of Colorado–Denver	$3,551	$15,179	N/A	$6,958
Northern Arizona University	$3,584	$12,104	$5,374	N/A
Arizona State University	$3,595	$12,115	N/A	N/A
University of Arizona	$3,603	$12,373	$6,810	N/A
Jackson State University (MS)	$3,612	$8,116	$4,770	$3,084
Texas Woman's University	$3,612	$9,312	$4,682	$10,412
Texas A&M University–Commerce	$3,620	$10,700	$5,370	$6,993
University of Utah	$3,647	$11,293	$5,036	$7,286
Louisiana State U.–Baton Rouge	$3,670	$8,970	$5,216	$6,342

Cheapest public schools

National Universities, continued

	Tuition, fees (in-state)	Tuition, fees (out-of-state)	Room and board	Average financial aid package
Univ. of Arkansas–Little Rock	$3,672	$8,430	$2,700	N/A
University of Oklahoma	$3,741	$10,254	$5,485	$8,453
Colorado State University	$3,744	$14,216	$6,045	$7,948
Oklahoma State University	$3,748	$10,066	$5,468	$7,910
Tennessee State University	$3,788	$11,720	$3,990	$3,670
Texas Southern University	$3,832	$10,912	$5,920	N/A
University of Alaska–Fairbanks	$3,850	$9,580	$4,950	$9,137
East Tennessee State University	$3,860	$8,660	$4,565	$4,528
Alabama A&M University	$3,872	$6,704	$4,500	N/A
Mississippi State University	$3,874	$8,780	$5,770	$8,488
Univ. of Southern Mississippi	$3,874	$8,752	$4,450	N/A
University of Mississippi	$3,916	$8,826	$5,300	N/A
Georgia State University	$3,920	$13,544	$6,471	N/A
North Dakota State University	$3,956	$8,956	$4,496	$4,425
Middle Tennessee State Univ.	$4,010	$11,942	$4,486	$4,887
University of Colorado–Boulder	$4,020	$20,336	$6,754	$9,962
SUNY College Environmental Science and Forestry	$4,041	$8,941	$9,400	$8,300
Kansas State University	$4,059	$11,949	$5,080	$6,229
U. of North Carolina–Chapel Hill	$4,072	$15,920	$6,045	$9,324
Georgia Institute of Technology	$4,076	$16,870	$6,150	$7,872
University of Georgia	$4,078	$14,854	$5,756	$7,323
University of Kansas	$4,101	$11,577	$4,822	$6,486
University of Alabama–Huntsville	$4,126	$8,702	$5,000	$5,560
University of Alabama	$4,134	$11,294	$4,456	$7,549
University of Memphis	$4,142	$12,082	$5,300	N/A
Montana State University–Bozeman	$4,145	$12,707	$5,370	$6,919
University of North Dakota	$4,156	$9,902	$4,234	$8,150
University of South Dakota	$4,205	$8,917	$3,504	$5,644
North Carolina State U.–Raleigh	$4,220	$16,118	$5,918	$7,497
University of Houston	$4,233	$11,313	$5,870	$12,000
South Dakota State University	$4,254	$8,965	$3,522	$7,126
University of Montana	$4,260	$11,860	$5,292	$8,832
Old Dominion University (VA)	$4,264	$13,294	$5,498	$7,191
University of Alabama–Birmingham	$4,274	$9,494	N/A	$8,536
Portland State University (OR)	$4,278	$13,674	$8,175	$7,712
University of Louisville (KY)	$4,344	$11,856	$3,872	$7,510
SUNY–Stony Brook	$4,358	$9,258	$7,346	$8,326
Wayne State University (MI)	$4,364	$9,395	$6,500	$7,336
Indiana State University	$4,422	$10,890	$4,998	$6,528
University of Texas–Arlington	$4,423	$11,503	$4,829	$8,014
Auburn University (AL)	$4,426	$12,886	$5,970	$6,696
University of Tennessee	$4,450	$13,532	$4,580	$6,954
University of Kentucky	$4,547	$11,227	$4,285	$7,421
University of Texas–Austin	$4,548	$11,668	$6,082	$8,750

Liberal Arts Colleges

	Tuition, fees (in-state)	Tuition, fees (out-of-state)	Room and board	Average financial aid package
University of Hawaii–Hilo	$2,426	$7,994	$4,600	$4,887
California State University–Monterey Bay	$2,474	$7,196	$5,600	$7,151
Western State College of Colorado	$2,479	$9,043	$5,680	$8,800
Mesa State College (CO)	$2,515	$8,168	$6,266	$6,206
Fort Lewis College (CO)	$2,789	$11,329	$5,664	$7,318
U. of North Carolina–Asheville	$3,101	$11,926	$4,978	$7,372
University of Virginia–Wise	$3,580	$12,468	$5,586	$5,798
Evergreen State College (WA)	$3,811	$13,492	$5,772	$10,006
Texas A&M Univ.–Galveston	$4,098	$11,178	$4,870	$9,281
Univ. of Maine–Presque Isle	$4,190	$9,740	$4,965	$6,854

Universities–Master's (North)

	Tuition, fees (in-state)	Tuition, fees (out-of-state)	Room and board	Average financial aid package
Univ. of the District of Columbia	$2,070	$4,710	N/A	$8,000
CUNY–City College	$3,384	$6,984	N/A	N/A
CUNY–Lehman College	$3,460	$7,060	N/A	$3,531
Salem State College (MA)	$3,938	$10,078	$5,428	$3,833
Rhode Island College	$3,995	$10,195	$6,340	N/A
Bowie State University (MD)	$4,064	$10,480	$5,288	$7,377
Buffalo State College	$4,109	$9,009	$5,640	$3,037
Worcester State College (MA)	$4,123	$10,203	$5,668	$6,868
SUNY Col. Arts & Sci.–New Paltz	$4,166	$9,066	$6,110	$2,446
Fitchburg State College (MA)	$4,186	$10,266	$5,436	$6,135
Coppin State University (MD)	$4,234	$9,777	$6,068	$6,606
SUNY College–Brockport	$4,271	$9,171	$6,860	$8,062
Delaware State University	$4,296	$9,096	N/A	$7,926
CUNY–Baruch College	$4,300	$11,100	N/A	$4,930
CUNY–College of Staten Island	$4,308	$8,908	N/A	$5,225
Framingham State College (MA)	$4,324	$10,404	$5,058	$4,700
CUNY–Hunter College	$4,329	$8,969	N/A	$5,842
Bridgewater State College (MA)	$4,342	$10,482	$5,922	$7,766
CUNY–Brooklyn College	$4,353	$8,993	N/A	$5,400
CUNY–Queens College	$4,361	$9,001	N/A	$8,600
Southern Connecticut State Univ.	$4,662	$10,584	$7,050	$6,865
Westfield State College (MA)	$4,857	$10,937	$5,378	N/A
Univ. of Maryland–Eastern Shore	$5,009	$9,881	$5,630	$9,500
Eastern Connecticut State Univ.	$5,045	$10,967	$6,752	$10,728
Western Connecticut State Univ.	$5,045	$10,967	$6,580	$6,343
SUNY–Oswego	$5,176	$11,126	$7,540	$8,411
SUNY College–Potsdam	$5,190	$11,140	$6,970	$11,203
University of Southern Maine	$5,198	$12,878	$5,738	$8,938
SUNY–Plattsburgh	$5,213	$11,163	$6,340	$8,447
SUNY College–Cortland	$5,235	$11,185	$6,860	$8,718
SUNY College–Oneonta	$5,256	$11,206	$7,230	$8,015
Frostburg State University (MD)	$5,342	$12,242	$5,772	$6,285
Cheyney U. of Pennsylvania	$5,353	$12,301	$5,383	N/A

Cheapest public schools

Universities–Master's (South)

	Tuition, fees (in-state)	Tuition, fees (out-of-state)	Room and board	Average financial aid package
Grambling State University (LA)	$1,591	$4,266	$1,678	N/A
Southern University–New Orleans	$2,266	$6,004	$7,019	N/A
Fayetteville State University (NC)	$2,465	$10,387	$3,820	N/A
University of West Florida	$2,470	$10,660	$6,000	N/A
U. of North Carolina–Pembroke	$2,495	$11,414	$4,364	$6,005
North Carolina A&T State Univ.	$2,561	$11,482	$4,768	N/A
Augusta State University (GA)	$2,592	$9,228	N/A	N/A
Armstrong Atlantic State University (GA)	$2,602	$9,238	N/A	N/A
McNeese State University (LA)	$2,619	$8,685	$3,720	N/A
Georgia Southwestern State University	$2,666	$9,002	$4,204	$6,141
Columbus State University (GA)	$2,676	$9,312	$5,270	$3,995
Florida A&M University	$2,702	$13,058	$5,492	N/A
Southern Univ. and A&M College (LA)	$2,702	$8,494	$4,360	$7,098
Fort Valley State University (GA)	$2,720	$9,356	$4,178	$7,476
Valdosta State University (GA)	$2,765	$9,097	$4,850	$6,484
Albany State University (GA)	$2,774	$9,410	N/A	N/A
State University of West Georgia	$2,774	$9,410	$4,406	$7,337
Kennesaw State University (GA)	$2,778	$8,606	N/A	$3,907
North Georgia College and State University	$2,808	$9,444	$4,160	N/A
Kentucky State University	$2,828	$8,472	$5,394	N/A
Savannah State University (GA)	$2,830	$9,466	$4,498	N/A
Florida Gulf Coast University	$2,837	$13,192	$7,000	N/A
Louisiana State U.–Shreveport	$2,884	$7,214	$6,403	N/A
University of Louisiana–Monroe	$2,910	$8,862	$4,790	N/A
Georgia Southern University	$2,912	$9,548	$5,628	$6,488
University of North Florida	$2,913	$13,268	$5,856	$2,237
Appalachian State University (NC)	$2,927	$12,277	$4,435	$5,778
Southeastern Louisiana University	$2,951	$8,279	$3,840	N/A
Nicholls State University (LA)	$2,993	$8,441	$3,402	N/A
Northwestern State U. of La.	$3,005	$9,083	$3,326	N/A
Western Carolina University (NC)	$3,034	$12,395	$4,406	$7,682
U. of North Carolina–Charlotte	$3,134	$13,171	$5,700	$8,210
Eastern Kentucky University	$3,198	$8,790	$4,510	$6,183
North Carolina Central Univ.	$3,218	$12,587	$4,311	$7,050
Arkansas Tech University	$3,256	$6,332	$3,576	N/A
Southern Arkansas University	$3,290	$4,850	$3,460	$6,612
Mississippi Univ. for Women	$3,298	$7,965	$3,230	$5,920

Universities–Master's (Midwest)

	Tuition, fees (in-state)	Tuition, fees (out-of-state)	Room and board	Average financial aid package
Fort Hays State University (KS)	$2,524	$8,148	$4,844	N/A
Emporia State University (KS)	$2,776	$8,914	$4,222	$5,430
Pittsburg State University (KS)	$2,962	$8,784	$4,166	$6,666
Minot State University (ND)	$3,225	$7,757	$3,274	$5,933
Chadron State College (NE)	$3,240	$5,850	$3,862	N/A
Peru State College (NE)	$3,310	$5,920	$4,950	N/A
Wayne State College (NE)	$3,462	$6,072	$3,920	N/A
Univ. of Wisconsin–Platteville	$3,722	$13,768	$3,978	N/A

Universities–Master's (Midwest), continued

	Tuition, fees (in-state)	Tuition, fees (out-of-state)	Room and board	Average financial aid package
Univ. of Wisconsin–Oshkosh	$3,750	$14,320	$3,970	$2,500
Lincoln University (MO)	$3,753	$6,585	$3,790	$5,000
Metropolitan State University (MN)	$3,852	$8,232	$8,984	N/A
Univ. of Nebraska–Kearney	$3,885	$7,148	$4,436	$6,490
University of Southern Indiana	$3,885	$9,188	$5,140	$5,134
Northeastern Illinois University	$3,957	$7,257	N/A	$5,591
Southern Illinois U.–Edwardsville	$4,015	$7,213	$5,338	$7,890
University of Nebraska–Omaha	$4,082	$10,922	$3,998	N/A
Purdue University–Calumet (IN)	$4,095	$9,821	N/A	$5,297
Washburn University (KS)	$4,112	$9,212	$4,972	$5,174
Univ. of Wisconsin–Stevens Point	$4,151	$14,197	$3,964	$6,308
Minnesota State University–Moorhead	$4,160	$4,160	$4,340	$4,193
Northern State University (SD)	$4,208	$8,920	$3,306	$4,996
Univ. of Wisconsin–Whitewater	$4,223	$14,879	$3,702	$5,970
Univ. of Wisconsin–River Falls	$4,230	$14,276	$3,806	N/A
Univ. of Wisconsin–Eau Claire	$4,313	$14,360	$4,150	$6,577
Univ. of Wisconsin–La Crosse	$4,358	$14,404	$4,150	$4,099

Universities–Master's (West)

	Tuition, fees (in-state)	Tuition, fees (out-of-state)	Room and board	Average financial aid package
San Francisco State University	$1,788	$10,740	$8,090	$8,638
Calif. State Poly. Univ.–Pomona	$1,968	$9,348	$6,747	$8,258
New Mexico Highlands University	$2,278	$9,776	$3,264	$7,924
California State Univ.–Bakersfield	$2,341	$9,109	$5,698	N/A
California State U.–Long Beach	$2,362	$10,822	$5,800	$7,635
California State Univ.–Hayward	$2,385	$9,153	$6,453	$7,251
Calif. State U.–Dominguez Hills	$2,410	$9,178	$5,022	$7,860
California State University–San Marcos	$2,414	$9,831	N/A	N/A
Southeastern Oklahoma State U.	$2,418	$5,808	$2,877	$1,318
University of Texas–Brownsville	$2,431	$10,684	N/A	$3,048
California State U.–Los Angeles	$2,440	$9,208	N/A	$7,416
California State U.–Northridge	$2,444	$13,348	$7,965	N/A
Humboldt State University (CA)	$2,461	$4,922	$6,409	N/A
Eastern New Mexico University	$2,472	$8,028	$4,290	$7,207
Western New Mexico University	$2,472	$9,347	$5,880	$5,927
California State U.–Stanislaus	$2,508	$10,968	$7,742	$7,472
California State U.–Sacramento	$2,513	$13,019	$6,523	$8,066
California State U.–Fullerton	$2,516	$10,976	N/A	$6,916
University of Central Oklahoma	$2,524	$6,069	$3,670	N/A
East Central University (OK)	$2,548	$5,768	$2,774	N/A
San Jose State University (CA)	$2,563	$11,023	$8,465	N/A
Calif. State U.–San Bernardino	$2,580	$7,302	$8,253	N/A
Weber State University (UT)	$2,632	$7,958	$6,150	$5,450
Northwestern Oklahoma State U.	$2,649	$4,329	$2,720	$4,660
Northeastern State University (OK)	$2,700	$6,600	$3,624	$8,100
California State Univ.–Fresno	$2,704	$9,104	$7,180	$5,449

Cheapest public schools

Universities–Master's (West), continued

	Tuition, fees (in-state)	Tuition, fees (out-of-state)	Room and board	Average financial aid package
Adams State College (CO)	$2,712	$8,342	$5,730	$4,586
Southwestern Oklahoma State U.	$2,758	$6,658	$2,910	$3,788
University of Texas–Pan American	$2,779	$9,259	$4,333	N/A
Cameron University (OK)	$2,781	$3,903	$3,782	$4,924
Southern Utah University	$2,794	$8,158	$3,380	N/A

Comprehensive Colleges– Bachelor's (North)

	Tuition, fees (in-state)	Tuition, fees (out-of-state)	Room and board	Average financial aid package
CUNY–New York City College of Technology	$3,550	$7,150	N/A	N/A
University of Maine–Fort Kent	$3,994	$9,064	$4,880	N/A
University of Maine–Machias	$4,115	$10,115	$5,150	N/A
CUNY–Medgar Evers College	$4,232	$8,872	N/A	N/A
CUNY–York College	$4,242	$8,882	$6,976	N/A
SUNY–Farmingdale	$4,251	$10,151	$8,194	N/A
University of Maine–Augusta	$4,665	$9,645	N/A	$6,778

Comprehensive Colleges– Bachelor's (South)

	Tuition, fees (in-state)	Tuition, fees (out-of-state)	Room and board	Average financial aid package
West Virginia University–Parkersburg	$1,548	$4,944	N/A	N/A
Winston-Salem State University (NC)	$2,336	$10,207	$4,892	$3,356
Clayton College and State University (GA)	$2,441	$9,077	N/A	$5,944
Elizabeth City State Univ. (NC)	$2,553	$10,817	$4,608	N/A
West Virginia State University	$2,665	$6,334	$4,400	N/A
Bluefield State College (WV)	$2,806	$6,894	N/A	$5,000
Glenville State College (WV)	$2,952	$5,124	$4,860	$7,554
Fairmont State University (WV)	$3,130	$7,038	$5,360	$5,121

Comprehensive Colleges–Bachelor's (Midwest)

	Tuition, fees (in-state)	Tuition, fees (out-of-state)	Room and board	Average financial aid package
Dickinson State University (ND)	$3,139	$7,405	$3,350	N/A
Missouri Southern State University	$3,976	$7,786	$4,340	$6,722
Mayville State University (ND)	$3,992	$8,293	$3,344	N/A
Valley City State University (ND)	$4,026	$8,454	$3,254	$5,736
Central State University (OH)	$4,287	$9,282	$6,069	N/A
Dakota State University (SD)	$4,378	$9,089	$3,250	$5,839

Comprehensive Colleges–Bachelor's (West)

	Tuition, fees (in-state)	Tuition, fees (out-of-state)	Room and board	Average financial aid package
University of Houston–Downtown	$2,088	$7,752	N/A	N/A
Langston University (OK)	$2,262	$5,152	$6,720	$7,738
Utah Valley State College	$2,450	$7,630	N/A	$6,120
Oklahoma Panhandle State Univ.	$2,500	$5,142	$2,870	N/A

Great deals at great schools

To determine which schools offer the best value, *U.S. News* uses a formula that relates a school's academic quality to the net cost of attendance for a student who receives the average level of financial aid. The higher the quality of the program (as indicated by its *U.S. News* ranking) and the lower the cost, the better the deal. We considered only schools ranked in the top half of their peer groups. The methodology we used is described in detail below.

National Universities

		% receiving grants based on need	Average cost after receiving grants based on need	Average discount from total cost			% receiving grants based on need	Average cost after receiving grants based on need	Average discount from total cost
1	California Institute of Technology	58%	$12,538	66%	26	Rensselaer Polytechnic Inst. (NY)	70%	$19,389	51%
2	Princeton University (NJ)	49%	$15,980	60%	27	Emory University (GA)	36%	$20,210	48%
3	Harvard University (MA)	48%	$16,532	60%	28	Howard University (DC)	36%	$11,245	45%
4	Yale University (CT)	40%	$16,446	59%	29	Tufts University (MA)	37%	$19,468	52%
5	Massachusetts Inst. of Technology	59%	$18,805	54%	30	Clark University (MA)	60%	$15,803	53%
6	Stanford University (CA)	47%	$18,221	56%	31	Univ. of Southern California	43%	$19,768	51%
7	Columbia University (NY)	41%	$17,095	58%	32	University of Rochester (NY)	58%	$20,319	47%
8	Duke University (NC)	38%	$18,871	53%	33	Lehigh University (PA)	44%	$19,917	47%
9	Dartmouth College (NH)	47%	$19,078	53%	34	Carnegie Mellon University (PA)	48%	$23,984	38%
10	University of Pennsylvania	42%	$20,163	51%	35	Pepperdine University (CA)	52%	$19,408	49%
11	Johns Hopkins University (MD)	37%	$19,623	51%	36	Wake Forest University (NC)	32%	$20,701	43%
12	Washington University in St. Louis	45%	$21,142	48%	37	University of the Pacific (CA)	66%	$17,401	50%
13	University of Chicago	47%	$21,126	48%	38	North Carolina State U.–Raleigh	42%	$14,346	41%
14	Rice University (TX)	36%	$18,322	36%	39	Yeshiva University (NY)	41%	$18,523	42%
15	Brown University (RI)	41%	$20,673	49%	40	SUNY Col Envir Science and Forestry	80%	$16,891	15%
16	University of Notre Dame (IN)	45%	$19,632	47%	41	Michigan State University	57%	$17,043	30%
17	Cornell University (NY)	44%	$21,167	48%	42	University of Georgia	10%	$13,447	42%
18	University of Texas–Austin	51%	$14,196	33%	43	Worcester Polytechnic Inst. (MA)	72%	$24,085	40%
19	U. of North Carolina–Chapel Hill	30%	$15,510	37%	44	College of William and Mary (VA)	31%	$19,374	33%
20	Vanderbilt University (TN)	36%	$19,374	52%	45	Boston College	37%	$21,681	45%
21	University of Virginia	22%	$16,774	45%	46	Brandeis University (MA)	46%	$23,767	41%
22	Loyola University Chicago	73%	$14,056	56%	47	Illinois Institute of Technology	57%	$17,436	44%
23	Northwestern University (IL)	41%	$22,036	46%	48	University of California–Berkeley	35%	$24,034	30%
24	Case Western Reserve Univ. (OH)	54%	$18,285	46%	49	University of Miami (FL)	54%	$21,433	43%
25	Brigham Young Univ.–Provo (UT)	29%	$10,254	19%	50	St. Louis University	67%	$21,139	37%

To be considered, a university or college had to finish in the top half of its categories in the *U.S. News* "America's Best Colleges 2005" rankings. The best values rankings were based on three variables:

1. Ratio of quality to price: A school's ranking—its overall score in the "America's Best Colleges" survey—was divided by the cost to a student receiving an average grant meeting financial need. The higher the ratio, the better the value.
2. Percentage of all undergraduates receiving grants meeting financial need during the 2003–2004 year.
3. Average discount: percentage of a school's 2003–2004 total costs (tuition, room and board, fees, books, and other expenses) covered by the average need-based grant to undergraduates. In the case of public institutions, 2003–2004 out-of-state tuition and percentage of out-of-state students receiving grants meeting need were used.

Overall rank was determined first by standardizing the scores achieved by every school in each of the three variables and weighting those scores. The first variable—the ratio of quality to price—accounted for 60 percent of the overall score; the percentage of all undergraduates receiving grants accounted for 25 percent; and the average discount accounted for 15 percent. The weighted scores for each school were totaled. The school with the highest total weighted points became No. 1 in its category. The scores for the other schools were then ranked in descending order.

Liberal Arts Colleges

		% receiving grants based on need	Average cost after receiving grants based on need	Average discount from total cost
1	Williams College (MA)	40%	$14,585	62%
2	Amherst College (MA)	47%	$17,195	58%
3	Swarthmore College (PA)	49%	$17,765	56%
4	Pomona College (CA)	51%	$17,306	56%
5	Wellesley College (MA)	55%	$17,888	55%
6	Wabash College (IN)	70%	$14,511	51%
7	Grinnell College (IA)	60%	$16,744	48%
8	Colgate University (NY)	42%	$15,859	59%
9	Bryn Mawr College (PA)	58%	$17,107	56%
10	Washington and Lee University (VA)	22%	$13,991	56%
11	Macalester College (MN)	69%	$16,921	50%
12	Claremont McKenna College (CA)	55%	$17,401	55%
13	Centre College (KY)	64%	$14,861	49%
14	Carleton College (MN)	58%	$19,424	47%
15	Bowdoin College (ME)	45%	$18,363	54%
16	Middlebury College (VT)	40%	$17,690	56%
17	Smith College (MA)	56%	$18,986	53%
18	Colby College (ME)	37%	$16,704	58%
19	Mount Holyoke College (MA)	67%	$19,356	51%
20	Wesleyan University (CT)	46%	$18,833	54%
21	Haverford College (PA)	41%	$18,343	55%
22	Hanover College (IN)	86%	$14,881	46%
23	Vassar College (NY)	52%	$19,559	50%
24	Lafayette College (PA)	51%	$17,277	54%
25	Wells College (NY)	77%	$13,287	44%
26	Agnes Scott College (GA)	64%	$15,738	49%
27	Sewanee–University of the South (TN)	45%	$16,045	51%
28	Hamilton College (NY)	55%	$19,559	50%
29	Furman University (SC)	43%	$15,304	51%
30	Trinity College (CT)	40%	$17,588	56%
31	Occidental College (CA)	54%	$17,471	55%
32	Knox College (IL)	73%	$16,361	49%
33	Beloit College (WI)	73%	$17,538	44%
34	Lake Forest College (IL)	77%	$15,353	51%
35	Willamette University (OR)	64%	$17,217	50%
36	Albion College (MI)	64%	$14,819	50%
37	Thomas Aquinas College (CA)	61%	$13,320	43%
38	College of Wooster (OH)	63%	$16,780	49%
39	Wofford College (SC)	52%	$14,780	50%
40	Gettysburg College (PA)	58%	$17,915	51%

Universities–Master's (North)

		% receiving grants based on need	Average cost after receiving grants based on need	Average discount from total cost
1	Gallaudet University (DC)	72%	$9,858	56%
2	Alfred University (NY)	87%	$14,702	53%
3	Le Moyne College (NY)	80%	$14,120	50%
4	Hood College (MD)	77%	$15,796	47%
5	Col. of Notre Dame of Maryland	70%	$14,108	51%
6	Villanova University (PA)	38%	$22,912	38%
7	St. Michael's College (VT)	63%	$18,857	40%
8	Rochester Inst. of Technology (NY)	64%	$20,360	33%
9	Lebanon Valley College (PA)	78%	$16,638	46%
10	Ithaca College (NY)	65%	$20,953	38%
11	St. Bonaventure University (NY)	71%	$16,129	38%
12	University of Scranton (PA)	64%	$22,393	32%
13	Nazareth College of Rochester (NY)	80%	$17,382	35%
14	Providence College (RI)	49%	$23,804	27%
15	St. Francis University (PA)	85%	$16,123	44%

Great deals at great schools

Universities–Master's (South)

		% receiving grants based on need	Average cost after receiving grants based on need	Average discount from total cost
1	University of Richmond (VA)	31%	$16,398	49%
2	Murray State University (KY)	57%	$8,957	26%
3	Mississippi Univ. for Women	25%	$7,695	44%
4	Converse College (SC)	69%	$13,424	51%
5	Rollins College (FL)	41%	$16,911	55%
6	Stetson University (FL)	57%	$16,936	46%
7	Mercer University (GA)	70%	$16,843	43%
8	The Citadel (SC)	33%	$14,006	37%
9	Mississippi College	39%	$11,331	43%
10	Centenary College of Louisiana	62%	$15,537	41%
11	Harding University (AR)	46%	$12,356	31%
12	Spring Hill College (AL)	68%	$16,891	42%
13	Carson-Newman College (TN)	67%	$12,725	39%
14	Meredith College (NC)	57%	$15,530	39%
15	Loyola University New Orleans	54%	$18,226	40%

Universities–Master's (Midwest)

		% receiving grants based on need	Average cost after receiving grants based on need	Average discount from total cost
1	Valparaiso University (IN)	67%	$16,578	41%
2	University of Evansville (IN)	67%	$14,335	47%
3	Drake University (IA)	58%	$16,504	41%
4	Drury University (MO)	87%	$14,504	32%
5	Creighton University (NE)	50%	$17,895	39%
6	Bradley University (IL)	70%	$17,326	33%
7	Aquinas College (MI)	72%	$11,208	53%
8	John Carroll University (OH)	71%	$18,739	38%
9	Doane College (NE)	80%	$13,458	40%
10	Butler University (IN)	58%	$18,850	39%
11	Dominican University (IL)	77%	$16,056	37%
12	Xavier University (OH)	48%	$19,791	33%
13	North Central College (IL)	68%	$16,371	41%
14	Baldwin-Wallace College (OH)	75%	$18,043	35%
15	University of Detroit Mercy	71%	$16,144	46%

Universities–Master's (West)

		% receiving grants based on need	Average cost after receiving grants based on need	Average discount from total cost
1	Trinity University (TX)	39%	$17,645	38%
2	Whitworth College (WA)	70%	$19,093	38%
3	University of Portland (OR)	58%	$18,271	41%
4	Seattle Pacific University	62%	$16,942	42%
5	Pacific University (OR)	75%	$15,696	43%
6	Gonzaga University (WA)	51%	$19,597	36%
7	St. Mary's College of California	55%	$19,275	45%
8	Westminster College (UT)	70%	$15,558	39%
9	Abilene Christian University (TX)	61%	$14,758	33%
10	George Fox University (OR)	78%	$17,303	39%
11	Santa Clara University (CA)	41%	$24,311	37%
12	St. Mary's Univ. of San Antonio	64%	$18,165	29%
13	LeTourneau University (TX)	70%	$15,988	31%
14	University of Redlands (CA)	68%	$24,092	35%
15	Chapman University (CA)	61%	$22,327	40%

Comprehensive Colleges–Bachelor's (North)

		% receiving grants based on need	Average cost after receiving grants based on need	Average discount from total cost
1	Grove City College (PA)	35%	$11,306	29%
2	Elizabethtown College (PA)	72%	$17,710	41%
3	College of St. Elizabeth (NJ)	70%	$14,845	48%
4	Stonehill College (MA)	63%	$21,605	34%
5	Elmira College (NY)	80%	$19,782	43%
6	Cedar Crest College (PA)	83%	$18,362	39%
7	Wilson College (PA)	71%	$14,034	46%
8	Utica College (NY)	91%	$17,743	41%
9	Mercyhurst College (PA)	75%	$18,449	33%
10	Neumann College (PA)	84%	$14,890	45%

Comprehensive Colleges–Bachelor's (South)

		% receiving grants based on need	Average cost after receiving grants based on need	Average discount from total cost
1	Claflin University (SC)	94%	$9,258	51%
2	Berry College (GA)	56%	$14,454	41%
3	University of the Ozarks (AR)	53%	$10,987	46%
4	Maryville College (TN)	79%	$16,085	44%
5	Covenant College (GA)	72%	$14,029	46%
6	Kentucky Wesleyan College	88%	$13,198	41%
7	LaGrange College (GA)	68%	$13,744	41%
8	John Brown University (AR)	33%	$11,519	48%
9	Florida Southern College	70%	$14,304	43%
10	Lenoir-Rhyne College (NC)	81%	$14,716	41%

Comprehensive Colleges–Bachelor's (Midwest)

		% receiving grants based on need	Average cost after receiving grants based on need	Average discount from total cost
1	Wartburg College (IA)	79%	$14,607	43%
2	Simpson College (IA)	88%	$15,077	43%
3	Augustana College (SD)	70%	$13,966	42%
4	Central College (IA)	81%	$15,301	43%
5	St. Norbert College (WI)	65%	$16,436	40%
6	Mount Union College (OH)	80%	$14,643	42%
7	Manchester College (IN)	77%	$12,724	50%
8	Buena Vista University (IA)	91%	$15,291	44%
9	Taylor University (IN)	53%	$16,402	37%
10	Franklin College (IN)	82%	$14,522	41%

Comprehensive Colleges–Bachelor's (West)

		% receiving grants based on need	Average cost after receiving grants based on need	Average discount from total cost
1	Brigham Young University–Hawaii	33%	$6,985	28%
2	Texas Lutheran University	58%	$11,977	48%
3	Carroll College (MT)	63%	$14,106	36%
4	Howard Payne University (TX)	74%	$11,375	37%
5	East Texas Baptist University	65%	$11,287	32%
6	Rocky Mountain College (MT)	60%	$13,639	38%
7	Western Baptist College (OR)	82%	$17,420	31%
8	Northwest Christian College (OR)	76%	$14,579	40%
9	Master's Col. and Seminary (CA)	62%	$17,101	37%
10	Oklahoma Baptist University	57%	$15,367	18%

Schools that award the largest need-based financial aid packages

The schools at the top of this list handed out the largest need-based financial aid packages, on average, during the 2003–2004 school year. The typical aid package has three components: need-based grants, need-based loans, and work-study. In order to qualify, students must file an annual aid application that demonstrates financial need. The table also lists the percentage of undergraduates receiving the average need-based aid package, the average need-based grant, and average need-based loan awarded to undergraduates, and the average percentage of a student's demonstrated need that was met by the school during the 2003–2004 academic year. In addition, some colleges give out merit awards, which are based on academic ability or other talents and not on financial need. The table lists the percentage of undergraduates receiving such awards and the average amount of the award during the 2003–2004 academic year.

National Universities	Average amount of aid package	% students receiving need-based package	Average need-based grant	Average need-based loan	Average % of need met	Average merit award	% students receiving merit awards
George Washington University (DC)	$29,206	39%	$16,744	$7,317	94%	$12,291	20%
Vanderbilt University (TN)	$28,495	38%	$20,673	$4,850	99%	$18,011	12%
Cornell University (NY)	$27,339	47%	$19,911	$7,248	100%	$0	0%
Columbia University (NY)	$27,079	42%	$23,555	$4,626	100%	N/A	N/A
Stanford University (CA)	$27,000	48%	$23,000	$2,600	100%	$2,800	10%
Yale University (CT)	$26,978	40%	$23,574	$2,591	100%	$0	0%
Harvard University (MA)	$26,939	48%	$24,418	$2,447	100%	$0	0%
University of Southern California	$26,465	48%	$20,414	$5,363	100%	$11,318	17%
Johns Hopkins University (MD)	$26,257	40%	$20,599	$3,931	95%	$13,096	5%
California Institute of Technology	$26,230	59%	$23,873	$1,212	100%	$24,729	11%
Duke University (NC)	$26,162	40%	$21,607	$5,050	100%	$9,370	14%
University of Pennsylvania	$26,029	46%	$20,707	$4,163	100%	N/A	N/A
Dartmouth College (NH)	$25,945	51%	$21,529	$4,800	100%	$311	0.2%
Tulane University (LA)	$25,837	42%	$18,025	$6,131	91%	$15,306	29%
Princeton University (NJ)	$25,460	49%	$23,660	$0	100%	N/A	N/A
University of Chicago	$25,388	48%	$19,864	$5,017	100%	$10,826	12%
Boston University	$25,338	47%	$16,953	$4,826	90%	$14,324	13%
Emory University (GA)	$25,238	38%	$18,962	$4,715	100%	$16,422	6%
Pepperdine University (CA)	$25,169	55%	$18,482	$5,476	88%	$17,237	10%
Massachusetts Institute of Technology	$24,875	61%	$22,225	$3,931	100%	$0	0%
Rensselaer Polytechnic Institute (NY)	$24,842	70%	$19,861	$5,810	92%	$13,824	14%
Northwestern University (IL)	$24,508	44%	$18,857	$3,876	100%	$4,793	0.4%
Washington University in St. Louis	$24,461	45%	$19,641	$6,214	100%	$9,231	14%
Brown University (RI)	$24,402	43%	$19,877	$4,642	100%	N/A	0%
American University (DC)	$24,370	44%	$12,699	$7,454	79%	$12,410	13%
University of La Verne (CA)	$24,188	81%	$10,027	$5,413	85%	$7,144	11%
Tufts University (MA)	$24,084	41%	$20,932	$4,202	100%	$500	2%
Case Western Reserve University (OH)	$23,571	55%	$15,695	$5,908	94%	$12,352	34%
Lehigh University (PA)	$23,533	46%	$17,403	$4,476	100%	$13,193	8%
University of Notre Dame (IN)	$23,412	48%	$17,160	$5,101	100%	$7,963	3%
Boston College	$23,215	42%	$17,698	$4,521	100%	$7,305	3%
Clark University (MA)	$23,136	60%	$18,012	$3,711	97%	$12,056	8%
University of Miami (FL)	$22,940	55%	$16,363	$5,113	82%	$12,776	21%
University of Rochester (NY)	$22,854	59%	$17,801	$4,981	100%	$10,022	34%
Georgetown University (DC)	$22,344	41%	$15,663	$3,859	100%	$3,500	0.1%
Southern Methodist University (TX)	$22,255	39%	$13,355	$3,511	92%	$5,485	30%

National Universities, continued

	Average amount of aid package	% students receiving need-based package	Average need-based grant	Average need-based loan	Average % of need met	Average merit award	% students receiving merit awards
Brandeis University (MA)	$22,199	48%	$16,420	$6,052	82%	$16,883	23%
University of the Pacific (CA)	$22,096	68%	$17,379	$4,721	N/A	$7,766	10%
Carnegie Mellon University (PA)	$21,658	51%	$15,007	$6,065	85%	$10,949	10%
Wake Forest University (NC)	$21,413	33%	$15,699	$6,380	91%	$10,201	30%
University of San Diego	$21,295	52%	$15,830	$4,741	94%	$11,712	13%
Worcester Polytechnic Institute (MA)	$21,030	74%	$15,776	$6,104	90%	$17,352	8%
Polytechnic University (NY)	$20,600	83%	$8,407	$5,062	87%	$16,341	15%
Florida Institute of Technology	$20,497	61%	$13,798	$4,868	83%	$7,280	21%
Loyola University Chicago	$20,488	75%	$17,942	$4,457	78%	$8,557	17%
Illinois Institute of Technology	$20,282	57%	$13,485	$4,807	87%	$9,981	40%
Andrews University (MI)	$20,162	65%	$6,426	$4,359	100%	$4,562	32%
Alliant International University (CA)	$19,668	57%	$8,838	$7,000	88%	$3,141	7%
University of San Francisco	$19,440	60%	$13,635	$4,989	72%	$13,247	4%
University of Hartford (CT)	$19,230	64%	$10,189	$5,185	74%	$8,302	8%
University of Tulsa (OK)	$19,097	50%	$4,220	$6,228	96%	$9,334	27%
Syracuse University (NY)	$18,720	58%	$12,793	$5,200	80%	$7,240	17%
New York University	$18,686	56%	$12,371	$5,068	67%	$6,497	12%
Widener University (PA)	$18,668	81%	$11,379	$5,781	91%	$8,117	13%
St. Louis University	$18,526	70%	$12,459	$5,222	62%	$8,692	17%
Fordham University (NY)	$18,363	66%	$13,771	$4,262	77%	$8,276	8%
Stevens Institute of Technology (NJ)	$18,336	70%	$12,871	$4,298	85%	$9,663	13%
University of Denver	$17,190	46%	$13,361	$5,188	69%	$7,180	30%
Marquette University (WI)	$16,853	60%	$10,774	$5,591	86%	$6,674	21%
Clarkson University (NY)	$16,730	82%	$8,469	$8,000	88%	$6,909	7%
St. John's University (NY)	$15,763	81%	$6,993	$4,222	72%	$8,000	N/A
Yeshiva University (NY)	$15,709	47%	$13,541	$4,967	72%	$5,632	7%
University of St. Thomas (MN)	$15,688	55%	$8,809	$3,767	81%	$6,404	11%
Biola University (CA)	$15,434	66%	$10,045	$2,918	73%	$10,005	11%
Northeastern University (MA)	$15,396	64%	$11,050	$4,836	63%	$12,627	12%
Duquesne University (PA)	$15,179	67%	$10,303	$4,478	83%	$8,113	19%
University of Vermont	$14,960	56%	$10,079	$5,980	82%	$2,132	12%
Catholic University of America (DC)	$14,945	81%	$4,478	$4,648	57%	$8,533	10%
Nova Southeastern University (FL)	$14,294	76%	$7,356	$5,535	50%	$2,604	21%
University of New Hampshire	$14,267	55%	$2,281	$3,354	80%	$5,414	19%
Seton Hall University (NJ)	$13,980	63%	$4,498	$3,026	69%	$11,763	15%
DePaul University (IL)	$13,691	75%	$8,989	$4,331	67%	$7,070	2%
Adelphi University (NY)	$13,500	68%	$5,043	$4,239	N/A	$6,971	20%
University of California–Berkeley	$13,481	50%	$9,441	$4,648	89%	$3,066	6%
University of Dayton (OH)	$13,181	60%	$8,403	$3,651	84%	$3,141	32%
University of California–Santa Cruz	$12,999	45%	$8,744	$4,284	91%	$4,975	3%
Pace University (NY)	$12,919	84%	$4,780	$4,120	87%	$5,644	5%
Rice University (TX)	$12,903	37%	$10,461	$3,103	100%	$3,101	19%
Pennsylvania State University–University Park	$12,773	50%	$4,569	$4,217	63%	$6,212	21%
Howard University (DC)	$12,708	64%	$9,250	$7,152	46%	$8,104	17%
Texas Christian University	$12,614	43%	$8,877	$4,970	94%	$7,979	20%
Temple University (PA)	$12,453	67%	$4,687	$3,602	86%	$3,676	20%
University of California–San Diego	$12,420	49%	$8,137	$4,761	87%	$5,875	3%
University of Virginia	$12,408	23%	$9,564	$4,368	92%	$5,667	18%
New School University (NY)	$12,350	57%	$9,412	$4,355	63%	$5,428	5%
Baylor University (TX)	$12,282	46%	$7,954	$2,429	66%	$5,419	28%
University of California–Los Angeles	$12,122	54%	$8,474	$5,198	82%	$3,680	4%
University of Houston	$12,000	58%	$7,800	$4,200	81%	$2,800	19%

Schools that award the largest need-based financial aid packages

National Universities, continued

	Average amount of aid package	% students receiving need-based package	Average need-based grant	Average need-based loan	Average % of need met	Average merit award	% students receiving merit awards
University of Illinois–Chicago	$11,600	52%	$7,032	$3,819	90%	$3,009	7%
University of Missouri–Kansas City	$11,547	61%	$4,309	$6,347	64%	$3,890	13%
University of California–Santa Barbara	$11,439	45%	$7,429	$5,274	81%	$3,913	2%
University of Michigan–Ann Arbor	$11,375	40%	$7,512	$4,780	90%	$4,744	21%
University of California–Riverside	$11,310	62%	$7,514	$4,836	84%	$4,966	1%
University of California–Irvine	$11,251	49%	$7,987	$4,554	83%	$5,965	4%
University of Florida	$10,922	40%	$4,459	$4,284	87%	$3,770	47%
Hofstra University (NY)	$10,649	56%	$6,897	$4,105	N/A	$5,400	7%
SUNY–Binghamton	$10,629	50%	$4,752	$4,214	84%	$2,471	2%
Texas Woman's University	$10,412	58%	$3,934	$3,720	98%	$2,100	5%
University of Wisconsin–Madison	$10,302	32%	$5,655	$4,248	N/A	$2,773	15%
Rutgers–New Brunswick (NJ)	$10,288	50%	$6,738	$4,064	82%	$4,954	10%
University of Massachusetts–Amherst	$10,275	51%	$5,491	$3,962	88%	$5,447	2%
Drexel University (PA)	$10,266	70%	$4,873	$6,749	46%	$6,469	17%
University of Pittsburgh	$10,003	56%	$5,183	$4,641	77%	$7,188	12%
University of Colorado–Boulder	$9,962	27%	$4,740	$4,190	73%	$5,210	19%
University of California–Davis	$9,864	47%	$6,965	$4,248	76%	$2,179	7%
University of Delaware	$9,750	39%	$5,600	$4,600	79%	$4,070	20%
Washington State University	$9,705	52%	$5,504	$4,640	95%	$3,245	5%
University of Massachusetts–Boston	$9,552	61%	$4,729	$5,393	91%	$3,026	1%
University of Missouri–Rolla	$9,550	53%	$5,760	$4,050	84%	$6,010	30%
University of Rhode Island	$9,430	51%	$5,501	$4,862	56%	$4,543	4%
University of Washington	$9,430	48%	$6,300	$4,600	88%	$3,260	2%
University of South Carolina–Columbia	$9,371	45%	$3,060	$3,962	91%	$4,037	43%
University of North Carolina–Chapel Hill	$9,324	32%	$5,589	$3,674	100%	$5,426	14%
University of Missouri–Columbia	$9,278	43%	$5,417	$3,973	86%	$4,497	24%

Liberal Arts Colleges

	Average amount of aid package	% students receiving need-based package	Average need-based grant	Average need-based loan	Average % of need met	Average merit award	% students receiving merit awards
Wesleyan University (CT)	$28,950	49%	$21,776	$5,478	100%	$0	0%
Pitzer College (CA)	$27,950	42%	$21,101	$4,941	100%	$10,000	3%
Occidental College (CA)	$27,814	61%	$21,647	$5,435	100%	$17,292	18%
Smith College (MA)	$27,378	56%	$20,988	$4,401	100%	$8,943	4%
Pomona College (CA)	$26,452	51%	$22,274	$2,822	100%	$0	0%
Williams College (MA)	$26,212	42%	$23,665	$4,576	100%	$0	0%
Swarthmore College (PA)	$26,088	49%	$22,251	$3,141	100%	$28,500	1%
Barnard College (NY)	$26,045	42%	$21,533	$3,951	100%	$0	0%
St. Lawrence University (NY)	$26,013	70%	$18,585	$6,134	90%	$9,151	10%
Middlebury College (VT)	$25,899	40%	$22,160	$2,922	100%	$0	0%
Sarah Lawrence College (NY)	$25,826	49%	$21,014	$3,080	95%	$6,418	12%
Trinity College (CT)	$25,648	42%	$22,337	$4,111	97%	$12,927	0.2%
Whittier College (CA)	$25,619	69%	$12,005	N/A	100%	N/A	N/A
Mount Holyoke College (MA)	$25,469	70%	$20,062	$4,867	100%	$10,950	5%
Colgate University (NY)	$25,421	44%	$22,956	$2,772	100%	$0	0%
Amherst College (MA)	$25,366	48%	$23,703	$2,233	100%	$0	0%

Liberal Arts Colleges, continued

	Average amount of aid package	% students receiving need-based package	Average need-based grant	Average need-based loan	Average % of need met	Average merit award	% students receiving merit awards
Bowdoin College (ME)	$25,295	45%	$21,437	$3,890	100%	$1,000	3%
Bryn Mawr College (PA)	$25,139	62%	$21,583	$4,421	99%	$0	0%
Haverford College (PA)	$25,073	43%	$22,203	$3,947	100%	N/A	0%
Hampshire College (MA)	$24,615	54%	$18,260	$4,030	100%	$4,990	2%
Wellesley College (MA)	$24,468	57%	$21,628	$3,196	100%	N/A	0%
Bates College (ME)	$24,457	40%	$21,234	$3,335	100%	N/A	N/A
Gettysburg College (PA)	$24,317	60%	$18,531	$4,527	100%	$7,805	5%
Reed College (OR)	$24,309	54%	$20,880	$4,119	100%	$0	0%
Vassar College (NY)	$24,305	53%	$19,511	$3,009	100%	$0	0%
Scripps College (CA)	$24,124	48%	$19,475	$3,720	100%	$14,396	10%
Skidmore College (NY)	$24,114	42%	$18,765	$3,608	94%	$10,000	1%
Colby College (ME)	$24,111	40%	$22,766	$2,991	100%	N/A	N/A
Claremont McKenna College (CA)	$23,906	55%	$21,329	$3,832	100%	$6,022	10%
Connecticut College	$23,900	46%	$21,198	$4,119	100%	$0	0%
Union College (NY)	$23,798	49%	$19,590	$4,351	100%	$11,998	5%
Colorado College	$23,278	45%	$19,275	$3,866	92%	$16,100	14%
Hamilton College (NY)	$22,980	58%	$19,451	$3,952	99%	$9,665	4%
Dickinson College (PA)	$22,973	53%	$18,568	$4,564	97%	$10,842	12%
Hobart and William Smith Colleges (NY)	$22,933	61%	$18,765	$3,817	90%	$16,640	15%
Bard College (NY)	$22,828	62%	$18,336	$4,330	90%	$12,905	2%
Hartwick College (NY)	$22,776	84%	$14,158	$4,627	77%	$11,475	8%
Denison University (OH)	$22,756	49%	$16,876	$4,495	98%	$10,372	51%
Chatham College (PA)	$22,742	90%	$7,158	$4,275	72%	$5,717	16%
Harvey Mudd College (CA)	$22,740	55%	$18,438	$4,500	100%	$6,563	24%
Oberlin College (OH)	$22,576	58%	$17,488	$4,013	100%	$11,472	10%
Lafayette College (PA)	$22,407	54%	$20,044	$4,437	99%	$12,445	7%
Kenyon College (OH)	$22,151	41%	$18,731	$3,644	98%	$12,502	24%
Ohio Wesleyan University	$22,149	58%	$16,141	$4,497	89%	$11,847	38%
Ursinus College (PA)	$22,129	96%	$15,874	$5,155	90%	$11,500	8%
College of the Atlantic (ME)	$21,823	86%	$18,900	$4,077	85%	$2,250	1%
Bennington College (VT)	$21,821	65%	$17,520	$3,780	75%	$4,589	14%
College of Wooster (OH)	$21,812	64%	$15,970	$4,664	95%	$10,643	34%
College of the Holy Cross (MA)	$21,793	43%	$16,044	$6,447	100%	$11,661	5%
Lawrence University (WI)	$21,596	60%	$15,380	$4,888	100%	$9,662	31%
Macalester College (MN)	$21,386	69%	$17,061	$3,483	100%	$5,242	6%
Agnes Scott College (GA)	$21,264	64%	$15,042	$3,924	97%	$10,451	26%
Hiram College (OH)	$21,218	N/A	$8,163	$6,960	95%	$8,635	N/A
Earlham College (IN)	$21,215	65%	$12,829	$4,300	95%	$6,153	16%
Carleton College (MN)	$21,208	58%	$16,911	$3,510	100%	$3,139	8%
Wheaton College (MA)	$21,159	58%	$16,164	$4,635	92%	$7,625	11%
Wittenberg University (OH)	$21,143	72%	$16,768	$4,691	89%	$9,599	24%
Drew University (NJ)	$21,033	49%	$15,603	$4,898	84%	$11,785	26%
Willamette University (OR)	$21,027	64%	$17,365	$2,846	86%	$10,995	32%
Washington and Lee University (VA)	$20,923	29%	$17,829	$4,307	99%	$8,663	22%
Franklin and Marshall College (PA)	$20,915	47%	$17,205	$4,805	97%	$13,067	20%
Oglethorpe University (GA)	$20,779	58%	$12,198	$2,288	86%	$10,542	34%
Knox College (IL)	$20,770	73%	$15,483	$5,266	97%	$10,280	21%
Grinnell College (IA)	$20,298	60%	$15,616	$4,884	100%	$8,890	28%
DePauw University (IN)	$20,208	58%	$16,693	$4,241	99%	$12,134	45%
Mills College (CA)	$20,190	90%	$13,640	$5,215	86%	$8,705	4%
Wofford College (SC)	$20,014	52%	$14,581	$3,890	88%	$8,268	21%
Randolph-Macon Woman's College (VA)	$19,958	66%	$14,203	$4,281	89%	$15,351	33%

Schools that award the largest need-based financial aid packages

Liberal Arts Colleges, continued

	Average amount of aid package	% students receiving need-based package	Average need-based grant	Average need-based loan	Average % of need met	Average merit award	% students receiving merit awards
Wabash College (IN)	$19,944	70%	$14,921	$2,564	100%	$11,261	25%
Furman University (SC)	$19,647	43%	$16,061	$2,934	87%	$10,875	24%
Sewanee–University of the South (TN)	$19,633	45%	$16,520	$3,496	100%	$12,155	13%
Allegheny College (PA)	$19,624	74%	$13,733	$4,538	94%	$8,883	22%
Lake Forest College (IL)	$19,466	77%	$16,147	$3,315	100%	$10,606	12%
Cornell College (IA)	$19,455	77%	$15,585	$4,210	98%	$11,210	23%
Washington College (MD)	$19,395	50%	$15,023	$3,500	88%	$10,717	34%
Presbyterian College (SC)	$19,217	62%	$16,206	$3,800	83%	$10,178	36%
University of Puget Sound (WA)	$19,217	59%	$13,011	$5,825	83%	$6,766	26%
Antioch College (OH)	$19,214	74%	$11,293	$3,424	82%	$7,520	26%
Bucknell University (PA)	$19,000	50%	$16,500	$5,200	100%	$6,777	0.3%
Kalamazoo College (MI)	$19,000	50%	$12,970	$5,600	N/A	$9,450	49%
McDaniel College (MD)	$18,978	63%	$7,823	$4,505	92%	$7,876	25%
West Virginia Wesleyan College	$18,927	75%	$15,165	$2,959	91%	$9,631	21%
Coe College (IA)	$18,882	79%	$13,274	$5,412	88%	$10,264	18%
Albion College (MI)	$18,706	64%	$14,791	$4,285	95%	$10,289	33%
Lewis and Clark College (OR)	$18,654	63%	$17,314	$4,600	79%	$7,229	5%
Beloit College (WI)	$18,635	73%	$14,026	$3,344	100%	$8,372	15%
Eckerd College (FL)	$18,550	56%	N/A	N/A	85%	N/A	N/A
St. Anselm College (NH)	$18,380	67%	$13,108	$3,158	75%	$5,602	12%
Juniata College (PA)	$18,258	79%	$14,190	$3,954	88%	$10,760	30%
St. Olaf College (MN)	$18,172	63%	$12,210	$4,707	100%	$5,717	19%
Rhodes College (TN)	$18,022	39%	$12,301	$4,428	80%	$9,198	33%
Goucher College (MD)	$18,020	59%	$15,009	$3,835	74%	$9,613	6%
Roanoke College (VA)	$17,852	70%	$13,649	$4,464	91%	$9,396	25%
Southwestern University (TX)	$17,781	55%	$10,653	$4,679	97%	$6,259	23%
Whitman College (WA)	$17,750	42%	$12,775	$3,625	90%	$7,450	7%
Illinois Wesleyan University	$17,641	55%	$12,294	$4,728	92%	$7,858	33%
St. John's University (MN)	$17,585	61%	$8,242	$4,547	86%	$5,849	28%

Universities–Master's (North)

	Average amount of aid package	% students receiving need-based package	Average need-based grant	Average need-based loan	Average % of need met	Average merit award	% students receiving merit awards
Bentley College (MA)	$22,572	51%	$13,530	$5,029	95%	$10,651	10%
Alfred University (NY)	$21,746	88%	$16,504	$4,992	92%	$8,526	9%
Ithaca College (NY)	$20,381	69%	$12,903	$5,275	89%	$8,086	9%
Manhattanville College (NY)	$19,872	65%	$9,137	$4,133	80%	$8,271	22%
College of Notre Dame of Maryland	$19,127	81%	$14,417	$4,749	100%	$9,640	16%
Villanova University (PA)	$18,217	46%	$14,296	$4,778	76%	$10,338	5%
Fairleigh Dickinson University (NJ)	$18,183	70%	$7,775	$3,246	N/A	$4,953	23%
Regis College (MA)	$17,940	79%	$9,242	$4,874	57%	$8,985	10%
Le Moyne College (NY)	$17,840	83%	$13,980	$4,358	85%	$8,411	9%
Rider University (NJ)	$17,733	66%	$8,196	$4,564	79%	$7,427	15%
Fairfield University (CT)	$17,603	53%	$10,642	$4,462	78%	$9,483	8%
St. Michael's College (VT)	$17,529	65%	$12,743	$4,805	86%	$6,784	15%

Universities–Master's (North), continued

	Average amount of aid package	% students receiving need-based package	Average need-based grant	Average need-based loan	Average % of need met	Average merit award	% students receiving merit awards
Hood College (MD)	$17,518	77%	$13,899	$4,731	90%	$14,337	22%
Loyola College in Maryland	$17,375	48%	$10,030	$5,395	97%	$9,670	16%
American International College (MA)	$17,269	96%	$9,309	$4,531	81%	$2,256	3%
University of New England (ME)	$17,240	85%	$8,249	$9,248	77%	$6,264	12%
St. Francis University (PA)	$17,128	85%	$12,421	$4,531	82%	$9,562	12%
Lebanon Valley College (PA)	$17,055	79%	$14,062	$4,111	86%	$9,062	16%
Canisius College (NY)	$16,917	75%	$11,650	$4,030	80%	$8,787	19%
Rivier College (NH)	$16,705	81%	$11,826	$6,475	75%	$6,000	10%
Emmanuel College (MA)	$16,474	78%	$9,973	$4,108	78%	$11,494	8%
Rochester Institute of Technology (NY)	$16,300	68%	$9,900	$4,700	90%	$5,800	9%
St. Joseph College (CT)	$16,273	87%	$11,151	$5,756	72%	$12,346	9%
Arcadia University (PA)	$16,134	89%	$6,149	$4,015	74%	$6,391	7%
Chestnut Hill College (PA)	$16,125	86%	$9,205	$5,500	51%	$7,225	7%
La Salle University (PA)	$15,998	74%	$11,273	$4,340	74%	$9,222	17%
St. Peter's College (NJ)	$15,921	80%	$4,441	$2,190	72%	$7,709	8%
Wilkes University (PA)	$15,863	85%	$11,152	$4,008	83%	$7,916	10%
University of New Haven (CT)	$15,758	75%	$10,288	$6,787	79%	$12,573	10%
Salve Regina University (RI)	$15,618	67%	$10,505	$5,079	73%	$9,688	14%
Niagara University (NY)	$15,400	84%	$10,355	$4,505	84%	$7,039	15%
New York Institute of Technology	$15,327	71%	$6,284	$4,530	N/A	$6,095	12%
Simmons College (MA)	$15,175	68%	$11,452	$2,880	56%	$12,454	1%
Wheelock College (MA)	$15,167	74%	$10,143	$4,897	71%	$12,716	15%
Springfield College (MA)	$15,142	77%	$10,475	$4,209	82%	$12,279	13%
Mount St. Mary's University (MD)	$15,125	62%	$11,425	$4,147	79%	$13,127	34%
St. Joseph's College (ME)	$15,022	85%	$9,531	$5,584	80%	$10,430	14%
College of Mount St. Vincent (NY)	$15,000	86%	$7,000	$4,100	74%	$0	0%
Assumption College (MA)	$14,955	70%	$10,387	$4,953	76%	$7,336	7%
Roberts Wesleyan College (NY)	$14,890	87%	$9,454	$5,093	80%	$8,790	13%
St. Bonaventure University (NY)	$14,782	71%	$10,090	$4,170	85%	$6,260	21%
Wagner College (NY)	$14,768	63%	$10,955	$4,542	73%	$7,439	26%
University of Scranton (PA)	$14,666	66%	$10,625	$4,073	72%	$8,085	5%
Providence College (RI)	$14,600	50%	$8,900	$4,833	85%	$10,500	10%
Philadelphia University	$14,577	71%	$9,274	$4,269	73%	$4,016	23%
Gwynedd-Mercy College (PA)	$14,523	68%	$10,800	$4,656	82%	$6,482	17%
Bryant College (RI)	$14,521	65%	$6,654	$4,713	73%	$7,247	47%
Marywood University (PA)	$14,499	83%	$10,319	$4,185	75%	$6,929	15%
Nazareth College of Rochester (NY)	$14,497	81%	$9,354	$4,670	80%	$6,046	13%
Trinity College (DC)	$14,406	84%	$10,606	$4,709	65%	$11,641	6%
King's College (PA)	$14,394	78%	$6,395	$4,182	76%	$8,085	13%
Anna Maria College (MA)	$14,378	80%	$9,385	$5,548	80%	$11,383	12%
Manhattan College (NY)	$14,185	68%	$5,395	$3,582	70%	$7,184	12%
Gallaudet University (DC)	$14,057	73%	$12,342	$3,028	76%	$10,996	4%
St. Joseph's University (PA)	$13,845	59%	$7,605	$4,890	80%	$6,580	20%
Sacred Heart University (CT)	$13,393	69%	$8,762	$5,215	72%	$9,864	15%
Geneva College (PA)	$13,180	85%	$9,326	$3,845	80%	$7,226	12%
Quinnipiac University (CT)	$13,160	60%	$8,534	$4,264	67%	$4,928	8%
Long Island University–Brooklyn (NY)	$13,159	81%	$8,213	$4,105	48%	$14,105	2%
Iona College (NY)	$13,144	74%	$2,925	$3,116	27%	$9,051	17%
Emerson College (MA)	$13,083	54%	$10,469	$4,232	85%	$13,005	16%
Nyack College (NY)	$13,031	83%	$8,419	$4,632	62%	$5,924	13%
Lincoln University (PA)	$13,000	90%	$1,965	$3,804	85%	$3,895	10%
St. John Fisher College (NY)	$13,000	84%	$9,417	$5,861	80%	$4,478	13%

Schools that award the largest need-based financial aid packages

Universities–Master's (North), continued

	Average amount of aid package	% students receiving need-based package	Average need-based grant	Average need-based loan	Average % of need met	Average merit award	% students receiving merit awards
Touro College (NY)	$13,000	56%	$4,000	$2,625	85%	$2,000	10%
Monmouth University (NJ)	$12,958	67%	$7,604	$4,288	66%	$4,619	26%
Cabrini College (PA)	$12,877	74%	$5,253	$5,269	48%	$4,260	23%
College Misericordia (PA)	$12,854	79%	$5,317	$2,769	75%	$5,954	8%
Gannon University (PA)	$12,740	85%	$10,140	$3,002	80%	$3,940	15%
La Roche College (PA)	$12,661	60%	$3,689	$4,592	84%	$4,500	7%
Immaculata University (PA)	$12,621	67%	$9,692	$3,598	70%	$11,672	18%
DeSales University (PA)	$12,586	59%	$9,187	$2,964	70%	$4,518	16%
Suffolk University (MA)	$12,457	53%	$6,417	$4,666	67%	$4,450	9%

Universities–Master's (South)

	Average amount of aid package	% students receiving need-based package	Average need-based grant	Average need-based loan	Average % of need met	Average merit award	% students receiving merit awards
Rollins College (FL)	$26,005	42%	$20,887	$3,923	92%	$7,982	13%
Mercer University (GA)	$21,250	70%	$12,688	$6,486	89%	$14,016	19%
Stetson University (FL)	$19,406	58%	$14,369	$5,002	83%	$11,283	32%
Lynn University (FL)	$19,285	53%	$11,449	$9,208	74%	$11,083	44%
Mary Baldwin College (VA)	$19,276	78%	$9,786	$3,196	89%	$12,432	19%
University of Richmond (VA)	$19,189	32%	$15,742	$3,432	97%	$11,596	14%
Campbell University (NC)	$18,024	68%	$4,997	$4,187	100%	$5,592	15%
St. Leo University (FL)	$17,695	70%	$12,077	$3,691	88%	$5,760	18%
Loyola University New Orleans	$16,895	55%	$11,964	$3,878	82%	$8,868	32%
Spring Hill College (AL)	$16,836	70%	$12,057	$3,835	79%	$7,936	11%
Converse College (SC)	$16,521	70%	$13,836	$4,120	88%	$16,158	26%
Wheeling Jesuit University (WV)	$16,062	79%	$4,852	$4,361	91%	$5,252	21%
Lynchburg College (VA)	$15,969	64%	$11,958	$4,441	84%	$7,856	36%
Jacksonville University (FL)	$15,853	66%	$12,438	$4,014	82%	$5,234	28%
Barry University (FL)	$14,739	74%	$6,221	$4,424	67%	$5,829	9%
Brenau University (GA)	$14,512	69%	$11,856	$3,648	82%	$7,965	19%
Mississippi College	$14,197	56%	$8,616	$6,462	84%	$9,838	42%
University of Tampa (FL)	$14,162	59%	$6,704	$3,533	84%	$6,520	11%
Meredith College (NC)	$13,574	58%	$9,935	$3,636	76%	$4,397	28%
Marymount University (VA)	$13,276	57%	$6,436	$3,942	75%	$6,870	17%
Centenary College of Louisiana	$13,207	64%	$10,913	$3,687	78%	$9,575	23%
Christian Brothers University (TN)	$12,767	63%	$5,526	$4,026	70%	$8,450	30%
Shenandoah University (VA)	$12,712	66%	$6,655	$4,671	84%	$3,589	11%
Warren Wilson College (NC)	$12,695	52%	$7,372	$3,430	73%	$3,014	14%
Embry Riddle Aeronautical University (FL)	$12,563	65%	$3,727	$5,514	0%	$3,588	14%
Charleston Southern University (SC)	$12,546	80%	$8,731	$4,179	71%	$9,723	14%
Cumberland University (TN)	$12,532	70%	$5,369	$3,457	65%	$4,675	2%
Carson-Newman College (TN)	$12,525	74%	$8,095	$3,752	72%	$4,585	21%
Campbellsville University (KY)	$12,431	92%	$9,191	$3,483	74%	$9,428	7%
Cumberland College (KY)	$12,416	82%	$4,921	$3,541	90%	$5,810	10%
Elon University (NC)	$11,368	35%	$5,779	$4,031	71%	$3,512	19%
Queens University of Charlotte (NC)	$11,243	59%	$8,588	$2,937	72%	$7,886	33%
Averett University (VA)	$10,980	84%	$8,292	$3,914	66%	$9,712	15%
Palm Beach Atlantic University (FL)	$10,659	71%	$2,059	$3,256	63%	$1,684	31%

Universities–Master's (South), continued

	Average amount of aid package	% students receiving need-based package	Average need-based grant	Average need-based loan	Average % of need met	Average merit award	% students receiving merit awards
Union University (TN)	$10,492	58%	$3,719	$3,782	N/A	$4,884	8%
Trevecca Nazarene University (TN)	$10,450	49%	$4,320	$4,430	45%	$3,150	12%
Pfeiffer University (NC)	$10,426	72%	$7,618	$3,239	82%	$8,834	14%
Tuskegee University (AL)	$9,960	71%	$4,000	$4,281	85%	$1,768	21%
Samford University (AL)	$9,908	49%	$5,757	$3,358	72%	$3,700	26%
Liberty University (VA)	$9,689	76%	$4,736	$3,267	66%	$5,199	14%
Gardner-Webb University (NC)	$9,512	70%	$5,163	$4,118	79%	$5,031	27%
Alcorn State University (MS)	$9,500	96%	$4,500	$5,500	76%	$4,250	43%
Tusculum College (TN)	$9,408	65%	$4,850	$3,410	63%	$4,535	49%
Freed-Hardeman University (TN)	$9,025	71%	$5,761	$3,689	59%	$10,088	20%
Troy State University–Troy (AL)	$9,000	95%	$5,000	$4,000	58%	$0	0%
David Lipscomb University (TN)	$8,909	53%	$1,698	$5,755	79%	$5,826	58%
College of Charleston (SC)	$8,696	38%	$2,854	$3,500	63%	$10,338	8%
Harding University (AR)	$8,673	47%	$5,444	$4,380	64%	$7,246	38%
Piedmont College (GA)	$8,642	84%	$3,049	$5,744	74%	$2,542	10%

Universities–Master's (Midwest)

	Average amount of aid package	% students receiving need-based package	Average need-based grant	Average need-based loan	Average % of need met	Average merit award	% students receiving merit awards
Maharishi University of Management (IA)	$22,649	78%	$17,720	$8,061	92%	$5,950	8%
Hamline University (MN)	$21,384	75%	$7,097	$2,691	87%	$13,030	20%
Rockford College (IL)	$20,000	59%	$8,000	$5,000	70%	$9,000	40%
Creighton University (NE)	$18,340	50%	$11,637	$6,805	87%	$7,568	28%
College of St. Catherine (MN)	$18,319	49%	$6,954	$4,752	77%	$14,651	27%
North Central College (IL)	$18,212	78%	$11,475	$5,239	87%	$7,673	20%
University of Detroit Mercy	$18,195	77%	$14,002	$4,645	80%	$11,476	7%
Valparaiso University (IN)	$17,404	68%	$11,310	$5,345	92%	$7,573	24%
University of Evansville (IN)	$17,375	70%	$12,915	$4,283	91%	$7,764	21%
Heidelberg College (OH)	$16,974	84%	$10,089	$4,300	95%	$5,553	16%
Capital University (OH)	$16,856	81%	$9,890	$4,589	80%	$8,628	17%
Anderson University (IN)	$16,684	78%	$10,784	$4,959	96%	$7,516	21%
John Carroll University (OH)	$16,588	71%	$11,469	$4,312	85%	$3,308	22%
Ashland University (OH)	$16,446	79%	$11,333	$4,055	90%	$5,680	14%
Drake University (IA)	$16,354	58%	$11,441	$5,606	98%	$8,936	31%
Rockhurst University (MO)	$16,260	71%	$5,773	$6,254	92%	$6,993	8%
Butler University (IN)	$16,000	61%	$12,000	$5,000	79%	$8,200	27%
University of Dubuque (IA)	$15,986	93%	$8,515	$8,042	83%	$15,657	7%
College of St. Scholastica (MN)	$15,945	82%	$5,510	$4,639	85%	$7,253	14%
Ursuline College (OH)	$15,872	77%	$7,996	N/A	78%	$4,212	7%
Webster University (MO)	$15,845	69%	$4,707	$4,132	N/A	$8,378	19%
Aurora University (IL)	$15,470	79%	$5,496	$3,663	82%	$7,653	18%
Aquinas College (MI)	$15,461	72%	$12,661	$2,800	92%	$8,266	28%
Fontbonne University (MO)	$15,150	76%	$8,650	$5,500	75%	$5,000	20%
University of Indianapolis	$15,035	76%	$8,013	$3,864	82%	$7,730	11%
Quincy University (IL)	$14,835	72%	$9,365	$4,373	85%	$3,867	21%

Schools that award the largest need-based financial aid packages

Universities–Master's (Midwest), continued	Average amount of aid package	% students receiving need-based package	Average need-based grant	Average need-based loan	Average % of need met	Average merit award	% students receiving merit awards
Bethel College (MN)	$14,810	68%	$8,933	$4,477	83%	$3,529	23%
Baker University (KS)	$14,534	72%	$5,958	$6,000	N/A	$5,150	28%
St. Xavier University (IL)	$14,282	83%	$8,775	$3,932	82%	$3,683	14%
Concordia University Wisconsin	$14,124	98%	$11,000	$3,500	80%	$5,200	10%
Concordia University (NE)	$14,099	89%	$4,932	$3,733	92%	$5,488	11%
Bradley University (IL)	$13,805	73%	$8,664	$4,523	85%	$8,939	23%
St. Mary's University of Minnesota	$13,719	62%	$5,804	$4,589	73%	$4,920	24%
University of St. Francis (IL)	$13,695	69%	$8,401	$4,109	81%	$4,806	23%
Xavier University (OH)	$13,616	49%	$9,759	$4,118	75%	$8,237	35%
Marian College of Fond du Lac (WI)	$13,560	79%	$5,220	$4,115	91%	$4,299	12%
Viterbo University (WI)	$13,534	81%	$8,859	$4,317	70%	$5,629	15%
William Woods University (MO)	$13,532	55%	$2,034	$2,547	84%	$3,554	33%
Lewis University (IL)	$13,302	71%	$5,814	$3,941	78%	$4,800	10%
Baldwin-Wallace College (OH)	$13,257	75%	$9,733	$3,778	95%	$7,181	25%
Augsburg College (MN)	$12,966	70%	$9,419	$4,430	70%	$16,973	15%
Doane College (NE)	$12,953	80%	$8,872	$4,149	99%	$7,159	19%
Benedictine College (KS)	$12,668	71%	$7,843	$4,618	74%	$5,298	6%
University of St. Francis (IN)	$12,668	83%	$9,101	$3,101	79%	$8,913	12%
Dominican University (IL)	$12,518	78%	$9,254	$3,623	77%	$5,600	33%
St. Ambrose University (IA)	$12,467	76%	$4,788	$4,316	43%	$5,297	19%
Mount Marty College (SD)	$12,417	87%	$7,863	$4,468	75%	$5,764	12%
Cornerstone University (MI)	$12,302	77%	$6,225	$4,102	80%	$3,004	15%
Olivet Nazarene University (IL)	$12,233	74%	$8,760	$4,362	76%	$4,870	22%
Spring Arbor University (MI)	$11,773	50%	$3,283	$3,875	78%	$1,668	7%
Marygrove College (MI)	$11,641	87%	$6,571	N/A	N/A	N/A	N/A
Roosevelt University (IL)	$11,600	70%	$6,200	N/A	75%	$6,030	38%
Benedictine University (IL)	$11,489	41%	$5,273	$3,692	68%	$6,632	27%
College of Mount St. Joseph (OH)	$11,400	65%	$8,000	$3,500	90%	$3,800	28%
Malone College (OH)	$11,365	74%	$7,708	$3,517	75%	$3,995	9%
Mount Mary College (WI)	$11,347	62%	$6,983	$4,194	71%	$6,037	19%
Concordia University–River Forest (IL)	$11,333	76%	$5,179	$3,670	45%	$39,000	13%
MidAmerica Nazarene University (KS)	$11,189	74%	$6,434	$5,038	66%	$3,506	14%

Universities–Master's (West)

	Average amount of aid package	% students receiving need-based package	Average need-based grant	Average need-based loan	Average % of need met	Average merit award	% students receiving merit awards
University of Redlands (CA)	$23,120	69%	$13,162	$4,926	90%	$9,525	6%
Holy Names University (CA)	$22,883	67%	$9,796	$4,015	72%	$19,970	0.3%
Regis University (CO)	$20,738	54%	$10,698	$5,732	97%	$5,876	32%
St. Mary's College of California	$20,460	62%	$15,625	$4,303	76%	$7,944	3%
Dominican University of California (CA)	$19,762	73%	$14,879	$4,159	23%	$9,765	20%
Seattle University	$19,380	66%	$9,058	$4,590	86%	$1,282	7%
University of Portland (OR)	$19,304	59%	$12,719	$5,213	83%	$16,102	33%
Chapman University (CA)	$18,358	62%	$14,873	$2,998	100%	$13,436	22%
Notre Dame de Namur University (CA)	$18,211	72%	$14,336	$3,757	71%	$6,953	11%
College of Santa Fe (NM)	$18,190	68%	$9,879	$4,363	82%	$3,427	19%
Loyola Marymount University (CA)	$18,095	57%	$11,116	$4,807	78%	$6,811	3%
Santa Clara University (CA)	$17,748	47%	$14,080	$4,766	84%	$5,025	11%
Whitworth College (WA)	$17,443	73%	$11,552	$4,559	84%	$6,947	20%
Pacific University (OR)	$17,369	76%	$11,834	$4,892	89%	$8,259	18%
Pacific Lutheran University (WA)	$17,229	71%	$7,135	$6,802	88%	$6,135	17%
Gonzaga University (WA)	$17,077	62%	$11,113	$5,407	84%	$6,618	30%
California Lutheran University	$16,800	66%	$11,360	$3,360	86%	$2,150	7%
Seattle Pacific University	$16,249	63%	$12,206	$5,566	80%	$8,832	28%
Eastern Washington University	$16,216	61%	$4,910	$3,837	40%	$3,474	2%
Trinity University (TX)	$15,486	41%	$10,905	$4,215	86%	$6,358	37%
Woodbury University (CA)	$15,369	65%	$11,938	$4,041	61%	$8,481	17%
Oral Roberts University (OK)	$15,213	71%	$7,645	$8,712	92%	$6,947	19%
Walla Walla College (WA)	$15,012	74%	$6,456	$4,953	83%	$4,173	4%
George Fox University (OR)	$14,902	81%	$10,967	$3,642	78%	$8,584	15%
St. Martin's College (WA)	$14,451	83%	$9,895	$4,160	80%	$10,336	14%
Westminster College (UT)	$14,130	70%	$9,761	$3,921	89%	$7,385	25%
Concordia University (CA)	$13,979	71%	$7,327	$3,817	86%	$5,397	15%
Point Loma Nazarene University (CA)	$13,791	59%	$10,018	$4,536	71%	$8,728	26%
St. Mary's University of San Antonio	$13,454	72%	$7,492	$4,488	69%	$8,897	7%
Chaminade University of Honolulu	$12,701	73%	$9,044	$3,771	66%	$4,693	8%
University of the Incarnate Word (TX)	$12,667	68%	$6,718	$4,878	66%	$4,099	18%
Azusa Pacific University (CA)	$12,616	64%	$8,335	$3,984	72%	$3,485	35%
Northwest Nazarene University (ID)	$12,598	71%	$2,887	$4,711	76%	$8,153	11%
Simpson College (CA)	$12,507	87%	$7,507	$5,000	72%	$3,050	4%
LeTourneau University (TX)	$11,613	75%	$7,067	$4,096	70%	$3,801	6%
St. Edward's University (TX)	$11,577	60%	$7,793	$4,221	69%	$4,770	3%
Hardin-Simmons University (TX)	$11,521	65%	$4,733	$3,913	66%	$3,111	8%
University of Mary Hardin-Baylor (TX)	$11,228	69%	$4,922	$4,516	75%	$3,141	21%
University of St. Thomas (TX)	$10,983	57%	$7,775	$3,712	68%	$6,795	19%
California Baptist University	$10,700	85%	$5,250	$3,750	78%	$3,650	3%
Oklahoma City University	$10,680	42%	$7,037	$3,313	82%	$5,567	9%
Abilene Christian University (TX)	$10,457	62%	$7,127	$4,015	74%	$4,419	24%
Houston Baptist University	$10,411	37%	$7,358	$3,097	59%	$9,829	10%
Hawaii Pacific University	$10,392	38%	$3,866	$4,611	77%	$4,074	18%
Heritage College (WA)	$10,161	87%	$7,643	$3,344	67%	$5,387	3%
Alaska Pacific University	$10,113	49%	$4,443	$4,340	78%	$6,701	20%
Eastern Oregon University	$9,461	66%	$3,624	$3,667	64%	$1,656	1%
University of Great Falls (MT)	$9,311	83%	$3,412	$4,017	77%	$2,888	9%

Schools that award the largest need-based financial aid packages

Comprehensive Colleges–Bachelor's (North)	Average amount of aid package	% students receiving need-based package	Average need-based grant	Average need-based loan	Average % of need met	Average merit award	% students receiving merit awards
Elmira College (NY)	$20,384	80%	$15,038	$5,647	85%	$15,850	18%
Colby-Sawyer College (NH)	$17,721	67%	$12,409	$3,875	87%	$3,669	11%
Merrimack College (MA)	$17,000	76%	$9,000	$7,000	70%	$5,000	3%
College of St. Elizabeth (NJ)	$16,697	74%	$13,765	$4,088	80%	$10,402	17%
Elizabethtown College (PA)	$16,402	72%	$12,540	$3,875	88%	$12,892	8%
Delaware Valley College (PA)	$16,030	73%	$11,458	$3,834	85%	$7,407	19%
Marymount College–Tarrytown (NY)	$15,968	69%	$10,406	$5,752	71%	$7,242	25%
Stonehill College (MA)	$15,639	66%	$10,999	$4,940	82%	$10,069	22%
Lasell College (MA)	$15,429	82%	$11,291	$3,472	73%	$12,126	10%
Cedar Crest College (PA)	$15,309	86%	$11,808	$3,707	79%	$12,868	10%
Neumann College (PA)	$15,000	90%	$12,000	$3,000	60%	N/A	N/A
Cazenovia College (NY)	$14,600	79%	$10,000	$3,750	80%	$4,520	9%
Keuka College (NY)	$14,560	89%	$9,413	$5,230	80%	$11,505	6%
Roger Williams University (RI)	$14,500	69%	$8,300	$4,200	87%	$6,000	8%
Wilson College (PA)	$14,228	71%	$11,876	$3,797	80%	$14,243	24%
Curry College (MA)	$14,025	66%	$9,830	$3,644	68%	$3,732	2%
Daemen College (NY)	$13,742	86%	$6,414	$4,061	90%	$5,849	7%
Thiel College (PA)	$13,200	86%	$8,920	$3,648	81%	$3,845	14%
Bloomfield College (NJ)	$13,116	85%	$9,316	$2,874	84%	$4,263	6%
Messiah College (PA)	$12,798	72%	$5,476	$3,947	65%	$5,228	18%
Mercyhurst College (PA)	$12,686	78%	$9,050	$3,554	92%	$5,010	19%
Unity College (ME)	$12,407	80%	$6,931	$4,903	79%	$9,034	16%
Endicott College (MA)	$12,062	64%	$5,411	$3,990	62%	$6,845	13%

Comprehensive Colleges–Bachelor's (South)	Average amount of aid package	% students receiving need-based package	Average need-based grant	Average need-based loan	Average % of need met	Average merit award	% students receiving merit awards
Berea College (KY)	$24,668	100%	$23,110	$1,509	82%	$0	0%
Maryville College (TN)	$19,013	79%	$12,475	$3,301	92%	$11,668	21%
Columbia College (SC)	$18,516	93%	$6,167	$4,427	92%	$6,458	6%
Alderson-Broaddus College (WV)	$18,231	96%	$10,663	$5,406	88%	$7,265	2%
Covenant College (GA)	$16,865	73%	$12,011	$4,176	85%	$3,798	20%
Coker College (SC)	$16,531	84%	$5,885	$3,775	97%	$5,269	16%
Davis and Elkins College (WV)	$15,769	77%	$2,999	$3,692	89%	$13,136	7%
Florida Southern College	$15,001	74%	$10,988	$4,937	65%	$10,453	11%
Thomas More College (KY)	$14,451	97%	$4,696	$2,619	90%	$5,923	16%
Claflin University (SC)	$14,000	95%	$9,780	$3,500	N/A	N/A	N/A
Bethune-Cookman College (FL)	$13,750	87%	$6,575	$3,430	74%	$7,815	3%
Anderson College (SC)	$13,694	84%	$6,760	$4,242	79%	$5,333	6%
Dillard University (LA)	$13,443	86%	$3,603	$3,337	85%	$3,924	6%
Berry College (GA)	$13,396	57%	$10,046	$3,271	86%	$11,228	41%
Lenoir-Rhyne College (NC)	$13,095	81%	$10,229	$4,431	57%	$5,282	16%
Ouachita Baptist University (AR)	$13,022	54%	$5,197	$3,674	88%	$6,111	31%
Wingate University (NC)	$12,748	67%	$4,134	$3,359	56%	$4,918	N/A
University of the Ozarks (AR)	$12,685	53%	$9,322	$3,114	77%	$11,784	38%
LaGrange College (GA)	$12,589	69%	$9,556	$3,445	75%	$6,710	28%
Brevard College (NC)	$12,400	68%	$9,975	$3,840	79%	$3,415	16%
Catawba College (NC)	$12,272	64%	$4,075	$4,131	N/A	$6,347	10%

Comprehensive Colleges– Bachelor's (South), continued

	Average amount of aid package	% students receiving need-based package	Average need-based grant	Average need-based loan	Average % of need met	Average merit award	% students receiving merit awards
Asbury College (KY)	$12,170	69%	$7,041	$3,991	78%	$6,648	10%
Peace College (NC)	$12,126	65%	$9,064	$2,907	72%	$7,541	33%
Pikeville College (KY)	$11,622	77%	$5,545	$3,660	84%	$5,591	6%
Mars Hill College (NC)	$11,609	79%	$8,749	$3,575	72%	$6,884	25%
Kentucky Wesleyan College	$11,416	88%	$9,177	$2,949	75%	$8,739	12%
High Point University (NC)	$11,400	76%	$4,000	$5,200	87%	$3,000	4%
John Brown University (AR)	$11,400	66%	$10,693	$5,935	65%	$3,923	22%
Ferrum College (VA)	$11,370	87%	$9,035	$2,931	53%	$2,589	11%
Belmont Abbey College (NC)	$11,294	74%	$8,215	$3,487	62%	$8,710	27%
Benedict College (SC)	$11,000	96%	N/A	N/A	95%	N/A	N/A
Morris College (SC)	$11,000	99%	$1,500	$3,500	83%	$0	0%
Belhaven College (MS)	$10,980	60%	$5,500	$4,304	51%	$3,843	8%
Virginia Intermont College	$10,935	78%	$3,014	$4,172	10%	$4,699	9%
Chowan College (NC)	$10,595	86%	$7,361	$3,507	70%	$10,077	14%
Warner Southern College (FL)	$10,255	64%	$3,093	$3,946	N/A	$3,475	16%
Toccoa Falls College (GA)	$10,132	80%	$3,960	$3,773	46%	$4,720	16%
Bryan College (TN)	$10,117	71%	$2,780	$4,668	68%	$4,422	21%
Shorter College (GA)	$10,051	68%	$7,313	$3,653	68%	$9,535	31%
North Greenville College (SC)	$10,000	67%	$4,000	$1,000	60%	$5,000	33%

Comprehensive Colleges– Bachelor's (Midwest)

	Average amount of aid package	% students receiving need-based package	Average need-based grant	Average need-based loan	Average % of need met	Average merit award	% students receiving merit awards
Ohio Northern University	$20,347	83%	$14,487	$4,842	88%	$10,438	17%
Notre Dame College of Ohio	$19,141	N/A	$12,233	$4,281	94%	$3,444	N/A
Buena Vista University (IA)	$19,049	92%	$12,115	$4,614	95%	$13,033	3%
Marietta College (OH)	$17,761	81%	$6,200	$3,258	91%	$6,400	16%
St. Mary's College (IN)	$17,358	67%	$8,283	$2,773	79%	$6,721	21%
Simpson College (IA)	$17,124	88%	$11,381	$3,757	87%	$7,800	11%
Wartburg College (IA)	$17,031	79%	$11,123	$6,460	95%	$19,090	19%
Briar Cliff University (IA)	$16,995	76%	$4,856	$4,885	92%	$2,895	73%
Bluffton University (OH)	$16,776	71%	$10,829	$4,777	93%	$7,030	10%
MacMurray College (IL)	$16,659	93%	$11,651	$3,858	93%	$5,200	6%
Loras College (IA)	$16,479	76%	$6,449	$5,329	92%	$6,330	11%
McPherson College (KS)	$16,475	84%	$5,258	$5,690	92%	$7,524	13%
Wilmington College (OH)	$16,395	86%	$11,185	$4,864	87%	$6,490	10%
Millikin University (IL)	$16,233	67%	$9,951	$3,784	88%	$6,535	27%
Manchester College (IN)	$16,033	77%	$12,666	$3,422	92%	$5,424	11%
Central College (IA)	$16,020	81%	$11,650	$4,493	82%	$8,710	18%
Bethel College (KS)	$15,772	86%	$4,534	$5,875	90%	$5,776	11%
Waldorf College (IA)	$15,752	84%	$11,062	$4,677	85%	$8,717	15%
Morningside College (IA)	$15,716	89%	$5,645	$3,815	81%	$5,794	11%
St. Norbert College (WI)	$15,507	66%	$10,899	$4,562	89%	$9,259	30%
Elmhurst College (IL)	$15,400	70%	$11,297	$4,538	95%	$8,871	15%
Mount Union College (OH)	$15,324	80%	$10,617	$4,438	85%	$7,428	18%
Bethany College (KS)	$15,310	82%	$4,881	$5,012	93%	$4,086	6%
Carroll College (WI)	$14,718	82%	$10,220	$3,980	100%	$7,084	18%

Schools that award the largest need-based financial aid packages

Comprehensive Colleges–Bachelor's (Midwest), continued	Average amount of aid package	% students receiving need-based package	Average need-based grant	Average need-based loan	Average % of need met	Average merit award	% students receiving merit awards
Dordt College (IA)	$14,665	80%	$7,820	$4,354	85%	$7,331	14%
Clarke College (IA)	$14,654	84%	$10,751	$4,039	100%	$9,948	14%
Dana College (NE)	$14,623	83%	$4,077	$4,619	85%	$5,186	17%
Tabor College (KS)	$14,427	72%	$3,491	$6,063	87%	$4,335	24%
Iowa Wesleyan College	$14,391	92%	$8,107	$3,460	78%	$6,005	4%
Northland College (WI)	$14,321	83%	$8,937	$3,708	79%	$7,832	7%
Augustana College (SD)	$14,299	70%	$9,932	$4,759	87%	$6,695	28%
Graceland University (IA)	$14,192	67%	$9,610	$5,172	85%	$8,506	19%
Cedarville University (OH)	$14,188	61%	$1,651	$4,053	43%	$7,300	22%
Midland Lutheran College (NE)	$14,166	85%	$10,191	$4,433	91%	$8,994	15%
Eureka College (IL)	$13,978	99%	$10,212	$2,904	97%	$7,251	11%
Concordia University (MI)	$13,807	85%	$9,494	$5,051	86%	$8,259	13%
St. Joseph's College (IN)	$13,800	78%	$7,850	$4,000	85%	$5,000	6%
Huntington College (IN)	$13,794	73%	$8,574	$4,164	69%	$5,282	7%
Marian College (IN)	$13,717	79%	$7,633	$3,019	78%	$9,301	5%
Greenville College (IL)	$13,704	84%	$9,179	$4,121	79%	$6,885	16%
Mount Mercy College (IA)	$13,649	89%	$8,788	$4,878	81%	$9,624	10%
Northwestern College (MN)	$13,499	84%	$9,760	$4,248	73%	$5,051	13%

Comprehensive Colleges–Bachelor's (West)	Average amount of aid package	% students receiving need-based package	Average need-based grant	Average need-based loan	Average % of need met	Average merit award	% students receiving merit awards
Menlo College (CA)	$18,427	62%	$14,599	$4,530	73%	$10,675	24%
Linfield College (OR)	$16,638	71%	$4,400	$4,617	83%	$8,902	19%
Sierra Nevada College (NV)	$14,500	83%	$9,800	$5,500	65%	$9,000	17%
Master's College and Seminary (CA)	$14,157	66%	$10,059	$4,119	74%	$8,145	20%
Northwest Christian College (OR)	$14,157	81%	$9,531	$4,180	75%	$8,804	7%
Carroll College (MT)	$13,799	68%	$8,020	$4,558	85%	$5,907	27%
Rocky Mountain College (MT)	$13,276	64%	$8,476	$4,233	74%	$6,869	8%
McMurry University (TX)	$12,932	80%	$6,002	$3,917	78%	$5,421	11%
Western Baptist College (OR)	$12,689	82%	$7,978	$5,741	71%	$8,192	13%
Texas Lutheran University	$12,271	73%	$10,993	$4,126	80%	$9,491	24%
Oklahoma Christian University	$11,748	67%	$1,737	$3,841	57%	$2,234	22%
Oklahoma Baptist University	$11,464	64%	$3,301	$3,834	70%	$4,389	29%
Concordia University–Austin (TX)	$11,423	66%	$9,652	$3,440	83%	$5,565	8%
Oklahoma Wesleyan University	$11,318	90%	$3,296	$5,423	55%	$2,941	9%
Lubbock Christian University (TX)	$11,040	66%	$7,324	$3,451	75%	$9,730	11%
Pacific Union College (CA)	$10,958	72%	$6,424	$4,250	72%	$7,606	2%
Northwest College (WA)	$10,592	78%	$6,853	$3,798	57%	$9,059	17%
Howard Payne University (TX)	$10,464	76%	$6,760	$3,516	82%	$4,331	17%

Schools that award the largest amounts of need-based scholarships and grants

The schools listed on the following pages are those that gave, on average, the largest dollar amount of need-based scholarships and grants during the 2003–2004 academic year. The figures represent the average scholarship and grant amount. The grants and scholarships are awarded based on financial need, and the money comes from institutional, state, federal, or other sources. They are doled out annually, so students have to file a financial aid application form each year to determine eligibility. The table also includes the percentage of all students who received need-based grants and scholarships, a rough indication of the proportion of students who don't pay full price.

National Universities

	% receiving grants and scholarships based on need	Average amount of need-based scholarship and grant
Harvard University (MA)	48%	$24,418
California Institute of Technology	58%	$23,873
Princeton University (NJ)	49%	$23,660
Yale University (CT)	40%	$23,574
Columbia University (NY)	41%	$23,555
Stanford University (CA)	47%	$23,000
Massachusetts Institute of Technology	59%	$22,225
Duke University (NC)	38%	$21,607
Dartmouth College (NH)	47%	$21,529
Tufts University (MA)	37%	$20,932
University of Pennsylvania	42%	$20,707
Vanderbilt University (TN)	36%	$20,673
Johns Hopkins University (MD)	37%	$20,599
University of Southern California	43%	$20,414
Cornell University (NY)	44%	$19,911
Brown University (RI)	41%	$19,877
University of Chicago	47%	$19,864
Rensselaer Polytechnic Institute (NY)	70%	$19,861
Washington University in St. Louis	45%	$19,641
Emory University (GA)	36%	$18,962
Northwestern University (IL)	41%	$18,857
Pepperdine University (CA)	52%	$18,482
Tulane University (LA)	40%	$18,025
Clark University (MA)	60%	$18,012
Loyola University Chicago	73%	$17,942
University of Rochester (NY)	58%	$17,801
Boston College	37%	$17,698
Lehigh University (PA)	44%	$17,403
University of the Pacific (CA)	66%	$17,379
University of Notre Dame (IN)	45%	$17,160
Boston University	44%	$16,953
George Washington University (DC)	38%	$16,744
Brandeis University (MA)	46%	$16,420
University of Miami (FL)	54%	$16,363
University of San Diego	51%	$15,830
Worcester Polytechnic Institute (MA)	72%	$15,776
Wake Forest University (NC)	32%	$15,699
Case Western Reserve University (OH)	54%	$15,695
Georgetown University (DC)	35%	$15,663
Carnegie Mellon University (PA)	48%	$15,007
Florida Institute of Technology	54%	$13,798
Fordham University (NY)	62%	$13,771
University of San Francisco	50%	$13,635
Yeshiva University (NY)	41%	$13,541
Illinois Institute of Technology	57%	$13,485
University of Denver	44%	$13,361

Schools that award the largest amounts of need-based scholarships and grants

Liberal Arts Colleges

	% receiving grants and scholarships based on need	Average amount of need-based scholarship and grant
Amherst College (MA)	47%	$23,703
Williams College (MA)	40%	$23,665
Colgate University (NY)	42%	$22,956
Colby College (ME)	37%	$22,766
Trinity College (CT)	40%	$22,337
Pomona College (CA)	51%	$22,274
Swarthmore College (PA)	49%	$22,251
Haverford College (PA)	41%	$22,203
Middlebury College (VT)	40%	$22,160
Wesleyan University (CT)	46%	$21,776
Occidental College (CA)	54%	$21,647
Wellesley College (MA)	55%	$21,628
Bryn Mawr College (PA)	58%	$21,583
Barnard College (NY)	39%	$21,533
Bowdoin College (ME)	45%	$21,437
Claremont McKenna College (CA)	55%	$21,329
Bates College (ME)	38%	$21,234
Connecticut College	42%	$21,198
Pitzer College (CA)	42%	$21,101
Sarah Lawrence College (NY)	49%	$21,014
Smith College (MA)	56%	$20,988
Reed College (OR)	53%	$20,880
Mount Holyoke College (MA)	67%	$20,062

	% receiving grants and scholarships based on need	Average amount of need-based scholarship and grant
Lafayette College (PA)	51%	$20,044
Union College (NY)	49%	$19,590
Vassar College (NY)	52%	$19,511
Scripps College (CA)	47%	$19,475
Hamilton College (NY)	55%	$19,451
Colorado College	43%	$19,275
College of the Atlantic (ME)	75%	$18,900
Hobart and William Smith Colleges (NY)	61%	$18,765
Skidmore College (NY)	42%	$18,765
Kenyon College (OH)	41%	$18,731
St. Lawrence University (NY)	69%	$18,585
Dickinson College (PA)	51%	$18,568
Gettysburg College (PA)	58%	$18,531
Harvey Mudd College (CA)	52%	$18,438
Bard College (NY)	59%	$18,336
Hampshire College (MA)	54%	$18,260
Washington and Lee University (VA)	22%	$17,829
Bennington College (VT)	65%	$17,520
Oberlin College (OH)	53%	$17,488
Willamette University (OR)	64%	$17,365
Lewis and Clark College (OR)	63%	$17,314
Franklin and Marshall College (PA)	42%	$17,205
Macalester College (MN)	69%	$17,061

Universities–Master's (North)

	% receiving grants and scholarships based on need	Average amount of need-based scholarship and grant
Alfred University (NY)	87%	$16,504
College of Notre Dame of Maryland	70%	$14,417
Villanova University (PA)	38%	$14,296
Lebanon Valley College (PA)	78%	$14,062
Le Moyne College (NY)	80%	$13,980
Hood College (MD)	77%	$13,899
Bentley College (MA)	46%	$13,530
Ithaca College (NY)	65%	$12,903

	% receiving grants and scholarships based on need	Average amount of need-based scholarship and grant
St. Michael's College (VT)	63%	$12,743
St. Francis University (PA)	85%	$12,421
Gallaudet University (DC)	72%	$12,342
Rivier College (NH)	81%	$11,826
Canisius College (NY)	74%	$11,650
Simmons College (MA)	65%	$11,452
Mount St. Mary's University (MD)	62%	$11,425
La Salle University (PA)	73%	$11,273

Universities–Master's (South)

	% receiving grants and scholarships based on need	Average amount of need-based scholarship and grant
Rollins College (FL)	41%	$20,887
University of Richmond (VA)	31%	$15,742
Stetson University (FL)	57%	$14,369
Converse College (SC)	69%	$13,836
Mercer University (GA)	70%	$12,688
Jacksonville University (FL)	66%	$12,438
St. Leo University (FL)	70%	$12,077
Spring Hill College (AL)	68%	$12,057
Loyola University New Orleans	54%	$11,964
Lynchburg College (VA)	64%	$11,958
Brenau University (GA)	69%	$11,856
Lynn University (FL)	52%	$11,449
Centenary College of Louisiana	62%	$10,913
Meredith College (NC)	57%	$9,935
Mary Baldwin College (VA)	77%	$9,786
Campbellsville University (KY)	91%	$9,191

Universities–Master's (Midwest)

	% receiving grants and scholarships based on need	Average amount of need-based scholarship and grant
Maharishi University of Management (IA)	78%	$17,720
University of Detroit Mercy	71%	$14,002
University of Evansville (IN)	67%	$12,915
Aquinas College (MI)	72%	$12,661
Butler University (IN)	58%	$12,000
Creighton University (NE)	50%	$11,637
North Central College (IL)	68%	$11,475
John Carroll University (OH)	71%	$11,469
Drake University (IA)	58%	$11,441
Ashland University (OH)	79%	$11,333
Valparaiso University (IN)	67%	$11,310
Concordia University Wisconsin	89%	$11,000
Anderson University (IN)	78%	$10,784
Heidelberg College (OH)	83%	$10,089
Capital University (OH)	79%	$9,890
Xavier University (OH)	48%	$9,759

Universities–Master's (West)

	% receiving grants and scholarships based on need	Average amount of need-based scholarship and grant
St. Mary's College of California	55%	$15,625
Dominican University of California (CA)	72%	$14,879
Chapman University (CA)	61%	$14,873
Notre Dame de Namur University (CA)	71%	$14,336
Santa Clara University (CA)	41%	$14,080
University of Redlands (CA)	68%	$13,162
University of Portland (OR)	58%	$12,719
Seattle Pacific University	62%	$12,206
Woodbury University (CA)	63%	$11,938
Pacific University (OR)	75%	$11,834
Whitworth College (WA)	70%	$11,552
California Lutheran University	66%	$11,360
Loyola Marymount University (CA)	49%	$11,116
Gonzaga University (WA)	51%	$11,113

Schools that award the largest amounts of need-based scholarships and grants

Comprehensive Colleges–Bachelor's (North)

	% receiving grants and scholarships based on need	Average amount of need-based scholarship and grant
Elmira College (NY)	80%	$15,038
College of St. Elizabeth (NJ)	70%	$13,765
Elizabethtown College (PA)	72%	$12,540
Utica College (NY)	91%	$12,477
Colby-Sawyer College (NH)	62%	$12,409
Neumann College (PA)	84%	$12,000

	% receiving grants and scholarships based on need	Average amount of need-based scholarship and grant
Wilson College (PA)	71%	$11,876
Cedar Crest College (PA)	83%	$11,808
Delaware Valley College (PA)	73%	$11,458
Lasell College (MA)	82%	$11,291
Stonehill College (MA)	63%	$10,999

Comprehensive Colleges–Bachelor's (South)

	% receiving grants and scholarships based on need	Average amount of need-based scholarship and grant
Berea College (KY)	100%	$23,110
Maryville College (TN)	79%	$12,475
Covenant College (GA)	72%	$12,011
Florida Southern College	70%	$10,988
John Brown University (AR)	33%	$10,693
Alderson-Broaddus College (WV)	96%	$10,663

	% receiving grants and scholarships based on need	Average amount of need-based scholarship and grant
Lenoir-Rhyne College (NC)	81%	$10,229
Berry College (GA)	56%	$10,046
Brevard College (NC)	67%	$9,975
Claflin University (SC)	94%	$9,780
LaGrange College (GA)	68%	$9,556

Comprehensive Colleges–Bachelor's (Midwest)

	% receiving grants and scholarships based on need	Average amount of need-based scholarship and grant
Ohio Northern University	82%	$14,487
Manchester College (IN)	77%	$12,666
Notre Dame College of Ohio	N/A	$12,233
Buena Vista University (IA)	91%	$12,115
MacMurray College (IL)	93%	$11,651
Central College (IA)	81%	$11,650

	% receiving grants and scholarships based on need	Average amount of need-based scholarship and grant
Simpson College (IA)	88%	$11,381
Elmhurst College (IL)	60%	$11,297
Wilmington College (OH)	85%	$11,185
Wartburg College (IA)	79%	$11,123
Waldorf College (IA)	83%	$11,062

Comprehensive Colleges–Bachelor's (West)

	% receiving grants and scholarships based on need	Average amount of need-based scholarship and grant
Menlo College (CA)	59%	$14,599
Texas Lutheran University	58%	$10,993
Master's College and Seminary (CA)	62%	$10,059
Sierra Nevada College (NV)	83%	$9,800
Concordia University–Austin (TX)	55%	$9,652
Northwest Christian College (OR)	76%	$9,531
Rocky Mountain College (MT)	60%	$8,476
Carroll College (MT)	63%	$8,020
Bethany College (CA)	47%	$8,000
Western Baptist College (OR)	82%	$7,978
Vanguard University of Southern California	77%	$7,400

Schools that give merit-based scholarships and grants to the most students

The schools listed on the following pages are those that gave merit-based awards to the largest percentages of students during the 2003–2004 academic year. Merit award is defined here as money given to students with no financial need. It is often given out on the basis of high test scores or top grades and doesn't include athletic scholarships. The tables also list the average dollar amount of each school's merit awards during the 2003–2004 academic year. Despite the growing popularity of merit aid to attract desirable students, a few schools continue to give only need-based awards.

National Universities

	Average amount of merit award	% receiving merit awards
University of North Carolina–Greensboro	$3,437	50%
University of Florida	$3,770	47%
University of South Carolina–Columbia	$4,037	43%
Illinois Institute of Technology	$9,981	40%
University of Louisiana–Lafayette	$2,631	40%
University of Wyoming	$3,421	39%
University of Nevada–Reno	$2,754	39%
West Virginia University	$3,324	36%
Louisiana State University–Baton Rouge	$3,765	36%
Case Western Reserve University (OH)	$12,352	34%
University of Rochester (NY)	$10,022	34%
Clemson University (SC)	$6,598	33%
New Mexico Institute of Mining and Technology	$3,853	33%
Andrews University (MI)	$4,562	32%
University of Dayton (OH)	$3,141	32%
University of New Mexico	$3,173	31%
University of Missouri–Rolla	$6,010	30%
Wake Forest University (NC)	$10,201	30%
University of Denver	$7,180	30%
Southern Methodist University (TX)	$5,485	30%
Tulane University (LA)	$15,306	29%
Georgia Institute of Technology	$4,559	28%
Brigham Young University–Provo (UT)	$2,991	28%
University of Alabama	$4,126	28%
Baylor University (TX)	$5,419	28%

	Average amount of merit award	% receiving merit awards
University of Nevada–Las Vegas	$2,094	27%
University of Tulsa (OK)	$9,334	27%
Texas Tech University	$2,187	26%
University of Texas–Austin	$4,560	26%
Michigan Technological University	$3,617	24%
East Carolina University (NC)	$5,659	24%
University of Missouri–Columbia	$4,497	24%
Louisiana Tech University	$5,289	24%
Michigan State University	$4,172	23%
University of South Dakota	$5,415	23%
Brandeis University (MA)	$16,883	23%
University of Alabama–Huntsville	$2,070	23%
Oklahoma State University	$2,851	23%
University of Alabama–Birmingham	$5,455	22%
North Carolina State University–Raleigh	$6,852	22%
University of Iowa	$4,192	22%
Nova Southeastern University (FL)	$2,604	21%
Florida Institute of Technology	$7,280	21%
New Mexico State University	$2,716	21%
University of Michigan–Ann Arbor	$4,744	21%
Pennsylvania State University–University Park	$6,212	21%
Mississippi State University	$2,128	21%
Marquette University (WI)	$6,674	21%
University of Miami (FL)	$12,776	21%
University of Arkansas	$5,645	21%

Liberal Arts Colleges

	Average amount of merit award	% receiving merit awards
Denison University (OH)	$10,372	51%
Kalamazoo College (MI)	$9,450	49%
Birmingham-Southern College (AL)	$10,425	48%
DePauw University (IN)	$12,134	45%
Hendrix College (AR)	$12,567	42%
Hampden-Sydney College (VA)	$14,307	42%
Sweet Briar College (VA)	$10,040	41%
Wesleyan College (GA)	$12,507	39%
Millsaps College (MS)	$11,659	39%
Ohio Wesleyan University	$11,847	38%
Transylvania University (KY)	$9,575	38%
Randolph-Macon College (VA)	$11,012	37%
Presbyterian College (SC)	$10,178	36%
Austin College (TX)	$8,473	36%
St. Andrews Presbyterian College (NC)	$9,671	34%
Oglethorpe University (GA)	$10,542	34%
College of Wooster (OH)	$10,643	34%
Washington College (MD)	$10,717	34%
Randolph-Macon Woman's College (VA)	$15,351	33%
Albion College (MI)	$10,289	33%
Illinois Wesleyan University	$7,858	33%
Rhodes College (TN)	$9,198	33%
Westminster College (MO)	$6,573	32%

	Average amount of merit award	% receiving merit awards
St. Mary's College of Maryland	$4,500	32%
Willamette University (OR)	$10,995	32%
Huntingdon College (AL)	$6,107	31%
Lawrence University (WI)	$9,662	31%
Hollins University (VA)	$7,558	31%
University of Dallas	$9,960	31%
Lyon College (AR)	$10,132	30%
Juniata College (PA)	$10,760	30%
Centre College (KY)	$8,013	30%
Westmont College (CA)	$8,450	30%
Albertson College (ID)	$8,259	30%
St. John's University (MN)	$5,849	28%
College of St. Benedict (MN)	$5,681	28%
Grinnell College (IA)	$8,890	28%
Greensboro College (NC)	$4,473	27%
Gordon College (MA)	$10,895	27%
Agnes Scott College (GA)	$10,451	26%
Antioch College (OH)	$7,520	26%
Drew University (NJ)	$11,785	26%
Hope College (MI)	$6,650	26%
Gustavus Adolphus College (MN)	$5,506	26%
University of Puget Sound (WA)	$6,766	26%

Universities–Master's (North)

	Average amount of merit award	% receiving merit awards
Bryant College (RI)	$7,247	47%
Buffalo State College	$1,429	43%
Mount St. Mary's University (MD)	$13,127	34%
SUNY College–Oneonta	$5,750	33%
Shippensburg University of Pennsylvania	$727	27%
Wagner College (NY)	$7,439	26%
Monmouth University (NJ)	$4,619	26%
Coppin State University (MD)	$4,383	25%

	Average amount of merit award	% receiving merit awards
Long Island University–C.W. Post Campus (NY)	$7,000	25%
SUNY–Plattsburgh	$4,552	24%
Philadelphia University	$4,016	23%
Fairleigh Dickinson University (NJ)	$4,953	23%
Cabrini College (PA)	$4,260	23%
Point Park University (PA)	$6,706	22%
Manhattanville College (NY)	$8,271	22%
Hood College (MD)	$14,337	22%

Schools that give merit-based scholarships and grants to the most students

Universities–Master's (South)

	Average amount of merit award	% receiving merit awards
David Lipscomb University (TN)	$5,826	58%
Tusculum College (TN)	$4,535	49%
Lynn University (FL)	$11,083	44%
Alcorn State University (MS)	$4,250	43%
Mississippi College	$9,838	42%
Harding University (AR)	$7,246	38%
Lynchburg College (VA)	$7,856	36%
Murray State University (KY)	$2,550	33%
Queens University of Charlotte (NC)	$7,886	33%
Loyola University New Orleans	$8,868	32%
Stetson University (FL)	$11,283	32%
Palm Beach Atlantic University (FL)	$1,684	31%
Christian Brothers University (TN)	$8,450	30%
Meredith College (NC)	$4,397	28%
Jacksonville University (FL)	$5,234	28%
Gardner-Webb University (NC)	$5,031	27%
Converse College (SC)	$16,158	26%
Samford University (AL)	$3,700	26%

Universities–Master's (Midwest)

	Average amount of merit award	% receiving merit awards
Washburn University (KS)	$515	45%
Rockford College (IL)	$9,000	40%
Truman State University (MO)	$4,314	40%
Roosevelt University (IL)	$6,030	38%
Xavier University (OH)	$8,237	35%
Dominican University (IL)	$5,600	33%
William Woods University (MO)	$3,554	33%
Drake University (IA)	$8,936	31%
Central Missouri State University	$2,257	30%
Creighton University (NE)	$7,568	28%
Aquinas College (MI)	$8,266	28%
College of Mount St. Joseph (OH)	$3,800	28%
Baker University (KS)	$5,150	28%
Benedictine University (IL)	$6,632	27%
Butler University (IN)	$8,200	27%
College of St. Catherine (MN)	$14,651	27%

Universities–Master's (West)

	Average amount of merit award	% receiving merit awards
Trinity University (TX)	$6,358	37%
Azusa Pacific University (CA)	$3,485	35%
University of Portland (OR)	$16,102	33%
Regis University (CO)	$5,876	32%
Central Washington University	$4,543	32%
Gonzaga University (WA)	$6,618	30%
Seattle Pacific University	$8,832	28%
Point Loma Nazarene University (CA)	$8,728	26%
Westminster College (UT)	$7,385	25%
University of Texas–Tyler	$1,699	25%
Adams State College (CO)	$1,824	25%
Abilene Christian University (TX)	$4,419	24%
Texas Wesleyan University	N/A	23%
Lamar University (TX)	$1,300	23%

Comprehensive Colleges–Bachelor's (North)

College	Average amount of merit award	% receiving merit awards
Felician College (NJ)	$7,626	50%
Marymount College–Tarrytown (NY)	$7,242	25%
Wilson College (PA)	$14,243	24%
Stonehill College (MA)	$10,069	22%
Ramapo College of New Jersey	$8,468	21%
St. Francis College (NY)	N/A	20%
Grove City College (PA)	$2,572	19%
Delaware Valley College (PA)	$7,407	19%
St. Joseph's College, New York	$3,985	19%
Mercyhurst College (PA)	$5,010	19%
Villa Julie College (MD)	$5,387	19%
Messiah College (PA)	$5,228	18%
Elmira College (NY)	$15,850	18%

Comprehensive Colleges–Bachelor's (South)

College	Average amount of merit award	% receiving merit awards
Flagler College (FL)	$3,665	41%
Berry College (GA)	$11,228	41%
University of the Ozarks (AR)	$11,784	38%
Livingstone College (NC)	$5,287	37%
Thomas University (GA)	$2,138	34%
Peace College (NC)	$7,541	33%
North Greenville College (SC)	$5,000	33%
Shorter College (GA)	$9,535	31%
Ouachita Baptist University (AR)	$6,111	31%
Johnson C. Smith University (NC)	N/A	30%
Alice Lloyd College (KY)	$4,712	30%

Comprehensive Colleges–Bachelor's (Midwest)

College	Average amount of merit award	% receiving merit awards
Kansas Wesleyan University	$4,224	87%
Briar Cliff University (IA)	$2,895	73%
Mount Vernon Nazarene University (OH)	$1,406	42%
Missouri Baptist College	$707	33%
Calvin College (MI)	$4,890	32%
St. Norbert College (WI)	$9,259	30%
Augustana College (SD)	$6,695	28%
Millikin University (IL)	$6,535	27%
Taylor University (IN)	$3,137	25%
Valley City State University (ND)	$1,403	25%
Lakeland College (WI)	$6,342	24%
Tabor College (KS)	$4,335	24%

Schools that give merit-based scholarships and grants to the most students

Comprehensive Colleges– Bachelor's (West)	Average amount of merit award	% receiving merit awards
Langston University (OK)	$2,226	30%
Oklahoma Baptist University	$4,389	29%
Carroll College (MT)	$5,907	27%
Patten College (CA)	$7,524	25%
Texas Lutheran University	$9,491	24%
Menlo College (CA)	$10,675	24%
Oklahoma Christian University	$2,234	22%
Vanguard University of Southern California	$4,051	22%

	Average amount of merit award	% receiving merit awards
Master's College and Seminary (CA)	$8,145	20%
Linfield College (OR)	$8,902	19%
East Texas Baptist University	$3,372	17%
St. Gregory's University (OK)	$3,953	17%
Howard Payne University (TX)	$4,331	17%
Sierra Nevada College (NV)	$9,000	17%
Northwest College (WA)	$9,059	17%

Schools whose graduates have the most and least debt

How mired in debt will you be when you get your diploma? This table shows the percentage of 2003 graduates who took on student loan debt and the average cumulative amount they borrowed. The data include any loans taken out by students from the colleges themselves, from financial institutions, and from federal, state, and local governments. Parents' loans are not included.

Most debt

National Universities	% of grads with debt	Average amount of debt		% of grads with debt	Average amount of debt
Pepperdine University (CA)	59%	$32,102	Drexel University (PA)	81%	$22,234
Worcester Polytechnic Institute (MA)	75%	$30,564	University of San Francisco	61%	$22,075
University of Miami (FL)	58%	$29,046	Temple University (PA)	69%	$22,041
University of San Diego	43%	$26,559	University of Tennessee	49%	$21,713
George Washington University (DC)	51%	$25,943	DePaul University (IL)	67%	$21,695
Florida Institute of Technology	50%	$25,692	Nova Southeastern University (FL)	61%	$21,607
University of Notre Dame (IN)	56%	$25,653	Georgetown University (DC)	47%	$21,500
Virginia Tech	37%	$25,611	University of Dayton (OH)	60%	$21,467
Andrews University (MI)	59%	$24,966	University of Toledo (OH)	63%	$21,272
University of Hartford (CT)	67%	$24,878	University of New Hampshire	69%	$21,251
Biola University (CA)	74%	$24,805	Carnegie Mellon University (PA)	52%	$21,235
New York University	58%	$24,620	Tulane University (LA)	52%	$20,755
Cornell University (NY)	39%	$24,570	Union Institute and University (OH)	98%	$20,696
Wake Forest University (NC)	39%	$24,549	Montana State University–Bozeman	62%	$20,618
Adelphi University (NY)	70%	$24,528	University of Memphis	29%	$20,491
Rensselaer Polytechnic Institute (NY)	72%	$23,725	University of Missouri–Columbia	46%	$20,428
Case Western Reserve University (OH)	55%	$23,534	College of William and Mary (VA)	27%	$20,355
Vanderbilt University (TN)	35%	$23,334	Polytechnic University (NY)	76%	$20,219
University of Denver	59%	$23,138	University of Pittsburgh	60%	$20,154
University of Vermont	51%	$23,114	Wilmington College (DE)	32%	$20,150
University of St. Thomas (MN)	68%	$23,084	West Virginia University	67%	$20,145
Marquette University (WI)	52%	$22,924	Massachusetts Institute of Technology	54%	$20,079
University of North Dakota	68%	$22,733	Southern Methodist University (TX)	54%	$20,079
New School University (NY)	56%	$22,611	North Dakota State University	69%	$19,929
St. Louis University	67%	$22,247	Tennessee State University	47%	$19,841
Howard University (DC)	71%	$22,245			

Schools whose graduates have the most and least debt

Most debt

Liberal Arts Colleges

	% of grads with debt	Average amount of debt
Albright College (PA)	88%	$24,876
University of Puget Sound (WA)	63%	$23,782
Allegheny College (PA)	75%	$23,735
St. Lawrence University (NY)	70%	$23,091
College of St. Benedict (MN)	73%	$22,688
Ohio Wesleyan University	58%	$22,166
Coe College (IA)	83%	$22,157
Whittier College (CA)	93%	$22,104
Austin College (TX)	76%	$22,085
Randolph-Macon Woman's College (VA)	68%	$21,992
Eastern Mennonite University (VA)	93%	$21,900
Harvey Mudd College (CA)	67%	$21,881
St. John's University (MN)	75%	$21,598
Davidson College (NC)	32%	$21,530
Marymount Manhattan College (NY)	82%	$21,000
Pitzer College (CA)	60%	$20,900
Wesleyan University (CT)	37%	$20,846
University of Dallas	65%	$20,836
Franklin Pierce College (NH)	79%	$20,815
Illinois Wesleyan University	68%	$20,803
Houghton College (NY)	70%	$20,768
Smith College (MA)	72%	$20,570
Hobart and William Smith Colleges (NY)	70%	$20,508

	% of grads with debt	Average amount of debt
Agnes Scott College (GA)	67%	$20,321
Wesleyan College (GA)	78%	$20,200
Wheaton College (MA)	65%	$20,188
Hartwick College (NY)	72%	$20,100
Bridgewater College (VA)	80%	$20,099
Mills College (CA)	84%	$20,030
Fisk University (TN)	85%	$20,000
Talladega College (AL)	75%	$20,000
Albion College (MI)	61%	$19,802
Lane College (TN)	98%	$19,681
Kenyon College (OH)	60%	$19,587
Hope College (MI)	87%	$19,568
Westmont College (CA)	80%	$19,548
Concordia College–Moorhead (MN)	66%	$19,546
College of Wooster (OH)	63%	$19,494
Goucher College (MD)	66%	$19,304
Alma College (MI)	87%	$19,237
Dickinson College (PA)	81%	$19,207
Union College (NY)	64%	$19,195
Furman University (SC)	31%	$19,170
St. Anselm College (NH)	79%	$19,111
Coastal Carolina University (SC)	60%	$18,975

Universities–Master's (North)

	% of grads with debt	Average amount of debt
Touro College (NY)	20%	$35,010
Villanova University (PA)	56%	$30,015
Arcadia University (PA)	71%	$29,145
University of New England (ME)	80%	$28,421
Rider University (NJ)	66%	$27,113
Philadelphia University	68%	$25,702
Norwich University (VT)	95%	$25,505
Marywood University (PA)	87%	$25,016
Lincoln University (PA)	80%	$25,000
Trinity College (DC)	73%	$24,093
Gannon University (PA)	71%	$23,710
St. Joseph's College (ME)	95%	$23,350
Wagner College (NY)	72%	$23,144
Bryant College (RI)	69%	$22,909
Assumption College (MA)	87%	$22,825
Carlow College (PA)	73%	$22,785

	% of grads with debt	Average amount of debt
Providence College (RI)	65%	$22,500
Lebanon Valley College (PA)	73%	$22,027
Wheelock College (MA)	80%	$22,000
University of Southern Maine	54%	$21,720
La Salle University (PA)	74%	$21,364
Nazareth College of Rochester (NY)	83%	$21,307
Fairfield University (CT)	49%	$21,200
Manhattanville College (NY)	75%	$21,160
Long Island University–Brooklyn (NY)	87%	$20,921
Springfield College (MA)	90%	$20,869
Geneva College (PA)	93%	$20,860
Quinnipiac University (CT)	71%	$20,510
Johnson and Wales University (RI)	76%	$20,268
King's College (PA)	82%	$20,267
St. Michael's College (VT)	80%	$20,233
Regis College (MA)	87%	$20,174

Universities–Master's (South)

	% of grads with debt	Average amount of debt
Embry Riddle Aeronautical University (FL)	98%	$36,022
Alabama State University	80%	$26,825
Spalding University (KY)	96%	$25,000
Southern Arkansas University	45%	$24,722
Tuskegee University (AL)	83%	$23,000
University of Tampa (FL)	74%	$22,791
Valdosta State University (GA)	60%	$22,361
Freed-Hardeman University (TN)	80%	$22,135
Northwestern State University of Louisiana	85%	$22,000
Marymount University (VA)	71%	$21,366
Northern Kentucky University	28%	$20,787
North Carolina Central University	84%	$20,701
Barry University (FL)	66%	$20,661

	% of grads with debt	Average amount of debt
Stetson University (FL)	55%	$20,000
Mary Baldwin College (VA)	73%	$19,694
Shenandoah University (VA)	65%	$18,588
Averett University (VA)	38%	$18,507
Southern Wesleyan University (SC)	99%	$18,469
State University of West Georgia	51%	$18,230
Loyola University New Orleans	57%	$18,125
Fort Valley State University (GA)	85%	$18,116
Elon University (NC)	46%	$18,102
Converse College (SC)	52%	$18,036
David Lipscomb University (TN)	70%	$18,000
University of Mobile (AL)	98%	$18,000

Universities–Master's (Midwest)

	% of grads with debt	Average amount of debt
Rockford College (IL)	99%	$45,000
College of St. Scholastica (MN)	87%	$25,474
Capital University (OH)	78%	$25,171
MidAmerica Nazarene University (KS)	74%	$24,812
Lawrence Technological University (MI)	50%	$24,590
Augsburg College (MN)	69%	$24,546
College of St. Catherine (MN)	81%	$24,537
University of Michigan–Dearborn	34%	$23,753
Franciscan University of Steubenville (OH)	77%	$23,140
Creighton University (NE)	61%	$22,437
Drake University (IA)	58%	$22,115
Bethel University (MN)	73%	$22,062
Heidelberg College (OH)	74%	$22,032
Eastern Michigan University	55%	$22,000

	% of grads with debt	Average amount of debt
St. Mary's University of Minnesota	72%	$21,915
Ursuline College (OH)	77%	$21,800
Mount Marty College (SD)	67%	$21,492
Hamline University (MN)	77%	$21,489
University of Evansville (IN)	68%	$21,141
Mount Mary College (WI)	65%	$20,715
Benedictine College (KS)	74%	$20,684
Olivet Nazarene University (IL)	68%	$20,607
Valparaiso University (IN)	59%	$20,270
Edgewood College (WI)	65%	$19,551
Butler University (IN)	63%	$19,500
St. Xavier University (IL)	63%	$19,374
Winona State University (MN)	81%	$19,067

Schools whose graduates have the most and least debt

Most debt

Universities–Master's (West)

	% of grads with debt	Average amount of debt		% of grads with debt	Average amount of debt
University of Great Falls (MT)	89%	$29,483	University of Redlands (CA)	70%	$22,358
Hardin-Simmons University (TX)	76%	$26,729	St. Edward's University (TX)	64%	$22,331
Seattle University	79%	$26,096	LeTourneau University (TX)	77%	$22,295
Santa Clara University (CA)	66%	$25,492	Pacific Lutheran University (WA)	60%	$22,190
University of the Incarnate Word (TX)	67%	$24,998	Regis University (CO)	60%	$22,000
Abilene Christian University (TX)	70%	$24,167	Gonzaga University (WA)	73%	$21,591
Oral Roberts University (OK)	86%	$24,104	Pacific University (OR)	86%	$21,465
Azusa Pacific University (CA)	73%	$24,000	Walla Walla College (WA)	75%	$21,273
Alaska Pacific University	68%	$23,791	St. Mary's College of California	62%	$21,165
St. Mary's University of San Antonio	81%	$23,406	Chaminade University of Honolulu	69%	$21,105
Montana State University–Northern	80%	$23,000	Northwest Nazarene University (ID)	77%	$21,073
College of Santa Fe (NM)	60%	$22,641			

Comprehensive Colleges–Bachelor's (North)

	% of grads with debt	Average amount of debt		% of grads with debt	Average amount of debt
Felician College (NJ)	85%	$40,000	Merrimack College (MA)	70%	$21,125
Dominican College of Blauvelt (NY)	100%	$30,625	Grove City College (PA)	42%	$19,986
Centenary College (NJ)	89%	$24,274	Green Mountain College (VT)	82%	$19,638
Messiah College (PA)	67%	$23,249	Elmira College (NY)	64%	$19,480
Becker College (MA)	99%	$22,262	Thiel College (PA)	84%	$19,394
Mercyhurst College (PA)	85%	$22,125	Cedar Crest College (PA)	78%	$19,382

Comprehensive Colleges–Bachelor's (South)

	% of grads with debt	Average amount of debt		% of grads with debt	Average amount of debt
Lenoir-Rhyne College (NC)	89%	$26,704	Benedict College (SC)	92%	$21,950
Bethune-Cookman College (FL)	77%	$26,200	Lee University (TN)	71%	$21,615
Kentucky Christian College	87%	$25,587	Alderson-Broaddus College (WV)	80%	$21,334
Dillard University (LA)	98%	$25,247	Mountain State University (WV)	61%	$21,168
Edward Waters College (FL)	90%	$24,531	Bryan College (TN)	53%	$20,442
Thomas University (GA)	61%	$24,000	Columbia College (SC)	88%	$19,741
Wingate University (NC)	88%	$24,000	Claflin University (SC)	93%	$19,680
Crichton College (TN)	69%	$22,514	Asbury College (KY)	68%	$18,885
Catawba College (NC)	64%	$22,000	Kentucky Wesleyan College	91%	$18,606
Thomas More College (KY)	62%	$21,980			

Comprehensive Colleges–Bachelor's (Midwest)

	% of grads with debt	Average amount of debt
Alverno College (WI)	97%	$30,000
Ohio Northern University	87%	$29,713
Martin University (IN)	91%	$27,193
Concordia University (MI)	90%	$26,471
Central College (IA)	85%	$25,846
Cedarville University (OH)	58%	$24,542
Grace College and Seminary (IN)	94%	$23,035
Wartburg College (IA)	93%	$22,809
Buena Vista University (IA)	90%	$22,566
Crown College (MN)	83%	$21,789
Simpson College (IA)	86%	$21,581
Evangel University (MO)	90%	$21,467
Wilmington College (OH)	86%	$21,235
Tabor College (KS)	83%	$20,498
St. Mary's College (IN)	82%	$20,356
Bluffton University (OH)	72%	$20,039
Graceland University (IA)	74%	$19,772
Mount Mercy College (IA)	71%	$19,656
Urbana University (OH)	84%	$19,225
Northwestern College (MN)	69%	$19,184

Comprehensive Colleges–Bachelor's (West)

	% of grads with debt	Average amount of debt
Concordia University–Austin (TX)	54%	$29,449
Humphreys College (CA)	97%	$26,000
Oklahoma Christian University	76%	$25,100
Linfield College (OR)	64%	$24,357
Carroll College (MT)	76%	$22,868
Texas Lutheran University	62%	$21,500
Bethany College (CA)	75%	$21,000
Rocky Mountain College (MT)	87%	$20,571

Least debt

National Universities

	% of grads with debt	Average amount of debt
Princeton University (NJ)	25%	$6,500
University of Texas–El Paso	40%	$7,704
California Institute of Technology	49%	$7,906
Harvard University (MA)	51%	$8,830
New Mexico Institute of Mining and Technology	42%	$9,161
Clark Atlanta University	67%	$10,808
University of South Alabama	71%	$11,000
University of Southern Mississippi	61%	$11,202
Brigham Young University–Provo (UT)	39%	$11,301
Utah State University	47%	$11,500
University of North Carolina–Chapel Hill	24%	$11,519
University of Alaska–Fairbanks	50%	$11,623
University of Utah	42%	$12,400
Southern Illinois University–Carbondale	37%	$12,413
University of Texas–Dallas	49%	$12,605
Michigan Technological University	56%	$12,775
University of Central Florida	36%	$12,780
University of California–Los Angeles	44%	$12,830
University of Texas–Arlington	47%	$12,934
Rice University (TX)	40%	$12,942
San Diego State University	47%	$13,000
University of California–Santa Cruz	54%	$13,116
University of Georgia	47%	$13,193
Johns Hopkins University (MD)	46%	$13,300
University of California–Riverside	72%	$13,414
University of Virginia	31%	$13,522
University of Hawaii–Manoa	29%	$13,707
University of Florida	42%	$13,744

Schools whose graduates have the most and least debt

Least debt

National Universities, continued

	% of grads with debt	Average amount of debt
Illinois State University	59%	$13,780
University of Delaware	33%	$13,806
University of Nevada–Las Vegas	36%	$13,860
University of Houston	30%	$13,961
University of Maryland–College Park	34%	$14,076
Stevens Institute of Technology (NJ)	68%	$14,113
Texas Woman's University	16%	$14,173
University of California–San Diego	54%	$14,192
George Mason University (VA)	42%	$14,215
Louisiana Tech University	37%	$14,306

	% of grads with debt	Average amount of debt
SUNY–Stony Brook	50%	$14,427
University of Illinois–Chicago	39%	$14,439
University of Louisville (KY)	39%	$14,498
University of Maryland–Baltimore County	29%	$14,500
University of Rhode Island	58%	$14,500
SUNY–Binghamton	61%	$14,531
University of Tulsa (OK)	64%	$14,546
New Jersey Institute of Technology	50%	$14,600
Rutgers–Newark (NJ)	73%	$14,757

Liberal Arts Colleges

	% of grads with debt	Average amount of debt
University of Virginia–Wise	67%	$7,414
Christopher Newport University (VA)	71%	$8,035
California State University–Monterey Bay	49%	$8,263
Texas A&M University–Galveston	64%	$9,870
Erskine College (SC)	68%	$10,000
Christendom College (VA)	52%	$10,050
St. Augustine's College (NC)	55%	$10,416
Williams College (MA)	46%	$10,627
Amherst College (MA)	48%	$10,787
University of Maine–Presque Isle	52%	$11,128
Principia College (IL)	66%	$11,314
Blackburn College (IL)	85%	$11,500
Claremont McKenna College (CA)	45%	$11,620
Trinity College (CT)	46%	$11,632
Greensboro College (NC)	67%	$11,802
University of Hawaii–Hilo	37%	$11,806
St. Andrews Presbyterian College (NC)	72%	$11,878
Wellesley College (MA)	59%	$11,913
Birmingham-Southern College (AL)	48%	$12,200
Wofford College (SC)	64%	$12,281
Colgate University (NY)	43%	$12,769
King College (TN)	81%	$12,859
Evergreen State College (WA)	51%	$13,000

	% of grads with debt	Average amount of debt
University of Minnesota–Morris	96%	$13,167
Thomas Aquinas College (CA)	83%	$13,250
Lindsey Wilson College (KY)	72%	$13,265
Salem College (NC)	63%	$13,409
Swarthmore College (PA)	31%	$13,533
Reed College (OR)	51%	$13,692
Western State College of Colorado	61%	$13,700
Colorado College	41%	$13,850
College of the Atlantic (ME)	61%	$13,882
Occidental College (CA)	61%	$13,905
University of North Carolina–Asheville	46%	$13,961
Fort Lewis College (CO)	53%	$14,100
Mesa State College (CO)	41%	$14,123
Centre College (KY)	58%	$14,200
Pine Manor College (MA)	60%	$14,312
Scripps College (CA)	51%	$14,362
Richard Stockton College of New Jersey	63%	$14,372
Hendrix College (AR)	52%	$14,400
Bates College (ME)	50%	$14,401
Sewanee–University of the South (TN)	37%	$14,441
Emory and Henry College (VA)	67%	$14,466
Virginia Military Institute	32%	$14,500

Universities–Master's (North)

	% of grads with debt	Average amount of debt
Mercy College (NY)	81%	$8,176
Bridgewater State College (MA)	41%	$8,180
Fitchburg State College (MA)	30%	$8,500
Point Park University (PA)	90%	$9,835
William Paterson University of New Jersey	44%	$9,981
CUNY–Baruch College	19%	$10,100
Gallaudet University (DC)	51%	$10,273
CUNY–Lehman College	35%	$11,000
Framingham State College (MA)	48%	$11,000
College of New Jersey	48%	$11,157
Worcester State College (MA)	43%	$11,843
St. Thomas Aquinas College (NY)	67%	$12,000
Westfield State College (MA)	92%	$12,347
Lesley University (MA)	91%	$13,125
SUNY–Fredonia	78%	$13,125
University of Maryland–Eastern Shore	80%	$13,250

	% of grads with debt	Average amount of debt
CUNY–Brooklyn College	30%	$13,500
DeSales University (PA)	64%	$13,977
CUNY–Queens College	40%	$14,000
St. Francis University (PA)	90%	$14,100
Millersville University of Pennsylvania	73%	$14,418
Nyack College (NY)	77%	$14,563
Kutztown University of Pennsylvania	73%	$14,570
Frostburg State University (MD)	64%	$14,757
Emerson College (MA)	74%	$14,800
University of Massachusetts–Dartmouth	63%	$14,800
SUNY College of Arts and Sciences–New Paltz	75%	$15,000
Niagara University (NY)	75%	$15,402
Rutgers–Camden (NJ)	63%	$15,432
Shippensburg University of Pennsylvania	68%	$15,464
SUNY College of Arts and Sciences–Geneseo	75%	$15,500
Manhattan College (NY)	79%	$15,715

Universities–Master's (South)

	% of grads with debt	Average amount of debt
Hampton University (VA)	84%	$6,230
Alcorn State University (MS)	67%	$7,500
Cumberland University (TN)	72%	$7,603
Gardner-Webb University (NC)	57%	$7,865
Belmont University (TN)	56%	$8,450
Western Kentucky University	56%	$9,568
Campbell University (NC)	54%	$10,438
Georgia College and State University	57%	$10,759
Armstrong Atlantic State University (GA)	55%	$11,000
Wheeling Jesuit University (WV)	70%	$11,440
James Madison University (VA)	50%	$11,639
University of North Carolina–Pembroke	64%	$11,775

	% of grads with debt	Average amount of debt
Carson-Newman College (TN)	70%	$11,957
St. Leo University (FL)	75%	$12,000
University of North Florida	41%	$12,346
Cumberland College (KY)	71%	$12,503
Southeastern Louisiana University	58%	$12,527
University of Mary Washington (VA)	59%	$12,665
University of Tennessee–Martin	53%	$12,920
Mississippi University for Women	74%	$13,239
Tennessee Technological University	35%	$13,338
Spring Hill College (AL)	61%	$13,421
Piedmont College (GA)	70%	$13,702
Appalachian State University (NC)	48%	$14,000

Schools whose graduates have the most and least debt

Least debt

Universities–Master's (Midwest)

	% of grads with debt	Average amount of debt
Benedictine University (IL)	50%	$6,726
William Woods University (MO)	56%	$9,112
Pittsburg State University (KS)	93%	$9,792
Lincoln University (MO)	69%	$10,000
Northeastern Illinois University	26%	$10,125
Maryville University of St. Louis (MO)	82%	$11,167
Spring Arbor University (MI)	80%	$11,169
Washburn University (KS)	60%	$11,750
Doane College (NE)	77%	$12,539
Park University (MO)	30%	$12,800
Minot State University (ND)	97%	$12,815
Indiana University Southeast	47%	$12,973
Southwest Missouri State University	60%	$12,993
University of Wisconsin–Green Bay	86%	$13,000

	% of grads with debt	Average amount of debt
Dominican University (IL)	59%	$13,437
University of Southern Indiana	57%	$13,487
Southwest Baptist University (MO)	72%	$13,558
Aquinas College (MI)	66%	$13,638
Bemidji State University (MN)	71%	$13,690
Purdue University–Calumet (IN)	46%	$13,693
North Central College (IL)	72%	$13,726
Western Illinois University	63%	$13,800
College of Mount St. Joseph (OH)	80%	$13,900
Eastern Illinois University	60%	$13,997
University of Wisconsin–Stevens Point	64%	$14,013
Southeast Missouri State University	57%	$14,018
Baldwin-Wallace College (OH)	63%	$14,099

Universities–Master's (West)

	% of grads with debt	Average amount of debt
California State University–Long Beach	29%	$6,319
Cameron University (OK)	36%	$6,500
Northeastern State University (OK)	68%	$7,500
Sonoma State University (CA)	29%	$7,848
New Mexico Highlands University	60%	$8,494
Eastern New Mexico University	9%	$9,532
Northwestern Oklahoma State University	52%	$9,577
Weber State University (UT)	65%	$10,500
California State University–Sacramento	37%	$10,554
Point Loma Nazarene University (CA)	76%	$11,029
Midwestern State University (TX)	47%	$11,046
Stephen F. Austin State University (TX)	59%	$11,070

	% of grads with debt	Average amount of debt
California State Polytechnic University–Pomona	33%	$11,258
Texas A&M International University	54%	$12,100
University of Texas–Pan American	84%	$12,175
Western Oregon University	55%	$12,563
California State University–Hayward	35%	$12,584
California State University–Fullerton	37%	$12,720
Cal Poly–San Luis Obispo	46%	$12,781
California State University–Stanislaus	29%	$13,050
Montana State University–Billings	68%	$13,250
University of Mary Hardin-Baylor (TX)	72%	$13,437
Lamar University (TX)	54%	$13,500

Comprehensive Colleges–Bachelor's (North)

	% of grads with debt	Average amount of debt
Marymount College–Tarrytown (NY)	85%	$11,006
Daemen College (NY)	66%	$11,250
University of Maine–Augusta	63%	$11,993
Hilbert College (NY)	61%	$12,532
Albertus Magnus College (CT)	95%	$12,625
SUNY College–Old Westbury	51%	$13,295

	% of grads with debt	Average amount of debt
College of St. Elizabeth (NJ)	78%	$14,026
St. Joseph's College, New York	66%	$15,171
Bloomfield College (NJ)	67%	$15,177
Ramapo College of New Jersey	37%	$15,183
University of Maine–Farmington	75%	$15,471
Wilson College (PA)	73%	$15,609

Comprehensive Colleges–Bachelor's (South)

	% of grads with debt	Average amount of debt
Louisiana College	46%	$5,440
Alice Lloyd College (KY)	45%	$5,694
Berea College (KY)	75%	$6,275
Warner Southern College (FL)	36%	$6,465
Mid-Continent College (KY)	75%	$6,738
Davis and Elkins College (WV)	95%	$8,902
Blue Mountain College (MS)	64%	$9,072
Limestone College (SC)	86%	$9,500
Peace College (NC)	76%	$9,938
St. Paul's College (VA)	80%	$10,315

	% of grads with debt	Average amount of debt
Mars Hill College (NC)	90%	$10,395
Winston-Salem State University (NC)	90%	$10,500
Tennessee Wesleyan College	63%	$10,870
Fairmont State University (WV)	87%	$10,930
Berry College (GA)	48%	$12,000
Pikeville College (KY)	68%	$12,071
Virginia Intermont College	77%	$12,131
Bluefield College (VA)	80%	$12,177
Williams Baptist College (AR)	68%	$12,752

Comprehensive Colleges–Bachelor's (Midwest)

	% of grads with debt	Average amount of debt
Purdue University–North Central (IN)	42%	$9,841
Waldorf College (IA)	92%	$10,500
Indiana University–Kokomo	55%	$11,681
Manchester College (IN)	64%	$12,084
Judson College (IL)	79%	$12,386
College of St. Mary (NE)	100%	$13,595
Wisconsin Lutheran College	71%	$13,707
Kansas Wesleyan University	84%	$14,132
Marian College (IN)	77%	$14,187
Southwest Minnesota State University (MN)	77%	$14,420

	% of grads with debt	Average amount of debt
Culver-Stockton College (MO)	97%	$14,438
McPherson College (KS)	84%	$14,450
McKendree College (IL)	47%	$14,592
Valley City State University (ND)	56%	$14,700
Eureka College (IL)	92%	$14,997
Defiance College (OH)	70%	$15,151
Bethany College (KS)	83%	$15,167
Carroll College (WI)	57%	$15,195
Elmhurst College (IL)	79%	$15,225
Concordia University–St. Paul (MN)	78%	$15,300

Comprehensive Colleges–Bachelor's (West)

	% of grads with debt	Average amount of debt
Utah Valley State College	28%	$5,575
Brigham Young University–Hawaii	31%	$8,505
East Texas Baptist University	69%	$9,982
Wiley College (TX)	16%	$11,231

	% of grads with debt	Average amount of debt
University of Science and Arts of Oklahoma	58%	$12,268
Master's College and Seminary (CA)	57%	$13,131
Pacific Union College (CA)	60%	$13,500
University of Montana–Western	73%	$13,510

The U.S. News & World Report

College Cost and Financial Aid Directory

How to Use the Directory

In the following pages, you'll find key financial aid data for the more than 1,400 colleges and universities *U.S. News* surveys each year. The directory is organized by state, and schools are presented alphabetically within each state.

The vital statistics shown in each directory entry are explained below. The data were collected from the schools themselves during 2004. If a college did not supply the data requested, the information either does not appear or is marked as "N/A" for "not available." If a school did not return the full *U.S. News* questionnaire, only limited information appears. In some cases, data reported in previous years were used if current-year data were unavailable.

Address and stats

This section supplies the basics—college name and address and whether the institution is public or private. Use the financial aid office phone number to request information or ask questions about the financial aid process at the school. Visit the school's website to learn about specific financial aid available from the school, such as scholarships and grants and details about student loans.

- **Tuition and fees:** Figures cited for tuition (including any required fees) are for the 2004–2005 academic year. For public schools, we list both in-state and out-of-state tuition. We also include the charge for room and board for the 2004–2005 academic year. If data for the 2004–2005 academic year are not available, we provide figures for 2003–2004 or, in some cases, the school's estimate for 2004–2005.

- **SAT I verbal/math or ACT score (25th/75th percentile):** The SAT I or ACT composite scores shown represent the range within which half the students scored; 25 percent of students scored at or below the lower end of the range, and 25 percent scored at or above the upper end of the range. If no range was available, an average score was provided.

- **2005 U.S News College Ranking:** The school's rank indicates where it sits among its peers in the 2005 ranking of colleges and universities published by U.S. News at www.usnews.com and in its annual guide, "America's Best Colleges." You'll see the school's rank, followed by the category of institution it falls into. The categories are National Universities, Liberal Arts College, University–Master's, and Comprehensive College–Bachelor's. The master's and comprehensive schools further subdivide by location: North, South, West, and Midwest. Colleges and universities in the top half of their categories are ranked numerically. Others are placed in third and fourth tiers. You cannot compare the ranks of institutions in different categories because schools are assessed only against their peers. Schools that specialize in business, engineering, and art are labeled as such, but are not ranked; nor are the service academies, schools with fewer than 200 students, or schools with a high percentage of older or part-time students.

- **Acceptance rate:** The percentage of applicants accepted is a measure of how hard the school is to get into for the class entering in fall 2003.

Other expenses

This section includes estimates of the cost of books and supplies, transportation, and personal expenses for the 2004–2005 academic year.

Financial aid

Anyone planning to apply for financial aid for the fall of 2005 will find the necessary deadlines for all the required forms. The data on financial aid packages are for those awarded to undergraduates during the 2003–2004 school year and include the percentage of undergraduates who applied for aid; the percentage determined by the school to have financial need; and the percentage whose need was fully met by an aid package that excluded parent or other private loans. In addition, we give the average financial aid package (including grants, loans, and work-study) and the proportion of students awarded a package; the average amount of gift aid (scholarships or grants) and the proportion

awarded such aid; the average amount of self-help aid (work-study or loans) and the proportion awarded such aid; and the average need-based student loan. Also provided are data on the average percentage of need met, for students who received need-based aid; the average amount and proportion of students awarded aid based solely on merit; and the average athletic scholarship awarded and the proportion receiving such an award. Last, we include the amount of average debt for the students in the Class of 2003 who borrowed money to finance their education and the proportion of students who borrowed.

Student employment

This section provides data on the proportion of undergraduates who worked on campus during the 2003–2004 academic year and how much undergraduates can expect to earn per year from part time, on-campus work.

Cooperative education programs

All cooperative education programs offered by the school are listed. If the information was not available, this section does not appear.

Reserve Officers Training Corps (ROTC)

This section indicates whether the school offers Army, Navy, or Air Force ROTC programs on campus or at a cooperating institution. If the information was not available, this section does not appear.

Alabama

Alabama Agricultural and Mechanical University

PO Box 1357
Normal, AL 35762
Public; www.aamu.edu
Financial aid office: (256) 851-5400

■ **2004-2005 TUITION AND FEES:**
In state: $3,872; Out of state: $6,704
■ **ROOM AND BOARD:** $4,500

ACT Score (25th/75th percentile): 16-19
2005 U.S. News College Ranking:
National Universities, fourth tier
Acceptance Rate: 45%

Other expenses: Estimated books and supplies: $900. Transportation: $1,000. Personal expenses: $1,300. **Reserve Officers Training Corps (ROTC):** Army ROTC: Offered on campus.

Alabama State University

915 S. Jackson Street
Montgomery, AL 36101
Public; www.alasu.edu
Financial aid office: (334) 229-4323

■ **2004-2005 TUITION AND FEES:**
In state: $4,008; Out of state: $8,016
■ **ROOM AND BOARD:** $3,600

ACT Score (25th/75th percentile): 14-18
2005 U.S. News College Ranking:
Universities–Master's (South), fourth tier
Acceptance Rate: 37%

Other expenses: Estimated books and supplies: $1,000. Transportation: $930. Personal expenses: $1,380. **Financial aid:** Priority filing date for institution's financial aid form: May 1. In 2003-2004, 98% of undergraduates applied for financial aid. Of those, 90% were determined to have financial need; 12% had their need fully met. Average financial aid package (proportion receiving): $7,011 (86%). Average amount of gift aid, such as scholarships or grants (proportion receiving): $3,292 (71%). Average amount of self-help aid, such as work study or loans (proportion receiving): $3,348 (75%). Average need-based loan (excluding PLUS or other private loans): $3,059. Among students who received need-based aid, the average percentage

of need met: 61%. Among students who received aid based on merit, the average award (and the proportion receiving): $4,973 (2%). The average athletic scholarship (and the proportion receiving): $7,285 (5%). Average amount of debt of borrowers graduating in 2003: $26,825. Proportion who borrowed: 80%. **Student employment:** During the 2003-2004 academic year, 5% of undergraduates worked on campus. Average per-year earnings: $4,017. **Cooperative education programs:** art, business, computer science, education, humanities, natural science, social/behavioral science, vocational arts. **Reserve Officers Training Corps (ROTC):** Army ROTC: Offered at cooperating institution; Air Force ROTC: Offered on campus.

Auburn University

202 Martin Hall
Auburn University, AL 36849-5145
Public; www.auburn.edu
Financial aid office: (334) 844-4367

■ **2004-2005 TUITION AND FEES:**
In state: $4,828; Out of state: $14,048
■ **ROOM AND BOARD:** $6,686

ACT Score (25th/75th percentile): 22-27
2005 U.S. News College Ranking:
National Universities, 90
Acceptance Rate: 78%

Other expenses: Estimated books and supplies: $900. Transportation: $1,104. Personal expenses: $1,988. **Financial aid:** Priority filing date for institution's financial aid form: March 1. In 2003-2004, 49% of undergraduates applied for financial aid. Of those, 33% were determined to have financial need; 10% had their need fully met. Average financial aid package (proportion receiving): $6,696 (32%). Average amount of gift aid, such as scholarships or grants (proportion receiving): $3,177 (14%). Average amount of self-help aid, such as work study or loans (proportion receiving): $4,364 (26%). Average need-based loan (excluding PLUS or other private loans): $4,077. Among students who received need-based aid, the average percentage of need met: 57%. Among students who received aid based on merit, the average award (and the proportion receiving): $4,771 (5%). The average athletic scholarship (and the proportion receiving): $12,173 (0%). Average amount of

debt of borrowers graduating in 2003: $19,459. Proportion who borrowed: 64%. **Student employment:** During the 2003-2004 academic year, 13% of undergraduates worked on campus. Average per-year earnings: $4,500. **Cooperative education programs:** agriculture, art, business, computer science, engineering, humanities, natural science, social/behavioral science, technologies, other. **Reserve Officers Training Corps (ROTC):** Army ROTC: Offered on campus; Navy ROTC: Offered on campus; Air Force ROTC: Offered on campus.

Auburn University– Montgomery

PO Box 244023
Montgomery, AL 36124
Public; www.aum.edu
Financial aid office: (334) 244-3570

■ **2004-2005 TUITION AND FEES:**
In state: $4,460; Out of state: $12,920
■ **ROOM AND BOARD:** $4,890

ACT Score (25th/75th percentile): 17-22
2005 U.S. News College Ranking:
Universities–Master's (South), third tier

Financial aid: In 2003-2004, 76% of undergraduates applied for financial aid. Average financial aid package (proportion receiving): $5,309 (58%). Average amount of gift aid, such as scholarships or grants (proportion receiving): $3,322 (N/A). **Cooperative education programs:** art, business, computer science, education, engineering, health professions, natural science, social/behavioral science. **Reserve Officers Training Corps (ROTC):** Army ROTC: Offered on campus; Air Force ROTC: Offered at cooperating institution (Alabama State University).

Birmingham-Southern College

900 Arkadelphia Road
Birmingham, AL 35254
Private; www.bsc.edu
Financial aid office: (205) 226-4688

■ **2004-2005 TUITION AND FEES:** $20,050
■ **ROOM AND BOARD:** $6,990

ACT Score (25th/75th percentile): 24-30
2005 U.S. News College Ranking:
Liberal Arts Colleges, 70
Acceptance Rate: 89%

....

Other expenses: Estimated books and supplies: $1,000. Transportation: $1,200. Personal expenses: $1,500. **Financial aid:** Priority filing date for institution's financial aid form: March 1; deadline: August 1. In 2003-2004, 68% of undergraduates applied for financial aid. Of those, 41% were determined to have financial need; 34% had their need fully met. Average financial aid package (proportion receiving): $16,015 (41%). Average amount of gift aid, such as scholarships or grants (proportion receiving): $7,342 (41%). Average amount of self-help aid, such as work study or loans (proportion receiving): $5,404 (28%). Average need-based loan (excluding PLUS or other private loans): $4,560. Among students who received need-based aid, the average percentage of need met: 82%. Among students who received aid based on merit, the average award (and the proportion receiving): $10,425 (48%). The average athletic scholarship (and the proportion receiving): $15,329 (11%). Average amount of debt of borrowers graduating in 2003: $12,200. Proportion who borrowed: 48%. **Reserve Officers Training Corps (ROTC):** Army ROTC: Offered at cooperating institution (University of Alabama at Bahm); Air Force ROTC: Offered at cooperating institution (Samford University).

Concordia College

1804 Green Street
Selma, AL 36703-3323
Private; www.concordiaselma.edu
Financial aid office: (334) 874-5700

■ **2004-2005 TUITION AND FEES:** $6,097
■ **ROOM AND BOARD:** $3,200

2005 U.S. News College Ranking:
Comp. Colleges–Bachelor's (South), fourth tier

....

Faulkner University

5345 Atlanta Highway
Montgomery, AL 36109
Private; www.faulkner.edu
Financial aid office: (334) 386-7195

■ **2004-2005 TUITION AND FEES:** $9,715
■ **ROOM AND BOARD:** $5,000

ACT Score (25th/75th percentile): 20
2005 U.S. News College Ranking:
Comp. Colleges–Bachelor's (South), third tier
Acceptance Rate: 55%

....

Other expenses: Estimated books and supplies: $1,200. Transportation: $1,200. Personal expenses: $1,200. **Financial aid:** Priority filing date for institution's financial aid form: May 1. In 2003-2004, 93% of undergraduates applied for financial aid. Of those, 79% were determined to have financial need; 11% had their need fully met. Average financial aid package (proportion receiving): $7,100 (79%). Average amount of gift aid, such as scholarships or grants (proportion receiving): $2,800 (59%). Average amount of self-help aid, such as work study or loans (proportion receiving): $4,900 (71%). Average need-based loan (excluding PLUS or other private loans): $4,800. Among students who received need-based aid, the average percentage of need met: 62%. Among students who received aid based on merit, the average award (and the proportion receiving): $1,900 (3%). The average athletic scholarship (and the proportion receiving): $0 (0%). Average amount of debt of borrowers graduating in 2003: $18,600. Proportion who borrowed: 80%. **Student employment:** During the 2003-2004 academic year, 1% of undergraduates worked on campus. Average per-year earnings: $800. **Cooperative education programs:** computer science, education, natural science. **Reserve Officers Training Corps (ROTC):** Army ROTC: Offered at cooperating institution (Auburn University at Montgomery); Air Force ROTC: Offered at cooperating institution (Alabama State University).

Huntingdon College

1500 E. Fairview Avenue
Montgomery, AL 36106-2148
Private; www.huntingdon.edu
Financial aid office: (334) 833-4519

■ **2004-2005 TUITION AND FEES:** $14,560
■ **ROOM AND BOARD:** $6,000

ACT Score (25th/75th percentile): 21-27
2005 U.S. News College Ranking:
Liberal Arts Colleges, third tier
Acceptance Rate: 59%

....

Other expenses: Estimated books and supplies: $900. Transportation: $500. Personal expenses: $900. **Financial aid:** Priority filing date for institution's financial aid form: April 15. In 2003-2004, 93% of undergraduates applied for

financial aid. Of those, 65% were determined to have financial need; 82% had their need fully met. Average financial aid package (proportion receiving): $9,867 (65%). Average amount of gift aid, such as scholarships or grants (proportion receiving): $4,218 (65%). Average amount of self-help aid, such as work study or loans (proportion receiving): $2,775 (57%). Average need-based loan (excluding PLUS or other private loans): $3,031. Among students who received need-based aid, the average percentage of need met: 83%. Among students who received aid based on merit, the average award (and the proportion receiving): $6,107 (31%). The average athletic scholarship (and the proportion receiving): $0 (0%). Average amount of debt of borrowers graduating in 2003: $16,000. Proportion who borrowed: 68%. **Student employment:** During the 2003-2004 academic year, 5% of undergraduates worked on campus. Average per-year earnings: $2,500. **Reserve Officers Training Corps (ROTC):** Army ROTC: Offered at cooperating institution (Auburn University at Montgomery); Air Force ROTC: Offered at cooperating institution (Alabama State University).

Jacksonville State University

700 Pelham Road N
Jacksonville, AL 36265-1602
Public; www.jsu.edu
Financial aid office: (256) 782-5006

■ **2004-2005 TUITION AND FEES:**
In state: $4,060; Out of state: $8,100
■ **ROOM AND BOARD:** $3,312

ACT Score (25th/75th percentile): 17-22
2005 U.S. News College Ranking:
Universities–Master's (South), third tier
Acceptance Rate: 89%

....

Other expenses: Estimated books and supplies: $900. Transportation: $1,100. Personal expenses: $2,400. **Financial aid:** Priority filing date for institution's financial aid form: March 15. In 2003-2004, 95% of undergraduates applied for financial aid. Of those, 95% were determined to have financial need; Average financial aid package (proportion receiving): $3,988 (95%). Average amount of gift aid, such as scholarships or grants (proportion receiving): $3,061 (46%). Average amount of self-help aid, such as work study or loans (proportion receiving): $5,406 (53%). Average amount of debt of borrowers graduating in 2003: $17,125. Proportion who borrowed: 46%. Average per-year earnings: $3,476. **Cooperative education programs:**

art, business, computer science, engineering, technologies, vocational arts. **Reserve Officers Training Corps (ROTC):** Army ROTC: Offered on campus.

Judson College

PO Box 120
Marion, AL 36756
Private; home.judson.edu
Financial aid office: (334) 683-5170

■ **2004-2005 TUITION AND FEES:** $9,470
■ **ROOM AND BOARD:** $5,850

ACT Score (25th/75th percentile): 19-27
2005 U.S. News College Ranking:
Liberal Arts Colleges, fourth tier
Acceptance Rate: 78%

Other expenses: Estimated books and supplies: $800. Transportation: $500. Personal expenses: $1,600. **Financial aid:** Priority filing date for institution's financial aid form: March 1. In 2003-2004, 86% of undergraduates applied for financial aid. Of those, 66% were determined to have financial need; 26% had their need fully met. Average financial aid package (proportion receiving): $11,500 (66%). Average amount of gift aid, such as scholarships or grants (proportion receiving): $6,884 (66%). Average amount of self-help aid, such as work study or loans (proportion receiving): $4,616 (66%). Average need-based loan (excluding PLUS or other private loans): $3,462. Among students who received need-based aid, the average percentage of need met: 82%. Among students who received aid based on merit, the average award (and the proportion receiving): $3,395 (11%). The average athletic scholarship (and the proportion receiving): $2,500 (2%). Average amount of debt of borrowers graduating in 2003: $15,339. Proportion who borrowed: 81%. **Student employment:** During the 2003-2004 academic year, 2% of undergraduates worked on campus. Average per-year earnings: $405. **Reserve Officers Training Corps (ROTC):** Army ROTC: Offered at cooperating institution (Marion Military Institute).

Miles College

PO Box 3800
Birmingham, AL 35208
Private; www.miles.edu
Financial aid office: (205) 929-1665

■ **2004-2005 TUITION AND FEES:** $5,717
■ **ROOM AND BOARD:** $4,338

ACT Score (25th/75th percentile): 16
2005 U.S. News College Ranking:
Comp. Colleges–Bachelor's (South), third tier
Acceptance Rate: 39%

Other expenses: Estimated books and supplies: $450.

Oakwood College

7000 Adventist Boulevard
Huntsville, AL 35896
Private; www.oakwood.edu
Financial aid office: (256) 726-7210

■ **2004-2005 TUITION AND FEES:** $11,298
■ **ROOM AND BOARD:** $6,374

ACT Score (25th/75th percentile): 16-21
2005 U.S. News College Ranking:
Comp. Colleges–Bachelor's (South), 48
Acceptance Rate: 47%

Financial aid: Priority filing date for institution's financial aid form: March 31.

Samford University

800 Lakeshore Drive
Birmingham, AL 35229
Private; www.samford.edu
Financial aid office: (205) 726-2905

■ **2004-2005 TUITION AND FEES:** $13,944
■ **ROOM AND BOARD:** $5,506

ACT Score (25th/75th percentile): 22-28
2005 U.S. News College Ranking:
Universities–Master's (South), 5
Acceptance Rate: 90%

Other expenses: Estimated books and supplies: $936. Transportation: $946. Personal expenses: $3,106. **Financial aid:** Priority filing date for institution's financial aid form: March 1. In 2003-2004, 66% of undergraduates applied for financial aid. Of those, 49% were determined to have financial need; 23% had their need fully met. Average financial aid package (proportion receiving): $9,908 (49%). Average amount of gift aid, such as scholarships or grants (proportion receiving): $5,757 (44%). Average amount of self-help aid, such as work study or loans (proportion receiving): $4,378 (43%). Average need-based loan (excluding PLUS or other private loans): $3,358. Among students who received need-based aid, the average percentage of need met: 72%. Among students who

received aid based on merit, the average award (and the proportion receiving): $3,700 (26%). The average athletic scholarship (and the proportion receiving): $12,294 (8%). Average amount of debt of borrowers graduating in 2003: $15,842. Proportion who borrowed: 49%. **Student employment:** During the 2003-2004 academic year, 25% of undergraduates worked on campus. Average per-year earnings: $1,800. **Cooperative education programs:** art, business, computer science, health professions, home economics, humanities, natural science. **Reserve Officers Training Corps (ROTC):** Army ROTC: Offered at cooperating institution (University of Alabama at Birmingham); Air Force ROTC: Offered on campus.

Spring Hill College

4000 Dauphin Street
Mobile, AL 36608
Private; www.shc.edu
Financial aid office: (251) 380-3460

■ **2004-2005 TUITION AND FEES:** $19,950
■ **ROOM AND BOARD:** $7,192

ACT Score (25th/75th percentile): 20-27
2005 U.S. News College Ranking:
Universities–Master's (South), 11
Acceptance Rate: 80%

Other expenses: Estimated books and supplies: $1,100. Transportation: $990. Personal expenses: $990. **Financial aid:** Priority filing date for institution's financial aid form: March 1. In 2003-2004, 81% of undergraduates applied for financial aid. Of those, 70% were determined to have financial need; 16% had their need fully met. Average financial aid package (proportion receiving): $16,836 (70%). Average amount of gift aid, such as scholarships or grants (proportion receiving): $12,057 (68%). Average amount of self-help aid, such as work study or loans (proportion receiving): $4,424 (57%). Average need-based loan (excluding PLUS or other private loans): $3,835. Among students who received need-based aid, the average percentage of need met: 79%. Among students who received aid based on merit, the average award (and the proportion receiving): $7,936 (11%). The average athletic scholarship (and the proportion receiving): $4,491 (8%). Average amount of debt of borrowers graduating in 2003: $13,421. Proportion who borrowed: 61%. **Student employment:** During the 2003-2004 academic year, 9% of undergraduates worked on campus. Average per-year earnings: $846. **Reserve Officers Training Corps (ROTC):** Army

ROTC: Offered at cooperating institution (University of South Alabama); Air Force ROTC: Offered at cooperating institution (University of South Alabama).

Stillman College

PO Box 1430, 3600 Stillman Boulevard
Tuscaloosa, AL 35403
Private; www.stillman.edu
Financial aid office: (205) 366-8844

- ■ **2003-2004 TUITION AND FEES:** $8,718
- ■ **ROOM AND BOARD:** $4,429

ACT Score (25th/75th percentile): 15-19
2005 U.S. News College Ranking:
Comp. Colleges–Bachelor's (South), 40
Acceptance Rate: 47%

Other expenses: Estimated books and supplies: $700. Transportation: $475. Personal expenses: $1,400. **Financial aid:** Priority filing date for institution's financial aid form: April 15; deadline: July 1. **Cooperative education programs:** business, health professions, social/behavioral science. **Reserve Officers Training Corps (ROTC):** Army ROTC: Offered at cooperating institution (University of Alabama); Air Force ROTC: Offered at cooperating institution (University of Alabama).

Talladega College

627 W. Battle Street
Talladega, AL 35160
Private; www.talladega.edu
Financial aid office: (256) 761-6341

- ■ **2004-2005 TUITION AND FEES:** $11,842
- ■ **ROOM AND BOARD:** $2,120

ACT Score (25th/75th percentile): 15-20
2005 U.S. News College Ranking:
Liberal Arts Colleges, fourth tier
Acceptance Rate: 42%

Other expenses: Estimated books and supplies: $1,178. Transportation: $1,100. Personal expenses: $1,100. **Financial aid:** Priority filing date for institution's financial aid form: April 15; deadline: June 30. In 2003-2004, 100% of undergraduates applied for financial aid. Of those, 84% were determined to have financial need; 27% had their need fully met. Average financial aid package (proportion receiving): $5,000 (84%). Average amount of gift aid, such as scholarships or grants (proportion receiving): $375 (84%). Average

amount of self-help aid, such as work study or loans (proportion receiving): $150 (34%). Average need-based loan (excluding PLUS or other private loans): $5,335. Among students who received need-based aid, the average percentage of need met: 90%. Among students who received aid based on merit, the average award (and the proportion receiving): $1,394 (11%). The average athletic scholarship (and the proportion receiving): $5,000 (22%). Average amount of debt of borrowers graduating in 2003: $20,000. Proportion who borrowed: 75%. **Reserve Officers Training Corps (ROTC):** Army ROTC: Offered at cooperating institution (Jacksonville State University).

Troy State University–Dothan

PO Box 8368
Dothan, AL 36304
Public; www.tsud.edu
Financial aid office: (334) 983-6556

- ■ **2004-2005 TUITION AND FEES:**
  In state: $4,162; Out of state: $8,012

ACT Score (25th/75th percentile): 19-23
2005 U.S. News College Ranking:
Universities–Master's (South), fourth tier
Acceptance Rate: 70%

Financial aid: Priority filing date for institution's financial aid form: March 1. In 2003-2004, 86% of undergraduates applied for financial aid. Of those, 86% were determined to have financial need; 100% had their need fully met. Average financial aid package (proportion receiving): $0 (86%). Average amount of gift aid, such as scholarships or grants (proportion receiving): $3,174 (47%). Average amount of self-help aid, such as work study or loans (proportion receiving): $8,281 (60%). Average need-based loan (excluding PLUS or other private loans): $4,281. Among students who received need-based aid, the average percentage of need met: 55%. **Student employment:** During the 2003-2004 academic year, 1% of undergraduates worked on campus. Average per-year earnings: $2,500.

Troy State University– Montgomery

PO Drawer 4419
Montgomery, AL 36103-4419
Public; www.tsum.edu
Financial aid office: (334) 241-9520

- ■ **2003-2004 TUITION AND FEES:**
  In state: $3,600; Out of state: $7,130

2005 U.S. News College Ranking:
Universities–Master's (South), fourth tier
Acceptance Rate: 99%

Reserve Officers Training Corps (ROTC): Army ROTC: Offered at cooperating institution (ASU); Air Force ROTC: Offered at cooperating institution (AUM).

Troy State University–Troy

University Avenue
Troy, AL 36082
Public; www.troyst.edu
Financial aid office: (334) 670-3186

- ■ **2004-2005 TUITION AND FEES:**
  In state: $4,162; Out of state: $8,012
- ■ **ROOM AND BOARD:** $4,812

ACT Score (25th/75th percentile): 17-23
2005 U.S. News College Ranking:
Universities–Master's (South), 64
Acceptance Rate: 67%

Other expenses: Estimated books and supplies: $860. Transportation: $1,120. Personal expenses: $2,036. **Financial aid:** Priority filing date for institution's financial aid form: May 1. In 2003-2004, 95% of undergraduates applied for financial aid. Of those, 95% were determined to have financial need; Average financial aid package (proportion receiving): $9,000 (95%). Average amount of gift aid, such as scholarships or grants (proportion receiving): $5,000 (37%). Average amount of self-help aid, such as work study or loans (proportion receiving): $4,000 (55%). Average need-based loan (excluding PLUS or other private loans): $4,000. Among students who received need-based aid, the average percentage of need met: 58%. Among students who received aid based on merit, the average award (and the proportion receiving): $0 (0%). The average athletic scholarship (and the proportion receiving): $8,252 (7%). Average amount of debt of borrowers graduating in 2003: $14,762. Proportion who borrowed: 65%. **Student employment:** During the 2003-2004 academic year, 5% of undergraduates worked on campus. Average per-year earnings: $1,652. **Reserve Officers Training Corps (ROTC):** Army ROTC: Offered on campus; Air Force ROTC: Offered on campus.

Tuskegee University

PO Box 1239
Tuskegee, AL 36088
Private; www.tuskegee.edu
Financial aid office: (334) 727-8201

■ **2004-2005 TUITION AND FEES:** $11,600
■ **ROOM AND BOARD:** $5,940

ACT Score (25th/75th percentile): 17-20
2005 U.S. News College Ranking:
Universities–Master's (South), 31
Acceptance Rate: 81%

Other expenses: Estimated books and supplies: $873. Transportation: $381. Personal expenses: $1,596. **Financial aid:** Priority filing date for institution's financial aid form: March 31; deadline: March 31. In 2003-2004, 83% of undergraduates applied for financial aid. Of those, 71% were determined to have financial need; 75% had their need fully met. Average financial aid package (proportion receiving): $9,960 (71%). Average amount of gift aid, such as scholarships or grants (proportion receiving): $4,000 (61%). Average amount of self-help aid, such as work study or loans (proportion receiving): $7,840 (61%). Average need-based loan (excluding PLUS or other private loans): $4,281. Among students who received need-based aid, the average percentage of need met: 85%. Among students who received aid based on merit, the average award (and the proportion receiving): $1,768 (21%). The average athletic scholarship (and the proportion receiving): $11,060 (2%). Average amount of debt of borrowers graduating in 2003: $23,000. Proportion who borrowed: 83%. **Cooperative education programs:** agriculture, business, computer science, education, engineering, health professions. **Reserve Officers Training Corps (ROTC):** Army ROTC: Offered on campus; Air Force ROTC: Offered on campus.

University of Alabama

Box 870100
Tuscaloosa, AL 35487-0100
Public; www.ua.edu
Financial aid office: (205) 348-2976

■ **2004-2005 TUITION AND FEES:**
  In state: $4,630; Out of state: $12,664
■ **ROOM AND BOARD:** $4,734

ACT Score (25th/75th percentile): 21-26
2005 U.S. News College Ranking:
National Universities, 86
Acceptance Rate: 87%

Other expenses: Estimated books and supplies: $800. Transportation: $736. Personal expenses: $1,690. **Financial aid:** Priority filing date for institution's financial aid form: March 1. In 2003-2004, 73% of undergraduates applied for financial aid. Of those, 39% were determined to have financial need; 19% had their need fully met. Average financial aid package (proportion receiving): $7,549 (39%). Average amount of gift aid, such as scholarships or grants (proportion receiving): $3,355 (25%). Average amount of self-help aid, such as work study or loans (proportion receiving): $4,262 (32%). Average need-based loan (excluding PLUS or other private loans): $3,931. Among students who received need-based aid, the average percentage of need met: 71%. Among students who received aid based on merit, the average award (and the proportion receiving): $4,126 (28%). The average athletic scholarship (and the proportion receiving): $12,866 (1%). Average amount of debt of borrowers graduating in 2003: $19,319. Proportion who borrowed: 53%. **Cooperative education programs:** engineering. **Reserve Officers Training Corps (ROTC):** Army ROTC: Offered on campus; Air Force ROTC: Offered on campus.

University of Alabama–Birmingham

1530 Third Avenue S
Birmingham, AL 35294
Public; www.uab.edu
Financial aid office: (205) 934-8223

■ **2004-2005 TUITION AND FEES:**
  In state: $4,662; Out of state: $10,422

ACT Score (25th/75th percentile): 19-24
2005 U.S. News College Ranking:
National Universities, third tier
Acceptance Rate: 81%

Financial aid: Priority filing date for institution's financial aid form: April 1. In 2003-2004, 73% of undergraduates applied for financial aid. Of those, 54% were determined to have financial need; 13% had their need fully met. Average financial aid package (proportion receiving): $8,536 (53%). Average amount of gift aid, such as scholarships or grants (proportion receiving): $3,336 (34%). Average amount of self-help aid, such as work study or loans (proportion receiving): $4,080 (52%). Average

need-based loan (excluding PLUS or other private loans): $4,101. Among students who received need-based aid, the average percentage of need met: 43%. Among students who received aid based on merit, the average award (and the proportion receiving): $5,455 (22%). The average athletic scholarship (and the proportion receiving): $11,349 (3%). Average amount of debt of borrowers graduating in 2003: $18,299. Proportion who borrowed: 51%. **Cooperative education programs:** art, business, computer science, engineering, health professions, humanities, natural science, social/behavioral science. **Reserve Officers Training Corps (ROTC):** Army ROTC: Offered on campus; Air Force ROTC: Offered at cooperating institution (Samford University).

University of Alabama–Huntsville

301 Sparkman Drive
Huntsville, AL 35899
Public; www.uah.edu
Financial aid office: (256) 824-6241

■ **2004-2005 TUITION AND FEES:**
  In state: $4,516; Out of state: $9,518
■ **ROOM AND BOARD:** $5,200

ACT Score (25th/75th percentile): 22-27
2005 U.S. News College Ranking:
National Universities, third tier
Acceptance Rate: 88%

Other expenses: Estimated books and supplies: $720. Transportation: $815. Personal expenses: $1,200. **Financial aid:** Priority filing date for institution's financial aid form: April 1; deadline: July 31. In 2003-2004, 81% of undergraduates applied for financial aid. Of those, 45% were determined to have financial need; 16% had their need fully met. Average financial aid package (proportion receiving): $5,560 (41%). Average amount of gift aid, such as scholarships or grants (proportion receiving): $3,165 (25%). Average amount of self-help aid, such as work study or loans (proportion receiving): $3,500 (32%). Average need-based loan (excluding PLUS or other private loans): $3,493. Among students who received need-based aid, the average percentage of need met: 53%. Among students who received aid based on merit, the average award (and the proportion receiving): $2,070 (23%). The average athletic scholarship (and the proportion receiving): $5,522 (4%). Average amount of debt of borrowers graduating in 2003: $17,058. Proportion who borrowed: 47%. **Student employment:**

During the 2003-2004 academic year, 15% of undergraduates worked on campus. Average per-year earnings: $5,924. **Cooperative education programs:** art, business, computer science, education, engineering, health professions, humanities, natural science, social/behavioral science, technologies. **Reserve Officers Training Corps (ROTC):** Army ROTC: Offered at cooperating institution (Albama A&M University).

University of Mobile

PO Box 13220
Mobile, AL 36663-0220
Private; www.umobile.edu
Financial aid office: (251) 442-2385

■ **2004-2005 TUITION AND FEES:** $9,780
■ **ROOM AND BOARD:** $5,860

ACT Score (25th/75th percentile): 19-28
2005 U.S. News College Ranking:
Universities–Master's (South), third tier
Acceptance Rate: 67%

Other expenses: Estimated books and supplies: $500. **Financial aid:** Priority filing date for institution's financial aid form: March 31. In 2003-2004, 83% of undergraduates applied for financial aid. Of those, 61% were determined to have financial need; Average financial aid package (proportion receiving): $7,468 (61%). Average amount of gift aid, such as scholarships or grants (proportion receiving): $3,350 (58%). Average amount of self-help aid, such as work study or loans (proportion receiving): $0 (58%). Average need-based loan (excluding PLUS or other private loans): $4,500. Among students who received need-based aid, the average percentage of need met: 56%. Among students who received aid based on merit, the average award (and the proportion receiving): N/A (18%). The average athletic scholarship (and the proportion receiving): $3,400 (N/A). Average amount of debt of borrowers graduating in 2003: $18,000. Proportion who borrowed: 98%. **Cooperative education programs:** art, business, computer science, education, health professions, humanities, natural science, social/behavioral science. **Reserve Officers Training Corps (ROTC):** Army ROTC: Offered at cooperating institution (University of South Alabama); Air Force ROTC: Offered at cooperating institution (University of South Alabama).

University of Montevallo

Station 6030
Montevallo, AL 35115
Public; www.montevallo.edu
Financial aid office: (205) 665-6050

■ **2004-2005 TUITION AND FEES:**
  In state: $5,536; Out of state: $10,726
■ **ROOM AND BOARD:** $3,850

ACT Score (25th/75th percentile): 19-24
2005 U.S. News College Ranking:
Universities–Master's (South), 62
Acceptance Rate: 79%

Financial aid: Priority filing date for institution's financial aid form: April 15. In 2003-2004, 75% of undergraduates applied for financial aid. Of those, 56% were determined to have financial need; 34% had their need fully met. Average financial aid package (proportion receiving): $6,861 (55%). Average amount of gift aid, such as scholarships or grants (proportion receiving): $5,997 (27%). Average amount of self-help aid, such as work study or loans (proportion receiving): $3,601 (39%). Average need-based loan (excluding PLUS or other private loans): $2,702. Among students who received need-based aid, the average percentage of need met: 77%. Among students who received aid based on merit, the average award (and the proportion receiving): $3,767 (20%). The average athletic scholarship (and the proportion receiving): $6,381 (4%). Average amount of debt of borrowers graduating in 2003: $14,265. Proportion who borrowed: 55%. **Student employment:** During the 2003-2004 academic year, 16% of undergraduates worked on campus. Average per-year earnings: $2,500. **Cooperative education programs:** business. **Reserve Officers Training Corps (ROTC):** Army ROTC: Offered at cooperating institution (University of Alabama, Birmingham); Air Force ROTC: Offered at cooperating institution (Samford University).

University of North Alabama

UNA–Box 5121
Florence, AL 35632
Public; www.una.edu
Financial aid office: (256) 765-4278

■ **2004-2005 TUITION AND FEES:**
  In state: $4,610; Out of state: $8,620
■ **ROOM AND BOARD:** $5,200

ACT Score (25th/75th percentile): 18-24
2005 U.S. News College Ranking:
Universities–Master's (South), third tier
Acceptance Rate: 79%

Other expenses: Estimated books and supplies: $950. Transportation: $900. Personal expenses: $800. **Financial aid:** Priority filing date for institution's financial aid form: April 4. In 2003-2004, 61% of undergraduates applied for financial aid. Of those, 50% were determined to have financial need; 41% had their need fully met. Average financial aid package (proportion receiving): $4,323 (48%). Average amount of gift aid, such as scholarships or grants (proportion receiving): $2,881 (34%). Average amount of self-help aid, such as work study or loans (proportion receiving): $2,418 (44%). Average need-based loan (excluding PLUS or other private loans): $3,380. Among students who received need-based aid, the average percentage of need met: 41%. Among students who received aid based on merit, the average award (and the proportion receiving): $1,542 (12%). Average amount of debt of borrowers graduating in 2003: $17,495. Proportion who borrowed: 42%. **Reserve Officers Training Corps (ROTC):** Army ROTC: Offered on campus.

University of South Alabama

307 University Boulevard
Mobile, AL 36688-0002
Public; www.southalabama.edu
Financial aid office: (251) 460-6231

■ **2004-2005 TUITION AND FEES:**
  In state: $4,290; Out of state: $8,100
■ **ROOM AND BOARD:** $5,800

ACT Score (25th/75th percentile): 20-25
2005 U.S. News College Ranking:
National Universities, fourth tier
Acceptance Rate: 76%

Other expenses: Estimated books and supplies: $1,200. Transportation: $504. Personal expenses: $1,950. **Financial aid:** Priority filing date for institution's financial aid form: May 4. In 2003-2004, 49% of undergraduates applied for financial aid. Of those, 49% were determined to have financial need; 87% had their need fully met. Average financial aid package (proportion receiving): $2,867 (49%). Average amount of gift aid, such as scholarships or grants (proportion receiving): $1,758 (35%). Average amount of self-help aid, such as work study or loans (proportion receiving): $1,746 (42%). Average need-based loan (excluding PLUS or other private loans): $1,746. Among students who received need-based aid, the average percentage of need met: 30%. Average amount of debt of borrowers graduating in 2003: $11,000. Proportion who borrowed: 71%. **Cooperative education programs:** art, business, computer science, education, engineering, humanities, natural science, social/behavioral science. **Reserve Officers Training Corps (ROTC):** Army ROTC: Offered on campus; Air Force ROTC: Offered on campus.

University of West Alabama

Station 4
Livingston, AL 35470
Public; www.uwa.edu
Financial aid office: (205) 652-3576

■ **2004-2005 TUITION AND FEES:**
   In state: $4,196; Out of state: $7,922
■ **ROOM AND BOARD:** $3,032

ACT Score (25th/75th percentile): 17-22
2005 U.S. News College Ranking:
Universities–Master's (South), fourth tier
Acceptance Rate: 78%

Other expenses: Estimated books and supplies: $900. Transportation: $900. Personal expenses: $1,200. **Financial aid:** Priority filing date for institution's financial aid form: April 1. Average amount of debt of borrowers graduating in 2003: $16,043. Proportion who borrowed: 62%. **Student employment:** During the 2003-2004 academic year, 10% of undergraduates worked on campus. Average per-year earnings: $1,200. **Reserve Officers Training Corps (ROTC):** Air Force ROTC: Offered at cooperating institution (University of Alabama).

Alaska

Alaska Pacific University

4101 University Drive
Anchorage, AK 99508-3051
Private; www.alaskapacific.edu
Financial aid office: (907) 564-8342

■ **2004-2005 TUITION AND FEES:** $17,310
■ **ROOM AND BOARD:** $6,700

ACT Score (25th/75th percentile): 17-26
2005 U.S. News College Ranking:
Universities–Master's (West), 52
Acceptance Rate: 91%

Other expenses: Estimated books and supplies:
$840. Transportation: $350. Personal expenses:
$1,100. **Financial aid:** Priority filing date for institution's financial aid form: April 15. In 2003-2004, 80% of undergraduates applied for financial aid. Of those, 49% were determined to have financial need; 17% had their need fully met. Average financial aid package (proportion receiving): $10,113 (49%). Average amount of gift aid, such as scholarships or grants (proportion receiving): $4,443 (32%). Average amount of self-help aid, such as work study or loans (proportion receiving): $4,730 (35%). Average need-based loan (excluding PLUS or other private loans): $4,340. Among students who received need-based aid, the average percentage of need met: 78%. Among students who received aid based on merit, the average award (and the proportion receiving): $6,701 (20%). Average amount of debt of borrowers graduating in 2003: $23,791. Proportion who borrowed: 68%.

Sheldon Jackson College

801 Lincoln Street
Sitka, AK 99835
Private; www.sj-alaska.edu
Financial aid office: (907) 747-5207

■ **2004-2005 TUITION AND FEES:** $10,850
■ **ROOM AND BOARD:** $7,300

2005 U.S. News College Ranking:
Comp. Colleges–Bachelor's (West), unranked

University of Alaska–Anchorage

3211 Providence Drive
Anchorage, AK 99508
Public; www.uaa.alaska.edu
Financial aid office: (907) 786-1586

■ **2004-2005 TUITION AND FEES:**
In state: $3,584; Out of state: $9,314
■ **ROOM AND BOARD:** $6,430

ACT Score (25th/75th percentile): 890-1140
2005 U.S. News College Ranking:
Universities–Master's (West), third tier
Acceptance Rate: 77%

Other expenses: Estimated books and supplies: $923. Personal expenses: $1,715.
Financial aid: Priority filing date for institution's financial aid form: April 1; deadline: August 1. Average amount of debt of borrowers graduating in 2003: $15,621. Proportion who borrowed: 47%. **Student employment:** During the 2003-2004 academic year, 10% of undergraduates worked on campus. Average per-year earnings: $8. **Reserve Officers Training Corps (ROTC):** Air Force ROTC: Offered on campus.

University of Alaska–Fairbanks

PO Box 757500
Fairbanks, AK 99775-7500
Public; www.uaf.edu
Financial aid office: (907) 474-7256

■ **2004-2005 TUITION AND FEES:**
In state: $4,165; Out of state: $11,095
■ **ROOM AND BOARD:** $5,130

SAT I Score (25th/75th percentile): 900-1180
2005 U.S. News College Ranking:
National Universities, fourth tier
Acceptance Rate: 84%

Other expenses: Estimated books and supplies: $700. Transportation: $0. Personal expenses: $300. **Financial aid:** Priority filing date for institution's financial aid form: July 1.

In 2003-2004, 83% of undergraduates applied for financial aid. Of those, 44% were determined to have financial need; 33% had their need fully met. Average financial aid package (proportion receiving): $9,137 (41%). Average amount of gift aid, such as scholarships or grants (proportion receiving): $4,093 (28%). Average amount of self-help aid, such as work study or loans (proportion receiving): $8,299 (31%). Average need-based loan (excluding PLUS or other private loans): $6,505. Among students who received need-based aid, the average percentage of need met: 71%. Among students who received aid based on merit, the average award (and the proportion receiving): $2,915 (14%). The average athletic scholarship (and the proportion receiving): $7,452 (2%). Average amount of debt of borrowers graduating in 2003: $11,623. Proportion who borrowed: 50%. **Student employment:** During the 2003-2004 academic year, 16% of undergraduates worked on campus. Average per-year earnings: $10,880. **Cooperative education programs:** agriculture, art, business, computer science, education, engineering, health professions, humanities, natural science, social/behavioral science, technologies, vocational arts, other. **Reserve Officers Training Corps (ROTC):** Army ROTC: Offered on campus.

University of Alaska–Southeast

11120 Glacier Highway
Juneau, AK 99801
Public; www.uas.alaska.edu
Financial aid office: (907) 465-6255

■ **2004-2005 TUITION AND FEES:**
In state: $3,111; Out of state: $8,655
■ **ROOM AND BOARD:** $6,330

SAT I Score (25th/75th percentile): 870-1190
2005 U.S. News College Ranking:
Universities–Master's (West), fourth tier
Acceptance Rate: 44%

Arizona

Arizona State University

Tempe, AZ 85287
Public; www.asu.edu
Financial aid office: (480) 965-3355

■ **2004-2005 TUITION AND FEES:**
In state: $4,064; Out of state: $12,919
■ **ROOM AND BOARD:** $6,574

SAT I Score (25th/75th percentile): 970-1220
2005 U.S. News College Ranking:
National Universities, third tier
Acceptance Rate: 88%

Other expenses: Estimated books and supplies:
$838. Transportation: $1,200. Personal expenses: $2,526. **Financial aid:** Priority filing date for institution's financial aid form: March 1.
Cooperative education programs: business, engineering. **Reserve Officers Training Corps (ROTC):** Army ROTC: Offered on campus; Air Force ROTC: Offered on campus.

Arizona State University West

PO Box 37100
Phoenix, AZ 85069-7100
Public; www.west.asu.edu/admissions
Financial aid office: (602) 543-8178

■ **2004-2005 TUITION AND FEES:**
In state: $4,064; Out of state: $12,919
■ **ROOM AND BOARD:** $4,455

SAT I Score (25th/75th percentile): 930-1170
2005 U.S. News College Ranking:
Universities–Master's West, unranked
Acceptance Rate: 62%

Financial aid: Priority filing date for institution's financial aid form: March 1. **Student employment:** During the 2003-2004 academic year, 33% of undergraduates worked on campus.

Grand Canyon University

3300 W. Camelback Road
Phoenix, AZ 85017
Private; www.grand-canyon.edu
Financial aid office: (602) 589-2885

■ **2004-2005 TUITION AND FEES:** $14,500
■ **ROOM AND BOARD:** $7,160

SAT I Score (25th/75th percentile): 940-1160
2005 U.S. News College Ranking:
Universities–Master's (West), third tier
Acceptance Rate: 72%

Reserve Officers Training Corps (ROTC): Army ROTC: Offered on campus; Air Force ROTC: Offered at cooperating institution (Arizona State University).

Northern Arizona University

PO Box 4084
Flagstaff, AZ 86011-4084
Public; www.nau.edu
Financial aid office: (928) 523-1383

■ **2004-2005 TUITION AND FEES:**
In state: $4,103; Out of state: $13,919
■ **ROOM AND BOARD:** $5,420

SAT I Score (25th/75th percentile): 930-1180
2005 U.S. News College Ranking:
National Universities, fourth tier
Acceptance Rate: 81%

Financial aid: Priority filing date for institution's financial aid form: February 14. **Student employment:** During the 2003-2004 academic year, 24% of undergraduates worked on campus. Average per-year earnings: $1,962.
Cooperative education programs: business, education, other. **Reserve Officers Training Corps (ROTC):** Army ROTC: Offered on campus; Air Force ROTC: Offered on campus.

Prescott College

220 Grove Avenue
Prescott, AZ 86301
Private; www.prescott.edu
Financial aid office: (928) 778-2090

■ **2004-2005 TUITION AND FEES:** $16,405

SAT I Score (25th/75th percentile): 980-1250
2005 U.S. News College Ranking:
Universities–Master's (West), third tier
Acceptance Rate: 83%

Financial aid: Average amount of debt of borrowers graduating in 2003: $14,255. Proportion who borrowed: 66%.

University of Arizona

PO Box 210066
Tucson, AZ 85721-0066
Public; www.arizona.edu
Financial aid office: (520) 621-5200

■ **2004-2005 TUITION AND FEES:**
In state: $4,098; Out of state: $13,078
■ **ROOM AND BOARD:** $7,108

SAT I Score (25th/75th percentile): 990-1240
2005 U.S. News College Ranking:
National Universities, 98
Acceptance Rate: 85%

Other expenses: Estimated books and supplies:
$762. Transportation: $558. Personal expenses:
$2,366. **Financial aid:** Priority filing date for institution's financial aid form: March 1. In 2003-2004, 71% of undergraduates applied for financial aid. Of those, 41% were determined to have financial need; Average financial aid package (proportion receiving): N/A (41%). Average amount of debt of borrowers graduating in 2003: $16,881. Proportion who borrowed: 42%.
Reserve Officers Training Corps (ROTC): Army ROTC: Offered on campus; Navy ROTC: Offered on campus; Air Force ROTC: Offered on campus.

Arkansas

Arkansas Baptist College

1600 Bishop Street
Little Rock, AR 72202
Private; www.arbaptcol.edu
Financial aid office: (501) 374-0804

- **2003-2004 TUITION AND FEES:** $4,710
- **ROOM AND BOARD:** $6,060

2005 U.S. News College Ranking:
Liberal Arts Colleges, fourth tier

Other expenses: Estimated books and supplies: $900. Personal expenses: $3,500.

Arkansas State University

PO Box 10
State University, AR 72467
Public; www.astate.edu
Financial aid office: (870) 972-2310

- **2004-2005 TUITION AND FEES:**
  In state: $5,155; Out of state: $11,515
- **ROOM AND BOARD:** $4,000

ACT Score (25th/75th percentile): 18-25
2005 U.S. News College Ranking:
Universities–Master's (South), third tier
Acceptance Rate: 66%

Financial aid: Priority filing date for institution's financial aid form: February 15; deadline: July 1. Average amount of debt of borrowers graduating in 2003: $14,900. Proportion who borrowed: 63%. **Student employment:** During the 2003-2004 academic year, 18% of undergraduates worked on campus. Average per-year earnings: $3,000. **Cooperative education programs:** agriculture, business, education, health professions. **Reserve Officers Training Corps (ROTC):** Army ROTC: Offered on campus.

Arkansas Tech University

1509 N. Boulder Avenue
Russellville, AR 72801-2222
Public; www.atu.edu
Financial aid office: (479) 968-0399

- **2004-2005 TUITION AND FEES:**
  In state: $3,820; Out of state: $7,360
- **ROOM AND BOARD:** $3,726

ACT Score (25th/75th percentile): 19-25
2005 U.S. News College Ranking:
Universities–Master's (South), fourth tier
Acceptance Rate: 56%

Other expenses: Estimated books and supplies: $990. Personal expenses: $1,900. **Financial aid:** Priority filing date for institution's financial aid form: April 15. Average amount of debt of borrowers graduating in 2003: $17,026. **Reserve Officers Training Corps (ROTC):** Army ROTC: Offered at cooperating institution (UCA).

Harding University

Box 12234
Searcy, AR 72149
Private; www.harding.edu
Financial aid office: (501) 279-5278

- **2004-2005 TUITION AND FEES:** $10,780
- **ROOM AND BOARD:** $5,182

ACT Score (25th/75th percentile): 20-27
2005 U.S. News College Ranking:
Universities–Master's (South), 22
Acceptance Rate: 58%

Other expenses: Estimated books and supplies: $850. Transportation: $968. Personal expenses: $1,000. **Financial aid:** Priority filing date for institution's financial aid form: April 15. In 2003-2004, 95% of undergraduates applied for financial aid. Of those, 47% were determined to have financial need; 11% had their need fully met. Average financial aid package (proportion receiving): $8,673 (47%). Average amount of gift aid, such as scholarships or grants (proportion receiving): $5,444 (46%). Average amount of self-help aid, such as work study or loans (proportion receiving): $4,303 (46%). Average need-based loan (excluding PLUS or other private loans): $4,380. Among students who received need-based aid, the average percentage of need met: 64%. Among students who received aid based on merit, the average award (and the proportion receiving): $7,246 (38%). The average athletic scholarship (and the proportion receiving): $5,532 (2%). Average amount of debt of borrowers graduating in 2003: $21,550. **Student employment:** During the 2003-2004 academic year, 11% of undergraduates worked on campus. Average per-year earnings: $2,000. **Cooperative education programs:** art, business, computer science, education, engineering, health professions, home economics, humanities, natural science, social/behavioral science. **Reserve Officers Training Corps (ROTC):** Army ROTC: Offered at cooperating institution (University of Central Arkansas).

Henderson State University

1100 Henderson Street
Arkadelphia, AR 71999-0001
Public; www.getreddie.com
Financial aid office: (870) 230-5148

- **2004-2005 TUITION AND FEES:**
  In state: $4,109; Out of state: $7,749
- **ROOM AND BOARD:** $3,874

ACT Score (25th/75th percentile): 19-25
2005 U.S. News College Ranking:
Universities–Master's (South), third tier
Acceptance Rate: 63%

Financial aid: Priority filing date for institution's financial aid form: June 1; deadline: June 1. Average amount of debt of borrowers graduating in 2003: $16,500. Proportion who borrowed: 38%. **Reserve Officers Training Corps (ROTC):** Army ROTC: Offered on campus.

Hendrix College

1600 Washington Avenue
Conway, AR 72032
Private; www.hendrix.edu
Financial aid office: (501) 450-1368

- **2004-2005 TUITION AND FEES:** $16,710
- **ROOM AND BOARD:** $5,680

ACT Score (25th/75th percentile): 24-30
2005 U.S. News College Ranking:
Liberal Arts Colleges, 70
Acceptance Rate: 86%

....

Other expenses: Estimated books and supplies: $800. Transportation: $1,080. Personal expenses: $1,080. **Financial aid:** Priority filing date for institution's financial aid form: February 15. In 2003-2004, 65% of undergraduates applied for financial aid. Of those, 53% were determined to have financial need; 34% had their need fully met. Average financial aid package (proportion receiving): $13,995 (53%). Average amount of gift aid, such as scholarships or grants (proportion receiving): $9,949 (53%). Average amount of self-help aid, such as work study or loans (proportion receiving): $5,140 (43%). Average need-based loan (excluding PLUS or other private loans): $4,103. Among students who received need-based aid, the average percentage of need met: 86%. Among students who received aid based on merit, the average award (and the proportion receiving): $12,567 (42%). The average athletic scholarship (and the proportion receiving): $0 (0%). Average amount of debt of borrowers graduating in 2003: $14,400. Proportion who borrowed: 52%. **Student employment:** During the 2003-2004 academic year, 18% of undergraduates worked on campus. Average per-year earnings: $991. **Reserve Officers Training Corps (ROTC):** Army ROTC: Offered at cooperating institution (University of Central Arkansas).

John Brown University

2000 W. University Street
Siloam Springs, AR 72761
Private; www.jbu.edu
Financial aid office: (479) 524-7115

■ **2004-2005 TUITION AND FEES:** $14,434
■ **ROOM AND BOARD:** $5,324

ACT Score (25th/75th percentile): 22-28
2005 U.S. News College Ranking:
Comp. Colleges–Bachelor's (South), 8
Acceptance Rate: 79%

....

Other expenses: Estimated books and supplies: $600. Transportation: $1,500. Personal expenses: $1,350. **Financial aid:** Priority filing date for institution's financial aid form: March 1. In 2003-2004, 75% of undergraduates applied for financial aid. Of those, 66% were determined to have financial need; 10% had their need fully met. Average financial aid package (proportion receiving): $11,400 (66%). Average amount of

gift aid, such as scholarships or grants (proportion receiving): $10,693 (33%). Average amount of self-help aid, such as work study or loans (proportion receiving): $6,503 (61%). Average need-based loan (excluding PLUS or other private loans): $5,935. Among students who received need-based aid, the average percentage of need met: 65%. Among students who received aid based on merit, the average award (and the proportion receiving): $3,923 (22%). The average athletic scholarship (and the proportion receiving): $12,261 (2%). Average amount of debt of borrowers graduating in 2003: $14,200. Proportion who borrowed: 63%. **Student employment:** During the 2003-2004 academic year, 8% of undergraduates worked on campus. Average per-year earnings: $1,500. **Reserve Officers Training Corps (ROTC):** Army ROTC: Offered at cooperating institution (University of Arkansas).

Lyon College

PO Box 2317
Batesville, AR 72503-2317
Private; www.lyon.edu
Financial aid office: (870) 698-4257

■ **2004-2005 TUITION AND FEES:** $13,130
■ **ROOM AND BOARD:** $5,820

ACT Score (25th/75th percentile): 22-28
2005 U.S. News College Ranking:
Liberal Arts Colleges, third tier
Acceptance Rate: 72%

....

Other expenses: Estimated books and supplies: $700. Transportation: $900. Personal expenses: $900. **Financial aid:** Priority filing date for institution's financial aid form: March 15. In 2003-2004, 77% of undergraduates applied for financial aid. Of those, 67% were determined to have financial need; 32% had their need fully met. Average financial aid package (proportion receiving): $13,491 (67%). Average amount of gift aid, such as scholarships or grants (proportion receiving): $10,230 (66%). Average amount of self-help aid, such as work study or loans (proportion receiving): $4,354 (52%). Average need-based loan (excluding PLUS or other private loans): $3,868. Among students who received need-based aid, the average percentage of need met: 85%. Among students who received aid based on merit, the average award (and the proportion receiving): $10,132 (30%). The average athletic scholarship (and the proportion receiving): $7,666 (16%). Average amount of debt of borrowers graduating in 2003: $15,383. Proportion who borrowed:

91%. **Student employment:** During the 2003-2004 academic year, 8% of undergraduates worked on campus. Average per-year earnings: $1,545.

Ouachita Baptist University

410 Ouachita
Arkadelphia, AR 71998
Private; www.obu.edu
Financial aid office: (870) 245-5570

■ **2004-2005 TUITION AND FEES:** $15,170
■ **ROOM AND BOARD:** $4,800

ACT Score (25th/75th percentile): 20-26
2005 U.S. News College Ranking:
Comp. Colleges–Bachelor's (South), 5
Acceptance Rate: 80%

....

Other expenses: Estimated books and supplies: $775. Transportation: $850. Personal expenses: $1,400. **Financial aid:** Priority filing date for institution's financial aid form: February 15; deadline: June 1. In 2003-2004, 65% of undergraduates applied for financial aid. Of those, 54% were determined to have financial need; 39% had their need fully met. Average financial aid package (proportion receiving): $13,022 (54%). Average amount of gift aid, such as scholarships or grants (proportion receiving): $5,197 (47%). Average amount of self-help aid, such as work study or loans (proportion receiving): $3,809 (44%). Average need-based loan (excluding PLUS or other private loans): $3,674. Among students who received need-based aid, the average percentage of need met: 88%. Among students who received aid based on merit, the average award (and the proportion receiving): $6,111 (31%). The average athletic scholarship (and the proportion receiving): $9,406 (12%). Average amount of debt of borrowers graduating in 2003: $17,125. Proportion who borrowed: 48%. **Reserve Officers Training Corps (ROTC):** Army ROTC: Offered on campus.

Philander Smith College

812 W. 13th Street
Little Rock, AR 72202-3718
Private; www.philander.edu
Financial aid office: (501) 370-5350

■ **2003-2004 TUITION AND FEES:** $5,040

2005 U.S. News College Ranking:
Comp. Colleges–Bachelor's (South), fourth tier

....

Southern Arkansas University

Box 9392
Magnolia, AR 71754-9392
Public; www.saumag.edu
Financial aid office: (870) 235-4023

■ **2004-2005 TUITION AND FEES:**
In state: $3,878; Out of state: $5,698
■ **ROOM AND BOARD:** $3,600

ACT Score (25th/75th percentile): 17-22
2005 U.S. News College Ranking:
Universities–Master's (South), fourth tier
Acceptance Rate: 81%

Financial aid: Priority filing date for institution's financial aid form: July 1. In 2003-2004, 74% of undergraduates applied for financial aid. Of those, 65% were determined to have financial need; 97% had their need fully met. Average financial aid package (proportion receiving): $6,612 (63%). Average amount of gift aid, such as scholarships or grants (proportion receiving): $3,825 (54%). Average amount of self-help aid, such as work study or loans (proportion receiving): $4,263 (49%). Average need-based loan (excluding PLUS or other private loans): $3,259. Among students who received need-based aid, the average percentage of need met: 100%. Among students who received aid based on merit, the average award (and the proportion receiving): $3,002 (15%). The average athletic scholarship (and the proportion receiving): $3,119 (6%). Average amount of debt of borrowers graduating in 2003: $24,722. Proportion who borrowed: 45%. **Student employment:** During the 2003-2004 academic year, 28% of undergraduates worked on campus. Average per-year earnings: $2,700. **Cooperative education programs:** health professions.

University of Arkansas

232 Silas Hunt Hall
Fayetteville, AR 72701
Public; www.uark.edu
Financial aid office: (479) 575-3806

■ **2004-2005 TUITION AND FEES:**
In state: $5,135; Out of state: $12,425
■ **ROOM AND BOARD:** $5,927

ACT Score (25th/75th percentile): 22-28
2005 U.S. News College Ranking:
National Universities, 120
Acceptance Rate: 85%

Other expenses: Estimated books and supplies: $892. Transportation: $1,090. Personal expenses: $1,812. **Financial aid:** Priority filing date for institution's financial aid form: March 15. In 2003-2004, 55% of undergraduates applied for financial aid. Of those, 44% were determined to have financial need; 34% had their need fully met. Average financial aid package (proportion receiving): $8,260 (42%). Average amount of gift aid, such as scholarships or grants (proportion receiving): $3,550 (28%). Average amount of self-help aid, such as work study or loans (proportion receiving): $4,387 (30%). Average need-based loan (excluding PLUS or other private loans): $4,204. Among students who received need-based aid, the average percentage of need met: 74%. Among students who received aid based on merit, the average award (and the proportion receiving): $5,645 (21%). The average athletic scholarship (and the proportion receiving): $5,965 (4%). Average amount of debt of borrowers graduating in 2003: $17,204. Proportion who borrowed: 49%. **Student employment:** During the 2003-2004 academic year, 12% of undergraduates worked on campus. Average per-year earnings: $2,378. **Cooperative education programs:** agriculture, art, business, computer science, education, engineering, health professions, home economics, humanities, natural science, social/behavioral science, technologies, other. **Reserve Officers Training Corps (ROTC):** Army ROTC: Offered on campus; Air Force ROTC: Offered on campus.

University of Arkansas–Little Rock

2801 S. University Avenue
Little Rock, AR 72204-1099
Public; www.ualr.edu
Financial aid office: (501) 569-3035

■ **2004-2005 TUITION AND FEES:**
In state: $4,955; Out of state: $11,435

ACT Score (25th/75th percentile): 16-22
2005 U.S. News College Ranking:
National Universities, fourth tier
Acceptance Rate: 46%

Student employment: During the 2003-2004 academic year, 5% of undergraduates worked on campus. **Cooperative education programs:** business, computer science, engineering, health professions, humanities, natural science, social/behavioral science, technologies. **Reserve Officers Training Corps (ROTC):** Army ROTC: Offered at cooperating institution (University of Central Arkansas).

University of Arkansas–Monticello

UAM Box 3478
Monticello, AR 71656
Public; www.uamont.edu
Financial aid office: (870) 460-1050

■ **2004-2005 TUITION AND FEES:**
In state: $2,280; Out of state: $5,160
■ **ROOM AND BOARD:** $3,110

2005 U.S. News College Ranking:
Comp. Colleges–Bachelor's (South), fourth tier

University of Arkansas–Pine Bluff

1200 N. University Drive
Pine Bluff, AR 71601
Public; www.uapb.edu
Financial aid office: (870) 575-8302

■ **2004-2005 TUITION AND FEES:**
In state: $3,687; Out of state: $7,437
■ **ROOM AND BOARD:** $5,180

ACT Score (25th/75th percentile): 14-18
2005 U.S. News College Ranking:
Comp. Colleges–Bachelor's (South), fourth tier
Acceptance Rate: 68%

Other expenses: Estimated books and supplies: $1,000. Transportation: $1,000. Personal expenses: $1,956. **Reserve Officers Training Corps (ROTC):** Army ROTC: Offered on campus.

University of Central Arkansas

201 Donaghey Avenue
Conway, AR 72035
Public; www.uca.edu
Financial aid office: (501) 450-3140

■ **2004-2005 TUITION AND FEES:**
In state: $4,997; Out of state: $8,553
■ **ROOM AND BOARD:** $3,920

ACT Score (25th/75th percentile): 20-26
2005 U.S. News College Ranking:
Universities–Master's (South), third tier
Acceptance Rate: 70%

Other expenses: Estimated books and supplies: $1,000. Transportation: $1,500. Personal expenses: $1,899. **Financial aid:** Priority filing date for institution's financial aid form: February 15. Average financial aid package (proportion receiving): N/A (68%). Average amount of gift aid, such as scholarships or grants (proportion receiving): $1,713 (40%). Average amount of self-help aid, such as work study or loans (proportion receiving): N/A (6%). **Reserve Officers Training Corps (ROTC):** Army ROTC: Offered on campus.

University of the Ozarks

415 N. College Avenue
Clarksville, AR 72830
Private; www.ozarks.edu
Financial aid office: (479) 979-1221

■ **2004-2005 TUITION AND FEES:** $13,312
■ **ROOM AND BOARD:** $4,880

ACT Score (25th/75th percentile): 19-26
2005 U.S. News College Ranking:
Comp. Colleges–Bachelor's (South), 9
Acceptance Rate: 84%

Other expenses: Estimated books and supplies: $700. Transportation: $896. Personal expenses: $2,451. **Financial aid:** Priority filing date for institution's financial aid form: February 15. In 2003-2004, 88% of undergraduates applied for financial aid. Of those, 53% were determined to have financial need; 23% had their need fully met. Average financial aid package (proportion receiving): $12,685 (53%). Average amount of gift aid, such as scholarships or grants (proportion receiving): $9,322 (53%). Average amount of self-help aid, such as work study or loans (proportion receiving): $2,818 (49%). Average

need-based loan (excluding PLUS or other private loans): $3,114. Among students who received need-based aid, the average percentage of need met: 77%. Among students who received aid based on merit, the average award (and the proportion receiving): $11,784 (38%). The average athletic scholarship (and the proportion receiving): $0 (0%). Average amount of debt of borrowers graduating in 2003: $13,900. Proportion who borrowed: 35%. **Student employment:** During the 2003-2004 academic year, 29% of undergraduates worked on campus. Average per-year earnings: $2,000.

Williams Baptist College

PO Box 3665
Walnut Ridge, AR 72476
Private; www.wbcoll.edu
Financial aid office: (870) 759-4112

■ **2004-2005 TUITION AND FEES:** $8,600
■ **ROOM AND BOARD:** $4,000

ACT Score (25th/75th percentile): 22
2005 U.S. News College Ranking:
Comp. Colleges–Bachelor's (South), third tier
Acceptance Rate: 70%

Other expenses: Estimated books and supplies: $900. Transportation: $800. Personal expenses: $1,000. **Financial aid:** Priority filing date for institution's financial aid form: May 3. Average amount of debt of borrowers graduating in 2003: $12,752. Proportion who borrowed: 68%. **Reserve Officers Training Corps (ROTC):** Army ROTC: Offered at cooperating institution (Arkansas State University).

California

California College of the Arts

1111 Eighth Street
San Francisco, CA 94107
Private; www.cca.edu
Financial aid office: (415) 703-9573

■ **2004-2005 TUITION AND FEES:** $24,640

SAT I Score (25th/75th percentile): 960-1180
2005 U.S. News College Ranking:
Unranked Specialty School–Fine Arts
Acceptance Rate: 79%

Other expenses: Estimated books and supplies:
$1,300. Transportation: $650. Personal expenses: $1,880. **Financial aid:** Priority filing date for institution's financial aid form: March 1.
Average amount of debt of borrowers graduating in 2003: $23,073. Proportion who borrowed: 76%.

Alliant International University

10455 Pomerado Road
San Diego, CA 92131-1799
Private; www.alliant.edu
Financial aid office: (858) 635-4700

■ **2004-2005 TUITION AND FEES:** $19,240
■ **ROOM AND BOARD:** $7,430

2005 U.S. News College Ranking:
National Universities, fourth tier
Acceptance Rate: 60%

Other expenses: Estimated books and supplies:
$1,224. Transportation: $594. Personal expenses: $1,872. **Financial aid:** Priority filing date for institution's financial aid form: March 2. In 2003-2004, 62% of undergraduates applied for financial aid. Of those, 57% were determined to have financial need; 60% had their need fully met. Average financial aid package (proportion receiving): $19,668 (57%). Average amount of gift aid, such as scholarships or grants (proportion receiving): $8,838 (52%). Average amount of self-help aid, such as work study or loans (proportion receiving): $8,500 (55%). Average need-based loan (excluding PLUS or other private loans): $7,000. Among students who received need-based aid, the average percentage of need met: 88%. Among students who received aid based on merit, the average award

(and the proportion receiving): $3,141 (7%). The average athletic scholarship (and the proportion receiving): $7,640 (17%). Average amount of debt of borrowers graduating in 2003: $16,500. Proportion who borrowed: 42%. **Student employment:** During the 2003-2004 academic year, 7% of undergraduates worked on campus. Average per-year earnings: $1,200.

Art Center College of Design

1700 Lida Street
Pasadena, CA 91103
Private; www.artcenter.edu
Financial aid office: (626) 396-2215

■ **2004-2005 TUITION AND FEES:** $23,450

SAT I Score (25th/75th percentile): 1100
2005 U.S. News College Ranking:
Unranked Specialty School–Fine Arts
Acceptance Rate: 72%

Other expenses: Estimated books and supplies:
$4,860. Transportation: $2,144. Personal expenses: $3,230. **Financial aid:** Average financial aid package (proportion receiving): $21,214 (N/A). Average amount of gift aid, such as scholarships or grants (proportion receiving): $8,195 (N/A). Average amount of self-help aid, such as work study or loans (proportion receiving): $5,333 (N/A). Average need-based loan (excluding PLUS or other private loans): $3,964. Among students who received need-based aid, the average percentage of need met: 60%. Among students who received aid based on merit, the average award (and the proportion receiving): $31,450 (N/A). The average athletic scholarship (and the proportion receiving): $0 (N/A). Average amount of debt of borrowers graduating in 2003: $49,910. Proportion who borrowed: 70%. **Student employment:** During the 2003-2004 academic year, 25% of undergraduates worked on campus. Average per-year earnings: $1,000.

Azusa Pacific University

901 E. Alosta
Azusa, CA 91702
Private; www.apu.edu
Financial aid office: (626) 815-6000

■ **2004-2005 TUITION AND FEES:** $20,386
■ **ROOM AND BOARD:** $6,620

SAT I Score (25th/75th percentile): 980-1220
2005 U.S. News College Ranking:
Universities–Master's (West), 20
Acceptance Rate: 83%

Other expenses: Estimated books and supplies:
$1,224. Transportation: $594. **Financial aid:** Priority filing date for institution's financial aid form: March 2; deadline: July 1. In 2003-2004, 78% of undergraduates applied for financial aid. Of those, 65% were determined to have financial need; 12% had their need fully met. Average financial aid package (proportion receiving): $12,616 (64%). Average amount of gift aid, such as scholarships or grants (proportion receiving): $8,335 (64%). Average amount of self-help aid, such as work study or loans (proportion receiving): $4,720 (64%). Average need-based loan (excluding PLUS or other private loans): $3,984. Among students who received need-based aid, the average percentage of need met: 72%. Among students who received aid based on merit, the average award (and the proportion receiving): $3,485 (35%). The average athletic scholarship (and the proportion receiving): $8,200 (2%). Average amount of debt of borrowers graduating in 2003: $24,000. Proportion who borrowed: 73%. Average per-year earnings: $3,038. **Reserve Officers Training Corps (ROTC):** Army ROTC: Offered at cooperating institution (Reserve Officers' Training Corps).

Bethany College

800 Bethany Drive
Scotts Valley, CA 95066
Private; www.bethany.edu
Financial aid office: (831) 438-3800

■ **2004-2005 TUITION AND FEES:** $13,750
■ **ROOM AND BOARD:** $5,940

2005 U.S. News College Ranking:
Comp. Colleges–Bachelor's (West), third tier

Other expenses: Estimated books and supplies:
$1,260. Transportation: $612. Personal expenses: $1,818. **Financial aid:** Priority filing date for institution's financial aid form: March 2. In 2003-2004, 89% of undergraduates applied for financial aid. Of those, 82% were determined to have financial need; 8% had their need fully met. Average financial aid package (proportion receiving): $10,250 (82%). Average amount of

gift aid, such as scholarships or grants (proportion receiving): $8,000 (47%). Average amount of self-help aid, such as work study or loans (proportion receiving): $5,000 (67%). Average need-based loan (excluding PLUS or other private loans): $5,000. Among students who received need-based aid, the average percentage of need met: 50%. Among students who received aid based on merit, the average award (and the proportion receiving): $9,800 (6%). The average athletic scholarship (and the proportion receiving): $6,000 (2%). Average amount of debt of borrowers graduating in 2003: $21,000. Proportion who borrowed: 75%.

Biola University

13800 Biola Avenue
La Mirada, CA 90639
Private; www.biola.edu
Financial aid office: (562) 903-4742

- **2004-2005 TUITION AND FEES:** $21,032
- **ROOM AND BOARD:** $6,800

SAT I Score (25th/75th percentile): 1000-1250
2005 U.S. News College Ranking:
National Universities, fourth tier
Acceptance Rate: 81%

Other expenses: Estimated books and supplies: $1,000. Transportation: $612. Personal expenses: $1,476. **Financial aid:** Priority filing date for institution's financial aid form: March 2. In 2003-2004, 76% of undergraduates applied for financial aid. Of those, 66% were determined to have financial need; 14% had their need fully met. Average financial aid package (proportion receiving): $15,434 (66%). Average amount of gift aid, such as scholarships or grants (proportion receiving): $10,045 (56%). Average amount of self-help aid, such as work study or loans (proportion receiving): $4,257 (64%). Average need-based loan (excluding PLUS or other private loans): $2,918. Among students who received need-based aid, the average percentage of need met: 73%. Among students who received aid based on merit, the average award (and the proportion receiving): $10,005 (11%). The average athletic scholarship (and the proportion receiving): $1,563 (3%). Average amount of debt of borrowers graduating in 2003: $24,805. Proportion who borrowed: 74%. **Student employment:** During the 2003-2004 academic year, 34% of undergraduates worked on campus. Average per-year earnings: $3,318. **Cooperative education programs:** engineering. **Reserve Officers Training Corps (ROTC):** Army ROTC: Offered at cooperating institution (California State University, Fullerton);

Air Force ROTC: Offered at cooperating institution (Loyola Marymount University).

California Baptist University

8432 Magnolia Avenue
Riverside, CA 92504
Private; www.calbaptist.edu
Financial aid office: (909) 343-4236

- **2004-2005 TUITION AND FEES:** $15,900
- **ROOM AND BOARD:** $7,630

SAT I Score (25th/75th percentile): 900-1120
2005 U.S. News College Ranking:
Universities–Master's (West), third tier
Acceptance Rate: 84%

Other expenses: Estimated books and supplies: $1,120. Transportation: $544. Personal expenses: $1,616. **Financial aid:** Priority filing date for institution's financial aid form: March 2. In 2003-2004, 95% of undergraduates applied for financial aid. Of those, 91% were determined to have financial need; 58% had their need fully met. Average financial aid package (proportion receiving): $10,700 (85%). Average amount of gift aid, such as scholarships or grants (proportion receiving): $5,250 (78%). Average amount of self-help aid, such as work study or loans (proportion receiving): $3,700 (80%). Average need-based loan (excluding PLUS or other private loans): $3,750. Among students who received need-based aid, the average percentage of need met: 78%. Among students who received aid based on merit, the average award (and the proportion receiving): $3,650 (3%). The average athletic scholarship (and the proportion receiving): $6,260 (3%). Average amount of debt of borrowers graduating in 2003: $18,800. Proportion who borrowed: 93%. **Student employment:** During the 2003-2004 academic year, 22% of undergraduates worked on campus. Average per-year earnings: $3,800. **Reserve Officers Training Corps (ROTC):** Air Force ROTC: Offered at cooperating institution (California State University–San Bernardino).

California Institute of Technology

1200 E. California Boulevard
Pasadena, CA 91125
Private; www.caltech.edu
Financial aid office: (626) 395-6280

- **2004-2005 TUITION AND FEES:** $25,551
- **ROOM AND BOARD:** $8,013

SAT I Score (25th/75th percentile): 1460-1580
2005 U.S. News College Ranking:
National Universities, 8
Acceptance Rate: 17%

Other expenses: Estimated books and supplies: $1,029. Personal expenses: $3,813. **Financial aid:** Priority filing date for institution's financial aid form: January 15; deadline: January 15. In 2003-2004, 65% of undergraduates applied for financial aid. Of those, 59% were determined to have financial need; 100% had their need fully met. Average financial aid package (proportion receiving): $26,230 (59%). Average amount of gift aid, such as scholarships or grants (proportion receiving): $23,873 (58%). Average amount of self-help aid, such as work study or loans (proportion receiving): $2,212 (42%). Average need-based loan (excluding PLUS or other private loans): $1,212. Among students who received need-based aid, the average percentage of need met: 100%. Among students who received aid based on merit, the average award (and the proportion receiving): $24,729 (11%). The average athletic scholarship (and the proportion receiving): $0 (0%). Average amount of debt of borrowers graduating in 2003: $7,906. Proportion who borrowed: 49%. **Student employment:** During the 2003-2004 academic year, 22% of undergraduates worked on campus. Average per-year earnings: $4,600. **Reserve Officers Training Corps (ROTC):** Army ROTC: Offered at cooperating institution (University of Southern California); Air Force ROTC: Offered at cooperating institution (University of Southern California, California State University–San Bernardino, Harvey Mudd College).

California Institute of the Arts

24700 McBean Parkway
Valencia, CA 91355
Private; www.calarts.edu
Financial aid office: (661) 253-7869

- **2004-2005 TUITION AND FEES:** $25,995
- **ROOM AND BOARD:** $7,455

2005 U.S. News College Ranking:
Unranked Specialty School–Fine Arts
Acceptance Rate: 36%

Other expenses: Estimated books and supplies: $1,570. Transportation: $650. Personal expenses: $2,100. **Financial aid:** Priority filing date for institution's financial aid form: March 2. In 2003-2004, 83% of undergraduates applied for financial aid. Of those, 73% were determined to have financial need; 8% had their need fully met. Average financial aid package (proportion receiving): $20,922 (72%). Average amount of gift aid, such as scholarships or grants (proportion receiving): $10,769 (70%). Average amount of self-help aid, such as work study or loans (proportion receiving): $6,338 (64%). Average need-based loan (excluding PLUS or other private loans): $5,499. Among students who received need-based aid, the average percentage of need met: 78%. Among students who received aid based on merit, the average award (and the proportion receiving): $5,719 (7%). Average amount of debt of borrowers graduating in 2003: $29,167. Proportion who borrowed: 77%. Average per-year earnings: $2,600.

California Lutheran University

60 W. Olsen Road
Thousand Oaks, CA 91360
Private; www.clunet.edu
Financial aid office: (805) 493-3115

■ **2004-2005 TUITION AND FEES:** $22,020
■ **ROOM AND BOARD:** $7,570

SAT I Score (25th/75th percentile): 1000-1200
2005 U.S. News College Ranking:
Universities–Master's (West), 18
Acceptance Rate: 77%

Other expenses: Estimated books and supplies: $1,260. Transportation: $612. Personal expenses: $2,438. **Financial aid:** Priority filing date for institution's financial aid form: March 2. In 2003-2004, 80% of undergraduates applied for financial aid. Of those, 66% were determined to have financial need; 28% had their need fully met. Average financial aid package (proportion receiving): $16,800 (66%). Average amount of gift aid, such as scholarships or grants (proportion receiving): $11,360 (66%). Average amount of self-help aid, such as work study or loans (proportion receiving): $4,260 (55%). Average need-based loan (excluding PLUS or other private loans): $3,360. Among students who received need-based aid, the average percentage of need met: 86%. Among students who received aid based on merit, the average award (and the proportion receiving): $2,150 (7%). **Student employment:** During the 2003-2004 academic year, 40% of undergraduates worked on campus. Average per-year earnings: $1,200. **Cooperative education programs:** art, business, computer science, engineering, humanities, natural science, social/behavioral science, other. **Reserve Officers Training Corps (ROTC):** Army ROTC: Offered at cooperating institution (UCSB); Air Force ROTC: Offered at cooperating institution (UCLA).

California State Polytechnic University–Pomona

3801 W. Temple Avenue
Pomona, CA 91768-2557
Public; www.csupomona.edu
Financial aid office: (909) 869-3714

■ **2004-2005 TUITION AND FEES:**
In state: $2,046; Out of state: $10,506
■ **ROOM AND BOARD:** $6,747

SAT I Score (25th/75th percentile): 890-1140
2005 U.S. News College Ranking:
Universities–Master's (West), 35
Acceptance Rate: 30%

Other expenses: Estimated books and supplies: $1,224. Transportation: $612. Personal expenses: $1,310. **Financial aid:** Priority filing date for institution's financial aid form: March 2. In 2003-2004, 60% of undergraduates applied for financial aid. Of those, 51% were determined to have financial need; 41% had their need fully met. Average financial aid package (proportion receiving): $8,258 (50%). Average amount of gift aid, such as scholarships or grants (proportion receiving): $5,277 (45%). Average amount of self-help aid, such as work study or loans (proportion receiving): $3,897 (42%). Average need-based loan (excluding PLUS or other private loans): $3,751. Among students who received need-based aid, the average percentage of need met: 85%. Among students who received aid based on merit, the average award (and the proportion receiving): $1,798 (1%). The average athletic scholarship (and the proportion receiving): $3,085 (0%). Average amount of debt of borrowers graduating in 2003: $11,258. Proportion who borrowed: 33%. **Cooperative education programs:** agriculture, art, business, computer science, education, engineering, natural science, social/behavioral science. **Reserve Officers Training Corps (ROTC):** Army ROTC: Offered on campus; Air Force ROTC: Offered at cooperating institution (USC, CSUSB, Harvey Mudd).

California State University–Bakersfield

9001 Stockdale Highway
Bakersfield, CA 93311
Public; www.csub.edu
Financial aid office: (661) 664-3016

■ **2004-2005 TUITION AND FEES:**
In state: $2,624; Out of state: $9,392
■ **ROOM AND BOARD:** $5,810

SAT I Score (25th/75th percentile): 810-1080
2005 U.S. News College Ranking:
Universities–Master's (West), 58
Acceptance Rate: 59%

Other expenses: Estimated books and supplies: $1,260. Transportation: $888. Personal expenses: $1,854. **Financial aid:** Priority filing date for institution's financial aid form: March 2.

California State University–Chico

400 W. First Street
Chico, CA 95929-0722
Public; www.csuchico.edu
Financial aid office: (530) 898-6451

■ **2004-2005 TUITION AND FEES:**
In state: $3,154; Out of state: $13,324
■ **ROOM AND BOARD:** $7,493

SAT I Score (25th/75th percentile): 930-1140
2005 U.S. News College Ranking:
Universities–Master's (West), 32
Acceptance Rate: 73%

Other expenses: Estimated books and supplies: $1,195. Transportation: $736. Personal expenses: $1,852. **Financial aid:** Priority filing date for institution's financial aid form: March 2. **Student employment:** During the 2003-2004 academic year, 9% of undergraduates worked on campus. Average per-year earnings: $2,500. **Cooperative education programs:** agriculture, art, business, computer science, education, engineering, health professions, humanities, natural science, social/behavioral science, technologies.

California State University–Dominguez Hills

1000 E. Victoria Street
Carson, CA 90747
Public; www.csudh.edu
Financial aid office: (310) 243-3691

■ **2004-2005 TUITION AND FEES:**
In state: $2,483; Out of state: $9,251
■ **ROOM AND BOARD:** $7,063

SAT I Score (25th/75th percentile): 720-930
2005 U.S. News College Ranking:
Universities–Master's (West), fourth tier
Acceptance Rate: 48%

Other expenses: Estimated books and supplies: $900. Transportation: $600. Personal expenses: $1,854. **Financial aid:** Priority filing date for institution's financial aid form: March 2; deadline: April 15. In 2003-2004, 91% of undergraduates applied for financial aid. Of those, 89% were determined to have financial need; 11% had their need fully met. Average financial aid package (proportion receiving): $7,860 (88%). Average amount of gift aid, such as scholarships or grants (proportion receiving): $4,702 (84%). Average amount of self-help aid, such as work study or loans (proportion receiving): $3,810 (45%). Average need-based loan (excluding PLUS or other private loans): $4,301. Among students who received need-based aid, the average percentage of need met: 71%. Among students who received aid based on merit, the average award (and the proportion receiving): $3,133 (1%). The average athletic scholarship (and the proportion receiving): $2,479 (0%). Average amount of debt of borrowers graduating in 2003: $14,715. Proportion who borrowed: 47%. **Reserve Officers Training Corps (ROTC):** Army ROTC: Offered at cooperating institution (CSU LONG BEACH); Air Force ROTC: Offered at cooperating institution (LOYOLA MARYMOUNT UNIVERSITY).

California State University–Fresno

5150 N. Maple
Fresno, CA 93740
Public; www.csufresno.edu
Financial aid office: (559) 278-2182

■ **2004-2005 TUITION AND FEES:**
In state: $2,782; Out of state: $9,182
■ **ROOM AND BOARD:** $7,180

SAT I Score (25th/75th percentile): 820-1080
2005 U.S. News College Ranking:
Universities–Master's (West), 52
Acceptance Rate: 70%

Other expenses: Estimated books and supplies: $1,260. Transportation: $944. Personal expenses: $1,838. **Financial aid:** Priority filing date for institution's financial aid form: March 2. In 2003-2004, 80% of undergraduates applied for financial aid. Of those, 67% were determined to have financial need; 40% had their need fully met. Average financial aid package (proportion receiving): $5,449 (64%). Average amount of gift aid, such as scholarships or grants (proportion receiving): $2,903 (47%). Average amount of self-help aid, such as work study or loans (proportion receiving): $3,692

(28%). Average need-based loan (excluding PLUS or other private loans): $3,702. Among students who received need-based aid, the average percentage of need met: 82%. Among students who received aid based on merit, the average award (and the proportion receiving): $2,436 (2%). Average amount of debt of borrowers graduating in 2003: $15,000. Proportion who borrowed: 52%. **Reserve Officers Training Corps (ROTC):** Army ROTC: Offered on campus; Air Force ROTC: Offered on campus.

California State University–Fullerton

800 N. State College Boulevard
Fullerton, CA 92834
Public; www.fullerton.edu
Financial aid office: (714) 278-3128

■ **2004-2005 TUITION AND FEES:**
In state: $2,516; Out of state: $10,976

SAT I Score (25th/75th percentile): 860-1090
2005 U.S. News College Ranking:
Universities–Master's (West), 41
Acceptance Rate: 66%

Other expenses: Estimated books and supplies: $1,260. Transportation: $810. Personal expenses: $1,854. **Financial aid:** Priority filing date for institution's financial aid form: March 2. In 2003-2004, 56% of undergraduates applied for financial aid. Of those, 45% were determined to have financial need; 3% had their need fully met. Average financial aid package (proportion receiving): $6,916 (37%). Average amount of gift aid, such as scholarships or grants (proportion receiving): $6,052 (29%). Average amount of self-help aid, such as work study or loans (proportion receiving): $4,023 (19%). Average need-based loan (excluding PLUS or other private loans): $3,906. Among students who received need-based aid, the average percentage of need met: 67%. Among students who received aid based on merit, the average award (and the proportion receiving): $4,083 (7%). The average athletic scholarship (and the proportion receiving): $5,746 (1%). Average amount of debt of borrowers graduating in 2003: $12,720. Proportion who borrowed: 37%. Average per-year earnings: $6,000. **Reserve Officers Training Corps (ROTC):** Army ROTC: Offered on campus.

California State University–Hayward

25800 Carlos Bee Boulevard
Hayward, CA 94542
Public; www.csuhayward.edu
Financial aid office: (510) 885-2784

■ **2004-2005 TUITION AND FEES:**
In state: $902; Out of state: $6,938

SAT I Score (25th/75th percentile): 800-1060
2005 U.S. News College Ranking:
Universities–Master's (West), third tier
Acceptance Rate: 46%

Financial aid: Priority filing date for institution's financial aid form: March 2. In 2003-2004, 45% of undergraduates applied for financial aid. Of those, 42% were determined to have financial need; 7% had their need fully met. Average financial aid package (proportion receiving): $7,251 (42%). Average amount of gift aid, such as scholarships or grants (proportion receiving): $5,588 (35%). Average amount of self-help aid, such as work study or loans (proportion receiving): $5,207 (24%). Average need-based loan (excluding PLUS or other private loans): $5,309. Among students who received need-based aid, the average percentage of need met: 61%. Among students who received aid based on merit, the average award (and the proportion receiving): $0 (0%). The average athletic scholarship (and the proportion receiving): $0 (0%). Average amount of debt of borrowers graduating in 2003: $12,584. Proportion who borrowed: 35%. **Cooperative education programs:** art, business, computer science, health professions, humanities, natural science, social/behavioral science.

California State University–Long Beach

1250 Bellflower Boulevard
Long Beach, CA 90840
Public; www.csulb.edu
Financial aid office: (562) 985-8403

■ **2004-2005 TUITION AND FEES:**
In state: $2,658; Out of state: $12,828
■ **ROOM AND BOARD:** $5,800

SAT I Score (25th/75th percentile): 920-1130
2005 U.S. News College Ranking:
Universities–Master's (West), 32
Acceptance Rate: 49%

Other expenses: Estimated books and supplies: $1,260. Transportation: $696. Personal expenses: $1,714. **Financial aid:** Priority filing date for institution's financial aid form: March 2. In 2003-2004, 58% of undergraduates applied for financial aid. Of those, 48% were determined to have financial need; 43% had their need fully met. Average financial aid package (proportion receiving): $7,635 (45%). Average amount of gift aid, such as scholarships or grants (proportion receiving): $4,100 (38%). Average amount of self-help aid, such as work study or loans (proportion receiving): $4,050 (33%). Average need-based loan (excluding PLUS or other private loans): $3,270. Among students who received need-based aid, the average percentage of need met: 84%. Among students who received aid based on merit, the average award (and the proportion receiving): $1,737 (3%). Average amount of debt of borrowers graduating in 2003: $6,319. Proportion who borrowed: 29%. Average per-year earnings: $5,440. **Cooperative education programs:** art, business, computer science, education, engineering, health professions, humanities, natural science, social/behavioral science, technologies, other.

California State University– Los Angeles

5151 State University Drive
Los Angeles, CA 90032
Public; www.calstatela.edu
Financial aid office: (323) 343-1784

■ **2004-2005 TUITION AND FEES:**
   In state: $2,852; Out of state: $10,988

2005 U.S. News College Ranking:
Universities–Master's (West), third tier
Acceptance Rate: 54%
....

Financial aid: Priority filing date for institution's financial aid form: March 2. In 2003-2004, 74% of undergraduates applied for financial aid. Of those, 69% were determined to have financial need; 6% had their need fully met. Average financial aid package (proportion receiving): $7,416 (65%). Average amount of gift aid, such as scholarships or grants (proportion receiving): $6,523 (56%). Average amount of self-help aid, such as work study or loans (proportion receiving): $4,102 (41%). Average need-based loan (excluding PLUS or other private loans): $3,592. Among students who received need-based aid, the average percentage of need met: 75%. Among students who received aid based on merit, the average award (and the proportion receiving): $0 (0%).

Average per-year earnings: $7,200. **Cooperative education programs:** art, business, computer science, engineering, health professions, natural science, social/behavioral science, technologies. **Reserve Officers Training Corps (ROTC):** Army ROTC: Offered at cooperating institution (University of California, Los Angeles (UCLA) program); Air Force ROTC: Offered at cooperating institution (University of Southern California, California State University–San Bernardino, Harvey Mudd College).

California State University– Monterey Bay

Seaside, CA 93955-8001
Public; www.csumb.edu

■ **2004-2005 TUITION AND FEES:**
   In state: $2,677; Out of state: $7,195
■ **ROOM AND BOARD:** $5,725

SAT I Score (25th/75th percentile): 849-1105
2005 U.S. News College Ranking:
Liberal Arts Colleges, fourth tier
Acceptance Rate: 68%
....

Other expenses: Estimated books and supplies: $1,260. Transportation: $828. Personal expenses: $1,854. **Financial aid:** Priority filing date for institution's financial aid form: March 2. In 2003-2004, 73% of undergraduates applied for financial aid. Of those, 60% were determined to have financial need; 21% had their need fully met. Average financial aid package (proportion receiving): $7,151 (60%). Average amount of gift aid, such as scholarships or grants (proportion receiving): $5,738 (39%). Average amount of self-help aid, such as work study or loans (proportion receiving): $3,488 (37%). Average need-based loan (excluding PLUS or other private loans): $3,486. Among students who received need-based aid, the average percentage of need met: 75%. Among students who received aid based on merit, the average award (and the proportion receiving): $1,517 (2%). The average athletic scholarship (and the proportion receiving): $13,667 (1%). Average amount of debt of borrowers graduating in 2003: $8,263. Proportion who borrowed: 49%. Average per-year earnings: $5,000.

California State University– Northridge

18111 Nordhoff Street
Northridge, CA 91330
Public; www.csun.edu
Financial aid office: (818) 677-3827

■ **2004-2005 TUITION AND FEES:**
   In state: $2,778; Out of state: $12,948

ACT Score (25th/75th percentile): 18
2005 U.S. News College Ranking:
Universities–Master's (West), third tier
....

Financial aid: Priority filing date for institution's financial aid form: March 2.

California State University– Sacramento

6000 J Street
Sacramento, CA 95819
Public; www.csus.edu
Financial aid office: (916) 278-6554

■ **2004-2005 TUITION AND FEES:**
   In state: $2,824; Out of state: $15,328
■ **ROOM AND BOARD:** $6,574

SAT I Score (25th/75th percentile): 840-1080
2005 U.S. News College Ranking:
Universities–Master's (West), 58
Acceptance Rate: 52%
....

Financial aid: Priority filing date for institution's financial aid form: March 2. In 2003-2004, 61% of undergraduates applied for financial aid. Of those, 52% were determined to have financial need; 8% had their need fully met. Average financial aid package (proportion receiving): $8,066 (49%). Average amount of gift aid, such as scholarships or grants (proportion receiving): $2,098 (39%). Average amount of self-help aid, such as work study or loans (proportion receiving): $3,674 (31%). Average need-based loan (excluding PLUS or other private loans): $3,880. Among students who received need-based aid, the average percentage of need met: 68%. Among students who received aid based on merit, the average award (and the proportion receiving): $5,465 (5%). Average amount of debt of borrowers graduating in 2003: $10,554. Proportion who borrowed: 37%. **Cooperative education programs:** art, business, computer science, education, engineering, health professions, humanities, natural science, social/behavioral science.

Reserve Officers Training Corps (ROTC): Army ROTC: Offered at cooperating institution (UC Davis); Air Force ROTC: Offered on campus.

California State University–San Bernardino

5500 University Parkway
San Bernardino, CA 92407
Public; www.csusb.edu
Financial aid office: (909) 880-7800

■ **2004-2005 TUITION AND FEES:**
In state: $2,580; Out of state: $7,302
■ **ROOM AND BOARD:** $7,756

SAT I Score (25th/75th percentile): 770-1000
2005 U.S. News College Ranking:
Universities–Master's (West), third tier
Acceptance Rate: 61%

Other expenses: Estimated books and supplies: $1,260. Transportation: $612. Personal expenses: $1,818. **Reserve Officers Training Corps (ROTC):** Army ROTC: Offered on campus; Air Force ROTC: Offered on campus.

California State University–San Marcos

333 S. Twin Oaks Valley Road
San Marcos, CA 92096-0001
Public; www.csusm.edu
Financial aid office: (760) 750-4850

■ **2004-2005 TUITION AND FEES:**
In state: $2,776; Out of state: $10,912

SAT I Score (25th/75th percentile): 870-1090
2005 U.S. News College Ranking:
Universities–Master's (West), third tier
Acceptance Rate: 73%

Financial aid: Priority filing date for institution's financial aid form: March 2. **Reserve Officers Training Corps (ROTC):** Army ROTC: Offered at cooperating institution (San Diego State University); Navy ROTC: Offered at cooperating institution (San Diego State University); Air Force ROTC: Offered at cooperating institution (San Diego State University).

California State University–Stanislaus

801 W. Monte Vista Avenue
Turlock, CA 95382
Public; www.csustan.edu
Financial aid office: (209) 667-3336

■ **2004-2005 TUITION AND FEES:**
In state: $2,807; Out of state: $12,977
■ **ROOM AND BOARD:** $8,295

SAT I Score (25th/75th percentile): 840-1100
2005 U.S. News College Ranking:
Universities–Master's (West), 50
Acceptance Rate: 65%

Other expenses: Estimated books and supplies: $1,260. Transportation: $639. Personal expenses: $1,602. **Financial aid:** Priority filing date for institution's financial aid form: March 2. In 2003-2004, 75% of undergraduates applied for financial aid. Of those, 66% were determined to have financial need; 9% had their need fully met. Average financial aid package (proportion receiving): $7,472 (63%). Average amount of gift aid, such as scholarships or grants (proportion receiving): $4,285 (54%). Average amount of self-help aid, such as work study or loans (proportion receiving): $4,668 (35%). Average need-based loan (excluding PLUS or other private loans): $8,970. Among students who received need-based aid, the average percentage of need met: 59%. Among students who received aid based on merit, the average award (and the proportion receiving): $1,263 (2%). The average athletic scholarship (and the proportion receiving): $2,337 (3%). Average amount of debt of borrowers graduating in 2003: $13,050. Proportion who borrowed: 29%. **Student employment:** During the 2003-2004 academic year, 11% of undergraduates worked on campus. Average per-year earnings: $6,720. **Cooperative education programs:** art, business, computer science, education, engineering, social/behavioral science.

Cal Poly–San Luis Obispo

1 Grand Avenue
San Luis Obispo, CA 93407
Public; www.calpoly.edu
Financial aid office: (805) 756-2927

■ **2004-2005 TUITION AND FEES:**
In state: $3,804; Out of state: $10,284
■ **ROOM AND BOARD:** $7,801

SAT I Score (25th/75th percentile): 1090-1280
2005 U.S. News College Ranking:
Universities–Master's (West), 5
Acceptance Rate: 39%

Other expenses: Estimated books and supplies: $1,260. Transportation: $828. Personal expenses: $1,892. **Financial aid:** Priority filing date for institution's financial aid form: March 2; deadline: June 30. In 2003-2004, 54% of undergraduates applied for financial aid. Of those, 37% were determined to have financial need; 3% had their need fully met. Average financial aid package (proportion receiving): $6,998 (35%). Average amount of gift aid, such as scholarships or grants (proportion receiving): $1,448 (25%). Average amount of self-help aid, such as work study or loans (proportion receiving): $4,060 (29%). Average need-based loan (excluding PLUS or other private loans): $3,833. Among students who received need-based aid, the average percentage of need met: 71%. Among students who received aid based on merit, the average award (and the proportion receiving): $0 (0%). The average athletic scholarship (and the proportion receiving): $0 (0%). Average amount of debt of borrowers graduating in 2003: $12,781. Proportion who borrowed: 46%. **Reserve Officers Training Corps (ROTC):** Army ROTC: Offered on campus.

Chapman University

1 University Drive
Orange, CA 92866
Private; www.chapman.edu
Financial aid office: (888) 282-7759

■ **2004-2005 TUITION AND FEES:** $26,150
■ **ROOM AND BOARD:** $10,000

SAT I Score (25th/75th percentile): 1076-1299
2005 U.S. News College Ranking:
Universities–Master's (West), 12
Acceptance Rate: 62%

Other expenses: Estimated books and supplies: $1,000. Transportation: $700. Personal expenses: $1,550. **Financial aid:** Priority filing date for institution's financial aid form: March 2. In 2003-2004, 87% of undergraduates applied for financial aid. Of those, 62% were determined to have financial need; 100% had their need fully met. Average financial aid package (proportion receiving): $18,358 (62%). Average amount of gift aid, such as scholarships or grants (proportion receiving): $14,873 (61%). Average amount of self-help aid, such as work study or loans (proportion receiving): $3,485 (48%). Average need-based loan (excluding PLUS or other private loans): $2,998. Among students who received need-based aid, the average percentage of need met: 100%. Among students who received aid based on merit, the average award (and the proportion receiving): $13,436 (22%). The average athletic scholarship (and the proportion receiving): $0 (0%). Average amount of debt of borrowers graduating in 2003: $18,574. Proportion who borrowed: 44%. **Student employment:** During the 2003-2004 academic year, 32% of undergraduates worked on campus. Average per-year earnings: $3,000. **Cooperative education programs:** business. **Reserve Officers Training Corps (ROTC):** Army ROTC: Offered at cooperating institution (CSU Pomona, Claremont Colleges, CSU Fullerton); Air Force ROTC: Offered at cooperating institution (Loyola Marymount University).

Christian Heritage College

2100 Greenfield Drive
El Cajon, CA 92019
Private; www.christianheritage.edu
Financial aid office: (619) 590-1786

■ **2004-2005 TUITION AND FEES:** $14,840
■ **ROOM AND BOARD:** $5,990

SAT I Score (25th/75th percentile): 890-1180
2005 U.S. News College Ranking:
Liberal Arts Colleges, fourth tier
Acceptance Rate: 71%

Other expenses: Estimated books and supplies: $1,260. Transportation: $612.

Claremont McKenna College

890 Columbia Avenue
Claremont, CA 91711
Private; www.claremontmckenna.edu
Financial aid office: (909) 621-8356

■ **2004-2005 TUITION AND FEES:** $29,210
■ **ROOM AND BOARD:** $9,780

SAT I Score (25th/75th percentile): 1310-1480
2005 U.S. News College Ranking:
Liberal Arts Colleges, 13
Acceptance Rate: 31%

Other expenses: Estimated books and supplies: $850. Transportation: $0. Personal expenses: $1,000. **Financial aid:** In 2003-2004, 63% of undergraduates applied for financial aid. Of those, 55% were determined to have financial

need; 100% had their need fully met. Average financial aid package (proportion receiving): $23,906 (55%). Average amount of gift aid, such as scholarships or grants (proportion receiving): $21,329 (55%). Average amount of self-help aid, such as work study or loans (proportion receiving): $3,895 (53%). Average need-based loan (excluding PLUS or other private loans): $3,832. Among students who received need-based aid, the average percentage of need met: 100%. Among students who received aid based on merit, the average award (and the proportion receiving): $6,022 (10%). The average athletic scholarship (and the proportion receiving): $0 (0%). Average amount of debt of borrowers graduating in 2003: $11,620. Proportion who borrowed: 45%. **Student employment:** During the 2003-2004 academic year, 40% of undergraduates worked on campus. Average per-year earnings: $2,200. **Reserve Officers Training Corps (ROTC):** Army ROTC: Offered on campus; Air Force ROTC: Offered at cooperating institution (Harvey Mudd College).

Cogswell Polytechnical College

1175 Bordeaux Drive
Sunnyvale, CA 94089-1299
Private; www.cogswell.edu
Financial aid office: (408) 541-0100

■ **2004-2005 TUITION AND FEES:** $12,480

2005 U.S. News College Ranking:
Comp. Colleges–Bachelor's (West), third tier
Acceptance Rate: 77%

Concordia University

1530 Concordia W
Irvine, CA 92612-3299
Private; www.cui.edu
Financial aid office: (949) 854-8002

■ **2004-2005 TUITION AND FEES:** $18,800
■ **ROOM AND BOARD:** $6,670

SAT I Score (25th/75th percentile): 960-1180
2005 U.S. News College Ranking:
Universities–Master's (West), 47
Acceptance Rate: 67%

Other expenses: Estimated books and supplies: $900. Transportation: $600. Personal expenses: $1,800. **Financial aid:** Priority filing date for institution's financial aid form: March 2; deadline: April 1. In 2003-2004, 94% of undergradu-

ates applied for financial aid. Of those, 71% were determined to have financial need; 36% had their need fully met. Average financial aid package (proportion receiving): $13,979 (71%). Average amount of gift aid, such as scholarships or grants (proportion receiving): $7,327 (38%). Average amount of self-help aid, such as work study or loans (proportion receiving): $4,220 (54%). Average need-based loan (excluding PLUS or other private loans): $3,817. Among students who received need-based aid, the average percentage of need met: 86%. Among students who received aid based on merit, the average award (and the proportion receiving): $5,397 (15%). The average athletic scholarship (and the proportion receiving): $7,122 (9%). Average amount of debt of borrowers graduating in 2003: $16,500. Proportion who borrowed: 70%. **Student employment:** During the 2003-2004 academic year, 24% of undergraduates worked on campus. Average per-year earnings: $2,000.

Dominican University of California

50 Acacia Avenue
San Rafael, CA 94901-2298
Private; www.dominican.edu
Financial aid office: (415) 257-1321

■ **2004-2005 TUITION AND FEES:** $24,454
■ **ROOM AND BOARD:** $10,270

SAT I Score (25th/75th percentile): 910-1160
2005 U.S. News College Ranking:
Universities–Master's (West), 35
Acceptance Rate: 55%

Other expenses: Estimated books and supplies: $1,260. Transportation: $612. Personal expenses: $1,818. **Financial aid:** Priority filing date for institution's financial aid form: March 2. In 2003-2004, 82% of undergraduates applied for financial aid. Of those, 73% were determined to have financial need; 23% had their need fully met. Average financial aid package (proportion receiving): $19,762 (73%). Average amount of gift aid, such as scholarships or grants (proportion receiving): $14,879 (72%). Average amount of self-help aid, such as work study or loans (proportion receiving): $8,523 (69%). Average need-based loan (excluding PLUS or other private loans): $4,159. Among students who received need-based aid, the average percentage of need met: 23%. Among students who received aid based on merit, the average award (and the proportion receiving): $9,765 (20%). The average athletic scholarship (and the proportion receiving): $6,425 (8%). Average amount of debt of borrowers graduating in 2003:

$17,675. Proportion who borrowed: 76%. **Student employment:** During the 2003-2004 academic year, 9% of undergraduates worked on campus. Average per-year earnings: $1,952.

Fresno Pacific University

1717 S. Chestnut Avenue
Fresno, CA 93702
Private; www.fresno.edu
Financial aid office: (559) 453-2027

■ **2004-2005 TUITION AND FEES:** $18,800
■ **ROOM AND BOARD:** $6,100

SAT I Score (25th/75th percentile): 880-1140
2005 U.S. News College Ranking:
Universities–Master's (West), 29
Acceptance Rate: 62%

Financial aid: Priority filing date for institution's financial aid form: March 2. **Student employment:** During the 2003-2004 academic year, 37% of undergraduates worked on campus. Average per-year earnings: $78.

Golden Gate University

536 Mission Street
San Francisco, CA 94105
Private; www.ggu.edu
Financial aid office: (415) 442-7262

■ **2004-2005 TUITION AND FEES:** $10,320

2005 U.S. News College Ranking:
Unranked Specialty School–Business
Acceptance Rate: 64%

Financial aid: Average amount of debt of borrowers graduating in 2003: $17,830. Proportion who borrowed: 57%.

Harvey Mudd College

301 E. 12th Street
Claremont, CA 91711
Private; www.hmc.edu
Financial aid office: (909) 621-8055

■ **2004-2005 TUITION AND FEES:** $30,237
■ **ROOM AND BOARD:** $9,845

SAT I Score (25th/75th percentile): 1370-1550
2005 U.S. News College Ranking:
Liberal Arts Colleges, 16
Acceptance Rate: 40%

....

Other expenses: Estimated books and supplies: $800. Transportation: $500. Personal expenses: $900. **Financial aid:** Priority filing date for institution's financial aid form: February 1; deadline: February 1. In 2003-2004, 64% of undergraduates applied for financial aid. Of those, 55% were determined to have financial need; 100% had their need fully met. Average financial aid package (proportion receiving): $22,740 (55%). Average amount of gift aid, such as scholarships or grants (proportion receiving): $18,438 (52%). Average amount of self-help aid, such as work study or loans (proportion receiving): $5,966 (48%). Average need-based loan (excluding PLUS or other private loans): $4,500. Among students who received need-based aid, the average percentage of need met: 100%. Among students who received aid based on merit, the average award (and the proportion receiving): $6,563 (24%). The average athletic scholarship (and the proportion receiving): $0 (0%). Average amount of debt of borrowers graduating in 2003: $21,881. Proportion who borrowed: 67%. **Student employment:** During the 2003-2004 academic year, 35% of undergraduates worked on campus. Average per-year earnings: $1,080. **Reserve Officers Training Corps (ROTC):** Army ROTC: Offered at cooperating institution (Claremont McKenna College); Air Force ROTC: Offered on campus.

Holy Names University

3500 Mountain Boulevard
Oakland, CA 94619
Private; www.hnu.edu
Financial aid office: (510) 436-1327

■ **2004-2005 TUITION AND FEES:** $20,980
■ **ROOM AND BOARD:** $7,800

SAT I Score (25th/75th percentile): 890-1050
2005 U.S. News College Ranking:
Universities–Master's (West), 58
Acceptance Rate: 62%

....

Other expenses: Estimated books and supplies: $946. Transportation: $846. Personal expenses: $1,800. **Financial aid:** Priority filing date for institution's financial aid form: March 2; deadline: March 15. In 2003-2004, 72% of undergraduates applied for financial aid. Of those, 72% were determined to have financial need; 13% had their need fully met. Average financial aid package (proportion receiving): $22,883 (67%). Average amount of gift aid, such as scholarships or grants (proportion receiving): $9,796 (66%).

Average amount of self-help aid, such as work study or loans (proportion receiving): $5,810 (66%). Average need-based loan (excluding PLUS or other private loans): $4,015. Among students who received need-based aid, the average percentage of need met: 72%. Among students who received aid based on merit, the average award (and the proportion receiving): $19,970 (0%). The average athletic scholarship (and the proportion receiving): $9,434 (20%). Average amount of debt of borrowers graduating in 2003: $21,000. Proportion who borrowed: 95%. **Student employment:** During the 2003-2004 academic year, 0% of undergraduates worked on campus. Average per-year earnings: $0. **Reserve Officers Training Corps (ROTC):** Army ROTC: Offered at cooperating institution (University of California–Berkeley); Air Force ROTC: Offered at cooperating institution (University of California–Berkeley).

Hope International University

2500 E. Nutwood Avenue
Fullerton, CA 92831
Private; www.hiu.edu
Financial aid office: (714) 879-3901

■ **2004-2005 TUITION AND FEES:** $16,500
■ **ROOM AND BOARD:** $5,400

SAT I Score (25th/75th percentile): 840-1080
2005 U.S. News College Ranking:
Universities–Master's (West), fourth tier
Acceptance Rate: 69%

....

Financial aid: Priority filing date for institution's financial aid form: March 2. **Student employment:** During the 2003-2004 academic year, 22% of undergraduates worked on campus. Average per-year earnings: $2,500. **Cooperative education programs:** business, education, humanities, social/behavioral science.

Humboldt State University

1 Harpst Street
Arcata, CA 95521-8299
Public; www.humboldt.edu
Financial aid office: (707) 826-4321

■ **2004-2005 TUITION AND FEES:**
In state: $2,539; Out of state: $7,261
■ **ROOM AND BOARD:** $6,861

SAT I Score (25th/75th percentile): 940-1180
2005 U.S. News College Ranking:
Universities–Master's (West), 39
Acceptance Rate: 67%

Other expenses: Estimated books and supplies: $1,050. Transportation: $774. Personal expenses: $1,854. **Financial aid:** Priority filing date for institution's financial aid form: March 2.

Humphreys College

6650 Inglewood Avenue
Stockton, CA 95207
Private; www.humphreys.edu
Financial aid office: (209) 478-0800

- **2004-2005 TUITION AND FEES:** $10,080
- **ROOM AND BOARD:** $8,109

2005 U.S. News College Ranking:
Comp. Colleges–Bachelor's (West), fourth tier
Acceptance Rate: 81%

Other expenses: Estimated books and supplies: $1,260. Transportation: $990. Personal expenses: $2,214. **Financial aid:** Priority filing date for institution's financial aid form: March 2; deadline: June 1. In 2003-2004, 99% of undergraduates applied for financial aid. Of those, 89% were determined to have financial need; 100% had their need fully met. Average financial aid package (proportion receiving): $9,850 (89%). Average amount of gift aid, such as scholarships or grants (proportion receiving): $8 (2%). Average amount of self-help aid, such as work study or loans (proportion receiving): $9,850 (0%). Average need-based loan (excluding PLUS or other private loans): $0. Among students who received need-based aid, the average percentage of need met: 75%. Among students who received aid based on merit, the average award (and the proportion receiving): $9,600 (2%). The average athletic scholarship (and the proportion receiving): $0 (0%). Average amount of debt of borrowers graduating in 2003: $26,000. Proportion who borrowed: 97%. **Cooperative education programs:** computer science, social/behavioral science, vocational arts.

John F. Kennedy University

12 Altarinda Road
Orinda, CA 94563
Private; www.jfku.edu
Financial aid office: (925) 258-2385

- **TUITION AND FEES:** $0

2005 U.S. News College Ranking:
Universities–Master's (West), unranked

Laguna College of Art and Design

2222 Laguna Canyon Road
Laguna Beach, CA 92651
Private; www.lagunacollege.edu
Financial aid office: (949) 376-6000

- **2004-2005 TUITION AND FEES:** $16,000

2005 U.S. News College Ranking:
Unranked Specialty School–Fine Arts
Acceptance Rate: 38%

La Sierra University

4700 Pierce Street
Riverside, CA 92515
Private; www.lasierra.edu
Financial aid office: (909) 785-2175

- **2004-2005 TUITION AND FEES:** $17,244
- **ROOM AND BOARD:** $5,130

SAT I Score (25th/75th percentile): 860-1120
2005 U.S. News College Ranking:
Universities–Master's (West), third tier
Acceptance Rate: 57%

Loyola Marymount University

1 LMU Drive
Los Angeles, CA 90045-2659
Private; www.lmu.edu
Financial aid office: (310) 338-2753

- **2004-2005 TUITION AND FEES:** $25,744
- **ROOM AND BOARD:** $9,456

SAT I Score (25th/75th percentile): 1060-1250
2005 U.S. News College Ranking:
Universities–Master's (West), 3
Acceptance Rate: 59%

Other expenses: Estimated books and supplies: $820. Transportation: $594. Personal expenses: $2,286. **Financial aid:** Priority filing date for institution's financial aid form: February 15; deadline: July 30. In 2003-2004, 73% of undergraduates applied for financial aid. Of those, 57% were determined to have financial need; 30% had their need fully met. Average financial aid package (proportion receiving): $18,095 (57%). Average amount of gift aid, such as scholarships or grants (proportion receiving):

$11,116 (49%). Average amount of self-help aid, such as work study or loans (proportion receiving): $6,667 (46%). Average need-based loan (excluding PLUS or other private loans): $4,807. Among students who received need-based aid, the average percentage of need met: 78%. Among students who received aid based on merit, the average award (and the proportion receiving): $6,811 (3%). The average athletic scholarship (and the proportion receiving): $19,269 (4%). Average amount of debt of borrowers graduating in 2003: $19,933. Proportion who borrowed: 62%. Average per-year earnings: $2,600. **Reserve Officers Training Corps (ROTC):** Army ROTC: Offered at cooperating institution (UCLA); Navy ROTC: Offered at cooperating institution (UCLA); Air Force ROTC: Offered on campus.

Master's College and Seminary

21726 Placerita Canyon Road
Santa Clarita, CA 91321-1200
Private; www.masters.edu
Financial aid office: (661) 259-3540

- **2004-2005 TUITION AND FEES:** $18,170
- **ROOM AND BOARD:** $6,370

SAT I Score (25th/75th percentile): 1030-1240
2005 U.S. News College Ranking:
Comp. Colleges–Bachelor's (West), 5
Acceptance Rate: 54%

Other expenses: Estimated books and supplies: $1,260. Transportation: $612. Personal expenses: $1,818. **Financial aid:** Priority filing date for institution's financial aid form: March 2. In 2003-2004, 72% of undergraduates applied for financial aid. Of those, 66% were determined to have financial need; 22% had their need fully met. Average financial aid package (proportion receiving): $14,157 (66%). Average amount of gift aid, such as scholarships or grants (proportion receiving): $10,059 (62%). Average amount of self-help aid, such as work study or loans (proportion receiving): $5,422 (56%). Average need-based loan (excluding PLUS or other private loans): $4,119. Among students who received need-based aid, the average percentage of need met: 74%. Among students who received aid based on merit, the average award (and the proportion receiving): $8,145 (20%). The average athletic scholarship (and the proportion receiving): $7,097 (4%). Average amount of debt of borrowers graduating in 2003: $13,131. Proportion who borrowed: 57%. **Student employment:** During the 2003-2004 academic year, 23% of undergraduates worked on campus. Average per-year earnings: $1,330. **Cooperative education programs:** education, home economics.

Menlo College

1000 El Camino Real
Atherton, CA 94027
Private; www.menlo.edu
Financial aid office: (650) 543-3880

■ **2004-2005 TUITION AND FEES:** $23,000
■ **ROOM AND BOARD:** $9,350

SAT I Score (25th/75th percentile): 1030
2005 U.S. News College Ranking:
Comp. Colleges–Bachelor's (West), 12
Acceptance Rate: 55%

Other expenses: Estimated books and supplies: $1,200. Transportation: $612. Personal expenses: $1,818. **Financial aid:** Priority filing date for institution's financial aid form: March 2. In 2003-2004, 67% of undergraduates applied for financial aid. Of those, 62% were determined to have financial need; 15% had their need fully met. Average financial aid package (proportion receiving): $18,427 (62%). Average amount of gift aid, such as scholarships or grants (proportion receiving): $14,599 (59%). Average amount of self-help aid, such as work study or loans (proportion receiving): $5,126 (56%). Average need-based loan (excluding PLUS or other private loans): $4,530. Among students who received need-based aid, the average percentage of need met: 73%. Among students who received aid based on merit, the average award (and the proportion receiving): $10,675 (24%). The average athletic scholarship (and the proportion receiving): $0 (0%). Average amount of debt of borrowers graduating in 2003: $20,126. Proportion who borrowed: 69%. **Student employment:** During the 2003-2004 academic year, 10% of undergraduates worked on campus. Average per-year earnings: $1,000. **Reserve Officers Training Corps (ROTC):** Army ROTC: Offered at cooperating institution (San Jose State University); Navy ROTC: Offered at cooperating institution (San Jose State University); Air Force ROTC: Offered at cooperating institution (San Jose State University).

Mills College

5000 MacArthur Boulevard
Oakland, CA 94613
Private; www.mills.edu
Financial aid office: (510) 430-2000

■ **2004-2005 TUITION AND FEES:** $27,085
■ **ROOM AND BOARD:** $9,400

SAT I Score (25th/75th percentile): 1010-1260
2005 U.S. News College Ranking:
Liberal Arts Colleges, 70
Acceptance Rate: 73%

Other expenses: Estimated books and supplies: $930. Transportation: $0. Personal expenses: $1,629. **Financial aid:** Priority filing date for institution's financial aid form: February 15. In 2003-2004, 94% of undergraduates applied for financial aid. Of those, 90% were determined to have financial need; 39% had their need fully met. Average financial aid package (proportion receiving): $20,190 (90%). Average amount of gift aid, such as scholarships or grants (proportion receiving): $13,640 (90%). Average amount of self-help aid, such as work study or loans (proportion receiving): $9,500 (86%). Average need-based loan (excluding PLUS or other private loans): $5,215. Among students who received need-based aid, the average percentage of need met: 86%. Among students who received aid based on merit, the average award (and the proportion receiving): $8,705 (4%). The average athletic scholarship (and the proportion receiving): $0 (0%). Average amount of debt of borrowers graduating in 2003: $20,030. Proportion who borrowed: 84%. **Student employment:** During the 2003-2004 academic year, 25% of undergraduates worked on campus. Average per-year earnings: $2,457.

Mount St. Mary's College

12001 Chalon Road
Los Angeles, CA 90049
Private; www.msmc.la.edu
Financial aid office: (310) 954-4191

■ **2004-2005 TUITION AND FEES:** $21,486
■ **ROOM AND BOARD:** $8,244

SAT I Score (25th/75th percentile): 920-1090
2005 U.S. News College Ranking:
Universities–Master's (West), 15
Acceptance Rate: 63%

Other expenses: Estimated books and supplies: $936. Transportation: $649. Personal expenses: $1,604. **Financial aid:** Priority filing date for institution's financial aid form: March 1; deadline: May 15. In 2003-2004, 87% of undergraduates applied for financial aid.

National Hispanic University

14271 Story Road
San Jose, CA 95127-3823
Private; www.nhu.edu
Financial aid office: (408) 254-6900

■ **2004-2005 TUITION AND FEES:** $3,628

2005 U.S. News College Ranking:
Liberal Arts Colleges, fourth tier
Acceptance Rate: 67%

National University

11255 N. Torrey Pines Road
La Jolla, CA 92037
Private; www.nu.edu
Financial aid office: (858) 642-8512

■ **2004-2005 TUITION AND FEES:** $9,500

2005 U.S. News College Ranking:
Universities–Master's (West), unranked
Acceptance Rate: 100%

Financial aid: Priority filing date for institution's financial aid form: March 2; deadline: June 30. **Reserve Officers Training Corps (ROTC):** Navy ROTC: Offered at cooperating institution (SDSU); Air Force ROTC: Offered at cooperating institution (SDSU).

New College of California

50 Fell Street
San Francisco, CA 94102
Private; www.newcollege.edu
Financial aid office: (415) 437-3442

■ **2004-2005 TUITION AND FEES:** $12,162

2005 U.S. News College Ranking:
Universities–Master's (West), fourth tier

Notre Dame de Namur University

1500 Ralston Avenue
Belmont, CA 94002-1908
Private; www.ndnu.edu
Financial aid office: (650) 508-3509

■ **2004-2005 TUITION AND FEES:** $21,500
■ **ROOM AND BOARD:** $9,630

SAT I Score (25th/75th percentile): 870-1100
2005 U.S. News College Ranking:
Universities–Master's (West), 39
Acceptance Rate: 89%

Other expenses: Estimated books and supplies:
$1,260. Transportation: $612. Personal expenses: $1,934. **Financial aid:** In 2003-2004, 77% of undergraduates applied for financial aid. Of those, 72% were determined to have financial need; 14% had their need fully met. Average financial aid package (proportion receiving): $18,211 (72%). Average amount of gift aid, such as scholarships or grants (proportion receiving): $14,336 (71%). Average amount of self-help aid, such as work study or loans (proportion receiving): $5,019 (58%). Average need-based loan (excluding PLUS or other private loans): $3,757. Among students who received need-based aid, the average percentage of need met: 71%. Among students who received aid based on merit, the average award (and the proportion receiving): $6,953 (11%). The average athletic scholarship (and the proportion receiving): $6,863 (8%). Average amount of debt of borrowers graduating in 2003: $18,255. Proportion who borrowed: 65%. **Student employment:** During the 2003-2004 academic year, 10% of undergraduates worked on campus. Average per-year earnings: $2,000.

Occidental College

1600 Campus Road
Los Angeles, CA 90041-3314
Private; www.oxy.edu
Financial aid office: (323) 259-2548

■ **2004-2005 TUITION AND FEES:** $29,710
■ **ROOM AND BOARD:** $8,221

SAT I Score (25th/75th percentile): 1170-1370
2005 U.S. News College Ranking:
Liberal Arts Colleges, 42
Acceptance Rate: 44%

Other expenses: Estimated books and supplies: $914. Transportation: $600. Personal expenses: $1,596. **Financial aid:** Priority filing date for institution's financial aid form: February 1; deadline: February 1. In 2003-2004, 62% of undergraduates applied for financial aid. Of those, 54% were determined to have financial need; 100% had their need fully met. Average financial aid package (proportion receiving): $27,814 (61%). Average amount of gift aid, such as scholarships or grants (proportion receiving): $21,647 (54%). Average amount of self-help aid, such as work study or loans (proportion receiving): $7,123 (47%). Average need-based loan (excluding PLUS or other private loans): $5,435. Among students who received need-based aid, the average percentage of need met: 100%. Among students who received aid based on merit, the average award (and the proportion receiving): $17,292 (18%). The average athletic scholarship (and the proportion receiving): $0 (0%). Average amount of debt of borrowers graduating in 2003: $13,905. Proportion who borrowed: 61%. **Student employment:** During the 2003-2004 academic year, 10% of undergraduates worked on campus. **Reserve Officers Training Corps (ROTC):** Army ROTC: Offered at cooperating institution (University of Southern California, University of California–Los Angeles); Air Force ROTC: Offered at cooperating institution (University of Southern California, University of California–Los Angeles).

Otis College of Art and Design

9045 Lincoln Boulevard
Los Angeles, CA 90045
Private; www.otis.edu
Financial aid office: (310) 665-6880

■ **2004-2005 TUITION AND FEES:** $25,100

SAT I Score (25th/75th percentile): 880-1130
2005 U.S. News College Ranking:
Unranked Specialty School–Fine Arts
Acceptance Rate: 63%

Other expenses: Estimated books and supplies: $2,400. Transportation: $1,400. Personal expenses: $1,200. **Financial aid:** Priority filing date for institution's financial aid form: February 15. In 2003-2004, 74% of undergraduates applied for financial aid. Of those, 63% were determined to have financial need; 1% had their need fully met. Average financial aid package (proportion receiving): $12,774 (63%). Average amount of gift aid, such as scholarships or grants (proportion receiving): $8,962

(63%). Average amount of self-help aid, such as work study or loans (proportion receiving): $4,048 (56%). Average need-based loan (excluding PLUS or other private loans): $3,677. Among students who received need-based aid, the average percentage of need met: 17%. Among students who received aid based on merit, the average award (and the proportion receiving): $3,097 (10%). Average amount of debt of borrowers graduating in 2003: $25,700. Proportion who borrowed: 61%.

Pacific Union College

1 Angwin Avenue
Angwin, CA 94508
Private; www.puc.edu
Financial aid office: (707) 965-7200

■ **2004-2005 TUITION AND FEES:** $18,054
■ **ROOM AND BOARD:** $5,136

SAT I Score (25th/75th percentile): 830-1320
2005 U.S. News College Ranking:
Comp. Colleges–Bachelor's (West), 15
Acceptance Rate: 33%

Other expenses: Estimated books and supplies: $1,260. Transportation: $612. Personal expenses: $1,818. **Financial aid:** Priority filing date for institution's financial aid form: March 2. In 2003-2004, 83% of undergraduates applied for financial aid. Of those, 72% were determined to have financial need; 35% had their need fully met. Average financial aid package (proportion receiving): $10,958 (72%). Average amount of gift aid, such as scholarships or grants (proportion receiving): $6,424 (68%). Average amount of self-help aid, such as work study or loans (proportion receiving): $1,900 (71%). Average need-based loan (excluding PLUS or other private loans): $4,250. Among students who received need-based aid, the average percentage of need met: 72%. Among students who received aid based on merit, the average award (and the proportion receiving): $7,606 (2%). Average amount of debt of borrowers graduating in 2003: $13,500. Proportion who borrowed: 60%. **Student employment:** During the 2003-2004 academic year, 52% of undergraduates worked on campus. Average per-year earnings: $2,000. **Cooperative education programs:** education, social/behavioral science.

Patten College

2433 Coolidge Avenue
Oakland, CA 94601
Private; www.patten.edu
Financial aid office: (510) 261-8500

■ **2004-2005 TUITION AND FEES:** $11,520
■ **ROOM AND BOARD:** $5,800

SAT I Score (25th/75th percentile): 870-1085
2005 U.S. News College Ranking:
Comp. Colleges–Bachelor's (West), third tier
Acceptance Rate: 89%

Other expenses: Estimated books and supplies: $1,260. Transportation: $990. Personal expenses: $2,214. **Financial aid:** Priority filing date for institution's financial aid form: March 2. In 2003-2004, 88% of undergraduates applied for financial aid. Of those, 82% were determined to have financial need; 11% had their need fully met. Average financial aid package (proportion receiving): $5,580 (82%). Average amount of gift aid, such as scholarships or grants (proportion receiving): $4,640 (78%). Average amount of self-help aid, such as work study or loans (proportion receiving): $3,407 (66%). Average need-based loan (excluding PLUS or other private loans): $3,010. Among students who received need-based aid, the average percentage of need met: 34%. Among students who received aid based on merit, the average award (and the proportion receiving): $7,524 (25%). The average athletic scholarship (and the proportion receiving): $0 (0%). Average amount of debt of borrowers graduating in 2003: $19,034. Proportion who borrowed: 15%. **Student employment:** During the 2003-2004 academic year, 69% of undergraduates worked on campus. Average per-year earnings: $4,480. **Cooperative education programs:** business, health professions, other.

Pepperdine University

24255 Pacific Coast Highway
Malibu, CA 90263
Private; www.pepperdine.edu
Financial aid office: (310) 506-4301

■ **2004-2005 TUITION AND FEES:** $28,720
■ **ROOM AND BOARD:** $8,640

SAT I Score (25th/75th percentile): 1090-1300
2005 U.S. News College Ranking:
National Universities, 52
Acceptance Rate: 25%

Other expenses: Estimated books and supplies: $800. Transportation: $600. Personal expenses: $700. **Financial aid:** Priority filing date for institution's financial aid form: February 15; deadline: February 15. In 2003-2004, 64% of undergraduates applied for financial aid. Of those, 55% were determined to have financial need; 19% had their need fully met. Average financial aid package (proportion receiving): $25,169 (55%). Average amount of gift aid, such as scholarships or grants (proportion receiving): $18,482 (52%). Average amount of self-help aid, such as work study or loans (proportion receiving): $6,621 (47%). Average need-based loan (excluding PLUS or other private loans): $5,476. Among students who received need-based aid, the average percentage of need met: 88%. Among students who received aid based on merit, the average award (and the proportion receiving): $17,237 (10%). The average athletic scholarship (and the proportion receiving): $23,585 (5%). Average amount of debt of borrowers graduating in 2003: $32,102. Proportion who borrowed: 59%. **Student employment:** During the 2003-2004 academic year, 20% of undergraduates worked on campus. Average per-year earnings: $3,000. **Reserve Officers Training Corps (ROTC):** Army ROTC: Offered at cooperating institution (UCLA); Air Force ROTC: Offered at cooperating institution (USC, Loyola Marymount Univ.).

Pitzer College

1050 N. Mills Avenue
Claremont, CA 91711-6101
Private; www.pitzer.edu
Financial aid office: (909) 621-8208

■ **2004-2005 TUITION AND FEES:** $31,438
■ **ROOM AND BOARD:** $8,222

SAT I Score (25th/75th percentile): 1140-1330
2005 U.S. News College Ranking:
Liberal Arts Colleges, 59
Acceptance Rate: 50%

Other expenses: Estimated books and supplies: $950. Transportation: $300. Personal expenses: $1,000. **Financial aid:** Priority filing date for institution's financial aid form: February 1; deadline: February 1. In 2003-2004, 45% of undergraduates applied for financial aid. Of those, 42% were determined to have financial need; 100% had their need fully met. Average financial aid package (proportion receiving): $27,950 (42%). Average amount of gift aid, such as scholarships or grants (proportion receiving): $21,101 (42%). Average amount of

self-help aid, such as work study or loans (proportion receiving): $7,050 (41%). Average need-based loan (excluding PLUS or other private loans): $4,941. Among students who received need-based aid, the average percentage of need met: 100%. Among students who received aid based on merit, the average award (and the proportion receiving): $10,000 (3%). The average athletic scholarship (and the proportion receiving): $0 (0%). Average amount of debt of borrowers graduating in 2003: $20,900. Proportion who borrowed: 60%. **Student employment:** During the 2003-2004 academic year, 17% of undergraduates worked on campus. **Cooperative education programs:** business, health professions. **Reserve Officers Training Corps (ROTC):** Army ROTC: Offered at cooperating institution (Claremont McKenna College); Air Force ROTC: Offered at cooperating institution (Harvey Mudd College).

Point Loma Nazarene University

3900 Lomaland Drive
San Diego, CA 92106
Private; www.ptloma.edu
Financial aid office: (619) 849-2666

■ **2004-2005 TUITION AND FEES:** $19,540
■ **ROOM AND BOARD:** $6,940

SAT I Score (25th/75th percentile): 1040-1235
2005 U.S. News College Ranking:
Universities–Master's (West), 26
Acceptance Rate: 46%

Other expenses: Estimated books and supplies: $1,260. Transportation: $776. Personal expenses: $2,096. **Financial aid:** Priority filing date for institution's financial aid form: March 15. In 2003-2004, 70% of undergraduates applied for financial aid. Of those, 59% were determined to have financial need; 26% had their need fully met. Average financial aid package (proportion receiving): $13,791 (59%). Average amount of gift aid, such as scholarships or grants (proportion receiving): $10,018 (55%). Average amount of self-help aid, such as work study or loans (proportion receiving): $5,671 (47%). Average need-based loan (excluding PLUS or other private loans): $4,536. Among students who received need-based aid, the average percentage of need met: 71%. Among students who received aid based on merit, the average award (and the proportion receiving): $8,728 (26%). The average athletic scholarship (and the proportion receiving): $0 (0%). Average amount of debt of borrowers graduating in 2003: $11,029.

Proportion who borrowed: 76%. **Cooperative education programs:** art, business, computer science, education, health professions, home economics, humanities, natural science, social/behavioral science. **Reserve Officers Training Corps (ROTC):** Army ROTC: Offered at cooperating institution (San Diego State University); Navy ROTC: Offered at cooperating institution (University of San Diego); Air Force ROTC: Offered at cooperating institution (San Diego State University).

Pomona College

550 N. College Avenue
Claremont, CA 91711
Private; www.pomona.edu
Financial aid office: (909) 621-8205

■ **2004-2005 TUITION AND FEES:** $28,365
■ **ROOM AND BOARD:** $10,385

SAT I Score (25th/75th percentile): 1390-1520
2005 U.S. News College Ranking:
Liberal Arts Colleges, 5
Acceptance Rate: 21%

Other expenses: Estimated books and supplies: $850. Transportation: $600. Personal expenses: $1,000. **Financial aid:** Priority filing date for institution's financial aid form: February 1; deadline: February 1. In 2003-2004, 61% of undergraduates applied for financial aid. Of those, 51% were determined to have financial need; 100% had their need fully met. Average financial aid package (proportion receiving): $26,452 (51%). Average amount of gift aid, such as scholarships or grants (proportion receiving): $22,274 (51%). Average amount of self-help aid, such as work study or loans (proportion receiving): $4,178 (51%). Average need-based loan (excluding PLUS or other private loans): $2,822. Among students who received need-based aid, the average percentage of need met: 100%. Among students who received aid based on merit, the average award (and the proportion receiving): $0 (0%). The average athletic scholarship (and the proportion receiving): $0 (0%). Average amount of debt of borrowers graduating in 2003: $15,500. Proportion who borrowed: 60%.

San Diego State University

5500 Campanile Drive
San Diego, CA 92182
Public; www.sdsu.edu
Financial aid office: (619) 594-6323

■ **2004-2005 TUITION AND FEES:**
In state: $2,936; Out of state: $8,714
■ **ROOM AND BOARD:** $9,391

SAT I Score (25th/75th percentile): 970-1180
2005 U.S. News College Ranking:
National Universities, fourth tier
Acceptance Rate: 50%

Other expenses: Estimated books and supplies: $1,260. Transportation: $761. Personal expenses: $2,232. **Financial aid:** In 2003-2004, 62% of undergraduates applied for financial aid. Of those, 46% were determined to have financial need; 25% had their need fully met. Average financial aid package (proportion receiving): $8,500 (43%). Average amount of gift aid, such as scholarships or grants (proportion receiving): $4,000 (34%). Average amount of self-help aid, such as work study or loans (proportion receiving): $4,000 (39%). Average need-based loan (excluding PLUS or other private loans): $2,800. Among students who received need-based aid, the average percentage of need met: 86%. Among students who received aid based on merit, the average award (and the proportion receiving): $1,400 (1%). The average athletic scholarship (and the proportion receiving): $8,500 (2%). Average amount of debt of borrowers graduating in 2003: $13,000. Proportion who borrowed: 47%. Average per-year earnings: $3,000. **Reserve Officers Training Corps (ROTC):** Army ROTC: Offered on campus; Navy ROTC: Offered on campus; Air Force ROTC: Offered on campus.

San Francisco Art Institute

800 Chestnut Street
San Francisco, CA 94133
Private; www.sfai.edu
Financial aid office: (415) 749-4520

■ **2004-2005 TUITION AND FEES:** $24,240
■ **ROOM AND BOARD:** $9,450

2005 U.S. News College Ranking:
Unranked Specialty School–Fine Arts
Acceptance Rate: 87%

Other expenses: Estimated books and supplies: $1,800. Transportation: $405. Personal expenses: $3,220. **Student employment:** During the 2003-2004 academic year, 20% of undergraduates worked on campus. Average per-year earnings: $4,000.

San Francisco Conservatory of Music

1201 Ortega Street
San Francisco, CA 94122
Private; www.sfcm.edu
Financial aid office: (415) 759-3414

■ **2004-2005 TUITION AND FEES:** $25,080
■ **ROOM AND BOARD:** $8,100

ACT Score (25th/75th percentile): 18-27
2005 U.S. News College Ranking:
Unranked Specialty School–Fine Arts
Acceptance Rate: 56%

Other expenses: Estimated books and supplies: $580. Transportation: $950. Personal expenses: $1,900. **Financial aid:** Priority filing date for institution's financial aid form: March 1; deadline: March 1. **Student employment:** During the 2003-2004 academic year, 17% of undergraduates worked on campus. Average per-year earnings: $3,000.

San Francisco State University

1600 Holloway Avenue
San Francisco, CA 94132
Public; www.sfsu.edu
Financial aid office: (415) 338-7000

■ **2004-2005 TUITION AND FEES:**
In state: $2,498; Out of state: $10,958
■ **ROOM AND BOARD:** $7,810

SAT I Score (25th/75th percentile): 870-1130
2005 U.S. News College Ranking:
Universities–Master's (West), third tier
Acceptance Rate: 64%

Other expenses: Estimated books and supplies: $1,224. Transportation: $1,116. Personal expenses: $2,400. **Financial aid:** Priority filing date for institution's financial aid form: March 3. In 2003-2004, 55% of undergraduates applied for financial aid. Of those, 50% were determined to have financial need; 14% had their need fully met. Average financial aid package (proportion receiving): $8,638 (47%). Average amount of gift aid, such as scholarships or grants (proportion receiving): $5,280 (35%). Average amount of self-help aid, such as work study or loans (proportion receiving): $5,641 (39%). Average need-based loan (excluding PLUS or other private loans): $4,814. Among students who received need-based aid, the average percentage of need met: 69%. Among students who received aid based on merit, the average award (and the proportion receiving): $1,053 (0%). The average athletic scholarship (and the proportion receiving): $1,765 (1%). Average amount of debt of borrowers graduating in 2003: $16,088. Proportion who borrowed: 44%. **Reserve Officers Training Corps (ROTC):** Army ROTC: Offered at cooperating institution (University of San Francisco); Navy ROTC: Offered at cooperating institution (University of California, Berkeley); Air Force ROTC: Offered at cooperating institution (University of California, Berkeley).

San Jose State University

1 Washington Square
San Jose, CA 95192
Public; www.sjsu.edu
Financial aid office: (408) 283-7500

■ **2004-2005 TUITION AND FEES:**
In state: $2,944; Out of state: $12,520

SAT I Score (25th/75th percentile): 850-1100
2005 U.S. News College Ranking:
Universities–Master's (West), 44
Acceptance Rate: 52%

Student employment: During the 2003-2004 academic year, 5% of undergraduates worked on campus. Average per-year earnings: $6,000. **Cooperative education programs:** business, computer science, engineering, technologies. **Reserve Officers Training Corps (ROTC):** Army ROTC: Offered on campus; Air Force ROTC: Offered on campus.

Santa Clara University

500 El Camino Real
Santa Clara, CA 95053
Private; www.scu.edu
Financial aid office: (408) 554-4505

■ **2004-2005 TUITION AND FEES:** $27,135
■ **ROOM AND BOARD:** $9,693

SAT I Score (25th/75th percentile): 1090-1280
2005 U.S. News College Ranking:
Universities–Master's (West), 2
Acceptance Rate: 66%

Other expenses: Estimated books and supplies: $1,260. Transportation: $612. Personal expenses: $1,818. **Financial aid:** Priority filing date for institution's financial aid form: February 1. In 2003-2004, 74% of undergraduates applied for financial aid. Of those, 56% were determined to have financial need; 58% had their need fully met. Average financial aid package (proportion receiving): $17,748 (47%). Average amount of gift aid, such as scholarships or grants (proportion receiving): $14,080 (41%). Average amount of self-help aid, such as work study or loans (proportion receiving): $5,025 (36%). Average need-based loan (excluding PLUS or other private loans): $4,766. Among students who received need-based aid, the average percentage of need met: 84%. Among students who received aid based on merit, the average award (and the proportion receiving): $5,025 (11%). The average athletic scholarship (and the proportion receiving): $10,000 (4%). Average amount of debt of borrowers graduating in 2003: $25,492. Proportion who borrowed: 66%. **Student employment:** During the 2003-2004 academic year, 30% of undergraduates worked on campus. Average per-year earnings: $2,350. **Cooperative education programs:** engineering. **Reserve Officers Training Corps (ROTC):** Army ROTC: Offered on campus; Air Force ROTC: Offered at cooperating institution (San Jose State University).

Scripps College

1030 Columbia Avenue
Claremont, CA 91711
Private; www.scrippscol.edu
Financial aid office: (909) 621-8275

■ **2004-2005 TUITION AND FEES:** $29,000
■ **ROOM AND BOARD:** $9,000

SAT I Score (25th/75th percentile): 1230-1400
2005 U.S. News College Ranking:
Liberal Arts Colleges, 26
Acceptance Rate: 54%

Other expenses: Estimated books and supplies: $800. Transportation: $0. Personal expenses: $1,000. **Financial aid:** Priority filing date for institution's financial aid form: February 1. In 2003-2004, 58% of undergraduates applied for financial aid. Of those, 48% were determined to have financial need; 100% had their need fully met. Average financial aid package (proportion receiving): $24,124 (48%). Average amount of gift aid, such as scholarships or grants (proportion receiving): $19,475 (47%). Average amount of self-help aid, such as work

study or loans (proportion receiving): $4,920 (43%). Average need-based loan (excluding PLUS or other private loans): $3,720. Among students who received need-based aid, the average percentage of need met: 100%. Among students who received aid based on merit, the average award (and the proportion receiving): $14,396 (10%). The average athletic scholarship (and the proportion receiving): $0 (0%). Average amount of debt of borrowers graduating in 2003: $14,362. Proportion who borrowed: 51%. **Student employment:** During the 2003-2004 academic year, 5% of undergraduates worked on campus. Average per-year earnings: $3,600. **Reserve Officers Training Corps (ROTC):** Army ROTC: Offered at cooperating institution (Claremont McKenna College).

Simpson University

2211 College View Drive
Redding, CA 96003-8606
Private; www.simpsonuniversity.edu
Financial aid office: (530) 226-4617

■ **2004-2005 TUITION AND FEES:** $15,500
■ **ROOM AND BOARD:** $5,900

SAT I Score (25th/75th percentile): 880-1120
2005 U.S. News College Ranking:
Universities–Master's (West), third tier
Acceptance Rate: 68%

Other expenses: Estimated books and supplies: $1,120. Transportation: $544. Personal expenses: $1,616. **Financial aid:** Priority filing date for institution's financial aid form: March 2. In 2003-2004, 96% of undergraduates applied for financial aid. Of those, 87% were determined to have financial need; 5% had their need fully met. Average financial aid package (proportion receiving): $12,507 (87%). Average amount of gift aid, such as scholarships or grants (proportion receiving): $7,507 (84%). Average amount of self-help aid, such as work study or loans (proportion receiving): $6,000 (84%). Average need-based loan (excluding PLUS or other private loans): $5,000. Among students who received need-based aid, the average percentage of need met: 72%. Among students who received aid based on merit, the average award (and the proportion receiving): $3,050 (4%). The average athletic scholarship (and the proportion receiving): $0 (0%). Average amount of debt of borrowers graduating in 2003: $17,600. Proportion who borrowed: 84%. **Student employment:** During the 2003-2004 academic year, 15% of undergraduates worked on campus. Average per-year earnings: $1,900.

Sonoma State University

1801 E. Cotati Avenue
Rohnert Park, CA 94928
Public; www.sonoma.edu
Financial aid office: (707) 664-2287

■ **2004-2005 TUITION AND FEES:**
In state: $3,010; Out of state: $11,470
■ **ROOM AND BOARD:** $8,805

SAT I Score (25th/75th percentile): 940-1140
2005 U.S. News College Ranking:
Universities–Master's (West), 37
Acceptance Rate: 84%

Other expenses: Estimated books and supplies: $1,260. Transportation: $810. Personal expenses: $1,854. **Financial aid:** Priority filing date for institution's financial aid form: January 31. In 2003-2004, 56% of undergraduates applied for financial aid. Of those, 38% were determined to have financial need; 31% had their need fully met. Average financial aid package (proportion receiving): $6,838 (49%). Average amount of gift aid, such as scholarships or grants (proportion receiving): $5,005 (24%). Average amount of self-help aid, such as work study or loans (proportion receiving): $4,281 (7%). Average need-based loan (excluding PLUS or other private loans): $3,937. Among students who received need-based aid, the average percentage of need met: 68%. Among students who received aid based on merit, the average award (and the proportion receiving): $6,182 (2%). The average athletic scholarship (and the proportion receiving): $1,334 (2%). Average amount of debt of borrowers graduating in 2003: $7,848. Proportion who borrowed: 29%. **Student employment:** During the 2003-2004 academic year, 10% of undergraduates worked on campus. Average per-year earnings: $1,950. **Cooperative education programs:** natural science, social/behavioral science. **Reserve Officers Training Corps (ROTC):** Army ROTC: Offered at cooperating institution (UC San Francisco); Navy ROTC: Offered at cooperating institution (UC San Francisco); Air Force ROTC: Offered at cooperating institution (UC San Francisco).

Southern California Institute of Architecture

960 E. Third Street
Los Angeles, CA 90013
Private; www.sciarc.edu
Financial aid office: (213) 613-2200

■ **2004-2005 TUITION AND FEES:** $18,376

SAT I Score (25th/75th percentile): 1000
2005 U.S. News College Ranking:
Unranked Specialty School–Fine Arts
Acceptance Rate: 73%

Stanford University

Stanford, CA 94305
Private; www.stanford.edu
Financial aid office: (650) 723-3058

■ **2004-2005 TUITION AND FEES:** $29,847
■ **ROOM AND BOARD:** $9,503

SAT I Score (25th/75th percentile): 1340-1560
2005 U.S. News College Ranking:
National Universities, 5
Acceptance Rate: 13%

Other expenses: Estimated books and supplies: $1,215. Transportation: $630. Personal expenses: $1,815. **Financial aid:** Priority filing date for institution's financial aid form: February 1. In 2003-2004, 57% of undergraduates applied for financial aid. Of those, 49% were determined to have financial need; 92% had their need fully met. Average financial aid package (proportion receiving): $27,000 (48%). Average amount of gift aid, such as scholarships or grants (proportion receiving): $23,000 (47%). Average amount of self-help aid, such as work study or loans (proportion receiving): $3,895 (35%). Average need-based loan (excluding PLUS or other private loans): $2,600. Among students who received need-based aid, the average percentage of need met: 100%. Among students who received aid based on merit, the average award (and the proportion receiving): $2,800 (10%). The average athletic scholarship (and the proportion receiving): $28,000 (5%). Average amount of debt of borrowers graduating in 2003: $16,045. Proportion who borrowed: 44%. **Reserve Officers Training Corps (ROTC):** Army ROTC: Offered at cooperating institution (Santa Clara University); Navy ROTC: Offered at cooperating institution (University of California–Berkeley); Air Force ROTC: Offered at cooperating institution (San Jose University).

St. Mary's College of California

1928 St. Mary's Road
Moraga, CA 94556
Private; www.stmarys-ca.edu
Financial aid office: (925) 631-4370

■ **2004-2005 TUITION AND FEES:** $23,470
■ **ROOM AND BOARD:** $9,530

SAT I Score (25th/75th percentile): 1020-1200
2005 U.S. News College Ranking:
Universities–Master's (West), 9
Acceptance Rate: 82%

Other expenses: Estimated books and supplies: $1,098. Transportation: $612. Personal expenses: $1,818. **Financial aid:** Priority filing date for institution's financial aid form: March 2; deadline: March 2. In 2003-2004, 69% of undergraduates applied for financial aid. Of those, 63% were determined to have financial need; 29% had their need fully met. Average financial aid package (proportion receiving): $20,460 (62%). Average amount of gift aid, such as scholarships or grants (proportion receiving): $15,625 (55%). Average amount of self-help aid, such as work study or loans (proportion receiving): $5,957 (61%). Average need-based loan (excluding PLUS or other private loans): $4,303. Among students who received need-based aid, the average percentage of need met: 76%. Among students who received aid based on merit, the average award (and the proportion receiving): $7,944 (3%). The average athletic scholarship (and the proportion receiving): $17,566 (4%). Average amount of debt of borrowers graduating in 2003: $21,165. Proportion who borrowed: 62%. **Student employment:** During the 2003-2004 academic year, 13% of undergraduates worked on campus. Average per-year earnings: $4,320. **Reserve Officers Training Corps (ROTC):** Army ROTC: Offered at cooperating institution (University of California–Berkeley); Air Force ROTC: Offered at cooperating institution (University of California–Berkeley).

Thomas Aquinas College

10000 N. Ojai Road
Santa Paula, CA 93060-9621
Private; www.thomasaquinas.edu
Financial aid office: (805) 525-4417

■ **2004-2005 TUITION AND FEES:** $17,700
■ **ROOM AND BOARD:** $5,500

SAT I Score (25th/75th percentile): 1193-1368
2005 U.S. News College Ranking:
Liberal Arts Colleges, 89
Acceptance Rate: 78%

Other expenses: Estimated books and supplies: $450. Transportation: $612. Personal expenses: $400. **Financial aid:** In 2003-2004, 75% of undergraduates applied for financial aid. Of those, 67% were determined to have financial need; 100% had their need fully met. Average financial aid package (proportion receiving): $14,936 (67%). Average amount of gift aid, such as scholarships or grants (proportion receiving): $10,124 (61%). Average amount of self-help aid, such as work study or loans (proportion receiving): $5,696 (66%). Average need-based loan (excluding PLUS or other private loans): $3,408. Among students who received need-based aid, the average percentage of need met: 100%. Among students who received aid based on merit, the average award (and the proportion receiving): $2,960 (2%). The average athletic scholarship (and the proportion receiving): $0 (0%). Average amount of debt of borrowers graduating in 2003: $13,250. Proportion who borrowed: 83%.

University of California–Berkeley

110 Sproul Hall
Berkeley, CA 94720
Public; www.berkeley.edu
Financial aid office: (510) 642-6442

■ **2004-2005 TUITION AND FEES:**
In state: $5,754; Out of state: $22,710
■ **ROOM AND BOARD:** $11,629

SAT I Score (25th/75th percentile): 1190-1440
2005 U.S. News College Ranking:
National Universities, 21
Acceptance Rate: 24%

Other expenses: Estimated books and supplies: $1,240. Transportation: $640. Personal expenses: $1,997. **Financial aid:** Priority filing date for institution's financial aid form: March 2; deadline: March 2. In 2003-2004, 62% of undergraduates applied for financial aid. Of those, 50% were determined to have financial need; 50% had their need fully met. Average financial aid package (proportion receiving): $13,481 (50%). Average amount of gift aid, such as scholarships or grants (proportion receiving): $9,441 (49%). Average amount of self-help aid, such as work study or loans (proportion receiving): $5,465 (38%). Average need-based loan (excluding

PLUS or other private loans): $4,648. Among students who received need-based aid, the average percentage of need met: 89%. Among students who received aid based on merit, the average award (and the proportion receiving): $3,066 (6%). The average athletic scholarship (and the proportion receiving): $10,089 (2%). Average amount of debt of borrowers graduating in 2003: $16,354. Proportion who borrowed: 33%. **Reserve Officers Training Corps (ROTC):** Army ROTC: Offered on campus; Navy ROTC: Offered on campus; Air Force ROTC: Offered on campus.

University of California–Davis

1 Shields Avenue
Davis, CA 95616
Public; www.ucdavis.edu
Financial aid office: (530) 752-2390

■ **2004-2005 TUITION AND FEES:**
In state: $6,351; Out of state: $23,307
■ **ROOM AND BOARD:** $10,234

SAT I Score (25th/75th percentile): 1080-1300
2005 U.S. News College Ranking:
National Universities, 42
Acceptance Rate: 60%

Other expenses: Estimated books and supplies: $1,414. Transportation: $699. Personal expenses: $1,881. **Financial aid:** Priority filing date for institution's financial aid form: March 2. In 2003-2004, 60% of undergraduates applied for financial aid. Of those, 48% were determined to have financial need; 12% had their need fully met. Average financial aid package (proportion receiving): $9,864 (47%). Average amount of gift aid, such as scholarships or grants (proportion receiving): $6,965 (45%). Average amount of self-help aid, such as work study or loans (proportion receiving): $4,402 (34%). Average need-based loan (excluding PLUS or other private loans): $4,248. Among students who received need-based aid, the average percentage of need met: 76%. Among students who received aid based on merit, the average award (and the proportion receiving): $2,179 (7%). The average athletic scholarship (and the proportion receiving): $0 (0%). **Student employment:** During the 2003-2004 academic year, 12% of undergraduates worked on campus. Average per-year earnings: $2,745. **Cooperative education programs:** education, health professions. **Reserve Officers Training Corps (ROTC):** Army ROTC: Offered on campus; Navy ROTC: Offered at cooperating institution (University of California–Berkeley); Air Force ROTC: Offered at cooperating institution (CSU - Sacramento).

University of California–Irvine

Irvine, CA 92697
Public; www.uci.edu
Financial aid office: (949) 824-5337

■ **2004-2005 TUITION AND FEES:**
In state: $6,895; Out of state: $23,851
■ **ROOM AND BOARD:** $8,768

SAT I Score (25th/75th percentile): 1086-1295
2005 U.S. News College Ranking:
National Universities, 43
Acceptance Rate: 54%

Other expenses: Estimated books and supplies: $1,523. Transportation: $1,193. Personal expenses: $2,097. **Financial aid:** Priority filing date for institution's financial aid form: March 2; deadline: May 1. In 2003-2004, 62% of undergraduates applied for financial aid. Of those, 50% were determined to have financial need; 22% had their need fully met. Average financial aid package (proportion receiving): $11,251 (49%). Average amount of gift aid, such as scholarships or grants (proportion receiving): $7,987 (48%). Average amount of self-help aid, such as work study or loans (proportion receiving): $4,601 (38%). Average need-based loan (excluding PLUS or other private loans): $4,554. Among students who received need-based aid, the average percentage of need met: 83%. Among students who received aid based on merit, the average award (and the proportion receiving): $5,965 (4%). The average athletic scholarship (and the proportion receiving): $7,163 (1%). **Reserve Officers Training Corps (ROTC):** Army ROTC: Offered at cooperating institution (Univ. of Southern California, Claremont Colleges, Extension Office at Cal State University Fullerton); Air Force ROTC: Offered at cooperating institution (Loyola Marymount University, UC Los Angeles, University of Southern California).

University of California–Los Angeles

405 Hilgard Avenue
Los Angeles, CA 90095
Public; www.ucla.edu
Financial aid office: (310) 206-0400

■ **2004-2005 TUITION AND FEES:**
In state: $6,585; Out of state: $23,541
■ **ROOM AND BOARD:** $11,187

SAT I Score (25th/75th percentile): 1160-1410
2005 U.S. News College Ranking:
National Universities, 25
Acceptance Rate: 24%

Other expenses: Estimated books and supplies: $1,452. Transportation: $714. Personal expenses: $1,419. **Financial aid:** Priority filing date for institution's financial aid form: March 2. In 2003-2004, 66% of undergraduates applied for financial aid. Of those, 54% were determined to have financial need; 46% had their need fully met. Average financial aid package (proportion receiving): $12,122 (54%). Average amount of gift aid, such as scholarships or grants (proportion receiving): $8,474 (52%). Average amount of self-help aid, such as work study or loans (proportion receiving): $5,155 (41%). Average need-based loan (excluding PLUS or other private loans): $5,198. Among students who received need-based aid, the average percentage of need met: 82%. Among students who received aid based on merit, the average award (and the proportion receiving): $3,680 (4%). The average athletic scholarship (and the proportion receiving): $11,488 (1%). Average amount of debt of borrowers graduating in 2003: $12,830. Proportion who borrowed: 44%. **Cooperative education programs:** engineering. **Reserve Officers Training Corps (ROTC):** Army ROTC: Offered on campus; Navy ROTC: Offered on campus; Air Force ROTC: Offered on campus.

University of California–Riverside

900 University Avenue
Riverside, CA 92521
Public; www.ucr.edu
Financial aid office: (909) 787-3878

■ **2004-2005 TUITION AND FEES:**
   In state: $5,931; Out of state: $24,095
■ **ROOM AND BOARD:** $9,800

SAT I Score (25th/75th percentile): 960-1190
2005 U.S. News College Ranking:
National Universities, 81
Acceptance Rate: 79%

Other expenses: Estimated books and supplies: $1,600. Transportation: $1,300. Personal expenses: $2,143. **Financial aid:** Priority filing date for institution's financial aid form: March 2; deadline: March 2. In 2003-2004, 75% of undergraduates applied for financial aid. Of those, 63% were determined to have financial need; 46% had their need fully met. Average

financial aid package (proportion receiving): $11,310 (62%). Average amount of gift aid, such as scholarships or grants (proportion receiving): $7,514 (60%). Average amount of self-help aid, such as work study or loans (proportion receiving): $5,139 (49%). Average need-based loan (excluding PLUS or other private loans): $4,836. Among students who received need-based aid, the average percentage of need met: 84%. Among students who received aid based on merit, the average award (and the proportion receiving): $4,966 (1%). The average athletic scholarship (and the proportion receiving): $7,818 (1%). Average amount of debt of borrowers graduating in 2003: $13,414. Proportion who borrowed: 72%. **Student employment:** During the 2003-2004 academic year, 12% of undergraduates worked on campus. Average per-year earnings: $2,135. **Cooperative education programs:** agriculture, art, business, computer science, education, engineering, health professions, humanities, natural science, social/behavioral science, technologies. **Reserve Officers Training Corps (ROTC):** Army ROTC: Offered at cooperating institution (Claremont McKenna College/California State University, San Bernardino); Air Force ROTC: Offered at cooperating institution (California State University, San Bernardino).

University of California–San Diego

9500 Gilman Drive
La Jolla, CA 92093
Public; www.ucsd.edu
Financial aid office: (858) 534-4480

■ **2004-2005 TUITION AND FEES:**
   In state: $6,851; Out of state: $23,807
■ **ROOM AND BOARD:** $8,996

SAT I Score (25th/75th percentile): 1150-1360
2005 U.S. News College Ranking:
National Universities, 35
Acceptance Rate: 41%

Other expenses: Estimated books and supplies: $1,407. Transportation: $1,025. Personal expenses: $2,096. **Financial aid:** Priority filing date for institution's financial aid form: March 2. In 2003-2004, 62% of undergraduates applied for financial aid. Of those, 51% were determined to have financial need; 49% had their need fully met. Average financial aid package (proportion receiving): $12,420 (49%). Average amount of gift aid, such as scholarships or grants (proportion receiving): $8,137 (47%). Average amount of self-help aid, such as

work study or loans (proportion receiving): $5,515 (40%). Average need-based loan (excluding PLUS or other private loans): $4,761. Among students who received need-based aid, the average percentage of need met: 87%. Among students who received aid based on merit, the average award (and the proportion receiving): $5,875 (3%). The average athletic scholarship (and the proportion receiving): $0 (0%). Average amount of debt of borrowers graduating in 2003: $14,192. Proportion who borrowed: 54%. **Student employment:** During the 2003-2004 academic year, 25% of undergraduates worked on campus. Average per-year earnings: $3,500.

University of California–Santa Barbara

Santa Barbara, CA 93106
Public; www.ucsb.edu
Financial aid office: (805) 893-2432

■ **2004-2005 TUITION AND FEES:**
   In state: $6,137; Out of state: $23,093
■ **ROOM AND BOARD:** $10,183

SAT I Score (25th/75th percentile): 1080-1300
2005 U.S. News College Ranking:
National Universities, 45
Acceptance Rate: 50%

Other expenses: Estimated books and supplies: $1,405. Transportation: $974. Personal expenses: $2,005. **Financial aid:** Priority filing date for institution's financial aid form: March 2; deadline: May 31. In 2003-2004, 62% of undergraduates applied for financial aid. Of those, 47% were determined to have financial need; 34% had their need fully met. Average financial aid package (proportion receiving): $11,439 (45%). Average amount of gift aid, such as scholarships or grants (proportion receiving): $7,429 (43%). Average amount of self-help aid, such as work study or loans (proportion receiving): $5,487 (37%). Average need-based loan (excluding PLUS or other private loans): $5,274. Among students who received need-based aid, the average percentage of need met: 81%. Among students who received aid based on merit, the average award (and the proportion receiving): $3,913 (2%). The average athletic scholarship (and the proportion receiving): $7,100 (1%). **Student employment:** During the 2003-2004 academic year, 17% of undergraduates worked on campus. **Reserve Officers Training Corps (ROTC):** Army ROTC: Offered on campus.

University of California–Santa Cruz

1156 High Street
Santa Cruz, CA 95064
Public; www.ucsc.edu
Financial aid office: (831) 459-4342

■ **2004-2005 TUITION AND FEES:**
  In state: $6,660; Out of state: $23,613
■ **ROOM AND BOARD:** $10,107

SAT I Score (25th/75th percentile): 1030-1260
2005 U.S. News College Ranking:
National Universities, 74
Acceptance Rate: 80%

....

Other expenses: Estimated books and supplies:
$1,302. Transportation: $813. Personal expenses: $1,362. **Financial aid:** Priority filing date for institution's financial aid form: March 2; deadline: March 2. In 2003-2004, 61% of undergraduates applied for financial aid. Of those, 47% were determined to have financial need; 56% had their need fully met. Average financial aid package (proportion receiving): $12,999 (45%). Average amount of gift aid, such as scholarships or grants (proportion receiving): $8,744 (43%). Average amount of self-help aid, such as work study or loans (proportion receiving): $5,363 (40%). Average need-based loan (excluding PLUS or other private loans): $4,284. Among students who received need-based aid, the average percentage of need met: 91%. Among students who received aid based on merit, the average award (and the proportion receiving): $4,975 (3%). The average athletic scholarship (and the proportion receiving): $0 (0%). Average amount of debt of borrowers graduating in 2003: $13,116. Proportion who borrowed: 54%. **Student employment:** During the 2003-2004 academic year, 28% of undergraduates worked on campus. Average per-year earnings: $1,687. **Reserve Officers Training Corps (ROTC):** Army ROTC: Offered at cooperating institution (Santa Clara University); Air Force ROTC: Offered at cooperating institution (UC Berkeley).

University of Judaism

15600 Mulholland Drive
Bel Air, CA 90077
Private; www.uj.edu
Financial aid office: (310) 476-9777

■ **2004-2005 TUITION AND FEES:** $18,250
■ **ROOM AND BOARD:** $10,060

SAT I Score (25th/75th percentile): 1030-1170
2005 U.S. News College Ranking:
Liberal Arts Colleges, third tier
Acceptance Rate: 87%

....

Student employment: During the 2003-2004 academic year, 45% of undergraduates worked on campus. Average per-year earnings: $2,500.

University of La Verne

1950 Third Street
La Verne, CA 91750
Private; www.ulv.edu
Financial aid office: (909) 593-3511

■ **2004-2005 TUITION AND FEES:** $21,500
■ **ROOM AND BOARD:** $8,510

SAT I Score (25th/75th percentile): 900-1090
2005 U.S. News College Ranking:
National Universities, third tier
Acceptance Rate: 56%

....

Other expenses: Estimated books and supplies: $1,224. Transportation: $594. Personal expenses: $1,872. **Financial aid:** Priority filing date for institution's financial aid form: March 2. In 2003-2004, 88% of undergraduates applied for financial aid. Of those, 81% were determined to have financial need; 30% had their need fully met. Average financial aid package (proportion receiving): $24,188 (81%). Average amount of gift aid, such as scholarships or grants (proportion receiving): $10,027 (76%). Average amount of self-help aid, such as work study or loans (proportion receiving): $5,171 (66%). Average need-based loan (excluding PLUS or other private loans): $5,413. Among students who received need-based aid, the average percentage of need met: 85%. Among students who received aid based on merit, the average award (and the proportion receiving): $7,144 (11%). The average athletic scholarship (and the proportion receiving): $0 (0%). **Student employment:** During the 2003-2004 academic year, 19% of undergraduates worked on campus. Average per-year earnings: $1,800.

University of Redlands

PO Box 3080
Redlands, CA 92373
Private; www.redlands.edu
Financial aid office: (909) 335-4047

■ **2004-2005 TUITION AND FEES:** $25,544
■ **ROOM AND BOARD:** $8,690

SAT I Score (25th/75th percentile): 1060-1240
2005 U.S. News College Ranking:
Universities–Master's (West), 5
Acceptance Rate: 71%

....

Other expenses: Estimated books and supplies: $1,000. Personal expenses: $2,300. **Financial aid:** Priority filing date for institution's financial aid form: February 15. In 2003-2004, 84% of undergraduates applied for financial aid. Of those, 69% were determined to have financial need; 40% had their need fully met. Average financial aid package (proportion receiving): $23,120 (69%). Average amount of gift aid, such as scholarships or grants (proportion receiving): $13,162 (68%). Average amount of self-help aid, such as work study or loans (proportion receiving): $6,029 (65%). Average need-based loan (excluding PLUS or other private loans): $4,926. Among students who received need-based aid, the average percentage of need met: 90%. Among students who received aid based on merit, the average award (and the proportion receiving): $9,525 (6%). The average athletic scholarship (and the proportion receiving): $0 (0%). Average amount of debt of borrowers graduating in 2003: $22,358. Proportion who borrowed: 70%. **Student employment:** During the 2003-2004 academic year, 45% of undergraduates worked on campus. Average per-year earnings: $1,287. **Reserve Officers Training Corps (ROTC):** Army ROTC: Offered at cooperating institution (CSUSB); Navy ROTC: Offered at cooperating institution; Air Force ROTC: Offered at cooperating institution.

University of San Diego

5998 Alcala Park
San Diego, CA 92110-2492
Private; www.SanDiego.edu
Financial aid office: (619) 260-4514

■ **2004-2005 TUITION AND FEES:** $25,064
■ **ROOM AND BOARD:** $11,260

SAT I Score (25th/75th percentile): 1060-1270
2005 U.S. News College Ranking:
National Universities, 106
Acceptance Rate: 51%

....

Other expenses: Estimated books and supplies: $1,260. Transportation: $612. Personal expenses: $1,814. **Financial aid:** Priority filing date for institution's financial aid form: February 20. In 2003-2004, 61% of undergraduates applied for financial aid. Of those, 52% were determined to have financial need; 50% had their need fully met. Average financial aid package (proportion receiving): $21,295 (52%). Average amount of gift aid, such as scholarships or grants (proportion receiving): $15,830 (51%). Average amount of self-help aid, such as work study or loans (proportion receiving): $5,707 (43%). Average need-based loan (excluding PLUS or other private loans): $4,741. Among students who received need-based aid, the average percentage of need met: 94%. Among students who received aid based on merit, the average award (and the proportion receiving): $11,712 (13%). The average athletic scholarship (and the proportion receiving): $15,403 (3%). Average amount of debt of borrowers graduating in 2003: $26,559. Proportion who borrowed: 43%. **Student employment:** During the 2003-2004 academic year, 18% of undergraduates worked on campus. Average per-year earnings: $2,912. **Reserve Officers Training Corps (ROTC):** Army ROTC: Offered at cooperating institution (San Diego State University); Navy ROTC: Offered on campus; Air Force ROTC: Offered at cooperating institution (San Diego State University).

University of San Francisco

Ignatian Heights
San Francisco, CA 94117-1080
Private; www.usfca.edu
Financial aid office: (415) 422-2620

■ **2004-2005 TUITION AND FEES:** $24,920
■ **ROOM AND BOARD:** $9,780

SAT I Score (25th/75th percentile): 1030-1240
2005 U.S. News College Ranking:
National Universities, 111
Acceptance Rate: 82%

Other expenses: Estimated books and supplies: $900. Transportation: $800. Personal expenses: $2,400. **Financial aid:** Priority filing date for institution's financial aid form: February 15. In 2003-2004, 66% of undergraduates applied for financial aid. Of those, 61% were determined to have financial need; 12% had their need fully met. Average financial aid package (proportion receiving): $19,440 (60%). Average amount of gift aid, such as scholarships or grants (proportion receiving): $13,635 (50%). Average amount of self-help aid, such as work study or loans (proportion receiving): $6,081 (53%). Average need-based loan (excluding PLUS or other private loans): $4,989. Among students who received need-based aid, the average percentage of need met: 72%. Among students who received aid based on merit, the average award (and the proportion receiving): $13,247 (4%). The average athletic scholarship (and the pro-

portion receiving): $20,195 (4%). Average amount of debt of borrowers graduating in 2003: $22,075. Proportion who borrowed: 61%. **Student employment:** During the 2003-2004 academic year, 9% of undergraduates worked on campus. Average per-year earnings: $2,900. **Reserve Officers Training Corps (ROTC):** Army ROTC: Offered on campus; Air Force ROTC: Offered at cooperating institution (University of California–Berkeley).

University of Southern California

University Park
Los Angeles, CA 90089
Private; www.usc.edu
Financial aid office: (213) 740-5445

■ **2004-2005 TUITION AND FEES:** $30,512
■ **ROOM AND BOARD:** $8,998

SAT I Score (25th/75th percentile): 1250-1420
2005 U.S. News College Ranking:
National Universities, 30
Acceptance Rate: 30%

Other expenses: Estimated books and supplies: $650. Transportation: $580. Personal expenses: $1,634. **Financial aid:** Priority filing date for institution's financial aid form: March 1. In 2003-2004, 58% of undergraduates applied for financial aid. Of those, 48% were determined to have financial need; 92% had their need fully met. Average financial aid package (proportion receiving): $26,465 (48%). Average amount of gift aid, such as scholarships or grants (proportion receiving): $20,414 (43%). Average amount of self-help aid, such as work study or loans (proportion receiving): $7,149 (45%). Average need-based loan (excluding PLUS or other private loans): $5,363. Among students who received need-based aid, the average percentage of need met: 100%. Among students who received aid based on merit, the average award (and the proportion receiving): $11,318 (17%). The average athletic scholarship (and the proportion receiving): $29,232 (2%). Average amount of debt of borrowers graduating in 2003: $19,176. Proportion who borrowed: 60%. **Cooperative education programs:** engineering. **Reserve Officers Training Corps (ROTC):** Army ROTC: Offered on campus; Navy ROTC: Offered on campus; Air Force ROTC: Offered on campus.

University of the Pacific

3601 Pacific Avenue
Stockton, CA 95211
Private; www.pacific.edu
Financial aid office: (209) 946-2421

■ **2004-2005 TUITION AND FEES:** $24,750
■ **ROOM AND BOARD:** $7,858

SAT I Score (25th/75th percentile): 1050-1278
2005 U.S. News College Ranking:
National Universities, 111
Acceptance Rate: 71%

Other expenses: Estimated books and supplies: $1,260. Transportation: $612. Personal expenses: $1,818. **Financial aid:** Priority filing date for institution's financial aid form: February 15. In 2003-2004, 77% of undergraduates applied for financial aid. Of those, 69% were determined to have financial need; 35% had their need fully met. Average financial aid package (proportion receiving): $22,096 (68%). Average amount of gift aid, such as scholarships or grants (proportion receiving): $17,379 (66%). Average amount of self-help aid, such as work study or loans (proportion receiving): $5,691 (63%). Average need-based loan (excluding PLUS or other private loans): $4,721. Among students who received aid based on merit, the average award (and the proportion receiving): $7,766 (10%). The average athletic scholarship (and the proportion receiving): $16,983 (6%). **Cooperative education programs:** business, education, engineering, health professions.

Vanguard University of Southern California

55 Fair Drive
Costa Mesa, CA 92626
Private; www.vanguard.edu
Financial aid office: (714) 556-3610

■ **2004-2005 TUITION AND FEES:** $18,828
■ **ROOM AND BOARD:** $6,060

SAT I Score (25th/75th percentile): 880-1130
2005 U.S. News College Ranking:
Comp. Colleges–Bachelor's (West), 10
Acceptance Rate: 80%

Other expenses: Estimated books and supplies: $1,224. Transportation: $594. Personal expenses: $1,872. **Financial aid:** Priority filing date for institution's financial aid form: March 2. In 2003-2004, 99% of undergraduates applied for financial aid. Of those, 77% were determined to have financial need; 22% had their need fully met. Average financial aid package (proportion receiving): $9,700 (77%). Average amount of gift aid, such as scholarships or grants (proportion receiving): $7,400 (77%). Average amount of self-help aid, such as work study or loans (proportion receiving): $3,277 (55%). Average need-based loan (excluding PLUS or other private loans): $4,281. Among students who received need-based aid, the average percentage of need met: 68%. Among students who received aid based on merit, the average award (and the proportion receiving): $4,051 (22%). The average athletic scholarship (and the proportion receiving): $12,858 (5%). Average amount of debt of borrowers graduating in 2003: $17,500. Proportion who borrowed: 75%. **Student employment:** During the 2003-2004 academic year, 20% of undergraduates worked on campus. Average per-year earnings: $2,300. **Reserve Officers Training Corps (ROTC):** Air Force ROTC: Offered at cooperating institution (Loyola Marymount).

Westmont College

995 La Paz Road
Santa Barbara, CA 93108
Private; www.westmont.edu
Financial aid office: (805) 565-6063

■ **2004-2005 TUITION AND FEES:** $26,240
■ **ROOM AND BOARD:** $8,610

SAT I Score (25th/75th percentile): 1100-1320
2005 U.S. News College Ranking:
Liberal Arts Colleges, third tier
Acceptance Rate: 85%

Other expenses: Estimated books and supplies: $1,260. Transportation: $612. Personal expenses: $1,818. **Financial aid:** Priority filing date for institution's financial aid form: March 1. In 2003-2004, 64% of undergraduates applied for financial aid. Of those, 56% were determined to have financial need; 8% had their need fully met. Average financial aid package (proportion receiving): $16,571 (56%). Average amount of gift aid, such as scholarships or grants (proportion receiving): $11,356 (56%). Average amount

of self-help aid, such as work study or loans (proportion receiving): $6,108 (49%). Average need-based loan (excluding PLUS or other private loans): $5,317. Among students who received need-based aid, the average percentage of need met: 68%. Among students who received aid based on merit, the average award (and the proportion receiving): $8,450 (30%). The average athletic scholarship (and the proportion receiving): $5,875 (4%). Average amount of debt of borrowers graduating in 2003: $19,548. Proportion who borrowed: 80%. **Student employment:** During the 2003-2004 academic year, 35% of undergraduates worked on campus. Average per-year earnings: $1,000. **Reserve Officers Training Corps (ROTC):** Army ROTC: Offered at cooperating institution (U.C. Santa Barbara); Air Force ROTC: Offered at cooperating institution (Loyola Marymount University).

Whittier College

13406 Philadelphia Street, PO Box 634
Whittier, CA 90608
Private; www.whittier.edu
Financial aid office: (562) 907-4285

■ **2004-2005 TUITION AND FEES:** $24,768
■ **ROOM AND BOARD:** $7,698

SAT I Score (25th/75th percentile): 970-1210
2005 U.S. News College Ranking:
Liberal Arts Colleges, third tier
Acceptance Rate: 88%

Other expenses: Estimated books and supplies: $656. Transportation: $584. Personal expenses: $1,380. **Financial aid:** Priority filing date for institution's financial aid form: February 1; deadline: March 2. In 2003-2004, 96% of undergraduates applied for financial aid. Average financial aid package (proportion receiving): $25,619 (69%). Average amount of gift aid, such as scholarships or grants (proportion receiving): $12,005 (56%). Average amount of self-help aid, such as work study or loans (proportion receiving): N/A (64%). Among students who received need-based aid, the average percentage of need met: 100%. Average amount of debt of borrowers graduating in

2003: $22,104. Proportion who borrowed: 93%. **Student employment:** During the 2003-2004 academic year, 7% of undergraduates worked on campus. Average per-year earnings: $676. **Reserve Officers Training Corps (ROTC):** Army ROTC: Offered at cooperating institution (USC, Cal State Fullerton, Loyola Marymount); Navy ROTC: Offered at cooperating institution (USC, Cal State Fullerton, Loyola Marymount); Air Force ROTC: Offered at cooperating institution (USC, Cal State Fullerton, Loyola Marymount).

Woodbury University

7500 Glenoaks Boulevard
Burbank, CA 91510
Private; www.woodbury.edu
Financial aid office: (818) 767-0888

■ **2004-2005 TUITION AND FEES:** $21,214
■ **ROOM AND BOARD:** $7,327

SAT I Score (25th/75th percentile): 967
2005 U.S. News College Ranking:
Universities–Master's (West), third tier
Acceptance Rate: 77%

Other expenses: Estimated books and supplies: $1,260. Transportation: $612. Personal expenses: $1,872. **Financial aid:** Priority filing date for institution's financial aid form: March 2. In 2003-2004, 92% of undergraduates applied for financial aid. Of those, 65% were determined to have financial need; 5% had their need fully met. Average financial aid package (proportion receiving): $15,369 (65%). Average amount of gift aid, such as scholarships or grants (proportion receiving): $11,938 (63%). Average amount of self-help aid, such as work study or loans (proportion receiving): $4,494 (55%). Average need-based loan (excluding PLUS or other private loans): $4,041. Among students who received need-based aid, the average percentage of need met: 61%. Among students who received aid based on merit, the average award (and the proportion receiving): $8,481 (17%). The average athletic scholarship (and the proportion receiving): $0 (0%). **Student employment:** During the 2003-2004 academic year, 10% of undergraduates worked on campus. Average per-year earnings: $2,000.

Colorado

Adams State College

208 Edgemont Boulevard
Alamosa, CO 81102
Public; www.adams.edu
Financial aid office: (719) 587-7306

- **2004-2005 TUITION AND FEES:**
  In state: $1,818; Out of state: $7,510
- **ROOM AND BOARD:** $5,920

ACT Score (25th/75th percentile): 17-22
2005 U.S. News College Ranking:
Universities–Master's (West), fourth tier
Acceptance Rate: 75%

Financial aid: Priority filing date for institution's financial aid form: March 1; deadline: April 15. In 2003-2004, 84% of undergraduates applied for financial aid. Of those, 70% were determined to have financial need; 60% had their need fully met. Average financial aid package (proportion receiving): $4,586 (69%). Average amount of gift aid, such as scholarships or grants (proportion receiving): $4,127 (63%). Average amount of self-help aid, such as work study or loans (proportion receiving): $3,055 (53%). Average need-based loan (excluding PLUS or other private loans): $3,568. Among students who received need-based aid, the average percentage of need met: 88%. Among students who received aid based on merit, the average award (and the proportion receiving): $1,824 (25%). The average athletic scholarship (and the proportion receiving): $2,652 (6%). Average amount of debt of borrowers graduating in 2003: $15,975. Proportion who borrowed: 66%.

Colorado Christian University

180 S. Garrison Street
Lakewood, CO 80226
Private; www.ccu.edu
Financial aid office: (303) 963-3230

- **2004-2005 TUITION AND FEES:** $15,950
- **ROOM AND BOARD:** $6,700

ACT Score (25th/75th percentile): 21-26
2005 U.S. News College Ranking:
Universities–Master's (West), third tier
Acceptance Rate: 76%

Financial aid: Priority filing date for institution's financial aid form: March 15. **Student employment:** During the 2003-2004 academic year, 5% of undergraduates worked on campus. Average per-year earnings: $1,500. **Cooperative education programs:** art. **Reserve Officers Training Corps (ROTC):** Army ROTC: Offered at cooperating institution (University of Colorado at Boulder); Air Force ROTC: Offered at cooperating institution (University of Colorado at Boulder).

Colorado College

14 E. Cache La Poudre Street
Colorado Springs, CO 80903
Private; www.ColoradoCollege.edu
Financial aid office: (719) 389-6651

- **2004-2005 TUITION AND FEES:** $29,009
- **ROOM AND BOARD:** $7,216

SAT I Score (25th/75th percentile): 1160-1360
2005 U.S. News College Ranking:
Liberal Arts Colleges, 33
Acceptance Rate: 56%

Other expenses: Estimated books and supplies: $844. Transportation: $720. Personal expenses: $900. **Financial aid:** Priority filing date for institution's financial aid form: February 15. In 2003-2004, 50% of undergraduates applied for financial aid. Of those, 45% were determined to have financial need; 54% had their need fully met. Average financial aid package (proportion receiving): $23,278 (45%). Average amount of gift aid, such as scholarships or grants (proportion receiving): $19,275 (43%). Average amount of self-help aid, such as work study or loans (proportion receiving): $4,717 (41%). Average need-based loan (excluding PLUS or other private loans): $3,866. Among students who received need-based aid, the average percentage of need met: 92%. Among students who received aid based on merit, the average award (and the proportion receiving): $16,100 (14%). The average athletic scholarship (and the proportion receiving): $27,999 (2%). Average amount of debt of borrowers graduating in 2003: $13,850. Proportion who borrowed: 41%. **Student employment:** During the 2003-2004 academic year, 22% of undergraduates worked on campus. Average per-year earnings: $2,000. **Cooperative education programs:** engineering.

Reserve Officers Training Corps (ROTC): Army ROTC: Offered at cooperating institution (University of Colorado at Colorado Springs).

Colorado School of Mines

1600 Maple Street, Undergraduate Admissions
Golden, CO 80401
Public; www.mines.edu
Financial aid office: (303) 273-3220

- **2004-2005 TUITION AND FEES:**
  In state: $6,747; Out of state: $20,744
- **ROOM AND BOARD:** $6,350

ACT Score (25th/75th percentile): 25-30
2005 U.S. News College Ranking:
Unranked Specialty School–Engineering
Acceptance Rate: 79%

Other expenses: Estimated books and supplies: $1,300. Transportation: $0. Personal expenses: $1,800. **Financial aid:** Priority filing date for institution's financial aid form: March 1. In 2003-2004, 75% of undergraduates applied for financial aid. Of those, 70% were determined to have financial need; 80% had their need fully met. Average financial aid package (proportion receiving): $13,100 (70%). Average amount of gift aid, such as scholarships or grants (proportion receiving): $6,900 (63%). Average amount of self-help aid, such as work study or loans (proportion receiving): $6,200 (70%). Average need-based loan (excluding PLUS or other private loans): $4,000. Among students who received need-based aid, the average percentage of need met: 90%. Among students who received aid based on merit, the average award (and the proportion receiving): $4,910 (9%). The average athletic scholarship (and the proportion receiving): $2,350 (13%). Average amount of debt of borrowers graduating in 2003: $18,000. Proportion who borrowed: 70%. **Student employment:** During the 2003-2004 academic year, 45% of undergraduates worked on campus. Average per-year earnings: $1,000. **Cooperative education programs:** business, computer science, engineering. **Reserve Officers Training Corps (ROTC):** Army ROTC: Offered on campus; Air Force ROTC: Offered on campus.

Colorado State University

Fort Collins, CO 80523
Public; www.colostate.edu
Financial aid office: (970) 491-6321

■ **2004-2005 TUITION AND FEES:**
In state: $3,790; Out of state: $14,377
■ **ROOM AND BOARD:** $6,216

ACT Score (25th/75th percentile): 22-26
2005 U.S. News College Ranking:
National Universities, 117
Acceptance Rate: 79%

Other expenses: Estimated books and supplies: $900. Transportation: $576. Personal expenses: $1,424. **Financial aid:** Priority filing date for institution's financial aid form: March 1. In 2003-2004, 56% of undergraduates applied for financial aid. Of those, 39% were determined to have financial need; 49% had their need fully met. Average financial aid package (proportion receiving): $7,948 (39%). Average amount of gift aid, such as scholarships or grants (proportion receiving): $4,288 (29%). Average amount of self-help aid, such as work study or loans (proportion receiving): $5,463 (33%). Average need-based loan (excluding PLUS or other private loans): $5,312. Among students who received need-based aid, the average percentage of need met: 82%. Among students who received aid based on merit, the average award (and the proportion receiving): $1,402 (4%). The average athletic scholarship (and the proportion receiving): $11,110 (1%). Average amount of debt of borrowers graduating in 2003: $16,075. Proportion who borrowed: 55%. **Reserve Officers Training Corps (ROTC):** Army ROTC: Offered on campus; Air Force ROTC: Offered on campus.

Colorado State University–Pueblo

2200 Bonforte Boulevard
Pueblo, CO 81001
Public; www.colostate-pueblo.edu
Financial aid office: (719) 549-2753

■ **2004-2005 TUITION AND FEES:**
In state: $2,930; Out of state: $13,031
■ **ROOM AND BOARD:** $5,805

ACT Score (25th/75th percentile): 17-21
2005 U.S. News College Ranking:
Universities–Master's (West), fourth tier
Acceptance Rate: 94%

Other expenses: Estimated books and supplies: $874. Transportation: $576. Personal expenses: $2,736. **Financial aid:** Priority filing date for institution's financial aid form: March 1. In 2003-2004, 72% of undergraduates applied for financial aid. Of those, 63% were determined to have financial need; 4% had their need fully met. Average financial aid package (proportion receiving): $6,601 (63%). Average amount of gift aid, such as scholarships or grants (proportion receiving): $4,387 (52%). Average amount of self-help aid, such as work study or loans (proportion receiving): $3,709 (51%). Average need-based loan (excluding PLUS or other private loans): $3,252. Among students who received need-based aid, the average percentage of need met: 61%. Among students who received aid based on merit, the average award (and the proportion receiving): $4,479 (16%). The average athletic scholarship (and the proportion receiving): $3,568 (2%). Average amount of debt of borrowers graduating in 2003: $18,159. Proportion who borrowed: 73%. **Student employment:** During the 2003-2004 academic year, 29% of undergraduates worked on campus. Average per-year earnings: $1,712. **Cooperative education programs:** art, computer science, engineering, technologies. **Reserve Officers Training Corps (ROTC):** Army ROTC: Offered on campus.

Fort Lewis College

1000 Rim Drive
Durango, CO 81301
Public; www.fortlewis.edu
Financial aid office: (970) 247-7142

■ **2004-2005 TUITION AND FEES:**
In state: $2,834; Out of state: $11,466
■ **ROOM AND BOARD:** $6,358

ACT Score (25th/75th percentile): 18-23
2005 U.S. News College Ranking:
Liberal Arts Colleges, fourth tier
Acceptance Rate: 78%

Other expenses: Estimated books and supplies: $850. Transportation: $1,080. Personal expenses: $2,210. **Financial aid:** Priority filing date for institution's financial aid form: February 15. In 2003-2004, 72% of undergraduates applied for financial aid. Of those, 59% were determined to have financial need; 20% had their need fully met. Average financial aid package (proportion receiving): $7,318 (55%). Average amount of gift aid, such as scholarships or grants (proportion receiving): $3,766 (34%). Average amount of self-help aid, such as work study or loans (proportion receiving): $4,981 (45%). Average need-based loan (excluding PLUS or other private loans): $3,874. Among students who received need-based aid, the average percentage of need met: 76%. Among students who received aid based on merit, the average award (and the proportion receiving): $1,990 (6%). The average athletic scholarship (and the proportion receiving): $1,852 (5%). Average amount of debt of borrowers graduating in 2003: $14,100. Proportion who borrowed: 53%. **Student employment:** During the 2003-2004 academic year, 9% of undergraduates worked on campus. Average per-year earnings: $1,500. **Cooperative education programs:** agriculture, art, business, computer science, education, engineering, health professions, humanities, natural science, social/behavioral science, technologies.

Mesa State College

1100 North Avenue
Grand Junction, CO 81501-3122
Public; www.mesastate.edu
Financial aid office: (970) 248-1396

■ **2004-2005 TUITION AND FEES:**
In state: $2,723; Out of state: $9,010
■ **ROOM AND BOARD:** $6,501

ACT Score (25th/75th percentile): 17-23
2005 U.S. News College Ranking:
Liberal Arts Colleges, fourth tier
Acceptance Rate: 93%

Financial aid: Priority filing date for institution's financial aid form: March 1. In 2003-2004, 79% of undergraduates applied for financial aid. Of those, 79% were determined to have financial need; Average financial aid package (proportion receiving): $6,206 (79%). Average amount of gift aid, such as scholarships or grants (proportion receiving): $2,678 (41%). Average amount of self-help aid, such as work study or loans (proportion receiving): $4,633 (46%). Average need-based loan (excluding PLUS or other private loans): $3,212. Among students who received need-based aid, the average percentage of need met: 59%. Average amount of debt of borrowers graduating in 2003: $14,123. Proportion who borrowed: 41%. **Student employment:** During the 2003-2004 academic year, 8% of undergraduates worked on campus. **Cooperative education programs:** art, business, computer science, education, health professions, natural science, social/behavioral science.

Metropolitan State College of Denver

PO Box 173362-CB-16
Denver, CO 80217-3362
Public; www.mscd.edu
Financial aid office: (303) 556-4741

■ **2004-2005 TUITION AND FEES:**
In state: $2,781; Out of state: $10,010

ACT Score (25th/75th percentile): 17-23
2005 U.S. News College Ranking:
Comp. Colleges–Bachelor's (West), fourth tier
Acceptance Rate: 79%

Financial aid: In 2003-2004, 59% of undergraduates applied for financial aid. Of those, 47% were determined to have financial need; 6% had their need fully met. Average financial aid package (proportion receiving): $6,856 (43%). Average amount of gift aid, such as scholarships or grants (proportion receiving): $4,566 (33%). Average amount of self-help aid, such as work study or loans (proportion receiving): $3,864 (36%). Average need-based loan (excluding PLUS or other private loans): $3,552. Among students who received need-based aid, the average percentage of need met: 65%. Among students who received aid based on merit, the average award (and the proportion receiving): $2,013 (6%). The average athletic scholarship (and the proportion receiving): $6,019 (1%). Average amount of debt of borrowers graduating in 2003: $16,117. Proportion who borrowed: 51%. **Student employment:** During the 2003-2004 academic year, 18% of undergraduates worked on campus. Average per-year earnings: $5,000. **Cooperative education programs:** business, computer science, education. **Reserve Officers Training Corps (ROTC):** Army ROTC: Offered at cooperating institution (University of Colorado, Boulder); Navy ROTC: Offered at cooperating institution (University of Colorado, Boulder); Air Force ROTC: Offered at cooperating institution (University of Colorado, Boulder).

Regis University

3333 Regis Boulevard, B-20
Denver, CO 80221
Private; www.regis.edu
Financial aid office: (303) 458-4066

■ **2004-2005 TUITION AND FEES:** $22,400
■ **ROOM AND BOARD:** $7,870

ACT Score (25th/75th percentile): 23
2005 U.S. News College Ranking:
Universities–Master's (West), 26
Acceptance Rate: 84%

Other expenses: Estimated books and supplies: $1,187. Transportation: $576. Personal expenses: $1,044. **Financial aid:** Priority filing date for institution's financial aid form: May 31. In 2003-2004, 65% of undergraduates applied for financial aid. Of those, 55% were determined to have financial need; 36% had their need fully met. Average financial aid package (proportion receiving): $20,738 (54%). Average amount of gift aid, such as scholarships or grants (proportion receiving): $10,698 (51%). Average amount of self-help aid, such as work study or loans (proportion receiving): $7,962 (49%). Average need-based loan (excluding PLUS or other private loans): $5,732. Among students who received need-based aid, the average percentage of need met: 97%. Among students who received aid based on merit, the average award (and the proportion receiving): $5,876 (32%). The average athletic scholarship (and the proportion receiving): $8,964 (9%). Average amount of debt of borrowers graduating in 2003: $22,000. Proportion who borrowed: 60%. **Reserve Officers Training Corps (ROTC):** Army ROTC: Offered at cooperating institution (University of Colorado); Navy ROTC: Offered at cooperating institution (University of Colorado); Air Force ROTC: Offered at cooperating institution (University of Colorado).

United States Air Force Academy

HQ USAFA/RRS
2304 Cadet Drive, Suite 200
USAF Academy, CO 80840-5025
Public; www.usafa.af.mil
Financial aid office: (719) 333-3160

■ **2004-2005 TUITION AND FEES:** $0

SAT I Score (25th/75th percentile): 1210-1370
2005 U.S. News College Ranking:
Unranked Specialty School–Military Academies
Acceptance Rate: 15%

Financial aid: Average amount of debt of borrowers graduating in 2003: $0.

University of Colorado– Boulder

Regent Administration Center
Room 125, 552 UCB
Boulder, CO 80309-0552
Public; www.colorado.edu
Financial aid office: (303) 492-5091

■ **2004-2005 TUITION AND FEES:**
In state: $4,341; Out of state: $21,453

ACT Score (25th/75th percentile): 23-28
2005 U.S. News College Ranking:
National Universities, 74
Acceptance Rate: 80%

Financial aid: Priority filing date for institution's financial aid form: April 1. In 2003-2004, 58% of undergraduates applied for financial aid. Of those, 27% were determined to have financial need; 31% had their need fully met. Average financial aid package (proportion receiving): $9,962 (27%). Average amount of gift aid, such as scholarships or grants (proportion receiving): $4,740 (19%). Average amount of self-help aid, such as work study or loans (proportion receiving): $4,572 (25%). Average need-based loan (excluding PLUS or other private loans): $4,190. Among students who received need-based aid, the average percentage of need met: 73%. Among students who received aid based on merit, the average award (and the proportion receiving): $5,210 (19%). The average athletic scholarship (and the proportion receiving): $18,141 (1%). Average amount of debt of borrowers graduating in 2003: $16,002. Proportion who borrowed: 44%. Average per-year earnings: $1,762. **Cooperative education programs:** engineering. **Reserve Officers Training Corps (ROTC):** Army ROTC: Offered on campus; Navy ROTC: Offered on campus; Air Force ROTC: Offered on campus.

University of Colorado– Colorado Springs

PO Box 7150
Colorado Springs, CO 80933-7150
Public; www.uccs.edu
Financial aid office: (719) 262-3460

■ **2004-2005 TUITION AND FEES:**
In state: $4,294; Out of state: $15,424
■ **ROOM AND BOARD:** $6,808

ACT Score (25th/75th percentile): 21-26
2005 U.S. News College Ranking:
Universities–Master's (West), 37
Acceptance Rate: 65%

....

Other expenses: Estimated books and supplies: $1,176. Transportation: $1,038. Personal expenses: $2,736. **Financial aid:** Priority filing date for institution's financial aid form: April 1. In 2003-2004, 76% of undergraduates applied for financial aid. Of those, 53% were determined to have financial need; 8% had their need fully met. Average financial aid package (proportion receiving): $6,859 (52%). Average amount of gift aid, such as scholarships or grants (proportion receiving): $3,872 (43%). Average amount of self-help aid, such as work study or loans (proportion receiving): $3,909 (39%). Average need-based loan (excluding PLUS or other private loans): $3,642. Among students who received need-based aid, the average percentage of need met: 60%. Among students who received aid based on merit, the average award (and the proportion receiving): $1,774 (9%). The average athletic scholarship (and the proportion receiving): $2,433 (1%). Average amount of debt of borrowers graduating in 2003: $16,724. Proportion who borrowed: 47%. **Student employment:** During the 2003-2004 academic year, 16% of undergraduates worked on campus. Average per-year earnings: $3,843. **Cooperative education programs:** art, business, computer science, education, engineering, health professions, natural science, social/behavioral science. **Reserve Officers Training Corps (ROTC):** Army ROTC: Offered on campus.

University of Colorado–Denver

Campus Box 167 PO Box 173364
Denver, CO 80217-3364
Public; www.cudenver.edu
Financial aid office: (303) 556-2886

■ **2004-2005 TUITION AND FEES:**
In state: $3,584; Out of state: $15,340

ACT Score (25th/75th percentile): 20-25
2005 U.S. News College Ranking:
National Universities, fourth tier
Acceptance Rate: 65%

....

Other expenses: Transportation: $0. Personal expenses: $0. **Financial aid:** Priority filing date for institution's financial aid form: April 1. In 2003-2004, 53% of undergraduates applied for financial aid. Of those, 43% were determined to have financial need; 12% had their need fully met. Average financial aid package (proportion

receiving): $6,958 (40%). Average amount of gift aid, such as scholarships or grants (proportion receiving): $4,407 (28%). Average amount of self-help aid, such as work study or loans (proportion receiving): $3,760 (33%). Average need-based loan (excluding PLUS or other private loans): $3,444. Among students who received need-based aid, the average percentage of need met: 71%. Among students who received aid based on merit, the average award (and the proportion receiving): $1,731 (2%). The average athletic scholarship (and the proportion receiving): $0 (0%). Average amount of debt of borrowers graduating in 2003: $16,644. Proportion who borrowed: 40%. **Reserve Officers Training Corps (ROTC):** Army ROTC: Offered at cooperating institution (CU-Boulder); Air Force ROTC: Offered at cooperating institution (CU-Boulder).

University of Denver

Office of Admissions,
University Hall, Room 110
Denver, CO 80208
Private; www.du.edu
Financial aid office: (303) 871-2337

■ **2004-2005 TUITION AND FEES:** $26,610
■ **ROOM AND BOARD:** $8,363

ACT Score (25th/75th percentile): 22-28
2005 U.S. News College Ranking:
National Universities, 90
Acceptance Rate: 79%

....

Other expenses: Estimated books and supplies: $1,187. Transportation: $576. Personal expenses: $1,044. **Financial aid:** Priority filing date for institution's financial aid form: February 15. In 2003-2004, 63% of undergraduates applied for financial aid. Of those, 53% were determined to have financial need; 8% had their need fully met. Average financial aid package (proportion receiving): $17,190 (46%). Average amount of gift aid, such as scholarships or grants (proportion receiving): $13,361 (44%). Average amount of self-help aid, such as work study or loans (proportion receiving): $5,316 (40%). Average need-based loan (excluding PLUS or other private loans): $5,188. Among students who received need-based aid, the average percentage of need met: 69%. Among students who received aid based on merit, the average award (and the proportion receiving): $7,180 (30%). The average athletic scholarship (and the proportion receiving): $21,102 (5%). Average amount of debt of borrowers graduating in 2003: $23,138. Proportion who borrowed: 59%.

Student employment: During the 2003-2004 academic year, 17% of undergraduates worked on campus. Average per-year earnings: $2,299. **Reserve Officers Training Corps (ROTC):** Army ROTC: Offered at cooperating institution (Univ of Colorado (Boulder)); Air Force ROTC: Offered at cooperating institution (Univ of Colorado (Boulder)).

University of Northern Colorado

Greeley, CO 80639
Public; www.unco.edu
Financial aid office: (970) 351-2502

■ **2004-2005 TUITION AND FEES:**
In state: $2,850; Out of state: $11,740
■ **ROOM AND BOARD:** $5,954

ACT Score (25th/75th percentile): 20-25
2005 U.S. News College Ranking:
National Universities, fourth tier
Acceptance Rate: 71%

....

Financial aid: Priority filing date for institution's financial aid form: March 1. In 2003-2004, 77% of undergraduates applied for financial aid. Of those, 45% were determined to have financial need; 23% had their need fully met. Average financial aid package (proportion receiving): $7,379 (35%). Average amount of gift aid, such as scholarships or grants (proportion receiving): $3,336 (18%). Average amount of self-help aid, such as work study or loans (proportion receiving): $3,587 (30%). Average need-based loan (excluding PLUS or other private loans): $3,463. Among students who received need-based aid, the average percentage of need met: 79%. Among students who received aid based on merit, the average award (and the proportion receiving): $2,364 (8%). The average athletic scholarship (and the proportion receiving): $3,883 (1%). **Student employment:** During the 2003-2004 academic year, 23% of undergraduates worked on campus. Average per-year earnings: $1,898. **Reserve Officers Training Corps (ROTC):** Army ROTC: Offered on campus; Air Force ROTC: Offered on campus.

Western State College of Colorado

600 N. Adams Street
Gunnison, CO 81231
Public; www.western.edu
Financial aid office: (970) 943-3085

■ **2004-2005 TUITION AND FEES:**
In state: $2,584; Out of state: $9,849
■ **ROOM AND BOARD:** $6,714

ACT Score (25th/75th percentile): 18-23
2005 U.S. News College Ranking:
Liberal Arts Colleges, fourth tier
Acceptance Rate: 75%

....

Other expenses: Estimated books and supplies: $800. Transportation: $765. Personal expenses: $1,008. **Financial aid:** Priority filing date for institution's financial aid form: March 4. In 2003-2004, 60% of undergraduates applied for financial aid. Of those, 36% were determined to have financial need; 21% had their need fully met. Average financial aid package (proportion receiving): $8,800 (30%). Average amount of gift aid, such as scholarships or grants (proportion receiving): $2,500 (26%). Average amount of self-help aid, such as work study or loans (proportion receiving): $2,000 (27%). Average need-based loan (excluding PLUS or other private loans): $4,880. Among students who received need-based aid, the average percentage of need met: 55%. Among students who received aid based on merit, the average award (and the proportion receiving): $1,000 (18%). The average athletic scholarship (and the proportion receiving): $2,200 (7%). Average amount of debt of borrowers graduating in 2003: $13,700. Proportion who borrowed: 61%. **Student employment:** During the 2003-2004 academic year, 30% of undergraduates worked on campus. Average per-year earnings: $1,500.
Cooperative education programs: art, business, computer science, education, humanities, natural science, social/behavioral science.

Connecticut

Albertus Magnus College

700 Prospect Street
New Haven, CT 06511
Private; www.albertus.edu
Financial aid office: (203) 773-8535

- **2004-2005 TUITION AND FEES:** $16,858
- **ROOM AND BOARD:** $7,550

SAT I Score (25th/75th percentile): 800-1040
2005 U.S. News College Ranking:
Comp. Colleges–Bachelor's (North), 34
Acceptance Rate: 96%

....

Other expenses: Estimated books and supplies:
$1,030. Personal expenses: $2,931. **Financial aid:**
Priority filing date for institution's financial aid
form: February 15. In 2003-2004, 100% of
undergraduates applied for financial aid. Of
those, 100% were determined to have financial
need; 70% had their need fully met. Average
financial aid package (proportion receiving):
$8,500 (100%). Average amount of gift aid,
such as scholarships or grants (proportion
receiving): $7,500 (61%). Average amount of
self-help aid, such as work study or loans (proportion receiving): $4,300 (78%). Average need-
based loan (excluding PLUS or other private
loans): $4,800. Among students who received
need-based aid, the average percentage of need
met: 87%. Among students who received aid
based on merit, the average award (and the proportion receiving): $7,000 (5%). The average
athletic scholarship (and the proportion receiving): $0 (0%). Average amount of debt of bor-
rowers graduating in 2003: $12,625. Proportion
who borrowed: 95%. **Student employment:**
During the 2003-2004 academic year, 20% of
undergraduates worked on campus.

Central Connecticut State University

1615 Stanley Street
New Britain, CT 06050
Public; www.ccsu.edu
Financial aid office: (860) 832-2200

- **2004-2005 TUITION AND FEES:**
  In state: $7,672; Out of state: $14,406
- **ROOM AND BOARD:** $6,992

SAT I Score (25th/75th percentile): 940-1120
2005 U.S. News College Ranking:
Universities–Master's (North), third tier
Acceptance Rate: 55%

....

Other expenses: Estimated books and supplies:
$1,100. Transportation: $500. Personal expenses: $1,744. **Financial aid:** Priority filing date for
institution's financial aid form: March 1; deadline: September 1. In 2003-2004, 69% of
undergraduates applied for financial aid. Of
those, 52% were determined to have financial
need; 12% had their need fully met. Average
financial aid package (proportion receiving):
$6,479 (50%). Average amount of gift aid, such
as scholarships or grants (proportion receiving):
$2,936 (30%). Average amount of self-help aid,
such as work study or loans (proportion receiving): $3,216 (41%). Average need-based loan
(excluding PLUS or other private loans): $3,388.
Among students who received need-based aid,
the average percentage of need met: 78%.
Among students who received aid based on
merit, the average award (and the proportion
receiving): $1,884 (2%). The average athletic
scholarship (and the proportion receiving):
$9,872 (1%). Average amount of debt of bor-
rowers graduating in 2003: $9,177. **Cooperative
education programs:** business, computer science, technologies, other. **Reserve Officers
Training Corps (ROTC):** Army ROTC: Offered at
cooperating institution (UCONN); Air Force
ROTC: Offered at cooperating institution
(UCONN).

Connecticut College

270 Mohegan Avenue
New London, CT 06320-4196
Private; www.conncoll.edu
Financial aid office: (860) 439-2058

- **2004-2005 TUITION/FEES/ROOM AND
  BOARD:** $39,975

SAT I Score (25th/75th percentile): 1205-1390
2005 U.S. News College Ranking:
Liberal Arts Colleges, 35
Acceptance Rate: 35%

....

Financial aid: In 2003-2004, 53% of undergraduates applied for financial aid. Of those, 46%
were determined to have financial need; 100%
had their need fully met. Average financial aid

package (proportion receiving): $23,900 (46%).
Average amount of gift aid, such as scholarships or grants (proportion receiving): $21,198
(42%). Average amount of self-help aid, such as
work study or loans (proportion receiving):
$5,303 (41%). Average need-based loan (exclud-
ing PLUS or other private loans): $4,119.
Among students who received need-based aid,
the average percentage of need met: 100%.
Among students who received aid based on
merit, the average award (and the proportion
receiving): $0 (0%). The average athletic schol-
arship (and the proportion receiving): $0 (0%).
Average amount of debt of borrowers graduating in 2003: $18,375. Proportion who borrowed:
46%. **Student employment:** During the 2003-
2004 academic year, 13% of undergraduates
worked on campus.

Eastern Connecticut State University

83 Windham Street
Willimantic, CT 06226
Public; www.easternct.edu
Financial aid office: (860) 465-5205

- **2004-2005 TUITION AND FEES:**
  In state: $5,704; Out of state: $12,438
- **ROOM AND BOARD:** $7,256

SAT I Score (25th/75th percentile): 940-1120
2005 U.S. News College Ranking:
Universities–Master's (North), third tier
Acceptance Rate: 59%

....

Other expenses: Estimated books and supplies:
$1,000. Transportation: $952. Personal expenses: $2,382. **Financial aid:** Priority filing date for
institution's financial aid form: March 15. In
2003-2004, 82% of undergraduates applied for
financial aid. Of those, 57% were determined to
have financial need; 24% had their need fully
met. Average financial aid package (proportion
receiving): $10,728 (55%). Average amount of
gift aid, such as scholarships or grants (proportion receiving): $1,998 (38%). Average amount
of self-help aid, such as work study or loans
(proportion receiving): $3,317 (52%). Average
need-based loan (excluding PLUS or other private loans): $3,456. Among students who
received need-based aid, the average percentage
of need met: 73%. Among students who
received aid based on merit, the average award

(and the proportion receiving): $2,682 (4%). The average athletic scholarship (and the proportion receiving): $0 (0%). **Cooperative education programs:** business, computer science, education, engineering, natural science, technologies, other. **Reserve Officers Training Corps (ROTC):** Army ROTC: Offered at cooperating institution (University of Connecticut); Air Force ROTC: Offered at cooperating institution (University of Connecticut).

Fairfield University

1073 N. Benson Road
Fairfield, CT 06824-5195
Private; www.fairfield.edu
Financial aid office: (203) 254-4125

■ **2004-2005 TUITION AND FEES:** $27,935
■ **ROOM AND BOARD:** $9,270

SAT I Score (25th/75th percentile): 1110-1280
2005 U.S. News College Ranking: Universities–Master's (North), 3
Acceptance Rate: 49%

Other expenses: Estimated books and supplies: $500. Transportation: $1,000. Personal expenses: $900. **Financial aid:** Priority filing date for institution's financial aid form: February 15. In 2003-2004, 66% of undergraduates applied for financial aid. Of those, 53% were determined to have financial need; 20% had their need fully met. Average financial aid package (proportion receiving): $17,603 (53%). Average amount of gift aid, such as scholarships or grants (proportion receiving): $10,642 (45%). Average amount of self-help aid, such as work study or loans (proportion receiving): $4,659 (45%). Average need-based loan (excluding PLUS or other private loans): $4,462. Among students who received need-based aid, the average percentage of need met: 78%. Among students who received aid based on merit, the average award (and the proportion receiving): $9,483 (8%). The average athletic scholarship (and the proportion receiving): $17,634 (4%). Average amount of debt of borrowers graduating in 2003: $21,200. Proportion who borrowed: 49%. **Student employment:** During the 2003-2004 academic year, 15% of undergraduates worked on campus. Average per-year earnings: $900. **Cooperative education programs:** engineering. **Reserve Officers Training Corps (ROTC):** Army ROTC: Offered at cooperating institution (Sacred Heart University).

Quinnipiac University

275 Mount Carmel Avenue
Hamden, CT 06518
Private; www.quinnipiac.edu
Financial aid office: (203) 582-8750

■ **2004-2005 TUITION AND FEES:** $22,500
■ **ROOM AND BOARD:** $9,900

SAT I Score (25th/75th percentile): 1050-1220
2005 U.S. News College Ranking: Universities–Master's (North), 13
Acceptance Rate: 52%

Other expenses: Estimated books and supplies: $800. Transportation: $300. Personal expenses: $900. **Financial aid:** Priority filing date for institution's financial aid form: March 1; deadline: April 15. In 2003-2004, 72% of undergraduates applied for financial aid. Of those, 60% were determined to have financial need; 12% had their need fully met. Average financial aid package (proportion receiving): $13,160 (60%). Average amount of gift aid, such as scholarships or grants (proportion receiving): $8,534 (57%). Average amount of self-help aid, such as work study or loans (proportion receiving): $5,155 (52%). Average need-based loan (excluding PLUS or other private loans): $4,264. Among students who received need-based aid, the average percentage of need met: 67%. Among students who received aid based on merit, the average award (and the proportion receiving): $4,928 (8%). The average athletic scholarship (and the proportion receiving): $16,809 (5%). Average amount of debt of borrowers graduating in 2003: $20,510. Proportion who borrowed: 71%. **Student employment:** During the 2003-2004 academic year, 20% of undergraduates worked on campus. Average per-year earnings: $1,900. **Reserve Officers Training Corps (ROTC):** Army ROTC: Offered at cooperating institution (Southern Connecticut State University); Air Force ROTC: Offered at cooperating institution (University of Connecticut).

Sacred Heart University

5151 Park Avenue
Fairfield, CT 06432
Private; www.sacredheart.edu
Financial aid office: (203) 371-7980

■ **2004-2005 TUITION AND FEES:** $21,990
■ **ROOM AND BOARD:** $9,500

SAT I Score (25th/75th percentile): 990-1150
2005 U.S. News College Ranking: Universities–Master's (North), 56
Acceptance Rate: 68%

Other expenses: Estimated books and supplies: $700. Transportation: $800. Personal expenses: $700. **Financial aid:** Priority filing date for institution's financial aid form: February 15; deadline: April 1. In 2003-2004, 83% of undergraduates applied for financial aid. Of those, 69% were determined to have financial need; 28% had their need fully met. Average financial aid package (proportion receiving): $13,393 (69%). Average amount of gift aid, such as scholarships or grants (proportion receiving): $8,762 (68%). Average amount of self-help aid, such as work study or loans (proportion receiving): $5,673 (60%). Average need-based loan (excluding PLUS or other private loans): $5,215. Among students who received need-based aid, the average percentage of need met: 72%. Among students who received aid based on merit, the average award (and the proportion receiving): $9,864 (15%). The average athletic scholarship (and the proportion receiving): $13,594 (4%). Average amount of debt of borrowers graduating in 2003: $18,213. Proportion who borrowed: 93%. **Student employment:** During the 2003-2004 academic year, 4% of undergraduates worked on campus. **Cooperative education programs:** business, computer science, natural science, social/behavioral science. **Reserve Officers Training Corps (ROTC):** Army ROTC: Offered on campus.

Southern Connecticut State University

501 Crescent Street
New Haven, CT 06515-1355
Public; www.southernct.edu
Financial aid office: (203) 392-5222

■ **2004-2005 TUITION AND FEES:**
   In state: $5,492; Out of state: $12,226
■ **ROOM AND BOARD:** $7,250

SAT I Score (25th/75th percentile): 870-1058
2005 U.S. News College Ranking: Universities–Master's (North), fourth tier
Acceptance Rate: 61%

Other expenses: Estimated books and supplies: $1,200. Transportation: $700. Personal expenses: $854. **Financial aid:** Priority filing date for institution's financial aid form: March 12. In 2003-2004, 77% of undergraduates applied for financial aid. Of those, 28% were determined to have financial need; 55% had their need fully met. Average financial aid package (proportion receiving): $6,865 (25%). Average amount of gift aid, such as scholarships or grants (proportion receiving): $4,138 (20%). Average amount of self-help aid, such as work study or loans (proportion receiving): $7,999 (17%). Average need-based loan (excluding PLUS or other private loans): $4,714. Among students who received need-based aid, the average percentage of need met: 84%. Among students who received aid based on merit, the average award (and the proportion receiving): $3,017 (7%). The average athletic scholarship (and the proportion receiving): $3,739 (1%). **Student employment:** During the 2003-2004 academic year, 2% of undergraduates worked on campus. Average per-year earnings: $3,500. **Cooperative education programs:** art, business, computer science, education, health professions, humanities, natural science, social/behavioral science, other. **Reserve Officers Training Corps (ROTC):** Army ROTC: Offered on campus; Air Force ROTC: Offered on campus.

St. Joseph College

1678 Asylum Avenue
West Hartford, CT 06117
Private; www.sjc.edu
Financial aid office: (860) 231-5223

■ **2004-2005 TUITION AND FEES:** $21,970
■ **ROOM AND BOARD:** $9,225

SAT I Score (25th/75th percentile): 870-1000
2005 U.S. News College Ranking:
Universities–Master's (North), 54
Acceptance Rate: 68%

Other expenses: Estimated books and supplies: $850. Transportation: $100. Personal expenses: $700. **Financial aid:** Priority filing date for institution's financial aid form: February 15; deadline: June 15. In 2003-2004, 93% of undergraduates applied for financial aid. Of those, 87% were determined to have financial need; 22% had their need fully met. Average financial aid package (proportion receiving): $16,273 (87%). Average amount of gift aid, such as scholarships or grants (proportion receiving): $11,151 (85%). Average amount of self-help aid, such as work study or loans (proportion receiving): $5,969 (79%). Average need-based loan (excluding PLUS or other private loans): $5,756. Among students who received need-based aid, the average percentage of need met: 72%. Among students who received aid based on merit, the average award (and the proportion receiving): $12,346 (9%). The average athletic

scholarship (and the proportion receiving): $0 (0%). Average amount of debt of borrowers graduating in 2003: $17,649. Proportion who borrowed: 74%. **Student employment:** During the 2003-2004 academic year, 28% of undergraduates worked on campus. Average per-year earnings: $1,500.

Teikyo Post University

800 Country Club Road, PO Box 2540
Waterbury, CT 06723
Private; www.teikyopost.edu
Financial aid office: (203) 596-4526

■ **2004-2005 TUITION AND FEES:** $18,800
■ **ROOM AND BOARD:** $7,950

SAT I Score (25th/75th percentile): 1038
2005 U.S. News College Ranking:
Comp. Colleges–Bachelor's (North), third tier
Acceptance Rate: 66%

Other expenses: Estimated books and supplies: $1,000. Transportation: $750. Personal expenses: $3,000. **Financial aid:** Priority filing date for institution's financial aid form: March 1. In 2003-2004, 100% of undergraduates applied for financial aid. Of those, 100% were determined to have financial need; Average financial aid package (proportion receiving): $8,385 (100%). Average amount of gift aid, such as scholarships or grants (proportion receiving): $4,500 (90%). Average amount of self-help aid, such as work study or loans (proportion receiving): $3,935 (90%). Average need-based loan (excluding PLUS or other private loans): $5,171. Among students who received need-based aid, the average percentage of need met: 75%. Among students who received aid based on merit, the average award (and the proportion receiving): $5,368 (0%). The average athletic scholarship (and the proportion receiving): $6,500 (1%). Average amount of debt of borrowers graduating in 2003: $17,500. Proportion who borrowed: 92%. **Student employment:** During the 2003-2004 academic year, 12% of undergraduates worked on campus. Average per-year earnings: $2,000. **Cooperative education programs:** business, computer science, social/behavioral science.

Trinity College

300 Summit Street
Hartford, CT 06106
Private; www.trincoll.edu
Financial aid office: (860) 297-2046

■ **2004-2005 TUITION AND FEES:** $31,940
■ **ROOM AND BOARD:** $8,260

SAT I Score (25th/75th percentile): 1210-1410
2005 U.S. News College Ranking:
Liberal Arts Colleges, 24
Acceptance Rate: 36%

Other expenses: Estimated books and supplies: $850. Transportation: $185. Personal expenses: $850. **Financial aid:** In 2003-2004, 48% of undergraduates applied for financial aid. Of those, 42% were determined to have financial need; 93% had their need fully met. Average financial aid package (proportion receiving): $25,648 (42%). Average amount of gift aid, such as scholarships or grants (proportion receiving): $22,337 (40%). Average amount of self-help aid, such as work study or loans (proportion receiving): $5,003 (35%). Average need-based loan (excluding PLUS or other private loans): $4,111. Among students who received need-based aid, the average percentage of need met: 97%. Among students who received aid based on merit, the average award (and the proportion receiving): $12,927 (0%). Average amount of debt of borrowers graduating in 2003: $11,632. Proportion who borrowed: 46%. **Student employment:** During the 2003-2004 academic year, 22% of undergraduates worked on campus. Average per-year earnings: $1,200. **Reserve Officers Training Corps (ROTC):** Army ROTC: Offered at cooperating institution (Univ. of Connecticut).

United States Coast Guard Academy

15 Mohegan Avenue
New London, CT 06320
Public; www.cga.edu

■ **2004-2005 TUITION AND FEES:** $0

SAT I Score (25th/75th percentile): 1170-1330
2005 U.S. News College Ranking:
Unranked Specialty School–Military Academies
Acceptance Rate: 7%

University of Bridgeport

126 Park Avenue
Bridgeport, CT 06601
Private; www.bridgeport.edu
Financial aid office: (203) 576-4568

■ **2004-2005 TUITION AND FEES:** $19,450
■ **ROOM AND BOARD:** $8,000

SAT I Score (25th/75th percentile): 750-980
2005 U.S. News College Ranking:
National Universities, fourth tier
Acceptance Rate: 84%

Financial aid: Priority filing date for institution's financial aid form: April 1. **Student employment:** During the 2003-2004 academic year, 50% of undergraduates worked on campus. Average per-year earnings: $2,000. **Cooperative education programs:** art, business, computer science, education, engineering, health professions, humanities, natural science, social/behavioral science, technologies. **Reserve Officers Training Corps (ROTC):** Army ROTC: Offered at cooperating institution.

University of Connecticut

2131 Hillside Road, Unit 3088
Storrs, CT 06269-3088
Public; www.uconn.edu
Financial aid office: (860) 486-2819

■ **2004-2005 TUITION AND FEES:**
In state: $7,308; Out of state: $19,036
■ **ROOM AND BOARD:** $7,300

SAT I Score (25th/75th percentile): 1080-1260
2005 U.S. News College Ranking:
National Universities, 66
Acceptance Rate: 53%

Other expenses: Estimated books and supplies: $725. Transportation: $725. Personal expenses: $1,500. **Financial aid:** Priority filing date for institution's financial aid form: March 1. In 2003-2004, 68% of undergraduates applied for financial aid. Of those, 49% were determined to have financial need; 30% had their need fully met. Average financial aid package (proportion receiving): $8,358 (48%). Average amount of gift aid, such as scholarships or grants (proportion receiving): $5,316 (35%). Average amount of self-help aid, such as work study or loans (proportion receiving): $3,708 (41%). Average need-based loan (excluding PLUS or other private loans): $3,340. Among students who received need-

based aid, the average percentage of need met: 75%. Among students who received aid based on merit, the average award (and the proportion receiving): $5,359 (12%). The average athletic scholarship (and the proportion receiving): $10,775 (3%). Average amount of debt of borrowers graduating in 2003: $17,185. Proportion who borrowed: 61%. **Student employment:** During the 2003-2004 academic year, 45% of undergraduates worked on campus. Average per-year earnings: $2,500. **Cooperative education programs:** art, computer science, social/behavioral science, other. **Reserve Officers Training Corps (ROTC):** Army ROTC: Offered on campus; Air Force ROTC: Offered on campus.

University of Hartford

200 Bloomfield Avenue
West Hartford, CT 06117-1599
Private; www.hartford.edu
Financial aid office: (860) 768-4296

■ **2004-2005 TUITION AND FEES:** $23,480
■ **ROOM AND BOARD:** $8,996

SAT I Score (25th/75th percentile): 970-1160
2005 U.S. News College Ranking:
National Universities, fourth tier
Acceptance Rate: 64%

Other expenses: Estimated books and supplies: $860. Transportation: $1,000. Personal expenses: $1,350. **Financial aid:** Priority filing date for institution's financial aid form: February 1. In 2003-2004, 72% of undergraduates applied for financial aid. Of those, 65% were determined to have financial need; 28% had their need fully met. Average financial aid package (proportion receiving): $19,230 (64%). Average amount of gift aid, such as scholarships or grants (proportion receiving): $10,189 (53%). Average amount of self-help aid, such as work study or loans (proportion receiving): $5,388 (55%). Average need-based loan (excluding PLUS or other private loans): $5,185. Among students who received need-based aid, the average percentage of need met: 74%. Among students who received aid based on merit, the average award (and the proportion receiving): $8,302 (8%). The average athletic scholarship (and the proportion receiving): $25,983 (3%). Average amount of debt of borrowers graduating in 2003: $24,878. Proportion who borrowed: 67%. **Reserve Officers Training Corps (ROTC):** Army ROTC: Offered at cooperating institution (University of Connecticut); Air Force ROTC: Offered at cooperating institution (University of Connecticut).

University of New Haven

300 Orange Avenue
West Haven, CT 06516
Private; www.newhaven.edu
Financial aid office: (203) 932-7315

■ **2004-2005 TUITION AND FEES:** $21,696
■ **ROOM AND BOARD:** $9,095

SAT I Score (25th/75th percentile): 910-1130
2005 U.S. News College Ranking:
Universities–Master's (North), third tier
Acceptance Rate: 67%

Other expenses: Estimated books and supplies: $750. Transportation: $300. Personal expenses: $1,000. **Financial aid:** Priority filing date for institution's financial aid form: March 2. In 2003-2004, 82% of undergraduates applied for financial aid. Of those, 75% were determined to have financial need; 39% had their need fully met. Average financial aid package (proportion receiving): $15,758 (75%). Average amount of gift aid, such as scholarships or grants (proportion receiving): $10,288 (68%). Average amount of self-help aid, such as work study or loans (proportion receiving): $6,861 (69%). Average need-based loan (excluding PLUS or other private loans): $6,787. Among students who received need-based aid, the average percentage of need met: 79%. Among students who received aid based on merit, the average award (and the proportion receiving): $12,573 (10%). The average athletic scholarship (and the proportion receiving): $12,771 (3%). **Student employment:** During the 2003-2004 academic year, 15% of undergraduates worked on campus. Average per-year earnings: $2,000. **Cooperative education programs:** computer science, engineering.

Wesleyan University

237 High Street
Middletown, CT 06459
Private; www.wesleyan.edu
Financial aid office: (860) 685-2800

■ **2004-2005 TUITION AND FEES:** $31,650
■ **ROOM AND BOARD:** $8,474

SAT I Score (25th/75th percentile): 1290-1460
2005 U.S. News College Ranking:
Liberal Arts Colleges, 9
Acceptance Rate: 27%

Other expenses: Estimated books and supplies: $1,105. Transportation: $275. Personal expenses: $1,105. **Financial aid:** In 2003-2004, 52% of undergraduates applied for financial aid. Of those, 49% were determined to have financial need; 100% had their need fully met. Average financial aid package (proportion receiving): $28,950 (49%). Average amount of gift aid, such as scholarships or grants (proportion receiving): $21,776 (46%). Average amount of self-help aid, such as work study or loans (proportion receiving): $7,174 (49%). Average need-based loan (excluding PLUS or other private loans): $5,478. Among students who received need-based aid, the average percentage of need met: 100%. Among students who received aid based on merit, the average award (and the proportion receiving): $0 (0%). The average athletic scholarship (and the proportion receiving): $0 (0%). Average amount of debt of borrowers graduating in 2003: $20,846. Proportion who borrowed: 37%. **Student employment:** During the 2003-2004 academic year, 79% of undergraduates worked on campus. Average per-year earnings: $2,025.

Western Connecticut State University

181 White Street
Danbury, CT 06810
Public; www.wcsu.edu
Financial aid office: (203) 837-8580

■ **2004-2005 TUITION AND FEES:**
  In state: $5,661; Out of state: $12,395
■ **ROOM AND BOARD:** $7,085

SAT I Score (25th/75th percentile): 870-1070
2005 U.S. News College Ranking:
Universities–Master's (North), fourth tier
Acceptance Rate: 55%

Other expenses: Estimated books and supplies: $1,000. Transportation: $730. Personal expenses: $1,750. **Financial aid:** In 2003-2004, 52% of undergraduates applied for financial aid. Of those, 39% were determined to have financial need; 40% had their need fully met. Average financial aid package (proportion receiving): $6,343 (38%). Average amount of gift aid, such as scholarships or grants (proportion receiving): $3,709 (30%). Average amount of self-help aid, such as work study or loans (proportion receiving): $4,119 (33%). Average need-based loan (excluding PLUS or other private loans): $4,024. Among students who received need-based aid, the average percentage of need met: 63%. Among students who received aid based

on merit, the average award (and the proportion receiving): $0 (0%). The average athletic scholarship (and the proportion receiving): $0 (0%). **Reserve Officers Training Corps (ROTC):** Army ROTC: Offered at cooperating institution (University of Connecticut); Air Force ROTC: Offered at cooperating institution (University of Connecticut).

Yale University

PO Box 208234
New Haven, CT 06520
Private; www.yale.edu/admit
Financial aid office: (203) 432-2700

■ **2004-2005 TUITION AND FEES:** $29,820
■ **ROOM AND BOARD:** $9,030

SAT I Score (25th/75th percentile): 1380-1580
2005 U.S. News College Ranking:
National Universities, 3
Acceptance Rate: 11%

Other expenses: Estimated books and supplies: $850. Transportation: $500. Personal expenses: $1,770. **Financial aid:** Priority filing date for institution's financial aid form: March 1; deadline: March 1. In 2003-2004, 49% of undergraduates applied for financial aid. Of those, 40% were determined to have financial need; 100% had their need fully met. Average financial aid package (proportion receiving): $26,978 (40%). Average amount of gift aid, such as scholarships or grants (proportion receiving): $23,574 (40%). Average amount of self-help aid, such as work study or loans (proportion receiving): $3,659 (40%). Average need-based loan (excluding PLUS or other private loans): $2,591. Among students who received need-based aid, the average percentage of need met: 100%. Among students who received aid based on merit, the average award (and the proportion receiving): $0 (0%). The average athletic scholarship (and the proportion receiving): $0 (0%). Average amount of debt of borrowers graduating in 2003: $16,911. Proportion who borrowed: 39%. **Student employment:** During the 2003-2004 academic year, 70% of undergraduates worked on campus. **Reserve Officers Training Corps (ROTC):** Army ROTC: Offered at cooperating institution (University of Connecticut); Air Force ROTC: Offered at cooperating institution (University of Connecticut).

Delaware State University

1200 N. Dupont Highway
Dover, DE 19901
Public; www.desu.edu
Financial aid office: (302) 857-6250

■ **2004-2005 TUITION AND FEES:**
  In state: $4,726; Out of state: $10,383
■ **ROOM AND BOARD:** $7,411

SAT I Score (25th/75th percentile): 670-930
2005 U.S. News College Ranking:
Universities–Master's (North), fourth tier
Acceptance Rate: 50%

Other expenses: Estimated books and supplies: $1,350. Transportation: $804. Personal expenses: $398. **Financial aid:** Priority filing date for institution's financial aid form: March 1. In 2003-2004, 90% of undergraduates applied for financial aid. Of those, 80% were determined to have financial need; 38% had their need fully met. Average financial aid package (proportion receiving): $7,926 (79%). Average amount of gift aid, such as scholarships or grants (proportion receiving): $2,456 (54%). Average amount of self-help aid, such as work study or loans (proportion receiving): $4,983 (66%). Average need-based loan (excluding PLUS or other private loans): $4,867. Among students who received need-based aid, the average percentage of need met: 73%. Among students who received aid based on merit, the average award (and the proportion receiving): $5,240 (19%). The average athletic scholarship (and the proportion receiving): $6,031 (1%). Average per-year earnings: $2,000. **Reserve Officers Training Corps (ROTC):** Army ROTC: Offered on campus; Air Force ROTC: Offered on campus.

Goldey Beacom College

4701 Limestone Road
Wilmington, DE 19808
Private; gbc.edu
Financial aid office: (302) 225-6265

■ **2004-2005 TUITION AND FEES:** $12,308
■ **ROOM AND BOARD:** $4,116

SAT I Score (25th/75th percentile): 908-1018
2005 U.S. News College Ranking:
Unranked Specialty School–Business
Acceptance Rate: 78%

University of Delaware

Newark, DE 19716
Public; www.udel.edu
Financial aid office: (302) 831-8761

■ **2004-2005 TUITION AND FEES:**
In state: $6,954; Out of state: $16,640
■ **ROOM AND BOARD:** $6,458

SAT I Score (25th/75th percentile): 1090-1270
2005 U.S. News College Ranking:
National Universities, 66
Acceptance Rate: 42%

Other expenses: Estimated books and supplies: $800. Personal expenses: $1,500.
Financial aid: Priority filing date for institution's financial aid form: February 1; deadline: March 15. In 2003-2004, 58% of undergraduates applied for financial aid. Of those, 39% were determined to have financial need; 46% had their need fully met. Average financial aid package (proportion receiving): $9,750 (39%). Average amount of gift aid, such as scholarships or grants (proportion receiving): $5,600 (29%). Average amount of self-help aid, such as work study or loans (proportion receiving): $5,000 (28%). Average need-based loan (excluding PLUS or other private loans): $4,600. Among students who received need-based aid, the average percentage of need met: 79%. Among students who received aid based on merit, the average award (and the proportion receiving): $4,070 (20%). The average athletic scholarship (and the proportion receiving): $12,500 (2%). Average amount of debt of borrowers graduating in 2003: $13,806. Proportion who borrowed: 33%. **Reserve Officers Training Corps (ROTC):** Army ROTC: Offered on campus; Air Force ROTC: Offered on campus.

Wesley College

120 N. State Street
Dover, DE 19901-3875
Private; www.wesley.edu
Financial aid office: (302) 736-2321

■ **2004-2005 TUITION AND FEES:** $14,364
■ **ROOM AND BOARD:** $6,480

SAT I Score (25th/75th percentile): 910-1060
2005 U.S. News College Ranking:
Comp. Colleges–Bachelor's (North), 23
Acceptance Rate: 68%

Other expenses: Estimated books and supplies: $1,000. Transportation: $500. Personal expenses: $915. **Financial aid:** Priority filing date for institution's financial aid form: April 15. In 2003-2004, 89% of undergraduates applied for financial aid. Of those, 76% were determined to have financial need; 86% had their need fully met. Average financial aid package (proportion receiving): $8,200 (76%). Average amount of gift aid, such as scholarships or grants (proportion receiving): $5,700 (54%). Average amount of self-help aid, such as work study or loans (proportion receiving): $3,600 (72%). Average need-based loan (excluding PLUS or other private loans): $3,400. Among students who received need-based aid, the average percentage of need met: 95%. Among students who received aid based on merit, the average award (and the proportion receiving): $9,150 (14%). The average athletic scholarship (and the proportion receiving): $0 (0%). Average amount of debt of borrowers graduating in 2003: $17,125. Proportion who borrowed: 80%. **Student employment:** During the 2003-2004 academic year, 4% of undergraduates worked on campus. Average per-year earnings: $2,575. **Reserve Officers Training Corps (ROTC):** Army ROTC: Offered at cooperating institution (Delaware State University).

Wilmington College

320 Dupont Highway
New Castle, DE 19720
Private; www.wilmcoll.edu
Financial aid office: (302) 328-9437

■ **2004-2005 TUITION AND FEES:** $7,340

2005 U.S. News College Ranking:
National Universities, fourth tier

Other expenses: Estimated books and supplies: $1,000. Transportation: $1,000.
Financial aid: Priority filing date for institution's financial aid form: April 15. In 2003-2004, 59% of undergraduates applied for financial aid. Of those, 49% were determined to have financial need; Average financial aid package (proportion receiving): $6,960 (46%). Average amount of gift aid, such as scholarships or grants (proportion receiving): $1,290 (22%). Average amount of self-help aid, such as work study or loans (proportion receiving): $4,094 (18%). Average need-based loan (excluding PLUS or other private loans): $3,847. Among students who received need-based aid, the average percentage of need met: 78%. Among students who received aid based on merit, the average award (and the proportion receiving): $1,204 (5%). The average athletic scholarship (and the proportion receiving): $1,476 (3%). Average amount of debt of borrowers graduating in 2003: $20,150. Proportion who borrowed: 32%. **Reserve Officers Training Corps (ROTC):** Army ROTC: Offered at cooperating institution.

District of Columbia

American University

4400 Massachusetts Avenue NW
Washington, DC 20016
Private; www.american.edu
Financial aid office: (202) 885-6100

■ **2004-2005 TUITION AND FEES:** $26,307
■ **ROOM AND BOARD:** $10,170

SAT I Score (25th/75th percentile): 1130-1320
2005 U.S. News College Ranking:
National Universities, 86
Acceptance Rate: 59%

Other expenses: Estimated books and supplies: $600. Transportation: $700. Personal expenses: $600. **Financial aid:** In 2003-2004, 57% of undergraduates applied for financial aid. Of those, 45% were determined to have financial need; 50% had their need fully met. Average financial aid package (proportion receiving): $24,370 (44%). Average amount of gift aid, such as scholarships or grants (proportion receiving): $12,699 (36%). Average amount of self-help aid, such as work study or loans (proportion receiving): $9,175 (41%). Average need-based loan (excluding PLUS or other private loans): $7,454. Among students who received need-based aid, the average percentage of need met: 79%. Among students who received aid based on merit, the average award (and the proportion receiving): $12,410 (13%). The average athletic scholarship (and the proportion receiving): $18,298 (3%). Average amount of debt of borrowers graduating in 2003: $18,716. Proportion who borrowed: 42%. **Cooperative education programs:** other. **Reserve Officers Training Corps (ROTC):** Army ROTC: Offered at cooperating institution (Georgetown University); Air Force ROTC: Offered at cooperating institution (Howard University).

Catholic University of America

Cardinal Station
Washington, DC 20064
Private; www.cua.edu
Financial aid office: (202) 319-5307

■ **2004-2005 TUITION AND FEES:** $24,750
■ **ROOM AND BOARD:** $9,498

SAT I Score (25th/75th percentile): 1050-1270
2005 U.S. News College Ranking:
National Universities, 111
Acceptance Rate: 82%

Other expenses: Estimated books and supplies: $1,000. Transportation: $800. Personal expenses: $1,500. **Financial aid:** Priority filing date for institution's financial aid form: January 15; deadline: February 1. In 2003-2004, 99% of undergraduates applied for financial aid. Of those, 88% were determined to have financial need; 18% had their need fully met. Average financial aid package (proportion receiving): $14,945 (81%). Average amount of gift aid, such as scholarships or grants (proportion receiving): $4,478 (22%). Average amount of self-help aid, such as work study or loans (proportion receiving): $5,506 (44%). Average need-based loan (excluding PLUS or other private loans): $4,648. Among students who received need-based aid, the average percentage of need met: 57%. Among students who received aid based on merit, the average award (and the proportion receiving): $8,533 (10%). **Cooperative education programs:** business, computer science, education, engineering, humanities, natural science, social/behavioral science, other. **Reserve Officers Training Corps (ROTC):** Army ROTC: Offered at cooperating institution (Georgetown University); Navy ROTC: Offered at cooperating institution (George Washington University); Air Force ROTC: Offered at cooperating institution (Howard University).

Corcoran College of Art and Design

500 17th Street NW
Washington, DC 20006-4804
Private; www.corcoran.edu
Financial aid office: (202) 639-1800

■ **2004-2005 TUITION AND FEES:** $21,300
■ **ROOM AND BOARD:** $9,800

SAT I Score (25th/75th percentile): 940-1150
2005 U.S. News College Ranking:
Unranked Specialty School–Fine Arts
Acceptance Rate: 63%

Other expenses: Estimated books and supplies: $2,300. Transportation: $1,050. Personal expenses: $2,279. **Financial aid:** Priority filing date for institution's financial aid form: March 15. In 2003-2004, 74% of undergraduates applied for financial aid. Of those, 74% were determined to have financial need; Average financial aid package (proportion receiving): $11,231 (74%). Average amount of gift aid, such as scholarships or grants (proportion receiving): $5,124 (52%). Average amount of self-help aid, such as work study or loans (proportion receiving): $4,912 (73%). Average need-based loan (excluding PLUS or other private loans): $8,622. Among students who received need-based aid, the average percentage of need met: 35%. Among students who received aid based on merit, the average award (and the proportion receiving): $2,430 (1%). The average athletic scholarship (and the proportion receiving): $0 (0%). Average amount of debt of borrowers graduating in 2003: $28,247. Proportion who borrowed: 76%. **Student employment:** During the 2003-2004 academic year, 17% of undergraduates worked on campus. Average per-year earnings: $1,250.

Gallaudet University

800 Florida Avenue NE
Washington, DC 20002
Private; www.gallaudet.edu
Financial aid office: (202) 651-5290

■ **2004-2005 TUITION AND FEES:** $9,960
■ **ROOM AND BOARD:** $8,270

2005 U.S. News College Ranking:
Universities–Master's (North), 22
Acceptance Rate: 69%

Other expenses: Estimated books and supplies: $834. Transportation: $1,214. Personal expenses: $2,938. **Financial aid:** Priority filing date for institution's financial aid form: July 1. In 2003-2004, 81% of undergraduates applied for financial aid. Of those, 76% were determined to have financial need; 26% had their need fully met. Average financial aid package (proportion receiving): $14,057 (73%). Average amount of gift aid, such as scholarships or grants (proportion receiving): $12,342 (72%). Average amount of self-help aid, such as work study or loans (proportion receiving): $3,118 (38%). Average need-based loan (excluding PLUS or other private loans): $3,028. Among students who received need-based aid, the average percentage of need met: 76%. Among students who received aid based on merit, the average award (and the proportion receiving): $10,996 (4%). The average athletic scholarship (and the proportion receiving): $0 (0%). Average amount of debt of borrowers graduating in 2003: $10,273. Proportion who borrowed: 51%.

Georgetown University

37th and O Streets NW
Washington, DC 20057
Private; www.georgetown.edu
Financial aid office: (202) 687-4547

■ **2004-2005 TUITION AND FEES:** $30,338
■ **ROOM AND BOARD:** $10,154

SAT I Score (25th/75th percentile): 1290-1460
2005 U.S. News College Ranking:
National Universities, 25
Acceptance Rate: 23%

Other expenses: Estimated books and supplies: $960. Transportation: $410. Personal expenses: $960. **Financial aid:** Priority filing date for institution's financial aid form: February 1; deadline: February 1. In 2003-2004, 45% of undergraduates applied for financial aid. Of those, 41% were determined to have financial need; 100% had their need fully met. Average financial aid package (proportion receiving): $22,344 (41%). Average amount of gift aid, such as scholarships or grants (proportion receiving): $15,663 (35%). Average amount of self-help aid, such as work study or loans (proportion receiving): $5,906 (36%). Average need-based loan (excluding PLUS or other private loans): $3,859. Among students who received need-based aid, the average percentage of need met: 100%. Among students who received aid based on merit, the average award (and the proportion receiving): $3,500 (0%). The average athletic scholarship (and the proportion receiving): $16,278 (2%). Average amount of debt of borrowers graduating in 2003: $21,500. Proportion who borrowed: 47%. **Student employment:** During the 2003-2004 academic year, 12% of undergraduates worked on campus. Average per-year earnings: $3,745. **Reserve Officers Training Corps (ROTC):** Army ROTC: Offered on campus; Navy ROTC: Offered at cooperating institution (George Washington University); Air Force ROTC: Offered at cooperating institution (Howard University).

George Washington University

2121 I Street NW
Washington, DC 20052
Private; www.gwu.edu
Financial aid office: (202) 994-6620

■ **2004-2005 TUITION AND FEES:** $30,820
■ **ROOM AND BOARD:** $10,210

SAT I Score (25th/75th percentile): 1180-1370
2005 U.S. News College Ranking:
National Universities, 52
Acceptance Rate: 39%

Other expenses: Estimated books and supplies: $850. Personal expenses: $1,030. **Financial aid:** Priority filing date for institution's financial aid form: February 1; deadline: February 1. In 2003-2004, 52% of undergraduates applied for financial aid. Of those, 39% were determined to have financial need; 80% had their need fully met. Average financial aid package (proportion receiving): $29,206 (39%). Average amount of gift aid, such as scholarships or grants (proportion receiving): $16,744 (38%). Average amount of self-help aid, such as work study or loans (proportion receiving): $8,220 (35%). Average need-based loan (excluding PLUS or other private loans): $7,317. Among students who received need-based aid, the average percentage of need met: 94%. Among students who received aid based on merit, the average award (and the proportion receiving): $12,291 (20%). The average athletic scholarship (and the proportion receiving): $20,898 (2%). Average amount of debt of borrowers graduating in 2003: $25,943. Proportion who borrowed: 51%. **Cooperative education programs:** art, business, computer science, engineering, humanities, natural science, social/behavioral science, technologies. **Reserve Officers Training Corps (ROTC):** Army ROTC: Offered at cooperating institution (Georgetown, Howard); Navy ROTC: Offered on campus; Air Force ROTC: Offered at cooperating institution (University of Maryland, Howard).

Howard University

2400 Sixth Street NW
Washington, DC 20059
Private; www.howard.edu
Financial aid office: (202) 806-2762

■ **2004-2005 TUITION AND FEES:** $11,645
■ **ROOM AND BOARD:** $5,870

SAT I Score (25th/75th percentile): 840-1360
2005 U.S. News College Ranking:
National Universities, 90
Acceptance Rate: 56%

Other expenses: Estimated books and supplies: $1,020. Transportation: $1,200. Personal expenses: $1,800. **Financial aid:** Priority filing date for institution's financial aid form: February 18; deadline: August 15. In 2003-2004, 74% of undergraduates applied for financial aid. Of those, 64% were determined to have financial need; 20% had their need fully met. Average financial aid package (proportion receiving): $12,708 (64%). Average amount of gift aid, such as scholarships or grants (proportion receiving): $9,250 (36%). Average amount of self-help aid, such as work study or loans (proportion receiving): $2,670 (62%). Average need-based loan (excluding PLUS or other private loans): $7,152. Among students who received need-based aid, the average percentage of need met: 46%. Among students who received aid based on merit, the average award (and the proportion receiving): $8,104 (17%). The average athletic scholarship (and the proportion receiving): $1,170 (3%). Average amount of debt of borrowers graduating in 2003: $22,245. Proportion who borrowed: 71%. **Student employment:** During the 2003-2004 academic year, 8% of undergraduates worked on campus. Average per-year earnings: $4,200. **Cooperative education programs:** business, computer science, engineering, other. **Reserve Officers Training Corps (ROTC):** Army ROTC: Offered on campus; Air Force ROTC: Offered on campus.

Southeastern University

501 I Street SW
Washington, DC 20024
Private; www.seu.edu
Financial aid office: (202) 488-8162

■ **2003-2004 TUITION AND FEES:** $9,755

2005 U.S. News College Ranking:
Universities–Master's (North), fourth tier
Acceptance Rate: 39%

Other expenses: Estimated books and supplies: $1,350. Transportation: $1,301. Personal expenses: $2,333. **Cooperative education programs:** computer science, education, health professions, technologies.

Trinity College

125 Michigan Avenue NE
Washington, DC 20017
Private; www.trinitydc.edu
Financial aid office: (202) 884-9545

■ **2004-2005 TUITION AND FEES:** $16,860
■ **ROOM AND BOARD:** $7,290

SAT I Score (25th/75th percentile): 730-970
2005 U.S. News College Ranking:
Universities–Master's (North), third tier
Acceptance Rate: 78%

....

Other expenses: Estimated books and supplies: $800. **Financial aid:** Priority filing date for institution's financial aid form: March 1. In 2003-2004, 87% of undergraduates applied for financial aid. Of those, 84% were determined to have financial need; 10% had their need fully met. Average financial aid package (proportion receiving): $14,406 (84%). Average amount of gift aid, such as scholarships or grants (proportion receiving): $10,606 (82%). Average amount of self-help aid, such as work study or loans (proportion receiving): $4,900 (70%). Average need-based loan (excluding PLUS or other private loans): $4,709. Among students who received need-based aid, the average percentage of need met: 65%. Among students who received aid based on merit, the average award (and the proportion receiving): $11,641 (6%). The average athletic scholarship (and the proportion receiving): $0 (0%). Average amount of debt of borrowers graduating in 2003: $24,093. Proportion who borrowed: 73%. **Student employment:** During the 2003-2004 academic year, 1% of undergraduates worked on campus. Average per-year earnings: $5,400. **Reserve Officers Training Corps (ROTC):** Army ROTC: Offered at cooperating institution (Howard University).

University of the District of Columbia

4200 Connecticut Avenue NW
Washington, DC 20008
Public; www.udc.edu
Financial aid office: (202) 274-5060

■ **2004-2005 TUITION AND FEES:**
   In state: $2,070; Out of state: $4,710

2005 U.S. News College Ranking:
Universities–Master's (North), fourth tier
Acceptance Rate: 85%

....

Other expenses: Estimated books and supplies: $1,100. Transportation: $1,500. Personal expenses: $1,900. **Financial aid:** Priority filing date for institution's financial aid form: May 1. In 2003-2004, 65% of undergraduates applied for financial aid. Of those, 39% were determined to have financial need; 6% had their need fully met. Average financial aid package (proportion receiving): $8,000 (23%). Average amount of gift aid, such as scholarships or grants (proportion receiving): $5,050 (3%). Average amount of self-help aid, such as work study or loans (proportion receiving): $4,625 (1%). Average need-based loan (excluding PLUS or other private loans): $4,500. Among students who received need-based aid, the average percentage of need met: 60%. Among students who received aid based on merit, the average award (and the proportion receiving): $500 (1%). The average athletic scholarship (and the proportion receiving): $2,500 (1%). Average amount of debt of borrowers graduating in 2003: $18,000. Proportion who borrowed: 61%. **Student employment:** During the 2003-2004 academic year, 3% of undergraduates worked on campus. Average per-year earnings: $4,000. **Reserve Officers Training Corps (ROTC):** Army ROTC: Offered at cooperating institution (Howard University); Navy ROTC: Offered at cooperating institution (George Washington University); Air Force ROTC: Offered at cooperating institution (Howard University).

Florida

Barry University

11300 N.E. Second Avenue
Miami Shores, FL 33161-6695
Private; www.barry.edu
Financial aid office: (800) 899-3673

- **2003-2004 TUITION AND FEES:** $21,350
- **ROOM AND BOARD:** $7,400

SAT I Score (25th/75th percentile): 850-1050
2005 U.S. News College Ranking:
Universities–Master's (South), 48
Acceptance Rate: 70%

....

Financial aid: In 2003-2004, 81% of undergraduates applied for financial aid. Of those, 75% were determined to have financial need; 9% had their need fully met. Average financial aid package (proportion receiving): $14,739 (74%). Average amount of gift aid, such as scholarships or grants (proportion receiving): $6,221 (56%). Average amount of self-help aid, such as work study or loans (proportion receiving): $5,678 (68%). Average need-based loan (excluding PLUS or other private loans): $4,424. Among students who received need-based aid, the average percentage of need met: 67%. Among students who received aid based on merit, the average award (and the proportion receiving): $5,829 (9%). The average athletic scholarship (and the proportion receiving): $13,475 (3%). Average amount of debt of borrowers graduating in 2003: $20,661. Proportion who borrowed: 66%. **Reserve Officers Training Corps (ROTC):** Army ROTC: Offered at cooperating institution (University of Miami); Air Force ROTC: Offered at cooperating institution.

Bethune-Cookman College

640 Dr. Mary McLeod Bethune Boulevard
Daytona Beach, FL 32114
Private; www.bethune.cookman.edu
Financial aid office: (386) 481-2620

- **2004-2005 TUITION AND FEES:** $10,611
- **ROOM AND BOARD:** $6,374

SAT I Score (25th/75th percentile): 820
2005 U.S. News College Ranking:
Comp. Colleges–Bachelor's (South), 48
Acceptance Rate: 67%

....

Other expenses: Estimated books and supplies: $760. Transportation: $740. Personal expenses: $2,300. **Financial aid:** Priority filing date for institution's financial aid form: April 1. In 2003-2004, 99% of undergraduates applied for financial aid. Of those, 87% were determined to have financial need; 21% had their need fully met. Average financial aid package (proportion receiving): $13,750 (87%). Average amount of gift aid, such as scholarships or grants (proportion receiving): $6,575 (71%). Average amount of self-help aid, such as work study or loans (proportion receiving): $3,600 (79%). Average need-based loan (excluding PLUS or other private loans): $3,430. Among students who received need-based aid, the average percentage of need met: 74%. Among students who received aid based on merit, the average award (and the proportion receiving): $7,815 (3%). The average athletic scholarship (and the proportion receiving): $12,760 (9%). Average amount of debt of borrowers graduating in 2003: $26,200. Proportion who borrowed: 77%. **Student employment:** During the 2003-2004 academic year, 10% of undergraduates worked on campus. Average per-year earnings: $2,500. **Cooperative education programs:** business, computer science, education, engineering, health professions, humanities, natural science, social/behavioral science. **Reserve Officers Training Corps (ROTC):** Army ROTC: Offered at cooperating institution (Embry-Riddle Aeronautical Univ); Air Force ROTC: Offered at cooperating institution (Embry-Riddle Aeronautical Univ).

Clearwater Christian College

3400 Gulf-to-Bay Boulevard
Clearwater, FL 33759-4595
Private; www.clearwater.edu
Financial aid office: (727) 726-1153

- **2004-2005 TUITION AND FEES:** $10,850
- **ROOM AND BOARD:** $4,820

ACT Score (25th/75th percentile): 20-26
2005 U.S. News College Ranking:
Comp. Colleges–Bachelor's (South), third tier
Acceptance Rate: 89%

....

Other expenses: Estimated books and supplies: $860. Transportation: $1,200. Personal expenses: $1,000. **Financial aid:** Priority filing date for institution's financial aid form: April 1. In 2003-

2004, 100% of undergraduates applied for financial aid. Of those, 100% were determined to have financial need; 3% had their need fully met. Average financial aid package (proportion receiving): $6,594 (86%). Average amount of gift aid, such as scholarships or grants (proportion receiving): $3,366 (46%). Average amount of self-help aid, such as work study or loans (proportion receiving): $3,484 (46%). Average need-based loan (excluding PLUS or other private loans): $3,434. Among students who received need-based aid, the average percentage of need met: 61%. Among students who received aid based on merit, the average award (and the proportion receiving): $0 (0%). The average athletic scholarship (and the proportion receiving): $0 (0%). Average amount of debt of borrowers graduating in 2003: $13,638. Proportion who borrowed: 48%. **Student employment:** During the 2003-2004 academic year, 51% of undergraduates worked on campus. Average per-year earnings: $2,500. **Reserve Officers Training Corps (ROTC):** Army ROTC: Offered at cooperating institution (University of South Florida); Navy ROTC: Offered at cooperating institution (University of South Florida); Air Force ROTC: Offered at cooperating institution (University of South Florida).

Eckerd College

4200 54th Avenue S
St. Petersburg, FL 33711
Private; www.eckerd.edu
Financial aid office: (727) 864-8334

- **2004-2005 TUITION AND FEES:** $24,362
- **ROOM AND BOARD:** $6,326

SAT I Score (25th/75th percentile): 1020-1260
2005 U.S. News College Ranking:
Liberal Arts Colleges, third tier
Acceptance Rate: 77%

....

Other expenses: Estimated books and supplies: $1,000. Transportation: $1,450. Personal expenses: $1,200. **Financial aid:** Priority filing date for institution's financial aid form: April 1. In 2003-2004, 65% of undergraduates applied for financial aid. Of those, 56% were determined to have financial need; 85% had their need fully met. Average financial aid package (proportion receiving): $18,550 (56%). Average amount of gift aid, such as scholarships or grants (proportion receiving): N/A (56%).

Average amount of self-help aid, such as work study or loans (proportion receiving): N/A (46%). Among students who received need-based aid, the average percentage of need met: 85%. Average amount of debt of borrowers graduating in 2003: $17,500. Proportion who borrowed: 57%. **Student employment:** During the 2003-2004 academic year, 47% of undergraduates worked on campus. Average per-year earnings: $3,250. **Reserve Officers Training Corps (ROTC):** Army ROTC: Offered at cooperating institution (University of South Florida); Air Force ROTC: Offered at cooperating institution (University of South Florida).

Edward Waters College

1658 Kings Road
Jacksonville, FL 32209
Private; www.ewc.edu
Financial aid office: (904) 470-8192

■ **2004-2005 TUITION AND FEES:** $9,176
■ **ROOM AND BOARD:** $6,474

2005 U.S. News College Ranking:
Comp. Colleges–Bachelor's (South), fourth tier
Acceptance Rate: 54%

Other expenses: Estimated books and supplies: $260. Transportation: $1,260. Personal expenses: $2,520. **Financial aid:** Priority filing date for institution's financial aid form: May 15; deadline: June 30. In 2003-2004, 93% of undergraduates applied for financial aid. Of those, 93% were determined to have financial need; 26% had their need fully met. Average financial aid package (proportion receiving): $6,064 (93%). Average amount of gift aid, such as scholarships or grants (proportion receiving): $2,939 (93%). Average amount of self-help aid, such as work study or loans (proportion receiving): $3,000 (91%). Average need-based loan (excluding PLUS or other private loans): $2,250. Among students who received need-based aid, the average percentage of need met: 79%. Among students who received aid based on merit, the average award (and the proportion receiving): $4,056 (2%). The average athletic scholarship (and the proportion receiving): $3,157 (4%). Average amount of debt of borrowers graduating in 2003: $24,531. Proportion who borrowed: 90%. **Student employment:** During the 2003-2004 academic year, 50% of undergraduates worked on campus. Average per-year earnings: $16,000. **Reserve Officers Training Corps (ROTC):** Army ROTC: Offered on campus.

Embry Riddle Aeronautical University

600 S. Clyde Morris Boulevard
Daytona Beach, FL 32114
Private; www.embryriddle.edu
Financial aid office: (800) 943-6279

■ **2004-2005 TUITION AND FEES:** $22,190
■ **ROOM AND BOARD:** $6,630

SAT I Score (25th/75th percentile): 1010-1230
2005 U.S. News College Ranking:
Universities–Master's (South), 19
Acceptance Rate: 82%

Other expenses: Estimated books and supplies: $900. Transportation: $2,070. Personal expenses: $1,220. **Financial aid:** Priority filing date for institution's financial aid form: April 15; deadline: June 30. In 2003-2004, 73% of undergraduates applied for financial aid. Of those, 66% were determined to have financial need; Average financial aid package (proportion receiving): $12,563 (65%). Average amount of gift aid, such as scholarships or grants (proportion receiving): $3,727 (24%). Average amount of self-help aid, such as work study or loans (proportion receiving): $5,794 (56%). Average need-based loan (excluding PLUS or other private loans): $5,514. Among students who received aid based on merit, the average award (and the proportion receiving): $3,588 (14%). The average athletic scholarship (and the proportion receiving): $11,685 (1%). Average amount of debt of borrowers graduating in 2003: $36,022. Proportion who borrowed: 98%. **Student employment:** During the 2003-2004 academic year, 20% of undergraduates worked on campus. Average per-year earnings: $1,800. **Cooperative education programs:** business, computer science, engineering, other. **Reserve Officers Training Corps (ROTC):** Army ROTC: Offered on campus; Navy ROTC: Offered on campus; Air Force ROTC: Offered on campus.

Flagler College

PO Box 1027
St. Augustine, FL 32085-1027
Private; www.flagler.edu
Financial aid office: (904) 819-6225

■ **2004-2005 TUITION AND FEES:** $8,000
■ **ROOM AND BOARD:** $4,760

SAT I Score (25th/75th percentile): 1040-1210
2005 U.S. News College Ranking:
Comp. Colleges–Bachelor's (South), 19
Acceptance Rate: 33%

Other expenses: Estimated books and supplies: $800. Transportation: $1,600. Personal expenses: $2,300. **Financial aid:** Priority filing date for institution's financial aid form: April 1. In 2003-2004, 66% of undergraduates applied for financial aid. Of those, 43% were determined to have financial need; 26% had their need fully met. Average financial aid package (proportion receiving): $7,404 (40%). Average amount of gift aid, such as scholarships or grants (proportion receiving): $2,712 (27%). Average amount of self-help aid, such as work study or loans (proportion receiving): $3,437 (40%). Average need-based loan (excluding PLUS or other private loans): $3,442. Among students who received need-based aid, the average percentage of need met: 73%. Among students who received aid based on merit, the average award (and the proportion receiving): $3,665 (41%). The average athletic scholarship (and the proportion receiving): $3,035 (4%). Average amount of debt of borrowers graduating in 2003: $14,971. Proportion who borrowed: 54%.

Florida A&M University

Tallahassee, FL 32307
Public; www.famu.edu
Financial aid office: (850) 599-3730

■ **2004-2005 TUITION AND FEES:**
  In state: $2,852; Out of state: $14,949
■ **ROOM AND BOARD:** $5,766

SAT I Score (25th/75th percentile): 880-1100
2005 U.S. News College Ranking:
Universities–Master's (South), third tier
Acceptance Rate: 71%

Florida Atlantic University

PO Box 3091
Boca Raton, FL 33431
Public; www.fau.edu
Financial aid office: (561) 297-3530

■ **2004-2005 TUITION AND FEES:**
  In state: $3,092; Out of state: $15,599
■ **ROOM AND BOARD:** $7,100

SAT I Score (25th/75th percentile): 930-1130
2005 U.S. News College Ranking:
National Universities, fourth tier
Acceptance Rate: 72%

....

Financial aid: Priority filing date for institution's financial aid form: March 1. In 2003-2004, 70% of undergraduates applied for financial aid. Of those, 48% were determined to have financial need; 17% had their need fully met. Average financial aid package (proportion receiving): $6,508 (46%). Average amount of gift aid, such as scholarships or grants (proportion receiving): $4,807 (40%). Average amount of self-help aid, such as work study or loans (proportion receiving): $3,634 (29%). Average need-based loan (excluding PLUS or other private loans): $3,456. Among students who received need-based aid, the average percentage of need met: 73%. Among students who received aid based on merit, the average award (and the proportion receiving): $2,040 (4%). The average athletic scholarship (and the proportion receiving): $7,794 (2%). **Cooperative education programs:** art, business, computer science, education, engineering, health professions, humanities, natural science, social/behavioral science. **Reserve Officers Training Corps (ROTC):** Army ROTC: Offered at cooperating institution (Florida International University); Air Force ROTC: Offered at cooperating institution (Florida International University).

Florida Gulf Coast University

10501 FGCU Boulevard S
Fort Myers, FL 33965-6565
Public; www.fgcu.edu
Financial aid office: (239) 590-7920

■ **2004-2005 TUITION AND FEES:**
In state: $3,150; Out of state: $15,248
■ **ROOM AND BOARD:** $6,630

SAT I Score (25th/75th percentile): 940-1120
2005 U.S. News College Ranking:
Universities—Master's (South), third tier
Acceptance Rate: 72%

....

Student employment: Average per-year earnings: $6,000.

Florida Institute of Technology

150 W. University Boulevard
Melbourne, FL 32901-6975
Private; www.fit.edu
Financial aid office: (321) 674-8070

■ **2004-2005 TUITION AND FEES:** $23,730
■ **ROOM AND BOARD:** $6,220

SAT I Score (25th/75th percentile): 1040-1270
2005 U.S. News College Ranking:
National Universities, third tier
Acceptance Rate: 85%

....

Other expenses: Estimated books and supplies: $1,200. Transportation: $250. Personal expenses: $400. **Financial aid:** Priority filing date for institution's financial aid form: March 15. In 2003-2004, 85% of undergraduates applied for financial aid. Of those, 61% were determined to have financial need; 24% had their need fully met. Average financial aid package (proportion receiving): $20,497 (61%). Average amount of gift aid, such as scholarships or grants (proportion receiving): $13,798 (54%). Average amount of self-help aid, such as work study or loans (proportion receiving): $5,454 (50%). Average need-based loan (excluding PLUS or other private loans): $4,868. Among students who received need-based aid, the average percentage of need met: 83%. Among students who received aid based on merit, the average award (and the proportion receiving): $7,280 (21%). The average athletic scholarship (and the proportion receiving): $18,428 (2%). Average amount of debt of borrowers graduating in 2003: $25,692. Proportion who borrowed: 50%. **Student employment:** During the 2003-2004 academic year, 12% of undergraduates worked on campus. Average per-year earnings: $6,193. **Cooperative education programs:** business, computer science, education, engineering, humanities, natural science, social/behavioral science, technologies, other. **Reserve Officers Training Corps (ROTC):** Army ROTC: Offered on campus.

Florida International University

University Park
Miami, FL 33199
Public; www.fiu.edu
Financial aid office: (305) 348-2431

■ **2004-2005 TUITION AND FEES:**
In state: $3,157; Out of state: $15,664

SAT I Score (25th/75th percentile): 1070-1220
2005 U.S. News College Ranking:
National Universities, fourth tier
Acceptance Rate: 43%

....

Other expenses: Estimated books and supplies: $1,200. Transportation: $2,500. Personal expenses: $2,500. **Financial aid:** In 2003-2004, 27% of undergraduates applied for financial aid. Of those, 23% were determined to have financial need; 11% had their need fully met. Average financial aid package (proportion receiving): $6,839 (22%). Average amount of gift aid, such as scholarships or grants (proportion receiving): $1,870 (18%). Average amount of self-help aid, such as work study or loans (proportion receiving): $3,266 (10%). Average need-based loan (excluding PLUS or other private loans): $3,394. Among students who received need-based aid, the average percentage of need met: 66%. Among students who received aid based on merit, the average award (and the proportion receiving): $2,286 (3%). The average athletic scholarship (and the proportion receiving): $4,643 (0%). **Reserve Officers Training Corps (ROTC):** Army ROTC: Offered on campus; Air Force ROTC: Offered on campus.

Florida Memorial College

15800 N.W. 42nd Avenue
Miami, FL 33054
Private; www.fmc.edu
Financial aid office: (305) 626-3745

■ **2004-2005 TUITION AND FEES:** $11,110
■ **ROOM AND BOARD:** $4,842

SAT I Score (25th/75th percentile): 950
2005 U.S. News College Ranking:
Comp. Colleges—Bachelor's (South), 48
Acceptance Rate: 45%

....

Cooperative education programs: art, computer science, humanities, natural science, social/behavioral science. **Reserve Officers Training Corps (ROTC):** Army ROTC: Offered at cooperating institution (Florida International University); Air Force ROTC: Offered at cooperating institution (University of Miami).

Florida Southern College

111 Lake Hollingsworth Drive
Lakeland, FL 33801-5698
Private; www.flsouthern.edu
Financial aid office: (863) 680-4140

■ **2004-2005 TUITION AND FEES:** $17,740
■ **ROOM AND BOARD:** $6,410

SAT I Score (25th/75th percentile): 900-1130
2005 U.S. News College Ranking:
Comp. Colleges–Bachelor's (South), 9
Acceptance Rate: 75%

....

Other expenses: Estimated books and supplies: $800. Transportation: $600. Personal expenses: $800. **Financial aid:** Priority filing date for institution's financial aid form: April 1; deadline: August 1. In 2003-2004, 86% of undergraduates applied for financial aid. Of those, 75% were determined to have financial need; 32% had their need fully met. Average financial aid package (proportion receiving): $15,001 (74%). Average amount of gift aid, such as scholarships or grants (proportion receiving): $10,988 (70%). Average amount of self-help aid, such as work study or loans (proportion receiving): $5,711 (61%). Average need-based loan (excluding PLUS or other private loans): $4,937. Among students who received need-based aid, the average percentage of need met: 65%. Among students who received aid based on merit, the average award (and the proportion receiving): $10,453 (11%). The average athletic scholarship (and the proportion receiving): $5,754 (3%). Average amount of debt of borrowers graduating in 2003: $13,703. Proportion who borrowed: 61%. **Cooperative education programs:** engineering. **Reserve Officers Training Corps (ROTC):** Army ROTC: Offered on campus.

Florida State University

Tallahassee, FL 32306
Public; www.fsu.edu
Financial aid office: (850) 644-1993

■ **2004-2005 TUITION AND FEES:**
   In state: $3,038; Out of state: $15,544
■ **ROOM AND BOARD:** $7,208

SAT I Score (25th/75th percentile): 1050-1250
2005 U.S. News College Ranking:
National Universities, 111
Acceptance Rate: 64%

....

Financial aid: Priority filing date for institution's financial aid form: February 15. In 2003-2004, 58% of undergraduates applied for financial aid. Of those, 41% were determined to have financial need; 28% had their need fully met. Average financial aid package (proportion receiving): $5,512 (41%). Average amount of gift aid, such as scholarships or grants (proportion receiving): $3,812 (31%). Average amount of self-help aid, such as work study or loans (proportion receiving): $3,526 (33%). Average need-based loan (excluding PLUS or other private loans): $3,719. Among students who received need-based aid, the average percentage of need met: 81%. Among students who received aid based on merit, the average award (and the proportion receiving): $2,454 (10%). The average athletic scholarship (and the proportion receiving): $4,667 (3%). Average amount of debt of borrowers graduating in 2003: $18,579. Proportion who borrowed: 82%. **Student employment:** During the 2003-2004 academic year, 9% of undergraduates worked on campus. Average per-year earnings: $3,765. **Cooperative education programs:** business, computer science, education, engineering, natural science, social/behavioral science, other. **Reserve Officers Training Corps (ROTC):** Army ROTC: Offered on campus; Navy ROTC: Offered at cooperating institution (Florida A&M); Air Force ROTC: Offered on campus.

International College

2655 Northbrooke Drive
Naples, FL 34119
Private; www.internationalcollege.edu
Financial aid office: (239) 513-1122

■ **2004-2005 TUITION AND FEES:** $8,540

2005 U.S. News College Ranking:
Comp. Colleges–Bachelor's (South), third tier
Acceptance Rate: 98%

....

Financial aid: Priority filing date for institution's financial aid form: September 1. In 2003-2004, 83% of undergraduates applied for financial aid. Of those, 76% were determined to have financial need; 48% had their need fully met. Average financial aid package (proportion receiving): $4,500 (76%). Average amount of gift aid, such as scholarships or grants (proportion receiving): $2,340 (74%). Average amount of self-help aid, such as work study or loans (proportion receiving): $2,600 (73%). Average need-based loan (excluding PLUS or other private loans): $2,600. Among students who received need-based aid, the average percentage

of need met: 70%. Among students who received aid based on merit, the average award (and the proportion receiving): $1,000 (2%). The average athletic scholarship (and the proportion receiving): $0 (0%). Average amount of debt of borrowers graduating in 2003: $18,100. Proportion who borrowed: 78%.

Jacksonville University

2800 University Boulevard N
Jacksonville, FL 32211
Private; www.jacksonville.edu
Financial aid office: (904) 256-7060

■ **2004-2005 TUITION AND FEES:** $18,830
■ **ROOM AND BOARD:** $6,290

SAT I Score (25th/75th percentile): 930-1170
2005 U.S. News College Ranking:
Universities–Master's (South), 52
Acceptance Rate: 70%

....

Other expenses: Estimated books and supplies: $600. Transportation: $800. Personal expenses: $600. **Financial aid:** Priority filing date for institution's financial aid form: February 1; deadline: March 15. In 2003-2004, 74% of undergraduates applied for financial aid. Of those, 66% were determined to have financial need; 38% had their need fully met. Average financial aid package (proportion receiving): $15,853 (66%). Average amount of gift aid, such as scholarships or grants (proportion receiving): $12,438 (66%). Average amount of self-help aid, such as work study or loans (proportion receiving): $4,383 (51%). Average need-based loan (excluding PLUS or other private loans): $4,014. Among students who received need-based aid, the average percentage of need met: 82%. Among students who received aid based on merit, the average award (and the proportion receiving): $5,234 (28%). The average athletic scholarship (and the proportion receiving): $14,308 (6%). Proportion who borrowed: 39%. **Reserve Officers Training Corps (ROTC):** Navy ROTC: Offered on campus.

Lynn University

3601 N. Military Trail
Boca Raton, FL 33431
Private; www.lynn.edu
Financial aid office: (800) 544-8035

■ **2004-2005 TUITION AND FEES:** $24,750
■ **ROOM AND BOARD:** $8,600

SAT I Score (25th/75th percentile): 800-1030
2005 U.S. News College Ranking:
Universities–Master's (South), fourth tier
Acceptance Rate: 77%

Other expenses: Estimated books and supplies: $950. Transportation: $1,100. Personal expenses: $1,200. Financial aid: Priority filing date for institution's financial aid form: March 1. In 2003-2004, 62% of undergraduates applied for financial aid. Of those, 53% were determined to have financial need; 32% had their need fully met. Average financial aid package (proportion receiving): $19,285 (53%). Average amount of gift aid, such as scholarships or grants (proportion receiving): $11,449 (52%). Average amount of self-help aid, such as work study or loans (proportion receiving): $9,755 (44%). Average need-based loan (excluding PLUS or other private loans): $9,208. Among students who received need-based aid, the average percentage of need met: 74%. Among students who received aid based on merit, the average award (and the proportion receiving): $11,083 (44%). The average athletic scholarship (and the proportion receiving): $17,525 (6%). Student employment: During the 2003-2004 academic year, 2% of undergraduates worked on campus. Average per-year earnings: $3,400. Reserve Officers Training Corps (ROTC): Air Force ROTC: Offered at cooperating institution (University of Miami).

Nova Southeastern University

3301 College Avenue
Ft. Lauderdale, FL 33314
Private; www.nova.edu
Financial aid office: (954) 262-3380

■ 2004-2005 TUITION AND FEES: $15,820
■ ROOM AND BOARD: $7,248

SAT I Score (25th/75th percentile): 880-1100
2005 U.S. News College Ranking:
National Universities, fourth tier
Acceptance Rate: 64%

Other expenses: Estimated books and supplies: $1,200. Transportation: $2,540. Personal expenses: $2,220. Financial aid: Priority filing date for institution's financial aid form: April 15. In 2003-2004, 100% of undergraduates applied for financial aid. Of those, 76% were determined to have financial need; 4% had their need fully met. Average financial aid package (proportion receiving): $14,294 (76%). Average amount of gift aid, such as scholarships or grants (proportion receiving): $7,356

(73%). Average amount of self-help aid, such as work study or loans (proportion receiving): $7,428 (67%). Average need-based loan (excluding PLUS or other private loans): $5,535. Among students who received need-based aid, the average percentage of need met: 50%. Among students who received aid based on merit, the average award (and the proportion receiving): $2,604 (21%). The average athletic scholarship (and the proportion receiving): $7,808 (5%). Average amount of debt of borrowers graduating in 2003: $21,607. Proportion who borrowed: 61%.

Palm Beach Atlantic University

901 S. Flagler Drive, PO Box 24708
West Palm Beach, FL 33416-4708
Private; www.pba.edu
Financial aid office: (561) 803-2000

■ 2004-2005 TUITION AND FEES: $16,360
■ ROOM AND BOARD: $6,055

SAT I Score (25th/75th percentile): 980-1170
2005 U.S. News College Ranking:
Universities–Master's (South), third tier
Acceptance Rate: 87%

Other expenses: Estimated books and supplies: $1,000. Transportation: $1,500. Personal expenses: $1,500. Financial aid: Priority filing date for institution's financial aid form: February 1. In 2003-2004, 83% of undergraduates applied for financial aid. Of those, 71% were determined to have financial need; 16% had their need fully met. Average financial aid package (proportion receiving): $10,659 (71%). Average amount of gift aid, such as scholarships or grants (proportion receiving): $2,059 (44%). Average amount of self-help aid, such as work study or loans (proportion receiving): $1,911 (58%). Average need-based loan (excluding PLUS or other private loans): $3,256. Among students who received need-based aid, the average percentage of need met: 63%. Among students who received aid based on merit, the average award (and the proportion receiving): $1,684 (31%). The average athletic scholarship (and the proportion receiving): $5,120 (4%). Average amount of debt of borrowers graduating in 2003: $14,181. Proportion who borrowed: 65%. Student employment: During the 2003-2004 academic year, 15% of undergraduates worked on campus.

Ringling School of Art and Design

2700 N. Tamiami Trail
Sarasota, FL 34234-5895
Private; www.ringling.edu
Financial aid office: (941) 351-5100

■ 2004-2005 TUITION AND FEES: $21,620
■ ROOM AND BOARD: $9,120

SAT I Score (25th/75th percentile): 1035
2005 U.S. News College Ranking:
Unranked Specialty School–Fine Arts
Acceptance Rate: 67%

Other expenses: Estimated books and supplies: $1,850. Transportation: $660. Personal expenses: $660. Financial aid: Priority filing date for institution's financial aid form: March 1. In 2003-2004, 92% of undergraduates applied for financial aid. Of those, 82% were determined to have financial need; 7% had their need fully met. Average financial aid package (proportion receiving): $10,172 (82%). Average amount of gift aid, such as scholarships or grants (proportion receiving): $5,676 (65%). Average amount of self-help aid, such as work study or loans (proportion receiving): $6,036 (76%). Average need-based loan (excluding PLUS or other private loans): $5,708. Among students who received need-based aid, the average percentage of need met: 25%. Among students who received aid based on merit, the average award (and the proportion receiving): $13,286 (13%). The average athletic scholarship (and the proportion receiving): $0 (0%). Proportion who borrowed: 73%.

Rollins College

1000 Holt Avenue
Winter Park, FL 32789-4499
Private; www.rollins.edu
Financial aid office: (407) 646-2395

■ 2004-2005 TUITION AND FEES: $27,700
■ ROOM AND BOARD: $8,570

SAT I Score (25th/75th percentile): 1080-1260
2005 U.S. News College Ranking:
Universities–Master's (South), 2
Acceptance Rate: 66%

Other expenses: Estimated books and supplies: $550. Transportation: $750. Personal expenses: $2,313. Financial aid: Priority filing date for institution's financial aid form: February 15;

deadline: March 1. In 2003-2004, 47% of undergraduates applied for financial aid. Of those, 42% were determined to have financial need; 60% had their need fully met. Average financial aid package (proportion receiving): $26,005 (42%). Average amount of gift aid, such as scholarships or grants (proportion receiving): $20,887 (41%). Average amount of self-help aid, such as work study or loans (proportion receiving): $5,372 (36%). Average need-based loan (excluding PLUS or other private loans): $3,923. Among students who received need-based aid, the average percentage of need met: 92%. Among students who received aid based on merit, the average award (and the proportion receiving): $7,982 (13%). The average athletic scholarship (and the proportion receiving): $15,787 (4%). Average amount of debt of borrowers graduating in 2003: $14,049. Proportion who borrowed: 52%.

Southeastern College of the Assemblies of God

1000 Longfellow Boulevard
Lakeland, FL 33801
Private; www.secollege.edu
Financial aid office: (863) 667-5026

■ **2004-2005 TUITION AND FEES:** $10,140
■ **ROOM AND BOARD:** $5,469

2005 U.S. News College Ranking:
Comp. Colleges–Bachelor's (South), fourth tier
Acceptance Rate: 85%

Financial aid: In 2003-2004, 88% of undergraduates applied for financial aid. Of those, 75% were determined to have financial need; 11% had their need fully met. Average financial aid package (proportion receiving): $7,328 (75%). Average amount of gift aid, such as scholarships or grants (proportion receiving): $4,850 (68%). Average amount of self-help aid, such as work study or loans (proportion receiving): $3,532 (62%). Average need-based loan (excluding PLUS or other private loans): $3,382. Among students who received need-based aid, the average percentage of need met: 59%. Among students who received aid based on merit, the average award (and the proportion receiving): $8,499 (22%). The average athletic scholarship (and the proportion receiving): $0 (0%). **Reserve Officers Training Corps (ROTC):** Army ROTC: Offered at cooperating institution (Florida Southern College).

Stetson University

421 N. Woodland Boulevard
Deland, FL 32723
Private; www.stetson.edu
Financial aid office: (386) 822-7120

■ **2004-2005 TUITION AND FEES:** $23,345
■ **ROOM AND BOARD:** $7,060

SAT I Score (25th/75th percentile): 1030-1230
2005 U.S. News College Ranking:
Universities–Master's (South), 4
Acceptance Rate: 76%

Other expenses: Estimated books and supplies: $800. Transportation: $660. Personal expenses: $960. **Financial aid:** Priority filing date for institution's financial aid form: March 15. In 2003-2004, 67% of undergraduates applied for financial aid. Of those, 58% were determined to have financial need; 30% had their need fully met. Average financial aid package (proportion receiving): $19,406 (58%). Average amount of gift aid, such as scholarships or grants (proportion receiving): $14,369 (57%). Average amount of self-help aid, such as work study or loans (proportion receiving): $6,052 (41%). Average need-based loan (excluding PLUS or other private loans): $5,002. Among students who received need-based aid, the average percentage of need met: 83%. Among students who received aid based on merit, the average award (and the proportion receiving): $11,283 (32%). The average athletic scholarship (and the proportion receiving): $14,852 (4%). Average amount of debt of borrowers graduating in 2003: $20,000. Proportion who borrowed: 55%. **Student employment:** During the 2003-2004 academic year, 6% of undergraduates worked on campus. Average per-year earnings: $3,250. **Cooperative education programs:** engineering, health professions, other. **Reserve Officers Training Corps (ROTC):** Army ROTC: Offered at cooperating institution (Embry Riddle).

St. Leo University

PO Box 6665
Saint Leo, FL 33574-6665
Private; www.saintleo.edu
Financial aid office: (352) 588-8270

■ **2004-2005 TUITION AND FEES:** $13,880
■ **ROOM AND BOARD:** $7,260

SAT I Score (25th/75th percentile): 888-1073
2005 U.S. News College Ranking:
Universities–Master's (South), third tier
Acceptance Rate: 59%

Other expenses: Estimated books and supplies: $1,200. Transportation: $900. Personal expenses: $900. **Financial aid:** Priority filing date for institution's financial aid form: March 1. In 2003-2004, 85% of undergraduates applied for financial aid. Of those, 70% were determined to have financial need; 29% had their need fully met. Average financial aid package (proportion receiving): $17,695 (70%). Average amount of gift aid, such as scholarships or grants (proportion receiving): $12,077 (70%). Average amount of self-help aid, such as work study or loans (proportion receiving): $5,025 (58%). Average need-based loan (excluding PLUS or other private loans): $3,691. Among students who received need-based aid, the average percentage of need met: 88%. Among students who received aid based on merit, the average award (and the proportion receiving): $5,760 (18%). The average athletic scholarship (and the proportion receiving): $7,001 (2%). Average amount of debt of borrowers graduating in 2003: $12,000. Proportion who borrowed: 75%. **Student employment:** During the 2003-2004 academic year, 34% of undergraduates worked on campus. Average per-year earnings: $1,650. **Reserve Officers Training Corps (ROTC):** Army ROTC: Offered on campus; Air Force ROTC: Offered at cooperating institution (University of South Florida).

St. Thomas University

16401 N.W. 37th Avenue
Miami Gardens, FL 33054
Private; www.stu.edu
Financial aid office: (305) 628-6547

■ **2004-2005 TUITION AND FEES:** $17,000

SAT I Score (25th/75th percentile): 770-988
2005 U.S. News College Ranking:
Universities–Master's (South), fourth tier
Acceptance Rate: 43%

Other expenses: Estimated books and supplies: $1,000. Transportation: $1,715. Personal expenses: $1,870. **Financial aid:** Priority filing date for institution's financial aid form: April 1. In 2003-2004, 93% of undergraduates applied for financial aid. Of those, 93% were determined to have financial need; Average financial aid package (proportion receiving): N/A (93%). Average amount of gift aid, such as scholarships or grants (proportion receiving): N/A

(77%). Among students who received aid based on merit, the average award (and the proportion receiving): $4,000 (16%). Average amount of debt of borrowers graduating in 2003: $17,000. Proportion who borrowed: 62%. **Student employment:** During the 2003-2004 academic year, 5% of undergraduates worked on campus. Average per-year earnings: $3,000.

University of Central Florida

4000 Central Florida Boulevard
Orlando, FL 32816
Public; www.ucf.edu
Financial aid office: (407) 823-2827

■ **2004-2005 TUITION AND FEES:**
   In state: $3,180; Out of state: $15,686
■ **ROOM AND BOARD:** $7,232

SAT I Score (25th/75th percentile): 1050-1230
2005 U.S. News College Ranking:
National Universities, fourth tier
Acceptance Rate: 60%

Financial aid: Priority filing date for institution's financial aid form: March 1; deadline: June 30. In 2003-2004, 55% of undergraduates applied for financial aid. Of those, 53% were determined to have financial need; 51% had their need fully met. Average financial aid package (proportion receiving): $5,397 (52%). Average amount of gift aid, such as scholarships or grants (proportion receiving): $3,709 (24%). Average amount of self-help aid, such as work study or loans (proportion receiving): $3,863 (23%). Average need-based loan (excluding PLUS or other private loans): $3,982. Among students who received need-based aid, the average percentage of need met: 71%. Among students who received aid based on merit, the average award (and the proportion receiving): $1,728 (6%). The average athletic scholarship (and the proportion receiving): $4,597 (1%). Average amount of debt of borrowers graduating in 2003: $12,780. Proportion who borrowed: 36%. **Student employment:** During the 2003-2004 academic year, 12% of undergraduates worked on campus. Average per-year earnings: $5,180. **Cooperative education programs:** art, business, computer science, education, engineering, health professions, humanities, natural science, social/behavioral science, technologies. **Reserve Officers Training Corps (ROTC):** Army ROTC: Offered on campus; Air Force ROTC: Offered on campus.

University of Florida

201 Criser Hall
Gainesville, FL 32611
Public; www.ufl.edu
Financial aid office: (352) 392-1271

■ **2003-2004 TUITION AND FEES:**
   In state: $2,780; Out of state: $13,283
■ **ROOM AND BOARD:** $5,800

SAT I Score (25th/75th percentile): 1140-1340
2005 U.S. News College Ranking:
National Universities, 50
Acceptance Rate: 52%

Other expenses: Estimated books and supplies: $790. Transportation: $310. Personal expenses: $2,470. **Financial aid:** Priority filing date for institution's financial aid form: March 15. In 2003-2004, 49% of undergraduates applied for financial aid. Of those, 40% were determined to have financial need; 29% had their need fully met. Average financial aid package (proportion receiving): $10,922 (40%). Average amount of gift aid, such as scholarships or grants (proportion receiving): $4,459 (25%). Average amount of self-help aid, such as work study or loans (proportion receiving): $4,397 (26%). Average need-based loan (excluding PLUS or other private loans): $4,284. Among students who received need-based aid, the average percentage of need met: 87%. Among students who received aid based on merit, the average award (and the proportion receiving): $3,770 (47%). The average athletic scholarship (and the proportion receiving): $9,482 (1%). Average amount of debt of borrowers graduating in 2003: $13,744. Proportion who borrowed: 42%. **Student employment:** During the 2003-2004 academic year, 20% of undergraduates worked on campus. Average per-year earnings: $2,000. **Cooperative education programs:** agriculture, business, computer science, engineering, natural science. **Reserve Officers Training Corps (ROTC):** Army ROTC: Offered on campus; Navy ROTC: Offered on campus; Air Force ROTC: Offered on campus.

University of Miami

PO Box 248025
Coral Gables, FL 33124
Private; www.miami.edu
Financial aid office: (305) 284-5212

■ **2004-2005 TUITION AND FEES:** $27,840
■ **ROOM AND BOARD:** $8,602

SAT I Score (25th/75th percentile): 1120-1340
2005 U.S. News College Ranking:
National Universities, 58
Acceptance Rate: 44%

Other expenses: Estimated books and supplies: $808. Transportation: $1,280. Personal expenses: $1,170. **Financial aid:** Priority filing date for institution's financial aid form: February 15. In 2003-2004, 62% of undergraduates applied for financial aid. Of those, 55% were determined to have financial need; 25% had their need fully met. Average financial aid package (proportion receiving): $22,940 (55%). Average amount of gift aid, such as scholarships or grants (proportion receiving): $16,363 (54%). Average amount of self-help aid, such as work study or loans (proportion receiving): $6,944 (45%). Average need-based loan (excluding PLUS or other private loans): $5,113. Among students who received need-based aid, the average percentage of need met: 82%. Among students who received aid based on merit, the average award (and the proportion receiving): $12,776 (21%). The average athletic scholarship (and the proportion receiving): $23,217 (2%). Average amount of debt of borrowers graduating in 2003: $29,046. Proportion who borrowed: 58%. **Student employment:** During the 2003-2004 academic year, 28% of undergraduates worked on campus. Average per-year earnings: $2,500. **Reserve Officers Training Corps (ROTC):** Army ROTC: Offered on campus; Air Force ROTC: Offered on campus.

University of North Florida

4567 St. Johns Bluff Road S
Jacksonville, FL 32224-2645
Public; www.unf.edu
Financial aid office: (904) 620-2604

■ **2004-2005 TUITION AND FEES:**
   In state: $3,100; Out of state: $14,850
■ **ROOM AND BOARD:** $6,278

SAT I Score (25th/75th percentile): 1000-1200
2005 U.S. News College Ranking:
Universities–Master's (South), 55
Acceptance Rate: 66%

Financial aid: Priority filing date for institution's financial aid form: April 1. In 2003-2004, 79% of undergraduates applied for financial aid. Of those, 65% were determined to have financial need; 23% had their need fully met. Average financial aid package (proportion receiving): $2,237 (64%). Average amount of gift aid, such as scholarships or grants (proportion receiving): $1,908 (28%). Average amount of self-help aid, such as work study or loans (proportion receiving): $3,612 (27%). Average need-based loan (excluding PLUS or other private loans): $3,634. Among students who received need-based aid, the average percentage of need met: 73%. Among students who received aid based on merit, the average award (and the proportion receiving): $3,168 (12%). The average athletic scholarship (and the proportion receiving): $3,877 (2%). Average amount of debt of borrowers graduating in 2003: $12,346. Proportion who borrowed: 41%. **Student employment:** During the 2003-2004 academic year, 5% of undergraduates worked on campus. Average per-year earnings: $6,476. **Cooperative education programs:** business, computer science, engineering, health professions, natural science, social/behavioral science. **Reserve Officers Training Corps (ROTC):** Navy ROTC: Offered at cooperating institution (Jacksonville University).

University of South Florida

4202 E. Fowler Avenue
Tampa, FL 33620-9951
Public; www.usf.edu
Financial aid office: (813) 974-4700

■ **2004-2005 TUITION AND FEES:**
  In state: $3,166; Out of state: $16,040
■ **ROOM AND BOARD:** $6,730

SAT I Score (25th/75th percentile): 980-1190
2005 U.S. News College Ranking:
National Universities, third tier
Acceptance Rate: 62%

Other expenses: Estimated books and supplies: $800. Transportation: $960. **Financial aid:** Priority filing date for institution's financial aid form: March 1. In 2003-2004, 61% of undergraduates applied for financial aid. Of those, 51% were determined to have financial need; 26% had their need fully met. Average financial aid package (proportion receiving): $8,799 (50%). Average amount of gift aid, such as scholarships or grants (proportion receiving): $3,681 (37%). Average amount of self-help aid, such as work study or loans (proportion receiving): $4,524 (30%). Average need-based loan (excluding PLUS or other private loans): $4,015. Among students who received need-based aid, the average percentage of need met: 81%. Among students who received aid based on merit, the average award (and the proportion receiving): $1,707 (7%). The average athletic scholarship (and the proportion receiving):

$2,765 (2%). Average amount of debt of borrowers graduating in 2003: $16,969. Proportion who borrowed: 50%. **Cooperative education programs:** art, business, computer science, health professions, technologies. **Reserve Officers Training Corps (ROTC):** Army ROTC: Offered on campus; Navy ROTC: Offered on campus; Air Force ROTC: Offered on campus.

University of Tampa

401 W. Kennedy Boulevard
Tampa, FL 33606-1490
Private; www.ut.edu
Financial aid office: (813) 253-6219

■ **2004-2005 TUITION AND FEES:** $18,172
■ **ROOM AND BOARD:** $6,666

SAT I Score (25th/75th percentile): 980-1160
2005 U.S. News College Ranking:
Universities–Master's (South), 40
Acceptance Rate: 61%

Other expenses: Estimated books and supplies: $843. Transportation: $661. Personal expenses: $1,183. **Financial aid:** Priority filing date for institution's financial aid form: March 1. In 2003-2004, 70% of undergraduates applied for financial aid. Of those, 59% were determined to have financial need; 24% had their need fully met. Average financial aid package (proportion receiving): $14,162 (59%). Average amount of gift aid, such as scholarships or grants (proportion receiving): $6,704 (58%). Average amount of self-help aid, such as work study or loans (proportion receiving): $4,069 (55%). Average need-based loan (excluding PLUS or other private loans): $3,533. Among students who received need-based aid, the average percentage of need met: 84%. Among students who received aid based on merit, the average award (and the proportion receiving): $6,520 (11%). The average athletic scholarship (and the proportion receiving): $3,870 (1%). Average amount of debt of borrowers graduating in 2003: $22,791. Proportion who borrowed: 74%. **Student employment:** During the 2003-2004 academic year, 22% of undergraduates worked on campus. Average per-year earnings: $2,000. **Reserve Officers Training Corps (ROTC):** Army ROTC: Offered on campus; Navy ROTC: Offered at cooperating institution (University of South Florida); Air Force ROTC: Offered at cooperating institution (University of South Florida).

University of West Florida

11000 University Parkway
Pensacola, FL 32514-5750
Public; uwf.edu
Financial aid office: (850) 474-3127

■ **2004-2005 TUITION AND FEES:**
  In state: $3,039; Out of state: $15,546
■ **ROOM AND BOARD:** $6,294

ACT Score (25th/75th percentile): 21-26
2005 U.S. News College Ranking:
Universities–Master's (South), 59
Acceptance Rate: 66%

Reserve Officers Training Corps (ROTC): Army ROTC: Offered on campus; Air Force ROTC: Offered on campus.

Warner Southern College

13895 US 27
Lake Wales, FL 33859
Private; www.warner.edu
Financial aid office: (863) 638-7202

■ **2004-2005 TUITION AND FEES:** $11,830
■ **ROOM AND BOARD:** $5,380

SAT I Score (25th/75th percentile): 718-1137
2005 U.S. News College Ranking:
Comp. Colleges–Bachelor's (South), third tier
Acceptance Rate: 71%

Other expenses: Estimated books and supplies: $1,000. Transportation: $910. Personal expenses: $4,175. **Financial aid:** Priority filing date for institution's financial aid form: May 1. In 2003-2004, 99% of undergraduates applied for financial aid. Of those, 64% were determined to have financial need; Average financial aid package (proportion receiving): $10,255 (64%). Average amount of gift aid, such as scholarships or grants (proportion receiving): $3,093 (46%). Average amount of self-help aid, such as work study or loans (proportion receiving): $3,929 (54%). Average need-based loan (excluding PLUS or other private loans): $3,946. Among students who received aid based on merit, the average award (and the proportion receiving): $3,475 (16%). The average athletic scholarship (and the proportion receiving): $4,199 (23%). Average amount of debt of borrowers graduating in 2003: $6,465. Proportion who borrowed: 36%. **Student employment:** During the 2003-2004 academic year, 16% of undergraduates worked on campus. Average per-year earnings: $1,000.

Webber International University

PO Box 96
Babson Park, FL 33827
Private; www.webber.edu
Financial aid office: (863) 638-2930

■ **2004-2005 TUITION AND FEES:** $12,900
■ **ROOM AND BOARD:** $4,520

SAT I Score (25th/75th percentile): 756-966
2005 U.S. News College Ranking:
Unranked Specialty School–Business
Acceptance Rate: 50%
....

Other expenses: Estimated books and supplies: $700. Transportation: $1,192. Personal expenses: $3,840. **Financial aid:** Priority filing date for institution's financial aid form: May 1; deadline: August 1. In 2003-2004, 66% of undergraduates applied for financial aid. Of those, 61% were determined to have financial need; 13% had their need fully met. Average financial aid package (proportion receiving): $11,999 (61%). Average amount of gift aid, such as scholarships or grants (proportion receiving): $8,273 (61%). Average amount of self-help aid, such as work study or loans (proportion receiving): $3,833 (59%). Average need-based loan (excluding PLUS or other private loans): $4,549. Among students who received need-based aid, the average percentage of need met: 72%. Among students who received aid based on merit, the average award (and the proportion receiving): $3,540 (7%). The average athletic scholarship (and the proportion receiving): $4,006 (24%). Average amount of debt of borrowers graduating in 2003: $12,454. Proportion who borrowed: 50%. **Student employment:** During the 2003-2004 academic year, 15% of undergraduates worked on campus. Average per-year earnings: $1,000.

Georgia

Agnes Scott College

141 E. College Avenue
Decatur, GA 30030
Private; www.agnesscott.edu
Financial aid office: (404) 471-6396

- **2004-2005 TUITION AND FEES:** $22,210
- **ROOM AND BOARD:** $8,200

SAT I Score (25th/75th percentile): 1080-1320
2005 U.S. News College Ranking:
Liberal Arts Colleges, 53
Acceptance Rate: 66%

Other expenses: Estimated books and supplies: $700. Transportation: $950. Personal expenses: $900. **Financial aid:** Priority filing date for institution's financial aid form: February 15; deadline: May 1. In 2003-2004, 77% of undergraduates applied for financial aid. Of those, 64% were determined to have financial need; 76% had their need fully met. Average financial aid package (proportion receiving): $21,264 (64%). Average amount of gift aid, such as scholarships or grants (proportion receiving): $15,042 (64%). Average amount of self-help aid, such as work study or loans (proportion receiving): $5,461 (54%). Average need-based loan (excluding PLUS or other private loans): $3,924. Among students who received need-based aid, the average percentage of need met: 97%. Among students who received aid based on merit, the average award (and the proportion receiving): $10,451 (26%). Average amount of debt of borrowers graduating in 2003: $20,321. Proportion who borrowed: 67%.
Student employment: During the 2003-2004 academic year, 7% of undergraduates worked on campus. Average per-year earnings: $2,000.
Reserve Officers Training Corps (ROTC): Army ROTC: Offered at cooperating institution (Georgia Institute of Technology); Air Force ROTC: Offered at cooperating institution (Georgia Institute of Technology).

Albany State University

504 College Drive
Albany, GA 31705
Public; asuweb.asurams.edu/asu/
Financial aid office: (229) 430-4650

- **2003-2004 TUITION AND FEES:**
  In state: $2,774; Out of state: $9,410

ACT Score (25th/75th percentile): 16-19
2005 U.S. News College Ranking:
Universities–Master's (South), fourth tier
Acceptance Rate: 24%

Other expenses: Estimated books and supplies: $800. Transportation: $480. Personal expenses: $964. **Reserve Officers Training Corps (ROTC):** Army ROTC: Offered on campus.

Armstrong Atlantic State University

11935 Abercorn Street
Savannah, GA 31419
Public; www.armstrong.edu
Financial aid office: (912) 921-5990

- **2004-2005 TUITION AND FEES:**
  In state: $2,734; Out of state: $9,702

SAT I Score (25th/75th percentile): 920-1120
2005 U.S. News College Ranking:
Universities–Master's (South), fourth tier
Acceptance Rate: 65%

Financial aid: Priority filing date for institution's financial aid form: March 15. Average amount of debt of borrowers graduating in 2003: $11,000. Proportion who borrowed: 55%.
Student employment: During the 2003-2004 academic year, 5% of undergraduates worked on campus. Average per-year earnings: $3,135.
Cooperative education programs: engineering.
Reserve Officers Training Corps (ROTC): Army ROTC: Offered on campus; Navy ROTC: Offered at cooperating institution (Savannah State University).

Atlanta College of Art

1280 Peachtree Street NE
Atlanta, GA 30309
Private; www.aca.edu
Financial aid office: (404) 733-5110

- **2004-2005 TUITION AND FEES:** $17,500
- **ROOM AND BOARD:** $5,100

SAT I Score (25th/75th percentile): 830-1140
2005 U.S. News College Ranking:
Unranked Specialty School–Fine Arts
Acceptance Rate: 64%

Other expenses: Estimated books and supplies: $900. Transportation: $0. Personal expenses: $1,245. **Financial aid:** Priority filing date for institution's financial aid form: March 15. In 2003-2004, 72% of undergraduates applied for financial aid. Of those, 67% were determined to have financial need; 12% had their need fully met. Average financial aid package (proportion receiving): $11,738 (67%). Average amount of gift aid, such as scholarships or grants (proportion receiving): $8,086 (65%). Average amount of self-help aid, such as work study or loans (proportion receiving): $4,251 (61%). Average need-based loan (excluding PLUS or other private loans): $3,925. Among students who received need-based aid, the average percentage of need met: 63%. Among students who received aid based on merit, the average award (and the proportion receiving): $13,799 (5%). The average athletic scholarship (and the proportion receiving): $0 (0%). Average amount of debt of borrowers graduating in 2003: $22,830. Proportion who borrowed: 61%.

Augusta State University

2500 Walton Way
Augusta, GA 30904-2200
Public; www.aug.edu
Financial aid office: (706) 737-1431

- **2004-2005 TUITION AND FEES:**
  In state: $1,351; Out of state: $4,654

SAT I Score (25th/75th percentile): 860-1070
2005 U.S. News College Ranking:
Universities–Master's (South), fourth tier
Acceptance Rate: 65%

Financial aid: Priority filing date for institution's financial aid form: April 15; deadline: June 1. Average amount of debt of borrowers graduating in 2003: $15,685. Proportion who borrowed: 45%. Student employment: During the 2003-2004 academic year, 5% of undergraduates worked on campus. Average per-year earnings: $5,000. Cooperative education programs: business, computer science, technologies, other. Reserve Officers Training Corps (ROTC): Army ROTC: Offered on campus.

Berry College

PO Box 490279
Mount Berry, GA 30149
Private; www.berry.edu
Financial aid office: (706) 236-1714

■ 2004-2005 TUITION AND FEES: $16,240
■ ROOM AND BOARD: $6,450

SAT I Score (25th/75th percentile): 1070-1280
2005 U.S. News College Ranking:
Comp. Colleges–Bachelor's (South), 2
Acceptance Rate: 83%

Other expenses: Estimated books and supplies: $800. Transportation: $440. Personal expenses: $1,870. Financial aid: Priority filing date for institution's financial aid form: April 1. In 2003-2004, 100% of undergraduates applied for financial aid. Of those, 57% were determined to have financial need; 24% had their need fully met. Average financial aid package (proportion receiving): $13,396 (57%). Average amount of gift aid, such as scholarships or grants (proportion receiving): $10,046 (56%). Average amount of self-help aid, such as work study or loans (proportion receiving): $4,302 (46%). Average need-based loan (excluding PLUS or other private loans): $3,271. Among students who received need-based aid, the average percentage of need met: 86%. Among students who received aid based on merit, the average award (and the proportion receiving): $11,228 (41%). The average athletic scholarship (and the proportion receiving): $9,627 (6%). Average amount of debt of borrowers graduating in 2003: $12,000. Proportion who borrowed: 48%. Student employment: During the 2003-2004 academic year, 78% of undergraduates worked on campus. Average per-year earnings: $2,800. Cooperative education programs:

business, computer science, humanities, natural science, social/behavioral science.

Brenau University

1 Centennial Circle
Gainesville, GA 30501
Private; www.brenau.edu
Financial aid office: (770) 534-6176

■ 2004-2005 TUITION AND FEES: $14,710
■ ROOM AND BOARD: $8,060

SAT I Score (25th/75th percentile): 983
2005 U.S. News College Ranking:
Universities–Master's (South), 42
Acceptance Rate: 74%

Other expenses: Estimated books and supplies: $850. Transportation: $750. Personal expenses: $1,200. Financial aid: Priority filing date for institution's financial aid form: March 15. In 2003-2004, 78% of undergraduates applied for financial aid. Of those, 69% were determined to have financial need; 31% had their need fully met. Average financial aid package (proportion receiving): $14,512 (69%). Average amount of gift aid, such as scholarships or grants (proportion receiving): $11,856 (69%). Average amount of self-help aid, such as work study or loans (proportion receiving): $3,709 (49%). Average need-based loan (excluding PLUS or other private loans): $3,648. Among students who received need-based aid, the average percentage of need met: 82%. Among students who received aid based on merit, the average award (and the proportion receiving): $7,965 (19%). The average athletic scholarship (and the proportion receiving): $7,381 (3%). Student employment: During the 2003-2004 academic year, 4% of undergraduates worked on campus. Average per-year earnings: $1,600.

Brewton-Parker College

Highway 280
Mount Vernon, GA 30445
Private; www.bpc.edu
Financial aid office: (912) 583-3215

■ 2004-2005 TUITION AND FEES: $11,820
■ ROOM AND BOARD: $4,900

SAT I Score (25th/75th percentile): 820-1070
2005 U.S. News College Ranking:
Comp. Colleges–Bachelor's (South), fourth tier
Acceptance Rate: 96%

Other expenses: Estimated books and supplies: $1,000. Transportation: $1,500. Personal expenses: $1,808. Financial aid: Priority filing date for institution's financial aid form: April 1. In 2003-2004, 97% of undergraduates applied for financial aid. Of those, 88% were determined to have financial need; 11% had their need fully met. Average financial aid package (proportion receiving): $8,709 (88%). Average amount of gift aid, such as scholarships or grants (proportion receiving): $6,302 (88%). Average amount of self-help aid, such as work study or loans (proportion receiving): $3,483 (61%). Average need-based loan (excluding PLUS or other private loans): $3,186. Among students who received need-based aid, the average percentage of need met: 57%. Among students who received aid based on merit, the average award (and the proportion receiving): $7,916 (12%). The average athletic scholarship (and the proportion receiving): $7,365 (1%). Average amount of debt of borrowers graduating in 2003: $18,094. Proportion who borrowed: 80%. Student employment: During the 2003-2004 academic year, 5% of undergraduates worked on campus. Average per-year earnings: $2.

Clark Atlanta University

223 James P. Brawley Drive SW
Atlanta, GA 30314
Private; www.cau.edu
Financial aid office: (404) 880-8111

■ 2004-2005 TUITION AND FEES: $14,036
■ ROOM AND BOARD: $8,130

SAT I Score (25th/75th percentile): 690-1190
2005 U.S. News College Ranking:
National Universities, fourth tier
Acceptance Rate: 53%

Financial aid: Priority filing date for institution's financial aid form: April 1; deadline: June 1. In 2003-2004, 99% of undergraduates applied for financial aid. Of those, 94% were determined to have financial need; 9% had their need fully met. Average financial aid package (proportion receiving): $3,204 (93%). Average amount of gift aid, such as scholarships or grants (proportion receiving): $2,492 (76%). Average amount of self-help aid, such as work study or loans (proportion receiving): $2,695 (29%). Average need-based loan (excluding PLUS or other private loans): $2,575. Among students who received need-based aid, the average percentage of need met: 25%. Among students who received aid based on merit, the average award (and the proportion receiving): $4,188 (10%). The average athletic scholarship (and the proportion receiving): $5,402 (0%). Average amount of debt of borrowers graduating in 2003: $10,808. Proportion who borrowed: 67%. **Student employment:** During the 2003-2004 academic year, 6% of undergraduates worked on campus. Average per-year earnings: $8,237. **Cooperative education programs:** other. **Reserve Officers Training Corps (ROTC):** Army ROTC: Offered on campus; Navy ROTC: Offered on campus; Air Force ROTC: Offered on campus.

Clayton College and State University

5900 N. Lee Street
Morrow, GA 30260
Public; www.clayton.edu
Financial aid office: (770) 961-3511

■ **2004-2005 TUITION AND FEES:**
In state: $2,802; Out of state: $9,770
■ **ROOM AND BOARD:** $7,620

SAT I Score (25th/75th percentile): 890-1100
2005 U.S. News College Ranking:
Comp. Colleges–Bachelor's (South), third tier
Acceptance Rate: 71%

Financial aid: Priority filing date for institution's financial aid form: July 23. In 2003-2004, 71% of undergraduates applied for financial aid. Of those, 55% were determined to have financial need; 25% had their need fully met. Average financial aid package (proportion receiving): $5,944 (55%). Average amount of gift aid, such as scholarships or grants (proportion receiving): $3,180 (37%). Average amount of self-help aid, such as work study or loans (proportion receiving): $3,118 (34%). Average need-based loan (excluding PLUS or other private loans): $3,410. Among students who received need-based aid, the average percentage of need met: 67%. Among students who received aid based on merit, the average award (and the proportion receiving): $3,210 (22%). The average athletic scholarship (and the proportion receiving): $2,148 (1%). Average amount of debt of borrowers graduating in 2003: $16,156. Proportion who borrowed: 29%. **Student employment:** During the 2003-2004 academic year, 4% of undergraduates worked on campus. Average per-year earnings: $7,000. **Reserve Officers Training Corps (ROTC):** Army ROTC: Offered at cooperating institution (Georgia State University); Navy ROTC: Offered at cooperating institution (Georgia Institute of

Technology); Air Force ROTC: Offered at cooperating institution (Georgia Institute of Technology).

Columbus State University

4225 University Avenue
Columbus, GA 31907
Public; www.colstate.edu
Financial aid office: (706) 568-2036

■ **2004-2005 TUITION AND FEES:**
In state: $2,808; Out of state: $9,776
■ **ROOM AND BOARD:** $5,310

SAT I Score (25th/75th percentile): 850-1070
2005 U.S. News College Ranking:
Universities–Master's (South), fourth tier
Acceptance Rate: 71%

Other expenses: Estimated books and supplies: $800. Transportation: $930. Personal expenses: $1,555. **Financial aid:** Priority filing date for institution's financial aid form: May 1. In 2003-2004, 72% of undergraduates applied for financial aid. Of those, 40% were determined to have financial need; 84% had their need fully met. Average financial aid package (proportion receiving): $3,995 (38%). Average amount of gift aid, such as scholarships or grants (proportion receiving): $3,284 (37%). Average amount of self-help aid, such as work study or loans (proportion receiving): $3,815 (37%). Average need-based loan (excluding PLUS or other private loans): $3,481. Among students who received need-based aid, the average percentage of need met: 69%. Among students who received aid based on merit, the average award (and the proportion receiving): $1,764 (18%). The average athletic scholarship (and the proportion receiving): $2,349 (3%). Average amount of debt of borrowers graduating in 2003: $14,237. Proportion who borrowed: 67%. **Student employment:** During the 2003-2004 academic year, 4% of undergraduates worked on campus. Average per-year earnings: $6. **Reserve Officers Training Corps (ROTC):** Army ROTC: Offered on campus.

Covenant College

14049 Scenic Highway
Lookout Mountain, GA 30750
Private; www.covenant.edu
Financial aid office: (706) 419-1126

■ **2004-2005 TUITION AND FEES:** $19,320
■ **ROOM AND BOARD:** $5,520

SAT I Score (25th/75th percentile): 1060-1320
2005 U.S. News College Ranking:
Comp. Colleges–Bachelor's (South), 6
Acceptance Rate: 61%

Other expenses: Estimated books and supplies: $1,000. Transportation: $600. Personal expenses: $560. **Financial aid:** Priority filing date for institution's financial aid form: March 1. In 2003-2004, 82% of undergraduates applied for financial aid. Of those, 73% were determined to have financial need; 26% had their need fully met. Average financial aid package (proportion receiving): $16,865 (73%). Average amount of gift aid, such as scholarships or grants (proportion receiving): $12,011 (72%). Average amount of self-help aid, such as work study or loans (proportion receiving): $4,406 (61%). Average need-based loan (excluding PLUS or other private loans): $4,176. Among students who received need-based aid, the average percentage of need met: 85%. Among students who received aid based on merit, the average award (and the proportion receiving): $3,798 (20%). The average athletic scholarship (and the proportion receiving): $5,902 (4%). Average amount of debt of borrowers graduating in 2003: $15,196. Proportion who borrowed: 51%. **Student employment:** During the 2003-2004 academic year, 7% of undergraduates worked on campus. Average per-year earnings: $1,500.

Emmanuel College

PO Box 129
Franklin Springs, GA 30639
Private; www.emmanuelcollege.edu
Financial aid office: (706) 245-2843

■ **2004-2005 TUITION AND FEES:** $9,600
■ **ROOM AND BOARD:** $4,300

SAT I Score (25th/75th percentile): 930
2005 U.S. News College Ranking:
Comp. Colleges–Bachelor's (South), third tier
Acceptance Rate: 49%

Other expenses: Estimated books and supplies: $850. Transportation: $1,752. Personal expenses: $1,407. **Financial aid:** Priority filing date for institution's financial aid form: May 1. In 2003-2004, 57% of undergraduates applied for financial aid. Of those, 46% were determined to have financial need; 34% had their need fully met. Average financial aid package (proportion receiving): $7,800 (46%). Average amount of gift aid, such as scholarships or grants (proportion receiving): $2,543 (42%). Average amount of self-help aid, such as work study or loans (proportion receiving): $3,659 (24%). Average need-based loan (excluding PLUS or other private loans): $3,312. Among students who received need-based aid, the average percentage of need met: 45%. Among students who received aid based on merit, the average award (and the proportion receiving): $2,386 (12%). The average athletic scholarship (and the proportion receiving): $3,825 (2%). Proportion who borrowed: 71%. **Cooperative education programs:** business, computer science, education, health professions, humanities, natural science, social/behavioral science.

Emory University

1380 S. Oxford Road NE
Atlanta, GA 30322
Private; www.emory.edu
Financial aid office: (404) 727-6039

■ **2004-2005 TUITION AND FEES:** $29,322
■ **ROOM AND BOARD:** $9,650

SAT I Score (25th/75th percentile): 1300-1460
2005 U.S. News College Ranking:
National Universities, 20
Acceptance Rate: 42%

Other expenses: Estimated books and supplies: $1,000. Transportation: $600. Personal expenses: $700. **Financial aid:** Priority filing date for institution's financial aid form: February 15; deadline: April 1. In 2003-2004, 46% of undergraduates applied for financial aid. Of those, 38% were determined to have financial need; 100% had their need fully met. Average financial aid package (proportion receiving): $25,238 (38%). Average amount of gift aid, such as scholarships or grants (proportion receiving): $18,962 (36%). Average amount of self-help aid, such as work study or loans (proportion receiving): $6,309 (34%). Average need-based loan (excluding PLUS or other private loans): $4,715. Among students who received need-based aid, the average percentage of need met: 100%. Among students who received aid based on merit, the average award (and the proportion receiving): $16,422 (6%). The average athletic scholarship (and the proportion receiving): $0 (0%). Average amount of debt of borrowers graduating in 2003: $18,803. Proportion who borrowed: 42%. **Student employment:** During the 2003-2004 academic year, 21% of undergraduates worked on campus. Average per-year earnings: $10,611. **Cooperative education programs:** business, education. **Reserve Officers Training Corps (ROTC):** Army ROTC: Offered at cooperating institution (Georgia Institute of Technology); Air Force ROTC: Offered at cooperating institution (Georgia Institute of Technology).

Fort Valley State University

1005 State University Drive
Fort Valley, GA 31030-4313
Public; www.fvsu.edu
Financial aid office: (478) 825-6351

■ **2004-2005 TUITION AND FEES:**
In state: $2,916; Out of state: $9,884
■ **ROOM AND BOARD:** $4,386

SAT I Score (25th/75th percentile): 891-1333
2005 U.S. News College Ranking:
Universities–Master's (South), third tier
Acceptance Rate: 48%

Other expenses: Estimated books and supplies: $1,200. Transportation: $570. **Financial aid:** Priority filing date for institution's financial aid form: April 15; deadline: July 19. In 2003-2004, 100% of undergraduates applied for financial aid. Of those, 95% were determined to have financial need; 60% had their need fully met. Average financial aid package (proportion receiving): $7,476 (94%). Average amount of gift aid, such as scholarships or grants (proportion receiving): $2,700 (74%). Average amount of self-help aid, such as work study or loans (proportion receiving): $2,438 (71%). Average need-based loan (excluding PLUS or other private loans): $3,033. Among students who received need-based aid, the average percentage of need met: 73%. Among students who received aid based on merit, the average award (and the proportion receiving): $1,653 (9%). The average athletic scholarship (and the proportion receiving): $2,441 (1%). Average amount of debt of borrowers graduating in 2003: $18,116. Proportion who borrowed: 85%. **Student employment:** During the 2003-2004 academic year, 2% of undergraduates worked on campus. Average per-year earnings: $6,000. **Cooperative education programs:** agriculture, computer science, health professions, home economics, natural science, technologies. **Reserve Officers Training Corps (ROTC):** Army ROTC: Offered on campus.

Georgia College and State University

Campus PO Box 52
Milledgeville, GA 31061
Public; www.gcsu.edu
Financial aid office: (478) 445-5149

■ **2004-2005 TUITION AND FEES:**
In state: $3,862; Out of state: $13,318
■ **ROOM AND BOARD:** $6,482

SAT I Score (25th/75th percentile): 1010-1160
2005 U.S. News College Ranking:
Universities–Master's (South), 52
Acceptance Rate: 62%

Other expenses: Estimated books and supplies: $800. **Financial aid:** Priority filing date for institution's financial aid form: March 1. In 2003-2004, 91% of undergraduates applied for financial aid. Of those, 19% were determined to have financial need; Average financial aid package (proportion receiving): $6,106 (19%). Average amount of gift aid, such as scholarships or grants (proportion receiving): $2,879 (7%). Average amount of self-help aid, such as work study or loans (proportion receiving): $3,566 (2%). Average need-based loan (excluding PLUS or other private loans): $3,493. Among students who received aid based on merit, the average award (and the proportion receiving): $5,361 (3%). The average athletic scholarship (and the proportion receiving): $3,301 (1%). Average amount of debt of borrowers graduating in 2003: $10,759. Proportion who borrowed: 57%. **Reserve Officers Training Corps (ROTC):** Army ROTC: Offered at cooperating institution (Georgia Military College).

Georgia Institute of Technology

225 North Avenue NW
Atlanta, GA 30332
Public; www.admission.gatech.edu
Financial aid office: (404) 894-4582

■ **2004-2005 TUITION AND FEES:**
In state: $4,278; Out of state: $17,558
■ **ROOM AND BOARD:** $6,150

SAT I Score (25th/75th percentile): 1250-1430
2005 U.S. News College Ranking:
National Universities, 41
Acceptance Rate: 63%

Financial aid: Priority filing date for institution's financial aid form: March 1; deadline: March 1. In 2003-2004, 79% of undergraduates applied for financial aid. Of those, 29% were determined to have financial need; 13% had their need fully met. Average financial aid package (proportion receiving): $7,872 (29%). Average amount of gift aid, such as scholarships or grants (proportion receiving): $3,729 (16%). Average amount of self-help aid, such as work study or loans (proportion receiving): $4,428 (20%). Average need-based loan (excluding PLUS or other private loans): $4,266. Among students who received need-based aid, the average percentage of need met: 67%. Among students who received aid based on merit, the average award (and the proportion receiving): $4,559 (28%). The average athletic scholarship (and the proportion receiving): $12,970 (2%). Average amount of debt of borrowers graduating in 2003: $16,576. Proportion who borrowed: 47%. **Cooperative education programs:** computer science, engineering, other. **Reserve Officers Training Corps (ROTC):** Army ROTC: Offered on campus; Navy ROTC: Offered on campus; Air Force ROTC: Offered on campus.

Georgia Southern University

PO Box 8033
Statesboro, GA 30460
Public; www.georgiasouthern.edu
Financial aid office: (912) 681-5413

■ **2004-2005 TUITION AND FEES:**
   In state: $2,912; Out of state: $9,548
■ **ROOM AND BOARD:** $5,628

SAT I Score (25th/75th percentile): 960-1140
2005 U.S. News College Ranking:
Universities–Master's (South), 58
Acceptance Rate: 54%

Other expenses: Estimated books and supplies: $970. Transportation: $840. Personal expenses: $1,710. **Financial aid:** Priority filing date for institution's financial aid form: March 31. In 2003-2004, 87% of undergraduates applied for financial aid. Of those, 50% were determined to have financial need; 24% had their need fully met. Average financial aid package (proportion receiving): $6,488 (49%). Average amount of gift aid, such as scholarships or grants (proportion receiving): $4,214 (41%). Average amount of self-help aid, such as work study or loans (proportion receiving): $3,772 (38%). Average need-based loan (excluding PLUS or other private loans): $3,690. Among students who

received need-based aid, the average percentage of need met: 74%. Among students who received aid based on merit, the average award (and the proportion receiving): $1,395 (3%). The average athletic scholarship (and the proportion receiving): $3,893 (2%). Average amount of debt of borrowers graduating in 2003: $17,557. Proportion who borrowed: 68%. **Student employment:** During the 2003-2004 academic year, 14% of undergraduates worked on campus. Average per-year earnings: $1,092. **Cooperative education programs:** business, computer science, engineering, health professions, natural science, technologies, other. **Reserve Officers Training Corps (ROTC):** Army ROTC: Offered on campus.

Georgia Southwestern State University

800 Wheatley Street
Americus, GA 31709
Public; www.gsw.edu
Financial aid office: (229) 928-1378

■ **2004-2005 TUITION AND FEES:**
   In state: $2,876; Out of state: $9,844
■ **ROOM AND BOARD:** $4,506

SAT I Score (25th/75th percentile): 910-1060
2005 U.S. News College Ranking:
Universities–Master's (South), third tier
Acceptance Rate: 74%

Other expenses: Estimated books and supplies: $900. **Financial aid:** Priority filing date for institution's financial aid form: April 1. In 2003-2004, 77% of undergraduates applied for financial aid. Of those, 61% were determined to have financial need; 9% had their need fully met. Average financial aid package (proportion receiving): $6,141 (60%). Average amount of gift aid, such as scholarships or grants (proportion receiving): $3,015 (44%). Average amount of self-help aid, such as work study or loans (proportion receiving): $3,236 (41%). Average need-based loan (excluding PLUS or other private loans): $3,147. Among students who received need-based aid, the average percentage of need met: 62%. Among students who received aid based on merit, the average award (and the proportion receiving): $1,913 (5%). The average athletic scholarship (and the proportion receiving): $3,335 (3%).

Georgia State University

33 Gilmer Street SE
Atlanta, GA 30303-3083
Public; www.gsu.edu/~wwwadm
Financial aid office: (404) 651-2227

■ **2004-2005 TUITION AND FEES:**
   In state: $4,312; Out of state: $14,898
■ **ROOM AND BOARD:** $7,118

SAT I Score (25th/75th percentile): 980-1200
2005 U.S. News College Ranking:
National Universities, fourth tier
Acceptance Rate: 56%

Financial aid: Priority filing date for institution's financial aid form: April 1; deadline: November 1. **Cooperative education programs:** art, business, computer science, education, health professions, humanities, natural science, social/behavioral science. **Reserve Officers Training Corps (ROTC):** Army ROTC: Offered on campus; Navy ROTC: Offered at cooperating institution (Georgia Institute of Technology); Air Force ROTC: Offered at cooperating institution (Georgia Institute of Technology).

Kennesaw State University

1000 Chastain Road, Campus Box 0115
Kennesaw, GA 30144-5591
Public; www.kennesaw.edu
Financial aid office: (770) 423-6074

■ **2004-2005 TUITION AND FEES:**
   In state: $2,898; Out of state: $9,866

SAT I Score (25th/75th percentile): 950-1140
2005 U.S. News College Ranking:
Universities–Master's (South), third tier
Acceptance Rate: 70%

Other expenses: Estimated books and supplies: $1,000. Transportation: $1,812. Personal expenses: $1,440. **Financial aid:** Priority filing date for institution's financial aid form: July 1. In 2003-2004, 77% of undergraduates applied for financial aid. Of those, 36% were determined to have financial need; 18% had their need fully met. Average financial aid package (proportion receiving): $3,907 (36%). Average amount of gift aid, such as scholarships or grants (proportion receiving): $1,324 (18%). Average amount of self-help aid, such as work study or loans (proportion receiving): $1,614 (31%). Average need-based loan (excluding PLUS or other private loans): $1,625. Among students who received need-based aid, the average percentage of need met: 20%. Among students who received aid based on merit, the average award (and the proportion receiving): $770 (7%). The average athletic scholarship (and the proportion receiving): $2,412 (1%). Average amount of debt of borrowers graduating in 2003: $14,332. Proportion who borrowed: 44%. **Student employment:** During the 2003-2004 academic year, 20% of undergraduates worked on campus. Average per-year earnings: $3,750. **Cooperative education programs:** art, business, computer science, health professions, humanities, natural science, social/behavioral science. **Reserve Officers Training Corps (ROTC):** Army ROTC: Offered at cooperating institution (Georgia Institute of Technology); Air Force ROTC: Offered at cooperating institution (Georia Institute of Technology).

LaGrange College

601 Broad Street
LaGrange, GA 30240
Private; www.lagrange.edu
Financial aid office: (706) 880-8229

■ **2004-2005 TUITION AND FEES:** $15,206
■ **ROOM AND BOARD:** $6,318

SAT I Score (25th/75th percentile): 920-1150
2005 U.S. News College Ranking:
Comp. Colleges–Bachelor's (South), 7
Acceptance Rate: 90%

Other expenses: Estimated books and supplies: $1,000. Transportation: $900. Personal expenses: $900. **Financial aid:** In 2003-2004, 97% of undergraduates applied for financial aid. Of those, 69% were determined to have financial need; 32% had their need fully met. Average financial aid package (proportion receiving): $12,589 (69%). Average amount of gift aid, such as scholarships or grants (proportion receiving): $9,556 (68%). Average amount of self-help aid, such as work study or loans (proportion receiving): $3,861 (50%). Average need-based loan (excluding PLUS or other private loans): $3,445. Among students who received need-based aid, the average percentage of need met: 75%. Among students who received aid based on merit, the average award (and the proportion receiving): $6,710 (28%). The average athletic scholarship (and the proportion receiving): $0 (0%). Average amount of debt of borrowers graduating in 2003: $16,147. Proportion who borrowed: 41%.

Mercer University

1400 Coleman Avenue
Macon, GA 31207-0003
Private; www.mercer.edu
Financial aid office: (478) 301-2670

■ **2004-2005 TUITION AND FEES:** $22,050
■ **ROOM AND BOARD:** $7,060

SAT I Score (25th/75th percentile): 1080-1280
2005 U.S. News College Ranking:
Universities–Master's (South), 8
Acceptance Rate: 79%

Other expenses: Estimated books and supplies: $800. Transportation: $500. Personal expenses: $715. **Financial aid:** Priority filing date for institution's financial aid form: April 1. In 2003-2004, 84% of undergraduates applied for financial aid. Of those, 70% were determined to have financial need; 52% had their need fully met. Average financial aid package (proportion receiving): $21,250 (70%). Average amount of gift aid, such as scholarships or grants (proportion receiving): $12,688 (70%). Average amount of self-help aid, such as work study or loans (proportion receiving): $7,051 (49%). Average need-based loan (excluding PLUS or other private loans): $6,486. Among students who received need-based aid, the average percentage of need met: 89%. Among students who received aid based on merit, the average award (and the proportion receiving): $14,016 (19%). The average athletic scholarship (and the proportion receiving): $11,305 (6%). Average amount of debt of borrowers graduating in 2003: $15,549. Proportion who borrowed: 67%. **Student employment:** During the 2003-2004 academic year, 33% of undergraduates worked on campus. Average per-year earnings: $1,400. **Cooperative education programs:** art, business, computer science, engineering, humanities, natural science, social/behavioral science, other. **Reserve Officers Training Corps (ROTC):** Army ROTC: Offered on campus.

Morehouse College

830 Westview Drive SW
Atlanta, GA 30314
Private; www.morehouse.edu
Financial aid office: (404) 681-2800

■ **2004-2005 TUITION AND FEES:** $15,740
■ **ROOM AND BOARD:** $8,748

SAT I Score (25th/75th percentile): 940-1170
2005 U.S. News College Ranking:
Liberal Arts Colleges, third tier
Acceptance Rate: 72%

Financial aid: Student employment: During the 2003-2004 academic year, 62% of undergraduates worked on campus. Average per-year earnings: $1,750. **Reserve Officers Training Corps (ROTC):** Army ROTC: Offered on campus; Navy ROTC: Offered on campus; Air Force ROTC: Offered at cooperating institution (Georgia Technical Institute).

North Georgia College and State University

College Circle
Dahlonega, GA 30597
Public; www.ngcsu.edu
Financial aid office: (706) 864-1412

■ **2004-2005 TUITION AND FEES:**
    In state: $1,393; Out of state: $5,573
■ **ROOM AND BOARD:** $2,204

SAT I Score (25th/75th percentile): 983-1160
2005 U.S. News College Ranking:
Universities–Master's (South), 43
Acceptance Rate: 59%

Financial aid: Priority filing date for institution's financial aid form: March 1; deadline: May 1. **Student employment:** During the 2003-2004 academic year, 12% of undergraduates worked on campus. Average per-year earnings: $3,000. **Reserve Officers Training Corps (ROTC):** Army ROTC: Offered on campus.

Oglethorpe University

4484 Peachtree Road NE
Atlanta, GA 30319-2797
Private; www.oglethorpe.edu
Financial aid office: (404) 364-8356

■ **2004-2005 TUITION AND FEES:** $20,900
■ **ROOM AND BOARD:** $7,100

SAT I Score (25th/75th percentile): 1070-1300
2005 U.S. News College Ranking:
Liberal Arts Colleges, third tier
Acceptance Rate: 66%

Financial aid: Priority filing date for institution's financial aid form: March 1; deadline: September 1. In 2003-2004, 68% of undergraduates applied for financial aid. Of those,

58% were determined to have financial need; 32% had their need fully met. Average financial aid package (proportion receiving): $20,779 (58%). Average amount of gift aid, such as scholarships or grants (proportion receiving): $12,198 (58%). Average amount of self-help aid, such as work study or loans (proportion receiving): $3,057 (58%). Average need-based loan (excluding PLUS or other private loans): $2,288. Among students who received need-based aid, the average percentage of need met: 86%. Among students who received aid based on merit, the average award (and the proportion receiving): $10,542 (34%). The average athletic scholarship (and the proportion receiving): $0 (0%). Average amount of debt of borrowers graduating in 2003: $16,273. Proportion who borrowed: 64%.

Paine College

1235 15th Street
Augusta, GA 30901-3182
Private; www.paine.edu
Financial aid office: (706) 821-8262

■ **2004-2005 TUITION AND FEES:** $9,626
■ **ROOM AND BOARD:** $4,460

SAT I Score (25th/75th percentile): 680-870
2005 U.S. News College Ranking:
Liberal Arts Colleges, fourth tier
....
Other expenses: Estimated books and supplies: $700. **Financial aid:** Priority filing date for institution's financial aid form: March 1. In 2003-2004, 97% of undergraduates applied for financial aid. Of those, 95% were determined to have financial need; 8% had their need fully met. Average financial aid package (proportion receiving): $9,003 (95%). Average amount of gift aid, such as scholarships or grants (proportion receiving): $5,590 (92%). Average amount of self-help aid, such as work study or loans (proportion receiving): $3,989 (85%). Average need-based loan (excluding PLUS or other private loans): $3,323. Among students who received need-based aid, the average percentage of need met: 61%. Among students who received aid based on merit, the average award (and the proportion receiving): $9,792 (5%). The average athletic scholarship (and the proportion receiving): $0 (0%). Average amount of debt of borrowers graduating in 2003: $17,275. Proportion who borrowed: 87%. **Student employment:** During the 2003-2004 academic year, 1% of undergraduates worked on campus. Average per-year earnings: $5,300. **Reserve Officers Training Corps (ROTC):** Army ROTC:

Offered at cooperating institution (Augusta State University).

Piedmont College

PO Box 10
Demorest, GA 30535
Private; www.piedmont.edu
Financial aid office: (706) 778-3000

■ **2004-2005 TUITION AND FEES:** $13,500
■ **ROOM AND BOARD:** $4,950

SAT I Score (25th/75th percentile): 880-1140
2005 U.S. News College Ranking:
Universities–Master's (South), third tier
Acceptance Rate: 54%
....
Other expenses: Estimated books and supplies: $1,200. Transportation: $1,400. Personal expenses: $2,370. **Financial aid:** Priority filing date for institution's financial aid form: May 1. In 2003-2004, 99% of undergraduates applied for financial aid. Of those, 87% were determined to have financial need; 44% had their need fully met. Average financial aid package (proportion receiving): $8,642 (84%). Average amount of gift aid, such as scholarships or grants (proportion receiving): $3,049 (58%). Average amount of self-help aid, such as work study or loans (proportion receiving): $5,744 (71%). Average need-based loan (excluding PLUS or other private loans): $5,744. Among students who received need-based aid, the average percentage of need met: 74%. Among students who received aid based on merit, the average award (and the proportion receiving): $2,542 (10%). The average athletic scholarship (and the proportion receiving): $0 (0%). Average amount of debt of borrowers graduating in 2003: $13,702. Proportion who borrowed: 70%.

Reinhardt College

7300 Reinhardt College Circle
Waleska, GA 30183-0128
Private; www.reinhardt.edu
Financial aid office: (770) 720-5667

■ **2004-2005 TUITION AND FEES:** $12,150
■ **ROOM AND BOARD:** $5,762

SAT I Score (25th/75th percentile): 880-1080
2005 U.S. News College Ranking:
Comp. Colleges–Bachelor's (South), third tier
Acceptance Rate: 68%
....

Other expenses: Estimated books and supplies: $1,100. Transportation: $2,100. Personal expenses: $900. **Financial aid:** Average amount of gift aid, such as scholarships or grants (proportion receiving): $2,250 (N/A). Among students who received need-based aid, the average percentage of need met: 72%. **Student employment:** During the 2003-2004 academic year, 20% of undergraduates worked on campus. Average per-year earnings: $2,200.

Savannah College of Art and Design

342 Bull Street, PO Box 3146
Savannah, GA 31402-3146
Private; www.scad.edu
Financial aid office: (912) 525-6119

■ **2004-2005 TUITION AND FEES:** $20,750
■ **ROOM AND BOARD:** $8,330

SAT I Score (25th/75th percentile): 960-1200
2005 U.S. News College Ranking:
Unranked Specialty School–Fine Arts
Acceptance Rate: 75%
....
Other expenses: Estimated books and supplies: $1,500. Transportation: $1,200. Personal expenses: $1,500. **Financial aid:** Priority filing date for institution's financial aid form: April 1. In 2003-2004, 61% of undergraduates applied for financial aid. Of those, 49% were determined to have financial need; 39% had their need fully met. Average financial aid package (proportion receiving): $8,727 (49%). Average amount of gift aid, such as scholarships or grants (proportion receiving): $3,307 (16%). Average amount of self-help aid, such as work study or loans (proportion receiving): $4,309 (44%). Average need-based loan (excluding PLUS or other private loans): $4,056. Among students who received need-based aid, the average percentage of need met: 24%. Among students who received aid based on merit, the average award (and the proportion receiving): $3,618 (26%). The average athletic scholarship (and the proportion receiving): $10,674 (2%). Average amount of debt of borrowers graduating in 2003: $18,000. Proportion who borrowed: 62%. **Student employment:** During the 2003-2004 academic year, 20% of undergraduates worked on campus. Average per-year earnings: $3,000.

Savannah State University

PO Box 20482
Savannah, GA 31404
Public; www.savstate.edu
Financial aid office: (912) 356-2253

■ **2004-2005 TUITION AND FEES:**
In state: $2,940; Out of state: $9,908
■ **ROOM AND BOARD:** $4,616

SAT I Score (25th/75th percentile): 810-950
2005 U.S. News College Ranking:
Universities–Master's (South), fourth tier
Acceptance Rate: 42%

Reserve Officers Training Corps (ROTC): Army
ROTC: Offered on campus; Navy ROTC:
Offered on campus.

Shorter College

315 Shorter Avenue
Rome, GA 30165-4298
Private; www.shorter.edu
Financial aid office: (706) 233-7227

■ **2004-2005 TUITION AND FEES:** $12,770
■ **ROOM AND BOARD:** $5,900

SAT I Score (25th/75th percentile): 950-1160
2005 U.S. News College Ranking:
Comp. Colleges–Bachelor's (South), 17
Acceptance Rate: 83%

Other expenses: Estimated books and supplies:
$800. Transportation: $1,000. Personal expenses: $2,500. **Financial aid:** Priority filing date for institution's financial aid form: April 1. In 2003-2004, 81% of undergraduates applied for financial aid. Of those, 68% were determined to have financial need; 26% had their need fully met. Average financial aid package (proportion receiving): $10,051 (68%). Average amount of gift aid, such as scholarships or grants (proportion receiving): $7,313 (68%). Average amount of self-help aid, such as work study or loans (proportion receiving): $3,912 (48%). Average need-based loan (excluding PLUS or other private loans): $3,653. Among students who received need-based aid, the average percentage of need met: 68%. Among students who received aid based on merit, the average award (and the proportion receiving): $9,535 (31%). The average athletic scholarship (and the proportion receiving): $5,571 (6%). Average amount of debt of borrowers graduating in 2003: $16,718. Proportion who bor-

rowed: 64%. **Student employment:** During the 2003-2004 academic year, 19% of undergraduates worked on campus. Average per-year earnings: $1,200.

Southern Polytechnic State University

1100 S. Marietta Parkway
Marietta, GA 30060-2896
Public; www.spsu.edu
Financial aid office: (770) 528-7290

■ **2004-2005 TUITION AND FEES:**
In state: $3,134; Out of state: $11,144
■ **ROOM AND BOARD:** $4,946

SAT I Score (25th/75th percentile): 1010-1190
2005 U.S. News College Ranking:
Unranked Specialty School–Engineering
Acceptance Rate: 85%

Financial aid: Priority filing date for institution's financial aid form: March 15. **Cooperative education programs:** business, computer science, technologies. **Reserve Officers Training Corps (ROTC):** Army ROTC: Offered at cooperating institution (Georgia Institute of Technology); Navy ROTC: Offered at cooperating institution (Georgia Institute of Technology); Air Force ROTC: Offered at cooperating institution (Georgia Institute of Technology).

Spelman College

350 Spelman Lane SW
Atlanta, GA 30314-4399
Private; www.spelman.edu
Financial aid office: (404) 681-3643

■ **2004-2005 TUITION AND FEES:** $14,940
■ **ROOM AND BOARD:** $8,040

SAT I Score (25th/75th percentile): 990-1160
2005 U.S. News College Ranking:
Liberal Arts Colleges, 66
Acceptance Rate: 39%

Financial aid: Priority filing date for institution's financial aid form: March 14. **Student employment:** During the 2003-2004 academic year, 11% of undergraduates worked on campus. Average per-year earnings: $2,700. **Reserve Officers Training Corps (ROTC):** Army ROTC: Offered at cooperating institution (Morehouse College); Navy ROTC: Offered at cooperating institution (Morehouse College);

Air Force ROTC: Offered at cooperating institution (Morehouse College).

State University of West Georgia

1600 Maple Street
Carrollton, GA 30118
Public; www.westga.edu
Financial aid office: (770) 836-6421

■ **2004-2005 TUITION AND FEES:**
In state: $2,906; Out of state: $9,874
■ **ROOM AND BOARD:** $4,550

SAT I Score (25th/75th percentile): 910-1100
2005 U.S. News College Ranking:
Universities–Master's (South), fourth tier
Acceptance Rate: 62%

Financial aid: Priority filing date for institution's financial aid form: April 1. In 2003-2004, 71% of undergraduates applied for financial aid. Of those, 53% were determined to have financial need; 22% had their need fully met. Average financial aid package (proportion receiving): $7,337 (47%). Average amount of gift aid, such as scholarships or grants (proportion receiving): $4,344 (43%). Average amount of self-help aid, such as work study or loans (proportion receiving): $3,521 (46%). Average need-based loan (excluding PLUS or other private loans): $2,715. Among students who received need-based aid, the average percentage of need met: 69%. Among students who received aid based on merit, the average award (and the proportion receiving): $1,833 (2%). The average athletic scholarship (and the proportion receiving): $3,035 (1%). Average amount of debt of borrowers graduating in 2003: $18,230. Proportion who borrowed: 51%. **Student employment:** During the 2003-2004 academic year, 20% of undergraduates worked on campus. Average per-year earnings: $4,320. **Cooperative education programs:** other. **Reserve Officers Training Corps (ROTC):** Army ROTC: Offered on campus.

Thomas University

1501 Millpond Road
Thomasville, GA 31792
Private; www.thomasu.edu
Financial aid office: (229) 227-6925

■ **2004-2005 TUITION AND FEES:** $9,800
■ **ROOM AND BOARD:** $4,800

ACT Score (25th/75th percentile): 17
2005 U.S. News College Ranking:
Comp. Colleges–Bachelor's (South), fourth tier
Acceptance Rate: 100%

....

Other expenses: Estimated books and supplies:
$1,100. Transportation: $2,125. Personal
expenses: $1,500. **Financial aid:** In 2003-2004,
86% of undergraduates applied for financial
aid. Of those, 86% were determined to have
financial need; 52% had their need fully met.
Average financial aid package (proportion
receiving): $5,284 (86%). Average amount of
gift aid, such as scholarships or grants (proportion receiving): $2,763 (42%). Average amount
of self-help aid, such as work study or loans
(proportion receiving): $2,720 (65%). Average
need-based loan (excluding PLUS or other private loans): $3,781. Among students who
received need-based aid, the average percentage
of need met: 52%. Among students who
received aid based on merit, the average award
(and the proportion receiving): $2,138 (34%).
The average athletic scholarship (and the proportion receiving): $4,981 (12%). Average
amount of debt of borrowers graduating in
2003: $24,000. Proportion who borrowed:
61%.

Toccoa Falls College

PO Box 800-899
Toccoa Falls, GA 30598
Private; www.tfc.edu
Financial aid office: (706) 886-6831

■ **2004-2005 TUITION AND FEES:** $11,900
■ **ROOM AND BOARD:** $4,450

SAT I Score (25th/75th percentile): 930-1160
2005 U.S. News College Ranking:
Comp. Colleges–Bachelor's (South), third tier
Acceptance Rate: 75%

....

Other expenses: Estimated books and supplies:
$800. **Financial aid:** Priority filing date for insti-
tution's financial aid form: March 1. In 2003-
2004, 88% of undergraduates applied for
financial aid. Of those, 80% were determined
to have financial need; 14% had their need fully
met. Average financial aid package (proportion
receiving): $10,132 (80%). Average amount of
gift aid, such as scholarships or grants (proportion receiving): $3,960 (64%). Average amount
of self-help aid, such as work study or loans
(proportion receiving): $4,363 (64%). Average
need-based loan (excluding PLUS or other private loans): $3,773. Among students who
received need-based aid, the average percentage

of need met: 46%. Among students who
received aid based on merit, the average award
(and the proportion receiving): $4,720 (16%).
The average athletic scholarship (and the proportion receiving): $0 (0%). Average amount of
debt of borrowers graduating in 2003: $16,152.
Proportion who borrowed: 63%. **Student
employment:** During the 2003-2004 academic
year, 12% of undergraduates worked on campus. Average per-year earnings: $1,875.

University of Georgia

212 Terrell Hall
Athens, GA 30602
Public; www.uga.edu
Financial aid office: (706) 542-6147

■ **2004-2005 TUITION AND FEES:**
   In state: $4,272; Out of state: $15,588
■ **ROOM AND BOARD:** $6,006

SAT I Score (25th/75th percentile): 1120-1300
2005 U.S. News College Ranking:
National Universities, 58
Acceptance Rate: 75%

....

Other expenses: Estimated books and supplies:
$750. Personal expenses: $1,740. **Financial aid:**
Priority filing date for institution's financial aid
form: March 1. In 2003-2004, 47% of undergraduates applied for financial aid. Of those,
28% were determined to have financial need;
32% had their need fully met. Average financial
aid package (proportion receiving): $7,323
(27%). Average amount of gift aid, such as
scholarships or grants (proportion receiving):
$5,664 (23%). Average amount of self-help aid,
such as work study or loans (proportion receiving): $3,911 (17%). Average need-based loan
(excluding PLUS or other private loans): $3,771.
Among students who received need-based aid,
the average percentage of need met: 73%.
Among students who received aid based on
merit, the average award (and the proportion
receiving): $1,927 (5%). The average athletic
scholarship (and the proportion receiving):
$8,706 (2%). Average amount of debt of bor-
rowers graduating in 2003: $13,193. Proportion
who borrowed: 47%. **Student employment:**
During the 2003-2004 academic year, 13% of
undergraduates worked on campus. Average
per-year earnings: $2,300. **Cooperative educa-
tion programs:** agriculture, natural science.
Reserve Officers Training Corps (ROTC): Army
ROTC: Offered on campus; Air Force ROTC:
Offered on campus.

Valdosta State University

1500 N. Patterson Street
Valdosta, GA 31698
Public; www.valdosta.edu
Financial aid office: (229) 333-5935

■ **2004-2005 TUITION AND FEES:**
   In state: $2,860; Out of state: $9,496
■ **ROOM AND BOARD:** $5,002

SAT I Score (25th/75th percentile): 930-1110
2005 U.S. News College Ranking:
Universities–Master's (South), third tier
Acceptance Rate: 68%

....

Other expenses: Estimated books and supplies:
$750. Transportation: $1,700. Personal expenses: $1,600. **Financial aid:** Priority filing date for
institution's financial aid form: May 1. In 2003-
2004, 87% of undergraduates applied for
financial aid. Of those, 51% were determined to
have financial need; 32% had their need fully
met. Average financial aid package (proportion
receiving): $6,484 (50%). Average amount of
gift aid, such as scholarships or grants (proportion receiving): $3,026 (30%). Average amount
of self-help aid, such as work study or loans
(proportion receiving): $3,279 (44%). Average
need-based loan (excluding PLUS or other private loans): $3,174. Among students who
received need-based aid, the average percentage
of need met: 70%. Among students who
received aid based on merit, the average award
(and the proportion receiving): $6,182 (13%).
The average athletic scholarship (and the proportion receiving): $3,330 (3%). Average
amount of debt of borrowers graduating in
2003: $22,361. Proportion who borrowed: 60%.
Student employment: During the 2003-2004
academic year, 11% of undergraduates worked
on campus. Average per-year earnings: $4,400.
Cooperative education programs: art, business,
computer science, education, engineering,
health professions, humanities, natural science,
social/behavioral science, technologies, other.
Reserve Officers Training Corps (ROTC): Air
Force ROTC: Offered on campus.

Wesleyan College

4760 Forsyth Road
Macon, GA 31210-4462
Private; www.wesleyancollege.edu
Financial aid office: (800) 447-6610

- **2004-2005 TUITION AND FEES:** $10,900
- **ROOM AND BOARD:** $7,450

SAT I Score (25th/75th percentile): 960-1210
2005 U.S. News College Ranking:
Liberal Arts Colleges, third tier
Acceptance Rate: 77%

Other expenses: Estimated books and supplies: $600. Transportation: $500. Personal expenses: $1,000. **Financial aid:** Priority filing date for institution's financial aid form: March 1; deadline: June 30. In 2003-2004, 72% of undergraduates applied for financial aid. Of those, 61% were determined to have financial need; 30% had their need fully met. Average financial aid package (proportion receiving): $10,974 (61%). Average amount of gift aid, such as scholarships or grants (proportion receiving): $8,029 (60%). Average amount of self-help aid, such as work study or loans (proportion receiving): $4,204 (44%). Average need-based loan (excluding PLUS or other private loans): $3,868. Among students who received need-based aid, the average percentage of need met: 82%. Among students who received aid based on merit, the average award (and the proportion receiving): $12,507 (39%). The average athletic scholarship (and the proportion receiving): $0 (0%). Average amount of debt of borrowers graduating in 2003: $20,200. Proportion who borrowed: 78%.

Hawaii

Brigham Young University–Hawaii

55-220 Kulanui Street
Laie Oahu, HI 96762-1294
Private; www.byuh.edu
Financial aid office: (808) 293-3530

- **2004-2005 TUITION AND FEES:** $2,610
- **ROOM AND BOARD:** $4,796

ACT Score (25th/75th percentile): 19-25
2005 U.S. News College Ranking:
Comp. Colleges–Bachelor's (West), 6
Acceptance Rate: 17%

Other expenses: Estimated books and supplies: $875. Transportation: $500. Personal expenses: $1,000. **Financial aid:** In 2003-2004, 95% of undergraduates applied for financial aid. Of those, 82% were determined to have financial need; 65% had their need fully met. Average financial aid package (proportion receiving): $3,000 (82%). Average amount of gift aid, such as scholarships or grants (proportion receiving): $2,700 (33%). Average amount of self-help aid, such as work study or loans (proportion receiving): $3,500 (33%). Average need-based loan (excluding PLUS or other private loans): $1,165. Among students who received need-based aid, the average percentage of need met: 80%. Among students who received aid based on merit, the average award (and the proportion receiving): $1,290 (16%). The average athletic scholarship (and the proportion receiving): $1,290 (8%). Average amount of debt of borrowers graduating in 2003: $8,505. Proportion who borrowed: 31%. **Student employment:** During the 2003-2004 academic year, 68% of undergraduates worked on campus. Average per-year earnings: $7,363. **Cooperative education programs:** business, computer science, education, social/behavioral science, technologies. **Reserve Officers Training Corps (ROTC):** Army ROTC: Offered at cooperating institution (University of Hawaii-Manoa); Air Force ROTC: Offered at cooperating institution (University of Hawaii-Manoa).

Chaminade University of Honolulu

3140 Waialae Avenue
Honolulu, HI 96816-1578
Private; www.chaminade.edu
Financial aid office: (808) 735-4780

- **2004-2005 TUITION AND FEES:** $13,970
- **ROOM AND BOARD:** $8,490

SAT I Score (25th/75th percentile): 855-1060
2005 U.S. News College Ranking:
Universities–Master's (West), fourth tier
Acceptance Rate: 96%

Other expenses: Estimated books and supplies: $720. Transportation: $360. Personal expenses: $1,104. **Financial aid:** Priority filing date for institution's financial aid form: March 1. In 2003-2004, 81% of undergraduates applied for financial aid. Of those, 73% were determined to have financial need; 18% had their need fully met. Average financial aid package (proportion receiving): $12,701 (73%). Average amount of gift aid, such as scholarships or grants (proportion receiving): $9,044 (73%). Average amount of self-help aid, such as work study or loans (proportion receiving): $4,446 (64%). Average need-based loan (excluding PLUS or other private loans): $3,771. Among students who received need-based aid, the average percentage of need met: 66%. Among students who received aid based on merit, the average award (and the proportion receiving): $4,693 (8%). The average athletic scholarship (and the proportion receiving): $8,207 (6%). Average amount of debt of borrowers graduating in 2003: $21,105. Proportion who borrowed: 69%. **Student employment:** During the 2003-2004 academic year, 5% of undergraduates worked on campus. Average per-year earnings: $1,875. **Cooperative education programs:** education, social/behavioral science. **Reserve Officers Training Corps (ROTC):** Army ROTC: Offered at cooperating institution (University of Hawaii at Manoa); Air Force ROTC: Offered at cooperating institution (University of Hawaii at Manoa).

Hawaii Pacific University

1164 Bishop Street
Honolulu, HI 96813
Private; www.hpu.edu
Financial aid office: (808) 544-0253

- **2004-2005 TUITION AND FEES:** $11,002
- **ROOM AND BOARD:** $9,020

SAT I Score (25th/75th percentile): 870-1130
2005 U.S. News College Ranking:
Universities–Master's (West), third tier
Acceptance Rate: 81%

Other expenses: Estimated books and supplies: $1,000. Transportation: $360. Personal expenses: $800. **Financial aid:** Priority filing date for institution's financial aid form: March 1. In 2003-2004, 63% of undergraduates applied for financial aid. Of those, 39% were determined to have financial need; 23% had their need fully met. Average financial aid package (proportion receiving): $10,392 (38%). Average amount of gift aid, such as scholarships or grants (proportion receiving): $3,866 (23%). Average amount of self-help aid, such as work study or loans (proportion receiving): $5,361 (35%). Average need-based loan (excluding PLUS or other private loans): $4,611. Among students who received need-based aid, the average percentage of need met: 77%. Among students who received aid based on merit, the average award (and the proportion receiving): $4,074 (18%). The average athletic scholarship (and the proportion receiving): $4,668 (4%). Average amount of debt of borrowers graduating in 2003: $17,759. Proportion who borrowed: 36%. **Student employment:** During the 2003-2004 academic year, 5% of undergraduates worked on campus. Average per-year earnings: $4,000. **Cooperative education programs:** business, computer science, education, health professions, humanities, natural science, social/behavioral science. **Reserve Officers Training Corps (ROTC):** Army ROTC: Offered at cooperating institution (University of Hawaii); Air Force ROTC: Offered at cooperating institution (University of Hawaii, Manoa).

University of Hawaii–Hilo

200 W. Kawili Street
Hilo, HI 96720-4091
Public; www.uhh.hawaii.edu
Financial aid office: (808) 974-7323

■ **2004-2005 TUITION AND FEES:**
  In state: $2,550; Out of state: $8,118
■ **ROOM AND BOARD:** $4,916

SAT I Score (25th/75th percentile): 890-1140
2005 U.S. News College Ranking:
Liberal Arts Colleges, fourth tier
Acceptance Rate: 66%
....

Other expenses: Estimated books and supplies:
$1,016. Transportation: $244. Personal expenses:
$990. **Financial aid:** Priority filing date for institution's financial aid form: March 1. In 2003-2004,
44% of undergraduates applied for financial aid.
Of those, 35% were determined to have financial
need; 21% had their need fully met. Average
financial aid package (proportion receiving):
$4,887 (32%). Average amount of gift aid, such as
scholarships or grants (proportion receiving):
$3,414 (23%). Average amount of self-help aid,
such as work study or loans (proportion receiving): $3,745 (20%). Average need-based loan
(excluding PLUS or other private loans): $2,747.
Among students who received need-based aid, the
average percentage of need met: 83%. Among
students who received aid based on merit, the
average award (and the proportion receiving):
$1,208 (5%). The average athletic scholarship (and
the proportion receiving): $4,631 (0%). Average
amount of debt of borrowers graduating in 2003:
$11,806. Proportion who borrowed: 37%. **Student
employment:** During the 2003-2004 academic
year, 23% of undergraduates worked on campus.
Average per-year earnings: $1,832.

University of Hawaii–Manoa

2444 Dole Street
Honolulu, HI 96822
Public; www.hawaii.edu
Financial aid office: (808) 956-7251

■ **2004-2005 TUITION AND FEES:**
  In state: $3,581; Out of state: $10,061
■ **ROOM AND BOARD:** $5,942

SAT I Score (25th/75th percentile): 990-1200
2005 U.S. News College Ranking:
National Universities, third tier
Acceptance Rate: 59%
....

Other expenses: Estimated books and supplies:
$1,017. Transportation: $243. Personal expenses: $1,166. **Financial aid:** Priority filing date for
institution's financial aid form: March 15. In
2003-2004, 55% of undergraduates applied for
financial aid. Of those, 34% were determined to
have financial need; 31% had their need fully
met. Average financial aid package (proportion
receiving): $5,846 (32%). Average amount of
gift aid, such as scholarships or grants (proportion receiving): $3,426 (26%). Average amount
of self-help aid, such as work study or loans
(proportion receiving): $3,657 (22%). Average
need-based loan (excluding PLUS or other private loans): $3,438. Among students who
received need-based aid, the average percentage
of need met: 71%. Among students who
received aid based on merit, the average award
(and the proportion receiving): $2,758 (9%).
The average athletic scholarship (and the proportion receiving): $10,777 (2%). Average
amount of debt of borrowers graduating in
2003: $13,707. Proportion who borrowed: 29%.
Student employment: During the 2003-2004
academic year, 42% of undergraduates worked
on campus. Average per-year earnings: $4,700.
Cooperative education programs: agriculture,
art, business, computer science, education,
engineering, health professions, humanities,
natural science, social/behavioral science, technologies, other. **Reserve Officers Training Corps
(ROTC):** Army ROTC: Offered on campus; Air
Force ROTC: Offered on campus.

Idaho

Albertson College

2112 Cleveland Boulevard
Caldwell, ID 83605
Private; www.albertson.edu
Financial aid office: (208) 459-5308

- **2004-2005 TUITION AND FEES:** $14,865
- **ROOM AND BOARD:** $5,250

ACT Score (25th/75th percentile): 22-27
2005 U.S. News College Ranking:
Liberal Arts Colleges, third tier
Acceptance Rate: 79%

Other expenses: Estimated books and supplies: $700. Transportation: $550. Personal expenses: $700. **Financial aid:** Priority filing date for institution's financial aid form: February 15. In 2003-2004, 64% of undergraduates applied for financial aid. Of those, 64% were determined to have financial need; 17% had their need fully met. Average financial aid package (proportion receiving): $14,200 (64%). Average amount of gift aid, such as scholarships or grants (proportion receiving): $4,435 (36%). Average amount of self-help aid, such as work study or loans (proportion receiving): $4,592 (52%). Average need-based loan (excluding PLUS or other private loans): $4,458. Among students who received need-based aid, the average percentage of need met: 83%. Among students who received aid based on merit, the average award (and the proportion receiving): $8,259 (30%). The average athletic scholarship (and the proportion receiving): $5,085 (21%). Average amount of debt of borrowers graduating in 2003: $17,181. Proportion who borrowed: 71%. **Student employment:** During the 2003-2004 academic year, 40% of undergraduates worked on campus. Average per-year earnings: $1,050. **Cooperative education programs:** computer science, engineering, health professions. **Reserve Officers Training Corps (ROTC):** Army ROTC: Offered on campus.

Boise State University

1910 University Drive
Boise, ID 83725
Public; www.BoiseState.edu
Financial aid office: (208) 426-1540

- **2004-2005 TUITION AND FEES:**
  In state: $3,520; Out of state: $10,576

ACT Score (25th/75th percentile): 18-27
2005 U.S. News College Ranking:
Universities–Master's (West), third tier
Acceptance Rate: 92%

Other expenses: Estimated books and supplies: $1,000. Transportation: $1,200. Personal expenses: $2,400. **Financial aid:** Priority filing date for institution's financial aid form: April 1. In 2003-2004, 69% of undergraduates applied for financial aid. Of those, 63% were determined to have financial need; 14% had their need fully met. Average financial aid package (proportion receiving): $6,978 (55%). Average amount of gift aid, such as scholarships or grants (proportion receiving): $3,072 (38%). Average amount of self-help aid, such as work study or loans (proportion receiving): $3,970 (44%). Average need-based loan (excluding PLUS or other private loans): $3,540. Among students who received need-based aid, the average percentage of need met: 75%. Among students who received aid based on merit, the average award (and the proportion receiving): $1,306 (12%). The average athletic scholarship (and the proportion receiving): $9,800 (3%). **Student employment:** During the 2003-2004 academic year, 8% of undergraduates worked on campus. Average per-year earnings: $2,000. **Reserve Officers Training Corps (ROTC):** Army ROTC: Offered on campus.

Idaho State University

741 S. Seventh Avenue
Pocatello, ID 83209
Public; www.isu.edu
Financial aid office: (208) 282-2756

- **2004-2005 TUITION AND FEES:**
  In state: $3,700; Out of state: $10,780
- **ROOM AND BOARD:** $4,680

ACT Score (25th/75th percentile): 18-23
2005 U.S. News College Ranking:
National Universities, fourth tier
Acceptance Rate: 74%

Other expenses: Estimated books and supplies: $800. Transportation: $810. Personal expenses: $1,602. **Financial aid:** Priority filing date for institution's financial aid form: March 15; deadline: June 30. Average amount of debt of borrowers graduating in 2003: $19,039. Proportion who borrowed: 45%. **Student employment:** During the 2003-2004 academic year, 16% of undergraduates worked on campus. Average per-year earnings: $3,120. **Cooperative education programs:** health professions, natural science, other. **Reserve Officers Training Corps (ROTC):** Army ROTC: Offered on campus.

Lewis-Clark State College

500 Eighth Avenue
Lewiston, ID 83501
Public; www.lcsc.edu
Financial aid office: (208) 792-2224

- **2004-2005 TUITION AND FEES:**
  In state: $3,757; Out of state: $9,997
- **ROOM AND BOARD:** $3,600

ACT Score (25th/75th percentile): 15-25
2005 U.S. News College Ranking:
Comp. Colleges–Bachelor's (West), third tier
Acceptance Rate: 64%

Other expenses: Estimated books and supplies: $1,500. Transportation: $1,780. Personal expenses: $1,450. **Financial aid:** Priority filing date for institution's financial aid form: March 1. In 2003-2004, 74% of undergraduates applied for financial aid. Of those, 65% were determined to have financial need; 15% had their need fully met. Average financial aid package (proportion receiving): $5,239 (64%). Average amount of gift aid, such as scholarships or grants (proportion receiving): $2,890 (53%). Average amount of self-help aid, such as work study or loans (proportion receiving): $3,462 (53%). Average need-based loan (excluding PLUS or other private loans): $3,365. Among students who received need-based aid, the average percentage of need met: 15%.

Among students who received aid based on merit, the average award (and the proportion receiving): $2,982 (7%). The average athletic scholarship (and the proportion receiving): $4,597 (6%). Proportion who borrowed: 61%. **Cooperative education programs:** business, computer science, education, health professions, humanities, natural science, social/behavioral science, technologies. **Reserve Officers Training Corps (ROTC):** Army ROTC: Offered on campus; Navy ROTC: Offered at cooperating institution (University of Idaho); Air Force ROTC: Offered at cooperating institution (University of Idaho).

Northwest Nazarene University

623 Holly Street
Nampa, ID 83686
Private; www.nnu.edu
Financial aid office: (208) 467-8347

■ **2004-2005 TUITION AND FEES:** $16,570
■ **ROOM AND BOARD:** $4,630

ACT Score (25th/75th percentile): 19-26
2005 U.S. News College Ranking:
Universities–Master's (West), 30
Acceptance Rate: 67%

Other expenses: Estimated books and supplies: $760. Transportation: $800. Personal expenses: $2,250. **Financial aid:** Priority filing date for institution's financial aid form: March 1. In 2003-2004, 82% of undergraduates applied for financial aid. Of those, 71% were determined to have financial need; 23% had their need fully met. Average financial aid package (proportion receiving): $12,598 (71%). Average amount of gift aid, such as scholarships or grants (proportion receiving): $2,887 (53%). Average amount of self-help aid, such as work study or loans (proportion receiving): $5,210 (60%). Average need-based loan (excluding PLUS or other private loans):

$4,711. Among students who received need-based aid, the average percentage of need met: 76%. Among students who received aid based on merit, the average award (and the proportion receiving): $8,153 (11%). The average athletic scholarship (and the proportion receiving): $4,230 (2%). Average amount of debt of borrowers graduating in 2003: $21,073. Proportion who borrowed: 77%. **Student employment:** During the 2003-2004 academic year, 28% of undergraduates worked on campus. Average per-year earnings: $2,286. **Reserve Officers Training Corps (ROTC):** Army ROTC: Offered on campus.

University of Idaho

875 Perimeter Drive, PO Box 442282
Moscow, ID 83844-2282
Public; www.uidaho.edu
Financial aid office: (208) 885-6312

■ **2004-2005 TUITION AND FEES:**
   In state: $3,632; Out of state: $11,652
■ **ROOM AND BOARD:** $5,034

ACT Score (25th/75th percentile): 20-26
2005 U.S. News College Ranking:
National Universities, third tier
Acceptance Rate: 81%

Financial aid: Priority filing date for institution's financial aid form: February 15. **Student employment:** During the 2003-2004 academic year, 35% of undergraduates worked on campus. Average per-year earnings: $2,340. **Cooperative education programs:** agriculture, art, business, computer science, education, engineering, health professions, home economics, humanities, natural science, social/behavioral science, technologies, vocational arts. **Reserve Officers Training Corps (ROTC):** Army ROTC: Offered on campus; Navy ROTC: Offered on campus; Air Force ROTC: Offered at cooperating institution (Washington State University).

Illinois

Augustana College

639 38th Street
Rock Island, IL 61201-2296
Private; www.augustana.edu
Financial aid office: (309) 794-7207

■ **2004-2005 TUITION AND FEES:** $22,131
■ **ROOM AND BOARD:** $6,042

ACT Score (25th/75th percentile): 24-29
2005 U.S. News College Ranking:
Liberal Arts Colleges, 89
Acceptance Rate: 68%

Other expenses: Estimated books and supplies:
$675. Transportation: $400. Personal expenses:
$800. **Financial aid:** Priority filing date for insti-
tution's financial aid form: April 1. In 2003-
2004, 80% of undergraduates applied for
financial aid. Of those, 67% were determined
to have financial need; 49% had their need
fully met. Average financial aid package (proportion receiving): $15,207 (67%). Average
amount of gift aid, such as scholarships or
grants (proportion receiving): $10,723 (67%).
Average amount of self-help aid, such as work
study or loans (proportion receiving): $4,135
(67%). Average need-based loan (excluding
PLUS or other private loans): $4,409. Among
students who received need-based aid, the average percentage of need met: 86%. Among students who received aid based on merit, the
average award (and the proportion receiving):
$6,976 (12%). Average amount of debt of bor-
rowers graduating in 2003: $17,076.
Proportion who borrowed: 76%. **Student
employment:** During the 2003-2004 academic
year, 60% of undergraduates worked on campus. Average per-year earnings: $1,500.

Aurora University

347 S. Gladstone
Aurora, IL 60506-4892
Private; www.aurora.edu
Financial aid office: (630) 844-5533

■ **2004-2005 TUITION AND FEES:** $14,750
■ **ROOM AND BOARD:** $6,614

ACT Score (25th/75th percentile): 19-24
2005 U.S. News College Ranking:
Universities–Master's (Midwest), third tier
Acceptance Rate: 56%

Other expenses: Estimated books and supplies:
$900. Transportation: $922. Personal expenses: $900. **Financial aid:** Priority filing date for
institution's financial aid form: April 15. In
2003-2004, 98% of undergraduates applied for
financial aid. Of those, 79% were determined
to have financial need; 35% had their need fully
met. Average financial aid package (proportion
receiving): $15,470 (79%). Average amount of
gift aid, such as scholarships or grants (proportion receiving): $5,496 (61%). Average amount
of self-help aid, such as work study or loans
(proportion receiving): $4,150 (63%). Average
need-based loan (excluding PLUS or other private loans): $3,663. Among students who
received need-based aid, the average percentage
of need met: 82%. Among students who
received aid based on merit, the average award
(and the proportion receiving): $7,653 (18%).
The average athletic scholarship (and the proportion receiving): $0 (0%). Average amount of
debt of borrowers graduating in 2003: $15,983.
Proportion who borrowed: 72%. **Student
employment:** During the 2003-2004 academic
year, 2% of undergraduates worked on campus.
Average per-year earnings: $6,000. **Reserve
Officers Training Corps (ROTC):** Army ROTC:
Offered at cooperating institution (Wheaton
College).

Benedictine University

5700 College Road
Lisle, IL 60532
Private; www.ben.edu
Financial aid office: (630) 829-6108

■ **2004-2005 TUITION AND FEES:** $18,055
■ **ROOM AND BOARD:** $6,600

ACT Score (25th/75th percentile): 20-26
2005 U.S. News College Ranking:
Universities–Master's (Midwest), 31
Acceptance Rate: 74%

Financial aid: Priority filing date for institution's financial aid form: April 15; deadline:
April 15. In 2003-2004, 49% of undergraduates
applied for financial aid. Of those, 41% were

determined to have financial need; 17% had
their need fully met. Average financial aid package (proportion receiving): $11,489 (41%).
Average amount of gift aid, such as scholarships or grants (proportion receiving): $5,273
(32%). Average amount of self-help aid, such as
work study or loans (proportion receiving):
$3,792 (35%). Average need-based loan (exclud-
ing PLUS or other private loans): $3,692.
Among students who received need-based aid,
the average percentage of need met: 68%.
Among students who received aid based on
merit, the average award (and the proportion
receiving): $6,632 (27%). Average amount of
debt of borrowers graduating in 2003: $6,726.
Proportion who borrowed: 50%. **Student
employment:** During the 2003-2004 academic
year, 18% of undergraduates worked on campus. Average per-year earnings: $5. **Reserve
Officers Training Corps (ROTC):** Army ROTC:
Offered on campus.

Blackburn College

700 College Avenue
Carlinville, IL 62626
Private; www.blackburn.edu
Financial aid office: (800) 233-3550

■ **2004-2005 TUITION AND FEES:** $14,600
■ **ROOM AND BOARD:** $3,580

ACT Score (25th/75th percentile): 20-24
2005 U.S. News College Ranking:
Liberal Arts Colleges, fourth tier
Acceptance Rate: 56%

Other expenses: Estimated books and supplies:
$700. Personal expenses: $800. **Financial aid:**
Priority filing date for institution's financial aid
form: April 1. In 2003-2004, 99% of undergraduates applied for financial aid. Of those,
88% were determined to have financial need;
53% had their need fully met. Average financial
aid package (proportion receiving): $9,652
(88%). Average amount of gift aid, such as
scholarships or grants (proportion receiving):
$7,199 (88%). Average amount of self-help aid,
such as work study or loans (proportion receiving): $2,677 (58%). Average need-based loan
(excluding PLUS or other private loans):
$2,677. Among students who received need-
based aid, the average percentage of need met:
89%. Among students who received aid based

on merit, the average award (and the proportion receiving): $4,449 (9%). The average athletic scholarship (and the proportion receiving): $0 (0%). Average amount of debt of borrowers graduating in 2003: $11,500. Proportion who borrowed: 85%. **Student employment:** During the 2003-2004 academic year, 80% of undergraduates worked on campus. Average per-year earnings: $2,055.

Bradley University

1501 W. Bradley Avenue
Peoria, IL 61625
Private; www.bradley.edu
Financial aid office: (309) 677-3089

■ **2004-2005 TUITION AND FEES:** $17,730
■ **ROOM AND BOARD:** $6,150

ACT Score (25th/75th percentile): 23-28
2005 U.S. News College Ranking:
Universities–Master's (Midwest), 6
Acceptance Rate: 69%

Other expenses: Estimated books and supplies: $1,000. Transportation: $250. Personal expenses: $1,870. **Financial aid:** Priority filing date for institution's financial aid form: March 1. In 2003-2004, 87% of undergraduates applied for financial aid. Of those, 73% were determined to have financial need; 63% had their need fully met. Average financial aid package (proportion receiving): $13,805 (73%). Average amount of gift aid, such as scholarships or grants (proportion receiving): $8,664 (70%). Average amount of self-help aid, such as work study or loans (proportion receiving): $5,223 (56%). Average need-based loan (excluding PLUS or other private loans): $4,523. Among students who received need-based aid, the average percentage of need met: 85%. Among students who received aid based on merit, the average award (and the proportion receiving): $8,939 (23%). The average athletic scholarship (and the proportion receiving): $11,509 (2%). Average amount of debt of borrowers graduating in 2003: $14,309. Proportion who borrowed: 74%. **Student employment:** During the 2003-2004 academic year, 11% of undergraduates worked on campus. Average per-year earnings: $2,500. **Cooperative education programs:** art, business, computer science, education, engineering, health professions, home economics, humanities, natural science, social/behavioral science. **Reserve Officers Training Corps (ROTC):** Army ROTC: Offered at cooperating institution (Illinois State University).

Chicago State University

9501 S. King Drive
Chicago, IL 60628
Public; www.csu.edu
Financial aid office: (773) 995-2304

■ **2004-2005 TUITION AND FEES:**
In state: $6,143; Out of state: $10,973
■ **ROOM AND BOARD:** $6,032

ACT Score (25th/75th percentile): 16-19
2005 U.S. News College Ranking:
Universities–Master's (Midwest), fourth tier
Acceptance Rate: 56%

Columbia College

600 S. Michigan Avenue
Chicago, IL 60605-1996
Private; www.colum.edu
Financial aid office: (312) 344-7140

■ **2004-2005 TUITION AND FEES:** $15,260
■ **ROOM AND BOARD:** $7,340

ACT Score (25th/75th percentile): 17-24
2005 U.S. News College Ranking:
Universities–Master's (Midwest), fourth tier
Acceptance Rate: 90%

Other expenses: Estimated books and supplies: $1,200. Transportation: $1,350. Personal expenses: $3,468. **Financial aid:** Priority filing date for institution's financial aid form: August 13. Average per-year earnings: $2,240.

Concordia University– River Forest

7400 Augusta Street
River Forest, IL 60305-1499
Private; www.curf.edu
Financial aid office: (708) 209-3113

■ **2004-2005 TUITION AND FEES:** $19,000
■ **ROOM AND BOARD:** $5,900

ACT Score (25th/75th percentile): 19-26
2005 U.S. News College Ranking:
Universities–Master's (Midwest), 48
Acceptance Rate: 56%

Other expenses: Estimated books and supplies: $900. Transportation: $600. Personal expenses: $400. **Financial aid:** Priority filing date for

institution's financial aid form: April 1; deadline: April 1. In 2003-2004, 96% of undergraduates applied for financial aid. Of those, 82% were determined to have financial need; 43% had their need fully met. Average financial aid package (proportion receiving): $11,333 (76%). Average amount of gift aid, such as scholarships or grants (proportion receiving): $5,179 (49%). Average amount of self-help aid, such as work study or loans (proportion receiving): $3,850 (51%). Average need-based loan (excluding PLUS or other private loans): $3,670. Among students who received need-based aid, the average percentage of need met: 45%. Among students who received aid based on merit, the average award (and the proportion receiving): $39,000 (13%). The average athletic scholarship (and the proportion receiving): $0 (0%). Average amount of debt of borrowers graduating in 2003: $14,800. Proportion who borrowed: 84%.

DePaul University

1 E. Jackson Boulevard
Chicago, IL 60604-2287
Private; www.depaul.edu
Financial aid office: (312) 362-8091

■ **2004-2005 TUITION AND FEES:** $19,740
■ **ROOM AND BOARD:** $9,343

ACT Score (25th/75th percentile): 21-26
2005 U.S. News College Ranking:
National Universities, third tier
Acceptance Rate: 73%

Other expenses: Estimated books and supplies: $1,000. Transportation: $48. **Financial aid:** Priority filing date for institution's financial aid form: May 1; deadline: May 1. In 2003-2004, 83% of undergraduates applied for financial aid. Of those, 75% were determined to have financial need; 10% had their need fully met. Average financial aid package (proportion receiving): $13,691 (75%). Average amount of gift aid, such as scholarships or grants (proportion receiving): $8,989 (60%). Average amount of self-help aid, such as work study or loans (proportion receiving): $5,729 (65%). Average need-based loan (excluding PLUS or other private loans): $4,331. Among students who received need-based aid, the average percentage of need met: 67%. Among students who received aid based on merit, the average award (and the proportion receiving): $7,070 (2%). The average athletic scholarship (and the proportion receiving): $16,127 (2%). Average amount of debt of borrowers graduating in

2003: $21,695. Proportion who borrowed: 67%. **Student employment:** During the 2003-2004 academic year, 13% of undergraduates worked on campus. Average per-year earnings: $1,939. **Reserve Officers Training Corps (ROTC):** Army ROTC: Offered on campus.

Dominican University

7900 W. Division
River Forest, IL 60305
Private; www.dom.edu
Financial aid office: (708) 524-6809

■ **2004-2005 TUITION AND FEES:** $19,000
■ **ROOM AND BOARD:** $5,890

ACT Score (25th/75th percentile): 20-26
2005 U.S. News College Ranking:
Universities–Master's (Midwest), 14
Acceptance Rate: 82%

Other expenses: Estimated books and supplies: $800. Transportation: $50. Personal expenses: $900. **Financial aid:** Priority filing date for institution's financial aid form: April 15. In 2003-2004, 88% of undergraduates applied for financial aid. Of those, 78% were determined to have financial need; 18% had their need fully met. Average financial aid package (proportion receiving): $12,518 (78%). Average amount of gift aid, such as scholarships or grants (proportion receiving): $9,254 (77%). Average amount of self-help aid, such as work study or loans (proportion receiving): $4,219 (62%). Average need-based loan (excluding PLUS or other private loans): $3,623. Among students who received need-based aid, the average percentage of need met: 77%. Among students who received aid based on merit, the average award (and the proportion receiving): $5,600 (33%). The average athletic scholarship (and the proportion receiving): $0 (0%). Average amount of debt of borrowers graduating in 2003: $13,437. Proportion who borrowed: 59%. **Student employment:** During the 2003-2004 academic year, 30% of undergraduates worked on campus. Average per-year earnings: $2,200.

Eastern Illinois University

600 Lincoln Avenue
Charleston, IL 61920-3099
Public; www.eiu.edu
Financial aid office: (217) 581-3713

■ **2004-2005 TUITION AND FEES:**
   In state: $5,479; Out of state: $13,138
■ **ROOM AND BOARD:** $7,150

ACT Score (25th/75th percentile): 20-24
2005 U.S. News College Ranking:
Universities–Master's (Midwest), 38
Acceptance Rate: 78%

Other expenses: Estimated books and supplies: $120. Transportation: $670. Personal expenses: $1,460. **Financial aid:** Priority filing date for institution's financial aid form: April 1. In 2003-2004, 70% of undergraduates applied for financial aid. Of those, 52% were determined to have financial need; 72% had their need fully met. Average financial aid package (proportion receiving): $8,766 (48%). Average amount of gift aid, such as scholarships or grants (proportion receiving): $2,587 (25%). Average amount of self-help aid, such as work study or loans (proportion receiving): $2,851 (32%). Average need-based loan (excluding PLUS or other private loans): $3,181. Among students who received need-based aid, the average percentage of need met: 19%. Among students who received aid based on merit, the average award (and the proportion receiving): $5,729 (3%). The average athletic scholarship (and the proportion receiving): $3,292 (0%). Average amount of debt of borrowers graduating in 2003: $13,997. Proportion who borrowed: 60%. **Student employment:** During the 2003-2004 academic year, 15% of undergraduates worked on campus. Average per-year earnings: $1,291. **Cooperative education programs:** business, engineering, health professions. **Reserve Officers Training Corps (ROTC):** Army ROTC: Offered on campus.

East-West University

816 S. Michigan Avenue
Chicago, IL 60605
Private; www.eastwest.edu
Financial aid office: (312) 939-0111

■ **2004-2005 TUITION AND FEES:** $10,815

2005 U.S. News College Ranking:
Comp. Colleges–Bachelor's (Midwest), fourth tier
Acceptance Rate: 73%

Other expenses: Estimated books and supplies: $1,200. Transportation: $450. Personal expenses: $500. **Financial aid:** Priority filing date for institution's financial aid form: June 30. 79% had their need fully met. Average financial aid package (proportion receiving): $9,170 (N/A). Average amount of gift aid, such as scholarships or grants (proportion receiving): $2,990 (N/A). Average need-based loan (excluding

PLUS or other private loans): $2,625. Among students who received need-based aid, the average percentage of need met: 90%.

Elmhurst College

190 Prospect Avenue
Elmhurst, IL 60126
Private; www.elmhurst.edu
Financial aid office: (630) 617-3080

■ **2004-2005 TUITION AND FEES:** $20,090
■ **ROOM AND BOARD:** $6,304

ACT Score (25th/75th percentile): 19-26
2005 U.S. News College Ranking:
Comp. Colleges–Bachelor's (Midwest), 10
Acceptance Rate: 73%

Other expenses: Estimated books and supplies: $1,000. Transportation: $0. Personal expenses: $1,006. **Financial aid:** Priority filing date for institution's financial aid form: April 15. In 2003-2004, 77% of undergraduates applied for financial aid. Of those, 70% were determined to have financial need; 82% had their need fully met. Average financial aid package (proportion receiving): $15,400 (70%). Average amount of gift aid, such as scholarships or grants (proportion receiving): $11,297 (60%). Average amount of self-help aid, such as work study or loans (proportion receiving): $5,412 (51%). Average need-based loan (excluding PLUS or other private loans): $4,538. Among students who received need-based aid, the average percentage of need met: 95%. Among students who received aid based on merit, the average award (and the proportion receiving): $8,871 (15%). The average athletic scholarship (and the proportion receiving): $0 (0%). Average amount of debt of borrowers graduating in 2003: $15,225. Proportion who borrowed: 79%. **Student employment:** During the 2003-2004 academic year, 14% of undergraduates worked on campus. Average per-year earnings: $3,000. **Reserve Officers Training Corps (ROTC):** Army ROTC: Offered at cooperating institution (Wheaton College); Air Force ROTC: Offered at cooperating institution (Illinois Institute of Technology).

Eureka College

300 E. College Avenue
Eureka, IL 61530-1500
Private; www.eureka.edu
Financial aid office: (309) 467-6311

■ **2004-2005 TUITION AND FEES:** $19,100
■ **ROOM AND BOARD:** $5,880

ACT Score (25th/75th percentile): 18-24
2005 U.S. News College Ranking:
Comp. Colleges–Bachelor's (Midwest), 33
Acceptance Rate: 94%

Other expenses: Estimated books and supplies: $750. Transportation: $100. Personal expenses: $150. Financial aid: Priority filing date for institution's financial aid form: April 15. In 2003-2004, 99% of undergraduates applied for financial aid. Of those, 99% were determined to have financial need; 42% had their need fully met. Average financial aid package (proportion receiving): $13,978 (99%). Average amount of gift aid, such as scholarships or grants (proportion receiving): $10,212 (98%). Average amount of self-help aid, such as work study or loans (proportion receiving): $3,216 (97%). Average need-based loan (excluding PLUS or other private loans): $2,904. Among students who received need-based aid, the average percentage of need met: 97%. Among students who received aid based on merit, the average award (and the proportion receiving): $7,251 (11%). The average athletic scholarship (and the proportion receiving): $0 (0%). Average amount of debt of borrowers graduating in 2003: $14,997. Proportion who borrowed: 92%. Student employment: During the 2003-2004 academic year, 14% of undergraduates worked on campus. Average per-year earnings: $1,734. Cooperative education programs: health professions. Reserve Officers Training Corps (ROTC): Army ROTC: Offered at cooperating institution.

Greenville College

315 E. College Avenue
Greenville, IL 62246-0159
Private; www.greenville.edu
Financial aid office: (618) 664-7110

■ 2004-2005 TUITION AND FEES: $16,834
■ ROOM AND BOARD: $5,760

ACT Score (25th/75th percentile): 19-25
2005 U.S. News College Ranking:
Comp. Colleges–Bachelor's (Midwest), 45
Acceptance Rate: 95%

Other expenses: Estimated books and supplies: $800. Transportation: $600. Personal expenses: $1,400. Financial aid: In 2003-2004, 90% of undergraduates applied for financial aid. Of those, 84% were determined to have financial need; 16% had their need fully met. Average financial aid package (proportion receiving): $13,704 (84%). Average amount of gift aid, such as scholarships or grants (proportion

receiving): $9,179 (84%). Average amount of self-help aid, such as work study or loans (proportion receiving): $5,072 (75%). Average need-based loan (excluding PLUS or other private loans): $4,121. Among students who received need-based aid, the average percentage of need met: 79%. Among students who received aid based on merit, the average award (and the proportion receiving): $6,885 (16%). Average amount of debt of borrowers graduating in 2003: $17,349. Proportion who borrowed: 83%. Student employment: During the 2003-2004 academic year, 26% of undergraduates worked on campus. Average per-year earnings: $1,000.

Illinois College

1101 W. College Avenue
Jacksonville, IL 62650-2299
Private; www.ic.edu
Financial aid office: (217) 245-3035

■ 2004-2005 TUITION AND FEES: $14,600
■ ROOM AND BOARD: $6,200

ACT Score (25th/75th percentile): 21-26
2005 U.S. News College Ranking:
Comp. Colleges–Bachelor's (Midwest), 16
Acceptance Rate: 72%

Other expenses: Estimated books and supplies: $800. Transportation: $400. Personal expenses: $900. Financial aid: Priority filing date for institution's financial aid form: March 1. In 2003-2004, 92% of undergraduates applied for financial aid. Of those, 79% were determined to have financial need; 31% had their need fully met. Average financial aid package (proportion receiving): $13,273 (79%). Average amount of gift aid, such as scholarships or grants (proportion receiving): $6,106 (69%). Average amount of self-help aid, such as work study or loans (proportion receiving): $4,978 (68%). Average need-based loan (excluding PLUS or other private loans): $4,044. Among students who received need-based aid, the average percentage of need met: 69%. Among students who received aid based on merit, the average award (and the proportion receiving): $5,074 (16%). The average athletic scholarship (and the proportion receiving): $0 (0%). Average amount of debt of borrowers graduating in 2003: $16,320. Proportion who borrowed: 86%. Student employment: During the 2003-2004 academic year, 15% of undergraduates worked on campus. Average per-year earnings: $1,500.

Illinois Institute of Technology

3300 S. Federal Street
Chicago, IL 60616-3793
Private; www.iit.edu
Financial aid office: (312) 567-7219

■ 2004-2005 TUITION AND FEES: $21,548
■ ROOM AND BOARD: $6,946

ACT Score (25th/75th percentile): 25-30
2005 U.S. News College Ranking:
National Universities, 106
Acceptance Rate: 59%

Other expenses: Estimated books and supplies: $1,000. Transportation: $1,200. Personal expenses: $2,100. Financial aid: Priority filing date for institution's financial aid form: April 15. In 2003-2004, 64% of undergraduates applied for financial aid. Of those, 58% were determined to have financial need; 23% had their need fully met. Average financial aid package (proportion receiving): $20,282 (57%). Average amount of gift aid, such as scholarships or grants (proportion receiving): $13,485 (57%). Average amount of self-help aid, such as work study or loans (proportion receiving): $5,389 (42%). Average need-based loan (excluding PLUS or other private loans): $4,807. Among students who received need-based aid, the average percentage of need met: 87%. Among students who received aid based on merit, the average award (and the proportion receiving): $9,981 (40%). The average athletic scholarship (and the proportion receiving): $5,448 (4%). Average amount of debt of borrowers graduating in 2003: $17,264. Proportion who borrowed: 52%. Student employment: During the 2003-2004 academic year, 21% of undergraduates worked on campus. Average per-year earnings: $2,300. Cooperative education programs: computer science, engineering. Reserve Officers Training Corps (ROTC): Army ROTC: Offered on campus; Navy ROTC: Offered on campus; Air Force ROTC: Offered on campus.

Illinois State University

Campus Box 2200
Normal, IL 61790-2200
Public; www.ilstu.edu
Financial aid office: (309) 438-2231

■ 2004-2005 TUITION AND FEES:
   In state: $6,328; Out of state: $11,548
■ ROOM AND BOARD: $5,576

ACT Score (25th/75th percentile): 21-26
2005 U.S. News College Ranking:
National Universities, third tier
Acceptance Rate: 75%

Other expenses: Estimated books and supplies: $786. Transportation: $794. Personal expenses: $2,304. **Financial aid:** Priority filing date for institution's financial aid form: March 1. In 2003-2004, 71% of undergraduates applied for financial aid. Of those, 46% were determined to have financial need; 53% had their need fully met. Average financial aid package (proportion receiving): $7,801 (45%). Average amount of gift aid, such as scholarships or grants (proportion receiving): $5,853 (30%). Average amount of self-help aid, such as work study or loans (proportion receiving): $4,309 (39%). Average need-based loan (excluding PLUS or other private loans): $4,176. Among students who received need-based aid, the average percentage of need met: 82%. Among students who received aid based on merit, the average award (and the proportion receiving): $3,465 (2%). The average athletic scholarship (and the proportion receiving): $7,851 (1%). Average amount of debt of borrowers graduating in 2003: $13,780. Proportion who borrowed: 59%. **Student employment:** During the 2003-2004 academic year, 18% of undergraduates worked on campus. Average per-year earnings: $2,250. **Cooperative education programs:** agriculture, health professions, home economics, natural science, social/behavioral science, technologies. **Reserve Officers Training Corps (ROTC):** Army ROTC: Offered on campus.

Illinois Wesleyan University

Box 2900
Bloomington, IL 61702-2900
Private; www.iwu.edu
Financial aid office: (309) 556-3096

■ **2004-2005 TUITION AND FEES:** $26,130
■ **ROOM AND BOARD:** $6,140

ACT Score (25th/75th percentile): 26-31
2005 U.S. News College Ranking:
Liberal Arts Colleges, 53
Acceptance Rate: 43%

Other expenses: Estimated books and supplies: $650. Transportation: $0. Personal expenses: $780. **Financial aid:** Priority filing date for institution's financial aid form: March 1. In 2003-2004, 63% of undergraduates applied for financial aid. Of those, 55% were determined to have financial need; 55% had their need fully

met. Average financial aid package (proportion receiving): $17,641 (55%). Average amount of gift aid, such as scholarships or grants (proportion receiving): $12,294 (55%). Average amount of self-help aid, such as work study or loans (proportion receiving): $6,120 (48%). Average need-based loan (excluding PLUS or other private loans): $4,728. Among students who received need-based aid, the average percentage of need met: 92%. Among students who received aid based on merit, the average award (and the proportion receiving): $7,858 (33%). The average athletic scholarship (and the proportion receiving): $0 (0%). Average amount of debt of borrowers graduating in 2003: $20,803. Proportion who borrowed: 68%. **Student employment:** During the 2003-2004 academic year, 44% of undergraduates worked on campus. Average per-year earnings: $1,715. **Reserve Officers Training Corps (ROTC):** Army ROTC: Offered at cooperating institution (Illinois State University).

Judson College

1151 N. State Street
Elgin, IL 60123-1498
Private; www.judsoncollege.edu
Financial aid office: (847) 695-2500

■ **2004-2005 TUITION AND FEES:** $17,150
■ **ROOM AND BOARD:** $6,200

ACT Score (25th/75th percentile): 19-25
2005 U.S. News College Ranking:
Comp. Colleges–Bachelor's (Midwest), 53
Acceptance Rate: 71%

Other expenses: Estimated books and supplies: $1,000. Transportation: $500. Personal expenses: $1,000. **Financial aid:** In 2003-2004, 91% of undergraduates applied for financial aid. Of those, 71% were determined to have financial need; Average financial aid package (proportion receiving): $8,183 (55%). Average amount of gift aid, such as scholarships or grants (proportion receiving): $3,016 (41%). Average amount of self-help aid, such as work study or loans (proportion receiving): N/A (63%). Among students who received need-based aid, the average percentage of need met: 33%. Average amount of debt of borrowers graduating in 2003: $12,386. Proportion who borrowed: 79%.

Kendall College

2408 Orrington Avenue
Evanston, IL 60201
Private; www.kendall.edu
Financial aid office: (847) 448-2060

■ **2004-2005 TUITION AND FEES:** $12,240

ACT Score (25th/75th percentile): 19
2005 U.S. News College Ranking:
Comp. Colleges–Bachelor's (Midwest), fourth tier
Acceptance Rate: 77%

Student employment: During the 2003-2004 academic year, 10% of undergraduates worked on campus. Average per-year earnings: $4,500.

Knox College

2 E. South Street
Galesburg, IL 61401
Private; www.knox.edu
Financial aid office: (309) 341-7130

■ **2004-2005 TUITION AND FEES:** $25,236
■ **ROOM AND BOARD:** $6,102

ACT Score (25th/75th percentile): 24-30
2005 U.S. News College Ranking:
Liberal Arts Colleges, 77
Acceptance Rate: 73%

Other expenses: Estimated books and supplies: $900. Transportation: $350. Personal expenses: $600. **Financial aid:** Priority filing date for institution's financial aid form: March 1. In 2003-2004, 83% of undergraduates applied for financial aid. Of those, 73% were determined to have financial need; 53% had their need fully met. Average financial aid package (proportion receiving): $20,770 (73%). Average amount of gift aid, such as scholarships or grants (proportion receiving): $15,483 (73%). Average amount of self-help aid, such as work study or loans (proportion receiving): $6,390 (57%). Average need-based loan (excluding PLUS or other private loans): $5,266. Among students who received need-based aid, the average percentage of need met: 97%. Among students who received aid based on merit, the average award (and the proportion receiving): $10,280 (21%). The average athletic scholarship (and the proportion receiving): $0 (0%). Average amount of debt of borrowers graduating in 2003: $18,221. Proportion who borrowed: 72%. **Student employment:** During the 2003-2004 academic year, 40% of undergraduates worked on campus. Average per-year earnings: $747.

Lake Forest College

555 N. Sheridan Road
Lake Forest, IL 60045
Private; www.lakeforest.edu
Financial aid office: (847) 735-5103

■ **2004-2005 TUITION AND FEES:** $25,828
■ **ROOM AND BOARD:** $6,222

ACT Score (25th/75th percentile): 23-29
2005 U.S. News College Ranking:
Liberal Arts Colleges, 105
Acceptance Rate: 68%

Other expenses: Estimated books and supplies: $700. Transportation: $300. Personal expenses: $750. **Financial aid:** Priority filing date for institution's financial aid form: March 1. In 2003-2004, 89% of undergraduates applied for financial aid. Of those, 77% were determined to have financial need; 100% had their need fully met. Average financial aid package (proportion receiving): $19,466 (77%). Average amount of gift aid, such as scholarships or grants (proportion receiving): $16,147 (77%). Average amount of self-help aid, such as work study or loans (proportion receiving): $4,360 (58%). Average need-based loan (excluding PLUS or other private loans): $3,315. Among students who received need-based aid, the average percentage of need met: 100%. Among students who received aid based on merit, the average award (and the proportion receiving): $10,606 (12%). The average athletic scholarship (and the proportion receiving): $0 (0%). Average amount of debt of borrowers graduating in 2003: $17,825. Proportion who borrowed: 58%. **Student employment:** During the 2003-2004 academic year, 55% of undergraduates worked on campus. Average per-year earnings: $1,800. **Cooperative education programs:** engineering.

Lewis University

1 University Parkway
Romeoville, IL 60446-2200
Private; www.lewisu.edu
Financial aid office: (815) 836-5263

■ **2004-2005 TUITION AND FEES:** $16,906
■ **ROOM AND BOARD:** $7,200

ACT Score (25th/75th percentile): 19-24
2005 U.S. News College Ranking:
Universities–Master's (Midwest), 52
Acceptance Rate: 66%

Other expenses: Estimated books and supplies: $500. Transportation: $570. Personal expenses: $1,320. **Financial aid:** Priority filing date for institution's financial aid form: May 1. In 2003-2004, 92% of undergraduates applied for financial aid. Of those, 71% were determined to have financial need; 38% had their need fully met. Average financial aid package (proportion receiving): $13,302 (71%). Average amount of gift aid, such as scholarships or grants (proportion receiving): $5,814 (48%). Average amount of self-help aid, such as work study or loans (proportion receiving): $3,909 (69%). Average need-based loan (excluding PLUS or other private loans): $3,941. Among students who received need-based aid, the average percentage of need met: 78%. Among students who received aid based on merit, the average award (and the proportion receiving): $4,800 (10%). The average athletic scholarship (and the proportion receiving): $5,695 (8%). Average amount of debt of borrowers graduating in 2003: $18,133. Proportion who borrowed: 60%. **Student employment:** During the 2003-2004 academic year, 20% of undergraduates worked on campus. Average per-year earnings: $3,000. **Reserve Officers Training Corps (ROTC):** Army ROTC: Offered at cooperating institution (Wheaton College); Air Force ROTC: Offered at cooperating institution (Illinois Institute of Technology).

Loyola University Chicago

820 N. Michigan Avenue
Chicago, IL 60611-9810
Private; www.luc.edu
Financial aid office: (773) 508-3177

■ **2004-2005 TUITION AND FEES:** $22,484
■ **ROOM AND BOARD:** $8,850

ACT Score (25th/75th percentile): 22-27
2005 U.S. News College Ranking:
National Universities, 111
Acceptance Rate: 82%

Other expenses: Estimated books and supplies: $800. Transportation: $500. Personal expenses: $1,600. **Financial aid:** Priority filing date for institution's financial aid form: March 1. In 2003-2004, 96% of undergraduates applied for financial aid. Of those, 76% were determined to have financial need; 17% had their need fully

met. Average financial aid package (proportion receiving): $20,488 (75%). Average amount of gift aid, such as scholarships or grants (proportion receiving): $17,942 (73%). Average amount of self-help aid, such as work study or loans (proportion receiving): $6,229 (64%). Average need-based loan (excluding PLUS or other private loans): $4,457. Among students who received need-based aid, the average percentage of need met: 78%. Among students who received aid based on merit, the average award (and the proportion receiving): $8,557 (17%). The average athletic scholarship (and the proportion receiving): $18,120 (0%). Average amount of debt of borrowers graduating in 2003: $16,168. Proportion who borrowed: 55%. **Reserve Officers Training Corps (ROTC):** Army ROTC: Offered at cooperating institution (University of Illinois-Chicago); Navy ROTC: Offered at cooperating institution (Northwestern University).

MacMurray College

447 E. College
Jacksonville, IL 62650
Private; www.mac.edu
Financial aid office: (217) 479-7041

■ **2004-2005 TUITION AND FEES:** $14,600
■ **ROOM AND BOARD:** $5,323

ACT Score (25th/75th percentile): 17-23
2005 U.S. News College Ranking:
Comp. Colleges–Bachelor's (Midwest), third tier
Acceptance Rate: 64%

Other expenses: Estimated books and supplies: $800. Transportation: $450. Personal expenses: $555. **Financial aid:** Priority filing date for institution's financial aid form: March 1. In 2003-2004, 99% of undergraduates applied for financial aid. Of those, 93% were determined to have financial need; 34% had their need fully met. Average financial aid package (proportion receiving): $16,659 (93%). Average amount of gift aid, such as scholarships or grants (proportion receiving): $11,651 (93%). Average amount of self-help aid, such as work study or loans (proportion receiving): $3,940 (88%). Average need-based loan (excluding PLUS or other private loans): $3,858. Among students who received need-based aid, the average percentage of need met: 93%. Among students who received aid based on merit, the average award (and the proportion receiving): $5,200 (6%). The average athletic scholarship (and the proportion receiving): $0 (0%). Average amount of debt of borrowers graduating in 2003: $17,477. Proportion who borrowed: 97%. **Student employment:** During the 2003-2004 academic year, 16% of undergraduates worked on campus. Average per-year earnings: $941.

McKendree College

701 College Road
Lebanon, IL 62254-1299
Private; www.mckendree.edu
Financial aid office: (618) 537-6828

■ **2004-2005 TUITION AND FEES:** $16,600
■ **ROOM AND BOARD:** $6,360

ACT Score (25th/75th percentile): 23-27
2005 U.S. News College Ranking:
Comp. Colleges–Bachelor's (Midwest), 29
Acceptance Rate: 70%

Other expenses: Estimated books and supplies: $1,000. Transportation: $700. Personal expenses: $700. **Financial aid:** Priority filing date for institution's financial aid form: May 31. In 2003-2004, 90% of undergraduates applied for financial aid. Of those, 80% were determined to have financial need; 27% had their need fully met. Average financial aid package (proportion receiving): $12,400 (80%). Average amount of gift aid, such as scholarships or grants (proportion receiving): $9,763 (78%). Average amount of self-help aid, such as work study or loans (proportion receiving): $3,906 (59%). Average need-based loan (excluding PLUS or other private loans): $3,211. Among students who received need-based aid, the average percentage of need met: 79%. Among students who received aid based on merit, the average award (and the proportion receiving): $8,371 (18%). The average athletic scholarship (and the proportion receiving): $5,066 (12%). Average amount of debt of borrowers graduating in 2003: $14,592. Proportion who borrowed: 47%. **Student employment:** During the 2003-2004 academic year, 24% of undergraduates worked on campus. Average per-year earnings: $2,000. **Cooperative education programs:** engineering, health professions. **Reserve Officers Training Corps (ROTC):** Army ROTC: Offered at cooperating institution (Southern Illinois University-Edwardsville); Air Force ROTC: Offered at cooperating institution (Southern Illinois University- Edwardsville).

Millikin University

1184 W. Main Street
Decatur, IL 62522-2084
Private; www.millikin.edu
Financial aid office: (217) 424-6343

■ **2004-2005 TUITION AND FEES:** $20,345
■ **ROOM AND BOARD:** $6,510

ACT Score (25th/75th percentile): 20-26
2005 U.S. News College Ranking:
Comp. Colleges–Bachelor's (Midwest), 14
Acceptance Rate: 74%

Other expenses: Estimated books and supplies: $800. Transportation: $200. Personal expenses: $0. **Financial aid:** Priority filing date for institution's financial aid form: April 15; deadline: June 1. In 2003-2004, 92% of undergraduates applied for financial aid. Of those, 72% were determined to have financial need; 71% had their need fully met. Average financial aid package (proportion receiving): $16,233 (67%). Average amount of gift aid, such as scholarships or grants (proportion receiving): $9,951 (61%). Average amount of self-help aid, such as work study or loans (proportion receiving): $1,500 (60%). Average need-based loan (excluding PLUS or other private loans): $3,784. Among students who received need-based aid, the average percentage of need met: 88%. Among students who received aid based on merit, the average award (and the proportion receiving): $6,535 (27%). The average athletic scholarship (and the proportion receiving): $0 (0%). Average amount of debt of borrowers graduating in 2003: $17,100. Proportion who borrowed: 88%. **Student employment:** During the 2003-2004 academic year, 6% of undergraduates worked on campus. Average per-year earnings: $1,100.

Monmouth College

700 E. Broadway
Monmouth, IL 61462
Private; www.monm.edu
Financial aid office: (309) 457-2129

■ **2004-2005 TUITION AND FEES:** $19,350
■ **ROOM AND BOARD:** $5,450

ACT Score (25th/75th percentile): 21-27
2005 U.S. News College Ranking:
Liberal Arts Colleges, third tier
Acceptance Rate: 73%

Other expenses: Estimated books and supplies: $650. Transportation: $350. Personal expenses: $510. **Financial aid:** Priority filing date for institution's financial aid form: March 1. In 2003-2004, 95% of undergraduates applied for financial aid. Of those, 82% were determined to have financial need; 36% had their need fully met. Average financial aid package (proportion receiving): $15,758 (82%). Average amount of gift aid, such as scholarships or grants (proportion receiving): $12,435 (82%). Average amount of self-help aid, such as work study or loans (proportion receiving): $4,642 (58%). Average need-based loan (excluding PLUS or other private loans): $3,921. Among students who received need-based aid, the average percentage of need met: 88%. Among students who received aid based on merit, the average award (and the proportion receiving): $9,687 (13%). The average athletic scholarship (and the proportion receiving): $0 (0%). Average amount of debt of borrowers graduating in 2003: $18,286. Proportion who borrowed: 87%. **Student employment:** During the 2003-2004 academic year, 33% of undergraduates worked on campus. Average per-year earnings: $1,400. **Reserve Officers Training Corps (ROTC):** Army ROTC: Offered at cooperating institution (Western Illinois University).

National-Louis University

122 S. Michigan Avenue
Chicago, IL 60603
Private; www.nl.edu
Financial aid office: (847) 465-0575

■ **2004-2005 TUITION AND FEES:** $16,240
■ **ROOM AND BOARD:** $6,360

ACT Score (25th/75th percentile): 16-19
2005 U.S. News College Ranking:
National Universities, fourth tier
Acceptance Rate: 96%

Other expenses: Estimated books and supplies: $500. **Student employment:** During the 2003-2004 academic year, 2% of undergraduates worked on campus. Average per-year earnings: $2,600. **Cooperative education programs:** art, business, computer science, education, health professions, humanities, natural science, social/behavioral science, technologies.

North Central College

30 N. Brainard Street, PO Box 3063
Naperville, IL 60566-7063
Private; www.noctrl.edu
Financial aid office: (630) 637-5600

■ **2004-2005 TUITION AND FEES:** $20,340
■ **ROOM AND BOARD:** $6,747

ACT Score (25th/75th percentile): 22-27
2005 U.S. News College Ranking:
Universities–Master's (Midwest), 14
Acceptance Rate: 71%

Other expenses: Estimated books and supplies: $800. Transportation: $325. Personal expenses: $1,182. **Financial aid:** In 2003-2004, 79% of undergraduates applied for financial aid. Of those, 68% were determined to have financial need; 41% had their need fully met. Average financial aid package (proportion receiving): $18,212 (78%). Average amount of gift aid, such as scholarships or grants (proportion receiving): $11,475 (68%). Average amount of self-help aid, such as work study or loans (proportion receiving): $5,607 (61%). Average need-based loan (excluding PLUS or other private loans): $5,239. Among students who received need-based aid, the average percentage of need met: 87%. Among students who received aid based on merit, the average award (and the proportion receiving): $7,673 (20%). The average athletic scholarship (and the proportion receiving): $0 (0%). Average amount of debt of borrowers graduating in 2003: $13,726. Proportion who borrowed: 72%. **Student employment:** During the 2003-2004 academic year, 37% of undergraduates worked on campus. Average per-year earnings: $3,500. **Reserve Officers Training Corps (ROTC):** Army ROTC: Offered at cooperating institution (Wheaton College); Navy ROTC: Offered at cooperating institution (Wheaton College).

Northeastern Illinois University

5500 N. St. Louis Avenue
Chicago, IL 60625
Public; www.neiu.edu
Financial aid office: (773) 442-5000

■ **2004-2005 TUITION AND FEES:**
In state: $4,226; Out of state: $7,756

ACT Score (25th/75th percentile): 16-20
2005 U.S. News College Ranking:
Universities–Master's (Midwest), fourth tier
Acceptance Rate: 71%

Financial aid: Priority filing date for institution's financial aid form: March 1. In 2003-2004, 68% of undergraduates applied for financial aid. Of those, 52% were determined to have financial need; 17% had their need fully met. Average financial aid package (proportion receiving): $5,591 (50%). Average amount of gift aid, such as scholarships or grants (proportion receiving): $4,922 (44%). Average amount of self-help aid, such as work study or loans (proportion receiving): $2,481 (16%). Average need-based loan (excluding PLUS or other private loans): $2,171. Among students who received need-based aid, the average percentage of need met: 67%. Among students who received aid based on merit, the average award (and the proportion receiving): $1,415 (3%). The average athletic scholarship (and the proportion receiving): $0 (0%). Average amount of debt of borrowers graduating in 2003: $10,125. Proportion who borrowed: 26%. **Reserve Officers Training Corps (ROTC):** Army ROTC: Offered at cooperating institution (University of Illinois at Chicago); Air Force ROTC: Offered at cooperating institution (Illinois Institute of Technology).

Northern Illinois University

PO Box 3001
DeKalb, IL 60115
Public; www.niu.edu
Financial aid office: (815) 753-1300

■ **2004-2005 TUITION AND FEES:**
In state: $6,137; Out of state: $10,749
■ **ROOM AND BOARD:** $5,750

ACT Score (25th/75th percentile): 19-24
2005 U.S. News College Ranking:
National Universities, fourth tier
Acceptance Rate: 62%

Student employment: During the 2003-2004 academic year, 17% of undergraduates worked on campus. Average per-year earnings: $3,628. **Reserve Officers Training Corps (ROTC):** Army ROTC: Offered on campus.

North Park University

3225 W. Foster Avenue
Chicago, IL 60625-4895
Private; www.northpark.edu
Financial aid office: (773) 244-5525

■ **2004-2005 TUITION AND FEES:** $20,600
■ **ROOM AND BOARD:** $6,980

ACT Score (25th/75th percentile): 19-26
2005 U.S. News College Ranking:
Universities–Master's (Midwest), 42
Acceptance Rate: 74%

Other expenses: Estimated books and supplies: $900. Personal expenses: $900. **Financial aid:** Priority filing date for institution's financial aid form: April 1; deadline: June 1.

Northwestern University

633 Clark Street
Evanston, IL 60208
Private; www.northwestern.edu
Financial aid office: (847) 491-7400

■ **2004-2005 TUITION AND FEES:** $30,085
■ **ROOM AND BOARD:** $9,393

SAT I Score (25th/75th percentile): 1310-1480
2005 U.S. News College Ranking:
National Universities, 11
Acceptance Rate: 33%

Other expenses: Estimated books and supplies: $1,353. Transportation: $426. Personal expenses: $1,611. **Financial aid:** In 2003-2004, 50% of undergraduates applied for financial aid. Of those, 44% were determined to have financial need; 100% had their need fully met. Average financial aid package (proportion receiving): $24,508 (44%). Average amount of gift aid, such as scholarships or grants (proportion receiving): $18,857 (41%). Average amount of self-help aid, such as work study or loans (proportion receiving): $5,652 (41%). Average need-based loan (excluding PLUS or other private loans): $3,876. Among students who received need-based aid, the average percentage of need met: 100%. Among students who received aid based on merit, the average award (and the proportion receiving): $4,793 (0%). The average athletic scholarship (and the proportion receiving): $26,484 (4%). Average amount of debt of borrowers graduating in 2003: $15,136. Proportion who borrowed: 50%. **Student employment:** During the 2003-2004 academic year, 32% of undergraduates worked on campus. Average per-year earnings: $1,842. **Cooperative education programs:** engineering. **Reserve Officers Training Corps (ROTC):** Army ROTC: Offered at cooperating institution (University of Illinois, Chicago); Navy ROTC: Offered on campus; Air Force ROTC: Offered at cooperating institution (Illinois Institute of Technology).

Olivet Nazarene University

1 University Avenue
Bourbonnais, IL 60914
Private; www.olivet.edu
Financial aid office: (815) 939-5249

■ **2004-2005 TUITION AND FEES:** $15,740
■ **ROOM AND BOARD:** $5,680

ACT Score (25th/75th percentile): 19-26
2005 U.S. News College Ranking:
Universities–Master's (Midwest), third tier
Acceptance Rate: 79%

Other expenses: Estimated books and supplies: $800. Transportation: $400. Personal expenses: $800. **Financial aid:** Priority filing date for institution's financial aid form: March 1. In 2003-2004, 84% of undergraduates applied for financial aid. Of those, 74% were determined to have financial need; 30% had their need fully met. Average financial aid package (proportion receiving): $12,233 (74%). Average amount of gift aid, such as scholarships or grants (proportion receiving): $8,760 (73%). Average amount of self-help aid, such as work study or loans (proportion receiving): $4,584 (64%). Average need-based loan (excluding PLUS or other private loans): $4,362. Among students who received need-based aid, the average percentage of need met: 76%. Among students who received aid based on merit, the average award (and the proportion receiving): $4,870 (22%). The average athletic scholarship (and the proportion receiving): $4,209 (15%). Average amount of debt of borrowers graduating in 2003: $20,607. Proportion who borrowed: 68%. **Student employment:** During the 2003-2004 academic year, 45% of undergraduates worked on campus. Average per-year earnings: $1,100. **Reserve Officers Training Corps (ROTC):** Army ROTC: Offered at cooperating institution (Wheaton College).

Principia College

1 Maybeck Place
Elsah, IL 62028
Private; www.prin.edu/college
Financial aid office: (618) 374-5186

■ **2004-2005 TUITION AND FEES:** $19,455
■ **ROOM AND BOARD:** $6,831

SAT I Score (25th/75th percentile): 1050-1310
2005 U.S. News College Ranking:
Liberal Arts Colleges, 96
Acceptance Rate: 85%

Other expenses: Estimated books and supplies: $750. Transportation: $700. Personal expenses: $750. **Financial aid:** In 2003-2004, 70% of undergraduates applied for financial aid. Of those, 67% were determined to have financial need; 99% had their need fully met. Average financial aid package (proportion receiving): $16,559 (67%). Average amount of gift aid, such as scholarships or grants (proportion receiving): $11,281 (67%). Average amount of self-help aid, such as work study or loans (proportion receiving): $4,652 (54%). Average need-based loan (excluding PLUS or other private loans): $3,400. Among students who received need-based aid, the average percentage of need met: 90%. Among students who received aid based on merit, the average award (and the proportion receiving): $14,010 (19%). Average amount of debt of borrowers graduating in 2003: $11,314. Proportion who borrowed: 66%. **Student employment:** During the 2003-2004 academic year, 50% of undergraduates worked on campus. Average per-year earnings: $1,500.

Quincy University

1800 College Avenue
Quincy, IL 62301
Private; www.quincy.edu
Financial aid office: (217) 228-5260

■ **2004-2005 TUITION AND FEES:** $17,650
■ **ROOM AND BOARD:** $5,725

ACT Score (25th/75th percentile): 19-24
2005 U.S. News College Ranking:
Universities–Master's (Midwest), third tier
Acceptance Rate: 94%

Other expenses: Estimated books and supplies: $1,000. Transportation: $800. Personal expenses: $1,000. **Financial aid:** Priority filing date for institution's financial aid form: April 15. In

2003-2004, 85% of undergraduates applied for financial aid. Of those, 73% were determined to have financial need; 26% had their need fully met. Average financial aid package (proportion receiving): $14,835 (72%). Average amount of gift aid, such as scholarships or grants (proportion receiving): $9,365 (71%). Average amount of self-help aid, such as work study or loans (proportion receiving): $4,940 (65%). Average need-based loan (excluding PLUS or other private loans): $4,373. Among students who received need-based aid, the average percentage of need met: 85%. Among students who received aid based on merit, the average award (and the proportion receiving): $3,867 (21%). The average athletic scholarship (and the proportion receiving): $8,506 (9%). Average amount of debt of borrowers graduating in 2003: $16,134. Proportion who borrowed: 80%. **Student employment:** During the 2003-2004 academic year, 17% of undergraduates worked on campus. Average per-year earnings: $1,000. **Cooperative education programs:** engineering.

Robert Morris College

401 S. State Street
Chicago, IL 60605
Private; www.robertmorris.edu
Financial aid office: (312) 935-4408

■ **2004-2005 TUITION AND FEES:** $14,250
■ **ROOM AND BOARD:** $6,300

2005 U.S. News College Ranking:
Unranked Specialty School–Business
Acceptance Rate: 76%

Other expenses: Estimated books and supplies: $1,350. Transportation: $1,170. Personal expenses: $1,632. **Financial aid:** In 2003-2004, 95% of undergraduates applied for financial aid. Of those, 93% were determined to have financial need; 4% had their need fully met. Average financial aid package (proportion receiving): $10,605 (93%). Average amount of gift aid, such as scholarships or grants (proportion receiving): $8,069 (91%). Average amount of self-help aid, such as work study or loans (proportion receiving): $3,355 (73%). Average need-based loan (excluding PLUS or other private loans): $3,340. Among students who received need-based aid, the average percentage of need met: 54%. Among students who received aid based on merit, the average award (and the proportion receiving): $7,631 (3%). The average athletic scholarship (and the proportion receiving): $5,560 (2%). Average amount of debt of borrowers graduating in 2003: $14,914. Proportion who borrowed: 90%. **Cooperative edu-**

cation programs: art, business, health professions, other. **Reserve Officers Training Corps (ROTC):** Army ROTC: Offered at cooperating institution (U of I Chicago).

Rockford College

5050 E. State Street
Rockford, IL 61108-2393
Private; www.rockford.edu
Financial aid office: (815) 226-3385

■ **2004-2005 TUITION AND FEES:** $21,715
■ **ROOM AND BOARD:** $6,780

ACT Score (25th/75th percentile): 22
2005 U.S. News College Ranking:
Universities–Master's (Midwest), 58
Acceptance Rate: 57%

Other expenses: Estimated books and supplies: $960. Transportation: $710. Personal expenses: $2,090. **Financial aid:** Priority filing date for institution's financial aid form: March 15. In 2003-2004, 99% of undergraduates applied for financial aid. Of those, 59% were determined to have financial need; 70% had their need fully met. Average financial aid package (proportion receiving): $20,000 (59%). Average amount of gift aid, such as scholarships or grants (proportion receiving): $8,000 (59%). Average amount of self-help aid, such as work study or loans (proportion receiving): $5,000 (59%). Average need-based loan (excluding PLUS or other private loans): $5,000. Among students who received need-based aid, the average percentage of need met: 70%. Among students who received aid based on merit, the average award (and the proportion receiving): $9,000 (40%). The average athletic scholarship (and the proportion receiving): $9,000 (N/A). Average amount of debt of borrowers graduating in 2003: $45,000. Proportion who borrowed: 99%. **Student employment:** During the 2003-2004 academic year, 50% of undergraduates worked on campus. Average per-year earnings: $2,000. **Reserve Officers Training Corps (ROTC):** Army ROTC: Offered at cooperating institution (Northern Illinois University).

Roosevelt University

430 S. Michigan Avenue
Chicago, IL 60605
Private; www.roosevelt.edu
Financial aid office: (312) 341-3565

■ **2004-2005 TUITION AND FEES:** $16,580
■ **ROOM AND BOARD:** $7,770

ACT Score (25th/75th percentile): 18-25
2005 U.S. News College Ranking:
Universities–Master's (Midwest), third tier
Acceptance Rate: 51%

Other expenses: Estimated books and supplies: $925. Transportation: $1,200. Personal expenses: $1,100. **Financial aid:** Priority filing date for institution's financial aid form: April 1. In 2003-2004, 86% of undergraduates applied for financial aid. Of those, 71% were determined to have financial need; Average financial aid package (proportion receiving): $11,600 (70%). Average amount of gift aid, such as scholarships or grants (proportion receiving): $6,200 (54%). Average amount of self-help aid, such as work study or loans (proportion receiving): $7,000 (52%). Among students who received need-based aid, the average percentage of need met: 75%. Among students who received aid based on merit, the average award (and the proportion receiving): $6,030 (38%). The average athletic scholarship (and the proportion receiving): $0 (0%). **Student employment:** During the 2003-2004 academic year, 25% of undergraduates worked on campus. Average per-year earnings: $2,200.

School of the Art Institute of Chicago

37 S. Wabash
Chicago, IL 60603
Private; www.artic.edu/saic
Financial aid office: (312) 899-5106

■ **2004-2005 TUITION AND FEES:** $25,500

2005 U.S. News College Ranking:
Unranked Specialty School–Fine Arts
Acceptance Rate: 83%

Other expenses: Estimated books and supplies: $2,300. Transportation: $910. Personal expenses: $1,500. **Financial aid:** Priority filing date for institution's financial aid form: March 15. In 2003-2004, 76% of undergraduates applied for financial aid. Of those, 59% were determined to have financial need; 4% had their need fully met. Average financial aid package (proportion receiving): $18,028 (59%). Average amount of gift aid, such as scholarships or grants (proportion receiving): $9,946 (53%). Average amount of self-help aid, such as work study or loans (proportion receiving): $3,238 (51%). Average need-based loan (excluding PLUS or other private loans): $4,633. Among students who received need-based aid, the average percentage of need met: 69%. Among students who received aid based on merit, the average award

(and the proportion receiving): $3,887 (32%). The average athletic scholarship (and the proportion receiving): $0 (0%). Average amount of debt of borrowers graduating in 2003: $20,983. Proportion who borrowed: 59%. **Student employment:** During the 2003-2004 academic year, 20% of undergraduates worked on campus. Average per-year earnings: $2,500. **Cooperative education programs:** art, business, computer science, technologies.

Shimer College

PO Box 500, 414 N. Sheridan
Waukegan, IL 60079
Private; www.shimer.edu
Financial aid office: (847) 249-7180

■ **2004-2005 TUITION AND FEES:** $18,535

SAT I Score (25th/75th percentile): 1100
2005 U.S. News College Ranking:
Liberal Arts Colleges, unranked
Acceptance Rate: 88%

Other expenses: Estimated books and supplies: $0. **Financial aid:** Priority filing date for institution's financial aid form: June 1; deadline: July 31. In 2003-2004, 97% of undergraduates applied for financial aid. Of those, 89% were determined to have financial need; Average financial aid package (proportion receiving): $17,704 (89%). Average amount of gift aid, such as scholarships or grants (proportion receiving): $4,030 (62%). Average amount of self-help aid, such as work study or loans (proportion receiving): $3,935 (75%). Average need-based loan (excluding PLUS or other private loans): $3,965. Among students who received need-based aid, the average percentage of need met: 73%. Among students who received aid based on merit, the average award (and the proportion receiving): $16,711 (4%). The average athletic scholarship (and the proportion receiving): $0 (0%).

Southern Illinois University–Carbondale

Mail Code 4512
Carbondale, IL 62901
Public; www.siuc.edu
Financial aid office: (618) 453-4334

■ **2004-2005 TUITION AND FEES:**
  In state: $5,980; Out of state: $10,540
■ **ROOM AND BOARD:** $5,178

ACT Score (25th/75th percentile): 19-24
2005 U.S. News College Ranking:
National Universities, third tier
Acceptance Rate: 77%

....

Other expenses: Estimated books and supplies: $840. Transportation: $1,200. Personal expenses: $1,200. **Financial aid:** Priority filing date for institution's financial aid form: April 1. In 2003-2004, 71% of undergraduates applied for financial aid. Of those, 58% were determined to have financial need; 80% had their need fully met. Average financial aid package (proportion receiving): $8,117 (56%). Average amount of gift aid, such as scholarships or grants (proportion receiving): $4,420 (46%). Average amount of self-help aid, such as work study or loans (proportion receiving): $3,541 (46%). Average need-based loan (excluding PLUS or other private loans): $3,496. Among students who received need-based aid, the average percentage of need met: 95%. Among students who received aid based on merit, the average award (and the proportion receiving): $3,102 (7%). The average athletic scholarship (and the proportion receiving): $8,602 (1%). Average amount of debt of borrowers graduating in 2003: $12,413. Proportion who borrowed: 37%. **Student employment:** During the 2003-2004 academic year, 25% of undergraduates worked on campus. Average per-year earnings: $1,596. **Cooperative education programs:** agriculture, art, business, education, engineering, health professions, home economics, humanities, natural science, social/behavioral science, technologies, vocational arts. **Reserve Officers Training Corps (ROTC):** Army ROTC: Offered on campus; Air Force ROTC: Offered on campus.

Southern Illinois University–Edwardsville

Box 1600
Edwardsville, IL 62026
Public; www.siue.edu
Financial aid office: (618) 650-3839

■ **2004-2005 TUITION AND FEES:**
 In state: $4,439; Out of state: $8,039
■ **ROOM AND BOARD:** $5,642

ACT Score (25th/75th percentile): 19-24
2005 U.S. News College Ranking:
Universities–Master's (Midwest), 58
Acceptance Rate: 81%

....

Other expenses: Estimated books and supplies: $632. Transportation: $1,643. Personal expenses: $1,360. **Financial aid:** Priority filing date for institution's financial aid form: March 1. In 2003-2004, 67% of undergraduates applied for financial aid. Of those, 52% were determined to have financial need; 19% had their need fully met. Average financial aid package (proportion receiving): $7,890 (50%). Average amount of gift aid, such as scholarships or grants (proportion receiving): $5,184 (38%). Average amount of self-help aid, such as work study or loans (proportion receiving): $4,088 (41%). Average need-based loan (excluding PLUS or other private loans): $3,236. Among students who received need-based aid, the average percentage of need met: 77%. Among students who received aid based on merit, the average award (and the proportion receiving): $3,389 (9%). The average athletic scholarship (and the proportion receiving): $1,826 (1%). Average amount of debt of borrowers graduating in 2003: $14,755. Proportion who borrowed: 20%. **Student employment:** During the 2003-2004 academic year, 14% of undergraduates worked on campus. Average per-year earnings: $2,812. **Cooperative education programs:** business, computer science, engineering, natural science, social/behavioral science. **Reserve Officers Training Corps (ROTC):** Army ROTC: Offered on campus; Air Force ROTC: Offered on campus.

St. Xavier University

3700 W. 103rd Street
Chicago, IL 60655
Private; www.sxu.edu
Financial aid office: (773) 298-3070

■ **2004-2005 TUITION AND FEES:** $17,320
■ **ROOM AND BOARD:** $6,724

ACT Score (25th/75th percentile): 19-23
2005 U.S. News College Ranking:
Universities–Master's (Midwest), 46
Acceptance Rate: 68%

....

Other expenses: Estimated books and supplies: $900. Transportation: $388. Personal expenses: $908. **Financial aid:** Priority filing date for institution's financial aid form: March 1. In 2003-2004, 92% of undergraduates applied for financial aid. Of those, 83% were determined to have financial need; 21% had their need fully met. Average financial aid package (proportion receiving): $14,282 (83%). Average amount of

gift aid, such as scholarships or grants (proportion receiving): $8,775 (82%). Average amount of self-help aid, such as work study or loans (proportion receiving): $6,642 (72%). Average need-based loan (excluding PLUS or other private loans): $3,932. Among students who received need-based aid, the average percentage of need met: 82%. Among students who received aid based on merit, the average award (and the proportion receiving): $3,683 (14%). The average athletic scholarship (and the proportion receiving): $6,719 (9%). Average amount of debt of borrowers graduating in 2003: $19,374. Proportion who borrowed: 63%. **Student employment:** During the 2003-2004 academic year, 18% of undergraduates worked on campus. Average per-year earnings: $2,500.

Trinity Christian College

6601 W. College Drive
Palos Heights, IL 60463
Private; www.trnty.edu
Financial aid office: (708) 239-4706

■ **2004-2005 TUITION AND FEES:** $16,250
■ **ROOM AND BOARD:** $6,044

ACT Score (25th/75th percentile): 19-26
2005 U.S. News College Ranking:
Comp. Colleges–Bachelor's (Midwest), 43
Acceptance Rate: 93%

....

Other expenses: Estimated books and supplies: $850. Transportation: $1,343. Personal expenses: $1,385. **Financial aid:** Priority filing date for institution's financial aid form: February 1; deadline: April 15. In 2003-2004, 80% of undergraduates applied for financial aid. Of those, 80% were determined to have financial need; Average financial aid package (proportion receiving): $8,469 (80%). Average amount of gift aid, such as scholarships or grants (proportion receiving): $3,078 (67%). Average amount of self-help aid, such as work study or loans (proportion receiving): $3,192 (47%). Average need-based loan (excluding PLUS or other private loans): $7,723. Among students who received need-based aid, the average percentage of need met: 66%. Average amount of debt of borrowers graduating in 2003: $17,125. Proportion who borrowed: 79%. **Student employment:** During the 2003-2004 academic year, 42% of undergraduates worked on campus. Average per-year earnings: $1,400.

University of Chicago

5801 S. Ellis Avenue
Chicago, IL 60637
Private; www.uchicago.edu
Financial aid office: (773) 702-8666

■ **2004-2005 TUITION AND FEES:** $30,729
■ **ROOM AND BOARD:** $9,624

SAT I Score (25th/75th percentile): 1300-1510
2005 U.S. News College Ranking:
National Universities, 14
Acceptance Rate: 40%

Other expenses: Estimated books and supplies: $2,560. **Financial aid:** In 2003-2004, 65% of undergraduates applied for financial aid. Of those, 48% were determined to have financial need; 100% had their need fully met. Average financial aid package (proportion receiving): $25,388 (48%). Average amount of gift aid, such as scholarships or grants (proportion receiving): $19,864 (47%). Average amount of self-help aid, such as work study or loans (proportion receiving): $6,789 (42%). Average need-based loan (excluding PLUS or other private loans): $5,017. Among students who received need-based aid, the average percentage of need met: 100%. Among students who received aid based on merit, the average award (and the proportion receiving): $10,826 (12%). The average athletic scholarship (and the proportion receiving): $0 (0%). **Reserve Officers Training Corps (ROTC):** Army ROTC: Offered at cooperating institution (University of Illinois Chicago); Air Force ROTC: Offered at cooperating institution (Illinios Institute of Technology).

University of Illinois–Chicago

601 S. Morgan M/C 102
Chicago, IL 60607
Public; www.uic.edu
Financial aid office: (312) 996-3126

■ **2004-2005 TUITION AND FEES:**
   In state: $7,432; Out of state: $17,904
■ **ROOM AND BOARD:** $6,884

ACT Score (25th/75th percentile): 20-26
2005 U.S. News College Ranking:
National Universities, third tier
Acceptance Rate: 61%

Other expenses: Estimated books and supplies: $900. Transportation: $160. Personal expenses: $2,000. **Financial aid:** Priority filing date for

institution's financial aid form: March 1. In 2003-2004, 70% of undergraduates applied for financial aid. Of those, 55% were determined to have financial need; 52% had their need fully met. Average financial aid package (proportion receiving): $11,600 (52%). Average amount of gift aid, such as scholarships or grants (proportion receiving): $7,032 (43%). Average amount of self-help aid, such as work study or loans (proportion receiving): $3,828 (28%). Average need-based loan (excluding PLUS or other private loans): $3,819. Among students who received need-based aid, the average percentage of need met: 90%. Among students who received aid based on merit, the average award (and the proportion receiving): $3,009 (7%). The average athletic scholarship (and the proportion receiving): $9,538 (1%). Average amount of debt of borrowers graduating in 2003: $14,439. Proportion who borrowed: 39%. **Student employment:** During the 2003-2004 academic year, 12% of undergraduates worked on campus. Average per-year earnings: $4,650. **Cooperative education programs:** business, other. **Reserve Officers Training Corps (ROTC):** Army ROTC: Offered on campus; Navy ROTC: Offered at cooperating institution (Illinois Institute of Technology); Air Force ROTC: Offered at cooperating institution (Illinois Institute of Technology).

University of Illinois–Springfield

1 University Plaza
Springfield, IL 62703-5407
Public; www.uis.edu
Financial aid office: (217) 206-6724

■ **2004-2005 TUITION AND FEES:**
   In state: $4,669; Out of state: $12,679
■ **ROOM AND BOARD:** $2,878

ACT Score (25th/75th percentile): 24-28
2005 U.S. News College Ranking:
Universities–Master's (Midwest), unranked
Acceptance Rate: 52%

Other expenses: Estimated books and supplies: $1,200. Transportation: $1,800. Personal expenses: $1,800. **Financial aid:** Priority filing date for institution's financial aid form: April 1; deadline: November 15. In 2003-2004, 74% of undergraduates applied for financial aid. Of those, 60% were determined to have financial need; 39% had their need fully met. Average financial aid package (proportion receiving): $7,226 (57%). Average amount of gift aid, such as scholarships or grants (proportion receiving):

$4,759 (39%). Average amount of self-help aid, such as work study or loans (proportion receiving): $3,821 (46%). Average need-based loan (excluding PLUS or other private loans): $3,805. Among students who received need-based aid, the average percentage of need met: 83%. Among students who received aid based on merit, the average award (and the proportion receiving): $2,915 (14%). The average athletic scholarship (and the proportion receiving): $5,214 (5%). Average amount of debt of borrowers graduating in 2003: $10,407. Proportion who borrowed: 48%.

University of Illinois–Urbana-Champaign

601 E. John Street
Champaign, IL 61820-5711
Public; www.uiuc.edu
Financial aid office: (217) 333-0100

■ **2004-2005 TUITION AND FEES:**
   In state: $7,476; Out of state: $19,504
■ **ROOM AND BOARD:** $6,848

ACT Score (25th/75th percentile): 25-31
2005 U.S. News College Ranking:
National Universities, 37
Acceptance Rate: 63%

Other expenses: Estimated books and supplies: $820. Transportation: $470. Personal expenses: $2,020. **Financial aid:** Priority filing date for institution's financial aid form: March 15. In 2003-2004, 58% of undergraduates applied for financial aid. Of those, 42% were determined to have financial need; 52% had their need fully met. Average financial aid package (proportion receiving): $8,521 (40%). Average amount of gift aid, such as scholarships or grants (proportion receiving): $6,195 (26%). Average amount of self-help aid, such as work study or loans (proportion receiving): $3,753 (33%). Average need-based loan (excluding PLUS or other private loans): $3,748. Among students who received need-based aid, the average percentage of need met: 90%. Among students who received aid based on merit, the average award (and the proportion receiving): $3,172 (12%). The average athletic scholarship (and the proportion receiving): $10,682 (1%). Average amount of debt of borrowers graduating in 2003: $15,100. Proportion who borrowed: 45%. **Student employment:** During the 2003-2004 academic year, 32% of undergraduates worked on campus. Average per-year earnings: $1,576. **Cooperative education programs:** computer science, engineering, natural science. **Reserve**

Officers Training Corps (ROTC): Army ROTC: Offered on campus; Navy ROTC: Offered on campus; Air Force ROTC: Offered on campus.

University of St. Francis

500 Wilcox Street
Joliet, IL 60435
Private; www.stfrancis.edu
Financial aid office: (815) 740-3403

■ 2004-2005 TUITION AND FEES: $17,670
■ ROOM AND BOARD: $6,180

ACT Score (25th/75th percentile): 20-24
2005 U.S. News College Ranking:
Universities–Master's (Midwest), 38
Acceptance Rate: 58%

Other expenses: Estimated books and supplies: $600. Transportation: $340. Personal expenses: $1,000. Financial aid: Priority filing date for institution's financial aid form: May 1. In 2003-2004, 98% of undergraduates applied for financial aid. Of those, 69% were determined to have financial need; 80% had their need fully met. Average financial aid package (proportion receiving): $13,695 (69%). Average amount of gift aid, such as scholarships or grants (proportion receiving): $8,401 (68%). Average amount of self-help aid, such as work study or loans (proportion receiving): $4,642 (52%). Average need-based loan (excluding PLUS or other private loans): $4,109. Among students who received need-based aid, the average percentage of need met: 81%. Among students who received aid based on merit, the average award (and the proportion receiving): $4,806 (23%). The average athletic scholarship (and the proportion receiving): $7,815 (7%). Average amount of debt of borrowers graduating in 2003: $16,359. Proportion who borrowed: 64%. Student employment: During the 2003-2004 academic year, 26% of undergraduates worked on campus. Average per-year earnings: $1,129. Reserve Officers Training Corps (ROTC): Army ROTC: Offered at cooperating institution (Wheaton College).

VanderCook College of Music

3140 S. Federal Street
Chicago, IL 60616
Private; www.vandercook.edu
Financial aid office: (312) 225-6288

■ 2004-2005 TUITION AND FEES: $15,760
■ ROOM AND BOARD: $10,094

ACT Score (25th/75th percentile): 20-24
2005 U.S. News College Ranking:
Unranked Specialty School–Fine Arts
Acceptance Rate: 81%

Cooperative education programs: education.

Western Illinois University

1 University Circle
Macomb, IL 61455
Public; www.wiu.edu
Financial aid office: (309) 298-2446

■ 2004-2005 TUITION AND FEES:
  In state: $5,485; Out of state: $9,400
■ ROOM AND BOARD: $5,366

ACT Score (25th/75th percentile): 19-24
2005 U.S. News College Ranking:
Universities–Master's (Midwest), 55
Acceptance Rate: 66%

Other expenses: Estimated books and supplies: $1,000. Transportation: $882. Personal expenses: $1,568. Financial aid: Priority filing date for institution's financial aid form: February 15. In 2003-2004, 71% of undergraduates applied for financial aid. Of those, 56% were determined to have financial need; 36% had their need fully met. Average financial aid package (proportion receiving): $7,428 (55%). Average amount of gift aid, such as scholarships or grants (proportion receiving): $4,794 (47%). Average amount of self-help aid, such as work study or loans (proportion receiving): $3,530 (49%). Average need-based loan (excluding PLUS or other private loans): $3,411. Among students who received need-based aid, the average percentage of need met: 68%. Among students who received aid based on merit, the average award (and the proportion receiving): $1,862 (6%). The average athletic scholarship (and the proportion receiving): $4,921 (3%). Average amount of debt of borrowers graduating in 2003: $13,800. Proportion who borrowed: 63%. Student employment: During the 2003-2004 academic year, 21% of undergraduates worked on campus. Average per-year earnings: $1,287. Reserve Officers Training Corps (ROTC): Army ROTC: Offered on campus.

Wheaton College

501 College Avenue
Wheaton, IL 60187
Private; www.wheaton.edu
Financial aid office: (630) 752-5021

■ 2004-2005 TUITION AND FEES: $20,000
■ ROOM AND BOARD: $6,466

SAT I Score (25th/75th percentile): 1230-1410
2005 U.S. News College Ranking:
Liberal Arts Colleges, 51
Acceptance Rate: 53%

Other expenses: Estimated books and supplies: $700. Personal expenses: $1,824. Financial aid: Priority filing date for institution's financial aid form: February 15. In 2003-2004, 73% of undergraduates applied for financial aid. Of those, 51% were determined to have financial need; 16% had their need fully met. Average financial aid package (proportion receiving): $16,040 (48%). Average amount of gift aid, such as scholarships or grants (proportion receiving): $10,582 (40%). Average amount of self-help aid, such as work study or loans (proportion receiving): $5,417 (44%). Average need-based loan (excluding PLUS or other private loans): $5,227. Among students who received need-based aid, the average percentage of need met: 86%. Among students who received aid based on merit, the average award (and the proportion receiving): $3,702 (18%). The average athletic scholarship (and the proportion receiving): $0 (0%). Average amount of debt of borrowers graduating in 2003: $16,476. Proportion who borrowed: 53%. Student employment: During the 2003-2004 academic year, 48% of undergraduates worked on campus. Average per-year earnings: $1,000. Reserve Officers Training Corps (ROTC): Army ROTC: Offered on campus; Air Force ROTC: Offered at cooperating institution (Illinois Inst of Technology).

Indiana

Anderson University

1100 E. Fifth Street
Anderson, IN 46012
Private; www.anderson.edu
Financial aid office: (765) 641-4180

- **2004-2005 TUITION AND FEES:** $17,990
- **ROOM AND BOARD:** $5,820

SAT I Score (25th/75th percentile): 940-1170
2005 U.S. News College Ranking:
Universities–Master's (Midwest), 42
Acceptance Rate: 71%

Other expenses: Estimated books and supplies: $750. Transportation: $700. Personal expenses: $1,300. **Financial aid:** Priority filing date for institution's financial aid form: March 1. In 2003-2004, 86% of undergraduates applied for financial aid. Of those, 78% were determined to have financial need; 22% had their need fully met. Average financial aid package (proportion receiving): $16,684 (78%). Average amount of gift aid, such as scholarships or grants (proportion receiving): $10,784 (78%). Average amount of self-help aid, such as work study or loans (proportion receiving): $6,575 (70%). Average need-based loan (excluding PLUS or other private loans): $4,959. Among students who received need-based aid, the average percentage of need met: 96%. Among students who received aid based on merit, the average award (and the proportion receiving): $7,516 (21%). The average athletic scholarship (and the proportion receiving): $0 (0%). Average amount of debt of borrowers graduating in 2003: $14,500. Proportion who borrowed: 91%. **Student employment:** During the 2003-2004 academic year, 49% of undergraduates worked on campus. Average per-year earnings: $2,600.

Ball State University

2000 University Avenue
Muncie, IN 47306
Public; www.bsu.edu
Financial aid office: (765) 285-5600

- **2004-2005 TUITION AND FEES:**
  In state: $5,124; Out of state: $14,272
- **ROOM AND BOARD:** $6,228

SAT I Score (25th/75th percentile): 920-1140
2005 U.S. News College Ranking:
National Universities, third tier
Acceptance Rate: 76%

Other expenses: Estimated books and supplies: $880. Transportation: $798. Personal expenses: $1,370. **Financial aid:** Priority filing date for institution's financial aid form: March 10. In 2003-2004, 74% of undergraduates applied for financial aid. Of those, 55% were determined to have financial need; 34% had their need fully met. Average financial aid package (proportion receiving): $6,836 (55%). Average amount of gift aid, such as scholarships or grants (proportion receiving): $4,442 (30%). Average amount of self-help aid, such as work study or loans (proportion receiving): $3,606 (44%). Average need-based loan (excluding PLUS or other private loans): $3,318. Among students who received need-based aid, the average percentage of need met: 69%. Among students who received aid based on merit, the average award (and the proportion receiving): $2,840 (7%). The average athletic scholarship (and the proportion receiving): $9,696 (2%). Average amount of debt of borrowers graduating in 2003: $17,053. Proportion who borrowed: 61%. **Student employment:** During the 2003-2004 academic year, 32% of undergraduates worked on campus. Average per-year earnings: $1,200. **Cooperative education programs:** computer science. **Reserve Officers Training Corps (ROTC):** Army ROTC: Offered on campus.

Bethel College

1001 W. McKinley Avenue
Mishawaka, IN 46545
Private; www.bethelcollege.edu
Financial aid office: (574) 257-3316

- **2004-2005 TUITION AND FEES:** $15,200
- **ROOM AND BOARD:** $4,930

SAT I Score (25th/75th percentile): 960-1200
2005 U.S. News College Ranking:
Comp. Colleges–Bachelor's (Midwest), 33
Acceptance Rate: 65%

Other expenses: Estimated books and supplies: $1,600. Transportation: $1,200. Personal expenses: $1,200. **Financial aid:** Priority filing date for institution's financial aid form: March

1. In 2003-2004, 99% of undergraduates applied for financial aid. Of those, 80% were determined to have financial need; 54% had their need fully met. Average financial aid package (proportion receiving): $12,313 (80%). Average amount of gift aid, such as scholarships or grants (proportion receiving): $3,310 (56%). Average amount of self-help aid, such as work study or loans (proportion receiving): $4,870 (78%). Average need-based loan (excluding PLUS or other private loans): $4,133. Among students who received need-based aid, the average percentage of need met: 90%. Among students who received aid based on merit, the average award (and the proportion receiving): $8,925 (7%). The average athletic scholarship (and the proportion receiving): $0 (0%). Average amount of debt of borrowers graduating in 2003: $16,509. Proportion who borrowed: 65%. **Student employment:** During the 2003-2004 academic year, 19% of undergraduates worked on campus. Average per-year earnings: $1,500. **Cooperative education programs:** engineering, technologies, vocational arts, other. **Reserve Officers Training Corps (ROTC):** Army ROTC: Offered at cooperating institution (University of Notre Dame); Air Force ROTC: Offered at cooperating institution (University of Notre Dame).

Butler University

4600 Sunset Avenue
Indianapolis, IN 46208
Private; www.butler.edu
Financial aid office: (317) 940-8200

- **2004-2005 TUITION AND FEES:** $22,470
- **ROOM AND BOARD:** $7,780

SAT I Score (25th/75th percentile): 1090-1280
2005 U.S. News College Ranking:
Universities–Master's (Midwest), 7
Acceptance Rate: 77%

Other expenses: Estimated books and supplies: $800. Transportation: $500. Personal expenses: $1,300. **Financial aid:** Priority filing date for institution's financial aid form: March 1; deadline: October 1. In 2003-2004, 92% of undergraduates applied for financial aid. Of those, 61% were determined to have financial need; 21% had their need fully met. Average financial aid package (proportion receiving): $16,000

(61%). Average amount of gift aid, such as scholarships or grants (proportion receiving): $12,000 (58%). Average amount of self-help aid, such as work study or loans (proportion receiving): $5,500 (47%). Average need-based loan (excluding PLUS or other private loans): $5,000. Among students who received need-based aid, the average percentage of need met: 79%. Among students who received aid based on merit, the average award (and the proportion receiving): $8,200 (27%). The average athletic scholarship (and the proportion receiving): $15,000 (3%). Average amount of debt of borrowers graduating in 2003: $19,500. Proportion who borrowed: 63%. **Student employment:** During the 2003-2004 academic year, 25% of undergraduates worked on campus. Average per-year earnings: $1,000. **Cooperative education programs:** business, engineering, health professions, other. **Reserve Officers Training Corps (ROTC):** Army ROTC: Offered on campus; Air Force ROTC: Offered at cooperating institution (Indiana University (Bloomington)).

Calumet College of St. Joseph

2400 New York Avenue
Whiting, IN 46394
Private; www.ccsj.edu
Financial aid office: (219) 473-4213

■ **2004-2005 TUITION AND FEES:** $9,450

2005 U.S. News College Ranking:
Comp. Colleges–Bachelor's (Midwest), fourth tier
Acceptance Rate: 75%

Financial aid: Priority filing date for institution's financial aid form: March 1. **Student employment:** During the 2003-2004 academic year, 10% of undergraduates worked on campus. **Cooperative education programs:** agriculture, art, business, computer science, education, engineering, health professions, humanities, natural science, social/behavioral science, technologies, vocational arts.

DePauw University

313 S. Locust Street
Greencastle, IN 46135
Private; www.depauw.edu
Financial aid office: (765) 658-4030

■ **2004-2005 TUITION AND FEES:** $25,460
■ **ROOM AND BOARD:** $7,300

SAT I Score (25th/75th percentile): 1130-1320
2005 U.S. News College Ranking:
Liberal Arts Colleges, 42
Acceptance Rate: 57%

Other expenses: Estimated books and supplies: $700. Transportation: $300. Personal expenses: $1,000. **Financial aid:** In 2003-2004, 71% of undergraduates applied for financial aid. Of those, 58% were determined to have financial need; 95% had their need fully met. Average financial aid package (proportion receiving): $20,208 (58%). Average amount of gift aid, such as scholarships or grants (proportion receiving): $16,693 (35%). Average amount of self-help aid, such as work study or loans (proportion receiving): $5,392 (38%). Average need-based loan (excluding PLUS or other private loans): $4,241. Among students who received need-based aid, the average percentage of need met: 99%. Among students who received aid based on merit, the average award (and the proportion receiving): $12,134 (45%). The average athletic scholarship (and the proportion receiving): $0 (0%). Average amount of debt of borrowers graduating in 2003: $15,635. Proportion who borrowed: 58%. **Student employment:** During the 2003-2004 academic year, 20% of undergraduates worked on campus. Average per-year earnings: $700. **Reserve Officers Training Corps (ROTC):** Army ROTC: Offered at cooperating institution (Rose-Hulman Institute of Technology); Air Force ROTC: Offered at cooperating institution (Indiana University).

Earlham College

801 National Road W
Richmond, IN 47374
Private; www.earlham.edu
Financial aid office: (765) 983-1217

■ **2004-2005 TUITION AND FEES:** $26,042
■ **ROOM AND BOARD:** $5,740

SAT I Score (25th/75th percentile): 1080-1330
2005 U.S. News College Ranking:
Liberal Arts Colleges, 70
Acceptance Rate: 77%

Other expenses: Estimated books and supplies: $850. Transportation: $500. Personal expenses: $1,000. **Financial aid:** Priority filing date for institution's financial aid form: March 1; deadline: March 1. In 2003-2004, 74% of undergraduates applied for financial aid. Of those, 66% were determined to have financial need; 22% had their need fully met. Average financial aid package (proportion receiving): $21,215

(65%). Average amount of gift aid, such as scholarships or grants (proportion receiving): $12,829 (62%). Average amount of self-help aid, such as work study or loans (proportion receiving): $5,367 (57%). Average need-based loan (excluding PLUS or other private loans): $4,300. Among students who received need-based aid, the average percentage of need met: 95%. Among students who received aid based on merit, the average award (and the proportion receiving): $6,153 (16%). The average athletic scholarship (and the proportion receiving): $0 (0%). Average amount of debt of borrowers graduating in 2003: $15,088. Proportion who borrowed: 70%. **Student employment:** During the 2003-2004 academic year, 74% of undergraduates worked on campus. Average per-year earnings: $1,000.

Franklin College

101 Branigin Boulevard
Franklin, IN 46131-2623
Private; www.franklincollege.edu
Financial aid office: (317) 738-8075

■ **2004-2005 TUITION AND FEES:** $18,275
■ **ROOM AND BOARD:** $5,500

SAT I Score (25th/75th percentile): 910-1130
2005 U.S. News College Ranking:
Comp. Colleges–Bachelor's (Midwest), 19
Acceptance Rate: 86%

Other expenses: Estimated books and supplies: $1,000. Transportation: $600. Personal expenses: $1,000. **Financial aid:** Priority filing date for institution's financial aid form: March 1; deadline: March 1. In 2003-2004, 93% of undergraduates applied for financial aid. Of those, 82% were determined to have financial need; 22% had their need fully met. Average financial aid package (proportion receiving): $13,337 (82%). Average amount of gift aid, such as scholarships or grants (proportion receiving): $10,073 (82%). Average amount of self-help aid, such as work study or loans (proportion receiving): N/A (64%). Among students who received need-based aid, the average percentage of need met: 88%. Among students who received aid based on merit, the average award (and the proportion receiving): $9,479 (18%). The average athletic scholarship (and the proportion receiving): $0 (0%). Average amount of debt of borrowers graduating in 2003: $18,054. Proportion who borrowed: 85%. **Student employment:** During the 2003-2004 academic year, 1% of undergraduates worked on campus. Average per-year earnings: $1,500. **Cooperative**

education programs: engineering, health professions, technologies, other. **Reserve Officers Training Corps (ROTC):** Army ROTC: Offered at cooperating institution (IUPUI).

Goshen College

1700 S. Main Street
Goshen, IN 46526
Private; www.goshen.edu
Financial aid office: (574) 535-7583

■ **2004-2005 TUITION AND FEES:** $18,200
■ **ROOM AND BOARD:** $6,200

SAT I Score (25th/75th percentile): 1030-1300
2005 U.S. News College Ranking:
Liberal Arts Colleges, third tier
Acceptance Rate: 61%

Other expenses: Estimated books and supplies: $800. Transportation: $450. Personal expenses: $1,100. **Financial aid:** Priority filing date for institution's financial aid form: February 15. In 2003-2004, 100% of undergraduates applied for financial aid. Of those, 71% were determined to have financial need; 35% had their need fully met. Average financial aid package (proportion receiving): $15,626 (71%). Average amount of gift aid, such as scholarships or grants (proportion receiving): $10,034 (70%). Average amount of self-help aid, such as work study or loans (proportion receiving): $5,708 (56%). Average need-based loan (excluding PLUS or other private loans): $5,189. Among students who received need-based aid, the average percentage of need met: 88%. Among students who received aid based on merit, the average award (and the proportion receiving): $7,486 (6%). The average athletic scholarship (and the proportion receiving): $3,675 (2%). Average amount of debt of borrowers graduating in 2003: $16,319. Proportion who borrowed: 73%.

Grace College and Seminary

200 Seminary Drive
Winona Lake, IN 46590
Private; www.grace.edu
Financial aid office: (574) 372-5100

■ **2004-2005 TUITION AND FEES:** $15,030
■ **ROOM AND BOARD:** $6,150

SAT I Score (25th/75th percentile): 960-1170
2005 U.S. News College Ranking:
Comp. Colleges–Bachelor's (Midwest), third tier
Acceptance Rate: 71%

Other expenses: Estimated books and supplies: $800. Transportation: $600. Personal expenses: $800. **Financial aid:** Priority filing date for institution's financial aid form: March 1. In 2003-2004, 86% of undergraduates applied for financial aid. Of those, 80% were determined to have financial need; 24% had their need fully met. Average financial aid package (proportion receiving): $12,437 (80%). Average amount of gift aid, such as scholarships or grants (proportion receiving): $7,359 (79%). Average amount of self-help aid, such as work study or loans (proportion receiving): $5,868 (71%). Average need-based loan (excluding PLUS or other private loans): $5,597. Among students who received need-based aid, the average percentage of need met: 85%. Among students who received aid based on merit, the average award (and the proportion receiving): $9,058 (15%). The average athletic scholarship (and the proportion receiving): $2,809 (8%). Average amount of debt of borrowers graduating in 2003: $23,035. Proportion who borrowed: 94%. **Student employment:** During the 2003-2004 academic year, 33% of undergraduates worked on campus. Average per-year earnings: $1,800.

Hanover College

Box 108
Hanover, IN 47243
Private; www.hanover.edu
Financial aid office: (812) 866-7030

■ **2004-2005 TUITION AND FEES:** $20,600
■ **ROOM AND BOARD:** $6,200

SAT I Score (25th/75th percentile): 1040-1260
2005 U.S. News College Ranking:
Liberal Arts Colleges, 89
Acceptance Rate: 79%

Other expenses: Estimated books and supplies: $800. Transportation: $600. Personal expenses: $800. **Financial aid:** Priority filing date for institution's financial aid form: March 10. In 2003-2004, 96% of undergraduates applied for financial aid. Of those, 86% were determined to have financial need; 37% had their need fully met. Average financial aid package (proportion receiving): $14,699 (86%). Average amount of gift aid, such as scholarships or grants (proportion receiving): $12,504 (86%). Average

amount of self-help aid, such as work study or loans (proportion receiving): $3,731 (50%). Average need-based loan (excluding PLUS or other private loans): $3,031. Among students who received need-based aid, the average percentage of need met: 72%. Among students who received aid based on merit, the average award (and the proportion receiving): $14,969 (14%). The average athletic scholarship (and the proportion receiving): $0 (0%). Average amount of debt of borrowers graduating in 2003: $14,978. Proportion who borrowed: 65%. **Student employment:** During the 2003-2004 academic year, 34% of undergraduates worked on campus. Average per-year earnings: $1,050.

Huntington College

2303 College Avenue
Huntington, IN 46750
Private; www.huntington.edu
Financial aid office: (260) 359-4015

■ **2004-2005 TUITION AND FEES:** $18,490
■ **ROOM AND BOARD:** $6,090

SAT I Score (25th/75th percentile): 1160-1270
2005 U.S. News College Ranking:
Comp. Colleges–Bachelor's (Midwest), 17
Acceptance Rate: 92%

Other expenses: Estimated books and supplies: $750. Transportation: $750. Personal expenses: $1,150. **Financial aid:** Priority filing date for institution's financial aid form: March 1. In 2003-2004, 83% of undergraduates applied for financial aid. Of those, 74% were determined to have financial need; 12% had their need fully met. Average financial aid package (proportion receiving): $13,794 (73%). Average amount of gift aid, such as scholarships or grants (proportion receiving): $8,574 (68%). Average amount of self-help aid, such as work study or loans (proportion receiving): $4,703 (63%). Average need-based loan (excluding PLUS or other private loans): $4,164. Among students who received need-based aid, the average percentage of need met: 69%. Among students who received aid based on merit, the average award (and the proportion receiving): $5,282 (7%). The average athletic scholarship (and the proportion receiving): $6,483 (8%). Average amount of debt of borrowers graduating in 2003: $16,952. Proportion who borrowed: 73%. **Student employment:** During the 2003-2004 academic year, 36% of undergraduates worked on campus. Average per-year earnings: $1,500.

Indiana Institute of Technology

1600 E. Washington Boulevard
Fort Wayne, IN 46803
Private; www.indianatech.edu
Financial aid office: (260) 422-5561

■ **2004-2005 TUITION AND FEES:** $16,680
■ **ROOM AND BOARD:** $6,272

SAT I Score (25th/75th percentile): 952
2005 U.S. News College Ranking:
Unranked Specialty School–Business
Acceptance Rate: 92%

Other expenses: Estimated books and supplies: $0. Transportation: $0. Personal expenses: $3,250. **Financial aid:** Priority filing date for institution's financial aid form: March 10. In 2003-2004, 83% of undergraduates applied for financial aid. Of those, 76% were determined to have financial need; 14% had their need fully met. Average financial aid package (proportion receiving): $8,622 (76%). Average amount of gift aid, such as scholarships or grants (proportion receiving): $7,206 (62%). Average amount of self-help aid, such as work study or loans (proportion receiving): $3,141 (65%). Average need-based loan (excluding PLUS or other private loans): $2,929. Among students who received need-based aid, the average percentage of need met: 69%. Among students who received aid based on merit, the average award (and the proportion receiving): $5,711 (8%). The average athletic scholarship (and the proportion receiving): $3,152 (4%). Average amount of debt of borrowers graduating in 2003: $15,020. Proportion who borrowed: 73%.

Indiana State University

210 N. Seventh Street
Terre Haute, IN 47809
Public; web.indstate.edu
Financial aid office: (812) 237-2215

■ **2004-2005 TUITION AND FEES:**
In state: $4,600; Out of state: $11,328
■ **ROOM AND BOARD:** $5,297

SAT I Score (25th/75th percentile): 840-1060
2005 U.S. News College Ranking:
National Universities, fourth tier
Acceptance Rate: 87%

Other expenses: Estimated books and supplies: $1,020. Transportation: $1,040. Personal expenses: $1,684. **Financial aid:** Priority filing

date for institution's financial aid form: March 1; deadline: March 1. In 2003-2004, 76% of undergraduates applied for financial aid. Of those, 61% were determined to have financial need; 16% had their need fully met. Average financial aid package (proportion receiving): $6,528 (57%). Average amount of gift aid, such as scholarships or grants (proportion receiving): $4,288 (36%). Average amount of self-help aid, such as work study or loans (proportion receiving): $3,574 (42%). Average need-based loan (excluding PLUS or other private loans): $3,536. Among students who received need-based aid, the average percentage of need met: 80%. Among students who received aid based on merit, the average award (and the proportion receiving): $2,799 (8%). The average athletic scholarship (and the proportion receiving): $7,337 (4%). Average amount of debt of borrowers graduating in 2003: $19,681. Proportion who borrowed: 62%. **Cooperative education programs:** business, computer science, education, health professions, home economics, technologies, other. **Reserve Officers Training Corps (ROTC):** Army ROTC: Offered on campus; Air Force ROTC: Offered on campus.

Indiana University–Bloomington

300 N. Jordan Avenue
Bloomington, IN 47405
Public; www.iub.edu
Financial aid office: (812) 855-0321

■ **2004-2005 TUITION AND FEES:**
In state: $6,777; Out of state: $18,590
■ **ROOM AND BOARD:** $6,006

SAT I Score (25th/75th percentile): 990-1220
2005 U.S. News College Ranking:
National Universities, 71
Acceptance Rate: 81%

Other expenses: Estimated books and supplies: $740. Transportation: $750. Personal expenses: $2,600. **Financial aid:** Priority filing date for institution's financial aid form: March 1. In 2003-2004, 66% of undergraduates applied for financial aid. Of those, 39% were determined to have financial need; 9% had their need fully met. Average financial aid package (proportion receiving): $7,425 (37%). Average amount of gift aid, such as scholarships or grants (proportion receiving): $4,877 (21%). Average amount of self-help aid, such as work study or loans (proportion receiving): $2,537 (16%). Average need-based loan (excluding PLUS or other private loans): $3,854. Among students who received need-

based aid, the average percentage of need met: 63%. Among students who received aid based on merit, the average award (and the proportion receiving): $3,586 (16%). The average athletic scholarship (and the proportion receiving): $13,779 (1%). Average amount of debt of borrowers graduating in 2003: $18,423. Proportion who borrowed: 48%. **Cooperative education programs:** business, computer science, education, health professions, humanities, natural science, social/behavioral science. **Reserve Officers Training Corps (ROTC):** Army ROTC: Offered on campus; Air Force ROTC: Offered on campus.

Indiana University East

2325 Chester Boulevard
Richmond, IN 47374-1289
Public; www.iue.edu
Financial aid office: (765) 973-8206

■ **2004-2005 TUITION AND FEES:**
In state: $4,601; Out of state: $10,991

SAT I Score (25th/75th percentile): 750-1000
2005 U.S. News College Ranking:
Comp. Colleges–Bachelor's (Midwest), fourth tier
Acceptance Rate: 79%

Other expenses: Estimated books and supplies: $800. Transportation: $1,400. Personal expenses: $1,300. **Financial aid:** Priority filing date for institution's financial aid form: March 1. In 2003-2004, 85% of undergraduates applied for financial aid. Of those, 72% were determined to have financial need; 5% had their need fully met. Average financial aid package (proportion receiving): $5,838 (67%). Average amount of gift aid, such as scholarships or grants (proportion receiving): $4,474 (53%). Average amount of self-help aid, such as work study or loans (proportion receiving): $3,117 (41%). Average need-based loan (excluding PLUS or other private loans): $2,880. Among students who received need-based aid, the average percentage of need met: 54%. Among students who received aid based on merit, the average award (and the proportion receiving): $600 (4%). Average amount of debt of borrowers graduating in 2003: $17,547. Proportion who borrowed: 63%.

Indiana University–Kokomo

2300 S. Washington Street, PO Box 9003
Kokomo, IN 46904-9003
Public; www.iuk.edu
Financial aid office: (765) 455-9216

■ **2004-2005 TUITION AND FEES:**
In state: $4,632; Out of state: $11,022

SAT I Score (25th/75th percentile): 840-1040
2005 U.S. News College Ranking:
Comp. Colleges–Bachelor's (Midwest), fourth tier
Acceptance Rate: 86%

Other expenses: Estimated books and supplies: $840. Transportation: $1,020. Personal expenses: $1,130. **Financial aid:** Priority filing date for institution's financial aid form: March 10. In 2003-2004, 61% of undergraduates applied for financial aid. Of those, 42% were determined to have financial need; 16% had their need fully met. Average financial aid package (proportion receiving): $5,654 (41%). Average amount of gift aid, such as scholarships or grants (proportion receiving): $4,283 (30%). Average amount of self-help aid, such as work study or loans (proportion receiving): $2,819 (27%). Average need-based loan (excluding PLUS or other private loans): $2,833. Among students who received need-based aid, the average percentage of need met: 70%. Among students who received aid based on merit, the average award (and the proportion receiving): $1,137 (5%). Average amount of debt of borrowers graduating in 2003: $11,681. Proportion who borrowed: 55%.

Indiana University Northwest

3400 Broadway
Gary, IN 46408
Public; www.iun.edu
Financial aid office: (219) 980-6778

■ **2004-2005 TUITION AND FEES:**
In state: $4,707; Out of state: $11,097

SAT I Score (25th/75th percentile): 770-1030
2005 U.S. News College Ranking:
Universities–Master's (Midwest), fourth tier
Acceptance Rate: 67%

Other expenses: Estimated books and supplies: $600. Transportation: $1,900. Personal expenses: $1,900. **Financial aid:** Priority filing date for institution's financial aid form: March 1. In 2003-2004, 68% of undergraduates applied for financial aid. Of those, 42% were determined to have

financial need; 12% had their need fully met. Average financial aid package (proportion receiving): $6,261 (41%). Average amount of gift aid, such as scholarships or grants (proportion receiving): $4,516 (30%). Average amount of self-help aid, such as work study or loans (proportion receiving): $3,211 (32%). Average need-based loan (excluding PLUS or other private loans): $2,842. Among students who received need-based aid, the average percentage of need met: 65%. Among students who received aid based on merit, the average award (and the proportion receiving): $1,428 (6%). Average amount of debt of borrowers graduating in 2003: $14,444. Proportion who borrowed: 58%. **Cooperative education programs:** business, computer science. **Reserve Officers Training Corps (ROTC):** Army ROTC: Offered on campus.

Indiana University-Purdue University—Fort Wayne

2101 E. Coliseum Boulevard
Fort Wayne, IN 46805-1499
Public; www.ipfw.edu
Financial aid office: (260) 481-6820

■ **2004-2005 TUITION AND FEES:**
In state: $4,780; Out of state: $11,024

SAT I Score (25th/75th percentile): 850-1080
2005 U.S. News College Ranking:
Universities–Master's (Midwest), fourth tier
Acceptance Rate: 97%

Other expenses: Estimated books and supplies: $950. Transportation: $1,684. Personal expenses: $2,836. **Financial aid:** Priority filing date for institution's financial aid form: March 10. In 2003-2004, 73% of undergraduates applied for financial aid. Of those, 57% were determined to have financial need; 10% had their need fully met. Average financial aid package (proportion receiving): $5,370 (55%). Average amount of gift aid, such as scholarships or grants (proportion receiving): $3,922 (35%). Average amount of self-help aid, such as work study or loans (proportion receiving): $2,976 (43%). Average need-based loan (excluding PLUS or other private loans): $2,955. Among students who received need-based aid, the average percentage of need met: 77%. Among students who received aid based on merit, the average award (and the proportion receiving): $1,036 (16%). The average athletic scholarship (and the proportion receiving): $2,789 (3%). Average amount of debt of borrowers graduating in 2003: $15,433. Proportion who borrowed: 52%. Average per-year earnings: $5,000. **Cooperative education programs:** business, computer science, engineering, natural science, technologies.

Indiana University-Purdue University—Indianapolis

425 N. University Boulevard
Indianapolis, IN 46202-5143
Public; www.iupui.edu
Financial aid office: (317) 274-4162

■ **2004-2005 TUITION AND FEES:**
In state: $5,930; Out of state: $15,767

SAT I Score (25th/75th percentile): 880-1090
2005 U.S. News College Ranking:
National Universities, fourth tier
Acceptance Rate: 77%

Other expenses: Estimated books and supplies: $840. Transportation: $2,998. Personal expenses: $2,972. **Financial aid:** Priority filing date for institution's financial aid form: March 1. In 2003-2004, 67% of undergraduates applied for financial aid. Of those, 57% were determined to have financial need; 4% had their need fully met. Average financial aid package (proportion receiving): $6,534 (52%). Average amount of gift aid, such as scholarships or grants (proportion receiving): $4,732 (35%). Average amount of self-help aid, such as work study or loans (proportion receiving): $3,719 (38%). Average need-based loan (excluding PLUS or other private loans): $3,643. Among students who received need-based aid, the average percentage of need met: 50%. Among students who received aid based on merit, the average award (and the proportion receiving): $1,686 (4%). The average athletic scholarship (and the proportion receiving): $3,686 (1%). Average amount of debt of borrowers graduating in 2003: $19,660. Proportion who borrowed: 58%. **Cooperative education programs:** art, business, computer science, education, health professions, humanities, natural science, social/behavioral science, technologies, vocational arts. **Reserve Officers Training Corps (ROTC):** Army ROTC: Offered on campus; Navy ROTC: Offered at cooperating institution (Purdue University); Air Force ROTC: Offered at cooperating institution (Indiana University South Bend).

Indiana University—South Bend

1700 Mishawaka Avenue, PO Box 7111
South Bend, IN 46634-7111
Public; www.iusb.edu
Financial aid office: (574) 237-4357

■ **2004-2005 TUITION AND FEES:**
In state: $4,755; Out of state: $11,826

SAT I Score (25th/75th percentile): 840-1070
2005 U.S. News College Ranking:
Universities–Master's (Midwest), fourth tier
Acceptance Rate: 83%

Other expenses: Estimated books and supplies: $976. Transportation: $1,932. Personal expenses: $1,604. **Financial aid:** Priority filing date for institution's financial aid form: March 1. In 2003-2004, 71% of undergraduates applied for financial aid. Of those, 52% were determined to have financial need; 7% had their need fully met. Average financial aid package (proportion receiving): $5,320 (34%). Average amount of gift aid, such as scholarships or grants (proportion receiving): $3,372 (34%). Average amount of self-help aid, such as work study or loans (proportion receiving): $3,458 (32%). Average need-based loan (excluding PLUS or other private loans): $3,407. Among students who received need-based aid, the average percentage of need met: 58%. Among students who received aid based on merit, the average award (and the proportion receiving): $2,309 (2%). The average athletic scholarship (and the proportion receiving): $3,450 (0%). Average amount of debt of borrowers graduating in 2003: $16,334. Proportion who borrowed: 57%. **Reserve Officers Training Corps (ROTC):** Army ROTC: Offered at cooperating institution (Notre Dame); Navy ROTC: Offered at cooperating institution (Notre Dame); Air Force ROTC: Offered at cooperating institution (Notre Dame).

Indiana University Southeast

4201 Grant Line Road
New Albany, IN 47150-6405
Public; www.ius.edu
Financial aid office: (812) 941-2246

■ **2004-2005 TUITION AND FEES:**
In state: $4,673; Out of state: $11,063

SAT I Score (25th/75th percentile): 840-1040
2005 U.S. News College Ranking:
Universities–Master's (Midwest), fourth tier
Acceptance Rate: 85%

Other expenses: Estimated books and supplies: $760. Transportation: $1,400. Personal expenses: $1,150. **Financial aid:** Priority filing date for institution's financial aid form: March 1. In 2003-2004, 68% of undergraduates applied for financial aid. Of those, 45% were determined to have financial need; 9% had their need fully met. Average financial aid package (proportion receiving): $5,556 (43%). Average amount of gift aid, such as scholarships or grants (proportion

receiving): $4,192 (30%). Average amount of self-help aid, such as work study or loans (proportion receiving): $3,220 (27%). Average need-based loan (excluding PLUS or other private loans): $3,209. Among students who received need-based aid, the average percentage of need met: 62%. Among students who received aid based on merit, the average award (and the proportion receiving): $1,702 (5%). The average athletic scholarship (and the proportion receiving): $976 (2%). Average amount of debt of borrowers graduating in 2003: $12,973. Proportion who borrowed: 47%. **Reserve Officers Training Corps (ROTC):** Army ROTC: Offered at cooperating institution (University of Louisville); Air Force ROTC: Offered at cooperating institution (University of Louisville).

Indiana Wesleyan University

4201 S. Washington Street
Marion, IN 46953-4999
Private; www.indwes.edu
Financial aid office: (765) 677-2116

■ **2004-2005 TUITION AND FEES:** $15,204
■ **ROOM AND BOARD:** $5,676

SAT I Score (25th/75th percentile): 971-1222
2005 U.S. News College Ranking:
Universities–Master's (Midwest), third tier
Acceptance Rate: 67%

Financial aid: Priority filing date for institution's financial aid form: March 1. **Cooperative education programs:** business, education, health professions, humanities, technologies.

Manchester College

604 E. College Avenue
North Manchester, IN 46962
Private; www.manchester.edu
Financial aid office: (260) 982-5066

■ **2004-2005 TUITION AND FEES:** $18,060
■ **ROOM AND BOARD:** $6,710

SAT I Score (25th/75th percentile): 895-1130
2005 U.S. News College Ranking:
Comp. Colleges–Bachelor's (Midwest), 33
Acceptance Rate: 79%

Other expenses: Estimated books and supplies: $550. Transportation: $550. Personal expenses: $900. **Financial aid:** In 2003-2004, 87% of undergraduates applied for financial aid. Of those, 78% were determined to have financial

need; 40% had their need fully met. Average financial aid package (proportion receiving): $16,033 (77%). Average amount of gift aid, such as scholarships or grants (proportion receiving): $12,666 (77%). Average amount of self-help aid, such as work study or loans (proportion receiving): $3,420 (77%). Average need-based loan (excluding PLUS or other private loans): $3,422. Among students who received need-based aid, the average percentage of need met: 92%. Among students who received aid based on merit, the average award (and the proportion receiving): $5,424 (11%). The average athletic scholarship (and the proportion receiving): $0 (0%). Average amount of debt of borrowers graduating in 2003: $12,084. Proportion who borrowed: 64%. **Student employment:** During the 2003-2004 academic year, 25% of undergraduates worked on campus. Average per-year earnings: $1,500.

Marian College

3200 Cold Spring Road
Indianapolis, IN 46222
Private; www.marian.edu
Financial aid office: (317) 955-6040

■ **2004-2005 TUITION AND FEES:** $18,240
■ **ROOM AND BOARD:** $6,000

SAT I Score (25th/75th percentile): 890-1100
2005 U.S. News College Ranking:
Comp. Colleges–Bachelor's (Midwest), third tier
Acceptance Rate: 74%

Other expenses: Estimated books and supplies: $700. Transportation: $360. Personal expenses: $900. **Financial aid:** Priority filing date for institution's financial aid form: March 15. In 2003-2004, 86% of undergraduates applied for financial aid. Of those, 79% were determined to have financial need; 33% had their need fully met. Average financial aid package (proportion receiving): $13,717 (79%). Average amount of gift aid, such as scholarships or grants (proportion receiving): $7,633 (68%). Average amount of self-help aid, such as work study or loans (proportion receiving): $5,731 (77%). Average need-based loan (excluding PLUS or other private loans): $3,019. Among students who received need-based aid, the average percentage of need met: 78%. Among students who received aid based on merit, the average award (and the proportion receiving): $9,301 (5%). The average athletic scholarship (and the proportion receiving): $4,811 (19%). Average amount of debt of borrowers graduating in

2003: $14,187. Proportion who borrowed: 77%.
Student employment: During the 2003-2004 academic year, 25% of undergraduates worked on campus. Average per-year earnings: $2,000. **Cooperative education programs:** art, business, computer science, education, health professions, humanities, natural science, social/behavioral science. **Reserve Officers Training Corps (ROTC):** Army ROTC: Offered at cooperating institution (IUPUI).

Martin University

PO Box 18567, 2171 Avondale Place
Indianapolis, IN 46218
Private; www.martin.edu
Financial aid office: (317) 543-3258

■ **2004-2005 TUITION AND FEES:** $8,840

2005 U.S. News College Ranking:
Comp. Colleges–Bachelor's (Midwest), fourth tier

Other expenses: Estimated books and supplies: $820. Transportation: $1,114. Personal expenses: $1,114. **Financial aid:** In 2003-2004, 87% of undergraduates applied for financial aid. Of those, 84% were determined to have financial need; 1% had their need fully met. Average financial aid package (proportion receiving): $8,779 (83%). Average amount of gift aid, such as scholarships or grants (proportion receiving): $6,705 (78%). Average amount of self-help aid, such as work study or loans (proportion receiving): $3,192 (75%). Average need-based loan (excluding PLUS or other private loans): $3,192. Among students who received need-based aid, the average percentage of need met: 69%. Among students who received aid based on merit, the average award (and the proportion receiving): $0 (0%). The average athletic scholarship (and the proportion receiving): $0 (0%). Average amount of debt of borrowers graduating in 2003: $27,193. Proportion who borrowed: 91%.

Oakland City University

143 N. Lucretia Street
Oakland City, IN 47660
Private; www.oak.edu
Financial aid office: (812) 749-1224

■ **2004-2005 TUITION AND FEES:** $12,920
■ **ROOM AND BOARD:** $4,800

SAT I Score (25th/75th percentile): 818-1043
2005 U.S. News College Ranking:
Universities–Master's (Midwest), fourth tier
Acceptance Rate: 99%

Purdue University–Calumet

2200 169th Street
Hammond, IN 46323-2094
Public; www.calumet.purdue.edu
Financial aid office: (219) 989-2301

■ **2004-2005 TUITION AND FEES:**
In state: $4,300; Out of state: $10,256

SAT I Score (25th/75th percentile): 790-1030
2005 U.S. News College Ranking:
Universities–Master's (Midwest), fourth tier
Acceptance Rate: 87%

Other expenses: Estimated books and supplies: $950. Transportation: $1,775. Personal expenses: $2,632. **Financial aid:** Priority filing date for institution's financial aid form: March 10. In 2003-2004, 67% of undergraduates applied for financial aid. Of those, 54% were determined to have financial need; 5% had their need fully met. Average financial aid package (proportion receiving): $5,297 (48%). Average amount of gift aid, such as scholarships or grants (proportion receiving): $4,169 (34%). Average amount of self-help aid, such as work study or loans (proportion receiving): $2,893 (33%). Average need-based loan (excluding PLUS or other private loans): $2,893. Among students who received need-based aid, the average percentage of need met: 49%. Among students who received aid based on merit, the average award (and the proportion receiving): $1,674 (2%). The average athletic scholarship (and the proportion receiving): $1,610 (0%). Average amount of debt of borrowers graduating in 2003: $13,693. Proportion who borrowed: 46%. **Student employment:** During the 2003-2004 academic year, 4% of undergraduates worked on campus. Average per-year earnings: $3,900. **Cooperative education programs:** engineering, technologies.

Purdue University–North Central

1401 S. U.S. Highway 421
Westville, IN 46391
Public; www.pnc.edu
Financial aid office: (219) 785-5279

■ **2004-2005 TUITION AND FEES:**
In state: $4,901; Out of state: $11,524

SAT I Score (25th/75th percentile): 830-1040
2005 U.S. News College Ranking:
Comp. Colleges–Bachelor's (Midwest), fourth tier
Acceptance Rate: 89%

Financial aid: Priority filing date for institution's financial aid form: March 1. In 2003-2004, 75% of undergraduates applied for financial aid. Of those, 61% were determined to have financial need; Among students who received aid based on merit, the average award (and the proportion receiving): $1,063 (1%). The average athletic scholarship (and the proportion receiving): $1,241 (2%). Average amount of debt of borrowers graduating in 2003: $9,841. Proportion who borrowed: 42%.

Purdue University–West Lafayette

Schleman Hall, 475 Stadium Mall Drive
West Lafayette, IN 47907-2050
Public; www.purdue.edu
Financial aid office: (765) 494-5090

■ **2004-2005 TUITION AND FEES:**
In state: $6,092; Out of state: $18,700
■ **ROOM AND BOARD:** $7,020

SAT I Score (25th/75th percentile): 1030-1260
2005 U.S. News College Ranking:
National Universities, 62
Acceptance Rate: 79%

Other expenses: Estimated books and supplies: $940. Transportation: $230. Personal expenses: $1,040. **Financial aid:** Priority filing date for institution's financial aid form: March 1. In 2003-2004, 60% of undergraduates applied for financial aid. Of those, 42% were determined to have financial need; 37% had their need fully met. Average financial aid package (proportion receiving): $8,796 (40%). Average amount of gift aid, such as scholarships or grants (proportion receiving): $6,879 (14%). Average amount of self-help aid, such as work study or loans (proportion receiving): $4,116 (36%). Average need-based loan (excluding PLUS or other private loans): $3,946. Among students who received need-based aid, the average percentage of need met: 90%. Among students who received aid based on merit, the average award (and the proportion receiving): $10,502 (13%). The average athletic scholarship (and the proportion receiving): $15,207 (1%). Average amount of debt of borrowers graduating in 2003: $16,641. Proportion who borrowed: 50%. **Student employment:** During the 2003-2004 academic year, 22% of undergraduates worked on campus. Average per-year earnings: $1,096. **Cooperative education programs:** agriculture, art, business, computer science, education, engineering, health professions, home economics, humanities, natural science, technologies, vocational arts. **Reserve Officers Training Corps (ROTC):** Army ROTC: Offered on campus; Navy ROTC: Offered on campus; Air Force ROTC: Offered on campus.

Rose-Hulman Institute of Technology

5500 Wabash Avenue
Terre Haute, IN 47803
Private; www.rose-hulman.edu
Financial aid office: (812) 877-8259

■ **2004-2005 TUITION AND FEES:** $26,136
■ **ROOM AND BOARD:** $7,065

SAT I Score (25th/75th percentile): 1210-1410
2005 U.S. News College Ranking:
Unranked Specialty School–Engineering
Acceptance Rate: 71%

Other expenses: Estimated books and supplies: $1,200. Transportation: $0. Personal expenses: $1,200. **Financial aid:** Priority filing date for institution's financial aid form: March 1. In 2003-2004, 84% of undergraduates applied for financial aid. Of those, 72% were determined to have financial need; 10% had their need fully met. Average financial aid package (proportion receiving): $15,261 (72%). Average amount of gift aid, such as scholarships or grants (proportion receiving): $5,746 (58%). Average amount of self-help aid, such as work study or loans (proportion receiving): $6,182 (62%). Average need-based loan (excluding PLUS or other private loans): $5,341. Among students who received need-based aid, the average percentage of need met: 83%. Among students who received aid based on merit, the average award (and the proportion receiving): $5,557 (23%). Average amount of debt of borrowers graduating in 2003: $27,000. Proportion who borrowed: 85%. **Student employment:** During the 2003-2004 academic year, 23% of undergraduates worked on campus. Average per-year earnings: $1,500. **Cooperative education programs:** computer science, engineering, natural science. **Reserve Officers Training Corps (ROTC):** Army ROTC: Offered on campus; Air Force ROTC: Offered on campus.

St. Joseph's College

PO Box 890
Rensselaer, IN 47978
Private; www.saintjoe.edu
Financial aid office: (219) 866-6163

■ **2004-2005 TUITION AND FEES:** $19,160
■ **ROOM AND BOARD:** $6,300

SAT I Score (25th/75th percentile): 875-1100
2005 U.S. News College Ranking:
Comp. Colleges–Bachelor's (Midwest), 40
Acceptance Rate: 76%

Other expenses: Estimated books and supplies: $700. Transportation: $400. Personal expenses: $650. **Financial aid:** Priority filing date for institution's financial aid form: March 1. In 2003-2004, 92% of undergraduates applied for financial aid. Of those, 78% were determined to have financial need; 45% had their need fully met. Average financial aid package (proportion receiving): $13,800 (78%). Average amount of gift aid, such as scholarships or grants (proportion receiving): $7,850 (60%). Average amount of self-help aid, such as work study or loans (proportion receiving): $4,000 (57%). Average need-based loan (excluding PLUS or other private loans): $4,000. Among students who received need-based aid, the average percentage of need met: 85%. Among students who received aid based on merit, the average award (and the proportion receiving): $5,000 (6%). The average athletic scholarship (and the proportion receiving): $10,200 (8%). Average amount of debt of borrowers graduating in 2003: $18,500. Proportion who borrowed: 83%. **Student employment:** During the 2003-2004 academic year, 45% of undergraduates worked on campus. Average per-year earnings: $1,200. **Cooperative education programs:** education, health professions, social/behavioral science.

St. Mary-of-the-Woods College

St. Mary-of-the-Woods, IN 47876
Private; www.smwc.edu
Financial aid office: (812) 535-5109

■ **2004-2005 TUITION AND FEES:** $17,860
■ **ROOM AND BOARD:** $6,560

SAT I Score (25th/75th percentile): 880-1100
2005 U.S. News College Ranking:
Comp. Colleges–Bachelor's (Midwest), 36
Acceptance Rate: 78%

Other expenses: Estimated books and supplies: $1,025. Transportation: $500. Personal expenses: $925. **Financial aid:** Priority filing date for institution's financial aid form: March 10. **Student employment:** During the 2003-2004 academic year, 60% of undergraduates worked on campus. Average per-year earnings: $800. **Reserve Officers Training Corps (ROTC):** Army ROTC: Offered at cooperating institution (Rose Hulman Institute of Technology); Air Force ROTC: Offered at cooperating institution (Indiana State University).

St. Mary's College

Notre Dame, IN 46556
Private; www.saintmarys.edu
Financial aid office: (574) 284-4557

■ **2004-2005 TUITION AND FEES:** $23,284
■ **ROOM AND BOARD:** $7,663

SAT I Score (25th/75th percentile): 1015-1220
2005 U.S. News College Ranking:
Comp. Colleges–Bachelor's (Midwest), 1
Acceptance Rate: 82%

Other expenses: Estimated books and supplies: $1,000. Transportation: $425. Personal expenses: $1,200. **Financial aid:** Priority filing date for institution's financial aid form: March 1. In 2003-2004, 72% of undergraduates applied for financial aid. Of those, 67% were determined to have financial need; 26% had their need fully met. Average financial aid package (proportion receiving): $17,358 (67%). Average amount of gift aid, such as scholarships or grants (proportion receiving): $8,283 (58%). Average amount of self-help aid, such as work study or loans (proportion receiving): $5,020 (51%). Average need-based loan (excluding PLUS or other private loans): $2,773. Among students who received need-based aid, the average percentage of need met: 79%. Among students who received aid based on merit, the average award (and the proportion receiving): $6,721 (21%). The average athletic scholarship (and the proportion receiving): $0 (0%). Average amount of debt of borrowers graduating in 2003: $20,356. Proportion who borrowed: 82%. **Student employment:** During the 2003-2004 academic year, 55% of undergraduates worked on campus. Average per-year earnings: $1,964. **Cooperative education programs:** engineering, health professions. **Reserve Officers Training Corps (ROTC):** Army ROTC: Offered at cooperating institution (University of Notre Dame); Navy ROTC: Offered at cooperating institution (University of Notre Dame); Air

Force ROTC: Offered at cooperating institution (University of Notre Dame).

Taylor University

236 W. Reade Avenue
Upland, IN 46989-1002
Private; www.taylor.edu
Financial aid office: (765) 998-5358

■ **2004-2005 TUITION AND FEES:** $19,674
■ **ROOM AND BOARD:** $5,452

ACT Score (25th/75th percentile): 23-28
2005 U.S. News College Ranking:
Comp. Colleges–Bachelor's (Midwest), 3
Acceptance Rate: 84%

Other expenses: Estimated books and supplies: $700. Personal expenses: $1,500. **Financial aid:** In 2003-2004, 68% of undergraduates applied for financial aid. Of those, 57% were determined to have financial need; 23% had their need fully met. Average financial aid package (proportion receiving): $13,351 (57%). Average amount of gift aid, such as scholarships or grants (proportion receiving): $9,618 (53%). Average amount of self-help aid, such as work study or loans (proportion receiving): $4,705 (51%). Average need-based loan (excluding PLUS or other private loans): $4,174. Among students who received need-based aid, the average percentage of need met: 81%. Among students who received aid based on merit, the average award (and the proportion receiving): $3,137 (25%). The average athletic scholarship (and the proportion receiving): $4,088 (3%). Average amount of debt of borrowers graduating in 2003: $15,467. Proportion who borrowed: 62%. **Student employment:** During the 2003-2004 academic year, 25% of undergraduates worked on campus. Average per-year earnings: $2,000.

Tri-State University

1 University Avenue
Angola, IN 46703
Private; www.tristate.edu
Financial aid office: (260) 665-4175

■ **2004-2005 TUITION AND FEES:** $19,260
■ **ROOM AND BOARD:** $5,700

SAT I Score (25th/75th percentile): 970-1210
2005 U.S. News College Ranking:
Comp. Colleges–Bachelor's (Midwest), 43
Acceptance Rate: 72%

Other expenses: Estimated books and supplies: $900. Personal expenses: $1,565. **Financial aid:** Priority filing date for institution's financial aid form: March 1; deadline: March 10. In 2003-2004, 100% of undergraduates applied for financial aid. Of those, 99% were determined to have financial need; 78% had their need fully met. Average financial aid package (proportion receiving): $12,100 (99%). Average amount of gift aid, such as scholarships or grants (proportion receiving): $3,362 (13%). Average amount of self-help aid, such as work study or loans (proportion receiving): $3,578 (65%). Average need-based loan (excluding PLUS or other private loans): $3,578. Among students who received need-based aid, the average percentage of need met: 75%. Among students who received aid based on merit, the average award (and the proportion receiving): $2,514 (3%). The average athletic scholarship (and the proportion receiving): $2,644 (27%). Average amount of debt of borrowers graduating in 2003: $16,510. Proportion who borrowed: 58%. **Student employment:** During the 2003-2004 academic year, 10% of undergraduates worked on campus. **Cooperative education programs:** business, computer science, engineering, natural science, technologies.

University of Evansville

1800 Lincoln Avenue
Evansville, IN 47722
Private; www.evansville.edu
Financial aid office: (812) 479-2364

■ **2004-2005 TUITION AND FEES:** $20,515
■ **ROOM AND BOARD:** $6,390

SAT I Score (25th/75th percentile): 1010-1260
2005 U.S. News College Ranking:
Universities–Master's (Midwest), 10
Acceptance Rate: 86%

Other expenses: Estimated books and supplies: $800. Transportation: $595. Personal expenses: $800. **Financial aid:** Priority filing date for institution's financial aid form: March 1; deadline: March 1. In 2003-2004, 96% of undergraduates applied for financial aid. Of those, 70% were determined to have financial need; 32% had their need fully met. Average financial aid package (proportion receiving): $17,375 (70%). Average amount of gift aid, such as scholar-

ships or grants (proportion receiving): $12,915 (67%). Average amount of self-help aid, such as work study or loans (proportion receiving): $4,646 (51%). Average need-based loan (excluding PLUS or other private loans): $4,283. Among students who received need-based aid, the average percentage of need met: 91%. Among students who received aid based on merit, the average award (and the proportion receiving): $7,764 (21%). The average athletic scholarship (and the proportion receiving): $19,763 (4%). Average amount of debt of borrowers graduating in 2003: $21,141. Proportion who borrowed: 68%. **Student employment:** During the 2003-2004 academic year, 34% of undergraduates worked on campus. Average per-year earnings: $1,300. **Cooperative education programs:** business, computer science, engineering, natural science, technologies.

University of Indianapolis

1400 E. Hanna Avenue
Indianapolis, IN 46227-3697
Private; www.uindy.edu
Financial aid office: (317) 788-3217

■ **2004-2005 TUITION AND FEES:** $17,300
■ **ROOM AND BOARD:** $6,150

SAT I Score (25th/75th percentile): 910-1140
2005 U.S. News College Ranking:
Universities–Master's (Midwest), 28
Acceptance Rate: 74%

Other expenses: Estimated books and supplies: $775. Transportation: $610. Personal expenses: $1,230. **Financial aid:** Priority filing date for institution's financial aid form: March 10. In 2003-2004, 85% of undergraduates applied for financial aid. Of those, 77% were determined to have financial need; 30% had their need fully met. Average financial aid package (proportion receiving): $15,035 (76%). Average amount of gift aid, such as scholarships or grants (proportion receiving): $8,013 (67%). Average amount of self-help aid, such as work study or loans (proportion receiving): $3,885 (58%). Average need-based loan (excluding PLUS or other private loans): $3,864. Among students who received need-based aid, the average percentage of need met: 82%. Among students who received aid based on merit, the average award (and the proportion receiving): $7,730 (11%). The average athletic scholarship (and the proportion receiving): $8,624 (14%). Average amount of debt of borrowers graduating in 2003: $18,968. Proportion who borrowed: 69%. **Student employment:** During the 2003-

2004 academic year, 50% of undergraduates worked on campus. Average per-year earnings: $1,400. **Cooperative education programs:** business, computer science, education, health professions, humanities, natural science, social/behavioral science. **Reserve Officers Training Corps (ROTC):** Army ROTC: Offered at cooperating institution (I.U.P.U.I.).

University of Notre Dame

Notre Dame, IN 46556
Private; www.nd.edu
Financial aid office: (574) 631-6436

■ **2004-2005 TUITION AND FEES:** $29,512
■ **ROOM AND BOARD:** $7,418

SAT I Score (25th/75th percentile): 1270-1460
2005 U.S. News College Ranking:
National Universities, 18
Acceptance Rate: 29%

Other expenses: Estimated books and supplies: $850. Transportation: $500. Personal expenses: $900. **Financial aid:** Priority filing date for institution's financial aid form: February 15; deadline: February 15. In 2003-2004, 56% of undergraduates applied for financial aid. Of those, 48% were determined to have financial need; 100% had their need fully met. Average financial aid package (proportion receiving): $23,412 (48%). Average amount of gift aid, such as scholarships or grants (proportion receiving): $17,160 (45%). Average amount of self-help aid, such as work study or loans (proportion receiving): $6,051 (41%). Average need-based loan (excluding PLUS or other private loans): $5,101. Among students who received need-based aid, the average percentage of need met: 100%. Among students who received aid based on merit, the average award (and the proportion receiving): $7,963 (3%). The average athletic scholarship (and the proportion receiving): $24,863 (4%). Average amount of debt of borrowers graduating in 2003: $25,653. Proportion who borrowed: 56%. **Reserve Officers Training Corps (ROTC):** Army ROTC: Offered on campus; Navy ROTC: Offered on campus; Air Force ROTC: Offered on campus.

University of Southern Indiana

8600 University Boulevard
Evansville, IN 47712
Public; www.usi.edu
Financial aid office: (812) 464-1767

■ **2004-2005 TUITION AND FEES:**
In state: $4,077; Out of state: $9,642
■ **ROOM AND BOARD:** $5,480

SAT I Score (25th/75th percentile): 830-1060
2005 U.S. News College Ranking:
Universities–Master's (Midwest), fourth tier
Acceptance Rate: 93%

Other expenses: Estimated books and supplies: $850. Transportation: $720. Personal expenses: $1,822. **Financial aid:** In 2003-2004, 79% of undergraduates applied for financial aid. Of those, 61% were determined to have financial need; 14% had their need fully met. Average financial aid package (proportion receiving): $5,134 (56%). Average amount of gift aid, such as scholarships or grants (proportion receiving): $4,060 (39%). Average amount of self-help aid, such as work study or loans (proportion receiving): $3,126 (37%). Average need-based loan (excluding PLUS or other private loans): $3,102. Among students who received need-based aid, the average percentage of need met: 59%. Among students who received aid based on merit, the average award (and the proportion receiving): $2,068 (7%). The average athletic scholarship (and the proportion receiving): $4,961 (1%). Average amount of debt of borrowers graduating in 2003: $13,487. Proportion who borrowed: 57%. **Student employment:** During the 2003-2004 academic year, 10% of undergraduates worked on campus. Average per-year earnings: $1,267. **Cooperative education programs:** business, computer science, engineering. **Reserve Officers Training Corps (ROTC):** Army ROTC: Offered on campus.

University of St. Francis

2701 Spring Street
Fort Wayne, IN 46808
Private; www.sf.edu
Financial aid office: (260) 434-3283

■ **2004-2005 TUITION AND FEES:** $16,460
■ **ROOM AND BOARD:** $5,450

SAT I Score (25th/75th percentile): 860-1070
2005 U.S. News College Ranking:
Universities–Master's (Midwest), third tier
Acceptance Rate: 74%

Other expenses: Estimated books and supplies: $1,000. Transportation: $1,000. Personal expenses: $2,100. **Financial aid:** Priority filing date for institution's financial aid form: March 10; deadline: June 30. In 2003-2004, 94% of undergraduates applied for financial aid. Of those, 83% were determined to have financial need; 31% had their need fully met. Average financial aid package (proportion receiving): $12,668 (83%). Average amount of gift aid, such as scholarships or grants (proportion receiving): $9,101 (82%). Average amount of self-help aid, such as work study or loans (proportion receiving): $4,046 (73%). Average need-based loan (excluding PLUS or other private loans): $3,101. Among students who received need-based aid, the average percentage of need met: 79%. Among students who received aid based on merit, the average award (and the proportion receiving): $8,913 (12%). The average athletic scholarship (and the proportion receiving): $4,490 (8%). Average amount of debt of borrowers graduating in 2003: $18,000. Proportion who borrowed: 100%. **Student employment:** During the 2003-2004 academic year, 0% of undergraduates worked on campus. Average per-year earnings: $0.

Valparaiso University

Kretzmann Hall, 1700 Chapel Drive
Valparaiso, IN 46383
Private; www.valpo.edu
Financial aid office: (219) 464-5015

■ **2004-2005 TUITION AND FEES:** $21,700
■ **ROOM AND BOARD:** $5,840

ACT Score (25th/75th percentile): 23-29
2005 U.S. News College Ranking:
Universities–Master's (Midwest), 2
Acceptance Rate: 82%

Other expenses: Estimated books and supplies: $800. Transportation: $500. Personal expenses: $870. **Financial aid:** Priority filing date for institution's financial aid form: March 1. In 2003-2004, 80% of undergraduates applied for financial aid. Of those, 68% were determined to have financial need; 51% had their need fully met. Average financial aid package (proportion receiving): $17,404 (68%). Average amount of gift aid, such as scholarships or grants (proportion receiving): $11,310 (67%). Average amount of self-help aid, such as work study or loans (proportion receiving): $6,288 (53%). Average need-based loan (excluding PLUS or other private loans): $5,345. Among students who received need-based aid, the average percentage of need met: 92%. Among students who received aid based on merit, the average award (and the proportion receiving): $7,573 (24%). The average athletic scholarship (and the proportion receiving): $12,855 (3%). Average amount of debt of borrowers graduating in 2003: $20,270. Proportion who borrowed: 59%. **Student employment:** During the 2003-2004 academic year, 40% of undergraduates worked on campus. Average per-year earnings: $1,000. **Cooperative education programs:** business, computer science, engineering, health professions, humanities, natural science, social/behavioral science, other. **Reserve Officers Training Corps (ROTC):** Air Force ROTC: Offered on campus.

Wabash College

PO Box 352
Crawfordsville, IN 47933
Private; www.wabash.edu
Financial aid office: (765) 361-6370

■ **2004-2005 TUITION AND FEES:** $22,275
■ **ROOM AND BOARD:** $7,053

SAT I Score (25th/75th percentile): 1070-1285
2005 U.S. News College Ranking:
Liberal Arts Colleges, 48
Acceptance Rate: 50%

....

Other expenses: Estimated books and supplies: $1,000. Personal expenses: $900. **Financial aid:** Priority filing date for institution's financial aid form: February 15; deadline: March 1. In 2003-2004, 79% of undergraduates applied for financial aid. Of those, 70% were determined to have financial need; 100% had their need fully met. Average financial aid package (proportion receiving): $19,944 (70%). Average amount of gift aid, such as scholarships or grants (proportion receiving): $14,921 (70%). Average amount of self-help aid, such as work study or loans (proportion receiving): $4,618 (66%). Average need-based loan (excluding PLUS or other private loans): $2,564. Among students who received need-based aid, the average percentage of need met: 100%. Among students who received aid based on merit, the average award (and the proportion receiving): $11,261 (25%). Average amount of debt of borrowers graduating in 2003: $17,818. Proportion who borrowed: 70%. **Student employment:** During the 2003-2004 academic year, 70% of undergraduates worked on campus. Average per-year earnings: $1,000. **Reserve Officers Training Corps (ROTC):** Army ROTC: Offered at cooperating institution (Purdue).

Iowa

Briar Cliff University

3303 Rebecca Street, Box 2100
Sioux City, IA 51104
Private; www.briarcliff.edu
Financial aid office: (712) 279-5239

- **2004-2005 TUITION AND FEES:** $16,995
- **ROOM AND BOARD:** $5,433

ACT Score (25th/75th percentile): 19-23
2005 U.S. News College Ranking:
Comp. Colleges–Bachelor's (Midwest),
third tier
Acceptance Rate: 80%

Other expenses: Estimated books and supplies: $720. Transportation: $870. Personal expenses: $1,935. **Financial aid:** Priority filing date for institution's financial aid form: March 15; deadline: July 5. In 2003-2004, 94% of undergraduates applied for financial aid. Of those, 76% were determined to have financial need; 99% had their need fully met. Average financial aid package (proportion receiving): $16,995 (76%). Average amount of gift aid, such as scholarships or grants (proportion receiving): $4,856 (70%). Average amount of self-help aid, such as work study or loans (proportion receiving): $7,100 (76%). Average need-based loan (excluding PLUS or other private loans): $4,885. Among students who received need-based aid, the average percentage of need met: 92%. Among students who received aid based on merit, the average award (and the proportion receiving): $2,895 (73%). The average athletic scholarship (and the proportion receiving): $3,120 (91%). Average amount of debt of borrowers graduating in 2003: $18,144. Proportion who borrowed: 84%. **Student employment:** During the 2003-2004 academic year, 23% of undergraduates worked on campus. Average per-year earnings: $670.

Buena Vista University

610 W. Fourth Street
Storm Lake, IA 50588
Private; www.bvu.edu
Financial aid office: (712) 749-2164

- **2004-2005 TUITION AND FEES:** $20,854
- **ROOM AND BOARD:** $5,822

ACT Score (25th/75th percentile): 20-25
2005 U.S. News College Ranking:
Comp. Colleges–Bachelor's (Midwest), 19
Acceptance Rate: 84%

Other expenses: Estimated books and supplies: $500. Personal expenses: $1,500. **Financial aid:** Priority filing date for institution's financial aid form: June 1. In 2003-2004, 96% of undergraduates applied for financial aid. Of those, 92% were determined to have financial need; 26% had their need fully met. Average financial aid package (proportion receiving): $19,049 (92%). Average amount of gift aid, such as scholarships or grants (proportion receiving): $12,115 (91%). Average amount of self-help aid, such as work study or loans (proportion receiving): $5,219 (81%). Average need-based loan (excluding PLUS or other private loans): $4,614. Among students who received need-based aid, the average percentage of need met: 95%. Among students who received aid based on merit, the average award (and the proportion receiving): $13,033 (3%). The average athletic scholarship (and the proportion receiving): $0 (0%). Average amount of debt of borrowers graduating in 2003: $22,566. Proportion who borrowed: 90%.

Central College

812 University Street
Pella, IA 50219
Private; www.central.edu
Financial aid office: (641) 628-5187

- **2004-2005 TUITION AND FEES:** $18,892
- **ROOM AND BOARD:** $6,486

ACT Score (25th/75th percentile): 21-27
2005 U.S. News College Ranking:
Comp. Colleges–Bachelor's (Midwest), 10
Acceptance Rate: 83%

Other expenses: Estimated books and supplies: $780. Transportation: $700. Personal expenses: $1,641. **Financial aid:** Priority filing date for institution's financial aid form: March 15. In 2003-2004, 89% of undergraduates applied for financial aid. Of those, 81% were determined to have financial need; 16% had their need fully met. Average financial aid package (proportion receiving): $16,020 (81%). Average amount of gift aid, such as scholarships or grants (propor-

tion receiving): $11,650 (81%). Average amount of self-help aid, such as work study or loans (proportion receiving): $4,625 (80%). Average need-based loan (excluding PLUS or other private loans): $4,493. Among students who received need-based aid, the average percentage of need met: 82%. Among students who received aid based on merit, the average award (and the proportion receiving): $8,710 (18%). The average athletic scholarship (and the proportion receiving): $0 (0%). Average amount of debt of borrowers graduating in 2003: $25,846. Proportion who borrowed: 85%. **Student employment:** During the 2003-2004 academic year, 56% of undergraduates worked on campus. Average per-year earnings: $1,200. **Cooperative education programs:** business.

Clarke College

1550 Clarke Drive
Dubuque, IA 52001
Private; www.clarke.edu
Financial aid office: (563) 588-6327

- **2004-2005 TUITION AND FEES:** $24,799
- **ROOM AND BOARD:** $6,289

ACT Score (25th/75th percentile): 19-24
2005 U.S. News College Ranking:
Comp. Colleges–Bachelor's (Midwest), 18
Acceptance Rate: 56%

Other expenses: Estimated books and supplies: $700. Transportation: $200. Personal expenses: $700. **Financial aid:** Priority filing date for institution's financial aid form: April 15. In 2003-2004, 91% of undergraduates applied for financial aid. Of those, 84% were determined to have financial need; 24% had their need fully met. Average financial aid package (proportion receiving): $14,654 (84%). Average amount of gift aid, such as scholarships or grants (proportion receiving): $10,751 (82%). Average amount of self-help aid, such as work study or loans (proportion receiving): $4,677 (74%). Average need-based loan (excluding PLUS or other private loans): $4,039. Among students who received need-based aid, the average percentage of need met: 100%. Among students who received aid based on merit, the average award (and the proportion receiving): $9,948 (14%). The average athletic scholarship (and the proportion receiving): $0 (0%). Average amount of debt of borrowers graduating in 2003: $17,399. Proportion who borrowed: 81%. **Reserve Officers Training Corps (ROTC):** Army ROTC: Offered at cooperating institution (university of dubuque).

Coe College

1220 First Avenue NE
Cedar Rapids, IA 52402
Private; www.coe.edu
Financial aid office: (319) 399-8540

■ **2004-2005 TUITION AND FEES:** $22,650
■ **ROOM AND BOARD:** $5,950

ACT Score (25th/75th percentile): 22-27
2005 U.S. News College Ranking:
Liberal Arts Colleges, 105
Acceptance Rate: 71%

Other expenses: Estimated books and supplies: $700. Transportation: $550. Personal expenses: $1,350. **Financial aid:** Priority filing date for institution's financial aid form: March 1. In 2003-2004, 86% of undergraduates applied for financial aid. Of those, 79% were determined to have financial need; 43% had their need fully met. Average financial aid package (proportion receiving): $18,882 (79%). Average amount of gift aid, such as scholarships or grants (proportion receiving): $13,274 (78%). Average amount of self-help aid, such as work study or loans (proportion receiving): $6,017 (66%). Average need-based loan (excluding PLUS or other private loans): $5,412. Among students who received need-based aid, the average percentage of need met: 88%. Among students who received aid based on merit, the average award (and the proportion receiving): $10,264 (18%). Average amount of debt of borrowers graduating in 2003: $22,157. Proportion who borrowed: 83%. **Cooperative education programs:** other. **Reserve Officers Training Corps (ROTC):** Army ROTC: Offered at cooperating institution (University of Iowa); Air Force ROTC: Offered at cooperating institution (University of Iowa).

Cornell College

600 First Street
Mount Vernon, IA 52314
Private; www.cornellcollege.edu
Financial aid office: (319) 895-4216

■ **2004-2005 TUITION AND FEES:** $22,650
■ **ROOM AND BOARD:** $6,240

ACT Score (25th/75th percentile): 23-29
2005 U.S. News College Ranking:
Liberal Arts Colleges, third tier
Acceptance Rate: 69%

Other expenses: Estimated books and supplies: $600. Transportation: $865. Personal expenses: $540. **Financial aid:** Priority filing date for institution's financial aid form: March 1; deadline: March 1. In 2003-2004, 87% of undergraduates applied for financial aid. Of those, 77% were determined to have financial need; 56% had their need fully met. Average financial aid package (proportion receiving): $19,455 (77%). Average amount of gift aid, such as scholarships or grants (proportion receiving): $15,585 (77%). Average amount of self-help aid, such as work study or loans (proportion receiving): $4,858 (61%). Average need-based loan (excluding PLUS or other private loans): $4,210. Among students who received need-based aid, the average percentage of need met: 98%. Among students who received aid based on merit, the average award (and the proportion receiving): $11,210 (23%). The average athletic scholarship (and the proportion receiving): $0 (0%). Average amount of debt of borrowers graduating in 2003: $17,850. Proportion who borrowed: 78%. **Student employment:** During the 2003-2004 academic year, 27% of undergraduates worked on campus. Average per-year earnings: $1,000. **Cooperative education programs:** engineering, health professions.

Dordt College

498 Fourth Avenue NE
Sioux Center, IA 51250
Private; www.dordt.edu
Financial aid office: (712) 722-6087

■ **2004-2005 TUITION AND FEES:** $16,670
■ **ROOM AND BOARD:** $4,650

ACT Score (25th/75th percentile): 21-28
2005 U.S. News College Ranking:
Comp. Colleges–Bachelor's (Midwest), 8
Acceptance Rate: 92%

Other expenses: Estimated books and supplies: $780. Transportation: $1,100. Personal expenses: $2,000. **Financial aid:** Priority filing date for institution's financial aid form: April 1. In 2003-2004, 87% of undergraduates applied for financial aid. Of those, 80% were determined to have financial need; 10% had their need fully met. Average financial aid package (proportion receiving): $14,665 (80%). Average amount of gift aid, such as scholarships or grants (propor-

tion receiving): $7,820 (80%). Average amount of self-help aid, such as work study or loans (proportion receiving): $6,845 (80%). Average need-based loan (excluding PLUS or other private loans): $4,354. Among students who received need-based aid, the average percentage of need met: 85%. Among students who received aid based on merit, the average award (and the proportion receiving): $7,331 (14%). The average athletic scholarship (and the proportion receiving): $2,245 (3%). Average amount of debt of borrowers graduating in 2003: $16,240. Proportion who borrowed: 79%. **Student employment:** During the 2003-2004 academic year, 32% of undergraduates worked on campus. Average per-year earnings: $1,300. **Cooperative education programs:** health professions.

Drake University

2507 University Avenue
Des Moines, IA 50311
Private; www.drake.edu
Financial aid office: (515) 271-2905

■ **2004-2005 TUITION AND FEES:** $20,550
■ **ROOM AND BOARD:** $5,920

ACT Score (25th/75th percentile): 23-28
2005 U.S. News College Ranking:
Universities–Master's (Midwest), 4
Acceptance Rate: 83%

Other expenses: Estimated books and supplies: $900. Transportation: $900. Personal expenses: $1,800. **Financial aid:** Priority filing date for institution's financial aid form: March 1. In 2003-2004, 70% of undergraduates applied for financial aid. Of those, 59% were determined to have financial need; 27% had their need fully met. Average financial aid package (proportion receiving): $16,354 (58%). Average amount of gift aid, such as scholarships or grants (proportion receiving): $11,441 (58%). Average amount of self-help aid, such as work study or loans (proportion receiving): $5,070 (58%). Average need-based loan (excluding PLUS or other private loans): $5,606. Among students who received need-based aid, the average percentage of need met: 98%. Among students who received aid based on merit, the average award (and the proportion receiving): $8,936 (31%). The average athletic scholarship (and the proportion receiving): $15,575 (3%). Average amount of debt of borrowers graduating in 2003: $22,115. Proportion who borrowed: 58%. **Student employment:** During the 2003-2004 academic year, 15% of undergraduates worked on campus. Average per-year earnings: $1,600. **Cooperative education programs:** computer science, education, other. **Reserve Officers Training Corps (ROTC):** Army ROTC: Offered on campus; Air Force ROTC: Offered at cooperating institution (Iowa State University).

The Franciscan University

400 N. Bluff Boulevard, PO Box 2967
Clinton, IA 52733-2967
Private; www.tfu.edu
Financial aid office: (563) 242-4023

■ **2004-2005 TUITION AND FEES:** $14,700
■ **ROOM AND BOARD:** $5,250

ACT Score (25th/75th percentile): 16-22
2005 U.S. News College Ranking:
Liberal Arts Colleges, fourth tier
Acceptance Rate: 77%

Other expenses: Estimated books and supplies: $600. Transportation: $400. Personal expenses: $600. **Financial aid:** Priority filing date for institution's financial aid form: March 1. In 2003-2004, 97% of undergraduates applied for financial aid. Of those, 89% were determined to have financial need; 27% had their need fully met. Average financial aid package (proportion receiving): $11,041 (89%). Average amount of gift aid, such as scholarships or grants (proportion receiving): $7,707 (89%). Average amount of self-help aid, such as work study or loans (proportion receiving): $4,181 (72%). Average need-based loan (excluding PLUS or other private loans): $3,935. Among students who received need-based aid, the average percentage of need met: 80%. Among students who received aid based on merit, the average award (and the proportion receiving): $8,632 (10%). The average athletic scholarship (and the proportion receiving): $3,967 (12%). Average amount of debt of borrowers graduating in 2003: $15,868. Proportion who borrowed: 88%.

Graceland University

1 University Place
Lamoni, IA 50140-1698
Private; www.graceland.edu
Financial aid office: (641) 784-5136

■ **2004-2005 TUITION AND FEES:** $15,150
■ **ROOM AND BOARD:** $5,150

ACT Score (25th/75th percentile): 18-24
2005 U.S. News College Ranking:
Comp. Colleges–Bachelor's (Midwest), third tier
Acceptance Rate: 58%

Other expenses: Estimated books and supplies: $1,000. Transportation: $400. Personal expenses: $1,300. **Financial aid:** In 2003-2004, 79% of undergraduates applied for financial aid. Of those, 68% were determined to have financial need; 31% had their need fully met. Average financial aid package (proportion receiving): $14,192 (67%). Average amount of gift aid, such as scholarships or grants (proportion receiving): $9,610 (65%). Average amount of self-help aid, such as work study or loans (proportion receiving): $5,802 (55%). Average need-based loan (excluding PLUS or other private loans): $5,172. Among students who received need-based aid, the average percentage of need met: 85%. Among students who received aid based on merit, the average award (and the proportion receiving): $8,506 (19%). The average athletic scholarship (and the proportion receiving): $3,059 (11%). Average amount of debt of borrowers graduating in 2003: $19,772. Proportion who borrowed: 74%. **Student employment:** During the 2003-2004 academic year, 38% of undergraduates worked on campus. Average per-year earnings: $814.

Grand View College

1200 Grandview Avenue
Des Moines, IA 50316
Private; www.gvc.edu
Financial aid office: (515) 263-2820

■ **2004-2005 TUITION AND FEES:** $15,342
■ **ROOM AND BOARD:** $5,204

ACT Score (25th/75th percentile): 18-23
2005 U.S. News College Ranking:
Comp. Colleges–Bachelor's (Midwest), fourth tier
Acceptance Rate: 95%

Other expenses: Estimated books and supplies: $800. Transportation: $600. Personal expenses: $2,002. **Financial aid:** Priority filing date for institution's financial aid form: March 1. In 2003-2004, 95% of undergraduates applied for financial aid. Of those, 94% were determined to have financial need; 16% had their need fully met. Average financial aid package (proportion receiving): $11,670 (94%). Average amount of gift aid, such as scholarships or grants (proportion receiving): $7,855 (93%). Average amount

of self-help aid, such as work study or loans (proportion receiving): $4,375 (82%). Average need-based loan (excluding PLUS or other private loans): $3,954. Among students who received need-based aid, the average percentage of need met: 76%. Among students who received aid based on merit, the average award (and the proportion receiving): $8,654 (12%). The average athletic scholarship (and the proportion receiving): $4,221 (4%). Average amount of debt of borrowers graduating in 2003: $18,938. Proportion who borrowed: 77%. **Student employment:** During the 2003-2004 academic year, 15% of undergraduates worked on campus. Average per-year earnings: $1,500. **Reserve Officers Training Corps (ROTC):** Army ROTC: Offered at cooperating institution (Drake University).

Grinnell College

Grinnell, IA 50112-1690
Private; www.grinnell.edu
Financial aid office: (641) 269-3250

■ **2004-2005 TUITION AND FEES:** $25,820
■ **ROOM AND BOARD:** $6,870

SAT I Score (25th/75th percentile): 1240-1450
2005 U.S. News College Ranking:
Liberal Arts Colleges, 16
Acceptance Rate: 63%

Other expenses: Estimated books and supplies: $400. Transportation: $500. Personal expenses: $400. **Financial aid:** Priority filing date for institution's financial aid form: February 1; deadline: February 1. In 2003-2004, 61% of undergraduates applied for financial aid. Of those, 60% were determined to have financial need; 100% had their need fully met. Average financial aid package (proportion receiving): $20,298 (60%). Average amount of gift aid, such as scholarships or grants (proportion receiving): $15,616 (60%). Average amount of self-help aid, such as work study or loans (proportion receiving): $5,548 (50%). Average need-based loan (excluding PLUS or other private loans): $4,884. Among students who received need-based aid, the average percentage of need met: 100%. Among students who received aid based on merit, the average award (and the proportion receiving): $8,890 (28%). The average athletic scholarship (and the proportion receiving): $0 (0%). Average amount of debt of borrowers graduating in 2003: $16,818. Proportion who borrowed: 52%. **Student employment:** During the 2003-2004 academic year, 55% of undergraduates worked on campus. Average per-year earnings: $2,025.

Iowa State University

100 Alumni Hall
Ames, IA 50011
Public; www.iastate.edu
Financial aid office: (515) 294-2223

■ **2004-2005 TUITION AND FEES:**
  In state: $5,426; Out of state: $15,128
■ **ROOM AND BOARD:** $6,121

ACT Score (25th/75th percentile): 22-27
2005 U.S. News College Ranking:
National Universities, 84
Acceptance Rate: 90%

Other expenses: Estimated books and supplies: $843. Transportation: $461. Personal expenses: $2,473. **Financial aid:** Priority filing date for institution's financial aid form: March 1. In 2003-2004, 78% of undergraduates applied for financial aid. Of those, 61% were determined to have financial need; 17% had their need fully met. Average financial aid package (proportion receiving): $7,657 (61%). Average amount of gift aid, such as scholarships or grants (proportion receiving): $3,049 (42%). Average amount of self-help aid, such as work study or loans (proportion receiving): $4,135 (51%). Average need-based loan (excluding PLUS or other private loans): $3,986. Among students who received need-based aid, the average percentage of need met: 65%. Among students who received aid based on merit, the average award (and the proportion receiving): $3,721 (7%). The average athletic scholarship (and the proportion receiving): $11,049 (1%). Average amount of debt of borrowers graduating in 2003: $17,065. Proportion who borrowed: 65%. **Student employment:** During the 2003-2004 academic year, 30% of undergraduates worked on campus. Average per-year earnings: $2,000.
Cooperative education programs: agriculture, business, computer science, education, engineering, home economics, humanities, natural science, social/behavioral science, technologies, other. **Reserve Officers Training Corps (ROTC):** Army ROTC: Offered on campus; Navy ROTC: Offered on campus; Air Force ROTC: Offered on campus.

Iowa Wesleyan College

601 N. Main Street
Mount Pleasant, IA 52641
Private; www.iwc.edu
Financial aid office: (319) 385-6242

■ **2004-2005 TUITION AND FEES:** $16,070
■ **ROOM AND BOARD:** $4,920

ACT Score (25th/75th percentile): 16-21
2005 U.S. News College Ranking:
Comp. Colleges–Bachelor's (Midwest), fourth tier
Acceptance Rate: 53%

Other expenses: Estimated books and supplies: $800. Transportation: $850. Personal expenses: $1,710. **Financial aid:** Priority filing date for institution's financial aid form: April 1. In 2003-2004, 97% of undergraduates applied for financial aid. Of those, 92% were determined to have financial need; 45% had their need fully met. Average financial aid package (proportion receiving): $14,391 (92%). Average amount of gift aid, such as scholarships or grants (proportion receiving): $8,107 (92%). Average amount of self-help aid, such as work study or loans (proportion receiving): $4,060 (92%). Average need-based loan (excluding PLUS or other private loans): $3,460. Among students who received need-based aid, the average percentage of need met: 78%. Among students who received aid based on merit, the average award (and the proportion receiving): $6,005 (4%). The average athletic scholarship (and the proportion receiving): $2,650 (2%). Average amount of debt of borrowers graduating in 2003: $17,568. Proportion who borrowed: 83%. **Student employment:** During the 2003-2004 academic year, 43% of undergraduates worked on campus. Average per-year earnings: $1,200. **Cooperative education programs:** health professions.

Loras College

1450 Alta Vista
Dubuque, IA 52004-0178
Private; www.loras.edu
Financial aid office: (563) 588-7136

■ **2004-2005 TUITION AND FEES:** $19,638
■ **ROOM AND BOARD:** $5,845

ACT Score (25th/75th percentile): 20-25
2005 U.S. News College Ranking:
Comp. Colleges–Bachelor's (Midwest), 19
Acceptance Rate: 79%

Other expenses: Estimated books and supplies: $1,000. Transportation: $600. Personal expenses: $600. **Financial aid:** Priority filing date for institution's financial aid form: April 15; deadline: August 1. In 2003-2004, 85% of undergraduates applied for financial aid. Of those, 76% were determined to have financial need; 33% had their need fully met. Average financial aid package (proportion receiving): $16,479 (76%). Average amount of gift aid, such as scholarships or grants (proportion receiving): $6,449 (65%). Average amount of self-help aid, such as work study or loans (proportion receiving): $4,768 (65%). Average need-based loan (excluding PLUS or other private loans): $5,329. Among students who received need-based aid, the average percentage of need met: 92%. Among students who received aid based on merit, the average award (and the proportion receiving): $6,330 (11%). The average athletic scholarship (and the proportion receiving): $0 (0%). Average amount of debt of borrowers graduating in 2003: $18,325. Proportion who borrowed: 83%. **Student employment:** During the 2003-2004 academic year, 40% of undergraduates worked on campus. Average per-year earnings: $1,500. **Reserve Officers Training Corps (ROTC):** Army ROTC: Offered at cooperating institution (University of Dubuque).

Luther College

700 College Drive
Decorah, IA 52101-1045
Private; www.luther.edu
Financial aid office: (563) 387-1018

■ **2004-2005 TUITION AND FEES:** $23,070
■ **ROOM AND BOARD:** $4,170

ACT Score (25th/75th percentile): 22-28
2005 U.S. News College Ranking:
Liberal Arts Colleges, 101
Acceptance Rate: 77%

Other expenses: Estimated books and supplies: $775. Transportation: $900. Personal expenses: $1,500. **Financial aid:** Priority filing date for institution's financial aid form: March 1. In 2003-2004, 84% of undergraduates applied for financial aid. Of those, 73% were determined to have financial need; 32% had their need fully met. Average financial aid package (proportion receiving): $16,612 (73%). Average amount of gift aid, such as scholarships or grants (proportion receiving): $11,104 (73%). Average amount of self-help aid, such as work study or loans (proportion receiving): $5,364 (63%). Average need-based loan (excluding PLUS or other private loans): $4,615. Among students who received need-based aid, the average percentage of need met: 86%. Among students who received aid based on merit, the average award (and the proportion receiving): $6,423 (9%). Average amount of debt of borrowers graduating in 2003: $17,312. Proportion who borrowed: 73%. **Student employment:** During the 2003-2004 academic year, 34% of undergraduates worked on campus. Average per-year earnings: $1,500.

Maharishi University of Management

Fairfield, IA 52557
Private; www.mum.edu
Financial aid office: (641) 472-1156

■ **2004-2005 TUITION AND FEES:** $24,430
■ **ROOM AND BOARD:** $6,000

ACT Score (25th/75th percentile): 19-25
2005 U.S. News College Ranking:
Universities–Master's (Midwest), third tier
Acceptance Rate: 63%

Other expenses: Estimated books and supplies: $800. Transportation: $900. Personal expenses: $1,500. **Financial aid:** Priority filing date for institution's financial aid form: April 15. In 2003-2004, 80% of undergraduates applied for financial aid. Of those, 78% were determined to have financial need; 41% had their need fully met. Average financial aid package (proportion receiving): $22,649 (78%). Average amount of gift aid, such as scholarships or grants (proportion receiving): $17,720 (78%). Average amount of self-help aid, such as work study or loans (proportion receiving): $8,892 (78%). Average need-based loan (excluding PLUS or other private loans): $8,061. Among students who received need-based aid, the average percentage of need met: 92%. Among students who received aid based on merit, the average award (and the proportion receiving): $5,950 (8%). The average athletic scholarship (and the proportion receiving): $0 (0%). Average amount of debt of borrowers graduating in 2003: $18,996. Proportion who borrowed: 84%. **Cooperative education programs:** business, computer science, education, engineering.

Morningside College

1501 Morningside Avenue
Sioux City, IA 51106
Private; www.morningside.edu
Financial aid office: (712) 274-5159

■ **2004-2005 TUITION AND FEES:** $17,170
■ **ROOM AND BOARD:** $5,400

ACT Score (25th/75th percentile): 19-25
2005 U.S. News College Ranking:
Comp. Colleges–Bachelor's (Midwest), 37
Acceptance Rate: 74%

Other expenses: Estimated books and supplies: $800. Transportation: $800. Personal expenses: $1,500. **Financial aid:** Priority filing date for institution's financial aid form: March 1. In 2003-2004, 96% of undergraduates applied for financial aid. Of those, 89% were determined to have financial need; 59% had their need fully met. Average financial aid package (proportion receiving): $15,716 (89%). Average amount of gift aid, such as scholarships or grants (proportion receiving): $5,645 (72%). Average amount of self-help aid, such as work study or loans (proportion receiving): $5,372 (78%). Average need-based loan (excluding PLUS or other private loans): $3,815. Among students who received need-based aid, the average percentage of need met: 81%. Among students who received aid based on merit, the average award (and the proportion receiving): $5,794 (11%). The average athletic scholarship (and the proportion receiving): $3,030 (35%). Average amount of debt of borrowers graduating in 2003: $19,025. Proportion who borrowed: 82%. **Student employment:** During the 2003-2004 academic year, 53% of undergraduates worked on campus. Average per-year earnings: $1,296. **Cooperative education programs:** health professions. **Reserve Officers Training Corps (ROTC):** Army ROTC: Offered at cooperating institution (University of South Dakota).

Mount Mercy College

1330 Elmhurst Drive NE
Cedar Rapids, IA 52402
Private; www.mtmercy.edu
Financial aid office: (319) 368-6467

■ **2004-2005 TUITION AND FEES:** $16,880
■ **ROOM AND BOARD:** $5,400

ACT Score (25th/75th percentile): 20-25
2005 U.S. News College Ranking:
Comp. Colleges–Bachelor's (Midwest), 37
Acceptance Rate: 84%

Other expenses: Estimated books and supplies: $800. Transportation: $880. Personal expenses: $1,990. **Financial aid:** Priority filing date for institution's financial aid form: March 1. In 2003-2004, 95% of undergraduates applied for financial aid. Of those, 89% were determined to have financial need; 33% had their need fully met. Average financial aid package (proportion receiving): $13,649 (89%). Average amount of gift aid, such as scholarships or grants (proportion receiving): $8,788 (88%). Average amount of self-help aid, such as work study or loans (proportion receiving): $5,590 (80%). Average need-based loan (excluding PLUS or other private loans): $4,878. Among students who received need-based aid, the average percentage of need met: 81%. Among students who received aid based on merit, the average award (and the proportion receiving): $9,624 (10%). The average athletic scholarship (and the proportion receiving): $0 (0%). Average amount of debt of borrowers graduating in 2003: $19,656. Proportion who borrowed: 71%. **Student employment:** During the 2003-2004 academic year, 10% of undergraduates worked on campus. Average per-year earnings: $1,000.

Northwestern College

101 Seventh Street SW
Orange City, IA 51041
Private; www.nwciowa.edu
Financial aid office: (712) 707-7131

■ **2004-2005 TUITION AND FEES:** $16,360
■ **ROOM AND BOARD:** $4,656

ACT Score (25th/75th percentile): 21-27
2005 U.S. News College Ranking:
Comp. Colleges–Bachelor's (Midwest), 19
Acceptance Rate: 83%

Other expenses: Estimated books and supplies: $900. Transportation: $1,400. Personal expenses: $2,584. **Financial aid:** Priority filing date for institution's financial aid form: April 1. In 2003-2004, 99% of undergraduates applied for financial aid. Of those, 99% were determined to have financial need; 45% had their need fully met. Average financial aid package (proportion receiving): $11,598 (98%). Average amount of gift aid, such as scholarships or grants (proportion receiving): $4,710 (72%). Average amount of self-help aid, such as work study or loans (proportion receiving): $5,552 (76%). Average need-based loan (excluding PLUS or other private loans): $5,336. Among students who received need-based aid, the average percentage of need met: 65%. Among students who received aid based on merit, the average award (and the proportion receiving): $1,000 (0%). The average athletic scholarship (and the proportion receiving): $5,000 (0%). **Student employment:** During the 2003-2004 academic year, 52% of undergraduates worked on campus. Average per-year earnings: $980.

Simpson College

701 N. C Street
Indianola, IA 50125
Private; www.simpson.edu
Financial aid office: (515) 961-1630

■ **2004-2005 TUITION AND FEES:** $19,635
■ **ROOM AND BOARD:** $5,561

ACT Score (25th/75th percentile): 22-26
2005 U.S. News College Ranking:
Comp. Colleges–Bachelor's (Midwest), 8
Acceptance Rate: 86%

Other expenses: Estimated books and supplies: $800. Transportation: $700. Personal expenses: $1,300. **Financial aid:** Priority filing date for institution's financial aid form: April 1. In 2003-2004, 99% of undergraduates applied for financial aid. Of those, 88% were determined to have financial need; 25% had their need fully met. Average financial aid package (proportion receiving): $17,124 (88%). Average amount of gift aid, such as scholarships or grants (proportion receiving): $11,381 (88%). Average amount of self-help aid, such as work study or loans (proportion receiving): $4,009 (75%). Average need-based loan (excluding PLUS or other private loans): $3,757. Among students who received need-based aid, the average percentage of need met: 87%. Among students who received aid based on merit, the average award (and the proportion receiving): $7,800 (11%). The average athletic scholarship (and the proportion receiving): $0 (0%). Average amount of debt of borrowers graduating in 2003: $21,581. Proportion who borrowed: 86%. **Student employment:** During the 2003-2004 academic year, 55% of undergraduates worked on campus. Average per-year earnings: $800. **Cooperative education programs:** computer science, engineering.

St. Ambrose University

518 W. Locust Street
Davenport, IA 52803-2898
Private; www.sau.edu
Financial aid office: (563) 333-6314

■ **2004-2005 TUITION AND FEES:** $17,640
■ **ROOM AND BOARD:** $6,350

ACT Score (25th/75th percentile): 19-25
2005 U.S. News College Ranking:
Universities–Master's (Midwest), 38
Acceptance Rate: 87%

Other expenses: Estimated books and supplies: $800. Transportation: $675. Personal expenses: $1,035. **Financial aid:** Priority filing date for institution's financial aid form: March 15. In 2003-2004, 96% of undergraduates applied for financial aid. Of those, 77% were determined to have financial need; 21% had their need fully met. Average financial aid package (proportion receiving): $12,467 (76%). Average amount of gift aid, such as scholarships or grants (proportion receiving): $4,788 (53%). Average amount of self-help aid, such as work study or loans (proportion receiving): $5,075 (64%). Average need-based loan (excluding PLUS or other private loans): $4,316. Among students who received need-based aid, the average percentage of need met: 43%. Among students who received aid based on merit, the average award (and the proportion receiving): $5,297 (19%). The average athletic scholarship (and the proportion receiving): $3,463 (6%). Average amount of debt of borrowers graduating in 2003: $16,732. Proportion who borrowed: 70%. **Student employment:** During the 2003-2004 academic year, 23% of undergraduates worked on campus. Average per-year earnings: $1,600. **Cooperative education programs:** art, business, computer science, engineering, health professions, humanities, natural science, social/behavioral science.

University of Dubuque

2000 University Avenue
Dubuque, IA 52001
Private; www.dbq.edu
Financial aid office: (563) 589-3396

■ **2004-2005 TUITION AND FEES:** $16,860
■ **ROOM AND BOARD:** $5,700

ACT Score (25th/75th percentile): 18-23
2005 U.S. News College Ranking:
Universities–Master's (Midwest), 63
Acceptance Rate: 82%

Other expenses: Estimated books and supplies: $850. Transportation: $900. Personal expenses: $1,500. **Financial aid:** Priority filing date for institution's financial aid form: April 1. In 2003-2004, 99% of undergraduates applied for financial aid. Of those, 93% were determined to have financial need; 40% had their need fully met. Average financial aid package (proportion receiving): $15,986 (93%). Average amount of gift aid, such as scholarships or grants (proportion receiving): $8,515 (88%). Average amount of self-help aid, such as work study or loans (proportion receiving): $8,625 (85%). Average need-based loan (excluding PLUS or other private loans): $8,042. Among students who received need-based aid, the average percentage of need met: 83%. Among students who received aid based on merit, the average award (and the proportion receiving): $15,657 (7%). The average athletic scholarship (and the proportion receiving): $0 (0%). Average amount of debt of borrowers graduating in 2003: $17,000. Proportion who borrowed: 85%. **Student employment:** During the 2003-2004 academic year, 50% of undergraduates worked on campus. Average per-year earnings: $1,500. **Cooperative education programs:** business, computer science, education, natural science, social/behavioral science, technologies, vocational arts. **Reserve Officers Training Corps (ROTC):** Army ROTC: Offered on campus.

University of Iowa

107 Calvin Hall
Iowa City, IA 52242-1396
Public; www.uiowa.edu
Financial aid office: (319) 335-1450

■ **2004-2005 TUITION AND FEES:**
In state: $5,396; Out of state: $16,048
■ **ROOM AND BOARD:** $6,350

ACT Score (25th/75th percentile): 22-27
2005 U.S. News College Ranking:
National Universities, 58
Acceptance Rate: 82%

Other expenses: Estimated books and supplies: $840. Transportation: $820. Personal expenses: $2,290. **Financial aid:** In 2003-2004, 70% of undergraduates applied for financial aid. Of those, 52% were determined to have financial need; 83% had their need fully met. Average financial aid package (proportion receiving): $7,386 (48%). Average amount of gift aid, such as scholarships or grants (proportion receiving): $4,497 (29%). Average amount of self-help aid, such as work study or loans (proportion receiving): $4,443 (39%). Average need-based loan (excluding PLUS or other private loans): $3,861. Among students who received need-based aid, the average percentage of need met: 88%. Among students who received aid based on merit, the average award (and the proportion receiving): $4,192 (22%). The average athletic scholarship (and the proportion receiving): $11,588 (3%). Average amount of debt of borrowers graduating in 2003: $16,750. Proportion who borrowed: 59%. **Cooperative education programs:** business, engineering. **Reserve Officers Training Corps (ROTC):** Army ROTC: Offered on campus; Air Force ROTC: Offered on campus.

University of Northern Iowa

1227 W. 27th Street
Cedar Falls, IA 50614
Public; www.uni.edu
Financial aid office: (319) 273-2700

- **2004-2005 TUITION AND FEES:**
  In state: $5,387; Out of state: $12,705
- **ROOM AND BOARD:** $5,275

ACT Score (25th/75th percentile): 20-25
2005 U.S. News College Ranking:
Universities–Master's (Midwest), 17
Acceptance Rate: 80%

Other expenses: Estimated books and supplies: $819. Transportation: $561. Personal expenses: $2,474. **Financial aid:** In 2003-2004, 78% of undergraduates applied for financial aid. Of those, 62% were determined to have financial need; 23% had their need fully met. Average financial aid package (proportion receiving): $6,705 (61%). Average amount of gift aid, such as scholarships or grants (proportion receiving): $3,122 (31%). Average amount of self-help aid, such as work study or loans (proportion receiving): $4,298 (57%). Average need-based loan (excluding PLUS or other private loans): $3,976. Among students who received need-based aid, the average percentage of need met: 71%. Among students who received aid based on merit, the average award (and the proportion receiving): $2,655 (7%). The average athletic scholarship (and the proportion receiving): $8,374 (2%). Average amount of debt of borrowers graduating in 2003: $16,716. Proportion who borrowed: 72%. **Student employment:** During the 2003-2004 academic year, 25% of under-

graduates worked on campus. Average per-year earnings: $1,250. **Cooperative education programs:** art, business, computer science, education, health professions, home economics, natural science, social/behavioral science, technologies, other. **Reserve Officers Training Corps (ROTC):** Army ROTC: Offered on campus.

Upper Iowa University

Box 1857
Fayette, IA 52142
Private; www.uiu.edu
Financial aid office: (563) 425-5274

- **2004-2005 TUITION AND FEES:** $16,556
- **ROOM AND BOARD:** $6,034

ACT Score (25th/75th percentile): 19-22
2005 U.S. News College Ranking:
Comp. Colleges–Bachelor's (Midwest), third tier
Acceptance Rate: 59%

Waldorf College

106 S. Sixth Street
Forest City, IA 50436
Private; www.waldorf.edu
Financial aid office: (641) 585-8120

- **2004-2005 TUITION AND FEES:** $15,870
- **ROOM AND BOARD:** $4,400

ACT Score (25th/75th percentile): 16-23
2005 U.S. News College Ranking:
Comp. Colleges–Bachelor's (Midwest), third tier
Acceptance Rate: 72%

Other expenses: Estimated books and supplies: $790. Transportation: $960. Personal expenses: $1,500. **Financial aid:** Priority filing date for institution's financial aid form: March 1. In 2003-2004, 87% of undergraduates applied for financial aid. Of those, 84% were determined to have financial need; 19% had their need fully met. Average financial aid package (proportion receiving): $15,752 (84%). Average amount of gift aid, such as scholarships or grants (proportion receiving): $11,062 (83%). Average amount of self-help aid, such as work study or loans (proportion receiving): $5,153 (77%). Average need-based loan (excluding PLUS or other private loans): $4,677. Among students who received need-based aid, the average percentage

of need met: 85%. Among students who received aid based on merit, the average award (and the proportion receiving): $8,717 (15%). The average athletic scholarship (and the proportion receiving): $0 (0%). Average amount of debt of borrowers graduating in 2003: $10,500. Proportion who borrowed: 92%. **Student employment:** During the 2003-2004 academic year, 36% of undergraduates worked on campus. Average per-year earnings: $535.

Wartburg College

PO Box 1003
Waverly, IA 50677-0903
Private; www.wartburg.edu
Financial aid office: (319) 352-8262

- **2004-2005 TUITION AND FEES:** $19,700
- **ROOM AND BOARD:** $5,515

ACT Score (25th/75th percentile): 21-27
2005 U.S. News College Ranking:
Comp. Colleges–Bachelor's (Midwest), 7
Acceptance Rate: 83%

Other expenses: Estimated books and supplies: $800. Transportation: $500. Personal expenses: $700. **Financial aid:** Priority filing date for institution's financial aid form: March 1. In 2003-2004, 88% of undergraduates applied for financial aid. Of those, 79% were determined to have financial need; 68% had their need fully met. Average financial aid package (proportion receiving): $17,031 (79%). Average amount of gift aid, such as scholarships or grants (proportion receiving): $11,123 (79%). Average amount of self-help aid, such as work study or loans (proportion receiving): $6,934 (67%). Average need-based loan (excluding PLUS or other private loans): $6,460. Among students who received need-based aid, the average percentage of need met: 95%. Among students who received aid based on merit, the average award (and the proportion receiving): $19,090 (19%). The average athletic scholarship (and the proportion receiving): $0 (0%). Average amount of debt of borrowers graduating in 2003: $22,809. Proportion who borrowed: 93%. **Student employment:** During the 2003-2004 academic year, 30% of undergraduates worked on campus. Average per-year earnings: $1,500.

William Penn University

201 Trueblood Avenue
Oskaloosa, IA 52577
Private; www.wmpenn.edu
Financial aid office: (641) 673-1040

■ **2004-2005 TUITION AND FEES:** $14,604
■ **ROOM AND BOARD:** $4,746

ACT Score (25th/75th percentile): 16-21
2005 U.S. News College Ranking:
Comp. Colleges–Bachelor's (Midwest),
fourth tier
Acceptance Rate: 75%

....

Other expenses: Estimated books and supplies:
$800. Transportation: $1,013. Personal expenses: $1,163. **Student employment:** During the
2003-2004 academic year, 1% of undergraduates worked on campus. Average per-year earnings: $1,000.

Kansas

Baker University

PO Box 65
Baldwin City, KS 66006
Private; www.bakeru.edu
Financial aid office: (785) 594-4595

- **2004-2005 TUITION AND FEES:** $15,550
- **ROOM AND BOARD:** $5,450

ACT Score (25th/75th percentile): 20-27
2005 U.S. News College Ranking:
Universities–Master's (Midwest), 46
Acceptance Rate: 82%

Other expenses: Estimated books and supplies: $1,000. Transportation: $1,840. Personal expenses: $1,400. **Financial aid:** Priority filing date for institution's financial aid form: March 1. In 2003-2004, 98% of undergraduates applied for financial aid. Of those, 72% were determined to have financial need; Average financial aid package (proportion receiving): $14,534 (72%). Average amount of gift aid, such as scholarships or grants (proportion receiving): $5,958 (68%). Average amount of self-help aid, such as work study or loans (proportion receiving): $6,700 (72%). Average need-based loan (excluding PLUS or other private loans): $6,000. Among students who received aid based on merit, the average award (and the proportion receiving): $5,150 (28%). The average athletic scholarship (and the proportion receiving): $5,000 (84%). Average amount of debt of borrowers graduating in 2003: $18,200. Proportion who borrowed: 70%. **Student employment:** During the 2003-2004 academic year, 1% of undergraduates worked on campus. Average per-year earnings: $260. **Reserve Officers Training Corps (ROTC):** Army ROTC: Offered at cooperating institution (University of Kansas); Air Force ROTC: Offered at cooperating institution (University of Kansas).

Benedictine College

1020 N. Second Street
Atchison, KS 66002
Private; www.benedictine.edu
Financial aid office: (913) 360-7484

- **2004-2005 TUITION AND FEES:** $15,126
- **ROOM AND BOARD:** $6,128

ACT Score (25th/75th percentile): 19-26
2005 U.S. News College Ranking:
Universities–Master's (Midwest), third tier
Acceptance Rate: 96%

Other expenses: Estimated books and supplies: $2,400. Transportation: $2,000. Personal expenses: $2,800. **Financial aid:** Priority filing date for institution's financial aid form: March 15. In 2003-2004, 99% of undergraduates applied for financial aid. Of those, 71% were determined to have financial need; 14% had their need fully met. Average financial aid package (proportion receiving): $12,668 (71%). Average amount of gift aid, such as scholarships or grants (proportion receiving): $7,843 (65%). Average amount of self-help aid, such as work study or loans (proportion receiving): $5,146 (66%). Average need-based loan (excluding PLUS or other private loans): $4,618. Among students who received need-based aid, the average percentage of need met: 74%. Among students who received aid based on merit, the average award (and the proportion receiving): $5,298 (6%). The average athletic scholarship (and the proportion receiving): $4,759 (3%). Average amount of debt of borrowers graduating in 2003: $20,684. Proportion who borrowed: 74%. **Student employment:** During the 2003-2004 academic year, 4% of undergraduates worked on campus. **Reserve Officers Training Corps (ROTC):** Army ROTC: Offered on campus.

Bethany College

421 N. First Street
Lindsborg, KS 67456-1897
Private; www.bethanylb.edu
Financial aid office: (785) 227-3311

- **2004-2005 TUITION AND FEES:** $14,950
- **ROOM AND BOARD:** $5,150

ACT Score (25th/75th percentile): 19-24
2005 U.S. News College Ranking:
Comp. Colleges–Bachelor's (Midwest), third tier
Acceptance Rate: 71%

Other expenses: Estimated books and supplies: $900. Transportation: $600. Personal expenses: $2,500. **Financial aid:** Priority filing date for institution's financial aid form: March 15. In

2003-2004, 95% of undergraduates applied for financial aid. Of those, 82% were determined to have financial need; 36% had their need fully met. Average financial aid package (proportion receiving): $15,310 (82%). Average amount of gift aid, such as scholarships or grants (proportion receiving): $4,881 (71%). Average amount of self-help aid, such as work study or loans (proportion receiving): $5,961 (68%). Average need-based loan (excluding PLUS or other private loans): $5,012. Among students who received need-based aid, the average percentage of need met: 93%. Among students who received aid based on merit, the average award (and the proportion receiving): $4,086 (6%). The average athletic scholarship (and the proportion receiving): $3,054 (8%). Average amount of debt of borrowers graduating in 2003: $15,167. Proportion who borrowed: 83%. **Student employment:** During the 2003-2004 academic year, 23% of undergraduates worked on campus. Average per-year earnings: $1,500. **Cooperative education programs:** education, engineering.

Bethel College

300 E. 27th Street
North Newton, KS 67117-0531
Private; www.bethelks.edu
Financial aid office: (316) 284-5232

- **2004-2005 TUITION AND FEES:** $14,700
- **ROOM AND BOARD:** $5,900

ACT Score (25th/75th percentile): 20-27
2005 U.S. News College Ranking:
Comp. Colleges–Bachelor's (Midwest), 28
Acceptance Rate: 72%

Other expenses: Estimated books and supplies: $800. Transportation: $600. Personal expenses: $1,835. **Financial aid:** In 2003-2004, 87% of undergraduates applied for financial aid. Of those, 86% were determined to have financial need; 34% had their need fully met. Average financial aid package (proportion receiving): $15,772 (86%). Average amount of gift aid, such as scholarships or grants (proportion receiving): $4,534 (66%). Average amount of self-help aid, such as work study or loans (proportion receiving): $6,682 (71%). Average need-based loan (excluding PLUS or other private loans): $5,875. Among students who received need-based aid, the average percentage of need met: 90%. Among students who received aid based on merit, the average award (and the proportion receiving): $5,776 (11%). The average athletic scholarship (and the proportion receiving): $2,468 (30%). Average amount of debt of borrowers graduating in 2003: $17,634. Proportion who borrowed: 85%. **Student employment:** During the 2003-2004 academic year, 31% of undergraduates worked on campus. Average per-year earnings: $1,200.

Central Christian College

1200 S. Main, PO Box 1403
McPherson, KS 67460-5799
Private; www.centralchristian.edu/index.html
Financial aid office: (620) 241-0723

■ **2004-2005 TUITION AND FEES:** $13,124
■ **ROOM AND BOARD:** $4,100

ACT Score (25th/75th percentile): 18-22
2005 U.S. News College Ranking:
Comp. Colleges–Bachelor's (Midwest),
fourth tier
Acceptance Rate: 47%

Other expenses: Estimated books and supplies: $600. Transportation: $1,000. Personal expenses: $1,000. **Financial aid:** Priority filing date for institution's financial aid form: March 1.
Cooperative education programs: business, health professions, social/behavioral science, other.

Emporia State University

1200 Commercial
Emporia, KS 66801-5087
Public; www.emporia.edu
Financial aid office: (620) 341-5457

■ **2004-2005 TUITION AND FEES:**
In state: $3,036; Out of state: $9,756
■ **ROOM AND BOARD:** $4,519

ACT Score (25th/75th percentile): 18-24
2005 U.S. News College Ranking:
Universities–Master's (Midwest), third tier
Acceptance Rate: 74%

Other expenses: Estimated books and supplies: $750. Transportation: $688. Personal expenses: $1,810. **Financial aid:** Priority filing date for institution's financial aid form: March 15. In 2003-2004, 88% of undergraduates applied for financial aid. Of those, 62% were determined

to have financial need; 28% had their need fully met. Average financial aid package (proportion receiving): $5,430 (62%). Average amount of gift aid, such as scholarships or grants (proportion receiving): $1,735 (41%). Average amount of self-help aid, such as work study or loans (proportion receiving): $1,889 (8%). Average need-based loan (excluding PLUS or other private loans): $2,899. Among students who received need-based aid, the average percentage of need met: 71%. Among students who received aid based on merit, the average award (and the proportion receiving): $880 (10%). The average athletic scholarship (and the proportion receiving): $1,930 (1%). Average amount of debt of borrowers graduating in 2003: $15,790. Proportion who borrowed: 66%. **Student employment:** During the 2003-2004 academic year, 11% of undergraduates worked on campus. Average per-year earnings: $2,310.

Fort Hays State University

600 Park Street
Hays, KS 67601-4099
Public; www.fhsu.edu
Financial aid office: (785) 628-4408

■ **2004-2005 TUITION AND FEES:**
In state: $2,900; Out of state: $9,025
■ **ROOM AND BOARD:** $5,060

ACT Score (25th/75th percentile): 18-24
2005 U.S. News College Ranking:
Universities–Master's (Midwest), third tier
Acceptance Rate: 94%

Financial aid: Priority filing date for institution's financial aid form: March 15.

Friends University

2100 W. University Street
Wichita, KS 67213
Private; www.friends.edu
Financial aid office: (316) 295-5200

■ **2004-2005 TUITION AND FEES:** $14,520
■ **ROOM AND BOARD:** $4,700

ACT Score (25th/75th percentile): 19-25
2005 U.S. News College Ranking:
Universities–Master's (Midwest), fourth tier
Acceptance Rate: 88%

Other expenses: Estimated books and supplies: $900. Transportation: $1,860. Personal expens-

es: $1,400. **Financial aid:** Priority filing date for institution's financial aid form: March 15. In 2003-2004, 93% of undergraduates applied for financial aid. Of those, 85% were determined to have financial need; 20% had their need fully met. Average financial aid package (proportion receiving): $8,180 (85%). Average amount of gift aid, such as scholarships or grants (proportion receiving): $5,211 (64%). Average amount of self-help aid, such as work study or loans (proportion receiving): $4,484 (81%). Average need-based loan (excluding PLUS or other private loans): $3,788. Among students who received need-based aid, the average percentage of need met: 60%. Among students who received aid based on merit, the average award (and the proportion receiving): $6,965 (11%). The average athletic scholarship (and the proportion receiving): $1,675 (4%). Average amount of debt of borrowers graduating in 2003: $16,447. Proportion who borrowed: 100%. **Student employment:** During the 2003-2004 academic year, 27% of undergraduates worked on campus. Average per-year earnings: $2,500.

Kansas State University

Anderson Hall
Manhattan, KS 66506
Public; www.ksu.edu
Financial aid office: (785) 532-6420

■ **2003-2004 TUITION AND FEES:**
In state: $4,059; Out of state: $11,949
■ **ROOM AND BOARD:** $5,080

ACT Score (25th/75th percentile): 21-26
2005 U.S. News College Ranking:
National Universities, third tier
Acceptance Rate: 60%

Other expenses: Estimated books and supplies: $1,000. Transportation: $200. Personal expenses: $3,000. **Financial aid:** Priority filing date for institution's financial aid form: March 1. In 2003-2004, 70% of undergraduates applied for financial aid. Of those, 53% were determined to have financial need; 23% had their need fully met. Average financial aid package (proportion receiving): $6,229 (51%). Average amount of gift aid, such as scholarships or grants (proportion receiving): $1,373 (29%). Average amount of self-help aid, such as work study or loans (proportion receiving): $3,106 (23%). Average need-based loan (excluding PLUS or other private loans): $2,917. Among students who received need-based aid, the average percentage of need met: 80%. Among students who received aid based on merit, the average award (and the proportion receiving): $1,292 (4%). The average athletic scholarship (and the proportion receiving): $7,794 (3%). **Student employment:** During the 2003-2004 academic year, 30% of undergraduates worked on campus. Average per-year earnings: $5,295. **Reserve Officers Training Corps (ROTC):** Army ROTC: Offered on campus; Air Force ROTC: Offered on campus.

Kansas Wesleyan University

100 E. Claflin
Salina, KS 67401
Private; www.kwu.edu
Financial aid office: (785) 827-5541

■ **2004-2005 TUITION AND FEES:** $15,000
■ **ROOM AND BOARD:** $5,400

ACT Score (25th/75th percentile): 20-24
2005 U.S. News College Ranking:
Comp. Colleges–Bachelor's (Midwest), third tier
Acceptance Rate: 51%

Other expenses: Estimated books and supplies: $800. Transportation: $600. Personal expenses: $500. **Financial aid:** Priority filing date for institution's financial aid form: March 15; deadline: August 26. In 2003-2004, 97% of undergraduates applied for financial aid. Of those, 87% were determined to have financial need; 96% had their need fully met. Average financial aid package (proportion receiving): $13,060 (87%). Average amount of gift aid, such as scholarships or grants (proportion receiving): $5,021 (87%). Average amount of self-help aid, such as work study or loans (proportion receiving): $3,815 (87%). Average need-based loan (excluding PLUS or other private loans): $3,486. Among students who received need-based aid, the average percentage of need met: 95%. Among students who received aid based on merit, the average award (and the proportion receiving): $4,224 (87%). Average amount of debt of borrowers graduating in 2003: $14,132. Proportion who borrowed: 84%. **Student employment:** During the 2003-2004 academic year, 35% of undergraduates worked on campus. Average per-year earnings: $800. **Cooperative education programs:** engineering, health professions.

McPherson College

PO Box 1402
McPherson, KS 67460
Private; www.mcpherson.edu
Financial aid office: (620) 241-0731

■ **2004-2005 TUITION AND FEES:** $14,645
■ **ROOM AND BOARD:** $5,620

ACT Score (25th/75th percentile): 19-23
2005 U.S. News College Ranking:
Comp. Colleges–Bachelor's (Midwest), third tier
Acceptance Rate: 73%

Other expenses: Estimated books and supplies: $750. Transportation: $960. Personal expenses: $2,525. **Financial aid:** Priority filing date for institution's financial aid form: April 1; deadline: April 1. In 2003-2004, 93% of undergraduates applied for financial aid. Of those, 85% were determined to have financial need; 28% had their need fully met. Average financial aid package (proportion receiving): $16,475 (84%). Average amount of gift aid, such as scholarships or grants (proportion receiving): $5,258 (67%). Average amount of self-help aid, such as work study or loans (proportion receiving): $6,483 (74%). Average need-based loan (excluding PLUS or other private loans): $5,690. Among students who received need-based aid, the average percentage of need met: 92%. Among students who received aid based on merit, the average award (and the proportion receiving): $7,524 (13%). The average athletic scholarship (and the proportion receiving): $3,192 (41%). Average amount of debt of borrowers graduating in 2003: $14,450. Proportion who borrowed: 84%. **Student employment:** During the 2003-2004 academic year, 12% of undergraduates worked on campus. Average per-year earnings: $1,000. **Cooperative education programs:** business, computer science, education, health professions, humanities, natural science, social/behavioral science, technologies, other.

MidAmerica Nazarene University

2030 E. College Way
Olathe, KS 66062
Private; www.mnu.edu
Financial aid office: (913) 791-3298

■ **2004-2005 TUITION AND FEES:** $13,630
■ **ROOM AND BOARD:** $5,990

ACT Score (25th/75th percentile): 19-26
2005 U.S. News College Ranking:
Universities–Master's (Midwest), third tier
Acceptance Rate: 41%

Other expenses: Estimated books and supplies: $1,300. Transportation: $1,427. Personal expenses: $1,212. **Financial aid:** Priority filing date for institution's financial aid form: March 1. In 2003-2004, 82% of undergraduates applied for financial aid. Of those, 74% were determined to have financial need; 9% had their need fully met. Average financial aid package (proportion receiving): $11,189 (74%). Average amount of gift aid, such as scholarships or grants (proportion receiving): $6,434 (64%). Average amount of self-help aid, such as work study or loans (proportion receiving): $5,277 (55%). Average need-based loan (excluding PLUS or other private loans): $5,038. Among students who received need-based aid, the average percentage of need met: 66%. Among students who received aid based on merit, the average award (and the proportion receiving): $3,506 (14%). The average athletic scholarship (and the proportion receiving): $6,636 (7%). Average amount of debt of borrowers graduating in 2003: $24,812. Proportion who borrowed: 74%. Average per-year earnings: $1,500. **Reserve Officers Training Corps (ROTC):** Army ROTC: Offered at cooperating institution (University of Kansas); Air Force ROTC: Offered at cooperating institution (University of Kansas).

Newman University

3100 McCormick Avenue
Wichita, KS 67213
Private; www.newmanu.edu
Financial aid office: (316) 942-4291

■ **2004-2005 TUITION AND FEES:** $14,794
■ **ROOM AND BOARD:** $5,060

ACT Score (25th/75th percentile): 19-25
2005 U.S. News College Ranking:
Universities–Master's (Midwest), fourth tier

Other expenses: Estimated books and supplies: $852. Personal expenses: $3,997. **Financial aid:** Priority filing date for institution's financial aid form: March 1. In 2003-2004, 97% of undergraduates applied for financial aid. Of those, 73% were determined to have financial need; 12% had their need fully met. Average financial aid package (proportion receiving): $9,191 (73%). Average amount of gift aid, such as scholarships or grants (proportion receiving): $3,551 (57%). Average amount of self-help aid, such as work study or loans (proportion receiving): $3,914 (62%). Average need-based loan (excluding PLUS or other private loans): $3,919. Among students who received need-based aid, the average percentage of need met: 60%. Among students who received aid based on merit, the average award (and the proportion receiving): $3,056 (5%). The average athletic scholarship (and the proportion receiving): $3,076 (24%). Average amount of debt of borrowers graduating in 2003: $16,699. Proportion who borrowed: 71%. **Student employment:** During the 2003-2004 academic year, 82% of undergraduates worked on campus. Average per-year earnings: $2,000. **Cooperative education programs:** computer science.

Ottawa University

1001 S. Cedar Street
Ottawa, KS 66067-3399
Private; www.ottawa.edu
Financial aid office: (785) 242-5200

■ **2004-2005 TUITION AND FEES:** $13,850
■ **ROOM AND BOARD:** $5,450

ACT Score (25th/75th percentile): 18-24
2005 U.S. News College Ranking:
Comp. Colleges–Bachelor's (Midwest),
fourth tier
Acceptance Rate: 73%

Pittsburg State University

1701 S. Broadway
Pittsburg, KS 66762
Public; www.pittstate.edu
Financial aid office: (620) 235-4240

■ **2004-2005 TUITION AND FEES:**
  In state: $3,294; Out of state: $9,652
■ **ROOM AND BOARD:** $4,334

ACT Score (25th/75th percentile): 19-24
2005 U.S. News College Ranking:
Universities–Master's (Midwest), third tier
Acceptance Rate: 89%

Other expenses: Estimated books and supplies: $800. Transportation: $780. Personal expenses: $1,980. **Financial aid:** Priority filing date for institution's financial aid form: March 1. In 2003-2004, 68% of undergraduates applied for financial aid. Of those, 57% were determined to

have financial need; 15% had their need fully met. Average financial aid package (proportion receiving): $6,666 (55%). Average amount of gift aid, such as scholarships or grants (proportion receiving): $3,219 (42%). Average amount of self-help aid, such as work study or loans (proportion receiving): $3,723 (46%). Average need-based loan (excluding PLUS or other private loans): $3,679. Among students who received need-based aid, the average percentage of need met: 88%. Among students who received aid based on merit, the average award (and the proportion receiving): $1,793 (8%). The average athletic scholarship (and the proportion receiving): $3,435 (2%). Average amount of debt of borrowers graduating in 2003: $9,792. Proportion who borrowed: 93%. **Student employment:** During the 2003-2004 academic year, 12% of undergraduates worked on campus. Average per-year earnings: $2,795. **Cooperative education programs:** business, education, engineering, health professions, social/behavioral science, technologies, vocational arts. **Reserve Officers Training Corps (ROTC):** Army ROTC: Offered on campus.

Southwestern College

100 College Street
Winfield, KS 67156-2499
Private; www.sckans.edu
Financial aid office: (620) 229-6215

■ **2004-2005 TUITION AND FEES:** $15,350
■ **ROOM AND BOARD:** $5,098

ACT Score (25th/75th percentile): 20-25
2005 U.S. News College Ranking:
Comp. Colleges–Bachelor's (Midwest), 40
Acceptance Rate: 98%

Other expenses: Estimated books and supplies: $600. Transportation: $1,988. Personal expenses: $2,333. **Financial aid:** Priority filing date for institution's financial aid form: April 1. In 2003-2004, 90% of undergraduates applied for financial aid. Of those, 85% were determined to have financial need; 14% had their need fully met. Average financial aid package (proportion receiving): $12,287 (85%). Average amount of gift aid, such as scholarships or grants (proportion receiving): $7,686 (74%). Average amount of self-help aid, such as work study or loans (proportion receiving): $8,732 (79%). Average need-based loan (excluding PLUS or other private loans): $5,009. Among students who received need-based aid, the average percentage of need met: 80%. Among students who received aid based on merit, the average award

(and the proportion receiving): $4,567 (5%). The average athletic scholarship (and the proportion receiving): $1,902 (3%). Average amount of debt of borrowers graduating in 2003: $16,568. Proportion who borrowed: 65%. **Student employment:** During the 2003-2004 academic year, 20% of undergraduates worked on campus. Average per-year earnings: $900.

Sterling College

PO Box 98
Sterling, KS 67579
Private; www.sterling.edu
Financial aid office: (620) 278-4207

■ **2004-2005 TUITION AND FEES:** $13,807
■ **ROOM AND BOARD:** $5,789

ACT Score (25th/75th percentile): 19-26
2005 U.S. News College Ranking:
Comp. Colleges–Bachelor's (Midwest),
third tier
Acceptance Rate: 57%

Other expenses: Estimated books and supplies: $550. Transportation: $1,100. Personal expenses: $500. **Financial aid:** Priority filing date for institution's financial aid form: April 1. In 2003-2004, 90% of undergraduates applied for financial aid. Of those, 76% were determined to have financial need; 23% had their need fully met. Average financial aid package (proportion receiving): N/A (100%). Average amount of gift aid, such as scholarships or grants (proportion receiving): N/A (76%). **Student employment:** During the 2003-2004 academic year, 42% of undergraduates worked on campus. Average per-year earnings: $1,100.

Tabor College

400 S. Jefferson
Hillsboro, KS 67063
Private; www.tabor.edu
Financial aid office: (620) 947-3121

■ **2004-2005 TUITION AND FEES:** $15,130
■ **ROOM AND BOARD:** $5,410

ACT Score (25th/75th percentile): 20-28
2005 U.S. News College Ranking:
Comp. Colleges–Bachelor's (Midwest), 45
Acceptance Rate: 100%

Other expenses: Estimated books and supplies: $600. Transportation: $1,000. Personal expenses: $1,980. **Financial aid:** Priority filing date for institution's financial aid form: March 1. In 2003-2004, 97% of undergraduates applied for financial aid. Of those, 72% were determined to have financial need; 32% had their need fully met. Average financial aid package (proportion receiving): $14,427 (72%). Average amount of gift aid, such as scholarships or grants (proportion receiving): $3,491 (63%). Average amount of self-help aid, such as work study or loans (proportion receiving): $6,232 (65%). Average need-based loan (excluding PLUS or other private loans): $6,063. Among students who received need-based aid, the average percentage of need met: 87%. Among students who received aid based on merit, the average award (and the proportion receiving): $4,335 (24%). The average athletic scholarship (and the proportion receiving): $2,056 (49%). Average amount of debt of borrowers graduating in 2003: $20,498. Proportion who borrowed: 83%. **Student employment:** During the 2003-2004 academic year, 27% of undergraduates worked on campus. Average per-year earnings: $675.

University of Kansas

1502 Iowa Street
Lawrence, KS 66045-7576
Public; www.ku.edu
Financial aid office: (785) 864-4700

■ **2004-2005 TUITION AND FEES:**
   In state: $4,737; Out of state: $12,691
■ **ROOM AND BOARD:** $5,216

ACT Score (25th/75th percentile): 21-27
2005 U.S. News College Ranking:
National Universities, 90
Acceptance Rate: 68%

Other expenses: Estimated books and supplies: $750. Transportation: $1,304. Personal expenses: $2,032. **Financial aid:** Priority filing date for institution's financial aid form: March 1. In 2003-2004, 53% of undergraduates applied for financial aid. Of those, 38% were determined to have financial need; 28% had their need fully met. Average financial aid package (proportion receiving): $6,486 (37%). Average amount of gift aid, such as scholarships or grants (proportion receiving): $3,333 (29%). Average amount of self-help aid, such as work study or loans (proportion receiving): $3,722 (31%). Average need-based loan (excluding PLUS or other private loans): $3,551. Among students who received need-based aid, the average percentage of need met: 69%. Among students who received aid based on merit, the average award

(and the proportion receiving): $3,995 (11%). The average athletic scholarship (and the proportion receiving): $10,972 (1%). Average amount of debt of borrowers graduating in 2003: $18,271. Proportion who borrowed: 39%. **Student employment:** During the 2003-2004 academic year, 16% of undergraduates worked on campus. Average per-year earnings: $3,300. **Cooperative education programs:** engineering. **Reserve Officers Training Corps (ROTC):** Army ROTC: Offered on campus; Navy ROTC: Offered on campus; Air Force ROTC: Offered on campus.

University of St. Mary

4100 S. Fourth Street Trafficway
Leavenworth, KS 66048
Private; www.stmary.edu
Financial aid office: (800) 752-7043

■ **2004-2005 TUITION AND FEES:** $14,590
■ **ROOM AND BOARD:** $5,540

ACT Score (25th/75th percentile): 18-24
2005 U.S. News College Ranking:
Universities–Master's (Midwest), fourth tier
Acceptance Rate: 47%

Other expenses: Estimated books and supplies: $900. Transportation: $900. Personal expenses: $1,650. **Financial aid:** Priority filing date for institution's financial aid form: May 1. **Reserve Officers Training Corps (ROTC):** Army ROTC: Offered at cooperating institution (University of Kansas); Air Force ROTC: Offered at cooperating institution (University of Kansas).

Washburn University

1700 S.W. College
Topeka, KS 66621
Public; www.washburn.edu
Financial aid office: (785) 231-1010

■ **2004-2005 TUITION AND FEES:**
   In state: $4,502; Out of state: $10,112
■ **ROOM AND BOARD:** $5,006

ACT Score (25th/75th percentile): 19-25
2005 U.S. News College Ranking:
Universities–Master's (Midwest), 28
Acceptance Rate: 100%

Other expenses: Estimated books and supplies: $880. Transportation: $1,694. Personal expenses: $1,308. **Financial aid:** Priority filing date for institution's financial aid form: March 1. In

2003-2004, 72% of undergraduates applied for financial aid. Of those, 60% were determined to have financial need; 8% had their need fully met. Average financial aid package (proportion receiving): $5,174 (53%). Average amount of gift aid, such as scholarships or grants (proportion receiving): $1,371 (35%). Average amount of self-help aid, such as work study or loans (proportion receiving): $2,586 (36%). Average need-based loan (excluding PLUS or other private loans): $2,499. Among students who received need-based aid, the average percentage of need met: 42%. Among students who received aid based on merit, the average award (and the proportion receiving): $515 (45%). The average athletic scholarship (and the proportion receiving): $5,086 (7%). Average amount of debt of borrowers graduating in 2003: $11,750. Proportion who borrowed: 60%. **Student employment:** During the 2003-2004 academic year, 10% of undergraduates worked on campus. Average per-year earnings: $3,000. **Cooperative education programs:** computer science, education, engineering, health professions, social/behavioral science. **Reserve Officers Training Corps (ROTC):** Army ROTC: Offered on campus; Navy ROTC: Offered at cooperating institution (University of Kansas); Air Force ROTC: Offered on campus.

Wichita State University

1845 Fairmount
Wichita, KS 67260
Public; www.wichita.edu
Financial aid office: (316) 978-3430

■ **2004-2005 TUITION AND FEES:**
   In state: $3,908; Out of state: $11,361
■ **ROOM AND BOARD:** $4,900

ACT Score (25th/75th percentile): 19-25
2005 U.S. News College Ranking:
National Universities, fourth tier
Acceptance Rate: 63%

Financial aid: Priority filing date for institution's financial aid form: March 15. In 2003-2004, 66% of undergraduates applied for financial aid. Of those, 65% were determined to have financial need; 15% had their need fully met. Average financial aid package (proportion receiving): $5,702 (61%). Average amount of gift aid, such as scholarships or grants (proportion receiving): $2,560 (32%). Average amount of self-help aid, such as work study or loans (proportion receiving): $3,133 (42%). Average need-based loan (excluding PLUS or other private loans): $3,113. Among students who received need-based aid, the average percentage of need met: 50%. Among students who received aid based on merit, the average award (and the proportion receiving): $1,507 (12%). The average athletic scholarship (and the proportion receiving): $4,951 (1%). Average amount of debt of borrowers graduating in 2003: $17,768. Proportion who borrowed: 62%. **Student employment:** During the 2003-2004 academic year, 12% of undergraduates worked on campus. Average per-year earnings: $5,168. **Cooperative education programs:** art, business, computer science, education, engineering, health professions, humanities, natural science, social/behavioral science.

Kentucky

Alice Lloyd College

100 Purpose Road
Pippa Passes, KY 41844
Private; www.alc.edu
Financial aid office: (606) 368-6059

■ **2004-2005 TUITION AND FEES:** $990
■ **ROOM AND BOARD:** $3,430

ACT Score (25th/75th percentile): 19-22
2005 U.S. News College Ranking:
Comp. Colleges–Bachelor's (South), third tier
Acceptance Rate: 58%

....

Other expenses: Estimated books and supplies: $850. Transportation: $1,400. Personal expenses: $1,300. **Financial aid:** Priority filing date for institution's financial aid form: March 15; deadline: August 15. In 2003-2004, 100% of undergraduates applied for financial aid. Of those, 70% were determined to have financial need; 16% had their need fully met. Average financial aid package (proportion receiving): $8,200 (70%). Average amount of gift aid, such as scholarships or grants (proportion receiving): $6,552 (70%). Average amount of self-help aid, such as work study or loans (proportion receiving): $1,648 (70%). Average need-based loan (excluding PLUS or other private loans): $596. Among students who received need-based aid, the average percentage of need met: 70%. Among students who received aid based on merit, the average award (and the proportion receiving): $4,712 (30%). The average athletic scholarship (and the proportion receiving): $7,399 (5%). Average amount of debt of borrowers graduating in 2003: $5,694. Proportion who borrowed: 45%. **Student employment:** During the 2003-2004 academic year, 4% of undergraduates worked on campus. Average per-year earnings: $1,751.

Asbury College

1 Macklem Drive
Wilmore, KY 40390
Private; www.asbury.edu
Financial aid office: (800) 888-1818

■ **2004-2005 TUITION AND FEES:** $17,808
■ **ROOM AND BOARD:** $4,498

SAT I Score (25th/75th percentile): 1020-1270
2005 U.S. News College Ranking:
Comp. Colleges–Bachelor's (South), 3
Acceptance Rate: 73%

....

Other expenses: Estimated books and supplies: $650. Transportation: $1,027. Personal expenses: $1,038. **Financial aid:** Priority filing date for institution's financial aid form: March 1. In 2003-2004, 82% of undergraduates applied for financial aid. Of those, 70% were determined to have financial need; 22% had their need fully met. Average financial aid package (proportion receiving): $12,170 (69%). Average amount of gift aid, such as scholarships or grants (proportion receiving): $7,041 (69%). Average amount of self-help aid, such as work study or loans (proportion receiving): $4,580 (61%). Average need-based loan (excluding PLUS or other private loans): $3,991. Among students who received need-based aid, the average percentage of need met: 78%. Among students who received aid based on merit, the average award (and the proportion receiving): $6,648 (10%). The average athletic scholarship (and the proportion receiving): $275 (0%). Average amount of debt of borrowers graduating in 2003: $18,885. Proportion who borrowed: 68%. Average per-year earnings: $1,300. **Reserve Officers Training Corps (ROTC):** Army ROTC: Offered at cooperating institution (University of Kentucky); Air Force ROTC: Offered at cooperating institution (University of Kentucky).

Bellarmine University

2001 Newburg Road
Louisville, KY 40205
Private; www.bellarmine.edu
Financial aid office: (502) 452-8124

■ **2004-2005 TUITION AND FEES:** $19,980
■ **ROOM AND BOARD:** $6,160

ACT Score (25th/75th percentile): 21-26
2005 U.S. News College Ranking:
Universities–Master's (South), 18
Acceptance Rate: 82%

....

Financial aid: Priority filing date for institution's financial aid form: March 1. **Student employment:** During the 2003-2004 academic year, 10% of undergraduates worked on campus. Average per-year earnings: $3,000.

Reserve Officers Training Corps (ROTC): Army ROTC: Offered at cooperating institution (University of Louisville); Air Force ROTC: Offered at cooperating institution (University of Louisville).

Berea College

CPO Box 2142
Berea, KY 40404
Private; www.berea.edu
Financial aid office: (859) 985-3310

■ **2004-2005 TUITION AND FEES:** $516
■ **ROOM AND BOARD:** $4,748

ACT Score (25th/75th percentile): 20-25
2005 U.S. News College Ranking:
Comp. Colleges–Bachelor's (South), 1
Acceptance Rate: 25%

....

Other expenses: Estimated books and supplies: $700. Transportation: $376. Personal expenses: $1,300. **Financial aid:** Priority filing date for institution's financial aid form: April 15; deadline: August 1. In 2003-2004, 100% of undergraduates applied for financial aid. Of those, 100% were determined to have financial need; 16% had their need fully met. Average financial aid package (proportion receiving): $24,668 (100%). Average amount of gift aid, such as scholarships or grants (proportion receiving): $23,110 (100%). Average amount of self-help aid, such as work study or loans (proportion receiving): $1,558 (100%). Average need-based loan (excluding PLUS or other private loans): $1,509. Among students who received need-based aid, the average percentage of need met: 82%. Among students who received aid based on merit, the average award (and the proportion receiving): $0 (0%). The average athletic scholarship (and the proportion receiving): $0 (0%). Average amount of debt of borrowers graduating in 2003: $6,275. Proportion who borrowed: 75%. **Student employment:** During the 2003-2004 academic year, 100% of undergraduates worked on campus. Average per-year earnings: $1,558.

Brescia University

717 Frederica Street
Owensboro, KY 42301
Private; www.brescia.edu
Financial aid office: (270) 686-4290

■ **2004-2005 TUITION AND FEES:** $11,600
■ **ROOM AND BOARD:** $5,000

2005 U.S. News College Ranking:
Comp. Colleges–Bachelor's (South), 32

Other expenses: Estimated books and supplies: $800. Transportation: $800. Personal expenses: $1,000. **Financial aid:** Priority filing date for institution's financial aid form: March 15. In 2003-2004, 100% of undergraduates applied for financial aid. Of those, 100% were determined to have financial need; 29% had their need fully met. Average financial aid package (proportion receiving): $7,187 (100%). Average amount of gift aid, such as scholarships or grants (proportion receiving): $5,901 (39%). Average amount of self-help aid, such as work study or loans (proportion receiving): $3,162 (68%). Average need-based loan (excluding PLUS or other private loans): $3,013. Among students who received need-based aid, the average percentage of need met: 58%. Among students who received aid based on merit, the average award (and the proportion receiving): $9,599 (23%). The average athletic scholarship (and the proportion receiving): $5,502 (39%). Average amount of debt of borrowers graduating in 2003: $28,500.

Campbellsville University

1 University Drive
Campbellsville, KY 42718
Private; www.campbellsville.edu
Financial aid office: (270) 789-5013

■ **2004-2005 TUITION AND FEES:** $13,952
■ **ROOM AND BOARD:** $5,440

ACT Score (25th/75th percentile): 18-24
2005 U.S. News College Ranking:
Universities–Master's (South), 64
Acceptance Rate: 80%

Other expenses: Estimated books and supplies: $800. Transportation: $900. Personal expenses: $1,600. **Financial aid:** In 2003-2004, 98% of undergraduates applied for financial aid. Of those, 92% were determined to have financial need; 16% had their need fully met. Average financial aid package (proportion receiving):

$12,431 (92%). Average amount of gift aid, such as scholarships or grants (proportion receiving): $9,191 (91%). Average amount of self-help aid, such as work study or loans (proportion receiving): $4,349 (70%). Average need-based loan (excluding PLUS or other private loans): $3,483. Among students who received need-based aid, the average percentage of need met: 74%. Among students who received aid based on merit, the average award (and the proportion receiving): $9,428 (7%). The average athletic scholarship (and the proportion receiving): $6,188 (4%). **Student employment:** During the 2003-2004 academic year, 10% of undergraduates worked on campus. Average per-year earnings: $1,500.

Centre College

600 W. Walnut Street
Danville, KY 40422
Private; www.centre.edu
Financial aid office: (859) 238-5365

■ **2004-2005 TUITION AND FEES:** $21,800
■ **ROOM AND BOARD:** $7,300

ACT Score (25th/75th percentile): 25-30
2005 U.S. News College Ranking:
Liberal Arts Colleges, 42
Acceptance Rate: 75%

Other expenses: Estimated books and supplies: $800. Transportation: $300. Personal expenses: $700. **Financial aid:** In 2003-2004, 74% of undergraduates applied for financial aid. Of those, 64% were determined to have financial need; 40% had their need fully met. Average financial aid package (proportion receiving): $17,012 (64%). Average amount of gift aid, such as scholarships or grants (proportion receiving): $14,139 (64%). Average amount of self-help aid, such as work study or loans (proportion receiving): $4,329 (50%). Average need-based loan (excluding PLUS or other private loans): $3,875. Among students who received need-based aid, the average percentage of need met: 90%. Among students who received aid based on merit, the average award (and the proportion receiving): $8,013 (30%). The average athletic scholarship (and the proportion receiving): $0 (0%). Average amount of debt of borrowers graduating in 2003: $14,200. Proportion who borrowed: 58%. **Student employment:** During the 2003-2004 academic year, 49% of undergraduates worked on campus. Average per-year earnings: $500. **Reserve Officers Training Corps (ROTC):** Army ROTC: Offered at cooperating institution (University of

Kentucky); Air Force ROTC: Offered at cooperating institution (University of Kentucky).

Cumberland College

6178 College Station Drive
Williamsburg, KY 40769
Private; www.cumberlandcollege.edu
Financial aid office: (800) 532-0828

■ **2004-2005 TUITION AND FEES:** $11,858
■ **ROOM AND BOARD:** $5,126

ACT Score (25th/75th percentile): 18-23
2005 U.S. News College Ranking:
Universities–Master's (South), 60
Acceptance Rate: 72%

Other expenses: Estimated books and supplies: $800. Transportation: $700. Personal expenses: $1,630. **Financial aid:** Priority filing date for institution's financial aid form: March 1. In 2003-2004, 89% of undergraduates applied for financial aid. Of those, 82% were determined to have financial need; 41% had their need fully met. Average financial aid package (proportion receiving): $12,416 (82%). Average amount of gift aid, such as scholarships or grants (proportion receiving): $4,921 (61%). Average amount of self-help aid, such as work study or loans (proportion receiving): $4,381 (61%). Average need-based loan (excluding PLUS or other private loans): $3,541. Among students who received need-based aid, the average percentage of need met: 90%. Among students who received aid based on merit, the average award (and the proportion receiving): $5,810 (10%). The average athletic scholarship (and the proportion receiving): $2,063 (5%). Average amount of debt of borrowers graduating in 2003: $12,503. Proportion who borrowed: 71%. **Student employment:** During the 2003-2004 academic year, 12% of undergraduates worked on campus. Average per-year earnings: $2,992. **Cooperative education programs:** art, business, computer science, education, health professions, social/behavioral science. **Reserve Officers Training Corps (ROTC):** Army ROTC: Offered on campus.

Eastern Kentucky University

521 Lancaster Avenue
Richmond, KY 40475
Public; www.eku.edu
Financial aid office: (859) 622-2361

■ **2004-2005 TUITION AND FEES:**
   In state: $3,792; Out of state: $10,464
■ **ROOM AND BOARD:** $4,658

ACT Score (25th/75th percentile): 18-23
2005 U.S. News College Ranking:
Universities–Master's (South), third tier
Acceptance Rate: 76%

Other expenses: Estimated books and supplies:
$800. Transportation: $500. Personal expenses:
$1,000. **Financial aid:** Priority filing date for
institution's financial aid form: April 1. In
2003-2004, 69% of undergraduates applied for
financial aid. Of those, 55% were determined to
have financial need; 28% had their need fully
met. Average financial aid package (proportion
receiving): $6,183 (54%). Average amount of
gift aid, such as scholarships or grants (proportion receiving): $3,877 (47%). Average amount
of self-help aid, such as work study or loans
(proportion receiving): $2,999 (44%). Average
need-based loan (excluding PLUS or other private loans): $2,547. Among students who
received need-based aid, the average percentage
of need met: 87%. Among students who
received aid based on merit, the average award
(and the proportion receiving): $1,835 (25%).
The average athletic scholarship (and the proportion receiving): $7,201 (3%). Average
amount of debt of borrowers graduating in
2003: $15,508. Proportion who borrowed: 42%.
Student employment: During the 2003-2004
academic year, 7% of undergraduates worked
on campus. Average per-year earnings: $3,672.
Cooperative education programs: agriculture,
business, computer science, education, health
professions, home economics, humanities, natural science, social/behavioral science, technologies, vocational arts, other. **Reserve Officers
Training Corps (ROTC):** Army ROTC: Offered
on campus; Air Force ROTC: Offered at cooperating institution (University of Kentucky).

Georgetown College

400 E. College Street
Georgetown, KY 40324
Private; www.georgetowncollege.edu
Financial aid office: (502) 863-8027

■ **2004-2005 TUITION AND FEES:** $17,290
■ **ROOM AND BOARD:** $5,450

ACT Score (25th/75th percentile): 21-26
2005 U.S. News College Ranking:
Liberal Arts Colleges, third tier
Acceptance Rate: 80%

Other expenses: Estimated books and supplies:
$1,050. Transportation: $500. Personal expenses: $1,000. **Financial aid:** Priority filing date for
institution's financial aid form: March 15; deadline: August 1. In 2003-2004, 80% of undergraduates applied for financial aid. Of those,
70% were determined to have financial need;
48% had their need fully met. Average financial
aid package (proportion receiving): $17,314
(70%). Average amount of gift aid, such as
scholarships or grants (proportion receiving):
$12,569 (70%). Average amount of self-help
aid, such as work study or loans (proportion
receiving): $3,907 (47%). Among students who
received need-based aid, the average percentage
of need met: 90%. Among students who
received aid based on merit, the average award
(and the proportion receiving): $7,258 (25%).
The average athletic scholarship (and the proportion receiving): $5,261 (12%). Average
amount of debt of borrowers graduating in
2003: $15,481. Proportion who borrowed: 65%.
Student employment: During the 2003-2004
academic year, 50% of undergraduates worked
on campus. Average per-year earnings: $1,400.
Reserve Officers Training Corps (ROTC): Army
ROTC: Offered at cooperating institution
(University of Kentucky); Air Force ROTC:
Offered at cooperating institution (University of
Kentucky).

Kentucky Christian College

100 Academic Parkway
Grayson, KY 41143
Private; www.kcc.edu
Financial aid office: (606) 474-3226

■ **2004-2005 TUITION AND FEES:** $10,640
■ **ROOM AND BOARD:** $4,355

ACT Score (25th/75th percentile): 18-25
2005 U.S. News College Ranking:
Comp. Colleges–Bachelor's (South), 48
Acceptance Rate: 76%

Other expenses: Estimated books and supplies:
$850. Transportation: $1,260. Personal expenses:
$2,012. **Financial aid:** Priority filing date for insti-
tution's financial aid form: April 1. In 2003-2004,
90% of undergraduates applied for financial aid.
Of those, 79% were determined to have financial
need; 18% had their need fully met. Average
financial aid package (proportion receiving):
$6,856 (79%). Average amount of gift aid, such
as scholarships or grants (proportion receiving):
$4,207 (54%). Average amount of self-help aid,
such as work study or loans (proportion receiving): $4,494 (69%). Average need-based loan
(excluding PLUS or other private loans): $3,790.
Among students who received need-based aid, the
average percentage of need met: 79%. Among
students who received aid based on merit, the
average award (and the proportion receiving):
$3,999 (21%). The average athletic scholarship
(and the proportion receiving): $0 (0%). Average
amount of debt of borrowers graduating in 2003:
$25,587. Proportion who borrowed: 87%. Average
per-year earnings: $1,760. **Cooperative education
programs:** health professions.

Kentucky State University

400 E. Main Street
Frankfort, KY 40601
Public; www.kysu.edu
Financial aid office: (502) 597-5960

■ **2003-2004 TUITION AND FEES:**
   In state: $2,828; Out of state: $8,472
■ **ROOM AND BOARD:** $5,394

2005 U.S. News College Ranking:
Universities–Master's (South), fourth tier
Acceptance Rate: 47%

Other expenses: Estimated books and supplies:
$1,000. Personal expenses: $542.

Kentucky Wesleyan College

3000 Frederica Street, PO Box 1039
Owensboro, KY 42302
Private; www.kwc.edu
Financial aid office: (270) 926-3111

■ **2004-2005 TUITION AND FEES:** $12,510
■ **ROOM AND BOARD:** $5,450

ACT Score (25th/75th percentile): 19-23
2005 U.S. News College Ranking:
Comp. Colleges–Bachelor's (South), 19
Acceptance Rate: 75%

....

Other expenses: Estimated books and supplies: $1,250. Transportation: $2,000. Personal expenses: $2,000. **Financial aid:** Priority filing date for institution's financial aid form: March 15. In 2003-2004, 100% of undergraduates applied for financial aid. Of those, 88% were determined to have financial need; 27% had their need fully met. Average financial aid package (proportion receiving): $11,416 (88%). Average amount of gift aid, such as scholarships or grants (proportion receiving): $9,177 (88%). Average amount of self-help aid, such as work study or loans (proportion receiving): $3,433 (57%). Average need-based loan (excluding PLUS or other private loans): $2,949. Among students who received need-based aid, the average percentage of need met: 75%. Among students who received aid based on merit, the average award (and the proportion receiving): $8,739 (12%). The average athletic scholarship (and the proportion receiving): $0 (0%). Average amount of debt of borrowers graduating in 2003: $18,606. Proportion who borrowed: 91%. **Student employment:** During the 2003-2004 academic year, 12% of undergraduates worked on campus. Average per-year earnings: $1,100. **Cooperative education programs:** business, computer science, natural science, social/behavioral science.

Lindsey Wilson College

210 Lindsey Wilson Street
Columbia, KY 42728
Private; www.lindsey.edu
Financial aid office: (270) 384-8022

■ **2004-2005 TUITION AND FEES:** $13,140
■ **ROOM AND BOARD:** $5,698

ACT Score (25th/75th percentile): 16-21
2005 U.S. News College Ranking:
Liberal Arts Colleges, fourth tier

....

Other expenses: Estimated books and supplies: $600. Transportation: $500. Personal expenses: $800. **Financial aid:** Priority filing date for institution's financial aid form: March 15. In 2003-2004, 99% of undergraduates applied for financial aid. Of those, 93% were determined to have financial need; 13% had their need fully met. Average financial aid package (proportion receiving): $4,120 (93%). Average amount of gift aid, such as scholarships or grants (propor-

tion receiving): $175 (93%). Average amount of self-help aid, such as work study or loans (proportion receiving): $1,098 (26%). Average need-based loan (excluding PLUS or other private loans): $2,379. Average amount of debt of borrowers graduating in 2003: $13,265. Proportion who borrowed: 72%. **Student employment:** During the 2003-2004 academic year, 0% of undergraduates worked on campus. Average per-year earnings: $0.

Mid-Continent College

99 Powell Road E
Mayfield, KY 42066
Private; www.midcontinent.edu
Financial aid office: (270) 247-8521

■ **2004-2005 TUITION AND FEES:** $9,350
■ **ROOM AND BOARD:** $5,485

ACT Score (25th/75th percentile): 17-19
2005 U.S. News College Ranking:
Comp. Colleges–Bachelor's (South), fourth tier
Acceptance Rate: 88%

....

Financial aid: Priority filing date for institution's financial aid form: March 15. In 2003-2004, 88% of undergraduates applied for financial aid. Of those, 76% were determined to have financial need; 19% had their need fully met. Average financial aid package (proportion receiving): $6,199 (76%). Average amount of gift aid, such as scholarships or grants (proportion receiving): $4,620 (71%). Average amount of self-help aid, such as work study or loans (proportion receiving): $2,834 (51%). Average need-based loan (excluding PLUS or other private loans): $2,577. Among students who received need-based aid, the average percentage of need met: 63%. Among students who received aid based on merit, the average award (and the proportion receiving): $5,445 (18%). Average amount of debt of borrowers graduating in 2003: $6,738. Proportion who borrowed: 75%. **Student employment:** During the 2003-2004 academic year, 10% of undergraduates worked on campus. Average per-year earnings: $800.

Midway College

512 E. Stephens Street
Midway, KY 40347
Private; www.Midway.edu
Financial aid office: (859) 846-5745

■ **2004-2005 TUITION AND FEES:** $12,825
■ **ROOM AND BOARD:** $5,800

ACT Score (25th/75th percentile): 18-21
2005 U.S. News College Ranking:
Comp. Colleges–Bachelor's (South), third tier
Acceptance Rate: 74%

....

Financial aid: Priority filing date for institution's financial aid form: March 15; deadline: April 15. In 2003-2004, 82% of undergraduates applied for financial aid. Of those, 71% were determined to have financial need; 33% had their need fully met. Average financial aid package (proportion receiving): $9,028 (68%). Average amount of gift aid, such as scholarships or grants (proportion receiving): $6,626 (66%). Average amount of self-help aid, such as work study or loans (proportion receiving): $4,778 (58%). Average need-based loan (excluding PLUS or other private loans): $3,298. Among students who received need-based aid, the average percentage of need met: 84%. Among students who received aid based on merit, the average award (and the proportion receiving): $2,974 (4%). The average athletic scholarship (and the proportion receiving): $3,600 (2%). Average amount of debt of borrowers graduating in 2003: $12,910. Proportion who borrowed: 63%. **Cooperative education programs:** education. **Reserve Officers Training Corps (ROTC):** Army ROTC: Offered at cooperating institution (University of Kentucky).

Morehead State University

Morehead, KY 40351
Public; www.moreheadstate.edu
Financial aid office: (606) 783-2011

■ **2004-2005 TUITION AND FEES:**
In state: $3,840; Out of state: $10,200
■ **ROOM AND BOARD:** $4,410

ACT Score (25th/75th percentile): 16-22
2005 U.S. News College Ranking:
Universities–Master's (South), 64
Acceptance Rate: 71%

....

Other expenses: Estimated books and supplies: $700. Transportation: $400. Personal expenses: $800. **Financial aid:** Priority filing date for institution's financial aid form: March 15. In 2003-2004, 81% of undergraduates applied for financial aid. Of those, 67% were determined to have financial need; 46% had their need fully met. Average financial aid package (proportion receiving): $6,799 (66%). Average amount of gift aid, such as scholarships or grants (proportion receiving): $4,085 (51%). Average amount of self-help aid, such as work study or loans (proportion receiving): $2,894 (42%). Average need-based loan (excluding PLUS or other private loans): $2,762. Among students who received need-based aid, the average percentage of need met: 90%. Among students who received aid based on merit, the average award (and the proportion receiving): $2,589 (19%). The average athletic scholarship (and the proportion receiving): $4,479 (3%). Average amount of debt of borrowers graduating in 2003: $14,191. Proportion who borrowed: 56%. **Student employment:** During the 2003-2004 academic year, 11% of undergraduates worked on campus. Average per-year earnings: $1,397. **Reserve Officers Training Corps (ROTC):** Army ROTC: Offered on campus.

Murray State University

PO Box 9
Murray, KY 42071
Public; www.murraystate.edu
Financial aid office: (270) 762-2546

■ **2004-2005 TUITION AND FEES:**
   In state: $3,984; Out of state: $6,592
■ **ROOM AND BOARD:** $4,510

ACT Score (25th/75th percentile): 20-25
2005 U.S. News College Ranking:
Universities–Master's (South), 21
Acceptance Rate: 63%

Other expenses: Estimated books and supplies: $700. Transportation: $350. Personal expenses: $790. **Financial aid:** Priority filing date for institution's financial aid form: April 1. In 2003-2004, 86% of undergraduates applied for financial aid. Of those, 48% were determined to have financial need; 90% had their need fully met. Average financial aid package (proportion receiving): $4,610 (44%). Average amount of gift aid, such as scholarships or grants (proportion receiving): $2,180 (30%). Average amount of self-help aid, such as work study or loans (proportion receiving): $2,430 (42%). Average need-based loan (excluding PLUS or other private loans): $1,950. Among students who received need-based aid, the average percentage of need met: 89%. Among students who received aid based on merit, the average award (and the proportion receiving): $2,550 (33%). The average athletic scholarship (and the proportion receiving): $7,220 (3%). Average amount of debt of borrowers graduating in 2003: $14,034. Proportion who borrowed: 55%. **Student employment:** During the 2003-2004 academic year, 18% of undergraduates worked on campus. Average per-year earnings: $3,000. **Cooperative education programs:**

agriculture, art, business, computer science, education, engineering, health professions, home economics, humanities, natural science, social/behavioral science, technologies, other. **Reserve Officers Training Corps (ROTC):** Army ROTC: Offered on campus.

Northern Kentucky University

Nunn Drive
Highland Heights, KY 41099
Public; www.nku.edu
Financial aid office: (859) 572-5143

■ **2004-2005 TUITION AND FEES:**
   In state: $4,368; Out of state: $9,096
■ **ROOM AND BOARD:** $5,256

ACT Score (25th/75th percentile): 18-22
2005 U.S. News College Ranking:
Universities–Master's (South), third tier
Acceptance Rate: 89%

Other expenses: Estimated books and supplies: $800. Transportation: $700. Personal expenses: $800. **Financial aid:** Priority filing date for institution's financial aid form: March 1. In 2003-2004, 75% of undergraduates applied for financial aid. Of those, 64% were determined to have financial need; Average financial aid package (proportion receiving): $7,378 (51%). Average amount of gift aid, such as scholarships or grants (proportion receiving): $3,744 (26%). Average amount of self-help aid, such as work study or loans (proportion receiving): $3,555 (37%). Average need-based loan (excluding PLUS or other private loans): $5,306. Among students who received need-based aid, the average percentage of need met: 85%. Among students who received aid based on merit, the average award (and the proportion receiving): $2,872 (10%). The average athletic scholarship (and the proportion receiving): $3,622 (2%). Average amount of debt of borrowers graduating in 2003: $20,787. Proportion who borrowed: 28%. **Student employment:** During the 2003-2004 academic year, 10% of undergraduates worked on campus. Average per-year earnings: $1,635. **Cooperative education programs:** art, business, computer science, education, humanities, natural science, social/behavioral science, technologies, other. **Reserve Officers Training Corps (ROTC):** Army ROTC: Offered on campus; Air Force ROTC: Offered at cooperating institution (University of Cincinnati).

Pikeville College

147 Sycamore Street
Pikeville, KY 41501-1194
Private; www.pc.edu
Financial aid office: (606) 218-5253

■ **2004-2005 TUITION AND FEES:** $10,500
■ **ROOM AND BOARD:** $5,000

ACT Score (25th/75th percentile): 17-23
2005 U.S. News College Ranking:
Comp. Colleges–Bachelor's (South), 48
Acceptance Rate: 100%

Other expenses: Estimated books and supplies: $1,500. Transportation: $1,500. Personal expenses: $1,500. **Financial aid:** Priority filing date for institution's financial aid form: March 15; deadline: August 19. In 2003-2004, 92% of undergraduates applied for financial aid. Of those, 77% were determined to have financial need; 52% had their need fully met. Average financial aid package (proportion receiving): $11,622 (77%). Average amount of gift aid, such as scholarships or grants (proportion receiving): $5,545 (71%). Average amount of self-help aid, such as work study or loans (proportion receiving): $1,640 (58%). Average need-based loan (excluding PLUS or other private loans): $3,660. Among students who received need-based aid, the average percentage of need met: 84%. Among students who received aid based on merit, the average award (and the proportion receiving): $5,591 (6%). The average athletic scholarship (and the proportion receiving): $6,836 (21%). Average amount of debt of borrowers graduating in 2003: $12,071. Proportion who borrowed: 68%. **Student employment:** During the 2003-2004 academic year, 2% of undergraduates worked on campus. Average per-year earnings: $1,500.

Spalding University

851 S. Fourth Street
Louisville, KY 40203-2188
Private; www.spalding.edu
Financial aid office: (502) 585-9911

■ **2004-2005 TUITION AND FEES:** $13,950
■ **ROOM AND BOARD:** $4,572

ACT Score (25th/75th percentile): 19-23
2005 U.S. News College Ranking:
Universities–Master's (South), 63
Acceptance Rate: 76%

Other expenses: Estimated books and supplies: $750. Transportation: $150. Personal expenses: $1,296. **Financial aid:** Priority filing date for institution's financial aid form: March 1. Average amount of debt of borrowers graduating in 2003: $25,000. Proportion who borrowed: 96%. **Student employment:** During the 2003-2004 academic year, 20% of undergraduates worked on campus. Average per-year earnings: $2,500. **Reserve Officers Training Corps (ROTC):** Army ROTC: Offered at cooperating institution (University Of Louisville).

Thomas More College

333 Thomas More Parkway
Crestview Hills, KY 41017-3495
Private; www.thomasmore.edu
Financial aid office: (859) 344-3319

■ **2004-2005 TUITION AND FEES:** $17,320
■ **ROOM AND BOARD:** $5,950

ACT Score (25th/75th percentile): 19-24
2005 U.S. News College Ranking:
Comp. Colleges–Bachelor's (South), 22
Acceptance Rate: 61%

Other expenses: Estimated books and supplies: $800. Transportation: $500. Personal expenses: $2,300. **Financial aid:** Priority filing date for institution's financial aid form: March 15; deadline: March 15. In 2003-2004, 97% of undergraduates applied for financial aid. Of those, 97% were determined to have financial need; 100% had their need fully met. Average financial aid package (proportion receiving): $14,451 (97%). Average amount of gift aid, such as scholarships or grants (proportion receiving): $4,696 (87%). Average amount of self-help aid, such as work study or loans (proportion receiving): $4,694 (53%). Average need-based loan (excluding PLUS or other private loans): $2,619. Among students who received need-based aid, the average percentage of need met: 90%. Among students who received aid based on merit, the average award (and the proportion receiving): $5,923 (16%). The average athletic scholarship (and the proportion receiving): $0 (0%). Average amount of debt of borrowers graduating in 2003: $21,980. Proportion who borrowed: 62%. **Student employment:** During the 2003-2004 academic year, 16% of undergraduates worked on campus. Average per-year earnings: $1,035. **Cooperative education programs:** art, business, computer science, education, humanities, natural science, social/behavioral science, technologies. **Reserve Officers**

Training Corps (ROTC): Army ROTC: Offered at cooperating institution (Xavier University); Air Force ROTC: Offered at cooperating institution (University of Cincinnati).

Transylvania University

300 N. Broadway
Lexington, KY 40508-1797
Private; www.transy.edu
Financial aid office: (859) 233-8239

■ **2004-2005 TUITION AND FEES:** $18,590
■ **ROOM AND BOARD:** $6,340

ACT Score (25th/75th percentile): 23-28
2005 U.S. News College Ranking:
Liberal Arts Colleges, 105
Acceptance Rate: 86%

Other expenses: Estimated books and supplies: $750. Transportation: $500. Personal expenses: $1,250. **Financial aid:** Priority filing date for institution's financial aid form: March 1. In 2003-2004, 71% of undergraduates applied for financial aid. Of those, 61% were determined to have financial need; 31% had their need fully met. Average financial aid package (proportion receiving): $15,115 (61%). Average amount of gift aid, such as scholarships or grants (proportion receiving): $11,343 (61%). Average amount of self-help aid, such as work study or loans (proportion receiving): $4,744 (49%). Average need-based loan (excluding PLUS or other private loans): $3,790. Among students who received need-based aid, the average percentage of need met: 87%. Among students who received aid based on merit, the average award (and the proportion receiving): $9,575 (38%). The average athletic scholarship (and the proportion receiving): $0 (0%). Average amount of debt of borrowers graduating in 2003: $16,005. Proportion who borrowed: 59%. **Student employment:** During the 2003-2004 academic year, 5% of undergraduates worked on campus. Average per-year earnings: $5,663. **Reserve Officers Training Corps (ROTC):** Army ROTC: Offered at cooperating institution (University of Kentucky); Air Force ROTC: Offered at cooperating institution (University of Kentucky).

University of Kentucky

105 Gillis Building
Lexington, KY 40506-0033
Public; www.uky.edu
Financial aid office: (859) 257-3172

■ **2004-2005 TUITION AND FEES:**
In state: $5,315; Out of state: $12,095
■ **ROOM AND BOARD:** $4,735

ACT Score (25th/75th percentile): 22-27
2005 U.S. News College Ranking:
National Universities, 120
Acceptance Rate: 81%

Other expenses: Estimated books and supplies: $600. Transportation: $570. Personal expenses: $1,290. **Financial aid:** Priority filing date for institution's financial aid form: February 15. In 2003-2004, 53% of undergraduates applied for financial aid. Of those, 38% were determined to have financial need; 34% had their need fully met. Average financial aid package (proportion receiving): $7,421 (38%). Average amount of gift aid, such as scholarships or grants (proportion receiving): $4,533 (29%). Average amount of self-help aid, such as work study or loans (proportion receiving): $3,153 (25%). Average need-based loan (excluding PLUS or other private loans): $3,632. Among students who received need-based aid, the average percentage of need met: 79%. Among students who received aid based on merit, the average award (and the proportion receiving): $3,728 (4%). The average athletic scholarship (and the proportion receiving): $9,989 (3%). Average amount of debt of borrowers graduating in 2003: $16,584. Proportion who borrowed: 57%. **Reserve Officers Training Corps (ROTC):** Army ROTC: Offered on campus; Air Force ROTC: Offered on campus.

University of Louisville

2301 S. Third Street
Louisville, KY 40292
Public; www.louisville.edu
Financial aid office: (502) 852-5511

■ **2004-2005 TUITION AND FEES:**
In state: $5,040; Out of state: $13,752
■ **ROOM AND BOARD:** $4,640

ACT Score (25th/75th percentile): 20-26
2005 U.S. News College Ranking:
National Universities, third tier
Acceptance Rate: 79%

Other expenses: Estimated books and supplies: $800. Transportation: $2,592. Personal expenses: $4,692. **Financial aid:** Priority filing date for institution's financial aid form: March 15. In 2003-2004, 58% of undergraduates applied for financial aid. Of those, 52% were determined to have financial need; 11% had their need fully met. Average financial aid package (proportion receiving): $7,510 (51%). Average amount of gift aid, such as scholarships or grants (proportion receiving): $4,827 (42%). Average amount of self-help aid, such as work study or loans (proportion receiving): $2,988 (37%). Average need-based loan (excluding PLUS or other private loans): $3,801. Among students who received need-based aid, the average percentage of need met: 53%. Among students who received aid based on merit, the average award (and the proportion receiving): $4,304 (15%). The average athletic scholarship (and the proportion receiving): $14,753 (2%). Average amount of debt of borrowers graduating in 2003: $14,498. Proportion who borrowed: 39%. **Cooperative education programs:** business, computer science, engineering. **Reserve Officers Training Corps (ROTC):** Army ROTC: Offered on campus; Air Force ROTC: Offered on campus.

Western Kentucky University

1 Big Red Way
Bowling Green, KY 42101-3576
Public; www.wku.edu
Financial aid office: (270) 745-2756

■ **2004-2005 TUITION AND FEES:**
   In state: $4,468; Out of state: $9,316
■ **ROOM AND BOARD:** $4,350

ACT Score (25th/75th percentile): 18-23
2005 U.S. News College Ranking:
Universities–Master's (South), 47
Acceptance Rate: 93%

....

Other expenses: Estimated books and supplies: $600. Transportation: $600. Personal expenses: $1,600. **Financial aid:** Priority filing date for institution's financial aid form: April 1. In 2003-2004, 70% of undergraduates applied for financial aid. Of those, 53% were determined to have financial need; 41% had their need fully met. Average financial aid package (proportion receiving): $6,970 (52%). Average amount of gift aid, such as scholarships or grants (proportion receiving): $3,560 (34%). Average amount of self-help aid, such as work study or loans (proportion receiving): $3,216 (36%). Average need-based loan (excluding PLUS or other private loans): $3,084. Among students who received need-based aid, the average percentage of need met: 42%. Among students who received aid based on merit, the average award (and the proportion receiving): $2,094 (25%). The average athletic scholarship (and the proportion receiving): $5,437 (3%). Average amount of debt of borrowers graduating in 2003: $9,568. Proportion who borrowed: 56%. **Student employment:** During the 2003-2004 academic year, 10% of undergraduates worked on campus. Average per-year earnings: $1,470. **Cooperative education programs:** agriculture, art, business, computer science, education, engineering, health professions, home economics, humanities, natural science, social/behavioral science, technologies, other. **Reserve Officers Training Corps (ROTC):** Army ROTC: Offered on campus; Air Force ROTC: Offered at cooperating institution (Tennessee State University).

Louisiana

Centenary College of Louisiana

PO Box 41188
Shreveport, LA 71134-1188
Private; www.centenary.edu
Financial aid office: (318) 869-5137

■ **2004-2005 TUITION AND FEES:** $17,360
■ **ROOM AND BOARD:** $6,180

ACT Score (25th/75th percentile): 23-28
2005 U.S. News College Ranking:
Universities–Master's (South), 11
Acceptance Rate: 74%

Other expenses: Estimated books and supplies: $1,000. Transportation: $900. Personal expenses: $1,550. **Financial aid:** Priority filing date for institution's financial aid form: February 15. In 2003-2004, 98% of undergraduates applied for financial aid. Of those, 66% were determined to have financial need; 38% had their need fully met. Average financial aid package (proportion receiving): $13,207 (64%). Average amount of gift aid, such as scholarships or grants (proportion receiving): $10,913 (62%). Average amount of self-help aid, such as work study or loans (proportion receiving): $4,217 (39%). Average need-based loan (excluding PLUS or other private loans): $3,687. Among students who received need-based aid, the average percentage of need met: 78%. Among students who received aid based on merit, the average award (and the proportion receiving): $9,575 (23%). The average athletic scholarship (and the proportion receiving): $13,003 (21%). Average amount of debt of borrowers graduating in 2003: $15,659. Proportion who borrowed: 53%. **Student employment:** During the 2003-2004 academic year, 7% of undergraduates worked on campus. Average per-year earnings: $1,000. **Cooperative education programs:** engineering, social/behavioral science. **Reserve Officers Training Corps (ROTC):** Army ROTC: Offered at cooperating institution (Northwestern State (Louisiana) University).

Dillard University

2601 Gentilly Boulevard
New Orleans, LA 70122
Private; www.dillard.edu
Financial aid office: (504) 816-4677

■ **2004-2005 TUITION AND FEES:** $11,550
■ **ROOM AND BOARD:** $6,840

ACT Score (25th/75th percentile): 17-21
2005 U.S. News College Ranking:
Comp. Colleges–Bachelor's (South), 21
Acceptance Rate: 64%

Other expenses: Estimated books and supplies: $1,000. Transportation: $883. Personal expenses: $1,533. **Financial aid:** Priority filing date for institution's financial aid form: March 1; deadline: May 1. In 2003-2004, 93% of undergraduates applied for financial aid. Of those, 86% were determined to have financial need; 100% had their need fully met. Average financial aid package (proportion receiving): $13,443 (86%). Average amount of gift aid, such as scholarships or grants (proportion receiving): $3,603 (66%). Average amount of self-help aid, such as work study or loans (proportion receiving): $3,146 (80%). Average need-based loan (excluding PLUS or other private loans): $3,337. Among students who received need-based aid, the average percentage of need met: 85%. Among students who received aid based on merit, the average award (and the proportion receiving): $3,924 (6%). The average athletic scholarship (and the proportion receiving): $11,588 (0%). Average amount of debt of borrowers graduating in 2003: $25,247. Proportion who borrowed: 98%. **Reserve Officers Training Corps (ROTC):** Army ROTC: Offered at cooperating institution (Tulane University); Air Force ROTC: Offered at cooperating institution (Tulane University).

Grambling State University

Box 607
Grambling, LA 71245
Public; www.gram.edu
Financial aid office: (318) 274-6056

■ **2004-2005 TUITION AND FEES:**
  In state: $1,639; Out of state: $4,314
■ **ROOM AND BOARD:** $1,784

ACT Score (25th/75th percentile): 14-18
2005 U.S. News College Ranking:
Universities–Master's (South), fourth tier
Acceptance Rate: 62%

Other expenses: Estimated books and supplies: $1,000. Transportation: $883. Personal expenses: $2,338. **Financial aid:** Priority filing date for institution's financial aid form: June 1; deadline: June 1. Average per-year earnings: $1,100. **Cooperative education programs:** business, computer science, engineering, home economics. **Reserve Officers Training Corps (ROTC):** Army ROTC: Offered on campus; Air Force ROTC: Offered on campus.

Louisiana College

1140 College Drive
Pineville, LA 71360
Private; www.lacollege.edu
Financial aid office: (318) 487-7386

■ **2004-2005 TUITION AND FEES:** $9,700
■ **ROOM AND BOARD:** $3,886

ACT Score (25th/75th percentile): 21-26
2005 U.S. News College Ranking:
Comp. Colleges–Bachelor's (South), 25
Acceptance Rate: 85%

Other expenses: Estimated books and supplies: $1,000. Transportation: $883. Personal expenses: $1,533. **Financial aid:** Priority filing date for institution's financial aid form: March 31. In 2003-2004, 100% of undergraduates applied for financial aid. Of those, 67% were determined to have financial need; 30% had their need fully met. Average financial aid package (proportion receiving): $9,475 (67%). Average amount of gift aid, such as scholarships or grants (proportion receiving): $1,017 (64%). Average amount of self-help aid, such as work study or loans (proportion receiving): $1,683 (46%). Average need-based loan (excluding PLUS or other private loans): $1,957. Among students who received need-based aid, the average percentage of need met: 72%. Among students who received aid based on merit, the average award (and the proportion receiving): $0 (0%). The average athletic scholarship (and the proportion receiving): $0 (0%). Average amount of debt of borrowers graduating in 2003: $5,440. Proportion who borrowed: 46%.

Student employment: During the 2003-2004 academic year, 5% of undergraduates worked on campus. Average per-year earnings: $2,300. **Reserve Officers Training Corps (ROTC):** Army ROTC: Offered on campus.

Louisiana State University–Baton Rouge

156 Thomas Boyd Hall
Baton Rouge, LA 70803
Public; www.lsu.edu
Financial aid office: (225) 578-3103

■ **2004-2005 TUITION AND FEES:**
   In state: $4,226; Out of state: $11,026
■ **ROOM AND BOARD:** $5,882

ACT Score (25th/75th percentile): 22-27
2005 U.S. News College Ranking:
National Universities, third tier
Acceptance Rate: 81%

Financial aid: In 2003-2004, 75% of undergraduates applied for financial aid. Of those, 45% were determined to have financial need; 17% had their need fully met. Average financial aid package (proportion receiving): $6,342 (43%). Average amount of gift aid, such as scholarships or grants (proportion receiving): $4,431 (37%). Average amount of self-help aid, such as work study or loans (proportion receiving): $3,780 (28%). Average need-based loan (excluding PLUS or other private loans): $3,862. Among students who received need-based aid, the average percentage of need met: 67%. Among students who received aid based on merit, the average award (and the proportion receiving): $3,765 (36%). The average athletic scholarship (and the proportion receiving): $9,693 (2%). **Student employment:** During the 2003-2004 academic year, 21% of undergraduates worked on campus. Average per-year earnings: $2,100. **Cooperative education programs:** agriculture, business, computer science, engineering, natural science, technologies, other. **Reserve Officers Training Corps (ROTC):** Army ROTC: Offered on campus; Navy ROTC: Offered at cooperating institution (Southern University A&M College); Air Force ROTC: Offered on campus.

Louisiana State University–Shreveport

1 University Place
Shreveport, LA 71115
Public; www.lsus.edu
Financial aid office: (318) 797-5363

■ **2004-2005 TUITION AND FEES:**
   In state: $3,270; Out of state: $7,600

ACT Score (25th/75th percentile): 18-23
2005 U.S. News College Ranking:
Universities–Master's (South), fourth tier
Acceptance Rate: 100%

Average per-year earnings: $6,240. **Cooperative education programs:** health professions. **Reserve Officers Training Corps (ROTC):** Army ROTC: Offered at cooperating institution (Northwestern State University).

Louisiana Tech University

Box 3178, Tech Station
Ruston, LA 71272
Public; www.latech.edu
Financial aid office: (318) 257-2643

■ **2004-2005 TUITION AND FEES:**
   In state: $3,069; Out of state: $6,864
■ **ROOM AND BOARD:** $3,915

ACT Score (25th/75th percentile): 20-25
2005 U.S. News College Ranking:
National Universities, fourth tier
Acceptance Rate: 92%

Other expenses: Estimated books and supplies: $900. Transportation: $864. Personal expenses: $1,500. **Financial aid:** Priority filing date for institution's financial aid form: April 15. In 2003-2004, 70% of undergraduates applied for financial aid. Of those, 45% were determined to have financial need; 15% had their need fully met. Average financial aid package (proportion receiving): $6,233 (45%). Average amount of gift aid, such as scholarships or grants (proportion receiving): $4,486 (40%). Average amount of self-help aid, such as work study or loans (proportion receiving): $3,171 (33%). Average need-based loan (excluding PLUS or other private loans): $2,877. Among students who received need-based aid, the average percentage of need met: 67%. Among students who received aid based on merit, the average award (and the proportion receiving): $5,289 (24%). The average athletic scholarship (and the proportion receiving):

$2,723 (0%). Average amount of debt of borrowers graduating in 2003: $14,306. Proportion who borrowed: 37%. **Student employment:** During the 2003-2004 academic year, 15% of undergraduates worked on campus. Average per-year earnings: $2,500. **Cooperative education programs:** agriculture, engineering, natural science, other. **Reserve Officers Training Corps (ROTC):** Army ROTC: Offered at cooperating institution (Grambling State University); Air Force ROTC: Offered on campus.

Loyola University New Orleans

6363 St. Charles Avenue
New Orleans, LA 70118-6195
Private; www.loyno.edu
Financial aid office: (504) 865-3231

■ **2004-2005 TUITION AND FEES:** $21,078
■ **ROOM AND BOARD:** $7,994

ACT Score (25th/75th percentile): 25-28
2005 U.S. News College Ranking:
Universities–Master's (South), 6
Acceptance Rate: 69%

Other expenses: Estimated books and supplies: $1,000. Personal expenses: $1,424. **Financial aid:** Priority filing date for institution's financial aid form: February 15. In 2003-2004, 68% of undergraduates applied for financial aid. Of those, 55% were determined to have financial need; 45% had their need fully met. Average financial aid package (proportion receiving): $16,895 (55%). Average amount of gift aid, such as scholarships or grants (proportion receiving): $11,964 (54%). Average amount of self-help aid, such as work study or loans (proportion receiving): $4,867 (40%). Average need-based loan (excluding PLUS or other private loans): $3,878. Among students who received need-based aid, the average percentage of need met: 82%. Among students who received aid based on merit, the average award (and the proportion receiving): $8,868 (32%). The average athletic scholarship (and the proportion receiving): $0 (0%). Average amount of debt of borrowers graduating in 2003: $18,125. Proportion who borrowed: 57%. **Student employment:** During the 2003-2004 academic year, 15% of undergraduates worked on campus. Average per-year earnings: $2,417. **Reserve Officers Training Corps (ROTC):** Army ROTC: Offered at cooperating institution (Tulane University); Navy ROTC: Offered at cooperating institution (Tulane University); Air Force ROTC: Offered at cooperating institution (Tulane University).

McNeese State University

4100 Ryan Street
Lake Charles, LA 70609
Public; www.mcneese.edu
Financial aid office: (337) 475-5065

■ **2004-2005 TUITION AND FEES:**
In state: $3,098; Out of state: $6,066
■ **ROOM AND BOARD:** $2,468

ACT Score (25th/75th percentile): 18-23
2005 U.S. News College Ranking:
Universities–Master's (South), fourth tier
Acceptance Rate: 88%

Financial aid: Priority filing date for institution's financial aid form: May 1. **Student employment:** During the 2003-2004 academic year, 10% of undergraduates worked on campus. Average per-year earnings: $2,000. **Cooperative education programs:** engineering, technologies.

Nicholls State University

PO Box 2004, University Station
Thibodaux, LA 70310
Public; www.nicholls.edu
Financial aid office: (985) 448-4048

■ **2004-2005 TUITION AND FEES:**
In state: $3,239; Out of state: $8,687
■ **ROOM AND BOARD:** $3,534

ACT Score (25th/75th percentile): 17-22
2005 U.S. News College Ranking:
Universities–Master's (South), fourth tier
Acceptance Rate: 99%

Other expenses: Estimated books and supplies: $1,000. Transportation: $864. Personal expenses: $1,500. **Financial aid:** Priority filing date for institution's financial aid form: April 17. **Student employment:** During the 2003-2004 academic year, 9% of undergraduates worked on campus. Average per-year earnings: $1,636.

Northwestern State University of Louisiana

College Avenue
Natchitoches, LA 71497
Public; www.nsula.edu
Financial aid office: (318) 357-5961

■ **2004-2005 TUITION AND FEES:**
In state: $3,241; Out of state: $9,319
■ **ROOM AND BOARD:** $3,426

ACT Score (25th/75th percentile): 17-22
2005 U.S. News College Ranking:
Universities–Master's (South), fourth tier
Acceptance Rate: 98%

Financial aid: Priority filing date for institution's financial aid form: May 1. Average amount of debt of borrowers graduating in 2003: $22,000. Proportion who borrowed: 85%. **Student employment:** During the 2003-2004 academic year, 8% of undergraduates worked on campus. Average per-year earnings: $1,524. **Reserve Officers Training Corps (ROTC):** Army ROTC: Offered on campus.

Our Lady of Holy Cross College

4123 Woodland Drive
New Orleans, LA 70131
Private; www.olhcc.edu
Financial aid office: (504) 398-2165

■ **2004-2005 TUITION AND FEES:** $6,240

ACT Score (25th/75th percentile): 20
2005 U.S. News College Ranking:
Comp. Colleges–Bachelor's (South), third tier
Acceptance Rate: 97%

Other expenses: Estimated books and supplies: $0. Transportation: $0. Personal expenses: $0. **Financial aid:** Priority filing date for institution's financial aid form: April 15; deadline: July 23. In 2003-2004, 73% of undergraduates applied for financial aid. Of those, 63% were determined to have financial need; 4% had their need fully met. Average financial aid package (proportion receiving): $4,128 (63%). Average amount of gift aid, such as scholarships or grants (proportion receiving): $3,301 (54%). Average amount of self-help aid, such as work study or loans (proportion receiving): $2,865 (29%). Average need-based loan (excluding PLUS or other private loans): $2,865. Among students who received need-based aid, the average percentage of need met: 35%. Among students who received aid based on merit, the average award (and the proportion receiving): $4,664 (13%). The average athletic scholarship (and the proportion receiving): $0 (0%). Average amount of debt of borrowers graduating in 2003: $17,355. Proportion who borrowed: 98%. **Student employment:** During the 2003-2004 academic year, 1% of undergraduates worked on campus. **Reserve Officers Training Corps (ROTC):** Army ROTC: Offered at cooperating institution (Tulane University); Navy ROTC: Offered at cooperating institution (Tulane University); Air Force ROTC: Offered at cooperating institution (Tulane University).

Southeastern Louisiana University

SLU 10752
Hammond, LA 70402
Public; www.selu.edu
Financial aid office: (985) 549-2244

■ **2004-2005 TUITION AND FEES:**
In state: $3,191; Out of state: $8,519
■ **ROOM AND BOARD:** $4,290

ACT Score (25th/75th percentile): 18-22
2005 U.S. News College Ranking:
Universities–Master's (South), fourth tier
Acceptance Rate: 96%

Other expenses: Estimated books and supplies: $1,000. Transportation: $864. Personal expenses: $1,500. **Financial aid:** Priority filing date for institution's financial aid form: May 1. Average amount of debt of borrowers graduating in 2003: $12,527. Proportion who borrowed: 58%. **Student employment:** During the 2003-2004 academic year, 18% of undergraduates worked on campus. Average per-year earnings: $1,244. **Cooperative education programs:** art, business, computer science, education, health professions, home economics, humanities, natural science, social/behavioral science, technologies, vocational arts. **Reserve Officers Training Corps (ROTC):** Army ROTC: Offered at cooperating institution (Louisiana State University).

Southern University and A&M College

PO Box 9374
Baton Rouge, LA 70813
Public; www.subr.edu
Financial aid office: (225) 771-2790

- **2004-2005 TUITION AND FEES:**
  In state: $3,168; Out of state: $8,960
- **ROOM AND BOARD:** $4,310

ACT Score (25th/75th percentile): 16-19
2005 U.S. News College Ranking:
Universities–Master's (South), fourth tier
Acceptance Rate: 57%

....

Other expenses: Estimated books and supplies: $1,400. Transportation: $1,302. Personal expenses: $1,875. **Financial aid:** Priority filing date for institution's financial aid form: March 31; deadline: July 1. In 2003-2004, 94% of undergraduates applied for financial aid. Of those, 85% were determined to have financial need; 8% had their need fully met. Average financial aid package (proportion receiving): $7,098 (76%). Average amount of gift aid, such as scholarships or grants (proportion receiving): $3,680 (69%). Average amount of self-help aid, such as work study or loans (proportion receiving): $4,280 (62%). Average need-based loan (excluding PLUS or other private loans): $4,280. Among students who received need-based aid, the average percentage of need met: 65%. Among students who received aid based on merit, the average award (and the proportion receiving): $4,280 (3%). The average athletic scholarship (and the proportion receiving): $3,430 (10%). Average amount of debt of borrowers graduating in 2003: $17,000. Proportion who borrowed: 75%. **Cooperative education programs:** engineering. **Reserve Officers Training Corps (ROTC):** Army ROTC: Offered on campus; Navy ROTC: Offered on campus; Air Force ROTC: Offered at cooperating institution (Louisiana State University).

Southern University–New Orleans

6400 Press Drive
New Orleans, LA 70126
Public; www.suno.edu
Financial aid office: (504) 286-5263

- **2004-2005 TUITION AND FEES:**
  In state: $2,872

ACT Score (25th/75th percentile): 15
2005 U.S. News College Ranking:
Universities–Master's (South), fourth tier
Acceptance Rate: 69%

....

Tulane University

6823 St. Charles Avenue, 218 Gibson Hall
New Orleans, LA 70118
Private; www.tulane.edu
Financial aid office: (504) 865-5723

- **2004-2005 TUITION AND FEES:** $31,210
- **ROOM AND BOARD:** $7,925

SAT I Score (25th/75th percentile): 1240-1420
2005 U.S. News College Ranking:
National Universities, 43
Acceptance Rate: 55%

....

Other expenses: Estimated books and supplies: $800. Transportation: $800. Personal expenses: $800. **Financial aid:** Priority filing date for institution's financial aid form: February 1; deadline: February 1. In 2003-2004, 53% of undergraduates applied for financial aid. Of those, 42% were determined to have financial need; 64% had their need fully met. Average financial aid package (proportion receiving): $25,837 (42%). Average amount of gift aid, such as scholarships or grants (proportion receiving): $18,025 (40%). Average amount of self-help aid, such as work study or loans (proportion receiving): $6,808 (30%). Average need-based loan (excluding PLUS or other private loans): $6,131. Among students who received need-based aid, the average percentage of need met: 91%. Among students who received aid based on merit, the average award (and the proportion receiving): $15,306 (29%). The average athletic scholarship (and the proportion receiving): $28,469 (3%). Average amount of debt of borrowers graduating in 2003: $20,755. Proportion who borrowed: 52%. **Student employment:** During the 2003-2004 academic year, 25% of undergraduates worked

on campus. Average per-year earnings: $2,800. **Reserve Officers Training Corps (ROTC):** Army ROTC: Offered on campus; Navy ROTC: Offered on campus; Air Force ROTC: Offered on campus.

University of Louisiana–Lafayette

PO Drawer 41008
Lafayette, LA 70504-1008
Public; www.louisiana.edu
Financial aid office: (337) 482-6506

- **2004-2005 TUITION AND FEES:**
  In state: $3,124; Out of state: $9,304
- **ROOM AND BOARD:** $3,126

ACT Score (25th/75th percentile): 18-23
2005 U.S. News College Ranking:
National Universities, fourth tier
Acceptance Rate: 87%

....

Other expenses: Estimated books and supplies: $1,000. Transportation: $883. Personal expenses: $1,533. **Financial aid:** Priority filing date for institution's financial aid form: May 1. In 2003-2004, 88% of undergraduates applied for financial aid. Of those, 66% were determined to have financial need; 69% had their need fully met. Average financial aid package (proportion receiving): $4,500 (57%). Average amount of gift aid, such as scholarships or grants (proportion receiving): $2,200 (34%). Average amount of self-help aid, such as work study or loans (proportion receiving): $800 (34%). Average need-based loan (excluding PLUS or other private loans): $4,200. Among students who received need-based aid, the average percentage of need met: 88%. Among students who received aid based on merit, the average award (and the proportion receiving): $2,631 (40%). The average athletic scholarship (and the proportion receiving): $3,837 (3%). Average amount of debt of borrowers graduating in 2003: $15,000. **Student employment:** During the 2003-2004 academic year, 5% of undergraduates worked on campus. Average per-year earnings: $1,364. **Reserve Officers Training Corps (ROTC):** Army ROTC: Offered on campus.

University of Louisiana–Monroe

700 University Avenue
Monroe, LA 71209
Public; www.ulm.edu
Financial aid office: (318) 342-5320

■ **2004-2005 TUITION AND FEES:**
In state: $3,075; Out of state: $9,028
■ **ROOM AND BOARD:** $5,080

ACT Score (25th/75th percentile): 17-23
2005 U.S. News College Ranking:
Universities–Master's (South), fourth tier
Acceptance Rate: 99%

Reserve Officers Training Corps (ROTC): Army ROTC: Offered on campus.

University of New Orleans

2000 Lakeshore Drive
New Orleans, LA 70148
Public; www.uno.edu
Financial aid office: (504) 280-6603

■ **2004-2005 TUITION AND FEES:**
In state: $3,464; Out of state: $10,508
■ **ROOM AND BOARD:** $4,122

ACT Score (25th/75th percentile): 18-23
2005 U.S. News College Ranking:
National Universities, fourth tier
Acceptance Rate: 70%

Other expenses: Estimated books and supplies: $1,150. Transportation: $882. Personal expenses: $1,490. **Financial aid:** Priority filing date for institution's financial aid form: May 15. In 2003-2004, 78% of undergraduates applied for financial aid. Of those, 61% were determined to have financial need; 6% had their need fully met. Average financial aid package (proportion receiving): $5,605 (56%). Average amount of gift aid, such as scholarships or grants (proportion receiving): $3,134 (37%). Average amount of self-help aid, such as work study or loans (proportion receiving): $3,488 (38%). Average need-based loan (excluding PLUS or other private loans): $3,436. Among students who received need-based aid, the average percentage of need met: 70%. Among students who received aid based on merit, the average award

(and the proportion receiving): $1,319 (2%). The average athletic scholarship (and the proportion receiving): $7,838 (1%). **Student employment:** During the 2003-2004 academic year, 12% of undergraduates worked on campus. Average per-year earnings: $2,137. **Reserve Officers Training Corps (ROTC):** Army ROTC: Offered at cooperating institution (Tulane University); Navy ROTC: Offered at cooperating institution (Tulane University); Air Force ROTC: Offered at cooperating institution (Tulane University).

Xavier University of Louisiana

1 Drexel Drive
New Orleans, LA 70125
Private; www.xula.edu
Financial aid office: (504) 520-7517

■ **2004-2005 TUITION AND FEES:** $11,400
■ **ROOM AND BOARD:** $6,200

ACT Score (25th/75th percentile): 18-23
2005 U.S. News College Ranking:
Universities–Master's (South), 25
Acceptance Rate: 84%

Other expenses: Estimated books and supplies: $1,000. Transportation: $864. Personal expenses: $1,500. **Financial aid:** Priority filing date for institution's financial aid form: January 1. In 2003-2004, 90% of undergraduates applied for financial aid. Of those, 80% were determined to have financial need; Average financial aid package (proportion receiving): $4,695 (80%). Average amount of gift aid, such as scholarships or grants (proportion receiving): $3,886 (56%). Average amount of self-help aid, such as work study or loans (proportion receiving): $2,166 (54%). Average need-based loan (excluding PLUS or other private loans): $4,400. Among students who received need-based aid, the average percentage of need met: 74%. Among students who received aid based on merit, the average award (and the proportion receiving): $3,046 (3%). The average athletic scholarship (and the proportion receiving): $6,074 (2%). Average amount of debt of borrowers graduating in 2003: $15,292. Proportion who borrowed: 66%. **Reserve Officers Training Corps (ROTC):** Army ROTC: Offered at cooperating institution (Tulane University); Navy ROTC: Offered at cooperating institution (Tulane University); Air Force ROTC: Offered at cooperating institution (Tulane University).

Maine

Bates College

23 Campus Avenue
Lewiston, ME 04240
Private; www.bates.edu
Financial aid office: (207) 786-6096

■ **2004-2005 TUITION/FEES/ROOM AND BOARD:** $39,900

SAT I Score (25th/75th percentile): 1270-1410
2005 U.S. News College Ranking:
Liberal Arts Colleges, 22
Acceptance Rate: 31%

Financial aid: Priority filing date for institution's financial aid form: February 1. In 2003-2004, 48% of undergraduates applied for financial aid. Of those, 43% were determined to have financial need; 88% had their need fully met. Average financial aid package (proportion receiving): $24,457 (40%). Average amount of gift aid, such as scholarships or grants (proportion receiving): $21,234 (38%). Average amount of self-help aid, such as work study or loans (proportion receiving): $4,716 (36%). Average need-based loan (excluding PLUS or other private loans): $3,335. Among students who received need-based aid, the average percentage of need met: 100%. Average amount of debt of borrowers graduating in 2003: $14,401. Proportion who borrowed: 50%. **Student employment:** During the 2003-2004 academic year, 54% of undergraduates worked on campus. Average per-year earnings: $2,730.

Bowdoin College

5700 College Station (President's Office)
Brunswick, ME 04011-8448
Private; www.bowdoin.edu
Financial aid office: (207) 725-3273

■ **2004-2005 TUITION AND FEES:** $31,626
■ **ROOM AND BOARD:** $8,054

SAT I Score (25th/75th percentile): 1290-1440
2005 U.S. News College Ranking:
Liberal Arts Colleges, 7
Acceptance Rate: 24%

Other expenses: Estimated books and supplies: $880. Personal expenses: $1,190. **Financial aid:**

In 2003-2004, 54% of undergraduates applied for financial aid. Of those, 45% were determined to have financial need; 100% had their need fully met. Average financial aid package (proportion receiving): $25,295 (45%). Average amount of gift aid, such as scholarships or grants (proportion receiving): $21,437 (45%). Average amount of self-help aid, such as work study or loans (proportion receiving): $4,864 (41%). Average need-based loan (excluding PLUS or other private loans): $3,890. Among students who received need-based aid, the average percentage of need met: 100%. Among students who received aid based on merit, the average award (and the proportion receiving): $1,000 (3%). The average athletic scholarship (and the proportion receiving): $0 (0%). Average amount of debt of borrowers graduating in 2003: $14,830. Proportion who borrowed: 46%. **Student employment:** During the 2003-2004 academic year, 44% of undergraduates worked on campus. Average per-year earnings: $1,500.

Colby College

4000 Mayflower Hill
Waterville, ME 04901-8840
Private; www.colby.edu
Financial aid office: (207) 872-3168

■ **2004-2005 TUITION/FEES/ROOM AND BOARD:** $39,800

SAT I Score (25th/75th percentile): 1270-1420
2005 U.S. News College Ranking:
Liberal Arts Colleges, 19
Acceptance Rate: 34%

Financial aid: In 2003-2004, 46% of undergraduates applied for financial aid. Of those, 40% were determined to have financial need; 100% had their need fully met. Average financial aid package (proportion receiving): $24,111 (40%). Average amount of gift aid, such as scholarships or grants (proportion receiving): $22,766 (37%). Average amount of self-help aid, such as work study or loans (proportion receiving): $3,862 (32%). Average need-based loan (excluding PLUS or other private loans): $2,991. Among students who received need-based aid, the average percentage of need met: 100%. Average amount of debt of borrowers graduating in 2003: $17,809. Proportion who

borrowed: 42%. **Student employment:** During the 2003-2004 academic year, 41% of undergraduates worked on campus. Average per-year earnings: $905. **Reserve Officers Training Corps (ROTC):** Army ROTC: Offered at cooperating institution (University of Maine).

College of the Atlantic

105 Eden Street
Bar Harbor, ME 04609
Private; www.coa.edu
Financial aid office: (800) 528-0025

■ **2004-2005 TUITION AND FEES:** $23,961
■ **ROOM AND BOARD:** $6,543

SAT I Score (25th/75th percentile): 1090-1320
2005 U.S. News College Ranking:
Liberal Arts Colleges, third tier
Acceptance Rate: 69%

Other expenses: Estimated books and supplies: $800. Transportation: $160. Personal expenses: $200. **Financial aid:** Priority filing date for institution's financial aid form: February 15; deadline: February 15. In 2003-2004, 88% of undergraduates applied for financial aid. Of those, 86% were determined to have financial need; 74% had their need fully met. Average financial aid package (proportion receiving): $21,823 (86%). Average amount of gift aid, such as scholarships or grants (proportion receiving): $18,900 (75%). Average amount of self-help aid, such as work study or loans (proportion receiving): $4,664 (74%). Average need-based loan (excluding PLUS or other private loans): $4,077. Among students who received need-based aid, the average percentage of need met: 85%. Among students who received aid based on merit, the average award (and the proportion receiving): $2,250 (1%). The average athletic scholarship (and the proportion receiving): $0 (0%). Average amount of debt of borrowers graduating in 2003: $13,882. Proportion who borrowed: 61%. **Student employment:** During the 2003-2004 academic year, 20% of undergraduates worked on campus. Average per-year earnings: $3,500. **Cooperative education programs:** education.

Husson College

1 College Circle
Bangor, ME 04401
Private; www.husson.edu
Financial aid office: (207) 941-7156

■ **2004-2005 TUITION AND FEES:** $11,050
■ **ROOM AND BOARD:** $5,850

ACT Score (25th/75th percentile): 18-28
2005 U.S. News College Ranking:
Universities–Master's (North), fourth tier
Acceptance Rate: 97%

Other expenses: Estimated books and supplies: $930. Transportation: $460. Personal expenses: $1,180. **Financial aid:** Priority filing date for institution's financial aid form: April 15; deadline: April 15. In 2003-2004, 71% of undergraduates applied for financial aid. Of those, 59% were determined to have financial need; 24% had their need fully met. Average financial aid package (proportion receiving): $8,287 (59%). Average amount of gift aid, such as scholarships or grants (proportion receiving): $5,799 (54%). Average amount of self-help aid, such as work study or loans (proportion receiving): $3,695 (48%). Average need-based loan (excluding PLUS or other private loans): $3,143. Among students who received need-based aid, the average percentage of need met: 75%. Among students who received aid based on merit, the average award (and the proportion receiving): $5,291 (16%). The average athletic scholarship (and the proportion receiving): $0 (0%). Average amount of debt of borrowers graduating in 2003: $17,125. Proportion who borrowed: 96%. **Student employment:** During the 2003-2004 academic year, 42% of undergraduates worked on campus. Average per-year earnings: $1,625. **Reserve Officers Training Corps (ROTC):** Army ROTC: Offered at cooperating institution (University of Maine Orono); Navy ROTC: Offered at cooperating institution (University of Maine Orono).

Maine College of Art

97 Spring Street
Portland, ME 04101
Private; www.meca.edu
Financial aid office: (207) 775-3052

■ **2004-2005 TUITION AND FEES:** $22,343
■ **ROOM AND BOARD:** $8,254

SAT I Score (25th/75th percentile): 960-1170
2005 U.S. News College Ranking:
Unranked Specialty School–Fine Arts
Acceptance Rate: 87%

Financial aid: Priority filing date for institution's financial aid form: March 1; deadline: April 15. In 2003-2004, 88% of undergraduates applied for financial aid. Of those, 80% were determined to have financial need; 12% had their need fully met. Average financial aid package (proportion receiving): $12,591 (80%). Average amount of gift aid, such as scholarships or grants (proportion receiving): $8,691 (80%). Average amount of self-help aid, such as work study or loans (proportion receiving): $4,355 (72%). Average need-based loan (excluding PLUS or other private loans): $3,935. Among students who received need-based aid, the average percentage of need met: 58%. Among students who received aid based on merit, the average award (and the proportion receiving): $8,422 (19%). The average athletic scholarship (and the proportion receiving): $0 (0%). Average amount of debt of borrowers graduating in 2003: $21,429. Proportion who borrowed: 91%. **Student employment:** During the 2003-2004 academic year, 1% of undergraduates worked on campus. Average per-year earnings: $1,500. **Cooperative education programs:** art, education.

St. Joseph's College

278 Whites Bridge Road
Standish, ME 04084
Private; www.sjcme.edu
Financial aid office: (800) 752-1266

■ **2004-2005 TUITION AND FEES:** $19,615
■ **ROOM AND BOARD:** $8,160

SAT I Score (25th/75th percentile): 880-1110
2005 U.S. News College Ranking:
Universities–Master's (North), third tier
Acceptance Rate: 79%

Other expenses: Estimated books and supplies: $800. Transportation: $400. Personal expenses: $1,255. **Financial aid:** Priority filing date for institution's financial aid form: March 1. In 2003-2004, 92% of undergraduates applied for financial aid. Of those, 85% were determined to have financial need; 31% had their need fully met. Average financial aid package (proportion receiving): $15,022 (85%). Average amount of gift aid, such as scholarships or grants (proportion receiving): $9,531 (85%). Average amount of self-help aid, such as work study or loans (proportion receiving): $6,119 (76%). Average need-based loan (excluding PLUS or other pri-

vate loans): $5,584. Among students who received need-based aid, the average percentage of need met: 80%. Among students who received aid based on merit, the average award (and the proportion receiving): $10,430 (14%). The average athletic scholarship (and the proportion receiving): $0 (0%). Average amount of debt of borrowers graduating in 2003: $23,350. Proportion who borrowed: 95%. **Student employment:** During the 2003-2004 academic year, 8% of undergraduates worked on campus. Average per-year earnings: $1,200. **Cooperative education programs:** education, health professions. **Reserve Officers Training Corps (ROTC):** Army ROTC: Offered at cooperating institution (University of New Hampshire).

Thomas College

180 W. River Road
Waterville, ME 04901
Private; www.thomas.edu
Financial aid office: (207) 859-1105

■ **2004-2005 TUITION AND FEES:** $15,520
■ **ROOM AND BOARD:** $6,760

SAT I Score (25th/75th percentile): 830-1030
2005 U.S. News College Ranking:
Unranked Specialty School–Business
Acceptance Rate: 73%

Other expenses: Estimated books and supplies: $700. Transportation: $1,000. Personal expenses: $1,000. **Financial aid:** Priority filing date for institution's financial aid form: February 15. In 2003-2004, 94% of undergraduates applied for financial aid. Of those, 87% were determined to have financial need; 3% had their need fully met. Average financial aid package (proportion receiving): $11,366 (87%). Average amount of gift aid, such as scholarships or grants (proportion receiving): $5,919 (87%). Average amount of self-help aid, such as work study or loans (proportion receiving): $1,700 (80%). Average need-based loan (excluding PLUS or other private loans): $5,447. Among students who received need-based aid, the average percentage of need met: 85%. Among students who received aid based on merit, the average award (and the proportion receiving): $9,128 (7%). The average athletic scholarship (and the proportion receiving): $0 (0%). Average amount of debt of borrowers graduating in 2003: $21,125. Proportion who borrowed: 78%. **Student employment:** During the 2003-2004 academic year, 4% of undergraduates worked on campus. Average per-year earnings: $1,250.

Unity College

90 Quaker Hill Road
Unity, ME 04988
Private; www.unity.edu
Financial aid office: (207) 948-3131

■ **2004-2005 TUITION AND FEES:** $16,190
■ **ROOM AND BOARD:** $6,250

SAT I Score (25th/75th percentile): 870-1110
2005 U.S. News College Ranking:
Comp. Colleges–Bachelor's (North), fourth tier
Acceptance Rate: 89%

Other expenses: Estimated books and supplies: $400. Transportation: $350. Personal expenses: $550. **Financial aid:** In 2003-2004, 91% of undergraduates applied for financial aid. Of those, 80% were determined to have financial need; 29% had their need fully met. Average financial aid package (proportion receiving): $12,407 (80%). Average amount of gift aid, such as scholarships or grants (proportion receiving): $6,931 (78%). Average amount of self-help aid, such as work study or loans (proportion receiving): $5,918 (76%). Average need-based loan (excluding PLUS or other private loans): $4,903. Among students who received need-based aid, the average percentage of need met: 79%. Among students who received aid based on merit, the average award (and the proportion receiving): $9,034 (16%). The average athletic scholarship (and the proportion receiving): $0 (0%). **Student employment:** During the 2003-2004 academic year, 7% of undergraduates worked on campus. Average per-year earnings: $1,800.

University of Maine–Augusta

46 University Drive
Augusta, ME 04330
Public; www.uma.edu
Financial aid office: (207) 621-3163

■ **2004-2005 TUITION AND FEES:**
   In state: $4,665; Out of state: $10,305

SAT I Score (25th/75th percentile): 952
2005 U.S. News College Ranking:
Comp. Colleges–Bachelor's (North), fourth tier
Acceptance Rate: 92%

Other expenses: Estimated books and supplies: $1,000. Transportation: $1,200. Personal expenses: $1,600. **Financial aid:** Priority filing date for institution's financial aid form: March 1. In 2003-2004, 89% of undergraduates applied for finan-

cial aid. Of those, 90% were determined to have financial need; 14% had their need fully met. Average financial aid package (proportion receiving): $6,778 (83%). Average amount of gift aid, such as scholarships or grants (proportion receiving): $4,788 (73%). Average amount of self-help aid, such as work study or loans (proportion receiving): $3,553 (60%). Average need-based loan (excluding PLUS or other private loans): $3,409. Among students who received need-based aid, the average percentage of need met: 67%. Among students who received aid based on merit, the average award (and the proportion receiving): $3,856 (5%). The average athletic scholarship (and the proportion receiving): $2,174 (0%). Average amount of debt of borrowers graduating in 2003: $11,993. Proportion who borrowed: 63%. Average per-year earnings: $3,930. **Reserve Officers Training Corps (ROTC):** Army ROTC: Offered at cooperating institution (University of Maine); Navy ROTC: Offered at cooperating institution (University of Maine); Air Force ROTC: Offered at cooperating institution (University of Maine).

University of Maine–Farmington

111 South Street
Farmington, ME 04938
Public; www.umf.maine.edu
Financial aid office: (207) 778-7100

■ **2004-2005 TUITION AND FEES:**
   In state: $5,150; Out of state: $11,840
■ **ROOM AND BOARD:** $5,568

SAT I Score (25th/75th percentile): 950-1160
2005 U.S. News College Ranking:
Comp. Colleges–Bachelor's (North), 19
Acceptance Rate: 72%

Other expenses: Estimated books and supplies: $600. Transportation: $510. Personal expenses: $1,728. **Financial aid:** Priority filing date for institution's financial aid form: March 1. In 2003-2004, 81% of undergraduates applied for financial aid. Of those, 67% were determined to have financial need; 15% had their need fully met. Average financial aid package (proportion receiving): $8,879 (67%). Average amount of gift aid, such as scholarships or grants (proportion receiving): $4,049 (55%). Average amount of self-help aid, such as work study or loans (proportion receiving): $4,305 (60%). Average need-based loan (excluding PLUS or other private loans): $3,744. Among students who received need-based aid, the average percentage of need met: 77%. Among students who

received aid based on merit, the average award (and the proportion receiving): $2,780 (3%). The average athletic scholarship (and the proportion receiving): $0 (0%). Average amount of debt of borrowers graduating in 2003: $15,471. Proportion who borrowed: 75%. **Student employment:** During the 2003-2004 academic year, 45% of undergraduates worked on campus. Average per-year earnings: $1,590.

University of Maine–Fort Kent

23 University Drive
Fort Kent, ME 04743
Public; www.umfk.maine.edu
Financial aid office: (888) 879-8635

■ **2004-2005 TUITION AND FEES:**
   In state: $4,514; Out of state: $10,154
■ **ROOM AND BOARD:** $5,511

2005 U.S. News College Ranking:
Comp. Colleges–Bachelor's (North), fourth tier
Acceptance Rate: 86%

Financial aid: Priority filing date for institution's financial aid form: March 15. Average per-year earnings: $1,500. **Cooperative education programs:** business, social/behavioral science.

University of Maine–Machias

9 O'Brien Avenue
Machias, ME 04654
Public; www.umm.maine.edu
Financial aid office: (207) 255-1203

■ **2003-2004 TUITION AND FEES:**
   In state: $4,115; Out of state: $10,115
■ **ROOM AND BOARD:** $5,150

SAT I Score (25th/75th percentile): 840-1040
2005 U.S. News College Ranking:
Comp. Colleges–Bachelor's (North), third tier
Acceptance Rate: 82%

Other expenses: Estimated books and supplies: $650. Transportation: $900. Personal expenses: $1,600. **Financial aid:** Priority filing date for institution's financial aid form: March 1. **Student employment:** During the 2003-2004 academic year, 13% of undergraduates worked on campus. Average per-year earnings: $1,720. **Cooperative education programs:** business, natural science, social/behavioral science, other.

University of Maine–Orono

168 College Avenue
Orono, ME 04469
Public; www.umaine.edu
Financial aid office: (207) 581-1324

■ **2004-2005 TUITION AND FEES:**
In state: $6,394; Out of state: $15,784
■ **ROOM AND BOARD:** $6,412

SAT I Score (25th/75th percentile): 970-1190
2005 U.S. News College Ranking:
National Universities, third tier
Acceptance Rate: 76%

Other expenses: Estimated books and supplies: $700. Transportation: $500. Personal expenses: $1,100. **Financial aid:** Priority filing date for institution's financial aid form: March 1. In 2003-2004, 81% of undergraduates applied for financial aid. Of those, 67% were determined to have financial need; 26% had their need fully met. Average financial aid package (proportion receiving): $8,853 (65%). Average amount of gift aid, such as scholarships or grants (proportion receiving): $4,931 (51%). Average amount of self-help aid, such as work study or loans (proportion receiving): $4,659 (58%). Average need-based loan (excluding PLUS or other private loans): $4,220. Among students who received need-based aid, the average percentage of need met: 86%. Among students who received aid based on merit, the average award (and the proportion receiving): $5,096 (17%). The average athletic scholarship (and the proportion receiving): $11,551 (0%). Average amount of debt of borrowers graduating in 2003: $18,922. Proportion who borrowed: 74%. **Student employment:** During the 2003-2004 academic year, 11% of undergraduates worked on campus. Average per-year earnings: $2,150. **Cooperative education programs:** agriculture, business, computer science, education, engineering, health professions, humanities, natural science, social/behavioral science, technologies, other. **Reserve Officers Training Corps (ROTC):** Army ROTC: Offered on campus; Navy ROTC: Offered on campus.

University of Maine–Presque Isle

181 Main Street
Presque Isle, ME 04769
Public; www.umpi.maine.edu
Financial aid office: (207) 768-9510

■ **2004-2005 TUITION AND FEES:**
In state: $4,460; Out of state: $10,400
■ **ROOM AND BOARD:** $5,114

2005 U.S. News College Ranking:
Liberal Arts Colleges, fourth tier
Acceptance Rate: 87%

Other expenses: Estimated books and supplies: $700. Transportation: $1,100. Personal expenses: $1,100. **Financial aid:** Priority filing date for institution's financial aid form: April 1. In 2003-2004, 72% of undergraduates applied for financial aid. Of those, 65% were determined to have financial need; 36% had their need fully met. Average financial aid package (proportion receiving): $6,854 (62%). Average amount of gift aid, such as scholarships or grants (proportion receiving): $4,501 (57%). Average amount of self-help aid, such as work study or loans (proportion receiving): $3,311 (47%). Average need-based loan (excluding PLUS or other private loans): $2,821. Among students who received need-based aid, the average percentage of need met: 87%. Among students who received aid based on merit, the average award (and the proportion receiving): $4,219 (7%). The average athletic scholarship (and the proportion receiving): $0 (0%). Average amount of debt of borrowers graduating in 2003: $11,128. Proportion who borrowed: 52%. **Student employment:** During the 2003-2004 academic year, 8% of undergraduates worked on campus. Average per-year earnings: $800. **Cooperative education programs:** business, education, health professions, other.

University of New England

Hills Beach Road
Biddeford, ME 04005
Private; www.une.edu
Financial aid office: (207) 283-0171

■ **2004-2005 TUITION AND FEES:** $20,875
■ **ROOM AND BOARD:** $8,050

SAT I Score (25th/75th percentile): 920-1140
2005 U.S. News College Ranking:
Universities–Master's (North), 68
Acceptance Rate: 97%

Other expenses: Estimated books and supplies: $800. Transportation: $1,025. Personal expenses: $925. **Financial aid:** In 2003-2004, 91% of undergraduates applied for financial aid. Of those, 85% were determined to have financial need; 9% had their need fully met. Average financial aid package (proportion receiving): $17,240 (85%). Average amount of gift aid, such as scholarships or grants (proportion receiving): $8,249 (84%). Average amount of self-help aid, such as work study or loans (proportion receiving): $9,765 (79%). Average need-based loan (excluding PLUS or other private loans): $9,248. Among students who received need-based aid, the average percentage of need met: 77%. Among students who received aid based on merit, the average award (and the proportion receiving): $6,264 (12%). The average athletic scholarship (and the proportion receiving): $0 (0%). Average amount of debt of borrowers graduating in 2003: $28,421. Proportion who borrowed: 80%. **Reserve Officers Training Corps (ROTC):** Army ROTC: Offered at cooperating institution (UNH).

University of Southern Maine

37 College Avenue
Gorham, ME 04038
Public; www.usm.maine.edu
Financial aid office: (207) 780-5250

■ **2004-2005 TUITION AND FEES:**
In state: $5,468; Out of state: $13,598
■ **ROOM AND BOARD:** $6,502

SAT I Score (25th/75th percentile): 940-1130
2005 U.S. News College Ranking:
Universities–Master's (North), third tier
Acceptance Rate: 72%

Other expenses: Estimated books and supplies: $807. Transportation: $1,285. Personal expenses: $1,714. **Financial aid:** Priority filing date for institution's financial aid form: February 15. In 2003-2004, 87% of undergraduates applied for financial aid. Of those, 76% were determined to have financial need; 24% had their need fully met. Average financial aid package (proportion receiving): $8,938 (73%). Average amount of gift aid, such as scholarships or grants (proportion receiving): $3,833 (55%). Average amount of self-help aid, such as work study or loans (proportion receiving): $5,672 (66%). Average need-based loan (excluding PLUS or other private loans): $4,382. Among students who received need-based aid, the average percentage of need met: 81%. Among students who received aid based on merit, the average award (and the proportion receiving): $4,267 (9%). The average athletic scholarship (and the proportion receiving): $0 (0%). Average amount of debt of borrowers graduating in 2003: $21,720. Proportion who borrowed: 54%. **Cooperative education programs:** art, business, computer science, education, engineering, health professions, humanities, natural science, social/behavioral science, technologies, vocational arts. **Reserve Officers Training Corps (ROTC):** Army ROTC: Offered at cooperating institution (UNH); Air Force ROTC: Offered at cooperating institution (UNH).

Maryland

Bowie State University

14000 Jericho Park Road
Bowie, MD 20715-9465
Public; www.bowiestate.edu
Financial aid office: (301) 860-3540

■ **2004-2005 TUITION AND FEES:**
In state: $4,722; Out of state: $12,065
■ **ROOM AND BOARD:** $6,020

SAT I Score (25th/75th percentile): 790-960
2005 U.S. News College Ranking:
Universities–Master's (North), fourth tier
Acceptance Rate: 64%

Other expenses: Estimated books and supplies: $1,236. Transportation: $1,111. Personal expenses: $1,667. **Financial aid:** In 2003-2004, 86% of undergraduates applied for financial aid. Of those, 66% were determined to have financial need; 11% had their need fully met. Average financial aid package (proportion receiving): $7,377 (61%). Average amount of gift aid, such as scholarships or grants (proportion receiving): $4,312 (47%). Average amount of self-help aid, such as work study or loans (proportion receiving): $3,728 (45%). Average need-based loan (excluding PLUS or other private loans): $3,728. Among students who received need-based aid, the average percentage of need met: 60%. Among students who received aid based on merit, the average award (and the proportion receiving): $4,361 (11%). The average athletic scholarship (and the proportion receiving): $2,307 (6%). **Reserve Officers Training Corps (ROTC):** Army ROTC: Offered on campus; Air Force ROTC: Offered at cooperating institution (University of Maryland–College Park).

Capitol College

11301 Springfield Road
Laurel, MD 20708
Private; www.capitol-college.edu
Financial aid office: (301) 369-2800

■ **2004-2005 TUITION AND FEES:** $17,444
■ **ROOM AND BOARD:** $3,850

SAT I Score (25th/75th percentile): 750-1110
2005 U.S. News College Ranking:
Unranked Specialty School–Engineering
Acceptance Rate: 89%

Other expenses: Estimated books and supplies: $1,000. Transportation: $1,100. Personal expenses: $1,500. **Financial aid:** Priority filing date for institution's financial aid form: March 1; deadline: March 1. In 2003-2004, 87% of undergraduates applied for financial aid. Of those, 83% were determined to have financial need; 36% had their need fully met. Average financial aid package (proportion receiving): $8,758 (72%). Average amount of gift aid, such as scholarships or grants (proportion receiving): $6,357 (67%). Average amount of self-help aid, such as work study or loans (proportion receiving): $5,140 (71%). Average need-based loan (excluding PLUS or other private loans): $4,706. Among students who received need-based aid, the average percentage of need met: 56%. Among students who received aid based on merit, the average award (and the proportion receiving): $5,077 (17%). The average athletic scholarship (and the proportion receiving): $0 (0%). Average amount of debt of borrowers graduating in 2003: $19,594. Proportion who borrowed: 38%. **Cooperative education programs:** business, computer science, engineering, technologies.

College of Notre Dame of Maryland

4701 N. Charles Street
Baltimore, MD 21210
Private; www.ndm.edu
Financial aid office: (410) 532-5369

■ **2004-2005 TUITION AND FEES:** $20,300
■ **ROOM AND BOARD:** $7,800

SAT I Score (25th/75th percentile): 930-1120
2005 U.S. News College Ranking:
Universities–Master's (North), 33
Acceptance Rate: 73%

Other expenses: Estimated books and supplies: $800. Transportation: $250. Personal expenses: $800. **Financial aid:** Priority filing date for institution's financial aid form: February 15. In 2003-2004, 89% of undergraduates applied for financial aid. Of those, 81% were determined to

have financial need; 54% had their need fully met. Average financial aid package (proportion receiving): $19,127 (81%). Average amount of gift aid, such as scholarships or grants (proportion receiving): $14,417 (70%). Average amount of self-help aid, such as work study or loans (proportion receiving): $5,492 (59%). Average need-based loan (excluding PLUS or other private loans): $4,749. Among students who received need-based aid, the average percentage of need met: 100%. Among students who received aid based on merit, the average award (and the proportion receiving): $9,640 (16%). The average athletic scholarship (and the proportion receiving): $0 (0%). Average amount of debt of borrowers graduating in 2003: $17,178. Proportion who borrowed: 68%. Average per-year earnings: $1,500. **Reserve Officers Training Corps (ROTC):** Army ROTC: Offered at cooperating institution (Loyola College).

Columbia Union College

7600 Flower Avenue
Takoma Park, MD 20912
Private; www.cuc.edu
Financial aid office: (301) 891-4005

■ **2004-2005 TUITION AND FEES:** $16,433
■ **ROOM AND BOARD:** $5,560

SAT I Score (25th/75th percentile): 730-1022
2005 U.S. News College Ranking:
Comp. Colleges–Bachelor's (North), third tier
Acceptance Rate: 54%

Other expenses: Estimated books and supplies: $950. Transportation: $800. Personal expenses: $1,250. **Financial aid:** Priority filing date for institution's financial aid form: March 1. **Student employment:** During the 2003-2004 academic year, 33% of undergraduates worked on campus. Average per-year earnings: $5,500. **Cooperative education programs:** business, computer science, natural science.

Coppin State University

2500 W. North Avenue
Baltimore, MD 21216-3698
Public; www.coppin.edu
Financial aid office: (410) 951-3636

■ **2004-2005 TUITION AND FEES:**
In state: $4,599; Out of state: $10,771
■ **ROOM AND BOARD:** $6,236

SAT I Score (25th/75th percentile): 750-1000
2005 U.S. News College Ranking:
Universities–Master's (North), fourth tier
Acceptance Rate: 56%

Other expenses: Estimated books and supplies: $800. Transportation: $600. Personal expenses: $2,785. **Financial aid:** Priority filing date for institution's financial aid form: March 1. In 2003-2004, 80% of undergraduates applied for financial aid. Of those, 78% were determined to have financial need; 20% had their need fully met. Average financial aid package (proportion receiving): $6,606 (78%). Average amount of gift aid, such as scholarships or grants (proportion receiving): $4,663 (67%). Average amount of self-help aid, such as work study or loans (proportion receiving): $3,348 (66%). Average need-based loan (excluding PLUS or other private loans): $3,282. Among students who received need-based aid, the average percentage of need met: 74%. Among students who received aid based on merit, the average award (and the proportion receiving): $4,383 (25%). The average athletic scholarship (and the proportion receiving): $3,248 (5%). Average amount of debt of borrowers graduating in 2003: $17,844. Proportion who borrowed: 90%. Average per-year earnings: $4,220. **Cooperative education programs:** business, computer science, natural science, social/behavioral science. **Reserve Officers Training Corps (ROTC):** Army ROTC: Offered at cooperating institution (Cross Enrollment with Morgan State University).

Frostburg State University

101 Braddock Road
Frostburg, MD 21532
Public; www.frostburg.edu
Financial aid office: (301) 687-4301

■ **2004-2005 TUITION AND FEES:**
In state: $5,830; Out of state: $13,374
■ **ROOM AND BOARD:** $6,408

SAT I Score (25th/75th percentile): 920-1120
2005 U.S. News College Ranking:
Universities–Master's (North), third tier
Acceptance Rate: 79%

Other expenses: Estimated books and supplies: $1,000. Transportation: $500. Personal expenses: $1,000. **Financial aid:** Priority filing date for institution's financial aid form: March 1. In 2003-2004, 71% of undergraduates applied for financial aid. Of those, 51% were determined to have financial need; 36% had their need fully met. Average financial aid package (proportion receiving): $6,285 (50%). Average amount of gift aid, such as scholarships or grants (proportion receiving): $3,993 (34%). Average amount of self-help aid, such as work study or loans (proportion receiving): $3,261 (38%). Average need-based loan (excluding PLUS or other private loans): $3,144. Among students who received need-based aid, the average percentage of need met: 78%. Among students who received aid based on merit, the average award (and the proportion receiving): $3,523 (10%). The average athletic scholarship (and the proportion receiving): $0 (0%). Average amount of debt of borrowers graduating in 2003: $14,757. Proportion who borrowed: 64%. **Cooperative education programs:** engineering.

Goucher College

1021 Dulaney Valley Road
Baltimore, MD 21204
Private; www.goucher.edu
Financial aid office: (410) 337-6141

■ **2004-2005 TUITION AND FEES:** $26,150
■ **ROOM AND BOARD:** $8,425

SAT I Score (25th/75th percentile): 1110-1310
2005 U.S. News College Ranking:
Liberal Arts Colleges, 96
Acceptance Rate: 65%

Other expenses: Estimated books and supplies: $800. Transportation: $530. Personal expenses: $800. **Financial aid:** Priority filing date for institution's financial aid form: February 15; deadline: February 15. In 2003-2004, 67% of undergraduates applied for financial aid. Of those, 60% were determined to have financial need; 21% had their need fully met. Average financial aid package (proportion receiving): $18,020 (59%). Average amount of gift aid, such as scholarships or grants (proportion receiving): $15,009 (56%). Average amount of self-help aid, such as work study or loans (proportion receiving): $4,145 (49%). Average need-based

loan (excluding PLUS or other private loans): $3,835. Among students who received need-based aid, the average percentage of need met: 74%. Among students who received aid based on merit, the average award (and the proportion receiving): $9,613 (6%). The average athletic scholarship (and the proportion receiving): $0 (0%). Average amount of debt of borrowers graduating in 2003: $19,304. Proportion who borrowed: 66%. **Student employment:** During the 2003-2004 academic year, 8% of undergraduates worked on campus.

Hood College

401 Rosemont Avenue
Frederick, MD 21701
Private; www.hood.edu
Financial aid office: (301) 696-3411

■ **2004-2005 TUITION AND FEES:** $21,275
■ **ROOM AND BOARD:** $7,520

SAT I Score (25th/75th percentile): 960-1210
2005 U.S. News College Ranking:
Universities–Master's (North), 19
Acceptance Rate: 50%

Other expenses: Estimated books and supplies: $825. Transportation: $400. Personal expenses: $720. **Financial aid:** Priority filing date for institution's financial aid form: February 15. In 2003-2004, 88% of undergraduates applied for financial aid. Of those, 77% were determined to have financial need; 42% had their need fully met. Average financial aid package (proportion receiving): $17,518 (77%). Average amount of gift aid, such as scholarships or grants (proportion receiving): $13,899 (77%). Average amount of self-help aid, such as work study or loans (proportion receiving): $5,203 (55%). Average need-based loan (excluding PLUS or other private loans): $4,731. Among students who received need-based aid, the average percentage of need met: 90%. Among students who received aid based on merit, the average award (and the proportion receiving): $14,337 (22%). The average athletic scholarship (and the proportion receiving): $0 (0%). Average amount of debt of borrowers graduating in 2003: $17,392. Proportion who borrowed: 61%. **Student employment:** During the 2003-2004 academic year, 2% of undergraduates worked on campus. Average per-year earnings: $1,500.

Johns Hopkins University

3400 N. Charles Street
Baltimore, MD 21218
Private; www.jhu.edu
Financial aid office: (410) 516-8028

■ **2004-2005 TUITION AND FEES:** $30,140
■ **ROOM AND BOARD:** $9,516

SAT I Score (25th/75th percentile): 1290-1470
2005 U.S. News College Ranking:
National Universities, 14
Acceptance Rate: 30%

Other expenses: Estimated books and supplies: $850. Transportation: $700. Personal expenses: $800. **Financial aid:** Priority filing date for institution's financial aid form: February 1; deadline: February 15. In 2003-2004, 55% of undergraduates applied for financial aid. Of those, 41% were determined to have financial need; 85% had their need fully met. Average financial aid package (proportion receiving): $26,257 (40%). Average amount of gift aid, such as scholarships or grants (proportion receiving): $20,599 (37%). Average amount of self-help aid, such as work study or loans (proportion receiving): $5,239 (40%). Average need-based loan (excluding PLUS or other private loans): $3,931. Among students who received need-based aid, the average percentage of need met: 95%. Among students who received aid based on merit, the average award (and the proportion receiving): $13,096 (5%). The average athletic scholarship (and the proportion receiving): $23,395 (1%). Average amount of debt of borrowers graduating in 2003: $13,300. Proportion who borrowed: 46%. **Student employment:** During the 2003-2004 academic year, 55% of undergraduates worked on campus. Average per-year earnings: $5,000. **Reserve Officers Training Corps (ROTC):** Army ROTC: Offered on campus; Air Force ROTC: Offered at cooperating institution (University of Maryland, College Park).

Loyola College in Maryland

4501 N. Charles Street
Baltimore, MD 21210
Private; www.loyola.edu
Financial aid office: (410) 617-2576

■ **2004-2005 TUITION AND FEES:** $27,450
■ **ROOM AND BOARD:** $8,830

SAT I Score (25th/75th percentile): 1130-1310
2005 U.S. News College Ranking:
Universities–Master's (North), 3
Acceptance Rate: 71%

Other expenses: Estimated books and supplies: $780. Transportation: $330. Personal expenses: $990. **Financial aid:** Priority filing date for institution's financial aid form: February 15; deadline: February 15. In 2003-2004, 59% of undergraduates applied for financial aid. Of those, 48% were determined to have financial need; 97% had their need fully met. Average financial aid package (proportion receiving): $17,375 (48%). Average amount of gift aid, such as scholarships or grants (proportion receiving): $10,030 (32%). Average amount of self-help aid, such as work study or loans (proportion receiving): $7,345 (42%). Average need-based loan (excluding PLUS or other private loans): $5,395. Among students who received need-based aid, the average percentage of need met: 97%. Among students who received aid based on merit, the average award (and the proportion receiving): $9,670 (16%). The average athletic scholarship (and the proportion receiving): $20,680 (5%). Average amount of debt of borrowers graduating in 2003: $15,870. Proportion who borrowed: 71%. **Student employment:** During the 2003-2004 academic year, 11% of undergraduates worked on campus. Average per-year earnings: $1,950. **Reserve Officers Training Corps (ROTC):** Army ROTC: Offered on campus; Air Force ROTC: Offered at cooperating institution (University of Maryland–College Park).

Maryland Institute College of Art

1300 Mount Royal Avenue
Baltimore, MD 21217
Private; www.mica.edu
Financial aid office: (410) 225-2285

■ **2004-2005 TUITION AND FEES:** $25,204
■ **ROOM AND BOARD:** $7,080

SAT I Score (25th/75th percentile): 1030-1270
2005 U.S. News College Ranking:
Unranked Specialty School–Fine Arts
Acceptance Rate: 50%

Other expenses: Estimated books and supplies: $1,400. Transportation: $700. Personal expenses: $600. **Financial aid: Reserve Officers Training Corps (ROTC):** Army ROTC: Offered at cooperating institution (Johns Hopkins University).

McDaniel College

2 College Hill
Westminster, MD 21157
Private; www.mcdaniel.edu
Financial aid office: (410) 857-2233

■ **2004-2005 TUITION AND FEES:** $24,800
■ **ROOM AND BOARD:** $5,600

SAT I Score (25th/75th percentile): 1020-1200
2005 U.S. News College Ranking:
Liberal Arts Colleges, third tier
Acceptance Rate: 83%

Other expenses: Estimated books and supplies: $900. Transportation: $400. Personal expenses: $670. **Financial aid:** Priority filing date for institution's financial aid form: March 1. In 2003-2004, 74% of undergraduates applied for financial aid. Of those, 63% were determined to have financial need; 30% had their need fully met. Average financial aid package (proportion receiving): $18,978 (63%). Average amount of gift aid, such as scholarships or grants (proportion receiving): $7,823 (62%). Average amount of self-help aid, such as work study or loans (proportion receiving): $5,585 (58%). Average need-based loan (excluding PLUS or other private loans): $4,505. Among students who received need-based aid, the average percentage of need met: 92%. Among students who received aid based on merit, the average award (and the proportion receiving): $7,876 (25%). The average athletic scholarship (and the proportion receiving): $0 (0%). Average amount of debt of borrowers graduating in 2003: $17,784. Proportion who borrowed: 57%. **Student employment:** During the 2003-2004 academic year, 12% of undergraduates worked on campus. Average per-year earnings: $872. **Reserve Officers Training Corps (ROTC):** Army ROTC: Offered on campus.

Morgan State University

1700 E. Cold Spring Lane
Baltimore, MD 21251
Public; www.morgan.edu
Financial aid office: (443) 885-3170

■ **2004-2005 TUITION AND FEES:**
   In state: $5,718; Out of state: $12,958
■ **ROOM AND BOARD:** $6,780

SAT I Score (25th/75th percentile): 820-990
2005 U.S. News College Ranking:
Universities–Master's (North), fourth tier
Acceptance Rate: 34%

Other expenses: Estimated books and supplies: $2,100. Transportation: $350. Personal expenses: $2,300. **Financial aid:** In 2003-2004, 97% of undergraduates applied for financial aid. Of those, 97% were determined to have financial need; Average financial aid package (proportion receiving): N/A (97%). Average amount of gift aid, such as scholarships or grants (proportion receiving): N/A (97%). The average athletic scholarship (and the proportion receiving): $5,398 (7%). Average amount of debt of borrowers graduating in 2003: $18,000. Proportion who borrowed: 91%. **Student employment:** During the 2003-2004 academic year, 6% of undergraduates worked on campus. Average per-year earnings: $2,500. **Cooperative education programs:** art, business, computer science, education, engineering, health professions, home economics, humanities, natural science, social/behavioral science, technologies. **Reserve Officers Training Corps (ROTC):** Army ROTC: Offered on campus.

Mount St. Mary's University

16300 Old Emmitsburg Road
Emmitsburg, MD 21727
Private; www.msmary.edu
Financial aid office: (301) 447-5207

■ **2004-2005 TUITION AND FEES:** $21,680
■ **ROOM AND BOARD:** $7,640

SAT I Score (25th/75th percentile): 970-1200
2005 U.S. News College Ranking:
Universities–Master's (North), 27
Acceptance Rate: 90%

Other expenses: Estimated books and supplies: $800. Transportation: $300. Personal expenses: $600. **Financial aid:** Priority filing date for institution's financial aid form: February 15; deadline: February 15. In 2003-2004, 74% of undergraduates applied for financial aid. Of those, 62% were determined to have financial need; 29% had their need fully met. Average financial aid package (proportion receiving): $15,125 (62%). Average amount of gift aid, such as scholarships or grants (proportion receiving): $11,425 (62%). Average amount of self-help aid, such as work study or loans (proportion receiving): $4,701 (49%). Average need-based loan (excluding PLUS or other private loans): $4,147. Among students who received need-based aid, the aver-

age percentage of need met: 79%. Among students who received aid based on merit, the average award (and the proportion receiving): $13,127 (34%). The average athletic scholarship (and the proportion receiving): $9,800 (7%). Average amount of debt of borrowers graduating in 2003: $15,940. Proportion who borrowed: 78%. **Reserve Officers Training Corps (ROTC):** Army ROTC: Offered at cooperating institution (McDaniel College).

Salisbury University

1101 Camden Avenue
Salisbury, MD 21801
Public; www.salisbury.edu
Financial aid office: (410) 543-6165

■ **2004-2005 TUITION AND FEES:**
In state: $5,976; Out of state: $13,554
■ **ROOM AND BOARD:** $7,050

SAT I Score (25th/75th percentile): 1040-1220
2005 U.S. News College Ranking:
Universities–Master's (North), 45
Acceptance Rate: 52%

Financial aid: Priority filing date for institution's financial aid form: February 1; deadline: May 31. In 2003-2004, 63% of undergraduates applied for financial aid. Of those, 41% were determined to have financial need; 22% had their need fully met. Average financial aid package (proportion receiving): $5,629 (40%). Average amount of gift aid, such as scholarships or grants (proportion receiving): $3,467 (22%). Average amount of self-help aid, such as work study or loans (proportion receiving): $3,481 (32%). Average need-based loan (excluding PLUS or other private loans): $3,433. Among students who received need-based aid, the average percentage of need met: 63%. Among students who received aid based on merit, the average award (and the proportion receiving): $3,129 (7%). **Student employment:** During the 2003-2004 academic year, 18% of undergraduates worked on campus. Average per-year earnings: $3,000. **Cooperative education programs:** natural science, social/behavioral science. **Reserve Officers Training Corps (ROTC):** Army ROTC: Offered at cooperating institution (Delaware State University).

St. John's College

PO Box 2800
Annapolis, MD 21404
Private; www.sjca.edu
Financial aid office: (410) 626-2502

■ **2004-2005 TUITION AND FEES:** $30,770
■ **ROOM AND BOARD:** $7,610

SAT I Score (25th/75th percentile): 1260-1440
2005 U.S. News College Ranking:
Liberal Arts Colleges, third tier
Acceptance Rate: 73%

St. Mary's College of Maryland

18952 E. Fisher Road
St. Mary's City, MD 20686-3001
Public; www.smcm.edu
Financial aid office: (240) 895-3000

■ **2004-2005 TUITION AND FEES:**
In state: $9,680; Out of state: $17,160
■ **ROOM AND BOARD:** $7,400

SAT I Score (25th/75th percentile): 1160-1360
2005 U.S. News College Ranking:
Liberal Arts Colleges, 87
Acceptance Rate: 55%

Other expenses: Estimated books and supplies: $1,000. Transportation: $300. Personal expenses: $1,500. **Financial aid:** Priority filing date for institution's financial aid form: March 1; deadline: March 1. In 2003-2004, 77% of undergraduates applied for financial aid. Of those, 44% were determined to have financial need; Average financial aid package (proportion receiving): $7,195 (44%). Average amount of gift aid, such as scholarships or grants (proportion receiving): $4,000 (26%). Average amount of self-help aid, such as work study or loans (proportion receiving): $5,500 (26%). Average need-based loan (excluding PLUS or other private loans): $5,500. Among students who received need-based aid, the average percentage of need met: 60%. Among students who received aid based on merit, the average award (and the proportion receiving): $4,500 (32%). The average athletic scholarship (and the proportion receiving): $0 (0%). Average amount of debt of borrowers graduating in 2003: $17,125. Proportion who borrowed: 68%. **Student employment:** During the 2003-2004 academic year, 29% of undergraduates worked on campus. Average per-year earnings: $1,005. **Cooperative education programs:** computer science.

Towson University

8000 York Road
Towson, MD 21252-0001
Public; www.towson.edu
Financial aid office: (410) 704-4236

■ **2004-2005 TUITION AND FEES:**
  In state: $6,672; Out of state: $15,352
■ **ROOM AND BOARD:** $6,468

SAT I Score (25th/75th percentile): 1003-1180
2005 U.S. News College Ranking:
Universities–Master's (North), 38
Acceptance Rate: 52%

Other expenses: Estimated books and supplies:
$800. Transportation: $1,500. Personal expenses: $1,500. **Financial aid:** Priority filing date for institution's financial aid form: January 31; deadline: March 1. In 2003-2004, 49% of undergraduates applied for financial aid. Of those, 33% were determined to have financial need; 21% had their need fully met. Average financial aid package (proportion receiving): $8,090 (31%). Average amount of gift aid, such as scholarships or grants (proportion receiving): $4,363 (17%). Average amount of self-help aid, such as work study or loans (proportion receiving): $3,972 (30%). Average need-based loan (excluding PLUS or other private loans): $3,845. Among students who received need-based aid, the average percentage of need met: 49%. Among students who received aid based on merit, the average award (and the proportion receiving): $4,006 (6%). The average athletic scholarship (and the proportion receiving): $8,130 (3%). Average amount of debt of borrowers graduating in 2003: $15,750. Proportion who borrowed: 48%. **Reserve Officers Training Corps (ROTC):** Army ROTC: Offered at cooperating institution (Loyola College).

United States Naval Academy

121 Blake Road
Annapolis, MD 21402
Public; www.usna.edu

■ **2004-2005 TUITION AND FEES:** $0

SAT I Score (25th/75th percentile): 1210-1380
2005 U.S. News College Ranking:
Unranked Specialty School–Military Academies
Acceptance Rate: 10%

Student employment: During the 2003-2004 academic year, 0% of undergraduates worked on campus. Average per-year earnings: $0.

University of Maryland–Baltimore County

1000 Hilltop Circle
Baltimore, MD 21250
Public; www.umbc.edu
Financial aid office: (410) 455-2387

■ **2004-2005 TUITION AND FEES:**
  In state: $8,020; Out of state: $15,620
■ **ROOM AND BOARD:** $7,880

SAT I Score (25th/75th percentile): 1120-1310
2005 U.S. News College Ranking:
National Universities, third tier
Acceptance Rate: 58%

Financial aid: Priority filing date for institution's financial aid form: February 15. In 2003-2004, 80% of undergraduates applied for financial aid. Of those, 66% were determined to have financial need; 58% had their need fully met. Average financial aid package (proportion receiving): $6,023 (53%). Average amount of gift aid, such as scholarships or grants (proportion receiving): $3,677 (36%). Average amount of self-help aid, such as work study or loans (proportion receiving): $3,895 (47%). Average need-based loan (excluding PLUS or other private loans): $4,404. Among students who received need-based aid, the average percentage of need met: 60%. Among students who received aid based on merit, the average award (and the proportion receiving): $6,341 (17%). The average athletic scholarship (and the proportion receiving): $8,925 (4%). Average amount of debt of borrowers graduating in 2003: $14,500. Proportion who borrowed: 29%. **Cooperative education programs:** computer science, engineering, natural science, social/behavioral science, technologies. **Reserve Officers Training Corps (ROTC):** Army ROTC: Offered at cooperating institution (John's Hopkins); Air Force ROTC: Offered at cooperating institution (University of Maryland at College Park).

University of Maryland–College Park

College Park, MD 20742-5025
Public; www.maryland.edu
Financial aid office: (301) 314-9000

■ **2004-2005 TUITION AND FEES:**
  In state: $7,410; Out of state: $18,710
■ **ROOM AND BOARD:** $7,931

SAT I Score (25th/75th percentile): 1170-1360
2005 U.S. News College Ranking:
National Universities, 56
Acceptance Rate: 43%

Other expenses: Estimated books and supplies: $909. Transportation: $674. Personal expenses: $2,022. **Financial aid:** Priority filing date for institution's financial aid form: February 15. In 2003-2004, 66% of undergraduates applied for financial aid. Of those, 42% were determined to have financial need; 24% had their need fully met. Average financial aid package (proportion receiving): $8,798 (39%). Average amount of gift aid, such as scholarships or grants (proportion receiving): $4,657 (27%). Average amount of self-help aid, such as work study or loans (proportion receiving): $3,878 (28%). Average need-based loan (excluding PLUS or other private loans): $3,795. Among students who received need-based aid, the average percentage of need met: 68%. Among students who received aid based on merit, the average award (and the proportion receiving): $5,794 (14%). The average athletic scholarship (and the proportion receiving): $14,479 (2%). Average amount of debt of borrowers graduating in 2003: $14,076. Proportion who borrowed: 34%. **Student employment:** During the 2003-2004 academic year, 17% of undergraduates worked on campus. Average per-year earnings: $4,900. **Cooperative education programs:** engineering. **Reserve Officers Training Corps (ROTC):** Army ROTC: Offered on campus; Navy ROTC: Offered at cooperating institution (George Washington University); Air Force ROTC: Offered on campus.

University of Maryland–Eastern Shore

J.T. Williams Hall, Room 2106
Princess Anne, MD 21853
Public; www.umes.edu
Financial aid office: (410) 651-6172

■ **2004-2005 TUITION AND FEES:**
In state: $5,105; Out of state: $10,440
■ **ROOM AND BOARD:** $5,630

2005 U.S. News College Ranking:
Universities–Master's (North), third tier
Acceptance Rate: 58%

Other expenses: Estimated books and supplies: $1,200. Transportation: $1,000. Personal expenses: $1,600. **Financial aid:** Priority filing date for institution's financial aid form: March 1. In 2003-2004, 98% of undergraduates applied for financial aid. Of those, 79% were determined to have financial need; 83% had their need fully met. Average financial aid package (proportion receiving): $9,500 (78%). Average amount of gift aid, such as scholarships or grants (proportion receiving): $3,500 (76%). Average amount of self-help aid, such as work study or loans (proportion receiving): $3,700 (72%). Average need-based loan (excluding PLUS or other private loans): $3,800. Among students who received need-based aid, the average percentage of need met: 85%. Among students who received aid based on merit, the average award (and the proportion receiving): $3,200 (8%). The average athletic scholarship (and the proportion receiving): $8,600 (3%). Average amount of debt of borrowers graduating in 2003: $13,250. Proportion who borrowed: 80%. **Student employment:** During the 2003-2004 academic year, 10% of undergraduates worked on campus. Average per-year earnings: $5,356. **Cooperative education programs:** agriculture, art, business, computer science, education, engineering, health professions, home economics, humanities, natural science, social/behavioral science, technologies, vocational arts. **Reserve Officers Training Corps (ROTC):** Army ROTC: Offered on campus.

University of Maryland–University College

3501 University Boulevard E
Adelphi, MD 20783
Public; umuc.edu
Financial aid office: (301) 985-7510

■ **2004-2005 TUITION AND FEES:**
In state: $6,750; Out of state: $12,330

2005 U.S. News College Ranking:
Universities–Master's (North), unranked
Acceptance Rate: 100%

Financial aid: Priority filing date for institution's financial aid form: June 1.

Villa Julie College

1525 Greenspring Valley Road
Stevenson, MD 21153
Private; www.vjc.edu
Financial aid office: (443) 334-2559

■ **2004-2005 TUITION AND FEES:** $14,653
■ **ROOM AND BOARD:** $6,250

SAT I Score (25th/75th percentile): 1000-1190
2005 U.S. News College Ranking:
Comp. Colleges–Bachelor's (North), 16
Acceptance Rate: 63%

Other expenses: Estimated books and supplies: $1,000. Transportation: $576. Personal expenses: $1,700. **Financial aid:** Priority filing date for institution's financial aid form: February 15. In 2003-2004, 73% of undergraduates applied for financial aid. Of those, 60% were determined to have financial need; 25% had their need fully met. Average financial aid package (proportion receiving): $9,343 (59%). Average amount of gift aid, such as scholarships or grants (proportion receiving): $7,262 (52%). Average amount of self-help aid, such as work study or loans (proportion receiving): $2,327 (38%). Average need-based loan (excluding PLUS or other private loans): $2,164. Among students who received need-based aid, the average percentage of need met: 74%. Among students who received aid based on merit, the average award (and the proportion receiving): $5,387 (19%). The average athletic scholarship (and the proportion receiving): $0 (0%). Average amount of debt of borrowers graduating in 2003: $16,832. Proportion who borrowed: 38%. Average per-year earnings: $1,774. **Cooperative education programs:** other. **Reserve Officers Training Corps (ROTC):** Army ROTC:

Offered at cooperating institution (Johns Hopkins University).

Washington College

300 Washington Avenue
Chestertown, MD 21620
Private; www.washcoll.edu
Financial aid office: (410) 778-7214

■ **2004-2005 TUITION AND FEES:** $26,550
■ **ROOM AND BOARD:** $6,000

SAT I Score (25th/75th percentile): 1060-1250
2005 U.S. News College Ranking:
Liberal Arts Colleges, 89
Acceptance Rate: 61%

Other expenses: Estimated books and supplies: $1,200. Transportation: $0. Personal expenses: $1,000. **Financial aid:** Priority filing date for institution's financial aid form: February 15. In 2003-2004, 59% of undergraduates applied for financial aid. Of those, 50% were determined to have financial need; 54% had their need fully met. Average financial aid package (proportion receiving): $19,395 (50%). Average amount of gift aid, such as scholarships or grants (proportion receiving): $15,023 (49%). Average amount of self-help aid, such as work study or loans (proportion receiving): $4,070 (50%). Average need-based loan (excluding PLUS or other private loans): $3,500. Among students who received need-based aid, the average percentage of need met: 88%. Among students who received aid based on merit, the average award (and the proportion receiving): $10,717 (34%). The average athletic scholarship (and the proportion receiving): $0 (0%). Average amount of debt of borrowers graduating in 2003: $17,756. Proportion who borrowed: 59%. **Student employment:** During the 2003-2004 academic year, 35% of undergraduates worked on campus. Average per-year earnings: $2,000.

Massachusetts

American International College

1000 State Street
Springfield, MA 01109
Private; www.aic.edu
Financial aid office: (413) 205-3259

- **2004-2005 TUITION AND FEES:** $18,000
- **ROOM AND BOARD:** $8,510

SAT I Score (25th/75th percentile): 830-1010
2005 U.S. News College Ranking:
Universities–Master's (North), fourth tier
Acceptance Rate: 77%

Other expenses: Estimated books and supplies: $800. Transportation: $200. Personal expenses: $1,050. **Financial aid:** Priority filing date for institution's financial aid form: April 15. In 2003-2004, 100% of undergraduates applied for financial aid. Of those, 96% were determined to have financial need; 38% had their need fully met. Average financial aid package (proportion receiving): $17,269 (96%). Average amount of gift aid, such as scholarships or grants (proportion receiving): $9,309 (90%). Average amount of self-help aid, such as work study or loans (proportion receiving): $6,900 (90%). Average need-based loan (excluding PLUS or other private loans): $4,531. Among students who received need-based aid, the average percentage of need met: 81%. Among students who received aid based on merit, the average award (and the proportion receiving): $2,256 (3%). The average athletic scholarship (and the proportion receiving): $14,410 (13%). Average amount of debt of borrowers graduating in 2003: $19,425. Proportion who borrowed: 85%. **Student employment:** During the 2003-2004 academic year, 15% of undergraduates worked on campus. Average per-year earnings: $2,400. **Reserve Officers Training Corps (ROTC):** Army ROTC: Offered at cooperating institution (Western New England College); Air Force ROTC: Offered at cooperating institution (Western New England).

Amherst College

Amherst College, PO Box 5000
Amherst, MA 01002
Private; www.amherst.edu
Financial aid office: (413) 542-2296

- **2004-2005 TUITION AND FEES:** $31,360
- **ROOM AND BOARD:** $8,160

SAT I Score (25th/75th percentile): 1320-1540
2005 U.S. News College Ranking:
Liberal Arts Colleges, 2
Acceptance Rate: 18%

Other expenses: Estimated books and supplies: $900. Transportation: $1,000. Personal expenses: $1,600. **Financial aid:** Priority filing date for institution's financial aid form: March 10. In 2003-2004, 53% of undergraduates applied for financial aid. Of those, 48% were determined to have financial need; 100% had their need fully met. Average financial aid package (proportion receiving): $25,366 (48%). Average amount of gift aid, such as scholarships or grants (proportion receiving): $23,703 (47%). Average amount of self-help aid, such as work study or loans (proportion receiving): $3,424 (43%). Average need-based loan (excluding PLUS or other private loans): $2,233. Among students who received need-based aid, the average percentage of need met: 100%. Among students who received aid based on merit, the average award (and the proportion receiving): $0 (0%). The average athletic scholarship (and the proportion receiving): $0 (0%). Average amount of debt of borrowers graduating in 2003: $10,787. Proportion who borrowed: 48%. **Student employment:** During the 2003-2004 academic year, 60% of undergraduates worked on campus. Average per-year earnings: $1,600.

Anna Maria College

Sunset Lane
Paxton, MA 01612
Private; www.annamaria.edu
Financial aid office: (508) 849-3366

- **2004-2005 TUITION AND FEES:** $20,335
- **ROOM AND BOARD:** $7,415

SAT I Score (25th/75th percentile): 830-1040
2005 U.S. News College Ranking:
Universities–Master's (North), fourth tier
Acceptance Rate: 88%

Financial aid: Priority filing date for institution's financial aid form: February 1. In 2003-2004, 86% of undergraduates applied for financial aid. Of those, 80% were determined to have financial need; 31% had their need fully met. Average financial aid package (proportion receiving): $14,378 (80%). Average amount of gift aid, such as scholarships or grants (proportion receiving): $9,385 (78%). Average amount of self-help aid, such as work study or loans (proportion receiving): $5,850 (70%). Average need-based loan (excluding PLUS or other private loans): $5,548. Among students who received need-based aid, the average percentage of need met: 80%. Among students who received aid based on merit, the average award (and the proportion receiving): $11,383 (12%). The average athletic scholarship (and the proportion receiving): $0 (0%). Average amount of debt of borrowers graduating in 2003: $18,869. Proportion who borrowed: 61%. **Reserve Officers Training Corps (ROTC):** Air Force ROTC: Offered at cooperating institution (Worcester Polytechnic Institute).

Art Institute of Boston

700 Beacon Street
Boston, MA 02215-2598
Private; www.aiboston.edu
Financial aid office: (617) 349-8710

- **2004-2005 TUITION AND FEES:** $18,710
- **ROOM AND BOARD:** $9,370

SAT I Score (25th/75th percentile): 940-1150
2005 U.S. News College Ranking:
Unranked Specialty School–Fine Arts
Acceptance Rate: 77%

Other expenses: Estimated books and supplies: $1,575. Transportation: $450. Personal expenses: $2,125. **Financial aid:** Priority filing date for institution's financial aid form: March 12. In 2003-2004, 74% of undergraduates applied for financial aid. Of those, 55% were determined to have financial need; 5% had their need fully met. Average financial aid package (proportion receiving): $7,792 (55%). Average amount of gift aid, such as scholarships or grants (proportion receiving): $4,298 (34%). Average amount of self-help aid, such as work study or loans (proportion receiving): $6,005 (55%). Average need-based loan (excluding PLUS or other private loans): $4,823. Among students who received need-based aid, the average percentage of need met: 60%. Among students who received aid based on merit, the average award (and the proportion receiving): $3,162 (5%). Average amount of debt of borrowers graduating in 2003: $14,110. Proportion who borrowed: 74%. **Student employment:** During the 2003-2004 academic year, 10% of undergraduates worked on campus. Average per-year earnings: $3,465.

Assumption College

500 Salisbury Street
Worcester, MA 01609
Private; www.assumption.edu
Financial aid office: (508) 767-7158

■ **2004-2005 TUITION AND FEES:** $22,425
■ **ROOM AND BOARD:** $8,640

SAT I Score (25th/75th percentile): 980-1170
2005 U.S. News College Ranking:
Universities–Master's (North), 31
Acceptance Rate: 79%

Other expenses: Estimated books and supplies: $850. Transportation: $400. Personal expenses: $1,130. **Financial aid:** Priority filing date for institution's financial aid form: February 28. In 2003-2004, 80% of undergraduates applied for financial aid. Of those, 70% were determined to have financial need; 29% had their need fully met. Average financial aid package (proportion receiving): $14,955 (70%). Average amount of gift aid, such as scholarships or grants (proportion receiving): $10,387 (69%). Average amount of self-help aid, such as work study or loans (proportion receiving): $5,346 (62%). Average need-based loan (excluding PLUS or other private loans): $4,953. Among students who received need-based aid, the average percentage of need met: 76%. Among students who received aid based on merit, the average award (and the proportion receiving): $7,336 (7%). The average athletic scholarship (and the proportion receiving): $28,791 (1%). Average amount of debt of borrowers graduating in 2003: $22,825. Proportion who borrowed: 87%. **Student employment:** During the 2003-2004 academic year, 33% of undergraduates worked on campus. Average per-year earn-

ings: $1,000. **Reserve Officers Training Corps (ROTC):** Army ROTC: Offered on campus; Air Force ROTC: Offered at cooperating institution (Worcester Polytechnic Institute).

Atlantic Union College

PO Box 1000
South Lancaster, MA 01561
Private; www.atlanticuc.edu
Financial aid office: (978) 368-2280

■ **2004-2005 TUITION AND FEES:** $12,780
■ **ROOM AND BOARD:** $3,780

2005 U.S. News College Ranking:
Comp. Colleges–Bachelor's (North), fourth tier
Acceptance Rate: 36%

Other expenses: Estimated books and supplies: $900.

Babson College

231 Forest Street
Babson Park, MA 02457-0310
Private; www.babson.edu
Financial aid office: (781) 239-4219

■ **2004-2005 TUITION AND FEES:** $28,832
■ **ROOM AND BOARD:** $10,376

SAT I Score (25th/75th percentile): 1170-1320
2005 U.S. News College Ranking:
Unranked Specialty School–Business
Acceptance Rate: 37%

Other expenses: Estimated books and supplies: $856. Transportation: $500. Personal expenses: $1,648. **Financial aid:** Priority filing date for institution's financial aid form: February 15; deadline: February 15. In 2003-2004, 47% of undergraduates applied for financial aid. Of those, 44% were determined to have financial need; 91% had their need fully met. Average financial aid package (proportion receiving): $22,870 (44%). Average amount of gift aid, such as scholarships or grants (proportion receiving): $17,461 (41%). Average amount of self-help aid, such as work study or loans (proportion receiving): $5,409 (40%). Average need-based loan (excluding PLUS or other private loans): $4,178. Among students who received need-based aid, the average percentage of need met: 98%. Among students who received aid based on merit, the average award (and the proportion receiving): $8,559 (5%). The average athletic scholarship (and the pro-

portion receiving): $0 (0%). Average amount of debt of borrowers graduating in 2003: $20,531. Proportion who borrowed: 53%. **Student employment:** During the 2003-2004 academic year, 30% of undergraduates worked on campus. Average per-year earnings: $2,200. **Reserve Officers Training Corps (ROTC):** Army ROTC: Offered at cooperating institution (Boston University); Navy ROTC: Offered at cooperating institution (Boston University); Air Force ROTC: Offered at cooperating institution (Boston University).

Bay Path College

588 Longmeadow Street
Longmeadow, MA 01106
Private; www.baypath.edu
Financial aid office: (413) 565-1261

■ **2004-2005 TUITION AND FEES:** $18,440
■ **ROOM AND BOARD:** $8,260

SAT I Score (25th/75th percentile): 910-1100
2005 U.S. News College Ranking:
Comp. Colleges–Bachelor's (North), 26
Acceptance Rate: 82%

Other expenses: Estimated books and supplies: $800. Transportation: $400. Personal expenses: $900. **Financial aid:** Priority filing date for institution's financial aid form: March 15. In 2003-2004, 95% of undergraduates applied for financial aid. Of those, 87% were determined to have financial need; 9% had their need fully met. Average financial aid package (proportion receiving): $9,267 (87%). Average amount of gift aid, such as scholarships or grants (proportion receiving): $5,990 (86%). Average amount of self-help aid, such as work study or loans (proportion receiving): $3,487 (82%). Average need-based loan (excluding PLUS or other private loans): $3,231. Among students who received need-based aid, the average percentage of need met: 71%. Among students who received aid based on merit, the average award (and the proportion receiving): $8,574 (13%). The average athletic scholarship (and the proportion receiving): $0 (0%). Average amount of debt of borrowers graduating in 2003: $17,000. Proportion who borrowed: 64%. **Reserve Officers Training Corps (ROTC):** Army ROTC: Offered at cooperating institution (Western New England College); Air Force ROTC: Offered at cooperating institution (Western New England College).

Becker College

61 Sever Street
Worcester, MA 01609
Private; www.beckercollege.edu
Financial aid office: (508) 791-9241

■ **2004-2005 TUITION AND FEES:** $17,200
■ **ROOM AND BOARD:** $8,000

2005 U.S. News College Ranking:
Comp. Colleges–Bachelor's (North), fourth tier
Acceptance Rate: 83%

Other expenses: Estimated books and supplies: $1,000. Transportation: $600. Personal expenses: $1,170. **Financial aid:** Priority filing date for institution's financial aid form: March 1. In 2003-2004, 98% of undergraduates applied for financial aid. Of those, 90% were determined to have financial need; 10% had their need fully met. Average financial aid package (proportion receiving): $9,298 (90%). Average amount of gift aid, such as scholarships or grants (proportion receiving): $5,693 (86%). Average amount of self-help aid, such as work study or loans (proportion receiving): $3,925 (89%). Average need-based loan (excluding PLUS or other private loans): $3,206. Among students who received need-based aid, the average percentage of need met: 52%. Among students who received aid based on merit, the average award (and the proportion receiving): $11,697 (9%). The average athletic scholarship (and the proportion receiving): $0 (0%). Average amount of debt of borrowers graduating in 2003: $22,262. Proportion who borrowed: 99%. Average per-year earnings: $3,000. **Cooperative education programs:** business, health professions. **Reserve Officers Training Corps (ROTC):** Army ROTC: Offered at cooperating institution (Worcester Polytechnic Institute).

Benjamin Franklin Institute of Technology

41 Berkeley Street
Boston, MA 02116
Private; www.bfit.edu
Financial aid office: (617) 423-4630

■ **2004-2005 TUITION AND FEES:** $12,500

2005 U.S. News College Ranking:
Unranked Specialty School–Engineering
Acceptance Rate: 91%

Financial aid: Priority filing date for institution's financial aid form: April 15.

Bentley College

175 Forest Street
Waltham, MA 02452-4705
Private; www.bentley.edu
Financial aid office: (781) 891-3441

■ **2004-2005 TUITION AND FEES:** $25,544
■ **ROOM AND BOARD:** $9,860

SAT I Score (25th/75th percentile): 1100-1270
2005 U.S. News College Ranking:
Universities–Master's (North), 8
Acceptance Rate: 46%

Other expenses: Estimated books and supplies: $920. Personal expenses: $1,020. **Financial aid:** In 2003-2004, 64% of undergraduates applied for financial aid. Of those, 51% were determined to have financial need; 37% had their need fully met. Average financial aid package (proportion receiving): $22,572 (51%). Average amount of gift aid, such as scholarships or grants (proportion receiving): $13,530 (46%). Average amount of self-help aid, such as work study or loans (proportion receiving): $6,486 (47%). Average need-based loan (excluding PLUS or other private loans): $5,029. Among students who received need-based aid, the average percentage of need met: 95%. Among students who received aid based on merit, the average award (and the proportion receiving): $10,651 (10%). The average athletic scholarship (and the proportion receiving): $29,166 (1%). Average amount of debt of borrowers graduating in 2003: $19,560. Proportion who borrowed: 61%. **Student employment:** During the 2003-2004 academic year, 14% of undergraduates worked on campus. Average per-year earnings: $1,400. **Reserve Officers Training Corps (ROTC):** Army ROTC: Offered at cooperating institution (Boston University).

Berklee College of Music

1140 Boylston Street
Boston, MA 02215
Private; www.berklee.edu
Financial aid office: (617) 747-2274

■ **2004-2005 TUITION AND FEES:** $23,480
■ **ROOM AND BOARD:** $10,900

2005 U.S. News College Ranking:
Unranked Specialty School–Fine Arts
Acceptance Rate: 78%

Other expenses: Estimated books and supplies: $500. **Financial aid:** Priority filing date for insti-

tution's financial aid form: March 4. In 2003-2004, 53% of undergraduates applied for financial aid. Of those, 53% were determined to have financial need; Average financial aid package (proportion receiving): $14,402 (53%). Average amount of gift aid, such as scholarships or grants (proportion receiving): $4,125 (23%). Average amount of self-help aid, such as work study or loans (proportion receiving): $3,638 (52%). Average need-based loan (excluding PLUS or other private loans): $3,785. Among students who received need-based aid, the average percentage of need met: 61%. Among students who received aid based on merit, the average award (and the proportion receiving): $6,608 (24%).

Boston Architectural Center

320 Newbury Street
Boston, MA 02115
Private; www.the-bac.edu
Financial aid office: (617) 585-0125

■ **2004-2005 TUITION AND FEES:** $8,220

2005 U.S. News College Ranking:
Unranked Specialty School–Fine Arts
Acceptance Rate: 89%

Other expenses: Estimated books and supplies: $1,189. Transportation: $941. Personal expenses: $2,675. **Financial aid:** Priority filing date for institution's financial aid form: April 15. 3% had their need fully met. Average financial aid package (proportion receiving): $3,635 (N/A). Average amount of gift aid, such as scholarships or grants (proportion receiving): $2,856 (N/A). Average amount of self-help aid, such as work study or loans (proportion receiving): $3,002 (N/A). Average need-based loan (excluding PLUS or other private loans): $3,002. Among students who received need-based aid, the average percentage of need met: 27%. Among students who received aid based on merit, the average award (and the proportion receiving): $4,326 (N/A). The average athletic scholarship (and the proportion receiving): $0 (N/A). Average amount of debt of borrowers graduating in 2003: $31,433. Proportion who borrowed: 65%. **Student employment:** During the 2003-2004 academic year, 0% of undergraduates worked on campus. **Cooperative education programs:** art, computer science.

Boston College

140 Commonwealth Avenue
Chestnut Hill, MA 02467
Private; www.bc.edu
Financial aid office: (617) 552-3320

■ 2004-2005 TUITION AND FEES: $29,396
■ ROOM AND BOARD: $10,580

SAT I Score (25th/75th percentile): 1230-1400
2005 U.S. News College Ranking:
National Universities, 37
Acceptance Rate: 31%

Other expenses: Estimated books and supplies:
$650. Personal expenses: $1,000. Financial aid:
Priority filing date for institution's financial aid
form: February 1. In 2003-2004, 53% of undergraduates applied for financial aid. Of those,
42% were determined to have financial need;
100% had their need fully met. Average financial aid package (proportion receiving): $23,215
(42%). Average amount of gift aid, such as
scholarships or grants (proportion receiving):
$17,698 (37%). Average amount of self-help
aid, such as work study or loans (proportion
receiving): $6,057 (38%). Average need-based
loan (excluding PLUS or other private loans):
$4,521. Among students who received need-
based aid, the average percentage of need met:
100%. Among students who received aid based
on merit, the average award (and the proportion receiving): $7,305 (3%). The average athlet-
ic scholarship (and the proportion receiving):
$30,182 (2%). Student employment: During the
2003-2004 academic year, 17% of undergraduates worked on campus. Average per-year earnings: $2,000. Reserve Officers Training Corps
(ROTC): Army ROTC: Offered at cooperating
institution (Northeastern University); Navy
ROTC: Offered at cooperating institution
(Boston University); Air Force ROTC: Offered
at cooperating institution (Boston University).

Boston Conservatory

8 The Fenway
Boston, MA 02215
Private; www.bostonconservatory.edu
Financial aid office: (617) 912-9147

■ 2004-2005 TUITION AND FEES: $22,740
■ ROOM AND BOARD: $10,430

2005 U.S. News College Ranking:
Unranked Specialty School–Fine Arts
Acceptance Rate: 43%

Other expenses: Estimated books and supplies:
$500. Transportation: $500. Personal expenses:
$1,413. Financial aid: Priority filing date for
institution's financial aid form: February 1;
deadline: February 1. In 2003-2004, 91% of
undergraduates applied for financial aid. Of
those, 64% were determined to have financial
need; 34% had their need fully met. Average
financial aid package (proportion receiving):
$14,500 (64%). Average amount of gift aid,
such as scholarships or grants (proportion
receiving): $4,188 (16%). Average amount of
self-help aid, such as work study or loans (proportion receiving): $4,326 (52%). Average need-
based loan (excluding PLUS or other private
loans): $4,310. Among students who received
need-based aid, the average percentage of need
met: 50%. Among students who received aid
based on merit, the average award (and the proportion receiving): $8,892 (13%). The average
athletic scholarship (and the proportion receiving): $0 (0%).

Boston University

121 Bay State Road
Boston, MA 02215
Private; www.bu.edu
Financial aid office: (617) 353-2965

■ 2004-2005 TUITION AND FEES: $30,402
■ ROOM AND BOARD: $9,680

SAT I Score (25th/75th percentile): 1220-1380
2005 U.S. News College Ranking:
National Universities, 56
Acceptance Rate: 52%

Other expenses: Estimated books and supplies:
$721. Transportation: $342. Personal expenses:
$1,155. Financial aid: Priority filing date for
institution's financial aid form: February 15. In
2003-2004, 51% of undergraduates applied for
financial aid. Of those, 47% were determined to
have financial need; 50% had their need fully
met. Average financial aid package (proportion
receiving): $25,338 (47%). Average amount of
gift aid, such as scholarships or grants (proportion receiving): $16,953 (44%). Average amount
of self-help aid, such as work study or loans
(proportion receiving): $5,921 (43%). Average
need-based loan (excluding PLUS or other private loans): $4,826. Among students who
received need-based aid, the average percentage
of need met: 90%. Among students who
received aid based on merit, the average award
(and the proportion receiving): $14,324 (13%).
The average athletic scholarship (and the pro-

portion receiving): $28,275 (1%). Average
amount of debt of borrowers graduating in
2003: $17,535. Proportion who borrowed: 59%.
Student employment: During the 2003-2004
academic year, 14% of undergraduates worked
on campus. Average per-year earnings: $1,400.
Cooperative education programs: engineering.
Reserve Officers Training Corps (ROTC): Army
ROTC: Offered on campus; Navy ROTC:
Offered on campus; Air Force ROTC: Offered
on campus.

Brandeis University

415 South Street
Waltham, MA 02454-9110
Private; www.brandeis.edu
Financial aid office: (781) 736-3700

■ 2004-2005 TUITION AND FEES: $31,072
■ ROOM AND BOARD: $8,656

SAT I Score (25th/75th percentile): 1250-1440
2005 U.S. News College Ranking:
National Universities, 32
Acceptance Rate: 44%

Other expenses: Estimated books and supplies:
$700. Personal expenses: $1,000. Financial aid:
Priority filing date for institution's financial aid
form: January 31. In 2003-2004, 57% of undergraduates applied for financial aid. Of those,
48% were determined to have financial need;
26% had their need fully met. Average financial aid package (proportion receiving): $22,199
(48%). Average amount of gift aid, such as
scholarships or grants (proportion receiving):
$16,420 (46%). Average amount of self-help
aid, such as work study or loans (proportion
receiving): $7,238 (43%). Average need-based
loan (excluding PLUS or other private loans):
$6,052. Among students who received need-
based aid, the average percentage of need met:
82%. Among students who received aid based
on merit, the average award (and the proportion receiving): $16,883 (23%). The average ath-
letic scholarship (and the proportion receiving):
$0 (0%). Student employment: During the
2003-2004 academic year, 51% of undergraduates worked on campus. Reserve Officers
Training Corps (ROTC): Army ROTC: Offered at
cooperating institution (Boston University); Air
Force ROTC: Offered at cooperating institution
(Boston University).

Bridgewater State College

Boyden Hall
Bridgewater, MA 02325
Public; www.bridgew.edu
Financial aid office: (508) 531-1341

■ **2004-2005 TUITION AND FEES:**
In state: $5,248; Out of state: $11,388
■ **ROOM AND BOARD:** $6,512

SAT I Score (25th/75th percentile): 920-1110
2005 U.S. News College Ranking:
Universities–Master's (North), fourth tier
Acceptance Rate: 72%

Other expenses: Estimated books and supplies: $800. Transportation: $750. Personal expenses: $1,500. **Financial aid:** Priority filing date for institution's financial aid form: March 1. In 2003-2004, 63% of undergraduates applied for financial aid. Of those, 46% were determined to have financial need; 47% had their need fully met. Average financial aid package (proportion receiving): $7,766 (45%). Average amount of gift aid, such as scholarships or grants (proportion receiving): $3,340 (38%). Average amount of self-help aid, such as work study or loans (proportion receiving): $3,695 (34%). Average need-based loan (excluding PLUS or other private loans): $3,442. Among students who received need-based aid, the average percentage of need met: 80%. Among students who received aid based on merit, the average award (and the proportion receiving): $5,442 (14%). The average athletic scholarship (and the proportion receiving): $0 (0%). Average amount of debt of borrowers graduating in 2003: $8,180. Proportion who borrowed: 41%. **Student employment:** During the 2003-2004 academic year, 17% of undergraduates worked on campus. Average per-year earnings: $2,000. **Reserve Officers Training Corps (ROTC):** Army ROTC: Offered at cooperating institution (Stonehill College/Boston University); Air Force ROTC: Offered at cooperating institution (Boston University).

Clark University

950 Main Street
Worcester, MA 01610-1477
Private; www.clarku.edu
Financial aid office: (508) 793-7478

■ **2004-2005 TUITION AND FEES:** $28,265
■ **ROOM AND BOARD:** $5,400

SAT I Score (25th/75th percentile): 1090-1300
2005 U.S. News College Ranking:
National Universities, 74
Acceptance Rate: 63%

Other expenses: Estimated books and supplies: $800. Transportation: $200. Personal expenses: $700. **Financial aid:** In 2003-2004, 78% of undergraduates applied for financial aid. Of those, 62% were determined to have financial need; 74% had their need fully met. Average financial aid package (proportion receiving): $23,136 (60%). Average amount of gift aid, such as scholarships or grants (proportion receiving): $18,012 (60%). Average amount of self-help aid, such as work study or loans (proportion receiving): $4,991 (56%). Average need-based loan (excluding PLUS or other loans): $3,711. Among students who received need-based aid, the average percentage of need met: 97%. Among students who received aid based on merit, the average award (and the proportion receiving): $12,056 (8%). Average amount of debt of borrowers graduating in 2003: $18,375. Proportion who borrowed: 88%. **Student employment:** During the 2003-2004 academic year, 45% of undergraduates worked on campus. Average per-year earnings: $1,700. **Reserve Officers Training Corps (ROTC):** Army ROTC: Offered at cooperating institution (Worcester Polytechnic Inst.); Navy ROTC: Offered at cooperating institution (College of the Holy Cross); Air Force ROTC: Offered at cooperating institution (Worcester Polytechnic Inst.).

College of the Holy Cross

1 College Street
Worcester, MA 01610
Private; www.holycross.edu
Financial aid office: (508) 793-2266

■ **2004-2005 TUITION AND FEES:** $29,686
■ **ROOM AND BOARD:** $8,860

SAT I Score (25th/75th percentile): 1210-1350
2005 U.S. News College Ranking:
Liberal Arts Colleges, 31
Acceptance Rate: 42%

Other expenses: Estimated books and supplies: $700. Transportation: $300. Personal expenses: $900. **Financial aid:** Priority filing date for institution's financial aid form: February 1; deadline: February 1. In 2003-2004, 63% of undergraduates applied for financial aid. Of those, 43% were determined to have financial need; 100% had their need fully met. Average

financial aid package (proportion receiving): $21,793 (43%). Average amount of gift aid, such as scholarships or grants (proportion receiving): $16,044 (40%). Average amount of self-help aid, such as work study or loans (proportion receiving): $7,100 (39%). Average need-based loan (excluding PLUS or other private loans): $6,447. Among students who received need-based aid, the average percentage of need met: 100%. Among students who received aid based on merit, the average award (and the proportion receiving): $11,661 (5%). The average athletic scholarship (and the proportion receiving): $34,684 (1%). Average amount of debt of borrowers graduating in 2003: $17,253. Proportion who borrowed: 58%. **Student employment:** During the 2003-2004 academic year, 17% of undergraduates worked on campus. Average per-year earnings: $1,700. **Reserve Officers Training Corps (ROTC):** Army ROTC: Offered at cooperating institution (Worcester Polytechnic Institute); Navy ROTC: Offered on campus; Air Force ROTC: Offered at cooperating institution (Worcester Polytechnic Institute).

Curry College

1071 Blue Hill Avenue
Milton, MA 02186
Private; www.curry.edu
Financial aid office: (617) 333-2146

■ **2004-2005 TUITION AND FEES:** $21,530
■ **ROOM AND BOARD:** $8,700

SAT I Score (25th/75th percentile): 893-1067
2005 U.S. News College Ranking:
Comp. Colleges–Bachelor's (North), third tier
Acceptance Rate: 68%

Other expenses: Estimated books and supplies: $700. Transportation: $1,000. Personal expenses: $1,128. **Financial aid:** Priority filing date for institution's financial aid form: March 1. In 2003-2004, 67% of undergraduates applied for financial aid. Of those, 67% were determined to have financial need; 8% had their need fully met. Average financial aid package (proportion receiving): $14,025 (66%). Average amount of gift aid, such as scholarships or grants (proportion receiving): $9,830 (59%). Average amount of self-help aid, such as work study or loans (proportion receiving): $4,210 (64%). Average need-based loan (excluding PLUS or other private loans): $3,644. Among students who received need-based aid, the average percentage of need met: 68%. Among students who received aid based on merit, the average award (and the proportion receiving): $3,732 (2%). The average athletic scholarship (and the proportion receiving): $0 (0%). Average amount of debt of borrowers graduating in 2003: $17,046. Proportion who borrowed: 43%. **Student employment:** During the 2003-2004 academic year, 8% of undergraduates worked on campus. Average per-year earnings: $1,200. **Reserve Officers Training Corps (ROTC):** Army ROTC: Offered at cooperating institution (Stonehill College).

Eastern Nazarene College

23 E. Elm Avenue
Quincy, MA 02170
Private; www.enc.edu
Financial aid office: (617) 745-3869

■ **2004-2005 TUITION AND FEES:** $17,439
■ **ROOM AND BOARD:** $5,920

SAT I Score (25th/75th percentile): 920-1180
2005 U.S. News College Ranking:
Universities–Master's (North), fourth tier
Acceptance Rate: 40%

Other expenses: Estimated books and supplies: $1,000. **Student employment:** During the 2003-2004 academic year, 55% of undergraduates worked on campus. Average per-year earnings: $4,500. **Cooperative education programs:** health professions. **Reserve Officers Training Corps (ROTC):** Army ROTC: Offered at cooperating institution (Boston University); Air Force ROTC: Offered at cooperating institution (Boston University).

Elms College (College of Our Lady of the Elms)

291 Springfield Street
Chicopee, MA 01013
Private; www.elms.edu
Financial aid office: (413) 594-2761

■ **2004-2005 TUITION AND FEES:** $19,970
■ **ROOM AND BOARD:** $7,750

SAT I Score (25th/75th percentile): 860-1140
2005 U.S. News College Ranking:
Universities–Master's (North), fourth tier
Acceptance Rate: 90%

Other expenses: Estimated books and supplies: $600. Transportation: $600. Personal expenses: $900. **Financial aid:** Priority filing date for institution's financial aid form: March 1. **Student employment:** During the 2003-2004

academic year, 0% of undergraduates worked on campus. Average per-year earnings: $0. **Reserve Officers Training Corps (ROTC):** Army ROTC: Offered at cooperating institution (University of Massachusetts–Amherst); Air Force ROTC: Offered at cooperating institution (University of Massachusetts–Amherst).

Emerson College

120 Boylston Street
Boston, MA 02116-4624
Private; www.emerson.edu
Financial aid office: (617) 824-8655

■ **2004-2005 TUITION AND FEES:** $23,380
■ **ROOM AND BOARD:** $10,118

SAT I Score (25th/75th percentile): 1110-1300
2005 U.S. News College Ranking:
Universities–Master's (North), 16
Acceptance Rate: 48%

Other expenses: Estimated books and supplies: $680. Personal expenses: $1,065. **Financial aid:** Priority filing date for institution's financial aid form: March 1. In 2003-2004, 64% of undergraduates applied for financial aid. Of those, 54% were determined to have financial need; 86% had their need fully met. Average financial aid package (proportion receiving): $13,083 (54%). Average amount of gift aid, such as scholarships or grants (proportion receiving): $10,469 (43%). Average amount of self-help aid, such as work study or loans (proportion receiving): $4,859 (52%). Average need-based loan (excluding PLUS or other private loans): $4,232. Among students who received need-based aid, the average percentage of need met: 85%. Among students who received aid based on merit, the average award (and the proportion receiving): $13,005 (16%). The average athletic scholarship (and the proportion receiving): $0 (0%). Average amount of debt of borrowers graduating in 2003: $14,800. Proportion who borrowed: 74%. **Student employment:** During the 2003-2004 academic year, 25% of undergraduates worked on campus. Average per-year earnings: $1,600.

Emmanuel College

400 The Fenway
Boston, MA 02115
Private; www.emmanuel.edu
Financial aid office: (617) 735-9938

■ **2004-2005 TUITION AND FEES:** $20,500
■ **ROOM AND BOARD:** $9,000

SAT I Score (25th/75th percentile): 940-1150
2005 U.S. News College Ranking:
Universities–Master's (North), 54
Acceptance Rate: 63%

Other expenses: Estimated books and supplies: $750. Transportation: $270. Personal expenses: $1,810. **Financial aid:** Priority filing date for institution's financial aid form: April 1. In 2003-2004, 92% of undergraduates applied for financial aid. Of those, 80% were determined to have financial need; 22% had their need fully met. Average financial aid package (proportion receiving): $16,474 (78%). Average amount of gift aid, such as scholarships or grants (proportion receiving): $9,973 (63%). Average amount of self-help aid, such as work study or loans (proportion receiving): $5,261 (70%). Average need-based loan (excluding PLUS or other private loans): $4,108. Among students who received need-based aid, the average percentage of need met: 78%. Among students who received aid based on merit, the average award (and the proportion receiving): $11,494 (8%). Average amount of debt of borrowers graduating in 2003: $15,763. Proportion who borrowed: 69%.

Endicott College

376 Hale Street
Beverly, MA 01915
Private; www.endicott.edu
Financial aid office: (978) 232-2070

■ **2004-2005 TUITION AND FEES:** $18,428
■ **ROOM AND BOARD:** $9,300

SAT I Score (25th/75th percentile): 970-1110
2005 U.S. News College Ranking:
Comp. Colleges–Bachelor's (North), 21
Acceptance Rate: 48%

Other expenses: Estimated books and supplies: $600. Transportation: $1,000. Personal expenses: $1,000. **Financial aid:** Priority filing date for institution's financial aid form: March 15. In 2003-2004, 83% of undergraduates applied for financial aid. Of those, 64% were determined to have financial need; 13% had their need fully met. Average financial aid package (proportion receiving): $12,062 (64%). Average amount of gift aid, such as scholarships or grants (proportion receiving): $5,411 (51%). Average amount of self-help aid, such as work study or loans (proportion receiving): $4,614 (60%). Average need-based loan (excluding PLUS or other private loans): $3,990. Among students who received need-based aid, the average percentage of need met: 62%. Among students who received aid based on merit, the average award (and the proportion receiving): $6,845 (13%). The average athletic scholarship (and the proportion receiving): $0 (0%). Average amount of debt of borrowers graduating in 2003: $17,125. Proportion who borrowed: 53%. **Student employment:** During the 2003-2004 academic year, 21% of undergraduates worked on campus. Average per-year earnings: $1,500. **Reserve Officers Training Corps (ROTC):** Army ROTC: Offered at cooperating institution (MIT).

Fitchburg State College

160 Pearl Street
Fitchburg, MA 01420-2697
Public; www.fsc.edu
Financial aid office: (978) 665-3156

■ **2004-2005 TUITION AND FEES:**
In state: $4,588; Out of state: $10,668
■ **ROOM AND BOARD:** $5,762

SAT I Score (25th/75th percentile): 920-1110
2005 U.S. News College Ranking:
Universities–Master's (North), third tier
Acceptance Rate: 60%

Other expenses: Estimated books and supplies: $600. Transportation: $350. Personal expenses: $1,580. **Financial aid:** Priority filing date for institution's financial aid form: March 1. In 2003-2004, 80% of undergraduates applied for financial aid. Of those, 51% were determined to have financial need; 96% had their need fully met. Average financial aid package (proportion receiving): $6,135 (49%). Average amount of gift aid, such as scholarships or grants (proportion receiving): $3,620 (40%). Average amount of self-help aid, such as work study or loans (proportion receiving): $3,370 (46%). Average need-based loan (excluding PLUS or other private loans): $3,060. Among students who received need-based aid, the average percentage of need met: 99%. Among students who received aid based on merit, the average award (and the proportion receiving): $1,910 (3%). The average athletic scholarship (and the proportion receiving): $0 (0%). Average amount of debt of borrowers graduating in 2003: $8,500. Proportion who borrowed: 30%. **Reserve Officers Training Corps (ROTC):** Army ROTC: Offered at cooperating institution (Worcester Polytech Institute).

Framingham State College

100 State Street, PO Box 9101
Framingham, MA 01701-9101
Public; www.framingham.edu
Financial aid office: (508) 626-4534

■ **2004-2005 TUITION AND FEES:**
In state: $4,740; Out of state: $10,820
■ **ROOM AND BOARD:** $5,539

SAT I Score (25th/75th percentile): 950-1140
2005 U.S. News College Ranking:
Universities–Master's (North), fourth tier
Acceptance Rate: 55%

Other expenses: Estimated books and supplies: $700. Transportation: $700. Personal expenses: $1,200. **Financial aid:** Priority filing date for institution's financial aid form: March 1. In 2003-2004, 56% of undergraduates applied for financial aid. Of those, 34% were determined to have financial need; 59% had their need fully met. Average financial aid package (proportion receiving): $4,700 (34%). Average amount of gift aid, such as scholarships or grants (proportion receiving): $3,475 (30%). Average amount of self-help aid, such as work study or loans (proportion receiving): $2,100 (29%). Average need-based loan (excluding PLUS or other private loans): $1,900. Among students who received need-based aid, the average percentage of need met: 91%. Among students who received aid based on merit, the average award (and the proportion receiving): $1,550 (3%). Average amount of debt of borrowers graduating in 2003: $11,000. Proportion who borrowed: 48%. **Student employment:** During the 2003-2004 academic year, 10% of undergraduates worked on campus. Average per-year earnings: $1,000. **Reserve Officers Training Corps (ROTC):** Army ROTC: Offered at cooperating institution (Boston College; WPI).

Gordon College

255 Grapevine Road
Wenham, MA 01984
Private; www.gordon.edu
Financial aid office: (978) 867-4035

■ **2004-2005 TUITION AND FEES:** $21,448
■ **ROOM AND BOARD:** $6,092

SAT I Score (25th/75th percentile): 1110-1310
2005 U.S. News College Ranking:
Liberal Arts Colleges, third tier
Acceptance Rate: 78%

Other expenses: Estimated books and supplies: $800. Transportation: $400. Personal expenses: $1,000. **Financial aid:** Priority filing date for institution's financial aid form: March 1. In 2003-2004, 80% of undergraduates applied for financial aid. Of those, 70% were determined to have financial need; 16% had their need fully met. Average financial aid package (proportion receiving): $14,375 (70%). Average amount of gift aid, such as scholarships or grants (proportion receiving): $9,609 (68%). Average amount of self-help aid, such as work study or loans (proportion receiving): $5,639 (63%). Average need-based loan (excluding PLUS or other private loans): $4,598. Among students who received need-based aid, the average percentage of need met: 75%. Among students who received aid based on merit, the average award (and the proportion receiving): $10,895 (27%). The average athletic scholarship (and the proportion receiving): $0 (0%). Average amount of debt of borrowers graduating in 2003: $17,441. Proportion who borrowed: 53%. **Student employment:** During the 2003-2004 academic year, 65% of undergraduates worked on campus. Average per-year earnings: $3,600. **Cooperative education programs:** engineering, health professions. **Reserve Officers Training Corps (ROTC):** Air Force ROTC: Offered at cooperating institution (University of Massachusetts at Lowell and Boston University).

Hampshire College

893 West Street
Amherst, MA 01002
Private; www.hampshire.edu
Financial aid office: (413) 559-5484

■ **2004-2005 TUITION AND FEES:** $30,978
■ **ROOM AND BOARD:** $8,113

SAT I Score (25th/75th percentile): 1160-1360
2005 U.S. News College Ranking:
Liberal Arts Colleges, 101
Acceptance Rate: 55%

Other expenses: Estimated books and supplies: $500. Personal expenses: $500. **Financial aid:** Priority filing date for institution's financial aid form: February 1. In 2003-2004, 64% of undergraduates applied for financial aid. Of those, 55% were determined to have financial need; 90% had their need fully met. Average financial aid package (proportion receiving): $24,615 (54%). Average amount of gift aid, such as scholarships or grants (proportion receiving): $18,260 (54%). Average amount of self-help aid, such as work study or loans (proportion receiving): $6,355 (54%). Average need-based loan (excluding PLUS or other private loans): $4,030. Among students who received need-based aid, the average percentage of need met: 100%. Among students who received aid based on merit, the average award (and the proportion receiving): $4,990 (2%). The average athletic scholarship (and the proportion receiving): $0 (0%). Average amount of debt of borrowers graduating in 2003: $16,975. Proportion who borrowed: 57%. **Student employment:** During the 2003-2004 academic year, 9% of undergraduates worked on campus. Average per-year earnings: $2,400.

Harvard University

Undergraduate Admissions Office, Byerly Hall, 8 Garden Street
Cambridge, MA 02138
Private; www.college.harvard.edu
Financial aid office: (617) 495-1581

■ **2004-2005 TUITION AND FEES:** $30,620
■ **ROOM AND BOARD:** $9,260

SAT I Score (25th/75th percentile): 1400-1590
2005 U.S. News College Ranking:
National Universities, 1
Acceptance Rate: 10%

Other expenses: Estimated books and supplies: $900. Transportation: $500. Personal expenses: $1,670. **Financial aid:** Priority filing date for institution's financial aid form: February 1. In 2003-2004, 54% of undergraduates applied for financial aid. Of those, 48% were determined to have financial need; 100% had their need fully met. Average financial aid package (proportion receiving): $26,939 (48%). Average amount of gift aid, such as scholarships or grants (proportion receiving): $24,418 (48%). Average amount of self-help aid, such as work study or loans (proportion receiving): $3,187 (40%). Average need-based loan (excluding PLUS or other private loans): $2,447. Among students who received need-based aid, the average percentage of need met: 100%. Among students who received aid based on merit, the average award (and the proportion receiving): $0 (0%). The average athletic scholarship (and the proportion receiving): $0 (0%). Average amount of debt of borrowers graduating in 2003: $8,830. Proportion who borrowed: 51%. **Student employment:** During the 2003-2004 academic year, 50% of undergraduates worked on campus. Average per-year earnings: $1,500. **Reserve Officers Training Corps (ROTC):** Army ROTC: Offered at cooperating institution

(Massachusetts Institute of Technology); Navy ROTC: Offered at cooperating institution (Massachusetts Institute of Technology); Air Force ROTC: Offered at cooperating institution (Massachusetts Institute of Technology).

Lasell College

1844 Commonwealth Avenue
Newton, MA 02466
Private; www.lasell.edu
Financial aid office: (617) 243-2227

■ **2004-2005 TUITION AND FEES:** $18,500
■ **ROOM AND BOARD:** $8,600

SAT I Score (25th/75th percentile): 850-1030
2005 U.S. News College Ranking:
Comp. Colleges–Bachelor's (North), 31
Acceptance Rate: 75%

Other expenses: Estimated books and supplies: $1,000. Transportation: $500. Personal expenses: $2,000. **Financial aid:** Priority filing date for institution's financial aid form: March 15. In 2003-2004, 91% of undergraduates applied for financial aid. Of those, 82% were determined to have financial need; 9% had their need fully met. Average financial aid package (proportion receiving): $15,429 (82%). Average amount of gift aid, such as scholarships or grants (proportion receiving): $11,291 (82%). Average amount of self-help aid, such as work study or loans (proportion receiving): $4,474 (76%). Average need-based loan (excluding PLUS or other private loans): $3,472. Among students who received need-based aid, the average percentage of need met: 73%. Among students who received aid based on merit, the average award (and the proportion receiving): $12,126 (10%). The average athletic scholarship (and the proportion receiving): $0 (0%). Average amount of debt of borrowers graduating in 2003: $18,500. Proportion who borrowed: 85%. Average per-year earnings: $1,500.

Lesley University

29 Everett Street
Cambridge, MA 02138
Private; www.lesley.edu
Financial aid office: (617) 349-8710

■ **2004-2005 TUITION AND FEES:** $21,275
■ **ROOM AND BOARD:** $9,370

SAT I Score (25th/75th percentile): 960-1130
2005 U.S. News College Ranking:
Universities–Master's (North), 38
Acceptance Rate: 77%

Other expenses: Estimated books and supplies: $700. Transportation: $450. Personal expenses: $2,065. **Financial aid:** Priority filing date for institution's financial aid form: February 1. In 2003-2004, 88% of undergraduates applied for financial aid. Of those, 82% were determined to have financial need; 25% had their need fully met. Average financial aid package (proportion receiving): $12,015 (82%). Average amount of gift aid, such as scholarships or grants (proportion receiving): $8,310 (81%). Average amount of self-help aid, such as work study or loans (proportion receiving): $5,881 (82%). Average need-based loan (excluding PLUS or other private loans): $4,873. Among students who received need-based aid, the average percentage of need met: 94%. Among students who received aid based on merit, the average award (and the proportion receiving): $8,986 (6%). Average amount of debt of borrowers graduating in 2003: $13,125. Proportion who borrowed: 91%. **Student employment:** During the 2003-2004 academic year, 10% of undergraduates worked on campus. Average per-year earnings: $3,465.

Longy School of Music

1 Follen Street
Cambridge, MA 02138
Private; www.longy.edu
Financial aid office: (617) 876-0956

■ **2004-2005 TUITION AND FEES:** $20,115

2005 U.S. News College Ranking:
Unranked Specialty School–Fine Arts
Acceptance Rate: 100%

Financial aid: Priority filing date for institution's financial aid form: February 28. In 2003-2004, 36% of undergraduates applied for financial aid. Of those, 31% were determined to have financial need; 17% had their need fully met. Average financial aid package (proportion receiving): $10,654 (31%). Average amount of gift aid, such as scholarships or grants (proportion receiving): $7,277 (28%). Average amount of self-help aid, such as work study or loans (proportion receiving): $5,170 (31%). Average need-based loan (excluding PLUS or other private loans): $4,735. Among students who received need-based aid, the average percentage of need met: 48%. Among students who received aid based on merit, the average award (and the proportion receiving): $3,395 (59%). The average athletic scholarship (and the proportion receiving): $0 (0%). Average amount of debt of borrowers graduating in 2003: $21,204. Proportion who borrowed: 71%. **Student employment:** During the 2003-2004 academic year, 25% of undergraduates worked on campus. Average per-year earnings: $1,000.

Massachusetts College of Art

621 Huntington Avenue
Boston, MA 02115
Public; www.massart.edu
Financial aid office: (617) 879-7850

■ **2004-2005 TUITION AND FEES:**
  In state: $6,400; Out of state: $17,700
■ **ROOM AND BOARD:** $9,550

SAT I Score (25th/75th percentile): 980-1180
2005 U.S. News College Ranking:
Unranked Specialty School–Fine Arts
Acceptance Rate: 53%

Other expenses: Estimated books and supplies: $2,000. Personal expenses: $1,150.

Massachusetts College of Liberal Arts

375 Church Street
North Adams, MA 01247
Public; www.mcla.edu
Financial aid office: (413) 662-5219

■ **2004-2005 TUITION AND FEES:**
  In state: $5,397; Out of state: $14,342
■ **ROOM AND BOARD:** $6,400

SAT I Score (25th/75th percentile): 930-1160
2005 U.S. News College Ranking:
Liberal Arts Colleges, fourth tier
Acceptance Rate: 67%

Other expenses: Estimated books and supplies: $750. Transportation: $500. Personal expenses: $1,400. **Financial aid:** Priority filing date for institution's financial aid form: April 1. In 2003-2004, 92% of undergraduates applied for financial aid. Of those, 71% were determined to have financial need; 31% had their need fully met. Average financial aid package (proportion receiving): $6,865 (68%). Average amount of gift aid, such as scholarships or grants (proportion receiving): $4,167 (57%). Average amount of self-help aid, such as work study or loans (proportion receiving): $4,325 (58%). Average

need-based loan (excluding PLUS or other private loans): $3,452. Among students who received need-based aid, the average percentage of need met: 73%. Among students who received aid based on merit, the average award (and the proportion receiving): $3,620 (17%). The average athletic scholarship (and the proportion receiving): $0 (0%). Average amount of debt of borrowers graduating in 2003: $15,890. Proportion who borrowed: 69%. Average per-year earnings: $1,575.

Massachusetts Institute of Technology

77 Massachusetts Avenue
Cambridge, MA 02139
Private; web.mit.edu/admissions/www
Financial aid office: (617) 253-4971

■ **2004-2005 TUITION AND FEES:** $30,800
■ **ROOM AND BOARD:** $9,100

SAT I Score (25th/75th percentile): 1410-1560
2005 U.S. News College Ranking:
National Universities, 5
Acceptance Rate: 16%

Other expenses: Estimated books and supplies: $1,050. Personal expenses: $1,750. **Financial aid:** Priority filing date for institution's financial aid form: February 1; deadline: February 1. In 2003-2004, 69% of undergraduates applied for financial aid. Of those, 61% were determined to have financial need; 100% had their need fully met. Average financial aid package (proportion receiving): $24,875 (61%). Average amount of gift aid, such as scholarships or grants (proportion receiving): $22,225 (59%). Average amount of self-help aid, such as work study or loans (proportion receiving): $4,275 (54%). Average need-based loan (excluding PLUS or other private loans): $3,931. Among students who received need-based aid, the average percentage of need met: 100%. Among students who received aid based on merit, the average award (and the proportion receiving): $0 (0%). The average athletic scholarship (and the proportion receiving): $0 (0%). Average amount of debt of borrowers graduating in 2003: $20,079. Proportion who borrowed: 54%. **Student employment:** During the 2003-2004 academic year, 58% of undergraduates worked on campus. Average per-year earnings: $1,947. **Reserve Officers Training Corps (ROTC):** Army ROTC: Offered on campus; Navy ROTC: Offered on campus; Air Force ROTC: Offered on campus.

Merrimack College

315 Turnpike Street
North Andover, MA 01845
Private; www.merrimack.edu
Financial aid office: (978) 837-5196

■ **2004-2005 TUITION AND FEES:** $22,100
■ **ROOM AND BOARD:** $9,200

SAT I Score (25th/75th percentile): 1020-1160
2005 U.S. News College Ranking:
Comp. Colleges–Bachelor's (North), 7
Acceptance Rate: 60%

Other expenses: Estimated books and supplies: $800. Transportation: $800. Personal expenses: $500. **Financial aid:** In 2003-2004, 81% of undergraduates applied for financial aid. Of those, 76% were determined to have financial need; 71% had their need fully met. Average financial aid package (proportion receiving): $17,000 (76%). Average amount of gift aid, such as scholarships or grants (proportion receiving): $9,000 (75%). Average amount of self-help aid, such as work study or loans (proportion receiving): $8,000 (74%). Average need-based loan (excluding PLUS or other private loans): $7,000. Among students who received need-based aid, the average percentage of need met: 70%. Among students who received aid based on merit, the average award (and the proportion receiving): $5,000 (3%). The average athletic scholarship (and the proportion receiving): $22,000 (6%). Average amount of debt of borrowers graduating in 2003: $21,125. Proportion who borrowed: 70%. **Student employment:** During the 2003-2004 academic year, 22% of undergraduates worked on campus. Average per-year earnings: $1,500. **Cooperative education programs:** business, other. **Reserve Officers Training Corps (ROTC):** Army ROTC: Offered at cooperating institution (University of Massachusetts–Lowell); Air Force ROTC: Offered on campus.

Montserrat College of Art

PO Box 26, 23 Essex Street
Beverly, MA 01915
Private; www.montserrat.edu
Financial aid office: (978) 921-4242

■ **2004-2005 TUITION AND FEES:** $19,650
■ **ROOM AND BOARD:** $4,950

SAT I Score (25th/75th percentile): 880-1150
2005 U.S. News College Ranking:
Unranked Specialty School–Fine Arts
Acceptance Rate: 83%

....

Other expenses: Estimated books and supplies: $900. Transportation: $1,000. Personal expenses: $900. **Financial aid:** Priority filing date for institution's financial aid form: March 2; deadline: July 1. In 2003-2004, 91% of undergraduates applied for financial aid. Of those, 87% were determined to have financial need; 8% had their need fully met. Average financial aid package (proportion receiving): $8,770 (87%). Average amount of gift aid, such as scholarships or grants (proportion receiving): $5,851 (76%). Average amount of self-help aid, such as work study or loans (proportion receiving): $3,915 (81%). Average need-based loan (excluding PLUS or other private loans): $3,762. Among students who received need-based aid, the average percentage of need met: 47%. Among students who received aid based on merit, the average award (and the proportion receiving): $6,864 (12%). The average athletic scholarship (and the proportion receiving): $0 (0%). Average amount of debt of borrowers graduating in 2003: $24,006. Proportion who borrowed: 72%. **Student employment:** During the 2003-2004 academic year, 13% of undergraduates worked on campus. Average per-year earnings: $2,500. **Reserve Officers Training Corps (ROTC):** Air Force ROTC: Offered at cooperating institution (Salem State College).

Mount Holyoke College

50 College Street
South Hadley, MA 01075
Private; www.mtholyoke.edu
Financial aid office: (413) 538-2291

■ **2004-2005 TUITION AND FEES:** $30,938
■ **ROOM AND BOARD:** $9,060

SAT I Score (25th/75th percentile): 1210-1370
2005 U.S. News College Ranking:
Liberal Arts Colleges, 24
Acceptance Rate: 52%

....

Other expenses: Estimated books and supplies: $750. Personal expenses: $750. **Financial aid:** Priority filing date for institution's financial aid form: February 1; deadline: February 1. In 2003-2004, 81% of undergraduates applied for financial aid. Of those, 70% were determined to have financial need; 100% had their need fully met. Average financial aid package (proportion receiving): $25,469 (70%). Average amount of

gift aid, such as scholarships or grants (proportion receiving): $20,062 (67%). Average amount of self-help aid, such as work study or loans (proportion receiving): $6,147 (68%). Average need-based loan (excluding PLUS or other private loans): $4,867. Among students who received need-based aid, the average percentage of need met: 100%. Among students who received aid based on merit, the average award (and the proportion receiving): $10,950 (5%). The average athletic scholarship (and the proportion receiving): $0 (0%). Average amount of debt of borrowers graduating in 2003: $17,000. Proportion who borrowed: 73%. **Student employment:** During the 2003-2004 academic year, 67% of undergraduates worked on campus. Average per-year earnings: $1,800. **Cooperative education programs:** other. **Reserve Officers Training Corps (ROTC):** Army ROTC: Offered at cooperating institution (University of Massachusetts Amherst); Air Force ROTC: Offered at cooperating institution (University of Massachusetts Amherst).

Mount Ida College

777 Dedham Street
Newton, MA 02159
Private; www.mountida.edu
Financial aid office: (617) 928-4785

■ **2004-2005 TUITION AND FEES:** $17,671
■ **ROOM AND BOARD:** $9,400

SAT I Score (25th/75th percentile): 730-940
2005 U.S. News College Ranking:
Comp. Colleges–Bachelor's (North), fourth tier
Acceptance Rate: 80%

....

Other expenses: Estimated books and supplies: $800. Transportation: $650. Personal expenses: $1,000. **Financial aid:** Priority filing date for institution's financial aid form: May 1. In 2003-2004, 91% of undergraduates applied for financial aid. Of those, 85% were determined to have financial need; 5% had their need fully met. Average financial aid package (proportion receiving): $10,749 (85%). Average amount of gift aid, such as scholarships or grants (proportion receiving): $7,635 (81%). Average amount of self-help aid, such as work study or loans (proportion receiving): $3,625 (82%). Average need-based loan (excluding PLUS or other private loans): $3,318. Among students who received need-based aid, the average percentage of need met: 51%. Among students who received aid based on merit, the average award (and the proportion receiving): $7,218 (14%). The average athletic scholarship (and the proportion receiving): $0 (0%). Average amount

of debt of borrowers graduating in 2003: $19,278. Proportion who borrowed: 73%. **Student employment:** During the 2003-2004 academic year, 9% of undergraduates worked on campus. Average per-year earnings: $10,000.

Newbury College

129 Fischer Avenue
Brookline, MA 02445-5796
Private; www.newbury.edu
Financial aid office: (617) 730-7100

■ **2004-2005 TUITION AND FEES:** $16,400
■ **ROOM AND BOARD:** $8,250

2005 U.S. News College Ranking:
Comp. Colleges–Bachelor's (North), fourth tier

....

New England Conservatory of Music

290 Huntington Avenue
Boston, MA 02115
Private; www.newenglandconservatory.edu
Financial aid office: (617) 585-1110

■ **2004-2005 TUITION AND FEES:** $26,300
■ **ROOM AND BOARD:** $10,650

2005 U.S. News College Ranking:
Unranked Specialty School–Fine Arts
Acceptance Rate: 38%

....

Other expenses: Estimated books and supplies: $700. Transportation: $316. Personal expenses: $2,100. **Financial aid:** Priority filing date for institution's financial aid form: December 1. In 2003-2004, 100% of undergraduates applied for financial aid. Of those, 92% were determined to have financial need; 8% had their need fully met. Average financial aid package (proportion receiving): $16,438 (92%). Average amount of gift aid, such as scholarships or grants (proportion receiving): $12,301 (71%). Average amount of self-help aid, such as work study or loans (proportion receiving): $5,573 (62%). Average need-based loan (excluding PLUS or other private loans): $4,316. Among students who received need-based aid, the average percentage of need met: 62%. Among students who received aid based on merit, the average award (and the proportion receiving): $6,131 (1%). The average athletic scholarship (and the proportion receiving): $0 (0%). Average amount of debt of borrowers graduating in 2003: $16,431. Proportion who borrowed: 89%. **Student**

employment: During the 2003-2004 academic year, 60% of undergraduates worked on campus. Average per-year earnings: $1,500.

Nichols College

Box 5000
Dudley, MA 01571
Private; www.nichols.edu
Financial aid office: (508) 213-2278

■ **2004-2005 TUITION AND FEES:** $20,810
■ **ROOM AND BOARD:** $8,052

SAT I Score (25th/75th percentile): 810-1000
2005 U.S. News College Ranking:
Unranked Specialty School–Business
Acceptance Rate: 82%

Other expenses: Estimated books and supplies: $800. Transportation: $500. Personal expenses: $1,171. **Financial aid:** Priority filing date for institution's financial aid form: March 1; deadline: June 1. In 2003-2004, 85% of undergraduates applied for financial aid. Of those, 76% were determined to have financial need; 34% had their need fully met. Average financial aid package (proportion receiving): $13,893 (76%). Average amount of gift aid, such as scholarships or grants (proportion receiving): $7,461 (75%). Average amount of self-help aid, such as work study or loans (proportion receiving): $7,181 (69%). Average need-based loan (excluding PLUS or other private loans): $6,594. Among students who received need-based aid, the average percentage of need met: 74%. Among students who received aid based on merit, the average award (and the proportion receiving): $9,419 (21%). The average athletic scholarship (and the proportion receiving): $0 (0%). Average amount of debt of borrowers graduating in 2003: $21,996. Proportion who borrowed: 62%.

Northeastern University

360 Huntington Avenue
Boston, MA 02115
Private; www.northeastern.edu
Financial aid office: (617) 373-3190

■ **2004-2005 TUITION AND FEES:** $26,990
■ **ROOM AND BOARD:** $10,800

SAT I Score (25th/75th percentile): 1120-1300
2005 U.S. News College Ranking:
National Universities, 120
Acceptance Rate: 47%

Financial aid: Priority filing date for institution's financial aid form: February 15. In 2003-2004, 73% of undergraduates applied for financial aid. Of those, 64% were determined to have financial need; 15% had their need fully met. Average financial aid package (proportion receiving): $15,396 (64%). Average amount of gift aid, such as scholarships or grants (proportion receiving): $11,050 (60%). Average amount of self-help aid, such as work study or loans (proportion receiving): $5,724 (58%). Average need-based loan (excluding PLUS or other private loans): $4,836. Among students who received need-based aid, the average percentage of need met: 63%. Among students who received aid based on merit, the average award (and the proportion receiving): $12,627 (12%). The average athletic scholarship (and the proportion receiving): $22,551 (1%). **Cooperative education programs:** art, business, computer science, education, engineering, health professions, humanities, natural science, social/behavioral science, technologies. **Reserve Officers Training Corps (ROTC):** Army ROTC: Offered on campus; Navy ROTC: Offered at cooperating institution (Boston University); Air Force ROTC: Offered at cooperating institution (Boston University).

Pine Manor College

400 Heath Street
Chestnut Hill, MA 02467
Private; www.pmc.edu
Financial aid office: (617) 731-7053

■ **2004-2005 TUITION AND FEES:** $14,544
■ **ROOM AND BOARD:** $9,000

SAT I Score (25th/75th percentile): 690-890
2005 U.S. News College Ranking:
Liberal Arts Colleges, fourth tier
Acceptance Rate: 71%

Other expenses: Estimated books and supplies: $956. Personal expenses: $1,500. **Financial aid:** Priority filing date for institution's financial aid form: May 1. In 2003-2004, 90% of undergraduates applied for financial aid. Of those, 85% were determined to have financial need; 16% had their need fully met. Average financial aid package (proportion receiving): $14,730 (85%). Average amount of gift aid, such as scholarships or grants (proportion receiving): $10,421 (84%). Average amount of self-help aid, such as work study or loans (proportion receiving): $4,543 (82%). Average need-based loan (excluding PLUS or other private loans): $3,575. Among students who received need-based aid, the average

percentage of need met: 78%. Among students who received aid based on merit, the average award (and the proportion receiving): $8,299 (12%). Average amount of debt of borrowers graduating in 2003: $14,312. Proportion who borrowed: 60%. **Student employment:** During the 2003-2004 academic year, 10% of undergraduates worked on campus.

Regis College

235 Wellesley Street
Weston, MA 02493-1571
Private; www.regiscollege.edu
Financial aid office: (781) 768-7180

■ **2004-2005 TUITION AND FEES:** $20,500
■ **ROOM AND BOARD:** $9,360

SAT I Score (25th/75th percentile): 800-1060
2005 U.S. News College Ranking:
Universities–Master's (North), 36
Acceptance Rate: 87%

Other expenses: Estimated books and supplies: $900. Transportation: $300. Personal expenses: $1,785. **Financial aid:** Priority filing date for institution's financial aid form: February 16. In 2003-2004, 86% of undergraduates applied for financial aid. Of those, 79% were determined to have financial need; 15% had their need fully met. Average financial aid package (proportion receiving): $17,940 (79%). Average amount of gift aid, such as scholarships or grants (proportion receiving): $9,242 (66%). Average amount of self-help aid, such as work study or loans (proportion receiving): $7,100 (77%). Average need-based loan (excluding PLUS or other private loans): $4,874. Among students who received need-based aid, the average percentage of need met: 57%. Among students who received aid based on merit, the average award (and the proportion receiving): $8,985 (10%). The average athletic scholarship (and the proportion receiving): $0 (0%). Average amount of debt of borrowers graduating in 2003: $20,174. Proportion who borrowed: 87%. **Student employment:** During the 2003-2004 academic year, 14% of undergraduates worked on campus. Average per-year earnings: $1,000. **Reserve Officers Training Corps (ROTC):** Army ROTC: Offered at cooperating institution (Boston College).

Salem State College

352 Lafayette Street
Salem, MA 01970
Public; www.salemstate.edu
Financial aid office: (978) 542-6139

■ **2004-2005 TUITION AND FEES:**
In state: $5,283; Out of state: $11,423
■ **ROOM AND BOARD:** $5,428

SAT I Score (25th/75th percentile): 840-1050
2005 U.S. News College Ranking:
Universities–Master's (North), fourth tier
Acceptance Rate: 82%

Other expenses: Estimated books and supplies: $800. Transportation: $540. Personal expenses: $900. **Financial aid:** Priority filing date for institution's financial aid form: April 1. In 2003-2004, 43% of undergraduates applied for financial aid. Of those, 42% were determined to have financial need; 40% had their need fully met. Average financial aid package (proportion receiving): $3,833 (42%). Average amount of gift aid, such as scholarships or grants (proportion receiving): N/A (3%). Average amount of self-help aid, such as work study or loans (proportion receiving): $2,074 (35%). Average need-based loan (excluding PLUS or other private loans): $1,881. Among students who received need-based aid, the average percentage of need met: 75%. Among students who received aid based on merit, the average award (and the proportion receiving): $783 (15%). The average athletic scholarship (and the proportion receiving): $0 (0%). **Reserve Officers Training Corps (ROTC):** Air Force ROTC: Offered at cooperating institution (U-Mass Lowell).

Simmons College

300 The Fenway
Boston, MA 02115
Private; www.simmons.edu
Financial aid office: (617) 521-2001

■ **2004-2005 TUITION AND FEES:** $24,490
■ **ROOM AND BOARD:** $9,820

SAT I Score (25th/75th percentile): 1000-1190
2005 U.S. News College Ranking:
Universities–Master's (North), 13
Acceptance Rate: 68%

Other expenses: Estimated books and supplies: $800. Transportation: $1,380. Personal expens-

es: $1,370. **Financial aid:** Priority filing date for institution's financial aid form: February 1; deadline: March 1. In 2003-2004, 76% of undergraduates applied for financial aid. Of those, 70% were determined to have financial need; 4% had their need fully met. Average financial aid package (proportion receiving): $15,175 (68%). Average amount of gift aid, such as scholarships or grants (proportion receiving): $11,452 (65%). Average amount of self-help aid, such as work study or loans (proportion receiving): $2,879 (61%). Average need-based loan (excluding PLUS or other private loans): $2,880. Among students who received need-based aid, the average percentage of need met: 56%. Among students who received aid based on merit, the average award (and the proportion receiving): $12,454 (1%). **Student employment:** During the 2003-2004 academic year, 50% of undergraduates worked on campus. Average per-year earnings: $2,000. **Reserve Officers Training Corps (ROTC):** Army ROTC: Offered at cooperating institution (Northeastern University); Navy ROTC: Offered at cooperating institution (Northeastern University); Air Force ROTC: Offered at cooperating institution (Northeastern University).

Simon's Rock College of Bard

84 Alford Road
Great Barrington, MA 01230
Private; www.simons-rock.edu
Financial aid office: (413) 528-7297

■ **2004-2005 TUITION AND FEES:** $30,687
■ **ROOM AND BOARD:** $8,088

2005 U.S. News College Ranking:
Comp. Colleges–Bachelor's (North), third tier
Acceptance Rate: 46%

Smith College

7 College Lane
Northampton, MA 01063
Private; www.smith.edu
Financial aid office: (413) 585-2530

■ **2004-2005 TUITION AND FEES:** $29,156
■ **ROOM AND BOARD:** $9,730

SAT I Score (25th/75th percentile): 1150-1370
2005 U.S. News College Ranking:
Liberal Arts Colleges, 13
Acceptance Rate: 52%

Financial aid: In 2003-2004, 68% of undergraduates applied for financial aid. Of those, 56% were determined to have financial need; 100% had their need fully met. Average financial aid package (proportion receiving): $27,378 (56%). Average amount of gift aid, such as scholarships or grants (proportion receiving): $20,988 (56%). Average amount of self-help aid, such as work study or loans (proportion receiving): $6,390 (56%). Average need-based loan (excluding PLUS or other private loans): $4,401. Among students who received need-based aid, the average percentage of need met: 100%. Among students who received aid based on merit, the average award (and the proportion receiving): $8,943 (4%). The average athletic scholarship (and the proportion receiving): $0 (0%). Average amount of debt of borrowers graduating in 2003: $20,570. Proportion who borrowed: 72%. **Student employment:** During the 2003-2004 academic year, 74% of undergraduates worked on campus. Average per-year earnings: $2,700. **Reserve Officers Training Corps (ROTC):** Army ROTC: Offered at cooperating institution (UMass–Amherst); Air Force ROTC: Offered at cooperating institution (UMass–Amherst).

Springfield College

263 Alden Street
Springfield, MA 01109
Private; www.springfieldcollege.edu
Financial aid office: (413) 748-3108

■ **2004-2005 TUITION AND FEES:** $20,360
■ **ROOM AND BOARD:** $7,380

SAT I Score (25th/75th percentile): 930-1120
2005 U.S. News College Ranking:
Universities–Master's (North), 50
Acceptance Rate: 74%

Other expenses: Estimated books and supplies: $900. Transportation: $400. Personal expenses: $1,200. **Financial aid:** Priority filing date for institution's financial aid form: March 15. In 2003-2004, 89% of undergraduates applied for financial aid. Of those, 77% were determined to have financial need; 19% had their need fully met. Average financial aid package (proportion receiving): $15,142 (77%). Average amount of gift aid, such as scholarships or grants (proportion receiving): $10,475 (76%). Average amount of self-help aid, such as work study or loans (proportion receiving): $5,356 (70%). Average need-based loan (excluding PLUS or other private loans): $4,209. Among students who received need-based aid, the average percentage of need met:

82%. Among students who received aid based on merit, the average award (and the proportion receiving): $12,279 (13%). The average athletic scholarship (and the proportion receiving): $0 (0%). Average amount of debt of borrowers graduating in 2003: $20,869. Proportion who borrowed: 90%. **Student employment:** During the 2003-2004 academic year, 11% of undergraduates worked on campus. Average per-year earnings: $1,600. **Reserve Officers Training Corps (ROTC):** Army ROTC: Offered at cooperating institution (Western New England College); Air Force ROTC: Offered at cooperating institution (Western New England College).

Stonehill College

320 Washington Street
Easton, MA 02357
Private; www.stonehill.edu
Financial aid office: (508) 565-1088

■ **2004-2005 TUITION AND FEES:** $23,008
■ **ROOM AND BOARD:** $10,206

SAT I Score (25th/75th percentile): 1110-1270
2005 U.S. News College Ranking:
Comp. Colleges–Bachelor's (North), 1
Acceptance Rate: 49%

Other expenses: Estimated books and supplies: $1,200. Transportation: $180. Personal expenses: $932. **Financial aid:** Priority filing date for institution's financial aid form: February 1; deadline: February 1. In 2003-2004, 78% of undergraduates applied for financial aid. Of those, 66% were determined to have financial need; 20% had their need fully met. Average financial aid package (proportion receiving): $15,639 (66%). Average amount of gift aid, such as scholarships or grants (proportion receiving): $10,999 (63%). Average amount of self-help aid, such as work study or loans (proportion receiving): $5,736 (59%). Average need-based loan (excluding PLUS or other private loans): $4,940. Among students who received need-based aid, the average percentage of need met: 82%. Among students who received aid based on merit, the average award (and the proportion receiving): $10,069 (22%). The average athletic scholarship (and the proportion receiving): $10,900 (2%). Average amount of debt of borrowers graduating in 2003: $16,237. Proportion who borrowed: 72%. **Student employment:** During the 2003-2004 academic year, 11% of undergraduates worked on campus. Average per-year earnings: $1,106. **Reserve Officers Training Corps (ROTC):** Army ROTC: Offered on campus.

Suffolk University

8 Ashburton Place, Beacon Hill
Boston, MA 02108
Private; www.suffolk.edu
Financial aid office: (617) 573-8470

■ **2004-2005 TUITION AND FEES:** $19,870
■ **ROOM AND BOARD:** $11,651

SAT I Score (25th/75th percentile): 940-1090
2005 U.S. News College Ranking:
Universities–Master's (North), 56
Acceptance Rate: 82%

Other expenses: Estimated books and supplies: $1,000. Transportation: $150. Personal expenses: $2,471. **Financial aid:** Priority filing date for institution's financial aid form: March 1; deadline: March 1. In 2003-2004, 63% of undergraduates applied for financial aid. Of those, 54% were determined to have financial need; 14% had their need fully met. Average financial aid package (proportion receiving): $12,457 (53%). Average amount of gift aid, such as scholarships or grants (proportion receiving): $6,417 (45%). Average amount of self-help aid, such as work study or loans (proportion receiving): $5,844 (51%). Average need-based loan (excluding PLUS or other private loans): $4,666. Among students who received need-based aid, the average percentage of need met: 67%. Among students who received aid based on merit, the average award (and the proportion receiving): $4,450 (9%). Average amount of debt of borrowers graduating in 2003: $18,821. Proportion who borrowed: 63%. **Student employment:** During the 2003-2004 academic year, 30% of undergraduates worked on campus. Average per-year earnings: $1,500. **Cooperative education programs:** art, business, computer science, education, engineering, health professions, humanities, natural science, social/behavioral science, other. **Reserve Officers Training Corps (ROTC):** Army ROTC: Offered at cooperating institution (Northeastern University).

Tufts University

Medford, MA 02155
Private; www.tufts.edu
Financial aid office: (617) 627-2000

■ **2004-2005 TUITION AND FEES:** $30,969
■ **ROOM AND BOARD:** $9,030

SAT I Score (25th/75th percentile): 1250-1420
2005 U.S. News College Ranking:
National Universities, 28
Acceptance Rate: 26%

Other expenses: Estimated books and supplies: $800. Transportation: $200. Personal expenses: $1,201. **Financial aid:** Priority filing date for institution's financial aid form: February 15; deadline: February 15. In 2003-2004, 47% of undergraduates applied for financial aid. Of those, 41% were determined to have financial need; 100% had their need fully met. Average financial aid package (proportion receiving): $24,084 (41%). Average amount of gift aid, such as scholarships or grants (proportion receiving): $20,932 (37%). Average amount of self-help aid, such as work study or loans (proportion receiving): $5,171 (38%). Average need-based loan (excluding PLUS or other private loans): $4,202. Among students who received need-based aid, the average percentage of need met: 100%. Among students who received aid based on merit, the average award (and the proportion receiving): $500 (2%). The average athletic scholarship (and the proportion receiving): $0 (0%). Average amount of debt of borrowers graduating in 2003: $14,925. Proportion who borrowed: 40%. **Student employment:** During the 2003-2004 academic year, 20% of undergraduates worked on campus. Average per-year earnings: $2,000. **Reserve Officers Training Corps (ROTC):** Army ROTC: Offered at cooperating institution (MIT); Navy ROTC: Offered at cooperating institution (MIT); Air Force ROTC: Offered at cooperating institution (MIT).

University of Massachusetts–Amherst

Whitmore, 181 President's Drive
Amherst, MA 01003-9291
Public; www.umass.edu
Financial aid office: (413) 545-0801

■ **2004-2005 TUITION AND FEES:**
   In state: $9,008; Out of state: $17,861
■ **ROOM AND BOARD:** $6,189

SAT I Score (25th/75th percentile): 1030-1240
2005 U.S. News College Ranking:
National Universities, 98
Acceptance Rate: 82%

Other expenses: Estimated books and supplies: $500. Transportation: $400. Personal expenses: $1,000. **Financial aid:** Priority filing date for institution's financial aid form: March 1. In 2003-2004, 69% of undergraduates applied for financial aid. Of those, 53% were determined to have financial need; 25% had their need fully met. Average financial aid package (proportion receiving): $10,275 (51%). Average amount of gift aid, such as scholarships or grants (proportion receiving): $5,491 (49%). Average amount of self-help aid, such as work study or loans (proportion receiving): $4,743 (47%). Average need-based loan (excluding PLUS or other private loans): $3,962. Among students who received need-based aid, the average percentage of need met: 88%. Among students who received aid based on merit, the average award (and the proportion receiving): $5,447 (2%). The average athletic scholarship (and the proportion receiving): $11,839 (1%). Average amount of debt of borrowers graduating in 2003: $15,374. Proportion who borrowed: 65%. **Cooperative education programs:** agriculture, art, business, computer science, education, engineering, health professions, humanities, natural science, social/behavioral science. **Reserve Officers Training Corps (ROTC):** Army ROTC: Offered on campus; Air Force ROTC: Offered on campus.

University of Massachusetts–Boston

100 Morrissey Boulevard
Boston, MA 02125-3393
Public; www.umb.edu
Financial aid office: (617) 287-6300

■ **2004-2005 TUITION AND FEES:**
In state: $4,012; Out of state: $9,378

SAT I Score (25th/75th percentile): 940-1140
2005 U.S. News College Ranking:
National Universities, fourth tier
Acceptance Rate: 55%

Financial aid: Priority filing date for institution's financial aid form: March 1. In 2003-2004, 71% of undergraduates applied for financial aid. Of those, 61% were determined to have financial need; 64% had their need fully met. Average financial aid package (proportion receiving): $9,552 (61%). Average amount of gift aid, such as scholarships or grants (proportion receiving): $4,729 (52%). Average amount of self-help aid, such as work study or loans (proportion receiving): $7,084 (58%). Average need-based loan (excluding PLUS or other private loans): $5,393. Among students who received need-based aid, the average percentage of need met: 91%. Among students who received aid based on merit, the average award (and the proportion receiving): $3,026 (1%). Average amount of debt of borrowers graduat-

ing in 2003: $17,213. Proportion who borrowed: 69%. Average per-year earnings: $3,000.

University of Massachusetts–Dartmouth

285 Old Westport Road
North Dartmouth, MA 02747-2300
Public; www.umassd.edu
Financial aid office: (508) 999-8632

■ **2004-2005 TUITION AND FEES:**
In state: $7,802; Out of state: $14,484
■ **ROOM AND BOARD:** $7,471

SAT I Score (25th/75th percentile): 970-1150
2005 U.S. News College Ranking:
Universities–Master's (North), 62
Acceptance Rate: 71%

Other expenses: Estimated books and supplies: $800. Transportation: $500. Personal expenses: $1,339. **Financial aid:** Priority filing date for institution's financial aid form: March 1. In 2003-2004, 79% of undergraduates applied for financial aid. Of those, 62% were determined to have financial need; 50% had their need fully met. Average financial aid package (proportion receiving): $7,500 (59%). Average amount of gift aid, such as scholarships or grants (proportion receiving): $4,733 (51%). Average amount of self-help aid, such as work study or loans (proportion receiving): $4,000 (60%). Average need-based loan (excluding PLUS or other private loans): $3,700. Among students who received need-based aid, the average percentage of need met: 84%. Among students who received aid based on merit, the average award (and the proportion receiving): $2,200 (4%). The average athletic scholarship (and the proportion receiving): $0 (0%). Average amount of debt of borrowers graduating in 2003: $14,800. Proportion who borrowed: 63%. **Cooperative education programs:** business, engineering. **Reserve Officers Training Corps (ROTC):** Army ROTC: Offered at cooperating institution (Providence College).

University of Massachusetts–Lowell

1 University Avenue
Lowell, MA 01854
Public; www.uml.edu
Financial aid office: (978) 934-4226

■ **2004-2005 TUITION AND FEES:**
In state: $7,891; Out of state: $15,004
■ **ROOM AND BOARD:** $6,011

SAT I Score (25th/75th percentile): 1000-1180
2005 U.S. News College Ranking:
National Universities, fourth tier
Acceptance Rate: 62%

Other expenses: Estimated books and supplies: $600. Transportation: $200. Personal expenses: $800. **Financial aid:** Priority filing date for institution's financial aid form: March 1. In 2003-2004, 65% of undergraduates applied for financial aid. Of those, 47% were determined to have financial need; 78% had their need fully met. Average financial aid package (proportion receiving): $8,001 (45%). Average amount of gift aid, such as scholarships or grants (proportion receiving): $3,911 (36%). Average amount of self-help aid, such as work study or loans (proportion receiving): $3,993 (37%). Average need-based loan (excluding PLUS or other private loans): $3,236. Among students who received need-based aid, the average percentage of need met: 95%. Among students who received aid based on merit, the average award (and the proportion receiving): $3,795 (4%). The average athletic scholarship (and the proportion receiving): $7,431 (2%). Average amount of debt of borrowers graduating in 2003: $15,258. Proportion who borrowed: 67%. **Student employment:** During the 2003-2004 academic year, 8% of undergraduates worked on campus. Average per-year earnings: $2,250. **Cooperative education programs:** engineering. **Reserve Officers Training Corps (ROTC):** Air Force ROTC: Offered on campus.

Wellesley College

106 Central Street
Wellesley, MA 02481-8203
Private; www.wellesley.edu
Financial aid office: (781) 283-2360

■ **2004-2005 TUITION AND FEES:** $29,796
■ **ROOM AND BOARD:** $9,202

SAT I Score (25th/75th percentile): 1260-1450
2005 U.S. News College Ranking:
Liberal Arts Colleges, 4
Acceptance Rate: 41%

Other expenses: Estimated books and supplies: $800. Transportation: $1,000. Personal expenses: $1,200. **Financial aid:** Priority filing date for institution's financial aid form: January 15. In 2003-2004, 66% of undergraduates applied for financial aid. Of those, 57% were determined to have financial need; 100% had their need fully met. Average financial aid package (proportion receiving): $24,468 (57%). Average amount of gift aid, such as scholarships or grants (proportion receiving): $21,628 (55%). Average amount of self-help aid, such as work study or loans (proportion receiving): $3,931 (52%). Average need-based loan (excluding PLUS or other private loans): $3,196. Among students who received need-based aid, the average percentage of need met: 100%. Average amount of debt of borrowers graduating in 2003: $11,913. Proportion who borrowed: 59%. **Student employment:** During the 2003-2004 academic year, 20% of undergraduates worked on campus. Average per-year earnings: $1,500. **Reserve Officers Training Corps (ROTC):** Army ROTC: Offered at cooperating institution (MIT); Air Force ROTC: Offered at cooperating institution (MIT).

Wentworth Institute of Technology

550 Huntington Avenue
Boston, MA 02115-5998
Private; www.wit.edu
Financial aid office: (617) 989-4020

■ **2004-2005 TUITION AND FEES:** $15,700
■ **ROOM AND BOARD:** $8,600

2005 U.S. News College Ranking:
Unranked Specialty School–Engineering
Acceptance Rate: 70%

Other expenses: Estimated books and supplies: $1,000. Transportation: $1,000. Personal expenses: $1,000. **Financial aid:** Priority filing date for institution's financial aid form: March 1. In 2003-2004, 100% of undergraduates applied for financial aid. Of those, 63% were determined to have financial need; 4% had their need fully met. Average financial aid package (proportion receiving): $7,625 (63%). Average amount of gift aid, such as scholarships or grants (proportion receiving): $1,125 (20%). Average amount of self-help aid, such as work study or loans (proportion receiving): $1,600 (63%). Average need-based loan (excluding PLUS or other private loans): $4,375. Among students who received need-based aid, the average percentage of need met: 46%. Among students who received aid based on merit, the average award (and the proportion receiving): $2,949 (17%). The average athletic scholarship (and the proportion receiving): $0 (0%). Average amount of debt of borrowers graduating in 2003: $18,781. Proportion who borrowed: 79%. **Reserve Officers Training Corps (ROTC):** Army ROTC: Offered at cooperating institution (Northeastern University).

Western New England College

1215 Wilbraham Road
Springfield, MA 01119-2684
Private; www.wnec.edu
Financial aid office: (413) 796-2080

■ **2004-2005 TUITION AND FEES:** $19,950
■ **ROOM AND BOARD:** $8,524

SAT I Score (25th/75th percentile): 960-1160
2005 U.S. News College Ranking:
Universities–Master's (North), 73
Acceptance Rate: 76%

Other expenses: Estimated books and supplies: $690. Transportation: $390. Personal expenses: $1,100. **Financial aid:** In 2003-2004, 95% of undergraduates applied for financial aid. Of those, 83% were determined to have financial need; 7% had their need fully met. Average financial aid package (proportion receiving): $12,334 (76%). Average amount of gift aid, such as scholarships or grants (proportion receiving): $7,887 (75%). Average amount of self-help aid, such as work study or loans (proportion receiving): $5,040 (69%). Average need-based loan (excluding PLUS or other private loans): $4,200. Among students who received need-based aid, the average percentage of need met: 67%. Among students who received aid based on merit, the average award (and the proportion receiving): $6,615 (10%). The average athletic scholarship (and the proportion receiving): $0 (0%). Proportion who borrowed: 85%. **Cooperative education programs:** business, computer science, education, engineering, humanities, natural science, social/behavioral science. **Reserve Officers Training Corps (ROTC):** Army ROTC: Offered on campus; Air Force ROTC: Offered at cooperating institution (UMass–Amherst).

Westfield State College

Western Avenue
Westfield, MA 01086
Public; www.wsc.mass.edu
Financial aid office: (413) 572-5218

■ **2004-2005 TUITION AND FEES:**
In state: $4,857; Out of state: $10,937
■ **ROOM AND BOARD:** $5,290

SAT I Score (25th/75th percentile): 940-1100
2005 U.S. News College Ranking:
Universities–Master's (North), fourth tier
Acceptance Rate: 66%

Other expenses: Estimated books and supplies: $650. Transportation: $400. Personal expenses: $5,052. **Financial aid:** Priority filing date for institution's financial aid form: March 1. Average amount of debt of borrowers graduating in 2003: $12,347. Proportion who borrowed: 92%. **Student employment:** During the 2003-2004 academic year, 5% of undergraduates worked on campus. Average per-year earnings: $2,500. **Cooperative education programs:** art, business, computer science, education, humanities, natural science, social/behavioral science. **Reserve Officers Training Corps (ROTC):** Army ROTC: Offered at cooperating institution (Western New England College); Air Force ROTC: Offered at cooperating institution (UMass–Amherst, Western New England College).

Wheaton College

East Main Street
Norton, MA 02766
Private; www.wheatoncollege.edu
Financial aid office: (508) 286-8232

■ **2004-2005 TUITION AND FEES:** $30,580
■ **ROOM AND BOARD:** $7,580

SAT I Score (25th/75th percentile): 1130-1290
2005 U.S. News College Ranking:
Liberal Arts Colleges, 62
Acceptance Rate: 43%

Other expenses: Estimated books and supplies: $1,060. Transportation: $300. Personal expenses: $640. **Financial aid:** In 2003-2004, 64% of undergraduates applied for financial aid. Of those, 58% were determined to have financial need; 55% had their need fully met. Average financial aid package (proportion receiving): $21,159 (58%). Average amount of gift aid, such as scholarships or grants (proportion receiving): $16,164 (55%). Average amount of self-help aid, such as work study or loans (proportion receiving): $6,382 (55%). Average need-based loan (excluding PLUS or other private loans): $4,635. Among students who received need-based aid, the average percentage of need met: 92%. Among students who received aid based on merit, the average award (and the proportion receiving): $7,625 (11%). The average athletic scholarship (and the proportion receiving): $0 (0%). Average amount of debt of borrowers graduating in 2003: $20,188. Proportion who borrowed: 65%. **Student employment:** During the 2003-2004 academic year, 20% of undergraduates worked on campus. Average per-year earnings: $800. **Reserve Officers Training Corps (ROTC):** Army ROTC: Offered at cooperating institution (Stonehill College).

Wheelock College

200 The Riverway
Boston, MA 02215
Private; www.wheelock.edu
Financial aid office: (617) 879-2206

■ **2004-2005 TUITION AND FEES:** $22,500
■ **ROOM AND BOARD:** $9,000

SAT I Score (25th/75th percentile): 940-1160
2005 U.S. News College Ranking:
Universities–Master's (North), 42
Acceptance Rate: 67%

....

Other expenses: Estimated books and supplies:
$660. Transportation: $510. Personal expenses:
$500. **Financial aid:** Priority filing date for insti-
tution's financial aid form: February 15. In
2003-2004, 81% of undergraduates applied for
financial aid. Of those, 74% were determined to
have financial need; 12% had their need fully
met. Average financial aid package (proportion
receiving): $15,167 (74%). Average amount of
gift aid, such as scholarships or grants (proportion receiving): $10,143 (71%). Average amount
of self-help aid, such as work study or loans
(proportion receiving): $5,685 (69%). Average
need-based loan (excluding PLUS or other private loans): $4,897. Among students who
received need-based aid, the average percentage
of need met: 71%. Among students who
received aid based on merit, the average award
(and the proportion receiving): $12,716 (15%).
The average athletic scholarship (and the proportion receiving): $0 (0%). Average amount of
debt of borrowers graduating in 2003:
$22,000. Proportion who borrowed: 80%.
Student employment: During the 2003-2004
academic year, 30% of undergraduates worked
on campus. Average per-year earnings: $8.

Williams College

988 Main Street
Williamstown, MA 01267
Private; www.williams.edu
Financial aid office: (413) 597-4181

■ **2004-2005 TUITION AND FEES:** $29,990
■ **ROOM AND BOARD:** $8,110

SAT I Score (25th/75th percentile): 1310-1510
2005 U.S. News College Ranking:
Liberal Arts Colleges, 1
Acceptance Rate: 21%

....

Other expenses: Estimated books and supplies:
$800. Transportation: $500. Personal expenses:
$1,200. **Financial aid:** In 2003-2004, 49% of
undergraduates applied for financial aid. Of
those, 42% were determined to have financial
need; 100% had their need fully met. Average
financial aid package (proportion receiving):
$26,212 (42%). Average amount of gift aid,
such as scholarships or grants (proportion
receiving): $23,665 (40%). Average amount of
self-help aid, such as work study or loans (proportion receiving): $5,258 (36%). Average need-
based loan (excluding PLUS or other private
loans): $4,576. Among students who received
need-based aid, the average percentage of need
met: 100%. Among students who received aid
based on merit, the average award (and the proportion receiving): $0 (0%). The average athlet-
ic scholarship (and the proportion receiving):
$0 (0%). Average amount of debt of borrowers
graduating in 2003: $10,627. Proportion who
borrowed: 46%. **Student employment:** During
the 2003-2004 academic year, 56% of undergraduates worked on campus. Average per-year
earnings: $1,700.

Worcester Polytechnic Institute

100 Institute Road
Worcester, MA 01609
Private; www.wpi.edu
Financial aid office: (508) 831-5469

■ **2004-2005 TUITION AND FEES:** $29,730
■ **ROOM AND BOARD:** $9,164

SAT I Score (25th/75th percentile): 1180-1370
2005 U.S. News College Ranking:
National Universities, 55
Acceptance Rate: 71%

....

Other expenses: Estimated books and supplies:
$706. Transportation: $400. Personal expenses:
$720. **Financial aid:** Priority filing date for insti-
tution's financial aid form: March 1. In 2003-
2004, 81% of undergraduates applied for financial aid. Of those, 75% were determined to have
financial need; 27% had their need fully met.
Average financial aid package (proportion receiving): $21,030 (74%). Average amount of gift aid,
such as scholarships or grants (proportion receiving): $15,776 (72%). Average amount of self-help
aid, such as work study or loans (proportion
receiving): $6,376 (67%). Average need-based
loan (excluding PLUS or other private loans):
$6,104. Among students who received need-
based aid, the average percentage of need met:
90%. Among students who received aid based
on merit, the average award (and the proportion

receiving): $17,352 (8%). The average athletic
scholarship (and the proportion receiving): $0
(0%). Average amount of debt of borrowers graduating in 2003: $30,564. Proportion who bor-
rowed: 75%. **Student employment:** During the
2003-2004 academic year, 28% of undergraduates worked on campus. Average per-year earnings: $2,240. **Cooperative education programs:**
business, computer science, engineering, natural
science, social/behavioral science. **Reserve
Officers Training Corps (ROTC):** Army ROTC:
Offered on campus; Navy ROTC: Offered at
cooperating institution (College of the Holy
Cross); Air Force ROTC: Offered on campus.

Worcester State College

486 Chandler Street
Worcester, MA 01602-2597
Public; www.worcester.edu
Financial aid office: (508) 929-8056

■ **2004-2005 TUITION AND FEES:**
  In state: $4,574; Out of state: $10,654
■ **ROOM AND BOARD:** $6,896

SAT I Score (25th/75th percentile): 900-1080
2005 U.S. News College Ranking:
Universities–Master's (North), fourth tier
Acceptance Rate: 56%

....

Financial aid: Priority filing date for institution's financial aid form: March 1. In 2003-
2004, 63% of undergraduates applied for
financial aid. Of those, 45% were determined to
have financial need; 46% had their need fully
met. Average financial aid package (proportion
receiving): $6,868 (43%). Average amount of
gift aid, such as scholarships or grants (proportion receiving): $1,836 (34%). Average amount
of self-help aid, such as work study or loans
(proportion receiving): $1,783 (42%). Average
need-based loan (excluding PLUS or other private loans): $1,532. Among students who
received need-based aid, the average percentage
of need met: 79%. Among students who
received aid based on merit, the average award
(and the proportion receiving): $1,541 (1%). The
average athletic scholarship (and the proportion
receiving): $0 (0%). Average amount of debt of
borrowers graduating in 2003: $11,843.
Proportion who borrowed: 43%. **Cooperative
education programs:** other. **Reserve Officers
Training Corps (ROTC):** Army ROTC: Offered at
cooperating institution (Worcester Polytechnic
Institute); Navy ROTC: Offered at cooperating
institution (College of Holy Cross); Air Force
ROTC: Offered at cooperating institution
(Worcester Polytechnic Institute).

Michigan

Adrian College

110 S. Madison Street
Adrian, MI 49221
Private; www.adrian.edu
Financial aid office: (517) 264-3107

- **2004-2005 TUITION AND FEES:** $17,600
- **ROOM AND BOARD:** $6,180

ACT Score (25th/75th percentile): 18-24
2005 U.S. News College Ranking:
Liberal Arts Colleges, fourth tier
Acceptance Rate: 88%

Other expenses: Estimated books and supplies: $540. Transportation: $647. Personal expenses: $828. **Financial aid:** Priority filing date for institution's financial aid form: March 1; deadline: March 1. In 2003-2004, 98% of undergraduates applied for financial aid. Of those, 78% were determined to have financial need; 82% had their need fully met. Average financial aid package (proportion receiving): $15,434 (78%). Average amount of gift aid, such as scholarships or grants (proportion receiving): $8,923 (76%). Average amount of self-help aid, such as work study or loans (proportion receiving): $5,476 (71%). Average need-based loan (excluding PLUS or other private loans): $4,267. Among students who received need-based aid, the average percentage of need met: 98%. Among students who received aid based on merit, the average award (and the proportion receiving): $7,551 (20%). The average athletic scholarship (and the proportion receiving): $0 (0%). Average amount of debt of borrowers graduating in 2003: $15,948. Proportion who borrowed: 89%. **Student employment:** During the 2003-2004 academic year, 60% of undergraduates worked on campus. Average per-year earnings: $1,700.

Albion College

611 E. Porter
Albion, MI 49224
Private; www.albion.edu
Financial aid office: (517) 629-0440

- **2004-2005 TUITION AND FEES:** $22,918
- **ROOM AND BOARD:** $6,536

ACT Score (25th/75th percentile): 23-28
2005 U.S. News College Ranking:
Liberal Arts Colleges, 83
Acceptance Rate: 87%

Other expenses: Estimated books and supplies: $700. Transportation: $350. Personal expenses: $350. **Financial aid:** Priority filing date for institution's financial aid form: February 15. In 2003-2004, 72% of undergraduates applied for financial aid. Of those, 64% were determined to have financial need; 62% had their need fully met. Average financial aid package (proportion receiving): $18,706 (64%). Average amount of gift aid, such as scholarships or grants (proportion receiving): $14,791 (64%). Average amount of self-help aid, such as work study or loans (proportion receiving): $4,898 (51%). Average need-based loan (excluding PLUS or other private loans): $4,285. Among students who received need-based aid, the average percentage of need met: 95%. Among students who received aid based on merit, the average award (and the proportion receiving): $10,289 (33%). The average athletic scholarship (and the proportion receiving): $0 (0%). Average amount of debt of borrowers graduating in 2003: $19,802. Proportion who borrowed: 61%. **Student employment:** During the 2003-2004 academic year, 41% of undergraduates worked on campus. Average per-year earnings: $930. **Reserve Officers Training Corps (ROTC):** Army ROTC: Offered at cooperating institution (Western Michigan University).

Alma College

614 W. Superior Street
Alma, MI 48801-1599
Private; www.alma.edu
Financial aid office: (989) 463-7347

- **2004-2005 TUITION AND FEES:** $19,986
- **ROOM AND BOARD:** $7,032

ACT Score (25th/75th percentile): 22-27
2005 U.S. News College Ranking:
Liberal Arts Colleges, third tier
Acceptance Rate: 77%

Other expenses: Estimated books and supplies: $700. Transportation: $750. Personal expenses: $700. **Financial aid:** Priority filing date for institution's financial aid form: March 1. In 2003-

2004, 99% of undergraduates applied for financial aid. Of those, 78% were determined to have financial need; 33% had their need fully met. Average financial aid package (proportion receiving): $16,461 (78%). Average amount of gift aid, such as scholarships or grants (proportion receiving): $12,568 (78%). Average amount of self-help aid, such as work study or loans (proportion receiving): $5,111 (60%). Average need-based loan (excluding PLUS or other private loans): $5,111. Among students who received need-based aid, the average percentage of need met: 86%. Among students who received aid based on merit, the average award (and the proportion receiving): $11,301 (20%). The average athletic scholarship (and the proportion receiving): $0 (0%). Average amount of debt of borrowers graduating in 2003: $19,237. Proportion who borrowed: 87%. **Student employment:** During the 2003-2004 academic year, 35% of undergraduates worked on campus. Average per-year earnings: $900. **Reserve Officers Training Corps (ROTC):** Army ROTC: Offered at cooperating institution (Central Michigan University).

Andrews University

Berrien Springs, MI 49104
Private; www.andrews.edu
Financial aid office: (269) 471-3334

- **2004-2005 TUITION AND FEES:** $15,470
- **ROOM AND BOARD:** $5,320

ACT Score (25th/75th percentile): 19-26
2005 U.S. News College Ranking:
National Universities, third tier
Acceptance Rate: 60%

Other expenses: Estimated books and supplies: $1,000. Transportation: $750. Personal expenses: $500. **Financial aid:** Priority filing date for institution's financial aid form: March 15. In 2003-2004, 99% of undergraduates applied for financial aid. Of those, 65% were determined to have financial need; 67% had their need fully met. Average financial aid package (proportion receiving): $20,162 (65%). Average amount of gift aid, such as scholarships or grants (proportion receiving): $6,426 (47%). Average amount of self-help aid, such as work study or loans (proportion receiving): $5,094 (56%). Average need-based loan (excluding PLUS or other private loans): $4,359. Among students who received need-based aid, the average percentage of need met: 100%. Among students who received aid based on merit, the average award (and the proportion receiving): $4,562 (32%). The average athletic scholarship (and the proportion receiving): $0 (0%). Average amount of debt of borrowers graduating in 2003: $24,966. Proportion who borrowed: 59%. **Student employment:** During the 2003-2004 academic year, 70% of undergraduates worked on campus. Average per-year earnings: $2,400. **Cooperative education programs:** agriculture, art, business, computer science, education, engineering, health professions, natural science, technologies.

Aquinas College

1607 Robinson Road SE
Grand Rapids, MI 49506-1799
Private; www.aquinas.edu
Financial aid office: (616) 459-8281

■ **2004-2005 TUITION AND FEES:** $16,992
■ **ROOM AND BOARD:** $5,600

ACT Score (25th/75th percentile): 20-26
2005 U.S. News College Ranking:
Universities–Master's (Midwest), 48
Acceptance Rate: 79%

Other expenses: Estimated books and supplies: $690. Transportation: $647. Personal expenses: $678. **Financial aid:** In 2003-2004, 80% of undergraduates applied for financial aid. Of those, 72% were determined to have financial need; 41% had their need fully met. Average financial aid package (proportion receiving): $15,461 (72%). Average amount of gift aid, such as scholarships or grants (proportion receiving): $12,661 (72%). Average amount of self-help aid, such as work study or loans (proportion receiving): $2,800 (72%). Average need-based loan (excluding PLUS or other private loans): $2,800. Among students who received need-based aid, the average percentage of need met: 92%. Among students who received aid based on merit, the average award (and the proportion receiving): $8,266 (28%). The average athletic scholarship (and the proportion receiving): $2,404 (4%). Average amount of debt of borrowers graduating in 2003: $13,638. Proportion who borrowed: 66%. **Student employment:** During the 2003-2004 academic year, 16% of undergraduates worked on campus. Average per-year earnings: $2,986.

Baker College of Flint

1050 W. Bristol Road
Flint, MI 48507
Private; www.baker.edu
Financial aid office: (810) 766-4202

■ **2004-2005 TUITION AND FEES:** $8,160

2005 U.S. News College Ranking:
Comp. Colleges–Bachelor's (Midwest), fourth tier
Acceptance Rate: 100%

Calvin College

3201 Burton Street SE
Grand Rapids, MI 49546
Private; www.calvin.edu
Financial aid office: (616) 526-6137

■ **2004-2005 TUITION AND FEES:** $17,770
■ **ROOM AND BOARD:** $6,185

ACT Score (25th/75th percentile): 23-28
2005 U.S. News College Ranking:
Comp. Colleges–Bachelor's (Midwest), 2
Acceptance Rate: 99%

Other expenses: Estimated books and supplies: $700. Transportation: $785. Personal expenses: $900. **Financial aid:** Priority filing date for institution's financial aid form: February 15. In 2003-2004, 69% of undergraduates applied for financial aid. Of those, 59% were determined to have financial need; 30% had their need fully met. Average financial aid package (proportion receiving): $13,270 (59%). Average amount of gift aid, such as scholarships or grants (proportion receiving): $7,740 (59%). Average amount of self-help aid, such as work study or loans (proportion receiving): $5,690 (53%). Average need-based loan (excluding PLUS or other private loans): $4,980. Among students who received need-based aid, the average percentage of need met: 89%. Among students who received aid based on merit, the average award (and the proportion receiving): $4,890 (32%). The average athletic scholarship (and the proportion receiving): $0 (0%). Average amount of debt of borrowers graduating in 2003: $17,440. Proportion who borrowed: 69%. **Student employment:** During the 2003-2004 academic year, 40% of undergraduates worked on campus. Average per-year earnings: $1,800. **Reserve Officers Training Corps (ROTC):** Army ROTC: Offered at cooperating institution (Western Michigan).

Central Michigan University

105 Warriner Hall
Mount Pleasant, MI 48859
Public; www.cmich.edu
Financial aid office: (989) 774-3674

■ **2003-2004 TUITION AND FEES:**
    In state: $5,218; Out of state: $11,590
■ **ROOM AND BOARD:** $5,924

ACT Score (25th/75th percentile): 19-24
2005 U.S. News College Ranking:
National Universities, fourth tier
Acceptance Rate: 70%

Other expenses: Estimated books and supplies: $750. Transportation: $500. Personal expenses: $1,110. **Financial aid:** Priority filing date for institution's financial aid form: February 15. In 2003-2004, 70% of undergraduates applied for financial aid. Of those, 54% were determined to have financial need; 42% had their need fully met. Average financial aid package (proportion receiving): $8,539 (53%). Average amount of gift aid, such as scholarships or grants (proportion receiving): $3,021 (40%). Average amount of self-help aid, such as work study or loans (proportion receiving): $4,138 (47%). Average need-based loan (excluding PLUS or other private loans): $3,886. Among students who received need-based aid, the average percentage of need met: 95%. Among students who received aid based on merit, the average award (and the proportion receiving): $3,159 (20%). The average athletic scholarship (and the proportion receiving): $6,373 (2%). Average amount of debt of borrowers graduating in 2003: $15,872. Proportion who borrowed: 63%. **Student employment:** During the 2003-2004 academic year, 21% of undergraduates worked on campus. Average per-year earnings: $1,800. **Cooperative education programs:** art, business, computer science, education, engineering, health professions, home economics, humanities, natural science, social/behavioral science, technologies, vocational arts. **Reserve Officers Training Corps (ROTC):** Army ROTC: Offered on campus.

Cleary University

3601 Plymouth Road
Ann Arbor, MI 48105
Private; www.cleary.edu
Financial aid office: (517) 548-3670

■ **2004-2005 TUITION AND FEES:** $11,760

ACT Score (25th/75th percentile): 22
2005 U.S. News College Ranking:
Unranked Specialty School–Business
Acceptance Rate: 97%

Other expenses: Estimated books and supplies: $0. Transportation: $2,537. **Financial aid:** Priority filing date for institution's financial aid form: March 20; deadline: July 15. In 2003-2004, 54% of undergraduates applied for financial aid. Of those, 48% were determined to have financial need; 3% had their need fully met. Average financial aid package (proportion receiving): $9,271 (48%). Average amount of gift aid, such as scholarships or grants (proportion receiving): $1,041 (35%). Average amount of self-help aid, such as work study or loans (proportion receiving): $1,455 (43%). Average need-based loan (excluding PLUS or other private loans): $1,460. Among students who received need-based aid, the average percentage of need met: 39%. Among students who received aid based on merit, the average award (and the proportion receiving): $2,888 (9%). The average athletic scholarship (and the proportion receiving): $0 (0%). Average amount of debt of borrowers graduating in 2003: $10,500. Proportion who borrowed: 36%. **Student employment:** During the 2003-2004 academic year, 2% of undergraduates worked on campus.

College for Creative Studies

201 E. Kirby
Detroit, MI 48202
Private; www.ccscad.edu
Financial aid office: (313) 664-7495

■ **2004-2005 TUITION AND FEES:** $21,376
■ **ROOM AND BOARD:** $3,500

2005 U.S. News College Ranking:
Unranked Specialty School–Fine Arts
Acceptance Rate: 74%

Other expenses: Estimated books and supplies: $2,500. Personal expenses: $1,000. **Financial aid:** Priority filing date for institution's financial aid form: February 21. Average amount of debt of borrowers graduating in 2003: $26,482. Proportion who borrowed: 67%.

Concordia University

4090 Geddes Road
Ann Arbor, MI 48105
Private; www.cuaa.edu
Financial aid office: (734) 995-7408

■ **2004-2005 TUITION AND FEES:** $17,595
■ **ROOM AND BOARD:** $6,745

ACT Score (25th/75th percentile): 20-25
2005 U.S. News College Ranking:
Comp. Colleges–Bachelor's (Midwest), 47
Acceptance Rate: 75%

Other expenses: Estimated books and supplies: $600. Transportation: $250. Personal expenses: $1,000. **Financial aid:** Priority filing date for institution's financial aid form: May 1. In 2003-2004, 92% of undergraduates applied for financial aid. Of those, 85% were determined to have financial need; 32% had their need fully met. Average financial aid package (proportion receiving): $13,807 (85%). Average amount of gift aid, such as scholarships or grants (proportion receiving): $9,494 (85%). Average amount of self-help aid, such as work study or loans (proportion receiving): $5,428 (68%). Average need-based loan (excluding PLUS or other private loans): $5,051. Among students who received need-based aid, the average percentage of need met: 86%. Among students who received aid based on merit, the average award (and the proportion receiving): $8,259 (13%). The average athletic scholarship (and the proportion receiving): $3,019 (8%). Average amount of debt of borrowers graduating in 2003: $26,471. Proportion who borrowed: 90%. **Reserve Officers Training Corps (ROTC):** Army ROTC: Offered at cooperating institution (University of Michigan); Air Force ROTC: Offered at cooperating institution (University of Michigan).

Cornerstone University

1001 E. Beltline NE
Grand Rapids, MI 49525
Private; www.cornerstone.edu
Financial aid office: (616) 222-1424

■ **2004-2005 TUITION AND FEES:** $14,700
■ **ROOM AND BOARD:** $5,284

ACT Score (25th/75th percentile): 20-26
2005 U.S. News College Ranking:
Universities–Master's (Midwest), fourth tier
Acceptance Rate: 76%

Other expenses: Estimated books and supplies: $950. Transportation: $1,020. Personal expenses: $1,078. **Financial aid:** Priority filing date for institution's financial aid form: March 1; deadline: March 1. In 2003-2004, 98% of undergraduates applied for financial aid. Of those, 77% were determined to have financial need; 15% had their need fully met. Average financial aid package (proportion receiving): $12,302 (77%). Average amount of gift aid, such as scholarships or grants (proportion receiving): $6,225 (77%). Average amount of self-help aid, such as work study or loans (proportion receiving): $4,431 (70%). Average need-based loan (excluding PLUS or other private loans): $4,102. Among students who received need-based aid, the average percentage of need met: 80%. Among students who received aid based on merit, the average award (and the proportion receiving): $3,004 (15%). The average athletic scholarship (and the proportion receiving): $5,301 (11%). Average amount of debt of borrowers graduating in 2003: $17,218. Proportion who borrowed: 74%.

Davenport University

415 E. Fulton Street
Grand Rapids, MI 49503
Private; www.davenport.edu
Financial aid office: (616) 732-1130

■ **2004-2005 TUITION AND FEES:** $8,376
■ **ROOM AND BOARD:** $4,050

2005 U.S. News College Ranking:
Unranked Specialty School–Business

Cooperative education programs: business.

Eastern Michigan University

Ypsilanti, MI 48197
Public; www.emich.edu
Financial aid office: (734) 487-0455

■ **2004-2005 TUITION AND FEES:**
  In state: $5,720; Out of state: $15,710
■ **ROOM AND BOARD:** $6,055

ACT Score (25th/75th percentile): 18-23
2005 U.S. News College Ranking:
Universities–Master's (Midwest), third tier
Acceptance Rate: 79%

Other expenses: Estimated books and supplies: $900. Transportation: $800. Personal expenses: $900. **Financial aid:** Priority filing date for institution's financial aid form: March 15. In

2003-2004, 83% of undergraduates applied for financial aid. Of those, 52% were determined to have financial need; 19% had their need fully met. Average financial aid package (proportion receiving): $9,504 (52%). Average amount of gift aid, such as scholarships or grants (proportion receiving): $3,884 (40%). Average amount of self-help aid, such as work study or loans (proportion receiving): $4,400 (51%). Average need-based loan (excluding PLUS or other private loans): $6,406. Among students who received need-based aid, the average percentage of need met: 55%. Among students who received aid based on merit, the average award (and the proportion receiving): $2,050 (10%). The average athletic scholarship (and the proportion receiving): $10,553 (3%). Average amount of debt of borrowers graduating in 2003: $22,000. Proportion who borrowed: 55%. **Student employment:** During the 2003-2004 academic year, 20% of undergraduates worked on campus. Average per-year earnings: $3,200. **Cooperative education programs:** art, business, computer science, engineering, health professions, home economics, humanities, natural science, social/behavioral science, technologies. **Reserve Officers Training Corps (ROTC):** Army ROTC: Offered on campus; Navy ROTC: Offered at cooperating institution (University of Michigan–Ann Arbor); Air Force ROTC: Offered at cooperating institution (University of Michigan–Ann Arbor).

Ferris State University

1201 S. State Street
Big Rapids, MI 49307
Public; www.ferris.edu
Financial aid office: (231) 591-2110

■ **2004-2005 TUITION AND FEES:**
  In state: $6,350; Out of state: $12,438
■ **ROOM AND BOARD:** $6,800

ACT Score (25th/75th percentile): 17-23
2005 U.S. News College Ranking:
Universities–Master's (Midwest), fourth tier
Acceptance Rate: 73%

Other expenses: Estimated books and supplies: $1,000. Transportation: $1,182. Personal expenses: $784. **Financial aid:** Priority filing date for institution's financial aid form: March 15. In 2003-2004, 92% of undergraduates applied for financial aid. Of those, 80% were determined to have financial need; 4% had their need fully met. Average financial aid package (proportion receiving): $8,000 (69%). Average amount of gift aid, such as scholar-

ships or grants (proportion receiving): $3,500 (42%). Average amount of self-help aid, such as work study or loans (proportion receiving): $3,900 (59%). Average need-based loan (excluding PLUS or other private loans): $3,500. Among students who received need-based aid, the average percentage of need met: 80%. Among students who received aid based on merit, the average award (and the proportion receiving): $2,000 (3%). The average athletic scholarship (and the proportion receiving): $5,000 (3%). Average amount of debt of borrowers graduating in 2003: $14,500. Proportion who borrowed: 85%. **Student employment:** During the 2003-2004 academic year, 13% of undergraduates worked on campus. Average per-year earnings: $2,000. **Cooperative education programs:** other. **Reserve Officers Training Corps (ROTC):** Army ROTC: Offered on campus.

Grand Valley State University

1 Campus Drive
Allendale, MI 49401
Public; www.gvsu.edu
Financial aid office: (616) 331-3234

■ **2004-2005 TUITION AND FEES:**
  In state: $5,782; Out of state: $12,510
■ **ROOM AND BOARD:** $6,160

ACT Score (25th/75th percentile): 21-25
2005 U.S. News College Ranking:
Universities–Master's (Midwest), 52
Acceptance Rate: 73%

Other expenses: Estimated books and supplies: $800. Transportation: $400. Personal expenses: $600. **Financial aid:** Priority filing date for institution's financial aid form: February 15. In 2003-2004, 75% of undergraduates applied for financial aid. Of those, 56% were determined to have financial need; 91% had their need fully met. Average financial aid package (proportion receiving): $6,614 (56%). Average amount of gift aid, such as scholarships or grants (proportion receiving): $3,114 (31%). Average amount of self-help aid, such as work study or loans (proportion receiving): $3,507 (55%). Average need-based loan (excluding PLUS or other private loans): $3,215. Among students who received need-based aid, the average percentage of need met: 92%. Among students who received aid based on merit, the average award (and the proportion receiving): $1,990 (13%). Average amount of debt of borrowers graduating in 2003: $15,611. Proportion who borrowed: 72%. **Student employment:** During the 2003-

2004 academic year, 16% of undergraduates worked on campus. Average per-year earnings: $1,800. **Cooperative education programs:** education, engineering.

Hillsdale College

33 E. College Street
Hillsdale, MI 49242
Private; www.hillsdale.edu
Financial aid office: (517) 437-7341

■ **2004-2005 TUITION AND FEES:** $16,800
■ **ROOM AND BOARD:** $6,700

ACT Score (25th/75th percentile): 24-29
2005 U.S. News College Ranking:
Liberal Arts Colleges, 96
Acceptance Rate: 77%

Other expenses: Estimated books and supplies: $600. Transportation: $1,000. Personal expenses: $1,000. **Financial aid:** Priority filing date for institution's financial aid form: February 15; deadline: April 15. **Student employment:** During the 2003-2004 academic year, 75% of undergraduates worked on campus. Average per-year earnings: $1,250.

Hope College

PO Box 9000
Holland, MI 49422-9000
Private; www.hope.edu
Financial aid office: (616) 395-7765

■ **2004-2005 TUITION AND FEES:** $20,420
■ **ROOM AND BOARD:** $6,318

ACT Score (25th/75th percentile): 23-28
2005 U.S. News College Ranking:
Liberal Arts Colleges, 96
Acceptance Rate: 83%

Other expenses: Estimated books and supplies: $660. Transportation: $295. Personal expenses: $1,060. **Financial aid:** Priority filing date for institution's financial aid form: March 1. In 2003-2004, 72% of undergraduates applied for financial aid. Of those, 63% were determined to have financial need; 31% had their need fully met. Average financial aid package (proportion receiving): $17,033 (62%). Average amount of gift aid, such as scholarships or grants (proportion receiving): $11,432 (54%). Average amount of self-help aid, such as work study or loans (proportion receiving): $5,602 (51%). Average need-based loan (excluding PLUS or other private loans): $4,838. Among students who received need-based aid, the average percentage of need met: 88%. Among students who received aid based on merit, the average award (and the proportion receiving): $6,650 (26%). The average athletic scholarship (and the proportion receiving): $0 (0%). Average amount of debt of borrowers graduating in 2003: $19,568. Proportion who borrowed: 87%. **Student employment:** During the 2003-2004 academic year, 23% of undergraduates worked on campus. Average per-year earnings: $3,300.

Kalamazoo College

1200 Academy Street
Kalamazoo, MI 49006
Private; www.kzoo.edu
Financial aid office: (269) 337-7192

■ **2004-2005 TUITION AND FEES:** $24,351
■ **ROOM AND BOARD:** $6,609

ACT Score (25th/75th percentile): 26-30
2005 U.S. News College Ranking:
Liberal Arts Colleges, 53
Acceptance Rate: 70%

Other expenses: Estimated books and supplies: $825. Transportation: $360. Personal expenses: $875. **Financial aid:** Priority filing date for institution's financial aid form: February 15. In 2003-2004, 61% of undergraduates applied for financial aid. Of those, 50% were determined to have financial need; 74% had their need fully met. Average financial aid package (proportion receiving): $19,000 (50%). Average amount of gift aid, such as scholarships or grants (proportion receiving): $12,970 (48%). Average amount of self-help aid, such as work study or loans (proportion receiving): $5,795 (45%). Average need-based loan (excluding PLUS or other private loans): $5,600. Among students who received aid based on merit, the average award (and the proportion receiving): $9,450 (49%). Average amount of debt of borrowers graduating in 2003: $18,782. Proportion who borrowed: 60%. **Student employment:** During the 2003-2004 academic year, 20% of undergraduates worked on campus. Average per-year earnings: $900. **Reserve Officers Training Corps (ROTC):** Army ROTC: Offered at cooperating institution (Western Michigan University).

Kettering University

1700 W. Third Avenue
Flint, MI 48504
Private; www.kettering.edu
Financial aid office: (810) 762-7859

■ **2004-2005 TUITION AND FEES:** $21,608
■ **ROOM AND BOARD:** $4,670

ACT Score (25th/75th percentile): 23-28
2005 U.S. News College Ranking:
Unranked Specialty School–Engineering
Acceptance Rate: 71%

Other expenses: Estimated books and supplies: $800. Transportation: $3,996. Personal expenses: $2,645. **Financial aid:** Priority filing date for institution's financial aid form: February 14. In 2003-2004, 78% of undergraduates applied for financial aid. Of those, 74% were determined to have financial need; 11% had their need fully met. Average financial aid package (proportion receiving): $9,664 (73%). Average amount of gift aid, such as scholarships or grants (proportion receiving): $6,073 (72%). Average amount of self-help aid, such as work study or loans (proportion receiving): $4,743 (56%). Average need-based loan (excluding PLUS or other private loans): $3,964. Among students who received need-based aid, the average percentage of need met: 54%. Among students who received aid based on merit, the average award (and the proportion receiving): $5,385 (14%). Average amount of debt of borrowers graduating in 2003: $33,605. Proportion who borrowed: 55%. **Cooperative education programs:** business, computer science, engineering, natural science, other.

Lake Superior State University

650 W. Easterday Avenue
Sault Ste. Marie, MI 49783-1699
Public; www.lssu.edu
Financial aid office: (906) 635-2678

■ **2004-2005 TUITION AND FEES:**
   In state: $5,418; Out of state: $10,836
■ **ROOM AND BOARD:** $6,228

ACT Score (25th/75th percentile): 18-24
2005 U.S. News College Ranking:
Universities–Master's (Midwest), fourth tier
Acceptance Rate: 89%

Financial aid: In 2003-2004, 84% of undergraduates applied for financial aid. Of those,

63% were determined to have financial need; 47% had their need fully met. Average financial aid package (proportion receiving): N/A (63%). Among students who received need-based aid, the average percentage of need met: 74%. The average athletic scholarship (and the proportion receiving): $5,580 (5%).

Lawrence Technological University

21000 W. Ten Mile Road
Southfield, MI 48075
Private; www.ltu.edu
Financial aid office: (248) 204-2120

■ **2004-2005 TUITION AND FEES:** $17,210
■ **ROOM AND BOARD:** $7,035

ACT Score (25th/75th percentile): 20-26
2005 U.S. News College Ranking:
Universities–Master's (Midwest), 42
Acceptance Rate: 76%

Other expenses: Estimated books and supplies: $1,127. Transportation: $1,520. Personal expenses: $1,774. **Financial aid:** Priority filing date for institution's financial aid form: April 1. In 2003-2004, 85% of undergraduates applied for financial aid. Of those, 57% were determined to have financial need; 22% had their need fully met. Average financial aid package (proportion receiving): $11,137 (57%). Average amount of gift aid, such as scholarships or grants (proportion receiving): $6,590 (52%). Average amount of self-help aid, such as work study or loans (proportion receiving): $4,675 (57%). Average need-based loan (excluding PLUS or other private loans): $4,218. Among students who received need-based aid, the average percentage of need met: 73%. Among students who received aid based on merit, the average award (and the proportion receiving): $6,472 (23%). The average athletic scholarship (and the proportion receiving): $0 (0%). Average amount of debt of borrowers graduating in 2003: $24,590. Proportion who borrowed: 50%. **Student employment:** During the 2003-2004 academic year, 7% of undergraduates worked on campus. Average per-year earnings: $7,218. **Cooperative education programs:** business, computer science, engineering, natural science, technologies. **Reserve Officers Training Corps (ROTC):** Army ROTC: Offered at cooperating institution (University of Michigan–Ann Arbor); Navy ROTC: Offered at cooperating institution (University of Michigan–Ann Arbor); Air Force ROTC: Offered at cooperating institution (University of Michigan–Ann Arbor).

Madonna University

36600 Schoolcraft Road
Livonia, MI 48150
Private; www.madonna.edu
Financial aid office: (734) 432-5662

■ **2004-2005 TUITION AND FEES:** $9,700
■ **ROOM AND BOARD:** $5,612

ACT Score (25th/75th percentile): 21-25
2005 U.S. News College Ranking:
Universities–Master's (Midwest), third tier
Acceptance Rate: 86%

Other expenses: Estimated books and supplies:
$808. Transportation: $730. Personal expenses:
$908. **Financial aid:** Priority filing date for insti-
tution's financial aid form: February 21. In
2003-2004, 86% of undergraduates applied for
financial aid. Of those, 73% were determined to
have financial need; 12% had their need fully
met. Average financial aid package (proportion
receiving): $6,343 (73%). Average amount of
gift aid, such as scholarships or grants (proportion receiving): $4,075 (66%). Average amount
of self-help aid, such as work study or loans
(proportion receiving): $3,180 (61%). Average
need-based loan (excluding PLUS or other private loans): $3,078. Among students who
received need-based aid, the average percentage
of need met: 58%. Among students who
received aid based on merit, the average award
(and the proportion receiving): $5,038 (24%).
The average athletic scholarship (and the proportion receiving): $1,779 (5%). Average
amount of debt of borrowers graduating in
2003: $15,778. Proportion who borrowed: 30%.
Student employment: During the 2003-2004
academic year, 17% of undergraduates worked
on campus. Average per-year earnings: $2,270.
Cooperative education programs: business,
computer science, health professions, technologies.

Marygrove College

8425 W. McNichols Road
Detroit, MI 48221
Private; www.marygrove.edu
Financial aid office: (313) 927-1245

■ **2004-2005 TUITION AND FEES:** $12,340
■ **ROOM AND BOARD:** $6,000

ACT Score (25th/75th percentile): 16-19
2005 U.S. News College Ranking:
Universities–Master's (Midwest), fourth tier
Acceptance Rate: 60%

Other expenses: Estimated books and supplies:
$700. **Financial aid:** Average financial aid pack-
age (proportion receiving): $11,641 (87%).
Average amount of gift aid, such as scholarships or grants (proportion receiving): $6,571
(N/A). **Cooperative education programs:** business, education, health professions,
social/behavioral science.

Michigan State University

East Lansing, MI 48824
Public; www.admis.msu.edu
Financial aid office: (517) 353-5940

■ **2004-2005 TUITION AND FEES:**
In state: $7,396; Out of state: $18,192
■ **ROOM AND BOARD:** $5,502

ACT Score (25th/75th percentile): 22-27
2005 U.S. News College Ranking:
National Universities, 71
Acceptance Rate: 71%

Other expenses: Estimated books and supplies:
$826. Transportation: $344. Personal expenses:
$1,076. **Financial aid:** Priority filing date for
institution's financial aid form: June 30. In
2003-2004, 58% of undergraduates applied for
financial aid. Of those, 41% were determined to
have financial need; 33% had their need fully
met. Average financial aid package (proportion
receiving): $8,487 (41%). Average amount of
gift aid, such as scholarships or grants (proportion receiving): $3,518 (36%). Average amount
of self-help aid, such as work study or loans
(proportion receiving): $4,489 (36%). Average
need-based loan (excluding PLUS or other private loans): $4,883. Among students who
received need-based aid, the average percentage
of need met: 83%. Among students who
received aid based on merit, the average award
(and the proportion receiving): $4,172 (23%).
The average athletic scholarship (and the proportion receiving): $13,838 (1%). Average
amount of debt of borrowers graduating in
2003: $18,814. Proportion who borrowed: 58%.
Cooperative education programs: engineering.
Reserve Officers Training Corps (ROTC): Army
ROTC: Offered on campus; Air Force ROTC:
Offered on campus.

Michigan Technological University

1400 Townsend Drive
Houghton, MI 49931
Public; www.mtu.edu
Financial aid office: (906) 487-2622

■ **2004-2005 TUITION AND FEES:**
In state: $7,610; Out of state: $18,782
■ **ROOM AND BOARD:** $6,096

ACT Score (25th/75th percentile): 23-28
2005 U.S. News College Ranking:
National Universities, 120
Acceptance Rate: 93%

Other expenses: Estimated books and supplies:
$900. Transportation: $600. Personal expenses: $1,000. **Financial aid:** Priority filing date for
institution's financial aid form: February 21. In
2003-2004, 63% of undergraduates applied for
financial aid. Of those, 48% were determined
to have financial need; 34% had their need fully
met. Average financial aid package (proportion
receiving): $8,213 (47%). Average amount of
gift aid, such as scholarships or grants (proportion receiving): $5,523 (42%). Average amount
of self-help aid, such as work study or loans
(proportion receiving): $5,960 (41%). Average
need-based loan (excluding PLUS or other private loans): $4,296. Among students who
received need-based aid, the average percentage
of need met: 76%. Among students who
received aid based on merit, the average award
(and the proportion receiving): $3,617 (24%).
The average athletic scholarship (and the proportion receiving): $6,214 (3%). Average
amount of debt of borrowers graduating in
2003: $12,775. Proportion who borrowed: 56%.
Student employment: During the 2003-2004
academic year, 24% of undergraduates worked
on campus. Average per-year earnings: $6,371.
Cooperative education programs: business,
computer science, engineering, health professions, humanities, natural science,
social/behavioral science, technologies, other.
Reserve Officers Training Corps (ROTC): Army
ROTC: Offered on campus; Air Force ROTC:
Offered on campus.

Northern Michigan University

1401 Presque Isle Avenue
Marquette, MI 49855
Public; www.nmu.edu
Financial aid office: (906) 227-2327

■ **2004-2005 TUITION AND FEES:**
In state: $5,992; Out of state: $9,400
■ **ROOM AND BOARD:** $6,182

ACT Score (25th/75th percentile): 23
2005 U.S. News College Ranking:
Universities–Master's (Midwest), 55
Acceptance Rate: 84%

Financial aid: Priority filing date for institution's financial aid form: February 20. In 2003-2004, 92% of undergraduates applied for financial aid. Of those, 62% were determined to have financial need; 13% had their need fully met. Average financial aid package (proportion receiving): $7,191 (60%). Average amount of gift aid, such as scholarships or grants (proportion receiving): $3,635 (46%). Average amount of self-help aid, such as work study or loans (proportion receiving): $4,359 (54%). Average need-based loan (excluding PLUS or other private loans): $3,736. Among students who received need-based aid, the average percentage of need met: 78%. Among students who received aid based on merit, the average award (and the proportion receiving): $19,591 (0%). The average athletic scholarship (and the proportion receiving): N/A (4%). Average amount of debt of borrowers graduating in 2003: $15,232. Proportion who borrowed: 72%. Average per-year earnings: $3,500. **Reserve Officers Training Corps (ROTC):** Army ROTC: Offered on campus.

Northwood University

4000 Whiting Drive
Midland, MI 48640
Private; www.northwood.edu
Financial aid office: (989) 837-4230

■ **2004-2005 TUITION AND FEES:** $14,529
■ **ROOM AND BOARD:** $6,507

ACT Score (25th/75th percentile): 18-23
2005 U.S. News College Ranking:
Unranked Specialty School–Business
Acceptance Rate: 87%

Other expenses: Estimated books and supplies: $1,265. Transportation: $623. Personal expenses: $1,118. **Financial aid:** In 2003-2004, 78% of undergraduates applied for financial aid. Of those, 67% were determined to have financial need; 17% had their need fully met. Average financial aid package (proportion receiving): $11,175 (67%). Average amount of gift aid, such as scholarships or grants (proportion receiving): $4,525 (56%). Average amount of self-help aid, such as work study or loans (proportion receiving): $3,930 (51%). Average need-based loan (excluding PLUS or other private loans): $3,664. Among students who received need-based aid, the average percentage of need met: 76%. Among students who received aid based on merit, the average award (and the proportion receiving): $3,959 (24%). The average athletic scholarship (and the proportion receiving): $7,103 (15%). Average amount of debt of borrowers graduating in 2003: $11,229. Proportion who borrowed: 51%. **Student employment:** During the 2003-2004 academic year, 23% of undergraduates worked on campus. Average per-year earnings: $2,000. **Cooperative education programs:** business.

Oakland University

Rochester, MI 48309-4401
Public; www.oakland.edu
Financial aid office: (248) 370-2550

■ **2004-2005 TUITION AND FEES:**
In state: $5,354; Out of state: $11,954
■ **ROOM AND BOARD:** $5,790

ACT Score (25th/75th percentile): 18-24
2005 U.S. News College Ranking:
National Universities, fourth tier
Acceptance Rate: 80%

Financial aid: Priority filing date for institution's financial aid form: February 15. In 2003-2004, 51% of undergraduates applied for financial aid. Of those, 34% were determined to have financial need; 28% had their need fully met. Average financial aid package (proportion receiving): $5,556 (33%). Average amount of gift aid, such as scholarships or grants (proportion receiving): $3,052 (21%). Average amount of self-help aid, such as work study or loans (proportion receiving): $3,614 (24%). Average need-based loan (excluding PLUS or other private loans): $3,637. Among students who received need-based aid, the average percentage of need met: 84%. Among students who received aid based on merit, the average award (and the proportion receiving): $3,520 (6%). The average athletic scholarship (and the proportion receiving): $7,248 (2%). **Student employment:** During the 2003-2004 academic year, 8% of undergraduates worked on campus. Average per-year earnings: $1,933. **Cooperative education programs:** business, computer science, engineering. **Reserve Officers Training Corps (ROTC):** Air Force ROTC: Offered at cooperating institution (University of Michigan–Ann Arbor).

Olivet College

320 S. Main Street
Olivet, MI 49076
Private; www.olivetcollege.edu
Financial aid office: (269) 749-7645

■ **2004-2005 TUITION AND FEES:** $15,994
■ **ROOM AND BOARD:** $5,330

ACT Score (25th/75th percentile): 18-24
2005 U.S. News College Ranking:
Liberal Arts Colleges, fourth tier
Acceptance Rate: 59%

Other expenses: Estimated books and supplies: $900. Transportation: $776. Personal expenses: $1,000. **Financial aid:** Priority filing date for institution's financial aid form: March 1. In 2003-2004, 91% of undergraduates applied for financial aid. Of those, 86% were determined to have financial need; 12% had their need fully met. Average financial aid package (proportion receiving): $12,230 (86%). Average amount of gift aid, such as scholarships or grants (proportion receiving): $8,631 (86%). Average amount of self-help aid, such as work study or loans (proportion receiving): $4,048 (77%). Average need-based loan (excluding PLUS or other private loans): $3,573. Among students who received need-based aid, the average percentage of need met: 78%. Among students who received aid based on merit, the average award (and the proportion receiving): $8,691 (10%). The average athletic scholarship (and the proportion receiving): $0 (0%). Average amount of debt of borrowers graduating in 2003: $17,877. Proportion who borrowed: 83%. **Student employment:** During the 2003-2004 academic year, 4% of undergraduates worked on campus. Average per-year earnings: $1,600.

Rochester College

800 W. Avon Road
Rochester Hills, MI 48307
Private; www.rc.edu
Financial aid office: (248) 218-2028

- **2003-2004 TUITION AND FEES:** $10,924
- **ROOM AND BOARD:** $5,799

ACT Score (25th/75th percentile): 18-23
2005 U.S. News College Ranking:
Comp. Colleges–Bachelor's (Midwest),
fourth tier
Acceptance Rate: 78%

Other expenses: Estimated books and supplies:
$600. Transportation: $655. Personal expenses:
$720. **Financial aid:** Priority filing date for insti-
tution's financial aid form: April 1; deadline:
July 1. **Student employment:** During the 2003-
2004 academic year, 10% of undergraduates
worked on campus. Average per-year earnings:
$1,380.

Saginaw Valley State University

7400 Bay Road
University Center, MI 48710
Public; www.svsu.edu
Financial aid office: (989) 964-4103

- **2004-2005 TUITION AND FEES:**
  In state: $4,188; Out of state: $9,778
- **ROOM AND BOARD:** $6,000

ACT Score (25th/75th percentile): 18-24
2005 U.S. News College Ranking:
Universities–Master's (Midwest), fourth tier
Acceptance Rate: 90%

Other expenses: Estimated books and supplies:
$800. Personal expenses: $858. **Financial aid:**
Priority filing date for institution's financial aid
form: February 14. **Student employment:**
During the 2003-2004 academic year, 6% of
undergraduates worked on campus. Average
per-year earnings: $2,000.

Siena Heights University

1247 E. Siena Heights Drive
Adrian, MI 49221
Private; www.sienahts.edu
Financial aid office: (517) 264-7130

- **2004-2005 TUITION AND FEES:** $15,520
- **ROOM AND BOARD:** $5,455

ACT Score (25th/75th percentile): 18-19
2005 U.S. News College Ranking:
Universities–Master's (Midwest), fourth tier
Acceptance Rate: 64%

Spring Arbor University

106 E. Main Street
Spring Arbor, MI 49283-9799
Private; www.arbor.edu
Financial aid office: (517) 750-6463

- **2004-2005 TUITION AND FEES:** $16,096
- **ROOM AND BOARD:** $5,610

ACT Score (25th/75th percentile): 20-26
2005 U.S. News College Ranking:
Universities–Master's (Midwest), 68
Acceptance Rate: 86%

Other expenses: Estimated books and supplies:
$605. Transportation: $665. Personal expenses:
$745. **Financial aid:** Priority filing date for insti-
tution's financial aid form: February 15. In
2003-2004, 65% of undergraduates applied for
financial aid. Of those, 51% were determined to
have financial need; 38% had their need fully
met. Average financial aid package (proportion
receiving): $11,773 (50%). Average amount of
gift aid, such as scholarships or grants (proportion receiving): $3,283 (48%). Average amount
of self-help aid, such as work study or loans
(proportion receiving): $3,764 (19%). Average
need-based loan (excluding PLUS or other private loans): $3,875. Among students who
received need-based aid, the average percentage
of need met: 78%. Among students who
received aid based on merit, the average award
(and the proportion receiving): $1,668 (7%).
The average athletic scholarship (and the proportion receiving): $2,575 (6%). Average
amount of debt of borrowers graduating in
2003: $11,169. Proportion who borrowed: 80%.
Student employment: During the 2003-2004
academic year, 30% of undergraduates worked
on campus. Average per-year earnings: $1,000.
Reserve Officers Training Corps (ROTC): Army

ROTC: Offered at cooperating institution
(Eastern Michigan University).

University of Detroit Mercy

PO Box 19900
Detroit, MI 48219-0900
Private; www.udmercy.edu
Financial aid office: (313) 993-3350

- **2004-2005 TUITION AND FEES:** $20,970
- **ROOM AND BOARD:** $7,040

ACT Score (25th/75th percentile): 19-25
2005 U.S. News College Ranking:
Universities–Master's (Midwest), 24
Acceptance Rate: 81%

Other expenses: Estimated books and supplies:
$1,300. Transportation: $750. Personal expenses: $2,644. **Financial aid:** Priority filing date for
institution's financial aid form: March 1. In
2003-2004, 83% of undergraduates applied for
financial aid. Of those, 77% were determined to
have financial need; 16% had their need fully
met. Average financial aid package (proportion
receiving): $18,195 (77%). Average amount of
gift aid, such as scholarships or grants (proportion receiving): $14,002 (71%). Average amount
of self-help aid, such as work study or loans
(proportion receiving): $6,098 (68%). Average
need-based loan (excluding PLUS or other private loans): $4,645. Among students who
received need-based aid, the average percentage
of need met: 80%. Among students who
received aid based on merit, the average award
(and the proportion receiving): $11,476 (7%).
The average athletic scholarship (and the proportion receiving): $5,657 (1%). **Cooperative
education programs:** business, computer science, engineering, health professions, humanities, natural science, social/behavioral science.

University of Michigan–
Ann Arbor

Ann Arbor, MI 48109
Public; www.umich.edu
Financial aid office: (734) 763-4119

- **2004-2005 TUITION AND FEES:**
  In state: $8,868; Out of state: $26,854
- **ROOM AND BOARD:** $6,972

ACT Score (25th/75th percentile): 26-30
2005 U.S. News College Ranking:
National Universities, 22
Acceptance Rate: 53%

Other expenses: Estimated books and supplies: $956. Personal expenses: $2,076. **Financial aid:** Priority filing date for institution's financial aid form: February 15; deadline: April 30. In 2003-2004, 50% of undergraduates applied for financial aid. Of those, 40% were determined to have financial need; 90% had their need fully met. Average financial aid package (proportion receiving): $11,375 (40%). Average amount of gift aid, such as scholarships or grants (proportion receiving): $7,512 (24%). Average amount of self-help aid, such as work study or loans (proportion receiving): $6,141 (40%). Average need-based loan (excluding PLUS or other private loans): $4,780. Among students who received need-based aid, the average percentage of need met: 90%. Among students who received aid based on merit, the average award (and the proportion receiving): $4,744 (21%). The average athletic scholarship (and the proportion receiving): $22,067 (2%). Average amount of debt of borrowers graduating in 2003: $19,407. Proportion who borrowed: 39%. **Reserve Officers Training Corps (ROTC):** Army ROTC: Offered on campus; Navy ROTC: Offered on campus; Air Force ROTC: Offered on campus.

University of Michigan–Dearborn

4901 Evergreen
Dearborn, MI 48128-1491
Public; www.umd.umich.edu
Financial aid office: (313) 593-5300

■ **2004-2005 TUITION AND FEES:**
In state: $6,791; Out of state: $14,381

ACT Score (25th/75th percentile): 21-26
2005 U.S. News College Ranking:
Universities–Master's (Midwest), 25
Acceptance Rate: 67%

Other expenses: Estimated books and supplies: $800. Transportation: $1,246. Personal expenses: $1,329. **Financial aid:** Priority filing date for institution's financial aid form: April 1. In 2003-2004, 69% of undergraduates applied for financial aid. Of those, 43% were determined to have financial need; 18% had their need fully met. Average financial aid package (proportion receiving): $7,306 (42%). Average amount of gift aid, such as scholarships or grants (proportion receiving): $3,695 (28%). Average amount of self-help

aid, such as work study or loans (proportion receiving): $4,303 (38%). Average need-based loan (excluding PLUS or other private loans): $4,154. Among students who received need-based aid, the average percentage of need met: 30%. Among students who received aid based on merit, the average award (and the proportion receiving): $2,119 (12%). The average athletic scholarship (and the proportion receiving): $1,774 (1%). Average amount of debt of borrowers graduating in 2003: $23,753. Proportion who borrowed: 34%. **Cooperative education programs:** art, business, humanities, natural science, social/behavioral science. **Reserve Officers Training Corps (ROTC):** Army ROTC: Offered at cooperating institution (University of Michigan–Ann Arbor); Navy ROTC: Offered at cooperating institution (University of Michigan–Ann Arbor); Air Force ROTC: Offered at cooperating institution (University of Michigan–Ann Arbor).

University of Michigan–Flint

303 E. Kearsley
Flint, MI 48502-1950
Public; www.umflint.edu
Financial aid office: (810) 762-3444

■ **2003-2004 TUITION AND FEES:**
In state: $5,274; Out of state: $10,274

ACT Score (25th/75th percentile): 19-24
2005 U.S. News College Ranking:
Universities–Master's (Midwest), 68
Acceptance Rate: 81%

Financial aid: Priority filing date for institution's financial aid form: March 1. Average amount of debt of borrowers graduating in 2003: $18,941. Proportion who borrowed: 66%. **Cooperative education programs:** business, computer science, engineering, humanities, natural science, social/behavioral science.

Walsh College of Accountancy and Business Adm.

PO Box 7006
Troy, MI 48007-7006
Private; www.walshcollege.edu
Financial aid office: (248) 823-1665

■ **2004-2005 TUITION AND FEES:** $8,784

2005 U.S. News College Ranking:
Unranked Specialty School–Business
Acceptance Rate: 81%

Financial aid: In 2003-2004, 52% of undergraduates applied for financial aid. Of those, 50% were determined to have financial need; Average financial aid package (proportion receiving): $10,012 (50%). Average amount of gift aid, such as scholarships or grants (proportion receiving): $4,204 (34%). Average amount of self-help aid, such as work study or loans (proportion receiving): $7,021 (50%). Average need-based loan (excluding PLUS or other private loans): $7,021. Among students who received need-based aid, the average percentage of need met: 48%. Among students who received aid based on merit, the average award (and the proportion receiving): $2,571 (17%). Average amount of debt of borrowers graduating in 2003: $8,908. Proportion who borrowed: 45%.

Wayne State University

656 W. Kirby
Detroit, MI 48202
Public; www.wayne.edu
Financial aid office: (313) 577-3378

■ **2004-2005 TUITION AND FEES:**
In state: $5,399; Out of state: $11,567
■ **ROOM AND BOARD:** $6,700

ACT Score (25th/75th percentile): 16-24
2005 U.S. News College Ranking:
National Universities, fourth tier
Acceptance Rate: 68%

Other expenses: Estimated books and supplies: $816. Transportation: $1,530. Personal expenses: $1,939. **Financial aid:** Priority filing date for institution's financial aid form: March 1. In 2003-2004, 63% of undergraduates applied for financial aid. Of those, 57% were determined to have financial need; 11% had their need fully met. Average financial aid package (proportion receiving): $7,336 (53%). Average amount of gift aid, such as scholarships or grants (proportion receiving): $3,618 (39%). Average amount of self-help aid, such as work study or loans (proportion receiving): $4,200 (46%). Average need-based loan (excluding PLUS or other private loans): $3,816. Among students who received need-based aid, the average percentage of need met: 70%. Among students who received aid based on merit, the average award (and the proportion receiving): $3,602 (2%). The average athletic scholarship (and the proportion receiving): $5,398 (3%). Average amount of debt of borrowers graduating in 2003: $19,414. Proportion who borrowed: 45%. **Student employment:** During the 2003-2004 academic year, 7% of undergraduates worked

on campus. Average per-year earnings: $7,857.
Cooperative education programs: art, business,
computer science, education, engineering,
health professions, humanities, natural science,
social/behavioral science. **Reserve Officers
Training Corps (ROTC):** Air Force ROTC:
Offered at cooperating institution (University of
Michigan–Ann Arbor).

Western Michigan University

1903 W. Michigan Avenue
Kalamazoo, MI 49008
Public; www.wmich.edu
Financial aid office: (269) 387-6000

■ **2004-2005 TUITION AND FEES:**
 In state: $5,668; Out of state: $13,823
■ **ROOM AND BOARD:** $6,496

ACT Score (25th/75th percentile): 20-25
2005 U.S. News College Ranking:
National Universities, third tier
Acceptance Rate: 82%

Other expenses: Estimated books and supplies:
$846. Transportation: $684. Personal expenses:
$1,930. **Financial aid:** Priority filing date for
institution's financial aid form: March 15. In
2003-2004, 56% of undergraduates applied for
financial aid. Of those, 53% were determined to
have financial need; 23% had their need fully
met. Average financial aid package (proportion
receiving): $7,300 (53%). Average amount of
gift aid, such as scholarships or grants (proportion receiving): $4,100 (49%). Average amount
of self-help aid, such as work study or loans

(proportion receiving): $3,860 (39%). Average
need-based loan (excluding PLUS or other private loans): $3,800. Among students who
received need-based aid, the average percentage
of need met: 69%. Among students who
received aid based on merit, the average award
(and the proportion receiving): $2,400 (13%).
The average athletic scholarship (and the proportion receiving): $10,000 (1%). Average
amount of debt of borrowers graduating in
2003: $16,100. Proportion who borrowed:
46%. **Student employment:** During the 2003-
2004 academic year, 13% of undergraduates
worked on campus. Average per-year earnings:
$4,320. **Reserve Officers Training Corps (ROTC):**
Army ROTC: Offered on campus.

William Tyndale College

35700 W. 12 Mile Road
Farmington Hills, MI 48331-3147
Private; www.WilliamTyndale.edu
Financial aid office: (800) 483-0707

■ **2004-2005 TUITION AND FEES:** $9,850
■ **ROOM AND BOARD:** $3,600

ACT Score (25th/75th percentile): 23-24
2005 U.S. News College Ranking:
Comp. Colleges–Bachelor's (Midwest),
fourth tier
Acceptance Rate: 50%

Other expenses: Estimated books and supplies:
$1,328. **Financial aid:** Priority filing date for
institution's financial aid form: February 15;
deadline: June 1.

Minnesota

Augsburg College

2211 Riverside Avenue S
Minneapolis, MN 55454
Private; www.augsburg.edu
Financial aid office: (612) 330-1046

- **2004-2005 TUITION AND FEES:** $20,758
- **ROOM AND BOARD:** $6,080

ACT Score (25th/75th percentile): 20-25
2005 U.S. News College Ranking:
Universities–Master's (Midwest), 20
Acceptance Rate: 82%

Other expenses: Estimated books and supplies:
$1,000. Transportation: $0. Personal expenses:
$1,670. **Financial aid:** Priority filing date for
institution's financial aid form: April 15; deadline: August 1. In 2003-2004, 80% of undergraduates applied for financial aid. Of those,
70% were determined to have financial need;
24% had their need fully met. Average financial
aid package (proportion receiving): $12,966
(70%). Average amount of gift aid, such as
scholarships or grants (proportion receiving):
$9,419 (63%). Average amount of self-help aid,
such as work study or loans (proportion receiving): $4,995 (63%). Average need-based loan
(excluding PLUS or other private loans):
$4,430. Among students who received need-
based aid, the average percentage of need met:
70%. Among students who received aid based
on merit, the average award (and the proportion receiving): $16,973 (15%). The average ath-
letic scholarship (and the proportion receiving):
$0 (0%). Average amount of debt of borrowers
graduating in 2003: $24,546. Proportion who
borrowed: 69%. **Student employment:** During
the 2003-2004 academic year, 37% of undergraduates worked on campus. Average per-year
earnings: $1,858. **Reserve Officers Training
Corps (ROTC):** Army ROTC: Offered at cooperating institution (The University of Minnesota);
Navy ROTC: Offered at cooperating institution
(The University of Minnesota); Air Force
ROTC: Offered at cooperating institution (The
University of St. Thomas).

Bemidji State University

1500 Birchmont Drive NE
Bemidji, MN 56601
Public; www.bemidjistate.edu
Financial aid office: (218) 755-4143

- **2004-2005 TUITION AND FEES:**
  In state: $5,652; Out of state: $11,146
- **ROOM AND BOARD:** $5,004

ACT Score (25th/75th percentile): 21-23
2005 U.S. News College Ranking:
Universities–Master's (Midwest), 68
Acceptance Rate: 74%

Other expenses: Estimated books and supplies:
$800. Transportation: $750. Personal expenses:
$1,230. **Financial aid:** Priority filing date for
institution's financial aid form: May 15. In
2003-2004, 76% of undergraduates applied for
financial aid. Of those, 61% were determined to
have financial need; 36% had their need fully
met. Average financial aid package (proportion
receiving): $7,072 (60%). Average amount of
gift aid, such as scholarships or grants (proportion receiving): $3,782 (46%). Average amount
of self-help aid, such as work study or loans
(proportion receiving): $3,647 (50%). Average
need-based loan (excluding PLUS or other private loans): $3,255. Among students who
received need-based aid, the average percentage
of need met: 79%. Among students who
received aid based on merit, the average award
(and the proportion receiving): $6,108 (14%).
The average athletic scholarship (and the proportion receiving): $3,373 (4%). Average
amount of debt of borrowers graduating in
2003: $13,690. Proportion who borrowed: 71%.
Student employment: During the 2003-2004
academic year, 70% of undergraduates worked
on campus. Average per-year earnings: $2,700.

Bethel University

3900 Bethel Drive
St. Paul, MN 55112
Private; www.bethel.edu
Financial aid office: (800) 255-8706

- **2004-2005 TUITION AND FEES:** $19,990
- **ROOM AND BOARD:** $6,430

ACT Score (25th/75th percentile): 21-27
2005 U.S. News College Ranking:
Universities–Master's (Midwest), 19
Acceptance Rate: 91%

Other expenses: Estimated books and supplies:
$800. Transportation: $0. Personal expenses:
$1,570. **Financial aid:** Priority filing date for
institution's financial aid form: April 15. In
2003-2004, 94% of undergraduates applied for
financial aid. Of those, 68% were determined
to have financial need; 25% had their need fully
met. Average financial aid package (proportion
receiving): $14,810 (68%). Average amount of
gift aid, such as scholarships or grants (proportion receiving): $8,933 (68%). Average amount
of self-help aid, such as work study or loans
(proportion receiving): $6,046 (64%). Average
need-based loan (excluding PLUS or other private loans): $4,477. Among students who
received need-based aid, the average percentage
of need met: 83%. Among students who
received aid based on merit, the average award
(and the proportion receiving): $3,529 (23%).
Average amount of debt of borrowers graduating in 2003: $22,062. Proportion who bor-
rowed: 73%. **Student employment:** During the
2003-2004 academic year, 38% of undergraduates worked on campus. Average per-year earnings: $2,200. **Cooperative education programs:**
business, education, engineering, health professions, natural science. **Reserve Officers Training
Corps (ROTC):** Army ROTC: Offered at cooperating institution (University of Minnesota); Air
Force ROTC: Offered at cooperating institution
(University of St. Thomas).

Carleton College

1 N. College Street
Northfield, MN 55057
Private; www.carleton.edu
Financial aid office: (507) 646-4138

- **2004-2005 TUITION AND FEES:** $30,666
- **ROOM AND BOARD:** $6,309

SAT I Score (25th/75th percentile): 1300-1480
2005 U.S. News College Ranking:
Liberal Arts Colleges, 5
Acceptance Rate: 30%

Other expenses: Estimated books and supplies:
$600. Transportation: $700. Personal expens-

es: $600. **Financial aid:** Priority filing date for institution's financial aid form: February 15; deadline: February 15. In 2003-2004, 95% of undergraduates applied for financial aid. Of those, 58% were determined to have financial need; 100% had their need fully met. Average financial aid package (proportion receiving): $21,208 (58%). Average amount of gift aid, such as scholarships or grants (proportion receiving): $16,911 (58%). Average amount of self-help aid, such as work study or loans (proportion receiving): $4,297 (58%). Average need-based loan (excluding PLUS or other private loans): $3,510. Among students who received need-based aid, the average percentage of need met: 100%. Among students who received aid based on merit, the average award (and the proportion receiving): $3,139 (8%). Average amount of debt of borrowers graduating in 2003: $15,689. Proportion who borrowed: 56%. **Student employment:** During the 2003-2004 academic year, 61% of undergraduates worked on campus. Average per-year earnings: $2,500. **Cooperative education programs:** education, engineering, other.

College of St. Benedict

37 S. College Avenue
St. Joseph, MN 56374
Private; www.csbsju.edu
Financial aid office: (320) 363-5388

■ **2004-2005 TUITION AND FEES:** $22,148
■ **ROOM AND BOARD:** $6,208

ACT Score (25th/75th percentile): 22-27
2005 U.S. News College Ranking:
Liberal Arts Colleges, 101
Acceptance Rate: 90%

Other expenses: Estimated books and supplies: $800. Transportation: $200. Personal expenses: $700. **Financial aid:** Priority filing date for institution's financial aid form: March 15. In 2003-2004, 99% of undergraduates applied for financial aid. Of those, 67% were determined to have financial need; 91% had their need fully met. Average financial aid package (proportion receiving): $17,036 (67%). Average amount of gift aid, such as scholarships or grants (proportion receiving): $10,989 (66%). Average amount of self-help aid, such as work study or loans (proportion receiving): $5,929 (62%). Average need-based loan (excluding PLUS or other private loans): $5,064. Among students who received need-based aid, the average percentage of need met: 90%. Among students who received aid based on merit, the average

award (and the proportion receiving): $5,681 (28%). The average athletic scholarship (and the proportion receiving): $0 (0%). Average amount of debt of borrowers graduating in 2003: $22,688. Proportion who borrowed: 73%. **Student employment:** During the 2003-2004 academic year, 60% of undergraduates worked on campus. Average per-year earnings: $2,314. **Reserve Officers Training Corps (ROTC):** Army ROTC: Offered at cooperating institution (Saint John's University).

College of St. Catherine

2004 Randolph Avenue
St. Paul, MN 55105
Private; www.stkate.edu
Financial aid office: (651) 690-6540

■ **2004-2005 TUITION AND FEES:** $19,750
■ **ROOM AND BOARD:** $5,808

ACT Score (25th/75th percentile): 21-26
2005 U.S. News College Ranking:
Universities–Master's (Midwest), 17
Acceptance Rate: 77%

Other expenses: Estimated books and supplies: $640. Transportation: $100. Personal expenses: $934. **Financial aid:** Priority filing date for institution's financial aid form: April 15. In 2003-2004, 84% of undergraduates applied for financial aid. Of those, 49% were determined to have financial need; 21% had their need fully met. Average financial aid package (proportion receiving): $18,319 (49%). Average amount of gift aid, such as scholarships or grants (proportion receiving): $6,954 (43%). Average amount of self-help aid, such as work study or loans (proportion receiving): $5,150 (42%). Average need-based loan (excluding PLUS or other private loans): $4,752. Among students who received need-based aid, the average percentage of need met: 77%. Among students who received aid based on merit, the average award (and the proportion receiving): $14,651 (27%). Average amount of debt of borrowers graduating in 2003: $24,537. Proportion who borrowed: 81%. **Student employment:** During the 2003-2004 academic year, 34% of undergraduates worked on campus. Average per-year earnings: $2,158. **Reserve Officers Training Corps (ROTC):** Air Force ROTC: Offered at cooperating institution (University of St. Thomas).

College of St. Scholastica

1200 Kenwood Avenue
Duluth, MN 55811
Private; www.css.edu
Financial aid office: (218) 723-6047

■ **2004-2005 TUITION AND FEES:** $20,760
■ **ROOM AND BOARD:** $5,916

ACT Score (25th/75th percentile): 21-27
2005 U.S. News College Ranking:
Universities–Master's (Midwest), 20
Acceptance Rate: 88%

Other expenses: Estimated books and supplies: $750. Transportation: $218. Personal expenses: $898. **Financial aid:** Priority filing date for institution's financial aid form: March 15. In 2003-2004, 89% of undergraduates applied for financial aid. Of those, 82% were determined to have financial need; 85% had their need fully met. Average financial aid package (proportion receiving): $15,945 (82%). Average amount of gift aid, such as scholarships or grants (proportion receiving): $5,510 (73%). Average amount of self-help aid, such as work study or loans (proportion receiving): $5,180 (63%). Average need-based loan (excluding PLUS or other private loans): $4,639. Among students who received need-based aid, the average percentage of need met: 85%. Among students who received aid based on merit, the average award (and the proportion receiving): $7,253 (14%). The average athletic scholarship (and the proportion receiving): $0 (0%). Average amount of debt of borrowers graduating in 2003: $25,474. Proportion who borrowed: 87%. **Student employment:** During the 2003-2004 academic year, 29% of undergraduates worked on campus. Average per-year earnings: $1,782. **Reserve Officers Training Corps (ROTC):** Air Force ROTC: Offered at cooperating institution (University of Minnesota–Duluth).

College of Visual Arts

344 Summit Avenue
St. Paul, MN 55102
Private; www.cva.edu
Financial aid office: (651) 224-3416

■ **2004-2005 TUITION AND FEES:** $17,530

ACT Score (25th/75th percentile): 19-24
2005 U.S. News College Ranking:
Unranked Specialty School–Fine Arts
Acceptance Rate: 50%

Other expenses: Estimated books and supplies: $2,132. Transportation: $350. Personal expenses: $2,162.

Concordia College–Moorhead

901 Eighth Street S
Moorhead, MN 56562
Private; www.cord.edu
Financial aid office: (218) 299-3010

■ **2004-2005 TUITION AND FEES:** $17,770
■ **ROOM AND BOARD:** $4,690

ACT Score (25th/75th percentile): 21-27
2005 U.S. News College Ranking:
Liberal Arts Colleges, third tier
Acceptance Rate: 84%

Other expenses: Estimated books and supplies: $700. Transportation: $350. Personal expenses: $900. **Financial aid:** Priority filing date for institution's financial aid form: April 15. In 2003-2004, 46% of undergraduates applied for financial aid. Of those, 41% were determined to have financial need; 75% had their need fully met. Average financial aid package (proportion receiving): $13,200 (41%). Average amount of gift aid, such as scholarships or grants (proportion receiving): $7,427 (39%). Average amount of self-help aid, such as work study or loans (proportion receiving): $5,042 (39%). Average need-based loan (excluding PLUS or other private loans): $4,060. Among students who received need-based aid, the average percentage of need met: 93%. Among students who received aid based on merit, the average award (and the proportion receiving): $5,418 (13%). The average athletic scholarship (and the proportion receiving): $0 (0%). Average amount of debt of borrowers graduating in 2003: $19,546. Proportion who borrowed: 66%. **Student employment:** During the 2003-2004 academic year, 42% of undergraduates worked on campus. Average per-year earnings: $626. **Cooperative education programs:** art, business, computer science, education, health professions, natural science, social/behavioral science. **Reserve Officers Training Corps (ROTC):** Army ROTC: Offered at cooperating institution (North Dakota State University); Air Force ROTC: Offered at cooperating institution (North Dakota State University).

Concordia University–St. Paul

275 Syndicate Street N
St. Paul, MN 55104
Private; www.csp.edu
Financial aid office: (651) 641-8204

■ **2004-2005 TUITION AND FEES:** $19,928
■ **ROOM AND BOARD:** $6,156

ACT Score (25th/75th percentile): 18-24
2005 U.S. News College Ranking:
Comp. Colleges–Bachelor's (Midwest), 49
Acceptance Rate: 64%

Other expenses: Estimated books and supplies: $600. Transportation: $1,000. Personal expenses: $900. **Financial aid:** Priority filing date for institution's financial aid form: April 15. In 2003-2004, 84% of undergraduates applied for financial aid. Of those, 75% were determined to have financial need; 22% had their need fully met. Average financial aid package (proportion receiving): $11,339 (75%). Average amount of gift aid, such as scholarships or grants (proportion receiving): $8,644 (56%). Average amount of self-help aid, such as work study or loans (proportion receiving): $4,684 (61%). Average need-based loan (excluding PLUS or other private loans): $4,534. Among students who received need-based aid, the average percentage of need met: 62%. Among students who received aid based on merit, the average award (and the proportion receiving): $5,645 (5%). The average athletic scholarship (and the proportion receiving): $5,508 (2%). Average amount of debt of borrowers graduating in 2003: $15,300. Proportion who borrowed: 78%. **Reserve Officers Training Corps (ROTC):** Army ROTC: Offered at cooperating institution (University of Minnesota); Navy ROTC: Offered at cooperating institution (University of Minnesota); Air Force ROTC: Offered at cooperating institution (University of St. Thomas).

Crown College

8700 College View Drive
St. Bonifacius, MN 55375
Private; www.crown.edu
Financial aid office: (952) 446-4177

■ **2004-2005 TUITION AND FEES:** $14,354
■ **ROOM AND BOARD:** $6,142

ACT Score (25th/75th percentile): 18-24
2005 U.S. News College Ranking:
Comp. Colleges–Bachelor's (Midwest), third tier
Acceptance Rate: 82%

Other expenses: Estimated books and supplies: $800. Transportation: $800. Personal expenses: $1,890. **Financial aid:** Priority filing date for institution's financial aid form: April 1; deadline: August 1. In 2003-2004, 73% of undergraduates applied for financial aid. Of those, 70% were determined to have financial need; 8% had their need fully met. Average financial aid package (proportion receiving): $10,054 (70%). Average amount of gift aid, such as scholarships or grants (proportion receiving): $4,378 (54%). Average amount of self-help aid, such as work study or loans (proportion receiving): $5,232 (53%). Average need-based loan (excluding PLUS or other private loans): $4,504. Among students who received need-based aid, the average percentage of need met: 62%. Among students who received aid based on merit, the average award (and the proportion receiving): $2,124 (3%). Average amount of debt of borrowers graduating in 2003: $21,789. Proportion who borrowed: 83%.

Gustavus Adolphus College

800 W. College Avenue
St. Peter, MN 56082
Private; www.gac.edu
Financial aid office: (507) 933-7527

■ **2004-2005 TUITION AND FEES:** $22,720
■ **ROOM AND BOARD:** $5,810

ACT Score (25th/75th percentile): 23-28
2005 U.S. News College Ranking:
Liberal Arts Colleges, 77
Acceptance Rate: 77%

Other expenses: Estimated books and supplies: $800. Transportation: $370. Personal expenses: $630. **Financial aid:** Priority filing date for institution's financial aid form: April 15; deadline: June 15. In 2003-2004, 81% of undergraduates applied for financial aid. Of those, 68% were determined to have financial need; Average financial aid package (proportion receiving): $15,439 (68%). Average amount of gift aid, such as scholarships or grants (proportion receiving): $10,796 (67%). Average amount of self-help aid, such as work study or loans (proportion receiving): $5,028 (57%). Average need-based loan (excluding PLUS or other private loans): $4,201. Among students who received need-based aid, the average percentage of need met: 87%. Among students who received aid based on merit, the average award (and the proportion receiving): $5,506 (26%). The average athletic scholarship (and the proportion receiving): $0 (0%). Average amount of debt of borrowers graduating in 2003: $17,700. Proportion who borrowed: 70%. **Student employment:** During the 2003-2004 academic year, 5% of undergraduates worked on campus. Average per-year earnings: $5,000. **Reserve Officers Training Corps (ROTC):** Army ROTC: Offered at cooperating institution (Minnesota State University–Mankato).

Hamline University

1536 Hewitt Avenue
St. Paul, MN 55104-1284
Private; www.hamline.edu
Financial aid office: (651) 523-3000

■ **2004-2005 TUITION AND FEES:** $20,910
■ **ROOM AND BOARD:** $6,536

ACT Score (25th/75th percentile): 22-28
2005 U.S. News College Ranking:
Universities–Master's (Midwest), 8
Acceptance Rate: 75%

Other expenses: Estimated books and supplies: $1,325. Transportation: $500. Personal expenses: $0. **Financial aid:** Priority filing date for institution's financial aid form: March 1. In 2003-2004, 96% of undergraduates applied for financial aid. Of those, 75% were determined to have financial need; 51% had their need fully met. Average financial aid package (proportion receiving): $21,384 (75%). Average amount of gift aid, such as scholarships or grants (proportion receiving): $7,097 (69%). Average amount of self-help aid, such as work study or loans (proportion receiving): $4,071 (65%). Average need-based loan (excluding PLUS or other private loans): $2,691. Among students who received need-based aid, the average percentage of need met: 87%. Among students who received aid based on merit, the average award (and the proportion receiving): $13,030 (20%). The average athletic scholarship (and the proportion receiving): $0 (0%). Average amount of debt of borrowers graduating in 2003: $21,489. Proportion who borrowed: 77%. **Student employment:** During the 2003-2004 academic year, 25% of undergraduates worked on campus. Average per-year earnings: $2,500. **Reserve Officers Training Corps (ROTC):** Air Force ROTC: Offered at cooperating institution (University of Saint Thomas).

Macalester College

1600 Grand Avenue
St. Paul, MN 55105
Private; www.macalester.edu
Financial aid office: (651) 696-6214

■ **2004-2005 TUITION AND FEES:** $26,806
■ **ROOM AND BOARD:** $7,350

SAT I Score (25th/75th percentile): 1260-1430
2005 U.S. News College Ranking:
Liberal Arts Colleges, 26
Acceptance Rate: 44%

Other expenses: Estimated books and supplies: $805. Transportation: $500. Personal expenses: $745. **Financial aid:** Priority filing date for institution's financial aid form: February 9; deadline: April 15. In 2003-2004, 75% of undergraduates applied for financial aid. Of those, 69% were determined to have financial need; 100% had their need fully met. Average financial aid package (proportion receiving): $21,386 (69%). Average amount of gift aid, such as scholarships or grants (proportion receiving): $17,061 (69%). Average amount of self-help aid, such as work study or loans (proportion receiving): $4,328 (69%). Average need-based loan (excluding PLUS or other private loans): $3,483. Among students who received need-based aid, the average percentage of need met: 100%. Among students who received aid based on merit, the average award (and the proportion receiving): $5,242 (6%). The average athletic scholarship (and the proportion receiving): $0 (0%). **Student employment:** During the 2003-2004 academic year, 67% of undergraduates worked on campus. Average per-year earnings: $2,000. **Cooperative education programs:** engineering, other. **Reserve Officers Training Corps (ROTC):** Navy ROTC: Offered at cooperating institution (University of Minnesota); Air Force ROTC: Offered at cooperating institution (University of St. Thomas).

Metropolitan State University

700 E. Seventh Street
St. Paul, MN 55106
Public; www.metrostate.edu
Financial aid office: (651) 772-7670

■ **2003-2004 TUITION AND FEES:**
In state: $3,852; Out of state: $8,232
■ **ROOM AND BOARD:** $8,984

2005 U.S. News College Ranking:
Universities–Master's (Midwest), fourth tier
Acceptance Rate: 74%

Other expenses: Estimated books and supplies: $1,500. Personal expenses: $3,952.

Minneapolis College of Art and Design

2501 Stevens Avenue S
Minneapolis, MN 55404
Private; www.mcad.edu
Financial aid office: (612) 874-3782

■ **2004-2005 TUITION AND FEES:** $23,910
■ **ROOM AND BOARD:** $3,660

ACT Score (25th/75th percentile): 25
2005 U.S. News College Ranking:
Unranked Specialty School–Fine Arts
Acceptance Rate: 75%

Other expenses: Estimated books and supplies: $1,800. Transportation: $900. Personal expenses: $500. **Financial aid:** Priority filing date for institution's financial aid form: March 15. In 2003-2004, 85% of undergraduates applied for financial aid. Of those, 78% were determined to have financial need; 11% had their need fully met. Average financial aid package (proportion receiving): $11,794 (78%). Average amount of gift aid, such as scholarships or grants (proportion receiving): $7,649 (74%). Average amount of self-help aid, such as work study or loans (proportion receiving): $4,094 (75%). Average need-based loan (excluding PLUS or other private loans): $3,699. Among students who received need-based aid, the average percentage of need met: 84%. Among students who received aid based on merit, the average award (and the proportion receiving): $10,736 (11%). The average athletic scholarship (and the proportion receiving): $0 (0%). Average amount of debt of borrowers graduating in 2003: $28,719. Proportion who borrowed: 79%. **Student employment:** During the 2003-2004 academic year, 15% of undergraduates worked on campus. Average per-year earnings: $1,150.

Minnesota State University–Mankato

309 Wigley Administration Center
Mankato, MN 56001
Public; www.mnsu.edu
Financial aid office: (507) 389-1185

■ **2004-2005 TUITION AND FEES:**
In state: $5,088; Out of state: $9,998
■ **ROOM AND BOARD:** $4,716

ACT Score (25th/75th percentile): 19-24
2005 U.S. News College Ranking:
Universities–Master's (Midwest), third tier
Acceptance Rate: 88%

Other expenses: Estimated books and supplies: $706. Personal expenses: $2,496. **Financial aid:** Priority filing date for institution's financial aid form: March 15. In 2003-2004, 73% of undergraduates applied for financial aid. Of those, 52% were determined to have financial need; 46% had their need fully met. Average financial aid package (proportion receiving): $6,417 (52%). Average amount of gift aid, such as scholarships or grants (proportion receiving): $3,352 (34%). Average amount of self-help aid, such as work study or loans (proportion receiving): $4,096 (48%). Average need-based loan (excluding PLUS or other private loans): $3,787. Among students who received need-based aid, the average percentage of need met: 81%. Among students who received aid based on merit, the average award (and the proportion receiving): $1,472 (5%). The average athletic scholarship (and the proportion receiving): $3,503 (2%). Average amount of debt of borrowers graduating in 2003: $15,500. Proportion who borrowed: 75%. **Student employment:** During the 2003-2004 academic year, 24% of undergraduates worked on campus. Average per-year earnings: $2,400. **Cooperative education programs:** business, computer science, education, engineering, health professions, humanities, natural science, social/behavioral science. **Reserve Officers Training Corps (ROTC):** Army ROTC: Offered on campus.

Minnesota State University–Moorhead

1104 Seventh Avenue S
Moorhead, MN 56563
Public; www.mnstate.edu
Financial aid office: (218) 477-2251

■ **2004-2005 TUITION AND FEES:**
In state: $4,896; Out of state: $4,896
■ **ROOM AND BOARD:** $4,530

ACT Score (25th/75th percentile): 18-24
2005 U.S. News College Ranking:
Universities–Master's (Midwest), third tier
Acceptance Rate: 86%

Other expenses: Estimated books and supplies: $800. Transportation: $900. Personal expenses: $2,274. **Financial aid:** Priority filing

date for institution's financial aid form: February 15. In 2003-2004, 75% of undergraduates applied for financial aid. Of those, 49% were determined to have financial need; Average financial aid package (proportion receiving): $4,193 (49%). Average amount of gift aid, such as scholarships or grants (proportion receiving): $3,564 (28%). Average amount of self-help aid, such as work study or loans (proportion receiving): $3,702 (49%). Average need-based loan (excluding PLUS or other private loans): $3,497. Among students who received aid based on merit, the average award (and the proportion receiving): $779 (11%). The average athletic scholarship (and the proportion receiving): $1,398 (2%). Average amount of debt of borrowers graduating in 2003: $18,228. Proportion who borrowed: 65%. **Student employment:** During the 2003-2004 academic year, 6% of undergraduates worked on campus. Average per-year earnings: $3,700. **Reserve Officers Training Corps (ROTC):** Army ROTC: Offered at cooperating institution (North Dakota State University); Air Force ROTC: Offered at cooperating institution (North Dakota State University).

Northwestern College

3003 Snelling Avenue N
St. Paul, MN 55113-1598
Private; www.nwc.edu
Financial aid office: (651) 631-5212

■ **2004-2005 TUITION AND FEES:** $18,370
■ **ROOM AND BOARD:** $6,020

ACT Score (25th/75th percentile): 21-26
2005 U.S. News College Ranking:
Comp. Colleges–Bachelor's (Midwest), 29
Acceptance Rate: 96%

Other expenses: Estimated books and supplies: $600. Transportation: $680. Personal expenses: $1,900. **Financial aid:** Priority filing date for institution's financial aid form: March 1; deadline: July 1. In 2003-2004, 97% of undergraduates applied for financial aid. Of those, 84% were determined to have financial need; 10% had their need fully met. Average financial aid package (proportion receiving): $13,499 (84%). Average amount of gift aid, such as scholarships or grants (proportion receiving): $9,760 (83%). Average amount of self-help aid, such as work study or loans (proportion receiving): $4,615 (69%). Average need-based loan (excluding PLUS or other private loans): $4,248. Among students who

received need-based aid, the average percentage of need met: 73%. Among students who received aid based on merit, the average award (and the proportion receiving): $5,051 (13%). The average athletic scholarship (and the proportion receiving): $0 (0%). Average amount of debt of borrowers graduating in 2003: $19,184. Proportion who borrowed: 69%. **Student employment:** During the 2003-2004 academic year, 10% of undergraduates worked on campus. Average per-year earnings: $2,100. **Reserve Officers Training Corps (ROTC):** Army ROTC: Offered at cooperating institution (University of Minnesota); Air Force ROTC: Offered at cooperating institution (University of St. Thomas).

Southwest Minnesota State University

1501 State Street
Marshall, MN 56258
Public; www.southwestmsu.edu
Financial aid office: (507) 537-6281

■ **2004-2005 TUITION AND FEES:**
In state: $5,212; Out of state: $5,212
■ **ROOM AND BOARD:** $4,760

ACT Score (25th/75th percentile): 18-24
2005 U.S. News College Ranking:
Comp. Colleges–Bachelor's (Midwest), third tier
Acceptance Rate: 47%

Other expenses: Estimated books and supplies: $900. Transportation: $300. Personal expenses: $1,800. **Financial aid:** Priority filing date for institution's financial aid form: April 1. In 2003-2004, 77% of undergraduates applied for financial aid. Of those, 62% were determined to have financial need; 45% had their need fully met. Average financial aid package (proportion receiving): $5,926 (61%). Average amount of gift aid, such as scholarships or grants (proportion receiving): $3,178 (45%). Average amount of self-help aid, such as work study or loans (proportion receiving): $3,494 (51%). Average need-based loan (excluding PLUS or other private loans): $3,231. Among students who received need-based aid, the average percentage of need met: 68%. Among students who received aid based on merit, the average award (and the proportion receiving): $1,319 (12%). The average athletic scholarship (and the proportion receiving): $1,921 (8%). Average amount of debt of borrowers graduating in 2003: $14,420. Proportion who borrowed: 77%. **Student employment:** During the 2003-2004 academic year, 19% of undergraduates worked on campus. Average per-year earnings: $1,300. **Cooperative education programs:** agriculture, business, technologies.

St. Cloud State University

720 S. Fourth Avenue
St. Cloud, MN 56301
Public; www.stcloudstate.edu
Financial aid office: (320) 308-2047

■ **2004-2005 TUITION AND FEES:**
In state: $5,201; Out of state: $10,559
■ **ROOM AND BOARD:** $4,088

ACT Score (25th/75th percentile): 19-24
2005 U.S. News College Ranking:
Universities–Master's (Midwest), third tier
Acceptance Rate: 76%

Other expenses: Estimated books and supplies: $1,000. **Financial aid:** In 2003-2004, 63% of undergraduates applied for financial aid. Of those, 44% were determined to have financial need; 95% had their need fully met. Average financial aid package (proportion receiving): $6,590 (44%). Average amount of gift aid, such as scholarships or grants (proportion receiving): $1,937 (30%). Average amount of self-help aid, such as work study or loans (proportion receiving): $2,426 (42%). Average need-based loan (excluding PLUS or other private loans): $2,841. Among students who received need-based aid, the average percentage of need met: 96%. Among students who received aid based on merit, the average award (and the proportion receiving): $478 (19%). The average athletic scholarship (and the proportion receiving): $2,096 (2%). Average amount of debt of borrowers graduating in 2003: $17,112. Proportion who borrowed: 61%. **Reserve Officers Training Corps (ROTC):** Army ROTC: Offered on campus.

St. John's University

PO Box 7155
Collegeville, MN 56321
Private; www.csbsju.edu
Financial aid office: (320) 363-3664

■ **2004-2005 TUITION AND FEES:** $22,148
■ **ROOM AND BOARD:** $6,027

ACT Score (25th/75th percentile): 23-28
2005 U.S. News College Ranking:
Liberal Arts Colleges, 77
Acceptance Rate: 89%

Other expenses: Estimated books and supplies: $800. Transportation: $200. Personal expenses: $700. **Financial aid:** Priority filing date for institution's financial aid form: March 15. In 2003-2004, 79% of undergraduates applied for financial aid. Of those, 61% were determined to have financial need; 56% had their need fully met. Average financial aid package (proportion receiving): $17,585 (61%). Average amount of gift aid, such as scholarships or grants (proportion receiving): $8,242 (52%). Average amount of self-help aid, such as work study or loans (proportion receiving): $5,556 (55%). Average need-based loan (excluding PLUS or other private loans): $4,547. Among students who received need-based aid, the average percentage of need met: 86%. Among students who received aid based on merit, the average award (and the proportion receiving): $5,849 (28%). Average amount of debt of borrowers graduating in 2003: $21,598. Proportion who borrowed: 75%. **Student employment:** During the 2003-2004 academic year, 60% of undergraduates worked on campus. Average per-year earnings: $2,395. **Reserve Officers Training Corps (ROTC):** Army ROTC: Offered on campus.

St. Mary's University of Minnesota

700 Terrace Heights
Winona, MN 55987-1399
Private; www.smumn.edu
Financial aid office: (507) 457-1438

■ **2004-2005 TUITION AND FEES:** $17,135
■ **ROOM AND BOARD:** $5,450

ACT Score (25th/75th percentile): 19-25
2005 U.S. News College Ranking:
Universities–Master's (Midwest), 31
Acceptance Rate: 75%

Other expenses: Estimated books and supplies: $1,050. Transportation: $275. Personal expenses: $800. **Financial aid:** Priority filing date for institution's financial aid form: March 15. In 2003-2004, 84% of undergraduates applied for financial aid. Of those, 62% were determined to have financial need; 69% had their need fully met. Average financial aid package (proportion receiving): $13,719 (62%). Average amount of gift aid, such as scholarships or grants (proportion receiving): $5,804 (62%).

Average amount of self-help aid, such as work study or loans (proportion receiving): $5,872 (62%). Average need-based loan (excluding PLUS or other private loans): $4,589. Among students who received need-based aid, the average percentage of need met: 73%. Among students who received aid based on merit, the average award (and the proportion receiving): $4,920 (24%). Average amount of debt of borrowers graduating in 2003: $21,915. Proportion who borrowed: 72%. **Student employment:** During the 2003-2004 academic year, 11% of undergraduates worked on campus. Average per-year earnings: $800. **Cooperative education programs:** health professions. **Reserve Officers Training Corps (ROTC):** Army ROTC: Offered at cooperating institution (University of Wisconsin, LaCrosse).

St. Olaf College

1520 St. Olaf Avenue
Northfield, MN 55057
Private; www.stolaf.edu
Financial aid office: (507) 646-3019

■ **2004-2005 TUITION AND FEES:** $25,150
■ **ROOM AND BOARD:** $5,800

ACT Score (25th/75th percentile): 25-30
2005 U.S. News College Ranking:
Liberal Arts Colleges, 62
Acceptance Rate: 75%

Other expenses: Estimated books and supplies: $950. Transportation: $650. Personal expenses: $700. **Financial aid:** Priority filing date for institution's financial aid form: February 15; deadline: April 15. In 2003-2004, 72% of undergraduates applied for financial aid. Of those, 63% were determined to have financial need; 100% had their need fully met. Average financial aid package (proportion receiving): $18,172 (63%). Average amount of gift aid, such as scholarships or grants (proportion receiving): $12,210 (63%). Average amount of self-help aid, such as work study or loans (proportion receiving): $5,364 (63%). Average need-based loan (excluding PLUS or other private loans): $4,707. Among students who received need-based aid, the average percentage of need met: 100%. Among students who received aid based on merit, the average award (and the proportion receiving): $5,717 (19%). The average athletic scholarship (and the proportion receiving): $0 (0%). Average amount of debt of borrowers graduating in 2003: $18,024. Proportion who borrowed: 78%.

University of Minnesota–Crookston

2900 University Avenue
Crookston, MN 56716
Public; www.crk.umn.edu
Financial aid office: (218) 281-8576

■ **2004-2005 TUITION AND FEES:**
In state: $7,608; Out of state: $7,608
■ **ROOM AND BOARD:** $4,800

ACT Score (25th/75th percentile): 18-23
2005 U.S. News College Ranking:
Comp. Colleges–Bachelor's (Midwest),
third tier
Acceptance Rate: 89%

Financial aid: Priority filing date for institution's financial aid form: March 31. In 2003-2004, 82% of undergraduates applied for financial aid. Of those, 70% were determined to have financial need; 43% had their need fully met. Average financial aid package (proportion receiving): $8,856 (70%). Average amount of gift aid, such as scholarships or grants (proportion receiving): $4,589 (59%). Average amount of self-help aid, such as work study or loans (proportion receiving): $6,645 (63%). Average need-based loan (excluding PLUS or other private loans): $6,452. Among students who received need-based aid, the average percentage of need met: 79%. Among students who received aid based on merit, the average award (and the proportion receiving): $2,459 (11%). **Student employment:** During the 2003-2004 academic year, 7% of undergraduates worked on campus. Average per-year earnings: $1,700. **Reserve Officers Training Corps (ROTC):** Air Force ROTC: Offered on campus.

University of Minnesota–Duluth

1049 University Drive
Duluth, MN 55812-2496
Public; www.d.umn.edu
Financial aid office: (218) 726-8000

■ **2004-2005 TUITION AND FEES:**
In state: $8,288; Out of state: $19,393
■ **ROOM AND BOARD:** $5,282

ACT Score (25th/75th percentile): 20-25
2005 U.S. News College Ranking:
Universities–Master's (Midwest), 42
Acceptance Rate: 75%

Other expenses: Estimated books and supplies: $1,200. Personal expenses: $2,000. **Financial aid:** In 2003-2004, 73% of undergraduates applied for financial aid. Of those, 55% were determined to have financial need; 81% had their need fully met. Average financial aid package (proportion receiving): $7,662 (53%). Average amount of gift aid, such as scholarships or grants (proportion receiving): $5,183 (37%). Average amount of self-help aid, such as work study or loans (proportion receiving): $3,981 (46%). Average need-based loan (excluding PLUS or other private loans): $3,844. Among students who received need-based aid, the average percentage of need met: 52%. Among students who received aid based on merit, the average award (and the proportion receiving): $2,052 (10%). The average athletic scholarship (and the proportion receiving): $3,454 (2%). Average amount of debt of borrowers graduating in 2003: $16,432. Proportion who borrowed: 70%. **Student employment:** During the 2003-2004 academic year, 14% of undergraduates worked on campus. Average per-year earnings: $2,500. **Reserve Officers Training Corps (ROTC):** Air Force ROTC: Offered on campus.

University of Minnesota–Morris

600 E. Fourth Street
Morris, MN 56267
Public; www.mrs.umn.edu
Financial aid office: (320) 589-6035

■ **2004-2005 TUITION AND FEES:**
In state: $8,996; Out of state: $8,996
■ **ROOM AND BOARD:** $5,230

ACT Score (25th/75th percentile): 23-28
2005 U.S. News College Ranking:
Liberal Arts Colleges, third tier
Acceptance Rate: 83%

Other expenses: Estimated books and supplies: $600. Transportation: $500. Personal expenses: $1,200. **Financial aid:** Priority filing date for institution's financial aid form: March 1. In 2003-2004, 82% of undergraduates applied for financial aid. Of those, 66% were determined to have financial need; 37% had their need fully met. Average financial aid package (proportion receiving): $9,754 (65%). Average amount of gift aid, such as scholarships or grants (proportion receiving): $5,050 (60%). Average amount of self-help aid, such as work study or loans (proportion receiving): $5,804 (57%). Average need-based loan (excluding PLUS or other pri-

vate loans): $5,773. Among students who received need-based aid, the average percentage of need met: 81%. Among students who received aid based on merit, the average award (and the proportion receiving): $2,394 (18%). The average athletic scholarship (and the proportion receiving): $840 (3%). Average amount of debt of borrowers graduating in 2003: $13,167. Proportion who borrowed: 96%. **Student employment:** During the 2003-2004 academic year, 43% of undergraduates worked on campus. Average per-year earnings: $1,200.

University of Minnesota–Twin Cities

100 Church Street SE
Minneapolis, MN 55455-0213
Public; www1.umn.edu/twincities
Financial aid office: (612) 624-1665

■ **2004-2005 TUITION AND FEES:**
In state: $8,029; Out of state: $19,659

ACT Score (25th/75th percentile): 22-28
2005 U.S. News College Ranking:
National Universities, 66
Acceptance Rate: 76%

Financial aid: In 2003-2004, 66% of undergraduates applied for financial aid. Of those, 51% were determined to have financial need; 34% had their need fully met. Average financial aid package (proportion receiving): $9,027 (50%). Average amount of gift aid, such as scholarships or grants (proportion receiving): $6,074 (36%). Average amount of self-help aid, such as work study or loans (proportion receiving): $6,284 (45%). Average need-based loan (excluding PLUS or other private loans): $5,720. Among students who received need-based aid, the average percentage of need met: 76%. Among students who received aid based on merit, the average award (and the proportion receiving): $4,238 (10%). **Reserve Officers Training Corps (ROTC):** Army ROTC: Offered on campus; Navy ROTC: Offered on campus; Air Force ROTC: Offered on campus.

University of St. Thomas

2115 Summit Avenue
St. Paul, MN 55105-1096
Private; www.stthomas.edu
Financial aid office: (651) 962-6550

■ **2004-2005 TUITION AND FEES:** $20,488
■ **ROOM AND BOARD:** $7,360

ACT Score (25th/75th percentile): 22-27
2005 U.S. News College Ranking:
National Universities, 120
Acceptance Rate: 87%

....

Other expenses: Estimated books and supplies: $800. Transportation: $680. Personal expenses: $1,450. **Financial aid:** Priority filing date for institution's financial aid form: April 1. In 2003-2004, 69% of undergraduates applied for financial aid. Of those, 55% were determined to have financial need; 24% had their need fully met. Average financial aid package (proportion receiving): $15,688 (55%). Average amount of gift aid, such as scholarships or grants (proportion receiving): $8,809 (53%). Average amount of self-help aid, such as work study or loans (proportion receiving): $5,228 (47%). Average need-based loan (excluding PLUS or other private loans): $3,767. Among students who received need-based aid, the average percentage of need met: 81%. Among students who received aid based on merit, the average award (and the proportion receiving): $6,404 (11%). The average athletic scholarship (and the proportion receiving): $0 (0%). Average amount of debt of borrowers graduating in 2003: $23,084. Proportion who borrowed: 68%. **Reserve Officers Training Corps (ROTC):** Army ROTC: Offered at cooperating institution (University of Minnesota); Navy ROTC: Offered at cooperating institution (University of Minnesota); Air Force ROTC: Offered on campus.

Winona State University

PO Box 5838
Winona, MN 55987-5838
Public; www.winona.edu
Financial aid office: (507) 457-5090

■ **2004-2005 TUITION AND FEES:**
 In state: $5,320; Out of state: $9,860
■ **ROOM AND BOARD:** $4,960

ACT Score (25th/75th percentile): 20-24
2005 U.S. News College Ranking:
Universities–Master's (Midwest), 68
Acceptance Rate: 81%

....

Other expenses: Estimated books and supplies: $980. Transportation: $520. Personal expenses: $1,000. **Financial aid:** In 2003-2004, 72% of undergraduates applied for financial aid. Of those, 50% were determined to have financial need; 17% had their need fully met. Average financial aid package (proportion receiving): $5,236 (50%). Average amount of gift aid, such as scholarships or grants (proportion receiving): $3,025 (31%). Average amount of self-help aid, such as work study or loans (proportion receiving): $3,077 (41%). Average need-based loan (excluding PLUS or other private loans): $2,860. Among students who received need-based aid, the average percentage of need met: 57%. Among students who received aid based on merit, the average award (and the proportion receiving): $1,660 (15%). Average amount of debt of borrowers graduating in 2003: $19,067. Proportion who borrowed: 81%. **Student employment:** During the 2003-2004 academic year, 33% of undergraduates worked on campus. Average per-year earnings: $2,800. **Cooperative education programs:** art, business, computer science, education, engineering, health professions, humanities, natural science, social/behavioral science, technologies. **Reserve Officers Training Corps (ROTC):** Army ROTC: Offered at cooperating institution (Univ. of Wisconsin-La Crosse); Air Force ROTC: Offered at cooperating institution (Univ. of Wisconsin–La Crosse).

Mississippi

Alcorn State University

1000 ASU Drive #359
Alcorn State, MS 39096
Public; www.alcorn.edu
Financial aid office: (601) 877-6190

■ **2004-2005 TUITION AND FEES:**
In state: $3,872; Out of state: $6,237

ACT Score (25th/75th percentile): 16-20
2005 U.S. News College Ranking:
Universities–Master's (South), third tier
Acceptance Rate: 22%

Financial aid: Priority filing date for institution's financial aid form: April 1. In 2003-2004, 97% of undergraduates applied for financial aid. Of those, 96% were determined to have financial need; 92% had their need fully met. Average financial aid package (proportion receiving): $9,500 (96%). Average amount of gift aid, such as scholarships or grants (proportion receiving): $4,500 (89%). Average amount of self-help aid, such as work study or loans (proportion receiving): $2,800 (89%). Average need-based loan (excluding PLUS or other private loans): $5,500. Among students who received need-based aid, the average percentage of need met: 76%. Among students who received aid based on merit, the average award (and the proportion receiving): $4,250 (43%). The average athletic scholarship (and the proportion receiving): $6,209 (9%). Average amount of debt of borrowers graduating in 2003: $7,500. Proportion who borrowed: 67%. **Cooperative education programs:** other. **Reserve Officers Training Corps (ROTC):** Army ROTC: Offered on campus.

Belhaven College

1500 Peachtree Street
Jackson, MS 39202
Private; www.belhaven.edu
Financial aid office: (601) 968-5934

■ **2004-2005 TUITION AND FEES:** $13,440
■ **ROOM AND BOARD:** $5,240

ACT Score (25th/75th percentile): 21-27
2005 U.S. News College Ranking:
Comp. Colleges–Bachelor's (South), 28
Acceptance Rate: 56%

Other expenses: Estimated books and supplies: $1,400. Transportation: $900. Personal expenses: $4,110. **Financial aid:** Priority filing date for institution's financial aid form: March 1. In 2003-2004, 92% of undergraduates applied for financial aid. Of those, 60% were determined to have financial need; 7% had their need fully met. Average financial aid package (proportion receiving): $10,980 (60%). Average amount of gift aid, such as scholarships or grants (proportion receiving): $5,500 (58%). Average amount of self-help aid, such as work study or loans (proportion receiving): $4,390 (53%). Average need-based loan (excluding PLUS or other private loans): $4,304. Among students who received need-based aid, the average percentage of need met: 51%. Among students who received aid based on merit, the average award (and the proportion receiving): $3,843 (8%). The average athletic scholarship (and the proportion receiving): $2,879 (16%). Average amount of debt of borrowers graduating in 2003: $18,126. Proportion who borrowed: 87%. **Student employment:** During the 2003-2004 academic year, 6% of undergraduates worked on campus. Average per-year earnings: $1,545.

Blue Mountain College

PO Box 160
Blue Mountain, MS 38610-0160
Private; www.bmc.edu
Financial aid office: (662) 685-4771

■ **2004-2005 TUITION AND FEES:** $6,820
■ **ROOM AND BOARD:** $3,326

ACT Score (25th/75th percentile): 17-22
2005 U.S. News College Ranking:
Comp. Colleges–Bachelor's (South), 48
Acceptance Rate: 64%

Other expenses: Estimated books and supplies: $600. Personal expenses: $1,500. **Financial aid:** Priority filing date for institution's financial aid form: March 1; deadline: July 15. In 2003-2004, 89% of undergraduates applied for financial aid. Of those, 75% were determined to have financial need; 32% had their need fully met. Average financial aid package (proportion receiving): N/A (75%). Average amount of gift aid, such as scholarships or grants (proportion receiving): $2,511 (54%). Average amount of self-help aid, such as

work study or loans (proportion receiving): $3,244 (54%). Average need-based loan (excluding PLUS or other private loans): $3,752. Among students who received need-based aid, the average percentage of need met: 32%. Among students who received aid based on merit, the average award (and the proportion receiving): $2,526 (10%). The average athletic scholarship (and the proportion receiving): $6,935 (6%). Average amount of debt of borrowers graduating in 2003: $9,072. Proportion who borrowed: 64%.

Delta State University

Highway 8 W
Cleveland, MS 38733
Public; www.deltastate.edu
Financial aid office: (662) 846-4670

■ **2004-2005 TUITION AND FEES:**
In state: $3,582; Out of state: $8,522
■ **ROOM AND BOARD:** $4,244

ACT Score (25th/75th percentile): 17-22
2005 U.S. News College Ranking:
Universities–Master's (South), third tier

Financial aid: Priority filing date for institution's financial aid form: April 1. **Student employment:** During the 2003-2004 academic year, 4% of undergraduates worked on campus. Average per-year earnings: $1,200.

Jackson State University

1400 J.R. Lynch Street
Jackson, MS 39217
Public; www.jsums.edu
Financial aid office: (601) 979-2227

■ **2004-2005 TUITION AND FEES:**
In state: $3,841; Out of state: $8,570
■ **ROOM AND BOARD:** $4,974

ACT Score (25th/75th percentile): 18
2005 U.S. News College Ranking:
National Universities, fourth tier
Acceptance Rate: 42%

Other expenses: Estimated books and supplies: $1,200. Transportation: $1,050. Personal expenses: $2,650. **Financial aid:** Priority filing date for institution's financial aid form: April

15; deadline: April 15. In 2003-2004, 72% of undergraduates applied for financial aid. Of those, 69% were determined to have financial need; 10% had their need fully met. Average financial aid package (proportion receiving): $3,084 (67%). Average amount of gift aid, such as scholarships or grants (proportion receiving): N/A (56%). Average amount of self-help aid, such as work study or loans (proportion receiving): $3,411 (59%). Average need-based loan (excluding PLUS or other private loans): $3,773. Among students who received need-based aid, the average percentage of need met: 27%. Among students who received aid based on merit, the average award (and the proportion receiving): $2,383 (2%). The average athletic scholarship (and the proportion receiving): $5,631 (2%). **Reserve Officers Training Corps (ROTC):** Army ROTC: Offered on campus.

Millsaps College

1701 N. State Street
Jackson, MS 39210-0001
Private; go.millsaps.edu
Financial aid office: (601) 974-1220

■ **2004-2005 TUITION AND FEES:** $19,518
■ **ROOM AND BOARD:** $7,206

ACT Score (25th/75th percentile): 23-28
2005 U.S. News College Ranking:
Liberal Arts Colleges, 89
Acceptance Rate: 84%

Other expenses: Estimated books and supplies: $800. Transportation: $450. Personal expenses: $900. **Financial aid:** Priority filing date for institution's financial aid form: March 1. In 2003-2004, 65% of undergraduates applied for financial aid. Of those, 56% were determined to have financial need; 29% had their need fully met. Average financial aid package (proportion receiving): $16,463 (56%). Average amount of gift aid, such as scholarships or grants (proportion receiving): $12,512 (56%). Average amount of self-help aid, such as work study or loans (proportion receiving): $4,968 (45%). Average need-based loan (excluding PLUS or other private loans): $4,124. Among students who received need-based aid, the average percentage of need met: 85%. Among students who received aid based on merit, the average award (and the proportion receiving): $11,659 (39%). The average athletic scholarship (and the proportion receiving): $0 (0%). Average amount of debt of borrowers graduating in 2003: $15,942. Proportion who borrowed: 67%. **Student employment:** During the 2003-2004 academic

year, 27% of undergraduates worked on campus. Average per-year earnings: $800. **Cooperative education programs:** business, engineering, health professions. **Reserve Officers Training Corps (ROTC):** Army ROTC: Offered at cooperating institution (Jackson State University).

Mississippi College

MC Box 4001
Clinton, MS 39058
Private; www.mc.edu
Financial aid office: (601) 925-3319

■ **2004-2005 TUITION AND FEES:** $11,836
■ **ROOM AND BOARD:** $5,612

ACT Score (25th/75th percentile): 20-26
2005 U.S. News College Ranking:
Universities–Master's (South), 26
Acceptance Rate: 58%

Other expenses: Estimated books and supplies: $735. Transportation: $746. Personal expenses: $1,746. **Financial aid:** Priority filing date for institution's financial aid form: March 1. In 2003-2004, 99% of undergraduates applied for financial aid. Of those, 56% were determined to have financial need; 41% had their need fully met. Average financial aid package (proportion receiving): $14,197 (56%). Average amount of gift aid, such as scholarships or grants (proportion receiving): $8,616 (39%). Average amount of self-help aid, such as work study or loans (proportion receiving): $6,603 (39%). Average need-based loan (excluding PLUS or other private loans): $6,462. Among students who received need-based aid, the average percentage of need met: 84%. Among students who received aid based on merit, the average award (and the proportion receiving): $9,838 (42%). The average athletic scholarship (and the proportion receiving): $0 (0%). Average amount of debt of borrowers graduating in 2003: $17,545. Proportion who borrowed: 59%. **Student employment:** During the 2003-2004 academic year, 20% of undergraduates worked on campus. Average per-year earnings: $2,100. **Reserve Officers Training Corps (ROTC):** Army ROTC: Offered at cooperating institution (Jackson State University).

Mississippi State University

PO Box 6334
Mississippi State, MS 39762
Public; www.msstate.edu
Financial aid office: (662) 325-2450

■ **2004-2005 TUITION AND FEES:**
In state: $4,106; Out of state: $9,306
■ **ROOM AND BOARD:** $5,994

ACT Score (25th/75th percentile): 20-27
2005 U.S. News College Ranking:
National Universities, third tier
Acceptance Rate: 75%

Other expenses: Estimated books and supplies: $750. Transportation: $1,000. Personal expenses: $995. **Financial aid:** Priority filing date for institution's financial aid form: April 1. In 2003-2004, 61% of undergraduates applied for financial aid. Of those, 52% were determined to have financial need; 49% had their need fully met. Average financial aid package (proportion receiving): $8,488 (51%). Average amount of gift aid, such as scholarships or grants (proportion receiving): $3,326 (44%). Average amount of self-help aid, such as work study or loans (proportion receiving): $3,966 (41%). Average need-based loan (excluding PLUS or other private loans): $3,547. Among students who received need-based aid, the average percentage of need met: 69%. Among students who received aid based on merit, the average award (and the proportion receiving): $2,128 (21%). The average athletic scholarship (and the proportion receiving): $6,222 (3%). Average amount of debt of borrowers graduating in 2003: $17,109. Proportion who borrowed: 48%. Average per-year earnings: $4,500. **Cooperative education programs:** agriculture, art, business, computer science, education, engineering, health professions, home economics, humanities, natural science, social/behavioral science, technologies, vocational arts, other. **Reserve Officers Training Corps (ROTC):** Army ROTC: Offered on campus; Air Force ROTC: Offered on campus.

Mississippi University for Women

W Box 1600
Columbus, MS 39701
Public; www.muw.edu
Financial aid office: (662) 329-7114

■ **2004-2005 TUITION AND FEES:**
In state: $3,298; Out of state: $7,965
■ **ROOM AND BOARD:** $3,378

ACT Score (25th/75th percentile): 18-24
2005 U.S. News College Ranking:
Universities–Master's (South), 33
Acceptance Rate: 60%

....

Other expenses: Estimated books and supplies:
$600. Transportation: $1,500. Personal expenses: $900. **Financial aid:** Priority filing date for institution's financial aid form: March 1. In 2003-2004, 92% of undergraduates applied for financial aid. Of those, 72% were determined to have financial need; 54% had their need fully met. Average financial aid package (proportion receiving): $5,920 (72%). Average amount of gift aid, such as scholarships or grants (proportion receiving): $3,750 (51%). Average amount of self-help aid, such as work study or loans (proportion receiving): $3,400 (43%). Average need-based loan (excluding PLUS or other private loans): $2,750. Among students who received need-based aid, the average percentage of need met: 79%. Among students who received aid based on merit, the average award (and the proportion receiving): $2,800 (20%). The average athletic scholarship (and the proportion receiving): $6,500 (1%). Average amount of debt of borrowers graduating in 2003: $13,239. Proportion who borrowed: 74%. **Student employment:** During the 2003-2004 academic year, 20% of undergraduates worked on campus. Average per-year earnings: $3,200. **Reserve Officers Training Corps (ROTC):** Army ROTC: Offered at cooperating institution (Mississippi State University); Air Force ROTC: Offered at cooperating institution (Mississippi State University).

Mississippi Valley State University

14000 Highway 82 W
Itta Bena, MS 38941-1400
Public; www.mvsu.edu
Financial aid office: (662) 254-3335

■ **2004-2005 TUITION AND FEES:**
In state: $3,411; Out of state: $7,965
■ **ROOM AND BOARD:** $3,354

ACT Score (25th/75th percentile): 17-22
2005 U.S. News College Ranking:
Comp. Colleges–Bachelor's (South), third tier
Acceptance Rate: 99%

....

Reserve Officers Training Corps (ROTC): Army ROTC: Offered on campus.

Rust College

150 Rust Avenue
Holly Springs, MS 38635
Private; www.rustcollege.edu
Financial aid office: (662) 252-8000

■ **2004-2005 TUITION AND FEES:** $6,000
■ **ROOM AND BOARD:** $2,598

ACT Score (25th/75th percentile): 14-19
2005 U.S. News College Ranking:
Comp. Colleges–Bachelor's (South), fourth tier
Acceptance Rate: 47%

....

Financial aid: Priority filing date for institution's financial aid form: May 1. **Student employment:** During the 2003-2004 academic year, 54% of undergraduates worked on campus. Average per-year earnings: $1,600.

Tougaloo College

500 W. County Line Road
Tougaloo, MS 39174
Private; www.tougaloo.edu
Financial aid office: (601) 977-7767

■ **2004-2005 TUITION AND FEES:** $8,860
■ **ROOM AND BOARD:** $5,100

ACT Score (25th/75th percentile): 16-17
2005 U.S. News College Ranking:
Liberal Arts Colleges, fourth tier
Acceptance Rate: 24%

....

University of Mississippi

PO Box 1848
University, MS 38677-1848
Public; www.olemiss.edu
Financial aid office: (662) 915-7175

■ **2004-2005 TUITION AND FEES:**
In state: $4,110; Out of state: $9,264
■ **ROOM AND BOARD:** $5,610

ACT Score (25th/75th percentile): 20-26
2005 U.S. News College Ranking:
National Universities, third tier
Acceptance Rate: 80%

....

Other expenses: Estimated books and supplies: $900. Transportation: $1,422. Personal expenses: $1,562. **Cooperative education programs:** engineering. **Reserve Officers Training Corps (ROTC):** Army ROTC: Offered on campus; Navy ROTC: Offered on campus; Air Force ROTC: Offered on campus.

University of Southern Mississippi

118 College Drive
Hattiesburg, MS 39406
Public; www.usm.edu
Financial aid office: (601) 266-4774

■ **2004-2005 TUITION AND FEES:**
In state: $2,035; Out of state: $2,585

ACT Score (25th/75th percentile): 18-24
2005 U.S. News College Ranking:
National Universities, fourth tier
Acceptance Rate: 49%

....

Financial aid: Priority filing date for institution's financial aid form: March 15. Average amount of debt of borrowers graduating in 2003: $11,202. Proportion who borrowed: 61%. **Student employment:** During the 2003-2004 academic year, 14% of undergraduates worked on campus. Average per-year earnings: $3,000. **Cooperative education programs:** computer science, engineering, other. **Reserve Officers Training Corps (ROTC):** Army ROTC: Offered on campus; Air Force ROTC: Offered on campus.

William Carey College

498 Tuscan Avenue
Hattiesburg, MS 39401-5499
Private; www.wmcarey.edu
Financial aid office: (601) 318-6153

■ **2004-2005 TUITION AND FEES:** $8,115
■ **ROOM AND BOARD:** $3,390

ACT Score (25th/75th percentile): 18-25
2005 U.S. News College Ranking:
Universities–Master's (South), third tier
Acceptance Rate: 59%

Other expenses: Estimated books and supplies: $1,350. Transportation: $1,602. Personal expenses: $1,350. **Financial aid:** Priority filing date for institution's financial aid form: April 1. In 2003-2004, 100% of undergraduates applied for financial aid. Of those, 93% were determined to have financial need; 96% had their need fully met. Average financial aid package (proportion receiving): $8,000 (93%). Average amount of gift aid, such as scholarships or grants (proportion receiving): $5,500 (93%). Average amount of self-help aid, such as work study or loans (proportion receiving): $3,500 (90%). Average need-based loan (excluding PLUS or other private loans): $3,500. Among students who received need-based aid, the average percentage of need met: 75%. Among students who received aid based on merit, the average award (and the proportion receiving): $4,000 (19%). The average athletic scholarship (and the proportion receiving): $5,000 (0%). Average amount of debt of borrowers graduating in 2003: $15,000. Proportion who borrowed: 75%. **Student employment:** During the 2003-2004 academic year, 20% of undergraduates worked on campus. Average per-year earnings: $1,500.

Missouri

Avila University

11901 Wornall Road
Kansas City, MO 64145
Private; www.Avila.edu
Financial aid office: (816) 501-3600

- **2004-2005 TUITION AND FEES:** $15,870
- **ROOM AND BOARD:** $5,400

ACT Score (25th/75th percentile): 18-25
2005 U.S. News College Ranking:
Universities–Master's (Midwest), third tier
Acceptance Rate: 42%

Student employment: During the 2003-2004 academic year, 6% of undergraduates worked on campus. Average per-year earnings: $710. **Cooperative education programs:** health professions. **Reserve Officers Training Corps (ROTC):** Army ROTC: Offered at cooperating institution (University of Missouri–Kansas City).

Central Methodist University

411 Central Methodist Square
Fayette, MO 65248
Private; www.centralmethodist.edu
Financial aid office: (660) 248-6244

- **2004-2005 TUITION AND FEES:** $14,490
- **ROOM AND BOARD:** $5,120

ACT Score (25th/75th percentile): 19-23
2005 U.S. News College Ranking:
Comp. Colleges–Bachelor's (Midwest), third tier
Acceptance Rate: 73%

Other expenses: Estimated books and supplies: $750. Transportation: $750. Personal expenses: $2,250. **Financial aid:** Priority filing date for institution's financial aid form: March 15. In 2003-2004, 80% of undergraduates applied for financial aid. Of those, 80% were determined to have financial need; 4% had their need fully met. Average financial aid package (proportion receiving): $10,109 (80%). Average amount of gift aid, such as scholarships or grants (proportion receiving): $3,515 (80%). Average amount of self-help aid, such as work study or loans (proportion receiving): $2,288 (65%). Average need-based loan (excluding PLUS or other pri-

vate loans): $2,095. Among students who received need-based aid, the average percentage of need met: 33%. Among students who received aid based on merit, the average award (and the proportion receiving): $5,862 (3%). The average athletic scholarship (and the proportion receiving): $6,023 (1%). Average amount of debt of borrowers graduating in 2003: $17,037. Proportion who borrowed: 66%. **Reserve Officers Training Corps (ROTC):** Army ROTC: Offered at cooperating institution (University of Missouri–Columbia); Air Force ROTC: Offered at cooperating institution (University of Missouri–Columbia).

Central Missouri State University

Warrensburg, MO 64093
Public; www.cmsu.edu
Financial aid office: (660) 543-4040

- **2004-2005 TUITION AND FEES:**
  In state: $5,340; Out of state: $10,260
- **ROOM AND BOARD:** $4,988

ACT Score (25th/75th percentile): 19-24
2005 U.S. News College Ranking:
Universities–Master's (Midwest), third tier
Acceptance Rate: 76%

Other expenses: Estimated books and supplies: $500. Transportation: $900. Personal expenses: $1,500. **Financial aid:** Priority filing date for institution's financial aid form: March 1. In 2003-2004, 81% of undergraduates applied for financial aid. Of those, 64% were determined to have financial need; 37% had their need fully met. Average financial aid package (proportion receiving): $6,723 (63%). Average amount of gift aid, such as scholarships or grants (proportion receiving): $3,284 (38%). Average amount of self-help aid, such as work study or loans (proportion receiving): $0 (56%). Average need-based loan (excluding PLUS or other private loans): $4,009. Among students who received need-based aid, the average percentage of need met: 88%. Among students who received aid based on merit, the average award (and the proportion receiving): $2,257 (30%). The average athletic scholarship (and the proportion receiving): $4,583 (5%). Average amount of debt of borrowers graduating in 2003: $14,478. Proportion who borrowed: 60%. Average per-

year earnings: $1,545. **Cooperative education programs:** education, technologies, other. **Reserve Officers Training Corps (ROTC):** Army ROTC: Offered on campus; Air Force ROTC: Offered at cooperating institution (University of Missouri-Columbia).

College of the Ozarks

PO Box 17
Point Lookout, MO 65726
Private; www.cofo.edu
Financial aid office: (417) 334-6411

- **2004-2005 TUITION AND FEES:** $13,150
- **ROOM AND BOARD:** $3,550

ACT Score (25th/75th percentile): 21-26
2005 U.S. News College Ranking:
Comp. Colleges–Bachelor's (Midwest), 31
Acceptance Rate: 14%

Other expenses: Estimated books and supplies: $800. Transportation: $1,959. Personal expenses: $290. **Financial aid:** Priority filing date for institution's financial aid form: March 15. **Student employment:** During the 2003-2004 academic year, 100% of undergraduates worked on campus. Average per-year earnings: $2,900. **Reserve Officers Training Corps (ROTC):** Army ROTC: Offered on campus.

Columbia College

1001 Rogers Street
Columbia, MO 65216
Private; www.ccis.edu
Financial aid office: (573) 875-7390

- **2004-2005 TUITION AND FEES:** $11,589
- **ROOM AND BOARD:** $4,913

ACT Score (25th/75th percentile): 19-25
2005 U.S. News College Ranking:
Comp. Colleges–Bachelor's (Midwest), 37
Acceptance Rate: 59%

Other expenses: Estimated books and supplies: $600. Transportation: $1,200. Personal expenses: $1,200. **Financial aid:** Priority filing date for institution's financial aid form: March 15. In 2003-2004, 78% of undergraduates applied for financial aid. Of those, 58% were determined to have financial need; 65% had their need fully met. Average financial aid package (proportion receiving): $7,426 (57%). Average amount of gift aid, such as scholarships or grants (proportion receiving): $3,541 (46%). Average amount of self-help aid, such as work study or loans (proportion receiving): $3,237 (42%). Average need-based loan (excluding PLUS or other private loans): $3,934. Among students who received need-based aid, the average percentage of need met: 85%. Among students who received aid based on merit, the average award (and the proportion receiving): $8,780 (21%). The average athletic scholarship (and the proportion receiving): $11,020 (12%). **Reserve Officers Training Corps (ROTC):** Army ROTC: Offered at cooperating institution (University of Missouri–Columbia); Navy ROTC: Offered at cooperating institution (University of Missouri–Columbia); Air Force ROTC: Offered at cooperating institution (University of Missouri–Columbia).

Culver-Stockton College

1 College Hill
Canton, MO 63435
Private; www.culver.edu
Financial aid office: (217) 231-6307

- **2004-2005 TUITION AND FEES:** $13,390
- **ROOM AND BOARD:** $5,775

ACT Score (25th/75th percentile): 18-24
2005 U.S. News College Ranking:
Comp. Colleges–Bachelor's (Midwest), 49
Acceptance Rate: 72%

Other expenses: Estimated books and supplies: $700. Transportation: $1,905. Personal expenses: $320. **Financial aid:** Priority filing date for institution's financial aid form: June 15; deadline: June 15. In 2003-2004, 92% of undergraduates applied for financial aid. Of those, 85% were determined to have financial need; 30% had their need fully met. Average financial aid package (proportion receiving): $11,676 (85%). Average amount of gift aid, such as scholarships or grants (proportion receiving): $8,328 (85%). Average amount of self-help aid, such as work study or loans (proportion receiving): $3,961 (72%). Average need-based loan (excluding PLUS or other private loans): $3,647. Among students who received need-based aid, the average percentage of need met: 82%. Among students who received aid based on merit, the average award (and the proportion receiving): $8,123 (14%). The average athletic scholarship (and the proportion receiving): $2,703 (10%). Average amount of debt of bor-

rowers graduating in 2003: $14,438. Proportion who borrowed: 97%. **Student employment:** During the 2003-2004 academic year, 43% of undergraduates worked on campus. Average per-year earnings: $4,748.

Drury University

900 N. Benton Avenue
Springfield, MO 65802
Private; www.drury.edu
Financial aid office: (417) 873-7312

- **2004-2005 TUITION AND FEES:** $13,904
- **ROOM AND BOARD:** $5,128

ACT Score (25th/75th percentile): 22-29
2005 U.S. News College Ranking:
Universities–Master's (Midwest), 12
Acceptance Rate: 77%

Other expenses: Estimated books and supplies: $1,000. Transportation: $800. Personal expenses: $1,500. **Financial aid:** Priority filing date for institution's financial aid form: March 15. In 2003-2004, 97% of undergraduates applied for financial aid. Of those, 90% were determined to have financial need; 90% had their need fully met. Average financial aid package (proportion receiving): $7,695 (90%). Average amount of gift aid, such as scholarships or grants (proportion receiving): $6,895 (87%). Average amount of self-help aid, such as work study or loans (proportion receiving): $5,845 (84%). Average need-based loan (excluding PLUS or other private loans): $5,450. Among students who received need-based aid, the average percentage of need met: 83%. Among students who received aid based on merit, the average award (and the proportion receiving): $2,955 (14%). The average athletic scholarship (and the proportion receiving): $6,975 (4%). Average amount of debt of borrowers graduating in 2003: $14,200. Proportion who borrowed: 40%. **Student employment:** During the 2003-2004 academic year, 25% of undergraduates worked on campus. Average per-year earnings: $2,000. **Cooperative education programs:** other. **Reserve Officers Training Corps (ROTC):** Army ROTC: Offered at cooperating institution (Southwest Missouri State University).

Evangel University

1111 N. Glenstone
Springfield, MO 65802
Private; www.evangel.edu
Financial aid office: (417) 865-2815

- **2004-2005 TUITION AND FEES:** $11,970
- **ROOM AND BOARD:** $4,380

ACT Score (25th/75th percentile): 19-25
2005 U.S. News College Ranking:
Comp. Colleges–Bachelor's (Midwest), 49
Acceptance Rate: 81%

Other expenses: Estimated books and supplies: $800. Transportation: $1,750. Personal expenses: $1,750. **Financial aid:** Priority filing date for institution's financial aid form: February 15. In 2003-2004, 84% of undergraduates applied for financial aid. Of those, 75% were determined to have financial need; 8% had their need fully met. Average financial aid package (proportion receiving): $8,525 (75%). Average amount of gift aid, such as scholarships or grants (proportion receiving): $4,972 (65%). Average amount of self-help aid, such as work study or loans (proportion receiving): $4,586 (69%). Average need-based loan (excluding PLUS or other private loans): $3,902. Among students who received need-based aid, the average percentage of need met: 45%. Among students who received aid based on merit, the average award (and the proportion receiving): $5,858 (20%). The average athletic scholarship (and the proportion receiving): $4,985 (5%). Average amount of debt of borrowers graduating in 2003: $21,467. Proportion who borrowed: 90%. **Student employment:** During the 2003-2004 academic year, 3% of undergraduates worked on campus. Average per-year earnings: $1,600. **Reserve Officers Training Corps (ROTC):** Army ROTC: Offered on campus.

Fontbonne University

6800 Wydown Boulevard
St. Louis, MO 63105
Private; www.fontbonne.edu
Financial aid office: (314) 889-1414

- **2004-2005 TUITION AND FEES:** $15,420
- **ROOM AND BOARD:** $6,000

ACT Score (25th/75th percentile): 20-25
2005 U.S. News College Ranking:
Universities–Master's (Midwest), third tier
Acceptance Rate: 81%

Other expenses: Estimated books and supplies: $650. Transportation: $950. Personal expenses: $1,300. Financial aid: Priority filing date for institution's financial aid form: April 1. In 2003-2004, 80% of undergraduates applied for financial aid. Of those, 76% were determined to have financial need; 76% had their need fully met. Average financial aid package (proportion receiving): $15,150 (76%). Average amount of gift aid, such as scholarships or grants (proportion receiving): $8,650 (72%). Average amount of self-help aid, such as work study or loans (proportion receiving): $5,500 (76%). Average need-based loan (excluding PLUS or other private loans): $5,500. Among students who received need-based aid, the average percentage of need met: 75%. Among students who received aid based on merit, the average award (and the proportion receiving): $5,000 (20%). The average athletic scholarship (and the proportion receiving): $0 (0%). Average amount of debt of borrowers graduating in 2003: $14,500. Proportion who borrowed: 85%.

Hannibal-LaGrange College

2800 Palmyra Road
Hannibal, MO 63401
Private; www.hlg.edu
Financial aid office: (573) 221-3675

■ **2004-2005 TUITION AND FEES:** $10,870
■ **ROOM AND BOARD:** $4,050

ACT Score (25th/75th percentile): 19-25
2005 U.S. News College Ranking:
Comp. Colleges–Bachelor's (Midwest), third tier
Acceptance Rate: 94%

Other expenses: Estimated books and supplies: $880. Financial aid: Priority filing date for institution's financial aid form: July 1. In 2003-2004, 96% of undergraduates applied for financial aid. Of those, 66% were determined to have financial need; Average financial aid package (proportion receiving): $8,918 (66%). Average amount of gift aid, such as scholarships or grants (proportion receiving): $3,172 (40%). Average amount of self-help aid, such as work study or loans (proportion receiving): $3,800 (56%). Average need-based loan (excluding PLUS or other private loans): $3,882. Among students who received aid based on merit, the average award (and the proportion receiving): $2,483 (16%). The average athletic scholarship (and the proportion receiving): $3,516 (21%). Average amount of debt of

borrowers graduating in 2003: $16,588. Proportion who borrowed: 91%. **Student employment:** During the 2003-2004 academic year, 12% of undergraduates worked on campus. Average per-year earnings: $1,100. **Cooperative education programs:** engineering.

Kansas City Art Institute

4415 Warwick Boulevard
Kansas City, MO 64111
Private; www.kcai.edu
Financial aid office: (816) 802-3448

■ **2004-2005 TUITION AND FEES:** $21,326
■ **ROOM AND BOARD:** $7,800

ACT Score (25th/75th percentile): 20-25
2005 U.S. News College Ranking:
Unranked Specialty School–Fine Arts
Acceptance Rate: 81%

Financial aid: Priority filing date for institution's financial aid form: March 15; deadline: August 1. **Student employment:** During the 2003-2004 academic year, 32% of undergraduates worked on campus. Average per-year earnings: $1,000.

Lincoln University

PO Box 29
Jefferson City, MO 65102-0029
Public; www.lincolnu.edu
Financial aid office: (573) 681-6156

■ **2004-2005 TUITION AND FEES:**
In state: $4,065; Out of state: $6,897
■ **ROOM AND BOARD:** $3,790

ACT Score (25th/75th percentile): 14-20
2005 U.S. News College Ranking:
Universities–Master's (Midwest), fourth tier
Acceptance Rate: 96%

Financial aid: Priority filing date for institution's financial aid form: March 1; deadline: June 30. In 2003-2004, 82% of undergraduates applied for financial aid. Of those, 64% were determined to have financial need; 45% had their need fully met. Average financial aid package (proportion receiving): $5,000 (63%). Average amount of gift aid, such as scholarships or grants (proportion receiving): $1,100 (17%). Average amount of self-help aid, such as work study or loans (proportion receiving): $1,100 (12%). Average need-based loan (excluding PLUS or other private loans): $3,200.

Among students who received need-based aid, the average percentage of need met: 40%. Among students who received aid based on merit, the average award (and the proportion receiving): $1,000 (6%). The average athletic scholarship (and the proportion receiving): $6,500 (8%). Average amount of debt of borrowers graduating in 2003: $10,000. Proportion who borrowed: 69%. **Cooperative education programs:** agriculture, social/behavioral science. **Reserve Officers Training Corps (ROTC):** Army ROTC: Offered on campus.

Lindenwood University

209 S. Kingshighway
St. Charles, MO 63301-1695
Private; www.lindenwood.edu
Financial aid office: (636) 949-4923

■ **2004-2005 TUITION AND FEES:** $11,400
■ **ROOM AND BOARD:** $5,920

ACT Score (25th/75th percentile): 19-26
2005 U.S. News College Ranking:
Universities–Master's (Midwest), fourth tier
Acceptance Rate: 46%

Other expenses: Estimated books and supplies: $2,600. Transportation: $2,200. Personal expenses: $5,700. **Financial aid:** Priority filing date for institution's financial aid form: March 15. **Student employment:** During the 2003-2004 academic year, 50% of undergraduates worked on campus. Average per-year earnings: $1,800. **Cooperative education programs:** agriculture, business, computer science, education, engineering, humanities, natural science, social/behavioral science, technologies. **Reserve Officers Training Corps (ROTC):** Army ROTC: Offered on campus.

Maryville University of St. Louis

13550 Conway Road
St Louis, MO 63141-7299
Private; www.maryville.edu
Financial aid office: (314) 529-9360

■ **2004-2005 TUITION AND FEES:** $16,300
■ **ROOM AND BOARD:** $7,000

ACT Score (25th/75th percentile): 21-27
2005 U.S. News College Ranking:
Universities–Master's (Midwest), 37
Acceptance Rate: 73%

Other expenses: Estimated books and supplies: $950. Transportation: $1,585. Personal expenses: $1,475. **Financial aid:** Priority filing date for institution's financial aid form: April 1. In 2003-2004, 82% of undergraduates applied for financial aid. Of those, 71% were determined to have financial need; 9% had their need fully met. Average financial aid package (proportion receiving): $10,822 (70%). Average amount of gift aid, such as scholarships or grants (proportion receiving): $5,999 (65%). Average amount of self-help aid, such as work study or loans (proportion receiving): $5,014 (66%). Average need-based loan (excluding PLUS or other private loans): $4,591. Among students who received need-based aid, the average percentage of need met: 42%. Among students who received aid based on merit, the average award (and the proportion receiving): $6,687 (15%). The average athletic scholarship (and the proportion receiving): $0 (0%). Average amount of debt of borrowers graduating in 2003: $11,167. Proportion who borrowed: 82%. **Student employment:** During the 2003-2004 academic year, 11% of undergraduates worked on campus. Average per-year earnings: $1,616. **Cooperative education programs:** art, business, computer science, education, health professions, humanities, natural science, social/behavioral science. **Reserve Officers Training Corps (ROTC):** Army ROTC: Offered at cooperating institution (Washington University).

Missouri Baptist College

1 College Park Drive
St. Louis, MO 63141
Private; www.mobap.edu
Financial aid office: (314) 392-2366

■ **2004-2005 TUITION AND FEES:** $6,355
■ **ROOM AND BOARD:** $2,900

ACT Score (25th/75th percentile): 19-24
2005 U.S. News College Ranking:
Comp. Colleges–Bachelor's (Midwest), fourth tier
Acceptance Rate: 71%

Other expenses: Estimated books and supplies: $1,825. Transportation: $4,930. Personal expenses: $2,250. **Financial aid:** Priority filing date for institution's financial aid form: April 1; deadline: November 15. In 2003-2004, 83% of undergraduates applied for financial aid. Of those, 83% were determined to have financial need; Average financial aid package (proportion receiving): $7,400 (83%). Average amount of

gift aid, such as scholarships or grants (proportion receiving): $6,693 (67%). Average amount of self-help aid, such as work study or loans (proportion receiving): $3,006 (52%). Average need-based loan (excluding PLUS or other private loans): $3,776. Among students who received need-based aid, the average percentage of need met: 40%. Among students who received aid based on merit, the average award (and the proportion receiving): $707 (33%). The average athletic scholarship (and the proportion receiving): $5,670 (25%). **Reserve Officers Training Corps (ROTC):** Army ROTC: Offered at cooperating institution (Washington University).

Missouri Southern State University

3950 E. Newman Road
Joplin, MO 64801-1595
Public; www.mssu.edu
Financial aid office: (417) 625-9325

■ **2004-2005 TUITION AND FEES:**
In state: $3,976; Out of state: $7,786
■ **ROOM AND BOARD:** $4,770

ACT Score (25th/75th percentile): 19-24
2005 U.S. News College Ranking:
Comp. Colleges–Bachelor's (Midwest), fourth tier
Acceptance Rate: 74%

Other expenses: Estimated books and supplies: $600. Transportation: $600. Personal expenses: $1,500. **Financial aid:** Priority filing date for institution's financial aid form: February 15. In 2003-2004, 91% of undergraduates applied for financial aid. Of those, 79% were determined to have financial need; Average financial aid package (proportion receiving): $6,722 (79%). Average amount of gift aid, such as scholarships or grants (proportion receiving): $4,636 (66%). Average amount of self-help aid, such as work study or loans (proportion receiving): $2,139 (61%). Average need-based loan (excluding PLUS or other private loans): $3,249. Among students who received need-based aid, the average percentage of need met: 69%. Among students who received aid based on merit, the average award (and the proportion receiving): $2,560 (17%). The average athletic scholarship (and the proportion receiving): $4,334 (6%). Average amount of debt of borrowers graduating in 2003: $15,448. Proportion who borrowed: 57%. **Cooperative education programs:** health professions, technologies.

Missouri Valley College

500 E. College
Marshall, MO 65340
Private; www.moval.edu
Financial aid office: (660) 831-4171

■ **2004-2005 TUITION AND FEES:** $13,500
■ **ROOM AND BOARD:** $5,200

ACT Score (25th/75th percentile): 19-27
2005 U.S. News College Ranking:
Comp. Colleges–Bachelor's (Midwest), fourth tier
Acceptance Rate: 67%

Other expenses: Estimated books and supplies: $1,500. Transportation: $1,700. Personal expenses: $3,100. **Financial aid:** In 2003-2004, 92% of undergraduates applied for financial aid. Of those, 92% were determined to have financial need; Average financial aid package (proportion receiving): $12,141 (92%). Average amount of gift aid, such as scholarships or grants (proportion receiving): $9,999 (92%). Average amount of self-help aid, such as work study or loans (proportion receiving): $4,320 (92%). Average need-based loan (excluding PLUS or other private loans): $2,455. Among students who received need-based aid, the average percentage of need met: 80%. Among students who received aid based on merit, the average award (and the proportion receiving): N/A (1%). The average athletic scholarship (and the proportion receiving): $0 (0%). **Reserve Officers Training Corps (ROTC):** Army ROTC: Offered at cooperating institution (Wentworth Military Academy).

Missouri Western State College

4525 Downs Drive
St. Joseph, MO 64507
Public; www.mwsc.edu
Financial aid office: (816) 271-4361

■ **2003-2004 TUITION AND FEES:**
In state: $4,464; Out of state: $8,040
■ **ROOM AND BOARD:** $4,500

ACT Score (25th/75th percentile): 16-22
2005 U.S. News College Ranking:
Comp. Colleges–Bachelor's (Midwest), fourth tier
Acceptance Rate: 100%

Other expenses: Estimated books and supplies: $700. Transportation: $600. Personal expenses: $2,100. **Financial aid:** Priority filing date for

institution's financial aid form: March 1.
Reserve Officers Training Corps (ROTC): Army ROTC: Offered on campus.

Northwest Missouri State University

800 University Drive
Maryville, MO 64468
Public; www.nwmissouri.edu
Financial aid office: (660) 562-1363

■ **2004-2005 TUITION AND FEES:**
 In state: $5,325; Out of state: $9,180
■ **ROOM AND BOARD:** $5,080

ACT Score (25th/75th percentile): 19-24
2005 U.S. News College Ranking:
Universities–Master's (Midwest), third tier
Acceptance Rate: 88%

Other expenses: Estimated books and supplies: $450. Transportation: $1,000. Personal expenses: $1,200. **Financial aid:** In 2003-2004, 64% of undergraduates applied for financial aid. Of those, 50% were determined to have financial need; 28% had their need fully met. Average financial aid package (proportion receiving): $6,821 (49%). Average amount of gift aid, such as scholarships or grants (proportion receiving): $2,652 (25%). Average amount of self-help aid, such as work study or loans (proportion receiving): $4,777 (43%). Average need-based loan (excluding PLUS or other private loans): $3,483. Among students who received need-based aid, the average percentage of need met: 77%. Among students who received aid based on merit, the average award (and the proportion receiving): $2,183 (6%). The average athletic scholarship (and the proportion receiving): $3,102 (0%). Average amount of debt of borrowers graduating in 2003: $17,947. Proportion who borrowed: 67%. **Student employment:** During the 2003-2004 academic year, 21% of undergraduates worked on campus. Average per-year earnings: $3,300. **Cooperative education programs:** education. **Reserve Officers Training Corps (ROTC):** Army ROTC: Offered at cooperating institution (MO Western St College).

Park University

8700 N.W. River Park Drive
Parkville, MO 64152
Private; www.park.edu
Financial aid office: (816) 584-6190

■ **2004-2005 TUITION AND FEES:** $6,480

ACT Score (25th/75th percentile): 18-23
2005 U.S. News College Ranking:
Universities–Master's (Midwest), fourth tier

Other expenses: Estimated books and supplies: $1,200. Transportation: $450. Personal expenses: $1,350. **Financial aid:** Priority filing date for institution's financial aid form: April 1. In 2003-2004, 71% of undergraduates applied for financial aid. Of those, 63% were determined to have financial need; 73% had their need fully met. Average financial aid package (proportion receiving): $4,800 (57%). Average amount of gift aid, such as scholarships or grants (proportion receiving): $2,812 (40%). Average amount of self-help aid, such as work study or loans (proportion receiving): $2,798 (46%). Average need-based loan (excluding PLUS or other private loans): $4,120. Among students who received need-based aid, the average percentage of need met: 68%. Among students who received aid based on merit, the average award (and the proportion receiving): $3,590 (10%). The average athletic scholarship (and the proportion receiving): $2,702 (4%). Average amount of debt of borrowers graduating in 2003: $12,800. Proportion who borrowed: 30%. **Reserve Officers Training Corps (ROTC):** Army ROTC: Offered on campus.

Rockhurst University

1100 Rockhurst Road
Kansas City, MO 64110-2561
Private; www.rockhurst.edu
Financial aid office: (816) 501-4100

■ **2004-2005 TUITION AND FEES:** $18,490
■ **ROOM AND BOARD:** $5,500

ACT Score (25th/75th percentile): 21-27
2005 U.S. News College Ranking:
Universities–Master's (Midwest), 14
Acceptance Rate: 80%

Other expenses: Estimated books and supplies: $1,400. Transportation: $980. Personal expenses: $980. **Financial aid:** Priority filing date for institution's financial aid form: March 1; deadline: June 30. In 2003-2004, 90% of undergraduates applied for financial aid. Of those, 76% were determined to have financial need; 6% had their need fully met. Average financial aid package (proportion receiving): $16,260 (71%). Average amount of gift aid, such as scholarships or grants (proportion receiving): $5,773 (52%). Average amount of self-help aid, such as work study or loans (proportion receiving): $4,027 (45%). Average need-based loan

(excluding PLUS or other private loans): $6,254. Among students who received need-based aid, the average percentage of need met: 92%. Among students who received aid based on merit, the average award (and the proportion receiving): $6,993 (8%). The average athletic scholarship (and the proportion receiving): $12,355 (10%). Average amount of debt of borrowers graduating in 2003: $14,556. Proportion who borrowed: 56%. **Student employment:** During the 2003-2004 academic year, 30% of undergraduates worked on campus. Average per-year earnings: $4,000. **Cooperative education programs:** art, business, computer science, education, health professions, humanities, natural science, social/behavioral science, technologies, other. **Reserve Officers Training Corps (ROTC):** Army ROTC: Offered at cooperating institution (University of MO at KC).

Southeast Missouri State University

1 University Plaza
Cape Girardeau, MO 63701
Public; www.semo.edu
Financial aid office: (573) 651-2253

■ **2004-2005 TUITION AND FEES:**
 In state: $4,875; Out of state: $8,460
■ **ROOM AND BOARD:** $5,187

ACT Score (25th/75th percentile): 19-25
2005 U.S. News College Ranking:
Universities–Master's (Midwest), third tier
Acceptance Rate: 83%

Other expenses: Estimated books and supplies: $400. Transportation: $794. Personal expenses: $1,967. **Financial aid:** Priority filing date for institution's financial aid form: March 1. In 2003-2004, 69% of undergraduates applied for financial aid. Of those, 53% were determined to have financial need; 16% had their need fully met. Average financial aid package (proportion receiving): $6,210 (52%). Average amount of gift aid, such as scholarships or grants (proportion receiving): $4,085 (38%). Average amount of self-help aid, such as work study or loans (proportion receiving): $3,733 (43%). Average need-based loan (excluding PLUS or other private loans): $3,506. Among students who received need-based aid, the average percentage of need met: 68%. Among students who received aid based on merit, the average award (and the proportion receiving): $3,422 (12%). The average athletic scholarship (and the proportion receiving): $7,572 (2%). Average amount of debt of borrowers graduating in

2003: $14,018. Proportion who borrowed: 57%. **Student employment:** During the 2003-2004 academic year, 18% of undergraduates worked on campus. Average per-year earnings: $1,022. **Reserve Officers Training Corps (ROTC):** Air Force ROTC: Offered on campus.

Southwest Baptist University

1600 University Avenue
Bolivar, MO 65613
Private; www.sbuniv.edu
Financial aid office: (417) 328-1820

■ **2004-2005 TUITION AND FEES:** $12,480
■ **ROOM AND BOARD:** $3,750

ACT Score (25th/75th percentile): 19-26
2005 U.S. News College Ranking:
Universities–Master's (Midwest), fourth tier
Acceptance Rate: 86%

Other expenses: Estimated books and supplies: $1,200. Transportation: $1,750. Personal expenses: $500. **Financial aid:** Priority filing date for institution's financial aid form: March 15. In 2003-2004, 81% of undergraduates applied for financial aid. Of those, 72% were determined to have financial need; 20% had their need fully met. Average financial aid package (proportion receiving): $9,976 (72%). Average amount of gift aid, such as scholarships or grants (proportion receiving): $3,633 (45%). Average amount of self-help aid, such as work study or loans (proportion receiving): $4,582 (58%). Average need-based loan (excluding PLUS or other private loans): $4,106. Among students who received need-based aid, the average percentage of need met: 70%. Among students who received aid based on merit, the average award (and the proportion receiving): $4,550 (21%). The average athletic scholarship (and the proportion receiving): $7,326 (11%). Average amount of debt of borrowers graduating in 2003: $13,558. Proportion who borrowed: 72%. **Student employment:** During the 2003-2004 academic year, 20% of undergraduates worked on campus. Average per-year earnings: $3,000. **Reserve Officers Training Corps (ROTC):** Army ROTC: Offered at cooperating institution (Southwest Missouri State University).

Southwest Missouri State University

901 S. National
Springfield, MO 65804-0094
Public; www.smsu.edu
Financial aid office: (417) 836-5262

■ **2004-2005 TUITION AND FEES:**
In state: $5,128; Out of state: $9,748
■ **ROOM AND BOARD:** $4,660

ACT Score (25th/75th percentile): 21-26
2005 U.S. News College Ranking:
Universities–Master's (Midwest), 55
Acceptance Rate: 86%

Other expenses: Estimated books and supplies: $800. Transportation: $1,000. Personal expenses: $2,374. **Financial aid:** Priority filing date for institution's financial aid form: March 30. In 2003-2004, 77% of undergraduates applied for financial aid. Of those, 49% were determined to have financial need; 7% had their need fully met. Average financial aid package (proportion receiving): $7,253 (47%). Average amount of gift aid, such as scholarships or grants (proportion receiving): $3,034 (25%). Average amount of self-help aid, such as work study or loans (proportion receiving): $3,847 (41%). Average need-based loan (excluding PLUS or other private loans): $3,847. Among students who received need-based aid, the average percentage of need met: 63%. Among students who received aid based on merit, the average award (and the proportion receiving): $4,527 (9%). The average athletic scholarship (and the proportion receiving): $7,664 (3%). Average amount of debt of borrowers graduating in 2003: $12,993. Proportion who borrowed: 60%. **Student employment:** During the 2003-2004 academic year, 16% of undergraduates worked on campus. **Reserve Officers Training Corps (ROTC):** Army ROTC: Offered on campus.

Stephens College

1200 E. Broadway Box 2121
Columbia, MO 65215
Private; www.stephens.edu
Financial aid office: (573) 876-7106

■ **2004-2005 TUITION AND FEES:** $18,230
■ **ROOM AND BOARD:** $7,180

ACT Score (25th/75th percentile): 21-26
2005 U.S. News College Ranking:
Liberal Arts Colleges, fourth tier
Acceptance Rate: 79%

Other expenses: Estimated books and supplies: $750. Transportation: $700. Personal expenses: $1,845. **Financial aid:** Priority filing date for institution's financial aid form: March 15. In 2003-2004, 77% of undergraduates applied for financial aid. Of those, 72% were determined to have financial need; 31% had their need fully met. Average financial aid package (proportion receiving): $16,576 (72%). Average amount of gift aid, such as scholarships or grants (proportion receiving): $5,477 (55%). Average amount of self-help aid, such as work study or loans (proportion receiving): $5,156 (64%). Average need-based loan (excluding PLUS or other private loans): $3,885. Among students who received need-based aid, the average percentage of need met: 82%. Among students who received aid based on merit, the average award (and the proportion receiving): $8,532 (19%). The average athletic scholarship (and the proportion receiving): $0 (0%). **Student employment:** During the 2003-2004 academic year, 48% of undergraduates worked on campus. Average per-year earnings: $1,200. **Reserve Officers Training Corps (ROTC):** Army ROTC: Offered at cooperating institution (University of Missouri–Columbia); Navy ROTC: Offered at cooperating institution (University of Missouri–Columbia); Air Force ROTC: Offered at cooperating institution (University of Missouri–Columbia).

St. Louis University

221 N. Grand Boulevard
St. Louis, MO 63103
Private; www.slu.edu
Financial aid office: (314) 977-2350

■ **2004-2005 TUITION AND FEES:** $23,558
■ **ROOM AND BOARD:** $7,960

ACT Score (25th/75th percentile): 23-29
2005 U.S. News College Ranking:
National Universities, 81
Acceptance Rate: 71%

Other expenses: Estimated books and supplies: $1,040. Transportation: $1,550. Personal expenses: $1,050. **Financial aid:** Priority filing date for institution's financial aid form: March 1. In 2003-2004, 81% of undergraduates applied for financial aid. Of those, 71% were determined to have financial need; 11% had their need fully met. Average financial aid package (proportion receiving): $18,526 (70%). Average amount of gift aid, such as scholarships or grants (proportion receiving): $12,459 (67%). Average amount of self-help aid, such as work study or loans (proportion receiving): $2,748 (58%). Average need-based loan (excluding PLUS or other private loans): $5,222. Among students who received need-based aid, the average percentage of need met: 62%. Among students who received aid based on merit, the average award (and the proportion receiving): $8,692 (17%). The average athletic scholarship (and the proportion receiving): $15,121 (1%). Average amount of debt of borrowers graduating in 2003: $22,247. Proportion who borrowed: 67%. **Student employment:** During the 2003-2004 academic year, 25% of undergraduates worked on campus. Average per-year earnings: $3,000. **Reserve Officers Training Corps (ROTC):** Air Force ROTC: Offered on campus.

Truman State University

McClain Hall 205
Kirksville, MO 63501
Public; www.truman.edu
Financial aid office: (660) 785-4130

■ **2004-2005 TUITION AND FEES:**
 In state: $5,466; Out of state: $9,566
■ **ROOM AND BOARD:** $5,175

ACT Score (25th/75th percentile): 25-30
2005 U.S. News College Ranking:
Universities–Master's (Midwest), 9
Acceptance Rate: 84%

Other expenses: Estimated books and supplies: $600. Transportation: $1,300. Personal expenses: $2,500. **Financial aid:** Priority filing date for institution's financial aid form: April 1. In 2003-2004, 56% of undergraduates applied for financial aid. Of those, 45% were determined to have financial need; 49% had their need fully met. Average financial aid package (proportion receiving): $6,017 (40%). Average amount of gift aid, such as scholarships or grants (proportion receiving): $3,008 (16%). Average amount of self-help aid, such as work study or loans (proportion receiving): $3,893 (29%). Average need-based loan (excluding PLUS or other private loans): $3,753. Among students who received need-based aid, the average percentage of need met: 78%. Among students who received aid based on merit, the average award (and the proportion receiving): $4,314 (40%). The average athletic scholarship (and the pro-

portion receiving): $3,936 (5%). Average amount of debt of borrowers graduating in 2003: $16,008. Proportion who borrowed: 43%. **Student employment:** During the 2003-2004 academic year, 39% of undergraduates worked on campus. Average per-year earnings: $899. **Reserve Officers Training Corps (ROTC):** Army ROTC: Offered on campus.

University of Missouri–Columbia

305 Jesse Hall
Columbia, MO 65211
Public; www.missouri.edu
Financial aid office: (573) 882-7506

■ **2004-2005 TUITION AND FEES:**
 In state: $7,100; Out of state: $16,547
■ **ROOM AND BOARD:** $6,220

ACT Score (25th/75th percentile): 23-28
2005 U.S. News College Ranking:
National Universities, 86
Acceptance Rate: 89%

Other expenses: Estimated books and supplies: $900. Personal expenses: $2,618. **Financial aid:** Priority filing date for institution's financial aid form: March 1. In 2003-2004, 62% of undergraduates applied for financial aid. Of those, 44% were determined to have financial need; 28% had their need fully met. Average financial aid package (proportion receiving): $9,278 (43%). Average amount of gift aid, such as scholarships or grants (proportion receiving): $5,417 (36%). Average amount of self-help aid, such as work study or loans (proportion receiving): $4,267 (36%). Average need-based loan (excluding PLUS or other private loans): $3,973. Among students who received need-based aid, the average percentage of need met: 86%. Among students who received aid based on merit, the average award (and the proportion receiving): $4,497 (24%). The average athletic scholarship (and the proportion receiving): $8,881 (4%). Average amount of debt of borrowers graduating in 2003: $20,428. Proportion who borrowed: 46%. **Cooperative education programs:** agriculture, business, computer science, education, engineering, other. **Reserve Officers Training Corps (ROTC):** Army ROTC: Offered on campus; Navy ROTC: Offered on campus; Air Force ROTC: Offered on campus.

University of Missouri–Kansas City

5100 Rockhill Road
Kansas City, MO 64110
Public; www.umkc.edu
Financial aid office: (816) 235-1154

■ **2004-2005 TUITION AND FEES:**
 In state: $7,181; Out of state: $16,628
■ **ROOM AND BOARD:** $5,660

ACT Score (25th/75th percentile): 20-27
2005 U.S. News College Ranking:
National Universities, third tier
Acceptance Rate: 93%

Other expenses: Estimated books and supplies: $968. Transportation: $990. Personal expenses: $3,250. **Financial aid:** Priority filing date for institution's financial aid form: March 1. In 2003-2004, 86% of undergraduates applied for financial aid. Of those, 61% were determined to have financial need; 52% had their need fully met. Average financial aid package (proportion receiving): $11,547 (61%). Average amount of gift aid, such as scholarships or grants (proportion receiving): $4,309 (40%). Average amount of self-help aid, such as work study or loans (proportion receiving): $7,579 (55%). Average need-based loan (excluding PLUS or other private loans): $6,347. Among students who received need-based aid, the average percentage of need met: 64%. Among students who received aid based on merit, the average award (and the proportion receiving): $3,890 (13%). The average athletic scholarship (and the proportion receiving): $8,694 (3%). Average amount of debt of borrowers graduating in 2003: $15,714. Proportion who borrowed: 80%. **Student employment:** During the 2003-2004 academic year, 6% of undergraduates worked on campus. Average per-year earnings: $2,930. **Reserve Officers Training Corps (ROTC):** Army ROTC: Offered on campus; Air Force ROTC: Offered at cooperating institution (University of Missouri–Colombia).

University of Missouri–Rolla

207 Parker Hall, 1870 Miner Circle
Rolla, MO 65409-0910
Public; www.umr.edu
Financial aid office: (573) 341-4282

■ **2004-2005 TUITION AND FEES:**
 In state: $7,299; Out of state: $16,746
■ **ROOM AND BOARD:** $5,646

ACT Score (25th/75th percentile): 25-30
2005 U.S. News College Ranking:
National Universities, 106
Acceptance Rate: 79%

....

Other expenses: Estimated books and supplies: $875. Personal expenses: $2,007. **Financial aid:** Priority filing date for institution's financial aid form: March 1. In 2003-2004, 68% of undergraduates applied for financial aid. Of those, 53% were determined to have financial need; 17% had their need fully met. Average financial aid package (proportion receiving): $9,550 (53%). Average amount of gift aid, such as scholarships or grants (proportion receiving): $5,760 (45%). Average amount of self-help aid, such as work study or loans (proportion receiving): $4,180 (41%). Average need-based loan (excluding PLUS or other private loans): $4,050. Among students who received need-based aid, the average percentage of need met: 84%. Among students who received aid based on merit, the average award (and the proportion receiving): $6,010 (30%). The average athletic scholarship (and the proportion receiving): $9,970 (1%). Average amount of debt of borrowers graduating in 2003: $17,820. Proportion who borrowed: 64%. **Student employment:** During the 2003-2004 academic year, 21% of undergraduates worked on campus. Average per-year earnings: $1,296. **Cooperative education programs:** business, computer science, engineering, humanities, natural science, social/behavioral science. **Reserve Officers Training Corps (ROTC):** Army ROTC: Offered on campus; Air Force ROTC: Offered on campus.

University of Missouri– St. Louis

8001 Natural Bridge Road
St. Louis, MO 63121-4400
Public; www.umsl.edu
Financial aid office: (314) 516-5526

■ **2004-2005 TUITION AND FEES:** In state: $7,378; Out of state: $16,825
■ **ROOM AND BOARD:** $6,194

ACT Score (25th/75th percentile): 21-26
2005 U.S. News College Ranking:
National Universities, fourth tier
Acceptance Rate: 48%

....

Other expenses: Estimated books and supplies: $850. Transportation: $2,946. Personal expenses: $3,228. **Financial aid:** Priority filing date for institution's financial aid form: April 1. In 2003-2004, 61% of undergraduates applied for financial aid. Of those, 52% were determined to

have financial need; 2% had their need fully met. Average financial aid package (proportion receiving): $9,103 (52%). Average amount of gift aid, such as scholarships or grants (proportion receiving): $3,363 (41%). Average amount of self-help aid, such as work study or loans (proportion receiving): $4,347 (47%). Average need-based loan (excluding PLUS or other private loans): $4,215. Among students who received need-based aid, the average percentage of need met: 68%. Among students who received aid based on merit, the average award (and the proportion receiving): $4,679 (9%). The average athletic scholarship (and the proportion receiving): $6,281 (1%). Average amount of debt of borrowers graduating in 2003: $15,958. Proportion who borrowed: 62%. **Student employment:** During the 2003-2004 academic year, 10% of undergraduates worked on campus. Average per-year earnings: $6,800. **Cooperative education programs:** business, computer science, health professions. **Reserve Officers Training Corps (ROTC):** Army ROTC: Offered at cooperating institution (Washington University); Air Force ROTC: Offered at cooperating institution (St. Louis University).

Washington University in St. Louis

Campus Box 1089, 1 Brookings Drive
St. Louis, MO 63130-4899
Private; admissions.wustl.edu
Financial aid office: (888) 547-6670

■ **2004-2005 TUITION AND FEES:** $30,546
■ **ROOM AND BOARD:** $9,640

SAT I Score (25th/75th percentile): 1320-1480
2005 U.S. News College Ranking:
National Universities, 11
Acceptance Rate: 20%

....

Other expenses: Estimated books and supplies: $1,000. Personal expenses: $1,600. **Financial aid:** In 2003-2004, 72% of undergraduates applied for financial aid. Of those, 46% were determined to have financial need; 99% had their need fully met. Average financial aid package (proportion receiving): $24,461 (45%). Average amount of gift aid, such as scholarships or grants (proportion receiving): $19,641 (45%). Average amount of self-help aid, such as work study or loans (proportion receiving): $7,166 (36%). Average need-based loan (excluding PLUS or other private loans): $6,214. Among students who received need-based aid, the average percentage of need met: 100%. Among students who received aid based on

merit, the average award (and the proportion receiving): $9,231 (14%). Proportion who borrowed: 41%. **Student employment:** During the 2003-2004 academic year, 10% of undergraduates worked on campus. Average per-year earnings: $2,000. **Cooperative education programs:** business, engineering. **Reserve Officers Training Corps (ROTC):** Army ROTC: Offered on campus; Air Force ROTC: Offered at cooperating institution (St. Louis University).

Webster University

470 E. Lockwood Avenue
St. Louis, MO 63119
Private; www.webster.edu
Financial aid office: (314) 968-6992

■ **2004-2005 TUITION AND FEES:** $16,250
■ **ROOM AND BOARD:** $6,610

ACT Score (25th/75th percentile): 21-27
2005 U.S. News College Ranking:
Universities–Master's (Midwest), 25
Acceptance Rate: 58%

....

Other expenses: Estimated books and supplies: $800. **Financial aid:** Priority filing date for institution's financial aid form: April 1. In 2003-2004, 80% of undergraduates applied for financial aid. Of those, 69% were determined to have financial need; Average financial aid package (proportion receiving): $15,845 (69%). Average amount of gift aid, such as scholarships or grants (proportion receiving): $4,707 (60%). Average amount of self-help aid, such as work study or loans (proportion receiving): $5,231 (62%). Average need-based loan (excluding PLUS or other private loans): $4,132. Among students who received aid based on merit, the average award (and the proportion receiving): $8,378 (19%). The average athletic scholarship (and the proportion receiving): $0 (0%). Average amount of debt of borrowers graduating in 2003: $17,752. Proportion who borrowed: 50%. **Student employment:** During the 2003-2004 academic year, 22% of undergraduates worked on campus. Average per-year earnings: $2,330. **Cooperative education programs:** computer science. **Reserve Officers Training Corps (ROTC):** Army ROTC: Offered at cooperating institution (Washington Univ., St. Louis Univ.); Air Force ROTC: Offered at cooperating institution (St. Louis Univ.).

Westminster College

501 Westminster Avenue
Fulton, MO 65251
Private; www.wcmo.edu
Financial aid office: (573) 592-5364

■ **2004-2005 TUITION AND FEES:** $17,450
■ **ROOM AND BOARD:** $5,650

ACT Score (25th/75th percentile): 21-26
2005 U.S. News College Ranking:
Liberal Arts Colleges, third tier
Acceptance Rate: 72%

Other expenses: Estimated books and supplies:
$800. Transportation: $375. Personal expenses:
$1,900. **Financial aid:** Priority filing date for institution's financial aid form: February 28; deadline:
February 15. In 2003-2004, 74% of undergraduates applied for financial aid. Of those, 64% were determined to have financial need; 35% had their need fully met. Average financial aid package (proportion receiving): $14,689 (64%). Average amount of gift aid, such as scholarships or grants (proportion receiving): $11,329 (64%). Average amount of self-help aid, such as work study or loans (proportion receiving): $3,246 (50%). Average need-based loan (excluding PLUS or other private loans): $2,369. Among students who received need-based aid, the average percentage of need met: 88%. Among students who received aid based on merit, the average award (and the proportion receiving): $6,573 (32%). The average athletic scholarship (and the proportion receiving): $0 (0%). Average amount of debt of borrowers graduating in 2003: $15,597. Proportion who borrowed: 62%. **Student employment:** During the 2003-2004 academic year, 13% of undergraduates worked on campus. Average per-year earnings: $1,300. **Reserve Officers Training Corps (ROTC):** Army ROTC: Offered at cooperating institution (University of Missouri–Columbia); Navy ROTC: Offered at cooperating institution (University of Missouri–Columbia); Air Force ROTC: Offered at cooperating institution (University of Missouri–Columbia).

William Jewell College

500 College Hill
Liberty, MO 64068
Private; www.jewell.edu
Financial aid office: (800) 753-7009

■ **2004-2005 TUITION AND FEES:** $17,500
■ **ROOM AND BOARD:** $5,100

ACT Score (25th/75th percentile): 22-28
2005 U.S. News College Ranking:
Liberal Arts Colleges, third tier
Acceptance Rate: 95%

Other expenses: Estimated books and supplies: $750. Transportation: $800. Personal expenses: $1,800. **Financial aid:** Priority filing date for institution's financial aid form: March 1. In 2003-2004, 80% of undergraduates applied for financial aid. Of those, 68% were determined to have financial need; Average financial aid package (proportion receiving): $13,859 (68%). Average amount of gift aid, such as scholarships or grants (proportion receiving): $9,320 (67%). Average amount of self-help aid, such as work study or loans (proportion receiving): $5,209 (53%). Average need-based loan (excluding PLUS or other private loans): $4,349. Average amount of debt of borrowers graduating in 2003: $17,306. **Student employment:** During the 2003-2004 academic year, 16% of undergraduates worked on campus. Average per-year earnings: $1,000. **Cooperative education programs:** engineering.

William Woods University

1 University Avenue
Fulton, MO 65251
Private; www.williamwoods.edu
Financial aid office: (573) 592-4232

■ **2004-2005 TUITION AND FEES:** $14,720
■ **ROOM AND BOARD:** $5,700

ACT Score (25th/75th percentile): 19-25
2005 U.S. News College Ranking:
Universities–Master's (Midwest), third tier
Acceptance Rate: 83%

Other expenses: Estimated books and supplies: $1,000. **Financial aid:** Priority filing date for institution's financial aid form: March 1; deadline: April 1. In 2003-2004, 89% of undergraduates applied for financial aid. Of those, 55% were determined to have financial need; 30% had their need fully met. Average financial aid package (proportion receiving): $13,532 (55%). Average amount of gift aid, such as scholarships or grants (proportion receiving): $2,034 (39%). Average amount of self-help aid, such as work study or loans (proportion receiving): $1,155 (51%). Average need-based loan (excluding PLUS or other private loans): $2,547. Among students who received need-based aid, the average percentage of need met: 84%. Among students who received aid based on merit, the average award (and the proportion receiving): $3,554 (33%). The average athletic scholarship (and the proportion receiving): $6,726 (10%). Average amount of debt of borrowers graduating in 2003: $9,112. Proportion who borrowed: 56%. **Student employment:** During the 2003-2004 academic year, 27% of undergraduates worked on campus. Average per-year earnings: $930. **Reserve Officers Training Corps (ROTC):** Army ROTC: Offered at cooperating institution (University of Missouri); Navy ROTC: Offered at cooperating institution (University of Missouri); Air Force ROTC: Offered at cooperating institution (University of Missouri).

Montana

Carroll College

1601 N. Benton Avenue
Helena, MT 59625-0002
Private; www.carroll.edu
Financial aid office: (406) 447-5423

■ **2004-2005 TUITION AND FEES:** $15,750
■ **ROOM AND BOARD:** $6,000

ACT Score (25th/75th percentile): 21-27
2005 U.S. News College Ranking:
Comp. Colleges–Bachelor's (West), 4
Acceptance Rate: 83%

....

Other expenses: Estimated books and supplies:
$600. Transportation: $350. Personal expenses:
$700. **Financial aid:** Priority filing date for insti-
tution's financial aid form: March 1. In 2003-
2004, 100% of undergraduates applied for
financial aid. Of those, 68% were determined
to have financial need; 21% had their need fully
met. Average financial aid package (proportion
receiving): $13,799 (68%). Average amount of
gift aid, such as scholarships or grants (proportion receiving): $8,020 (63%). Average amount
of self-help aid, such as work study or loans
(proportion receiving): $6,506 (34%). Average
need-based loan (excluding PLUS or other private loans): $4,558. Among students who
received need-based aid, the average percentage
of need met: 85%. Among students who
received aid based on merit, the average award
(and the proportion receiving): $5,907 (27%).
The average athletic scholarship (and the proportion receiving): $7,959 (8%). Average
amount of debt of borrowers graduating in
2003: $22,868. Proportion who borrowed:
76%. **Student employment:** During the 2003-
2004 academic year, 9% of undergraduates
worked on campus. Average per-year earnings:
$1,510. **Cooperative education programs:** busi-
ness, computer science, engineering, natural
science, social/behavioral science. **Reserve
Officers Training Corps (ROTC):** Army ROTC:
Offered on campus.

Montana State University–Billings

1500 University Drive
Billings, MT 59101
Public; www.msubillings.edu
Financial aid office: (406) 657-2188

■ **2004-2005 TUITION AND FEES:**
In state: $4,550; Out of state: $12,831

ACT Score (25th/75th percentile): 18-23
2005 U.S. News College Ranking:
Universities–Master's (West), third tier
Acceptance Rate: 96%

....

Other expenses: Estimated books and supplies:
$900. Transportation: $900. Personal expenses: $1,570. **Financial aid:** Priority filing date for
institution's financial aid form: March 1; deadline: July 1. In 2003-2004, 86% of undergraduates applied for financial aid. Of those, 71%
were determined to have financial need; 21%
had their need fully met. Average financial aid
package (proportion receiving): $7,109 (68%).
Average amount of gift aid, such as scholarships or grants (proportion receiving): $3,937
(55%). Average amount of self-help aid, such as
work study or loans (proportion receiving):
$3,330 (56%). Average need-based loan (exclud-
ing PLUS or other private loans): $3,145.
Among students who received need-based aid,
the average percentage of need met: 67%.
Among students who received aid based on
merit, the average award (and the proportion
receiving): $7,918 (4%). The average athletic
scholarship (and the proportion receiving):
$5,336 (2%). Average amount of debt of bor-
rowers graduating in 2003: $13,250. Proportion
who borrowed: 68%. **Student employment:**
During the 2003-2004 academic year, 11% of
undergraduates worked on campus. Average
per-year earnings: $925. **Cooperative education
programs:** art, business, computer science, education, health professions, humanities, natural
science, social/behavioral science, technologies,
vocational arts.

Montana State University–Bozeman

Bozeman, MT 59717
Public; www.montana.edu
Financial aid office: (406) 994-2845

■ **2004-2005 TUITION AND FEES:**
In state: $4,577; Out of state: $14,177
■ **ROOM AND BOARD:** $5,500

ACT Score (25th/75th percentile): 20-26
2005 U.S. News College Ranking:
National Universities, fourth tier
Acceptance Rate: 81%

....

Other expenses: Estimated books and supplies:
$930. Transportation: $2,470. **Financial aid:**
Priority filing date for institution's financial aid
form: March 1. In 2003-2004, 76% of undergraduates applied for financial aid. Of those,
52% were determined to have financial need;
10% had their need fully met. Average financial
aid package (proportion receiving): $6,919
(52%). Average amount of gift aid, such as
scholarships or grants (proportion receiving):
$3,569 (41%). Average amount of self-help aid,
such as work study or loans (proportion receiving): $4,097 (45%). Average need-based loan
(excluding PLUS or other private loans):
$3,914. Among students who received need-
based aid, the average percentage of need met:
66%. Among students who received aid based
on merit, the average award (and the proportion receiving): $3,255 (6%). The average athlet-
ic scholarship (and the proportion receiving):
$4,602 (1%). Average amount of debt of bor-
rowers graduating in 2003: $20,618.
Proportion who borrowed: 62%. **Student
employment:** During the 2003-2004 academic
year, 20% of undergraduates worked on campus. Average per-year earnings: $2,000.
Reserve Officers Training Corps (ROTC): Army
ROTC: Offered on campus; Air Force ROTC:
Offered on campus.

Montana State University–Northern

PO Box 7751
Havre, MT 59501
Public; www.msun.edu
Financial aid office: (406) 265-3787

■ **2004-2005 TUITION AND FEES:**
In state: $4,480; Out of state: $13,000
■ **ROOM AND BOARD:** $6,000

ACT Score (25th/75th percentile): 16-21
2005 U.S. News College Ranking:
Universities–Master's (West), fourth tier

Other expenses: Estimated books and supplies: $1,000. Transportation: $2,000. **Financial aid:** Priority filing date for institution's financial aid form: March 1. In 2003-2004, 100% of undergraduates applied for financial aid. Of those, 75% were determined to have financial need; Average financial aid package (proportion receiving): $8,925 (75%). Average amount of gift aid, such as scholarships or grants (proportion receiving): $8,032 (38%). Average amount of self-help aid, such as work study or loans (proportion receiving): $566 (56%). Average need-based loan (excluding PLUS or other private loans): $3,875. Among students who received need-based aid, the average percentage of need met: 75%. Among students who received aid based on merit, the average award (and the proportion receiving): $0 (0%). The average athletic scholarship (and the proportion receiving): $5,790 (0%). Average amount of debt of borrowers graduating in 2003: $23,000. Proportion who borrowed: 80%.

Montana Tech of the University of Montana

1300 W. Park Street
Butte, MT 59701
Public; www.mtech.edu
Financial aid office: (406) 496-4212

■ **2004-2005 TUITION AND FEES:**
In state: $4,607; Out of state: $13,007
■ **ROOM AND BOARD:** $5,128

ACT Score (25th/75th percentile): 20-25
2005 U.S. News College Ranking:
Unranked Specialty School–Engineering
Acceptance Rate: 98%

Other expenses: Estimated books and supplies: $800. Transportation: $1,600. Personal expenses: $1,600. **Financial aid:** Priority filing date for institution's financial aid form: March 1. In 2003-2004, 87% of undergraduates applied for financial aid. Of those, 73% were determined to have financial need; 73% had their need fully met. Average financial aid package (proportion receiving): $5,500 (67%). Average amount of gift aid, such as scholarships or grants (proportion receiving): $1,000 (53%). Average amount of self-help aid, such as work study or loans (proportion receiving): $4,000 (60%). Average need-based loan (excluding PLUS or other private loans): $4,000. Among students who received need-based aid, the average percentage of need met: 80%. Among students who received aid based on merit, the average award (and the proportion receiving): $1,000 (33%). The average athletic scholarship (and the proportion receiving): $3,500 (20%). Average amount of debt of borrowers graduating in 2003: $15,000. Proportion who borrowed: 80%. **Student employment:** During the 2003-2004 academic year, 20% of undergraduates worked on campus. Average per-year earnings: $2,000.

Rocky Mountain College

1511 Poly Drive
Billings, MT 59102
Private; www.rocky.edu
Financial aid office: (406) 657-1031

■ **2004-2005 TUITION AND FEES:** $14,715
■ **ROOM AND BOARD:** $5,480

ACT Score (25th/75th percentile): 19-25
2005 U.S. News College Ranking:
Comp. Colleges–Bachelor's (West), 9
Acceptance Rate: 85%

Financial aid: Priority filing date for institution's financial aid form: April 1. In 2003-2004, 77% of undergraduates applied for financial aid. Of those, 64% were determined to have financial need; 18% had their need fully met. Average financial aid package (proportion receiving): $13,276 (64%). Average amount of gift aid, such as scholarships or grants (proportion receiving): $8,476 (60%). Average amount of self-help aid, such as work study or loans (proportion receiving): $5,127 (58%). Average need-based loan (excluding PLUS or other private loans): $4,233. Among students who received need-based aid, the average percentage of need met: 74%. Among students who received aid based on merit, the average award (and the proportion receiving): $6,869 (8%). The average athletic scholarship (and the proportion receiving): $8,650 (3%). Average

amount of debt of borrowers graduating in 2003: $20,571. Proportion who borrowed: 87%. **Student employment:** During the 2003-2004 academic year, 22% of undergraduates worked on campus. Average per-year earnings: $595.

University of Great Falls

1301 20th Street S
Great Falls, MT 59405
Private; www.ugf.edu
Financial aid office: (406) 791-5235

■ **2004-2005 TUITION AND FEES:** $12,860
■ **ROOM AND BOARD:** $5,500

ACT Score (25th/75th percentile): 17-22
2005 U.S. News College Ranking:
Universities–Master's (West), fourth tier
Acceptance Rate: 80%

Other expenses: Estimated books and supplies: $750. Transportation: $0. Personal expenses: $500. **Financial aid:** Priority filing date for institution's financial aid form: March 1. In 2003-2004, 91% of undergraduates applied for financial aid. Of those, 83% were determined to have financial need; 18% had their need fully met. Average financial aid package (proportion receiving): $9,311 (83%). Average amount of gift aid, such as scholarships or grants (proportion receiving): $3,412 (58%). Average amount of self-help aid, such as work study or loans (proportion receiving): $4,279 (74%). Average need-based loan (excluding PLUS or other private loans): $4,017. Among students who received need-based aid, the average percentage of need met: 77%. Among students who received aid based on merit, the average award (and the proportion receiving): $2,888 (9%). The average athletic scholarship (and the proportion receiving): $3,957 (10%). Average amount of debt of borrowers graduating in 2003: $29,483. Proportion who borrowed: 89%. **Student employment:** During the 2003-2004 academic year, 3% of undergraduates worked on campus. Average per-year earnings: $3,000. **Cooperative education programs:** business, computer science, education, social/behavioral science.

University of Montana

32 Campus Drive
Missoula, MT 59812
Public; www.umt.edu
Financial aid office: (406) 243-5373

■ **2004-2005 TUITION AND FEES:**
  In state: $4,546; Out of state: $12,786
■ **ROOM AND BOARD:** $5,432

ACT Score (25th/75th percentile): 20-25
2005 U.S. News College Ranking:
National Universities, third tier
Acceptance Rate: 93%

Other expenses: Estimated books and supplies:
$800. Personal expenses: $3,248. **Financial aid:**
Priority filing date for institution's financial aid
form: February 15. In 2003-2004, 75% of
undergraduates applied for financial aid. Of
those, 58% were determined to have financial
need; 54% had their need fully met. Average
financial aid package (proportion receiving):
$8,832 (57%). Average amount of gift aid, such
as scholarships or grants (proportion receiving): $2,981 (41%). Average amount of self-
help aid, such as work study or loans (proportion receiving): $4,140 (50%). Average need-
based loan (excluding PLUS or other private
loans): $4,312. Among students who received
need-based aid, the average percentage of need
met: 83%. Among students who received aid
based on merit, the average award (and the
proportion receiving): $2,020 (13%). The aver-
age athletic scholarship (and the proportion
receiving): $4,293 (2%). Average amount of
debt of borrowers graduating in 2003: $18,175.
Proportion who borrowed: 56%. Average per-
year earnings: $1,330. **Cooperative education
programs:** art, business, computer science,
education, humanities, natural science,
social/behavioral science, technologies, other.
Reserve Officers Training Corps (ROTC): Army
ROTC: Offered on campus.

University of Montana–Western

710 S. Atlantic
Dillon, MT 59725
Public; www.umwestern.edu
Financial aid office: (406) 683-7511

■ **2004-2005 TUITION AND FEES:**
  In state: $4,222; Out of state: $11,656
■ **ROOM AND BOARD:** $4,530

ACT Score (25th/75th percentile): 16-22
2005 U.S. News College Ranking:
Comp. Colleges–Bachelor's (West), third tier
Acceptance Rate: 100%

Other expenses: Estimated books and supplies: $700. Transportation: $1,000. Personal
expenses: $2,190. **Financial aid:** Priority filing
date for institution's financial aid form: March
1. In 2003-2004, 83% of undergraduates
applied for financial aid. Of those, 83% were
determined to have financial need; Average
financial aid package (proportion receiving):
$4,991 (83%). Average amount of gift aid,
such as scholarships or grants (proportion
receiving): $3,557 (61%). Average amount of
self-help aid, such as work study or loans (proportion receiving): $3,156 (13%). Average
need-based loan (excluding PLUS or other private loans): $3,742. Among students who
received need-based aid, the average percentage of need met: 38%. Among students who
received aid based on merit, the average award
(and the proportion receiving): $3,167 (1%).
The average athletic scholarship (and the proportion receiving): $1,000 (13%). Average
amount of debt of borrowers graduating in
2003: $13,510. Proportion who borrowed: 73%.
Student employment: During the 2003-2004
academic year, 10% of undergraduates worked
on campus. Average per-year earnings:
$2,000. **Cooperative education programs:**
business, social/behavioral science.

Nebraska

Bellevue University

1000 Galvin Road S
Bellevue, NE 68005
Private; www.bellevue.edu
Financial aid office: (402) 293-3763

■ **2004-2005 TUITION AND FEES:** $4,740

ACT Score (25th/75th percentile): 19-23
2005 U.S. News College Ranking:
Universities–Master's (Midwest), fourth tier
Acceptance Rate: 94%

Other expenses: Estimated books and supplies:
$900. Transportation: $1,080. Personal expenses: $1,800. **Financial aid:** Average amount of gift aid, such as scholarships or grants (proportion receiving): $2,441 (N/A). Average need-based loan (excluding PLUS or other private loans): $2,944. Among students who received aid based on merit, the average award (and the proportion receiving): $956 (N/A). **Student employment:** During the 2003-2004 academic year, 1% of undergraduates worked on campus. Average per-year earnings: $2,000.

Chadron State College

1000 Main Street
Chadron, NE 69337
Public; www.csc.edu
Financial aid office: (308) 432-6230

■ **2004-2005 TUITION AND FEES:**
   In state: $3,496; Out of state: $6,346
■ **ROOM AND BOARD:** $3,986

ACT Score (25th/75th percentile): 17-24
2005 U.S. News College Ranking:
Universities–Master's (Midwest), third tier
Acceptance Rate: 100%

Financial aid: Priority filing date for institution's financial aid form: June 1.

College of St. Mary

1901 S. 72nd Street
Omaha, NE 68124-2377
Private; www.csm.edu
Financial aid office: (402) 399-2362

■ **2004-2005 TUITION AND FEES:** $17,000
■ **ROOM AND BOARD:** $5,700

ACT Score (25th/75th percentile): 19-25
2005 U.S. News College Ranking:
Comp. Colleges–Bachelor's (Midwest),
third tier
Acceptance Rate: 67%

Other expenses: Estimated books and supplies:
$600. Transportation: $1,125. Personal expenses: $1,320. **Financial aid:** Priority filing date for institution's financial aid form: March 1; deadline: March 15. In 2003-2004, 76% of undergraduates applied for financial aid. Of those, 71% were determined to have financial need; 13% had their need fully met. Average financial aid package (proportion receiving): $11,276 (71%). Average amount of gift aid, such as scholarships or grants (proportion receiving): $7,356 (63%). Average amount of self-help aid, such as work study or loans (proportion receiving): $5,070 (66%). Average need-based loan (excluding PLUS or other private loans): $4,698. Among students who received need-based aid, the average percentage of need met: 61%. Among students who received aid based on merit, the average award (and the proportion receiving): $8,363 (12%). The average athletic scholarship (and the proportion receiving): $4,917 (5%). Average amount of debt of borrowers graduating in 2003: $13,595. Proportion who borrowed: 100%. **Reserve Officers Training Corps (ROTC):** Army ROTC: Offered at cooperating institution (Creighton University); Air Force ROTC: Offered at cooperating institution (University of Nebraska at Omaha).

Concordia University

800 N. Columbia
Seward, NE 68434
Private; www.cune.edu
Financial aid office: (402) 643-7270

■ **2004-2005 TUITION AND FEES:** $16,880
■ **ROOM AND BOARD:** $4,580

ACT Score (25th/75th percentile): 20-27
2005 U.S. News College Ranking:
Universities–Master's (Midwest), 36
Acceptance Rate: 92%

Other expenses: Estimated books and supplies:
$600. Transportation: $900. Personal expenses: $1,200. **Financial aid:** Priority filing date for institution's financial aid form: March 1; deadline: May 1. In 2003-2004, 89% of undergraduates applied for financial aid. Of those, 89% were determined to have financial need; 77% had their need fully met. Average financial aid package (proportion receiving): $14,099 (89%). Average amount of gift aid, such as scholarships or grants (proportion receiving): $4,932 (71%). Average amount of self-help aid, such as work study or loans (proportion receiving): $3,415 (51%). Average need-based loan (excluding PLUS or other private loans): $3,733. Among students who received need-based aid, the average percentage of need met: 92%. Among students who received aid based on merit, the average award (and the proportion receiving): $5,488 (11%). The average athletic scholarship (and the proportion receiving): $3,181 (24%). Average amount of debt of borrowers graduating in 2003: $14,280. Proportion who borrowed: 68%. **Student employment:** During the 2003-2004 academic year, 34% of undergraduates worked on campus. Average per-year earnings: $885. **Reserve Officers Training Corps (ROTC):** Army ROTC: Offered at cooperating institution (University of Nebraska–Lincoln); Air Force ROTC: Offered at cooperating institution (University of Nebraska–Lincoln).

Creighton University

2500 California Plaza
Omaha, NE 68178
Private; www.creighton.edu
Financial aid office: (402) 280-2731

■ **2004-2005 TUITION AND FEES:** $20,510
■ **ROOM AND BOARD:** $7,372

ACT Score (25th/75th percentile): 23-28
2005 U.S. News College Ranking:
Universities–Master's (Midwest), 1
Acceptance Rate: 88%

....

Other expenses: Estimated books and supplies: $1,000. Transportation: $800. Personal expenses: $1,400. **Financial aid:** Priority filing date for institution's financial aid form: April 15. In 2003-2004, 60% of undergraduates applied for financial aid. Of those, 50% were determined to have financial need; 51% had their need fully met. Average financial aid package (proportion receiving): $18,340 (50%). Average amount of gift aid, such as scholarships or grants (proportion receiving): $11,637 (50%). Average amount of self-help aid, such as work study or loans (proportion receiving): $7,131 (43%). Average need-based loan (excluding PLUS or other private loans): $6,805. Among students who received need-based aid, the average percentage of need met: 87%. Among students who received aid based on merit, the average award (and the proportion receiving): $7,568 (28%). The average athletic scholarship (and the proportion receiving): $14,078 (3%). Average amount of debt of borrowers graduating in 2003: $22,437. Proportion who borrowed: 61%. **Student employment:** During the 2003-2004 academic year, 20% of undergraduates worked on campus. Average per-year earnings: $1,500. **Reserve Officers Training Corps (ROTC):** Army ROTC: Offered on campus; Air Force ROTC: Offered at cooperating institution (University of Nebraska–Omaha).

Dana College

2848 College Drive
Blair, NE 68008-1099
Private; www.dana.edu
Financial aid office: (402) 426-7226

■ **2004-2005 TUITION AND FEES:** $16,800
■ **ROOM AND BOARD:** $4,700

ACT Score (25th/75th percentile): 19-23
2005 U.S. News College Ranking:
Comp. Colleges–Bachelor's (Midwest), 53
Acceptance Rate: 98%

....

Other expenses: Estimated books and supplies: $750. Transportation: $300. Personal expenses: $1,150. **Financial aid:** Priority filing date for institution's financial aid form: March 15. In 2003-2004, 92% of undergraduates applied for financial aid. Of those, 83% were determined to have financial need; 25% had their need fully met. Average financial aid package (proportion

receiving): $14,623 (83%). Average amount of gift aid, such as scholarships or grants (proportion receiving): $4,077 (51%). Average amount of self-help aid, such as work study or loans (proportion receiving): $5,061 (68%). Average need-based loan (excluding PLUS or other private loans): $4,619. Among students who received need-based aid, the average percentage of need met: 85%. Among students who received aid based on merit, the average award (and the proportion receiving): $5,186 (17%). The average athletic scholarship (and the proportion receiving): $6,136 (58%). Average amount of debt of borrowers graduating in 2003: $16,182. Proportion who borrowed: 80%. Average per-year earnings: $1,500. **Reserve Officers Training Corps (ROTC):** Army ROTC: Offered at cooperating institution (Creighton Universtiy); Navy ROTC: Offered at cooperating institution (University of Nebraska–Omaha).

Doane College

1014 Boswell Avenue
Crete, NE 68333
Private; www.doane.edu
Financial aid office: (402) 826-8260

■ **2004-2005 TUITION AND FEES:** $15,970
■ **ROOM AND BOARD:** $4,720

ACT Score (25th/75th percentile): 20-26
2005 U.S. News College Ranking:
Universities–Master's (Midwest), 30
Acceptance Rate: 86%

....

Other expenses: Estimated books and supplies: $700. Transportation: $600. Personal expenses: $1,030. **Financial aid:** Priority filing date for institution's financial aid form: March 1. In 2003-2004, 89% of undergraduates applied for financial aid. Of those, 80% were determined to have financial need; 73% had their need fully met. Average financial aid package (proportion receiving): $12,953 (80%). Average amount of gift aid, such as scholarships or grants (proportion receiving): $8,872 (80%). Average amount of self-help aid, such as work study or loans (proportion receiving): $4,102 (78%). Average need-based loan (excluding PLUS or other private loans): $4,149. Among students who received need-based aid, the average percentage of need met: 99%. Among students who received aid based on merit, the average award (and the proportion receiving): $7,159 (19%). Average amount of debt of borrowers graduating in 2003: $12,539. Proportion who borrowed: 77%. **Student employment:** During the 2003-2004 academic year, 14% of undergradu-

ates worked on campus. Average per-year earnings: $500. **Cooperative education programs:** engineering, health professions. **Reserve Officers Training Corps (ROTC):** Army ROTC: Offered at cooperating institution (University of Nebraska); Air Force ROTC: Offered at cooperating institution (University of Nebraska).

Grace University

1311 S. Ninth Street
Omaha, NE 68108-3629
Private; www.graceuniversity.edu
Financial aid office: (402) 449-2920

■ **2004-2005 TUITION AND FEES:** $11,370
■ **ROOM AND BOARD:** $5,300

ACT Score (25th/75th percentile): 18-26
2005 U.S. News College Ranking:
Comp. Colleges–Bachelor's (Midwest), fourth tier
Acceptance Rate: 64%

....

Other expenses: Estimated books and supplies: $800. Transportation: $1,200. Personal expenses: $2,000. **Financial aid:** Priority filing date for institution's financial aid form: March 1. **Student employment:** During the 2003-2004 academic year, 25% of undergraduates worked on campus. Average per-year earnings: $3,000. **Cooperative education programs:** business, computer science, health professions, technologies. **Reserve Officers Training Corps (ROTC):** Air Force ROTC: Offered at cooperating institution (University of Nebraska–Omaha).

Hastings College

800 Turner Avenue
Hastings, NE 68901-7696
Private; www.hastings.edu
Financial aid office: (402) 461-7391

■ **2004-2005 TUITION AND FEES:** $16,290
■ **ROOM AND BOARD:** $4,760

ACT Score (25th/75th percentile): 20-26
2005 U.S. News College Ranking:
Liberal Arts Colleges, third tier
Acceptance Rate: 80%

....

Student employment: During the 2003-2004 academic year, 60% of undergraduates worked on campus. Average per-year earnings: $650.

Midland Lutheran College

900 N. Clarkson Street
Fremont, NE 68025
Private; www.mlc.edu
Financial aid office: (402) 941-6520

■ **2004-2005 TUITION AND FEES:** $17,210
■ **ROOM AND BOARD:** $4,560

ACT Score (25th/75th percentile): 19-25
2005 U.S. News College Ranking:
Comp. Colleges–Bachelor's (Midwest), 49
Acceptance Rate: 79%

Other expenses: Estimated books and supplies: $600. Transportation: $200. Personal expenses: $1,380. **Financial aid:** In 2003-2004, 92% of undergraduates applied for financial aid. Of those, 85% were determined to have financial need; 43% had their need fully met. Average financial aid package (proportion receiving): $14,166 (85%). Average amount of gift aid, such as scholarships or grants (proportion receiving): $10,191 (85%). Average amount of self-help aid, such as work study or loans (proportion receiving): $4,628 (82%). Average need-based loan (excluding PLUS or other private loans): $4,433. Among students who received need-based aid, the average percentage of need met: 91%. Among students who received aid based on merit, the average award (and the proportion receiving): $8,994 (15%). The average athletic scholarship (and the proportion receiving): $4,772 (43%). Average amount of debt of borrowers graduating in 2003: $18,915. Proportion who borrowed: 90%. **Student employment:** During the 2003-2004 academic year, 65% of undergraduates worked on campus. Average per-year earnings: $1,000.

Nebraska Wesleyan University

5000 St. Paul Avenue
Lincoln, NE 68504-2794
Private; www.nebrwesleyan.edu
Financial aid office: (402) 465-2212

■ **2004-2005 TUITION AND FEES:** $17,390
■ **ROOM AND BOARD:** $5,005

ACT Score (25th/75th percentile): 21-27
2005 U.S. News College Ranking:
Liberal Arts Colleges, third tier
Acceptance Rate: 93%

Other expenses: Estimated books and supplies: $800. Transportation: $400. Personal expens-

es: $1,800. **Financial aid:** In 2003-2004, 82% of undergraduates applied for financial aid. Of those, 74% were determined to have financial need; 17% had their need fully met. Average financial aid package (proportion receiving): $12,708 (74%). Average amount of gift aid, such as scholarships or grants (proportion receiving): $8,552 (73%). Average amount of self-help aid, such as work study or loans (proportion receiving): $4,429 (67%). Average need-based loan (excluding PLUS or other private loans): $4,079. Among students who received need-based aid, the average percentage of need met: 76%. Among students who received aid based on merit, the average award (and the proportion receiving): $4,938 (22%). The average athletic scholarship (and the proportion receiving): $0 (0%). Average amount of debt of borrowers graduating in 2003: $16,698. Proportion who borrowed: 70%. **Student employment:** During the 2003-2004 academic year, 25% of undergraduates worked on campus. Average per-year earnings: $1,100. **Reserve Officers Training Corps (ROTC):** Army ROTC: Offered at cooperating institution (University of Nebraska–Lincoln); Air Force ROTC: Offered at cooperating institution (University of Nebraska–Lincoln).

Peru State College

Box 10
Peru, NE 68421-0010
Public; www.peru.edu
Financial aid office: (402) 872-2228

■ **2004-2005 TUITION AND FEES:**
In state: $3,550; Out of state: $6,400
■ **ROOM AND BOARD:** $4,676

ACT Score (25th/75th percentile): 20
2005 U.S. News College Ranking:
Universities–Master's (Midwest), fourth tier
Acceptance Rate: 67%

Other expenses: Estimated books and supplies: $600. Transportation: $1,600. Personal expenses: $1,000. **Financial aid:** Priority filing date for institution's financial aid form: March 1. Average amount of debt of borrowers graduating in 2003: $15,000. Proportion who borrowed: 50%. **Cooperative education programs:** art, business, computer science, education, humanities, natural science, social/behavioral science. **Reserve Officers Training Corps (ROTC):** Army ROTC: Offered at cooperating institution (Creighton University); Air Force ROTC: Offered at cooperating institution (University of Nebraska–Omaha).

Union College

3800 S. 48th Street
Lincoln, NE 68506
Private; www.ucollege.edu
Financial aid office: (402) 486-2505

■ **2004-2005 TUITION AND FEES:** $13,880
■ **ROOM AND BOARD:** $4,366

ACT Score (25th/75th percentile): 18-25
2005 U.S. News College Ranking:
Comp. Colleges–Bachelor's (Midwest), third tier
Acceptance Rate: 49%

Financial aid: Priority filing date for institution's financial aid form: May 1. **Student employment:** During the 2003-2004 academic year, 51% of undergraduates worked on campus. Average per-year earnings: $1,635.

University of Nebraska–Kearney

905 W. 25th Street
Kearney, NE 68849
Public; www.unk.edu
Financial aid office: (308) 865-8520

■ **2004-2005 TUITION AND FEES:**
In state: $4,260; Out of state: $7,913
■ **ROOM AND BOARD:** $4,990

ACT Score (25th/75th percentile): 19-25
2005 U.S. News College Ranking:
Universities–Master's (Midwest), 63
Acceptance Rate: 84%

Other expenses: Estimated books and supplies: $754. Transportation: $532. Personal expenses: $2,186. **Financial aid:** Priority filing date for institution's financial aid form: March 1. In 2003-2004, 73% of undergraduates applied for financial aid. Of those, 58% were determined to have financial need; 41% had their need fully met. Average financial aid package (proportion receiving): $6,490 (57%). Average amount of gift aid, such as scholarships or grants (proportion receiving): $3,361 (36%). Average amount of self-help aid, such as work study or loans (proportion receiving): $3,605 (48%). Average need-based loan (excluding PLUS or other private loans): $3,429. Among students who received need-based aid, the average percentage of need met: 79%. Among students who received aid based on merit, the average award (and the proportion receiving): $1,346 (2%). The average athletic scholarship (and the proportion receiving):

$1,920 (1%). Average amount of debt of borrowers graduating in 2003: $14,930. Proportion who borrowed: 68%. **Cooperative education programs:** health professions.

University of Nebraska–Lincoln

14th and R Streets
Lincoln, NE 68588
Public; www.unl.edu
Financial aid office: (402) 472-2030

■ **2004-2005 TUITION AND FEES:**
In state: $5,340; Out of state: $13,830
■ **ROOM AND BOARD:** $5,504

ACT Score (25th/75th percentile): 21-27
2005 U.S. News College Ranking:
National Universities, 98
Acceptance Rate: 76%

Other expenses: Estimated books and supplies: $850. Transportation: $720. Personal expenses: $1,834. **Financial aid:** Priority filing date for institution's financial aid form: April 1. In 2003-2004, 62% of undergraduates applied for financial aid. Of those, 44% were determined to have financial need; 30% had their need fully met. Average financial aid package (proportion receiving): $6,947 (43%). Average amount of gift aid, such as scholarships or grants (proportion receiving): $4,142 (32%). Average amount of self-help aid, such as work study or loans (proportion receiving): $4,027 (36%). Average need-based loan (excluding PLUS or other private loans): $3,680. Among students who received need-based aid, the average percentage of need met: 76%. Among students who received aid based on merit, the average award (and the proportion receiving): $3,102 (6%). The average athletic scholarship (and the proportion receiving): $7,204 (1%). Average amount of debt of borrowers graduating in 2003: $16,376. Proportion who borrowed: 72%. Average per-year earnings: $3,120. **Cooperative education programs:** computer science, engineering. **Reserve Officers Training Corps (ROTC):** Army ROTC: Offered on campus; Navy ROTC: Offered on campus; Air Force ROTC: Offered on campus.

University of Nebraska–Omaha

6001 Dodge Street
Omaha, NE 68182
Public; www.unomaha.edu
Financial aid office: (402) 554-2327

■ **2004-2005 TUITION AND FEES:**
In state: $4,533; Out of state: $12,198
■ **ROOM AND BOARD:** $4,241

ACT Score (25th/75th percentile): 20-25
2005 U.S. News College Ranking:
Universities–Master's (Midwest), third tier
Acceptance Rate: 85%

Other expenses: Estimated books and supplies: $700. Transportation: $880. Personal expenses: $1,860. **Financial aid:** Priority filing date for institution's financial aid form: March 1. In 2003-2004, 62% of undergraduates applied for financial aid. Of those, 45% were determined to have financial need; Average financial aid package (proportion receiving): N/A (45%). Average amount of gift aid, such as scholarships or grants (proportion receiving): N/A (30%). Average amount of self-help aid, such as work study or loans (proportion receiving): N/A (27%). Average amount of debt of borrowers graduating in 2003: $16,900. Proportion who borrowed: 48%. **Student employment:** During the 2003-2004 academic year, 5% of undergraduates worked on campus. Average per-year earnings: $3,629. **Cooperative education programs:** agriculture, engineering, health professions, home economics. **Reserve Officers Training Corps (ROTC):** Army ROTC: Offered at cooperating institution (Creighton University); Air Force ROTC: Offered on campus.

Wayne State College

1111 Main Street
Wayne, NE 68787
Public; www.wsc.edu
Financial aid office: (402) 375-7230

■ **2004-2005 TUITION AND FEES:**
In state: $3,672; Out of state: $6,522
■ **ROOM AND BOARD:** $4,120

ACT Score (25th/75th percentile): 18-24
2005 U.S. News College Ranking:
Universities–Master's (Midwest), third tier
Acceptance Rate: 100%

Other expenses: Estimated books and supplies: $800. Transportation: $812. Personal expenses: $871. **Financial aid:** Priority filing date for institution's financial aid form: May 1. **Cooperative education programs:** agriculture, art, business, computer science, education, health professions, home economics, humanities, natural science, social/behavioral science, technologies. **Reserve Officers Training Corps (ROTC):** Army ROTC: Offered at cooperating institution (University of South Dakota).

York College

1125 E. Eighth Street
York, NE 68467
Private; www.york.edu
Financial aid office: (402) 363-5624

■ **2004-2005 TUITION AND FEES:** $11,930
■ **ROOM AND BOARD:** $3,800

ACT Score (25th/75th percentile): 17-27
2005 U.S. News College Ranking:
Comp. Colleges–Bachelor's (Midwest), third tier
Acceptance Rate: 63%

Other expenses: Estimated books and supplies: $800. Transportation: $1,200. Personal expenses: $2,270. **Financial aid:** Priority filing date for institution's financial aid form: April 1. In 2003-2004, 88% of undergraduates applied for financial aid. Of those, 80% were determined to have financial need; 25% had their need fully met. Average financial aid package (proportion receiving): $10,339 (80%). Average amount of gift aid, such as scholarships or grants (proportion receiving): $5,701 (78%). Average amount of self-help aid, such as work study or loans (proportion receiving): $4,638 (80%). Average need-based loan (excluding PLUS or other private loans): $3,820. Among students who received need-based aid, the average percentage of need met: 63%. Among students who received aid based on merit, the average award (and the proportion receiving): $4,477 (8%). The average athletic scholarship (and the proportion receiving): $4,756 (6%). Average amount of debt of borrowers graduating in 2003: $16,803. Proportion who borrowed: 81%. **Student employment:** During the 2003-2004 academic year, 0% of undergraduates worked on campus. Average per-year earnings: $0. **Reserve Officers Training Corps (ROTC):** Army ROTC: Offered at cooperating institution (University of Nebraska–Lincoln); Navy ROTC: Offered at cooperating institution (University of Nebraska at Lincoln); Air Force ROTC: Offered at cooperating institution (University of Nebraska–Lincoln).

Nevada

Sierra Nevada College

999 Tahoe Boulevard
Incline Village, NV 89451
Private; www.sierranevada.edu
Financial aid office: (775) 831-1314

■ **2004-2005 TUITION AND FEES:** $19,675
■ **ROOM AND BOARD:** $7,450

SAT I Score (25th/75th percentile): 960-1120
2005 U.S. News College Ranking:
Comp. Colleges–Bachelor's (West), third tier
Acceptance Rate: 69%

Other expenses: Estimated books and supplies: $750. Transportation: $500. Personal expenses: $2,035. **Financial aid:** Priority filing date for institution's financial aid form: May 1; deadline: August 1. In 2003-2004, 83% of undergraduates applied for financial aid. Of those, 83% were determined to have financial need; 28% had their need fully met. Average financial aid package (proportion receiving): $14,500 (83%). Average amount of gift aid, such as scholarships or grants (proportion receiving): $9,800 (83%). Average amount of self-help aid, such as work study or loans (proportion receiving): $5,500 (83%). Average need-based loan (excluding PLUS or other private loans): $5,500. Among students who received need-based aid, the average percentage of need met: 65%. Among students who received aid based on merit, the average award (and the proportion receiving): $9,000 (17%). The average athletic scholarship (and the proportion receiving): $25,000 (1%). Average amount of debt of borrowers graduating in 2003: $18,000. Proportion who borrowed: 89%. **Student employment:** During the 2003-2004 academic year, 70% of undergraduates worked on campus. Average per-year earnings: $2,000. **Cooperative education programs:** computer science, health professions. **Reserve Officers Training Corps (ROTC):** Army ROTC: Offered at cooperating institution (Univ. of Nevada, Reno).

University of Nevada–Las Vegas

4505 S. Maryland Parkway
Las Vegas, NV 89154
Public; www.unlv.edu
Financial aid office: (702) 895-3697

■ **2004-2005 TUITION AND FEES:**
In state: $3,020; Out of state: $8,670
■ **ROOM AND BOARD:** $9,140

SAT I Score (25th/75th percentile): 900-1140
2005 U.S. News College Ranking:
National Universities, fourth tier
Acceptance Rate: 80%

Other expenses: Estimated books and supplies: $850. Transportation: $610. Personal expenses: $1,800. **Financial aid:** Priority filing date for institution's financial aid form: February 1. In 2003-2004, 53% of undergraduates applied for financial aid. Of those, 44% were determined to have financial need; 46% had their need fully met. Average financial aid package (proportion receiving): $6,911 (40%). Average amount of gift aid, such as scholarships or grants (proportion receiving): $3,030 (23%). Average amount of self-help aid, such as work study or loans (proportion receiving): $5,057 (27%). Average need-based loan (excluding PLUS or other private loans): $3,993. Among students who received need-based aid, the average percentage of need met: 74%. Among students who received aid based on merit, the average award (and the proportion receiving): $2,094 (27%). The average athletic scholarship (and the proportion receiving): $6,490 (3%). Average amount of debt of borrowers graduating in 2003: $13,860. Proportion who borrowed: 36%. **Student employment:** During the 2003-2004 academic year, 15% of undergraduates worked on campus. Average per-year earnings: $4,000. **Cooperative education programs:** business, education, engineering, health professions, other. **Reserve Officers Training Corps (ROTC):** Army ROTC: Offered on campus.

University of Nevada–Reno

Reno, NV 89557
Public; www.unr.edu
Financial aid office: (775) 784-4666

■ **2004-2005 TUITION AND FEES:**
In state: $3,036; Out of state: $11,710
■ **ROOM AND BOARD:** $8,385

ACT Score (25th/75th percentile): 20-25
2005 U.S. News College Ranking:
National Universities, third tier
Acceptance Rate: 88%

Other expenses: Estimated books and supplies: $1,200. Transportation: $1,800. Personal expenses: $3,105. **Financial aid:** Priority filing date for institution's financial aid form: February 1. In 2003-2004, 42% of undergraduates applied for financial aid. Of those, 32% were determined to have financial need; 11% had their need fully met. Average financial aid package (proportion receiving): $7,003 (30%). Average amount of gift aid, such as scholarships or grants (proportion receiving): $3,296 (17%). Average amount of self-help aid, such as work study or loans (proportion receiving): $4,101 (20%). Average need-based loan (excluding PLUS or other private loans): $3,854. Among students who received need-based aid, the average percentage of need met: 61%. Among students who received aid based on merit, the average award (and the proportion receiving): $2,754 (39%). The average athletic scholarship (and the proportion receiving): $9,648 (4%). Average amount of debt of borrowers graduating in 2003: $16,000. Proportion who borrowed: 45%. **Student employment:** During the 2003-2004 academic year, 14% of undergraduates worked on campus. Average per-year earnings: $4,500. **Reserve Officers Training Corps (ROTC):** Army ROTC: Offered on campus.

New Hampshire

Colby-Sawyer College

541 Main Street
New London, NH 03257
Private; www.colby-sawyer.edu
Financial aid office: (603) 526-3717

- **2004-2005 TUITION AND FEES:** $23,310
- **ROOM AND BOARD:** $8,950

SAT I Score (25th/75th percentile): 920-1110
2005 U.S. News College Ranking:
Comp. Colleges–Bachelor's (North), 11
Acceptance Rate: 82%

Other expenses: Estimated books and supplies: $750. Transportation: $900. Personal expenses: $0. **Financial aid:** Priority filing date for institution's financial aid form: March 1; deadline: March 1. In 2003-2004, 72% of undergraduates applied for financial aid. Of those, 67% were determined to have financial need; 6% had their need fully met. Average financial aid package (proportion receiving): $17,721 (67%). Average amount of gift aid, such as scholarships or grants (proportion receiving): $12,409 (62%). Average amount of self-help aid, such as work study or loans (proportion receiving): $4,289 (63%). Average need-based loan (excluding PLUS or other private loans): $3,875. Among students who received need-based aid, the average percentage of need met: 87%. Among students who received aid based on merit, the average award (and the proportion receiving): $3,669 (11%). The average athletic scholarship (and the proportion receiving): $0 (0%). Average amount of debt of borrowers graduating in 2003: $18,930. Proportion who borrowed: 59%. **Reserve Officers Training Corps (ROTC):** Army ROTC: Offered at cooperating institution (University of New Hampshire); Air Force ROTC: Offered at cooperating institution (University of New Hampshire).

College for Lifelong Learning

125 N. State Street
Concord, NH 03301-6400
Public; www.cll.edu

- **2004-2005 TUITION AND FEES:**
  In state: $4,563; Out of state: $5,043

2005 U.S. News College Ranking:
Liberal Arts Colleges, unranked

Daniel Webster College

20 University Drive
Nashua, NH 03063
Private; www.dwc.edu
Financial aid office: (603) 577-6590

- **2004-2005 TUITION AND FEES:** $21,630
- **ROOM AND BOARD:** $8,170

SAT I Score (25th/75th percentile): 970-1190
2005 U.S. News College Ranking:
Comp. Colleges–Bachelor's (North), third tier
Acceptance Rate: 77%

Dartmouth College

6016 McNutt Hall
Hanover, NH 03755
Private; www.dartmouth.edu
Financial aid office: (603) 646-2451

- **2004-2005 TUITION AND FEES:** $30,465
- **ROOM AND BOARD:** $9,000

SAT I Score (25th/75th percentile): 1330-1530
2005 U.S. News College Ranking:
National Universities, 9
Acceptance Rate: 18%

Other expenses: Estimated books and supplies: $2,386. Transportation: $565. **Financial aid:** In 2003-2004, 60% of undergraduates applied for financial aid. Of those, 51% were determined to have financial need; 100% had their need fully met. Average financial aid package (proportion receiving): $25,945 (51%). Average amount of gift aid, such as scholarships or grants (proportion receiving): $21,529 (47%). Average amount of self-help aid, such as work study or loans (proportion receiving): $6,063 (48%). Average need-based loan (excluding PLUS or other private loans): $4,800. Among students who received need-based aid, the average percentage of need met: 100%. Among students who received aid based on merit, the average award (and the proportion receiving): $311 (0%). The average athletic scholarship (and the proportion receiving): $0 (0%). Average amount of debt of borrowers graduating in 2003: $16,922. Proportion who borrowed: 51%. **Student employment:** During the 2003-2004 academic year, 35% of undergraduates worked on cam-

pus. Average per-year earnings: $2,075. **Reserve Officers Training Corps (ROTC):** Army ROTC: Offered at cooperating institution (Norwich University).

Franklin Pierce College

20 College Road
Rindge, NH 03461
Private; www.fpc.edu
Financial aid office: (603) 899-4186

- **2004-2005 TUITION AND FEES:** $22,510
- **ROOM AND BOARD:** $7,655

SAT I Score (25th/75th percentile): 905-1110
2005 U.S. News College Ranking:
Liberal Arts Colleges, fourth tier
Acceptance Rate: 87%

Other expenses: Estimated books and supplies: $826. Transportation: $520. Personal expenses: $1,094. **Financial aid:** Priority filing date for institution's financial aid form: May 1. In 2003-2004, 79% of undergraduates applied for financial aid. Of those, 73% were determined to have financial need; 8% had their need fully met. Average financial aid package (proportion receiving): $16,123 (73%). Average amount of gift aid, such as scholarships or grants (proportion receiving): $11,126 (72%). Average amount of self-help aid, such as work study or loans (proportion receiving): $5,533 (67%). Average need-based loan (excluding PLUS or other private loans): $4,712. Among students who received need-based aid, the average percentage of need met: 72%. Among students who received aid based on merit, the average award (and the proportion receiving): $10,109 (23%). The average athletic scholarship (and the proportion receiving): $13,136 (3%). Average amount of debt of borrowers graduating in 2003: $20,815. Proportion who borrowed: 79%. **Student employment:** During the 2003-2004 academic year, 52% of undergraduates worked on campus. Average per-year earnings: $1,500. **Reserve Officers Training Corps (ROTC):** Army ROTC: Offered at cooperating institution (University of New Hampshire); Air Force ROTC: Offered at cooperating institution (University of New Hampshire).

Keene State College

229 Main Street
Keene, NH 03435
Public; www.keene.edu
Financial aid office: (603) 358-2280

■ **2004-2005 TUITION AND FEES:**
In state: $6,920; Out of state: $13,360
■ **ROOM AND BOARD:** $5,966

SAT I Score (25th/75th percentile): 910-1100
2005 U.S. News College Ranking:
Universities–Master's (North), third tier
Acceptance Rate: 71%

Financial aid: Student employment: During the 2003-2004 academic year, 13% of undergraduates worked on campus. Average per-year earnings: $780. **Cooperative education programs:** computer science, education, natural science, social/behavioral science, technologies, other. **Reserve Officers Training Corps (ROTC):** Air Force ROTC: Offered at cooperating institution (University of Massachusetts–Lowell).

New England College

7 Main Street
Henniker, NH 03242
Private; www.nec.edu
Financial aid office: (603) 428-2414

■ **2004-2005 TUITION AND FEES:** $21,944
■ **ROOM AND BOARD:** $8,052

SAT I Score (25th/75th percentile): 810-1020
2005 U.S. News College Ranking:
Comp. Colleges–Bachelor's (North), third tier
Acceptance Rate: 97%

Other expenses: Estimated books and supplies: $600. Transportation: $900. Personal expenses: $1,200. **Financial aid:** Priority filing date for institution's financial aid form: February 15. **Student employment:** During the 2003-2004 academic year, 3% of undergraduates worked on campus. Average per-year earnings: $2,000. **Reserve Officers Training Corps (ROTC):** Army ROTC: Offered at cooperating institution; Air Force ROTC: Offered at cooperating institution.

Plymouth State University

17 High Street
Plymouth, NH 03264-1595
Public; www.plymouth.edu
Financial aid office: (603) 535-2338

■ **2003-2004 TUITION AND FEES:**
In state: $6,240; Out of state: $12,290
■ **ROOM AND BOARD:** $6,058

SAT I Score (25th/75th percentile): 860-1060
2005 U.S. News College Ranking:
Universities–Master's (North), third tier
Acceptance Rate: 71%

Other expenses: Estimated books and supplies: $700. Transportation: $250. Personal expenses: $1,002. **Financial aid:** Priority filing date for institution's financial aid form: March 1. In 2003-2004, 77% of undergraduates applied for financial aid. Of those, 58% were determined to have financial need; 6% had their need fully met. Average financial aid package (proportion receiving): $6,940 (58%). Average amount of gift aid, such as scholarships or grants (proportion receiving): $4,085 (35%). Average amount of self-help aid, such as work study or loans (proportion receiving): $4,605 (56%). Average need-based loan (excluding PLUS or other private loans): $3,649. Among students who received need-based aid, the average percentage of need met: 68%. Among students who received aid based on merit, the average award (and the proportion receiving): $1,942 (7%). The average athletic scholarship (and the proportion receiving): $0 (0%). Average amount of debt of borrowers graduating in 2003: $17,629. Proportion who borrowed: 72%. **Student employment:** During the 2003-2004 academic year, 16% of undergraduates worked on campus. Average per-year earnings: $854. **Reserve Officers Training Corps (ROTC):** Army ROTC: Offered at cooperating institution (University of New Hampshire); Air Force ROTC: Offered at cooperating institution (University of New Hampshire).

Rivier College

420 Main Street
Nashua, NH 03060
Private; www.rivier.edu
Financial aid office: (603) 897-8533

■ **2004-2005 TUITION AND FEES:** $19,825
■ **ROOM AND BOARD:** $7,273

SAT I Score (25th/75th percentile): 790-1050
2005 U.S. News College Ranking:
Universities–Master's (North), third tier
Acceptance Rate: 77%

Other expenses: Estimated books and supplies: $800. Transportation: $450. Personal expenses: $1,500. **Financial aid:** Priority filing date for institution's financial aid form: February 1. In 2003-2004, 90% of undergraduates applied for financial aid. Of those, 81% were determined to have financial need; 23% had their need fully met. Average financial aid package (proportion receiving): $16,705 (81%). Average amount of gift aid, such as scholarships or grants (proportion receiving): $11,826 (81%). Average amount of self-help aid, such as work study or loans (proportion receiving): $7,910 (81%). Average need-based loan (excluding PLUS or other private loans): $6,475. Among students who received need-based aid, the average percentage of need met: 75%. Among students who received aid based on merit, the average award (and the proportion receiving): $6,000 (10%). The average athletic scholarship (and the proportion receiving): $0 (0%). Average amount of debt of borrowers graduating in 2003: $19,418. Proportion who borrowed: 75%. **Reserve Officers Training Corps (ROTC):** Air Force ROTC: Offered at cooperating institution (Daniel Webster College).

Southern New Hampshire University

2500 N. River Road
Manchester, NH 03106
Private; www.snhu.edu
Financial aid office: (603) 645-9645

■ **2004-2005 TUITION AND FEES:** $19,314
■ **ROOM AND BOARD:** $7,866

SAT I Score (25th/75th percentile): 867-1079
2005 U.S. News College Ranking:
Unranked Specialty School–Business
Acceptance Rate: 71%

Other expenses: Estimated books and supplies: $750. Transportation: $350. Personal expenses: $900. **Financial aid:** Priority filing date for institution's financial aid form: March 15. 12% had their need fully met. Average financial aid package (proportion receiving): $11,966 (N/A). Average amount of gift aid, such as scholarships or grants (proportion receiving): $5,655 (N/A). Average amount of self-help aid, such as work study or loans (proportion receiving): $4,913 (N/A). Average need-based loan (excluding PLUS or other private loans): $4,214. Among students who received need-based aid, the average percentage of need met: 69%. Among students who received aid based on merit, the average award (and the proportion receiving): $3,426 (N/A). The average athletic scholarship (and the proportion receiving): $13,413 (N/A). **Reserve Officers Training Corps (ROTC):** Army ROTC: Offered at cooperating institution (University of New Hampshire); Air Force ROTC: Offered at cooperating institution (University of New Hampshire).

St. Anselm College

100 St. Anselm Drive
Manchester, NH 03102-1310
Private; www.anselm.edu
Financial aid office: (603) 641-7203

■ **2004-2005 TUITION AND FEES:** $23,350
■ **ROOM AND BOARD:** $8,580

SAT I Score (25th/75th percentile): 1020-1200
2005 U.S. News College Ranking:
Liberal Arts Colleges, third tier
Acceptance Rate: 71%

....

Other expenses: Estimated books and supplies: $800. Transportation: $500. Personal expenses: $1,000. **Financial aid:** Priority filing date for institution's financial aid form: March 1. In 2003-2004, 90% of undergraduates applied for financial aid. Of those, 67% were determined to have financial need; 3% had their need fully met. Average financial aid package (proportion receiving): $18,380 (67%). Average amount of gift aid, such as scholarships or grants (proportion receiving): $13,108 (67%). Average amount of self-help aid, such as work study or loans (proportion receiving): $2,483 (64%). Average need-based loan (excluding PLUS or other private loans): $3,158. Among students who received need-based aid, the average percentage of need met: 75%. Among students who received aid based on merit, the average award (and the proportion receiving): $5,602 (12%). The average athletic scholarship (and the proportion receiving): $30,044 (1%). Average amount of debt of borrowers graduating in 2003: $19,111. Proportion who borrowed: 79%. **Student employment:** During the 2003-2004 academic year, 12% of undergraduates worked

on campus. Average per-year earnings: $900. **Reserve Officers Training Corps (ROTC):** Army ROTC: Offered at cooperating institution (University of New Hampshire); Air Force ROTC: Offered at cooperating institution (University of New Hampshire).

University of New Hampshire

Thompson Hall
Durham, NH 03824
Public; www.unh.edu
Financial aid office: (603) 862-3600

■ **2004-2005 TUITION AND FEES:**
In state: $9,226; Out of state: $20,256
■ **ROOM AND BOARD:** $6,612

SAT I Score (25th/75th percentile): 1010-1230
2005 U.S. News College Ranking:
National Universities, 98
Acceptance Rate: 69%

....

Other expenses: Estimated books and supplies: $1,300. Transportation: $300. Personal expenses: $1,800. **Financial aid:** Priority filing date for institution's financial aid form: March 1. In 2003-2004, 68% of undergraduates applied for financial aid. Of those, 56% were determined to have financial need; 20% had their need fully met. Average financial aid package (proportion receiving): $14,267 (55%). Average amount of gift aid, such as scholarships or grants (proportion receiving): $2,281 (34%). Average amount of self-help aid, such as work study or loans (proportion receiving): $2,928 (52%). Average need-based loan (excluding PLUS or other private loans): $3,354. Among students who received need-based aid, the average percentage of need met: 80%. Among students who received aid based on merit, the average award (and the proportion receiving): $5,414 (19%). The average athletic scholarship (and the proportion receiving): $18,700 (2%). Average amount of debt of borrowers graduating in 2003: $21,251. Proportion who borrowed: 69%. **Student employment:** During the 2003-2004 academic year, 34% of undergraduates worked on campus. Average per-year earnings: $1,331. **Reserve Officers Training Corps (ROTC):** Army ROTC: Offered on campus; Air Force ROTC: Offered on campus.

New Jersey

Bloomfield College

467 Franklin Street
Bloomfield, NJ 07003
Private; www.bloomfield.edu
Financial aid office: (973) 748-9000

- **2004-2005 TUITION AND FEES:** $13,900
- **ROOM AND BOARD:** $6,750

SAT I Score (25th/75th percentile): 730-920
2005 U.S. News College Ranking:
Comp. Colleges–Bachelor's (North), third tier
Acceptance Rate: 56%

Other expenses: Estimated books and supplies: $500. Transportation: $300. Personal expenses: $1,496. **Financial aid:** Priority filing date for institution's financial aid form: March 15. In 2003-2004, 97% of undergraduates applied for financial aid. Of those, 86% were determined to have financial need; 68% had their need fully met. Average financial aid package (proportion receiving): $13,116 (85%). Average amount of gift aid, such as scholarships or grants (proportion receiving): $9,316 (82%). Average amount of self-help aid, such as work study or loans (proportion receiving): $1,436 (64%). Average need-based loan (excluding PLUS or other private loans): $2,874. Among students who received need-based aid, the average percentage of need met: 84%. Among students who received aid based on merit, the average award (and the proportion receiving): $4,263 (6%). The average athletic scholarship (and the proportion receiving): $8,631 (3%). Average amount of debt of borrowers graduating in 2003: $15,177. Proportion who borrowed: 67%. **Student employment:** During the 2003-2004 academic year, 5% of undergraduates worked on campus. Average per-year earnings: $1,600. **Reserve Officers Training Corps (ROTC):** Army ROTC: Offered at cooperating institution (Seton Hall University).

Caldwell College

9 Ryerson Avenue
Caldwell, NJ 07006
Private; www.caldwell.edu
Financial aid office: (973) 618-3221

- **2004-2005 TUITION AND FEES:** $18,010
- **ROOM AND BOARD:** $7,350

SAT I Score (25th/75th percentile): 810-1020
2005 U.S. News College Ranking:
Comp. Colleges–Bachelor's (North), 22
Acceptance Rate: 69%

Other expenses: Estimated books and supplies: $800. Transportation: $600. Personal expenses: $1,000. **Financial aid:** Priority filing date for institution's financial aid form: April 15. In 2003-2004, 85% of undergraduates applied for financial aid. Of those, 81% were determined to have financial need; 4% had their need fully met. Average financial aid package (proportion receiving): $9,685 (81%). Average amount of gift aid, such as scholarships or grants (proportion receiving): $4,555 (69%). Average amount of self-help aid, such as work study or loans (proportion receiving): $4,785 (65%). Average need-based loan (excluding PLUS or other private loans): $3,875. Among students who received need-based aid, the average percentage of need met: 84%. Among students who received aid based on merit, the average award (and the proportion receiving): $6,835 (12%). The average athletic scholarship (and the proportion receiving): $7,835 (17%). Average amount of debt of borrowers graduating in 2003: $16,350. Proportion who borrowed: 81%. **Student employment:** During the 2003-2004 academic year, 12% of undergraduates worked on campus. Average per-year earnings: $1,000. **Cooperative education programs:** art, business, computer science, education, humanities, social/behavioral science. **Reserve Officers Training Corps (ROTC):** Army ROTC: Offered at cooperating institution (Seton Hall University).

Centenary College

400 Jefferson Street
Hackettstown, NJ 07840
Private; www.centenarycollege.edu
Financial aid office: (908) 852-1400

- **2004-2005 TUITION AND FEES:** $19,210
- **ROOM AND BOARD:** $7,500

SAT I Score (25th/75th percentile): 800-1010
2005 U.S. News College Ranking:
Comp. Colleges–Bachelor's (North), third tier
Acceptance Rate: 76%

Other expenses: Estimated books and supplies: $910. Transportation: $600. Personal expenses: $1,200. **Financial aid:** Priority filing date for institution's financial aid form: April 15. In 2003-2004, 59% of undergraduates applied for financial aid. Of those, 48% were determined to have financial need; 31% had their need fully met. Average financial aid package (proportion receiving): $11,862 (48%). Average amount of gift aid, such as scholarships or grants (proportion receiving): $9,082 (43%). Average amount of self-help aid, such as work study or loans (proportion receiving): $3,872 (10%). Average need-based loan (excluding PLUS or other private loans): $4,907. Among students who received need-based aid, the average percentage of need met: 69%. Among students who received aid based on merit, the average award (and the proportion receiving): $11,123 (9%). The average athletic scholarship (and the proportion receiving): $0 (0%). Average amount of debt of borrowers graduating in 2003: $24,274. Proportion who borrowed: 89%.

College of New Jersey

PO Box 7718, 2000 Pennington Road
Ewing, NJ 08628-0718
Public; www.tcnj.edu
Financial aid office: (609) 771-2211

- **2004-2005 TUITION AND FEES:**
  In state: $11,464; Out of state: $14,745
- **ROOM AND BOARD:** $8,093

SAT I Score (25th/75th percentile): 1180-1360
2005 U.S. News College Ranking:
Universities–Master's (North), 5
Acceptance Rate: 48%

Financial aid: Priority filing date for institution's financial aid form: March 1; deadline: October 1. In 2003-2004, 67% of undergraduates applied for financial aid. Of those, 46% were determined to have financial need; 14% had their need fully met. Average financial aid package (proportion receiving): $7,658 (43%). Average amount of gift aid, such as scholarships or grants (proportion receiving): $5,984 (19%). Average amount of self-help aid, such as work study or loans (proportion receiving): $3,922 (34%). Average need-based loan (excluding PLUS or other private loans): $3,847. Among students who received need-based aid, the average percentage of need met: 71%. Among students who received aid based on merit, the average award (and the proportion receiving): $4,554 (10%). The average athletic scholarship (and the proportion receiving): $0 (0%). Average amount of debt of borrowers graduating in 2003: $11,157. Proportion who borrowed: 48%. **Student employment:** During the 2003-2004 academic year, 27% of undergraduates worked on campus. Average per-year earnings: $2,247. **Reserve Officers Training Corps (ROTC):** Army ROTC: Offered on campus; Air Force ROTC: Offered at cooperating institution (RUTGERS).

College of St. Elizabeth

2 Convent Road
Morristown, NJ 07960-6989
Private; www.cse.edu
Financial aid office: (973) 290-4445

■ **2004-2005 TUITION AND FEES:** $18,077
■ **ROOM AND BOARD:** $8,618

SAT I Score (25th/75th percentile): 820-1040
2005 U.S. News College Ranking:
Comp. Colleges–Bachelor's (North), 9
Acceptance Rate: 81%

Other expenses: Estimated books and supplies: $1,200. Transportation: $1,000. Personal expenses: $1,250. **Financial aid:** Priority filing date for institution's financial aid form: March 1. In 2003-2004, 80% of undergraduates applied for financial aid. Of those, 74% were determined to have financial need; 21% had their need fully met. Average financial aid package (proportion receiving): $16,697 (74%). Average amount of gift aid, such as scholarships or grants (proportion receiving): $13,765 (70%). Average amount of self-help aid, such as work study or loans (proportion receiving): $4,572 (59%). Average need-based loan (excluding PLUS or other private loans): $4,088. Among students who received need-based aid, the average percentage of need met: 80%. Among students who received aid based on merit, the average award (and the proportion receiving): $10,402 (17%). The average athletic scholarship (and the proportion receiving): $0 (0%). Average amount of debt of borrowers graduating in 2003: $14,026. Proportion who borrowed: 78%. **Student employment:** During the 2003-2004 academic year, 30% of undergraduates worked on campus. Average per-year earnings: $2,000. **Cooperative education programs:** health professions.

Drew University

36 Madison Avenue
Madison, NJ 07940-1493
Private; www.drew.edu
Financial aid office: (973) 408-3112

■ **2004-2005 TUITION AND FEES:** $29,546
■ **ROOM AND BOARD:** $8,018

SAT I Score (25th/75th percentile): 1110-1320
2005 U.S. News College Ranking:
Liberal Arts Colleges, 59
Acceptance Rate: 69%

Other expenses: Estimated books and supplies: $1,090. Personal expenses: $2,438. **Financial aid:** In 2003-2004, 61% of undergraduates applied for financial aid. Of those, 50% were determined to have financial need; 35% had their need fully met. Average financial aid package (proportion receiving): $21,033 (49%). Average amount of gift aid, such as scholarships or grants (proportion receiving): $15,603 (49%). Average amount of self-help aid, such as work study or loans (proportion receiving): $5,737 (40%). Average need-based loan (excluding PLUS or other private loans): $4,898. Among students who received need-based aid, the average percentage of need met: 84%. Among students who received aid based on merit, the average award (and the proportion receiving): $11,785 (26%). The average athletic scholarship (and the proportion receiving): $0 (0%). Average amount of debt of borrowers graduating in 2003: $16,381. Proportion who borrowed: 58%. **Student employment:** During the 2003-2004 academic year, 29% of undergraduates worked on campus. Average per-year earnings: $1,200. **Cooperative education programs:** other. **Reserve Officers Training Corps (ROTC):** Army ROTC: Offered at cooperating institution (Seton Hall University); Air Force ROTC: Offered at cooperating institution (New Jersey Institute of Technology).

Fairleigh Dickinson University

1000 River Road
Teaneck, NJ 07666
Private; www.fdu.edu
Financial aid office: (201) 692-2823

■ **2004-2005 TUITION AND FEES:** $21,734
■ **ROOM AND BOARD:** $9,056

SAT I Score (25th/75th percentile): 910-1100
2005 U.S. College Ranking:
Universities–Master's (North), 62
Acceptance Rate: 71%

Other expenses: Estimated books and supplies: $784. Transportation: $1,172. Personal expenses: $2,290. **Financial aid:** Priority filing date for institution's financial aid form: February 15; deadline: February 15. In 2003-2004, 77% of undergraduates applied for financial aid. Of those, 70% were determined to have financial need; Average financial aid package (proportion receiving): $18,183 (70%). Average amount of gift aid, such as scholarships or grants (proportion receiving): $7,775 (61%). Average amount of self-help aid, such as work study or loans (proportion receiving): $5,881 (64%). Average need-based loan (excluding PLUS or other private loans): $3,246. Among students who received aid based on merit, the average award (and the proportion receiving): $4,953 (23%). The average athletic scholarship (and the proportion receiving): $12,196 (3%). **Reserve Officers Training Corps (ROTC):** Army ROTC: Offered at cooperating institution (Seton Hall University); Air Force ROTC: Offered at cooperating institution (New Jersey Institute of Technology).

Felician College

262 S. Main Street
Lodi, NJ 07644
Private; www.felician.edu
Financial aid office: (201) 559-6010

■ **2004-2005 TUITION AND FEES:** $17,100
■ **ROOM AND BOARD:** $7,200

SAT I Score (25th/75th percentile): 795-995
2005 U.S. News College Ranking:
Comp. Colleges–Bachelor's (North), third tier
Acceptance Rate: 72%

Other expenses: Estimated books and supplies: $2,000. Transportation: $2,000. Personal expenses: $1,500. **Financial aid:** In 2003-2004, 100% of undergraduates applied for financial aid. Of those, 100% were determined to have financial need; 16% had their need fully met. Average financial aid package (proportion receiving): $11,130 (100%). Average amount of gift aid, such as scholarships or grants (proportion receiving): $6,000 (50%). Average amount of self-help aid, such as work study or loans (proportion receiving): $3,800 (73%). Average need-based loan (excluding PLUS or other private loans): $6,625. Among students who received need-based aid, the average percentage of need met: 85%. Among students who received aid based on merit, the average award (and the proportion receiving): $7,626 (50%). The average athletic scholarship (and the proportion receiving): $7,626 (7%). Average amount of debt of borrowers graduating in 2003: $40,000. Proportion who borrowed: 85%.

Georgian Court University

900 Lakewood Avenue
Lakewood, NJ 08701-2697
Private; www.georgian.edu
Financial aid office: (732) 364-2200

■ **2004-2005 TUITION AND FEES:** $17,924
■ **ROOM AND BOARD:** $7,200

SAT I Score (25th/75th percentile): 830-1030
2005 U.S. News College Ranking:
Universities–Master's (North), third tier
Acceptance Rate: 86%

Other expenses: Estimated books and supplies: $1,000. Transportation: $1,000. Personal expenses: $2,000. **Financial aid:** In 2003-2004, 91% of undergraduates applied for financial aid. Of those, 82% were determined to have financial need; 16% had their need fully met. Average financial aid package (proportion receiving): $11,166 (82%). Average amount of gift aid, such as scholarships or grants (proportion receiving): $8,410 (70%). Average amount of self-help aid, such as work study or loans (proportion receiving): $4,819 (68%). Average need-based loan (excluding PLUS or other private loans): $4,466. Among students who received need-based aid, the average percentage of need met: 60%. Among students who received aid based on merit, the average award (and the proportion receiving): $10,879 (10%). The average athletic scholarship (and the proportion receiving): $0 (0%). Average amount of debt of borrowers graduating in 2003: $17,319. Proportion who borrowed: 79%. **Student employment:** During the 2003-2004 academic year, 12% of undergraduates worked on campus. Average per-year earnings: $1,575.

Kean University

PO Box 411
Union, NJ 07083
Public; www.kean.edu
Financial aid office: (908) 737-3190

■ **2004-2005 TUITION AND FEES:**
In state: $7,149; Out of state: $9,654
■ **ROOM AND BOARD:** $7,953

SAT I Score (25th/75th percentile): 830-1030
2005 U.S. News College Ranking:
Universities–Master's (North), third tier
Acceptance Rate: 64%

Other expenses: Estimated books and supplies: $1,000. Transportation: $800. Personal expenses: $1,250. **Financial aid:** Priority filing date for institution's financial aid form: March 15; deadline: June 30. In 2003-2004, 94% of undergraduates applied for financial aid. Of those, 77% were determined to have financial need; 23% had their need fully met. Average financial aid package (proportion receiving): $7,324 (74%). Average amount of gift aid, such as scholarships or grants (proportion receiving): $5,141 (52%). Average amount of self-help aid, such as work study or loans (proportion receiving): $3,724 (73%). Average need-based loan (excluding PLUS or other private loans): $3,579. Among students who received need-based aid, the average percentage of need met: 31%. Among students who received aid based on merit, the average award (and the proportion receiving): $1,563 (5%). The average athletic scholarship (and the proportion receiving): $0 (0%). **Cooperative education programs:** art, business, computer science, education, health professions, humanities, natural science, social/behavioral science, technologies. **Reserve Officers Training Corps (ROTC):** Army ROTC: Offered at cooperating institution (Seton Hall University); Air Force ROTC: Offered at cooperating institution (NJ Inst. of Technology).

Monmouth University

400 Cedar Avenue
West Long Branch, NJ 07764-1898
Private; www.monmouth.edu
Financial aid office: (732) 571-3463

■ **2004-2005 TUITION AND FEES:** $19,704
■ **ROOM AND BOARD:** $7,911

SAT I Score (25th/75th percentile): 980-1140
2005 U.S. News College Ranking:
Universities–Master's (North), 76
Acceptance Rate: 66%

Other expenses: Estimated books and supplies: $900. Transportation: $509. Personal expenses: $1,768. **Financial aid:** In 2003-2004, 81% of undergraduates applied for financial aid. Of those, 67% were determined to have financial need; 14% had their need fully met. Average financial aid package (proportion receiving): $12,958 (67%). Average amount of gift aid, such as scholarships or grants (proportion receiving): $7,604 (30%). Average amount of self-help aid, such as work study or loans (proportion receiving): $4,800 (57%). Average need-based loan (excluding PLUS or other private loans): $4,288. Among students who received need-based aid, the average percentage of need met: 66%. Among students who received aid based on merit, the average award (and the proportion receiving): $4,619 (26%). The average athletic scholarship (and the proportion receiving): $8,962 (2%). Average amount of debt of borrowers graduating in 2003: $18,500. Proportion who borrowed: 66%. **Student employment:** During the 2003-2004 academic year, 28% of undergraduates worked on campus. Average per-year earnings: $1,549. **Reserve Officers Training Corps (ROTC):** Air Force ROTC: Offered at cooperating institution (Rutgers, The State University of New Jersey, New Brunswick).

Montclair State University

1 Normal Avenue
Upper Montclair, NJ 07043
Public; www.montclair.edu
Financial aid office: (973) 655-4461

■ **2004-2005 TUITION AND FEES:**
In state: $7,169; Out of state: $10,694

SAT I Score (25th/75th percentile): 930-1130
2005 U.S. News College Ranking:
Universities–Master's (North), 62
Acceptance Rate: 51%

Other expenses: Estimated books and supplies: $1,000. Transportation: $800. Personal expenses: $1,940. **Financial aid:** Priority filing date for institution's financial aid form: March 1. In 2003-2004, 66% of undergraduates applied for financial aid. Of those, 52% were determined to have financial need; 41% had their need fully met. Average financial aid package (proportion receiving): $8,341 (49%). Average amount of gift aid, such as scholarships or grants (proportion receiving): $2,181 (33%). Average amount of self-help aid, such as work study or loans (proportion receiving): $2,987 (39%). Average need-based loan (excluding PLUS or other private loans): $3,307. Among students who received need-based aid, the average percentage of need met: 82%. Among students who received aid based on merit, the average award (and the proportion receiving): $2,859 (6%). The average athletic scholarship (and the proportion receiving): $0 (0%). Average amount of debt of borrowers graduating in 2003: $15,918. Proportion who borrowed: 49%. **Cooperative education programs:** business, education, social/behavioral science.

New Jersey City University

2039 Kennedy Boulevard
Jersey City, NJ 07305
Public; www.njcu.edu
Financial aid office: (201) 200-3173

■ **2004-2005 TUITION AND FEES:**
    In state: $6,550; Out of state: $11,230
■ **ROOM AND BOARD:** $6,958

SAT I Score (25th/75th percentile): 700-980
2005 U.S. News College Ranking:
Universities–Master's (North), fourth tier
Acceptance Rate: 52%

New Jersey Institute of Technology

University Heights
Newark, NJ 07102-1982
Public; www.njit.edu
Financial aid office: (973) 596-3479

■ **2003-2004 TUITION AND FEES:**
    In state: $8,500; Out of state: $13,868
■ **ROOM AND BOARD:** $7,896

SAT I Score (25th/75th percentile): 1040-1250
2005 U.S. News College Ranking:
National Universities, third tier
Acceptance Rate: 68%

Other expenses: Estimated books and supplies: $1,000. Transportation: $500. Personal expenses: $1,200. **Financial aid:** Priority filing date for institution's financial aid form: March 15; deadline: May 15. In 2003-2004, 100% of undergraduates applied for financial aid. Of those, 60% were determined to have financial need;

33% had their need fully met. Average financial aid package (proportion receiving): $5,400 (57%). Average amount of gift aid, such as scholarships or grants (proportion receiving): $3,700 (51%). Average amount of self-help aid, such as work study or loans (proportion receiving): $2,500 (35%). Average need-based loan (excluding PLUS or other private loans): $1,500. Among students who received need-based aid, the average percentage of need met: 90%. Among students who received aid based on merit, the average award (and the proportion receiving): $2,472 (10%). Average amount of debt of borrowers graduating in 2003: $14,600. Proportion who borrowed: 50%. **Student employment:** During the 2003-2004 academic year, 25% of undergraduates worked on campus. Average per-year earnings: $2,000. **Cooperative education programs:** business, computer science, engineering, natural science, social/behavioral science, technologies. **Reserve Officers Training Corps (ROTC):** Army ROTC: Offered on campus; Air Force ROTC: Offered on campus.

Princeton University

Box 430
Princeton, NJ 08544
Private; www.princeton.edu
Financial aid office: (609) 258-3330

■ **2004-2005 TUITION AND FEES:** $29,910
■ **ROOM AND BOARD:** $8,387

SAT I Score (25th/75th percentile): 1370-1560
2005 U.S. News College Ranking:
National Universities, 1
Acceptance Rate: 10%

Other expenses: Estimated books and supplies: $990. Personal expenses: $2,093. **Financial aid:** Priority filing date for institution's financial aid form: February 1. In 2003-2004, 53% of undergraduates applied for financial aid. Of those, 49% were determined to have financial need; 100% had their need fully met. Average financial aid package (proportion receiving): $25,460 (49%). Average amount of gift aid, such as scholarships or grants (proportion receiving): $23,660 (49%). Average amount of self-help aid, such as work study or loans (proportion receiving): $2,810 (33%). Average need-based loan (excluding PLUS or other private loans): $0. Among students who received need-based aid, the average percentage of need met: 100%. Average amount of debt of borrowers graduating in 2003: $6,500. Proportion who borrowed: 25%. **Student employment:** During the 2003-

2004 academic year, 45% of undergraduates worked on campus. Average per-year earnings: $1,180. **Reserve Officers Training Corps (ROTC):** Army ROTC: Offered on campus; Air Force ROTC: Offered at cooperating institution (Rutgers University).

Ramapo College of New Jersey

505 Ramapo Valley Road
Mahwah, NJ 07430-1680
Public; www.ramapo.edu
Financial aid office: (201) 684-7549

■ **2004-2005 TUITION AND FEES:**
    In state: $6,949; Out of state: $11,151
■ **ROOM AND BOARD:** $8,269

SAT I Score (25th/75th percentile): 1060-1230
2005 U.S. News College Ranking:
Comp. Colleges–Bachelor's (North), 9
Acceptance Rate: 43%

Other expenses: Estimated books and supplies: $950. Transportation: $250. Personal expenses: $1,300. **Financial aid:** Priority filing date for institution's financial aid form: March 1. In 2003-2004, 64% of undergraduates applied for financial aid. Of those, 49% were determined to have financial need; 15% had their need fully met. Average financial aid package (proportion receiving): $9,351 (47%). Average amount of gift aid, such as scholarships or grants (proportion receiving): $6,721 (25%). Average amount of self-help aid, such as work study or loans (proportion receiving): $4,119 (39%). Average need-based loan (excluding PLUS or other private loans): $4,026. Among students who received need-based aid, the average percentage of need met: 79%. Among students who received aid based on merit, the average award (and the proportion receiving): $8,468 (21%). The average athletic scholarship (and the proportion receiving): $0 (0%). Average amount of debt of borrowers graduating in 2003: $15,183. Proportion who borrowed: 37%. **Cooperative education programs:** art, business, computer science, education, health professions, humanities, natural science, social/behavioral science, vocational arts. **Reserve Officers Training Corps (ROTC):** Air Force ROTC: Offered at cooperating institution (New Jersey Institute of Technology).

Richard Stockton College of New Jersey

PO Box 195
Pomona, NJ 08240-0195
Public; www.stockton.edu
Financial aid office: (609) 652-4201

■ **2004-2005 TUITION AND FEES:**
  In state: $6,660; Out of state: $9,600
■ **ROOM AND BOARD:** $7,379

SAT I Score (25th/75th percentile): 1030-1190
2005 U.S. News College Ranking:
Liberal Arts Colleges, fourth tier
Acceptance Rate: 43%

Other expenses: Estimated books and supplies: $850. Transportation: $965. Personal expenses: $1,275. **Financial aid:** Priority filing date for institution's financial aid form: March 1. In 2003-2004, 71% of undergraduates applied for financial aid. Of those, 55% were determined to have financial need; 73% had their need fully met. Average financial aid package (proportion receiving): $9,541 (53%). Average amount of gift aid, such as scholarships or grants (proportion receiving): $5,459 (31%). Average amount of self-help aid, such as work study or loans (proportion receiving): $3,894 (43%). Average need-based loan (excluding PLUS or other private loans): $3,770. Among students who received need-based aid, the average percentage of need met: 61%. Among students who received aid based on merit, the average award (and the proportion receiving): $1,908 (6%). The average athletic scholarship (and the proportion receiving): $0 (0%). Average amount of debt of borrowers graduating in 2003: $14,372. Proportion who borrowed: 63%. **Student employment:** During the 2003-2004 academic year, 5% of undergraduates worked on campus.

Rider University

2083 Lawrenceville Road
Lawrenceville, NJ 08648-3099
Private; www.rider.edu
Financial aid office: (609) 896-5360

■ **2004-2005 TUITION AND FEES:** $22,300
■ **ROOM AND BOARD:** $8,400

SAT I Score (25th/75th percentile): 950-1140
2005 U.S. News College Ranking:
Universities–Master's (North), 36
Acceptance Rate: 78%

Other expenses: Estimated books and supplies: $1,000. Transportation: $1,200. Personal expenses: $850. **Financial aid:** Priority filing date for institution's financial aid form: March 1; deadline: June 1. In 2003-2004, 75% of undergraduates applied for financial aid. Of those, 66% were determined to have financial need; 10% had their need fully met. Average financial aid package (proportion receiving): $17,733 (66%). Average amount of gift aid, such as scholarships or grants (proportion receiving): $8,196 (49%). Average amount of self-help aid, such as work study or loans (proportion receiving): $6,109 (57%). Average need-based loan (excluding PLUS or other private loans): $4,564. Among students who received need-based aid, the average percentage of need met: 79%. Among students who received aid based on merit, the average award (and the proportion receiving): $7,427 (15%). The average athletic scholarship (and the proportion receiving): $9,944 (7%). Average amount of debt of borrowers graduating in 2003: $27,113. Proportion who borrowed: 66%. **Student employment:** During the 2003-2004 academic year, 31% of undergraduates worked on campus. Average per-year earnings: $1,200. **Reserve Officers Training Corps (ROTC):** Army ROTC: Offered at cooperating institution (Princeton University).

Rowan University

201 Mullica Hill Road
Glassboro, NJ 08028
Public; www.rowan.edu
Financial aid office: (856) 256-4250

■ **2004-2005 TUITION AND FEES:**
  In state: $3,985; Out of state: $6,899

SAT I Score (25th/75th percentile): 1020-1210
2005 U.S. News College Ranking:
Universities–Master's (North), 34
Acceptance Rate: 52%

Financial aid: In 2003-2004, 98% of undergraduates applied for financial aid. Of those, 78% were determined to have financial need; 38% had their need fully met. Average financial aid package (proportion receiving): $7,775 (78%). Average amount of gift aid, such as scholarships or grants (proportion receiving): $4,817 (50%). Average amount of self-help aid, such as work study or loans (proportion receiving): $3,487 (45%). Average need-based loan (excluding PLUS or other private loans): $3,355. Among students who received need-based aid, the average percentage of need met: 91%. Among students who received aid based on merit, the average award (and the proportion receiving): $1,592 (15%). **Reserve Officers Training Corps (ROTC):** Army ROTC: Offered at cooperating institution (Drexel University).

Rutgers–Camden

406 Penn Street
Camden, NJ 08102
Public; www.rutgers.edu
Financial aid office: (856) 225-6039

■ **2004-2005 TUITION AND FEES:**
  In state: $8,389; Out of state: $15,424
■ **ROOM AND BOARD:** $7,862

SAT I Score (25th/75th percentile): 990-1210
2005 U.S. News College Ranking:
Universities–Master's (North), 34
Acceptance Rate: 59%

Financial aid: Priority filing date for institution's financial aid form: March 15. In 2003-2004, 77% of undergraduates applied for financial aid. Of those, 64% were determined to have financial need; 41% had their need fully met. Average financial aid package (proportion receiving): $9,063 (63%). Average amount of gift aid, such as scholarships or grants (proportion receiving): $6,245 (48%). Average amount of self-help aid, such as work study or loans (proportion receiving): $4,156 (52%). Average need-based loan (excluding PLUS or other private loans): $3,745. Among students who received need-based aid, the average percentage of need met: 86%. Among students who received aid based on merit, the average award (and the proportion receiving): $4,218 (3%). The average athletic scholarship (and the proportion receiving): $0 (0%). Average amount of debt of borrowers graduating in 2003: $15,432. Proportion who borrowed: 63%. **Student employment:** During the 2003-2004 academic year, 8% of undergraduates worked on campus. Average per-year earnings: $2,450. **Reserve Officers Training Corps (ROTC):** Army ROTC: Offered at cooperating institution (At the University of Pennsylvania); Air Force ROTC: Offered at cooperating institution (At the University of Pennsylvania).

Rutgers–Newark

249 University Avenue
Newark, NJ 07102-1896
Public; rutgers-newark.rutgers.edu
Financial aid office: (973) 353-5151

■ **2004-2005 TUITION AND FEES:**
In state: $8,209; Out of state: $15,244
■ **ROOM AND BOARD:** $8,570

SAT I Score (25th/75th percentile): 990-1190
2005 U.S. News College Ranking:
National Universities, third tier
Acceptance Rate: 48%

Financial aid: Priority filing date for institution's financial aid form: March 15. In 2003-2004, 72% of undergraduates applied for financial aid. Of those, 63% were determined to have financial need; 26% had their need fully met. Average financial aid package (proportion receiving): $9,164 (62%). Average amount of gift aid, such as scholarships or grants (proportion receiving): $6,769 (50%). Average amount of self-help aid, such as work study or loans (proportion receiving): $4,004 (46%). Average need-based loan (excluding PLUS or other private loans): $3,432. Among students who received need-based aid, the average percentage of need met: 79%. Among students who received aid based on merit, the average award (and the proportion receiving): $3,590 (4%). The average athletic scholarship (and the proportion receiving): $5,700 (0%). Average amount of debt of borrowers graduating in 2003: $14,757. Proportion who borrowed: 73%. **Student employment:** During the 2003-2004 academic year, 13% of undergraduates worked on campus. Average per-year earnings: $1,600. **Reserve Officers Training Corps (ROTC):** Army ROTC: Offered at cooperating institution (On the Rutgers-New Brunswick Campus); Air Force ROTC: Offered at cooperating institution (On the Rutgers–New Brunswick Campus).

Rutgers–New Brunswick

65 Davidson Road, Room 202
Piscataway, NJ 08854-8097
Public; www.rutgers.edu
Financial aid office: (732) 932-7057

■ **2004-2005 TUITION AND FEES:**
In state: $8,564; Out of state: $15,599
■ **ROOM AND BOARD:** $8,357

SAT I Score (25th/75th percentile): 1110-1310
2005 U.S. News College Ranking:
National Universities, 58
Acceptance Rate: 54%

Financial aid: Priority filing date for institution's financial aid form: March 15. In 2003-2004, 63% of undergraduates applied for financial aid. Of those, 50% were determined to have financial need; 31% had their need fully met. Average financial aid package (proportion receiving): $10,288 (50%). Average amount of gift aid, such as scholarships or grants (proportion receiving): $6,738 (33%). Average amount of self-help aid, such as work study or loans (proportion receiving): $4,540 (43%). Average need-based loan (excluding PLUS or other private loans): $4,064. Among students who received need-based aid, the average percentage of need met: 82%. Among students who received aid based on merit, the average award (and the proportion receiving): $4,954 (10%). The average athletic scholarship (and the proportion receiving): $10,176 (1%). Average amount of debt of borrowers graduating in 2003: $15,018. Proportion who borrowed: 56%. **Student employment:** During the 2003-2004 academic year, 26% of undergraduates worked on campus. Average per-year earnings: $1,600. **Cooperative education programs:** agriculture, art, business, computer science, health professions, natural science, technologies. **Reserve Officers Training Corps (ROTC):** Army ROTC: Offered on campus; Air Force ROTC: Offered on campus.

Seton Hall University

400 S. Orange Avenue
South Orange, NJ 07079
Private; www.shu.edu
Financial aid office: (973) 761-9332

■ **2004-2005 TUITION AND FEES:** $22,440
■ **ROOM AND BOARD:** $9,832

SAT I Score (25th/75th percentile): 990-1210
2005 U.S. News College Ranking:
National Universities, 120
Acceptance Rate: 82%

Other expenses: Estimated books and supplies: $1,200. Transportation: $1,200. Personal expenses: $1,800. **Financial aid:** Priority filing date for institution's financial aid form: February 15. In 2003-2004, 73% of undergraduates applied for financial aid. Of those, 64% were determined to have financial need; 16% had their need fully met. Average financial aid

package (proportion receiving): $13,980 (63%). Average amount of gift aid, such as scholarships or grants (proportion receiving): $4,498 (37%). Average amount of self-help aid, such as work study or loans (proportion receiving): $3,354 (49%). Average need-based loan (excluding PLUS or other private loans): $3,026. Among students who received need-based aid, the average percentage of need met: 69%. Among students who received aid based on merit, the average award (and the proportion receiving): $11,763 (15%). The average athletic scholarship (and the proportion receiving): $18,478 (3%). Average amount of debt of borrowers graduating in 2003: $16,763. Proportion who borrowed: 69%. **Student employment:** During the 2003-2004 academic year, 22% of undergraduates worked on campus. Average per-year earnings: $1,500. **Cooperative education programs:** art, business, computer science, education, health professions, humanities, natural science, social/behavioral science. **Reserve Officers Training Corps (ROTC):** Army ROTC: Offered on campus.

Stevens Institute of Technology

1 Castle Point on Hudson
Hoboken, NJ 07030
Private; www.stevens.edu
Financial aid office: (201) 216-5555

■ **2004-2005 TUITION AND FEES:** $28,360
■ **ROOM AND BOARD:** $8,930

SAT I Score (25th/75th percentile): 1190-1370
2005 U.S. News College Ranking:
National Universities, 81
Acceptance Rate: 51%

Other expenses: Estimated books and supplies: $900. Personal expenses: $750. **Financial aid:** Priority filing date for institution's financial aid form: February 15. In 2003-2004, 93% of undergraduates applied for financial aid. Of those, 82% were determined to have financial need; 14% had their need fully met. Average financial aid package (proportion receiving): $18,336 (70%). Average amount of gift aid, such as scholarships or grants (proportion receiving): $12,871 (54%). Average amount of self-help aid, such as work study or loans (proportion receiving): $5,041 (58%). Average need-based loan (excluding PLUS or other private loans): $4,298. Among students who received need-based aid, the average percentage of need met: 85%. Among students who received aid based on merit, the average award (and the proportion receiving): $9,663 (13%). The average athletic scholarship (and the proportion receiving): $0 (0%). Average amount of debt of borrowers graduating in 2003: $14,113. Proportion who borrowed: 68%. **Cooperative education programs:** computer science, engineering, health professions, natural science, technologies. **Reserve Officers Training Corps (ROTC):** Army ROTC: Offered at cooperating institution (Seton Hall University); Air Force ROTC: Offered at cooperating institution (New Jersey Institute of Technology).

St. Peter's College

2641 Kennedy Boulevard
Jersey City, NJ 07306-5997
Private; www.spc.edu
Financial aid office: (201) 915-4929

■ **2004-2005 TUITION AND FEES:** $19,750
■ **ROOM AND BOARD:** $8,430

SAT I Score (25th/75th percentile): 830-1040
2005 U.S. News College Ranking:
Universities–Master's (North), third tier
Acceptance Rate: 64%

Other expenses: Estimated books and supplies: $700. Transportation: $700. Personal expenses: $600. **Financial aid:** In 2003-2004, 91% of undergraduates applied for financial aid. Of those, 82% were determined to have financial need; 21% had their need fully met. Average financial aid package (proportion receiving): $15,921 (80%). Average amount of gift aid, such as scholarships or grants (proportion receiving): $4,441 (63%). Average amount of self-help aid, such as work study or loans (proportion receiving): $4,441 (50%). Average need-based loan (excluding PLUS or other private loans): $2,190. Among students who received need-based aid, the average percentage of need

met: 72%. Among students who received aid based on merit, the average award (and the proportion receiving): $7,709 (8%). The average athletic scholarship (and the proportion receiving): $11,106 (1%). Proportion who borrowed: 1%. **Student employment:** During the 2003-2004 academic year, 20% of undergraduates worked on campus. Average per-year earnings: $2,000. **Cooperative education programs:** art, business, computer science, education, humanities, natural science, social/behavioral science, other. **Reserve Officers Training Corps (ROTC):** Army ROTC: Offered at cooperating institution (Seton Hall University); Air Force ROTC: Offered at cooperating institution (New Jersey Institute of Technology (NJIT)).

Thomas Edison State College

101 W. State Street
Trenton, NJ 08608-1176
Public; www.tesc.edu
Financial aid office: (609) 633-9658

■ **2004-2005 TUITION AND FEES:**
In state: $3,945; Out of state: $4,380

2005 U.S. News College Ranking:
Universities–Master's (North), unranked

William Paterson University of New Jersey

300 Pompton Road
Wayne, NJ 07470
Public; ww2.wpunj.edu
Financial aid office: (973) 720-2202

■ **2004-2005 TUITION AND FEES:**
In state: $7,952; Out of state: $12,690
■ **ROOM AND BOARD:** $8,340

SAT I Score (25th/75th percentile): 920-1100
2005 U.S. News College Ranking:
Universities–Master's (North), third tier
Acceptance Rate: 61%

Financial aid: Priority filing date for institution's financial aid form: April 1; deadline: April 1. In 2003-2004, 66% of undergraduates applied for financial aid. Of those, 51% were determined to have financial need; 27% had their need fully met. Average financial aid package (proportion receiving): $8,608 (48%). Average amount of gift aid, such as scholarships or grants (proportion receiving): $5,346 (29%). Average amount of self-help aid, such as work study or loans (proportion receiving): $3,747 (37%). Average need-based loan (excluding PLUS or other private loans): $3,607. Among students who received need-based aid, the average percentage of need met: 84%. Among students who received aid based on merit, the average award (and the proportion receiving): $3,750 (3%). The average athletic scholarship (and the proportion receiving): $0 (0%). Average amount of debt of borrowers graduating in 2003: $9,981. Proportion who borrowed: 44%. **Student employment:** During the 2003-2004 academic year, 2% of undergraduates worked on campus. **Reserve Officers Training Corps (ROTC):** Air Force ROTC: Offered at cooperating institution (New Jersey Institute of Technology).

New Mexico

College of Santa Fe

1600 St. Michael's Drive
Santa Fe, NM 87505
Private; www.csf.edu
Financial aid office: (505) 473-6454

■ **2004-2005 TUITION AND FEES:** $20,840
■ **ROOM AND BOARD:** $6,250

SAT I Score (25th/75th percentile): 1000-1240
2005 U.S. News College Ranking:
Universities–Master's (West), 30
Acceptance Rate: 81%

Other expenses: Estimated books and supplies: $816. Transportation: $592. Personal expenses: $1,146. **Financial aid:** Priority filing date for institution's financial aid form: March 15. In 2003-2004, 76% of undergraduates applied for financial aid. Of those, 68% were determined to have financial need; 15% had their need fully met. Average financial aid package (proportion receiving): $18,190 (68%). Average amount of gift aid, such as scholarships or grants (proportion receiving): $9,879 (62%). Average amount of self-help aid, such as work study or loans (proportion receiving): $5,566 (65%). Average need-based loan (excluding PLUS or other private loans): $4,363. Among students who received need-based aid, the average percentage of need met: 82%. Among students who received aid based on merit, the average award (and the proportion receiving): $3,427 (19%). The average athletic scholarship (and the proportion receiving): $22,957 (1%). Average amount of debt of borrowers graduating in 2003: $22,641. Proportion who borrowed: 60%. **Student employment:** During the 2003-2004 academic year, 40% of undergraduates worked on campus. Average per-year earnings: $2,000. **Cooperative education programs:** art, business, other. **Reserve Officers Training Corps (ROTC):** Air Force ROTC: Offered at cooperating institution (University of New Mexico).

College of the Southwest

6610 Lovington Highway
Hobbs, NM 88240
Private; www.csw.edu
Financial aid office: (505) 392-6561

■ **2003-2004 TUITION AND FEES:** $6,475
■ **ROOM AND BOARD:** $4,500

ACT Score (25th/75th percentile): 18
2005 U.S. News College Ranking:
Universities–Master's (West), third tier
Acceptance Rate: 49%

Other expenses: Estimated books and supplies: $800. Transportation: $720. Personal expenses: $800. **Financial aid:** Priority filing date for institution's financial aid form: April 1; deadline: August 1. In 2003-2004, 96% of undergraduates applied for financial aid. Of those, 76% were determined to have financial need; 2% had their need fully met. Average financial aid package (proportion receiving): $3,562 (72%). Average amount of gift aid, such as scholarships or grants (proportion receiving): $2,156 (67%). Average amount of self-help aid, such as work study or loans (proportion receiving): $1,720 (10%). Average need-based loan (excluding PLUS or other private loans): $2,056. Among students who received need-based aid, the average percentage of need met: 62%. Among students who received aid based on merit, the average award (and the proportion receiving): $2,200 (7%). The average athletic scholarship (and the proportion receiving): $2,761 (10%). Average amount of debt of borrowers graduating in 2003: $15,652. Proportion who borrowed: 66%.

Eastern New Mexico University

Station 2
Portales, NM 88130
Public; www.enmu.edu
Financial aid office: (800) 367-3668

■ **2004-2005 TUITION AND FEES:**
   In state: $2,616; Out of state: $8,172
■ **ROOM AND BOARD:** $4,340

ACT Score (25th/75th percentile): 16-22
2005 U.S. News College Ranking:
Universities–Master's (West), fourth tier
Acceptance Rate: 74%

Financial aid: In 2003-2004, 71% of undergraduates applied for financial aid. Of those, 70% were determined to have financial need; 30% had their need fully met. Average financial aid package (proportion receiving): $7,207 (70%). Average amount of gift aid, such as scholarships or grants (proportion receiving): $3,586 (61%). Average amount of self-help aid, such as work study or loans (proportion receiving): $3,392 (48%). Average need-based loan (excluding PLUS or other private loans): $4,077. Among students who received need-based aid, the average percentage of need met: 57%. Among students who received aid based on merit, the average award (and the proportion receiving): $3,174 (5%). The average athletic scholarship (and the proportion receiving): $2,809 (8%). Average amount of debt of borrowers graduating in 2003: $9,532. Proportion who borrowed: 9%. **Cooperative education programs:** other.

New Mexico Highlands University

Box 9000
Las Vegas, NM 87701
Public; www.nmhu.edu
Financial aid office: (505) 454-3430

■ **2004-2005 TUITION AND FEES:**
   In state: $2,280; Out of state: $10,272
■ **ROOM AND BOARD:** $3,264

ACT Score (25th/75th percentile): 17
2005 U.S. News College Ranking:
Universities–Master's (West), fourth tier
Acceptance Rate: 100%

Other expenses: Estimated books and supplies: $758. Transportation: $2,110. Personal expenses: $1,616. **Financial aid:** Priority filing date for institution's financial aid form: March 1. In 2003-2004, 91% of undergraduates applied for financial aid. Of those, 80% were determined to have financial need; 17% had their need fully met. Average financial aid package (proportion receiving): $7,924 (79%). Average amount of gift aid, such as scholarships or grants (proportion receiving): $3,622 (66%). Average amount of self-help aid, such as work study or loans (proportion receiving): $4,194 (58%). Average need-based loan (excluding PLUS or other private loans): $3,364. Among students who received need-based aid, the average percentage of need met: 69%. Among students who received aid based on merit, the average award (and the proportion receiving): $2,216 (9%). The average athletic scholarship (and the proportion receiving): $1,789 (5%). Average amount of debt of borrowers graduating in 2003: $8,494. Proportion who borrowed: 60%.

New Mexico Institute of Mining and Technology

801 Leroy Place
Socorro, NM 87801
Public; www.nmt.edu
Financial aid office: (505) 835-5333

■ **2004-2005 TUITION AND FEES:**
In state: $3,280; Out of state: $9,911
■ **ROOM AND BOARD:** $4,670

ACT Score (25th/75th percentile): 23-29
2005 U.S. News College Ranking:
National Universities, third tier
Acceptance Rate: 98%

Other expenses: Estimated books and supplies: $800. Personal expenses: $2,254. **Financial aid:** Priority filing date for institution's financial aid form: June 1. In 2003-2004, 87% of undergraduates applied for financial aid. Of those, 42% were determined to have financial need; 51% had their need fully met. Average financial aid package (proportion receiving): $7,641 (42%). Average amount of gift aid, such as scholarships or grants (proportion receiving): $6,738 (29%). Average amount of self-help aid, such as work study or loans (proportion receiving): $6,955 (31%). Average need-based loan (excluding PLUS or other private loans): $7,170. Among students who received need-based aid, the average percentage of need met: 90%. Among students who received aid based on merit, the average award (and the proportion receiving): $3,853 (33%). The average athletic scholarship (and the proportion receiving): $0 (0%). Average amount of debt of borrowers graduating in 2003: $9,161. Proportion who borrowed: 42%.

New Mexico State University

Box 30001, MSC 3004
Las Cruces, NM 88003-8001
Public; www.nmsu.edu
Financial aid office: (505) 646-4105

■ **2004-2005 TUITION AND FEES:**
In state: $3,666; Out of state: $12,210

ACT Score (25th/75th percentile): 18-23
2005 U.S. News College Ranking:
National Universities, third tier
Acceptance Rate: 84%

Financial aid: Priority filing date for institution's financial aid form: March 1. In 2003-2004, 70% of undergraduates applied for financial aid. Of those, 61% were determined to have financial need; 20% had their need fully met. Average financial aid package (proportion receiving): $8,292 (58%). Average amount of gift aid, such as scholarships or grants (proportion receiving): $5,697 (53%). Average amount of self-help aid, such as work study or loans (proportion receiving): $3,979 (40%). Average need-based loan (excluding PLUS or other private loans): $3,882. Among students who received need-based aid, the average percentage of need met: 73%. Among students who received aid based on merit, the average award (and the proportion receiving): $2,716 (21%). The average athletic scholarship (and the proportion receiving): $10,759 (1%). **Student employment:** During the 2003-2004 academic year, 30% of undergraduates worked on campus. Average per-year earnings: $3,000. **Cooperative education programs:** agriculture, business, computer science, education, engineering, home economics, natural science, technologies. **Reserve Officers Training Corps (ROTC):** Army ROTC: Offered on campus; Air Force ROTC: Offered on campus.

St. John's College

1160 Camino Cruz Blanca
Santa Fe, NM 87505
Private; www.sjcsf.edu
Financial aid office: (505) 984-6073

■ **2004-2005 TUITION AND FEES:** $30,770
■ **ROOM AND BOARD:** $7,610

2005 U.S. News College Ranking:
Liberal Arts Colleges, third tier
Acceptance Rate: 81%

University of New Mexico

Student Services Center Room 140 MSC06 3720
Albuquerque, NM 87131-0001
Public; www.unm.edu
Financial aid office: (505) 277-3012

■ **2004-2005 TUITION AND FEES:**
In state: $3,738; Out of state: $12,500
■ **ROOM AND BOARD:** $5,576

ACT Score (25th/75th percentile): 19-24
2005 U.S. News College Ranking:
National Universities, third tier
Acceptance Rate: 75%

Other expenses: Estimated books and supplies: $792. Transportation: $1,396. Personal expenses: $1,562. **Financial aid:** Priority filing date for institution's financial aid form: March 1. In 2003-2004, 58% of undergraduates applied for financial aid. Of those, 50% were determined to have financial need; 16% had their need fully met. Average financial aid package (proportion receiving): $7,829 (48%). Average amount of gift aid, such as scholarships or grants (proportion receiving): $4,796 (42%). Average amount of self-help aid, such as work study or loans (proportion receiving): $4,076 (35%). Average need-based loan (excluding PLUS or other private loans): $3,261. Among students who received need-based aid, the average percentage of need met: 75%. Among students who received aid based on merit, the average award (and the proportion receiving): $3,173 (31%). **Cooperative education programs:** business, engineering, other. **Reserve Officers Training Corps (ROTC):** Army ROTC: Offered on campus; Navy ROTC: Offered on campus; Air Force ROTC: Offered on campus.

Western New Mexico University

Box 680
Silver City, NM 88062
Public; www.wnmu.edu
Financial aid office: (505) 538-6173

■ **2004-2005 TUITION AND FEES:**
In state: $2,678; Out of state: $9,686
■ **ROOM AND BOARD:** $4,466

ACT Score (25th/75th percentile): 13-24
2005 U.S. News College Ranking:
Universities–Master's (West), fourth tier
Acceptance Rate: 100%

....

Other expenses: Estimated books and supplies: $1,000. Transportation: $1,500. Personal expenses: $1,840. **Financial aid:** Priority filing date for institution's financial aid form: April 1. In 2003-2004, 91% of undergraduates applied for financial aid. Of those, 77% were determined to have financial need; 18% had their need fully met. Average financial aid package (proportion receiving): $5,927 (77%). Average amount of gift aid, such as scholarships or grants (proportion receiving): $3,593 (71%). Average amount of self-help aid, such as work study or loans (proportion receiving): $2,783 (28%). Average need-based loan (excluding PLUS or other private loans): $2,770. Among students who received need-based aid, the average percentage of need met: 74%. Among students who received aid based on merit, the average award (and the proportion receiving): $990 (8%). The average athletic scholarship (and the proportion receiving): $3,086 (8%).
Student employment: During the 2003-2004 academic year, 15% of undergraduates worked on campus. Average per-year earnings: $3,000.
Cooperative education programs: art, business, computer science, social/behavioral science, technologies, vocational arts.

New York

Adelphi University

1 South Avenue
Garden City, NY 11530
Private; www.adelphi.edu
Financial aid office: (516) 877-3365

■ **2004-2005 TUITION AND FEES:** $18,700
■ **ROOM AND BOARD:** $8,500

SAT I Score (25th/75th percentile): 980-1190
2005 U.S. News College Ranking:
National Universities, third tier
Acceptance Rate: 71%

Other expenses: Estimated books and supplies:
$1,000. Transportation: $1,100. Personal expenses: $1,000. **Financial aid:** Priority filing date for institution's financial aid form: March 1. In 2003-2004, 73% of undergraduates applied for financial aid. Of those, 68% were determined to have financial need; Average financial aid package (proportion receiving): $13,500 (68%). Average amount of gift aid, such as scholarships or grants (proportion receiving): $5,043 (61%). Average amount of self-help aid, such as work study or loans (proportion receiving): $5,187 (59%). Average need-based loan (excluding PLUS or other private loans): $4,239. Among students who received aid based on merit, the average award (and the proportion receiving): $6,971 (20%). The average athletic scholarship (and the proportion receiving): $10,689 (2%). Average amount of debt of borrowers graduating in 2003: $24,528. Proportion who borrowed: 70%. **Student employment:** During the 2003-2004 academic year, 23% of undergraduates worked on campus. Average per-year earnings: $1,176. **Reserve Officers Training Corps (ROTC):** Army ROTC: Offered at cooperating institution (Hofstra University); Air Force ROTC: Offered at cooperating institution (New York Institute of Technology).

Alfred University

1 Saxon Drive
Alfred, NY 14802-1205
Private; www.alfred.edu
Financial aid office: (607) 871-2159

■ **2004-2005 TUITION AND FEES:** $21,186
■ **ROOM AND BOARD:** $9,374

SAT I Score (25th/75th percentile): 1000-1200
2005 U.S. News College Ranking:
Universities–Master's (North), 16
Acceptance Rate: 69%

Other expenses: Estimated books and supplies:
$800. Transportation: $350. Personal expenses:
$850. **Financial aid:** In 2003-2004, 93% of undergraduates applied for financial aid. Of those, 88% were determined to have financial need; 85% had their need fully met. Average financial aid package (proportion receiving): $21,746 (88%). Average amount of gift aid, such as scholarships or grants (proportion receiving): $16,504 (87%). Average amount of self-help aid, such as work study or loans (proportion receiving): $5,954 (80%). Average need-based loan (excluding PLUS or other private loans): $4,992. Among students who received need-based aid, the average percentage of need met: 92%. Among students who received aid based on merit, the average award (and the proportion receiving): $8,526 (9%). The average athletic scholarship (and the proportion receiving): $0 (0%). Average amount of debt of borrowers graduating in 2003: $18,200. Proportion who borrowed: 90%. **Student employment:** During the 2003-2004 academic year, 50% of undergraduates worked on campus. Average per-year earnings: $1,000. **Reserve Officers Training Corps (ROTC):** Army ROTC: Offered at cooperating institution (St. Bonaventure University).

Bard College

PO Box 5000
Annandale on Hudson, NY 12504
Private; www.bard.edu
Financial aid office: (845) 758-7525

■ **2004-2005 TUITION AND FEES:** $30,548
■ **ROOM AND BOARD:** $8,908

SAT I Score (25th/75th percentile): 1240-1440
2005 U.S. News College Ranking:
Liberal Arts Colleges, 35
Acceptance Rate: 39%

Other expenses: Estimated books and supplies:
$750. Transportation: $550. Personal expenses:
$400. **Financial aid:** Priority filing date for institution's financial aid form: February 1; deadline: March 1. In 2003-2004, 65% of under-

graduates applied for financial aid. Of those, 62% were determined to have financial need; 49% had their need fully met. Average financial aid package (proportion receiving): $22,828 (62%). Average amount of gift aid, such as scholarships or grants (proportion receiving): $18,336 (59%). Average amount of self-help aid, such as work study or loans (proportion receiving): $5,507 (55%). Average need-based loan (excluding PLUS or other private loans): $4,330. Among students who received need-based aid, the average percentage of need met: 90%. Among students who received aid based on merit, the average award (and the proportion receiving): $12,905 (2%). The average athletic scholarship (and the proportion receiving): $0 (0%). Average amount of debt of borrowers graduating in 2003: $16,000. Proportion who borrowed: 63%. **Student employment:** During the 2003-2004 academic year, 45% of undergraduates worked on campus. Average per-year earnings: $1,500.

Barnard College

3009 Broadway
New York, NY 10027
Private; www.barnard.edu
Financial aid office: (212) 854-2154

■ **2004-2005 TUITION AND FEES:** $28,340
■ **ROOM AND BOARD:** $10,596

SAT I Score (25th/75th percentile): 1280-1430
2005 U.S. News College Ranking:
Liberal Arts Colleges, 29
Acceptance Rate: 31%

Other expenses: Estimated books and supplies:
$1,000. Transportation: $500. Personal expenses:
$1,200. **Financial aid:** In 2003-2004, 49% of undergraduates applied for financial aid. Of those, 42% were determined to have financial need; 100% had their need fully met. Average financial aid package (proportion receiving): $26,045 (42%). Average amount of gift aid, such as scholarships or grants (proportion receiving): $21,533 (39%). Average amount of self-help aid, such as work study or loans (proportion receiving): $5,192 (42%). Average need-based loan (excluding PLUS or other private loans): $3,951. Among students who received need-based aid, the average percentage of need met: 100%. Among students who received aid based on

merit, the average award (and the proportion receiving): $0 (0%). The average athletic scholarship (and the proportion receiving): $0 (0%). Average amount of debt of borrowers graduating in 2003: $16,275. Proportion who borrowed: 43%. **Student employment:** During the 2003-2004 academic year, 38% of undergraduates worked on campus. Average per-year earnings: $3,000.

Boricua College

3755 Broadway
New York, NY 10032
Private; www.boricuacollege.edu
Financial aid office: (212) 694-1000

■ **2004-2005 TUITION AND FEES:** $8,300

2005 U.S. News College Ranking:
Comp. Colleges–Bachelor's (North), fourth tier
Acceptance Rate: 75%

Buffalo State College

1300 Elmwood Avenue
Buffalo, NY 14222
Public; www.buffalostate.edu
Financial aid office: (716) 878-4901

■ **2004-2005 TUITION AND FEES:**
In state: $5,137; Out of state: $11,087
■ **ROOM AND BOARD:** $6,258

SAT I Score (25th/75th percentile): 910-1090
2005 U.S. News College Ranking:
Universities–Master's (North), fourth tier
Acceptance Rate: 53%

Other expenses: Estimated books and supplies: $900. Transportation: $900. Personal expenses: $900. **Financial aid:** Priority filing date for institution's financial aid form: March 15. In 2003-2004, 90% of undergraduates applied for financial aid. Of those, 75% were determined to have financial need; Average financial aid package (proportion receiving): $3,037 (67%). Average amount of gift aid, such as scholarships or grants (proportion receiving): $1,043 (55%). Average amount of self-help aid, such as work study or loans (proportion receiving): $1,537 (37%). Average need-based loan (excluding PLUS or other private loans): $1,559. Among students who received need-based aid, the average percentage of need met: 62%. Among students who received aid based on merit, the average award (and the proportion receiving): $1,429 (43%). Average amount of

debt of borrowers graduating in 2003: $15,776. Proportion who borrowed: 65%. **Student employment:** During the 2003-2004 academic year, 3% of undergraduates worked on campus. **Reserve Officers Training Corps (ROTC):** Army ROTC: Offered at cooperating institution (Canisius College).

Canisius College

2001 Main Street
Buffalo, NY 14208-1098
Private; www.canisius.edu
Financial aid office: (716) 888-2300

■ **2004-2005 TUITION AND FEES:** $21,811
■ **ROOM AND BOARD:** $8,480

SAT I Score (25th/75th percentile): 1000-1210
2005 U.S. News College Ranking:
Universities–Master's (North), 25
Acceptance Rate: 83%

Other expenses: Estimated books and supplies: $700. Transportation: $430. Personal expenses: $700. **Financial aid:** Priority filing date for institution's financial aid form: February 15. In 2003-2004, 84% of undergraduates applied for financial aid. Of those, 75% were determined to have financial need; 27% had their need fully met. Average financial aid package (proportion receiving): $16,917 (75%). Average amount of gift aid, such as scholarships or grants (proportion receiving): $11,650 (74%). Average amount of self-help aid, such as work study or loans (proportion receiving): $4,923 (58%). Average need-based loan (excluding PLUS or other private loans): $4,030. Among students who received need-based aid, the average percentage of need met: 80%. Among students who received aid based on merit, the average award (and the proportion receiving): $8,787 (19%). The average athletic scholarship (and the proportion receiving): $13,239 (3%). Average amount of debt of borrowers graduating in 2003: $18,938. Proportion who borrowed: 71%. **Student employment:** During the 2003-2004 academic year, 25% of undergraduates worked on campus. Average per-year earnings: $1,200. **Reserve Officers Training Corps (ROTC):** Army ROTC: Offered on campus.

Cazenovia College

22 Sullivan Street
Cazenovia, NY 13035-1804
Private; www.cazenovia.edu
Financial aid office: (315) 655-7208

■ **2004-2005 TUITION AND FEES:** $18,105
■ **ROOM AND BOARD:** $7,235

SAT I Score (25th/75th percentile): 860-1050
2005 U.S. News College Ranking:
Comp. Colleges–Bachelor's (North), 34
Acceptance Rate: 84%

Financial aid: Priority filing date for institution's financial aid form: March 15. In 2003-2004, 92% of undergraduates applied for financial aid. Of those, 79% were determined to have financial need; 23% had their need fully met. Average financial aid package (proportion receiving): $14,600 (79%). Average amount of gift aid, such as scholarships or grants (proportion receiving): $10,000 (77%). Average amount of self-help aid, such as work study or loans (proportion receiving): $2,450 (77%). Average need-based loan (excluding PLUS or other private loans): $3,750. Among students who received need-based aid, the average percentage of need met: 80%. Among students who received aid based on merit, the average award (and the proportion receiving): $4,520 (9%). Average amount of debt of borrowers graduating in 2003: $16,466. Proportion who borrowed: 78%. **Reserve Officers Training Corps (ROTC):** Army ROTC: Offered at cooperating institution; Air Force ROTC: Offered at cooperating institution.

Clarkson University

Box 5605
Potsdam, NY 13699
Private; www.clarkson.edu
Financial aid office: (315) 268-6479

■ **2004-2005 TUITION AND FEES:** $24,500
■ **ROOM AND BOARD:** $9,068

SAT I Score (25th/75th percentile): 1070-1270
2005 U.S. News College Ranking:
National Universities, third tier
Acceptance Rate: 81%

Other expenses: Estimated books and supplies: $1,000. Transportation: $1,074. Personal expenses: $1,000. **Financial aid:** Priority filing date for institution's financial aid form: March

1. In 2003-2004, 86% of undergraduates applied for financial aid. Of those, 82% were determined to have financial need; 26% had their need fully met. Average financial aid package (proportion receiving): $16,730 (82%). Average amount of gift aid, such as scholarships or grants (proportion receiving): $8,469 (82%). Average amount of self-help aid, such as work study or loans (proportion receiving): $8,500 (75%). Average need-based loan (excluding PLUS or other private loans): $8,000. Among students who received need-based aid, the average percentage of need met: 88%. Among students who received aid based on merit, the average award (and the proportion receiving): $6,909 (7%). The average athletic scholarship (and the proportion receiving): $27,021 (1%). Average amount of debt of borrowers graduating in 2003: $18,148. Proportion who borrowed: 83%. **Student employment:** During the 2003-2004 academic year, 52% of undergraduates worked on campus. Average per-year earnings: $1,000. **Reserve Officers Training Corps (ROTC):** Army ROTC: Offered on campus; Air Force ROTC: Offered on campus.

Colgate University

13 Oak Drive
Hamilton, NY 13346
Private; www.colgate.edu
Financial aid office: (315) 228-7431

■ **2004-2005 TUITION AND FEES:** $31,440
■ **ROOM AND BOARD:** $7,620

SAT I Score (25th/75th percentile): 1270-1430
2005 U.S. News College Ranking:
Liberal Arts Colleges, 16
Acceptance Rate: 31%

Other expenses: Estimated books and supplies: $830. Transportation: $100. Personal expenses: $830. **Financial aid:** Priority filing date for institution's financial aid form: February 1; deadline: February 1. In 2003-2004, 46% of undergraduates applied for financial aid. Of those, 44% were determined to have financial need; 100% had their need fully met. Average financial aid package (proportion receiving): $25,421 (44%). Average amount of gift aid, such as scholarships or grants (proportion receiving): $22,956 (42%). Average amount of self-help aid, such as work study or loans (proportion receiving): $4,064 (32%). Average need-based loan (excluding PLUS or other private loans): $2,772. Among students who received need-based aid, the average percentage of need met: 100%. Among stu-

dents who received aid based on merit, the average award (and the proportion receiving): $0 (0%). The average athletic scholarship (and the proportion receiving): $0 (0%). Average amount of debt of borrowers graduating in 2003: $12,769. Proportion who borrowed: 43%. **Student employment:** During the 2003-2004 academic year, 49% of undergraduates worked on campus. Average per-year earnings: $1,700.

College of Aeronautics

La Guardia Airport, 86-01 23rd Avenue
Flushing, NY 11369
Private; www.aero.edu
Financial aid office: (800) 776-2376

■ **2004-2005 TUITION AND FEES:** $10,920

SAT I Score (25th/75th percentile): 820-1060
2005 U.S. News College Ranking:
Unranked Specialty School–Engineering
Acceptance Rate: 78%

Financial aid: In 2003-2004, 86% of undergraduates applied for financial aid. Of those, 86% were determined to have financial need; 30% had their need fully met. Average financial aid package (proportion receiving): $10,000 (86%). Average amount of gift aid, such as scholarships or grants (proportion receiving): $1,500 (86%). Average amount of self-help aid, such as work study or loans (proportion receiving): $3,000 (86%). Average need-based loan (excluding PLUS or other private loans): $2,625. Among students who received need-based aid, the average percentage of need met: 50%. Among students who received aid based on merit, the average award (and the proportion receiving): $1,250 (3%). Average amount of debt of borrowers graduating in 2003: $18,000. Proportion who borrowed: 85%. **Student employment:** During the 2003-2004 academic year, 10% of undergraduates worked on campus. Average per-year earnings: $5,000. **Reserve Officers Training Corps (ROTC):** Air Force ROTC: Offered at cooperating institution (Manhattan College).

College of Mount St. Vincent

6301 Riverdale Avenue
Riverdale, NY 10471
Private; www.mountsaintvincent.edu
Financial aid office: (718) 405-3290

■ **2004-2005 TUITION AND FEES:** $19,600
■ **ROOM AND BOARD:** $8,000

SAT I Score (25th/75th percentile): 920-1100
2005 U.S. News College Ranking:
Universities–Master's (North), 83
Acceptance Rate: 75%

Other expenses: Estimated books and supplies: $800. Transportation: $200. Personal expenses: $900. **Financial aid:** Priority filing date for institution's financial aid form: February 15. In 2003-2004, 98% of undergraduates applied for financial aid. Of those, 86% were determined to have financial need; 1% had their need fully met. Average financial aid package (proportion receiving): $15,000 (86%). Average amount of gift aid, such as scholarships or grants (proportion receiving): $7,000 (86%). Average amount of self-help aid, such as work study or loans (proportion receiving): $5,200 (86%). Average need-based loan (excluding PLUS or other private loans): $4,100. Among students who received need-based aid, the average percentage of need met: 74%. Among students who received aid based on merit, the average award (and the proportion receiving): $0 (0%). The average athletic scholarship (and the proportion receiving): $0 (0%). Average amount of debt of borrowers graduating in 2003: $17,000. Proportion who borrowed: 80%. **Student employment:** During the 2003-2004 academic year, 5% of undergraduates worked on campus. Average per-year earnings: $800. **Reserve Officers Training Corps (ROTC):** Air Force ROTC: Offered at cooperating institution (Manhattan College).

College of New Rochelle

Castle Place
New Rochelle, NY 10805-2338
Private; www.cnr.edu
Financial aid office: (914) 654-5224

■ **2003-2004 TUITION AND FEES:** $14,400
■ **ROOM AND BOARD:** $7,150

SAT I Score (25th/75th percentile): 850-1040
2005 U.S. News College Ranking:
Universities–Master's (North), fourth tier
Acceptance Rate: 67%

Other expenses: Estimated books and supplies: $600. Personal expenses: $3,000.

College of St. Rose

432 Western Avenue
Albany, NY 12203-1490
Private; www.strose.edu
Financial aid office: (518) 454-5168

■ **2004-2005 TUITION AND FEES:** $16,780
■ **ROOM AND BOARD:** $7,472

SAT I Score (25th/75th percentile): 950-1140
2005 U.S. News College Ranking:
Universities–Master's (North), 56
Acceptance Rate: 74%

Other expenses: Estimated books and supplies: $1,000. Transportation: $500. Personal expenses: $1,500. **Financial aid:** Priority filing date for institution's financial aid form: March 1; deadline: October 1. In 2003-2004, 98% of undergraduates applied for financial aid. Of those, 86% were determined to have financial need; 16% had their need fully met. Average financial aid package (proportion receiving): $10,999 (86%). Average amount of gift aid, such as scholarships or grants (proportion receiving): $7,544 (82%). Average amount of self-help aid, such as work study or loans (proportion receiving): $4,019 (83%). Average need-based loan (excluding PLUS or other private loans): $3,770. Among students who received need-based aid, the average percentage of need met: 71%. Among students who received aid based on merit, the average award (and the proportion receiving): $4,170 (10%). The average athletic scholarship (and the proportion receiving): $5,279 (1%). **Student employment:** During the 2003-2004 academic year, 0% of undergraduates worked on campus.

Columbia University

212 Hamilton Hall
New York, NY 10027
Private; www.columbia.edu
Financial aid office: (212) 854-3711

■ **2004-2005 TUITION AND FEES:** $31,472
■ **ROOM AND BOARD:** $9,066

SAT I Score (25th/75th percentile): 1310-1510
2005 U.S. News College Ranking:
National Universities, 9
Acceptance Rate: 11%

Financial aid: In 2003-2004, 49% of undergraduates applied for financial aid. Of those, 42% were determined to have financial need;

100% had their need fully met. Average financial aid package (proportion receiving): $27,079 (42%). Average amount of gift aid, such as scholarships or grants (proportion receiving): $23,555 (41%). Average amount of self-help aid, such as work study or loans (proportion receiving): $6,106 (39%). Average need-based loan (excluding PLUS or other private loans): $4,626. Among students who received need-based aid, the average percentage of need met: 100%. Average amount of debt of borrowers graduating in 2003: $16,085. Proportion who borrowed: 41%. **Reserve Officers Training Corps (ROTC):** Army ROTC: Offered at cooperating institution (John Jay College); Navy ROTC: Offered at cooperating institution (John Jay College); Air Force ROTC: Offered at cooperating institution (John Jay College).

Concordia College

171 White Plains Road
Bronxville, NY 10708
Private; www.concordia-ny.edu
Financial aid office: (914) 337-9300

■ **2004-2005 TUITION AND FEES:** $18,700
■ **ROOM AND BOARD:** $7,600

SAT I Score (25th/75th percentile): 910-1070
2005 U.S. News College Ranking:
Comp. Colleges–Bachelor's (North), 26
Acceptance Rate: 74%

Student employment: During the 2003-2004 academic year, 30% of undergraduates worked on campus. Average per-year earnings: $1,100. **Cooperative education programs:** health professions.

Cooper Union

30 Cooper Square
New York, NY 10003
Private; www.cooper.edu
Financial aid office: (212) 353-4113

■ **2004-2005 TUITION AND FEES:** $28,900
■ **ROOM AND BOARD:** $9,000

SAT I Score (25th/75th percentile): 1250-1450
2005 U.S. News College Ranking:
Unranked Specialty School–Engineering
Acceptance Rate: 12%

Other expenses: Estimated books and supplies: $1,400. Transportation: $700. Personal expenses: $1,575. **Financial aid:** Priority filing date for

institution's financial aid form: May 1; deadline: May 1. In 2003-2004, 34% of undergraduates applied for financial aid. Of those, 32% were determined to have financial need; 84% had their need fully met. Average financial aid package (proportion receiving): $6,491 (32%). Average amount of gift aid, such as scholarships or grants (proportion receiving): $3,302 (29%). Average amount of self-help aid, such as work study or loans (proportion receiving): $2,847 (28%). Average need-based loan (excluding PLUS or other private loans): $3,323. Among students who received need-based aid, the average percentage of need met: 89%. Among students who received aid based on merit, the average award (and the proportion receiving): $26,000 (100%). The average athletic scholarship (and the proportion receiving): $0 (0%). Average amount of debt of borrowers graduating in 2003: $11,030. Proportion who borrowed: 30%. **Student employment:** During the 2003-2004 academic year, 64% of undergraduates worked on campus. Average per-year earnings: $1,114.

Cornell University

349 Pine Tree Road
Ithaca, NY 14850
Private; www.cornell.edu
Financial aid office: (607) 255-5145

■ **2004-2005 TUITION AND FEES:** $30,167
■ **ROOM AND BOARD:** $9,882

SAT I Score (25th/75th percentile): 1280-1470
2005 U.S. News College Ranking:
National Universities, 14
Acceptance Rate: 31%

Other expenses: Estimated books and supplies: $660. Transportation: $855. Personal expenses: $1,340. **Financial aid:** In 2003-2004, 51% of undergraduates applied for financial aid. Of those, 47% were determined to have financial need; 100% had their need fully met. Average financial aid package (proportion receiving): $27,339 (47%). Average amount of gift aid, such as scholarships or grants (proportion receiving): $19,911 (44%). Average amount of self-help aid, such as work study or loans (proportion receiving): $9,097 (45%). Average need-based loan (excluding PLUS or other private loans): $7,248. Among students who received need-based aid, the average percentage of need met: 100%. Among students who received aid based on merit, the average award (and the proportion receiving): $0 (0%). The average athletic scholarship (and the proportion receiving): $0 (0%). Average amount of debt of borrowers graduating in 2003: $24,570. Proportion who borrowed: 39%. **Student employment:** During the 2003-2004 academic year, 43% of undergraduates worked on campus. Average per-year earnings: $1,800. **Cooperative education programs:** agriculture, engineering. **Reserve Officers Training Corps (ROTC):** Army ROTC: Offered on campus; Navy ROTC: Offered on campus; Air Force ROTC: Offered on campus.

CUNY–Baruch College

1 Bernard Baruch Way
New York, NY 10010
Public; www.baruch.cuny.edu
Financial aid office: (646) 312-1360

■ **2003-2004 TUITION AND FEES:**
  In state: $4,300; Out of state: $11,100

SAT I Score (25th/75th percentile): 980-1200
2005 U.S. News College Ranking:
Universities–Master's (North), 45
Acceptance Rate: 36%

Other expenses: Estimated books and supplies: $692. Transportation: $578. Personal expenses: $2,667. **Financial aid:** Priority filing date for institution's financial aid form: March 15; deadline: April 30. In 2003-2004, 90% of undergraduates applied for financial aid. Of those, 87% were determined to have financial need; 24% had their need fully met. Average financial aid package (proportion receiving): $4,930 (78%). Average amount of gift aid, such as scholarships or grants (proportion receiving): $4,300 (72%). Average amount of self-help aid, such as work study or loans (proportion receiving): $3,700 (35%). Average need-based loan (excluding PLUS or other private loans): $2,860. Among students who received need-based aid, the average percentage of need met: 64%. Among students who received aid based on merit, the average award (and the proportion receiving): $1,800 (7%). The average athletic scholarship (and the proportion receiving): $0 (0%). Average amount of debt of borrowers graduating in 2003: $10,100. Proportion who borrowed: 19%. **Student employment:** During the 2003-2004 academic year, 6% of undergraduates worked on campus. Average per-year earnings: $2,500. **Cooperative education programs:** business. **Reserve Officers Training Corps (ROTC):** Army ROTC: Offered at cooperating institution (Fordham).

CUNY–Brooklyn College

2900 Bedford Avenue
Brooklyn, NY 11210
Public; www.brooklyn.cuny.edu
Financial aid office: (718) 951-5045

■ **2004-2005 TUITION AND FEES:**
  In state: $4,353; Out of state: $8,993

SAT I Score (25th/75th percentile): 940-1150
2005 U.S. News College Ranking:
Universities–Master's (North), 76
Acceptance Rate: 36%

Other expenses: Estimated books and supplies: $800. Transportation: $800. Personal expenses: $4,000. **Financial aid:** Priority filing date for institution's financial aid form: April 1. In 2003-2004, 82% of undergraduates applied for financial aid. Of those, 78% were determined to have financial need; 97% had their need fully met. Average financial aid package (proportion receiving): $5,400 (77%). Average amount of gift aid, such as scholarships or grants (proportion receiving): $3,300 (71%). Average amount of self-help aid, such as work study or loans (proportion receiving): $2,200 (69%). Average need-based loan (excluding PLUS or other private loans): $2,850. Among students who received need-based aid, the average percentage of need met: 99%. Among students who received aid based on merit, the average award (and the proportion receiving): $4,000 (10%). The average athletic scholarship (and the proportion receiving): $0 (0%). Average amount of debt of borrowers graduating in 2003: $13,500. Proportion who borrowed: 30%. **Student employment:** During the 2003-2004 academic year, 0% of undergraduates worked on campus. Average per-year earnings: $8. **Cooperative education programs:** business.

CUNY–City College

160 Convent Avenue
New York, NY 10031
Public; www.ccny.cuny.edu
Financial aid office: (212) 650-5819

■ **2004-2005 TUITION AND FEES:**
  In state: $4,179; Out of state: $10,979

SAT I Score (25th/75th percentile): 830-1100
2005 U.S. News College Ranking:
Universities–Master's (North), 76
Acceptance Rate: 35%

Other expenses: Estimated books and supplies: $800. Transportation: $700. **Financial aid:** Priority filing date for institution's financial aid form: April 1. Among students who received need-based aid, the average percentage of need met: 70%. Average amount of debt of borrowers graduating in 2003: $16,000. Proportion who borrowed: 70%. **Cooperative education programs:** art, engineering.

CUNY–College of Staten Island

2800 Victory Boulevard
Staten Island, NY 10314
Public; www.csi.cuny.edu
Financial aid office: (718) 982-2030

■ **2004-2005 TUITION AND FEES:**
  In state: $4,308; Out of state: $8,908

SAT I Score (25th/75th percentile): 910-1100
2005 U.S. News College Ranking:
Universities–Master's (North), fourth tier
Acceptance Rate: 88%

Financial aid: In 2003-2004, 71% of undergraduates applied for financial aid. Of those, 56% were determined to have financial need; 6% had their need fully met. Average financial aid package (proportion receiving): $5,225 (54%). Average amount of gift aid, such as scholarships or grants (proportion receiving): N/A (53%). Average amount of self-help aid, such as work study or loans (proportion receiving): $2,029 (23%). Average need-based loan (excluding PLUS or other private loans): $3,348. Among students who received need-based aid, the average percentage of need met: 52%. Among students who received aid based on merit, the average award (and the proportion receiving): $1,795 (3%). **Student employment:** During the 2003-2004 academic year, 1% of undergraduates worked on campus. Average per-year earnings: $3,708.

CUNY–Hunter College

695 Park Avenue
New York, NY 10021
Public; www.hunter.cuny.edu
Financial aid office: (212) 772-4820

■ **2004-2005 TUITION AND FEES:**
  In state: $4,329; Out of state: $8,969

SAT I Score (25th/75th percentile): 960-1170
2005 U.S. News College Ranking:
Universities–Master's (North), 50
Acceptance Rate: 30%

....

Other expenses: Estimated books and supplies: $798. Transportation: $714. Personal expenses: $5,838. **Financial aid:** Priority filing date for institution's financial aid form: May 1. In 2003-2004, 90% of undergraduates applied for financial aid. Of those, 77% were determined to have financial need; 41% had their need fully met. Average financial aid package (proportion receiving): $5,842 (60%). Average amount of gift aid, such as scholarships or grants (proportion receiving): $165 (5%). Average amount of self-help aid, such as work study or loans (proportion receiving): $1,055 (25%). Average need-based loan (excluding PLUS or other private loans): $4,091. Among students who received need-based aid, the average percentage of need met: 100%. Among students who received aid based on merit, the average award (and the proportion receiving): $807 (1%).

CUNY–Lehman College

250 Bedford Park Boulevard W
Bronx, NY 10468
Public; www.lehman.cuny.edu
Financial aid office: (718) 960-8545

■ **2004-2005 TUITION AND FEES:**
In state: $4,270; Out of state: $8,910

SAT I Score (25th/75th percentile): 820-1010
2005 U.S. News College Ranking:
Universities–Master's (North), fourth tier
Acceptance Rate: 30%

....

Financial aid: In 2003-2004, 84% of undergraduates applied for financial aid. Of those, 83% were determined to have financial need; 2% had their need fully met. Average financial aid package (proportion receiving): $3,531 (83%). Average amount of gift aid, such as scholarships or grants (proportion receiving): $1,313 (78%). Average amount of self-help aid, such as work study or loans (proportion receiving): $1,088 (33%). Average need-based loan (excluding PLUS or other private loans): $1,525. Among students who received need-based aid, the average percentage of need met: 65%. Among students who received aid based on merit, the average award (and the proportion receiving): $1,352 (2%). The average athletic scholarship (and the proportion receiving): $0 (0%). Average amount of debt of borrowers graduating in 2003: $11,000. Proportion who borrowed: 35%. **Student employment:** During the 2003-2004 academic year, 2%

of undergraduates worked on campus. Average per-year earnings: $3,400. **Reserve Officers Training Corps (ROTC):** Army ROTC: Offered at cooperating institution (Fordham University).

CUNY–Medgar Evers College

1650 Bedford Avenue
Brooklyn, NY 11225
Public; www.mec.cuny.edu
Financial aid office: (718) 270-6038

■ **2004-2005 TUITION AND FEES:**
In state: $4,232; Out of state: $8,872

SAT I Score (25th/75th percentile): 675-880
2005 U.S. News College Ranking:
Comp. Colleges–Bachelor's (North), fourth tier
Acceptance Rate: 76%

....

Other expenses: Estimated books and supplies: $500. **Financial aid:** Priority filing date for institution's financial aid form: March 15. Average financial aid package (proportion receiving): N/A (72%). Average amount of gift aid, such as scholarships or grants (proportion receiving): N/A (72%). Average amount of self-help aid, such as work study or loans (proportion receiving): N/A (20%). Among students who received aid based on merit, the average award (and the proportion receiving): $500 (0%). The average athletic scholarship (and the proportion receiving): $0 (0%). **Cooperative education programs:** art, business, computer science, education, health professions, natural science, social/behavioral science.

CUNY–New York City College of Technology

300 Jay Street
Brooklyn, NY 11201
Public; www.citytech.cuny.edu
Financial aid office: (718) 260-5700

■ **2004-2005 TUITION AND FEES:**
In state: $4,538; Out of state: $9,178

SAT I Score (25th/75th percentile): 870-940
2005 U.S. News College Ranking:
Comp. Colleges–Bachelor's (North), fourth tier
Acceptance Rate: 77%

....

Student employment: During the 2003-2004 academic year, 2% of undergraduates worked on campus. Average per-year earnings: $10,000. **Cooperative education programs:** art, business, computer science, education, engineering, health professions, technologies.

CUNY–Queens College

65-30 Kissena Boulevard
Flushing, NY 11367
Public; www.qc.edu
Financial aid office: (718) 997-5101

■ **2004-2005 TUITION AND FEES:**
In state: $4,361; Out of state: $9,001

SAT I Score (25th/75th percentile): 1010-1070
2005 U.S. News College Ranking:
Universities–Master's (North), 50
Acceptance Rate: 40%

....

Financial aid: Priority filing date for institution's financial aid form: February 1. In 2003-2004, 81% of undergraduates applied for financial aid. Of those, 61% were determined to have financial need; 69% had their need fully met. Average financial aid package (proportion receiving): $8,600 (54%). Average amount of gift aid, such as scholarships or grants (proportion receiving): $5,000 (47%). Average amount of self-help aid, such as work study or loans (proportion receiving): $3,500 (35%). Average need-based loan (excluding PLUS or other private loans): $4,500. Among students who received need-based aid, the average percentage of need met: 95%. Among students who received aid based on merit, the average award (and the proportion receiving): $5,500 (3%). The average athletic scholarship (and the proportion receiving): $5,166 (1%). Average amount of debt of borrowers graduating in 2003: $14,000. Proportion who borrowed: 40%. **Student employment:** During the 2003-2004 academic year, 15% of undergraduates worked on campus. Average per-year earnings: $4,000. **Cooperative education programs:** art, business, computer science, education, humanities, natural science, social/behavioral science, other. **Reserve Officers Training Corps (ROTC):** Army ROTC: Offered at cooperating institution (St. John's University); Navy ROTC: Offered at cooperating institution (St. John's University).

CUNY–York College

94-20 Guy R. Brewer Boulevard
Jamaica, NY 11451
Public; www.york.cuny.edu
Financial aid office: (718) 262-2230

■ **2004-2005 TUITION AND FEES:**
In state: $4,000

SAT I Score (25th/75th percentile): 753-930
2005 U.S. News College Ranking:
Comp. Colleges–Bachelor's (North), fourth tier
Acceptance Rate: 31%

....

Cooperative education programs: business, health professions, natural science.

Daemen College

4380 Main Street
Amherst, NY 14226-3592
Private; www.daemen.edu
Financial aid office: (716) 839-8254

■ **2004-2005 TUITION AND FEES:** $16,020
■ **ROOM AND BOARD:** $7,370

SAT I Score (25th/75th percentile): 910-1090
2005 U.S. News College Ranking:
Comp. Colleges–Bachelor's (North), third tier
Acceptance Rate: 70%

....

Other expenses: Estimated books and supplies: $800. Transportation: $700. Personal expenses: $800. **Financial aid:** Priority filing date for institution's financial aid form: March 15. In 2003-2004, 94% of undergraduates applied for financial aid. Of those, 86% were determined to have financial need; 27% had their need fully met. Average financial aid package (proportion receiving): $13,742 (86%). Average amount of gift aid, such as scholarships or grants (proportion receiving): $6,414 (79%). Average amount of self-help aid, such as work study or loans (proportion receiving): $4,929 (73%). Average need-based loan (excluding PLUS or other private loans): $4,061. Among students who received need-based aid, the average percentage of need met: 90%. Among students who received aid based on merit, the average award (and the proportion receiving): $5,849 (7%). The average athletic scholarship (and the proportion receiving): $6,570 (5%). Average amount of debt of borrowers graduating in 2003: $11,250. Proportion who borrowed: 66%. **Student employment:** During the 2003-2004 academic year, 6% of undergraduates worked on campus. Average per-year earnings: $800. **Cooperative education programs:** art, business, education, health professions, humanities, natural science, social/behavioral science. **Reserve Officers Training Corps (ROTC):** Army ROTC: Offered at cooperating institution (Canisius College).

Dominican College of Blauvelt

470 Western Highway
Orangeburg, NY 10962-1210
Private; www.dc.edu
Financial aid office: (845) 359-7800

■ **2004-2005 TUITION AND FEES:** $17,250
■ **ROOM AND BOARD:** $8,470

SAT I Score (25th/75th percentile): 780-980
2005 U.S. News College Ranking:
Comp. Colleges–Bachelor's (North), third tier
Acceptance Rate: 88%

....

Other expenses: Estimated books and supplies: $1,350. Personal expenses: $1,900. **Financial aid:** Priority filing date for institution's financial aid form: February 15. In 2003-2004, 97% of undergraduates applied for financial aid. Of those, 82% were determined to have financial need; 16% had their need fully met. Average financial aid package (proportion receiving): $10,957 (82%). Average amount of gift aid, such as scholarships or grants (proportion receiving): $7,875 (70%). Average amount of self-help aid, such as work study or loans (proportion receiving): $4,445 (70%). Average need-based loan (excluding PLUS or other private loans): $3,987. Among students who received need-based aid, the average percentage of need met: 68%. Among students who received aid based on merit, the average award (and the proportion receiving): $14,373 (11%). The average athletic scholarship (and the proportion receiving): $6,743 (1%). Average amount of debt of borrowers graduating in 2003: $30,625. Proportion who borrowed: 100%.

Dowling College

Idle Hour Boulevard
Oakdale Long Island, NY 11769
Private; www.dowling.edu
Financial aid office: (631) 244-3303

■ **2004-2005 TUITION AND FEES:** $15,330

SAT I Score (25th/75th percentile): 820-1090
2005 U.S. News College Ranking:
Universities–Master's (North), fourth tier
Acceptance Rate: 97%

....

Other expenses: Estimated books and supplies: $750. Transportation: $1,350. Personal expenses: $1,066. **Financial aid:** Priority filing date for institution's financial aid form: June 1. In 2003-2004, 92% of undergraduates applied for financial aid.

Of those, 71% were determined to have financial need; 19% had their need fully met. Average financial aid package (proportion receiving): $12,209 (69%). Average amount of gift aid, such as scholarships or grants (proportion receiving): $5,772 (63%). Average amount of self-help aid, such as work study or loans (proportion receiving): $6,120 (63%). Average need-based loan (excluding PLUS or other private loans): $5,500. Among students who received need-based aid, the average percentage of need met: 76%. Among students who received aid based on merit, the average award (and the proportion receiving): $4,918 (10%). The average athletic scholarship (and the proportion receiving): $10,768 (4%). Average amount of debt of borrowers graduating in 2003: $16,410. Proportion who borrowed: 85%. **Student employment:** During the 2003-2004 academic year, 0% of undergraduates worked on campus. Average per-year earnings: $0. **Cooperative education programs:** art, business, computer science, engineering, natural science, social/behavioral science, other. **Reserve Officers Training Corps (ROTC):** Army ROTC: Offered at cooperating institution (Hoftstra University); Air Force ROTC: Offered at cooperating institution (Manhatten College).

Elmira College

1 Park Place
Elmira, NY 14901
Private; www.elmira.edu
Financial aid office: (607) 735-1728

■ **2004-2005 TUITION AND FEES:** $27,030
■ **ROOM AND BOARD:** $8,330

SAT I Score (25th/75th percentile): 1030-1250
2005 U.S. News College Ranking:
Comp. Colleges–Bachelor's (North), 6
Acceptance Rate: 67%

....

Other expenses: Estimated books and supplies: $450. Personal expenses: $550. **Financial aid:** Priority filing date for institution's financial aid form: February 1. In 2003-2004, 85% of undergraduates applied for financial aid. Of those, 80% were determined to have financial need; 16% had their need fully met. Average financial aid package (proportion receiving): $20,384 (80%). Average amount of gift aid, such as scholarships or grants (proportion receiving): $15,038 (80%). Average amount of self-help aid, such as work study or loans (proportion receiving): $6,245 (69%). Average need-based loan (excluding PLUS or other private loans): $5,647. Among students who received need-based aid, the average percentage of need met:

85%. Among students who received aid based on merit, the average award (and the proportion receiving): $15,850 (18%). Average amount of debt of borrowers graduating in 2003: $19,480. Proportion who borrowed: 64%. **Student employment:** During the 2003-2004 academic year, 23% of undergraduates worked on campus. Average per-year earnings: $1,000. **Reserve Officers Training Corps (ROTC):** Army ROTC: Offered at cooperating institution (Cornell University); Air Force ROTC: Offered at cooperating institution (Cornell University).

Excelsior College

7 Columbia Circle
Albany, NY 12203
Private; www.excelsior.edu
Financial aid office: (518) 464-8500

- **2003-2004 TUITION AND FEES:** $6,110

2005 U.S. News College Ranking:
Liberal Arts Colleges, unranked

Financial aid: Priority filing date for institution's financial aid form: July 1.

Fordham University

113 W. 60th Street
New York, NY 10023
Private; www.fordham.edu
Financial aid office: (718) 817-3800

- **2004-2005 TUITION AND FEES:** $26,757
- **ROOM AND BOARD:** $10,248

SAT I Score (25th/75th percentile): 1090-1282
2005 U.S. News College Ranking:
National Universities, 70
Acceptance Rate: 54%

Other expenses: Estimated books and supplies: $725. Transportation: $705. Personal expenses: $1,375. **Financial aid:** Priority filing date for institution's financial aid form: February 1; deadline: February 1. In 2003-2004, 74% of undergraduates applied for financial aid. Of those, 66% were determined to have financial need; 23% had their need fully met. Average financial aid package (proportion receiving): $18,363 (66%). Average amount of gift aid, such as scholarships or grants (proportion receiving): $13,771 (62%). Average amount of self-help aid, such as work study or loans (proportion receiving): $5,163 (54%). Average need-based loan (excluding PLUS or other private loans): $4,262. Among

students who received need-based aid, the average percentage of need met: 77%. Among students who received aid based on merit, the average award (and the proportion receiving): $8,276 (8%). The average athletic scholarship (and the proportion receiving): $13,327 (2%). Average amount of debt of borrowers graduating in 2003: $16,590. Proportion who borrowed: 66%. **Reserve Officers Training Corps (ROTC):** Army ROTC: Offered on campus; Navy ROTC: Offered at cooperating institution (SUNY Maritime College); Air Force ROTC: Offered at cooperating institution (Manhattan College).

Hamilton College

198 College Hill Road
Clinton, NY 13323
Private; www.hamilton.edu
Financial aid office: (315) 859-4434

- **2004-2005 TUITION AND FEES:** $31,700
- **ROOM AND BOARD:** $7,825

SAT I Score (25th/75th percentile): 1240-1400
2005 U.S. News College Ranking:
Liberal Arts Colleges, 19
Acceptance Rate: 33%

Financial aid: Priority filing date for institution's financial aid form: February 1. In 2003-2004, 66% of undergraduates applied for financial aid. Of those, 58% were determined to have financial need; 100% had their need fully met. Average financial aid package (proportion receiving): $22,980 (58%). Average amount of gift aid, such as scholarships or grants (proportion receiving): $19,451 (55%). Average amount of self-help aid, such as work study or loans (proportion receiving): $4,952 (43%). Average need-based loan (excluding PLUS or other private loans): $3,952. Among students who received need-based aid, the average percentage of need met: 99%. Among students who received aid based on merit, the average award (and the proportion receiving): $9,665 (4%). Average amount of debt of borrowers graduating in 2003: $16,894. Proportion who borrowed: 77%. **Student employment:** During the 2003-2004 academic year, 33% of undergraduates worked on campus. Average per-year earnings: $1,000. **Reserve Officers Training Corps (ROTC):** Army ROTC: Offered at cooperating institution (Syracuse University); Air Force ROTC: Offered at cooperating institution (Syracuse University).

Hartwick College

1 Hartwick Drive
Oneonta, NY 13820-4020
Private; www.hartwick.edu
Financial aid office: (607) 431-4130

- **2004-2005 TUITION AND FEES:** $26,260
- **ROOM AND BOARD:** $7,280

SAT I Score (25th/75th percentile): 1030-1210
2005 U.S. News College Ranking:
Liberal Arts Colleges, third tier
Acceptance Rate: 88%

Other expenses: Estimated books and supplies: $700. Transportation: $400. Personal expenses: $300. **Financial aid:** Priority filing date for institution's financial aid form: February 15. In 2003-2004, 88% of undergraduates applied for financial aid. Of those, 84% were determined to have financial need; 32% had their need fully met. Average financial aid package (proportion receiving): $22,776 (84%). Average amount of gift aid, such as scholarships or grants (proportion receiving): $14,158 (79%). Average amount of self-help aid, such as work study or loans (proportion receiving): $7,754 (60%). Average need-based loan (excluding PLUS or other private loans): $4,627. Among students who received need-based aid, the average percentage of need met: 77%. Among students who received aid based on merit, the average award (and the proportion receiving): $11,475 (8%). The average athletic scholarship (and the proportion receiving): $19,915 (2%). Average amount of debt of borrowers graduating in 2003: $20,100. Proportion who borrowed: 72%. **Student employment:** During the 2003-2004 academic year, 80% of undergraduates worked on campus. Average per-year earnings: $1,400. **Reserve Officers Training Corps (ROTC):** Army ROTC: Offered at cooperating institution (RPI); Air Force ROTC: Offered at cooperating institution (Siena College).

Hilbert College

5200 S. Park Avenue
Hamburg, NY 14075-1597
Private; www.hilbert.edu
Financial aid office: (716) 649-7900

- **2004-2005 TUITION AND FEES:** $14,300
- **ROOM AND BOARD:** $5,380

SAT I Score (25th/75th percentile): 840-1020
2005 U.S. News College Ranking:
Comp. Colleges–Bachelor's (North), fourth tier
Acceptance Rate: 94%

Other expenses: Estimated books and supplies: $700. Transportation: $700. Personal expenses: $930. **Financial aid:** Priority filing date for institution's financial aid form: April 1. In 2003-2004, 84% of undergraduates applied for financial aid. Of those, 75% were determined to have financial need; 27% had their need fully met. Average financial aid package (proportion receiving): $9,851 (75%). Average amount of gift aid, such as scholarships or grants (proportion receiving): $6,204 (73%). Average amount of self-help aid, such as work study or loans (proportion receiving): $4,161 (68%). Average need-based loan (excluding PLUS or other private loans): $4,001. Among students who received need-based aid, the average percentage of need met: 78%. Among students who received aid based on merit, the average award (and the proportion receiving): $7,870 (12%). The average athletic scholarship (and the proportion receiving): $0 (0%). Average amount of debt of borrowers graduating in 2003: $12,532. Proportion who borrowed: 61%. **Reserve Officers Training Corps (ROTC):** Army ROTC: Offered at cooperating institution (Canisius College).

Hobart and William Smith Colleges

337 Pulteney Street
Geneva, NY 14456
Private; www.hws.edu
Financial aid office: (315) 781-3315

■ **2004-2005 TUITION AND FEES:** $30,643
■ **ROOM AND BOARD:** $7,987

SAT I Score (25th/75th percentile): 1080-1250
2005 U.S. News College Ranking:
Liberal Arts Colleges, 68
Acceptance Rate: 62%

Other expenses: Estimated books and supplies: $850. Transportation: $210. Personal expenses: $600. **Financial aid:** Priority filing date for institution's financial aid form: February 15; deadline: March 15. In 2003-2004, 69% of undergraduates applied for financial aid. Of those, 61% were determined to have financial need; 77% had their need fully met. Average financial aid package (proportion receiving): $22,933 (61%). Average amount of gift aid, such as scholarships or grants (proportion

receiving): $18,765 (61%). Average amount of self-help aid, such as work study or loans (proportion receiving): $4,872 (54%). Average need-based loan (excluding PLUS or other private loans): $3,817. Among students who received need-based aid, the average percentage of need met: 90%. Among students who received aid based on merit, the average award (and the proportion receiving): $16,640 (15%). The average athletic scholarship (and the proportion receiving): $0 (0%). Average amount of debt of borrowers graduating in 2003: $20,508. Proportion who borrowed: 70%. **Student employment:** During the 2003-2004 academic year, 57% of undergraduates worked on campus. Average per-year earnings: $1,800.

Hofstra University

100 Hofstra University
Hempstead, NY 11549
Private; www.hofstra.edu
Financial aid office: (516) 463-6680

■ **2004-2005 TUITION AND FEES:** $20,012
■ **ROOM AND BOARD:** $9,000

SAT I Score (25th/75th percentile): 1030-1220
2005 U.S. News College Ranking:
National Universities, third tier
Acceptance Rate: 68%

Financial aid: Priority filing date for institution's financial aid form: February 15. In 2003-2004, 71% of undergraduates applied for financial aid. Of those, 57% were determined to have financial need; 32% had their need fully met. Average financial aid package (proportion receiving): $10,649 (56%). Average amount of gift aid, such as scholarships or grants (proportion receiving): $6,897 (35%). Average amount of self-help aid, such as work study or loans (proportion receiving): $4,885 (51%). Average need-based loan (excluding PLUS or other private loans): $4,105. Among students who received aid based on merit, the average award (and the proportion receiving): $5,400 (7%). The average athletic scholarship (and the proportion receiving): $18,762 (3%). Average amount of debt of borrowers graduating in 2003: $17,763. Proportion who borrowed: 46%. **Student employment:** During the 2003-2004 academic year, 46% of undergraduates worked on campus. Average per-year earnings: $2,500. **Reserve Officers Training Corps (ROTC):** Army ROTC: Offered on campus.

Houghton College

1 Willard Avenue
Houghton, NY 14744
Private; www.houghton.edu
Financial aid office: (585) 567-9328

■ **2004-2005 TUITION AND FEES:** $18,660
■ **ROOM AND BOARD:** $6,320

SAT I Score (25th/75th percentile): 1080-1290
2005 U.S. News College Ranking:
Liberal Arts Colleges, third tier
Acceptance Rate: 84%

Other expenses: Estimated books and supplies: $750. Transportation: $500. Personal expenses: $1,500. **Financial aid:** Priority filing date for institution's financial aid form: March 1. In 2003-2004, 79% of undergraduates applied for financial aid. Of those, 73% were determined to have financial need; 29% had their need fully met. Average financial aid package (proportion receiving): $14,126 (73%). Average amount of gift aid, such as scholarships or grants (proportion receiving): $9,595 (70%). Average amount of self-help aid, such as work study or loans (proportion receiving): $5,434 (66%). Average need-based loan (excluding PLUS or other private loans): $4,628. Among students who received need-based aid, the average percentage of need met: 72%. Among students who received aid based on merit, the average award (and the proportion receiving): $7,293 (17%). Average amount of debt of borrowers graduating in 2003: $20,768. Proportion who borrowed: 70%. **Student employment:** During the 2003-2004 academic year, 48% of undergraduates worked on campus. Average per-year earnings: $1,500. **Reserve Officers Training Corps (ROTC):** Army ROTC: Offered at cooperating institution (St. Bonaventure University).

Iona College

715 North Avenue
New Rochelle, NY 10801
Private; www.iona.edu/info
Financial aid office: (914) 633-2497

■ **2004-2005 TUITION AND FEES:** $19,530
■ **ROOM AND BOARD:** $9,698

SAT I Score (25th/75th percentile): 1040-1230
2005 U.S. News College Ranking:
Universities–Master's (North), 68
Acceptance Rate: 64%

Other expenses: Estimated books and supplies: $700. Transportation: $600. Personal expenses: $1,250. **Financial aid:** Priority filing date for institution's financial aid form: March 15; deadline: April 15. In 2003-2004, 93% of undergraduates applied for financial aid. Of those, 75% were determined to have financial need; 20% had their need fully met. Average financial aid package (proportion receiving): $13,144 (74%). Average amount of gift aid, such as scholarships or grants (proportion receiving): $2,925 (35%). Average amount of self-help aid, such as work study or loans (proportion receiving): $3,740 (57%). Average need-based loan (excluding PLUS or other private loans): $3,116. Among students who received need-based aid, the average percentage of need met: 27%. Among students who received aid based on merit, the average award (and the proportion receiving): $9,051 (17%). The average athletic scholarship (and the proportion receiving): $8,415 (7%). Average amount of debt of borrowers graduating in 2003: $18,646. Proportion who borrowed: 76%. **Student employment:** During the 2003-2004 academic year, 12% of undergraduates worked on campus. Average per-year earnings: $1,421. **Reserve Officers Training Corps (ROTC):** Army ROTC: Offered at cooperating institution (Fordham University); Air Force ROTC: Offered at cooperating institution (Manhattan College).

Ithaca College

100 Job Hall
Ithaca, NY 14850-7020
Private; www.ithaca.edu
Financial aid office: (607) 274-3131

■ **2004-2005 TUITION AND FEES:** $23,690
■ **ROOM AND BOARD:** $9,704

SAT I Score (25th/75th percentile): 1090-1280
2005 U.S. News College Ranking:
Universities–Master's (North), 8
Acceptance Rate: 63%

Financial aid: Priority filing date for institution's financial aid form: February 1. In 2003-2004, 77% of undergraduates applied for financial aid. Of those, 69% were determined to have financial need; 45% had their need fully met. Average financial aid package (proportion receiving): $20,381 (69%). Average amount of gift aid, such as scholarships or grants (proportion receiving): $12,903 (65%). Average amount of self-help aid, such as work study or loans (proportion receiving): $6,912 (65%). Average need-based loan (excluding PLUS or other pri-

vate loans): $5,275. Among students who received need-based aid, the average percentage of need met: 89%. Among students who received aid based on merit, the average award (and the proportion receiving): $8,086 (9%). **Student employment:** During the 2003-2004 academic year, 48% of undergraduates worked on campus. Average per-year earnings: $2,200. **Reserve Officers Training Corps (ROTC):** Army ROTC: Offered at cooperating institution (Cornell University); Air Force ROTC: Offered at cooperating institution (Cornell University).

Juilliard School

60 Lincoln Center Plaza
New York, NY 10023-6588
Private; www.juilliard.edu
Financial aid office: (212) 799-5000

■ **2004-2005 TUITION AND FEES:** $23,350
■ **ROOM AND BOARD:** $9,030

2005 U.S. News College Ranking:
Unranked Specialty School–Fine Arts
Acceptance Rate: 7%

Financial aid: Priority filing date for institution's financial aid form: March 1; deadline: April 1. In 2003-2004, 94% of undergraduates applied for financial aid. Of those, 77% were determined to have financial need; 22% had their need fully met. Average financial aid package (proportion receiving): $21,298 (77%). Average amount of gift aid, such as scholarships or grants (proportion receiving): $15,760 (76%). Average amount of self-help aid, such as work study or loans (proportion receiving): $5,856 (76%). Average need-based loan (excluding PLUS or other private loans): $5,473. Among students who received need-based aid, the average percentage of need met: 83%. Among students who received aid based on merit, the average award (and the proportion receiving): $4,698 (12%). The average athletic scholarship (and the proportion receiving): $0 (0%). Average amount of debt of borrowers graduating in 2003: $21,447. Proportion who borrowed: 68%.

Keuka College

Keuka Park, NY 14478
Private; www.keuka.edu
Financial aid office: (315) 279-5232

■ **2004-2005 TUITION AND FEES:** $17,080
■ **ROOM AND BOARD:** $7,880

SAT I Score (25th/75th percentile): 895-1080
2005 U.S. News College Ranking:
Comp. Colleges–Bachelor's (North), 26
Acceptance Rate: 82%

Other expenses: Estimated books and supplies: $800. Transportation: $750. Personal expenses: $1,000. **Financial aid:** Priority filing date for institution's financial aid form: March 15. In 2003-2004, 94% of undergraduates applied for financial aid. Of those, 89% were determined to have financial need; 23% had their need fully met. Average financial aid package (proportion receiving): $14,560 (89%). Average amount of gift aid, such as scholarships or grants (proportion receiving): $9,413 (87%). Average amount of self-help aid, such as work study or loans (proportion receiving): $5,792 (82%). Average need-based loan (excluding PLUS or other private loans): $5,230. Among students who received need-based aid, the average percentage of need met: 80%. Among students who received aid based on merit, the average award (and the proportion receiving): $11,505 (6%). Average amount of debt of borrowers graduating in 2003: $18,645. Proportion who borrowed: 85%. **Student employment:** During the 2003-2004 academic year, 42% of undergraduates worked on campus. Average per-year earnings: $5.

Le Moyne College

1419 Salt Springs Road
Syracuse, NY 13214-1399
Private; www.lemoyne.edu
Financial aid office: (315) 445-4400

■ **2004-2005 TUITION AND FEES:** $20,150
■ **ROOM AND BOARD:** $7,890

SAT I Score (25th/75th percentile): 1020-1200
2005 U.S. News College Ranking:
Universities–Master's (North), 22
Acceptance Rate: 72%

Other expenses: Estimated books and supplies: $550. Transportation: $200. Personal expenses: $950. **Financial aid:** Priority filing date for institution's financial aid form: February 1. In 2003-2004, 90% of undergraduates applied for financial aid. Of those, 83% were determined to have financial need; 43% had their need fully met. Average financial aid package (proportion receiving): $17,840 (83%). Average amount of gift aid, such as scholarships or grants (proportion receiving): $13,980 (80%). Average amount of self-help aid, such as work study or loans (proportion receiving): $4,780 (73%).

Average need-based loan (excluding PLUS or other private loans): $4,358. Among students who received need-based aid, the average percentage of need met: 85%. Among students who received aid based on merit, the average award (and the proportion receiving): $8,411 (9%). The average athletic scholarship (and the proportion receiving): $6,898 (7%). Average amount of debt of borrowers graduating in 2003: $19,490. Proportion who borrowed: 86%. **Student employment:** During the 2003-2004 academic year, 18% of undergraduates worked on campus. Average per-year earnings: $700. **Reserve Officers Training Corps (ROTC):** Army ROTC: Offered at cooperating institution (Syracuse Unversity); Air Force ROTC: Offered at cooperating institution (Syracuse University).

Long Island University– Brooklyn

1 University Plaza
Brooklyn, NY 11201
Private; www.brooklyn.liu.edu
Financial aid office: (718) 488-1037

■ **2004-2005 TUITION AND FEES:** $18,830
■ **ROOM AND BOARD:** $8,100

SAT I Score (25th/75th percentile): 820-1100
2005 U.S. News College Ranking:
Universities–Master's (North), fourth tier
Acceptance Rate: 58%

Other expenses: Estimated books and supplies: $1,500. Transportation: $500. Personal expenses: $800. **Financial aid:** In 2003-2004, 86% of undergraduates applied for financial aid. Of those, 83% were determined to have financial need; 52% had their need fully met. Average financial aid package (proportion receiving): $13,159 (81%). Average amount of gift aid, such as scholarships or grants (proportion receiving): $8,213 (80%). Average amount of self-help aid, such as work study or loans (proportion receiving): $8,625 (75%). Average need-based loan (excluding PLUS or other private loans): $4,105. Among students who received need-based aid, the average percentage of need met: 48%. Among students who received aid based on merit, the average award (and the proportion receiving): $14,105 (2%). The average athletic scholarship (and the proportion receiving): $15,718 (4%). Average amount of debt of borrowers graduating in 2003: $20,921. Proportion who borrowed: 87%. **Student employment:** During the 2003-2004 academic year, 30% of undergraduates worked on campus. Average per-year earnings: $4,000.

Long Island University– C.W. Post Campus

720 Northern Boulevard
Brookville, NY 11548-1300
Private; www.liu.edu
Financial aid office: (516) 299-2338

■ **2004-2005 TUITION AND FEES:** $21,890
■ **ROOM AND BOARD:** $8,240

SAT I Score (25th/75th percentile): 880-1090
2005 U.S. News College Ranking:
Universities–Master's (North), third tier
Acceptance Rate: 76%

Financial aid: Priority filing date for institution's financial aid form: March 1; deadline: March 1. In 2003-2004, 86% of undergraduates applied for financial aid. Of those, 73% were determined to have financial need; Average financial aid package (proportion receiving): $8,791 (73%). Average amount of gift aid, such as scholarships or grants (proportion receiving): $4,400 (62%). Average amount of self-help aid, such as work study or loans (proportion receiving): $6,500 (73%). Average need-based loan (excluding PLUS or other private loans): $4,000. Among students who received need-based aid, the average percentage of need met: 75%. Among students who received aid based on merit, the average award (and the proportion receiving): $7,000 (25%). The average athletic scholarship (and the proportion receiving): $6,500 (4%). **Student employment:** During the 2003-2004 academic year, 14% of undergraduates worked on campus. **Cooperative education programs:** art, business, computer science, education, engineering, health professions, humanities, natural science, social/behavioral science, technologies. **Reserve Officers Training Corps (ROTC):** Army ROTC: Offered at cooperating institution (Hofstra University); Air Force ROTC: Offered at cooperating institution (Manhattan College).

Long Island University– Southampton College

239 Montauk Highway
Southampton, NY 11968
Private; www.southampton.liu.edu
Financial aid office: (631) 287-8321

■ **2004-2005 TUITION AND FEES:** $21,970
■ **ROOM AND BOARD:** $9,250

SAT I Score (25th/75th percentile): 1052
2005 U.S. News College Ranking:
Liberal Arts Colleges, fourth tier
Acceptance Rate: 63%

Financial aid: Priority filing date for institution's financial aid form: March 1; deadline: April 1. **Student employment:** During the 2003-2004 academic year, 40% of undergraduates worked on campus. Average per-year earnings: $1,250. **Cooperative education programs:** art, business, computer science, education, humanities, natural science, social/behavioral science.

Manhattan College

Manhattan College Parkway
Riverdale, NY 10471
Private; www.manhattan.edu
Financial aid office: (718) 862-7100

■ **2004-2005 TUITION AND FEES:** $20,635
■ **ROOM AND BOARD:** $8,400

SAT I Score (25th/75th percentile): 1010-1200
2005 U.S. News College Ranking:
Universities–Master's (North), 15
Acceptance Rate: 53%

Other expenses: Estimated books and supplies: $1,000. Transportation: $600. Personal expenses: $1,000. **Financial aid:** Priority filing date for institution's financial aid form: March 1. In 2003-2004, 79% of undergraduates applied for financial aid. Of those, 69% were determined to have financial need; 3% had their need fully met. Average financial aid package (proportion receiving): $14,185 (68%). Average amount of gift aid, such as scholarships or grants (proportion receiving): $5,395 (63%). Average amount of self-help aid, such as work study or loans (proportion receiving): $4,562 (61%). Average need-based loan (excluding PLUS or other private loans): $3,582. Among students who received need-based aid, the average percentage of need met: 70%. Among students who received aid based on merit, the average award (and the proportion receiving): $7,184 (12%). The average athletic scholarship (and the proportion receiving): $13,069 (3%). Average amount of debt of borrowers graduating in 2003: $15,715. Proportion who borrowed: 79%. **Student employment:** During the 2003-2004 academic year, 23% of undergraduates worked on campus. Average per-year earnings: $1,518. **Cooperative education programs:** art, business, computer science, education, engineering, health professions, humanities, natural science, social/behavioral science, technologies. **Reserve**

Officers Training Corps (ROTC): Army ROTC: Offered at cooperating institution (Fordham University); Air Force ROTC: Offered on campus.

Manhattan School of Music

120 Claremont Avenue
New York, NY 10027
Private; www.msmnyc.edu
Financial aid office: (212) 749-2802

■ **2004-2005 TUITION AND FEES:** $24,960
■ **ROOM AND BOARD:** $12,000

2005 U.S. News College Ranking:
Unranked Specialty School–Fine Arts
Acceptance Rate: 32%

Other expenses: Estimated books and supplies: $800. Transportation: $1,500. Personal expenses: $1,200. **Financial aid:** Priority filing date for institution's financial aid form: March 1; deadline: March 1. In 2003-2004, 69% of undergraduates applied for financial aid. Of those, 60% were determined to have financial need; 6% had their need fully met. Average financial aid package (proportion receiving): $12,795 (60%). Average amount of gift aid, such as scholarships or grants (proportion receiving): $11,105 (49%). Average amount of self-help aid, such as work study or loans (proportion receiving): $4,480 (51%). Average need-based loan (excluding PLUS or other private loans): $3,988. Among students who received need-based aid, the average percentage of need met: 45%. Among students who received aid based on merit, the average award (and the proportion receiving): $13,746 (26%). The average athletic scholarship (and the proportion receiving): $0 (0%). Average amount of debt of borrowers graduating in 2003: $11,250. Proportion who borrowed: 48%. **Student employment:** During the 2003-2004 academic year, 10% of undergraduates worked on campus. Average per-year earnings: $1,200.

Manhattanville College

2900 Purchase Street
Purchase, NY 10577
Private; www.mville.edu
Financial aid office: (914) 323-5357

■ **2004-2005 TUITION AND FEES:** $24,570
■ **ROOM AND BOARD:** $10,130

SAT I Score (25th/75th percentile): 970-1160
2005 U.S. News College Ranking:
Universities–Master's (North), 42
Acceptance Rate: 55%

Other expenses: Estimated books and supplies: $800. Transportation: $750. Personal expenses: $800. **Financial aid:** Priority filing date for institution's financial aid form: March 1; deadline: March 1. In 2003-2004, 72% of undergraduates applied for financial aid. Of those, 65% were determined to have financial need; 21% had their need fully met. Average financial aid package (proportion receiving): $19,872 (65%). Average amount of gift aid, such as scholarships or grants (proportion receiving): $9,137 (58%). Average amount of self-help aid, such as work study or loans (proportion receiving): $4,689 (55%). Average need-based loan (excluding PLUS or other private loans): $4,133. Among students who received need-based aid, the average percentage of need met: 80%. Among students who received aid based on merit, the average award (and the proportion receiving): $8,271 (22%). The average athletic scholarship (and the proportion receiving): $0 (0%). Average amount of debt of borrowers graduating in 2003: $21,160. Proportion who borrowed: 75%. **Student employment:** During the 2003-2004 academic year, 25% of undergraduates worked on campus. Average per-year earnings: $1,250. **Cooperative education programs:** computer science, health professions, social/behavioral science.

Marist College

3399 North Road
Poughkeepsie, NY 12601
Private; www.marist.edu
Financial aid office: (845) 575-3230

■ **2004-2005 TUITION AND FEES:** $19,978
■ **ROOM AND BOARD:** $8,948

SAT I Score (25th/75th percentile): 1130-1280
2005 U.S. News College Ranking:
Universities–Master's (North), 18
Acceptance Rate: 50%

Other expenses: Estimated books and supplies: $1,120. Transportation: $1,300. Personal expenses: $600. **Financial aid:** Priority filing date for institution's financial aid form: February 15; deadline: February 15. In 2003-2004, 79% of undergraduates applied for financial aid. Of those, 65% were determined to have financial need; 18% had their need fully met. Average financial aid package (proportion

receiving): $12,126 (65%). Average amount of gift aid, such as scholarships or grants (proportion receiving): $6,342 (60%). Average amount of self-help aid, such as work study or loans (proportion receiving): $5,510 (54%). Average need-based loan (excluding PLUS or other private loans): $4,560. Among students who received need-based aid, the average percentage of need met: 70%. Among students who received aid based on merit, the average award (and the proportion receiving): $5,272 (6%). The average athletic scholarship (and the proportion receiving): $9,308 (5%). Average amount of debt of borrowers graduating in 2003: $20,124. Proportion who borrowed: 66%. **Student employment:** During the 2003-2004 academic year, 13% of undergraduates worked on campus. Average per-year earnings: $2,000.

Marymount College–Tarrytown

100 Marymount Avenue
Tarrytown, NY 10591-3796
Private; www.marymt.edu
Financial aid office: (914) 332-8345

■ **2004-2005 TUITION AND FEES:** $19,491
■ **ROOM AND BOARD:** $9,760

SAT I Score (25th/75th percentile): 880-1090
2005 U.S. News College Ranking:
Comp. Colleges–Bachelor's (North), 19
Acceptance Rate: 82%

Other expenses: Estimated books and supplies: $750. Transportation: $1,422. Personal expenses: $1,265. **Financial aid:** Priority filing date for institution's financial aid form: March 1. In 2003-2004, 77% of undergraduates applied for financial aid. Of those, 69% were determined to have financial need; 16% had their need fully met. Average financial aid package (proportion receiving): $15,968 (69%). Average amount of gift aid, such as scholarships or grants (proportion receiving): $10,406 (67%). Average amount of self-help aid, such as work study or loans (proportion receiving): $6,323 (54%). Average need-based loan (excluding PLUS or other private loans): $5,752. Among students who received need-based aid, the average percentage of need met: 71%. Among students who received aid based on merit, the average award (and the proportion receiving): $7,242 (25%). The average athletic scholarship (and the proportion receiving): $0 (0%). Average amount of debt of borrowers graduating in 2003: $11,006. Proportion who borrowed: 85%.

Marymount Manhattan College

221 E. 71st Street
New York, NY 10021
Private; marymount.mmm.edu/home.htm
Financial aid office: (212) 517-0480

■ **2004-2005 TUITION AND FEES:** $17,352
■ **ROOM AND BOARD:** $12,366

SAT I Score (25th/75th percentile): 890-1160
2005 U.S. News College Ranking:
Liberal Arts Colleges, fourth tier
Acceptance Rate: 80%

Other expenses: Estimated books and supplies: $1,000. Transportation: $600. Personal expenses: $1,500. **Financial aid:** Priority filing date for institution's financial aid form: March 15. In 2003-2004, 88% of undergraduates applied for financial aid. Of those, 71% were determined to have financial need; Average financial aid package (proportion receiving): $8,695 (71%). Average amount of gift aid, such as scholarships or grants (proportion receiving): $7,425 (71%). Average amount of self-help aid, such as work study or loans (proportion receiving): $5,010 (61%). Average need-based loan (excluding PLUS or other private loans): $4,581. Among students who received need-based aid, the average percentage of need met: 56%. Among students who received aid based on merit, the average award (and the proportion receiving): $3,802 (13%). The average athletic scholarship (and the proportion receiving): $0 (0%). Average amount of debt of borrowers graduating in 2003: $21,000. Proportion who borrowed: 82%. **Student employment:** During the 2003-2004 academic year, 17% of undergraduates worked on campus. Average per-year earnings: $1,500.

Medaille College

18 Agassiz Circle
Buffalo, NY 14214
Private; www.medaille.edu
Financial aid office: (716) 884-3281

■ **2004-2005 TUITION AND FEES:** $14,320
■ **ROOM AND BOARD:** $6,800

SAT I Score (25th/75th percentile): 830-1020
2005 U.S. News College Ranking:
Comp. Colleges–Bachelor's (North), fourth tier
Acceptance Rate: 68%

Other expenses: Estimated books and supplies: $930. Transportation: $1,500. Personal expenses: $1,100. **Financial aid:** Priority filing date for institution's financial aid form: April 1. In 2003-2004, 88% of undergraduates applied for financial aid. Of those, 82% were determined to have financial need; 10% had their need fully met. Average financial aid package (proportion receiving): $10,000 (82%). Average amount of gift aid, such as scholarships or grants (proportion receiving): $4,200 (67%). Average amount of self-help aid, such as work study or loans (proportion receiving): $4,100 (73%). Average need-based loan (excluding PLUS or other private loans): $4,100. Among students who received need-based aid, the average percentage of need met: 75%. Among students who received aid based on merit, the average award (and the proportion receiving): $1,000 (2%). The average athletic scholarship (and the proportion receiving): $0 (0%). Average amount of debt of borrowers graduating in 2003: $18,000. Proportion who borrowed: 85%. **Student employment:** During the 2003-2004 academic year, 1% of undergraduates worked on campus. Average per-year earnings: $1,800. **Reserve Officers Training Corps (ROTC):** Army ROTC: Offered at cooperating institution (Canisius College).

Mercy College

555 Broadway
Dobbs Ferry, NY 10522
Private; www.mercy.edu
Financial aid office: (914) 378-3421

■ **2004-2005 TUITION AND FEES:** $12,430
■ **ROOM AND BOARD:** $8,755

SAT I Score (25th/75th percentile): 1000
2005 U.S. News College Ranking:
Universities–Master's (North), fourth tier

Other expenses: Estimated books and supplies: $1,100. **Financial aid:** Average amount of debt of borrowers graduating in 2003: $8,176. Proportion who borrowed: 81%. **Student employment:** During the 2003-2004 academic year, 40% of undergraduates worked on campus. Average per-year earnings: $13,000. **Cooperative education programs:** business, education, health professions, natural science, social/behavioral science, technologies. **Reserve Officers Training Corps (ROTC):** Army ROTC: Offered on campus; Navy ROTC: Offered on campus; Air Force ROTC: Offered on campus.

Molloy College

1000 Hempstead Avenue, PO Box 5002
Rockville Centre, NY 11571
Private; www.molloy.edu
Financial aid office: (516) 256-2217

■ **2004-2005 TUITION AND FEES:** $15,700

SAT I Score (25th/75th percentile): 908-1093
2005 U.S. News College Ranking:
Universities–Master's (North), third tier
Acceptance Rate: 67%

Financial aid: Priority filing date for institution's financial aid form: May 1; deadline: July 1. In 2003-2004, 71% of undergraduates applied for financial aid. Of those, 61% were determined to have financial need; 16% had their need fully met. Average financial aid package (proportion receiving): $9,453 (61%). Average amount of gift aid, such as scholarships or grants (proportion receiving): $5,593 (52%). Average amount of self-help aid, such as work study or loans (proportion receiving): $4,997 (56%). Average need-based loan (excluding PLUS or other private loans): $4,323. Among students who received need-based aid, the average percentage of need met: 58%. Among students who received aid based on merit, the average award (and the proportion receiving): $11,889 (11%). The average athletic scholarship (and the proportion receiving): $5,673 (2%). Average amount of debt of borrowers graduating in 2003: $17,500. Proportion who borrowed: 85%. **Student employment:** During the 2003-2004 academic year, 2% of undergraduates worked on campus. Average per-year earnings: $7,200. **Reserve Officers Training Corps (ROTC):** Army ROTC: Offered at cooperating institution (St. John's University; Hofstra University); Navy ROTC: Offered at cooperating institution (SUNY Maritime (Nursing majors only)); Air Force ROTC: Offered at cooperating institution (New York Institute of Technology).

Mount St. Mary College

330 Powell Avenue
Newburgh, NY 12550
Private; www.msmc.edu
Financial aid office: (845) 569-3298

■ **2004-2005 TUITION AND FEES:** $15,690
■ **ROOM AND BOARD:** $7,640

SAT I Score (25th/75th percentile): 920-1100
2005 U.S. News College Ranking:
Universities–Master's (North), third tier
Acceptance Rate: 82%

Financial aid: Priority filing date for institution's financial aid form: March 15. In 2003-2004, 88% of undergraduates applied for financial aid. Of those, 75% were determined to have financial need; 26% had their need fully met. Average financial aid package (proportion receiving): $12,303 (73%). Average amount of gift aid, such as scholarships or grants (proportion receiving): $5,065 (59%). Average amount of self-help aid, such as work study or loans (proportion receiving): $4,250 (60%). Average need-based loan (excluding PLUS or other private loans): $4,017. Among students who received need-based aid, the average percentage of need met: 71%. Among students who received aid based on merit, the average award (and the proportion receiving): $0 (0%). The average athletic scholarship (and the proportion receiving): $0 (0%). Average amount of debt of borrowers graduating in 2003: $20,000. Proportion who borrowed: 70%. Student employment: During the 2003-2004 academic year, 12% of undergraduates worked on campus. Average per-year earnings: $1,300. Cooperative education programs: business, computer science, education, health professions, humanities, natural science, social/behavioral science, technologies.

Nazareth College of Rochester

4245 East Avenue
Rochester, NY 14618-3790
Private; www.naz.edu
Financial aid office: (585) 389-2310

■ 2004-2005 TUITION AND FEES: $18,676
■ ROOM AND BOARD: $7,840

SAT I Score (25th/75th percentile): 1025-1225
2005 U.S. News College Ranking:
Universities–Master's (North), 27
Acceptance Rate: 83%

Other expenses: Estimated books and supplies: $750. Transportation: $150. Personal expenses: $1,000. Financial aid: Priority filing date for institution's financial aid form: February 15; deadline: May 1. In 2003-2004, 90% of undergraduates applied for financial aid. Of those, 81% were determined to have financial need; Average financial aid package (proportion receiving): $14,497 (81%). Average amount of gift aid, such as scholarships or grants (propor-

tion receiving): $9,354 (80%). Average amount of self-help aid, such as work study or loans (proportion receiving): $5,377 (72%). Average need-based loan (excluding PLUS or other private loans): $4,670. Among students who received need-based aid, the average percentage of need met: 80%. Among students who received aid based on merit, the average award (and the proportion receiving): $6,046 (13%). Average amount of debt of borrowers graduating in 2003: $21,307. Proportion who borrowed: 83%. Student employment: During the 2003-2004 academic year, 16% of undergraduates worked on campus. Average per-year earnings: $1,400. Reserve Officers Training Corps (ROTC): Army ROTC: Offered at cooperating institution (Rochester Institute of Technology); Air Force ROTC: Offered at cooperating institution (Rochester Institute of Technology).

New School University

66 W. 12th Street
New York, NY 10011
Private; www.newschool.edu
Financial aid office: (212) 229-8930

■ 2004-2005 TUITION AND FEES: $25,470
■ ROOM AND BOARD: $10,810

SAT I Score (25th/75th percentile): 1080-1280
2005 U.S. News College Ranking:
National Universities, 120
Acceptance Rate: 50%

Other expenses: Estimated books and supplies: $918. Transportation: $744. Personal expenses: $1,742. Financial aid: Priority filing date for institution's financial aid form: March 1. In 2003-2004, 62% of undergraduates applied for financial aid. Of those, 57% were determined to have financial need; 6% had their need fully met. Average financial aid package (proportion receiving): $12,350 (57%). Average amount of gift aid, such as scholarships or grants (proportion receiving): $9,412 (54%). Average amount of self-help aid, such as work study or loans (proportion receiving): $4,641 (39%). Average need-based loan (excluding PLUS or other private loans): $4,355. Among students who received need-based aid, the average percentage of need met: 63%. Among students who received aid based on merit, the average award (and the proportion receiving): $5,428 (5%). The average athletic scholarship (and the proportion receiving): $0 (0%). Average amount of debt of borrowers graduating in 2003: $22,611. Proportion who borrowed: 56%.

New York Institute of Technology

PO Box 8000
Old Westbury, NY 11568-8000
Private; www.nyit.edu
Financial aid office: (516) 686-7680

■ 2004-2005 TUITION AND FEES: $18,190
■ ROOM AND BOARD: $7,380

SAT I Score (25th/75th percentile): 980-1210
2005 U.S. News College Ranking:
Universities–Master's (North), 68
Acceptance Rate: 76%

Other expenses: Estimated books and supplies: $800. Transportation: $500. Personal expenses: $2,100. Financial aid: Priority filing date for institution's financial aid form: March 1. In 2003-2004, 83% of undergraduates applied for financial aid. Of those, 72% were determined to have financial need; 89% had their need fully met. Average financial aid package (proportion receiving): $15,327 (71%). Average amount of gift aid, such as scholarships or grants (proportion receiving): $6,284 (34%). Average amount of self-help aid, such as work study or loans (proportion receiving): $5,444 (66%). Average need-based loan (excluding PLUS or other private loans): $4,530. Among students who received aid based on merit, the average award (and the proportion receiving): $6,095 (12%). The average athletic scholarship (and the proportion receiving): $14,815 (4%). Average amount of debt of borrowers graduating in 2003: $17,125. Student employment: During the 2003-2004 academic year, 13% of undergraduates worked on campus. Average per-year earnings: $2,200. Reserve Officers Training Corps (ROTC): Army ROTC: Offered on campus; Air Force ROTC: Offered on campus.

New York University

70 Washington Square S
New York, NY 10012
Private; www.nyu.edu
Financial aid office: (212) 998-4444

■ 2004-2005 TUITION AND FEES: $30,095
■ ROOM AND BOARD: $11,390

SAT I Score (25th/75th percentile): 1210-1410
2005 U.S. News College Ranking:
National Universities, 32
Acceptance Rate: 32%

Other expenses: Estimated books and supplies: $700. Personal expenses: $1,000. **Financial aid:** In 2003-2004, 65% of undergraduates applied for financial aid. Of those, 56% were determined to have financial need; Average financial aid package (proportion receiving): $18,686 (56%). Average amount of gift aid, such as scholarships or grants (proportion receiving): $12,371 (52%). Average amount of self-help aid, such as work study or loans (proportion receiving): $7,791 (50%). Average need-based loan (excluding PLUS or other private loans): $5,068. Among students who received need-based aid, the average percentage of need met: 67%. Among students who received aid based on merit, the average award (and the proportion receiving): $6,497 (12%). Average amount of debt of borrowers graduating in 2003: $24,620. Proportion who borrowed: 58%. **Student employment:** During the 2003-2004 academic year, 16% of undergraduates worked on campus. Average per-year earnings: $2,393.

Niagara University

Niagara University, NY 14109
Private; www.niagara.edu
Financial aid office: (716) 286-8686

- **2004-2005 TUITION AND FEES:** $18,420
- **ROOM AND BOARD:** $8,050

SAT I Score (25th/75th percentile): 950-1150
2005 U.S. News College Ranking: Universities–Master's (North), 56
Acceptance Rate: 80%

Other expenses: Estimated books and supplies: $750. Transportation: $600. Personal expenses: $750. **Financial aid:** Priority filing date for institution's financial aid form: February 15. In 2003-2004, 88% of undergraduates applied for financial aid. Of those, 84% were determined to have financial need; 29% had their need fully met. Average financial aid package (proportion receiving): $15,400 (84%). Average amount of gift aid, such as scholarships or grants (proportion receiving): $10,355 (80%). Average amount of self-help aid, such as work study or loans (proportion receiving): $5,135 (69%). Average need-based loan (excluding PLUS or other private loans): $4,505. Among students who received need-based aid, the average percentage of need met: 84%. Among students who received aid based on merit, the average award (and the proportion receiving): $7,039 (15%). The average athletic scholarship (and the proportion receiving): $12,958 (3%). Average amount of debt of borrowers graduat-

ing in 2003: $15,402. Proportion who borrowed: 75%. **Student employment:** During the 2003-2004 academic year, 17% of undergraduates worked on campus. Average per-year earnings: $1,800. **Cooperative education programs:** business, computer science, social/behavioral science. **Reserve Officers Training Corps (ROTC):** Army ROTC: Offered on campus.

Nyack College

1 South Boulevard
Nyack, NY 10960
Private; www.nyackcollege.edu
Financial aid office: (845) 358-1710

- **2004-2005 TUITION AND FEES:** $14,790
- **ROOM AND BOARD:** $7,250

SAT I Score (25th/75th percentile): 808-1090
2005 U.S. News College Ranking: Universities–Master's (North), fourth tier
Acceptance Rate: 63%

Other expenses: Estimated books and supplies: $750. Transportation: $720. Personal expenses: $1,760. **Financial aid:** In 2003-2004, 88% of undergraduates applied for financial aid. Of those, 83% were determined to have financial need; 16% had their need fully met. Average financial aid package (proportion receiving): $13,031 (83%). Average amount of gift aid, such as scholarships or grants (proportion receiving): $8,419 (83%). Average amount of self-help aid, such as work study or loans (proportion receiving): $5,113 (76%). Average need-based loan (excluding PLUS or other private loans): $4,632. Among students who received need-based aid, the average percentage of need met: 62%. Among students who received aid based on merit, the average award (and the proportion receiving): $5,924 (13%). The average athletic scholarship (and the proportion receiving): $5,786 (3%). Average amount of debt of borrowers graduating in 2003: $14,563. Proportion who borrowed: 77%.

Pace University

1 Pace Plaza
New York, NY 10038
Private; www.pace.edu
Financial aid office: (212) 346-1300

- **2004-2005 TUITION AND FEES:** $22,712
- **ROOM AND BOARD:** $8,400

SAT I Score (25th/75th percentile): 980-1170
2005 U.S. News College Ranking: National Universities, third tier
Acceptance Rate: 71%

Financial aid: Priority filing date for institution's financial aid form: February 15. In 2003-2004, 91% of undergraduates applied for financial aid. Of those, 85% were determined to have financial need; 7% had their need fully met. Average financial aid package (proportion receiving): $12,919 (84%). Average amount of gift aid, such as scholarships or grants (proportion receiving): $4,780 (70%). Average amount of self-help aid, such as work study or loans (proportion receiving): $4,111 (60%). Average need-based loan (excluding PLUS or other private loans): $4,120. Among students who received need-based aid, the average percentage of need met: 87%. Among students who received aid based on merit, the average award (and the proportion receiving): $5,644 (5%). The average athletic scholarship (and the proportion receiving): $10,409 (1%). Average amount of debt of borrowers graduating in 2003: $17,202. Proportion who borrowed: 67%. **Student employment:** During the 2003-2004 academic year, 10% of undergraduates worked on campus. Average per-year earnings: $1,694. **Cooperative education programs:** business, computer science, education, health professions, social/behavioral science. **Reserve Officers Training Corps (ROTC):** Air Force ROTC: Offered at cooperating institution (Manhattan College).

Polytechnic University

6 Metrotech Center
Brooklyn, NY 11201
Private; www.poly.edu
Financial aid office: (718) 260-3300

- **2004-2005 TUITION AND FEES:** $27,170
- **ROOM AND BOARD:** $8,000

SAT I Score (25th/75th percentile): 1060-1270
2005 U.S. News College Ranking: National Universities, third tier
Acceptance Rate: 73%

Other expenses: Estimated books and supplies: $750. Transportation: $1,389. Personal expenses: $1,575. **Financial aid:** In 2003-2004, 98% of undergraduates applied for financial aid. Of those, 83% were determined to have financial need; 37% had their need fully met. Average financial aid package (proportion receiving): $20,600 (83%). Average amount of gift aid, such as scholarships or grants (proportion receiving): $8,407 (75%). Average amount of self-help aid, such as work study or loans (proportion receiving): $5,355 (64%). Average need-based loan (excluding PLUS or other private loans): $5,062. Among students who received need-based aid, the average percentage of need met: 87%. Among students who received aid based on merit, the average award (and the proportion receiving): $16,341 (15%). The average athletic scholarship (and the proportion receiving): $0 (0%). Average amount of debt of borrowers graduating in 2003: $20,219. Proportion who borrowed: 76%. **Student employment:** During the 2003-2004 academic year, 15% of undergraduates worked on campus. **Cooperative education programs:** computer science, engineering. **Reserve Officers Training Corps (ROTC):** Army ROTC: Offered at cooperating institution (Fordham University); Air Force ROTC: Offered at cooperating institution (Fordham University).

Pratt Institute

200 Willoughby Avenue
Brooklyn, NY 11205
Private; www.pratt.edu
Financial aid office: (718) 636-3599

■ **2004-2005 TUITION AND FEES:** $25,680
■ **ROOM AND BOARD:** $8,320

SAT I Score (25th/75th percentile): 1020-1240
2005 U.S. News College Ranking:
Unranked Specialty School–Fine Arts
Acceptance Rate: 47%

Other expenses: Estimated books and supplies: $3,000. Transportation: $0. Personal expenses: $1,650. **Financial aid:** Priority filing date for institution's financial aid form: February 1. In 2003-2004, 89% of undergraduates applied for financial aid. Of those, 78% were determined to have financial need; Average financial aid package (proportion receiving): $14,605 (78%). Average amount of gift aid, such as scholarships or grants (proportion receiving): $5,870 (76%). Average amount of self-help aid, such as work study or loans (proportion receiving): $4,105 (70%). Average need-based loan (excluding PLUS or other private loans): $3,780. Among students who received need-based aid, the average percentage of need met: 58%. Among students who received aid based on merit, the average award (and the proportion receiving): $6,960 (9%). **Student employment:** During the 2003-2004 academic year, 31% of undergraduates worked on campus. Average per-year earnings: $2,170.

Rensselaer Polytechnic Institute

110 Eighth Street
Troy, NY 12180-3590
Private; www.rpi.edu
Financial aid office: (518) 276-6813

■ **2004-2005 TUITION AND FEES:** $29,786
■ **ROOM AND BOARD:** $9,133

SAT I Score (25th/75th percentile): 1220-1400
2005 U.S. News College Ranking:
National Universities, 46
Acceptance Rate: 80%

Other expenses: Estimated books and supplies: $1,631. **Financial aid:** Priority filing date for institution's financial aid form: February 15. In 2003-2004, 78% of undergraduates applied for financial aid. Of those, 70% were determined to have financial need; 64% had their need fully met. Average financial aid package (proportion receiving): $24,842 (70%). Average amount of gift aid, such as scholarships or grants (proportion receiving): $19,861 (70%). Average amount of self-help aid, such as work study or loans (proportion receiving): $7,790 (51%). Average need-based loan (excluding PLUS or other private loans): $5,810. Among students who received need-based aid, the average percentage of need met: 92%. Among students who received aid based on merit, the average award (and the proportion receiving): $13,824 (14%). The average athletic scholarship (and the proportion receiving): $39,200 (0%). Average amount of debt of borrowers graduating in 2003: $23,725. Proportion who borrowed: 72%. **Student employment:** During the 2003-2004 academic year, 33% of undergraduates worked on campus. Average per-year earnings: $1,100. **Cooperative education programs:** business, computer science, engineering, humanities, natural science, social/behavioral science, technologies, other. **Reserve Officers Training Corps (ROTC):** Army ROTC: Offered on campus; Navy ROTC: Offered on campus; Air Force ROTC: Offered on campus.

Roberts Wesleyan College

2301 Westside Drive
Rochester, NY 14624-1997
Private; www.roberts.edu
Financial aid office: (585) 594-6150

■ **2004-2005 TUITION AND FEES:** $17,840
■ **ROOM AND BOARD:** $6,604

SAT I Score (25th/75th percentile): 882-1304
2005 U.S. News College Ranking:
Universities–Master's (North), 76
Acceptance Rate: 80%

Other expenses: Estimated books and supplies: $650. Transportation: $658. Personal expenses: $1,125. **Financial aid:** Priority filing date for institution's financial aid form: March 15. In 2003-2004, 92% of undergraduates applied for financial aid. Of those, 87% were determined to have financial need; 19% had their need fully met. Average financial aid package (proportion receiving): $14,890 (87%). Average amount of gift aid, such as scholarships or grants (proportion receiving): $9,454 (87%). Average amount of self-help aid, such as work study or loans (proportion receiving): $5,859 (81%). Average need-based loan (excluding PLUS or other private loans): $5,093. Among students who received need-based aid, the average percentage of need met: 80%. Among students who received aid based on merit, the average award (and the proportion receiving): $8,790 (13%). The average athletic scholarship (and the proportion receiving): $5,320 (4%). **Student employment:** During the 2003-2004 academic year, 14% of undergraduates worked on campus. Average per-year earnings: $1,600. **Reserve Officers Training Corps (ROTC):** Army ROTC: Offered at cooperating institution; Air Force ROTC: Offered at cooperating institution.

Rochester Institute of Technology

1 Lomb Memorial Drive
Rochester, NY 14623
Private; www.rit.edu
Financial aid office: (585) 475-2186

■ **2004-2005 TUITION AND FEES:** $21,804
■ **ROOM AND BOARD:** $8,136

SAT I Score (25th/75th percentile): 1110-1310
2005 U.S. News College Ranking:
Universities–Master's (North), 6
Acceptance Rate: 69%

Other expenses: Estimated books and supplies: $600. Transportation: $300. Personal expenses: $725. **Financial aid:** Priority filing date for institution's financial aid form: March 1. In 2003-2004, 76% of undergraduates applied for financial aid. Of those, 68% were determined to have financial need; 85% had their need fully met. Average financial aid package (proportion receiving): $16,300 (68%). Average amount of gift aid, such as scholarships or grants (proportion receiving): $9,900 (64%). Average amount of self-help aid, such as work study or loans (proportion receiving): $5,900 (61%). Average need-based loan (excluding PLUS or other private loans): $4,700. Among students who received need-based aid, the average percentage of need met: 90%. Among students who received aid based on merit, the average award (and the proportion receiving): $5,800 (9%). The average athletic scholarship (and the proportion receiving): $0 (0%). Proportion who borrowed: 77%. **Student employment:** During the 2003-2004 academic year, 25% of undergraduates worked on campus. Average per-year earnings: $2,000. **Cooperative education programs:** business, computer science, engineering, natural science, social/behavioral science, technologies, other. **Reserve Officers Training Corps (ROTC):** Army ROTC: Offered on campus; Navy ROTC: Offered at cooperating institution (University of Rochester); Air Force ROTC: Offered on campus.

Russell Sage College

45 Ferry Street
Troy, NY 12180-4115
Private; www.sage.edu
Financial aid office: (518) 244-4525

- **2004-2005 TUITION AND FEES:** $22,120
- **ROOM AND BOARD:** $7,050

SAT I Score (25th/75th percentile): 960-1140
2005 U.S. News College Ranking:
Comp. Colleges–Bachelor's (North), 4
Acceptance Rate: 82%

Other expenses: Estimated books and supplies: $900. Transportation: $600. Personal expenses: $1,100. **Financial aid:** Priority filing date for institution's financial aid form: March 1. In 2003-2004, 98% of undergraduates applied for financial aid. Of those, 85% were determined to have financial need; Average financial aid package (proportion receiving): N/A (85%). Average amount of gift aid, such as scholarships or grants (proportion receiving): N/A (83%). Average amount of self-help aid, such as work study or loans (proportion receiving): N/A (85%). Among students who received aid based on merit, the average award (and the proportion receiving): $8,300 (5%). The average athletic scholarship (and the proportion receiving): $0 (0%). Average amount of debt of borrowers graduating in 2003: $19,200. Proportion who borrowed: 89%. **Student employment:** During the 2003-2004 academic year, 12% of undergraduates worked on campus. Average per-year

earnings: $900. **Reserve Officers Training Corps (ROTC):** Army ROTC: Offered at cooperating institution (Siena College/R.P.I.); Air Force ROTC: Offered at cooperating institution (R.P.I.).

Sarah Lawrence College

1 Mead Way
Bronxville, NY 10708-5999
Private; www.sarahlawrence.edu
Financial aid office: (914) 395-2570

- **2004-2005 TUITION AND FEES:** $32,416
- **ROOM AND BOARD:** $10,918

SAT I Score (25th/75th percentile): 1140-1340
2005 U.S. News College Ranking:
Liberal Arts Colleges, 48
Acceptance Rate: 41%

Other expenses: Estimated books and supplies: $600. Personal expenses: $800. **Financial aid:** Priority filing date for institution's financial aid form: February 1; deadline: February 1. In 2003-2004, 60% of undergraduates applied for financial aid. Of those, 59% were determined to have financial need; 59% had their need fully met. Average financial aid package (proportion receiving): $25,826 (49%). Average amount of gift aid, such as scholarships or grants (proportion receiving): $21,014 (49%). Average amount of self-help aid, such as work study or loans (proportion receiving): $4,738 (49%). Average need-based loan (excluding PLUS or other private loans): $3,080. Among students who received need-based aid, the average percentage of need met: 95%. Among students who received aid based on merit, the average award (and the proportion receiving): $6,418 (12%). The average athletic scholarship (and the proportion receiving): $0 (0%). Average amount of debt of borrowers graduating in 2003: $15,023. Proportion who borrowed: 55%. **Student employment:** During the 2003-2004 academic year, 43% of undergraduates worked on campus. Average per-year earnings: $1,000.

Siena College

515 Loudon Road
Loudonville, NY 12211
Private; www.siena.edu
Financial aid office: (518) 783-2427

- **2004-2005 TUITION AND FEES:** $19,130
- **ROOM AND BOARD:** $7,575

SAT I Score (25th/75th percentile): 1020-1210
2005 U.S. News College Ranking:
Liberal Arts Colleges, third tier
Acceptance Rate: 63%

Other expenses: Estimated books and supplies: $825. Transportation: $595. Personal expenses: $755. **Financial aid:** Priority filing date for institution's financial aid form: February 1. In 2003-2004, 82% of undergraduates applied for financial aid. Of those, 68% were determined to have financial need; 16% had their need fully met. Average financial aid package (proportion receiving): $13,175 (68%). Average amount of gift aid, such as scholarships or grants (proportion receiving): $9,555 (67%). Average amount of self-help aid, such as work study or loans (proportion receiving): $4,203 (55%). Average need-based loan (excluding PLUS or other private loans): $4,183. Among students who received need-based aid, the average percentage of need met: 80%. Among students who received aid based on merit, the average award (and the proportion receiving): $5,956 (13%). The average athletic scholarship (and the proportion receiving): $11,278 (8%). Average amount of debt of borrowers graduating in 2003: $16,200. Proportion who borrowed: 70%. **Student employment:** During the 2003-2004 academic year, 15% of undergraduates worked on campus. Average per-year earnings: $1,133. **Reserve Officers Training Corps (ROTC):** Army ROTC: Offered on campus; Air Force ROTC: Offered at cooperating institution (Rensselear Polytechnic Institute).

Skidmore College

815 N. Broadway
Saratoga Springs, NY 12866
Private; www.skidmore.edu
Financial aid office: (518) 580-5750

- **2004-2005 TUITION AND FEES:** $31,105
- **ROOM AND BOARD:** $8,710

SAT I Score (25th/75th percentile): 1170-1340
2005 U.S. News College Ranking:
Liberal Arts Colleges, 45
Acceptance Rate: 46%

Financial aid: In 2003-2004, 45% of undergraduates applied for financial aid. Of those, 42% were determined to have financial need; 87% had their need fully met. Average financial aid package (proportion receiving): $24,114 (42%). Average amount of gift aid, such as scholarships or grants (proportion receiving): $18,765 (42%). Average amount of self-help aid, such as work study or loans (proportion receiving): $5,349 (42%). Average need-based loan (excluding PLUS or other private loans): $3,608. Among students who received need-based aid, the average percentage of need met: 94%. Among students who received aid based on merit, the average award (and the proportion receiving): $10,000 (1%). The average athletic scholarship (and the proportion receiving): $0 (0%). Average amount of debt of borrowers graduating in 2003: $16,228. Proportion who borrowed: 46%. **Student employment:** During the 2003-2004 academic year, 55% of undergraduates worked on campus. Average per-year earnings: $800. **Reserve Officers Training Corps (ROTC):** Army ROTC: Offered at cooperating institution (R.P.I., Siena); Air Force ROTC: Offered at cooperating institution (R.P.I.).

St. Bonaventure University

Route 417
St. Bonaventure, NY 14778
Private; www.sbu.edu
Financial aid office: (716) 375-2528

■ **2004-2005 TUITION AND FEES:** $19,485
■ **ROOM AND BOARD:** $6,910

SAT I Score (25th/75th percentile): 960-1160
2005 U.S. News College Ranking:
Universities–Master's (North), 27
Acceptance Rate: 87%

Other expenses: Estimated books and supplies: $600. Transportation: $400. Personal expenses: $700. **Financial aid:** Priority filing date for institution's financial aid form: February 1. In 2003-2004, 83% of undergraduates applied for financial aid. Of those, 71% were determined to have financial need; 33% had their need fully met. Average financial aid package (proportion receiving): $14,782 (71%). Average amount of gift aid, such as scholarships or grants (proportion receiving): $10,090 (71%). Average amount of self-help aid, such as work study or loans (proportion receiving): $4,735 (60%). Average need-based loan (excluding PLUS or other private loans): $4,170. Among students who received need-based aid, the average percentage of need met: 85%. Among students who received aid based on merit, the average award (and the proportion receiving): $6,260 (21%). The average athletic scholarship (and the proportion receiving): $12,770 (4%). Average amount of debt of borrowers graduating in 2003: $16,900. Proportion who borrowed: 72%. **Student employment:** During the 2003-2004 academic year, 36% of undergraduates

worked on campus. Average per-year earnings: $1,500. **Reserve Officers Training Corps (ROTC):** Army ROTC: Offered on campus.

St. Francis College

180 Remsen Street
Brooklyn, NY 11201
Private; www.stfranciscollege.edu
Financial aid office: (718) 489-5255

■ **2004-2005 TUITION AND FEES:** $11,780

SAT I Score (25th/75th percentile): 810-1090
2005 U.S. News College Ranking:
Comp. Colleges–Bachelor's (North), 24
Acceptance Rate: 88%

Other expenses: Transportation: $700. **Financial aid:** Priority filing date for institution's financial aid form: February 15. In 2003-2004, 82% of undergraduates applied for financial aid. Of those, 50% were determined to have financial need; Average financial aid package (proportion receiving): N/A (50%). Average amount of gift aid, such as scholarships or grants (proportion receiving): N/A (50%). Average amount of self-help aid, such as work study or loans (proportion receiving): $1,500 (28%). Among students who received aid based on merit, the average award (and the proportion receiving): N/A (20%). The average athletic scholarship (and the proportion receiving): N/A (7%). **Student employment:** During the 2003-2004 academic year, 5% of undergraduates worked on campus. Average per-year earnings: $2,330. **Cooperative education programs:** computer science, health professions. **Reserve Officers Training Corps (ROTC):** Army ROTC: Offered at cooperating institution (Polytechnic University); Air Force ROTC: Offered at cooperating institution (Manhattan College).

St. John Fisher College

3690 East Avenue
Rochester, NY 14618
Private; www.sjfc.edu
Financial aid office: (585) 385-8042

■ **2004-2005 TUITION AND FEES:** $18,450
■ **ROOM AND BOARD:** $7,900

SAT I Score (25th/75th percentile): 970-1140
2005 U.S. News College Ranking:
Universities–Master's (North), 62
Acceptance Rate: 71%

Other expenses: Estimated books and supplies: $700. Transportation: $200. Personal expenses: $600. **Financial aid:** Priority filing date for institution's financial aid form: February 15. In 2003-2004, 93% of undergraduates applied for financial aid. Of those, 84% were determined to have financial need; 53% had their need fully met. Average financial aid package (proportion receiving): $13,000 (84%). Average amount of gift aid, such as scholarships or grants (proportion receiving): $9,417 (83%). Average amount of self-help aid, such as work study or loans (proportion receiving): $6,812 (75%). Average need-based loan (excluding PLUS or other private loans): $5,861. Among students who received need-based aid, the average percentage of need met: 80%. Among students who received aid based on merit, the average award (and the proportion receiving): $4,478 (13%). The average athletic scholarship (and the proportion receiving): $0 (0%). Average amount of debt of borrowers graduating in 2003: $18,400. Proportion who borrowed: 85%. **Student employment:** During the 2003-2004 academic year, 9% of undergraduates worked on campus. Average per-year earnings: $1,549. **Cooperative education programs:** engineering, other. **Reserve Officers Training Corps (ROTC):** Army ROTC: Offered at cooperating institution (Rochester Institute Of Technology); Navy ROTC: Offered at cooperating institution (University of Rochester); Air Force ROTC: Offered at cooperating institution (Rochester Institute of Technology).

St. John's University

8000 Utopia Parkway
Jamaica, NY 11439
Private; www.stjohns.edu
Financial aid office: (718) 990-2000

■ **2004-2005 TUITION AND FEES:** $21,630
■ **ROOM AND BOARD:** $10,550

SAT I Score (25th/75th percentile): 930-1140
2005 U.S. News College Ranking:
National Universities, third tier
Acceptance Rate: 68%

Financial aid: Priority filing date for institution's financial aid form: February 1. In 2003-2004, 88% of undergraduates applied for financial aid. Of those, 81% were determined to have financial need; 12% had their need fully met. Average financial aid package (proportion receiving): $15,763 (81%). Average amount of gift aid, such as scholarships or grants (proportion receiving): $6,993 (71%). Average amount of self-help aid, such as work study or loans (proportion receiving): $5,634 (77%). Average need-based loan (excluding PLUS or other private loans): $4,222. Among students who received need-based aid, the average percentage of need met: 72%. Among students who received aid based on merit, the average award (and the proportion receiving): $8,000 (N/A). The average athletic scholarship (and the proportion receiving): $18,713 (2%). Average amount of debt of borrowers graduating in 2003: $18,037. Proportion who borrowed: 68%. **Student employment:** During the 2003-2004 academic year, 3% of undergraduates worked on campus. Average per-year earnings: $8,000. **Reserve Officers Training Corps (ROTC):** Army ROTC: Offered on campus.

St. Joseph's College, New York

245 Clinton Avenue
Brooklyn, NY 11205-3688
Private; www.sjcny.edu
Financial aid office: (718) 636-6808

■ **2004-2005 TUITION AND FEES:** $11,944

SAT I Score (25th/75th percentile): 968-1156
2005 U.S. News College Ranking:
Comp. Colleges–Bachelor's (North), 15
Acceptance Rate: 73%

Financial aid: Priority filing date for institution's financial aid form: February 25. In 2003-2004, 70% of undergraduates applied for financial aid. Of those, 53% were determined to have financial need; 63% had their need fully met. Average financial aid package (proportion receiving): $10,332 (53%). Average amount of gift aid, such as scholarships or grants (proportion receiving): $5,956 (53%). Average amount of self-help aid, such as work study or loans (proportion receiving): $3,299 (41%). Average need-based loan (excluding PLUS or other private loans): $3,782. Among students who received need-based aid, the average percentage of need met: 68%. Among students who received aid based on merit, the average award (and the proportion receiving): $3,985 (19%). The average athletic scholarship (and the proportion receiving): $0 (0%). Average amount of debt of borrowers graduating in 2003: $15,171. Proportion who borrowed: 66%. **Student employment:** During the 2003-2004 academic year, 2% of undergraduates worked on campus. Average per-year earnings: $1,900.

St. Lawrence University

23 Romoda Drive
Canton, NY 13617
Private; www.stlawu.edu
Financial aid office: (315) 229-5265

■ **2004-2005 TUITION AND FEES:** $30,230
■ **ROOM AND BOARD:** $7,755

SAT I Score (25th/75th percentile): 1040-1250
2005 U.S. News College Ranking:
Liberal Arts Colleges, 62
Acceptance Rate: 57%

Other expenses: Estimated books and supplies: $650. Transportation: $500. Personal expenses: $300. **Financial aid:** Priority filing date for institution's financial aid form: February 15; deadline: February 15. In 2003-2004, 77% of undergraduates applied for financial aid. Of those, 71% were determined to have financial need; 37% had their need fully met. Average financial aid package (proportion receiving): $26,013 (70%). Average amount of gift aid, such as scholarships or grants (proportion receiving): $18,585 (69%). Average amount of self-help aid, such as work study or loans (proportion receiving): $6,971 (63%). Average need-based loan (excluding PLUS or other private loans): $6,134. Among students who received need-based aid, the average percentage of need met: 90%. Among students who received aid based on merit, the average award (and the proportion receiving): $9,151 (10%). The average athletic scholarship (and the proportion receiving): $34,009 (2%). Average amount of debt of borrowers graduating in 2003: $23,091. Proportion who borrowed: 70%. **Student employment:** During the 2003-2004 academic year, 38% of undergraduates worked on campus. Average per-year earnings: $1,110. **Reserve Officers Training Corps (ROTC):** Army ROTC: Offered at cooperating institution (Clarkson University); Air Force ROTC: Offered at cooperating institution (Clarkson University).

St. Thomas Aquinas College

125 Route 340
Sparkill, NY 10976
Private; www.stac.edu
Financial aid office: (845) 398-4097

■ **2004-2005 TUITION AND FEES:** $15,700
■ **ROOM AND BOARD:** $8,590

SAT I Score (25th/75th percentile): 820-1040
2005 U.S. News College Ranking:
Universities–Master's (North), fourth tier
Acceptance Rate: 75%

Other expenses: Estimated books and supplies: $750. Transportation: $750. Personal expenses: $1,000. **Financial aid:** Priority filing date for institution's financial aid form: February 15. In 2003-2004, 86% of undergraduates applied for financial aid. Of those, 68% were determined to have financial need; 14% had their need fully met. Average financial aid package (proportion receiving): $9,443 (66%). Average amount of gift aid, such as scholarships or grants (proportion receiving): $6,382 (62%). Average amount of self-help aid, such as work study or loans (proportion receiving): $4,100 (52%). Average need-based loan (excluding PLUS or other private loans): $3,760. Among students who received need-based aid, the average percentage of need met: 61%. Among students who received aid based on merit, the average award (and the proportion receiving): $4,736 (10%). The average athletic scholarship (and the proportion receiving): $5,297 (3%). Average amount of debt of borrowers graduating in 2003: $12,000. Proportion who borrowed: 67%. **Student employment:** During the 2003-2004 academic year, 10% of undergraduates worked on campus. Average per-year earnings: $1,500. **Cooperative education programs:** engineering, health professions. **Reserve Officers Training Corps (ROTC):** Air Force ROTC: Offered at cooperating institution (Manhattan College).

SUNY–Albany

1400 Washington Avenue
Albany, NY 12222
Public; www.albany.edu
Financial aid office: (518) 442-5757

■ **2004-2005 TUITION AND FEES:**
  In state: $5,770; Out of state: $11,720
■ **ROOM AND BOARD:** $7,181

SAT I Score (25th/75th percentile): 1030-1230
2005 U.S. News College Ranking:
National Universities, third tier
Acceptance Rate: 56%

Other expenses: Estimated books and supplies: $800. Transportation: $300. Personal expenses: $1,242. **Financial aid:** In 2003-2004, 74% of undergraduates applied for financial aid. Of those, 57% were determined to have financial need; 19% had their need fully met. Average financial aid package (proportion receiving): $8,251 (57%). Average amount of gift aid, such as scholarships or grants (proportion receiving): $4,456 (50%). Average amount of self-help aid, such as work study or loans (proportion receiving): $4,583 (48%). Average need-based loan (excluding PLUS or other private loans): $4,283. Among students who received need-based aid, the average percentage of need met: 71%. Among students who received aid based on merit, the average award (and the proportion receiving): $3,534 (5%). The average athletic scholarship (and the proportion receiving): $7,925 (2%). Average amount of debt of borrowers graduating in 2003: $16,700. Proportion who borrowed: 69%. **Reserve Officers Training Corps (ROTC):** Army ROTC: Offered on campus; Air Force ROTC: Offered at cooperating institution (Rensselaer Polytechnic Institute).

SUNY–Binghamton

PO Box 6000
Binghamton, NY 13902-6000
Public; www.binghamton.edu
Financial aid office: (607) 777-2428

- **2004-2005 TUITION AND FEES:**
  In state: $5,756; Out of state: $11,706
- **ROOM AND BOARD:** $7,710

SAT I Score (25th/75th percentile): 1150-1320
2005 U.S. News College Ranking:
National Universities, 74
Acceptance Rate: 45%

Other expenses: Estimated books and supplies: $800. Transportation: $260. **Financial aid:** Priority filing date for institution's financial aid form: March 1. In 2003-2004, 69% of undergraduates applied for financial aid. Of those, 50% were determined to have financial need; 72% had their need fully met. Average financial aid package (proportion receiving): $10,629 (50%). Average amount of gift aid, such as scholarships or grants (proportion receiving): $4,752 (45%). Average amount of self-help aid, such as work study or loans (proportion receiving): $4,646 (46%). Average need-based loan (excluding PLUS or other private loans): $4,214. Among students who received need-based aid, the average percentage of need met: 84%. Among students who received aid based on merit, the average award (and the proportion receiving): $2,471 (2%). The average athletic scholarship (and the proportion receiving): $8,754 (2%). Average amount of debt of borrowers graduating in 2003: $14,531. Proportion

who borrowed: 61%. **Student employment:** During the 2003-2004 academic year, 13% of undergraduates worked on campus. Average per-year earnings: $1,000. **Reserve Officers Training Corps (ROTC):** Air Force ROTC: Offered at cooperating institution (Cornell University).

SUNY College–Brockport

350 New Campus Drive
Brockport, NY 14420
Public; www.brockport.edu
Financial aid office: (585) 395-2501

- **2004-2005 TUITION AND FEES:**
  In state: $5,221; Out of state: $11,171
- **ROOM AND BOARD:** $7,230

SAT I Score (25th/75th percentile): 970-1150
2005 U.S. News College Ranking:
Universities–Master's (North), third tier
Acceptance Rate: 51%

Other expenses: Estimated books and supplies: $900. Transportation: $130. Personal expenses: $1,719. **Financial aid:** Priority filing date for institution's financial aid form: March 15. In 2003-2004, 98% of undergraduates applied for financial aid. Of those, 77% were determined to have financial need; 61% had their need fully met. Average financial aid package (proportion receiving): $8,062 (75%). Average amount of gift aid, such as scholarships or grants (proportion receiving): $2,846 (66%). Average amount of self-help aid, such as work study or loans (proportion receiving): $3,730 (67%). Average need-based loan (excluding PLUS or other private loans): $3,537. Among students who received need-based aid, the average percentage of need met: 98%. Among students who received aid based on merit, the average award (and the proportion receiving): $2,882 (11%). The average athletic scholarship (and the proportion receiving): $0 (0%). Average amount of debt of borrowers graduating in 2003: $16,902. Proportion who borrowed: 77%. **Student employment:** During the 2003-2004 academic year, 28% of undergraduates worked on campus. Average per-year earnings: $1,298. **Reserve Officers Training Corps (ROTC):** Army ROTC: Offered on campus; Air Force ROTC: Offered at cooperating institution (Rochester Institute of Technology).

SUNY College–Cortland

PO Box 2000
Cortland, NY 13045
Public; www.cortland.edu
Financial aid office: (607) 753-4717

- **2004-2005 TUITION AND FEES:**
  In state: $5,300; Out of state: $11,250
- **ROOM AND BOARD:** $7,290

SAT I Score (25th/75th percentile): 990-1140
2005 U.S. News College Ranking:
Universities–Master's (North), third tier
Acceptance Rate: 49%

Financial aid: In 2003-2004, 85% of undergraduates applied for financial aid. Of those, 65% were determined to have financial need; 22% had their need fully met. Average financial aid package (proportion receiving): $8,718 (64%). Average amount of gift aid, such as scholarships or grants (proportion receiving): $3,488 (57%). Average amount of self-help aid, such as work study or loans (proportion receiving): $3,217 (57%). Average need-based loan (excluding PLUS or other private loans): $3,680. Among students who received need-based aid, the average percentage of need met: 77%. Among students who received aid based on merit, the average award (and the proportion receiving): $6,118 (16%). The average athletic scholarship (and the proportion receiving): $0 (0%). **Reserve Officers Training Corps (ROTC):** Army ROTC: Offered at cooperating institution (Cornell University); Air Force ROTC: Offered at cooperating institution (Cornell University).

SUNY College Environmental Science and Forestry

1 Forestry Drive
Syracuse, NY 13210
Public; www.esf.edu
Financial aid office: (315) 470-6706

- **2004-2005 TUITION AND FEES:**
  In state: $4,991; Out of state: $10,941
- **ROOM AND BOARD:** $9,790

SAT I Score (25th/75th percentile): 1040-1220
2005 U.S. News College Ranking:
National Universities, 98
Acceptance Rate: 57%

Other expenses: Estimated books and supplies: $800. Transportation: $300. Personal expenses: $450. **Financial aid:** Priority filing date for institution's financial aid form: March 1. In 2003-2004, 87% of undergraduates applied for financial aid. Of those, 72% were determined to have financial need; 100% had their need fully met. Average financial aid package (proportion receiving): $8,300 (72%). Average amount of gift aid, such as scholarships or grants (proportion receiving): $5,300 (72%). Average amount of self-help aid, such as work study or loans (proportion receiving): $6,700 (72%). Average need-based loan (excluding PLUS or other private loans): $5,500. Among students who received need-based aid, the average percentage of need met: 100%. Among students who received aid based on merit, the average award (and the proportion receiving): $2,500 (12%). Average amount of debt of borrowers graduating in 2003: $19,000. Proportion who borrowed: 92%. **Reserve Officers Training Corps (ROTC):** Army ROTC: Offered at cooperating institution (Syracuse University); Air Force ROTC: Offered at cooperating institution (Syracuse University).

SUNY College of A&T–Cobleskill

Cobleskill, NY 12043
Public; www.cobleskill.edu
Financial aid office: (518) 255-5623

■ **2003-2004 TUITION AND FEES:**
  In state: $5,243; Out of state: $7,893
■ **ROOM AND BOARD:** $6,970

SAT I Score (25th/75th percentile): 820-1010
2005 U.S. News College Ranking:
Comp. Colleges–Bachelor's (North), fourth tier
Acceptance Rate: 79%

Other expenses: Estimated books and supplies: $1,000. Personal expenses: $1,400.

SUNY College of Arts and Sciences–Geneseo

1 College Circle
Geneseo, NY 14454-1401
Public; www.geneseo.edu
Financial aid office: (585) 245-5731

■ **2004-2005 TUITION AND FEES:**
  In state: $5,390; Out of state: $11,340
■ **ROOM AND BOARD:** $6,350

SAT I Score (25th/75th percentile): 1180-1330
2005 U.S. News College Ranking:
Universities–Master's (North), 12
Acceptance Rate: 42%

Other expenses: Estimated books and supplies: $700. Transportation: $650. Personal expenses: $650. **Financial aid:** Priority filing date for institution's financial aid form: February 15. In 2003-2004, 90% of undergraduates applied for financial aid. Of those, 49% were determined to have financial need; 86% had their need fully met. Average financial aid package (proportion receiving): $8,402 (49%). Average amount of gift aid, such as scholarships or grants (proportion receiving): $3,391 (46%). Average amount of self-help aid, such as work study or loans (proportion receiving): $3,704 (46%). Average need-based loan (excluding PLUS or other private loans): $3,454. Among students who received need-based aid, the average percentage of need met: 87%. Among students who received aid based on merit, the average award (and the proportion receiving): $1,454 (11%). The average athletic scholarship (and the proportion receiving): $0 (0%). Average amount of debt of borrowers graduating in 2003: $15,500. Proportion who borrowed: 75%. **Student employment:** During the 2003-2004 academic year, 11% of undergraduates worked on campus. Average per-year earnings: $1,500. **Reserve Officers Training Corps (ROTC):** Army ROTC: Offered at cooperating institution (Rochester Institute of Technology); Air Force ROTC: Offered at cooperating institution (Rochester Institute of Technology).

SUNY College of Arts and Sciences–New Paltz

75 S. Manheim Boulevard, Suite 9
New Paltz, NY 12561-2443
Public; www.newpaltz.edu
Financial aid office: (845) 257-3250

■ **2004-2005 TUITION AND FEES:**
  In state: $7,695; Out of state: $11,295
■ **ROOM AND BOARD:** $6,420

SAT I Score (25th/75th percentile): 1010-1200
2005 U.S. News College Ranking:
Universities–Master's (North), 50
Acceptance Rate: 34%

Other expenses: Estimated books and supplies: $1,100. Transportation: $600. Personal expenses: $125. **Financial aid:** Priority filing date for institution's financial aid form: March 15; deadline: March 15. In 2003-2004, 77% of undergrad-

uates applied for financial aid. Of those, 56% were determined to have financial need; 29% had their need fully met. Average financial aid package (proportion receiving): $2,446 (56%). Average amount of gift aid, such as scholarships or grants (proportion receiving): $2,229 (49%). Average amount of self-help aid, such as work study or loans (proportion receiving): $2,591 (47%). Average need-based loan (excluding PLUS or other private loans): $859. Among students who received need-based aid, the average percentage of need met: 74%. Among students who received aid based on merit, the average award (and the proportion receiving): $1,525 (3%). The average athletic scholarship (and the proportion receiving): $0 (0%). Average amount of debt of borrowers graduating in 2003: $15,000. Proportion who borrowed: 75%.

SUNY College–Old Westbury

PO Box 210
Old Westbury, NY 11568
Public; www.oldwestbury.edu
Financial aid office: (516) 876-3222

■ **2004-2005 TUITION AND FEES:**
  In state: $5,035; Out of state: $10,985
■ **ROOM AND BOARD:** $7,914

SAT I Score (25th/75th percentile): 870-1029
2005 U.S. News College Ranking:
Comp. Colleges–Bachelor's (North), third tier
Acceptance Rate: 57%

Other expenses: Estimated books and supplies: $675. Transportation: $750. Personal expenses: $1,210. **Financial aid:** Priority filing date for institution's financial aid form: April 15; deadline: April 15. In 2003-2004, 74% of undergraduates applied for financial aid. Of those, 66% were determined to have financial need; 21% had their need fully met. Average financial aid package (proportion receiving): $7,275 (62%). Average amount of gift aid, such as scholarships or grants (proportion receiving): $4,974 (57%). Average amount of self-help aid, such as work study or loans (proportion receiving): $2,775 (45%). Average need-based loan (excluding PLUS or other private loans): $2,659. Among students who received need-based aid, the average percentage of need met: 61%. Among students who received aid based on merit, the average award (and the proportion receiving): $5,478 (1%). The average athletic scholarship (and the proportion receiving): $0 (0%). Average amount of debt of borrowers graduating in 2003: $13,295. Proportion who borrowed: 51%. **Student employment:** During the 2003-2004 academic year, 14%

of undergraduates worked on campus. Average per-year earnings: $900. **Reserve Officers Training Corps (ROTC):** Air Force ROTC: Offered at cooperating institution (Manhattan College).

SUNY College–Oneonta

Ravine Parkway
Oneonta, NY 13820
Public; www.oneonta.edu
Financial aid office: (607) 436-2532

■ **2004-2005 TUITION AND FEES:**
    In state: $5,332; Out of state: $11,592
■ **ROOM AND BOARD:** $7,030

SAT I Score (25th/75th percentile): 1010-1150
2005 U.S. News College Ranking:
Universities–Master's (North), third tier
Acceptance Rate: 48%

Other expenses: Estimated books and supplies: $850. Transportation: $1,007. Personal expenses: $1,070. **Financial aid:** Priority filing date for institution's financial aid form: March 1. In 2003-2004, 79% of undergraduates applied for financial aid. Of those, 61% were determined to have financial need; 18% had their need fully met. Average financial aid package (proportion receiving): $8,015 (60%). Average amount of gift aid, such as scholarships or grants (proportion receiving): $3,201 (54%). Average amount of self-help aid, such as work study or loans (proportion receiving): $4,128 (50%). Average need-based loan (excluding PLUS or other private loans): $4,017. Among students who received need-based aid, the average percentage of need met: 67%. Among students who received aid based on merit, the average award (and the proportion receiving): $5,750 (33%). The average athletic scholarship (and the proportion receiving): $2,575 (0%). Average amount of debt of borrowers graduating in 2003: $16,065. Proportion who borrowed: 74%. **Student employment:** During the 2003-2004 academic year, 13% of undergraduates worked on campus. Average per-year earnings: $1,200.

SUNY College–Potsdam

44 Pierrepont Avenue
Potsdam, NY 13676
Public; www.potsdam.edu
Financial aid office: (315) 267-2162

■ **2004-2005 TUITION AND FEES:**
    In state: $5,350; Out of state: $11,300
■ **ROOM AND BOARD:** $7,270

SAT I Score (25th/75th percentile): 960-1180
2005 U.S. News College Ranking:
Universities–Master's (North), third tier
Acceptance Rate: 69%

Other expenses: Estimated books and supplies: $900. Transportation: $600. Personal expenses: $1,200. **Financial aid:** Priority filing date for institution's financial aid form: March 1; deadline: May 1. In 2003-2004, 83% of undergraduates applied for financial aid. Of those, 68% were determined to have financial need; 83% had their need fully met. Average financial aid package (proportion receiving): $11,203 (68%). Average amount of gift aid, such as scholarships or grants (proportion receiving): $4,231 (62%). Average amount of self-help aid, such as work study or loans (proportion receiving): $4,328 (59%). Average need-based loan (excluding PLUS or other private loans): $4,115. Among students who received need-based aid, the average percentage of need met: 83%. Among students who received aid based on merit, the average award (and the proportion receiving): $6,660 (4%). The average athletic scholarship (and the proportion receiving): $0 (0%). Average amount of debt of borrowers graduating in 2003: $17,601. Proportion who borrowed: 84%. **Reserve Officers Training Corps (ROTC):** Army ROTC: Offered at cooperating institution (Clarkson University); Air Force ROTC: Offered at cooperating institution (Clarkson University).

SUNY–Empire State College

1 Union Avenue
Saratoga Springs, NY 12866
Public; www.esc.edu
Financial aid office: (518) 587-2100

■ **2004-2005 TUITION AND FEES:**
    In state: $2,175; Out of state: $5,145

2005 U.S. News College Ranking:
Universities–Master's (North), unranked

SUNY–Farmingdale

2350 Broadhollow Road
Farmingdale, NY 11735-1021
Public; www.farmingdale.edu
Financial aid office: (631) 420-2328

■ **2003-2004 TUITION AND FEES:**
    In state: $4,251; Out of state: $10,151
■ **ROOM AND BOARD:** $8,194

SAT I Score (25th/75th percentile): 870-1065
2005 U.S. News College Ranking:
Comp. Colleges–Bachelor's (North), third tier
Acceptance Rate: 55%

Other expenses: Estimated books and supplies: $1,050. Transportation: $550. Personal expenses: $800. **Reserve Officers Training Corps (ROTC):** Army ROTC: Offered at cooperating institution; Air Force ROTC: Offered at cooperating institution.

SUNY–Fredonia

Fredonia, NY 14063-1136
Public; www.fredonia.edu
Financial aid office: (716) 673-3253

■ **2004-2005 TUITION AND FEES:**
    In state: $5,462; Out of state: $11,412
■ **ROOM AND BOARD:** $6,880

SAT I Score (25th/75th percentile): 1030-1180
2005 U.S. News College Ranking:
Universities–Master's (North), 62
Acceptance Rate: 57%

Other expenses: Estimated books and supplies: $850. Transportation: $600. Personal expenses: $808. **Financial aid:** Priority filing date for institution's financial aid form: February 1. In 2003-2004, 84% of undergraduates applied for financial aid. Of those, 63% were determined to have financial need; 80% had their need fully met. Average financial aid package (proportion receiving): $7,165 (63%). Average amount of gift aid, such as scholarships or grants (proportion receiving): $3,279 (59%). Average amount of self-help aid, such as work study or loans (proportion receiving): $4,174 (57%). Average need-based loan (excluding PLUS or other private loans): $4,063. Among students who received need-based aid, the average percentage of need met: 74%. Among students who received aid based on merit, the average award (and the proportion receiving): $1,447 (16%). The average athletic scholarship (and the proportion receiving): $0 (0%). Average amount of debt of borrowers graduating in 2003: $13,125. Proportion who borrowed: 78%. **Student employment:** During the 2003-2004 academic year, 8% of undergraduates worked on campus. **Cooperative education programs:** agriculture, engineering. **Reserve Officers Training Corps (ROTC):** Army ROTC: Offered at cooperating institution (St. Boneventure University).

SUNY–Oswego

7060 State Route 104
Oswego, NY 13126
Public; www.oswego.edu
Financial aid office: (315) 312-2248

■ **2004-2005 TUITION AND FEES:**
In state: $2,619; Out of state: $5,594

SAT I Score (25th/75th percentile): 1040-1190
2005 U.S. News College Ranking:
Universities–Master's (North), third tier
Acceptance Rate: 57%

Financial aid: In 2003-2004, 86% of undergraduates applied for financial aid. Of those, 69% were determined to have financial need; 31% had their need fully met. Average financial aid package (proportion receiving): $8,411 (68%). Average amount of gift aid, such as scholarships or grants (proportion receiving): $3,572 (63%). Average amount of self-help aid, such as work study or loans (proportion receiving): $4,995 (61%). Average need-based loan (excluding PLUS or other private loans): $4,774. Among students who received need-based aid, the average percentage of need met: 84%. Among students who received aid based on merit, the average award (and the proportion receiving): $5,388 (14%). Average amount of debt of borrowers graduating in 2003: $16,880. Proportion who borrowed: 85%. **Student employment:** During the 2003-2004 academic year, 27% of undergraduates worked on campus. Average per-year earnings: $1,100. **Cooperative education programs:** agriculture, art, business, computer science, education. **Reserve Officers Training Corps (ROTC):** Army ROTC: Offered at cooperating institution (Syracuse University).

SUNY–Plattsburgh

101 Broad Street
Plattsburgh, NY 12901-2697
Public; www.plattsburgh.edu
Financial aid office: (518) 564-4061

■ **2004-2005 TUITION AND FEES:**
In state: $5,240; Out of state: $11,190
■ **ROOM AND BOARD:** $6,712

SAT I Score (25th/75th percentile): 960-1120
2005 U.S. News College Ranking:
Universities–Master's (North), third tier
Acceptance Rate: 60%

Other expenses: Estimated books and supplies: $850. Transportation: $500. Personal expenses: $1,576. **Financial aid:** Priority filing date for institution's financial aid form: March 1. In 2003-2004, 78% of undergraduates applied for financial aid. Of those, 62% were determined to have financial need; 39% had their need fully met. Average financial aid package (proportion receiving): $8,447 (61%). Average amount of gift aid, such as scholarships or grants (proportion receiving): $4,040 (56%). Average amount of self-help aid, such as work study or loans (proportion receiving): $5,497 (54%). Average need-based loan (excluding PLUS or other private loans): $5,389. Among students who received need-based aid, the average percentage of need met: 87%. Among students who received aid based on merit, the average award (and the proportion receiving): $4,552 (24%). The average athletic scholarship (and the proportion receiving): $0 (0%). Average amount of debt of borrowers graduating in 2003: $15,738. Proportion who borrowed: 73%. **Student employment:** During the 2003-2004 academic year, 19% of undergraduates worked on campus. Average per-year earnings: $1,600. **Cooperative education programs:** business, computer science, humanities, technologies.

SUNY–Purchase College

735 Anderson Hill Road
Purchase, NY 10577
Public; www.purchase.edu
Financial aid office: (914) 251-6350

■ **2004-2005 TUITION AND FEES:**
In state: $5,536; Out of state: $11,486
■ **ROOM AND BOARD:** $7,426

SAT I Score (25th/75th percentile): 1018-1210
2005 U.S. News College Ranking:
Universities–Master's (North), third tier
Acceptance Rate: 33%

Other expenses: Estimated books and supplies: $1,500. Transportation: $325. Personal expenses: $600. **Financial aid:** Priority filing date for institution's financial aid form: March 15. In 2003-2004, 62% of undergraduates applied for financial aid. Of those, 48% were determined to have financial need; 18% had their need fully met. Average financial aid package (proportion receiving): $7,235 (48%). Average amount of gift aid, such as scholarships or grants (proportion receiving): $3,975 (42%). Average amount of self-help aid, such as work study or loans (proportion receiving): $3,919 (46%). Average need-based loan (excluding PLUS or other pri-

vate loans): $3,643. Among students who received need-based aid, the average percentage of need met: 69%. Among students who received aid based on merit, the average award (and the proportion receiving): $11,242 (14%). Average amount of debt of borrowers graduating in 2003: $13,873.

SUNY–Stony Brook

Administration Building
Stony Brook, NY 11794
Public; www.stonybrook.edu
Financial aid office: (631) 632-6840

■ **2004-2005 TUITION AND FEES:**
In state: $5,336; Out of state: $11,286
■ **ROOM AND BOARD:** $7,774

SAT I Score (25th/75th percentile): 1070-1270
2005 U.S. News College Ranking:
National Universities, 106
Acceptance Rate: 51%

Other expenses: Estimated books and supplies: $900. Transportation: $500. Personal expenses: $1,000. **Financial aid:** Priority filing date for institution's financial aid form: March 1. In 2003-2004, 72% of undergraduates applied for financial aid. Of those, 59% were determined to have financial need; 14% had their need fully met. Average financial aid package (proportion receiving): $8,326 (57%). Average amount of gift aid, such as scholarships or grants (proportion receiving): $6,638 (52%). Average amount of self-help aid, such as work study or loans (proportion receiving): $4,983 (45%). Average need-based loan (excluding PLUS or other private loans): $3,469. Among students who received need-based aid, the average percentage of need met: 68%. Among students who received aid based on merit, the average award (and the proportion receiving): $2,776 (8%). The average athletic scholarship (and the proportion receiving): $8,226 (2%). Average amount of debt of borrowers graduating in 2003: $14,427. Proportion who borrowed: 50%. **Reserve Officers Training Corps (ROTC):** Army ROTC: Offered at cooperating institution (Hofstra); Air Force ROTC: Offered at cooperating institution (New York Institute of Technology).

Syracuse University

201 Tolley Administration Building
Syracuse, NY 13244
Private; www.syracuse.edu
Financial aid office: (315) 443-1513

■ 2004-2005 TUITION AND FEES: $26,824
■ ROOM AND BOARD: $9,960

SAT I Score (25th/75th percentile): 1150-1320
2005 U.S. News College Ranking:
National Universities, 52
Acceptance Rate: 62%

Other expenses: Estimated books and supplies:
$1,190. Transportation: $516. Personal expenses:
$992. Financial aid: In 2003-2004, 66% of
undergraduates applied for financial aid. Of
those, 58% were determined to have financial
need; 25% had their need fully met. Average
financial aid package (proportion receiving):
$18,720 (58%). Average amount of gift aid, such
as scholarships or grants (proportion receiving):
$12,793 (52%). Average amount of self-help aid,
such as work study or loans (proportion receiving): $6,800 (52%). Average need-based loan
(excluding PLUS or other private loans): $5,200.
Among students who received need-based aid,
the average percentage of need met: 80%.
Among students who received aid based on
merit, the average award (and the proportion
receiving): $7,240 (17%). The average athletic
scholarship (and the proportion receiving):
$27,150 (3%). Average amount of debt of borrow-
ers graduating in 2003: $19,000. Proportion who
borrowed: 70%. Student employment: During the
2003-2004 academic year, 20% of undergraduates worked on campus. Average per-year earnings: $1,500. Cooperative education programs:
education, engineering, other. Reserve Officers
Training Corps (ROTC): Army ROTC: Offered on
campus; Air Force ROTC: Offered on campus.

Touro College

27-33 W. 23rd Street
New York, NY 10001
Private; www.touro.edu
Financial aid office: (718) 252-7800

■ 2004-2005 TUITION AND FEES: $10,800
■ ROOM AND BOARD: $7,955

SAT I Score (25th/75th percentile): 1050-1270
2005 U.S. News College Ranking:
Universities–Master's (North), third tier
Acceptance Rate: 79%

Other expenses: Estimated books and supplies:
$807. Financial aid: Priority filing date for insti-
tution's financial aid form: May 15; deadline:
August 15. In 2003-2004, 75% of undergraduates applied for financial aid. Of those, 56%
were determined to have financial need;
Average financial aid package (proportion
receiving): $13,000 (56%). Average amount of
gift aid, such as scholarships or grants (proportion receiving): $4,000 (56%). Average amount
of self-help aid, such as work study or loans
(proportion receiving): $4,500 (39%). Average
need-based loan (excluding PLUS or other private loans): $2,625. Among students who
received need-based aid, the average percentage
of need met: 85%. Among students who
received aid based on merit, the average award
(and the proportion receiving): $2,000 (10%).
The average athletic scholarship (and the proportion receiving): $0 (0%). Average amount of
debt of borrowers graduating in 2003: $35,010.
Proportion who borrowed: 20%.

Union College

807 Union Street
Schenectady, NY 12308
Private; www.union.edu
Financial aid office: (518) 388-6123

■ 2003-2004 TUITION AND FEES: $28,928
■ ROOM AND BOARD: $7,077

SAT I Score (25th/75th percentile): 1150-1350
2005 U.S. News College Ranking:
Liberal Arts Colleges, 40
Acceptance Rate: 44%

Other expenses: Estimated books and supplies:
$450. Transportation: $250. Personal expenses:
$795. Financial aid: Priority filing date for insti-
tution's financial aid form: February 1; deadline: February 1. In 2003-2004, 54% of undergraduates applied for financial aid. Of those,
49% were determined to have financial need;
98% had their need fully met. Average financial aid package (proportion receiving): $23,798
(49%). Average amount of gift aid, such as
scholarships or grants (proportion receiving):
$19,590 (49%). Average amount of self-help
aid, such as work study or loans (proportion
receiving): $4,941 (45%). Average need-based
loan (excluding PLUS or other private loans):
$4,351. Among students who received need-
based aid, the average percentage of need met:
100%. Among students who received aid based
on merit, the average award (and the proportion receiving): $11,998 (5%). Average amount
of debt of borrowers graduating in 2003:

$19,195. Proportion who borrowed: 64%.
Student employment: During the 2003-2004
academic year, 16% of undergraduates worked
on campus. Average per-year earnings: $1,150.
Cooperative education programs: engineering.
Reserve Officers Training Corps (ROTC): Army
ROTC: Offered at cooperating institution (Siena
College); Navy ROTC: Offered at cooperating
institution (Rensselaer Polytechnic Institute);
Air Force ROTC: Offered at cooperating institu-
tion (Rensselaer Polytechnic Institute).

United States Merchant Marine Academy

300 Steamboat Road
Kings Point, NY 11024
Public; www.usmma.edu
Financial aid office: (516) 773-5295

■ 2004-2005 TUITION AND FEES:
In state: $2,002; Out of state: $2,002
■ ROOM AND BOARD: $0

SAT I Score (25th/75th percentile): 1155-1355
2005 U.S. News College Ranking:
Unranked Specialty School–Military Academies
Acceptance Rate: 20%

Other expenses: Estimated books and supplies:
$0. Financial aid: In 2003-2004, 26% of under-
graduates applied for financial aid. Of those,
13% were determined to have financial need;
Average financial aid package (proportion
receiving): $1,381 (24%). Average amount of
gift aid, such as scholarships or grants (proportion receiving): $1,111 (2%). Average amount of
self-help aid, such as work study or loans (proportion receiving): $2,429 (9%). Average need-
based loan (excluding PLUS or other private
loans): $1,381. Among students who received
need-based aid, the average percentage of need
met: 100%. Among students who received aid
based on merit, the average award (and the proportion receiving): $0 (0%). The average athlet-
ic scholarship (and the proportion receiving):
$0 (0%). Average amount of debt of borrowers
graduating in 2003: $9,000. Proportion who
borrowed: 33%. Student employment: During
the 2003-2004 academic year, 1% of undergraduates worked on campus. Average per-year
earnings: $500. Cooperative education pro-
grams: other. Reserve Officers Training Corps
(ROTC): Navy ROTC: Offered on campus.

United States Military Academy

600 Thayer Road
West Point, NY 10996-2101
Public; www.usma.edu
Financial aid office: (845) 938-4262

■ **2004-2005 TUITION AND FEES:** $0

SAT I Score (25th/75th percentile): 1170-1350
2005 U.S. News College Ranking:
Unranked Specialty School–Military Academies
Acceptance Rate: 10%

Financial aid: Average financial aid package (proportion receiving): $0 (N/A). Average amount of gift aid, such as scholarships or grants (proportion receiving): $0 (N/A). Average amount of self-help aid, such as work study or loans (proportion receiving): $0 (N/A). Average need-based loan (excluding PLUS or other private loans): $0. Among students who received aid based on merit, the average award (and the proportion receiving): $0 (N/A). The average athletic scholarship (and the proportion receiving): $0 (N/A). Average amount of debt of borrowers graduating in 2003: $0. **Student employment:** During the 2003-2004 academic year, 0% of undergraduates worked on campus. Average per-year earnings: $0.

University at Buffalo–SUNY

3435 Main Street
Buffalo, NY 14214
Public; www.buffalo.edu
Financial aid office: (716) 645-6018

■ **2004-2005 TUITION AND FEES:**
In state: $5,861; Out of state: $11,811
■ **ROOM AND BOARD:** $6,816

SAT I Score (25th/75th percentile): 1030-1230
2005 U.S. News College Ranking:
National Universities, 120
Acceptance Rate: 62%

Other expenses: Estimated books and supplies: $795. Transportation: $530. Personal expenses: $764. **Financial aid:** Priority filing date for institution's financial aid form: March 1. In 2003-2004, 73% of undergraduates applied for financial aid. Of those, 71% were determined to have financial need; 67% had their need fully met. Average financial aid package (proportion receiving): $7,520 (54%). Average amount of gift aid, such as scholarships or grants (propor-

tion receiving): $3,573 (35%). Average amount of self-help aid, such as work study or loans (proportion receiving): $4,450 (52%). Average need-based loan (excluding PLUS or other private loans): $3,040. Among students who received need-based aid, the average percentage of need met: 71%. Among students who received aid based on merit, the average award (and the proportion receiving): $2,930 (2%). The average athletic scholarship (and the proportion receiving): $7,900 (1%). Average amount of debt of borrowers graduating in 2003: $16,418. Proportion who borrowed: 70%. **Cooperative education programs:** art, business, computer science, engineering, health professions, natural science, social/behavioral science, technologies, other. **Reserve Officers Training Corps (ROTC):** Army ROTC: Offered at cooperating institution (Canisius College).

University of Rochester

Wilson Boulevard
Rochester, NY 14627
Private; www.rochester.edu
Financial aid office: (585) 275-3226

■ **2004-2005 TUITION AND FEES:** $28,968
■ **ROOM AND BOARD:** $9,595

SAT I Score (25th/75th percentile): 1210-1400
2005 U.S. News College Ranking:
National Universities, 37
Acceptance Rate: 49%

Other expenses: Estimated books and supplies: $550. Transportation: $300. Personal expenses: $900. **Financial aid:** Priority filing date for institution's financial aid form: February 1; deadline: February 1. In 2003-2004, 69% of undergraduates applied for financial aid. Of those, 59% were determined to have financial need; 100% had their need fully met. Average financial aid package (proportion receiving): $22,854 (59%). Average amount of gift aid, such as scholarships or grants (proportion receiving): $17,801 (58%). Average amount of self-help aid, such as work study or loans (proportion receiving): $6,275 (51%). Average need-based loan (excluding PLUS or other private loans): $4,981. Among students who received need-based aid, the average percentage of need met: 100%. Among students who received aid based on merit, the average award (and the proportion receiving): $10,022 (34%). The average athletic scholarship (and the proportion receiving): $0 (0%). Average amount of debt of borrowers graduating in 2003: $19,782. Proportion who borrowed: 68%. **Student employment:**

During the 2003-2004 academic year, 49% of undergraduates worked on campus. Average per-year earnings: $2,500. **Cooperative education programs:** engineering. **Reserve Officers Training Corps (ROTC):** Army ROTC: Offered at cooperating institution (Rochester Institute of Technology); Navy ROTC: Offered on campus; Air Force ROTC: Offered at cooperating institution (Rochester Institute of Technology).

Utica College

1600 Burrstone Road
Utica, NY 13502
Private; www.utica.edu
Financial aid office: (315) 792-3179

■ **2004-2005 TUITION AND FEES:** $21,270
■ **ROOM AND BOARD:** $8,600

SAT I Score (25th/75th percentile): 880-1080
2005 U.S. News College Ranking:
Comp. Colleges–Bachelor's (North), 12
Acceptance Rate: 77%

Other expenses: Estimated books and supplies: $850. Transportation: $500. Personal expenses: $786. **Financial aid:** Priority filing date for institution's financial aid form: February 15. In 2003-2004, 99% of undergraduates applied for financial aid. Of those, 92% were determined to have financial need; 17% had their need fully met. Average financial aid package (proportion receiving): N/A (92%). Average amount of gift aid, such as scholarships or grants (proportion receiving): $12,477 (91%). Average amount of self-help aid, such as work study or loans (proportion receiving): $5,006 (86%). Average need-based loan (excluding PLUS or other private loans): $4,107. Among students who received aid based on merit, the average award (and the proportion receiving): $8,038 (1%). The average athletic scholarship (and the proportion receiving): $0 (0%). **Student employment:** During the 2003-2004 academic year, 54% of undergraduates worked on campus. Average per-year earnings: $1,194. **Cooperative education programs:** business, computer science, education, health professions, humanities, natural science, social/behavioral science, technologies. **Reserve Officers Training Corps (ROTC):** Army ROTC: Offered on campus; Air Force ROTC: Offered at cooperating institution (Syracuse Universtiy).

Vassar College

124 Raymond Avenue
Poughkeepsie, NY 12604
Private; www.vassar.edu
Financial aid office: (845) 437-5320

■ **2004-2005 TUITION AND FEES:** $31,350
■ **ROOM AND BOARD:** $7,680

SAT I Score (25th/75th percentile): 1300-1450
2005 U.S. News College Ranking:
Liberal Arts Colleges, 12
Acceptance Rate: 29%

Other expenses: Estimated books and supplies:
$820. Transportation: $340. Personal expenses:
$880. **Financial aid:** Priority filing date for insti-
tution's financial aid form: February 1; deadline: February 1. In 2003-2004, 64% of undergraduates applied for financial aid. Of those,
53% were determined to have financial need;
100% had their need fully met. Average financial aid package (proportion receiving): $24,305
(53%). Average amount of gift aid, such as
scholarships or grants (proportion receiving):
$19,511 (52%). Average amount of self-help aid,
such as work study or loans (proportion receiving): $4,794 (53%). Average need-based loan
(excluding PLUS or other private loans):
$3,009. Among students who received need-
based aid, the average percentage of need met:
100%. Among students who received aid based
on merit, the average award (and the proportion receiving): $0 (0%). The average athletic
scholarship (and the proportion receiving): $0
(0%). Average amount of debt of borrowers
graduating in 2003: $18,729. Proportion who
borrowed: 57%. **Student employment:** During
the 2003-2004 academic year, 71% of undergraduates worked on campus. Average per-year
earnings: $1,066.

Wagner College

1 Campus Road
Staten Island, NY 10301
Private; www.wagner.edu
Financial aid office: (718) 390-3183

■ **2004-2005 TUITION AND FEES:** $23,900
■ **ROOM AND BOARD:** $7,500

SAT I Score (25th/75th percentile): 1050-1250
2005 U.S. News College Ranking:
Universities–Master's (North), 25
Acceptance Rate: 66%

Other expenses: Estimated books and supplies:
$701. Transportation: $701. Personal expenses:
$1,219. **Financial aid:** Priority filing date for
institution's financial aid form: February 15. In
2003-2004, 75% of undergraduates applied for
financial aid. Of those, 63% were determined to
have financial need; 25% had their need fully
met. Average financial aid package (proportion
receiving): $14,768 (63%). Average amount of
gift aid, such as scholarships or grants (proportion receiving): $10,955 (62%). Average amount
of self-help aid, such as work study or loans
(proportion receiving): $5,155 (48%). Average
need-based loan (excluding PLUS or other private loans): $4,542. Among students who
received need-based aid, the average percentage
of need met: 73%. Among students who
received aid based on merit, the average award
(and the proportion receiving): $7,439 (26%).
Average amount of debt of borrowers graduating in 2003: $23,144. Proportion who bor-
rowed: 72%. **Student employment:** During the
2003-2004 academic year, 20% of undergraduates worked on campus. Average per-year earnings: $1,200. **Reserve Officers Training Corps
(ROTC):** Army ROTC: Offered at cooperating
institution (St. John's University).

Webb Institute

298 Crescent Beach Road
Glen Cove, NY 11542-1398
Private; www.webb-institute.edu
Financial aid office: (516) 671-2213

■ **2004-2005 TUITION AND FEES:** $0
■ **ROOM AND BOARD:** $7,550

SAT I Score (25th/75th percentile): 1340-1470
2005 U.S. News College Ranking:
Unranked Specialty School–Engineering
Acceptance Rate: 32%

Other expenses: Estimated books and supplies:
$600. Transportation: $2,000. Personal
expenses: $600. **Financial aid:** Priority filing
date for institution's financial aid form: July 1;
deadline: August 1. In 2003-2004, 15% of
undergraduates applied for financial aid. Of
those, 15% were determined to have financial
need; 9% had their need fully met. Average
financial aid package (proportion receiving):
$4,650 (15%). Average amount of gift aid, such
as scholarships or grants (proportion receiving):
$1,850 (3%). Average amount of self-help aid,
such as work study or loans (proportion receiving): $0 (0%). Average need-based loan (exclud-
ing PLUS or other private loans): $4,230.
Among students who received need-based aid,

the average percentage of need met: 90%.
Among students who received aid based on
merit, the average award (and the proportion
receiving): $0 (0%). The average athletic schol-
arship (and the proportion receiving): $0 (0%).
Average amount of debt of borrowers graduating in 2003: $14,450. Proportion who bor-
rowed: 19%.

Wells College

170 Main Street
Aurora, NY 13026
Private; www.wells.edu
Financial aid office: (315) 364-3289

■ **2004-2005 TUITION AND FEES:** $14,900
■ **ROOM AND BOARD:** $7,000

SAT I Score (25th/75th percentile): 990-1240
2005 U.S. News College Ranking:
Liberal Arts Colleges, 105
Acceptance Rate: 84%

Other expenses: Estimated books and supplies:
$700. Transportation: $0. Personal expenses:
$700. **Financial aid:** Priority filing date for insti-
tution's financial aid form: February 15. In
2003-2004, 88% of undergraduates applied for
financial aid. Of those, 77% were determined to
have financial need; 36% had their need fully
met. Average financial aid package (proportion
receiving): $15,475 (77%). Average amount of
gift aid, such as scholarships or grants (proportion receiving): $10,235 (77%). Average amount
of self-help aid, such as work study or loans
(proportion receiving): $5,380 (76%). Average
need-based loan (excluding PLUS or other private loans): $4,775. Among students who
received need-based aid, the average percentage
of need met: 91%. Among students who
received aid based on merit, the average award
(and the proportion receiving): $4,756 (12%).
The average athletic scholarship (and the proportion receiving): $0 (0%). Average amount of
debt of borrowers graduating in 2003: $17,125.
Proportion who borrowed: 92%. **Student
employment:** During the 2003-2004 academic
year, 56% of undergraduates worked on campus. Average per-year earnings: $1,400. **Reserve
Officers Training Corps (ROTC):** Air Force
ROTC: Offered at cooperating institution
(Cornell University).

Yeshiva University

500 W. 185th Street
New York, NY 10033
Private; www.yu.edu
Financial aid office: (212) 960-5269

■ **2004-2005 TUITION AND FEES:** $23,630
■ **ROOM AND BOARD:** $7,330

SAT I Score (25th/75th percentile): 1170-1350
2005 U.S. News College Ranking:
National Universities, 46
Acceptance Rate: 78%

....

Other expenses: Estimated books and supplies: $1,100. Transportation: $1,125. Personal expenses: $3,009. **Financial aid:** Priority filing date for institution's financial aid form: February 15. In 2003-2004, 56% of undergraduates applied for financial aid. Of those, 47% were determined to have financial need; 28% had their need fully met. Average financial aid package (proportion receiving): $15,709 (47%). Average amount of gift aid, such as scholarships or grants (proportion receiving): $13,541 (41%). Average amount of self-help aid, such as work study or loans (proportion receiving): $5,195 (35%). Average need-based loan (excluding PLUS or other private loans): $4,967. Among students who received need-based aid, the average percentage of need met: 72%. Among students who received aid based on merit, the average award (and the proportion receiving): $5,632 (7%). The average athletic scholarship (and the proportion receiving): $0 (0%). Average amount of debt of borrowers graduating in 2003: $16,642. Proportion who borrowed: 49%. **Student employment:** During the 2003-2004 academic year, 5% of undergraduates worked on campus. Average per-year earnings: $2,000.

North Carolina

Appalachian State University

Boone, NC 28608
Public; www.appstate.edu
Financial aid office: (828) 262-2190

■ **2004-2005 TUITION AND FEES:**
In state: $3,199; Out of state: $12,641
■ **ROOM AND BOARD:** $4,608

SAT I Score (25th/75th percentile): 1020-1210
2005 U.S. News College Ranking:
Universities–Master's (South), 11
Acceptance Rate: 66%

Other expenses: Estimated books and supplies: $500. Transportation: $1,100. Personal expenses: $1,200. **Financial aid:** Priority filing date for institution's financial aid form: March 15. In 2003-2004, 59% of undergraduates applied for financial aid. Of those, 35% were determined to have financial need; 36% had their need fully met. Average financial aid package (proportion receiving): $5,778 (34%). Average amount of gift aid, such as scholarships or grants (proportion receiving): $3,399 (30%). Average amount of self-help aid, such as work study or loans (proportion receiving): $3,464 (27%). Average need-based loan (excluding PLUS or other private loans): $3,328. Among students who received need-based aid, the average percentage of need met: 76%. Among students who received aid based on merit, the average award (and the proportion receiving): $2,751 (9%). The average athletic scholarship (and the proportion receiving): $6,305 (2%). Average amount of debt of borrowers graduating in 2003: $14,000. Proportion who borrowed: 48%. **Student employment:** During the 2003-2004 academic year, 14% of undergraduates worked on campus. Average per-year earnings: $3,500. **Reserve Officers Training Corps (ROTC):** Army ROTC: Offered on campus.

Barber Scotia College

145 Cabarrus Avenue W
Concord, NC 28025
Private; www.b-sc.edu
Financial aid office: (704) 789-2923

■ **2004-2005 TUITION AND FEES:** $9,200
■ **ROOM AND BOARD:** $4,452

ACT Score (25th/75th percentile): 12-17
2005 U.S. News College Ranking:
Liberal Arts Colleges, fourth tier
Acceptance Rate: 51%

Student employment: During the 2003-2004 academic year, 35% of undergraduates worked on campus. **Cooperative education programs:** home economics, social/behavioral science.

Barton College

Box 5000
Wilson, NC 27893
Private; www.barton.edu
Financial aid office: (252) 399-6323

■ **2004-2005 TUITION AND FEES:** $15,363
■ **ROOM AND BOARD:** $5,420

SAT I Score (25th/75th percentile): 820-1130
2005 U.S. News College Ranking:
Comp. Colleges–Bachelor's (South), 41
Acceptance Rate: 74%

Student employment: During the 2003-2004 academic year, 28% of undergraduates worked on campus. Average per-year earnings: $1,200. **Cooperative education programs:** natural science.

Belmont Abbey College

100 Belmont-Mount Holly Road
Belmont, NC 28012
Private; www.belmontabbeycollege.edu
Financial aid office: (704) 825-6718

■ **2004-2005 TUITION AND FEES:** $15,778
■ **ROOM AND BOARD:** $8,100

SAT I Score (25th/75th percentile): 860-1110
2005 U.S. News College Ranking:
Comp. Colleges–Bachelor's (South), 32
Acceptance Rate: 69%

Other expenses: Estimated books and supplies: $900. Transportation: $1,800. Personal expenses: $1,800. **Financial aid:** Priority filing date for institution's financial aid form: April 1. In 2003-2004, 82% of undergraduates applied for financial aid. Of those, 74% were determined to have financial need; 16% had their need fully

met. Average financial aid package (proportion receiving): $11,294 (74%). Average amount of gift aid, such as scholarships or grants (proportion receiving): $8,215 (73%). Average amount of self-help aid, such as work study or loans (proportion receiving): $3,746 (63%). Average need-based loan (excluding PLUS or other private loans): $3,487. Among students who received need-based aid, the average percentage of need met: 62%. Among students who received aid based on merit, the average award (and the proportion receiving): $8,710 (27%). The average athletic scholarship (and the proportion receiving): $5,634 (7%). Average amount of debt of borrowers graduating in 2003: $18,000. Proportion who borrowed: 78%. **Student employment:** During the 2003-2004 academic year, 5% of undergraduates worked on campus. Average per-year earnings: $3,500. **Reserve Officers Training Corps (ROTC):** Army ROTC: Offered at cooperating institution (University of North Carolina–Charlotte); Navy ROTC: Offered at cooperating institution (University of North Carolina–Charlotte); Air Force ROTC: Offered at cooperating institution (University of North Carolina–Charlotte).

Bennett College

900 E. Washington Street
Greensboro, NC 27401
Private; www.bennett.edu
Financial aid office: (336) 517-2205

■ **2004-2005 TUITION AND FEES:** $11,801
■ **ROOM AND BOARD:** $5,452

SAT I Score (25th/75th percentile): 808
2005 U.S. News College Ranking:
Liberal Arts Colleges, fourth tier
Acceptance Rate: 74%

Other expenses: Estimated books and supplies: $1,800. Transportation: $2,600. Personal expenses: $2,000. **Financial aid:** Priority filing date for institution's financial aid form: March 15. In 2003-2004, 97% of undergraduates applied for financial aid. Of those, 94% were determined to have financial need; 87% had their need fully met. Average financial aid package (proportion receiving): $15,000 (91%). Average amount of gift aid, such as scholarships or grants (proportion receiving): $3,500 (46%). Average amount of self-help aid, such as work study or loans (proportion receiving): $2,000 (28%). Average need-based loan (excluding PLUS or other private loans): $2,000. Among students who received need-based aid, the average percentage of need met: 91%. Among students who received aid based on merit, the average award (and the proportion receiving): $1,972 (9%). Proportion who borrowed: 97%. **Cooperative education programs:** engineering. **Reserve Officers Training Corps (ROTC):** Army ROTC: Offered at cooperating institution (North Carolina State A&T).

Brevard College

400 N. Broad Street
Brevard, NC 28712-3306
Private; www.brevard.edu
Financial aid office: (828) 884-8287

■ **2004-2005 TUITION AND FEES:** $14,740
■ **ROOM AND BOARD:** $5,560

SAT I Score (25th/75th percentile): 770-1193
2005 U.S. News College Ranking:
Comp. Colleges–Bachelor's (South), 41
Acceptance Rate: 82%

Other expenses: Estimated books and supplies: $800. Transportation: $750. Personal expenses: $1,000. **Financial aid:** Priority filing date for institution's financial aid form: April 15. In 2003-2004, 79% of undergraduates applied for financial aid. Of those, 68% were determined to have financial need; 19% had their need fully met. Average financial aid package (proportion receiving): $12,400 (68%). Average amount of gift aid, such as scholarships or grants (proportion receiving): $9,975 (67%). Average amount of self-help aid, such as work study or loans (proportion receiving): $3,950 (59%). Average need-based loan (excluding PLUS or other private loans): $3,840. Among students who received need-based aid, the average percentage of need met: 79%. Among students who received aid based on merit, the average award (and the proportion receiving): $3,415 (16%). The average athletic scholarship (and the proportion receiving): $6,500 (3%). Average amount of debt of borrowers graduating in 2003: $16,950. Proportion who borrowed: 55%.

Campbell University

PO Box 546
Buies Creek, NC 27506
Private; www.campbell.edu
Financial aid office: (910) 893-1310

■ **2004-2005 TUITION AND FEES:** $14,420
■ **ROOM AND BOARD:** $5,132

SAT I Score (25th/75th percentile): 1005-1250
2005 U.S. News College Ranking:
Universities–Master's (South), 55
Acceptance Rate: 58%

Other expenses: Estimated books and supplies: $1,000. Transportation: $900. Personal expenses: $3,052. **Financial aid:** Priority filing date for institution's financial aid form: March 15. In 2003-2004, 78% of undergraduates applied for financial aid. Of those, 68% were determined to have financial need; 100% had their need fully met. Average financial aid package (proportion receiving): $18,024 (68%). Average amount of gift aid, such as scholarships or grants (proportion receiving): $4,997 (47%). Average amount of self-help aid, such as work study or loans (proportion receiving): $4,609 (61%). Average need-based loan (excluding PLUS or other private loans): $4,187. Among students who received need-based aid, the average percentage of need met: 100%. Among students who received aid based on merit, the average award (and the proportion receiving): $5,592 (15%). The average athletic scholarship (and the proportion receiving): $9,600 (6%). Average amount of debt of borrowers graduating in 2003: $10,438. Proportion who borrowed: 54%. **Student employment:** During the 2003-2004 academic year, 15% of undergraduates worked on campus. Average per-year earnings: $1,200. **Cooperative education programs:** education. **Reserve Officers Training Corps (ROTC):** Army ROTC: Offered on campus.

Catawba College

2300 W. Innes Street
Salisbury, NC 28144
Private; www.catawba.edu
Financial aid office: (704) 637-4416

■ **2004-2005 TUITION AND FEES:** $17,600
■ **ROOM AND BOARD:** $5,900

SAT I Score (25th/75th percentile): 950-1130
2005 U.S. News College Ranking:
Comp. Colleges–Bachelor's (South), 22
Acceptance Rate: 64%

Other expenses: Estimated books and supplies: $800. Transportation: $1,200. Personal expenses: $1,200. **Financial aid:** Priority filing date for institution's financial aid form: March 1. In 2003-2004, 76% of undergraduates applied for financial aid. Of those, 64% were determined to have financial need; 36% had their need fully met. Average financial aid package (proportion receiving): $12,272 (64%). Average amount of gift aid, such as scholarships or grants (proportion receiving): $4,075 (41%). Average amount of self-help aid, such as work study or loans (proportion receiving): $4,400 (55%). Average need-based loan (excluding PLUS or other private loans): $4,131. Among students who received aid based on merit, the average award (and the proportion receiving): $6,347 (10%). The average athletic scholarship (and the proportion receiving): $6,496 (4%). Average amount of debt of borrowers graduating in 2003: $22,000. Proportion who borrowed: 64%. **Student employment:** During the 2003-2004 academic year, 0% of undergraduates worked on campus. **Reserve Officers Training Corps (ROTC):** Army ROTC: Offered at cooperating institution (UNC Charlotte); Air Force ROTC: Offered at cooperating institution (UNC Charlotte).

Chowan College

200 Jones Drive
Murfreesboro, NC 27855
Private; www.chowan.edu
Financial aid office: (252) 398-1229

■ **2004-2005 TUITION AND FEES:** $14,100
■ **ROOM AND BOARD:** $6,100

SAT I Score (25th/75th percentile): 760-970
2005 U.S. News College Ranking:
Comp. Colleges–Bachelor's (South), fourth tier
Acceptance Rate: 67%

Other expenses: Estimated books and supplies: $864. Transportation: $536. Personal expenses: $1,000. **Financial aid:** Priority filing date for institution's financial aid form: May 1; deadline: August 1. In 2003-2004, 93% of undergraduates applied for financial aid. Of those, 86% were determined to have financial need; 12% had their need fully met. Average financial aid package (proportion receiving): $10,595 (86%). Average amount of gift aid, such as scholarships or grants (proportion receiving): $7,361 (86%). Average amount of self-help aid, such as work study or loans (proportion receiving): $3,728 (76%). Average need-based loan (excluding PLUS or other private loans): $3,507. Among students who received need-based aid, the average percentage of need met: 70%. Among students who received aid based on merit, the average award (and the proportion receiving): $10,077 (14%). The average athletic scholarship (and the proportion receiving): $0 (0%). Average amount of debt of borrowers graduating in 2003: $17,953. Proportion who borrowed: 86%.

Davidson College

209 Ridge Road
Davidson, NC 28035
Private; www.davidson.edu
Financial aid office: (704) 894-2232

■ **2004-2005 TUITION AND FEES:** $27,171
■ **ROOM AND BOARD:** $7,732

SAT I Score (25th/75th percentile): 1270-1440
2005 U.S. News College Ranking:
Liberal Arts Colleges, 7
Acceptance Rate: 32%

Other expenses: Estimated books and supplies: $1,000. Transportation: $350. Personal expenses: $1,177. **Financial aid:** Priority filing date for institution's financial aid form: February 15. In 2003-2004, 41% of undergraduates applied for financial aid. Of those, 34% were determined to have financial need; 99% had their need fully met. Average financial aid package (proportion receiving): $17,395 (34%). Average amount of gift aid, such as scholarships or grants (proportion receiving): $14,902 (32%). Average amount of self-help aid, such as work study or loans (proportion receiving): $4,092 (29%). Average need-based loan (excluding PLUS or other private loans): $3,903. Among students who received need-based aid, the average percentage of need met: 100%. Among students who received aid based on merit, the average award (and the proportion receiving): $7,633 (15%). The average athletic scholarship (and the proportion receiving): $10,660 (11%). Average amount of debt of borrowers graduating in 2003: $21,530. Proportion who borrowed: 32%. **Reserve Officers Training Corps (ROTC):** Army ROTC: Offered on campus; Air Force ROTC: Offered at cooperating institution (University of North Carolina–Charlotte).

Duke University

2138 Campus Drive, Box 90586
Durham, NC 27708
Private; www.duke.edu
Financial aid office: (919) 684-6225

■ **2004-2005 TUITION AND FEES:** $30,720
■ **ROOM AND BOARD:** $8,525

SAT I Score (25th/75th percentile): 1330-1520
2005 U.S. News College Ranking:
National Universities, 5
Acceptance Rate: 25%

Other expenses: Estimated books and supplies: $940. Transportation: $420. Personal expenses: $1,640. **Financial aid:** In 2003-2004, 44% of undergraduates applied for financial aid. Of those, 40% were determined to have financial need; 100% had their need fully met. Average financial aid package (proportion receiving): $26,162 (40%). Average amount of gift aid, such as scholarships or grants (proportion receiving): $21,607 (38%). Average amount of self-help aid, such as work study or loans (proportion receiving): $6,346 (37%). Average need-based loan (excluding PLUS or other private loans): $5,050. Among students who received need-based aid, the average percentage of need met: 100%. Among students who received aid based on merit, the average award (and the proportion receiving): $9,370 (14%). The average athletic scholarship (and the proportion receiving): $25,124 (4%). Average amount of debt of borrowers graduating in 2003: $19,737. Proportion who borrowed: 39%. **Reserve Officers Training Corps (ROTC):** Army ROTC: Offered on campus; Navy ROTC: Offered on campus; Air Force ROTC: Offered on campus.

East Carolina University

East Fifth Street
Greenville, NC 27858-4353
Public; www.ecu.edu
Financial aid office: (252) 328-6610

■ **2004-2005 TUITION AND FEES:**
In state: $3,454; Out of state: $13,668
■ **ROOM AND BOARD:** $5,400

SAT I Score (25th/75th percentile): 950-1130
2005 U.S. News College Ranking:
National Universities, third tier
Acceptance Rate: 77%

Financial aid: Priority filing date for institution's financial aid form: April 15. In 2003-2004, 66% of undergraduates applied for financial aid. Of those, 33% were determined to have financial need; 46% had their need fully met. Average financial aid package (proportion receiving): N/A (32%). Average amount of gift aid, such as scholarships or grants (proportion receiving): $3,072 (24%). Average amount of self-help aid, such as work study or loans (proportion receiving): $3,600 (27%). Average need-based loan (excluding PLUS or other private loans): $3,511. Among students who received aid based on merit, the average award (and the proportion receiving): $5,659 (24%). The average athletic scholarship (and the proportion receiving): $9,331 (1%). Average amount of debt of borrowers graduating in 2003: $18,318. Proportion who borrowed: 61%. **Cooperative education programs:** other. **Reserve Officers Training Corps (ROTC):** Army ROTC: Offered on campus; Air Force ROTC: Offered on campus.

Elizabeth City State University

1704 Weeksville Road
Elizabeth City, NC 27909
Public; www.ecsu.edu
Financial aid office: (252) 335-3283

■ **2004-2005 TUITION AND FEES:**
In state: $2,950; Out of state: $11,214
■ **ROOM AND BOARD:** $4,608

SAT I Score (25th/75th percentile): 720-900
2005 U.S. News College Ranking:
Comp. Colleges–Bachelor's (South), 43
Acceptance Rate: 76%

Other expenses: Estimated books and supplies: $600. Transportation: $400. Personal expenses: $400. **Financial aid:** Priority filing date for institution's financial aid form: March 15. Average financial aid package (proportion receiving): N/A (98%). **Cooperative education programs:** education, technologies. **Reserve Officers Training Corps (ROTC):** Army ROTC: Offered on campus.

Elon University

2700 Campus Box
Elon, NC 27244
Private; www.elon.edu
Financial aid office: (336) 278-7640

■ **2004-2005 TUITION AND FEES:** $17,555
■ **ROOM AND BOARD:** $6,010

SAT I Score (25th/75th percentile): 1070-1250
2005 U.S. News College Ranking:
Universities–Master's (South), 6
Acceptance Rate: 45%

Other expenses: Estimated books and supplies: $900. Transportation: $800. Personal expenses: $1,400. **Financial aid:** Priority filing date for institution's financial aid form: February 15. In 2003-2004, 47% of undergraduates applied for financial aid. Of those, 35% were determined to have financial need; Average financial aid package (proportion receiving): $11,368 (35%). Average amount of gift aid, such as scholarships or grants (proportion receiving): $5,779 (32%). Average amount of self-help aid, such as work study or loans (proportion receiving): $5,589 (29%). Average need-based loan (excluding PLUS or other private loans): $4,031. Among students who received need-based aid, the average percentage of need met: 71%. Among students who received aid based on merit, the average award (and the proportion receiving): $3,512 (19%). The average athletic scholarship (and the proportion receiving): $11,392 (4%). Average amount of debt of borrowers graduating in 2003: $18,102. Proportion who borrowed: 46%. **Student employment:** During the 2003-2004 academic year, 17% of undergraduates worked on campus. Average per-year earnings: $2,245. **Cooperative education programs:** art, business, computer science, education, engineering, health professions, humanities, natural science, social/behavioral science, technologies. **Reserve Officers Training Corps (ROTC):** Army ROTC: Offered at cooperating institution (North Carolina A&T University); Air Force ROTC: Offered at cooperating institution (North Carolina A&T University).

Fayetteville State University

1200 Murchison Road
Fayetteville, NC 28301
Public; www.uncfsu.edu
Financial aid office: (910) 672-1325

■ **2004-2005 TUITION AND FEES:**
In state: $2,279; Out of state: $11,715
■ **ROOM AND BOARD:** $4,120

SAT I Score (25th/75th percentile): 770-950
2005 U.S. News College Ranking:
Universities–Master's (South), fourth tier
Acceptance Rate: 85%

Financial aid: Priority filing date for institution's financial aid form: March 1; deadline: March 1. **Student employment:** During the 2003-2004 academic year, 10% of undergraduates worked on campus. Average per-year earnings: $1,500. **Cooperative education programs:** business, natural science, social/behavioral science. **Reserve Officers Training Corps (ROTC):** Army ROTC: Offered at cooperating institution (Methodist College); Air Force ROTC: Offered on campus.

Gardner-Webb University

PO Box 997
Boiling Springs, NC 28017
Private; www.gardner-webb.edu
Financial aid office: (704) 406-4243

■ **2004-2005 TUITION AND FEES:** $15,130
■ **ROOM AND BOARD:** $5,340

SAT I Score (25th/75th percentile): 900-1140
2005 U.S. News College Ranking:
Universities–Master's (South), third tier
Acceptance Rate: 74%

Other expenses: Estimated books and supplies: $820. Transportation: $640. Personal expenses: $270. **Financial aid:** Priority filing date for institution's financial aid form: March 15. In 2003-2004, 80% of undergraduates applied for financial aid. Of those, 70% were determined to have financial need; 33% had their need fully met. Average financial aid package (proportion receiving): $9,512 (70%). Average amount of gift aid, such as scholarships or grants (proportion receiving): $5,163 (68%). Average amount of self-help aid, such as work study or loans (proportion receiving): $5,099 (57%). Average need-based loan (excluding PLUS or other private loans): $4,118. Among students who received need-

based aid, the average percentage of need met: 79%. Among students who received aid based on merit, the average award (and the proportion receiving): $5,031 (27%). The average athletic scholarship (and the proportion receiving): $10,646 (6%). Average amount of debt of borrowers graduating in 2003: $7,865. Proportion who borrowed: 57%. **Student employment:** During the 2003-2004 academic year, 48% of undergraduates worked on campus. Average per-year earnings: $1,114. **Reserve Officers Training Corps (ROTC):** Army ROTC: Offered on campus.

Greensboro College

815 W. Market Street
Greensboro, NC 27401-1875
Private; www.gborocollege.edu
Financial aid office: (336) 272-7102

■ **2004-2005 TUITION AND FEES:** $16,820
■ **ROOM AND BOARD:** $6,460

SAT I Score (25th/75th percentile): 860-1090
2005 U.S. News College Ranking:
Liberal Arts Colleges, fourth tier
Acceptance Rate: 74%

Other expenses: Estimated books and supplies: $900. Transportation: $300. Personal expenses: $900. **Financial aid:** Priority filing date for institution's financial aid form: April 15. In 2003-2004, 81% of undergraduates applied for financial aid. Of those, 65% were determined to have financial need; 41% had their need fully met. Average financial aid package (proportion receiving): $9,395 (65%). Average amount of gift aid, such as scholarships or grants (proportion receiving): $3,824 (49%). Average amount of self-help aid, such as work study or loans (proportion receiving): $3,960 (54%). Average need-based loan (excluding PLUS or other private loans): $4,011. Among students who received need-based aid, the average percentage of need met: 71%. Among students who received aid based on merit, the average award (and the proportion receiving): $4,473 (27%). Average amount of debt of borrowers graduating in 2003: $11,802. Proportion who borrowed: 67%. **Student employment:** During the 2003-2004 academic year, 1% of undergraduates worked on campus. Average per-year earnings: $800. **Cooperative education programs:** art, business, computer science, education, health professions, humanities, natural science, social/behavioral science, technologies. **Reserve Officers Training Corps (ROTC):** Army ROTC: Offered at cooperating institution (N.C. A&T University); Air Force ROTC: Offered at cooperating institution (N.C. A&T University).

Guilford College

5800 W. Friendly Avenue
Greensboro, NC 27410
Private; www.guilford.edu
Financial aid office: (336) 316-2165

■ **2004-2005 TUITION AND FEES:** $20,290
■ **ROOM AND BOARD:** $6,330

SAT I Score (25th/75th percentile): 1020-1270
2005 U.S. News College Ranking:
Liberal Arts Colleges, third tier
Acceptance Rate: 69%

Other expenses: Estimated books and supplies:
$750. Transportation: $600. Personal expenses:
$1,000. **Financial aid:** Priority filing date for
institution's financial aid form: March 1. In
2003-2004, 78% of undergraduates applied for
financial aid. Of those, 69% were determined
to have financial need; 26% had their need
fully met. Average financial aid package (proportion receiving): $12,795 (68%). Average
amount of gift aid, such as scholarships or
grants (proportion receiving): $9,105 (68%).
Average amount of self-help aid, such as work
study or loans (proportion receiving): $4,800
(57%). Average need-based loan (excluding
PLUS or other private loans): $4,691. Among
students who received need-based aid, the average percentage of need met: 75%. Among students who received aid based on merit, the
average award (and the proportion receiving):
$7,112 (25%). The average athletic scholarship
(and the proportion receiving): $0 (0%).
Student employment: During the 2003-2004
academic year, 11% of undergraduates worked
on campus. Average per-year earnings: $816.

High Point University

University Station 3598
High Point, NC 27262-3598
Private; www.highpoint.edu
Financial aid office: (336) 841-9128

■ **2004-2005 TUITION AND FEES:** $15,700
■ **ROOM AND BOARD:** $6,780

SAT I Score (25th/75th percentile): 920-1130
2005 U.S. News College Ranking:
Comp. Colleges–Bachelor's (South), 12
Acceptance Rate: 87%

Other expenses: Estimated books and supplies:
$1,000. Transportation: $580. Personal expenses: $1,700. **Financial aid:** Priority filing date for

institution's financial aid form: March 1. In
2003-2004, 91% of undergraduates applied for
financial aid. Of those, 76% were determined
to have financial need; 7% had their need fully
met. Average financial aid package (proportion
receiving): $11,400 (76%). Average amount of
gift aid, such as scholarships or grants (proportion receiving): $4,000 (36%). Average amount
of self-help aid, such as work study or loans
(proportion receiving): $7,500 (64%). Average
need-based loan (excluding PLUS or other private loans): $5,200. Among students who
received need-based aid, the average percentage
of need met: 87%. Among students who
received aid based on merit, the average award
(and the proportion receiving): $3,000 (4%).
The average athletic scholarship (and the proportion receiving): $12,000 (7%). Average
amount of debt of borrowers graduating in
2003: $15,000. Proportion who borrowed: 76%.
Student employment: During the 2003-2004
academic year, 55% of undergraduates worked
on campus. Average per-year earnings: $1,500.
Reserve Officers Training Corps (ROTC): Army
ROTC: Offered at cooperating institution
(North Carolina A&T); Air Force ROTC:
Offered at cooperating institution (North
Carolina A&T).

Johnson C. Smith University

100 Beatties Ford Road
Charlotte, NC 28216
Private; www.jcsu.edu
Financial aid office: (704) 378-1035

■ **2004-2005 TUITION AND FEES:** $13,712
■ **ROOM AND BOARD:** $5,298

SAT I Score (25th/75th percentile): 825-1009
2005 U.S. News College Ranking:
Comp. Colleges–Bachelor's (South), 34
Acceptance Rate: 48%

Other expenses: Estimated books and supplies:
$1,250. Transportation: $1,260. Personal
expenses: $2,520. **Financial aid:** Priority filing
date for institution's financial aid form: March
15; deadline: June 30. In 2003-2004, 100% of
undergraduates applied for financial aid. Of
those, 89% were determined to have financial
need; 3% had their need fully met. Average
financial aid package (proportion receiving):
$9,725 (89%). Average amount of gift aid, such
as scholarships or grants (proportion receiving):
$2,000 (70%). Average amount of self-help aid,
such as work study or loans (proportion receiving): $1,268 (26%). Average need-based loan
(excluding PLUS or other private loans):

$4,725. Among students who received need-
based aid, the average percentage of need met:
59%. Among students who received aid based
on merit, the average award (and the proportion receiving): N/A (30%). Average amount of
debt of borrowers graduating in 2003: $15,000.
Proportion who borrowed: 90%. **Student
employment:** During the 2003-2004 academic
year, 14% of undergraduates worked on campus. Average per-year earnings: $8,000.
Cooperative education programs: business,
computer science, education, engineering,
humanities, natural science, social/behavioral
science. **Reserve Officers Training Corps
(ROTC):** Army ROTC: Offered at cooperating
institution (University of North Carolina at
Charlotte); Air Force ROTC: Offered at cooperating institution (University of North Carolina
at Charlotte).

Lees-McRae College

PO Box 128
Banner Elk, NC 28604
Private; www.lmc.edu
Financial aid office: (828) 898-8793

■ **2004-2005 TUITION AND FEES:** $15,228
■ **ROOM AND BOARD:** $5,874

SAT I Score (25th/75th percentile): 860-1080
2005 U.S. News College Ranking:
Liberal Arts Colleges, fourth tier
Acceptance Rate: 80%

Financial aid: Priority filing date for institution's financial aid form: March 15; deadline:
March 15. In 2003-2004, 94% of undergraduates applied for financial aid. Of those, 58%
were determined to have financial need; 18%
had their need fully met. Average financial aid
package (proportion receiving): $9,082 (58%).
Average amount of gift aid, such as scholarships or grants (proportion receiving): $3,850
(37%). Average amount of self-help aid, such as
work study or loans (proportion receiving):
$1,943 (27%). Average need-based loan (exclud-
ing PLUS or other private loans): $3,288.
Among students who received need-based aid,
the average percentage of need met: 93%.
Student employment: During the 2003-2004
academic year, 27% of undergraduates worked
on campus. Average per-year earnings: $1,400.

Lenoir-Rhyne College

PO Box 7163
Hickory, NC 28603-7163
Private; www.lrc.edu
Financial aid office: (828) 328-7304

■ **2004-2005 TUITION AND FEES:** $17,550
■ **ROOM AND BOARD:** $6,300

SAT I Score (25th/75th percentile): 900-1150
2005 U.S. News College Ranking:
Comp. Colleges–Bachelor's (South), 15
Acceptance Rate: 81%

Other expenses: Estimated books and supplies: $1,000. Transportation: $1,000. Personal expenses: $1,500. **Financial aid:** Priority filing date for institution's financial aid form: March 1; deadline: September 1. In 2003-2004, 98% of undergraduates applied for financial aid. Of those, 81% were determined to have financial need; 15% had their need fully met. Average financial aid package (proportion receiving): $13,095 (81%). Average amount of gift aid, such as scholarships or grants (proportion receiving): $10,229 (81%). Average amount of self-help aid, such as work study or loans (proportion receiving): $4,278 (54%). Average need-based loan (excluding PLUS or other private loans): $4,431. Among students who received need-based aid, the average percentage of need met: 57%. Among students who received aid based on merit, the average award (and the proportion receiving): $5,282 (16%). The average athletic scholarship (and the proportion receiving): $4,767 (4%). Average amount of debt of borrowers graduating in 2003: $26,704. Proportion who borrowed: 89%. **Student employment:** During the 2003-2004 academic year, 27% of undergraduates worked on campus. Average per-year earnings: $762. **Reserve Officers Training Corps (ROTC):** Army ROTC: Offered at cooperating institution (Davidson College).

Livingstone College

701 W. Monroe Street
Salisbury, NC 28144
Private; www.livingstone.edu
Financial aid office: (704) 216-6069

■ **2004-2005 TUITION AND FEES:** $13,527
■ **ROOM AND BOARD:** $5,919

SAT I Score (25th/75th percentile): 680-890
2005 U.S. News College Ranking:
Comp. Colleges–Bachelor's (South), fourth tier
Acceptance Rate: 15%

Financial aid: Priority filing date for institution's financial aid form: May 1; deadline: May 1. In 2003-2004, 100% of undergraduates applied for financial aid. Average financial aid package (proportion receiving): $7,270 (87%). Average amount of gift aid, such as scholarships or grants (proportion receiving): $3,999 (79%). Average amount of self-help aid, such as work study or loans (proportion receiving): $3,762 (81%). Average need-based loan (excluding PLUS or other private loans): $3,471. Among students who received aid based on merit, the average award (and the proportion receiving): $5,287 (37%). The average athletic scholarship (and the proportion receiving): $7,031 (12%). **Student employment:** During the 2003-2004 academic year, 10% of undergraduates worked on campus. Average per-year earnings: $1,000. **Cooperative education programs:** education, engineering, other. **Reserve Officers Training Corps (ROTC):** Army ROTC: Offered at cooperating institution (University of North Carolina–Charlotte).

Mars Hill College

100 Athletic Street
Mars Hill, NC 28754
Private; www.mhc.edu
Financial aid office: (828) 689-1103

■ **2004-2005 TUITION AND FEES:** $15,922
■ **ROOM AND BOARD:** $6,248

SAT I Score (25th/75th percentile): 850-1080
2005 U.S. News College Ranking:
Comp. Colleges–Bachelor's (South), 45
Acceptance Rate: 81%

Other expenses: Estimated books and supplies: $1,100. Transportation: $400. Personal expenses: $1,500. **Financial aid:** Priority filing date for institution's financial aid form: April 15. In 2003-2004, 88% of undergraduates applied for financial aid. Of those, 79% were determined to have financial need; 27% had their need fully met. Average financial aid package (proportion receiving): $11,609 (79%). Average amount of gift aid, such as scholarships or grants (proportion receiving): $8,749 (79%). Average amount of self-help aid, such as work study or loans (proportion receiving): $3,990 (75%). Average need-based loan (excluding PLUS or other private loans): $3,575. Among students who received need-

based aid, the average percentage of need met: 72%. Among students who received aid based on merit, the average award (and the proportion receiving): $6,884 (25%). The average athletic scholarship (and the proportion receiving): $4,930 (10%). Average amount of debt of borrowers graduating in 2003: $10,395. Proportion who borrowed: 90%. **Cooperative education programs:** art, business, computer science, education, health professions, humanities, natural science, social/behavioral science.

Meredith College

3800 Hillsborough Street
Raleigh, NC 27607-5298
Private; www.meredith.edu
Financial aid office: (919) 760-8565

■ **2004-2005 TUITION AND FEES:** $19,000
■ **ROOM AND BOARD:** $5,350

SAT I Score (25th/75th percentile): 940-1130
2005 U.S. News College Ranking:
Universities–Master's (South), 16
Acceptance Rate: 87%

Other expenses: Estimated books and supplies: $750. Transportation: $400. Personal expenses: $1,250. **Financial aid:** Priority filing date for institution's financial aid form: February 15. In 2003-2004, 69% of undergraduates applied for financial aid. Of those, 58% were determined to have financial need; 10% had their need fully met. Average financial aid package (proportion receiving): $13,574 (58%). Average amount of gift aid, such as scholarships or grants (proportion receiving): $9,935 (57%). Average amount of self-help aid, such as work study or loans (proportion receiving): $4,166 (53%). Average need-based loan (excluding PLUS or other private loans): $3,636. Among students who received need-based aid, the average percentage of need met: 76%. Among students who received aid based on merit, the average award (and the proportion receiving): $4,397 (28%). Average amount of debt of borrowers graduating in 2003: $14,840. Proportion who borrowed: 40%. **Student employment:** During the 2003-2004 academic year, 12% of undergraduates worked on campus. Average per-year earnings: $1,300. **Cooperative education programs:** art, business, computer science, home economics, humanities, natural science, social/behavioral science, other. **Reserve Officers Training Corps (ROTC):** Army ROTC: Offered at cooperating institution (North Carolina State University); Air Force ROTC: Offered at cooperating institution (North Carolina State University).

Methodist College

5400 Ramsey Street
Fayetteville, NC 28311-1498
Private; www.methodist.edu
Financial aid office: (910) 630-7193

■ 2004-2005 TUITION AND FEES: $16,710
■ ROOM AND BOARD: $6,420

SAT I Score (25th/75th percentile): 870-1110
2005 U.S. News College Ranking:
Comp. Colleges–Bachelor's (South), third tier
Acceptance Rate: 76%

Other expenses: Estimated books and supplies:
$800. Reserve Officers Training Corps (ROTC):
Army ROTC: Offered on campus; Air Force
ROTC: Offered at cooperating institution
(Fayetteville State University).

Montreat College

PO Box 1267
Montreat, NC 28757-1267
Private; www.montreat.edu
Financial aid office: (828) 669-8012

■ 2004-2005 TUITION AND FEES: $15,108
■ ROOM AND BOARD: $4,866

SAT I Score (25th/75th percentile): 928-1143
2005 U.S. News College Ranking:
Unranked Specialty School–Business
Acceptance Rate: 78%

Other expenses: Estimated books and supplies:
$800. Transportation: $1,050. Personal expenses: $1,700. Financial aid: Priority filing date for
institution's financial aid form: March 15. In
2003-2004, 99% of undergraduates applied for
financial aid. Of those, 65% were determined to
have financial need; 23% had their need fully
met. Average financial aid package (proportion
receiving): $13,433 (65%). Average amount of
gift aid, such as scholarships or grants (proportion receiving): $7,598 (61%). Average amount
of self-help aid, such as work study or loans
(proportion receiving): $5,835 (54%). Average
need-based loan (excluding PLUS or other private loans): $3,097. Among students who
received need-based aid, the average percentage
of need met: 81%. Among students who
received aid based on merit, the average award
(and the proportion receiving): $6,126 (32%).
The average athletic scholarship (and the proportion receiving): $5,876 (4%). Average
amount of debt of borrowers graduating in

2003: $17,715. Proportion who borrowed: 87%.
Student employment: During the 2003-2004
academic year, 3% of undergraduates worked
on campus. Average per-year earnings: $1,700.

Mount Olive College

634 Henderson Street
Mount Olive, NC 28365
Private; www.moc.edu/index.cfm
Financial aid office: (919) 658-2502

■ 2004-2005 TUITION AND FEES: $11,220
■ ROOM AND BOARD: $4,600

SAT I Score (25th/75th percentile): 850-1040
2005 U.S. News College Ranking:
Comp. Colleges–Bachelor's (South), fourth tier
Acceptance Rate: 74%

Other expenses: Estimated books and supplies:
$510. Transportation: $714. Financial aid:
Priority filing date for institution's financial aid
form: March 1. Student employment: During
the 2003-2004 academic year, 18% of undergraduates worked on campus. Average per-year
earnings: $800. Cooperative education pro-
grams: business, computer science, education.

North Carolina A&T State University

1601 E. Market Street
Greensboro, NC 27411
Public; www.ncat.edu
Financial aid office: (336) 334-7973

■ 2004-2005 TUITION AND FEES:
In state: $2,722; Out of state: $12,089
■ ROOM AND BOARD: $4,968

SAT I Score (25th/75th percentile): 790-1010
2005 U.S. News College Ranking:
Universities–Master's (South), third tier
Acceptance Rate: 81%

Other expenses: Estimated books and supplies:
$800. Transportation: $1,200. Personal expenses: $1,700. Reserve Officers Training Corps
(ROTC): Army ROTC: Offered on campus; Air
Force ROTC: Offered on campus.

North Carolina Central University

1801 Fayetteville Street
Durham, NC 27707
Public; www.nccu.edu
Financial aid office: (919) 530-7412

■ 2004-2005 TUITION AND FEES:
In state: $3,524; Out of state: $12,968
■ ROOM AND BOARD: $4,311

SAT I Score (25th/75th percentile): 740-920
2005 U.S. News College Ranking:
Universities–Master's (South), fourth tier
Acceptance Rate: 81%

Other expenses: Estimated books and supplies:
$1,500. Transportation: $600. Personal expenses: $1,575. Financial aid: Priority filing date for
institution's financial aid form: March 15. In
2003-2004, 93% of undergraduates applied for
financial aid. Of those, 80% were determined to
have financial need; 21% had their need fully
met. Average financial aid package (proportion
receiving): $7,050 (80%). Average amount of gift
aid, such as scholarships or grants (proportion
receiving): $1,811 (67%). Average amount of self-
help aid, such as work study or loans (proportion
receiving): $2,538 (71%). Average need-based
loan (excluding PLUS or other private loans):
$2,918. Among students who received need-
based aid, the average percentage of need met:
71%. Among students who received aid based on
merit, the average award (and the proportion
receiving): $2,326 (5%). The average athletic
scholarship (and the proportion receiving):
$2,472 (3%). Average amount of debt of borrow-
ers graduating in 2003: $20,701. Proportion who
borrowed: 84%. Reserve Officers Training Corps
(ROTC): Army ROTC: Offered at cooperating
institution (Duke University); Air Force ROTC:
Offered on campus.

North Carolina School of the Arts

1533 S. Main Street
Winston-Salem, NC 27127-2189
Public; www.ncarts.edu
Financial aid office: (336) 770-3297

■ 2004-2005 TUITION AND FEES:
In state: $4,307; Out of state: $15,587
■ ROOM AND BOARD: $5,700

SAT I Score (25th/75th percentile): 1040-1260
2005 U.S. News College Ranking:
Unranked Specialty School–Fine Arts
Acceptance Rate: 40%

Other expenses: Estimated books and supplies: $1,030. Personal expenses: $1,954. **Financial aid:** Priority filing date for institution's financial aid form: March 1. In 2003-2004, 63% of undergraduates applied for financial aid. Of those, 51% were determined to have financial need; 12% had their need fully met. Average financial aid package (proportion receiving): $9,381 (51%). Average amount of gift aid, such as scholarships or grants (proportion receiving): $4,270 (50%). Average amount of self-help aid, such as work study or loans (proportion receiving): $3,558 (45%). Average need-based loan (excluding PLUS or other private loans): $3,332. Among students who received need-based aid, the average percentage of need met: 77%. Among students who received aid based on merit, the average award (and the proportion receiving): $2,994 (10%). Average amount of debt of borrowers graduating in 2003: $15,832. Proportion who borrowed: 59%. **Student employment:** During the 2003-2004 academic year, 15% of undergraduates worked on campus. Average per-year earnings: $750.

North Carolina State University–Raleigh

Box 7001
Raleigh, NC 27695
Public; www.ncsu.edu
Financial aid office: (919) 515-2421

■ **2004-2005 TUITION AND FEES:**
In state: $4,294; Out of state: $16,192
■ **ROOM AND BOARD:** $6,496

SAT I Score (25th/75th percentile): 1100-1300
2005 U.S. News College Ranking:
National Universities, 86
Acceptance Rate: 62%

Other expenses: Estimated books and supplies: $800. Transportation: $500. Personal expenses: $1,200. **Financial aid:** Priority filing date for institution's financial aid form: March 1. In 2003-2004, 51% of undergraduates applied for financial aid. Of those, 41% were determined to have financial need; 24% had their need fully met. Average financial aid package (proportion receiving): $7,497 (39%). Average amount of gift aid, such as scholarships or grants (proportion receiving): $5,356 (37%). Average amount of self-help aid, such as work study or loans (pro-

portion receiving): $3,033 (31%). Average need-based loan (excluding PLUS or other private loans): $2,763. Among students who received need-based aid, the average percentage of need met: 84%. Among students who received aid based on merit, the average award (and the proportion receiving): $6,852 (22%). The average athletic scholarship (and the proportion receiving): $11,850 (2%). Average amount of debt of borrowers graduating in 2003: $16,897. Proportion who borrowed: 38%. **Cooperative education programs:** agriculture, business, computer science, engineering, humanities, natural science, social/behavioral science. **Reserve Officers Training Corps (ROTC):** Army ROTC: Offered on campus; Navy ROTC: Offered on campus; Air Force ROTC: Offered on campus.

North Carolina Wesleyan College

3400 N. Wesleyan Boulevard
Rocky Mount, NC 27804
Private; www.ncwc.edu
Financial aid office: (919) 985-5291

■ **2004-2005 TUITION AND FEES:** $12,443
■ **ROOM AND BOARD:** $6,555

2005 U.S. News College Ranking:
Comp. Colleges–Bachelor's (South), third tier
Acceptance Rate: 83%

Other expenses: Estimated books and supplies: $800. Transportation: $432. Personal expenses: $863. **Financial aid:** Priority filing date for institution's financial aid form: March 15.

Peace College

15 E. Peace Street
Raleigh, NC 27604-1194
Private; www.peace.edu
Financial aid office: (919) 508-2249

■ **2004-2005 TUITION AND FEES:** $16,880
■ **ROOM AND BOARD:** $6,520

SAT I Score (25th/75th percentile): 688-1258
2005 U.S. News College Ranking:
Comp. Colleges–Bachelor's (South), 31
Acceptance Rate: 78%

Other expenses: Estimated books and supplies: $1,000. Transportation: $600. Personal expenses: $2,200. **Financial aid:** In 2003-2004, 77% of undergraduates applied for financial aid. Of those, 65% were determined to have financial need; 17% had their need fully met. Average

financial aid package (proportion receiving): $12,126 (65%). Average amount of gift aid, such as scholarships or grants (proportion receiving): $9,064 (65%). Average amount of self-help aid, such as work study or loans (proportion receiving): $3,691 (54%). Average need-based loan (excluding PLUS or other private loans): $2,907. Among students who received need-based aid, the average percentage of need met: 72%. Among students who received aid based on merit, the average award (and the proportion receiving): $7,541 (33%). The average athletic scholarship (and the proportion receiving): $0 (0%). Average amount of debt of borrowers graduating in 2003: $9,938. Proportion who borrowed: 76%. **Student employment:** During the 2003-2004 academic year, 51% of undergraduates worked on campus. Average per-year earnings: $2,000. **Reserve Officers Training Corps (ROTC):** Army ROTC: Offered at cooperating institution (North Carolina State University); Navy ROTC: Offered at cooperating institution (North Carolina State University); Air Force ROTC: Offered at cooperating institution (North Carolina State University).

Pfeiffer University

PO Box 960
Misenheimer, NC 28109
Private; www.pfeiffer.edu
Financial aid office: (800) 338-2060

■ **2004-2005 TUITION AND FEES:** $14,570
■ **ROOM AND BOARD:** $5,830

SAT I Score (25th/75th percentile): 880-1110
2005 U.S. News College Ranking:
Universities–Master's (South), third tier
Acceptance Rate: 72%

Other expenses: Estimated books and supplies: $1,000. Transportation: $700. Personal expenses: $1,000. **Financial aid:** Priority filing date for institution's financial aid form: April 15. In 2003-2004, 86% of undergraduates applied for financial aid. Of those, 72% were determined to have financial need; 25% had their need fully met. Average financial aid package (proportion receiving): $10,426 (72%). Average amount of gift aid, such as scholarships or grants (proportion receiving): $7,618 (71%). Average amount of self-help aid, such as work study or loans (proportion receiving): $3,409 (61%). Average need-based loan (excluding PLUS or other private loans): $3,239. Among students who received need-based aid, the average percentage of need met: 82%. Among students who received aid based on merit, the average award (and the proportion receiving): $8,834 (14%). The average athletic scholarship (and the proportion receiving): $3,038 (4%). Average amount of debt of borrowers graduating in 2003: $16,800. Proportion who borrowed: 78%. **Student employment:** During the 2003-2004 academic year, 23% of undergraduates worked on campus. **Cooperative education programs:** art, business, computer science, education, engineering, humanities, natural science, social/behavioral science, technologies. **Reserve Officers Training Corps (ROTC):** Army ROTC: Offered at cooperating institution (Davidson College).

Queens University of Charlotte

1900 Selwyn Avenue
Charlotte, NC 28274
Private; www.queens.edu
Financial aid office: (704) 337-2225

■ **2004-2005 TUITION AND FEES:** $17,008
■ **ROOM AND BOARD:** $6,190

SAT I Score (25th/75th percentile): 1000-1170
2005 U.S. News College Ranking:
Universities–Master's (South), 26
Acceptance Rate: 74%

Other expenses: Estimated books and supplies: $750. Transportation: $800. Personal expenses: $1,070. **Financial aid:** Priority filing date for institution's financial aid form: March 1. In 2003-2004, 73% of undergraduates applied for financial aid. Of those, 59% were determined to have financial need; 28% had their need fully met. Average financial aid package (proportion receiving): $11,243 (59%). Average amount of gift aid, such as scholarships or grants (proportion receiving): $8,588 (58%). Average amount of self-help aid, such as work study or loans (proportion receiving): $3,279 (50%). Average need-based loan (excluding PLUS or other private loans): $2,937. Among students who received need-based aid, the average percentage of need met: 72%. Among students who received aid based on merit, the average award (and the proportion receiving): $7,886 (33%). The average athletic scholarship (and the proportion receiving): $5,892 (8%). Average amount of debt of borrowers graduating in 2003: $16,320. Proportion who borrowed: 61%. **Student employment:** During the 2003-2004 academic year, 13% of undergraduates worked on campus. Average per-year earnings: $2,000. **Reserve Officers Training Corps (ROTC):** Army ROTC: Offered at cooperating institution (University of North Carolina); Air Force

ROTC: Offered at cooperating institution (University of North Carolina).

Salem College

PO Box 10548
Winston-Salem, NC 27108
Private; www.salem.edu
Financial aid office: (336) 721-2808

■ **2004-2005 TUITION AND FEES:** $16,490
■ **ROOM AND BOARD:** $8,870

SAT I Score (25th/75th percentile): 1020-1250
2005 U.S. News College Ranking:
Liberal Arts Colleges, third tier
Acceptance Rate: 70%

Other expenses: Estimated books and supplies: $600. Transportation: $1,000. Personal expenses: $2,000. **Financial aid:** Priority filing date for institution's financial aid form: March 15. In 2003-2004, 94% of undergraduates applied for financial aid. Of those, 80% were determined to have financial need; 100% had their need fully met. Average financial aid package (proportion receiving): $14,404 (80%). Average amount of gift aid, such as scholarships or grants (proportion receiving): $8,303 (68%). Average amount of self-help aid, such as work study or loans (proportion receiving): $6,101 (80%). Average need-based loan (excluding PLUS or other private loans): $4,501. Among students who received need-based aid, the average percentage of need met: 100%. Among students who received aid based on merit, the average award (and the proportion receiving): $10,104 (24%). The average athletic scholarship (and the proportion receiving): $0 (0%). Average amount of debt of borrowers graduating in 2003: $13,409. Proportion who borrowed: 63%. **Reserve Officers Training Corps (ROTC):** Army ROTC: Offered at cooperating institution (Wake Forest University).

Shaw University

118 E. South Street
Raleigh, NC 27601
Private; www.shawuniversity.edu
Financial aid office: (919) 546-8240

■ **2004-2005 TUITION AND FEES:** $9,438
■ **ROOM AND BOARD:** $6,050

SAT I Score (25th/75th percentile): 645-885
2005 U.S. News College Ranking:
Comp. Colleges–Bachelor's (South), third tier
Acceptance Rate: 44%

Other expenses: Estimated books and supplies: $700. Transportation: $500. Personal expenses: $1,000. **Financial aid:** Priority filing date for institution's financial aid form: March 1; deadline: June 1. Average amount of debt of borrowers graduating in 2003: $17,125. Proportion who borrowed: 98%. Average per-year earnings: $12,000. **Reserve Officers Training Corps (ROTC):** Army ROTC: Offered at cooperating institution (Saint Augustine's College); Air Force ROTC: Offered at cooperating institution (North Carolina State University).

St. Andrews Presbyterian College

1700 Dogwood Mile
Laurinburg, NC 28352
Private; www.sapc.edu
Financial aid office: (910) 277-5560

■ **2004-2005 TUITION AND FEES:** $15,725
■ **ROOM AND BOARD:** $5,630

SAT I Score (25th/75th percentile): 870-1105
2005 U.S. News College Ranking:
Liberal Arts Colleges, fourth tier
Acceptance Rate: 84%

Other expenses: Estimated books and supplies: $1,000. Transportation: $1,950. Personal expenses: $1,694. **Financial aid:** In 2003-2004, 77% of undergraduates applied for financial aid. Of those, 64% were determined to have financial need; 29% had their need fully met. Average financial aid package (proportion receiving): $12,819 (64%). Average amount of gift aid, such as scholarships or grants (proportion receiving): $9,786 (64%). Average amount of self-help aid, such as work study or loans (proportion receiving): $4,062 (49%). Average need-based loan (excluding PLUS or other private loans): $3,225. Among students who received need-based aid, the average percentage of need met: 81%. Among students who received aid based on merit, the average award (and the proportion receiving): $9,671 (34%). The average athletic scholarship (and the proportion receiving): $4,585 (14%). Average amount of debt of borrowers graduating in 2003: $11,878. Proportion who borrowed: 72%. **Student employment:** During the 2003-2004 academic year, 37% of undergraduates worked on campus. Average per-year earnings: $1,571.

St. Augustine's College

1315 Oakwood Avenue
Raleigh, NC 27610-2298
Private; www.st-aug.edu
Financial aid office: (919) 516-4131

- **2004-2005 TUITION AND FEES:** $10,388
- **ROOM AND BOARD:** $5,312

SAT I Score (25th/75th percentile): 660-840
2005 U.S. News College Ranking:
Liberal Arts Colleges, fourth tier
Acceptance Rate: 60%

Other expenses: Estimated books and supplies: $900. Transportation: $1,000. Personal expenses: $2,040. **Financial aid:** Priority filing date for institution's financial aid form: April 15. Average amount of debt of borrowers graduating in 2003: $10,416. Proportion who borrowed: 55%. **Student employment:** During the 2003-2004 academic year, 34% of undergraduates worked on campus. Average per-year earnings: $1,517. **Cooperative education programs:** art, business, computer science, education, health professions, humanities, natural science, social/behavioral science, technologies. **Reserve Officers Training Corps (ROTC):** Army ROTC: Offered on campus; Air Force ROTC: Offered at cooperating institution (North Carolina State University).

University of North Carolina–Asheville

1 University Heights
Asheville, NC 28804
Public; www.unca.edu
Financial aid office: (828) 251-6535

- **2004-2005 TUITION AND FEES:**
  In state: $3,392; Out of state: $12,592
- **ROOM AND BOARD:** $5,312

SAT I Score (25th/75th percentile): 1060-1270
2005 U.S. News College Ranking:
Liberal Arts Colleges, third tier
Acceptance Rate: 73%

Other expenses: Estimated books and supplies: $850. Transportation: $1,435. Personal expenses: $1,541. **Financial aid:** Priority filing date for institution's financial aid form: March 1. In 2003-2004, 67% of undergraduates applied for financial aid. Of those, 43% were determined to have financial need; 37% had their need fully met. Average financial aid package (proportion receiving): $7,372 (41%). Average amount of

gift aid, such as scholarships or grants (proportion receiving): $3,365 (36%). Average amount of self-help aid, such as work study or loans (proportion receiving): $3,582 (32%). Average need-based loan (excluding PLUS or other private loans): $3,538. Among students who received need-based aid, the average percentage of need met: 79%. Among students who received aid based on merit, the average award (and the proportion receiving): $2,981 (9%). The average athletic scholarship (and the proportion receiving): $5,959 (4%). Average amount of debt of borrowers graduating in 2003: $13,961. Proportion who borrowed: 46%. **Student employment:** During the 2003-2004 academic year, 20% of undergraduates worked on campus. Average per-year earnings: $1,504.

University of North Carolina–Chapel Hill

South Building, CB #9100
Chapel Hill, NC 27599
Public; www.unc.edu
Financial aid office: (919) 962-8396

- **2004-2005 TUITION AND FEES:**
  In state: $3,205; Out of state: $16,303
- **ROOM AND BOARD:** $6,245

SAT I Score (25th/75th percentile): 1190-1390
2005 U.S. News College Ranking:
National Universities, 29
Acceptance Rate: 37%

Other expenses: Estimated books and supplies: $900. Transportation: $500. Personal expenses: $1,200. **Financial aid:** Priority filing date for institution's financial aid form: March 1. In 2003-2004, 62% of undergraduates applied for financial aid. Of those, 33% were determined to have financial need; 73% had their need fully met. Average financial aid package (proportion receiving): $9,324 (32%). Average amount of gift aid, such as scholarships or grants (proportion receiving): $5,589 (30%). Average amount of self-help aid, such as work study or loans (proportion receiving): $3,853 (19%). Average need-based loan (excluding PLUS or other private loans): $3,674. Among students who received need-based aid, the average percentage of need met: 100%. Among students who received aid based on merit, the average award (and the proportion receiving): $5,426 (14%). The average athletic scholarship (and the proportion receiving): $11,919 (2%). Average amount of debt of borrowers graduating in 2003: $11,519. Proportion who borrowed: 24%. **Reserve Officers Training Corps (ROTC):** Army

ROTC: Offered on campus; Navy ROTC: Offered on campus; Air Force ROTC: Offered on campus.

University of North Carolina–Charlotte

9201 University City Boulevard
Charlotte, NC 28223-0001
Public; www.uncc.edu
Financial aid office: (704) 687-2461

- **2004-2005 TUITION AND FEES:**
  In state: $3,419; Out of state: $13,531
- **ROOM AND BOARD:** $5,900

SAT I Score (25th/75th percentile): 970-1160
2005 U.S. News College Ranking:
Universities–Master's (South), 26
Acceptance Rate: 72%

Other expenses: Estimated books and supplies: $900. Transportation: $1,150. Personal expenses: $1,250. **Financial aid:** Priority filing date for institution's financial aid form: April 1. In 2003-2004, 60% of undergraduates applied for financial aid. Of those, 47% were determined to have financial need; 32% had their need fully met. Average financial aid package (proportion receiving): $8,210 (46%). Average amount of gift aid, such as scholarships or grants (proportion receiving): $3,829 (38%). Average amount of self-help aid, such as work study or loans (proportion receiving): $3,855 (39%). Average need-based loan (excluding PLUS or other private loans): $3,779. Among students who received need-based aid, the average percentage of need met: 81%. Among students who received aid based on merit, the average award (and the proportion receiving): $1,691 (16%). The average athletic scholarship (and the proportion receiving): $5,533 (1%). Average amount of debt of borrowers graduating in 2003: $17,250. Proportion who borrowed: 56%. **Student employment:** During the 2003-2004 academic year, 14% of undergraduates worked on campus. Average per-year earnings: $1,586. **Cooperative education programs:** art, business, computer science, education, engineering, health professions, humanities, natural science, social/behavioral science, technologies. **Reserve Officers Training Corps (ROTC):** Army ROTC: Offered on campus; Air Force ROTC: Offered on campus.

University of North Carolina–Greensboro

1000 Spring Garden Street
Greensboro, NC 27412
Public; www.uncg.edu
Financial aid office: (336) 334-5702

■ **2004-2005 TUITION AND FEES:**
In state: $3,830; Out of state: $15,262
■ **ROOM AND BOARD:** $5,298

SAT I Score (25th/75th percentile): 940-1140
2005 U.S. News College Ranking:
National Universities, third tier
Acceptance Rate: 77%

Other expenses: Estimated books and supplies: $1,314. Transportation: $190. Personal expenses: $1,488. **Financial aid:** Priority filing date for institution's financial aid form: March 1. In 2003-2004, 92% of undergraduates applied for financial aid. Of those, 62% were determined to have financial need; 62% had their need fully met. Average financial aid package (proportion receiving): $9,269 (62%). Average amount of gift aid, such as scholarships or grants (proportion receiving): $6,721 (60%). Average amount of self-help aid, such as work study or loans (proportion receiving): $3,966 (60%). Average need-based loan (excluding PLUS or other private loans): $1,257. Among students who received need-based aid, the average percentage of need met: 88%. Among students who received aid based on merit, the average award (and the proportion receiving): $3,437 (50%). The average athletic scholarship (and the proportion receiving): $8,287 (2%). Average amount of debt of borrowers graduating in 2003: $16,942. Proportion who borrowed: 48%. **Reserve Officers Training Corps (ROTC):** Army ROTC: Offered at cooperating institution (NCAT); Air Force ROTC: Offered at cooperating institution (NCAT).

University of North Carolina–Pembroke

PO Box 1510
Pembroke, NC 28372
Public; www.uncp.edu
Financial aid office: (910) 521-6255

■ **2004-2005 TUITION AND FEES:**
In state: $1,689; Out of state: $11,129
■ **ROOM AND BOARD:** $4,560

SAT I Score (25th/75th percentile): 850-1030
2005 U.S. News College Ranking:
Universities–Master's (South), third tier
Acceptance Rate: 86%

Other expenses: Estimated books and supplies: $900. Transportation: $1,267. Personal expenses: $1,300. **Financial aid:** Priority filing date for institution's financial aid form: March 15. In 2003-2004, 83% of undergraduates applied for financial aid. Of those, 69% were determined to have financial need; 28% had their need fully met. Average financial aid package (proportion receiving): $6,005 (67%). Average amount of gift aid, such as scholarships or grants (proportion receiving): $3,894 (60%). Average amount of self-help aid, such as work study or loans (proportion receiving): $3,210 (52%). Average need-based loan (excluding PLUS or other private loans): $3,165. Among students who received need-based aid, the average percentage of need met: 73%. Among students who received aid based on merit, the average award (and the proportion receiving): $1,434 (3%). The average athletic scholarship (and the proportion receiving): $0 (0%). Average amount of debt of borrowers graduating in 2003: $11,775. Proportion who borrowed: 64%. **Reserve Officers Training Corps (ROTC):** Army ROTC: Offered on campus; Air Force ROTC: Offered on campus.

University of North Carolina–Wilmington

601 S. College Road
Wilmington, NC 28403
Public; www.uncwil.edu
Financial aid office: (910) 962-3177

■ **2004-2005 TUITION AND FEES:**
In state: $3,626; Out of state: $13,336
■ **ROOM AND BOARD:** $5,800

SAT I Score (25th/75th percentile): 1020-1200
2005 U.S. News College Ranking:
Universities–Master's (South), 22
Acceptance Rate: 54%

Other expenses: Estimated books and supplies: $1,000. Transportation: $1,300. Personal expenses: $700. **Financial aid:** Priority filing date for institution's financial aid form: April 1. In 2003-2004, 58% of undergraduates applied for financial aid. Of those, 38% were determined to have financial need; 61% had their need fully met. Average financial aid package (proportion receiving): $6,466 (38%). Average amount of gift aid, such as scholarships or grants (proportion receiving): $3,551 (31%). Average amount of self-help aid, such as work study or loans (proportion receiving): $4,169 (31%). Average need-based loan (excluding PLUS or other private loans): $3,982. Among students who received need-based aid, the average percentage of need met: 87%. The average athletic scholarship (and the proportion receiving): $6,838 (2%). Average amount of debt of borrowers graduating in 2003: $15,176. Proportion who borrowed: 46%.

Wake Forest University

Box 7305, Reynolda Station
Winston-Salem, NC 27109
Private; www.wfu.edu
Financial aid office: (336) 758-5154

■ **2004-2005 TUITION AND FEES:** $28,310
■ **ROOM AND BOARD:** $8,000

SAT I Score (25th/75th percentile): 1240-1390
2005 U.S. News College Ranking:
National Universities, 27
Acceptance Rate: 45%

Other expenses: Estimated books and supplies: $800. Transportation: $400. Personal expenses: $1,240. **Financial aid:** Priority filing date for institution's financial aid form: March 1. In 2003-2004, 41% of undergraduates applied for financial aid. Of those, 33% were determined to have financial need; 40% had their need fully met. Average financial aid package (proportion receiving): $21,413 (33%). Average amount of gift aid, such as scholarships or grants (proportion receiving): $15,699 (32%). Average amount of self-help aid, such as work study or loans (proportion receiving): $7,785 (27%). Average need-based loan (excluding PLUS or other private loans): $6,380. Among students who received need-based aid, the average percentage of need met: 91%. Among students who received aid based on merit, the average award (and the proportion receiving): $10,201 (30%). The average athletic scholarship (and the proportion receiving): $22,076 (6%). Average amount of debt of borrowers graduating in 2003: $24,549. Proportion who borrowed: 39%. **Student employment:** During the 2003-2004 academic year, 25% of undergraduates worked on campus. Average per-year earnings: $1,750. **Cooperative education programs:** engineering, health professions, other. **Reserve Officers Training Corps (ROTC):** Army ROTC: Offered on campus.

Warren Wilson College

PO Box 9000
Asheville, NC 28815
Private; www.warren-wilson.edu
Financial aid office: (828) 771-2082

■ **2004-2005 TUITION AND FEES:** $17,738
■ **ROOM AND BOARD:** $5,278

SAT I Score (25th/75th percentile): 1050-1290
2005 U.S. News College Ranking:
Universities–Master's (South), 40
Acceptance Rate: 79%

Other expenses: Estimated books and supplies: $784. Transportation: $1,000. Personal expenses: $1,000. **Financial aid:** Priority filing date for institution's financial aid form: April 1. In 2003-2004, 61% of undergraduates applied for financial aid. Of those, 52% were determined to have financial need; 17% had their need fully met. Average financial aid package (proportion receiving): $12,695 (52%). Average amount of gift aid, such as scholarships or grants (proportion receiving): $7,372 (47%). Average amount of self-help aid, such as work study or loans (proportion receiving): $5,010 (50%). Average need-based loan (excluding PLUS or other private loans): $3,430. Among students who received need-based aid, the average percentage of need met: 73%. Among students who received aid based on merit, the average award (and the proportion receiving): $3,014 (14%). The average athletic scholarship (and the proportion receiving): $0 (0%). Average amount of debt of borrowers graduating in 2003: $14,407. Proportion who borrowed: 55%. **Student employment:** During the 2003-2004 academic year, 100% of undergraduates worked on campus. Average per-year earnings: $2,742. **Cooperative education programs:** engineering, other.

Western Carolina University

Cullowhee, NC 28723
Public; www.wcu.edu
Financial aid office: (828) 227-7290

■ **2004-2005 TUITION AND FEES:**
In state: $3,448; Out of state: $12,884
■ **ROOM AND BOARD:** $4,528

SAT I Score (25th/75th percentile): 920-1110
2005 U.S. News College Ranking:
Universities–Master's (South), 55
Acceptance Rate: 74%

Other expenses: Estimated books and supplies: $530. Transportation: $807. Personal expenses: $1,080. **Financial aid:** Priority filing date for institution's financial aid form: March 31. In 2003-2004, 68% of undergraduates applied for financial aid. Of those, 48% were determined to have financial need; 58% had their need fully met. Average financial aid package (proportion receiving): $7,682 (48%). Average amount of gift aid, such as scholarships or grants (proportion receiving): $4,034 (47%). Average amount of self-help aid, such as work study or loans (proportion receiving): $4,419 (36%). Average need-based loan (excluding PLUS or other private loans): $4,352. Among students who received need-based aid, the average percentage of need met: 79%. Among students who received aid based on merit, the average award (and the proportion receiving): $2,644 (12%). The average athletic scholarship (and the proportion receiving): $7,251 (2%). Average amount of debt of borrowers graduating in 2003: $16,249. Proportion who borrowed: 46%. **Student employment:** During the 2003-2004 academic year, 12% of undergraduates worked on campus. Average per-year earnings: $2,001. **Cooperative education programs:** art, business, computer science, education, engineering, health professions, home economics, humanities, natural science, social/behavioral science, technologies.

Wingate University

Wingate, NC 28174
Private; www.wingate.edu
Financial aid office: (704) 233-8209

■ **2004-2005 TUITION AND FEES:** $16,000
■ **ROOM AND BOARD:** $6,200

SAT I Score (25th/75th percentile): 920-1150
2005 U.S. News College Ranking:
Comp. Colleges–Bachelor's (South), 18
Acceptance Rate: 82%

Financial aid: Priority filing date for institution's financial aid form: May 1. In 2003-2004, 99% of undergraduates applied for financial aid. Of those, 67% were determined to have financial need; 1% had their need fully met. Average financial aid package (proportion receiving): $12,748 (67%). Average amount of gift aid, such as scholarships or grants (proportion receiving): $4,134 (52%). Average amount of self-help aid, such as work study or loans (proportion receiving): $3,862 (67%). Average need-based loan (excluding PLUS or other private loans): $3,359. Among

students who received need-based aid, the average percentage of need met: 56%. Among students who received aid based on merit, the average award (and the proportion receiving): $4,918 (N/A). The average athletic scholarship (and the proportion receiving): $5,814 (20%). Average amount of debt of borrowers graduating in 2003: $24,000. Proportion who borrowed: 88%. **Reserve Officers Training Corps (ROTC):** Army ROTC: Offered at cooperating institution (University of North Carolina–Charlotte); Air Force ROTC: Offered at cooperating institution (University of North Carolina–Charlotte).

Winston-Salem State University

601 Martin Luther King Jr. Drive
Winston-Salem, NC 27110
Public; www.wssu.edu
Financial aid office: (336) 750-3280

■ **2004-2005 TUITION AND FEES:**
In state: $2,675; Out of state: $11,015
■ **ROOM AND BOARD:** $5,136

SAT I Score (25th/75th percentile): 780-940
2005 U.S. News College Ranking:
Comp. Colleges–Bachelor's (South), 34
Acceptance Rate: 77%

Other expenses: Estimated books and supplies: $1,100. Transportation: $750. Personal expenses: $1,500. **Financial aid:** Priority filing date for institution's financial aid form: May 1; deadline: April 1. In 2003-2004, 93% of undergraduates applied for financial aid. Of those, 90% were determined to have financial need; 3% had their need fully met. Average financial aid package (proportion receiving): $3,356 (84%). Average amount of gift aid, such as scholarships or grants (proportion receiving): $2,527 (80%). Average amount of self-help aid, such as work study or loans (proportion receiving): $1,374 (76%). Average need-based loan (excluding PLUS or other private loans): $3,317. Among students who received need-based aid, the average percentage of need met: 75%. Among students who received aid based on merit, the average award (and the proportion receiving): $3,107 (3%). The average athletic scholarship (and the proportion receiving): $2,381 (4%). Average amount of debt of borrowers graduating in 2003: $10,500. Proportion who borrowed: 90%. **Cooperative education programs:** business. **Reserve Officers Training Corps (ROTC):** Army ROTC: Offered on campus.

North Dakota

Dickinson State University

291 Campus Drive
Dickinson, ND 58601
Public; www.dickinsonstate.com
Financial aid office: (701) 483-2371

■ **2004-2005 TUITION AND FEES:**
In state: $3,775; Out of state: $8,852
■ **ROOM AND BOARD:** $3,518

ACT Score (25th/75th percentile): 16-26
2005 U.S. News College Ranking:
Comp. Colleges–Bachelor's (Midwest),
fourth tier
Acceptance Rate: 100%

Other expenses: Estimated books and supplies:
$750. Transportation: $1,425. Personal expenses: $1,425. **Financial aid:** Priority filing date for institution's financial aid form: March 15.
Student employment: During the 2003-2004 academic year, 9% of undergraduates worked on campus. Average per-year earnings: $1,500.
Cooperative education programs: business, social/behavioral science.

Jamestown College

6086 College Lane
Jamestown, ND 58405
Private; www.jc.edu
Financial aid office: (701) 252-3467

■ **2004-2005 TUITION AND FEES:** $9,400
■ **ROOM AND BOARD:** $3,970

ACT Score (25th/75th percentile): 19-25
2005 U.S. News College Ranking:
Comp. Colleges–Bachelor's (Midwest),
third tier
Acceptance Rate: 98%

Other expenses: Estimated books and supplies:
$1,000. Transportation: $1,500. Personal expenses: $1,300. **Financial aid:** In 2003-2004, 99% of undergraduates applied for financial aid. Of those, 87% were determined to have financial need; 18% had their need fully met. Average financial aid package (proportion receiving): $7,775 (87%). Average amount of gift aid, such as scholarships or grants (proportion receiving): $4,149 (87%). Average amount

of self-help aid, such as work study or loans (proportion receiving): $4,325 (73%). Average need-based loan (excluding PLUS or other private loans): $4,064. Among students who received need-based aid, the average percentage of need met: 68%. Among students who received aid based on merit, the average award (and the proportion receiving): $7,449 (13%). The average athletic scholarship (and the proportion receiving): $1,481 (7%). Average amount of debt of borrowers graduating in 2003: $16,986. Proportion who borrowed: 94%. **Cooperative education programs:** art, business, computer science, education, humanities, natural science.

Mayville State University

330 Third Street NE
Mayville, ND 58257
Public; www.mayvillestate.edu
Financial aid office: (701) 788-4767

■ **2004-2005 TUITION AND FEES:**
In state: $4,489; Out of state: $9,523
■ **ROOM AND BOARD:** $3,508

ACT Score (25th/75th percentile): 17-22
2005 U.S. News College Ranking:
Comp. Colleges–Bachelor's (Midwest),
fourth tier
Acceptance Rate: 99%

Other expenses: Estimated books and supplies:
$700. Transportation: $1,400. Personal expenses: $1,400. **Financial aid:** Priority filing date for institution's financial aid form: April 15.
Student employment: During the 2003-2004 academic year, 40% of undergraduates worked on campus. Average per-year earnings: $1,200.
Cooperative education programs: business, computer science, education, natural science, social/behavioral science. **Reserve Officers Training Corps (ROTC):** Air Force ROTC: Offered at cooperating institution (North Dakota State University).

Minot State University

500 University Avenue W
Minot, ND 58707
Public; www.minotstateu.edu
Financial aid office: (701) 858-3375

■ **2004-2005 TUITION AND FEES:**
In state: $3,712; Out of state: $8,990
■ **ROOM AND BOARD:** $3,402

ACT Score (25th/75th percentile): 18-24
2005 U.S. News College Ranking:
Universities–Master's (Midwest), fourth tier
Acceptance Rate: 86%

Other expenses: Estimated books and supplies:
$750. Transportation: $850. Personal expenses: $2,086. **Financial aid:** Priority filing date for institution's financial aid form: March 15. In 2003-2004, 81% of undergraduates applied for financial aid. Of those, 68% were determined to have financial need; 97% had their need fully met. Average financial aid package (proportion receiving): $5,933 (68%). Average amount of gift aid, such as scholarships or grants (proportion receiving): $2,726 (42%). Average amount of self-help aid, such as work study or loans (proportion receiving): $3,556 (57%). Average need-based loan (excluding PLUS or other private loans): $3,305. Among students who received need-based aid, the average percentage of need met: 95%. The average athletic scholarship (and the proportion receiving): $1,328 (4%). Average amount of debt of borrowers graduating in 2003: $12,815. Proportion who borrowed: 97%. **Student employment:** During the 2003-2004 academic year, 6% of undergraduates worked on campus. Average per-year earnings: $2,000. **Cooperative education programs:** business, education, health professions.

North Dakota State University

University Station, Box 5454
Fargo, ND 58105-5454
Public; www.ndsu.edu
Financial aid office: (800) 726-3188

■ **2004-2005 TUITION AND FEES:**
In state: $4,776; Out of state: $11,426
■ **ROOM AND BOARD:** $4,753

ACT Score (25th/75th percentile): 20-26
2005 U.S. News College Ranking:
National Universities, fourth tier
Acceptance Rate: 97%

....

Other expenses: Estimated books and supplies: $750. Transportation: $600. Personal expenses: $2,158. Financial aid: Priority filing date for institution's financial aid form: March 15. In 2003-2004, 74% of undergraduates applied for financial aid. Of those, 59% were determined to have financial need; 28% had their need fully met. Average financial aid package (proportion receiving): $4,425 (59%). Average amount of gift aid, such as scholarships or grants (proportion receiving): $3,036 (38%). Average amount of self-help aid, such as work study or loans (proportion receiving): $4,016 (51%). Average need-based loan (excluding PLUS or other private loans): $3,784. Among students who received need-based aid, the average percentage of need met: 67%. Among students who received aid based on merit, the average award (and the proportion receiving): $1,427 (10%). The average athletic scholarship (and the proportion receiving): $3,627 (1%). Average amount of debt of borrowers graduating in 2003: $19,929. Proportion who borrowed: 69%. Student employment: During the 2003-2004 academic year, 9% of undergraduates worked on campus. Average per-year earnings: $3,606. Cooperative education programs: agriculture, art, business, computer science, education, engineering, health professions, home economics, humanities, natural science, social/behavioral science, technologies. Reserve Officers Training Corps (ROTC): Army ROTC: Offered on campus; Air Force ROTC: Offered on campus.

University of Mary

7500 University Drive
Bismarck, ND 58504
Private; www.umary.edu
Financial aid office: (701) 355-8079

■ 2004-2005 TUITION AND FEES: $10,290
■ ROOM AND BOARD: $4,080

ACT Score (25th/75th percentile): 20-24
2005 U.S. News College Ranking:
Universities–Master's (Midwest), fourth tier
Acceptance Rate: 90%

....

Other expenses: Estimated books and supplies: $800. Transportation: $2,000. Personal expenses: $250. Financial aid: In 2003-2004,

90% of undergraduates applied for financial aid. Of those, 87% were determined to have financial need; Average financial aid package (proportion receiving): $10,500 (87%). Average amount of self-help aid, such as work study or loans (proportion receiving): $8,000 (87%). Average need-based loan (excluding PLUS or other private loans): $3,894. Among students who received need-based aid, the average percentage of need met: 75%. Among students who received aid based on merit, the average award (and the proportion receiving): $3,382 (22%). The average athletic scholarship (and the proportion receiving): $4,117 (26%). Student employment: During the 2003-2004 academic year, 3% of undergraduates worked on campus. Average per-year earnings: $857. Cooperative education programs: business, computer science.

University of North Dakota

PO Box 8135
Grand Forks, ND 58202
Public; www.und.edu
Financial aid office: (701) 777-3121

■ 2004-2005 TUITION AND FEES:
    In state: $4,828; Out of state: $11,523
■ ROOM AND BOARD: $4,455

ACT Score (25th/75th percentile): 20-26
2005 U.S. News College Ranking:
National Universities, third tier
Acceptance Rate: 76%

....

Other expenses: Estimated books and supplies: $700. Transportation: $800. Personal expenses: $2,000. Financial aid: Priority filing date for institution's financial aid form: March 15. In 2003-2004, 80% of undergraduates applied for financial aid. Of those, 55% were determined to have financial need; 51% had their need fully met. Average financial aid package (proportion receiving): $8,150 (55%). Average amount of gift aid, such as scholarships or grants (proportion receiving): $3,087 (24%). Average amount of self-help aid, such as work study or loans (proportion receiving): $4,823 (49%). Average need-based loan (excluding PLUS or other private loans): $4,036. Among students who received need-based aid, the average percentage of need met: 87%. Among students who received aid based on merit, the average award (and the proportion receiving): $2,300 (4%). The average athletic scholarship (and the proportion receiving): $3,933 (3%). Average amount of debt of

borrowers graduating in 2003: $22,733. Proportion who borrowed: 68%. Student employment: During the 2003-2004 academic year, 13% of undergraduates worked on campus. Average per-year earnings: $2,083. Cooperative education programs: art, business, computer science, education, engineering, health professions, home economics, humanities, natural science, social/behavioral science, technologies, vocational arts, other. Reserve Officers Training Corps (ROTC): Army ROTC: Offered on campus; Air Force ROTC: Offered on campus.

Valley City State University

101 College Street SW
Valley City, ND 58072
Public; www.vcsu.edu
Financial aid office: (701) 845-7412

■ 2004-2005 TUITION AND FEES:
    In state: $4,558; Out of state: $9,784
■ ROOM AND BOARD: $4,074

ACT Score (25th/75th percentile): 19-23
2005 U.S. News College Ranking:
Comp. Colleges–Bachelor's (Midwest), third tier
Acceptance Rate: 88%

....

Other expenses: Estimated books and supplies: $700. Transportation: $1,417. Personal expenses: $1,417. Financial aid: Priority filing date for institution's financial aid form: March 15. In 2003-2004, 79% of undergraduates applied for financial aid. Of those, 68% were determined to have financial need; 30% had their need fully met. Average financial aid package (proportion receiving): $5,736 (67%). Average amount of gift aid, such as scholarships or grants (proportion receiving): $2,900 (39%). Average amount of self-help aid, such as work study or loans (proportion receiving): $3,992 (54%). Average need-based loan (excluding PLUS or other private loans): $3,340. Among students who received need-based aid, the average percentage of need met: 79%. Among students who received aid based on merit, the average award (and the proportion receiving): $1,403 (25%). The average athletic scholarship (and the proportion receiving): $1,008 (9%). Average amount of debt of borrowers graduating in 2003: $14,700. Proportion who borrowed: 56%. Student employment: During the 2003-2004 academic year, 24% of undergraduates worked on campus. Average per-year earnings: $875.

Ohio

Antioch College

795 Livermore Street
Yellow Springs, OH 45387
Private; www.antioch-college.edu
Financial aid office: (937) 769-1120

■ **2004-2005 TUITION AND FEES:** $24,902
■ **ROOM AND BOARD:** $6,413

SAT I Score (25th/75th percentile): 1080-1290
2005 U.S. News College Ranking:
Liberal Arts Colleges, fourth tier
Acceptance Rate: 75%
....

Other expenses: Estimated books and supplies:
$750. Transportation: $500. Personal expenses:
$750. **Financial aid:** Priority filing date for institu-
tion's financial aid form: February 15; deadline:
March 1. In 2003-2004, 100% of undergraduates
applied for financial aid. Of those, 74% were
determined to have financial need; 50% had their
need fully met. Average financial aid package (proportion receiving): $19,214 (74%). Average
amount of gift aid, such as scholarships or grants
(proportion receiving): $11,293 (70%). Average
amount of self-help aid, such as work study or
loans (proportion receiving): $4,198 (74%).
Average need-based loan (excluding PLUS or
other private loans): $3,424. Among students who
received need-based aid, the average percentage of
need met: 82%. Among students who received aid
based on merit, the average award (and the proportion receiving): $7,520 (26%). The average ath-
letic scholarship (and the proportion receiving): $0
(0%). Proportion who borrowed: 70%.

Art Academy of Cincinnati

1125 St. Gregory Street
Cincinnati, OH 45202
Private; www.artacademy.edu
Financial aid office: (513) 562-8751

■ **2004-2005 TUITION AND FEES:** $18,050

ACT Score (25th/75th percentile): 17-26
2005 U.S. News College Ranking:
Unranked Specialty School–Fine Arts
Acceptance Rate: 69%
....

Other expenses: Estimated books and supplies:
$1,200. **Cooperative education programs:** art.

Ashland University

401 College Avenue
Ashland, OH 44805
Private; www.ashland.edu
Financial aid office: (419) 289-5002

■ **2004-2005 TUITION AND FEES:** $18,858
■ **ROOM AND BOARD:** $6,964

ACT Score (25th/75th percentile): 19-25
2005 U.S. News College Ranking:
Universities–Master's (Midwest), 50
Acceptance Rate: 86%
....

Other expenses: Estimated books and supplies:
$800. Transportation: $700. Personal expenses:
$1,630. **Financial aid:** Priority filing date for
institution's financial aid form: March 15; deadline: March 15. In 2003-2004, 92% of undergraduates applied for financial aid. Of those,
79% were determined to have financial need;
Average financial aid package (proportion
receiving): $16,446 (79%). Average amount of
gift aid, such as scholarships or grants (proportion receiving): $11,333 (79%). Average amount
of self-help aid, such as work study or loans
(proportion receiving): $5,370 (68%). Average
need-based loan (excluding PLUS or other private loans): $4,055. Among students who
received need-based aid, the average percentage
of need met: 90%. Among students who
received aid based on merit, the average award
(and the proportion receiving): $5,680 (14%).
The average athletic scholarship (and the proportion receiving): $10,588 (3%). Average
amount of debt of borrowers graduating in
2003: $18,250. Proportion who borrowed: 75%.
Reserve Officers Training Corps (ROTC): Air
Force ROTC: Offered at cooperating institution
(University of Akron).

Baldwin-Wallace College

275 Eastland Road
Berea, OH 44017
Private; www.bw.edu
Financial aid office: (440) 826-2108

■ **2004-2005 TUITION AND FEES:** $19,494
■ **ROOM AND BOARD:** $6,417

ACT Score (25th/75th percentile): 21-26
2005 U.S. News College Ranking:
Universities–Master's (Midwest), 10
Acceptance Rate: 82%
....

Other expenses: Estimated books and supplies:
$830. Personal expenses: $2,300. **Financial aid:**
Priority filing date for institution's financial aid
form: May 1; deadline: September 1. In 2003-
2004, 87% of undergraduates applied for
financial aid. Of those, 75% were determined to
have financial need; 75% had their need fully
met. Average financial aid package (proportion
receiving): $13,257 (75%). Average amount of
gift aid, such as scholarships or grants (proportion receiving): $9,733 (75%). Average amount
of self-help aid, such as work study or loans
(proportion receiving): $5,024 (63%). Average
need-based loan (excluding PLUS or other private loans): $3,778. Among students who
received need-based aid, the average percentage
of need met: 95%. Among students who
received aid based on merit, the average award
(and the proportion receiving): $7,181 (25%).
Average amount of debt of borrowers graduating in 2003: $14,099. Proportion who bor-
rowed: 63%. **Student employment:** During the
2003-2004 academic year, 40% of undergraduates worked on campus. Average per-year earnings: $515. **Reserve Officers Training Corps
(ROTC):** Air Force ROTC: Offered at cooperating institution (University of Akron).

Bluffton University

1 University Drive
Bluffton, OH 45817
Private; www.bluffton.edu
Financial aid office: (419) 358-3266

■ **2004-2005 TUITION AND FEES:** $18,350
■ **ROOM AND BOARD:** $6,304

ACT Score (25th/75th percentile): 21-25
2005 U.S. News College Ranking:
Comp. Colleges–Bachelor's (Midwest), 25
Acceptance Rate: 77%
....

Other expenses: Estimated books and supplies:
$900. Transportation: $800. Personal expenses: $1,144. **Financial aid:** Priority filing date for
institution's financial aid form: May 1; deadline:
October 1. In 2003-2004, 75% of undergraduates applied for financial aid. Of those, 71%

were determined to have financial need; 52% had their need fully met. Average financial aid package (proportion receiving): $16,776 (71%). Average amount of gift aid, such as scholarships or grants (proportion receiving): $10,829 (71%). Average amount of self-help aid, such as work study or loans (proportion receiving): $6,083 (64%). Average need-based loan (excluding PLUS or other private loans): $4,777. Among students who received need-based aid, the average percentage of need met: 93%. Among students who received aid based on merit, the average award (and the proportion receiving): $7,030 (10%). Average amount of debt of borrowers graduating in 2003: $20,039. Proportion who borrowed: 72%. **Student employment:** During the 2003-2004 academic year, 65% of undergraduates worked on campus. Average per-year earnings: $1,500. **Cooperative education programs:** business, education, home economics, social/behavioral science, technologies.

Bowling Green State University

110 McFall Center
Bowling Green, OH 43403
Public; www.bgsu.edu
Financial aid office: (419) 372-2651

■ **2004-2005 TUITION AND FEES:**
   In state: $7,794; Out of state: $15,100
■ **ROOM AND BOARD:** $6,588

ACT Score (25th/75th percentile): 19-24
2005 U.S. News College Ranking:
National Universities, third tier
Acceptance Rate: 90%

Other expenses: Estimated books and supplies: $902. Transportation: $778. Personal expenses: $1,614. **Financial aid:** Priority filing date for institution's financial aid form: February 15. In 2003-2004, 68% of undergraduates applied for financial aid. Of those, 55% were determined to have financial need; 13% had their need fully met. Average financial aid package (proportion receiving): $8,536 (55%). Average amount of gift aid, such as scholarships or grants (proportion receiving): $3,583 (34%). Average amount of self-help aid, such as work study or loans (proportion receiving): $3,559 (49%). Average need-based loan (excluding PLUS or other private loans): $3,441. Among students who received need-based aid, the average percentage of need met: 76%. Among students who received aid based on merit, the average award (and the proportion receiving): $4,864 (12%). The average athletic scholarship (and the pro-

portion receiving): $14,651 (2%). Average amount of debt of borrowers graduating in 2003: $17,967. Proportion who borrowed: 50%. **Student employment:** During the 2003-2004 academic year, 22% of undergraduates worked on campus. Average per-year earnings: $2,171. **Cooperative education programs:** art, business, computer science, education, health professions, home economics, humanities, natural science, social/behavioral science, technologies, other. **Reserve Officers Training Corps (ROTC):** Army ROTC: Offered on campus; Air Force ROTC: Offered on campus.

Capital University

2199 E. Main Street
Columbus, OH 43209
Private; www.capital.edu
Financial aid office: (614) 236-6511

■ **2004-2005 TUITION AND FEES:** $21,530
■ **ROOM AND BOARD:** $6,160

ACT Score (25th/75th percentile): 20-26
2005 U.S. News College Ranking:
Universities–Master's (Midwest), 13
Acceptance Rate: 84%

Other expenses: Estimated books and supplies: $960. Transportation: $560. **Financial aid:** Priority filing date for institution's financial aid form: March 1. In 2003-2004, 88% of undergraduates applied for financial aid. Of those, 81% were determined to have financial need; 23% had their need fully met. Average financial aid package (proportion receiving): $16,856 (81%). Average amount of gift aid, such as scholarships or grants (proportion receiving): $9,890 (79%). Average amount of self-help aid, such as work study or loans (proportion receiving): $5,997 (71%). Average need-based loan (excluding PLUS or other private loans): $4,589. Among students who received need-based aid, the average percentage of need met: 80%. Among students who received aid based on merit, the average award (and the proportion receiving): $8,628 (17%). The average athletic scholarship (and the proportion receiving): $0 (0%). Average amount of debt of borrowers graduating in 2003: $25,171. Proportion who borrowed: 78%. **Student employment:** During the 2003-2004 academic year, 30% of undergraduates worked on campus. Average per-year earnings: $2,000. **Reserve Officers Training Corps (ROTC):** Army ROTC: Offered on campus; Air Force ROTC: Offered at cooperating institution.

Case Western Reserve University

10900 Euclid Avenue
Cleveland, OH 44106
Private; www.case.edu
Financial aid office: (216) 368-3866

■ **2004-2005 TUITION AND FEES:** $26,762
■ **ROOM AND BOARD:** $8,202

SAT I Score (25th/75th percentile): 1220-1430
2005 U.S. News College Ranking:
National Universities, 35
Acceptance Rate: 75%

Other expenses: Estimated books and supplies: $1,000. Transportation: $800. Personal expenses: $1,206. **Financial aid:** Priority filing date for institution's financial aid form: February 1. In 2003-2004, 67% of undergraduates applied for financial aid. Of those, 55% were determined to have financial need; 92% had their need fully met. Average financial aid package (proportion receiving): $23,571 (55%). Average amount of gift aid, such as scholarships or grants (proportion receiving): $15,695 (54%). Average amount of self-help aid, such as work study or loans (proportion receiving): $6,498 (49%). Average need-based loan (excluding PLUS or other private loans): $5,908. Among students who received need-based aid, the average percentage of need met: 94%. Among students who received aid based on merit, the average award (and the proportion receiving): $12,352 (34%). Average amount of debt of borrowers graduating in 2003: $23,534. Proportion who borrowed: 55%. **Student employment:** During the 2003-2004 academic year, 43% of undergraduates worked on campus. Average per-year earnings: $2,800. **Cooperative education programs:** business, computer science, engineering, natural science. **Reserve Officers Training Corps (ROTC):** Army ROTC: Offered at cooperating institution (John Carroll University); Air Force ROTC: Offered at cooperating institution (University of Akron).

Cedarville University

251 N. Main Street
Cedarville, OH 45314
Private; www.cedarville.edu
Financial aid office: (937) 766-7866

■ **2004-2005 TUITION AND FEES:** $16,032
■ **ROOM AND BOARD:** $5,010

ACT Score (25th/75th percentile): 23-28
2005 U.S. News College Ranking:
Comp. Colleges–Bachelor's (Midwest), 13
Acceptance Rate: 81%

....

Other expenses: Estimated books and supplies: $740. Personal expenses: $970. Financial aid: Priority filing date for institution's financial aid form: March 1. In 2003-2004, 72% of undergraduates applied for financial aid. Of those, 61% were determined to have financial need; 49% had their need fully met. Average financial aid package (proportion receiving): $14,188 (61%). Average amount of gift aid, such as scholarships or grants (proportion receiving): $1,651 (31%). Average amount of self-help aid, such as work study or loans (proportion receiving): $3,749 (55%). Average need-based loan (excluding PLUS or other private loans): $4,053. Among students who received need-based aid, the average percentage of need met: 43%. Among students who received aid based on merit, the average award (and the proportion receiving): $7,300 (22%). The average athletic scholarship (and the proportion receiving): $3,199 (5%). Average amount of debt of borrowers graduating in 2003: $24,542. Proportion who borrowed: 58%. Student employment: During the 2003-2004 academic year, 41% of undergraduates worked on campus. Average per-year earnings: $710. Reserve Officers Training Corps (ROTC): Army ROTC: Offered at cooperating institution (Central State); Air Force ROTC: Offered at cooperating institution (Wright State University).

Central State University

PO Box 1004
Wilberforce, OH 45384
Public; www.centralstate.edu
Financial aid office: (937) 376-6579

■ 2004-2005 TUITION AND FEES:
  In state: $4,710; Out of state: $10,200
■ ROOM AND BOARD: $6,432

ACT Score (25th/75th percentile): 14-17
2005 U.S. News College Ranking:
Comp. Colleges–Bachelor's (Midwest), fourth tier
Acceptance Rate: 49%

....

Other expenses: Estimated books and supplies: $900. Transportation: $658. Personal expenses: $165. Financial aid: Priority filing date for institution's financial aid form: February 15. In 2003-2004, 95% of undergraduates applied for financial aid. Among students who received

need-based aid, the average percentage of need met: 95%. Student employment: During the 2003-2004 academic year, 11% of undergraduates worked on campus. Average per-year earnings: $4,800. Cooperative education programs: business, computer science, education, engineering, humanities. Reserve Officers Training Corps (ROTC): Army ROTC: Offered on campus; Air Force ROTC: Offered at cooperating institution (Wright State University).

Cleveland Institute of Art

11141 East Boulevard
Cleveland, OH 44106
Private; www.cia.edu
Financial aid office: (216) 421-7424

■ 2004-2005 TUITION AND FEES: $24,991
■ ROOM AND BOARD: $8,252

2005 U.S. News College Ranking:
Unranked Specialty School–Fine Arts
Acceptance Rate: 77%

....

Other expenses: Estimated books and supplies: $1,200. Transportation: $1,400. Personal expenses: $1,800. Financial aid: Priority filing date for institution's financial aid form: March 15. In 2003-2004, 86% of undergraduates applied for financial aid. Of those, 80% were determined to have financial need; 15% had their need fully met. Average financial aid package (proportion receiving): $23,429 (80%). Average amount of gift aid, such as scholarships or grants (proportion receiving): $4,902 (79%). Average amount of self-help aid, such as work study or loans (proportion receiving): $5,534 (80%). Average need-based loan (excluding PLUS or other private loans): $4,052. Among students who received need-based aid, the average percentage of need met: 63%. Among students who received aid based on merit, the average award (and the proportion receiving): $9,844 (6%). The average athletic scholarship (and the proportion receiving): $0 (0%). Average amount of debt of borrowers graduating in 2003: $22,775. Proportion who borrowed: 65%.

Cleveland Institute of Music

11021 East Boulevard
Cleveland, OH 44106
Private; www.cim.edu
Financial aid office: (216) 795-3192

■ 2004-2005 TUITION AND FEES: $24,986
■ ROOM AND BOARD: $7,574

2005 U.S. News College Ranking:
Unranked Specialty School–Fine Arts

....

Other expenses: Estimated books and supplies: $800. Transportation: $1,000. Personal expenses: $1,000. Financial aid: Priority filing date for institution's financial aid form: February 15; deadline: February 15.

Cleveland State University

1983 E. 24th Street
Cleveland, OH 44115
Public; www.csuohio.edu
Financial aid office: (216) 687-2054

■ 2004-2005 TUITION AND FEES:
  In state: $6,090; Out of state: $11,976
■ ROOM AND BOARD: $6,392

ACT Score (25th/75th percentile): 16-21
2005 U.S. News College Ranking:
National Universities, fourth tier
Acceptance Rate: 78%

....

Other expenses: Estimated books and supplies: $800. Transportation: $1,400. Personal expenses: $2,376. Financial aid: Priority filing date for institution's financial aid form: February 15. In 2003-2004, 74% of undergraduates applied for financial aid. Of those, 69% were determined to have financial need; 8% had their need fully met. Average financial aid package (proportion receiving): $6,893 (69%). Average amount of gift aid, such as scholarships or grants (proportion receiving): $4,663 (50%). Average amount of self-help aid, such as work study or loans (proportion receiving): $4,088 (59%). Average need-based loan (excluding PLUS or other private loans): $3,954. Among students who received need-based aid, the average percentage of need met: 54%. Among students who received aid based on merit, the average award (and the proportion receiving): $7,054 (9%). The average athletic scholarship (and the proportion receiving): $8,528 (2%). Cooperative education programs: art, business, computer science, education, engineering, health professions, humanities, natural science, social/behavioral science, technologies. Reserve Officers Training Corps (ROTC): Army ROTC: Offered on campus; Air Force ROTC: Offered at cooperating institution (Kent State University).

College of Mount St. Joseph

5701 Delhi Road
Cincinnati, OH 45233
Private; www.msj.edu
Financial aid office: (513) 244-4418

- **2004-2005 TUITION AND FEES:** $18,090
- **ROOM AND BOARD:** $6,195

ACT Score (25th/75th percentile): 18-24
2005 U.S. News College Ranking:
Universities–Master's (Midwest), 31
Acceptance Rate: 76%

....

Other expenses: Estimated books and supplies: $800. Transportation: $400. Personal expenses: $600. **Financial aid:** Priority filing date for institution's financial aid form: March 1. In 2003-2004, 94% of undergraduates applied for financial aid. Of those, 65% were determined to have financial need; 35% had their need fully met. Average financial aid package (proportion receiving): $11,400 (65%). Average amount of gift aid, such as scholarships or grants (proportion receiving): $8,000 (60%). Average amount of self-help aid, such as work study or loans (proportion receiving): $5,840 (55%). Average need-based loan (excluding PLUS or other private loans): $3,500. Among students who received need-based aid, the average percentage of need met: 90%. Among students who received aid based on merit, the average award (and the proportion receiving): $3,800 (28%). The average athletic scholarship (and the proportion receiving): $0 (0%). Average amount of debt of borrowers graduating in 2003: $13,900. Proportion who borrowed: 80%. **Student employment:** During the 2003-2004 academic year, 13% of undergraduates worked on campus. Average per-year earnings: $1,500. **Cooperative education programs:** art, business, computer science, education, health professions, humanities, natural science, social/behavioral science. **Reserve Officers Training Corps (ROTC):** Army ROTC: Offered at cooperating institution (Xavier University); Air Force ROTC: Offered at cooperating institution (University of Cincinnati).

College of Wooster

1189 Beall Avenue
Wooster, OH 44691
Private; www.wooster.edu
Financial aid office: (330) 263-2317

- **2004-2005 TUITION AND FEES:** $26,560
- **ROOM AND BOARD:** $6,640

SAT I Score (25th/75th percentile): 1090-1310
2005 U.S. News College Ranking:
Liberal Arts Colleges, 59
Acceptance Rate: 70%

....

Other expenses: Estimated books and supplies: $700. Transportation: $150. Personal expenses: $600. **Financial aid:** Priority filing date for institution's financial aid form: February 15. In 2003-2004, 71% of undergraduates applied for financial aid. Of those, 64% were determined to have financial need; 70% had their need fully met. Average financial aid package (proportion receiving): $21,812 (64%). Average amount of gift aid, such as scholarships or grants (proportion receiving): $15,970 (63%). Average amount of self-help aid, such as work study or loans (proportion receiving): $5,251 (53%). Average need-based loan (excluding PLUS or other private loans): $4,664. Among students who received need-based aid, the average percentage of need met: 95%. Among students who received aid based on merit, the average award (and the proportion receiving): $10,643 (34%). The average athletic scholarship (and the proportion receiving): $0 (0%). Average amount of debt of borrowers graduating in 2003: $19,494. Proportion who borrowed: 63%. **Cooperative education programs:** engineering, health professions, natural science, other.

Columbus College of Art and Design

107 N. Ninth Street
Columbus, OH 43215
Private; www.ccad.edu
Financial aid office: (614) 222-3275

- **2004-2005 TUITION AND FEES:** $19,320
- **ROOM AND BOARD:** $6,400

ACT Score (25th/75th percentile): 18-23
2005 U.S. News College Ranking:
Unranked Specialty School–Fine Arts
Acceptance Rate: 64%

....

Other expenses: Estimated books and supplies: $3,000. Transportation: $1,000. Personal expenses: $925. **Financial aid:** Priority filing date for institution's financial aid form: March 3; deadline: June 2. In 2003-2004, 94% of undergraduates applied for financial aid. Of those, 82% were determined to have financial need; 18% had their need fully met. Average financial aid package (proportion receiving): $12,897 (82%). Average amount of gift aid, such as scholarships or grants (proportion receiving): $8,613 (80%). Average amount of

self-help aid, such as work study or loans (proportion receiving): $5,401 (67%). Average need-based loan (excluding PLUS or other private loans): $5,117. Among students who received need-based aid, the average percentage of need met: 64%. Among students who received aid based on merit, the average award (and the proportion receiving): $10,034 (19%). The average athletic scholarship (and the proportion receiving): $0 (0%). Average amount of debt of borrowers graduating in 2003: $26,822. Proportion who borrowed: 99%. **Student employment:** During the 2003-2004 academic year, 10% of undergraduates worked on campus. Average per-year earnings: $2,790.

Defiance College

701 N. Clinton Street
Defiance, OH 43512
Private; www.defiance.edu
Financial aid office: (419) 783-2376

- **2004-2005 TUITION AND FEES:** $18,230
- **ROOM AND BOARD:** $5,590

SAT I Score (25th/75th percentile): 870-1130
2005 U.S. News College Ranking:
Comp. Colleges–Bachelor's (Midwest), third tier
Acceptance Rate: 76%

....

Other expenses: Estimated books and supplies: $700. Transportation: $650. Personal expenses: $1,200. **Financial aid:** Priority filing date for institution's financial aid form: March 1. In 2003-2004, 92% of undergraduates applied for financial aid. Of those, 83% were determined to have financial need; Average financial aid package (proportion receiving): $13,493 (83%). Average amount of gift aid, such as scholarships or grants (proportion receiving): $3,325 (49%). Average amount of self-help aid, such as work study or loans (proportion receiving): $4,384 (67%). Average need-based loan (excluding PLUS or other private loans): $4,256. Among students who received need-based aid, the average percentage of need met: 81%. Among students who received aid based on merit, the average award (and the proportion receiving): $9,879 (7%). The average athletic scholarship (and the proportion receiving): $0 (0%). Average amount of debt of borrowers graduating in 2003: $15,151. Proportion who borrowed: 70%. **Student employment:** During the 2003-2004 academic year, 40% of undergraduates worked on campus. Average per-year earnings: $5. **Cooperative education programs:** business, computer science, education.

Denison University

1 Main Street
Granville, OH 43023
Private; www.denison.edu
Financial aid office: (740) 587-6279

- ■ **2004-2005 TUITION AND FEES:** $27,310
- ■ **ROOM AND BOARD:** $7,670

SAT I Score (25th/75th percentile): 1130-1310
2005 U.S. News College Ranking:
Liberal Arts Colleges, 50
Acceptance Rate: 68%

Other expenses: Estimated books and supplies: $600. Transportation: $400. Personal expenses: $1,200. **Financial aid:** Priority filing date for institution's financial aid form: February 15. In 2003-2004, 57% of undergraduates applied for financial aid. Of those, 49% were determined to have financial need; 59% had their need fully met. Average financial aid package (proportion receiving): $22,756 (49%). Average amount of gift aid, such as scholarships or grants (proportion receiving): $16,876 (49%). Average amount of self-help aid, such as work study or loans (proportion receiving): $5,405 (37%). Average need-based loan (excluding PLUS or other private loans): $4,495. Among students who received need-based aid, the average percentage of need met: 98%. Among students who received aid based on merit, the average award (and the proportion receiving): $10,372 (51%). The average athletic scholarship (and the proportion receiving): $0 (0%). Average amount of debt of borrowers graduating in 2003: $15,009. Proportion who borrowed: 53%. **Student employment:** During the 2003-2004 academic year, 43% of undergraduates worked on campus. Average per-year earnings: $2,100. **Reserve Officers Training Corps (ROTC):** Army ROTC: Offered at cooperating institution (Capital University).

Franciscan University of Steubenville

1235 University Boulevard
Steubenville, OH 43952-1763
Private; www.franciscan.edu
Financial aid office: (740) 283-6226

- ■ **2004-2005 TUITION AND FEES:** $15,700
- ■ **ROOM AND BOARD:** $5,350

SAT I Score (25th/75th percentile): 1040-1270
2005 U.S. News College Ranking:
Universities–Master's (Midwest), 25
Acceptance Rate: 84%

Other expenses: Estimated books and supplies: $800. Transportation: $1,500. Personal expenses: $1,200. **Financial aid:** Priority filing date for institution's financial aid form: April 15. In 2003-2004, 82% of undergraduates applied for financial aid. Of those, 67% were determined to have financial need; 15% had their need fully met. Average financial aid package (proportion receiving): $10,631 (67%). Average amount of gift aid, such as scholarships or grants (proportion receiving): $6,565 (62%). Average amount of self-help aid, such as work study or loans (proportion receiving): $4,831 (63%). Average need-based loan (excluding PLUS or other private loans): $3,066. Among students who received need-based aid, the average percentage of need met: 62%. Among students who received aid based on merit, the average award (and the proportion receiving): $6,930 (21%). The average athletic scholarship (and the proportion receiving): $0 (0%). Average amount of debt of borrowers graduating in 2003: $23,140. Proportion who borrowed: 77%. **Student employment:** During the 2003-2004 academic year, 50% of undergraduates worked on campus. Average per-year earnings: $1,500.

Franklin University

201 S. Grant Avenue
Columbus, OH 43215
Private; www.franklin.edu
Financial aid office: (614) 797-4700

- ■ **2004-2005 TUITION AND FEES:** $6,990

2005 U.S. News College Ranking:
Unranked Specialty School–Business

Heidelberg College

310 E. Market Street
Tiffin, OH 44883
Private; www.heidelberg.edu
Financial aid office: (419) 448-2293

- ■ **2004-2005 TUITION AND FEES:** $14,900
- ■ **ROOM AND BOARD:** $6,710

ACT Score (25th/75th percentile): 21
2005 U.S. News College Ranking:
Universities–Master's (Midwest), 31
Acceptance Rate: 98%

Other expenses: Estimated books and supplies: $1,000. Transportation: $500. Personal expenses: $500. **Financial aid:** Priority filing date for institution's financial aid form: March 1. In 2003-2004, 91% of undergraduates applied for financial aid. Of those, 84% were determined to have financial need; 47% had their need fully met. Average financial aid package (proportion receiving): $16,974 (84%). Average amount of gift aid, such as scholarships or grants (proportion receiving): $10,089 (83%). Average amount of self-help aid, such as work study or loans (proportion receiving): $4,933 (83%). Average need-based loan (excluding PLUS or other private loans): $4,300. Among students who received need-based aid, the average percentage of need met: 95%. Among students who received aid based on merit, the average award (and the proportion receiving): $5,553 (16%). The average athletic scholarship (and the proportion receiving): $0 (0%). Average amount of debt of borrowers graduating in 2003: $22,032. Proportion who borrowed: 74%. **Student employment:** During the 2003-2004 academic year, 70% of undergraduates worked on campus. Average per-year earnings: $800. **Reserve Officers Training Corps (ROTC):** Army ROTC: Offered at cooperating institution (Bowling Green State University); Air Force ROTC: Offered at cooperating institution (Bowling Green State University).

Hiram College

PO Box 67
Hiram, OH 44234
Private; www.hiram.edu
Financial aid office: (330) 569-5107

- ■ **2004-2005 TUITION AND FEES:** $21,860
- ■ **ROOM AND BOARD:** $7,275

ACT Score (25th/75th percentile): 21-26
2005 U.S. News College Ranking:
Liberal Arts Colleges, third tier
Acceptance Rate: 88%

Other expenses: Estimated books and supplies: $600. Transportation: $864. Personal expenses: $1,372. **Financial aid:** 95% had their need fully met. Average financial aid package (proportion receiving): $21,218 (N/A). Average amount of gift aid, such as scholarships or grants (proportion receiving): $8,163 (N/A).

Average amount of self-help aid, such as work study or loans (proportion receiving): $8,484 (N/A). Average need-based loan (excluding PLUS or other private loans): $6,960. Among students who received need-based aid, the average percentage of need met: 95%. Among students who received aid based on merit, the average award (and the proportion receiving): $8,635 (N/A). The average athletic scholarship (and the proportion receiving): $0 (N/A). Average amount of debt of borrowers graduating in 2003: $17,125. **Student employment:** During the 2003-2004 academic year, 48% of undergraduates worked on campus. Average per-year earnings: $1,600.

John Carroll University

20700 N. Park Boulevard
University Heights, OH 44118
Private; www.jcu.edu
Financial aid office: (216) 397-4248

- **2004-2005 TUITION AND FEES:** $22,308
- **ROOM AND BOARD:** $7,236

ACT Score (25th/75th percentile): 21-26
2005 U.S. News College Ranking:
Universities–Master's (Midwest), 5
Acceptance Rate: 87%

Other expenses: Estimated books and supplies: $1,000. Transportation: $800. Personal expenses: $750. **Financial aid:** Priority filing date for institution's financial aid form: March 1; deadline: March 1. In 2003-2004, 84% of undergraduates applied for financial aid. Of those, 71% were determined to have financial need; 36% had their need fully met. Average financial aid package (proportion receiving): $16,588 (71%). Average amount of gift aid, such as scholarships or grants (proportion receiving): $11,469 (71%). Average amount of self-help aid, such as work study or loans (proportion receiving): $5,355 (61%). Average need-based loan (excluding PLUS or other private loans): $4,312. Among students who received need-based aid, the average percentage of need met: 85%. Among students who received aid based on merit, the average award (and the proportion receiving): $3,308 (22%). The average athletic scholarship (and the proportion receiving): $0 (0%). Average amount of debt of borrowers graduating in 2003: $18,108. Proportion who borrowed: 77%. **Student employment:** During the 2003-2004 academic year, 25% of undergraduates worked on campus. Average per-year earnings: $1,600. **Cooperative education programs:** art, business, computer science, natural

science, other. **Reserve Officers Training Corps (ROTC):** Army ROTC: Offered on campus.

Kent State University

PO Box 5190
Kent, OH 44242-0001
Public; www.kent.edu
Financial aid office: (330) 672-2972

- **2004-2005 TUITION AND FEES:**
  In state: $7,504; Out of state: $14,516
- **ROOM AND BOARD:** $6,410

ACT Score (25th/75th percentile): 19-24
2005 U.S. News College Ranking:
National Universities, fourth tier
Acceptance Rate: 89%

Other expenses: Estimated books and supplies: $990. Transportation: $1,122. Personal expenses: $2,040. **Financial aid:** Priority filing date for institution's financial aid form: March 1. In 2003-2004, 68% of undergraduates applied for financial aid. Of those, 58% were determined to have financial need; 16% had their need fully met. Average financial aid package (proportion receiving): $7,151 (58%). Average amount of gift aid, such as scholarships or grants (proportion receiving): $4,614 (39%). Average amount of self-help aid, such as work study or loans (proportion receiving): $4,164 (52%). Average need-based loan (excluding PLUS or other private loans): $3,925. Among students who received need-based aid, the average percentage of need met: 62%. Among students who received aid based on merit, the average award (and the proportion receiving): $3,455 (8%). The average athletic scholarship (and the proportion receiving): $10,999 (1%). Average amount of debt of borrowers graduating in 2003: $19,439. Proportion who borrowed: 66%. **Student employment:** During the 2003-2004 academic year, 23% of undergraduates worked on campus. Average per-year earnings: $3,520. **Cooperative education programs:** vocational arts. **Reserve Officers Training Corps (ROTC):** Army ROTC: Offered on campus; Air Force ROTC: Offered on campus.

Kenyon College

Ransom Hall
Gambier, OH 43022-9623
Private; www.kenyon.edu
Financial aid office: (740) 427-5430

- **2004-2005 TUITION AND FEES:** $32,170
- **ROOM AND BOARD:** $5,270

SAT I Score (25th/75th percentile): 1220-1410
2005 U.S. News College Ranking:
Liberal Arts Colleges, 29
Acceptance Rate: 46%

Other expenses: Estimated books and supplies: $1,090. Transportation: $780. Personal expenses: $0. **Financial aid:** Priority filing date for institution's financial aid form: February 15; deadline: March 1. In 2003-2004, 49% of undergraduates applied for financial aid. Of those, 41% were determined to have financial need; 100% had their need fully met. Average financial aid package (proportion receiving): $22,151 (41%). Average amount of gift aid, such as scholarships or grants (proportion receiving): $18,731 (41%). Average amount of self-help aid, such as work study or loans (proportion receiving): $4,222 (37%). Average need-based loan (excluding PLUS or other private loans): $3,644. Among students who received need-based aid, the average percentage of need met: 98%. Among students who received aid based on merit, the average award (and the proportion receiving): $12,502 (24%). Average amount of debt of borrowers graduating in 2003: $19,587. Proportion who borrowed: 60%. **Student employment:** During the 2003-2004 academic year, 30% of undergraduates worked on campus. Average per-year earnings: $583.

Lake Erie College

391 W. Washington Street
Painesville, OH 44077
Private; www.lec.edu
Financial aid office: (440) 375-7100

- **2004-2005 TUITION AND FEES:** $18,590
- **ROOM AND BOARD:** $6,014

ACT Score (25th/75th percentile): 16-23
2005 U.S. News College Ranking:
Universities–Master's (Midwest), third tier
Acceptance Rate: 55%

Other expenses: Estimated books and supplies: $530. Transportation: $1,145. Personal expenses: $990. **Student employment:** During the 2003-2004 academic year, 13% of undergraduates worked on campus. Average per-year earnings: $3,090.

Lourdes College

6832 Convent Boulevard
Sylvania, OH 43560-2898
Private; www.lourdes.edu
Financial aid office: (419) 824-3732

■ **2004-2005 TUITION AND FEES:** $11,880

ACT Score (25th/75th percentile): 19-23
2005 U.S. News College Ranking:
Comp. Colleges–Bachelor's (Midwest),
fourth tier
Acceptance Rate: 25%

Financial aid: Priority filing date for institution's
financial aid form: March 1. In 2003-2004, 94%
of undergraduates applied for financial aid. Of
those, 87% were determined to have financial
need; Average financial aid package (proportion
receiving): $11,936 (87%). Average amount of
gift aid, such as scholarships or grants (proportion receiving): $4,952 (72%). Average amount
of self-help aid, such as work study or loans
(proportion receiving): $4,028 (80%). Average
need-based loan (excluding PLUS or other private loans): $3,470. Among students who
received aid based on merit, the average award
(and the proportion receiving): $4,665 (2%).
The average athletic scholarship (and the proportion receiving): $0 (0%). **Reserve Officers
Training Corps (ROTC):** Army ROTC: Offered at
cooperating institution (University of Toledo);
Air Force ROTC: Offered at cooperating institution (Bowling Green State University).

Malone College

515 25th Street NW
Canton, OH 44709
Private; www.malone.edu
Financial aid office: (330) 471-8159

■ **2004-2005 TUITION AND FEES:** $15,880
■ **ROOM AND BOARD:** $5,920

ACT Score (25th/75th percentile): 19-25
2005 U.S. News College Ranking:
Universities–Master's (Midwest), third tier
Acceptance Rate: 85%

Other expenses: Estimated books and supplies:
$900. Transportation: $676. Personal expenses: $800. **Financial aid:** Priority filing date for
institution's financial aid form: March 1; deadline: July 31. In 2003-2004, 83% of undergraduates applied for financial aid. Of those, 74%
were determined to have financial need; 20%

had their need fully met. Average financial aid
package (proportion receiving): $11,365 (74%).
Average amount of gift aid, such as scholarships or grants (proportion receiving): $7,708
(73%). Average amount of self-help aid, such as
work study or loans (proportion receiving):
$4,150 (67%). Average need-based loan (exclud-
ing PLUS or other private loans): $3,517.
Among students who received need-based aid,
the average percentage of need met: 75%.
Among students who received aid based on
merit, the average award (and the proportion
receiving): $3,995 (9%). The average athletic
scholarship (and the proportion receiving):
$5,610 (4%). Average amount of debt of bor-
rowers graduating in 2003: $16,465.
Proportion who borrowed: 62%. **Student
employment:** During the 2003-2004 academic
year, 5% of undergraduates worked on campus.
Average per-year earnings: $700. **Cooperative
education programs:** art, business, computer
science, health professions, humanities, natural
science, social/behavioral science, technologies.
Reserve Officers Training Corps (ROTC): Army
ROTC: Offered at cooperating institution
(University of Akron); Air Force ROTC: Offered
at cooperating institution (University of Akron).

Marietta College

215 Fifth Street
Marietta, OH 45750
Private; www.marietta.edu
Financial aid office: (740) 376-4712

■ **2004-2005 TUITION AND FEES:** $21,730
■ **ROOM AND BOARD:** $6,186

ACT Score (25th/75th percentile): 20-27
2005 U.S. News College Ranking:
Comp. Colleges–Bachelor's (Midwest), 23
Acceptance Rate: 78%

Other expenses: Estimated books and supplies:
$614. Transportation: $510. Personal expenses:
$560. **Financial aid:** Priority filing date for insti-
tution's financial aid form: March 1; deadline:
May 1. In 2003-2004, 91% of undergraduates
applied for financial aid. Of those, 81% were
determined to have financial need; 49% had
their need fully met. Average financial aid package (proportion receiving): $17,761 (81%).
Average amount of gift aid, such as scholarships or grants (proportion receiving): $6,200
(63%). Average amount of self-help aid, such as
work study or loans (proportion receiving):
$4,633 (75%). Average need-based loan (exclud-
ing PLUS or other private loans): $3,258.
Among students who received need-based aid,

the average percentage of need met: 91%.
Among students who received aid based on
merit, the average award (and the proportion
receiving): $6,400 (16%). The average athletic
scholarship (and the proportion receiving): $0
(0%). Average amount of debt of borrowers
graduating in 2003: $17,810. Proportion who
borrowed: 70%. Average per-year earnings:
$2,000.

Miami University–Oxford

Oxford, OH 45056
Public; www.muohio.edu
Financial aid office: (513) 529-8734

■ **2004-2005 TUITION AND FEES:**
In state: $19,642; Out of state: $19,662
■ **ROOM AND BOARD:** $7,010

ACT Score (25th/75th percentile): 25-29
2005 U.S. News College Ranking:
National Universities, 62
Acceptance Rate: 71%

Other expenses: Estimated books and supplies:
$800. Transportation: $450. Personal expenses:
$2,076. **Financial aid:** Priority filing date for
institution's financial aid form: February 15. In
2003-2004, 48% of undergraduates applied for
financial aid. Of those, 33% were determined to
have financial need; 22% had their need fully
met. Average financial aid package (proportion
receiving): $7,090 (32%). Average amount of
gift aid, such as scholarships or grants (proportion receiving): $4,217 (14%). Average amount
of self-help aid, such as work study or loans
(proportion receiving): $4,117 (27%). Average
need-based loan (excluding PLUS or other private loans): $3,723. Among students who
received need-based aid, the average percentage
of need met: 67%. Among students who
received aid based on merit, the average award
(and the proportion receiving): $4,539 (14%).
The average athletic scholarship (and the proportion receiving): $14,105 (2%). Average
amount of debt of borrowers graduating in
2003: $18,302. Proportion who borrowed: 46%.
Student employment: During the 2003-2004
academic year, 25% of undergraduates worked
on campus. Average per-year earnings: $800.
Cooperative education programs: computer science, engineering. **Reserve Officers Training
Corps (ROTC):** Army ROTC: Offered at cooperating institution (Xavier University); Navy
ROTC: Offered on campus; Air Force ROTC:
Offered on campus.

Mount Union College

1972 Clark Avenue
Alliance, OH 44601
Private; www.muc.edu
Financial aid office: (877) 543-9185

- **2004-2005 TUITION AND FEES:** $18,810
- **ROOM AND BOARD:** $5,630

ACT Score (25th/75th percentile): 19-24
2005 U.S. News College Ranking:
Comp. Colleges–Bachelor's (Midwest), 14
Acceptance Rate: 75%

....

Other expenses: Estimated books and supplies: $600. Transportation: $760. Personal expenses: $740. **Financial aid:** Priority filing date for institution's financial aid form: May 1. In 2003-2004, 86% of undergraduates applied for financial aid. Of those, 80% were determined to have financial need; 18% had their need fully met. Average financial aid package (proportion receiving): $15,324 (80%). Average amount of gift aid, such as scholarships or grants (proportion receiving): $10,617 (80%). Average amount of self-help aid, such as work study or loans (proportion receiving): $5,217 (73%). Average need-based loan (excluding PLUS or other private loans): $4,438. Among students who received need-based aid, the average percentage of need met: 85%. Among students who received aid based on merit, the average award (and the proportion receiving): $7,428 (18%). The average athletic scholarship (and the proportion receiving): $0 (0%). Average amount of debt of borrowers graduating in 2003: $15,335. Proportion who borrowed: 76%. **Student employment:** During the 2003-2004 academic year, 45% of undergraduates worked on campus. Average per-year earnings: $1,173. **Cooperative education programs:** business, other. **Reserve Officers Training Corps (ROTC):** Army ROTC: Offered at cooperating institution (Kent State University); Air Force ROTC: Offered at cooperating institution (Kent State University).

Mount Vernon Nazarene University

800 Martinsburg Road
Mount Vernon, OH 43050
Private; www.mvnu.edu
Financial aid office: (740) 392-6868

- **2004-2005 TUITION AND FEES:** $15,126
- **ROOM AND BOARD:** $4,734

ACT Score (25th/75th percentile): 20-25
2005 U.S. News College Ranking:
Comp. Colleges–Bachelor's (Midwest), 47
Acceptance Rate: 86%

....

Other expenses: Estimated books and supplies: $900. Transportation: $800. Personal expenses: $970. **Financial aid:** Priority filing date for institution's financial aid form: March 15. In 2003-2004, 68% of undergraduates applied for financial aid. Of those, 54% were determined to have financial need; 26% had their need fully met. Average financial aid package (proportion receiving): $10,581 (53%). Average amount of gift aid, such as scholarships or grants (proportion receiving): $5,355 (53%). Average amount of self-help aid, such as work study or loans (proportion receiving): $2,820 (49%). Average need-based loan (excluding PLUS or other private loans): $831. Among students who received need-based aid, the average percentage of need met: 83%. Among students who received aid based on merit, the average award (and the proportion receiving): $1,406 (42%). The average athletic scholarship (and the proportion receiving): $2,112 (1%). Average amount of debt of borrowers graduating in 2003: $17,796. Proportion who borrowed: 79%. **Student employment:** During the 2003-2004 academic year, 61% of undergraduates worked on campus. Average per-year earnings: $1,100. **Cooperative education programs:** health professions, vocational arts.

Muskingum College

163 Stormont Street
New Concord, OH 43762
Private; www.muskingum.edu
Financial aid office: (740) 826-8139

- **2004-2005 TUITION AND FEES:** $15,470
- **ROOM AND BOARD:** $6,200

ACT Score (25th/75th percentile): 19-24
2005 U.S. News College Ranking:
Liberal Arts Colleges, third tier
Acceptance Rate: 80%

....

Other expenses: Estimated books and supplies: $1,000. Transportation: $400. Personal expenses: $800. **Financial aid:** Priority filing date for institution's financial aid form: March 15. In 2003-2004, 84% of undergraduates applied for financial aid. Of those, 78% were determined to have financial need; 39% had their need fully met. Average financial aid package (proportion receiving): $13,767 (78%). Average amount of gift aid, such as scholarships or grants (propor-

tion receiving): $9,809 (78%). Average amount of self-help aid, such as work study or loans (proportion receiving): $4,688 (66%). Average need-based loan (excluding PLUS or other private loans): $4,065. Among students who received need-based aid, the average percentage of need met: 86%. Among students who received aid based on merit, the average award (and the proportion receiving): $4,649 (17%). The average athletic scholarship (and the proportion receiving): $0 (0%). Average amount of debt of borrowers graduating in 2003: $18,036. Proportion who borrowed: 72%. **Student employment:** During the 2003-2004 academic year, 40% of undergraduates worked on campus. Average per-year earnings: $1,000.

Myers University

112 Prospect Avenue
Cleveland, OH 44115
Private; www.dnmyers.edu
Financial aid office: (216) 523-3818

- **2004-2005 TUITION AND FEES:** $11,700
- **ROOM AND BOARD:** $7,100

2005 U.S. News College Ranking:
Unranked Specialty School–Business
Acceptance Rate: 70%

....

Other expenses: Estimated books and supplies: $1,000. Transportation: $800. Personal expenses: $0. **Financial aid:** Priority filing date for institution's financial aid form: April 15. In 2003-2004, 91% of undergraduates applied for financial aid. Of those, 75% were determined to have financial need; 25% had their need fully met. Average financial aid package (proportion receiving): $9,684 (76%). Average amount of gift aid, such as scholarships or grants (proportion receiving): $3,831 (32%). Average amount of self-help aid, such as work study or loans (proportion receiving): $5,140 (75%). Average need-based loan (excluding PLUS or other private loans): $4,840. Among students who received need-based aid, the average percentage of need met: 65%. Among students who received aid based on merit, the average award (and the proportion receiving): $0 (0%). The average athletic scholarship (and the proportion receiving): $0 (0%). **Cooperative education programs:** business.

Notre Dame College of Ohio

4545 College Road
Cleveland, OH 44121
Private; www.notredamecollege.edu
Financial aid office: (216) 373-5263

■ 2004-2005 TUITION AND FEES: $18,350
■ ROOM AND BOARD: $6,210

ACT Score (25th/75th percentile): 20-26
2005 U.S. News College Ranking:
Comp. Colleges–Bachelor's (Midwest),
third tier
Acceptance Rate: 47%

Other expenses: Estimated books and supplies: $1,277. Transportation: $550. Personal expenses: $1,550. **Financial aid:** Priority filing date for institution's financial aid form: April 1. Average financial aid package (proportion receiving): $19,141 (N/A). Average amount of gift aid, such as scholarships or grants (proportion receiving): $12,233 (N/A). Average amount of self-help aid, such as work study or loans (proportion receiving): $6,981 (N/A). Average need-based loan (excluding PLUS or other private loans): $4,281. Among students who received need-based aid, the average percentage of need met: 94%. Among students who received aid based on merit, the average award (and the proportion receiving): $3,444 (N/A). The average athletic scholarship (and the proportion receiving): $5,666 (N/A). Average per-year earnings: $2,450.

Oberlin College

173 W. Lorain Street
Oberlin, OH 44074
Private; www.oberlin.edu
Financial aid office: (440) 775-8142

■ 2004-2005 TUITION AND FEES: $31,167
■ ROOM AND BOARD: $7,643

SAT I Score (25th/75th percentile): 1240-1440
2005 U.S. News College Ranking:
Liberal Arts Colleges, 23
Acceptance Rate: 36%

Other expenses: Estimated books and supplies: $761. Transportation: $650. Personal expenses: $1,094. **Financial aid:** Priority filing date for institution's financial aid form: January 15; deadline: January 15. In 2003-2004, 66% of undergraduates applied for financial aid. Of those, 58% were determined to have financial need; 100% had their need fully met. Average financial aid package (proportion receiving): $22,576 (58%). Average amount of gift aid, such as scholarships or grants (proportion receiving): $17,488 (53%). Average amount of self-help aid, such as work study or loans (proportion receiving): $4,606 (52%). Average need-based loan (excluding PLUS or other private loans): $4,013. Among students who received need-based aid, the average percentage of need met: 100%. Among students who received aid based on merit, the average award (and the proportion receiving): $11,472 (10%). The average athletic scholarship (and the proportion receiving): $0 (0%). Average amount of debt of borrowers graduating in 2003: $17,000. Proportion who borrowed: 58%. **Student employment:** During the 2003-2004 academic year, 60% of undergraduates worked on campus. Average per-year earnings: $1,500.

Ohio Dominican University

1216 Sunbury Road
Columbus, OH 43219
Private; www.ohiodominican.edu
Financial aid office: (614) 251-4640

■ 2004-2005 TUITION AND FEES: $18,000
■ ROOM AND BOARD: $5,900

ACT Score (25th/75th percentile): 18-23
2005 U.S. News College Ranking:
Comp. Colleges–Bachelor's (Midwest),
third tier
Acceptance Rate: 76%

Other expenses: Estimated books and supplies: $665. Transportation: $460. Personal expenses: $1,655. **Financial aid:** Priority filing date for institution's financial aid form: April 4; deadline: August 4. Proportion who borrowed: 89%. **Student employment:** During the 2003-2004 academic year, 17% of undergraduates worked on campus. Average per-year earnings: $2,000. **Reserve Officers Training Corps (ROTC):** Army ROTC: Offered at cooperating institution (Capital University).

Ohio Northern University

525 S. Main Street
Ada, OH 45810
Private; www.onu.edu
Financial aid office: (419) 772-2272

■ 2004-2005 TUITION AND FEES: $25,815
■ ROOM AND BOARD: $6,360

ACT Score (25th/75th percentile): 23-28
2005 U.S. News College Ranking:
Comp. Colleges–Bachelor's (Midwest), 5
Acceptance Rate: 80%

Other expenses: Estimated books and supplies: $900. Transportation: $600. Personal expenses: $1,200. **Financial aid:** Priority filing date for institution's financial aid form: April 15; deadline: June 1. In 2003-2004, 90% of undergraduates applied for financial aid. Of those, 83% were determined to have financial need; 29% had their need fully met. Average financial aid package (proportion receiving): $20,347 (83%). Average amount of gift aid, such as scholarships or grants (proportion receiving): $14,487 (82%). Average amount of self-help aid, such as work study or loans (proportion receiving): $5,821 (76%). Average need-based loan (excluding PLUS or other private loans): $4,842. Among students who received need-based aid, the average percentage of need met: 88%. Among students who received aid based on merit, the average award (and the proportion receiving): $10,438 (17%). The average athletic scholarship (and the proportion receiving): $0 (0%). Average amount of debt of borrowers graduating in 2003: $29,713. Proportion who borrowed: 87%. **Cooperative education programs:** computer science, engineering, technologies. **Reserve Officers Training Corps (ROTC):** Army ROTC: Offered at cooperating institution (Bowling Green State University); Air Force ROTC: Offered at cooperating institution (Bowling Green State University).

Ohio State University–Columbus

190 N. Oval Mall
Columbus, OH 43210
Public; www.osu.edu
Financial aid office: (614) 292-0300

■ 2004-2005 TUITION AND FEES:
    In state: $7,446; Out of state: $18,033
■ ROOM AND BOARD: $6,609

ACT Score (25th/75th percentile): 23-28
2005 U.S. News College Ranking:
National Universities, 62
Acceptance Rate: 72%

Other expenses: Estimated books and supplies: $1,044. Transportation: $120. Personal expenses: $3,165. **Financial aid:** Priority filing date for institution's financial aid form: March 1. In 2003-2004, 63% of undergraduates applied for financial aid. Of those, 50% were determined to have financial need; 23% had their need fully met. Average financial aid package (proportion receiving): $8,897 (50%). Average amount of gift aid, such as scholarships or grants (proportion receiving): $3,321 (38%). Average amount of self-help aid, such as work study or loans (proportion receiving): $5,076 (44%). Average need-based loan (excluding PLUS or other private loans): $4,361. Among students who received need-based aid, the average percentage of need met: 71%. Among students who received aid based on merit, the average award (and the proportion receiving): $3,741 (7%). The average athletic scholarship (and the proportion receiving): $16,640 (2%). Average amount of debt of borrowers graduating in 2003: $14,869. Proportion who borrowed: 47%. **Student employment:** During the 2003-2004 academic year, 15% of undergraduates worked on campus. Average per-year earnings: $5,088. **Cooperative education programs:** agriculture, art, business, computer science, engineering, humanities, natural science, social/behavioral science, vocational arts. **Reserve Officers Training Corps (ROTC):** Army ROTC: Offered on campus; Navy ROTC: Offered on campus; Air Force ROTC: Offered on campus.

Ohio University

Athens, OH 45701
Public; www.ohiou.edu
Financial aid office: (740) 593-4141

■ **2004-2005 TUITION AND FEES:**
   In state: $7,404; Out of state: $15,396
■ **ROOM AND BOARD:** $7,539

ACT Score (25th/75th percentile): 22-26
2005 U.S. News College Ranking:
National Universities, 98
Acceptance Rate: 79%

Other expenses: Estimated books and supplies: $840. Transportation: $1,947. Personal expenses: $738. **Financial aid:** Priority filing date for institution's financial aid form: March 15. In 2003-2004, 70% of undergraduates applied for financial aid. Of those, 49% were determined to have financial need; 11% had their need fully met. Average financial aid package (proportion receiving): $6,823 (48%). Average amount of gift aid, such as scholarships or grants (proportion receiving): $3,487 (23%). Average amount of self-help aid, such as work study or loans (proportion receiving): $4,115 (42%). Average need-based loan (excluding PLUS or other private loans): $3,927. Among students who received need-based aid, the average percentage

of need met: 54%. Among students who received aid based on merit, the average award (and the proportion receiving): $3,813 (8%). The average athletic scholarship (and the proportion receiving): $12,189 (2%). Average amount of debt of borrowers graduating in 2003: $16,307. Proportion who borrowed: 49%. **Student employment:** During the 2003-2004 academic year, 34% of undergraduates worked on campus. Average per-year earnings: $1,386. **Reserve Officers Training Corps (ROTC):** Army ROTC: Offered on campus; Air Force ROTC: Offered on campus.

Ohio Wesleyan University

61 S. Sandusky Street
Delaware, OH 43015
Private; web.owu.edu
Financial aid office: (740) 368-3050

■ **2004-2005 TUITION AND FEES:** $26,820
■ **ROOM AND BOARD:** $7,330

SAT I Score (25th/75th percentile): 1120-1310
2005 U.S. News College Ranking:
Liberal Arts Colleges, 89
Acceptance Rate: 74%

Other expenses: Estimated books and supplies: $2,300. Transportation: $60. Personal expenses: $238. **Financial aid:** Priority filing date for institution's financial aid form: March 15; deadline: May 15. In 2003-2004, 64% of undergraduates applied for financial aid. Of those, 58% were determined to have financial need; 32% had their need fully met. Average financial aid package (proportion receiving): $22,149 (58%). Average amount of gift aid, such as scholarships or grants (proportion receiving): $16,141 (58%). Average amount of self-help aid, such as work study or loans (proportion receiving): $5,911 (48%). Average need-based loan (excluding PLUS or other private loans): $4,497. Among students who received need-based aid, the average percentage of need met: 89%. Among students who received aid based on merit, the average award (and the proportion receiving): $11,847 (38%). The average athletic scholarship (and the proportion receiving): $0 (0%). Average amount of debt of borrowers graduating in 2003: $22,166. Proportion who borrowed: 58%. **Student employment:** During the 2003-2004 academic year, 40% of undergraduates worked on campus. Average per-year earnings: $1,500. **Reserve Officers Training Corps (ROTC):** Army ROTC: Offered at cooperating institution (Capital University).

Otterbein College

College Avenue and Grove Street
Westerville, OH 43081
Private; www.otterbein.edu
Financial aid office: (614) 823-1502

■ **2004-2005 TUITION AND FEES:** $21,342
■ **ROOM AND BOARD:** $6,189

ACT Score (25th/75th percentile): 21-27
2005 U.S. News College Ranking:
Comp. Colleges–Bachelor's (Midwest), 5
Acceptance Rate: 84%

Financial aid: Priority filing date for institution's financial aid form: February 1; deadline: April 15. **Student employment:** During the 2003-2004 academic year, 70% of undergraduates worked on campus. Average per-year earnings: $1,800. **Reserve Officers Training Corps (ROTC):** Army ROTC: Offered at cooperating institution (Ohio State University); Navy ROTC: Offered at cooperating institution (Ohio State University); Air Force ROTC: Offered at cooperating institution (Ohio State University).

Shawnee State University

940 Second Street
Portsmouth, OH 45662
Public; www.shawnee.edu
Financial aid office: (740) 351-3237

■ **2004-2005 TUITION AND FEES:**
   In state: $4,779; Out of state: $8,379
■ **ROOM AND BOARD:** $6,510

ACT Score (25th/75th percentile): 16-22
2005 U.S. News College Ranking:
Liberal Arts Colleges, fourth tier
Acceptance Rate: 100%

Other expenses: Estimated books and supplies: $1,200. Transportation: $750. Personal expenses: $1,554. **Student employment:** During the 2003-2004 academic year, 12% of undergraduates worked on campus. Average per-year earnings: $3,000.

Tiffin University

155 Miami Street
Tiffin, OH 44883
Private; www.tiffin.edu
Financial aid office: (419) 448-3357

■ **2004-2005 TUITION AND FEES:** $14,280
■ **ROOM AND BOARD:** $6,150

ACT Score (25th/75th percentile): 17-22
2005 U.S. News College Ranking:
Unranked Specialty School–Business
Acceptance Rate: 91%

Other expenses: Estimated books and supplies: $1,000. Transportation: $1,250. Personal expenses: $1,450. **Financial aid:** In 2003-2004, 93% of undergraduates applied for financial aid. Of those, 83% were determined to have financial need; 8% had their need fully met. Average financial aid package (proportion receiving): $9,033 (83%). Average amount of gift aid, such as scholarships or grants (proportion receiving): $4,843 (68%). Average amount of self-help aid, such as work study or loans (proportion receiving): $4,165 (81%). Average need-based loan (excluding PLUS or other private loans): $3,656. Among students who received need-based aid, the average percentage of need met: 7%. Among students who received aid based on merit, the average award (and the proportion receiving): $2,474 (10%). The average athletic scholarship (and the proportion receiving): $3,660 (6%). Average amount of debt of borrowers graduating in 2003: $17,125. Proportion who borrowed: 82%. **Student employment:** During the 2003-2004 academic year, 16% of undergraduates worked on campus. Average per-year earnings: $1,178. **Reserve Officers Training Corps (ROTC):** Army ROTC: Offered at cooperating institution (Bowling Green State University); Air Force ROTC: Offered at cooperating institution (Bowling Green State University).

Union Institute and University

440 E. McMillan Street
Cincinnati, OH 45206
Private; www.tui.edu
Financial aid office: (513) 487-1127

■ **2004-2005 TUITION AND FEES:** $10,162

2005 U.S. News College Ranking:
National Universities, fourth tier

Financial aid: Priority filing date for institution's financial aid form: March 15; deadline: June 4. Average amount of debt of borrowers graduating in 2003: $20,696. Proportion who borrowed: 98%.

University of Akron

302 Buchtel Common
Akron, OH 44325
Public; www.uakron.edu
Financial aid office: (330) 972-7032

■ **2004-2005 TUITION AND FEES:**
  In state: $6,808; Out of state: $14,298
■ **ROOM AND BOARD:** $6,326

ACT Score (25th/75th percentile): 16-23
2005 U.S. News College Ranking:
National Universities, fourth tier
Acceptance Rate: 71%

Other expenses: Estimated books and supplies: $800. Transportation: $984. Personal expenses: $1,520. **Financial aid:** Priority filing date for institution's financial aid form: February 1; deadline: March 1. In 2003-2004, 72% of undergraduates applied for financial aid. Of those, 68% were determined to have financial need; 9% had their need fully met. Average financial aid package (proportion receiving): $1,988 (68%). Average amount of gift aid, such as scholarships or grants (proportion receiving): $1,528 (37%). Average amount of self-help aid, such as work study or loans (proportion receiving): $2,509 (58%). Average need-based loan (excluding PLUS or other private loans): $2,509. Among students who received need-based aid, the average percentage of need met: 49%. Among students who received aid based on merit, the average award (and the proportion receiving): $2,105 (6%). The average athletic scholarship (and the proportion receiving): $4,701 (3%). **Student employment:** During the 2003-2004 academic year, 6% of undergraduates worked on campus. Average per-year earnings: $3,630. **Cooperative education programs:** business, computer science, engineering, health professions, technologies. **Reserve Officers Training Corps (ROTC):** Army ROTC: Offered on campus; Air Force ROTC: Offered on campus.

University of Cincinnati

PO Box 210063
Cincinnati, OH 45221-0063
Public; www.uc.edu
Financial aid office: (513) 556-6982

■ **2004-2005 TUITION AND FEES:**
  In state: $7,623; Out of state: $19,230
■ **ROOM AND BOARD:** $7,113

ACT Score (25th/75th percentile): 18-26
2005 U.S. News College Ranking:
National Universities, third tier
Acceptance Rate: 88%

Other expenses: Estimated books and supplies: $815. Transportation: $195. Personal expenses: $4,400. **Financial aid:** In 2003-2004, 59% of undergraduates applied for financial aid. Of those, 49% were determined to have financial need; 11% had their need fully met. Average financial aid package (proportion receiving): $7,524 (48%). Average amount of gift aid, such as scholarships or grants (proportion receiving): $3,325 (33%). Average amount of self-help aid, such as work study or loans (proportion receiving): $2,798 (47%). Average need-based loan (excluding PLUS or other private loans): $3,011. Among students who received need-based aid, the average percentage of need met: 56%. Among students who received aid based on merit, the average award (and the proportion receiving): $4,111 (4%). The average athletic scholarship (and the proportion receiving): $7,682 (0%). Proportion who borrowed: 54%. **Cooperative education programs:** art, business, engineering, other. **Reserve Officers Training Corps (ROTC):** Army ROTC: Offered on campus; Air Force ROTC: Offered on campus.

University of Dayton

300 College Park
Dayton, OH 45469
Private; www.udayton.edu
Financial aid office: (937) 229-4311

■ **2004-2005 TUITION AND FEES:** $20,250
■ **ROOM AND BOARD:** $6,300

ACT Score (25th/75th percentile): 22-28
2005 U.S. News College Ranking:
National Universities, 98
Acceptance Rate: 82%

Other expenses: Estimated books and supplies: $800. Transportation: $500. Personal expenses:

$1,770. **Financial aid:** Priority filing date for institution's financial aid form: March 31. In 2003-2004, 77% of undergraduates applied for financial aid. Of those, 62% were determined to have financial need; 60% had their need fully met. Average financial aid package (proportion receiving): $13,181 (60%). Average amount of gift aid, such as scholarships or grants (proportion receiving): $8,403 (59%). Average amount of self-help aid, such as work study or loans (proportion receiving): $3,927 (57%). Average need-based loan (excluding PLUS or other private loans): $3,651. Among students who received need-based aid, the average percentage of need met: 84%. Among students who received aid based on merit, the average award (and the proportion receiving): $3,141 (32%). The average athletic scholarship (and the proportion receiving): $11,939 (1%). Average amount of debt of borrowers graduating in 2003: $21,467. Proportion who borrowed: 60%. **Student employment:** During the 2003-2004 academic year, 51% of undergraduates worked on campus. Average per-year earnings: $1,145. **Cooperative education programs:** art, business, computer science, engineering, humanities, natural science, social/behavioral science, technologies, other. **Reserve Officers Training Corps (ROTC):** Army ROTC: Offered on campus; Air Force ROTC: Offered at cooperating institution (Wright State University).

University of Findlay

1000 N. Main Street
Findlay, OH 45840
Private; www.findlay.edu
Financial aid office: (419) 434-4791

- **2003-2004 TUITION AND FEES:** $19,662
- **ROOM AND BOARD:** $7,062

ACT Score (25th/75th percentile): 19-24
2005 U.S. News College Ranking:
Universities–Master's (Midwest), 63
Acceptance Rate: 55%

Other expenses: Estimated books and supplies: $800. Transportation: $780. Personal expenses: $500. **Financial aid:** Priority filing date for institution's financial aid form: August 1; deadline: September 1. In 2003-2004, 75% of undergraduates applied for financial aid. Of those, 63% were determined to have financial need; 20% had their need fully met. Average financial aid package (proportion receiving): $11,000 (63%). Average amount of gift aid, such as scholarships or grants (proportion receiving): $6,500 (63%). Average amount of self-help aid, such as

work study or loans (proportion receiving): $5,500 (63%). Average need-based loan (excluding PLUS or other private loans): $4,500. Among students who received need-based aid, the average percentage of need met: 75%. Among students who received aid based on merit, the average award (and the proportion receiving): $7,945 (12%). The average athletic scholarship (and the proportion receiving): $8,851 (12%). Proportion who borrowed: 85%. **Student employment:** During the 2003-2004 academic year, 11% of undergraduates worked on campus. Average per-year earnings: $1,700. **Cooperative education programs:** business, other. **Reserve Officers Training Corps (ROTC):** Army ROTC: Offered at cooperating institution (Bowling Green State University); Air Force ROTC: Offered at cooperating institution (Bowling Green State University).

University of Rio Grande

PO Box 500
Rio Grande, OH 45674
Private; www.rio.edu
Financial aid office: (740) 245-7218

- **2004-2005 TUITION AND FEES:** $11,840
- **ROOM AND BOARD:** $3,021

2005 U.S. News College Ranking:
Universities–Master's (Midwest), third tier

Student employment: During the 2003-2004 academic year, 15% of undergraduates worked on campus. Average per-year earnings: $3,000. **Cooperative education programs:** business.

University of Toledo

2801 W. Bancroft
Toledo, OH 43606
Public; www.utoledo.edu
Financial aid office: (419) 530-8700

- **2004-2005 TUITION AND FEES:**
  In state: $7,052; Out of state: $15,864
- **ROOM AND BOARD:** $7,568

ACT Score (25th/75th percentile): 18-24
2005 U.S. News College Ranking:
National Universities, fourth tier
Acceptance Rate: 96%

Financial aid: Priority filing date for institution's financial aid form: April 1. In 2003-2004, 84% of undergraduates applied for financial aid. Of those, 66% were determined to have financial

need; 11% had their need fully met. Average financial aid package (proportion receiving): $6,881 (64%). Average amount of gift aid, such as scholarships or grants (proportion receiving): $4,372 (46%). Average amount of self-help aid, such as work study or loans (proportion receiving): $4,100 (54%). Average need-based loan (excluding PLUS or other private loans): $3,770. Among students who received need-based aid, the average percentage of need met: 56%. Among students who received aid based on merit, the average award (and the proportion receiving): $3,130 (17%). The average athletic scholarship (and the proportion receiving): $13,520 (1%). Average amount of debt of borrowers graduating in 2003: $21,272. Proportion who borrowed: 63%. **Cooperative education programs:** business, education, engineering. **Reserve Officers Training Corps (ROTC):** Army ROTC: Offered on campus; Air Force ROTC: Offered at cooperating institution (Bowling Green State University).

Urbana University

579 College Way
Urbana, OH 43078
Private; www.urbana.edu
Financial aid office: (937) 484-1355

- **2004-2005 TUITION AND FEES:** $14,470
- **ROOM AND BOARD:** $5,636

2005 U.S. News College Ranking:
Comp. Colleges–Bachelor's (Midwest), fourth tier
Acceptance Rate: 58%

Other expenses: Estimated books and supplies: $1,000. Transportation: $0. Personal expenses: $1,000. **Financial aid:** Priority filing date for institution's financial aid form: April 1. In 2003-2004, 98% of undergraduates applied for financial aid. Of those, 65% were determined to have financial need; 8% had their need fully met. Average financial aid package (proportion receiving): $10,079 (65%). Average amount of gift aid, such as scholarships or grants (proportion receiving): $1,518 (46%). Average amount of self-help aid, such as work study or loans (proportion receiving): $1,901 (58%). Average need-based loan (excluding PLUS or other private loans): $2,869. Among students who received need-based aid, the average percentage of need met: 48%. Among students who received aid based on merit, the average award (and the proportion receiving): $2,609 (2%). The average athletic scholarship (and the proportion receiving): $4,251 (2%). Average amount of debt of borrowers graduating in 2003: $19,225. Proportion who borrowed: 84%.

Ursuline College

2550 Lander Road
Pepper Pike, OH 44124
Private; www.ursuline.edu
Financial aid office: (440) 646-8309

■ **2004-2005 TUITION AND FEES:** $18,150
■ **ROOM AND BOARD:** $5,896

ACT Score (25th/75th percentile): 17-21
2005 U.S. News College Ranking:
Universities–Master's (Midwest), third tier
Acceptance Rate: 70%

Other expenses: Estimated books and supplies: $800. Transportation: $404. Personal expenses: $700. **Financial aid:** Priority filing date for institution's financial aid form: March 1. In 2003-2004, 82% of undergraduates applied for financial aid. Of those, 77% were determined to have financial need; 23% had their need fully met. Average financial aid package (proportion receiving): $15,872 (77%). Average amount of gift aid, such as scholarships or grants (proportion receiving): $7,996 (75%). Average amount of self-help aid, such as work study or loans (proportion receiving): N/A (74%). Among students who received need-based aid, the average percentage of need met: 78%. Among students who received aid based on merit, the average award (and the proportion receiving): $4,212 (7%). The average athletic scholarship (and the proportion receiving): $2,600 (1%). Average amount of debt of borrowers graduating in 2003: $21,800. Proportion who borrowed: 77%. **Student employment:** During the 2003-2004 academic year, 0% of undergraduates worked on campus. Average per-year earnings: $0. **Reserve Officers Training Corps (ROTC):** Army ROTC: Offered at cooperating institution (John Carroll University).

Walsh University

2020 E. Maple Street
North Canton, OH 44720
Private; www.walsh.edu
Financial aid office: (330) 490-7150

■ **2004-2005 TUITION AND FEES:** $15,610
■ **ROOM AND BOARD:** $6,650

ACT Score (25th/75th percentile): 19-24
2005 U.S. News College Ranking:
Universities–Master's (Midwest), third tier
Acceptance Rate: 82%

Other expenses: Estimated books and supplies: $800. Transportation: $600. Personal expenses: $1,000. **Financial aid:** Priority filing date for institution's financial aid form: March 1. In 2003-2004, 88% of undergraduates applied for financial aid. Of those, 76% were determined to have financial need; 78% had their need fully met. Average financial aid package (proportion receiving): $10,364 (76%). Average amount of gift aid, such as scholarships or grants (proportion receiving): $5,602 (76%). Average amount of self-help aid, such as work study or loans (proportion receiving): $4,447 (69%). Average need-based loan (excluding PLUS or other private loans): $2,424. Among students who received need-based aid, the average percentage of need met: 81%. Among students who received aid based on merit, the average award (and the proportion receiving): $4,362 (14%). The average athletic scholarship (and the proportion receiving): $3,769 (25%). Average amount of debt of borrowers graduating in 2003: $18,450. Proportion who borrowed: 86%. **Student employment:** During the 2003-2004 academic year, 18% of undergraduates worked on campus. Average per-year earnings: $1,260. **Cooperative education programs:** business, computer science, education, health professions, humanities, natural science, social/behavioral science.

Wilberforce University

PO Box 1001
Wilberforce, OH 45384
Private; www.wilberforce.edu
Financial aid office: (800) 367-8565

■ **2004-2005 TUITION AND FEES:** $10,780
■ **ROOM AND BOARD:** $5,320

2005 U.S. News College Ranking:
Comp. Colleges–Bachelor's (Midwest), fourth tier
Acceptance Rate: 22%

Cooperative education programs: business, computer science, engineering, health professions, humanities, natural science, social/behavioral science, technologies. **Reserve Officers Training Corps (ROTC):** Army ROTC: Offered at cooperating institution (Central State University); Air Force ROTC: Offered at cooperating institution (Wright State University).

Wilmington College

Pyle Center Box 1327
Wilmington, OH 45177
Private; www.wilmington.edu
Financial aid office: (937) 382-6661

■ **2004-2005 TUITION AND FEES:** $18,728
■ **ROOM AND BOARD:** $6,718

ACT Score (25th/75th percentile): 18-24
2005 U.S. News College Ranking:
Comp. Colleges–Bachelor's (Midwest), 40
Acceptance Rate: 68%

Other expenses: Estimated books and supplies: $1,200. Transportation: $500. Personal expenses: $600. **Financial aid:** Priority filing date for institution's financial aid form: March 15. In 2003-2004, 91% of undergraduates applied for financial aid. Of those, 86% were determined to have financial need; 31% had their need fully met. Average financial aid package (proportion receiving): $16,395 (86%). Average amount of gift aid, such as scholarships or grants (proportion receiving): $11,185 (85%). Average amount of self-help aid, such as work study or loans (proportion receiving): $5,552 (76%). Average need-based loan (excluding PLUS or other private loans): $4,864. Among students who received need-based aid, the average percentage of need met: 87%. Among students who received aid based on merit, the average award (and the proportion receiving): $6,490 (10%). The average athletic scholarship (and the proportion receiving): $0 (0%). Average amount of debt of borrowers graduating in 2003: $21,235. Proportion who borrowed: 86%. **Student employment:** During the 2003-2004 academic year, 30% of undergraduates worked on campus. Average per-year earnings: $1,000.

Wittenberg University

PO Box 720
Springfield, OH 45501
Private; www.wittenberg.edu
Financial aid office: (937) 327-7321

■ **2004-2005 TUITION AND FEES:** $26,196
■ **ROOM AND BOARD:** $6,686

ACT Score (25th/75th percentile): 21-26
2005 U.S. News College Ranking:
Liberal Arts Colleges, 105
Acceptance Rate: 80%

Other expenses: Estimated books and supplies: $800. Transportation: $600. Personal expenses: $1,000. **Financial aid:** Priority filing date for institution's financial aid form: March 15; deadline: March 15. In 2003-2004, 81% of undergraduates applied for financial aid. Of those, 72% were determined to have financial need; 35% had their need fully met. Average financial aid package (proportion receiving): $21,143 (72%). Average amount of gift aid, such as scholarships or grants (proportion receiving): $16,768 (72%). Average amount of self-help aid, such as work study or loans (proportion receiving): $5,519 (57%). Average need-based loan (excluding PLUS or other private loans): $4,691. Among students who received need-based aid, the average percentage of need met: 89%. Among students who received aid based on merit, the average award (and the proportion receiving): $9,599 (24%). The average athletic scholarship (and the proportion receiving): $0 (0%). **Student employment:** During the 2003-2004 academic year, 78% of undergraduates worked on campus. Average per-year earnings: $1,800. **Reserve Officers Training Corps (ROTC):** Army ROTC: Offered at cooperating institution (Central State University); Air Force ROTC: Offered at cooperating institution (Wright State University).

Wright State University

3640 Colonel Glenn Highway
Dayton, OH 45435
Public; www.wright.edu
Financial aid office: (937) 873-5721

■ **2004-2005 TUITION AND FEES:**
In state: $6,246; Out of state: $12,261
■ **ROOM AND BOARD:** $6,069

ACT Score (25th/75th percentile): 18-24
2005 U.S. News College Ranking:
National Universities, fourth tier
Acceptance Rate: 91%

....

Cooperative education programs: art, business, computer science, education, engineering, humanities, technologies, vocational arts.
Reserve Officers Training Corps (ROTC): Army ROTC: Offered on campus; Air Force ROTC: Offered on campus.

Xavier University

3800 Victory Parkway
Cincinnati, OH 45207
Private; www.xavier.edu
Financial aid office: (513) 745-3142

■ **2004-2005 TUITION AND FEES:** $20,400
■ **ROOM AND BOARD:** $7,930

ACT Score (25th/75th percentile): 23-29
2005 U.S. News College Ranking:
Universities–Master's (Midwest), 2
Acceptance Rate: 78%

....

Other expenses: Estimated books and supplies: $900. Transportation: $600. Personal expenses: $1,200. **Financial aid:** Priority filing date for institution's financial aid form: February 15. In 2003-2004, 60% of undergraduates applied for financial aid. Of those, 49% were determined to have financial need; 22% had their need fully met. Average financial aid package (proportion receiving): $13,616 (49%). Average amount of gift aid, such as scholarships or grants (proportion receiving): $9,759 (48%). Average amount of self-help aid, such as work study or loans (proportion receiving): $4,968 (38%). Average need-based loan (excluding PLUS or other private loans): $4,118. Among students who received need-based

aid, the average percentage of need met: 75%. Among students who received aid based on merit, the average award (and the proportion receiving): $8,237 (35%). The average athletic scholarship (and the proportion receiving): $13,679 (4%). Average amount of debt of borrowers graduating in 2003: $17,981. Proportion who borrowed: 58%. **Student employment:** During the 2003-2004 academic year, 8% of undergraduates worked on campus. Average per-year earnings: $1,500. **Cooperative education programs:** business, computer science. **Reserve Officers Training Corps (ROTC):** Army ROTC: Offered on campus; Air Force ROTC: Offered at cooperating institution (University of Cincinnati).

Youngstown State University

1 University Plaza
Youngstown, OH 44555
Public; www.ysu.edu
Financial aid office: (330) 941-3399

■ **2004-2005 TUITION AND FEES:**
In state: $6,042; Out of state: $11,250
■ **ROOM AND BOARD:** $6,100

ACT Score (25th/75th percentile): 17-24
2005 U.S. News College Ranking:
Universities–Master's (Midwest), fourth tier
Acceptance Rate: 99%

....

Other expenses: Estimated books and supplies: $920. Transportation: $1,294. Personal expenses: $1,636. **Financial aid:** Priority filing date for institution's financial aid form: February 15; deadline: February 15. Average per-year earnings: $5,356. **Cooperative education programs:** business, engineering. **Reserve Officers Training Corps (ROTC):** Army ROTC: Offered on campus; Air Force ROTC: Offered at cooperating institution (Kent State University).

Oklahoma

Cameron University

2800 W. Gore Boulevard
Lawton, OK 73505-6377
Public; www.cameron.edu
Financial aid office: (580) 581-2293

- **2004-2005 TUITION AND FEES:**
  In state: $2,781; Out of state: $3,903
- **ROOM AND BOARD:** $3,782

ACT Score (25th/75th percentile): 18-23
2005 U.S. News College Ranking:
Universities–Master's (West), fourth tier
Acceptance Rate: 100%

Other expenses: Estimated books and supplies: $800. Transportation: $1,416. Personal expenses: $1,300. **Financial aid:** Priority filing date for institution's financial aid form: May 1. In 2003-2004, 74% of undergraduates applied for financial aid. Of those, 72% were determined to have financial need; Average financial aid package (proportion receiving): $4,924 (87%). Average amount of gift aid, such as scholarships or grants (proportion receiving): $3,137 (70%). Average amount of self-help aid, such as work study or loans (proportion receiving): $2,945 (40%). Average need-based loan (excluding PLUS or other private loans): $3,082. Among students who received need-based aid, the average percentage of need met: 75%. Among students who received aid based on merit, the average award (and the proportion receiving): $639 (16%). The average athletic scholarship (and the proportion receiving): $3,733 (3%). Average amount of debt of borrowers graduating in 2003: $6,500. Proportion who borrowed: 36%. **Student employment:** During the 2003-2004 academic year, 3% of undergraduates worked on campus. Average per-year earnings: $5,000. **Cooperative education programs:** computer science, education. **Reserve Officers Training Corps (ROTC):** Army ROTC: Offered on campus.

East Central University

14th Street and Francis Avenue
Ada, OK 74820
Public; www.ecok.edu
Financial aid office: (580) 332-8000

- **2004-2005 TUITION AND FEES:**
  In state: $2,996; Out of state: $4,173

2005 U.S. News College Ranking:
Universities–Master's (West), fourth tier
Acceptance Rate: 98%

Langston University

PO Box 907
Langston, OK 73050
Public; www.lunet.edu
Financial aid office: (405) 466-3282

- **2004-2005 TUITION AND FEES:**
  In state: $3,961; Out of state: $8,025
- **ROOM AND BOARD:** $5,750

2005 U.S. News College Ranking:
Comp. Colleges–Bachelor's (West), fourth tier

Financial aid: Priority filing date for institution's financial aid form: March 31. In 2003-2004, 89% of undergraduates applied for financial aid. Of those, 70% were determined to have financial need; 52% had their need fully met. Average financial aid package (proportion receiving): $7,738 (69%). Average amount of gift aid, such as scholarships or grants (proportion receiving): $970 (18%). Average amount of self-help aid, such as work study or loans (proportion receiving): $4,147 (61%). Average need-based loan (excluding PLUS or other private loans): $4,016. Among students who received need-based aid, the average percentage of need met: 74%. Among students who received aid based on merit, the average award (and the proportion receiving): $2,226 (30%).

Northeastern State University

600 N. Grand
Tahlequah, OK 74464
Public; www.nsuok.edu
Financial aid office: (918) 456-5511

- **2004-2005 TUITION AND FEES:**
  In state: $3,000; Out of state: $7,350
- **ROOM AND BOARD:** $3,080

ACT Score (25th/75th percentile): 18-23
2005 U.S. News College Ranking:
Universities–Master's (West), fourth tier
Acceptance Rate: 89%

Other expenses: Estimated books and supplies: $900. Transportation: $1,200. Personal expenses: $1,080. **Financial aid:** Priority filing date for institution's financial aid form: April 15. In 2003-2004, 85% of undergraduates applied for financial aid. Of those, 82% were determined to have financial need; 86% had their need fully met. Average financial aid package (proportion receiving): $8,100 (81%). Average amount of gift aid, such as scholarships or grants (proportion receiving): $4,050 (61%). Average amount of self-help aid, such as work study or loans (proportion receiving): $5,000 (65%). Average need-based loan (excluding PLUS or other private loans): $4,100. Among students who received need-based aid, the average percentage of need met: 69%. Among students who received aid based on merit, the average award (and the proportion receiving): $900 (19%). The average athletic scholarship (and the proportion receiving): $1,900 (3%). Average amount of debt of borrowers graduating in 2003: $7,500. Proportion who borrowed: 68%. **Student employment:** During the 2003-2004 academic year, 69% of undergraduates worked on campus. Average per-year earnings: $4,100. **Reserve Officers Training Corps (ROTC):** Army ROTC: Offered on campus.

Northwestern Oklahoma State University

709 Oklahoma Boulevard
Alva, OK 73717
Public; www.nwalva.edu
Financial aid office: (580) 327-8542

- **2004-2005 TUITION AND FEES:**
  In state: $2,787; Out of state: $4,610
- **ROOM AND BOARD:** $2,920

ACT Score (25th/75th percentile): 17-23
2005 U.S. News College Ranking:
Universities–Master's (West), fourth tier
Acceptance Rate: 99%

Other expenses: Estimated books and supplies: $800. Transportation: $950. Personal expenses: $1,200. **Financial aid:** In 2003-2004, 74% of undergraduates applied for financial aid. Of those, 57% were determined to have financial need; 41% had their need fully met. Average financial aid package (proportion receiving): $4,660 (56%). Average amount of gift aid, such as scholarships or grants (proportion receiving): $3,316 (44%). Average amount of self-help aid, such as work study or loans (proportion receiving): $2,101 (35%). Average need-based loan (excluding PLUS or other private loans): $2,256. Among students who received need-based aid, the average percentage of need met: 77%. Among students who received aid based on merit, the average award (and the proportion receiving): $1,853 (20%). The average athletic scholarship (and the proportion receiving): $1,960 (10%). Average amount of debt of borrowers graduating in 2003: $9,577. Proportion who borrowed: 52%.

Oklahoma Baptist University

500 W. University
Shawnee, OK 74804
Private; www.okbu.edu
Financial aid office: (405) 878-2016

■ **2004-2005 TUITION AND FEES:** $13,162
■ **ROOM AND BOARD:** $3,800

ACT Score (25th/75th percentile): 20-27
2005 U.S. News College Ranking:
Comp. Colleges–Bachelor's (West), 2
Acceptance Rate: 95%

Other expenses: Estimated books and supplies: $900. Transportation: $1,200. Personal expenses: $1,400. **Financial aid:** Priority filing date for institution's financial aid form: March 1. In 2003-2004, 93% of undergraduates applied for financial aid. Of those, 64% were determined to have financial need; 51% had their need fully met. Average financial aid package (proportion receiving): $11,464 (64%). Average amount of gift aid, such as scholarships or grants (proportion receiving): $3,301 (57%). Average amount of self-help aid, such as work study or loans (proportion receiving): $4,214 (42%). Average need-based loan (excluding PLUS or other private loans): $3,834. Among students who received need-based aid, the average percentage of need met: 70%. Among students who received aid based on merit, the average award (and the proportion receiving): $4,389 (29%). The average athletic scholarship (and the proportion receiving): $5,801 (11%). Average amount of debt of borrowers graduating in 2003: $15,192. Proportion who borrowed: 57%. **Student employment:** During the 2003-2004 academic year, 22% of undergraduates worked on campus. Average per-year earnings: $1,400. **Cooperative education programs:** business, computer science, education, health professions, social/behavioral science, other.

Oklahoma Christian University

Box 11000
Oklahoma City, OK 73136-1100
Private; www.oc.edu
Financial aid office: (405) 425-5190

■ **2004-2005 TUITION AND FEES:** $13,160
■ **ROOM AND BOARD:** $4,820

ACT Score (25th/75th percentile): 18-25
2005 U.S. News College Ranking:
Comp. Colleges–Bachelor's (West), 7
Acceptance Rate: 100%

Other expenses: Estimated books and supplies: $800. Transportation: $1,174. Personal expenses: $3,616. **Financial aid:** Priority filing date for institution's financial aid form: March 15; deadline: August 31. In 2003-2004, 100% of undergraduates applied for financial aid. Of those, 68% were determined to have financial need; 23% had their need fully met. Average financial aid package (proportion receiving): $11,748 (67%). Average amount of gift aid, such as scholarships or grants (proportion receiving): $1,737 (42%). Average amount of self-help aid, such as work study or loans (proportion receiving): $4,374 (54%). Average need-based loan (excluding PLUS or other private loans): $3,841. Among students who received need-based aid, the average percentage of need met: 57%. Among students who received aid based on merit, the average award (and the proportion receiving): $2,234 (22%). The average athletic scholarship (and the proportion receiving): $3,921 (18%). Average amount of debt of borrowers graduating in 2003: $25,100. Proportion who borrowed: 76%. **Student employment:** During the 2003-2004 academic year, 11% of undergraduates worked on campus. Average per-year earnings: $1,500. **Cooperative education programs:** other. **Reserve Officers Training Corps (ROTC):** Army ROTC: Offered at cooperating institution (University of Central Oklahoma); Air Force ROTC: Offered at cooperating institution (University of Oklahoma).

Oklahoma City University

2501 N. Blackwelder
Oklahoma City, OK 73106-1493
Private; www.okcu.edu
Financial aid office: (405) 521-5211

■ **2004-2005 TUITION AND FEES:** $15,740
■ **ROOM AND BOARD:** $5,950

ACT Score (25th/75th percentile): 21-27
2005 U.S. News College Ranking:
Universities–Master's (West), 23
Acceptance Rate: 78%

Other expenses: Estimated books and supplies: $1,050. Transportation: $1,100. Personal expenses: $1,000. **Financial aid:** Priority filing date for institution's financial aid form: March 1. In 2003-2004, 56% of undergraduates applied for financial aid. Of those, 45% were determined to have financial need; 21% had their need fully met. Average financial aid package (proportion receiving): $10,680 (42%). Average amount of gift aid, such as scholarships or grants (proportion receiving): $7,037 (40%). Average amount of self-help aid, such as work study or loans (proportion receiving): $3,797 (32%). Average need-based loan (excluding PLUS or other private loans): $3,313. Among students who received need-based aid, the average percentage of need met: 82%. Among students who received aid based on merit, the average award (and the proportion receiving): $5,567 (9%). The average athletic scholarship (and the proportion receiving): $10,321 (10%). Average amount of debt of borrowers graduating in 2003: $18,669. Proportion who borrowed: 43%. **Reserve Officers Training Corps (ROTC):** Army ROTC: Offered at cooperating institution (University of Central Oklahoma); Air Force ROTC: Offered at cooperating institution (University of Oklahoma).

Oklahoma Panhandle State University

PO Box 430
Goodwell, OK 73939-0430
Public; www.opsu.edu
Financial aid office: (580) 349-1580

■ **2004-2005 TUITION AND FEES:**
  In state: $830; Out of state: $830
■ **ROOM AND BOARD:** $5,120

2005 U.S. News College Ranking:
Comp. Colleges–Bachelor's (West), fourth tier
Acceptance Rate: 71%

Oklahoma State University

104 Whitehurst Hall
Stillwater, OK 74078
Public; www.okstate.edu
Financial aid office: (405) 744-6604

■ **2004-2005 TUITION AND FEES:**
In state: $2,910; Out of state: $10,200

ACT Score (25th/75th percentile): 21-26
2005 U.S. News College Ranking:
National Universities, third tier
Acceptance Rate: 89%

Financial aid: In 2003-2004, 66% of undergraduates applied for financial aid. Of those, 52% were determined to have financial need; 21% had their need fully met. Average financial aid package (proportion receiving): $7,910 (51%). Average amount of gift aid, such as scholarships or grants (proportion receiving): $3,414 (36%). Average amount of self-help aid, such as work study or loans (proportion receiving): $3,816 (38%). Average need-based loan (excluding PLUS or other private loans): $3,789. Among students who received need-based aid, the average percentage of need met: 78%. Among students who received aid based on merit, the average award (and the proportion receiving): $2,851 (23%). The average athletic scholarship (and the proportion receiving): $6,265 (1%). Average amount of debt of borrowers graduating in 2003: $16,268. Proportion who borrowed: 54%. **Reserve Officers Training Corps (ROTC):** Army ROTC: Offered on campus; Air Force ROTC: Offered on campus.

Oklahoma Wesleyan University

2201 Silver Lake Road
Bartlesville, OK 74006
Private; www.okwu.edu
Financial aid office: (918) 335-6282

■ **2004-2005 TUITION AND FEES:** $12,900
■ **ROOM AND BOARD:** $4,900

ACT Score (25th/75th percentile): 18-24
2005 U.S. News College Ranking:
Comp. Colleges–Bachelor's (West), 15
Acceptance Rate: 88%

Other expenses: Estimated books and supplies: $700. Transportation: $800. Personal expenses: $1,610. **Financial aid:** Priority filing date for institution's financial aid form: March 1. In

2003-2004, 91% of undergraduates applied for financial aid. Of those, 90% were determined to have financial need; 20% had their need fully met. Average financial aid package (proportion receiving): $11,318 (90%). Average amount of gift aid, such as scholarships or grants (proportion receiving): $3,296 (90%). Average amount of self-help aid, such as work study or loans (proportion receiving): $1,860 (90%). Average need-based loan (excluding PLUS or other private loans): $5,423. Among students who received need-based aid, the average percentage of need met: 55%. Among students who received aid based on merit, the average award (and the proportion receiving): $2,941 (9%). The average athletic scholarship (and the proportion receiving): $4,381 (3%). Average amount of debt of borrowers graduating in 2003: $15,352. Proportion who borrowed: 96%. **Student employment:** During the 2003-2004 academic year, 4% of undergraduates worked on campus. Average per-year earnings: $1,680. **Cooperative education programs:** technologies, vocational arts.

Oral Roberts University

7777 S. Lewis Avenue
Tulsa, OK 74171
Private; www.oru.edu
Financial aid office: (918) 495-7088

■ **2004-2005 TUITION AND FEES:** $13,970
■ **ROOM AND BOARD:** $5,900

ACT Score (25th/75th percentile): 20-26
2005 U.S. News College Ranking:
Universities–Master's (West), 41
Acceptance Rate: 64%

Other expenses: Estimated books and supplies: $1,000. Transportation: $1,300. Personal expenses: $1,500. **Financial aid:** Priority filing date for institution's financial aid form: March 15. In 2003-2004, 78% of undergraduates applied for financial aid. Of those, 71% were determined to have financial need; 51% had their need fully met. Average financial aid package (proportion receiving): $15,213 (71%). Average amount of gift aid, such as scholarships or grants (proportion receiving): $7,645 (65%). Average amount of self-help aid, such as work study or loans (proportion receiving): $9,064 (65%). Average need-based loan (excluding PLUS or other private loans): $8,712. Among students who received need-based aid, the average percentage of need met: 92%. Among students who received aid based on merit, the average award (and the proportion

receiving): $6,947 (19%). The average athletic scholarship (and the proportion receiving): $13,449 (4%). Average amount of debt of borrowers graduating in 2003: $24,104. Proportion who borrowed: 86%. **Student employment:** During the 2003-2004 academic year, 29% of undergraduates worked on campus. Average per-year earnings: $2,000. **Cooperative education programs:** art, business, computer science, education, engineering, health professions, other. **Reserve Officers Training Corps (ROTC):** Air Force ROTC: Offered at cooperating institution (OSU–Tulsa).

Southeastern Oklahoma State University

1405 N. Fourth, PMB 4225
Durant, OK 74701-0609
Public; www.sosu.edu
Financial aid office: (580) 745-2186

■ **2004-2005 TUITION AND FEES:**
In state: $2,667; Out of state: $6,307
■ **ROOM AND BOARD:** $3,138

ACT Score (25th/75th percentile): 17-22
2005 U.S. News College Ranking:
Universities–Master's (West), fourth tier
Acceptance Rate: 80%

Other expenses: Estimated books and supplies: $800. Transportation: $1,094. Personal expenses: $1,447. **Financial aid:** Priority filing date for institution's financial aid form: May 1. In 2003-2004, 74% of undergraduates applied for financial aid. Of those, 74% were determined to have financial need; 56% had their need fully met. Average financial aid package (proportion receiving): $1,318 (72%). Average amount of gift aid, such as scholarships or grants (proportion receiving): $1,241 (48%). Average amount of self-help aid, such as work study or loans (proportion receiving): $1,764 (43%). Average need-based loan (excluding PLUS or other private loans): $1,900. Among students who received need-based aid, the average percentage of need met: 75%. Among students who received aid based on merit, the average award (and the proportion receiving): $940 (21%). The average athletic scholarship (and the proportion receiving): $1,062 (6%). **Student employment:** During the 2003-2004 academic year, 20% of undergraduates worked on campus. Average per-year earnings: $1,200.

Southern Nazarene University

6729 N.W. 39th Expressway
Bethany, OK 73008
Private; www.snu.edu
Financial aid office: (405) 491-6310

■ **2004-2005 TUITION AND FEES:** $12,834
■ **ROOM AND BOARD:** $5,110

ACT Score (25th/75th percentile): 18-26
2005 U.S. News College Ranking:
Universities–Master's (West), 52
Acceptance Rate: 100%

Other expenses: Estimated books and supplies:
$850. Transportation: $400. Personal expenses:
$2,500. **Financial aid:** Priority filing date for
institution's financial aid form: March 1.
Student employment: During the 2003-2004
academic year, 10% of undergraduates worked
on campus. Average per-year earnings: $2,000.
Reserve Officers Training Corps (ROTC): Army
ROTC: Offered at cooperating institution
(University of Central Oklahoma); Air Force
ROTC: Offered at cooperating institution
(University of Oklahoma).

Southwestern Oklahoma State University

100 Campus Drive
Weatherford, OK 73096-3098
Public; www.swosu.edu
Financial aid office: (580) 774-3786

■ **2004-2005 TUITION AND FEES:**
  In state: $3,000; Out of state: $7,200
■ **ROOM AND BOARD:** $2,970

ACT Score (25th/75th percentile): 18-23
2005 U.S. News College Ranking:
Universities–Master's (West), fourth tier
Acceptance Rate: 93%

Financial aid: Priority filing date for institution's financial aid form: March 1; deadline:
March 1. In 2003-2004, 72% of undergraduates
applied for financial aid. Of those, 62% were
determined to have financial need; 31% had
their need fully met. Average financial aid package (proportion receiving): $3,788 (60%).
Average amount of gift aid, such as scholarships or grants (proportion receiving): $1,104
(42%). Average amount of self-help aid, such as
work study or loans (proportion receiving):
$1,320 (54%). Average need-based loan (exclud-
ing PLUS or other private loans): $1,418.

Among students who received need-based aid,
the average percentage of need met: 91%.
Among students who received aid based on
merit, the average award (and the proportion
receiving): $612 (6%). The average athletic
scholarship (and the proportion receiving):
$705 (7%).

St. Gregory's University

1900 W. MacArthur Street
Shawnee, OK 74804
Private; www.stgregorys.edu
Financial aid office: (405) 878-5412

■ **2004-2005 TUITION AND FEES:** $11,076
■ **ROOM AND BOARD:** $5,053

ACT Score (25th/75th percentile): 22
2005 U.S. News College Ranking:
Comp. Colleges–Bachelor's (West), third tier
Acceptance Rate: 80%

Other expenses: Estimated books and supplies:
$715. Transportation: $2,002. Personal expenses: $1,335. **Financial aid:** Priority filing date for
institution's financial aid form: April 15. In
2003-2004, 91% of undergraduates applied for
financial aid. Of those, 61% were determined to
have financial need; 22% had their need fully
met. Average financial aid package (proportion
receiving): $9,652 (61%). Average amount of
gift aid, such as scholarships or grants (proportion receiving): $5,391 (47%). Average amount
of self-help aid, such as work study or loans
(proportion receiving): $3,787 (41%). Average
need-based loan (excluding PLUS or other private loans): $3,536. Among students who
received need-based aid, the average percentage
of need met: 87%. Among students who
received aid based on merit, the average award
(and the proportion receiving): $3,953 (17%).
The average athletic scholarship (and the proportion receiving): $8,886 (10%). Average
amount of debt of borrowers graduating in
2003: $15,396. Proportion who borrowed: 68%.
Student employment: During the 2003-2004
academic year, 10% of undergraduates worked
on campus. **Cooperative education programs:**
business, education, health professions,
humanities, natural science, social/behavioral
science, technologies. **Reserve Officers Training
Corps (ROTC):** Air Force ROTC: Offered at
cooperating institution (University of Central
Oklahoma).

University of Central Oklahoma

100 N. University Drive
Edmond, OK 73034
Public; www.ucok.edu
Financial aid office: (405) 974-3334

■ **2004-2005 TUITION AND FEES:**
  In state: $2,649; Out of state: $6,549
■ **ROOM AND BOARD:** $3,670

ACT Score (25th/75th percentile): 19-23
2005 U.S. News College Ranking:
Universities–Master's (West), fourth tier
Acceptance Rate: 88%

Other expenses: Estimated books and supplies:
$1,000. Personal expenses: $2,000. **Financial
aid:** Priority filing date for institution's financial
aid form: May 31; deadline: June 30. **Reserve
Officers Training Corps (ROTC):** Army ROTC:
Offered on campus.

University of Oklahoma

660 Parrington Oval
Norman, OK 73019-0390
Public; www.ou.edu
Financial aid office: (405) 325-4521

■ **2004-2005 TUITION AND FEES:**
  In state: $4,140; Out of state: $11,658
■ **ROOM AND BOARD:** $5,814

ACT Score (25th/75th percentile): 24-28
2005 U.S. News College Ranking:
National Universities, 120
Acceptance Rate: 82%

Financial aid: Priority filing date for institution's financial aid form: March 1. In 2003-
2004, 55% of undergraduates applied for financial aid. Of those, 52% were determined to have
financial need; 82% had their need fully met.
Average financial aid package (proportion
receiving): $8,453 (52%). Average amount of
gift aid, such as scholarships or grants (proportion receiving): $3,699 (17%). Average amount
of self-help aid, such as work study or loans
(proportion receiving): $4,850 (36%). Average
need-based loan (excluding PLUS or other private loans): $4,749. Among students who
received need-based aid, the average percentage
of need met: 81%. Among students who
received aid based on merit, the average award
(and the proportion receiving): $3,688 (13%).
The average athletic scholarship (and the pro-

portion receiving): $11,102 (1%). Average amount of debt of borrowers graduating in 2003: $18,081. Proportion who borrowed: 52%. **Student employment:** During the 2003-2004 academic year, 2% of undergraduates worked on campus. Average per-year earnings: $5,943. **Cooperative education programs:** business, engineering, health professions. **Reserve Officers Training Corps (ROTC):** Army ROTC: Offered on campus; Navy ROTC: Offered on campus; Air Force ROTC: Offered on campus.

University of Science and Arts of Oklahoma

1727 W. Alabama
Chickasha, OK 73018-5322
Public; www.usao.edu
Financial aid office: (405) 574-1251

■ **2004-2005 TUITION AND FEES:**
  In state: $3,090; Out of state: $7,290
■ **ROOM AND BOARD:** $4,130

ACT Score (25th/75th percentile): 18-23
2005 U.S. News College Ranking:
Comp. Colleges–Bachelor's (West), third tier
Acceptance Rate: 86%

....

Other expenses: Estimated books and supplies: $900. Transportation: $1,500. Personal expenses: $1,248. **Financial aid:** Priority filing date for institution's financial aid form: March 15. In 2003-2004, 77% of undergraduates applied for financial aid. Of those, 73% were determined to have financial need; 15% had their need fully met. Average financial aid package (proportion receiving): $6,413 (73%). Average amount of gift aid, such as scholarships or grants (proportion receiving): $4,671 (66%). Average amount of self-help aid, such as work study or loans (proportion receiving): $3,339 (47%). Average need-based loan (excluding PLUS or other private loans): $2,756. Among students who received need-based aid, the average percentage of need met: 69%. Among students who received aid based on merit, the average award (and the proportion receiving): $1,887 (11%). The average athletic scholarship (and the proportion receiving): $4,361 (4%). Average

amount of debt of borrowers graduating in 2003: $12,268. Proportion who borrowed: 58%. **Student employment:** During the 2003-2004 academic year, 23% of undergraduates worked on campus. Average per-year earnings: $1,012.

University of Tulsa

600 S. College Avenue
Tulsa, OK 74104
Private; www.utulsa.edu
Financial aid office: (918) 631-2526

■ **2004-2005 TUITION AND FEES:** $16,830
■ **ROOM AND BOARD:** $5,896

ACT Score (25th/75th percentile): 22-29
2005 U.S. News College Ranking:
National Universities, 90
Acceptance Rate: 76%

....

Other expenses: Estimated books and supplies: $1,200. Transportation: $1,119. Personal expenses: $2,238. **Financial aid:** Priority filing date for institution's financial aid form: April 1. In 2003-2004, 87% of undergraduates applied for financial aid. Of those, 50% were determined to have financial need; 77% had their need fully met. Average financial aid package (proportion receiving): $19,097 (50%). Average amount of gift aid, such as scholarships or grants (proportion receiving): $4,220 (30%). Average amount of self-help aid, such as work study or loans (proportion receiving): $7,141 (39%). Average need-based loan (excluding PLUS or other private loans): $6,228. Among students who received need-based aid, the average percentage of need met: 96%. Among students who received aid based on merit, the average award (and the proportion receiving): $9,334 (27%). The average athletic scholarship (and the proportion receiving): $15,949 (13%). Average amount of debt of borrowers graduating in 2003: $14,546. Proportion who borrowed: 64%. **Student employment:** During the 2003-2004 academic year, 24% of undergraduates worked on campus. Average per-year earnings: $3,000. **Reserve Officers Training Corps (ROTC):** Air Force ROTC: Offered at cooperating institution (Oklahoma State University).

Oregon

Concordia University

2811 N.E. Holman
Portland, OR 97211
Private; www.cu-portland.edu
Financial aid office: (503) 280-8514

- **2003-2004 TUITION AND FEES:** $17,640
- **ROOM AND BOARD:** $7,500

2005 U.S. News College Ranking:
Universities–Master's (West), fourth tier
Acceptance Rate: 25%

Other expenses: Estimated books and supplies: $740. Personal expenses: $2,120.

Eastern Oregon University

1 University Boulevard
La Grande, OR 97850
Public; www.eou.edu
Financial aid office: (541) 962-3551

- **2004-2005 TUITION AND FEES:**
  In state: $5,517; Out of state: $5,517
- **ROOM AND BOARD:** $6,100

SAT I Score (25th/75th percentile): 880-1110
2005 U.S. News College Ranking:
Universities–Master's (West), fourth tier
Acceptance Rate: 98%

Other expenses: Estimated books and supplies: $1,068. Transportation: $750. Personal expenses: $1,146. **Financial aid:** Priority filing date for institution's financial aid form: March 1. In 2003-2004, 82% of undergraduates applied for financial aid. Of those, 67% were determined to have financial need; 34% had their need fully met. Average financial aid package (proportion receiving): $9,461 (66%). Average amount of gift aid, such as scholarships or grants (proportion receiving): $3,624 (48%). Average amount of self-help aid, such as work study or loans (proportion receiving): $4,103 (60%). Average need-based loan (excluding PLUS or other private loans): $3,667. Among students who received need-based aid, the average percentage of need met: 64%. Among students who received aid based on merit, the average award (and the proportion receiving): $1,656 (1%). The average athletic scholarship (and the proportion receiving): $0

(0%). Average amount of debt of borrowers graduating in 2003: $14,185. Proportion who borrowed: 61%. **Student employment:** During the 2003-2004 academic year, 14% of undergraduates worked on campus. Average per-year earnings: $2,000. **Cooperative education programs:** agriculture, health professions. **Reserve Officers Training Corps (ROTC):** Army ROTC: Offered on campus.

George Fox University

414 N. Meridian Street
Newberg, OR 97132
Private; www.georgefox.edu
Financial aid office: (503) 554-2233

- **2004-2005 TUITION AND FEES:** $20,590
- **ROOM AND BOARD:** $6,550

SAT I Score (25th/75th percentile): 1000-1223
2005 U.S. News College Ranking:
Universities–Master's (West), 15
Acceptance Rate: 88%

Other expenses: Estimated books and supplies: $700. Transportation: $350. Personal expenses: $900. **Financial aid:** Priority filing date for institution's financial aid form: February 1; deadline: June 1. In 2003-2004, 90% of undergraduates applied for financial aid. Of those, 81% were determined to have financial need; 14% had their need fully met. Average financial aid package (proportion receiving): $14,902 (81%). Average amount of gift aid, such as scholarships or grants (proportion receiving): $10,967 (78%). Average amount of self-help aid, such as work study or loans (proportion receiving): $4,826 (74%). Average need-based loan (excluding PLUS or other private loans): $3,642. Among students who received need-based aid, the average percentage of need met: 78%. Among students who received aid based on merit, the average award (and the proportion receiving): $8,584 (15%). The average athletic scholarship (and the proportion receiving): $0 (0%). Average amount of debt of borrowers graduating in 2003: $15,473. Proportion who borrowed: 72%. **Student employment:** During the 2003-2004 academic year, 11% of undergraduates worked on campus. Average per-year earnings: $2,070. **Reserve Officers Training Corps (ROTC):** Air Force ROTC: Offered at cooperating institution (University of Portland).

Lewis and Clark College

0615 S.W. Palatine Hill Road
Portland, OR 97219-7899
Private; www.lclark.edu
Financial aid office: (503) 768-7090

- **2004-2005 TUITION AND FEES:** $26,154
- **ROOM AND BOARD:** $7,330

SAT I Score (25th/75th percentile): 1180-1380
2005 U.S. News College Ranking:
Liberal Arts Colleges, 77
Acceptance Rate: 68%

Other expenses: Estimated books and supplies: $800. Transportation: $900. Personal expenses: $1,120. **Financial aid:** Priority filing date for institution's financial aid form: March 1. In 2003-2004, 69% of undergraduates applied for financial aid. Of those, 63% were determined to have financial need; 36% had their need fully met. Average financial aid package (proportion receiving): $18,654 (63%). Average amount of gift aid, such as scholarships or grants (proportion receiving): $17,314 (63%). Average amount of self-help aid, such as work study or loans (proportion receiving): $5,573 (46%). Average need-based loan (excluding PLUS or other private loans): $4,600. Among students who received need-based aid, the average percentage of need met: 79%. Among students who received aid based on merit, the average award (and the proportion receiving): $7,229 (5%). The average athletic scholarship (and the proportion receiving): $0 (0%). Average amount of debt of borrowers graduating in 2003: $17,055. Proportion who borrowed: 58%. **Student employment:** During the 2003-2004 academic year, 31% of undergraduates worked on campus. Average per-year earnings: $985.

Linfield College

900 S.E. Baker Street
McMinnville, OR 97128-6894
Private; www.linfield.edu
Financial aid office: (503) 883-2225

- **2004-2005 TUITION AND FEES:** $22,022
- **ROOM AND BOARD:** $6,370

SAT I Score (25th/75th percentile): 1010-1228
2005 U.S. News College Ranking:
Comp. Colleges–Bachelor's (West), 1
Acceptance Rate: 78%

....

Other expenses: Estimated books and supplies: $650. Transportation: $200. Personal expenses: $1,100. **Financial aid:** Priority filing date for institution's financial aid form: February 1; deadline: February 1. In 2003-2004, 71% of undergraduates applied for financial aid. Of those, 71% were determined to have financial need; 30% had their need fully met. Average financial aid package (proportion receiving): $16,638 (71%). Average amount of gift aid, such as scholarships or grants (proportion receiving): $4,400 (70%). Average amount of self-help aid, such as work study or loans (proportion receiving): $5,031 (68%). Average need-based loan (excluding PLUS or other private loans): $4,617. Among students who received need-based aid, the average percentage of need met: 83%. Among students who received aid based on merit, the average award (and the proportion receiving): $8,902 (19%). The average athletic scholarship (and the proportion receiving): $0 (0%). Average amount of debt of borrowers graduating in 2003: $24,357. Proportion who borrowed: 64%. **Student employment:** During the 2003-2004 academic year, 19% of undergraduates worked on campus. Average per-year earnings: $1,800. **Reserve Officers Training Corps (ROTC):** Air Force ROTC: Offered at cooperating institution (University of Portland).

Marylhurst University

PO Box 261
Marylhurst, OR 97036-0261
Private; www.marylhurst.edu
Financial aid office: (503) 699-6253

■ **2004-2005 TUITION AND FEES:** $13,455

2005 U.S. News College Ranking:
Universities–Master's (West), third tier
Acceptance Rate: 100%

....

Financial aid: Priority filing date for institution's financial aid form: March 1. In 2003-2004, 64% of undergraduates applied for financial aid. Of those, 51% were determined to have financial need; 14% had their need fully met. Average financial aid package (proportion receiving): $6,543 (55%). Average amount of gift aid, such as scholarships or grants (proportion receiving): $4,556 (48%). Average amount of self-help aid, such as work study or loans

(proportion receiving): $7,133 (51%). Average need-based loan (excluding PLUS or other private loans): $5,456. Among students who received need-based aid, the average percentage of need met: 57%. Among students who received aid based on merit, the average award (and the proportion receiving): $2,000 (2%). Average amount of debt of borrowers graduating in 2003: $17,906. Proportion who borrowed: 69%. **Student employment:** During the 2003-2004 academic year, 1% of undergraduates worked on campus. Average per-year earnings: $6,000. **Cooperative education programs:** art, business, social/behavioral science, other.

Northwest Christian College

828 E. 11th Avenue
Eugene, OR 97401
Private; www.nwcc.edu
Financial aid office: (541) 684-7210

■ **2004-2005 TUITION AND FEES:** $17,270
■ **ROOM AND BOARD:** $5,676

ACT Score (25th/75th percentile): 18-24
2005 U.S. News College Ranking:
Comp. Colleges–Bachelor's (West), 13
Acceptance Rate: 65%

....

Other expenses: Estimated books and supplies: $825. Transportation: $0. Personal expenses: $900. **Financial aid:** Priority filing date for institution's financial aid form: March 1. In 2003-2004, 86% of undergraduates applied for financial aid. Of those, 81% were determined to have financial need; 23% had their need fully met. Average financial aid package (proportion receiving): $14,157 (81%). Average amount of gift aid, such as scholarships or grants (proportion receiving): $9,531 (76%). Average amount of self-help aid, such as work study or loans (proportion receiving): $5,769 (73%). Average need-based loan (excluding PLUS or other private loans): $4,180. Among students who received need-based aid, the average percentage of need met: 75%. Among students who received aid based on merit, the average award (and the proportion receiving): $8,804 (7%). The average athletic scholarship (and the proportion receiving): $2,151 (1%). Average amount of debt of borrowers graduating in 2003: $17,764. Proportion who borrowed: 83%. **Reserve Officers Training Corps (ROTC):** Army ROTC: Offered at cooperating institution (University of Oregon).

Oregon Institute of Technology

3201 Campus Drive
Klamath Falls, OR 97601
Public; www.oit.edu
Financial aid office: (541) 885-1280

■ **2004-2005 TUITION AND FEES:**
In state: $4,963; Out of state: $14,409
■ **ROOM AND BOARD:** $6,441

SAT I Score (25th/75th percentile): 940-1170
2005 U.S. News College Ranking:
Unranked Specialty School–Engineering
Acceptance Rate: 54%

....

Other expenses: Estimated books and supplies: $1,000. Transportation: $600. Personal expenses: $1,500. **Financial aid:** Priority filing date for institution's financial aid form: March 1. In 2003-2004, 93% of undergraduates applied for financial aid. Of those, 88% were determined to have financial need; 45% had their need fully met. Average financial aid package (proportion receiving): $5,708 (86%). Average amount of gift aid, such as scholarships or grants (proportion receiving): $3,923 (48%). Average amount of self-help aid, such as work study or loans (proportion receiving): $5,174 (67%). Average need-based loan (excluding PLUS or other private loans): $4,288. Among students who received need-based aid, the average percentage of need met: 16%. Among students who received aid based on merit, the average award (and the proportion receiving): $8,261 (0%). The average athletic scholarship (and the proportion receiving): $1,585 (0%). Average amount of debt of borrowers graduating in 2003: $21,931. Proportion who borrowed: 75%. **Cooperative education programs:** business, computer science, engineering, health professions, natural science, social/behavioral science, technologies, vocational arts. **Reserve Officers Training Corps (ROTC):** Army ROTC: Offered at cooperating institution (Southern Oregon University).

Oregon State University

104 Kerr Administration Building
Corvallis, OR 97331
Public; oregonstate.edu
Financial aid office: (541) 737-2241

■ **2003-2004 TUITION AND FEES:**
In state: $4,869; Out of state: $17,625
■ **ROOM AND BOARD:** $6,336

SAT I Score (25th/75th percentile): 960-1200
2005 U.S. News College Ranking:
National Universities, third tier
Acceptance Rate: 88%

....

Other expenses: Estimated books and supplies: $1,350. Personal expenses: $2,082. Student employment: During the 2003-2004 academic year, 20% of undergraduates worked on campus. Reserve Officers Training Corps (ROTC): Army ROTC: Offered on campus; Navy ROTC: Offered on campus; Air Force ROTC: Offered on campus.

Pacific Northwest College of Art

1241 N.W. Johnson
Portland, OR 97209
Private; www.pnca.edu
Financial aid office: (503) 821-8976

■ 2004-2005 TUITION AND FEES: $16,200

2005 U.S. News College Ranking:
Unranked Specialty School–Fine Arts
Acceptance Rate: 91%

....

Pacific University

2043 College Way
Forest Grove, OR 97116
Private; www.pacificu.edu
Financial aid office: (503) 352-2222

■ 2004-2005 TUITION AND FEES: $20,664
■ ROOM AND BOARD: $5,764

SAT I Score (25th/75th percentile): 1010-1220
2005 U.S. News College Ranking:
Universities–Master's (West), 15
Acceptance Rate: 84%

....

Other expenses: Estimated books and supplies: $700. Transportation: $500. Personal expenses: $900. Financial aid: Priority filing date for institution's financial aid form: February 15. In 2003-2004, 97% of undergraduates applied for financial aid. Of those, 76% were determined to have financial need; 47% had their need fully met. Average financial aid package (proportion receiving): $17,369 (76%). Average amount of gift aid, such as scholarships or grants (proportion receiving): $11,834 (75%). Average amount of self-help aid, such as work study or loans (proportion receiving): $6,454 (66%). Average need-based loan (excluding PLUS or other pri-

vate loans): $4,892. Among students who received need-based aid, the average percentage of need met: 89%. Among students who received aid based on merit, the average award (and the proportion receiving): $8,259 (18%). The average athletic scholarship (and the proportion receiving): $0 (0%). Average amount of debt of borrowers graduating in 2003: $21,465. Proportion who borrowed: 86%. Student employment: During the 2003-2004 academic year, 1% of undergraduates worked on campus. Average per-year earnings: $3,000. Cooperative education programs: engineering, health professions, natural science. Reserve Officers Training Corps (ROTC): Army ROTC: Offered at cooperating institution (Portland State University); Air Force ROTC: Offered at cooperating institution (University of Portland).

Portland State University

PO Box 751
Portland, OR 97207-0751
Public; www.pdx.edu
Financial aid office: (503) 725-3461

■ 2003-2004 TUITION AND FEES:
    In state: $4,278; Out of state: $13,674
■ ROOM AND BOARD: $8,175

SAT I Score (25th/75th percentile): 920-1160
2005 U.S. News College Ranking:
National Universities, fourth tier
Acceptance Rate: 85%

....

Other expenses: Estimated books and supplies: $1,200. Transportation: $450. Personal expenses: $1,400. Financial aid: In 2003-2004, 62% of undergraduates applied for financial aid. Of those, 52% were determined to have financial need; 18% had their need fully met. Average financial aid package (proportion receiving): $7,712 (51%). Average amount of gift aid, such as scholarships or grants (proportion receiving): $3,755 (35%). Average amount of self-help aid, such as work study or loans (proportion receiving): $4,656 (45%). Average need-based loan (excluding PLUS or other private loans): $6,982. Among students who received need-based aid, the average percentage of need met: 67%. Among students who received aid based on merit, the average award (and the proportion receiving): $2,378 (3%). The average athletic scholarship (and the proportion receiving): $8,598 (1%). Average amount of debt of borrowers graduating in 2003: $17,456. Proportion who borrowed: 62%. Cooperative education programs: art, business, computer science, education, engineering, health professions,

humanities, natural science, social/behavioral science, technologies. Reserve Officers Training Corps (ROTC): Army ROTC: Offered on campus; Air Force ROTC: Offered at cooperating institution (University of Portland).

Reed College

3203 S.E. Woodstock Boulevard
Portland, OR 97202
Private; www.reed.edu
Financial aid office: (503) 777-7223

■ 2004-2005 TUITION AND FEES: $29,200
■ ROOM AND BOARD: $7,750

SAT I Score (25th/75th percentile): 1270-1460
2005 U.S. News College Ranking:
Liberal Arts Colleges, 53
Acceptance Rate: 46%

....

Other expenses: Estimated books and supplies: $950. Personal expenses: $900. Financial aid: Priority filing date for institution's financial aid form: January 15; deadline: January 15. In 2003-2004, 67% of undergraduates applied for financial aid. Of those, 54% were determined to have financial need; 95% had their need fully met. Average financial aid package (proportion receiving): $24,309 (54%). Average amount of gift aid, such as scholarships or grants (proportion receiving): $20,880 (53%). Average amount of self-help aid, such as work study or loans (proportion receiving): $4,229 (50%). Average need-based loan (excluding PLUS or other private loans): $4,119. Among students who received need-based aid, the average percentage of need met: 100%. Among students who received aid based on merit, the average award (and the proportion receiving): $0 (0%). The average athletic scholarship (and the proportion receiving): $0 (0%). Average amount of debt of borrowers graduating in 2003: $13,692. Proportion who borrowed: 51%.

Southern Oregon University

1250 Siskiyou Boulevard
Ashland, OR 97520
Public; www.sou.edu
Financial aid office: (541) 552-6754

■ 2004-2005 TUITION AND FEES:
    In state: $5,064; Out of state: $15,642
■ ROOM AND BOARD: $6,765

SAT I Score (25th/75th percentile): 910-1150
2005 U.S. News College Ranking:
Universities–Master's (West), third tier
Acceptance Rate: 90%

Other expenses: Estimated books and supplies:
$1,125. Transportation: $900. Personal expenses: $3,066. **Financial aid:** Priority filing date for institution's financial aid form: March 1. Average amount of debt of borrowers graduating in 2003: $14,617. Proportion who borrowed: 63%. **Cooperative education programs:** other. **Reserve Officers Training Corps (ROTC):** Army ROTC: Offered on campus.

University of Oregon

1217 University of Oregon
Eugene, OR 97403
Public; www.uoregon.edu
Financial aid office: (541) 346-1192

■ **2004-2005 TUITION AND FEES:**
   In state: $5,484; Out of state: $16,914
■ **ROOM AND BOARD:** $7,331

SAT I Score (25th/75th percentile): 989-1219
2005 U.S. News College Ranking:
National Universities, 117
Acceptance Rate: 84%

Financial aid: Priority filing date for institution's financial aid form: March 1. In 2003-2004, 61% of undergraduates applied for financial aid. Of those, 46% were determined to have financial need; 30% had their need fully met. Average financial aid package (proportion receiving): $8,058 (44%). Average amount of gift aid, such as scholarships or grants (proportion receiving): $3,779 (25%). Average amount of self-help aid, such as work study or loans (proportion receiving): $5,111 (40%). Average need-based loan (excluding PLUS or other private loans): $4,243. Among students who received need-based aid, the average percentage of need met: 77%. Among students who received aid based on merit, the average award (and the proportion receiving): $1,753 (6%). The average athletic scholarship (and the proportion receiving): N/A (2%). Average amount of debt of borrowers graduating in 2003: $17,111. Proportion who borrowed: 40%. **Reserve Officers Training Corps (ROTC):** Army ROTC: Offered on campus.

University of Portland

5000 N. Willamette Boulevard
Portland, OR 97203
Private; www.up.edu
Financial aid office: (503) 943-7311

■ **2004-2005 TUITION AND FEES:** $23,520
■ **ROOM AND BOARD:** $7,050

SAT I Score (25th/75th percentile): 1070-1280
2005 U.S. News College Ranking:
Universities–Master's (West), 8
Acceptance Rate: 72%

Other expenses: Estimated books and supplies: $700. Transportation: $800. Personal expenses: $800. **Financial aid:** Priority filing date for institution's financial aid form: March 1. In 2003-2004, 72% of undergraduates applied for financial aid. Of those, 59% were determined to have financial need; 33% had their need fully met. Average financial aid package (proportion receiving): $19,304 (59%). Average amount of gift aid, such as scholarships or grants (proportion receiving): $12,719 (58%). Average amount of self-help aid, such as work study or loans (proportion receiving): $5,532 (49%). Average need-based loan (excluding PLUS or other private loans): $5,213. Among students who received need-based aid, the average percentage of need met: 83%. Among students who received aid based on merit, the average award (and the proportion receiving): $16,102 (33%). The average athletic scholarship (and the proportion receiving): $17,348 (4%). Average amount of debt of borrowers graduating in 2003: $18,909. Proportion who borrowed: 67%. **Student employment:** During the 2003-2004 academic year, 45% of undergraduates worked on campus. Average per-year earnings: $2,000. **Reserve Officers Training Corps (ROTC):** Army ROTC: Offered on campus; Air Force ROTC: Offered on campus.

Warner Pacific College

2219 S.E. 68th Avenue
Portland, OR 97215
Private; www.warnerpacific.edu
Financial aid office: (503) 517-1017

■ **2004-2005 TUITION AND FEES:** $18,060
■ **ROOM AND BOARD:** $5,100

2005 U.S. News College Ranking:
Liberal Arts Colleges, fourth tier
Acceptance Rate: 44%

Other expenses: Estimated books and supplies: $818. Transportation: $743. Personal expenses: $2,640. **Financial aid:** Priority filing date for institution's financial aid form: March 1. **Reserve Officers Training Corps (ROTC):** Air Force ROTC: Offered at cooperating institution (University of Portland).

Western Baptist College

5000 Deer Park Drive SE
Salem, OR 97301
Private; www.wbc.edu
Financial aid office: (503) 375-7006

■ **2004-2005 TUITION AND FEES:** $17,035
■ **ROOM AND BOARD:** $6,070

SAT I Score (25th/75th percentile): 886-1304
2005 U.S. News College Ranking:
Comp. Colleges–Bachelor's (West), 8
Acceptance Rate: 84%

Other expenses: Estimated books and supplies: $700. Transportation: $1,400. Personal expenses: $1,500. **Financial aid:** Priority filing date for institution's financial aid form: February 15. In 2003-2004, 89% of undergraduates applied for financial aid. Of those, 82% were determined to have financial need; 25% had their need fully met. Average financial aid package (proportion receiving): $12,689 (82%). Average amount of gift aid, such as scholarships or grants (proportion receiving): $7,978 (82%). Average amount of self-help aid, such as work study or loans (proportion receiving): $5,741 (67%). Average need-based loan (excluding PLUS or other private loans): $5,741. Among students who received need-based aid, the average percentage of need met: 71%. Among students who received aid based on merit, the average award (and the proportion receiving): $8,192 (13%). The average athletic scholarship (and the proportion receiving): $5,203 (4%). Average amount of debt of borrowers graduating in 2003: $17,500. Proportion who borrowed: 63%. **Student employment:** During the 2003-2004 academic year, 15% of undergraduates worked on campus. Average per-year earnings: $1,500. **Reserve Officers Training Corps (ROTC):** Army ROTC: Offered at cooperating institution (Oregon State University); Air Force ROTC: Offered at cooperating institution (Oregon State University).

Western Oregon University

345 N. Monmouth Avenue
Monmouth, OR 97361-1394
Public; www.wou.edu
Financial aid office: (503) 838-8475

■ **2004-2005 TUITION AND FEES:**
    In state: $4,878; Out of state: $14,538
■ **ROOM AND BOARD:** $6,276

SAT I Score (25th/75th percentile): 870-1090
2005 U.S. News College Ranking:
Universities–Master's (West), third tier
Acceptance Rate: 94%

Other expenses: Estimated books and supplies: $1,125. Personal expenses: $2,475. **Financial aid:** Priority filing date for institution's financial aid form: March 1. In 2003-2004, 93% of undergraduates applied for financial aid. Of those, 76% were determined to have financial need; 11% had their need fully met. Average financial aid package (proportion receiving): $6,332 (76%). Average amount of gift aid, such as scholarships or grants (proportion receiving): $3,993 (57%). Average amount of self-help aid, such as work study or loans (proportion receiving): $3,724 (69%). Average need-based loan (excluding PLUS or other private loans): $3,478. Among students who received need-based aid, the average percentage of need met: 68%. Among students who received aid based on merit, the average award (and the proportion receiving): $7,011 (20%). The average athletic scholarship (and the proportion receiving): $1,647 (2%). Average amount of debt of borrowers graduating in 2003: $12,563. Proportion who borrowed: 55%. **Reserve Officers Training Corps (ROTC):** Army ROTC: Offered on campus; Air Force ROTC: Offered at cooperating institution (Oregon State University).

Willamette University

900 State Street
Salem, OR 97301
Private; www.willamette.edu
Financial aid office: (503) 370-6273

■ **2004-2005 TUITION AND FEES:** $26,852
■ **ROOM AND BOARD:** $6,800

SAT I Score (25th/75th percentile): 1140-1340
2005 U.S. News College Ranking:
Liberal Arts Colleges, 51
Acceptance Rate: 74%

Other expenses: Estimated books and supplies: $800. Transportation: $750. Personal expenses: $1,000. **Financial aid:** Priority filing date for institution's financial aid form: February 1. In 2003-2004, 74% of undergraduates applied for financial aid. Of those, 65% were determined to have financial need; 17% had their need fully met. Average financial aid package (proportion receiving): $21,027 (64%). Average amount of gift aid, such as scholarships or grants (proportion receiving): $17,365 (64%). Average amount of self-help aid, such as work study or loans (proportion receiving): $4,267 (56%). Average need-based loan (excluding PLUS or other private loans): $2,846. Among students who received need-based aid, the average percentage of need met: 86%. Among students who received aid based on merit, the average award (and the proportion receiving): $10,995 (32%). The average athletic scholarship (and the proportion receiving): $0 (0%). Average amount of debt of borrowers graduating in 2003: $18,689. Proportion who borrowed: 66%. **Student employment:** During the 2003-2004 academic year, 30% of undergraduates worked on campus. Average per-year earnings: $1,870. **Reserve Officers Training Corps (ROTC):** Air Force ROTC: Offered at cooperating institution (University of Portland).

Pennsylvania

Albright College

PO Box 15234, 13th and Bern Streets
Reading, PA 19612-5234
Private; www.albright.edu
Financial aid office: (610) 921-7515

■ **2004-2005 TUITION AND FEES:** $24,580
■ **ROOM AND BOARD:** $7,510

SAT I Score (25th/75th percentile): 910-1140
2005 U.S. News College Ranking:
Liberal Arts Colleges, third tier
Acceptance Rate: 72%

Other expenses: Estimated books and supplies: $800. Transportation: $200. Personal expenses: $1,000. **Financial aid:** Priority filing date for institution's financial aid form: March 1. In 2003-2004, 81% of undergraduates applied for financial aid. Of those, 74% were determined to have financial need; 16% had their need fully met. Average financial aid package (proportion receiving): $16,536 (74%). Average amount of gift aid, such as scholarships or grants (proportion receiving): $12,748 (72%). Average amount of self-help aid, such as work study or loans (proportion receiving): $4,790 (63%). Average need-based loan (excluding PLUS or other private loans): $4,206. Among students who received need-based aid, the average percentage of need met: 76%. Among students who received aid based on merit, the average award (and the proportion receiving): $11,053 (12%). The average athletic scholarship (and the proportion receiving): $0 (0%). Average amount of debt of borrowers graduating in 2003: $24,876. Proportion who borrowed: 88%. **Student employment:** During the 2003-2004 academic year, 17% of undergraduates worked on campus. Average per-year earnings: $1,800.

Allegheny College

520 N. Main Street
Meadville, PA 16335
Private; www.allegheny.edu
Financial aid office: (800) 835-7780

■ **2004-2005 TUITION AND FEES:** $25,550
■ **ROOM AND BOARD:** $6,160

SAT I Score (25th/75th percentile): 1090-1300
2005 U.S. News College Ranking:
Liberal Arts Colleges, 83
Acceptance Rate: 82%

Other expenses: Estimated books and supplies: $800. Transportation: $700. Personal expenses: $700. **Financial aid:** Priority filing date for institution's financial aid form: February 15. In 2003-2004, 82% of undergraduates applied for financial aid. Of those, 74% were determined to have financial need; 46% had their need fully met. Average financial aid package (proportion receiving): $19,624 (74%). Average amount of gift aid, such as scholarships or grants (proportion receiving): $13,733 (74%). Average amount of self-help aid, such as work study or loans (proportion receiving): $5,843 (62%). Average need-based loan (excluding PLUS or other private loans): $4,538. Among students who received need-based aid, the average percentage of need met: 94%. Among students who received aid based on merit, the average award (and the proportion receiving): $8,883 (22%). The average athletic scholarship (and the proportion receiving): $0 (0%). Average amount of debt of borrowers graduating in 2003: $23,735. Proportion who borrowed: 75%. **Student employment:** During the 2003-2004 academic year, 17% of undergraduates worked on campus. Average per-year earnings: $675.
Cooperative education programs: education, engineering, health professions, other.

Alvernia College

400 St. Bernardine Street
Reading, PA 19607-1799
Private; www.alvernia.edu
Financial aid office: (610) 796-8356

■ **2004-2005 TUITION AND FEES:** $17,675
■ **ROOM AND BOARD:** $7,330

SAT I Score (25th/75th percentile): 865-1092
2005 U.S. News College Ranking:
Comp. Colleges–Bachelor's (North), 29
Acceptance Rate: 82%

Reserve Officers Training Corps (ROTC): Army ROTC: Offered at cooperating institution (Lehigh University).

Arcadia University

450 S. Easton Road
Glenside, PA 19038-3295
Private; www.arcadia.edu
Financial aid office: (215) 572-2980

■ **2004-2005 TUITION AND FEES:** $22,720
■ **ROOM AND BOARD:** $8,960

SAT I Score (25th/75th percentile): 970-1190
2005 U.S. News College Ranking:
Universities–Master's (North), 27
Acceptance Rate: 81%

Other expenses: Estimated books and supplies: $800. Transportation: $250. Personal expenses: $650. **Financial aid:** Priority filing date for institution's financial aid form: March 1. In 2003-2004, 98% of undergraduates applied for financial aid. Of those, 91% were determined to have financial need; 17% had their need fully met. Average financial aid package (proportion receiving): $16,134 (89%). Average amount of gift aid, such as scholarships or grants (proportion receiving): $6,149 (74%). Average amount of self-help aid, such as work study or loans (proportion receiving): $4,802 (72%). Average need-based loan (excluding PLUS or other private loans): $4,015. Among students who received need-based aid, the average percentage of need met: 74%. Among students who received aid based on merit, the average award (and the proportion receiving): $6,391 (7%). The average athletic scholarship (and the proportion receiving): $0 (0%). Average amount of debt of borrowers graduating in 2003: $29,145. Proportion who borrowed: 71%. **Student employment:** During the 2003-2004 academic year, 45% of undergraduates worked on campus. Average per-year earnings: $1,200. **Cooperative education programs:** business, computer science, natural science.

Bloomsburg University of Pennsylvania

400 E. Second Street
Bloomsburg, PA 17815
Public; www.bloomu.edu
Financial aid office: (570) 389-4297

■ **2004-2005 TUITION AND FEES:**
In state: $6,090; Out of state: $13,306
■ **ROOM AND BOARD:** $5,200

SAT I Score (25th/75th percentile): 930-1110
2005 U.S. News College Ranking:
Universities–Master's (North), 68
Acceptance Rate: 70%

Financial aid: Priority filing date for institution's financial aid form: March 15. In 2003-2004, 80% of undergraduates applied for financial aid. Of those, 64% were determined to have financial need; 86% had their need fully met. Average financial aid package (proportion receiving): $10,026 (61%). Average amount of gift aid, such as scholarships or grants (proportion receiving): $3,570 (48%). Average amount of self-help aid, such as work study or loans (proportion receiving): $3,977 (56%). Average need-based loan (excluding PLUS or other private loans): $3,470. Among students who received need-based aid, the average percentage of need met: 65%. The average athletic scholarship (and the proportion receiving): $2,211 (3%). Average amount of debt of borrowers graduating in 2003: $15,743. Proportion who borrowed: 73%. **Student employment:** During the 2003-2004 academic year, 17% of undergraduates worked on campus. Average per-year earnings: $1,500. **Reserve Officers Training Corps (ROTC):** Army ROTC: Offered on campus; Air Force ROTC: Offered at cooperating institution (Wilkes University).

Bryn Athyn College

Box 717
Bryn Athyn, PA 19009
Private; www.newchurch.edu
Financial aid office: (215) 938-2630

■ **2004-2005 TUITION AND FEES:** $8,804
■ **ROOM AND BOARD:** $5,154

SAT I Score (25th/75th percentile): 1030-1310
2005 U.S. News College Ranking:
Comp. Colleges–Bachelor's (North), unranked
Acceptance Rate: 97%

Other expenses: Estimated books and supplies: $600. Personal expenses: $1,500. **Financial aid:** Priority filing date for institution's financial aid form: June 1; deadline: June 1. In 2003-2004, 69% of undergraduates applied for financial aid. Of those, 65% were determined to have financial need; 100% had their need fully met. Average financial aid package (proportion receiving): N/A (68%). Average amount of gift aid, such as scholarships or grants (proportion receiving): N/A (50%). Average amount of self-help aid, such as work study or loans (proportion receiving): $1,800 (11%). Average need-based loan (exclud-

ing PLUS or other private loans): $1,500. Among students who received need-based aid, the average percentage of need met: 100%. Among students who received aid based on merit, the average award (and the proportion receiving): $1,522 (8%). The average athletic scholarship (and the proportion receiving): $0 (0%). **Student employment:** During the 2003-2004 academic year, 40% of undergraduates worked on campus. Average per-year earnings: $1,800. **Cooperative education programs:** other.

Bryn Mawr College

101 N. Merion Avenue
Bryn Mawr, PA 19010
Private; www.brynmawr.edu
Financial aid office: (610) 526-5245

■ **2004-2005 TUITION AND FEES:** $28,630
■ **ROOM AND BOARD:** $9,700

SAT I Score (25th/75th percentile): 1200-1400
2005 U.S. News College Ranking:
Liberal Arts Colleges, 21
Acceptance Rate: 51%

Other expenses: Estimated books and supplies: $2,000. Transportation: $350. Personal expenses: $0. **Financial aid:** Priority filing date for institution's financial aid form: February 2; deadline: March 1. In 2003-2004, 68% of undergraduates applied for financial aid. Of those, 62% were determined to have financial need; 99% had their need fully met. Average financial aid package (proportion receiving): $25,139 (62%). Average amount of gift aid, such as scholarships or grants (proportion receiving): $21,583 (58%). Average amount of self-help aid, such as work study or loans (proportion receiving): $6,172 (49%). Average need-based loan (excluding PLUS or other private loans): $4,421. Among students who received need-based aid, the average percentage of need met: 99%. Among students who received aid based on merit, the average award (and the proportion receiving): $0 (0%). The average athletic scholarship (and the proportion receiving): $0 (0%). Average amount of debt of borrowers graduating in 2003: $17,827. Proportion who borrowed: 52%. **Student employment:** During the 2003-2004 academic year, 75% of undergraduates worked on campus. Average per-year earnings: $1,700. **Cooperative education programs:** engineering. **Reserve Officers Training Corps (ROTC):** Air Force ROTC: Offered at cooperating institution (St. Joseph's University).

Bucknell University

Lewisburg, PA 17837
Private; www.bucknell.edu
Financial aid office: (570) 577-1331

■ **2004-2005 TUITION AND FEES:** $30,730
■ **ROOM AND BOARD:** $6,578

SAT I Score (25th/75th percentile): 1230-1370
2005 U.S. News College Ranking:
Liberal Arts Colleges, 26
Acceptance Rate: 38%

Other expenses: Estimated books and supplies: $750. Transportation: $488. Personal expenses: $1,500. **Financial aid:** In 2003-2004, 52% of undergraduates applied for financial aid. Of those, 50% were determined to have financial need; 100% had their need fully met. Average financial aid package (proportion receiving): $19,000 (50%). Average amount of gift aid, such as scholarships or grants (proportion receiving): $16,500 (45%). Average amount of self-help aid, such as work study or loans (proportion receiving): $1,600 (50%). Average need-based loan (excluding PLUS or other private loans): $5,200. Among students who received need-based aid, the average percentage of need met: 100%. Among students who received aid based on merit, the average award (and the proportion receiving): $6,777 (0%). The average athletic scholarship (and the proportion receiving): $10,000 (0%). Average amount of debt of borrowers graduating in 2003: $16,695. Proportion who borrowed: 62%. **Student employment:** During the 2003-2004 academic year, 33% of undergraduates worked on campus. Average per-year earnings: $1,500. **Reserve Officers Training Corps (ROTC):** Army ROTC: Offered on campus.

Cabrini College

610 King of Prussia Road
Radnor, PA 19087-3698
Private; www.cabrini.edu
Financial aid office: (610) 902-8420

■ **2004-2005 TUITION AND FEES:** $22,250
■ **ROOM AND BOARD:** $8,980

SAT I Score (25th/75th percentile): 900-1085
2005 U.S. News College Ranking:
Universities–Master's (North), third tier
Acceptance Rate: 83%

Other expenses: Estimated books and supplies: $900. Transportation: $470. Personal expenses: $630. **Financial aid:** Priority filing date for institution's financial aid form: February 15. In 2003-2004, 96% of undergraduates applied for financial aid. Of those, 74% were determined to have financial need; 9% had their need fully met. Average financial aid package (proportion receiving): $12,877 (74%). Average amount of gift aid, such as scholarships or grants (proportion receiving): $5,253 (64%). Average amount of self-help aid, such as work study or loans (proportion receiving): $5,084 (72%). Average need-based loan (excluding PLUS or other private loans): $5,269. Among students who received need-based aid, the average percentage of need met: 48%. Among students who received aid based on merit, the average award (and the proportion receiving): $4,260 (23%). The average athletic scholarship (and the proportion receiving): $0 (0%). Average amount of debt of borrowers graduating in 2003: $17,050. Proportion who borrowed: 79%. **Student employment:** During the 2003-2004 academic year, 4% of undergraduates worked on campus. Average per-year earnings: $3,438. **Reserve Officers Training Corps (ROTC):** Army ROTC: Offered at cooperating institution (Valley Forge Military Academy).

California University of Pennsylvania

250 University Avenue, Box 94
California, PA 15419
Public; www.cup.edu
Financial aid office: (724) 938-4415

■ **2004-2005 TUITION AND FEES:**
   In state: $4,810; Out of state: $7,216
■ **ROOM AND BOARD:** $7,515

SAT I Score (25th/75th percentile): 870-1050
2005 U.S. News College Ranking:
Universities–Master's (North), fourth tier
Acceptance Rate: 75%

Student employment: During the 2003-2004 academic year, 25% of undergraduates worked on campus. Average per-year earnings: $328. **Cooperative education programs:** business, education. **Reserve Officers Training Corps (ROTC):** Army ROTC: Offered on campus.

Carlow College

3333 Fifth Avenue
Pittsburgh, PA 15213-3165
Private; www.carlow.edu
Financial aid office: (412) 578-6058

■ **2004-2005 TUITION AND FEES:** $16,428
■ **ROOM AND BOARD:** $6,538

SAT I Score (25th/75th percentile): 860-1080
2005 U.S. News College Ranking:
Universities–Master's (North), third tier
Acceptance Rate: 57%

Other expenses: Estimated books and supplies: $700. Transportation: $500. Personal expenses: $1,000. **Financial aid:** Priority filing date for institution's financial aid form: April 1. In 2003-2004, 93% of undergraduates applied for financial aid. Of those, 92% were determined to have financial need; 94% had their need fully met. Average financial aid package (proportion receiving): $12,037 (92%). Average amount of gift aid, such as scholarships or grants (proportion receiving): $7,112 (72%). Average amount of self-help aid, such as work study or loans (proportion receiving): $4,626 (74%). Average need-based loan (excluding PLUS or other private loans): $4,276. Among students who received need-based aid, the average percentage of need met: 87%. The average athletic scholarship (and the proportion receiving): $2,828 (6%). Average amount of debt of borrowers graduating in 2003: $22,785. Proportion who borrowed: 73%. **Cooperative education programs:** art, engineering, health professions. **Reserve Officers Training Corps (ROTC):** Army ROTC: Offered at cooperating institution (University of Pittsburgh); Navy ROTC: Offered at cooperating institution (Carnegie Mellon University); Air Force ROTC: Offered at cooperating institution (University of Pittsburgh).

Carnegie Mellon University

5000 Forbes Avenue
Pittsburgh, PA 15213
Private; www.cmu.edu
Financial aid office: (412) 268-8186

■ **2004-2005 TUITION AND FEES:** $31,036
■ **ROOM AND BOARD:** $8,554

SAT I Score (25th/75th percentile): 1280-1480
2005 U.S. News College Ranking:
National Universities, 22
Acceptance Rate: 38%

Other expenses: Estimated books and supplies: $910. Personal expenses: $1,280. **Financial aid:** Priority filing date for institution's financial aid form: February 15; deadline: May 1. In 2003-2004, 60% of undergraduates applied for financial aid. Of those, 51% were determined to have financial need; 47% had their need fully met. Average financial aid package (proportion receiving): $21,658 (51%). Average amount of gift aid, such as scholarships or grants (proportion receiving): $15,007 (48%). Average amount of self-help aid, such as work study or loans (proportion receiving): $7,936 (48%). Average need-based loan (excluding PLUS or other private loans): $6,065. Among students who received need-based aid, the average percentage of need met: 85%. Among students who received aid based on merit, the average award (and the proportion receiving): $10,949 (10%). The average athletic scholarship (and the proportion receiving): $0 (0%). Average amount of debt of borrowers graduating in 2003: $21,235. Proportion who borrowed: 52%. **Cooperative education programs:** computer science, engineering. **Reserve Officers Training Corps (ROTC):** Army ROTC: Offered on campus; Navy ROTC: Offered on campus; Air Force ROTC: Offered on campus.

Cedar Crest College

100 College Drive
Allentown, PA 18104-6196
Private; www.cedarcrest.edu
Financial aid office: (610) 740-3785

■ **2004-2005 TUITION AND FEES:** $21,930
■ **ROOM AND BOARD:** $7,565

SAT I Score (25th/75th percentile): 960-1200
2005 U.S. News College Ranking:
Comp. Colleges–Bachelor's (North), 8
Acceptance Rate: 73%

Other expenses: Estimated books and supplies: $1,000. Transportation: $0. Personal expenses: $500. **Financial aid:** In 2003-2004, 92% of undergraduates applied for financial aid. Of those, 86% were determined to have financial need; 17% had their need fully met. Average financial aid package (proportion receiving): $15,309 (86%). Average amount of gift aid, such as scholarships or grants (proportion receiving): $11,808 (83%). Average amount of self-help aid, such as work study or loans (proportion receiving): $4,434 (76%). Average need-based loan (excluding PLUS or other private loans): $3,707. Among students who received need-based aid, the average percentage of need met: 79%. Among students who received aid based on merit, the average award (and the proportion receiving): $12,868 (10%). The average athletic scholarship (and the proportion receiving): $0 (0%). Average amount of debt of borrowers graduating in 2003: $19,382. Proportion who borrowed: 78%. **Student employment:** During the 2003-2004 academic year, 60% of undergraduates worked on campus. Average per-year earnings: $1,500. **Reserve Officers Training Corps (ROTC):** Army ROTC: Offered at cooperating institution (Lehigh University).

Chatham College

Woodland Road
Pittsburgh, PA 15232
Private; www.chatham.edu
Financial aid office: (412) 365-1777

■ **2004-2005 TUITION AND FEES:** $21,996
■ **ROOM AND BOARD:** $7,050

SAT I Score (25th/75th percentile): 920-1170
2005 U.S. News College Ranking:
Liberal Arts Colleges, third tier
Acceptance Rate: 61%

Other expenses: Estimated books and supplies: $860. Transportation: $1,722. Personal expenses: $316. **Financial aid:** In 2003-2004, 95% of undergraduates applied for financial aid. Of those, 90% were determined to have financial need; Average financial aid package (proportion receiving): $22,742 (90%). Average amount of gift aid, such as scholarships or grants (proportion receiving): $7,158 (90%). Average amount of self-help aid, such as work study or loans (proportion receiving): $5,700 (90%). Average need-based loan (excluding PLUS or other private loans): $4,275. Among students who received need-based aid, the average percentage of need met: 72%. Among students who received aid based on merit, the average award (and the proportion receiving): $5,717 (16%). The average athletic scholarship (and the proportion receiving): $0 (0%). Average amount of debt of borrowers graduating in 2003: $18,655. Proportion who borrowed: 99%. **Student employment:** During the 2003-2004 academic year, 50% of undergraduates worked on campus. Average per-year earnings: $1,290. **Cooperative education programs:** art, business, education, natural science, social/behavioral science. **Reserve Officers Training Corps (ROTC):** Army ROTC:

Offered at cooperating institution (University of Pittsburgh); Navy ROTC: Offered at cooperating institution (Carnegie Mellon); Air Force ROTC: Offered at cooperating institution (University of Pittsburgh).

Chestnut Hill College

9601 Germantown Avenue
Philadelphia, PA 19118-2693
Private; www.chc.edu
Financial aid office: (215) 248-7182

■ **2004-2005 TUITION AND FEES:** $20,345
■ **ROOM AND BOARD:** $7,500

SAT I Score (25th/75th percentile): 840-1060
2005 U.S. News College Ranking:
Universities–Master's (North), 80
Acceptance Rate: 77%

Other expenses: Estimated books and supplies: $2,045. Transportation: $650. Personal expenses: $980. **Financial aid:** Priority filing date for institution's financial aid form: April 15; deadline: April 15. In 2003-2004, 95% of undergraduates applied for financial aid. Of those, 86% were determined to have financial need; Average financial aid package (proportion receiving): $16,125 (86%). Average amount of gift aid, such as scholarships or grants (proportion receiving): $9,205 (82%). Average amount of self-help aid, such as work study or loans (proportion receiving): $7,450 (82%). Average need-based loan (excluding PLUS or other private loans): $5,500. Among students who received need-based aid, the average percentage of need met: 51%. Among students who received aid based on merit, the average award (and the proportion receiving): $7,225 (7%). Average amount of debt of borrowers graduating in 2003: $17,125. Proportion who borrowed: 92%. **Cooperative education programs:** business, computer science, humanities, natural science, social/behavioral science.

Cheyney University of Pennsylvania

1837 University Circle
Cheyney, PA 19319
Public; www.cheyney.edu
Financial aid office: (610) 399-2302

■ **2004-2005 TUITION AND FEES:**
In state: $5,565; Out of state: $12,781
■ **ROOM AND BOARD:** $5,524

SAT I Score (25th/75th percentile): 751
2005 U.S. News College Ranking:
Universities–Master's (North), fourth tier
Acceptance Rate: 62%

Cooperative education programs: business, computer science, natural science, social/behavioral science. **Reserve Officers Training Corps (ROTC):** Army ROTC: Offered on campus.

Clarion University of Pennsylvania

840 Wood Street
Clarion, PA 16214
Public; www.clarion.edu
Financial aid office: (814) 393-2315

■ **2003-2004 TUITION AND FEES:**
In state: $5,998; Out of state: $9,448
■ **ROOM AND BOARD:** $4,560

SAT I Score (25th/75th percentile): 820-1040
2005 U.S. News College Ranking:
Universities–Master's (North), fourth tier
Acceptance Rate: 81%

Other expenses: Estimated books and supplies: $800. Personal expenses: $2,649.

College Misericordia

301 Lake Street
Dallas, PA 18612-1098
Private; www.misericordia.edu
Financial aid office: (570) 674-6280

■ **2004-2005 TUITION AND FEES:** $18,800
■ **ROOM AND BOARD:** $7,850

SAT I Score (25th/75th percentile): 920-1100
2005 U.S. News College Ranking:
Universities–Master's (North), 56
Acceptance Rate: 77%

Other expenses: Estimated books and supplies: $800. Transportation: $500. Personal expenses: $500. **Financial aid:** Priority filing date for institution's financial aid form: March 1; deadline: May 1. In 2003-2004, 87% of undergraduates applied for financial aid. Of those, 79% were determined to have financial need; 57% had their need fully met. Average financial aid package (proportion receiving): $12,854 (79%). Average amount of gift aid, such as scholarships or grants (proportion receiving): $5,317 (76%). Average amount of self-help aid, such as work study or loans (proportion receiving): $3,978 (68%). Average need-based loan (excluding PLUS or other private loans): $2,769. Among students who received need-based aid, the average percentage of need met: 75%. Among students who received aid based on merit, the average award (and the proportion receiving): $5,954 (8%). The average athletic scholarship (and the proportion receiving): $0 (0%). Average amount of debt of borrowers graduating in 2003: $16,495. Proportion who borrowed: 94%. **Student employment:** During the 2003-2004 academic year, 10% of undergraduates worked on campus. Average per-year earnings: $1,000. **Reserve Officers Training Corps (ROTC):** Army ROTC: Offered at cooperating institution (Kings College); Air Force ROTC: Offered at cooperating institution (Wilkes University).

Curtis Institute of Music

1726 Locust Street
Philadelphia, PA 19103
Private; www.curtis.edu
Financial aid office: (215) 717-3165

■ **2004-2005 TUITION AND FEES:** $1,000

2005 U.S. News College Ranking:
Unranked Specialty School–Fine Arts
Acceptance Rate: 3%

Delaware Valley College

700 E. Butler Avenue
Doylestown, PA 18901
Private; www.devalcol.edu
Financial aid office: (215) 489-2272

■ **2004-2005 TUITION AND FEES:** $20,738
■ **ROOM AND BOARD:** $7,742

SAT I Score (25th/75th percentile): 900-1093
2005 U.S. News College Ranking:
Comp. Colleges–Bachelor's (North), 32
Acceptance Rate: 82%

Other expenses: Estimated books and supplies: $800. Transportation: $400. Personal expenses: $1,100. **Financial aid:** Priority filing date for institution's financial aid form: April 1. In 2003-2004, 88% of undergraduates applied for financial aid. Of those, 74% were determined to have financial need; 38% had their need fully met. Average financial aid package (proportion receiving): $16,030 (73%). Average amount of gift aid,

such as scholarships or grants (proportion receiving): $11,458 (73%). Average amount of self-help aid, such as work study or loans (proportion receiving): $3,834 (63%). Average need-based loan (excluding PLUS or other private loans): $3,834. Among students who received need-based aid, the average percentage of need met: 85%. Among students who received aid based on merit, the average award (and the proportion receiving): $7,407 (19%). The average athletic scholarship (and the proportion receiving): $0 (0%). Average amount of debt of borrowers graduating in 2003: $17,790. Proportion who borrowed: 62%. **Student employment:** During the 2003-2004 academic year, 25% of undergraduates worked on campus. Average per-year earnings: $1,800. **Cooperative education programs:** agriculture, business, computer science, social/behavioral science.

DeSales University

2755 Station Avenue
Center Valley, PA 18034-9568
Private; www.desales.edu
Financial aid office: (610) 282-1100

■ **2004-2005 TUITION AND FEES:** $19,390
■ **ROOM AND BOARD:** $7,590

SAT I Score (25th/75th percentile): 970-1180
2005 U.S. News College Ranking:
Universities–Master's (North), 80
Acceptance Rate: 77%

Other expenses: Estimated books and supplies: $800. Personal expenses: $1,800. **Financial aid:** Priority filing date for institution's financial aid form: February 1; deadline: May 1. In 2003-2004, 71% of undergraduates applied for financial aid. Of those, 59% were determined to have financial need; 38% had their need fully met. Average financial aid package (proportion receiving): $12,586 (59%). Average amount of gift aid, such as scholarships or grants (proportion receiving): $9,187 (57%). Average amount of self-help aid, such as work study or loans (proportion receiving): $3,544 (58%). Average need-based loan (excluding PLUS or other private loans): $2,964. Among students who received need-based aid, the average percentage of need met: 70%. Among students who received aid based on merit, the average award (and the proportion receiving): $4,518 (16%). The average athletic scholarship (and the proportion receiving): $0 (0%). Average amount of debt of borrowers graduating in 2003: $13,977. Proportion who borrowed: 64%. **Student employment:** During the 2003-2004 academic year, 45% of undergradu-

ates worked on campus. Average per-year earnings: $725. **Reserve Officers Training Corps (ROTC):** Army ROTC: Offered at cooperating institution (Lehigh University).

Dickinson College

PO Box 1773
Carlisle, PA 17013-2896
Private; www.dickinson.edu
Financial aid office: (717) 245-1308

■ **2004-2005 TUITION AND FEES:** $30,300
■ **ROOM AND BOARD:** $7,600

SAT I Score (25th/75th percentile): 1180-1360
2005 U.S. News College Ranking:
Liberal Arts Colleges, 40
Acceptance Rate: 52%

Other expenses: Estimated books and supplies: $750. Transportation: $300. Personal expenses: $1,125. **Financial aid:** Priority filing date for institution's financial aid form: November 15; deadline: February 1. In 2003-2004, 60% of undergraduates applied for financial aid. Of those, 53% were determined to have financial need; 71% had their need fully met. Average financial aid package (proportion receiving): $22,973 (53%). Average amount of gift aid, such as scholarships or grants (proportion receiving): $18,568 (51%). Average amount of self-help aid, such as work study or loans (proportion receiving): $5,890 (47%). Average need-based loan (excluding PLUS or other private loans): $4,564. Among students who received need-based aid, the average percentage of need met: 97%. Among students who received aid based on merit, the average award (and the proportion receiving): $10,842 (12%). Average amount of debt of borrowers graduating in 2003: $19,207. Proportion who borrowed: 81%. **Student employment:** During the 2003-2004 academic year, 28% of undergraduates worked on campus. Average per-year earnings: $885. **Reserve Officers Training Corps (ROTC):** Army ROTC: Offered on campus.

Drexel University

3141 Chestnut Street
Philadelphia, PA 19104-2875
Private; www.drexel.edu
Financial aid office: (215) 895-2537

■ **2004-2005 TUITION AND FEES:** $22,180
■ **ROOM AND BOARD:** $7,320

SAT I Score (25th/75th percentile): 1100-1290
2005 U.S. News College Ranking:
National Universities, 106
Acceptance Rate: 70%

Other expenses: Estimated books and supplies: $1,500. Transportation: $600. Personal expenses: $2,400. Financial aid: In 2003-2004, 89% of undergraduates applied for financial aid. Of those, 70% were determined to have financial need; 12% had their need fully met. Average financial aid package (proportion receiving): $10,266 (70%). Average amount of gift aid, such as scholarships or grants (proportion receiving): $4,873 (36%). Average amount of self-help aid, such as work study or loans (proportion receiving): $5,912 (69%). Average need-based loan (excluding PLUS or other private loans): $6,749. Among students who received need-based aid, the average percentage of need met: 46%. Among students who received aid based on merit, the average award (and the proportion receiving): $6,469 (17%). The average athletic scholarship (and the proportion receiving): $19,955 (2%). Average amount of debt of borrowers graduating in 2003: $22,234. Proportion who borrowed: 81%. Student employment: During the 2003-2004 academic year, 8% of undergraduates worked on campus. Cooperative education programs: business, computer science, education, engineering, health professions, humanities, social/behavioral science, technologies, other. Reserve Officers Training Corps (ROTC): Army ROTC: Offered on campus; Navy ROTC: Offered at cooperating institution (University of Pennsylvania); Air Force ROTC: Offered at cooperating institution (St. Joseph's University).

Duquesne University

600 Forbes Avenue
Pittsburgh, PA 15282
Private; www.duq.edu
Financial aid office: (412) 396-6607

■ 2004-2005 TUITION AND FEES: $20,360
■ ROOM AND BOARD: $7,820

SAT I Score (25th/75th percentile): 1020-1220
2005 U.S. News College Ranking:
National Universities, third tier
Acceptance Rate: 84%

Other expenses: Estimated books and supplies: $600. Transportation: $550. Personal expenses: $600. Financial aid: In 2003-2004, 78% of undergraduates applied for financial aid. Of those, 67% were determined to have financial

need; 48% had their need fully met. Average financial aid package (proportion receiving): $15,179 (67%). Average amount of gift aid, such as scholarships or grants (proportion receiving): $10,303 (63%). Average amount of self-help aid, such as work study or loans (proportion receiving): $5,947 (59%). Average need-based loan (excluding PLUS or other private loans): $4,478. Among students who received need-based aid, the average percentage of need met: 83%. Among students who received aid based on merit, the average award (and the proportion receiving): $8,113 (19%). The average athletic scholarship (and the proportion receiving): $8,914 (6%). Average amount of debt of borrowers graduating in 2003: $15,437. Proportion who borrowed: 72%. Student employment: During the 2003-2004 academic year, 5% of undergraduates worked on campus. Average per-year earnings: $1,200. Reserve Officers Training Corps (ROTC): Army ROTC: Offered on campus; Navy ROTC: Offered at cooperating institution (Carnegie Mellon University); Air Force ROTC: Offered at cooperating institution (University of Pittsburgh).

Eastern University

1300 Eagle Road
St. Davids, PA 19087-3696
Private; www.eastern.edu
Financial aid office: (610) 341-5842

■ 2004-2005 TUITION AND FEES: $17,700
■ ROOM AND BOARD: $7,600

SAT I Score (25th/75th percentile): 980-1210
2005 U.S. News College Ranking:
Universities–Master's (North), third tier
Acceptance Rate: 78%

Average per-year earnings: $1,500. Reserve Officers Training Corps (ROTC): Army ROTC: Offered at cooperating institution (Valley Forge Military College); Air Force ROTC: Offered at cooperating institution (St. Joseph's University).

East Stroudsburg University of Pennsylvania

200 Prospect Street
East Stroudsburg, PA 18301-2999
Public; www.esu.edu
Financial aid office: (570) 422-2800

■ 2004-2005 TUITION AND FEES:
    In state: $5,979; Out of state: $12,877
■ ROOM AND BOARD: $4,464

SAT I Score (25th/75th percentile): 890-1070
2005 U.S. News College Ranking:
Universities–Master's (North), third tier
Acceptance Rate: 70%

Other expenses: Estimated books and supplies: $900. Transportation: $255. Personal expenses: $1,402. Financial aid: Priority filing date for institution's financial aid form: March 1; deadline: May 1. In 2003-2004, 78% of undergraduates applied for financial aid. Of those, 56% were determined to have financial need; 79% had their need fully met. Average financial aid package (proportion receiving): $5,203 (53%). Average amount of gift aid, such as scholarships or grants (proportion receiving): $3,249 (37%). Average amount of self-help aid, such as work study or loans (proportion receiving): $5,987 (46%). Average need-based loan (excluding PLUS or other private loans): $3,531. Among students who received need-based aid, the average percentage of need met: 89%. Among students who received aid based on merit, the average award (and the proportion receiving): $6,315 (20%). The average athletic scholarship (and the proportion receiving): $1,712 (3%). Average amount of debt of borrowers graduating in 2003: $19,677. Proportion who borrowed: 69%. Reserve Officers Training Corps (ROTC): Army ROTC: Offered at cooperating institution (Lehigh University); Air Force ROTC: Offered at cooperating institution (Wilkes University).

Edinboro University of Pennsylvania

Edinboro, PA 16444
Public; www.edinboro.edu
Financial aid office: (814) 732-5555

■ 2004-2005 TUITION AND FEES:
    In state: $5,764; Out of state: $8,064
■ ROOM AND BOARD: $5,086

SAT I Score (25th/75th percentile): 830-1050
2005 U.S. News College Ranking:
Universities–Master's (North), fourth tier
Acceptance Rate: 69%

Other expenses: Estimated books and supplies: $750. Transportation: $750. Personal expenses: $700. Financial aid: Priority filing date for institution's financial aid form: March 15; deadline: May 1. In 2003-2004, 89% of undergraduates applied for financial aid. Of those, 74% were determined to have financial need; 14% had their need fully met. Average financial aid package (proportion receiving): $6,036 (58%).

Average amount of gift aid, such as scholarships or grants (proportion receiving): $1,500 (58%). Average amount of self-help aid, such as work study or loans (proportion receiving): $3,900 (57%). Average need-based loan (excluding PLUS or other private loans): $4,281. Among students who received need-based aid, the average percentage of need met: 81%. Among students who received aid based on merit, the average award (and the proportion receiving): $2,200 (13%). The average athletic scholarship (and the proportion receiving): $900 (2%). Average amount of debt of borrowers graduating in 2003: $15,935. Proportion who borrowed: 72%. **Student employment:** During the 2003-2004 academic year, 19% of undergraduates worked on campus. Average per-year earnings: $1,829. **Cooperative education programs:** engineering, health professions. **Reserve Officers Training Corps (ROTC):** Army ROTC: Offered on campus; Air Force ROTC: Offered on campus.

Elizabethtown College

1 Alpha Drive
Elizabethtown, PA 17022-2298
Private; www.etown.edu
Financial aid office: (717) 361-1404

■ **2004-2005 TUITION AND FEES:** $23,710
■ **ROOM AND BOARD:** $6,600

SAT I Score (25th/75th percentile): 1010-1210
2005 U.S. News College Ranking:
Comp. Colleges–Bachelor's (North), 2
Acceptance Rate: 70%

Other expenses: Estimated books and supplies: $700. Transportation: $150. Personal expenses: $600. **Financial aid:** Priority filing date for institution's financial aid form: March 15; deadline: March 15. In 2003-2004, 81% of undergraduates applied for financial aid. Of those, 72% were determined to have financial need; 31% had their need fully met. Average financial aid package (proportion receiving): $16,402 (72%). Average amount of gift aid, such as scholarships or grants (proportion receiving): $12,540 (72%). Average amount of self-help aid, such as work study or loans (proportion receiving): $4,814 (64%). Average need-based loan (excluding PLUS or other private loans): $3,875. Among students who received need-based aid, the average percentage of need met: 88%. Among students who received aid based on merit, the average award (and the proportion receiving): $12,892 (8%). The average athletic scholarship (and the proportion receiving): $0 (0%). Average amount of debt of borrowers graduating in 2003: $19,025. Proportion who borrowed: 80%. **Student employment:** During the 2003-2004 academic year, 55% of undergraduates worked on campus. Average per-year earnings: $804. **Cooperative education programs:** engineering, health professions, other.

Franklin and Marshall College

PO Box 3003
Lancaster, PA 17604
Private; www.fandm.edu
Financial aid office: (717) 291-3991

■ **2004-2005 TUITION AND FEES:** $30,440
■ **ROOM AND BOARD:** $7,540

SAT I Score (25th/75th percentile): 1150-1350
2005 U.S. News College Ranking:
Liberal Arts Colleges, 38
Acceptance Rate: 58%

Other expenses: Estimated books and supplies: $650. Personal expenses: $750. **Financial aid:** Priority filing date for institution's financial aid form: February 1; deadline: March 1. In 2003-2004, 53% of undergraduates applied for financial aid. Of those, 47% were determined to have financial need; 97% had their need fully met. Average financial aid package (proportion receiving): $20,915 (47%). Average amount of gift aid, such as scholarships or grants (proportion receiving): $17,205 (42%). Average amount of self-help aid, such as work study or loans (proportion receiving): $5,903 (42%). Average need-based loan (excluding PLUS or other private loans): $4,805. Among students who received need-based aid, the average percentage of need met: 97%. Among students who received aid based on merit, the average award (and the proportion receiving): $13,067 (20%). The average athletic scholarship (and the proportion receiving): $0 (0%). Average amount of debt of borrowers graduating in 2003: $18,370. Proportion who borrowed: 51%. Average per-year earnings: $1,350. **Cooperative education programs:** engineering. **Reserve Officers Training Corps (ROTC):** Army ROTC: Offered at cooperating institution (Millersville University).

Gannon University

University Square
Erie, PA 16541
Private; www.gannon.edu
Financial aid office: (814) 871-7337

■ **2004-2005 TUITION AND FEES:** $17,500
■ **ROOM AND BOARD:** $7,070

SAT I Score (25th/75th percentile): 940-1160
2005 U.S. News College Ranking:
Universities–Master's (North), 45
Acceptance Rate: 84%

Other expenses: Estimated books and supplies: $950. Transportation: $800. Personal expenses: $950. **Financial aid:** Priority filing date for institution's financial aid form: March 15. In 2003-2004, 93% of undergraduates applied for financial aid. Of those, 85% were determined to have financial need; 44% had their need fully met. Average financial aid package (proportion receiving): $12,740 (85%). Average amount of gift aid, such as scholarships or grants (proportion receiving): $10,140 (84%). Average amount of self-help aid, such as work study or loans (proportion receiving): $6,050 (74%). Average need-based loan (excluding PLUS or other private loans): $3,002. Among students who received need-based aid, the average percentage of need met: 80%. Among students who received aid based on merit, the average award (and the proportion receiving): $3,940 (15%). The average athletic scholarship (and the proportion receiving): N/A (3%). Average amount of debt of borrowers graduating in 2003: $23,710. Proportion who borrowed: 71%. **Student employment:** During the 2003-2004 academic year, 12% of undergraduates worked on campus. Average per-year earnings: $1,700. **Cooperative education programs:** engineering. **Reserve Officers Training Corps (ROTC):** Army ROTC: Offered on campus.

Geneva College

3200 College Avenue
Beaver Falls, PA 15010
Private; www.geneva.edu
Financial aid office: (724) 847-6530

■ **2004-2005 TUITION AND FEES:** $16,590
■ **ROOM AND BOARD:** $6,600

SAT I Score (25th/75th percentile): 970-1210
2005 U.S. News College Ranking:
Universities–Master's (North), third tier
Acceptance Rate: 60%

Other expenses: Estimated books and supplies: $800. Transportation: $140. Personal expenses: $1,150. **Financial aid:** Priority filing date for institution's financial aid form: March 15. In 2003-2004, 92% of undergraduates applied for financial aid. Of those, 85% were determined to have financial need; 22% had their need fully met. Average financial aid package (proportion receiving): $13,180 (85%). Average amount of gift aid, such as scholarships or grants (proportion receiving): $9,326 (84%). Average amount of self-help aid, such as work study or loans (proportion receiving): $4,531 (74%). Average need-based loan (excluding PLUS or other private loans): $3,845. Among students who received need-based aid, the average percentage of need met: 80%. Among students who received aid based on merit, the average award (and the proportion receiving): $7,226 (12%). The average athletic scholarship (and the proportion receiving): $3,009 (5%). Average amount of debt of borrowers graduating in 2003: $20,860. Proportion who borrowed: 93%. Average per-year earnings: $1,500. **Cooperative education programs:** other. **Reserve Officers Training Corps (ROTC):** Army ROTC: Offered at cooperating institution (Slippery Rock University).

Gettysburg College

300 N. Washington Street
Gettysburg, PA 17325
Private; www.gettysburg.edu
Financial aid office: (717) 337-6611

■ **2004-2005 TUITION AND FEES:** $30,040
■ **ROOM AND BOARD:** $7,354

SAT I Score (25th/75th percentile): 1200-1340
2005 U.S. News College Ranking:
Liberal Arts Colleges, 45
Acceptance Rate: 46%

Other expenses: Estimated books and supplies: $500. Transportation: $500. Personal expenses: $0. **Financial aid:** Priority filing date for institution's financial aid form: January 15; deadline: February 15. In 2003-2004, 69% of undergraduates applied for financial aid. Of those, 60% were determined to have financial need; 100% had their need fully met. Average financial aid package (proportion receiving): $24,317 (60%). Average amount of gift aid, such as scholarships or grants (proportion receiving): $18,531 (58%). Average amount of self-help aid, such as work study or loans (proportion receiving): $5,786 (53%). Average need-based loan (excluding PLUS or other private loans): $4,527. Among students who received need-based aid, the average percentage of need met: 100%. Among students who received aid based on merit, the average award (and the proportion receiving): $7,805 (5%). The average athletic scholarship (and the proportion receiving): $0 (0%). Average amount of debt of borrowers graduating in 2003: $15,500. Proportion who borrowed: 75%. **Student employment:** During the 2003-2004 academic year, 30% of under-

graduates worked on campus. Average per-year earnings: $900. **Reserve Officers Training Corps (ROTC):** Army ROTC: Offered at cooperating institution (Dickinson College).

Gratz College

7605 Old York Road
Melrose Park, PA 19027
Private; www.gratzcollege.edu
Financial aid office: (215) 635-7300

■ **2004-2005 TUITION AND FEES:** $9,500

2005 U.S. News College Ranking:
Universities–Master's (North), unranked

Other expenses: Estimated books and supplies: $0. Transportation: $0. Personal expenses: $0. **Financial aid:** In 2003-2004, 88% of undergraduates applied for financial aid. Of those, 88% were determined to have financial need; Average financial aid package (proportion receiving): $5,500 (88%). Average amount of gift aid, such as scholarships or grants (proportion receiving): $2,647 (75%). Average amount of self-help aid, such as work study or loans (proportion receiving): $2,514 (63%). Average need-based loan (excluding PLUS or other private loans): $2,514. Among students who received need-based aid, the average percentage of need met: 80%. Among students who received aid based on merit, the average award (and the proportion receiving): $0 (0%). The average athletic scholarship (and the proportion receiving): $0 (0%). Average amount of debt of borrowers graduating in 2003: $0.

Grove City College

100 Campus Drive
Grove City, PA 16127
Private; www.gcc.edu
Financial aid office: (724) 458-3300

■ **2004-2005 TUITION AND FEES:** $9,952
■ **ROOM AND BOARD:** $5,094

SAT I Score (25th/75th percentile): 1152-1378
2005 U.S. News College Ranking:
Comp. Colleges–Bachelor's (North), 5
Acceptance Rate: 41%

Other expenses: Estimated books and supplies: $900. Transportation: $500. Personal expenses: $350. **Financial aid:** In 2003-2004, 69% of undergraduates applied for financial aid. Of those, 38% were determined to have financial

need; 8% had their need fully met. Average financial aid package (proportion receiving): $4,385 (38%). Average amount of gift aid, such as scholarships or grants (proportion receiving): $4,672 (35%). Average amount of self-help aid, such as work study or loans (proportion receiving): $0 (0%). Average need-based loan (excluding PLUS or other private loans): $0. Among students who received need-based aid, the average percentage of need met: 50%. Among students who received aid based on merit, the average award (and the proportion receiving): $2,572 (19%). The average athletic scholarship (and the proportion receiving): $0 (0%). Average amount of debt of borrowers graduating in 2003: $19,986. Proportion who borrowed: 42%. **Student employment:** During the 2003-2004 academic year, 30% of undergraduates worked on campus. Average per-year earnings: $1,000. **Reserve Officers Training Corps (ROTC):** Army ROTC: Offered at cooperating institution (Slippery Rock University).

Gwynedd-Mercy College

1325 Sumneytown Pike, PO Box 901
Gwynedd Valley, PA 19437-0901
Private; www.gmc.edu
Financial aid office: (215) 641-5570

■ **2004-2005 TUITION AND FEES:** $17,400
■ **ROOM AND BOARD:** $7,500

SAT I Score (25th/75th percentile): 870-1060
2005 U.S. News College Ranking:
Universities–Master's (North), third tier
Acceptance Rate: 58%

Other expenses: Estimated books and supplies: $700. Personal expenses: $1,000. **Financial aid:** Priority filing date for institution's financial aid form: March 15; deadline: July 15. In 2003-2004, 85% of undergraduates applied for financial aid. Of those, 70% were determined to have financial need; 74% had their need fully met. Average financial aid package (proportion receiving): $14,523 (68%). Average amount of gift aid, such as scholarships or grants (proportion receiving): $10,800 (64%). Average amount of self-help aid, such as work study or loans (proportion receiving): $5,363 (62%). Average need-based loan (excluding PLUS or other private loans): $4,656. Among students who received need-based aid, the average percentage of need met: 82%. Among students who received aid based on merit, the average award (and the proportion receiving): $6,482 (17%). Average amount of debt of borrowers graduating in 2003: $18,624. Proportion who borrowed: 82%.

Haverford College

370 Lancaster Avenue
Haverford, PA 19041-1392
Private; www.haverford.edu
Financial aid office: (610) 896-1350

- **2004-2005 TUITION AND FEES:** $30,270
- **ROOM AND BOARD:** $9,420

SAT I Score (25th/75th percentile): 1290-1450
2005 U.S. News College Ranking:
Liberal Arts Colleges, 9
Acceptance Rate: 30%

Other expenses: Estimated books and supplies: $1,074. Transportation: $151. Personal expenses: $1,468. **Financial aid:** In 2003-2004, 50% of undergraduates applied for financial aid. Of those, 43% were determined to have financial need; 100% had their need fully met. Average financial aid package (proportion receiving): $25,073 (43%). Average amount of gift aid, such as scholarships or grants (proportion receiving): $22,203 (41%). Average amount of self-help aid, such as work study or loans (proportion receiving): $4,582 (39%). Average need-based loan (excluding PLUS or other private loans): $3,947. Among students who received need-based aid, the average percentage of need met: 100%. Average amount of debt of borrowers graduating in 2003: $15,362. Proportion who borrowed: 36%. **Student employment:** During the 2003-2004 academic year, 20% of undergraduates worked on campus.

Holy Family University

9701 Frankford Avenue
Philadelphia, PA 19114-2094
Private; www.holyfamily.edu
Financial aid office: (215) 637-5538

- **2004-2005 TUITION AND FEES:** $16,490

SAT I Score (25th/75th percentile): 873-1078
2005 U.S. News College Ranking:
Universities–Master's (North), third tier
Acceptance Rate: 74%

Financial aid: Priority filing date for institution's financial aid form: March 1. Average amount of debt of borrowers graduating in 2003: $17,125. Proportion who borrowed: 60%. **Student employment:** During the 2003-2004 academic year, 0% of undergraduates worked on campus. **Cooperative education programs:** art, business, computer science, education,

health professions, humanities, natural science, social/behavioral science.

Immaculata University

1145 King Road
Immaculata, PA 19345-0702
Private; www.immaculata.edu
Financial aid office: (610) 647-4400

- **2004-2005 TUITION AND FEES:** $18,000
- **ROOM AND BOARD:** $8,250

SAT I Score (25th/75th percentile): 890-1140
2005 U.S. News College Ranking:
Universities–Master's (North), third tier
Acceptance Rate: 85%

Other expenses: Estimated books and supplies: $1,050. Transportation: $840. Personal expenses: $1,576. **Financial aid:** Priority filing date for institution's financial aid form: April 15; deadline: April 15. In 2003-2004, 76% of undergraduates applied for financial aid. Of those, 67% were determined to have financial need; 28% had their need fully met. Average financial aid package (proportion receiving): $12,621 (67%). Average amount of gift aid, such as scholarships or grants (proportion receiving): $9,692 (67%). Average amount of self-help aid, such as work study or loans (proportion receiving): $3,926 (51%). Average need-based loan (excluding PLUS or other private loans): $3,598. Among students who received need-based aid, the average percentage of need met: 70%. Among students who received aid based on merit, the average award (and the proportion receiving): $11,672 (18%). The average athletic scholarship (and the proportion receiving): $0 (0%). Average amount of debt of borrowers graduating in 2003: $17,125. Proportion who borrowed: 88%. **Student employment:** During the 2003-2004 academic year, 30% of undergraduates worked on campus. Average per-year earnings: $1,000.

Indiana University of Pennsylvania

1011 South Drive
Indiana, PA 15705
Public; www.iup.edu
Financial aid office: (724) 357-2218

- **2004-2005 TUITION AND FEES:**
  In state: $4,810; Out of state: $12,026
- **ROOM AND BOARD:** $4,866

SAT I Score (25th/75th percentile): 950-1140
2005 U.S. News College Ranking:
National Universities, fourth tier
Acceptance Rate: 60%

Financial aid: Priority filing date for institution's financial aid form: April 15. In 2003-2004, 83% of undergraduates applied for financial aid. Of those, 67% were determined to have financial need; 20% had their need fully met. Average financial aid package (proportion receiving): $7,067 (66%). Average amount of gift aid, such as scholarships or grants (proportion receiving): $3,639 (55%). Average amount of self-help aid, such as work study or loans (proportion receiving): $3,946 (60%). Average need-based loan (excluding PLUS or other private loans): $3,483. Among students who received need-based aid, the average percentage of need met: 76%. Among students who received aid based on merit, the average award (and the proportion receiving): $2,286 (3%). The average athletic scholarship (and the proportion receiving): $3,356 (2%). Average amount of debt of borrowers graduating in 2003: $17,825. Proportion who borrowed: 73%. **Student employment:** During the 2003-2004 academic year, 20% of undergraduates worked on campus. Average per-year earnings: $2,300. **Cooperative education programs:** health professions, natural science, other. **Reserve Officers Training Corps (ROTC):** Army ROTC: Offered on campus.

Juniata College

1700 Moore Street
Huntingdon, PA 16652
Private; www.juniata.edu
Financial aid office: (814) 641-3142

- **2004-2005 TUITION AND FEES:** $24,320
- **ROOM AND BOARD:** $6,770

SAT I Score (25th/75th percentile): 1070-1270
2005 U.S. News College Ranking:
Liberal Arts Colleges, 101
Acceptance Rate: 75%

Other expenses: Estimated books and supplies: $450. Transportation: $250. Personal expenses: $420. **Financial aid:** Priority filing date for institution's financial aid form: March 1; deadline: May 1. In 2003-2004, 88% of undergraduates applied for financial aid. Of those, 79% were determined to have financial need; 61% had their need fully met. Average financial aid package (proportion receiving): $18,258 (79%). Average amount of gift aid, such as scholarships or grants (proportion receiving): $14,190 (79%). Average amount of self-help aid, such as work study or loans (proportion receiving): $4,729 (67%). Average need-based loan (excluding PLUS or other private loans): $3,954. Among students who received need-based aid, the average percentage of need met: 88%. Among students who received aid based on merit, the average award (and the proportion receiving): $10,760 (30%). The average athletic scholarship (and the proportion receiving): $0 (0%). Average amount of debt of borrowers graduating in 2003: $17,572. Proportion who borrowed: 78%. **Student employment:** During the 2003-2004 academic year, 54% of undergraduates worked on campus. Average per-year earnings: $780. **Cooperative education programs:** engineering, health professions, other.

King's College

133 N. River Street
Wilkes-Barre, PA 18711
Private; www.kings.edu
Financial aid office: (570) 208-5868

■ **2004-2005 TUITION AND FEES:** $20,110
■ **ROOM AND BOARD:** $8,250

SAT I Score (25th/75th percentile): 940-1160
2005 U.S. News College Ranking:
Universities–Master's (North), 31
Acceptance Rate: 81%

Other expenses: Estimated books and supplies: $900. Transportation: $500. Personal expenses: $1,050. **Financial aid:** Priority filing date for institution's financial aid form: February 15. In 2003-2004, 90% of undergraduates applied for financial aid. Of those, 79% were determined to have financial need; 21% had their need fully met. Average financial aid package (proportion receiving): $14,394 (78%). Average amount of gift aid, such as scholarships or grants (proportion receiving): $6,395 (60%). Average amount of self-help aid, such as work study or loans (proportion receiving): $4,677 (63%). Average need-based loan (excluding PLUS or other private loans): $4,182. Among students who received need-based aid, the average percentage of need met: 76%. Among students who received aid based on merit, the average award (and the proportion receiving): $8,085 (13%). The average athletic scholarship (and the proportion receiving): $0 (0%). Average amount of debt of borrowers graduating in 2003: $20,267. Proportion who borrowed: 82%. **Student employment:** During the 2003-2004 academic year, 1% of undergraduates worked on campus.

Average per-year earnings: $1,800. **Reserve Officers Training Corps (ROTC):** Army ROTC: Offered on campus; Air Force ROTC: Offered on campus.

Kutztown University of Pennsylvania

15200 Kutztown Road
Kutztown, PA 19530-0730
Public; www.kutztown.edu
Financial aid office: (610) 683-4077

■ **2004-2005 TUITION AND FEES:**
In state: $6,256; Out of state: $13,472
■ **ROOM AND BOARD:** $5,274

SAT I Score (25th/75th percentile): 900-1080
2005 U.S. News College Ranking:
Universities–Master's (North), third tier
Acceptance Rate: 70%

Financial aid: Priority filing date for institution's financial aid form: February 15. In 2003-2004, 80% of undergraduates applied for financial aid. Of those, 58% were determined to have financial need; 56% had their need fully met. Average financial aid package (proportion receiving): $6,282 (58%). Average amount of gift aid, such as scholarships or grants (proportion receiving): $3,774 (42%). Average amount of self-help aid, such as work study or loans (proportion receiving): $3,545 (49%). Average need-based loan (excluding PLUS or other private loans): $3,378. Among students who received need-based aid, the average percentage of need met: 65%. Among students who received aid based on merit, the average award (and the proportion receiving): $1,721 (3%). The average athletic scholarship (and the proportion receiving): $1,329 (2%). Average amount of debt of borrowers graduating in 2003: $14,570. Proportion who borrowed: 73%. **Student employment:** During the 2003-2004 academic year, 22% of undergraduates worked on campus. Average per-year earnings: $1,200. **Reserve Officers Training Corps (ROTC):** Army ROTC: Offered at cooperating institution (Lehigh University).

Lafayette College

118 Markle Hall
Easton, PA 18042
Private; www.lafayette.edu
Financial aid office: (610) 330-5055

■ **2004-2005 TUITION AND FEES:** $28,625
■ **ROOM AND BOARD:** $8,786

SAT I Score (25th/75th percentile): 1180-1360
2005 U.S. News College Ranking:
Liberal Arts Colleges, 31
Acceptance Rate: 36%

Other expenses: Estimated books and supplies: $600. Transportation: $100. Personal expenses: $875. **Financial aid:** Priority filing date for institution's financial aid form: February 1; deadline: March 15. In 2003-2004, 62% of undergraduates applied for financial aid. Of those, 55% were determined to have financial need; 98% had their need fully met. Average financial aid package (proportion receiving): $22,407 (54%). Average amount of gift aid, such as scholarships or grants (proportion receiving): $20,044 (51%). Average amount of self-help aid, such as work study or loans (proportion receiving): $4,854 (38%). Average need-based loan (excluding PLUS or other private loans): $4,437. Among students who received need-based aid, the average percentage of need met: 99%. Among students who received aid based on merit, the average award (and the proportion receiving): $12,445 (7%). The average athletic scholarship (and the proportion receiving): $0 (0%). Average amount of debt of borrowers graduating in 2003: $17,204. Proportion who borrowed: 54%. **Student employment:** During the 2003-2004 academic year, 15% of undergraduates worked on campus. **Cooperative education programs:** health professions. **Reserve Officers Training Corps (ROTC):** Army ROTC: Offered at cooperating institution (Lehigh University).

La Roche College

9000 Babcock Boulevard
Pittsburgh, PA 15237
Private; www.laroche.edu
Financial aid office: (412) 536-1120

■ **2004-2005 TUITION AND FEES:** $16,382
■ **ROOM AND BOARD:** $6,862

SAT I Score (25th/75th percentile): 840-1070
2005 U.S. News College Ranking:
Universities–Master's (North), fourth tier
Acceptance Rate: 69%

Other expenses: Estimated books and supplies: $800. Transportation: $650. Personal expenses: $650. **Financial aid:** Priority filing date for institution's financial aid form: January 15; deadline: March 1. In 2003-2004, 66% of undergraduates applied for financial aid. Of those, 60% were determined to have financial need; 30% had their need fully met. Average financial aid package (proportion receiving): $12,661 (60%). Average amount of gift aid, such as scholarships or grants (proportion receiving): $3,689 (60%). Average amount of self-help aid, such as work study or loans (proportion receiving): $4,813 (55%). Average need-based loan (excluding PLUS or other private loans): $4,592. Among students who received need-based aid, the average percentage of need met: 84%. Among students who received aid based on merit, the average award (and the proportion receiving): $4,500 (7%). The average athletic scholarship (and the proportion receiving): $0 (0%). Average amount of debt of borrowers graduating in 2003: $18,000. Proportion who borrowed: 80%. **Student employment:** During the 2003-2004 academic year, 2% of undergraduates worked on campus. Average per-year earnings: $3,000. **Reserve Officers Training Corps (ROTC):** Army ROTC: Offered at cooperating institution (University of Pittsburgh); Air Force ROTC: Offered at cooperating institution (Duquesne University).

La Salle University

1900 W. Olney Avenue
Philadelphia, PA 19141-1199
Private; www.lasalle.edu
Financial aid office: (215) 951-1070

■ **2004-2005 TUITION AND FEES:** $24,610
■ **ROOM AND BOARD:** $8,570

SAT I Score (25th/75th percentile): 990-1210
2005 U.S. News College Ranking:
Universities–Master's (North), 21
Acceptance Rate: 68%

Other expenses: Estimated books and supplies: $500. Personal expenses: $1,119. **Financial aid:** Priority filing date for institution's financial aid form: February 15; deadline: March 15. In 2003-2004, 84% of undergraduates applied for financial aid. Of those, 75% were determined to have financial need; 20% had their need fully met. Average financial aid package (proportion receiving): $15,998 (74%). Average amount of gift aid, such as scholarships or grants (proportion receiving): $11,273 (73%). Average amount of self-help aid, such as work study or loans (proportion receiving): $4,637 (61%). Average need-based loan (excluding PLUS or other private loans): $4,340. Among students who received need-based aid, the average percentage of need met: 74%. Among students who received aid based on merit, the average award (and the proportion receiving): $9,222 (17%). The average athletic scholarship (and the proportion receiving): $11,131 (4%). Average amount of debt of borrowers graduating in

2003: $21,364. Proportion who borrowed: 74%. **Student employment:** During the 2003-2004 academic year, 13% of undergraduates worked on campus. Average per-year earnings: $2,781. **Cooperative education programs:** business, computer science, education, health professions, social/behavioral science. **Reserve Officers Training Corps (ROTC):** Army ROTC: Offered at cooperating institution (Drexel University); Air Force ROTC: Offered at cooperating institution (St. Joseph's University).

Lebanon Valley College

101 N. College Avenue
Annville, PA 17003
Private; www.lvc.edu
Financial aid office: (717) 867-6126

■ **2004-2005 TUITION AND FEES:** $23,600
■ **ROOM AND BOARD:** $6,590

SAT I Score (25th/75th percentile): 1010-1220
2005 U.S. News College Ranking:
Universities–Master's (North), 24
Acceptance Rate: 73%

Other expenses: Estimated books and supplies: $750. Transportation: $310. Personal expenses: $750. **Financial aid:** Priority filing date for institution's financial aid form: March 1. In 2003-2004, 87% of undergraduates applied for financial aid. Of those, 79% were determined to have financial need; 28% had their need fully met. Average financial aid package (proportion receiving): $17,055 (79%). Average amount of gift aid, such as scholarships or grants (proportion receiving): $14,062 (78%). Average amount of self-help aid, such as work study or loans (proportion receiving): $5,145 (68%). Average need-based loan (excluding PLUS or other private loans): $4,111. Among students who received need-based aid, the average percentage of need met: 86%. Among students who received aid based on merit, the average award (and the proportion receiving): $9,062 (16%). The average athletic scholarship (and the proportion receiving): $0 (0%). Average amount of debt of borrowers graduating in 2003: $22,027. Proportion who borrowed: 73%. **Student employment:** During the 2003-2004 academic year, 50% of undergraduates worked on campus. Average per-year earnings: $625. **Cooperative education programs:** engineering, health professions, other.

Lehigh University

27 Memorial Drive W
Bethlehem, PA 18015
Private; www.lehigh.edu
Financial aid office: (610) 758-3181

■ **2004-2005 TUITION AND FEES:** $29,340
■ **ROOM AND BOARD:** $8,230

SAT I Score (25th/75th percentile): 1220-1380
2005 U.S. News College Ranking:
National Universities, 37
Acceptance Rate: 40%

Other expenses: Estimated books and supplies: $800. Personal expenses: $1,210. **Financial aid:** In 2003-2004, 56% of undergraduates applied for financial aid. Of those, 46% were determined to have financial need; 57% had their need fully met. Average financial aid package (proportion receiving): $23,533 (46%). Average amount of gift aid, such as scholarships or grants (proportion receiving): $17,403 (44%). Average amount of self-help aid, such as work study or loans (proportion receiving): $5,585 (43%). Average need-based loan (excluding PLUS or other private loans): $4,476. Among students who received need-based aid, the average percentage of need met: 100%. Among students who received aid based on merit, the average award (and the proportion receiving): $13,193 (8%). The average athletic scholarship (and the proportion receiving): $27,687 (1%). Average amount of debt of borrowers graduating in 2003: $16,774. Proportion who borrowed: 52%. **Student employment:** During the 2003-2004 academic year, 1% of undergraduates worked on campus. Average per-year earnings: $950. **Cooperative education programs:** education, engineering. **Reserve Officers Training Corps (ROTC):** Army ROTC: Offered on campus.

Lincoln University

PO Box 179
Lincoln University, PA 19352
Public; www.lincoln.edu
Financial aid office: (800) 561-2606

■ **2004-2005 TUITION AND FEES:**
In state: $6,130; Out of state: $12,436
■ **ROOM AND BOARD:** $6,510

SAT I Score (25th/75th percentile): 740-950
2005 U.S. News College Ranking:
Universities–Master's (North), fourth tier
Acceptance Rate: 40%

Other expenses: Estimated books and supplies: $1,200. Transportation: $210. Personal expenses: $1,297. **Financial aid:** Priority filing date for institution's financial aid form: May 1; deadline: May 1. In 2003-2004, 95% of undergraduates applied for financial aid. Of those, 90% were determined to have financial need; 80% had their need fully met. Average financial aid package (proportion receiving): $13,000 (90%). Average amount of gift aid, such as scholarships or grants (proportion receiving): $1,965 (72%). Average amount of self-help aid, such as work study or loans (proportion receiving): $497 (81%). Average need-based loan (excluding PLUS or other private loans): $3,804. Among students who received need-based aid, the average percentage of need met: 85%. Among students who received aid based on merit, the average award (and the proportion receiving): $3,895 (10%). The average athletic scholarship (and the proportion receiving): $0 (0%). Average amount of debt of borrowers graduating in 2003: $25,000. Proportion who borrowed: 80%. **Student employment:** During the 2003-2004 academic year, 36% of undergraduates worked on campus. Average per-year earnings: $700. **Reserve Officers Training Corps (ROTC):** Army ROTC: Offered at cooperating institution (University of Delaware).

Lock Haven University of Pennsylvania

North Fairview Street
Lock Haven, PA 17745
Public; www.lhup.edu
Financial aid office: (570) 893-2344

■ **2004-2005 TUITION AND FEES:**
  In state: $6,090; Out of state: $11,322
■ **ROOM AND BOARD:** $4,716

SAT I Score (25th/75th percentile): 860-1060
2005 U.S. News College Ranking:
Universities–Master's (North), fourth tier
Acceptance Rate: 81%

Other expenses: Estimated books and supplies: $900. Personal expenses: $1,290. **Financial aid:** Priority filing date for institution's financial aid form: March 15. In 2003-2004, 95% of undergraduates applied for financial aid. Of those, 77% were determined to have financial need; 55% had their need fully met. Average financial aid package (proportion receiving): $6,120 (77%). Average amount of gift aid, such as scholarships or grants (proportion receiving): $4,568 (51%). Average amount of self-help aid, such as work study or loans (proportion receiv-

ing): $3,997 (67%). Average need-based loan (excluding PLUS or other private loans): $3,767. Among students who received need-based aid, the average percentage of need met: 77%. Among students who received aid based on merit, the average award (and the proportion receiving): $1,575 (2%). The average athletic scholarship (and the proportion receiving): $1,472 (3%). Average amount of debt of borrowers graduating in 2003: $17,021. Proportion who borrowed: 76%. **Cooperative education programs:** engineering. **Reserve Officers Training Corps (ROTC):** Army ROTC: Offered on campus.

Lycoming College

700 College Place
Williamsport, PA 17701
Private; www.lycoming.edu
Financial aid office: (570) 321-4040

■ **2004-2005 TUITION AND FEES:** $22,791
■ **ROOM AND BOARD:** $6,242

SAT I Score (25th/75th percentile): 990-1210
2005 U.S. News College Ranking:
Liberal Arts Colleges, third tier
Acceptance Rate: 80%

Other expenses: Estimated books and supplies: $800. Transportation: $600. Personal expenses: $2,200. **Financial aid:** Priority filing date for institution's financial aid form: April 15; deadline: May 1. In 2003-2004, 91% of undergraduates applied for financial aid. Of those, 83% were determined to have financial need; 24% had their need fully met. Average financial aid package (proportion receiving): $16,840 (83%). Average amount of gift aid, such as scholarships or grants (proportion receiving): $13,596 (83%). Average amount of self-help aid, such as work study or loans (proportion receiving): $4,727 (74%). Average need-based loan (excluding PLUS or other private loans): $4,083. Among students who received need-based aid, the average percentage of need met: 80%. Among students who received aid based on merit, the average award (and the proportion receiving): $8,650 (12%). The average athletic scholarship (and the proportion receiving): $0 (0%). Average amount of debt of borrowers graduating in 2003: $15,656. Proportion who borrowed: 93%. **Student employment:** During the 2003-2004 academic year, 33% of undergraduates worked on campus. Average per-year earnings: $1,105. **Reserve Officers Training Corps (ROTC):** Army ROTC: Offered at cooperating institution (Bucknell University).

Mansfield University of Pennsylvania

Alumni Hall
Mansfield, PA 16933
Public; www.mansfield.edu
Financial aid office: (570) 662-4878

■ **2004-2005 TUITION AND FEES:**
  In state: $6,218; Out of state: $9,356
■ **ROOM AND BOARD:** $5,704

SAT I Score (25th/75th percentile): 870-1060
2005 U.S. News College Ranking:
Universities–Master's (North), fourth tier
Acceptance Rate: 77%

Other expenses: Estimated books and supplies: $900. Transportation: $912. Personal expenses: $912. **Financial aid:** Priority filing date for institution's financial aid form: March 15; deadline: April 30. In 2003-2004, 82% of undergraduates applied for financial aid. Of those, 51% were determined to have financial need; 43% had their need fully met. Average financial aid package (proportion receiving): $6,985 (43%). Average amount of gift aid, such as scholarships or grants (proportion receiving): $3,482 (35%). Average amount of self-help aid, such as work study or loans (proportion receiving): $1,928 (38%). Average need-based loan (excluding PLUS or other private loans): $1,894. Among students who received need-based aid, the average percentage of need met: 85%. Among students who received aid based on merit, the average award (and the proportion receiving): $1,390 (11%). The average athletic scholarship (and the proportion receiving): $950 (6%). Average amount of debt of borrowers graduating in 2003: $15,800. Proportion who borrowed: 68%. **Student employment:** During the 2003-2004 academic year, 15% of undergraduates worked on campus. Average per-year earnings: $1,300.

Marywood University

2300 Adams Avenue
Scranton, PA 18509-1598
Private; www.marywood.edu
Financial aid office: (570) 348-6225

■ **2004-2005 TUITION AND FEES:** $20,540
■ **ROOM AND BOARD:** $8,582

SAT I Score (25th/75th percentile): 900-1120
2005 U.S. News College Ranking:
Universities–Master's (North), 42
Acceptance Rate: 79%

Other expenses: Estimated books and supplies: $700. Transportation: $500. Personal expenses: $700. **Financial aid:** Priority filing date for institution's financial aid form: February 15. In 2003-2004, 89% of undergraduates applied for financial aid. Of those, 83% were determined to have financial need; 18% had their need fully met. Average financial aid package (proportion receiving): $14,499 (83%). Average amount of gift aid, such as scholarships or grants (proportion receiving): $10,319 (83%). Average amount of self-help aid, such as work study or loans (proportion receiving): $6,855 (75%). Average need-based loan (excluding PLUS or other private loans): $4,185. Among students who received need-based aid, the average percentage of need met: 75%. Among students who received aid based on merit, the average award (and the proportion receiving): $6,929 (15%). The average athletic scholarship (and the proportion receiving): $0 (0%). Average amount of debt of borrowers graduating in 2003: $25,016. Proportion who borrowed: 87%. **Reserve Officers Training Corps (ROTC):** Army ROTC: Offered at cooperating institution (University of Scranton); Air Force ROTC: Offered at cooperating institution (Wilkes University).

Mercyhurst College

501 E. 38th Street
Erie, PA 16546
Private; www.mercyhurst.edu
Financial aid office: (814) 824-2288

■ **2004-2005 TUITION AND FEES:** $18,093
■ **ROOM AND BOARD:** $6,798

SAT I Score (25th/75th percentile): 990-1180
2005 U.S. News College Ranking:
Comp. Colleges–Bachelor's (North), 12
Acceptance Rate: 77%

Other expenses: Estimated books and supplies: $1,000. Personal expenses: $2,000. **Financial aid:** Priority filing date for institution's financial aid form: March 1; deadline: May 1. In 2003-2004, 99% of undergraduates applied for financial aid. Of those, 78% were determined to have financial need; 80% had their need fully met. Average financial aid package (proportion receiving): $12,686 (78%). Average amount of gift aid, such as scholarships or grants (proportion receiving): $9,050 (75%). Average amount

of self-help aid, such as work study or loans (proportion receiving): $3,900 (73%). Average need-based loan (excluding PLUS or other private loans): $3,554. Among students who received need-based aid, the average percentage of need met: 92%. Among students who received aid based on merit, the average award (and the proportion receiving): $5,010 (19%). The average athletic scholarship (and the proportion receiving): $8,592 (16%). Average amount of debt of borrowers graduating in 2003: $22,125. Proportion who borrowed: 85%. **Student employment:** During the 2003-2004 academic year, 35% of undergraduates worked on campus. Average per-year earnings: $1,200. **Cooperative education programs:** art, business, computer science, home economics, social/behavioral science. **Reserve Officers Training Corps (ROTC):** Army ROTC: Offered at cooperating institution (Gannon University).

Messiah College

1 College Avenue
Grantham, PA 17027-0800
Private; www.messiah.edu
Financial aid office: (717) 691-6007

■ **2004-2005 TUITION AND FEES:** $20,790
■ **ROOM AND BOARD:** $6,560

SAT I Score (25th/75th percentile): 1100-1300
2005 U.S. News College Ranking:
Comp. Colleges–Bachelor's (North), 3
Acceptance Rate: 79%

Other expenses: Estimated books and supplies: $810. Transportation: $600. Personal expenses: $1,100. **Financial aid:** Priority filing date for institution's financial aid form: April 1. In 2003-2004, 80% of undergraduates applied for financial aid. Of those, 72% were determined to have financial need; 17% had their need fully met. Average financial aid package (proportion receiving): $12,798 (72%). Average amount of gift aid, such as scholarships or grants (proportion receiving): $5,476 (62%). Average amount of self-help aid, such as work study or loans (proportion receiving): $4,519 (67%). Average need-based loan (excluding PLUS or other private loans): $3,947. Among students who received need-based aid, the average percentage of need met: 65%. Among students who received aid based on merit, the average award (and the proportion receiving): $5,228 (18%). The average athletic scholarship (and the proportion receiving): $0 (0%). Average amount of debt of borrowers graduating in 2003: $23,249. Proportion who borrowed: 67%. **Student**

employment: During the 2003-2004 academic year, 22% of undergraduates worked on campus. Average per-year earnings: $2,405.

Millersville University of Pennsylvania

PO Box 1002
Millersville, PA 17551-0302
Public; www.millersville.edu
Financial aid office: (717) 872-3026

■ **2004-2005 TUITION AND FEES:**
In state: $6,081; Out of state: $13,297
■ **ROOM AND BOARD:** $5,642

SAT I Score (25th/75th percentile): 960-1150
2005 U.S. News College Ranking:
Universities–Master's (North), 38
Acceptance Rate: 61%

Other expenses: Estimated books and supplies: $800. Transportation: $650. Personal expenses: $1,600. **Financial aid:** In 2003-2004, 75% of undergraduates applied for financial aid. Of those, 52% were determined to have financial need; 29% had their need fully met. Average financial aid package (proportion receiving): $6,494 (51%). Average amount of gift aid, such as scholarships or grants (proportion receiving): $3,666 (38%). Average amount of self-help aid, such as work study or loans (proportion receiving): $3,700 (46%). Average need-based loan (excluding PLUS or other private loans): $3,283. Among students who received need-based aid, the average percentage of need met: 94%. Among students who received aid based on merit, the average award (and the proportion receiving): $2,341 (3%). The average athletic scholarship (and the proportion receiving): $1,393 (1%). Average amount of debt of borrowers graduating in 2003: $14,418. Proportion who borrowed: 73%. **Student employment:** During the 2003-2004 academic year, 34% of undergraduates worked on campus. Average per-year earnings: $1,108. **Cooperative education programs:** art, business, computer science, education, engineering, health professions, humanities, natural science, social/behavioral science, technologies. **Reserve Officers Training Corps (ROTC):** Army ROTC: Offered on campus.

Moore College of Art and Design

20th and the Parkway
Philadelphia, PA 19103
Private; www.moore.edu
Financial aid office: (215) 965-4042

■ **2004-2005 TUITION AND FEES:** $21,250
■ **ROOM AND BOARD:** $8,013

SAT I Score (25th/75th percentile): 1005
2005 U.S. News College Ranking:
Unranked Specialty School–Fine Arts
Acceptance Rate: 47%

....

Other expenses: Estimated books and supplies: $2,000. **Financial aid:** Priority filing date for institution's financial aid form: March 1. In 2003-2004, 87% of undergraduates applied for financial aid. Of those, 81% were determined to have financial need; 3% had their need fully met. Average financial aid package (proportion receiving): $12,194 (81%). Average amount of gift aid, such as scholarships or grants (proportion receiving): $7,627 (81%). Average amount of self-help aid, such as work study or loans (proportion receiving): $5,023 (75%). Average need-based loan (excluding PLUS or other private loans): $4,487. Among students who received need-based aid, the average percentage of need met: 52%. Among students who received aid based on merit, the average award (and the proportion receiving): $7,619 (18%). The average athletic scholarship (and the proportion receiving): $0 (0%). Average amount of debt of borrowers graduating in 2003: $25,000. Proportion who borrowed: 79%.

Moravian College

1200 Main Street
Bethlehem, PA 18018
Private; www.moravian.edu
Financial aid office: (610) 861-1330

■ **2004-2005 TUITION AND FEES:** $23,574
■ **ROOM AND BOARD:** $7,310

SAT I Score (25th/75th percentile): 1030-1210
2005 U.S. News College Ranking:
Liberal Arts Colleges, third tier
Acceptance Rate: 68%

....

Other expenses: Estimated books and supplies: $730. Transportation: $400. Personal expenses: $1,275. **Financial aid:** Priority filing date for institution's financial aid form: February 14;

deadline: April 15. In 2003-2004, 86% of undergraduates applied for financial aid. Of those, 77% were determined to have financial need; 23% had their need fully met. Average financial aid package (proportion receiving): $15,931 (77%). Average amount of gift aid, such as scholarships or grants (proportion receiving): $11,243 (76%). Average amount of self-help aid, such as work study or loans (proportion receiving): $5,443 (68%). Average need-based loan (excluding PLUS or other private loans): $4,148. Among students who received need-based aid, the average percentage of need met: 78%. Among students who received aid based on merit, the average award (and the proportion receiving): $11,570 (18%). The average athletic scholarship (and the proportion receiving): $0 (0%). **Student employment:** During the 2003-2004 academic year, 10% of undergraduates worked on campus. Average per-year earnings: $1,050. **Reserve Officers Training Corps (ROTC):** Army ROTC: Offered at cooperating institution (Lehigh University).

Mount Aloysius College

7373 Admiral Peary Highway
Cresson, PA 16630
Private; www.mtaloy.edu
Financial aid office: (814) 886-6357

■ **2004-2005 TUITION AND FEES:** $14,100
■ **ROOM AND BOARD:** $5,960

SAT I Score (25th/75th percentile): 930
2005 U.S. News College Ranking:
Comp. Colleges–Bachelor's (North), 29
Acceptance Rate: 74%

....

Other expenses: Estimated books and supplies: $1,400. Personal expenses: $2,750. **Financial aid:** Priority filing date for institution's financial aid form: February 15; deadline: May 1. In 2003-2004, 98% of undergraduates applied for financial aid. Of those, 97% were determined to have financial need; Average financial aid package (proportion receiving): $9,000 (96%). Average amount of gift aid, such as scholarships or grants (proportion receiving): $2,500 (96%). Average amount of self-help aid, such as work study or loans (proportion receiving): $0 (96%). Average need-based loan (excluding PLUS or other private loans): $0. Among students who received need-based aid, the average percentage of need met: 83%. Among students who received aid based on merit, the average award (and the proportion receiving): $0 (0%). The average athletic scholarship (and the proportion receiving): $0 (0%). Average amount of

debt of borrowers graduating in 2003: $17,125. Proportion who borrowed: 90%. **Cooperative education programs:** art, business, computer science, education, health professions, humanities, natural science, social/behavioral science.

Muhlenberg College

2400 W. Chew Street
Allentown, PA 18104
Private; www.muhlenberg.edu
Financial aid office: (484) 664-3174

■ **2004-2005 TUITION AND FEES:** $26,800
■ **ROOM AND BOARD:** $7,025

SAT I Score (25th/75th percentile): 1110-1310
2005 U.S. News College Ranking:
Liberal Arts Colleges, 70
Acceptance Rate: 42%

....

Other expenses: Estimated books and supplies: $1,000. Transportation: $300. **Financial aid:** Priority filing date for institution's financial aid form: January 15; deadline: February 15. **Student employment:** During the 2003-2004 academic year, 26% of undergraduates worked on campus. Average per-year earnings: $1,800. **Reserve Officers Training Corps (ROTC):** Army ROTC: Offered at cooperating institution (Lehigh University).

Neumann College

1 Neumann Drive
Aston, PA 19014-1298
Private; www.neumann.edu
Financial aid office: (610) 558-5520

■ **2004-2005 TUITION AND FEES:** $17,190
■ **ROOM AND BOARD:** $7,740

SAT I Score (25th/75th percentile): 790-960
2005 U.S. News College Ranking:
Comp. Colleges–Bachelor's (North), 32
Acceptance Rate: 96%

....

Other expenses: Estimated books and supplies: $1,400. Transportation: $800. Personal expenses: $1,000. **Financial aid:** Priority filing date for institution's financial aid form: March 15; deadline: May 15. In 2003-2004, 93% of undergraduates applied for financial aid. Of those, 90% were determined to have financial need; 60% had their need fully met. Average financial aid package (proportion receiving): $15,000 (90%). Average amount of gift aid, such as scholarships or grants (proportion receiving): $12,000

(84%). Average amount of self-help aid, such as work study or loans (proportion receiving): $1,800 (12%). Average need-based loan (excluding PLUS or other private loans): $3,000. Among students who received need-based aid, the average percentage of need met: 60%. Average amount of debt of borrowers graduating in 2003: $18,000. Proportion who borrowed: 70%. **Student employment:** During the 2003-2004 academic year, 20% of undergraduates worked on campus. Average per-year earnings: $1,500. **Cooperative education programs:** business, computer science, education, health professions. **Reserve Officers Training Corps (ROTC):** Army ROTC: Offered at cooperating institution (Widner University).

Pennsylvania College of Technology

1 College Avenue
Williamsport, PA 17701
Public; www.pct.edu
Financial aid office: (570) 327-4766

■ **2004-2005 TUITION AND FEES:**
In state: $9,480; Out of state: $11,940
■ **ROOM AND BOARD:** $5,132

2005 U.S. News College Ranking:
Comp. Colleges–Bachelor's (North), fourth tier
Acceptance Rate: 87%
....

Cooperative education programs: health professions, technologies, vocational arts. **Reserve Officers Training Corps (ROTC):** Army ROTC: Offered at cooperating institution (Bucknell University).

Pennsylvania State–Erie, The Behrend College

5091 Station Road
Erie, PA 16563
Public; www.pennstatebehrend.psu.edu
Financial aid office: (814) 898-6162

■ **2004-2005 TUITION AND FEES:**
In state: $9,582; Out of state: $15,466

SAT I Score (25th/75th percentile): 970-1180
2005 U.S. News College Ranking:
Universities–Master's (North), 62
Acceptance Rate: 79%
....

Financial aid: Priority filing date for institution's financial aid form: February 15. In 2003-2004, 83% of undergraduates applied for finan-

cial aid. Of those, 70% were determined to have financial need; 7% had their need fully met. Average financial aid package (proportion receiving): $11,921 (69%). Average amount of gift aid, such as scholarships or grants (proportion receiving): $4,302 (49%). Average amount of self-help aid, such as work study or loans (proportion receiving): $4,194 (63%). Average need-based loan (excluding PLUS or other private loans): $3,867. Among students who received need-based aid, the average percentage of need met: 64%. Among students who received aid based on merit, the average award (and the proportion receiving): $5,861 (14%). The average athletic scholarship (and the proportion receiving): $0 (0%). Average amount of debt of borrowers graduating in 2003: $18,200. Proportion who borrowed: 70%. **Student employment:** During the 2003-2004 academic year, 16% of undergraduates worked on campus. Average per-year earnings: $1,900. **Cooperative education programs:** education. **Reserve Officers Training Corps (ROTC):** Army ROTC: Offered on campus.

Pennsylvania State University– University Park

University Park Campus
University Park, PA 16802
Public; www.psu.edu
Financial aid office: (814) 865-6301

■ **2004-2005 TUITION AND FEES:**
In state: $10,408; Out of state: $20,336

SAT I Score (25th/75th percentile): 1090-1300
2005 U.S. News College Ranking:
National Universities, 50
Acceptance Rate: 55%
....

Financial aid: Priority filing date for institution's financial aid form: February 15. In 2003-2004, 66% of undergraduates applied for financial aid. Of those, 51% were determined to have financial need; 10% had their need fully met. Average financial aid package (proportion receiving): $12,773 (50%). Average amount of gift aid, such as scholarships or grants (proportion receiving): $4,569 (30%). Average amount of self-help aid, such as work study or loans (proportion receiving): $4,465 (44%). Average need-based loan (excluding PLUS or other private loans): $4,217. Among students who received need-based aid, the average percentage of need met: 63%. Among students who received aid based on merit, the average award (and the proportion receiving): $6,212 (21%). The average athletic scholarship (and the pro-

portion receiving): $16,423 (1%). Average amount of debt of borrowers graduating in 2003: $18,200. Proportion who borrowed: 70%. **Cooperative education programs:** engineering, natural science, social/behavioral science, other. **Reserve Officers Training Corps (ROTC):** Army ROTC: Offered on campus; Navy ROTC: Offered on campus; Air Force ROTC: Offered on campus.

Philadelphia University

School House Lane and Henry Avenue
Philadelphia, PA 19144
Private; www.philau.edu
Financial aid office: (215) 951-2940

■ **2004-2005 TUITION AND FEES:** $21,000
■ **ROOM AND BOARD:** $7,782

SAT I Score (25th/75th percentile): 980-1160
2005 U.S. News College Ranking:
Universities–Master's (North), 80
Acceptance Rate: 70%
....

Other expenses: Estimated books and supplies: $1,200. Personal expenses: $2,356. **Financial aid:** Priority filing date for institution's financial aid form: April 15; deadline: April 15. In 2003-2004, 81% of undergraduates applied for financial aid. Of those, 71% were determined to have financial need; 12% had their need fully met. Average financial aid package (proportion receiving): $14,577 (71%). Average amount of gift aid, such as scholarships or grants (proportion receiving): $9,274 (67%). Average amount of self-help aid, such as work study or loans (proportion receiving): $5,416 (64%). Average need-based loan (excluding PLUS or other private loans): $4,269. Among students who received need-based aid, the average percentage of need met: 73%. Among students who received aid based on merit, the average award (and the proportion receiving): $4,016 (23%). The average athletic scholarship (and the proportion receiving): $13,139 (2%). Average amount of debt of borrowers graduating in 2003: $25,702. Proportion who borrowed: 68%. **Student employment:** During the 2003-2004 academic year, 7% of undergraduates worked on campus. Average per-year earnings: $2,000. **Cooperative education programs:** business, computer science, engineering, health professions, natural science, social/behavioral science, other.

Point Park University

201 Wood Street
Pittsburgh, PA 15222
Private; www.ppc.edu
Financial aid office: (412) 392-3930

■ **2004-2005 TUITION AND FEES:** $15,960
■ **ROOM AND BOARD:** $7,000

SAT I Score (25th/75th percentile): 920-1130
2005 U.S. News College Ranking:
Universities–Master's (North), fourth tier
Acceptance Rate: 81%

Other expenses: Estimated books and supplies: $1,000. Transportation: $1,200. Personal expenses: $1,000. **Financial aid:** Priority filing date for institution's financial aid form: May 1. In 2003-2004, 82% of undergraduates applied for financial aid. Of those, 75% were determined to have financial need; 23% had their need fully met. Average financial aid package (proportion receiving): $12,285 (75%). Average amount of gift aid, such as scholarships or grants (proportion receiving): $6,841 (74%). Average amount of self-help aid, such as work study or loans (proportion receiving): $6,059 (69%). Average need-based loan (excluding PLUS or other private loans): $4,772. Among students who received need-based aid, the average percentage of need met: 72%. Among students who received aid based on merit, the average award (and the proportion receiving): $6,706 (22%). The average athletic scholarship (and the proportion receiving): $7,890 (1%). Average amount of debt of borrowers graduating in 2003: $9,835. Proportion who borrowed: 90%. **Student employment:** During the 2003-2004 academic year, 0% of undergraduates worked on campus. Average per-year earnings: $0. **Cooperative education programs:** education. **Reserve Officers Training Corps (ROTC):** Army ROTC: Offered at cooperating institution (Duquesne University); Air Force ROTC: Offered at cooperating institution (University of Pittsburgh).

Robert Morris University

6001 University Boulevard
Moon Township, PA 15108-1189
Private; www.rmu.edu
Financial aid office: (412) 262-8545

■ **2004-2005 TUITION AND FEES:** $14,226
■ **ROOM AND BOARD:** $7,286

SAT I Score (25th/75th percentile): 890-1100
2005 U.S. News College Ranking:
Universities–Master's (North), third tier
Acceptance Rate: 91%

Other expenses: Estimated books and supplies: $1,000. Transportation: $1,000. Personal expenses: $1,500. **Financial aid:** Priority filing date for institution's financial aid form: May 1. In 2003-2004, 83% of undergraduates applied for financial aid. Of those, 74% were determined to have financial need; 21% had their need fully met. Average financial aid package (proportion receiving): $11,526 (74%). Average amount of gift aid, such as scholarships or grants (proportion receiving): $6,462 (68%). Average amount of self-help aid, such as work study or loans (proportion receiving): $6,080 (68%). Average need-based loan (excluding PLUS or other private loans): $4,977. Among students who received need-based aid, the average percentage of need met: 70%. Among students who received aid based on merit, the average award (and the proportion receiving): $7,366 (15%). The average athletic scholarship (and the proportion receiving): $9,703 (3%). **Cooperative education programs:** business, computer science, education, engineering. **Reserve Officers Training Corps (ROTC):** Army ROTC: Offered at cooperating institution (Duquesne University); Air Force ROTC: Offered at cooperating institution (University of Pittsburgh).

Rosemont College

1400 Montgomery Avenue
Rosemont, PA 19010-1699
Private; www.rosemont.edu
Financial aid office: (610) 527-0200

■ **2004-2005 TUITION AND FEES:** $19,365
■ **ROOM AND BOARD:** $8,400

SAT I Score (25th/75th percentile): 950-1220
2005 U.S. News College Ranking:
Liberal Arts Colleges, third tier
Acceptance Rate: 70%

Other expenses: Estimated books and supplies: $1,100. Transportation: $400. Personal expenses: $800. **Financial aid:** Priority filing date for institution's financial aid form: March 1; deadline: April 1. In 2003-2004, 91% of undergraduates applied for financial aid. Of those, 81% were determined to have financial need; 44% had their need fully met. Average financial aid package (proportion receiving): $14,593 (81%). Average amount of gift aid, such as scholar-

ships or grants (proportion receiving): $9,485 (72%). Average amount of self-help aid, such as work study or loans (proportion receiving): $5,244 (63%). Average need-based loan (excluding PLUS or other private loans): $4,391. Among students who received need-based aid, the average percentage of need met: 94%. Among students who received aid based on merit, the average award (and the proportion receiving): $9,210 (9%). The average athletic scholarship (and the proportion receiving): $0 (0%). Average amount of debt of borrowers graduating in 2003: $17,170. Proportion who borrowed: 70%. **Student employment:** During the 2003-2004 academic year, 47% of undergraduates worked on campus. Average per-year earnings: $2,000. **Reserve Officers Training Corps (ROTC):** Army ROTC: Offered at cooperating institution (Valley Forge Military); Navy ROTC: Offered at cooperating institution (Villanova University).

Seton Hill University

Seton Hill Drive
Greensburg, PA 15601
Private; www.setonhill.edu
Financial aid office: (724) 838-4293

■ **2004-2005 TUITION AND FEES:** $20,630
■ **ROOM AND BOARD:** $6,420

SAT I Score (25th/75th percentile): 920-1140
2005 U.S. News College Ranking:
Liberal Arts Colleges, fourth tier
Acceptance Rate: 84%

Other expenses: Estimated books and supplies: $1,000. Transportation: $200. Personal expenses: $2,400. **Financial aid:** In 2003-2004, 83% of undergraduates applied for financial aid. Of those, 80% were determined to have financial need; 19% had their need fully met. Average financial aid package (proportion receiving): $14,658 (80%). Average amount of gift aid, such as scholarships or grants (proportion receiving): $11,000 (61%). Average amount of self-help aid, such as work study or loans (proportion receiving): $4,501 (74%). Average need-based loan (excluding PLUS or other private loans): $3,449. Among students who received need-based aid, the average percentage of need met: 75%. Among students who received aid based on merit, the average award (and the proportion receiving): $7,667 (2%). The average athletic scholarship (and the proportion receiving): $16,011 (3%). Average amount of debt of borrowers graduating in 2003: $17,014. Proportion who borrowed: 67%. **Reserve**

Officers Training Corps (ROTC): Army ROTC: Offered at cooperating institution (University of Pittsburgh).

Shippensburg University of Pennsylvania

1871 Old Main Drive
Shippensburg, PA 17257-2299
Public; www.ship.edu
Financial aid office: (717) 477-1131

■ 2004-2005 TUITION AND FEES:
  In state: $5,986; Out of state: $13,252
■ ROOM AND BOARD: $5,274

SAT I Score (25th/75th percentile): 960-1150
2005 U.S. News College Ranking:
Universities–Master's (North), 45
Acceptance Rate: 67%

Financial aid: Priority filing date for institution's financial aid form: March 15. In 2003-2004, 73% of undergraduates applied for financial aid. Of those, 52% were determined to have financial need; 24% had their need fully met. Average financial aid package (proportion receiving): $5,980 (50%). Average amount of gift aid, such as scholarships or grants (proportion receiving): $3,596 (40%). Average amount of self-help aid, such as work study or loans (proportion receiving): $3,624 (43%). Average need-based loan (excluding PLUS or other private loans): $3,352. Among students who received need-based aid, the average percentage of need met: 72%. Among students who received aid based on merit, the average award (and the proportion receiving): $727 (27%). The average athletic scholarship (and the proportion receiving): $1,294 (3%). Average amount of debt of borrowers graduating in 2003: $15,464. Proportion who borrowed: 68%. Cooperative education programs: art, engineering, health professions. Reserve Officers Training Corps (ROTC): Army ROTC: Offered on campus.

Slippery Rock University of Pennsylvania

1 Morrow Way
Slippery Rock, PA 16057-1383
Public; www.sru.edu
Financial aid office: (724) 738-2044

■ 2004-2005 TUITION AND FEES:
  In state: $6,095; Out of state: $8,501
■ ROOM AND BOARD: $4,714

SAT I Score (25th/75th percentile): 890-1080
2005 U.S. News College Ranking:
Universities–Master's (North), third tier
Acceptance Rate: 81%

Financial aid: Priority filing date for institution's financial aid form: May 1. In 2003-2004, 87% of undergraduates applied for financial aid. Of those, 61% were determined to have financial need; 70% had their need fully met. Average financial aid package (proportion receiving): $6,402 (59%). Average amount of gift aid, such as scholarships or grants (proportion receiving): $2,767 (45%). Average amount of self-help aid, such as work study or loans (proportion receiving): $2,976 (52%). Average need-based loan (excluding PLUS or other private loans): $2,964. Among students who received need-based aid, the average percentage of need met: 85%. Among students who received aid based on merit, the average award (and the proportion receiving): $4,471 (21%). The average athletic scholarship (and the proportion receiving): $2,393 (3%). Average amount of debt of borrowers graduating in 2003: $19,195. Proportion who borrowed: 75%. Student employment: During the 2003-2004 academic year, 20% of undergraduates worked on campus. Average per-year earnings: $3,000. Reserve Officers Training Corps (ROTC): Army ROTC: Offered on campus.

St. Francis University

PO Box 600
Loretto, PA 15940
Private; www.francis.edu
Financial aid office: (814) 472-3010

■ 2004-2005 TUITION AND FEES: $20,440
■ ROOM AND BOARD: $7,420

SAT I Score (25th/75th percentile): 1040
2005 U.S. News College Ranking:
Universities–Master's (North), 45
Acceptance Rate: 87%

Other expenses: Estimated books and supplies: $500. Transportation: $0. Personal expenses: $1,356. Financial aid: Priority filing date for institution's financial aid form: May 1. In 2003-2004, 93% of undergraduates applied for financial aid. Of those, 85% were determined to have financial need; 32% had their need fully met. Average financial aid package (proportion receiving): $17,128 (85%). Average amount of gift aid, such as scholarships or grants (proportion receiving): $12,421 (85%). Average amount of self-help aid, such as work study or loans

(proportion receiving): $5,348 (75%). Average need-based loan (excluding PLUS or other private loans): $4,531. Among students who received need-based aid, the average percentage of need met: 82%. Among students who received aid based on merit, the average award (and the proportion receiving): $9,562 (12%). The average athletic scholarship (and the proportion receiving): $8,394 (9%). Average amount of debt of borrowers graduating in 2003: $14,100. Proportion who borrowed: 90%. Reserve Officers Training Corps (ROTC): Army ROTC: Offered at cooperating institution (Penn State Altoona, Indiana University of Pennsylvania).

St. Joseph's University

5600 City Avenue
Philadelphia, PA 19131
Private; www.sju.edu
Financial aid office: (610) 660-1556

■ 2004-2005 TUITION AND FEES: $25,905
■ ROOM AND BOARD: $9,610

SAT I Score (25th/75th percentile): 1040-1230
2005 U.S. News College Ranking:
Universities–Master's (North), 10
Acceptance Rate: 48%

Other expenses: Estimated books and supplies: $1,250. Transportation: $0. Personal expenses: $2,500. Financial aid: Priority filing date for institution's financial aid form: February 15; deadline: May 1. In 2003-2004, 71% of undergraduates applied for financial aid. Of those, 59% were determined to have financial need; 41% had their need fully met. Average financial aid package (proportion receiving): $13,845 (59%). Average amount of gift aid, such as scholarships or grants (proportion receiving): $7,605 (49%). Average amount of self-help aid, such as work study or loans (proportion receiving): $6,240 (59%). Average need-based loan (excluding PLUS or other private loans): $4,890. Among students who received need-based aid, the average percentage of need met: 80%. Among students who received aid based on merit, the average award (and the proportion receiving): $6,580 (20%). The average athletic scholarship (and the proportion receiving): $11,471 (7%). Average amount of debt of borrowers graduating in 2003: $15,734. Proportion who borrowed: 68%. Student employment: During the 2003-2004 academic year, 3% of undergraduates worked on campus. Cooperative education programs: business. Reserve Officers Training Corps (ROTC): Army ROTC: Offered at cooperating institution

(University of Pennsylvania, Temple University, Drexel University); Navy ROTC: Offered at cooperating institution (Villanova University, University of Pennsylvania); Air Force ROTC: Offered on campus.

St. Vincent College

300 Fraser Purchase Road
Latrobe, PA 15650-2690
Private; www.stvincent.edu
Financial aid office: (724) 537-4540

■ **2004-2005 TUITION AND FEES:** $20,822
■ **ROOM AND BOARD:** $6,424

SAT I Score (25th/75th percentile): 973-1180
2005 U.S. News College Ranking:
Liberal Arts Colleges, third tier
Acceptance Rate: 75%

Other expenses: Estimated books and supplies: $500. Personal expenses: $1,000. **Financial aid:** Priority filing date for institution's financial aid form: March 1; deadline: May 1. In 2003-2004, 98% of undergraduates applied for financial aid. Of those, 79% were determined to have financial need; 19% had their need fully met. Average financial aid package (proportion receiving): $15,577 (79%). Average amount of gift aid, such as scholarships or grants (proportion receiving): $10,699 (79%). Average amount of self-help aid, such as work study or loans (proportion receiving): $5,133 (62%). Average need-based loan (excluding PLUS or other private loans): $3,273. Among students who received need-based aid, the average percentage of need met: 87%. Among students who received aid based on merit, the average award (and the proportion receiving): $5,915 (18%). The average athletic scholarship (and the proportion receiving): $4,403 (22%). **Student employment:** During the 2003-2004 academic year, 41% of undergraduates worked on campus. Average per-year earnings: $825. **Reserve Officers Training Corps (ROTC):** Air Force ROTC: Offered at cooperating institution (University of Pittsburgh).

Susquehanna University

514 University Avenue
Selinsgrove, PA 17870
Private; www.susqu.edu
Financial aid office: (570) 372-4450

■ **2004-2005 TUITION AND FEES:** $24,810
■ **ROOM AND BOARD:** $6,840

SAT I Score (25th/75th percentile): 1060-1230
2005 U.S. News College Ranking:
Liberal Arts Colleges, third tier
Acceptance Rate: 70%

Other expenses: Estimated books and supplies: $700. Transportation: $210. Personal expenses: $700. **Financial aid:** Priority filing date for institution's financial aid form: March 1; deadline: May 1. In 2003-2004, 75% of undergraduates applied for financial aid. Of those, 65% were determined to have financial need; 23% had their need fully met. Average financial aid package (proportion receiving): $17,158 (65%). Average amount of gift aid, such as scholarships or grants (proportion receiving): $13,319 (64%). Average amount of self-help aid, such as work study or loans (proportion receiving): $4,734 (55%). Average need-based loan (excluding PLUS or other private loans): $3,703. Among students who received need-based aid, the average percentage of need met: 82%. Among students who received aid based on merit, the average award (and the proportion receiving): $8,142 (24%). The average athletic scholarship (and the proportion receiving): $0 (0%). Average amount of debt of borrowers graduating in 2003: $16,756. Proportion who borrowed: 81%. **Student employment:** During the 2003-2004 academic year, 22% of undergraduates worked on campus. Average per-year earnings: $1,500. **Reserve Officers Training Corps (ROTC):** Army ROTC: Offered at cooperating institution (Bucknell University).

Swarthmore College

500 College Avenue
Swarthmore, PA 19081
Private; www.swarthmore.edu
Financial aid office: (610) 328-8358

■ **2004-2005 TUITION AND FEES:** $30,094
■ **ROOM AND BOARD:** $9,314

SAT I Score (25th/75th percentile): 1340-1530
2005 U.S. News College Ranking:
Liberal Arts Colleges, 2
Acceptance Rate: 24%

Other expenses: Estimated books and supplies: $982. Transportation: $400. Personal expenses: $962. **Financial aid:** Priority filing date for institution's financial aid form: February 15; deadline: February 15. In 2003-2004, 55% of undergraduates applied for financial aid. Of those, 49% were determined to have financial need; 100% had their need fully met. Average financial aid package (proportion receiving):

$26,088 (49%). Average amount of gift aid, such as scholarships or grants (proportion receiving): $22,251 (49%). Average amount of self-help aid, such as work study or loans (proportion receiving): $4,039 (46%). Average need-based loan (excluding PLUS or other private loans): $3,141. Among students who received need-based aid, the average percentage of need met: 100%. Among students who received aid based on merit, the average award (and the proportion receiving): $28,500 (1%). The average athletic scholarship (and the proportion receiving): $0 (0%). Average amount of debt of borrowers graduating in 2003: $13,533. Proportion who borrowed: 31%. **Student employment:** During the 2003-2004 academic year, 80% of undergraduates worked on campus. Average per-year earnings: $1,520. **Reserve Officers Training Corps (ROTC):** Army ROTC: Offered at cooperating institution (Widener University); Navy ROTC: Offered at cooperating institution (University of Pennsylvania); Air Force ROTC: Offered at cooperating institution (St. Joseph's University).

Temple University

1801 N. Broad Street
Philadelphia, PA 19122-6096
Public; www.temple.edu
Financial aid office: (215) 204-8760

■ **2004-2005 TUITION AND FEES:**
In state: $9,102; Out of state: $16,268
■ **ROOM AND BOARD:** $7,522

SAT I Score (25th/75th percentile): 980-1180
2005 U.S. News College Ranking:
National Universities, third tier
Acceptance Rate: 60%

Financial aid: Priority filing date for institution's financial aid form: March 1. In 2003-2004, 90% of undergraduates applied for financial aid. Of those, 67% were determined to have financial need; 33% had their need fully met. Average financial aid package (proportion receiving): $12,453 (67%). Average amount of gift aid, such as scholarships or grants (proportion receiving): $4,687 (67%). Average amount of self-help aid, such as work study or loans (proportion receiving): $3,596 (58%). Average need-based loan (excluding PLUS or other private loans): $3,602. Among students who received need-based aid, the average percentage of need met: 86%. Among students who received aid based on merit, the average award (and the proportion receiving): $3,676 (20%). The average athletic scholarship (and the proportion receiving): $13,290 (1%). Average amount of debt of borrowers graduating in 2003: $22,041. Proportion who borrowed: 69%. **Student employment:** During the 2003-2004 academic year, 14% of undergraduates worked on campus. Average per-year earnings: $1,194. **Cooperative education programs:** business. **Reserve Officers Training Corps (ROTC):** Army ROTC: Offered on campus; Navy ROTC: Offered at cooperating institution (University of Pennsylvania); Air Force ROTC: Offered at cooperating institution (Saint Joseph's University).

Thiel College

75 College Avenue
Greenville, PA 16125
Private; www.thiel.edu
Financial aid office: (724) 589-2178

■ **2004-2005 TUITION AND FEES:** $16,526
■ **ROOM AND BOARD:** $6,554

SAT I Score (25th/75th percentile): 850-1080
2005 U.S. News College Ranking:
Comp. Colleges–Bachelor's (North), 24
Acceptance Rate: 76%

Other expenses: Estimated books and supplies: $700. Transportation: $825. Personal expenses: $1,930. **Financial aid:** Priority filing date for institution's financial aid form: March 1. In 2003-2004, 96% of undergraduates applied for financial aid. Of those, 86% were determined to have financial need; 21% had their need fully met. Average financial aid package (proportion receiving): $13,200 (86%). Average amount of gift aid, such as scholarships or grants (proportion receiving): $8,920 (86%). Average amount of self-help aid, such as work study or loans (proportion receiving): $4,258 (86%). Average need-based loan (excluding PLUS or other private loans): $3,648. Among students who received need-based aid, the average percentage of need met: 81%. Among students who received aid based on merit, the average award (and the proportion receiving): $3,845 (14%). The average athletic scholarship (and the proportion receiving): $0 (0%). Average amount of debt of borrowers graduating in 2003: $19,394. Proportion who borrowed: 84%. **Student employment:** During the 2003-2004 academic year, 45% of undergraduates worked on campus. Average per-year earnings: $1,225. **Cooperative education programs:** art, business, computer science, humanities, natural science, social/behavioral science.

University of Pennsylvania

3451 Walnut Street
Philadelphia, PA 19104
Private; www.upenn.edu
Financial aid office: (215) 898-1988

■ **2004-2005 TUITION AND FEES:** $30,716
■ **ROOM AND BOARD:** $8,918

SAT I Score (25th/75th percentile): 1330-1510
2005 U.S. News College Ranking:
National Universities, 4
Acceptance Rate: 20%

Other expenses: Estimated books and supplies: $830. Transportation: $500. Personal expenses: $1,636. **Financial aid:** Priority filing date for institution's financial aid form: February 15. In 2003-2004, 52% of undergraduates applied for financial aid. Of those, 46% were determined to have financial need; 100% had their need fully met. Average financial aid package (proportion receiving): $26,029 (46%). Average amount of gift aid, such as scholarships or grants (proportion receiving): $20,707 (42%). Average amount of self-help aid, such as work study or loans (proportion receiving): $6,815 (46%). Average need-based loan (excluding PLUS or other private loans): $4,163. Among students who received need-based aid, the average percentage of need met: 100%. Average amount of debt of borrowers graduating in 2003: $19,579. Proportion who borrowed: 43%. **Student employment:** During the 2003-2004 academic year, 36% of undergraduates worked on campus. Average per-year earnings: $1,656. **Reserve Officers Training Corps (ROTC):** Army ROTC: Offered on campus; Navy ROTC: Offered on campus; Air Force ROTC: Offered at cooperating institution (St. Joseph's University).

University of Pittsburgh

4200 Fifth Avenue
Pittsburgh, PA 15260
Public; www.pitt.edu
Financial aid office: (412) 624-7488

■ **2004-2005 TUITION AND FEES:**
   In state: $9,830; Out of state: $19,700
■ **ROOM AND BOARD:** $7,090

SAT I Score (25th/75th percentile): 1120-1310
2005 U.S. News College Ranking:
National Universities, 66
Acceptance Rate: 48%

Financial aid: Priority filing date for institution's financial aid form: March 1. In 2003-2004, 70% of undergraduates applied for financial aid. Of those, 57% were determined to have financial need; 40% had their need fully met. Average financial aid package (proportion receiving): $10,003 (56%). Average amount of gift aid, such as scholarships or grants (proportion receiving): $5,183 (38%). Average amount of self-help aid, such as work study or loans (proportion receiving): $5,290 (53%). Average need-based loan (excluding PLUS or other private loans): $4,641. Among students who received need-based aid, the average percentage of need met: 77%. Among students who received aid based on merit, the average award (and the proportion receiving): $7,188 (12%). The average athletic scholarship (and the proportion receiving): $14,752 (2%). Average amount of debt of borrowers graduating in 2003: $20,154. Proportion who borrowed: 60%. Average per-year earnings: $6,200. **Cooperative education programs:** engineering. **Reserve Officers Training Corps (ROTC):** Army ROTC: Offered on campus; Navy ROTC: Offered at cooperating institution (Carnegie Mellon University); Air Force ROTC: Offered on campus.

University of Pittsburgh– Bradford

300 Campus Drive
Bradford, PA 16701
Public; www.upb.pitt.edu
Financial aid office: (814) 362-7550

■ **2004-2005 TUITION AND FEES:**
   In state: $9,867; Out of state: $19,652
■ **ROOM AND BOARD:** $6,344

SAT I Score (25th/75th percentile): 900-1120
2005 U.S. News College Ranking:
Liberal Arts Colleges, fourth tier
Acceptance Rate: 82%

Other expenses: Estimated books and supplies: $800. Transportation: $800. Personal expenses: $800. **Financial aid:** Priority filing date for institution's financial aid form: March 1. In 2003-2004, 94% of undergraduates applied for financial aid. Of those, 80% were determined to have financial need; Average financial aid package (proportion receiving): N/A (80%). Average amount of gift aid, such as scholarships or grants (proportion receiving): N/A (62%). Average amount of self-help aid, such as work study or loans (proportion receiving): N/A (73%). Average amount of debt of borrowers graduating in 2003: $17,502. Proportion who borrowed: 74%. **Student employment:** During the 2003-2004 academic year, 1% of undergraduates worked on campus. Average per-year earnings: $3,584. **Reserve Officers Training Corps (ROTC):** Army ROTC: Offered at cooperating institution (St. Bonaventure University).

University of Pittsburgh–Greensburg

1150 Mt. Pleasant Road
Greensburg, PA 15601
Public; www.upg.pitt.edu
Financial aid office: (724) 836-9881

■ **2004-2005 TUITION AND FEES:**
  In state: $9,960; Out of state: $19,830
■ **ROOM AND BOARD:** $6,480

SAT I Score (25th/75th percentile): 970-1150
2005 U.S. News College Ranking:
Liberal Arts Colleges, fourth tier
Acceptance Rate: 89%

Financial aid: Priority filing date for institution's financial aid form: March 1; deadline: May 1. In 2003-2004, 87% of undergraduates applied for financial aid. Of those, 78% were determined to have financial need; Average financial aid package (proportion receiving): $10,815 (78%). Average amount of gift aid, such as scholarships or grants (proportion receiving): $6,315 (48%). Average amount of self-help aid, such as work study or loans (proportion receiving): N/A (70%). Average need-based loan (excluding PLUS or other private loans): $5,500. Among students who received need-based aid, the average percentage of need met: 70%. Among students who received aid based on merit, the average award (and the proportion receiving): $2,500 (2%). The average athletic scholarship (and the proportion receiving): $0 (0%). Average amount of debt of borrowers graduating in 2003: $17,125. Proportion who borrowed: 85%. **Student employment:** During the 2003-2004 academic year, 5% of undergraduates worked on campus. Average per-year earnings: $2,250. **Reserve Officers Training Corps (ROTC):** Army ROTC: Offered at cooperating institution (University of Pittsburgh, Oakland); Air Force ROTC: Offered at cooperating institution (University of Pittsburgh, Oakland).

University of Pittsburgh–Johnstown

450 Schoolhouse Road
Johnstown, PA 15904
Public; www.upj.pitt.edu
Financial aid office: (814) 269-7045

■ **2004-2005 TUITION AND FEES:**
  In state: $9,732; Out of state: $19,602
■ **ROOM AND BOARD:** $6,050

SAT I Score (25th/75th percentile): 940-1120
2005 U.S. News College Ranking:
Comp. Colleges–Bachelor's (North), third tier
Acceptance Rate: 84%

Other expenses: Estimated books and supplies: $800. Transportation: $1,250. Personal expenses: $1,100. **Financial aid:** Priority filing date for institution's financial aid form: April 1. In 2003-2004, 94% of undergraduates applied for financial aid. Of those, 76% were determined to have financial need; 15% had their need fully met. Average financial aid package (proportion receiving): $7,406 (73%). Average amount of gift aid, such as scholarships or grants (proportion receiving): $4,065 (57%). Average amount of self-help aid, such as work study or loans (proportion receiving): $3,985 (63%). Average need-based loan (excluding PLUS or other private loans): $3,618. Among students who received need-based aid, the average percentage of need met: 56%. Among students who received aid based on merit, the average award (and the proportion receiving): $2,806 (2%). The average athletic scholarship (and the proportion receiving): $6,581 (2%). Average amount of debt of borrowers graduating in 2003: $17,952. Proportion who borrowed: 81%. **Student employment:** During the 2003-2004 academic year, 8% of undergraduates worked on campus. Average per-year earnings: $1,719. **Cooperative education programs:** engineering.

University of Scranton

800 Linden Street
Scranton, PA 18510-4694
Private; www.scranton.edu
Financial aid office: (570) 941-7700

■ **2004-2005 TUITION AND FEES:** $22,474
■ **ROOM AND BOARD:** $9,524

SAT I Score (25th/75th percentile): 1030-1210
2005 U.S. News College Ranking:
Universities–Master's (North), 6
Acceptance Rate: 75%

Other expenses: Estimated books and supplies: $900. Transportation: $450. Personal expenses: $1,100. **Financial aid:** Priority filing date for institution's financial aid form: February 15. In 2003-2004, 77% of undergraduates applied for financial aid. Of those, 67% were determined to have financial need; 14% had their need fully met. Average financial aid package (proportion receiving): $14,666 (66%). Average amount of gift aid, such as scholarships or grants (proportion receiving): $10,625 (64%). Average amount of self-help aid, such as work study or loans (proportion receiving): $4,725 (56%). Average need-based loan (excluding PLUS or other private loans): $4,073. Among students who received need-based aid, the average percentage of need met: 72%. Among students who received aid based on merit, the average award (and the proportion receiving): $8,085 (5%). The average athletic scholarship (and the proportion receiving): $0 (0%). Average amount of debt of borrowers graduating in 2003: $15,800. Proportion who borrowed: 63%. **Student employment:** During the 2003-2004 academic year, 17% of undergraduates worked on campus. Average per-year earnings: $1,200. **Reserve Officers Training Corps (ROTC):** Army ROTC: Offered on campus; Air Force ROTC: Offered at cooperating institution (Wilkes University).

University of the Arts

320 S. Broad Street
Philadelphia, PA 19102
Private; www.uarts.edu
Financial aid office: (215) 717-6170

■ **2004-2005 TUITION AND FEES:** $22,910
■ **ROOM AND BOARD:** $7,800

SAT I Score (25th/75th percentile): 910-1140
2005 U.S. News College Ranking:
Unranked Specialty School–Fine Arts
Acceptance Rate: 51%

Other expenses: Estimated books and supplies: $2,000. Personal expenses: $2,190. **Financial aid:** Priority filing date for institution's financial aid form: March 1; deadline: March 1. In 2003-2004, 98% of undergraduates applied for financial aid. Of those, 90% were determined to have financial need; 40% had their need fully met. Average financial aid package (proportion receiving): $16,500 (90%). Average amount of gift aid, such as scholarships or grants (proportion receiving): $6,000 (40%). Average amount of self-help aid, such as work study or loans (proportion receiving): $4,800 (90%). Average need-based loan (excluding PLUS or other private loans): $4,500. Among students who received need-based aid, the average percentage of need met: 65%. Among students who received aid based on merit, the average award (and the proportion receiving): $7,400 (20%). **Student employment:** During the 2003-2004 academic year, 0% of undergraduates worked on campus.

Ursinus College

Box 1000
Collegeville, PA 19426
Private; www.ursinus.edu
Financial aid office: (610) 409-3600

■ **2004-2005 TUITION AND FEES:** $29,780
■ **ROOM AND BOARD:** $7,150

SAT I Score (25th/75th percentile): 1110-1320
2005 U.S. News College Ranking:
Liberal Arts Colleges, 70
Acceptance Rate: 74%

Other expenses: Estimated books and supplies: $600. Transportation: $200. Personal expenses: $900. **Financial aid:** In 2003-2004, 96% of undergraduates applied for financial aid. Of those, 96% were determined to have financial need; 53% had their need fully met. Average financial aid package (proportion receiving): $22,129 (96%). Average amount of gift aid, such as scholarships or grants (proportion receiving): $15,874 (77%). Average amount of self-help aid, such as work study or loans (proportion receiving): $6,255 (96%). Average need-based loan (excluding PLUS or other private loans): $5,155. Among students who received need-based aid, the average percentage of need met: 90%. Among students who received aid based on merit, the average award (and the proportion receiving): $11,500 (8%). The average athletic scholarship (and the proportion receiving): $0 (0%). Average amount of debt of borrowers graduating in 2003: $18,000. Proportion who borrowed: 78%. **Student employment:** During the 2003-2004 academic year, 44% of undergraduates worked on campus. Average per-year earnings: $2,600.

Villanova University

800 Lancaster Avenue
Villanova, PA 19085
Private; www.villanova.edu
Financial aid office: (610) 519-4010

■ **2004-2005 TUITION AND FEES:** $27,635
■ **ROOM AND BOARD:** $9,050

SAT I Score (25th/75th percentile): 1170-1330
2005 U.S. News College Ranking:
Universities–Master's (North), 1
Acceptance Rate: 53%

Other expenses: Estimated books and supplies: $950. Transportation: $600. Personal expenses: $900. **Financial aid:** In 2003-2004, 57% of undergraduates applied for financial aid. Of those, 47% were determined to have financial need; 14% had their need fully met. Average financial aid package (proportion receiving): $18,217 (46%). Average amount of gift aid, such as scholarships or grants (proportion receiving): $14,296 (38%). Average amount of self-help aid, such as work study or loans (proportion receiving): $5,743 (40%). Average need-based loan (excluding PLUS or other private loans): $4,778. Among students who received need-based aid, the average percentage of need met: 76%. Among students who received aid based on merit, the average award (and the proportion receiving): $10,338 (5%). The average athletic scholarship (and the proportion receiving): $28,461 (2%). Average amount of debt of borrowers graduating in 2003: $30,015. Proportion who borrowed: 56%. **Student employment:** During the 2003-2004 academic year, 17% of undergraduates worked on campus. Average per-year earnings: $1,500. **Reserve Officers Training Corps (ROTC):** Army ROTC: Offered on campus; Navy ROTC: Offered on campus; Air Force ROTC: Offered at cooperating institution (St. Joseph's University).

Washington and Jefferson College

60 S. Lincoln Street
Washington, PA 15301
Private; www.washjeff.edu
Financial aid office: (724) 223-6019

■ **2004-2005 TUITION AND FEES:** $24,620
■ **ROOM AND BOARD:** $6,710

SAT I Score (25th/75th percentile): 1030-1240
2005 U.S. News College Ranking:
Liberal Arts Colleges, 83
Acceptance Rate: 40%

Other expenses: Estimated books and supplies: $600. Transportation: $195. Personal expenses: $700. **Financial aid:** Priority filing date for institution's financial aid form: February 15. In 2003-2004, 83% of undergraduates applied for financial aid. Of those, 76% were determined to have financial need; 17% had their need fully met. Average financial aid package (proportion receiving): $15,658 (75%). Average amount of gift aid, such as scholarships or grants (proportion receiving): $9,984 (75%). Average amount of self-help aid, such as work study or loans (proportion receiving): $4,425 (49%). Average need-based loan (excluding PLUS or other private loans): $3,875. Among students who received need-based aid, the average percentage of need met: 72%. Among students who received aid based on merit, the average award (and the proportion receiving): $8,025 (18%). The average athletic scholarship (and the proportion receiving): $0 (0%). Average amount of debt of borrowers graduating in 2003: $16,384. Proportion who borrowed: 74%. **Student employment:** During the 2003-2004 academic year, 44% of undergraduates worked on campus. Average per-year earnings: $1,200. **Reserve Officers Training Corps (ROTC):** Army ROTC: Offered at cooperating institution (University of Pittsburgh); Air Force ROTC: Offered at cooperating institution (University of Pittsburgh).

Waynesburg College

51 W. College Street
Waynesburg, PA 15370
Private; www.waynesburg.edu
Financial aid office: (724) 852-3208

■ **2004-2005 TUITION AND FEES:** $14,540
■ **ROOM AND BOARD:** $5,800

2005 U.S. News College Ranking:
Universities–Master's (North), third tier
Acceptance Rate: 78%

Other expenses: Estimated books and supplies: $1,000. Transportation: $500. Personal expenses: $660. **Financial aid:** Priority filing date for institution's financial aid form: March 15. In 2003-2004, 92% of undergraduates applied for financial aid. Of those, 87% were determined to have financial need; 35% had their need fully met. Average financial aid package (proportion receiving): $11,000 (87%). Average amount of

gift aid, such as scholarships or grants (proportion receiving): $7,500 (82%). Average amount of self-help aid, such as work study or loans (proportion receiving): $4,400 (82%). Average need-based loan (excluding PLUS or other private loans): $4,200. Among students who received need-based aid, the average percentage of need met: 85%. Among students who received aid based on merit, the average award (and the proportion receiving): $4,200 (4%). The average athletic scholarship (and the proportion receiving): $0 (0%). Average amount of debt of borrowers graduating in 2003: $20,000. Proportion who borrowed: 88%.
Student employment: During the 2003-2004 academic year, 15% of undergraduates worked on campus. Average per-year earnings: $1,250.
Reserve Officers Training Corps (ROTC): Army ROTC: Offered at cooperating institution (West Virginia University).

West Chester University of Pennsylvania

West Chester, PA 19383
Public; www.wcupa.edu
Financial aid office: (610) 436-2627

■ **2004-2005 TUITION AND FEES:**
  In state: $4,810; Out of state: $12,026
■ **ROOM AND BOARD:** $5,932

SAT I Score (25th/75th percentile): 980-1150
2005 U.S. News College Ranking:
Universities–Master's (North), 68
Acceptance Rate: 46%

Financial aid: Priority filing date for institution's financial aid form: March 1. Average amount of debt of borrowers graduating in 2003: $17,500. Proportion who borrowed: 59%.
Student employment: During the 2003-2004 academic year, 12% of undergraduates worked on campus. **Cooperative education programs:** art, business, computer science, education, engineering, health professions, humanities, natural science, social/behavioral science.
Reserve Officers Training Corps (ROTC): Army ROTC: Offered at cooperating institution (Widener University); Air Force ROTC: Offered at cooperating institution (St. Joseph University).

Westminster College

South Market Street
New Wilmington, PA 16172
Private; www.westminster.edu
Financial aid office: (724) 946-7102

■ **2004-2005 TUITION AND FEES:** $21,470
■ **ROOM AND BOARD:** $6,360

SAT I Score (25th/75th percentile): 980-1200
2005 U.S. News College Ranking:
Liberal Arts Colleges, third tier
Acceptance Rate: 77%

Other expenses: Estimated books and supplies: $1,700. **Financial aid:** Priority filing date for institution's financial aid form: May 1. In 2003-2004, 87% of undergraduates applied for financial aid. Of those, 80% were determined to have financial need; 37% had their need fully met. Average financial aid package (proportion receiving): $17,237 (80%). Average amount of gift aid, such as scholarships or grants (proportion receiving): $7,719 (69%). Average amount of self-help aid, such as work study or loans (proportion receiving): $4,444 (64%). Average need-based loan (excluding PLUS or other private loans): $3,972. Among students who received need-based aid, the average percentage of need met: 90%. Among students who received aid based on merit, the average award (and the proportion receiving): $7,990 (18%). The average athletic scholarship (and the proportion receiving): $0 (0%). Average amount of debt of borrowers graduating in 2003: $16,353. Proportion who borrowed: 79%. **Student employment:** During the 2003-2004 academic year, 21% of undergraduates worked on campus. **Reserve Officers Training Corps (ROTC):** Army ROTC: Offered at cooperating institution (Youngstown State University).

Widener University

1 University Place
Chester, PA 19013
Private; www.widener.edu
Financial aid office: (610) 499-4174

■ **2004-2005 TUITION AND FEES:** $23,000
■ **ROOM AND BOARD:** $8,100

SAT I Score (25th/75th percentile): 890-1120
2005 U.S. News College Ranking:
National Universities, third tier
Acceptance Rate: 77%

Other expenses: Estimated books and supplies: $840. Transportation: $180. Personal expenses: $990. **Financial aid:** Priority filing date for institution's financial aid form: February 15; deadline: April 1. In 2003-2004, 83% of undergraduates applied for financial aid. Of those, 81% were determined to have financial need; 30% had their need fully met. Average financial aid package (proportion receiving): $18,668 (81%). Average amount of gift aid, such as scholarships or grants (proportion receiving): $11,379 (69%). Average amount of self-help aid, such as work study or loans (proportion receiving): $7,289 (69%). Average need-based loan (excluding PLUS or other private loans): $5,781. Among students who received need-based aid, the average percentage of need met: 91%. Among students who received aid based on merit, the average award (and the proportion receiving): $8,117 (13%). The average athletic scholarship (and the proportion receiving): $0 (0%). Average amount of debt of borrowers graduating in 2003: $18,465. Proportion who borrowed: 76%.
Student employment: During the 2003-2004 academic year, 40% of undergraduates worked on campus. Average per-year earnings: $2,500.
Cooperative education programs: business, computer science, engineering, other. **Reserve Officers Training Corps (ROTC):** Army ROTC: Offered on campus; Air Force ROTC: Offered at cooperating institution (St. Joseph's University).

Wilkes University

PO Box 111
Wilkes-Barre, PA 18766
Private; www.wilkes.edu
Financial aid office: (570) 408-4346

■ **2004-2005 TUITION AND FEES:** $20,408
■ **ROOM AND BOARD:** $8,924

SAT I Score (25th/75th percentile): 970-1210
2005 U.S. News College Ranking:
Universities–Master's (North), 73
Acceptance Rate: 81%

Other expenses: Estimated books and supplies: $900. Transportation: $500. Personal expenses: $900. **Financial aid:** Priority filing date for institution's financial aid form: March 1. In 2003-2004, 93% of undergraduates applied for financial aid. Of those, 85% were determined to have financial need; 28% had their need fully met. Average financial aid package (proportion receiving): $15,863 (85%). Average amount of gift aid, such as scholarships or grants (proportion receiving): $11,152 (82%). Average amount of self-help aid, such as work study or loans (proportion receiving): $5,101 (74%). Average need-based loan (excluding PLUS or other private loans): $4,008. Among students who received need-based aid, the average percentage of need met: 83%. Among students who received aid based on merit, the average award (and the proportion receiving): $7,916 (10%). The average athletic scholarship (and the proportion receiving): $0 (0%). Average amount of debt of borrowers graduating in 2003: $19,467. Proportion who borrowed: 82%. **Student employment:** During the 2003-2004 academic year, 36% of undergraduates worked on campus. Average per-year earnings: $700. **Reserve Officers Training Corps (ROTC):** Army ROTC: Offered at cooperating institution (King's College, University of Scranton); Air Force ROTC: Offered on campus.

Wilson College

1015 Philadelphia Avenue
Chambersburg, PA 17201
Private; www.wilson.edu
Financial aid office: (717) 262-2016

■ **2004-2005 TUITION AND FEES:** $18,407
■ **ROOM AND BOARD:** $7,308

SAT I Score (25th/75th percentile): 900-1160
2005 U.S. News College Ranking:
Comp. Colleges–Bachelor's (North), 18
Acceptance Rate: 67%

....

Other expenses: Estimated books and supplies: $800. Transportation: $400. Personal expenses: $800. **Financial aid:** Priority filing date for institution's financial aid form: April 30. In 2003-2004, 80% of undergraduates applied for financial aid. Of those, 71% were determined to have financial need; 17% had their need fully met. Average financial aid package (proportion receiving): $14,228 (71%). Average amount of gift aid, such as scholarships or grants (proportion receiving): $11,876 (71%). Average amount of self-help aid, such as work study or loans (proportion receiving): $4,123 (63%). Average need-based loan (excluding PLUS or other private loans): $3,797. Among students who received need-based aid, the average percentage of need met: 80%. Among students who received aid based on merit, the average award (and the proportion receiving): $14,243 (24%). The average athletic scholarship (and the pro-

portion receiving): $0 (0%). Average amount of debt of borrowers graduating in 2003: $15,609. Proportion who borrowed: 73%. **Student employment:** During the 2003-2004 academic year, 3% of undergraduates worked on campus. Average per-year earnings: $2,250.

York College of Pennsylvania

Country Club Road
York, PA 17405-7199
Private; www.ycp.edu
Financial aid office: (717) 849-1682

■ **2004-2005 TUITION AND FEES:** $9,184
■ **ROOM AND BOARD:** $6,250

SAT I Score (25th/75th percentile): 1050-1200
2005 U.S. News College Ranking:
Universities–Master's (North), 73
Acceptance Rate: 74%

....

Other expenses: Estimated books and supplies: $800. Transportation: $500. Personal expenses: $1,000. **Financial aid:** Priority filing date for institution's financial aid form: February 15. In 2003-2004, 74% of undergraduates applied for financial aid. Of those, 51% were determined to have financial need; 25% had their need fully met. Average financial aid package (proportion receiving): $6,717 (50%). Average amount of gift aid, such as scholarships or grants (proportion receiving): $3,727 (36%). Average amount of self-help aid, such as work study or loans (proportion receiving): $3,871 (46%). Average need-based loan (excluding PLUS or other private loans): $3,666. Among students who received need-based aid, the average percentage of need met: 73%. Among students who received aid based on merit, the average award (and the proportion receiving): $2,794 (8%). The average athletic scholarship (and the proportion receiving): $0 (0%). Average amount of debt of borrowers graduating in 2003: $15,913. Proportion who borrowed: 73%. **Student employment:** During the 2003-2004 academic year, 15% of undergraduates worked on campus. Average per-year earnings: $1,600. **Cooperative education programs:** education, engineering, health professions. **Reserve Officers Training Corps (ROTC):** Army ROTC: Offered at cooperating institution (Johns Hopkins University, Dickinson University).

Rhode Island

Brown University

Box 1920
Providence, RI 02912
Private; www.brown.edu
Financial aid office: (401) 863-2721

- **2004-2005 TUITION AND FEES:** $31,334
- **ROOM AND BOARD:** $8,474

SAT I Score (25th/75th percentile): 1290-1500
2005 U.S. News College Ranking:
National Universities, 13
Acceptance Rate: 16%

Other expenses: Estimated books and supplies: $1,040. Transportation: $300. Personal expenses: $1,352. **Financial aid:** In 2003-2004, 49% of undergraduates applied for financial aid. Of those, 43% were determined to have financial need; 98% had their need fully met. Average financial aid package (proportion receiving): $24,402 (43%). Average amount of gift aid, such as scholarships or grants (proportion receiving): $19,877 (41%). Average amount of self-help aid, such as work study or loans (proportion receiving): $5,714 (39%). Average need-based loan (excluding PLUS or other private loans): $4,642. Among students who received need-based aid, the average percentage of need met: 100%. Average amount of debt of borrowers graduating in 2003: $16,040. Proportion who borrowed: 36%. **Student employment:** During the 2003-2004 academic year, 43% of undergraduates worked on campus. **Reserve Officers Training Corps (ROTC):** Army ROTC: Offered at cooperating institution (Providence College).

Bryant College

1150 Douglas Pike
Smithfield, RI 02917
Private; www.bryant.edu
Financial aid office: (401) 232-6020

- **2004-2005 TUITION AND FEES:** $23,580
- **ROOM AND BOARD:** $8,974

SAT I Score (25th/75th percentile): 1010-1170
2005 U.S. News College Ranking:
Universities–Master's (North), 20
Acceptance Rate: 59%

Other expenses: Estimated books and supplies: $900. Transportation: $200. Personal expenses: $1,000. **Financial aid:** Priority filing date for institution's financial aid form: February 15. In 2003-2004, 74% of undergraduates applied for financial aid. Of those, 65% were determined to have financial need; 13% had their need fully met. Average financial aid package (proportion receiving): $14,521 (65%). Average amount of gift aid, such as scholarships or grants (proportion receiving): $6,654 (44%). Average amount of self-help aid, such as work study or loans (proportion receiving): $5,270 (58%). Average need-based loan (excluding PLUS or other private loans): $4,713. Among students who received need-based aid, the average percentage of need met: 73%. Among students who received aid based on merit, the average award (and the proportion receiving): $7,247 (47%). The average athletic scholarship (and the proportion receiving): $15,995 (2%). Average amount of debt of borrowers graduating in 2003: $22,909. Proportion who borrowed: 69%. **Student employment:** During the 2003-2004 academic year, 19% of undergraduates worked on campus. Average per-year earnings: $1,400. **Reserve Officers Training Corps (ROTC):** Army ROTC: Offered on campus.

Johnson and Wales University

8 Abbott Park Place
Providence, RI 02903-3703
Private; www.jwu.edu
Financial aid office: (401) 598-1468

- **2004-2005 TUITION AND FEES:** $17,460
- **ROOM AND BOARD:** $7,185

SAT I Score (25th/75th percentile): 810-1040
2005 U.S. News College Ranking:
Universities–Master's (North), third tier
Acceptance Rate: 85%

Other expenses: Estimated books and supplies: $825. Transportation: $750. Personal expenses: $639. **Financial aid:** In 2003-2004, 75% of undergraduates applied for financial aid. Of those, 66% were determined to have financial need; 69% had their need fully met. Average financial aid package (proportion receiving): $11,459 (64%). Average amount of gift aid, such as scholarships or grants (proportion receiving): $4,065 (49%). Average amount of

self-help aid, such as work study or loans (proportion receiving): $6,244 (59%). Average need-based loan (excluding PLUS or other private loans): $5,250. Among students who received need-based aid, the average percentage of need met: 69%. Among students who received aid based on merit, the average award (and the proportion receiving): $3,239 (4%). Average amount of debt of borrowers graduating in 2003: $20,268. Proportion who borrowed: 76%. **Student employment:** During the 2003-2004 academic year, 10% of undergraduates worked on campus. Average per-year earnings: $5,000. **Cooperative education programs:** business, computer science, technologies, other. **Reserve Officers Training Corps (ROTC):** Army ROTC: Offered at cooperating institution (Providence College).

Providence College

549 River Avenue
Providence, RI 02918
Private; www.providence.edu
Financial aid office: (401) 865-2286

- **2004-2005 TUITION AND FEES:** $23,639
- **ROOM AND BOARD:** $8,895

SAT I Score (25th/75th percentile): 1110-1300
2005 U.S. News College Ranking:
Universities–Master's (North), 2
Acceptance Rate: 53%

Other expenses: Estimated books and supplies: $650. Transportation: $200. Personal expenses: $1,250. **Financial aid:** In 2003-2004, 66% of undergraduates applied for financial aid. Of those, 50% were determined to have financial need; 19% had their need fully met. Average financial aid package (proportion receiving): $14,600 (50%). Average amount of gift aid, such as scholarships or grants (proportion receiving): $8,900 (49%). Average amount of self-help aid, such as work study or loans (proportion receiving): $5,400 (48%). Average need-based loan (excluding PLUS or other private loans): $4,833. Among students who received need-based aid, the average percentage of need met: 85%. Among students who received aid based on merit, the average award (and the proportion receiving): $10,500 (10%). The average athletic scholarship (and the proportion receiving): $19,660 (4%). Average amount of debt of borrowers graduating in 2003: $22,500. Proportion who borrowed: 65%. **Student employment:** During the 2003-2004 academic year, 19% of undergraduates worked on campus. Average per-year earnings: $1,800. **Reserve Officers Training Corps (ROTC):** Army ROTC: Offered on campus.

Rhode Island College

600 Mount Pleasant Avenue
Providence, RI 02908
Public; www.ric.edu
Financial aid office: (401) 456-8033

■ **2004-2005 TUITION AND FEES:**
   In state: $4,270; Out of state: $10,910
■ **ROOM AND BOARD:** $6,650

SAT I Score (25th/75th percentile): 890-1090
2005 U.S. News College Ranking:
Universities–Master's (North), third tier
Acceptance Rate: 73%

Other expenses: Estimated books and supplies: $750. Transportation: $400. Personal expenses: $1,000. **Financial aid:** Priority filing date for institution's financial aid form: March 1. **Reserve Officers Training Corps (ROTC):** Army ROTC: Offered at cooperating institution (Providence College).

Rhode Island School of Design

2 College Street
Providence, RI 02903
Private; www.risd.edu
Financial aid office: (401) 454-6636

■ **2004-2005 TUITION AND FEES:** $27,975
■ **ROOM AND BOARD:** $7,720

SAT I Score (25th/75th percentile): 1090-1310
2005 U.S. News College Ranking:
Unranked Specialty School–Fine Arts
Acceptance Rate: 35%

Other expenses: Estimated books and supplies: $2,200. Transportation: $700. Personal expenses: $1,905. **Financial aid:** In 2003-2004, 59% of undergraduates applied for financial aid. Of those, 48% were determined to have financial need; 9% had their need fully met. Average financial aid package (proportion receiving): $15,300 (47%). Average amount of gift aid, such as scholarships or grants (proportion receiving): $9,200 (42%). Average amount of self-help aid, such as work study or loans (pro-

portion receiving): $6,900 (47%). Average need-based loan (excluding PLUS or other private loans): $5,600. Among students who received need-based aid, the average percentage of need met: 69%. Among students who received aid based on merit, the average award (and the proportion receiving): $1,250 (2%). The average athletic scholarship (and the proportion receiving): $0 (0%). Average amount of debt of borrowers graduating in 2003: $22,700. Proportion who borrowed: 56%. **Student employment:** During the 2003-2004 academic year, 65% of undergraduates worked on campus. Average per-year earnings: $1,700.

Roger Williams University

1 Old Ferry Road
Bristol, RI 02809
Private; www.rwu.edu
Financial aid office: (401) 254-3100

■ **2004-2005 TUITION AND FEES:** $21,778
■ **ROOM AND BOARD:** $9,600

SAT I Score (25th/75th percentile): 980-1160
2005 U.S. News College Ranking:
Comp. Colleges–Bachelor's (North), 14
Acceptance Rate: 80%

Other expenses: Estimated books and supplies: $700. Transportation: $560. Personal expenses: $515. **Financial aid:** Priority filing date for institution's financial aid form: February 1. In 2003-2004, 81% of undergraduates applied for financial aid. Of those, 69% were determined to have financial need; 68% had their need fully met. Average financial aid package (proportion receiving): $14,500 (69%). Average amount of gift aid, such as scholarships or grants (proportion receiving): $8,300 (65%). Average amount of self-help aid, such as work study or loans (proportion receiving): $6,200 (71%). Average need-based loan (excluding PLUS or other private loans): $4,200. Among students who received need-based aid, the average percentage of need met: 87%. Among students who received aid based on merit, the average award (and the proportion receiving): $6,000 (8%). The average athletic scholarship (and the proportion receiving): $0 (0%). Average amount of debt of borrowers graduating in 2003: $17,125. Proportion who borrowed: 70%. **Student employment:** During the 2003-2004 academic year, 9% of undergraduates worked on campus. Average per-year earnings: $1,000. **Cooperative education programs:** business, computer science, education, humanities, natural science, social/behavioral science. **Reserve Officers**

Training Corps (ROTC): Army ROTC: Offered on campus.

Salve Regina University

100 Ochre Point Avenue
Newport, RI 02840-4192
Private; www.salve.edu
Financial aid office: (401) 341-2901

■ **2004-2005 TUITION AND FEES:** $22,200
■ **ROOM AND BOARD:** $9,000

SAT I Score (25th/75th percentile): 990-1140
2005 U.S. News College Ranking:
Universities–Master's (North), 38
Acceptance Rate: 55%

Other expenses: Estimated books and supplies: $800. Transportation: $700. Personal expenses: $1,000. **Financial aid:** Priority filing date for institution's financial aid form: March 1. In 2003-2004, 76% of undergraduates applied for financial aid. Of those, 67% were determined to have financial need; Average financial aid package (proportion receiving): $15,618 (67%). Average amount of gift aid, such as scholarships or grants (proportion receiving): $10,505 (62%). Average amount of self-help aid, such as work study or loans (proportion receiving): $6,243 (64%). Average need-based loan (excluding PLUS or other private loans): $5,079. Among students who received need-based aid, the average percentage of need met: 73%. Among students who received aid based on merit, the average award (and the proportion receiving): $9,688 (14%). The average athletic scholarship (and the proportion receiving): $0 (0%). Average amount of debt of borrowers graduating in 2003: $19,840. Proportion who borrowed: 77%. **Student employment:** During the 2003-2004 academic year, 28% of undergraduates worked on campus. Average per-year earnings: $1,200. **Reserve Officers Training Corps (ROTC):** Army ROTC: Offered at cooperating institution (University of Rhode Island).

University of Rhode Island

Admission
Kingston, RI 02881
Public; www.uri.edu
Financial aid office: (401) 874-9500

■ **2004-2005 TUITION AND FEES:**
   In state: $6,752; Out of state: $18,338
■ **ROOM AND BOARD:** $7,810

SAT I Score (25th/75th percentile): 1010-1200
2005 U.S. News College Ranking:
National Universities, third tier
Acceptance Rate: 70%

....

Financial aid: Priority filing date for institution's financial aid form: March 1. In 2003-2004, 83% of undergraduates applied for financial aid. Of those, 70% were determined to have financial need; 45% had their need fully met. Average financial aid package (proportion receiving): $9,430 (51%). Average amount of gift aid, such as scholarships or grants (proportion receiving): $5,501 (51%). Average amount of self-help aid, such as work study or loans (proportion receiving): $4,810 (46%). Average need-based loan (excluding PLUS or other private loans): $4,862. Among students who received need-based aid, the average percentage of need met: 56%. Among students who received aid based on merit, the average award (and the proportion receiving): $4,543 (4%). The average athletic scholarship (and the proportion receiving): $3,441 (0%). Average amount of debt of borrowers graduating in 2003: $14,500. Proportion who borrowed: 58%. **Cooperative education programs:** health professions. **Reserve Officers Training Corps (ROTC):** Army ROTC: Offered on campus.

South Carolina

Allen University

1530 Harden Street
Columbia, SC 29204
Private; www.allenuniversity.edu
Financial aid office: (803) 376-5736

- **2004-2005 TUITION AND FEES:** $7,518
- **ROOM AND BOARD:** $4,210

2005 U.S. News College Ranking:
Comp. Colleges–Bachelor's (South), fourth tier
Acceptance Rate: 61%

Other expenses: Estimated books and supplies: $800. Transportation: $1,000. Personal expenses: $1,100. **Financial aid:** Priority filing date for institution's financial aid form: April 15. In 2003-2004, 100% of undergraduates applied for financial aid. Of those, 100% were determined to have financial need; 10% had their need fully met. Average financial aid package (proportion receiving): $8,081 (80%). Average amount of gift aid, such as scholarships or grants (proportion receiving): $2,213 (80%). Average amount of self-help aid, such as work study or loans (proportion receiving): $1,000 (11%). Average need-based loan (excluding PLUS or other private loans): $4,833. Among students who received need-based aid, the average percentage of need met: 74%. Among students who received aid based on merit, the average award (and the proportion receiving): $3,609 (1%). The average athletic scholarship (and the proportion receiving): $1,039 (7%). Average amount of debt of borrowers graduating in 2003: $13,037. Proportion who borrowed: 78%.

Anderson College

316 Boulevard
Anderson, SC 29621
Private; www.ac.edu
Financial aid office: (864) 231-2070

- **2004-2005 TUITION AND FEES:** $14,225
- **ROOM AND BOARD:** $5,766

SAT I Score (25th/75th percentile): 930-1140
2005 U.S. News College Ranking:
Comp. Colleges–Bachelor's (South), third tier
Acceptance Rate: 79%

Other expenses: Estimated books and supplies: $1,500. Transportation: $1,890. Personal expenses: $2,163. **Financial aid:** Priority filing date for institution's financial aid form: March 1; deadline: July 30. In 2003-2004, 93% of undergraduates applied for financial aid. Of those, 84% were determined to have financial need; 35% had their need fully met. Average financial aid package (proportion receiving): $13,694 (84%). Average amount of gift aid, such as scholarships or grants (proportion receiving): $6,760 (82%). Average amount of self-help aid, such as work study or loans (proportion receiving): $1,752 (51%). Average need-based loan (excluding PLUS or other private loans): $4,242. Among students who received need-based aid, the average percentage of need met: 79%. Among students who received aid based on merit, the average award (and the proportion receiving): $5,333 (6%). The average athletic scholarship (and the proportion receiving): $3,572 (2%). Average amount of debt of borrowers graduating in 2003: $14,874. Proportion who borrowed: 76%. **Student employment:** During the 2003-2004 academic year, 33% of undergraduates worked on campus. Average per-year earnings: $1,670. **Reserve Officers Training Corps (ROTC):** Army ROTC: Offered at cooperating institution (Clemson University); Air Force ROTC: Offered at cooperating institution (Clemson University).

Benedict College

1600 Harden Street
Columbia, SC 29204
Private; www.benedict.edu
Financial aid office: (803) 253-5105

- **2004-2005 TUITION AND FEES:** $12,256
- **ROOM AND BOARD:** $5,674

SAT I Score (25th/75th percentile): 680-900
2005 U.S. News College Ranking:
Comp. Colleges–Bachelor's (South), third tier
Acceptance Rate: 72%

Other expenses: Estimated books and supplies: $1,300. Transportation: $600. Personal expenses: $600. **Financial aid:** In 2003-2004, 100% of undergraduates applied for financial aid. Of those, 100% were determined to have financial need; Average financial aid package (proportion receiving): $11,000 (96%). Average amount of

gift aid, such as scholarships or grants (proportion receiving): N/A (96%). Average amount of self-help aid, such as work study or loans (proportion receiving): N/A (96%). Among students who received need-based aid, the average percentage of need met: 95%. Average amount of debt of borrowers graduating in 2003: $21,950. Proportion who borrowed: 92%. **Cooperative education programs:** business, computer science, education, engineering. **Reserve Officers Training Corps (ROTC):** Army ROTC: Offered on campus; Air Force ROTC: Offered at cooperating institution (University of South Carolina).

Charleston Southern University

PO Box 118087, 9200 University Boulevard
Charleston, SC 29423
Private; www.csuniv.edu
Financial aid office: (843) 863-7050

- **2004-2005 TUITION AND FEES:** $15,292
- **ROOM AND BOARD:** $5,878

SAT I Score (25th/75th percentile): 930-1130
2005 U.S. News College Ranking:
Universities–Master's (South), third tier
Acceptance Rate: 80%

Other expenses: Estimated books and supplies: $1,070. Personal expenses: $1,360. **Financial aid:** Priority filing date for institution's financial aid form: April 15. In 2003-2004, 88% of undergraduates applied for financial aid. Of those, 80% were determined to have financial need; 21% had their need fully met. Average financial aid package (proportion receiving): $12,546 (80%). Average amount of gift aid, such as scholarships or grants (proportion receiving): $8,731 (79%). Average amount of self-help aid, such as work study or loans (proportion receiving): $4,876 (63%). Average need-based loan (excluding PLUS or other private loans): $4,179. Among students who received need-based aid, the average percentage of need met: 71%. Among students who received aid based on merit, the average award (and the proportion receiving): $9,723 (14%). The average athletic scholarship (and the proportion receiving): $7,845 (6%). **Student employment:** During the 2003-2004 academic year, 12% of undergraduates worked on campus. Average per-year earnings: $2,000. **Cooperative education programs:** engineering. **Reserve Officers Training Corps (ROTC):** Air Force ROTC: Offered on campus.

The Citadel

171 Moultrie Street
Charleston, SC 29409
Public; www.citadel.edu
Financial aid office: (843) 953-5187

■ **2004-2005 TUITION AND FEES:**
In state: $6,828; Out of state: $15,446
■ **ROOM AND BOARD:** $4,684

SAT I Score (25th/75th percentile): 1003-1210
2005 U.S. News College Ranking:
Universities–Master's (South), 8
Acceptance Rate: 67%

Other expenses: Estimated books and supplies: $1,620. Transportation: $1,101. Personal expenses: $1,493. **Financial aid:** Priority filing date for institution's financial aid form: February 28; deadline: February 28. In 2003-2004, 61% of undergraduates applied for financial aid. Of those, 46% were determined to have financial need; 20% had their need fully met. Average financial aid package (proportion receiving): $8,136 (45%). Average amount of gift aid, such as scholarships or grants (proportion receiving): $7,734 (34%). Average amount of self-help aid, such as work study or loans (proportion receiving): $3,643 (27%). Average need-based loan (excluding PLUS or other private loans): $3,643. Among students who received need-based aid, the average percentage of need met: 78%. Among students who received aid based on merit, the average award (and the proportion receiving): $4,681 (19%). The average athletic scholarship (and the proportion receiving): $10,004 (10%). Average amount of debt of borrowers graduating in 2003: $14,396. Proportion who borrowed: 62%. **Reserve Officers Training Corps (ROTC):** Army ROTC: Offered on campus; Navy ROTC: Offered on campus; Air Force ROTC: Offered on campus.

Claflin University

400 Magnolia Street
Orangeburg, SC 29115
Private; www.claflin.edu
Financial aid office: (803) 535-5334

■ **2004-2005 TUITION AND FEES:** $10,452
■ **ROOM AND BOARD:** $5,752

SAT I Score (25th/75th percentile): 845-1110
2005 U.S. News College Ranking:
Comp. Colleges–Bachelor's (South), 9
Acceptance Rate: 40%

Other expenses: Estimated books and supplies: $1,200. Transportation: $1,800. Personal expenses: $1,200. **Financial aid:** Priority filing date for institution's financial aid form: June 1; deadline: June 1. In 2003-2004, 98% of undergraduates applied for financial aid. Of those, 95% were determined to have financial need; Average financial aid package (proportion receiving): $14,000 (95%). Average amount of gift aid, such as scholarships or grants (proportion receiving): $9,780 (94%). Average amount of self-help aid, such as work study or loans (proportion receiving): $10,050 (82%). Average need-based loan (excluding PLUS or other private loans): $3,500. Average amount of debt of borrowers graduating in 2003: $19,680. Proportion who borrowed: 93%. **Student employment:** During the 2003-2004 academic year, 10% of undergraduates worked on campus. Average per-year earnings: $1,500. **Cooperative education programs:** engineering, health professions. **Reserve Officers Training Corps (ROTC):** Army ROTC: Offered at cooperating institution (SCSU).

Clemson University

105 Sikes Hall
Clemson, SC 29634
Public; www.clemson.edu
Financial aid office: (864) 656-2280

■ **2004-2005 TUITION AND FEES:**
In state: $8,012; Out of state: $15,610
■ **ROOM AND BOARD:** $5,292

SAT I Score (25th/75th percentile): 1120-1290
2005 U.S. News College Ranking:
National Universities, 74
Acceptance Rate: 61%

Other expenses: Estimated books and supplies: $798. Transportation: $2,234. Personal expenses: $1,704. **Financial aid:** Priority filing date for institution's financial aid form: April 1. In 2003-2004, 53% of undergraduates applied for financial aid. Of those, 40% were determined to have financial need; 28% had their need fully met. Average financial aid package (proportion receiving): $8,669 (39%). Average amount of gift aid, such as scholarships or grants (proportion receiving): $3,301 (18%). Average amount of self-help aid, such as work study or loans (proportion receiving): $4,523 (26%). Average

need-based loan (excluding PLUS or other private loans): $4,126. Among students who received need-based aid, the average percentage of need met: 69%. Among students who received aid based on merit, the average award (and the proportion receiving): $6,598 (33%). The average athletic scholarship (and the proportion receiving): $11,996 (3%). Average amount of debt of borrowers graduating in 2003: $15,125. Proportion who borrowed: 42%. **Student employment:** During the 2003-2004 academic year, 30% of undergraduates worked on campus. Average per-year earnings: $2,400. **Cooperative education programs:** agriculture, art, business, computer science, education, engineering, health professions, home economics, humanities, natural science, social/behavioral science, technologies, vocational arts. **Reserve Officers Training Corps (ROTC):** Army ROTC: Offered on campus; Air Force ROTC: Offered on campus.

Coastal Carolina University

PO Box 261954
Conway, SC 29528-6054
Public; www.coastal.edu
Financial aid office: (843) 349-2313

■ **2004-2005 TUITION AND FEES:**
In state: $6,100; Out of state: $14,200
■ **ROOM AND BOARD:** $5,970

SAT I Score (25th/75th percentile): 940-1130
2005 U.S. News College Ranking:
Liberal Arts Colleges, fourth tier
Acceptance Rate: 71%

Other expenses: Estimated books and supplies: $840. Transportation: $1,664. Personal expenses: $1,196. **Financial aid:** Priority filing date for institution's financial aid form: April 1. In 2003-2004, 75% of undergraduates applied for financial aid. Of those, 64% were determined to have financial need; 38% had their need fully met. Average financial aid package (proportion receiving): $7,381 (64%). Average amount of gift aid, such as scholarships or grants (proportion receiving): $3,187 (25%). Average amount of self-help aid, such as work study or loans (proportion receiving): $6,676 (43%). Average need-based loan (excluding PLUS or other private loans): $6,605. Among students who received need-based aid, the average percentage of need met: 62%. Among students who received aid based on merit, the average award (and the proportion receiving): $6,260 (24%). The average athletic scholarship (and the proportion receiving): $5,101 (5%). Average amount of debt of borrowers graduating in 2003: $18,975. Proportion who borrowed: 60%. **Student employment:** During the 2003-2004 academic year, 12% of undergraduates worked on campus. Average per-year earnings: $2,000. **Cooperative education programs:** business, computer science, education, humanities, natural science, social/behavioral science, technologies.

Coker College

300 E. College Avenue
Hartsville, SC 29550
Private; www.coker.edu
Financial aid office: (843) 383-8055

■ **2004-2005 TUITION AND FEES:** $16,800
■ **ROOM AND BOARD:** $5,326

SAT I Score (25th/75th percentile): 880-1090
2005 U.S. News College Ranking:
Comp. Colleges–Bachelor's (South), 13
Acceptance Rate: 61%

Other expenses: Estimated books and supplies: $1,000. Personal expenses: $650. **Financial aid:** Priority filing date for institution's financial aid form: April 1; deadline: June 1. In 2003-2004, 92% of undergraduates applied for financial aid. Of those, 84% were determined to have financial need; 40% had their need fully met. Average financial aid package (proportion receiving): $16,531 (84%). Average amount of gift aid, such as scholarships or grants (proportion receiving): $5,885 (79%). Average amount of self-help aid, such as work study or loans (proportion receiving): $4,281 (67%). Average need-based loan (excluding PLUS or other private loans): $3,775. Among students who received need-based aid, the average percentage of need met: 97%. Among students who received aid based on merit, the average award (and the proportion receiving): $5,269 (16%). The average athletic scholarship (and the proportion receiving): $5,597 (9%). Average amount of debt of borrowers graduating in 2003: $17,093. Proportion who borrowed: 84%. **Student employment:** During the 2003-2004 academic year, 1% of undergraduates worked on campus. Average per-year earnings: $800. **Cooperative education programs:** health professions.

College of Charleston

66 George Street
Charleston, SC 29424-0001
Public; www.cofc.edu
Financial aid office: (843) 953-5540

■ **2004-2005 TUITION AND FEES:**
    In state: $6,202; Out of state: $14,140
■ **ROOM AND BOARD:** $6,506

SAT I Score (25th/75th percentile): 1120-1280
2005 U.S. News College Ranking:
Universities–Master's (South), 11
Acceptance Rate: 60%

Financial aid: Priority filing date for institution's financial aid form: March 15. In 2003-2004, 51% of undergraduates applied for financial aid. Of those, 39% were determined to have financial need; 25% had their need fully met. Average financial aid package (proportion receiving): $8,696 (38%). Average amount of gift aid, such as scholarships or grants (proportion receiving): $2,854 (24%). Average amount of self-help aid, such as work study or loans (proportion receiving): $3,435 (32%). Average need-based loan (excluding PLUS or other private loans): $3,500. Among students who received need-based aid, the average percentage of need met: 63%. Among students who received aid based on merit, the average award (and the proportion receiving): $10,338 (8%). The average athletic scholarship (and the proportion receiving): $11,231 (2%). Average amount of debt of borrowers graduating in 2003: $16,626. Proportion who borrowed: 51%. **Student employment:** During the 2003-2004 academic year, 25% of undergraduates worked on campus. Average per-year earnings: $6,500. **Reserve Officers Training Corps (ROTC):** Air Force ROTC: Offered at cooperating institution (Charleston Southern University).

Columbia College

1301 Columbia College Drive
Columbia, SC 29203
Private; www.columbiacollegesc.edu
Financial aid office: (803) 786-3612

■ **2004-2005 TUITION AND FEES:** $17,990
■ **ROOM AND BOARD:** $5,619

SAT I Score (25th/75th percentile): 850-1060
2005 U.S. News College Ranking:
Comp. Colleges–Bachelor's (South), 16
Acceptance Rate: 86%

Other expenses: Estimated books and supplies: $800. Transportation: $1,250. Personal expenses: $2,150. **Financial aid:** Priority filing date for institution's financial aid form: March 15. In 2003-2004, 94% of undergraduates applied for financial aid. Of those, 93% were determined to have financial need; 68% had their need fully met. Average financial aid package (proportion receiving): $18,516 (93%). Average amount of gift aid, such as scholarships or grants (proportion receiving): $6,167 (95%). Average amount of self-help aid, such as work study or loans (proportion receiving): $4,427 (85%). Average need-based loan (excluding PLUS or other private loans): $4,427. Among students who received need-based aid, the average percentage of need met: 92%. Among students who received aid based on merit, the average award (and the proportion receiving): $6,458 (6%). The average athletic scholarship (and the proportion receiving): $2,500 (3%). Average amount of debt of borrowers graduating in 2003: $19,741. Proportion who borrowed: 88%. **Student employment:** During the 2003-2004 academic year, 6% of undergraduates worked on campus. Average per-year earnings: $1,000. **Reserve Officers Training Corps (ROTC):** Army ROTC: Offered at cooperating institution (University of South Carolina).

Converse College

580 E. Main Street
Spartanburg, SC 29302
Private; www.converse.edu
Financial aid office: (864) 596-9019

■ **2004-2005 TUITION AND FEES:** $19,960
■ **ROOM AND BOARD:** $6,110

SAT I Score (25th/75th percentile): 980-1210
2005 U.S. News College Ranking:
Universities–Master's (South), 17
Acceptance Rate: 69%

Other expenses: Estimated books and supplies: $750. Transportation: $500. Personal expenses: $1,350. **Financial aid:** Priority filing date for institution's financial aid form: March 1. In 2003-2004, 78% of undergraduates applied for financial aid. Of those, 70% were determined to have financial need; 41% had their need fully met. Average financial aid package (proportion receiving): $16,521 (70%). Average amount of gift aid, such as scholarships or grants (proportion receiving): $13,836 (69%). Average amount of self-help aid, such as work study or loans (proportion receiving): $4,547 (45%). Average need-based loan (excluding PLUS or other private loans): $4,120. Among students who received need-based aid, the average percentage of need met: 88%. Among students who received aid based on merit, the average award (and the proportion receiving): $16,158 (26%). The average athletic scholarship (and the proportion receiving): $7,205 (4%). Average amount of debt of borrowers graduating in 2003: $18,036. Proportion who borrowed: 52%. **Student employment:** During the 2003-2004 academic year, 5% of undergraduates worked on campus. **Reserve Officers Training Corps (ROTC):** Army ROTC: Offered at cooperating institution (Wofford).

Erskine College

2 Washington Street
Due West, SC 29639
Private; www.erskine.edu
Financial aid office: (864) 379-8832

■ **2004-2005 TUITION AND FEES:** $18,128
■ **ROOM AND BOARD:** $6,026

SAT I Score (25th/75th percentile): 1005-1243
2005 U.S. News College Ranking:
Liberal Arts Colleges, third tier
Acceptance Rate: 70%

Other expenses: Estimated books and supplies: $800. Transportation: $1,200. **Financial aid:** Priority filing date for institution's financial aid form: April 1. In 2003-2004, 95% of undergraduates applied for financial aid. Of those, 78% were determined to have financial need; 31% had their need fully met. Average financial aid package (proportion receiving): $16,500 (78%). Average amount of gift aid, such as scholarships or grants (proportion receiving): $8,456 (78%). Average amount of self-help aid, such as work study or loans (proportion receiving): $3,250 (78%). Average need-based loan (excluding PLUS or other private loans): $3,250. Among students who received need-based aid, the average percentage of need met: 84%. Among students who received aid based on merit, the average award (and the proportion receiving): $8,550 (18%). The average athletic scholarship (and the proportion receiving): $4,120 (22%). Average amount of debt of borrowers graduating in 2003: $10,000. Proportion who borrowed: 68%. **Student employment:** During the 2003-2004 academic

year, 11% of undergraduates worked on campus. Average per-year earnings: $1,000.

Francis Marion University

PO Box 100547
Florence, SC 29501
Public; www.fmarion.edu
Financial aid office: (843) 661-1190

■ **2004-2005 TUITION AND FEES:**
In state: $5,540; Out of state: $10,945
■ **ROOM AND BOARD:** $4,656

SAT I Score (25th/75th percentile): 860-1050
2005 U.S. News College Ranking:
Universities–Master's (South), third tier
Acceptance Rate: 76%

Other expenses: Estimated books and supplies: $781. Transportation: $1,292. Personal expenses: $2,098. **Financial aid:** Priority filing date for institution's financial aid form: March 1; deadline: June 30. In 2003-2004, 65% of undergraduates applied for financial aid. Of those, 56% were determined to have financial need; Average amount of debt of borrowers graduating in 2003: $18,841. **Student employment:** During the 2003-2004 academic year, 20% of undergraduates worked on campus. **Cooperative education programs:** engineering, natural science, other. **Reserve Officers Training Corps (ROTC):** Army ROTC: Offered on campus.

Furman University

3300 Poinsett Highway
Greenville, SC 29613
Private; www.engagefurman.com
Financial aid office: (864) 294-2204

■ **2004-2005 TUITION AND FEES:** $24,408
■ **ROOM AND BOARD:** $6,272

SAT I Score (25th/75th percentile): 1190-1370
2005 U.S. News College Ranking:
Liberal Arts Colleges, 38
Acceptance Rate: 60%

Other expenses: Estimated books and supplies: $750. Transportation: $950. Personal expenses: $689. **Financial aid:** In 2003-2004, 53% of undergraduates applied for financial aid. Of those, 43% were determined to have financial need; 43% had their need fully met. Average financial aid package (proportion receiving): $19,647 (43%). Average amount of gift aid,

such as scholarships or grants (proportion receiving): $16,061 (43%). Average amount of self-help aid, such as work study or loans (proportion receiving): $3,586 (27%). Average need-based loan (excluding PLUS or other private loans): $2,934. Among students who received need-based aid, the average percentage of need met: 87%. Among students who received aid based on merit, the average award (and the proportion receiving): $10,875 (24%). The average athletic scholarship (and the proportion receiving): $22,175 (8%). Average amount of debt of borrowers graduating in 2003: $19,170. Proportion who borrowed: 31%. **Student employment:** During the 2003-2004 academic year, 25% of undergraduates worked on campus. Average per-year earnings: $1,250. **Reserve Officers Training Corps (ROTC):** Army ROTC: Offered on campus.

Lander University

320 Stanley Avenue
Greenwood, SC 29649-2099
Public; www.lander.edu
Financial aid office: (864) 388-8340

■ **2004-2005 TUITION AND FEES:**
In state: $5,628; Out of state: $11,537
■ **ROOM AND BOARD:** $5,294

SAT I Score (25th/75th percentile): 900-1090
2005 U.S. News College Ranking:
Universities–Master's (South), third tier
Acceptance Rate: 81%

Financial aid: Priority filing date for institution's financial aid form: April 15. **Student employment:** During the 2003-2004 academic year, 20% of undergraduates worked on campus. Average per-year earnings: $1,000. **Cooperative education programs:** art, business, computer science, education, health professions, humanities, natural science, social/behavioral science. **Reserve Officers Training Corps (ROTC):** Army ROTC: Offered on campus.

Limestone College

1115 College Drive
Gaffney, SC 29340-3799
Private; www.limestone.edu
Financial aid office: (864) 488-4567

■ **2004-2005 TUITION AND FEES:** $13,200
■ **ROOM AND BOARD:** $5,400

SAT I Score (25th/75th percentile): 830-1050
2005 U.S. News College Ranking:
Comp. Colleges–Bachelor's (South), fourth tier
Acceptance Rate: 60%

···

Other expenses: Estimated books and supplies: $1,315. Transportation: $1,400. Personal expenses: $1,560. **Financial aid:** Priority filing date for institution's financial aid form: February 1. In 2003-2004, 97% of undergraduates applied for financial aid. Of those, 84% were determined to have financial need; 19% had their need fully met. Average financial aid package (proportion receiving): $9,350 (84%). Average amount of gift aid, such as scholarships or grants (proportion receiving): $6,404 (82%). Average amount of self-help aid, such as work study or loans (proportion receiving): $3,952 (67%). Average need-based loan (excluding PLUS or other private loans): $3,464. Among students who received need-based aid, the average percentage of need met: 60%. Among students who received aid based on merit, the average award (and the proportion receiving): $8,689 (14%). The average athletic scholarship (and the proportion receiving): $3,742 (11%). Average amount of debt of borrowers graduating in 2003: $9,500. Proportion who borrowed: 86%. **Student employment:** During the 2003-2004 academic year, 7% of undergraduates worked on campus. Average per-year earnings: $1,251. **Reserve Officers Training Corps (ROTC):** Army ROTC: Offered at cooperating institution (Wofford College).

Morris College

100 W. College Street
Sumter, SC 29150
Private; www.morris.edu
Financial aid office: (803) 934-3238

■ **2004-2005 TUITION AND FEES:** $7,785
■ **ROOM AND BOARD:** $3,724

2005 U.S. News College Ranking:
Comp. Colleges–Bachelor's (South), fourth tier
Acceptance Rate: 94%

···

Other expenses: Estimated books and supplies: $1,200. Transportation: $1,200. Personal expenses: $1,200. **Financial aid:** Priority filing date for institution's financial aid form: March 30. In 2003-2004, 99% of undergraduates applied for financial aid. Of those, 99% were determined to have financial need; 5% had their need fully met. Average financial aid package (proportion receiving): $11,000 (99%). Average amount of gift aid, such as scholarships or grants (proportion receiving): $1,500.

(99%). Average amount of self-help aid, such as work study or loans (proportion receiving): $5,200 (99%). Average need-based loan (excluding PLUS or other private loans): $3,500. Among students who received need-based aid, the average percentage of need met: 83%. Among students who received aid based on merit, the average award (and the proportion receiving): $0 (0%). The average athletic scholarship (and the proportion receiving): $0 (0%). Average amount of debt of borrowers graduating in 2003: $15,000. Proportion who borrowed: 99%. **Cooperative education programs:** business, health professions, humanities, natural science, social/behavioral science. **Reserve Officers Training Corps (ROTC):** Army ROTC: Offered on campus.

Newberry College

2100 College Street
Newberry, SC 29108
Private; www.newberry.edu
Financial aid office: (803) 321-5120

■ **2004-2005 TUITION AND FEES:** $17,470
■ **ROOM AND BOARD:** $5,890

SAT I Score (25th/75th percentile): 820-1090
2005 U.S. News College Ranking:
Comp. Colleges–Bachelor's (South), 43
Acceptance Rate: 58%

···

Student employment: During the 2003-2004 academic year, 8% of undergraduates worked on campus. Average per-year earnings: $500. **Cooperative education programs:** engineering, health professions, other. **Reserve Officers Training Corps (ROTC):** Army ROTC: Offered at cooperating institution (Presbyterian College).

North Greenville College

PO Box 1892
Tigerville, SC 29688
Private; www.ngc.edu
Financial aid office: (864) 977-7058

■ **2004-2005 TUITION AND FEES:** $9,760
■ **ROOM AND BOARD:** $5,550

SAT I Score (25th/75th percentile): 930-1150
2005 U.S. News College Ranking:
Comp. Colleges–Bachelor's (South), third tier
Acceptance Rate: 95%

···

Other expenses: Estimated books and supplies: $1,000. Transportation: $2,000. Personal

expenses: $2,690. **Financial aid:** In 2003-2004, 96% of undergraduates applied for financial aid. Of those, 67% were determined to have financial need; 40% had their need fully met. Average financial aid package (proportion receiving): $10,000 (67%). Average amount of gift aid, such as scholarships or grants (proportion receiving): $4,000 (64%). Average amount of self-help aid, such as work study or loans (proportion receiving): $5,000 (21%). Average need-based loan (excluding PLUS or other private loans): $1,000. Among students who received need-based aid, the average percentage of need met: 60%. Among students who received aid based on merit, the average award (and the proportion receiving): $5,000 (33%). The average athletic scholarship (and the proportion receiving): $2,000 (27%). Average amount of debt of borrowers graduating in 2003: $12,000. **Student employment:** During the 2003-2004 academic year, 0% of undergraduates worked on campus. Average per-year earnings: $0. **Reserve Officers Training Corps (ROTC):** Army ROTC: Offered at cooperating institution (Furman University).

Presbyterian College

503 S. Broad Street
Clinton, SC 29325
Private; www.presby.edu
Financial aid office: (864) 833-8289

■ **2004-2005 TUITION AND FEES:** $21,622
■ **ROOM AND BOARD:** $6,808

SAT I Score (25th/75th percentile): 1040-1240
2005 U.S. News College Ranking:
Liberal Arts Colleges, 89
Acceptance Rate: 78%

···

Other expenses: Estimated books and supplies: $1,039. Transportation: $1,301. Personal expenses: $2,597. **Financial aid:** Priority filing date for institution's financial aid form: March 15. In 2003-2004, 72% of undergraduates applied for financial aid. Of those, 62% were determined to have financial need; 32% had their need fully met. Average financial aid package (proportion receiving): $19,217 (62%). Average amount of gift aid, such as scholarships or grants (proportion receiving): $16,206 (62%). Average amount of self-help aid, such as work study or loans (proportion receiving): $3,858 (36%). Average need-based loan (excluding PLUS or other private loans): $3,800. Among students who received need-based aid, the average percentage of need met: 83%. Among students who received aid based on merit, the average award (and the proportion receiving): $10,178 (36%). The average athletic scholarship (and the proportion receiving): $7,587 (6%). Average amount of debt of borrowers graduating in 2003: $15,481. Proportion who borrowed: 68%. **Reserve Officers Training Corps (ROTC):** Army ROTC: Offered on campus.

South Carolina State University

300 College Street NE
Orangeburg, SC 29117
Public; www.scsu.edu
Financial aid office: (803) 536-7067

■ **2004-2005 TUITION AND FEES:**
In state: $3,085; Out of state: $6,489

SAT I Score (25th/75th percentile): 730-910
2005 U.S. News College Ranking:
National Universities, fourth tier
Acceptance Rate: 55%

Other expenses: Estimated books and supplies: $1,000. Transportation: $1,385. Personal expenses: $2,350. **Financial aid:** Priority filing date for institution's financial aid form: May 1. **Student employment:** During the 2003-2004 academic year, 3% of undergraduates worked on campus. Average per-year earnings: $1,500. **Reserve Officers Training Corps (ROTC):** Army ROTC: Offered on campus; Navy ROTC: Offered on campus.

Southern Wesleyan University

PO Box 1020, SWU, Wesleyan Drive
Central, SC 29630
Private; www.swu.edu
Financial aid office: (864) 644-5500

■ **2004-2005 TUITION AND FEES:** $14,750
■ **ROOM AND BOARD:** $5,200

SAT I Score (25th/75th percentile): 880-1160
2005 U.S. News College Ranking:
Universities–Master's (South), third tier
Acceptance Rate: 68%

Other expenses: Estimated books and supplies: $900. Transportation: $700. Personal expenses: $1,000. **Financial aid:** Priority filing date for institution's financial aid form: June 30; deadline: June 30. In 2003-2004, 43% of undergraduates applied for financial aid. Of those, 39% were determined to have financial need; 19% had their need fully met. Average financial aid package (proportion receiving): $8,524 (39%).

Average amount of gift aid, such as scholarships or grants (proportion receiving): $6,540 (32%). Average amount of self-help aid, such as work study or loans (proportion receiving): $3,769 (32%). Average need-based loan (excluding PLUS or other private loans): $3,339. Among students who received need-based aid, the average percentage of need met: 65%. Among students who received aid based on merit, the average award (and the proportion receiving): $9,004 (6%). The average athletic scholarship (and the proportion receiving): $5,103 (3%). Average amount of debt of borrowers graduating in 2003: $18,469. Proportion who borrowed: 99%. **Cooperative education programs:** health professions. **Reserve Officers Training Corps (ROTC):** Army ROTC: Offered at cooperating institution (Clemson University); Air Force ROTC: Offered at cooperating institution (Clemson University).

University of South Carolina–Aiken

471 University Parkway
Aiken, SC 29801
Public; www.usca.edu
Financial aid office: (803) 641-3476

■ **2004-2005 TUITION AND FEES:**
In state: $5,116; Out of state: $10,256
■ **ROOM AND BOARD:** $4,150

SAT I Score (25th/75th percentile): 890-1110
2005 U.S. News College Ranking:
Comp. Colleges–Bachelor's (South), 37
Acceptance Rate: 65%

Other expenses: Estimated books and supplies: $910. Transportation: $1,610. Personal expenses: $1,700. **Financial aid:** Priority filing date for institution's financial aid form: March 15. In 2003-2004, 81% of undergraduates applied for financial aid. Of those, 66% were determined to have financial need; 45% had their need fully met. Average financial aid package (proportion receiving): $4,150 (64%). Average amount of gift aid, such as scholarships or grants (proportion receiving): $2,825 (51%). Average amount of self-help aid, such as work study or loans (proportion receiving): $3,890 (48%). Average need-based loan (excluding PLUS or other private loans): $3,788. Among students who received need-based aid, the average percentage of need met: 47%. Among students who received aid based on merit, the average award (and the proportion receiving): $975 (12%). The average athletic scholarship (and the proportion receiving): $1,325 (7%). Average amount of debt

of borrowers graduating in 2003: $13,826. Proportion who borrowed: 75%. **Student employment:** During the 2003-2004 academic year, 5% of undergraduates worked on campus. **Cooperative education programs:** art, business, computer science, engineering, humanities, natural science, technologies.

University of South Carolina–Columbia

Columbia, SC 29208
Public; www.sc.edu
Financial aid office: (803) 777-8134

■ **2004-2005 TUITION AND FEES:**
In state: $6,356; Out of state: $16,724
■ **ROOM AND BOARD:** $5,590

SAT I Score (25th/75th percentile): 1030-1250
2005 U.S. News College Ranking:
National Universities, 117
Acceptance Rate: 64%

Other expenses: Estimated books and supplies: $720. Transportation: $1,335. Personal expenses: $2,420. **Financial aid:** Priority filing date for institution's financial aid form: April 1. In 2003-2004, 58% of undergraduates applied for financial aid. Of those, 45% were determined to have financial need; 31% had their need fully met. Average financial aid package (proportion receiving): $9,371 (45%). Average amount of gift aid, such as scholarships or grants (proportion receiving): $3,060 (24%). Average amount of self-help aid, such as work study or loans (proportion receiving): $4,273 (34%). Average need-based loan (excluding PLUS or other private loans): $3,962. Among students who received need-based aid, the average percentage of need met: 91%. Among students who received aid based on merit, the average award (and the proportion receiving): $4,037 (43%). The average athletic scholarship (and the proportion receiving): $10,757 (3%). Average amount of debt of borrowers graduating in 2003: $16,105. Proportion who borrowed: 71%. **Student employment:** During the 2003-2004 academic year, 16% of undergraduates worked on campus. Average per-year earnings: $2,858. **Cooperative education programs:** art, business, computer science, education, engineering, health professions, humanities, natural science, social/behavioral science. **Reserve Officers Training Corps (ROTC):** Army ROTC: Offered on campus; Navy ROTC: Offered on campus; Air Force ROTC: Offered on campus.

University of South Carolina–Upstate

800 University Way
Spartanburg, SC 29303
Public; www.uscs.edu
Financial aid office: (864) 503-5340

■ **2004-2005 TUITION AND FEES:**
   In state: $6,261; Out of state: $12,505
■ **ROOM AND BOARD:** $5,460

SAT I Score (25th/75th percentile): 890-1070
2005 U.S. News College Ranking:
Comp. Colleges–Bachelor's (South), 38
Acceptance Rate: 49%

Financial aid: Priority filing date for institution's financial aid form: March 1. In 2003-2004, 72% of undergraduates applied for financial aid. Of those, 58% were determined to have financial need; 13% had their need fully met. Average financial aid package (proportion receiving): $6,148 (57%). Average amount of gift aid, such as scholarships or grants (proportion receiving): $3,298 (37%). Average amount of self-help aid, such as work study or loans (proportion receiving): $3,416 (45%). Average need-based loan (excluding PLUS or other private loans): $3,352. Among students who received need-based aid, the average percentage of need met: 20%. Among students who received aid based on merit, the average award (and the proportion receiving): $4,203 (4%). The average athletic scholarship (and the proportion receiving): $2,763 (3%). **Student employment:** During the 2003-2004 academic year, 1% of undergraduates worked on campus. Average per-year earnings: $5,000. **Reserve Officers Training Corps (ROTC):** Army ROTC: Offered at cooperating institution (Wofford College).

Voorhees College

1411 Voorhees Road, PO Box 678
Denmark, SC 29042
Private; www.voorhees.edu
Financial aid office: (803) 703-7109

■ **2004-2005 TUITION AND FEES:** $7,276
■ **ROOM AND BOARD:** $4,572

ACT Score (25th/75th percentile): 12-17
2005 U.S. News College Ranking:
Comp. Colleges–Bachelor's (South), fourth tier
Acceptance Rate: 35%

Other expenses: Estimated books and supplies: $1,200. Transportation: $1,500. Personal expenses: $1,175. **Financial aid:** Priority filing date for institution's financial aid form: April 15. In 2003-2004, 93% of undergraduates applied for financial aid. Of those, 91% were determined to have financial need; 5% had their need fully met. Average financial aid package (proportion receiving): $7,947 (91%). Average amount of gift aid, such as scholarships or grants (proportion receiving): $5,188 (84%). Average amount of self-help aid, such as work study or loans (proportion receiving): $3,533 (83%). Average need-based loan (excluding PLUS or other private loans): $2,965. Among students who received need-based aid, the average percentage of need met: 55%. Among students who received aid based on merit, the average award (and the proportion receiving): $8,089 (4%). The average athletic scholarship (and the proportion receiving): $0 (0%). Average amount of debt of borrowers graduating in 2003: $13,283. Proportion who borrowed: 98%. **Student employment:** During the 2003-2004 academic year, 5% of undergraduates worked on campus. Average per-year earnings: $750. **Reserve Officers Training Corps (ROTC):** Army ROTC: Offered at cooperating institution (SCSU).

Winthrop University

701 Oakland Avenue
Rock Hill, SC 29733
Public; www.winthrop.edu
Financial aid office: (803) 323-2189

■ **2004-2005 TUITION AND FEES:**
   In state: $7,816; Out of state: $14,410
■ **ROOM AND BOARD:** $4,992

SAT I Score (25th/75th percentile): 960-1160
2005 U.S. News College Ranking:
Universities–Master's (South), 29
Acceptance Rate: 66%

Other expenses: Estimated books and supplies: $900. **Financial aid:** Priority filing date for institution's financial aid form: March 1. In 2003-2004, 71% of undergraduates applied for financial aid. Of those, 57% were determined to have financial need; 23% had their need fully met. Average financial aid package (proportion receiving): $7,995 (55%). Average amount of gift aid, such as scholarships or grants (proportion receiving): $4,713 (45%). Average amount of self-help aid, such as work study or loans (proportion receiving): $4,852 (45%). Average need-based loan (excluding PLUS or other pri-

vate loans): $4,754. Among students who received need-based aid, the average percentage of need met: 68%. Among students who received aid based on merit, the average award (and the proportion receiving): $5,070 (12%). The average athletic scholarship (and the proportion receiving): $4,821 (2%). Average amount of debt of borrowers graduating in 2003: $17,482. Proportion who borrowed: 60%. **Cooperative education programs:** business.

Wofford College

429 N. Church Street
Spartanburg, SC 29303-3663
Private; www.wofford.edu
Financial aid office: (864) 597-4160

■ **2003-2004 TUITION AND FEES:** $20,610
■ **ROOM AND BOARD:** $6,100

SAT I Score (25th/75th percentile): 1140-1340
2005 U.S. News College Ranking:
Liberal Arts Colleges, 66
Acceptance Rate: 80%

Other expenses: Estimated books and supplies: $851. Transportation: $690. Personal expenses: $1,110. **Financial aid:** Priority filing date for institution's financial aid form: March 15. In 2003-2004, 64% of undergraduates applied for financial aid. Of those, 53% were determined to have financial need; 50% had their need fully met. Average financial aid package (proportion receiving): $20,014 (52%). Average amount of gift aid, such as scholarships or grants (proportion receiving): $14,581 (52%). Average amount of self-help aid, such as work study or loans (proportion receiving): $4,371 (27%). Average need-based loan (excluding PLUS or other private loans): $3,890. Among students who received need-based aid, the average percentage of need met: 88%. Among students who received aid based on merit, the average award (and the proportion receiving): $8,268 (21%). The average athletic scholarship (and the proportion receiving): $10,873 (13%). Average amount of debt of borrowers graduating in 2003: $12,281. Proportion who borrowed: 64%. **Student employment:** During the 2003-2004 academic year, 21% of undergraduates worked on campus. Average per-year earnings: $1,368. **Reserve Officers Training Corps (ROTC):** Army ROTC: Offered on campus.

South Dakota

Augustana College

2001 S. Summit Avenue
Sioux Falls, SD 57197
Private; www.augie.edu
Financial aid office: (605) 274-5216

- **2004-2005 TUITION AND FEES:** $17,980
- **ROOM AND BOARD:** $5,096

ACT Score (25th/75th percentile): 22-28
2005 U.S. News College Ranking:
Comp. Colleges–Bachelor's (Midwest), 12
Acceptance Rate: 79%

Other expenses: Estimated books and supplies:
$800. Transportation: $300. Personal expenses:
$800. **Financial aid:** Priority filing date for institution's financial aid form: March 1. In 2003-2004,
82% of undergraduates applied for financial aid.
Of those, 70% were determined to have financial
need; 19% had their need fully met. Average
financial aid package (proportion receiving):
$14,299 (70%). Average amount of gift aid, such
as scholarships or grants (proportion receiving):
$9,932 (70%). Average amount of self-help aid,
such as work study or loans (proportion receiving): $5,286 (57%). Average need-based loan
(excluding PLUS or other private loans): $4,759.
Among students who received need-based aid,
the average percentage of need met: 87%. Among
students who received aid based on merit, the
average award (and the proportion receiving):
$6,695 (28%). The average athletic scholarship
(and the proportion receiving): $7,321 (7%).
Average amount of debt of borrowers graduating
in 2003: $18,315. Proportion who borrowed: 79%.
Student employment: During the 2003-2004 academic year, 4% of undergraduates worked on
campus. Average per-year earnings: $4,001.

Black Hills State University

1200 University Street, Unit 9500
Spearfish, SD 57799-9500
Public; www.bhsu.edu
Financial aid office: (605) 642-6145

- **2004-2005 TUITION AND FEES:**
  In state: $4,820; Out of state: $9,986
- **ROOM AND BOARD:** $3,449

ACT Score (25th/75th percentile): 18-23
2005 U.S. News College Ranking:
Comp. Colleges–Bachelor's (Midwest),
fourth tier
Acceptance Rate: 95%

Reserve Officers Training Corps (ROTC): Army
ROTC: Offered on campus.

Dakota State University

820 N. Washington Avenue
Madison, SD 57042
Public; www.dsu.edu
Financial aid office: (605) 256-5158

- **2004-2005 TUITION AND FEES:**
  In state: $4,614; Out of state: $9,457
- **ROOM AND BOARD:** $3,420

ACT Score (25th/75th percentile): 17-24
2005 U.S. News College Ranking:
Comp. Colleges–Bachelor's (Midwest),
third tier
Acceptance Rate: 93%

Other expenses: Estimated books and supplies:
$800. Transportation: $680. Personal expenses: $1,880. **Financial aid:** Priority filing date for
institution's financial aid form: March 1. In
2003-2004, 87% of undergraduates applied for
financial aid. Of those, 71% were determined to
have financial need; 29% had their need fully
met. Average financial aid package (proportion
receiving): $5,839 (70%). Average amount of
gift aid, such as scholarships or grants (proportion receiving): $2,797 (38%). Average amount
of self-help aid, such as work study or loans
(proportion receiving): $4,877 (65%). Average
need-based loan (excluding PLUS or other private loans): $4,552. Among students who
received need-based aid, the average percentage
of need met: 81%. Among students who
received aid based on merit, the average award
(and the proportion receiving): $5,016 (15%).
The average athletic scholarship (and the proportion receiving): $1,136 (9%). Average
amount of debt of borrowers graduating in
2003: $18,430. Proportion who borrowed: 82%.
Cooperative education programs: education.

Dakota Wesleyan University

1200 W. University Avenue
Mitchell, SD 57301
Private; www.dwu.edu
Financial aid office: (605) 995-2656

- **2004-2005 TUITION AND FEES:** $14,800
- **ROOM AND BOARD:** $4,476

ACT Score (25th/75th percentile): 20
2005 U.S. News College Ranking:
Comp. Colleges–Bachelor's (Midwest),
third tier
Acceptance Rate: 77%

Other expenses: Estimated books and supplies:
$800. Transportation: $600. Personal expenses: $1,200. **Financial aid:** Priority filing date for
institution's financial aid form: April 1. In
2003-2004, 100% of undergraduates applied
for financial aid. Of those, 93% were determined to have financial need; 57% had their
need fully met. Average financial aid package
(proportion receiving): $11,061 (93%). Average
amount of gift aid, such as scholarships or
grants (proportion receiving): $3,869 (93%).
Average amount of self-help aid, such as work
study or loans (proportion receiving): $4,816
(52%). Average need-based loan (excluding
PLUS or other private loans): $3,502. Among
students who received need-based aid, the average percentage of need met: 72%. Among students who received aid based on merit, the
average award (and the proportion receiving):
$4,871 (13%). The average athletic scholarship
(and the proportion receiving): $3,606 (7%).
Average amount of debt of borrowers graduating in 2003: $15,352. Proportion who borrowed:
96%. **Student employment:** During the 2003-
2004 academic year, 0% of undergraduates
worked on campus. Average per-year earnings:
$0.

Mount Marty College

1105 W. Eighth Street
Yankton, SD 57078
Private; www.mtmc.edu
Financial aid office: (605) 668-1589

- **2004-2005 TUITION AND FEES:** $14,936
- **ROOM AND BOARD:** $4,764

ACT Score (25th/75th percentile): 19-24
2005 U.S. News College Ranking:
Universities–Master's (Midwest), fourth tier
Acceptance Rate: 80%

....

Other expenses: Estimated books and supplies: $700. Transportation: $1,050. Personal expenses: $1,350. Financial aid: Priority filing date for institution's financial aid form: March 1. In 2003-2004, 93% of undergraduates applied for financial aid. Of those, 87% were determined to have financial need; 20% had their need fully met. Average financial aid package (proportion receiving): $12,417 (87%). Average amount of gift aid, such as scholarships or grants (proportion receiving): $7,863 (86%). Average amount of self-help aid, such as work study or loans (proportion receiving): $4,837 (84%). Average need-based loan (excluding PLUS or other private loans): $4,468. Among students who received need-based aid, the average percentage of need met: 75%. Among students who received aid based on merit, the average award (and the proportion receiving): $5,764 (12%). The average athletic scholarship (and the proportion receiving): $3,563 (4%). Average amount of debt of borrowers graduating in 2003: $21,492. Proportion who borrowed: 67%. Student employment: During the 2003-2004 academic year, 3% of undergraduates worked on campus. Average per-year earnings: $2,000. Reserve Officers Training Corps (ROTC): Army ROTC: Offered at cooperating institution (University of South Dakota).

Northern State University

1200 S. Jay Street
Aberdeen, SD 57401-7198
Public; www.northern.edu
Financial aid office: (605) 626-2640

■ 2004-2005 TUITION AND FEES:
   In state: $4,448; Out of state: $9,292
■ ROOM AND BOARD: $3,890

ACT Score (25th/75th percentile): 18-24
2005 U.S. News College Ranking:
Universities–Master's (Midwest), fourth tier
Acceptance Rate: 93%

....

Other expenses: Estimated books and supplies: $750. Transportation: $1,000. Personal expenses: $1,500. Financial aid: Priority filing date for institution's financial aid form: March 1. In 2003-2004, 78% of undergraduates applied for financial aid. Of those, 64% were determined to have financial need; 98% had their need fully met. Average financial aid package (pro-

portion receiving): $4,996 (63%). Average amount of gift aid, such as scholarships or grants (proportion receiving): $2,466 (49%). Average amount of self-help aid, such as work study or loans (proportion receiving): $3,132 (53%). Average need-based loan (excluding PLUS or other private loans): $3,132. Among students who received aid based on merit, the average award (and the proportion receiving): $1,195 (6%). The average athletic scholarship (and the proportion receiving): $2,750 (8%). Average amount of debt of borrowers graduating in 2003: $18,129. Proportion who borrowed: 82%. Student employment: During the 2003-2004 academic year, 10% of undergraduates worked on campus. Average per-year earnings: $2,000.

South Dakota School of Mines and Technology

501 E. St. Joseph Street
Rapid City, SD 57701
Public; www.sdsmt.edu
Financial aid office: (605) 394-2274

■ 2004-2005 TUITION AND FEES:
   In state: $4,534; Out of state: $9,378
■ ROOM AND BOARD: $3,684

ACT Score (25th/75th percentile): 21-27
2005 U.S. News College Ranking:
Unranked Specialty School–Engineering
Acceptance Rate: 94%

....

Other expenses: Estimated books and supplies: $850. Transportation: $1,000. Personal expenses: $1,500. Financial aid: Priority filing date for institution's financial aid form: March 15. In 2003-2004, 91% of undergraduates applied for financial aid. Of those, 54% were determined to have financial need; 30% had their need fully met. Average financial aid package (proportion receiving): $6,048 (53%). Average amount of gift aid, such as scholarships or grants (proportion receiving): $3,175 (39%). Average amount of self-help aid, such as work study or loans (proportion receiving): $3,538 (49%). Average need-based loan (excluding PLUS or other private loans): $3,199. Among students who received need-based aid, the average percentage of need met: 76%. Among students who received aid based on merit, the average award (and the proportion receiving): $2,439 (15%). The average athletic scholarship (and the proportion receiving): $1,395 (4%). Cooperative education programs: other. Reserve Officers Training Corps (ROTC): Army ROTC: Offered on campus.

South Dakota State University

Box 2201
Brookings, SD 57007
Public; www.sdstate.edu
Financial aid office: (605) 688-4695

■ 2004-2005 TUITION AND FEES:
   In state: $4,501; Out of state: $9,344
■ ROOM AND BOARD: $3,653

ACT Score (25th/75th percentile): 19-25
2005 U.S. News College Ranking:
National Universities, third tier
Acceptance Rate: 96%

....

Other expenses: Estimated books and supplies: $800. Transportation: $1,098. Personal expenses: $1,800. Financial aid: Priority filing date for institution's financial aid form: March 7. In 2003-2004, 84% of undergraduates applied for financial aid. Of those, 78% were determined to have financial need; 77% had their need fully met. Average financial aid package (proportion receiving): $7,126 (76%). Average amount of gift aid, such as scholarships or grants (proportion receiving): $3,015 (39%). Average amount of self-help aid, such as work study or loans (proportion receiving): $4,542 (76%). Average need-based loan (excluding PLUS or other private loans): $4,310. Among students who received need-based aid, the average percentage of need met: 85%. Among students who received aid based on merit, the average award (and the proportion receiving): $910 (12%). The average athletic scholarship (and the proportion receiving): $3,028 (4%). Average amount of debt of borrowers graduating in 2003: $16,660. Proportion who borrowed: 80%. Student employment: During the 2003-2004 academic year, 21% of undergraduates worked on campus. Cooperative education programs: agriculture, business, computer science, education, engineering, health professions, natural science, social/behavioral science. Reserve Officers Training Corps (ROTC): Army ROTC: Offered on campus; Air Force ROTC: Offered on campus.

University of Sioux Falls

1101 W. 22nd Street
Sioux Falls, SD 57105
Private; www.usiouxfalls.edu
Financial aid office: (605) 331-6623

■ 2004-2005 TUITION AND FEES: $15,100
■ ROOM AND BOARD: $4,350

ACT Score (25th/75th percentile): 16-26
2005 U.S. News College Ranking:
Universities–Master's (Midwest), third tier
Acceptance Rate: 96%

....

Other expenses: Estimated books and supplies:
$700. Transportation: $650. Personal expenses:
$1,630. **Financial aid:** Priority filing date for
institution's financial aid form: March 1.
Reserve Officers Training Corps (ROTC): Army
ROTC: Offered at cooperating institution
(University of South Dakota).

University of South Dakota

414 E. Clark Street
Vermillion, SD 57069
Public; www.usd.edu
Financial aid office: (605) 677-5446

■ **2004-2005 TUITION AND FEES:**
   In state: $4,452; Out of state: $9,296
■ **ROOM AND BOARD:** $3,741

ACT Score (25th/75th percentile): 20-25
2005 U.S. News College Ranking:
National Universities, third tier
Acceptance Rate: 83%

....

Other expenses: Estimated books and supplies:
$750. Transportation: $1,100. Personal expenses: $2,000. **Financial aid:** Priority filing date for
institution's financial aid form: March 15; deadline: March 15. In 2003-2004, 78% of undergraduates applied for financial aid. Of those,
62% were determined to have financial need;
39% had their need fully met. Average financial
aid package (proportion receiving): $5,644
(58%). Average amount of gift aid, such as
scholarships or grants (proportion receiving):
$2,939 (30%). Average amount of self-help aid,
such as work study or loans (proportion receiving): $4,714 (32%). Average need-based loan
(excluding PLUS or other private loans): $3,184.
Among students who received need-based aid,
the average percentage of need met: 81%.
Among students who received aid based on
merit, the average award (and the proportion
receiving): $5,415 (23%). The average athletic
scholarship (and the proportion receiving):
$2,880 (7%). Average amount of debt of bor-
rowers graduating in 2003: $18,810. Proportion
who borrowed: 80%. **Student employment:**
During the 2003-2004 academic year, 15% of
undergraduates worked on campus. Average
per-year earnings: $2,635. **Reserve Officers
Training Corps (ROTC):** Army ROTC: Offered
on campus.

Tennessee

Austin Peay State University

PO Box 4675
Clarksville, TN 37044
Public; www.apsu.edu
Financial aid office: (931) 221-7907

- **2004-2005 TUITION AND FEES:**
  In state: $4,224; Out of state: $12,712
- **ROOM AND BOARD:** $4,296

ACT Score (25th/75th percentile): 18-24
2005 U.S. News College Ranking:
Universities–Master's (South), third tier
Acceptance Rate: 93%

Other expenses: Estimated books and supplies: $1,350. Transportation: $1,569. Personal expenses: $2,500. **Financial aid:** Priority filing date for institution's financial aid form: April 1. In 2003-2004, 72% of undergraduates applied for financial aid. Of those, 65% were determined to have financial need; Average financial aid package (proportion receiving): N/A (63%). Average amount of gift aid, such as scholarships or grants (proportion receiving): N/A (42%). Average amount of self-help aid, such as work study or loans (proportion receiving): N/A (3%). Among students who received aid based on merit, the average award (and the proportion receiving): $2,824 (2%). The average athletic scholarship (and the proportion receiving): $5,215 (2%). **Cooperative education programs:** agriculture, art, business, computer science, education, engineering, health professions, humanities, natural science, social/behavioral science, technologies, vocational arts. **Reserve Officers Training Corps (ROTC):** Army ROTC: Offered on campus.

Belmont University

1900 Belmont Boulevard
Nashville, TN 37212
Private; www.belmont.edu
Financial aid office: (615) 460-6403

- **2004-2005 TUITION AND FEES:** $16,220
- **ROOM AND BOARD:** $8,730

ACT Score (25th/75th percentile): 22-27
2005 U.S. News College Ranking:
Universities–Master's (South), 19
Acceptance Rate: 75%

Other expenses: Estimated books and supplies: $900. Transportation: $950. Personal expenses: $1,500. **Financial aid:** Priority filing date for institution's financial aid form: March 1. In 2003-2004, 84% of undergraduates applied for financial aid. Of those, 54% were determined to have financial need; 18% had their need fully met. Average financial aid package (proportion receiving): $3,527 (52%). Average amount of gift aid, such as scholarships or grants (proportion receiving): $2,463 (35%). Average amount of self-help aid, such as work study or loans (proportion receiving): $3,417 (43%). Average need-based loan (excluding PLUS or other private loans): $3,765. Among students who received need-based aid, the average percentage of need met: 37%. Among students who received aid based on merit, the average award (and the proportion receiving): $6,503 (19%). The average athletic scholarship (and the proportion receiving): $11,937 (7%). Average amount of debt of borrowers graduating in 2003: $8,450. Proportion who borrowed: 56%. **Student employment:** During the 2003-2004 academic year, 15% of undergraduates worked on campus. Average per-year earnings: $1,500. **Reserve Officers Training Corps (ROTC):** Army ROTC: Offered at cooperating institution (Vanderbilt University); Navy ROTC: Offered at cooperating institution (Vanderbilt University).

Bethel College

325 Cherry Street
McKenzie, TN 38201
Private; www.bethel-college.edu
Financial aid office: (731) 352-4233

- **2003-2004 TUITION AND FEES:** $9,630
- **ROOM AND BOARD:** $5,080

ACT Score (25th/75th percentile): 9-28
2005 U.S. News College Ranking:
Liberal Arts Colleges, fourth tier
Acceptance Rate: 49%

Other expenses: Estimated books and supplies: $1,000. Transportation: $1,200. Personal expenses: $1,250. **Financial aid:** Priority filing date for institution's financial aid form: February 15; deadline: March 1. **Student employment:** During the 2003-2004 academic year, 2% of undergraduates worked on campus. Average per-year earnings: $1,064. **Cooperative education programs:** health professions.

Bryan College

PO Box 7000
Dayton, TN 37321-7000
Private; www.bryan.edu
Financial aid office: (423) 775-7339

- **2004-2005 TUITION AND FEES:** $14,100
- **ROOM AND BOARD:** $4,400

ACT Score (25th/75th percentile): 22-28
2005 U.S. News College Ranking:
Comp. Colleges–Bachelor's (South), 13
Acceptance Rate: 81%

Other expenses: Estimated books and supplies: $900. Transportation: $1,500. Personal expenses: $900. **Financial aid:** Priority filing date for institution's financial aid form: February 15. In 2003-2004, 80% of undergraduates applied for financial aid. Of those, 71% were determined to have financial need; 21% had their need fully met. Average financial aid package (proportion receiving): $10,117 (71%). Average amount of gift aid, such as scholarships or grants (proportion receiving): $2,780 (49%). Average amount of self-help aid, such as work study or loans (proportion receiving): $3,754 (57%). Average need-based loan (excluding PLUS or other private loans): $4,668. Among students who received need-based aid, the average percentage of need met: 68%. Among students who received aid based on merit, the average award (and the proportion receiving): $4,422 (21%). The average athletic scholarship (and the proportion receiving): $5,075 (13%). Average amount of debt of borrowers graduating in 2003: $20,442. Proportion who borrowed: 53%. **Student employment:** During the 2003-2004 academic year, 2% of undergraduates worked on campus. Average per-year earnings: $1,000.

Carson-Newman College

1646 Russell Avenue
Jefferson City, TN 37760
Private; www.cn.edu
Financial aid office: (865) 471-3247

■ **2004-2005 TUITION AND FEES:** $14,420
■ **ROOM AND BOARD:** $4,930

ACT Score (25th/75th percentile): 19-25
2005 U.S. News College Ranking:
Universities–Master's (South), 36
Acceptance Rate: 88%

Other expenses: Estimated books and supplies: $600. Transportation: $1,000. Personal expenses: $800. **Financial aid:** In 2003-2004, 84% of undergraduates applied for financial aid. Of those, 74% were determined to have financial need; 14% had their need fully met. Average financial aid package (proportion receiving): $12,525 (74%). Average amount of gift aid, such as scholarships or grants (proportion receiving): $8,095 (67%). Average amount of self-help aid, such as work study or loans (proportion receiving): $4,343 (58%). Average need-based loan (excluding PLUS or other private loans): $3,752. Among students who received need-based aid, the average percentage of need met: 72%. Among students who received aid based on merit, the average award (and the proportion receiving): $4,585 (21%). The average athletic scholarship (and the proportion receiving): $4,734 (5%). Average amount of debt of borrowers graduating in 2003: $11,957. Proportion who borrowed: 70%. **Reserve Officers Training Corps (ROTC):** Army ROTC: Offered on campus; Air Force ROTC: Offered on campus.

Christian Brothers University

650 East Parkway S
Memphis, TN 38104
Private; www.cbu.edu
Financial aid office: (901) 321-3305

■ **2004-2005 TUITION AND FEES:** $18,230
■ **ROOM AND BOARD:** $5,300

ACT Score (25th/75th percentile): 20-26
2005 U.S. News College Ranking:
Universities–Master's (South), 31
Acceptance Rate: 85%

Other expenses: Estimated books and supplies: $900. Personal expenses: $500. **Financial aid:** Priority filing date for institution's financial aid

form: March 1. In 2003-2004, 74% of undergraduates applied for financial aid. Of those, 63% were determined to have financial need; 15% had their need fully met. Average financial aid package (proportion receiving): $12,767 (63%). Average amount of gift aid, such as scholarships or grants (proportion receiving): $5,526 (33%). Average amount of self-help aid, such as work study or loans (proportion receiving): $4,174 (49%). Average need-based loan (excluding PLUS or other private loans): $4,026. Among students who received need-based aid, the average percentage of need met: 70%. Among students who received aid based on merit, the average award (and the proportion receiving): $8,450 (30%). The average athletic scholarship (and the proportion receiving): $7,250 (11%). Average amount of debt of borrowers graduating in 2003: $16,600. Proportion who borrowed: 71%. **Reserve Officers Training Corps (ROTC):** Army ROTC: Offered at cooperating institution (The University of Memphis); Navy ROTC: Offered at cooperating institution (The University of Memphis); Air Force ROTC: Offered at cooperating institution (The University of Memphis).

Crichton College

255 N. Highland
Memphis, TN 38111-1375
Private; www.crichton.edu
Financial aid office: (901) 320-9787

■ **2004-2005 TUITION AND FEES:** $12,095
■ **ROOM AND BOARD:** $3,800

ACT Score (25th/75th percentile): 20-26
2005 U.S. News College Ranking:
Comp. Colleges–Bachelor's (South), fourth tier
Acceptance Rate: 55%

Financial aid: Priority filing date for institution's financial aid form: March 31. In 2003-2004, 82% of undergraduates applied for financial aid. Of those, 66% were determined to have financial need; 22% had their need fully met. Average financial aid package (proportion receiving): $8,381 (66%). Average amount of gift aid, such as scholarships or grants (proportion receiving): $5,240 (40%). Average amount of self-help aid, such as work study or loans (proportion receiving): $4,218 (56%). Average need-based loan (excluding PLUS or other private loans): $4,031. Among students who received need-based aid, the average percentage of need met: 53%. Among students who received aid based on merit, the average award (and the proportion receiving): $6,173 (9%).

The average athletic scholarship (and the proportion receiving): $3,811 (7%). Average amount of debt of borrowers graduating in 2003: $22,514. Proportion who borrowed: 69%. **Student employment:** During the 2003-2004 academic year, 9% of undergraduates worked on campus. Average per-year earnings: $3,389.

Cumberland University

1 Cumberland Square
Lebanon, TN 37087-3408
Private; www.cumberland.edu
Financial aid office: (615) 444-2562

■ **2004-2005 TUITION AND FEES:** $12,280
■ **ROOM AND BOARD:** $4,680

ACT Score (25th/75th percentile): 17-22
2005 U.S. News College Ranking:
Universities–Master's (South), fourth tier
Acceptance Rate: 66%

Other expenses: Estimated books and supplies: $1,061. Transportation: $663. Personal expenses: $2,662. **Financial aid:** Priority filing date for institution's financial aid form: February 15; deadline: May 1. In 2003-2004, 80% of undergraduates applied for financial aid. Of those, 73% were determined to have financial need; 15% had their need fully met. Average financial aid package (proportion receiving): $12,532 (70%). Average amount of gift aid, such as scholarships or grants (proportion receiving): $5,369 (40%). Average amount of self-help aid, such as work study or loans (proportion receiving): $3,215 (49%). Average need-based loan (excluding PLUS or other private loans): $3,457. Among students who received need-based aid, the average percentage of need met: 65%. Among students who received aid based on merit, the average award (and the proportion receiving): $4,675 (2%). The average athletic scholarship (and the proportion receiving): $7,345 (6%). Average amount of debt of borrowers graduating in 2003: $7,603. Proportion who borrowed: 72%. **Reserve Officers Training Corps (ROTC):** Army ROTC: Offered at cooperating institution (Middle TN State University).

David Lipscomb University

3901-4001 Granny White Pike
Nashville, TN 37204-3951
Private; www.lipscomb.edu
Financial aid office: (615) 269-1791

■ **2004-2005 TUITION AND FEES:** $13,486
■ **ROOM AND BOARD:** $6,090

ACT Score (25th/75th percentile): 20-29
2005 U.S. News College Ranking:
Universities–Master's (South), 33
Acceptance Rate: 73%

Financial aid: Priority filing date for institution's financial aid form: March 1. In 2003-2004, 82% of undergraduates applied for financial aid. Of those, 58% were determined to have financial need; 24% had their need fully met. Average financial aid package (proportion receiving): $8,909 (53%). Average amount of gift aid, such as scholarships or grants (proportion receiving): $1,698 (30%). Average amount of self-help aid, such as work study or loans (proportion receiving): $5,755 (32%). Average need-based loan (excluding PLUS or other private loans): $5,755. Among students who received need-based aid, the average percentage of need met: 79%. Among students who received aid based on merit, the average award (and the proportion receiving): $5,826 (58%). The average athletic scholarship (and the proportion receiving): $5,736 (9%). Average amount of debt of borrowers graduating in 2003: $18,000. Proportion who borrowed: 70%. **Student employment:** During the 2003-2004 academic year, 18% of undergraduates worked on campus. Average per-year earnings: $2,800. **Cooperative education programs:** art, business, computer science, education, engineering, health professions, home economics, humanities, natural science, social/behavioral science, technologies. **Reserve Officers Training Corps (ROTC):** Army ROTC: Offered at cooperating institution (Vanderbilt University); Air Force ROTC: Offered at cooperating institution (Vanderbilt University).

East Tennessee State University

807 University Parkway
Johnson City, TN 37614-0000
Public; www.etsu.edu
Financial aid office: (423) 439-4300

■ **2004-2005 TUITION AND FEES:**
   In state: $4,172; Out of state: $9,452
■ **ROOM AND BOARD:** $4,752

ACT Score (25th/75th percentile): 19-25
2005 U.S. News College Ranking:
National Universities, fourth tier
Acceptance Rate: 82%

Other expenses: Estimated books and supplies: $919. Transportation: $2,400. Personal expenses: $1,973. **Financial aid:** Priority filing date for institution's financial aid form: April 15. 44% had their need fully met. Average financial aid package (proportion receiving): $4,528 (N/A). Average amount of gift aid, such as scholarships or grants (proportion receiving): $3,026 (N/A). Average amount of self-help aid, such as work study or loans (proportion receiving): $2,964 (N/A). Average need-based loan (excluding PLUS or other private loans): $3,546. Among students who received need-based aid, the average percentage of need met: 81%. Among students who received aid based on merit, the average award (and the proportion receiving): $2,822 (N/A). The average athletic scholarship (and the proportion receiving): $9,651 (N/A). Average amount of debt of borrowers graduating in 2003: $17,688. Proportion who borrowed: 57%. **Cooperative education programs:** art, business, computer science, education, health professions, home economics, humanities, natural science, social/behavioral science, technologies, other. **Reserve Officers Training Corps (ROTC):** Army ROTC: Offered on campus.

Fisk University

1000 17th Avenue N
Nashville, TN 37208-3051
Private; www.fisk.edu
Financial aid office: (615) 329-8585

■ **2004-2005 TUITION AND FEES:** $12,450
■ **ROOM AND BOARD:** $6,230

ACT Score (25th/75th percentile): 16-21
2005 U.S. News College Ranking:
Liberal Arts Colleges, third tier
Acceptance Rate: 66%

Other expenses: Estimated books and supplies: $1,000. Transportation: $1,000. Personal expenses: $1,500. **Financial aid:** Priority filing date for institution's financial aid form: March 1; deadline: June 1. In 2003-2004, 95% of undergraduates applied for financial aid. Of those, 95% were determined to have financial need; 6% had their need fully met. Average financial aid package (proportion receiving): $13,650 (94%). Average amount of gift aid, such as scholarships or grants (proportion receiving): $3,700 (93%). Average amount of self-help aid, such as work study or loans (proportion receiving): $3,700 (92%). Average need-based loan (excluding PLUS or other private loans): $3,750. Among students who received need-based aid, the average percentage of need met: 55%. Among students who received aid based on merit, the average award (and the proportion receiving): $8,200 (3%). The average athletic scholarship (and the proportion receiving): $0 (0%). Average amount of debt of borrowers graduating in 2003: $20,000. Proportion who borrowed: 85%. **Reserve Officers Training Corps (ROTC):** Army ROTC: Offered at cooperating institution (Vanderbilt University); Navy ROTC: Offered at cooperating institution (Vanderbilt University); Air Force ROTC: Offered at cooperating institution (Tennessee State University).

Freed-Hardeman University

158 E. Main Street
Henderson, TN 38340-2399
Private; www.fhu.edu
Financial aid office: (731) 989-6662

■ **2004-2005 TUITION AND FEES:** $11,960
■ **ROOM AND BOARD:** $5,960

ACT Score (25th/75th percentile): 20-26
2005 U.S. News College Ranking:
Universities–Master's (South), 52
Acceptance Rate: 99%

Other expenses: Estimated books and supplies: $1,300. Personal expenses: $1,580. **Financial aid:** Priority filing date for institution's financial aid form: April 1. In 2003-2004, 81% of undergraduates applied for financial aid. Of those, 71% were determined to have financial need; 11% had their need fully met. Average financial aid package (proportion receiving): $9,025

(71%). Average amount of gift aid, such as scholarships or grants (proportion receiving): $5,761 (63%). Average amount of self-help aid, such as work study or loans (proportion receiving): $4,320 (63%). Average need-based loan (excluding PLUS or other private loans): $3,689. Among students who received need-based aid, the average percentage of need met: 59%. Among students who received aid based on merit, the average award (and the proportion receiving): $10,088 (20%). The average athletic scholarship (and the proportion receiving): $0 (0%). Average amount of debt of borrowers graduating in 2003: $22,135. Proportion who borrowed: 80%. **Student employment:** During the 2003-2004 academic year, 33% of undergraduates worked on campus. Average per-year earnings: $1,000.

King College

1350 King College Road
Bristol, TN 37620
Private; www.king.edu
Financial aid office: (423) 652-4725

■ **2004-2005 TUITION AND FEES:** $17,040
■ **ROOM AND BOARD:** $5,460

ACT Score (25th/75th percentile): 22-27
2005 U.S. News College Ranking:
Liberal Arts Colleges, fourth tier
Acceptance Rate: 92%

Other expenses: Estimated books and supplies: $850. Transportation: $1,000. Personal expenses: $2,000. **Financial aid:** Priority filing date for institution's financial aid form: March 1. In 2003-2004, 80% of undergraduates applied for financial aid. Of those, 77% were determined to have financial need; 17% had their need fully met. Average financial aid package (proportion receiving): $14,354 (77%). Average amount of gift aid, such as scholarships or grants (proportion receiving): $10,866 (76%). Average amount of self-help aid, such as work study or loans (proportion receiving): $4,534 (60%). Average need-based loan (excluding PLUS or other private loans): $4,335. Among students who received need-based aid, the average percentage of need met: 74%. Among students who received aid based on merit, the average award (and the proportion receiving): $6,881 (20%). The average athletic scholarship (and the proportion receiving): $6,777 (12%). Average amount of debt of borrowers graduating in 2003: $12,859. Proportion who borrowed: 81%. **Student employment:** During the 2003-2004 academic year, 47% of undergradu-

ates worked on campus. Average per-year earnings: $1,236.

Lambuth University

705 Lambuth Boulevard
Jackson, TN 38301
Private; www.lambuth.edu
Financial aid office: (731) 425-3332

■ **2004-2005 TUITION AND FEES:** $12,490
■ **ROOM AND BOARD:** $5,436

ACT Score (25th/75th percentile): 20-25
2005 U.S. News College Ranking:
Comp. Colleges–Bachelor's (South), 28
Acceptance Rate: 65%

Other expenses: Estimated books and supplies: $1,200. Transportation: $1,500. Personal expenses: $1,874. **Financial aid:** Priority filing date for institution's financial aid form: February 15. In 2003-2004, 95% of undergraduates applied for financial aid. Of those, 69% were determined to have financial need; 20% had their need fully met. Average financial aid package (proportion receiving): $9,704 (69%). Average amount of gift aid, such as scholarships or grants (proportion receiving): $4,879 (67%). Average amount of self-help aid, such as work study or loans (proportion receiving): $4,879 (53%). Average need-based loan (excluding PLUS or other private loans): $4,519. Among students who received need-based aid, the average percentage of need met: 63%. Among students who received aid based on merit, the average award (and the proportion receiving): $5,563 (22%). The average athletic scholarship (and the proportion receiving): $9,109 (5%). Average amount of debt of borrowers graduating in 2003: $15,000. Proportion who borrowed: 85%. **Student employment:** During the 2003-2004 academic year, 9% of undergraduates worked on campus. Average per-year earnings: $1,000.

Lane College

545 Lane Avenue
Jackson, TN 38301-4598
Private; www.lanecollege.edu
Financial aid office: (731) 426-7535

■ **2004-2005 TUITION AND FEES:** $7,176
■ **ROOM AND BOARD:** $4,534

ACT Score (25th/75th percentile): 18-23
2005 U.S. News College Ranking:
Liberal Arts Colleges, fourth tier
Acceptance Rate: 17%

Other expenses: Estimated books and supplies: $550. Transportation: $405. Personal expenses: $675. **Financial aid:** Priority filing date for institution's financial aid form: April 1. In 2003-2004, 99% of undergraduates applied for financial aid. Of those, 96% were determined to have financial need; 27% had their need fully met. Average financial aid package (proportion receiving): $8,052 (95%). Average amount of gift aid, such as scholarships or grants (proportion receiving): $4,792 (87%). Average amount of self-help aid, such as work study or loans (proportion receiving): $3,498 (84%). Average need-based loan (excluding PLUS or other private loans): $2,850. Among students who received need-based aid, the average percentage of need met: 79%. Among students who received aid based on merit, the average award (and the proportion receiving): $0 (0%). The average athletic scholarship (and the proportion receiving): $2,452 (0%). Average amount of debt of borrowers graduating in 2003: $19,681. Proportion who borrowed: 98%.

Lee University

PO Box 3450
Cleveland, TN 37320
Private; www.leeuniversity.edu
Financial aid office: (423) 614-8300

■ **2004-2005 TUITION AND FEES:** $9,075
■ **ROOM AND BOARD:** $4,560

ACT Score (25th/75th percentile): 19-26
2005 U.S. News College Ranking:
Comp. Colleges–Bachelor's (South), 25
Acceptance Rate: 56%

Other expenses: Estimated books and supplies: $700. Transportation: $1,210. Personal expenses: $1,510. **Financial aid:** Priority filing date for institution's financial aid form: April 15. In 2003-2004, 71% of undergraduates applied for financial aid. Of those, 63% were determined to have financial need; 13% had their need fully met. Average financial aid package (proportion receiving): $7,539 (63%). Average amount of gift aid, such as scholarships or grants (proportion receiving): $4,993 (51%). Average amount of self-help aid, such as work study or loans (proportion receiving): $4,270 (53%). Average need-based loan (excluding PLUS or other private loans): $4,098. Among students who received need-based aid, the average percentage of need met: 56%. Among students who received aid based on merit, the average award (and the proportion receiving): $6,142 (22%). The average athletic scholarship (and the proportion receiving): $6,731 (3%). Average amount of debt of borrowers graduating in 2003: $21,615. Proportion who borrowed: 71%. **Student employment:** During the 2003-2004 academic year, 10% of undergraduates worked on campus. Average per-year earnings: $2,000.

LeMoyne-Owen College

807 Walker Avenue
Memphis, TN 38126
Private; www.lemoyne-owen.edu
Financial aid office: (901) 942-7313

■ **2004-2005 TUITION AND FEES:** $9,360
■ **ROOM AND BOARD:** $4,500

ACT Score (25th/75th percentile): 16
2005 U.S. News College Ranking:
Comp. Colleges–Bachelor's (South), fourth tier
Acceptance Rate: 45%
....

Other expenses: Estimated books and supplies: $1,000. Transportation: $750. Personal expenses: $1,955. **Financial aid:** Priority filing date for institution's financial aid form: April 1. In 2003-2004, 100% of undergraduates applied for financial aid. Of those, 85% were determined to have financial need; 3% had their need fully met. Average financial aid package (proportion receiving): $9,523 (85%). Average amount of gift aid, such as scholarships or grants (proportion receiving): $8,570 (33%). Average need-based loan (excluding PLUS or other private loans): $3,115. Among students who received need-based aid, the average percentage of need met: 50%. **Student employment:** During the 2003-2004 academic year, 15% of undergraduates worked on campus. Average per-year earnings: $1,500. **Reserve Officers Training Corps (ROTC):** Army ROTC: Offered at cooperating institution (University of Memphis); Navy ROTC: Offered at cooperating institution (University of Memphis); Air Force ROTC: Offered at cooperating institution (University of Memphis).

Lincoln Memorial University

Cumberland Gap Parkway
Harrogate, TN 37752-1901
Private; www.lmunet.edu
Financial aid office: (423) 869-6336

■ **2004-2005 TUITION AND FEES:** $12,600
■ **ROOM AND BOARD:** $4,910

ACT Score (25th/75th percentile): 18-22
2005 U.S. News College Ranking:
Universities–Master's (South), fourth tier
Acceptance Rate: 85%
....

Financial aid: Priority filing date for institution's financial aid form: April 1.

Martin Methodist College

433 W. Madison Street
Pulaski, TN 38478
Private; www.martinmethodist.edu
Financial aid office: (931) 363-9821

■ **2003-2004 TUITION AND FEES:** $13,000
■ **ROOM AND BOARD:** $4,000

ACT Score (25th/75th percentile): 17-22
2005 U.S. News College Ranking:
Comp. Colleges–Bachelor's (South), third tier
Acceptance Rate: 95%
....

Other expenses: Estimated books and supplies: $750. Transportation: $460. Personal expenses: $1,750. **Financial aid:** Priority filing date for institution's financial aid form: February 3; deadline: August 3. **Student employment:** During the 2003-2004 academic year, 15% of undergraduates worked on campus. Average per-year earnings: $1,500.

Maryville College

502 E. Lamar Alexander Parkway
Maryville, TN 37804-5907
Private; www.maryvillecollege.edu
Financial aid office: (865) 981-8100

■ **2004-2005 TUITION AND FEES:** $21,065
■ **ROOM AND BOARD:** $6,500

ACT Score (25th/75th percentile): 21-27
2005 U.S. News College Ranking:
Comp. Colleges–Bachelor's (South), 4
Acceptance Rate: 81%
....

Other expenses: Estimated books and supplies: $650. Transportation: $700. Personal expenses: $800. **Financial aid:** Priority filing date for institution's financial aid form: March 1. In 2003-2004, 100% of undergraduates applied for financial aid. Of those, 79% were determined to have financial need; 50% had their need fully met. Average financial aid package (proportion receiving): $19,013 (79%). Average amount of gift aid, such as scholarships or grants (proportion receiving): $12,475 (79%). Average amount of self-help aid, such as work study or loans (proportion receiving): $4,262 (64%). Average need-based loan (excluding PLUS or other private loans): $3,301. Among students who received need-based aid, the average percentage of need met: 92%. Among students who received aid based on merit, the average award (and the proportion receiving): $11,668 (21%). The average athletic scholarship (and the proportion receiving): $0 (0%). **Student employment:** During the 2003-2004 academic year, 15% of undergraduates worked on campus. Average per-year earnings: $1,200.

Memphis College of Art

Overton Park, 1930 Poplar Avenue
Memphis, TN 38104
Private; www.mca.edu
Financial aid office: (901) 272-5136

■ **2004-2005 TUITION AND FEES:** $15,860
■ **ROOM AND BOARD:** $7,400

ACT Score (25th/75th percentile): 17-23
2005 U.S. News College Ranking:
Unranked Specialty School–Fine Arts
Acceptance Rate: 76%
....

Other expenses: Estimated books and supplies: $1,500. Transportation: $1,365. Personal expenses: $1,175. **Financial aid:** Priority filing date for institution's financial aid form: March 1. In 2003-2004, 96% of undergraduates applied for financial aid. Of those, 90% were determined to have financial need; 79% had their need fully met. Average financial aid package (proportion receiving): $7,000 (90%). Average amount of gift aid, such as scholarships or grants (proportion receiving): $3,000 (35%). Average amount of self-help aid, such as work study or loans (proportion receiving): $5,500 (35%). Average need-based loan (excluding PLUS or other private loans): $5,500. Among students who received need-based aid, the average percentage of need met: 90%. Among students who received aid based on merit, the average award (and the proportion receiving): $5,500 (8%). The average athletic scholarship (and the proportion receiving): $0 (0%). Average amount of debt of borrowers graduating in 2003: $23,000. Proportion who borrowed: 95%.

Middle Tennessee State University

1301 E. Main Street, CAB Room 205
Murfreesboro, TN 37132
Public; www.mtsu.edu
Financial aid office: (615) 898-2830

■ **2004-2005 TUITION AND FEES:**
  In state: $4,130; Out of state: $12,618
■ **ROOM AND BOARD:** $4,676

ACT Score (25th/75th percentile): 20-24
2005 U.S. News College Ranking:
National Universities, fourth tier
Acceptance Rate: 75%

Other expenses: Estimated books and supplies: $1,000. Transportation: $1,800. Personal expenses: $1,350. **Financial aid:** Priority filing date for institution's financial aid form: May 1. In 2003-2004, 64% of undergraduates applied for financial aid. Of those, 43% were determined to have financial need; 55% had their need fully met. Average financial aid package (proportion receiving): $4,887 (41%). Average amount of gift aid, such as scholarships or grants (proportion receiving): $2,625 (24%). Average amount of self-help aid, such as work study or loans (proportion receiving): $3,791 (33%). Average need-based loan (excluding PLUS or other private loans): $4,538. Among students who received need-based aid, the average percentage of need met: 78%. Among students who received aid based on merit, the average award (and the proportion receiving): $2,339 (11%). The average athletic scholarship (and the proportion receiving): $10,045 (1%). Average amount of debt of borrowers graduating in 2003: $18,675. Proportion who borrowed: 8%. **Student employment:** During the 2003-2004 academic year, 7% of undergraduates worked on campus. Average per-year earnings: $3,400. **Cooperative education programs:** agriculture, business, computer science, education, engineering, humanities, social/behavioral science, technologies. **Reserve Officers Training Corps (ROTC):** Army ROTC: Offered on campus; Air Force ROTC: Offered at cooperating institution (Tennessee State University).

Milligan College

PO Box 500
Milligan College, TN 37682
Private; www.milligan.edu
Financial aid office: (423) 461-8949

■ **2004-2005 TUITION AND FEES:** $16,360
■ **ROOM AND BOARD:** $4,600

ACT Score (25th/75th percentile): 20-26
2005 U.S. News College Ranking:
Universities–Master's (South), 43
Acceptance Rate: 76%

Other expenses: Estimated books and supplies: $750. Transportation: $718. Personal expenses: $1,145. **Financial aid:** Priority filing date for institution's financial aid form: March 1. In 2003-2004, 100% of undergraduates applied for financial aid. Of those, 87% were determined to have financial need; 16% had their need fully met. Average financial aid package (proportion receiving): $7,223 (87%). Average amount of gift aid, such as scholarships or grants (proportion receiving): $3,929 (47%). Average amount of self-help aid, such as work study or loans (proportion receiving): $1,070 (67%). Average need-based loan (excluding PLUS or other private loans): $2,523. Among students who received need-based aid, the average percentage of need met: 55%. Among students who received aid based on merit, the average award (and the proportion receiving): $5,779 (9%). The average athletic scholarship (and the proportion receiving): $4,724 (2%). Average amount of debt of borrowers graduating in 2003: $17,712. Proportion who borrowed: 56%. **Reserve Officers Training Corps (ROTC):** Army ROTC: Offered at cooperating institution (East Tennessee State University).

Rhodes College

2000 N. Parkway
Memphis, TN 38112
Private; www.rhodes.edu
Financial aid office: (901) 843-3810

■ **2004-2005 TUITION AND FEES:** $24,274
■ **ROOM AND BOARD:** $6,638

SAT I Score (25th/75th percentile): 1190-1360
2005 U.S. News College Ranking:
Liberal Arts Colleges, 45
Acceptance Rate: 72%

Other expenses: Estimated books and supplies: $840. Transportation: $730. Personal expenses: $1,200. **Financial aid:** Priority filing date for institution's financial aid form: March 1. In 2003-2004, 51% of undergraduates applied for financial aid. Of those, 40% were determined to have financial need; 42% had their need fully met. Average financial aid package (proportion receiving): $18,022 (39%). Average amount of gift aid, such as scholarships or grants (proportion receiving): $12,301 (39%). Average amount of self-help aid, such as work study or loans (proportion receiving): $6,279 (27%). Average need-based loan (excluding PLUS or other private loans): $4,428. Among students who received need-based aid, the average percentage of need met: 80%. Among students who received aid based on merit, the average award (and the proportion receiving): $9,198 (33%). The average athletic scholarship (and the proportion receiving): $0 (0%). **Student employment:** During the 2003-2004 academic year, 30% of undergraduates worked on campus. Average per-year earnings: $1,340. **Cooperative education programs:** art, education. **Reserve Officers Training Corps (ROTC):** Army ROTC: Offered at cooperating institution (University of Memphis); Air Force ROTC: Offered at cooperating institution (University of Memphis).

Sewanee—University of the South

735 University Avenue
Sewanee, TN 37383
Private; www.sewanee.edu
Financial aid office: (931) 598-1312

■ **2004-2005 TUITION AND FEES:** $25,580
■ **ROOM AND BOARD:** $7,120

SAT I Score (25th/75th percentile): 1160-1320
2005 U.S. News College Ranking:
Liberal Arts Colleges, 33
Acceptance Rate: 72%

Other expenses: Estimated books and supplies: $600. Personal expenses: $1,110. **Financial aid:** Priority filing date for institution's financial aid form: March 1. In 2003-2004, 48% of undergraduates applied for financial aid. Of those, 45% were determined to have financial need; 100% had their need fully met. Average financial aid package (proportion receiving): $19,633 (45%). Average amount of gift aid, such as scholarships or grants (proportion receiving): $16,520 (45%). Average amount of self-help aid, such as work study or loans (proportion receiving): $4,996 (37%). Average need-based loan (excluding PLUS or other private loans): $3,496. Among students who received need-based aid, the average percentage of need met: 100%. Among students who received aid based on merit, the average award (and the proportion receiving): $12,155 (13%). The average athletic scholarship (and the proportion receiving): $0 (0%). Average amount of debt of borrowers graduating in 2003: $14,441. Proportion who borrowed: 37%.

Southern Adventist University

PO Box 370
Collegedale, TN 37315
Private; www.southern.edu
Financial aid office: (423) 238-2835

■ **2004-2005 TUITION AND FEES:** $13,410
■ **ROOM AND BOARD:** $4,390

ACT Score (25th/75th percentile): 18-25
2005 U.S. News College Ranking:
Comp. Colleges–Bachelor's (South), 34
Acceptance Rate: 76%

Other expenses: Estimated books and supplies: $900. Transportation: $1,000. Personal expenses: $1,500. **Financial aid:** Priority filing date for institution's financial aid form: March 31. **Student employment:** During the 2003-2004 academic year, 50% of undergraduates worked on campus. Average per-year earnings: $3,000.

Tennessee State University

3500 John Merritt Boulevard
Nashville, TN 37209-1561
Public; www.tnstate.edu
Financial aid office: (615) 963-5772

■ **2004-2005 TUITION AND FEES:**
In state: $4,038; Out of state: $12,526
■ **ROOM AND BOARD:** $4,350

ACT Score (25th/75th percentile): 17-22
2005 U.S. News College Ranking:
National Universities, fourth tier
Acceptance Rate: 59%

Other expenses: Estimated books and supplies: $1,030. Transportation: $1,744. Personal expenses: $3,589. **Financial aid:** Priority filing date for institution's financial aid form: April 1. 12% had their need fully met. Average financial aid package (proportion receiving): $3,670 (N/A). Average amount of gift aid, such as scholarships or grants (proportion receiving):

$1,178 (N/A). Average amount of self-help aid, such as work study or loans (proportion receiving): $1,814 (N/A). Average need-based loan (excluding PLUS or other private loans): $2,004. Among students who received need-based aid, the average percentage of need met: 81%. Among students who received aid based on merit, the average award (and the proportion receiving): $6,085 (N/A). The average athletic scholarship (and the proportion receiving): $9,884 (N/A). Average amount of debt of borrowers graduating in 2003: $19,841. Proportion who borrowed: 47%. **Student employment:** During the 2003-2004 academic year, 33% of undergraduates worked on campus. **Cooperative education programs:** business, computer science. **Reserve Officers Training Corps (ROTC):** Air Force ROTC: Offered on campus.

Tennessee Technological University

Campus Box 5006 USPS 077-460
Cookeville, TN 38505
Public; www.tntech.edu
Financial aid office: (931) 372-3073

■ **2004-2005 TUITION AND FEES:**
In state: $3,900; Out of state: $8,542
■ **ROOM AND BOARD:** $5,978

ACT Score (25th/75th percentile): 20-26
2005 U.S. News College Ranking:
Universities–Master's (South), 37
Acceptance Rate: 80%

Other expenses: Estimated books and supplies: $1,265. Transportation: $1,300. Personal expenses: $1,277. **Financial aid:** Priority filing date for institution's financial aid form: March 15. In 2003-2004, 74% of undergraduates applied for financial aid. Of those, 43% were determined to have financial need; 24% had their need fully met. Average financial aid package (proportion receiving): $3,689 (42%). Average amount of gift aid, such as scholarships or grants (proportion receiving): $2,633 (27%). Average amount of self-help aid, such as work study or loans (proportion receiving): $2,628 (30%). Average need-based loan (excluding PLUS or other private loans): $3,159. Among students who received need-based aid, the average percentage of need met: 77%. Among students who received aid based on merit, the average award (and the proportion receiving): $2,533 (18%). The average athletic scholarship (and the proportion receiving): $7,857 (3%). Average amount of debt of borrow-

ers graduating in 2003: $13,338. Proportion who borrowed: 35%. **Student employment:** During the 2003-2004 academic year, 10% of undergraduates worked on campus. Average per-year earnings: $3,160. **Cooperative education programs:** business, computer science, engineering. **Reserve Officers Training Corps (ROTC):** Army ROTC: Offered on campus; Air Force ROTC: Offered at cooperating institution (Tennessee State University).

Tennessee Wesleyan College

PO Box 40
Athens, TN 37371-0040
Private; www.twcnet.edu
Financial aid office: (423) 746-5209

■ **2004-2005 TUITION AND FEES:** $12,340
■ **ROOM AND BOARD:** $4,850

ACT Score (25th/75th percentile): 18-24
2005 U.S. News College Ranking:
Comp. Colleges–Bachelor's (South), third tier
Acceptance Rate: 83%

Other expenses: Estimated books and supplies: $1,000. Transportation: $1,000. Personal expenses: $1,000. **Financial aid:** In 2003-2004, 85% of undergraduates applied for financial aid. Of those, 77% were determined to have financial need; 16% had their need fully met. Average financial aid package (proportion receiving): $9,785 (77%). Average amount of gift aid, such as scholarships or grants (proportion receiving): $6,797 (76%). Average amount of self-help aid, such as work study or loans (proportion receiving): $3,856 (61%). Average need-based loan (excluding PLUS or other private loans): $3,681. Among students who received need-based aid, the average percentage of need met: 69%. Among students who received aid based on merit, the average award (and the proportion receiving): $4,990 (16%). The average athletic scholarship (and the proportion receiving): $6,224 (13%). Average amount of debt of borrowers graduating in 2003: $10,870. Proportion who borrowed: 63%. **Student employment:** During the 2003-2004 academic year, 22% of undergraduates worked on campus. Average per-year earnings: $1,000. **Cooperative education programs:** business, computer science.

Trevecca Nazarene University

333 Murfreesboro Road
Nashville, TN 37210
Private; www.trevecca.edu
Financial aid office: (615) 248-1242

- **2004-2005 TUITION AND FEES:** $12,792
- **ROOM AND BOARD:** $5,868

ACT Score (25th/75th percentile): 19-25
2005 U.S. News College Ranking:
Universities–Master's (South), third tier
Acceptance Rate: 67%

Other expenses: Estimated books and supplies: $823. Transportation: $880. Personal expenses: $1,315. **Financial aid:** Priority filing date for institution's financial aid form: March 1. In 2003-2004, 58% of undergraduates applied for financial aid. Of those, 49% were determined to have financial need; 86% had their need fully met. Average financial aid package (proportion receiving): $10,450 (49%). Average amount of gift aid, such as scholarships or grants (proportion receiving): $4,320 (21%). Average amount of self-help aid, such as work study or loans (proportion receiving): $4,430 (39%). Average need-based loan (excluding PLUS or other private loans): $4,430. Among students who received need-based aid, the average percentage of need met: 45%. Among students who received aid based on merit, the average award (and the proportion receiving): $3,150 (12%). The average athletic scholarship (and the proportion receiving): $5,340 (16%). Average amount of debt of borrowers graduating in 2003: $15,060. Proportion who borrowed: 60%. **Reserve Officers Training Corps (ROTC):** Army ROTC: Offered at cooperating institution (Vanderbilt University).

Tusculum College

PO Box 5035
Greeneville, TN 37743
Private; www.tusculum.edu
Financial aid office: (423) 636-7377

- **2004-2005 TUITION AND FEES:** $15,110
- **ROOM AND BOARD:** $5,950

ACT Score (25th/75th percentile): 18-23
2005 U.S. News College Ranking:
Universities–Master's (South), fourth tier
Acceptance Rate: 78%

Other expenses: Estimated books and supplies: $940. Transportation: $1,200. **Financial aid:** Priority filing date for institution's financial aid form: February 15. In 2003-2004, 84% of undergraduates applied for financial aid. Of those, 67% were determined to have financial need; 16% had their need fully met. Average financial aid package (proportion receiving): $9,408 (65%). Average amount of gift aid, such as scholarships or grants (proportion receiving): $4,850 (34%). Average amount of self-help aid, such as work study or loans (proportion receiving): $3,658 (54%). Average need-based loan (excluding PLUS or other private loans): $3,410. Among students who received need-based aid, the average percentage of need met: 63%. Among students who received aid based on merit, the average award (and the proportion receiving): $4,535 (49%). The average athletic scholarship (and the proportion receiving): $5,595 (12%). Average amount of debt of borrowers graduating in 2003: $16,393. Proportion who borrowed: 69%. **Student employment:** During the 2003-2004 academic year, 1% of undergraduates worked on campus.

Union University

1050 Union University Drive
Jackson, TN 38305
Private; www.uu.edu
Financial aid office: (731) 661-5015

- **2004-2005 TUITION AND FEES:** $15,370
- **ROOM AND BOARD:** $5,400

ACT Score (25th/75th percentile): 21-27
2005 U.S. News College Ranking:
Universities–Master's (South), 33
Acceptance Rate: 84%

Other expenses: Estimated books and supplies: $750. Transportation: $400. Personal expenses: $1,500. **Financial aid:** Priority filing date for institution's financial aid form: January 30. In 2003-2004, 95% of undergraduates applied for financial aid. Of those, 58% were determined to have financial need; Average financial aid package (proportion receiving): $10,492 (58%). Average amount of gift aid, such as scholarships or grants (proportion receiving): $3,719 (42%). Average amount of self-help aid, such as work study or loans (proportion receiving): $4,081 (41%). Average need-based loan (excluding PLUS or other private loans): $3,782. Among students who received aid based on merit, the average award (and the proportion receiving): $4,884 (8%). Average amount of debt of borrowers graduating in 2003: $15,328.

Proportion who borrowed: 11%. **Cooperative education programs:** business, education.

University of Memphis

Memphis, TN 38152
Public; www.memphis.edu
Financial aid office: (901) 678-4825

- **2004-2005 TUITION AND FEES:**
  In state: $4,392; Out of state: $13,116
- **ROOM AND BOARD:** $5,780

ACT Score (25th/75th percentile): 18-25
2005 U.S. News College Ranking:
National Universities, fourth tier
Acceptance Rate: 73%

Other expenses: Estimated books and supplies: $900. Transportation: $1,500. Personal expenses: $2,277. **Financial aid:** Priority filing date for institution's financial aid form: March 1; deadline: July 1. Average amount of debt of borrowers graduating in 2003: $20,491. Proportion who borrowed: 29%. **Reserve Officers Training Corps (ROTC):** Army ROTC: Offered on campus; Navy ROTC: Offered on campus; Air Force ROTC: Offered on campus.

University of Tennessee

800 Andy Holt Tower
Knoxville, TN 37996
Public; www.tennessee.edu
Financial aid office: (865) 974-3131

- **2004-2005 TUITION AND FEES:**
  In state: $4,748; Out of state: $14,528

ACT Score (25th/75th percentile): 21-26
2005 U.S. News College Ranking:
National Universities, 90
Acceptance Rate: 71%

Other expenses: Estimated books and supplies: $1,122. Transportation: $2,050. Personal expenses: $2,432. **Financial aid:** Priority filing date for institution's financial aid form: March 1. In 2003-2004, 54% of undergraduates applied for financial aid. Of those, 39% were determined to have financial need; 19% had their need fully met. Average financial aid package (proportion receiving): $6,954 (37%). Average amount of gift aid, such as scholarships or grants (proportion receiving): $5,115 (25%). Average amount of self-help aid, such as work study or loans (proportion receiving): $3,417 (31%). Average need-based loan (excluding PLUS or other private loans): $3,523. Among students who received need-based aid, the average percentage of need met: 64%. Among students who received aid based on merit, the average award (and the proportion receiving): $8,931 (1%). The average athletic scholarship (and the proportion receiving): $25,051 (1%). Average amount of debt of borrowers graduating in 2003: $21,713. Proportion who borrowed: 49%. **Student employment:** During the 2003-2004 academic year, 15% of undergraduates worked on campus. **Cooperative education programs:** business, engineering. **Reserve Officers Training Corps (ROTC):** Army ROTC: Offered on campus; Air Force ROTC: Offered on campus.

University of Tennessee– Chattanooga

615 McCallie Avenue
Chattanooga, TN 37403
Public; www.utc.edu
Financial aid office: (423) 425-4677

■ **2004-2005 TUITION AND FEES:**
In state: $4,094; Out of state: $12,350
■ **ROOM AND BOARD:** $7,500

ACT Score (25th/75th percentile): 18-24
2005 U.S. News College Ranking:
Universities–Master's (South), 43
Acceptance Rate: 52%

Financial aid: Priority filing date for institution's financial aid form: April 1. In 2003-2004, 71% of undergraduates applied for financial aid. Of those, 60% were determined to have financial need; 12% had their need fully met. Average financial aid package (proportion receiving): $8,200 (45%). Average amount of gift aid, such as scholarships or grants (proportion receiving): $3,500 (34%). Average amount of self-help aid, such as work study or loans (proportion receiving): $5,580 (29%). Average need-based loan (excluding PLUS or other private loans): $4,525. Among students who received need-based aid, the average percentage of need met: 78%. Among students who received aid based on merit, the average award

(and the proportion receiving): $3,800 (14%). The average athletic scholarship (and the proportion receiving): $12,500 (5%). Average amount of debt of borrowers graduating in 2003: $14,675. Proportion who borrowed: 47%. **Cooperative education programs:** business, engineering, health professions, home economics, social/behavioral science.

University of Tennessee– Martin

University Street
Martin, TN 38238
Public; www.utm.edu
Financial aid office: (731) 587-7040

■ **2004-2005 TUITION AND FEES:**
In state: $4,044; Out of state: $12,140
■ **ROOM AND BOARD:** $4,748

ACT Score (25th/75th percentile): 19-24
2005 U.S. News College Ranking:
Universities–Master's (South), 60
Acceptance Rate: 56%

Other expenses: Estimated books and supplies: $1,200. Transportation: $900. Personal expenses: $2,100. **Financial aid:** Priority filing date for institution's financial aid form: March 1. In 2003-2004, 90% of undergraduates applied for financial aid. Of those, 57% were determined to have financial need; 19% had their need fully met. Average financial aid package (proportion receiving): $7,154 (55%). Average amount of gift aid, such as scholarships or grants (proportion receiving): $3,793 (38%). Average amount of self-help aid, such as work study or loans (proportion receiving): $3,700 (43%). Average need-based loan (excluding PLUS or other private loans): $3,527. Among students who received need-based aid, the average percentage of need met: 73%. Among students who received aid based on merit, the average award (and the proportion receiving): $2,880 (22%). The average athletic scholarship (and the proportion receiving): $8,095 (3%). Average amount of debt of borrowers graduating in 2003: $12,920. Proportion who borrowed: 53%. **Student employment:** During the 2003-2004 academic year,

11% of undergraduates worked on campus. Average per-year earnings: $4,520. **Cooperative education programs:** agriculture, engineering, other. **Reserve Officers Training Corps (ROTC):** Army ROTC: Offered on campus.

Vanderbilt University

Nashville, TN 37240
Private; www.vanderbilt.edu
Financial aid office: (615) 322-3591

■ **2004-2005 TUITION AND FEES:** $29,990
■ **ROOM AND BOARD:** $9,826

SAT I Score (25th/75th percentile): 1250-1430
2005 U.S. News College Ranking:
National Universities, 18
Acceptance Rate: 40%

Financial aid: Priority filing date for institution's financial aid form: February 1. In 2003-2004, 41% of undergraduates applied for financial aid. Of those, 38% were determined to have financial need; 90% had their need fully met. Average financial aid package (proportion receiving): $28,495 (38%). Average amount of gift aid, such as scholarships or grants (proportion receiving): $20,673 (36%). Average amount of self-help aid, such as work study or loans (proportion receiving): $5,848 (28%). Average need-based loan (excluding PLUS or other private loans): $4,850. Among students who received need-based aid, the average percentage of need met: 99%. Among students who received aid based on merit, the average award (and the proportion receiving): $18,011 (12%). The average athletic scholarship (and the proportion receiving): $30,216 (4%). Average amount of debt of borrowers graduating in 2003: $23,334. Proportion who borrowed: 35%. **Student employment:** During the 2003-2004 academic year, 22% of undergraduates worked on campus. Average per-year earnings: $2,600. **Reserve Officers Training Corps (ROTC):** Army ROTC: Offered on campus; Navy ROTC: Offered on campus; Air Force ROTC: Offered at cooperating institution (University of Tennessee).

Texas

Abilene Christian University

ACU Box 29000
Abilene, TX 79699-9000
Private; www.acu.edu
Financial aid office: (325) 674-2643

■ 2004-2005 TUITION AND FEES: $14,200
■ ROOM AND BOARD: $5,270

SAT I Score (25th/75th percentile): 980-1210
2005 U.S. News College Ranking:
Universities–Master's (West), 20
Acceptance Rate: 53%

Other expenses: Estimated books and supplies: $1,000. Transportation: $1,165. Personal expenses: $1,610. Financial aid: Priority filing date for institution's financial aid form: March 1. In 2003-2004, 97% of undergraduates applied for financial aid. Of those, 63% were determined to have financial need; 49% had their need fully met. Average financial aid package (proportion receiving): $10,457 (62%). Average amount of gift aid, such as scholarships or grants (proportion receiving): $7,127 (61%). Average amount of self-help aid, such as work study or loans (proportion receiving): $4,072 (48%). Average need-based loan (excluding PLUS or other private loans): $4,015. Among students who received need-based aid, the average percentage of need met: 74%. Among students who received aid based on merit, the average award (and the proportion receiving): $4,419 (24%). The average athletic scholarship (and the proportion receiving): $10,380 (5%). Average amount of debt of borrowers graduating in 2003: $24,167. Proportion who borrowed: 70%. Student employment: During the 2003-2004 academic year, 20% of undergraduates worked on campus. Average per-year earnings: $1,500. Cooperative education programs: engineering, natural science.

Angelo State University

2601 West Avenue N
San Angelo, TX 76909
Public; www.angelo.edu
Financial aid office: (325) 942-2246

■ 2004-2005 TUITION AND FEES:
  In state: $3,780; Out of state: $11,520
■ ROOM AND BOARD: $4,656

ACT Score (25th/75th percentile): 17-22
2005 U.S. News College Ranking:
Universities–Master's (West), fourth tier
Acceptance Rate: 99%

Other expenses: Estimated books and supplies: $800. Transportation: $798. Personal expenses: $1,746. Financial aid: Priority filing date for institution's financial aid form: May 1. In 2003-2004, 78% of undergraduates applied for financial aid. Of those, 56% were determined to have financial need; 76% had their need fully met. Average financial aid package (proportion receiving): $4,448 (56%). Average amount of gift aid, such as scholarships or grants (proportion receiving): $2,266 (51%). Average amount of self-help aid, such as work study or loans (proportion receiving): $2,351 (42%). Average need-based loan (excluding PLUS or other private loans): $2,351. Among students who received need-based aid, the average percentage of need met: 64%. Among students who received aid based on merit, the average award (and the proportion receiving): $2,609 (4%). The average athletic scholarship (and the proportion receiving): $2,609 (1%). Average amount of debt of borrowers graduating in 2003: $15,000. Proportion who borrowed: 53%. Average per-year earnings: $2,750. Reserve Officers Training Corps (ROTC): Air Force ROTC: Offered on campus.

Austin College

900 N. Grand Avenue
Sherman, TX 75090-4400
Private; www.austincollege.edu
Financial aid office: (903) 813-2900

■ 2004-2005 TUITION AND FEES: $19,140
■ ROOM AND BOARD: $7,089

SAT I Score (25th/75th percentile): 1138-1340
2005 U.S. News College Ranking:
Liberal Arts Colleges, 70
Acceptance Rate: 72%

Other expenses: Estimated books and supplies: $800. Transportation: $250. Personal expenses: $950. Financial aid: Priority filing date for institution's financial aid form: April 1. In 2003-2004, 73% of undergraduates applied for financial aid. Of those, 60% were determined to have financial need; 69% had their need fully

met. Average financial aid package (proportion receiving): $17,454 (60%). Average amount of gift aid, such as scholarships or grants (proportion receiving): $11,753 (59%). Average amount of self-help aid, such as work study or loans (proportion receiving): $5,479 (46%). Average need-based loan (excluding PLUS or other private loans): $4,856. Among students who received need-based aid, the average percentage of need met: 96%. Among students who received aid based on merit, the average award (and the proportion receiving): $8,473 (36%). Average amount of debt of borrowers graduating in 2003: $22,085. Proportion who borrowed: 76%. Student employment: During the 2003-2004 academic year, 15% of undergraduates worked on campus. Average per-year earnings: $1,600.

Baylor University

1 Bear Place
Waco, TX 76798
Private; www.baylor.edu
Financial aid office: (254) 710-2611

■ 2004-2005 TUITION AND FEES: $19,880
■ ROOM AND BOARD: $6,256

SAT I Score (25th/75th percentile): 1070-1275
2005 U.S. News College Ranking:
National Universities, 84
Acceptance Rate: 82%

Other expenses: Estimated books and supplies: $1,356. Transportation: $1,370. Personal expenses: $1,778. Financial aid: Priority filing date for institution's financial aid form: March 1. In 2003-2004, 59% of undergraduates applied for financial aid. Of those, 46% were determined to have financial need; 18% had their need fully met. Average financial aid package (proportion receiving): $12,282 (46%). Average amount of gift aid, such as scholarships or grants (proportion receiving): $7,954 (42%). Average amount of self-help aid, such as work study or loans (proportion receiving): $5,441 (35%). Average need-based loan (excluding PLUS or other private loans): $2,429. Among students who received need-based aid, the average percentage of need met: 66%. Among students who received aid based on merit, the average award (and the proportion receiving): $5,419 (28%). The average athletic scholarship (and the proportion receiving): $12,024 (3%). **Student employment:** During the 2003-2004 academic year, 10% of undergraduates worked on campus. Average per-year earnings: $750. **Cooperative education programs:** health professions. **Reserve Officers Training Corps (ROTC):** Air Force ROTC: Offered on campus.

Concordia University–Austin

3400 I-35 N
Austin, TX 78705
Private; www.concordia.edu
Financial aid office: (512) 486-1283

■ **2004-2005 TUITION AND FEES:** $16,105
■ **ROOM AND BOARD:** $6,570

SAT I Score (25th/75th percentile): 880-1050
2005 U.S. News College Ranking:
Comp. Colleges–Bachelor's (West), 20
Acceptance Rate: 76%

Other expenses: Estimated books and supplies: $1,000. Transportation: $660. Personal expenses: $1,070. **Financial aid:** Priority filing date for institution's financial aid form: April 1; deadline: July 1. In 2003-2004, 83% of undergraduates applied for financial aid. Of those, 67% were determined to have financial need; 98% had their need fully met. Average financial aid package (proportion receiving): $11,423 (66%). Average amount of gift aid, such as scholarships or grants (proportion receiving): $9,652 (55%). Average amount of self-help aid, such as work study or loans (proportion receiving): $3,665 (50%). Average need-based loan (excluding PLUS or other private loans): $3,440. Among students who received need-based aid, the average percentage of need met: 83%. Among students who received aid based on merit, the average award (and the proportion receiving): $5,565 (8%). The average athletic scholarship (and the proportion receiving): $0 (0%). Average amount of debt of borrowers graduating in 2003: $29,449. Proportion who borrowed: 54%. **Reserve Officers Training Corps (ROTC):** Army ROTC: Offered at cooperating institution (University of Texas); Air Force ROTC: Offered at cooperating institution (University of Texas).

Dallas Baptist University

3000 Mountain Creek Parkway
Dallas, TX 75211-9299
Private; www.dbu.edu
Financial aid office: (214) 333-5460

■ **2004-2005 TUITION AND FEES:** $11,610
■ **ROOM AND BOARD:** $4,644

SAT I Score (25th/75th percentile): 945-1138
2005 U.S. News College Ranking:
Universities–Master's (West), third tier
Acceptance Rate: 68%

Other expenses: Estimated books and supplies: $930. Transportation: $639. Personal expenses: $1,422. **Financial aid:** Priority filing date for institution's financial aid form: March 15. In 2003-2004, 87% of undergraduates applied for financial aid. Of those, 63% were determined to have financial need; 41% had their need fully met. Average financial aid package (proportion receiving): $9,195 (62%). Average amount of gift aid, such as scholarships or grants (proportion receiving): $2,467 (43%). Average amount of self-help aid, such as work study or loans (proportion receiving): $3,060 (49%). Average need-based loan (excluding PLUS or other private loans): $3,242. Among students who received need-based aid, the average percentage of need met: 73%. Among students who received aid based on merit, the average award (and the proportion receiving): $8,310 (18%). The average athletic scholarship (and the proportion receiving): $5,184 (4%). Average amount of debt of borrowers graduating in 2003: $18,364. Proportion who borrowed: 52%. **Student employment:** During the 2003-2004 academic year, 20% of undergraduates worked on campus. Average per-year earnings: $2,880. **Reserve Officers Training Corps (ROTC):** Army ROTC: Offered at cooperating institution (Univ. of Texas at Arlington); Air Force ROTC: Offered at cooperating institution (Texas Christian University).

East Texas Baptist University

1209 N. Grove
Marshall, TX 75670
Private; www.etbu.edu
Financial aid office: (903) 923-2137

■ **2004-2005 TUITION AND FEES:** $12,000
■ **ROOM AND BOARD:** $3,873

ACT Score (25th/75th percentile): 18-23
2005 U.S. News College Ranking:
Comp. Colleges–Bachelor's (West), 13
Acceptance Rate: 96%

Other expenses: Estimated books and supplies: $800. Transportation: $651. Personal expenses: $1,247. **Financial aid:** Priority filing date for institution's financial aid form: June 1. In 2003-2004, 83% of undergraduates applied for financial aid. Of those, 78% were determined to have financial need; 26% had their need fully met. Average financial aid package (proportion receiving): $9,293 (78%). Average amount of gift aid, such as scholarships or grants (proportion receiving): $5,297 (65%). Average amount of self-help aid, such as work study or loans (proportion receiving): $3,895 (58%). Average need-based loan (excluding PLUS or other private loans): $4,481. Among students who received need-based aid, the average percentage of need met: 87%. Among students who received aid based on merit, the average award (and the proportion receiving): $3,372 (17%). Average amount of debt of borrowers graduating in 2003: $9,982. Proportion who borrowed: 69%. **Student employment:** During the 2003-2004 academic year, 20% of undergraduates worked on campus. Average per-year earnings: $1,604.

Hardin-Simmons University

2200 Hickory
Abilene, TX 79698-1000
Private; www.hsutx.edu
Financial aid office: (325) 670-5891

■ **2004-2005 TUITION AND FEES:** $13,376
■ **ROOM AND BOARD:** $3,922

SAT I Score (25th/75th percentile): 920-1140
2005 U.S. News College Ranking:
Universities–Master's (West), 41
Acceptance Rate: 53%

Other expenses: Estimated books and supplies: $750. Transportation: $1,056. Personal expenses: $1,482. **Financial aid:** Priority filing date for institution's financial aid form: March 15. In 2003-2004, 93% of undergraduates applied for financial aid. Of those, 65% were determined to have financial need; 20% had their need fully met. Average financial aid package (proportion receiving): $11,521 (65%). Average amount of gift aid, such as scholarships or grants (proportion receiving): $4,733 (50%). Average amount of self-help aid, such as work study or loans (proportion receiving): $4,951 (60%). Average need-based loan (excluding PLUS or other private loans): $3,913. Among students who received need-based aid, the average percentage of need met: 66%. Among students who received aid based on merit, the average award (and the proportion receiving): $3,111 (8%). The average athletic scholarship (and the proportion receiving): $0 (0%). Average amount of debt of borrowers graduating in 2003: $26,729. Proportion who borrowed: 76%. **Student employment:** During the 2003-2004 academic year, 1% of undergraduates worked on campus. Average per-year earnings: $3,500. **Cooperative education programs:** agriculture, other.

Houston Baptist University

7502 Fondren Road
Houston, TX 77074-3298
Private; www.hbu.edu
Financial aid office: (281) 649-3389

■ **2004-2005 TUITION AND FEES:** $12,915
■ **ROOM AND BOARD:** $4,566

SAT I Score (25th/75th percentile): 950-1190
2005 U.S. News College Ranking:
Universities–Master's (West), 58
Acceptance Rate: 62%

Other expenses: Estimated books and supplies: $1,272. Transportation: $822. Personal expenses: $1,646. **Financial aid:** Priority filing date for institution's financial aid form: March 1; deadline: April 15. In 2003-2004, 41% of undergraduates applied for financial aid. Of those, 37% were determined to have financial need; 12% had their need fully met. Average financial aid package (proportion receiving): $10,411 (37%). Average amount of gift aid, such as scholarships or grants (proportion receiving): $7,358 (35%). Average amount of self-help aid, such as work study or loans (proportion receiving): $4,026 (31%). Average need-based loan (excluding PLUS or other private loans): $3,097. Among students who received need-based aid, the average percentage of need met: 59%. Among students who received aid based on merit, the average award (and the proportion receiving): $9,829 (10%). The average athletic scholarship (and the proportion receiving): $12,616 (2%). Average amount of debt of borrowers graduating in 2003: $17,982. Proportion who borrowed: 74%. **Student employment:** During the 2003-2004 academic year, 17% of undergraduates worked on campus. Average per-year earnings: $2,000. **Reserve Officers Training Corps (ROTC):** Army ROTC: Offered at cooperating institution (University of Houston);

Navy ROTC: Offered at cooperating institution (Rice University).

Howard Payne University

1000 Fisk Avenue
Brownwood, TX 76801
Private; www.hputx.edu
Financial aid office: (325) 649-8014

■ **2004-2005 TUITION AND FEES:** $12,000
■ **ROOM AND BOARD:** $4,615

SAT I Score (25th/75th percentile): 890-1120
2005 U.S. News College Ranking:
Comp. Colleges–Bachelor's (West), 17
Acceptance Rate: 79%

Other expenses: Estimated books and supplies: $850. Transportation: $720. Personal expenses: $1,475. **Financial aid:** Priority filing date for institution's financial aid form: March 15. In 2003-2004, 88% of undergraduates applied for financial aid. Of those, 76% were determined to have financial need; 30% had their need fully met. Average financial aid package (proportion receiving): $10,464 (76%). Average amount of gift aid, such as scholarships or grants (proportion receiving): $6,760 (74%). Average amount of self-help aid, such as work study or loans (proportion receiving): $4,643 (58%). Average need-based loan (excluding PLUS or other private loans): $3,516. Among students who received need-based aid, the average percentage of need met: 82%. Among students who received aid based on merit, the average award (and the proportion receiving): $4,331 (17%). The average athletic scholarship (and the proportion receiving): $0 (0%). Average amount of debt of borrowers graduating in 2003: $17,735. Proportion who borrowed: 70%. Average per-year earnings: $1,200.

Huston-Tillotson College

900 Chicon Street
Austin, TX 78702
Private; www.htc.edu
Financial aid office: (512) 505-3027

■ **2004-2005 TUITION AND FEES:** $7,530
■ **ROOM AND BOARD:** $6,042

SAT I Score (25th/75th percentile): 710-850
2005 U.S. News College Ranking:
Comp. Colleges–Bachelor's (West), fourth tier
Acceptance Rate: 98%

Other expenses: Estimated books and supplies: $635. Transportation: $810. Personal expenses: $1,306. **Financial aid:** In 2003-2004, 91% of undergraduates applied for financial aid. Of those, 91% were determined to have financial need; 29% had their need fully met. Average financial aid package (proportion receiving): $9,211 (86%). Average amount of gift aid, such as scholarships or grants (proportion receiving): $1,710 (2%). Average amount of self-help aid, such as work study or loans (proportion receiving): $4,931 (49%). Average need-based loan (excluding PLUS or other private loans): $4,068. Among students who received need-based aid, the average percentage of need met: 81%. Among students who received aid based on merit, the average award (and the proportion receiving): $5,546 (1%). The average athletic scholarship (and the proportion receiving): $5,806 (9%). Average amount of debt of borrowers graduating in 2003: $17,500. Proportion who borrowed: 83%. **Reserve Officers Training Corps (ROTC):** Army ROTC: Offered at cooperating institution (University of Texas at Austin); Navy ROTC: Offered at cooperating institution (University of Texas at Austin); Air Force ROTC: Offered at cooperating institution (University of Texas at Austin).

Jarvis Christian College

PO Box 1470
Hawkins, TX 75765-1470
Private; www.jarvis.edu
Financial aid office: (903) 769-5740

■ **2004-2005 TUITION AND FEES:** $6,330
■ **ROOM AND BOARD:** $3,485

ACT Score (25th/75th percentile): 16
2005 U.S. News College Ranking:
Comp. Colleges–Bachelor's (West), fourth tier
Acceptance Rate: 66%

Other expenses: Estimated books and supplies: $800. Transportation: $500. Personal expenses: $1,000. **Student employment:** During the 2003-2004 academic year, 2% of undergraduates worked on campus. Average per-year earnings: $5,000. **Cooperative education programs:** business, health professions, social/behavioral science.

Lamar University

Lamar Station, Box 10001
Beaumont, TX 77710
Public; www.lamar.edu
Financial aid office: (409) 880-8450

- **2004-2005 TUITION AND FEES:**
  In state: $3,824; Out of state: $11,564
- **ROOM AND BOARD:** $5,162

SAT I Score (25th/75th percentile): 830-1050
2005 U.S. News College Ranking:
Universities–Master's (West), fourth tier
Acceptance Rate: 68%

Other expenses: Estimated books and supplies: $775. Transportation: $1,965. Personal expenses: $1,842. **Financial aid:** Priority filing date for institution's financial aid form: April 1. In 2003-2004, 67% of undergraduates applied for financial aid. Of those, 45% were determined to have financial need; 6% had their need fully met. Average financial aid package (proportion receiving): $1,215 (38%). Average amount of gift aid, such as scholarships or grants (proportion receiving): $0 (0%). Average amount of self-help aid, such as work study or loans (proportion receiving): $0 (15%). Average need-based loan (excluding PLUS or other private loans): $0. Among students who received need-based aid, the average percentage of need met: 15%. Among students who received aid based on merit, the average award (and the proportion receiving): $1,300 (23%). The average athletic scholarship (and the proportion receiving): $0 (0%). Average amount of debt of borrowers graduating in 2003: $13,500. Proportion who borrowed: 54%. **Cooperative education programs:** computer science, education, natural science.

LeTourneau University

PO Box 7001
Longview, TX 75607-7001
Private; www.letu.edu
Financial aid office: (903) 233-3430

- **2004-2005 TUITION AND FEES:** $15,030
- **ROOM AND BOARD:** $6,050

SAT I Score (25th/75th percentile): 1040-1300
2005 U.S. News College Ranking:
Universities–Master's (West), 23
Acceptance Rate: 80%

Other expenses: Estimated books and supplies: $1,075. Transportation: $1,075. Personal expenses: $980. **Financial aid:** Priority filing date for institution's financial aid form: February 15. In 2003-2004, 87% of undergraduates applied for financial aid. Of those, 75% were determined to have financial need; 16% had their need fully met. Average financial aid package (proportion receiving): $11,613 (75%). Average amount of gift aid, such as scholarships or grants (proportion receiving): $7,067 (70%). Average amount of self-help aid, such as work study or loans (proportion receiving): $6,092 (67%). Average need-based loan (excluding PLUS or other private loans): $4,096. Among students who received need-based aid, the average percentage of need met: 70%. Among students who received aid based on merit, the average award (and the proportion receiving): $3,801 (6%). The average athletic scholarship (and the proportion receiving): $0 (0%). Average amount of debt of borrowers graduating in 2003: $22,295. Proportion who borrowed: 77%. **Student employment:** During the 2003-2004 academic year, 38% of undergraduates worked on campus. Average per-year earnings: $1,239. **Cooperative education programs:** other.

Lubbock Christian University

5601 19th Street
Lubbock, TX 79407
Private; www.lcu.edu
Financial aid office: (800) 933-7601

- **2004-2005 TUITION AND FEES:** $11,994
- **ROOM AND BOARD:** $4,130

ACT Score (25th/75th percentile): 18-24
2005 U.S. News College Ranking:
Comp. Colleges–Bachelor's (West), 18
Acceptance Rate: 72%

Other expenses: Estimated books and supplies: $810. Transportation: $1,648. Personal expenses: $1,846. **Financial aid:** Priority filing date for institution's financial aid form: June 1. In 2003-2004, 73% of undergraduates applied for financial aid. Of those, 66% were determined to have financial need; 8% had their need fully met. Average financial aid package (proportion receiving): $11,040 (66%). Average amount of gift aid, such as scholarships or grants (proportion receiving): $7,324 (64%). Average amount of self-help aid, such as work study or loans (proportion receiving): $4,260 (61%). Average need-based loan (excluding PLUS or other private loans): $3,451. Among students who received need-based aid, the average percentage of need met: 75%. Among stu-

dents who received aid based on merit, the average award (and the proportion receiving): $9,730 (11%). The average athletic scholarship (and the proportion receiving): $6,925 (2%). Average amount of debt of borrowers graduating in 2003: $17,189. Proportion who borrowed: 68%. **Student employment:** During the 2003-2004 academic year, 18% of undergraduates worked on campus. Average per-year earnings: $1,745. **Cooperative education programs:** agriculture, engineering, health professions, other. **Reserve Officers Training Corps (ROTC):** Army ROTC: Offered at cooperating institution (Texas Tech University).

McMurry University

S. 14th and Sayles Boulevard
Abilene, TX 79697
Private; www.mcm.edu
Financial aid office: (325) 793-4713

- **2004-2005 TUITION AND FEES:** $13,550
- **ROOM AND BOARD:** $5,255

SAT I Score (25th/75th percentile): 840-1090
2005 U.S. News College Ranking:
Comp. Colleges–Bachelor's (West), 11
Acceptance Rate: 61%

Other expenses: Estimated books and supplies: $853. Transportation: $663. Personal expenses: $1,918. **Financial aid:** Priority filing date for institution's financial aid form: March 15. In 2003-2004, 89% of undergraduates applied for financial aid. Of those, 80% were determined to have financial need; 23% had their need fully met. Average financial aid package (proportion receiving): $12,932 (80%). Average amount of gift aid, such as scholarships or grants (proportion receiving): $6,002 (71%). Average amount of self-help aid, such as work study or loans (proportion receiving): $4,220 (66%). Average need-based loan (excluding PLUS or other private loans): $3,917. Among students who received need-based aid, the average percentage of need met: 78%. Among students who received aid based on merit, the average award (and the proportion receiving): $5,421 (11%). The average athletic scholarship (and the proportion receiving): $0 (0%). Average amount of debt of borrowers graduating in 2003: $15,125. Proportion who borrowed: 80%. **Student employment:** During the 2003-2004 academic year, 8% of undergraduates worked on campus. Average per-year earnings: $1,650. **Reserve Officers Training Corps (ROTC):** Air Force ROTC: Offered at cooperating institution (Angelo State University).

Midwestern State University

3410 Taft Boulevard
Wichita Falls, TX 76308-2099
Public; www.mwsu.edu
Financial aid office: (940) 397-4214

■ **2004-2005 TUITION AND FEES:**
In state: $3,740; Out of state: $12,800
■ **ROOM AND BOARD:** $4,844

SAT I Score (25th/75th percentile): 850-1080
2005 U.S. News College Ranking:
Universities–Master's (West), fourth tier
Acceptance Rate: 65%

Other expenses: Estimated books and supplies: $1,133. Transportation: $1,016. Personal expenses: $2,369. **Financial aid:** Priority filing date for institution's financial aid form: May 1; deadline: May 1. In 2003-2004, 82% of undergraduates applied for financial aid. Of those, 79% were determined to have financial need; 60% had their need fully met. Average financial aid package (proportion receiving): $4,035 (79%). Average amount of gift aid, such as scholarships or grants (proportion receiving): $3,937 (43%). Average amount of self-help aid, such as work study or loans (proportion receiving): $5,965 (48%). Average need-based loan (excluding PLUS or other private loans): $4,715. Among students who received need-based aid, the average percentage of need met: 81%. Among students who received aid based on merit, the average award (and the proportion receiving): $3,937 (16%). The average athletic scholarship (and the proportion receiving): $4,715 (16%). Average amount of debt of borrowers graduating in 2003: $11,046. Proportion who borrowed: 47%. **Reserve Officers Training Corps (ROTC):** Air Force ROTC: Offered at cooperating institution (University of North Texas).

Our Lady of the Lake University

411 S. W. 24th Street
San Antonio, TX 78207-4689
Private; www.ollusa.edu
Financial aid office: (210) 434-6711

■ **2004-2005 TUITION AND FEES:** $16,430
■ **ROOM AND BOARD:** $5,445

SAT I Score (25th/75th percentile): 870-1060
2005 U.S. News College Ranking:
Universities–Master's (West), 52
Acceptance Rate: 65%

Other expenses: Estimated books and supplies: $1,000. Transportation: $990. Personal expenses: $1,836. **Financial aid:** The average athletic scholarship (and the proportion receiving): $0 (N/A). **Reserve Officers Training Corps (ROTC):** Army ROTC: Offered at cooperating institution (St. Mary's University of San Antonio).

Paul Quinn College

3837 Simpson Stuart Road
Dallas, TX 75241
Private; www.pqc.edu
Financial aid office: (214) 302-3560

■ **2004-2005 TUITION AND FEES:** $6,490
■ **ROOM AND BOARD:** $4,750

ACT Score (25th/75th percentile): 8-16
2005 U.S. News College Ranking:
Comp. Colleges–Bachelor's (West), fourth tier
Acceptance Rate: 41%

Other expenses: Estimated books and supplies: $1,000. **Financial aid:** Priority filing date for institution's financial aid form: April 1. In 2003-2004, 99% of undergraduates applied for financial aid. Of those, 98% were determined to have financial need; 83% had their need fully met. Average financial aid package (proportion receiving): $9,900 (98%). Average amount of gift aid, such as scholarships or grants (proportion receiving): $2,954 (19%). Average amount of self-help aid, such as work study or loans (proportion receiving): $3,875 (60%). Average need-based loan (excluding PLUS or other private loans): $3,875. Among students who received need-based aid, the average percentage of need met: 83%. Among students who received aid based on merit, the average award (and the proportion receiving): $0 (0%). The average athletic scholarship (and the proportion receiving): $5,769 (11%). **Student employment:** During the 2003-2004 academic year, 5% of undergraduates worked on campus. Average per-year earnings: $4,800. **Cooperative education programs:** engineering, health professions.

Prairie View A&M University

PO Box 3089
Office of Admissions and Records
Prairie View, TX 77446-0188
Public; www.pvamu.edu
Financial aid office: (936) 857-2424

■ **2004-2005 TUITION AND FEES:**
In state: $4,274; Out of state: $11,744
■ **ROOM AND BOARD:** $5,975

SAT I Score (25th/75th percentile): 710-920
2005 U.S. News College Ranking:
Universities–Master's (West), fourth tier
Acceptance Rate: 98%

Other expenses: Estimated books and supplies: $771. Transportation: $2,757. Personal expenses: $1,818. **Financial aid:** Priority filing date for institution's financial aid form: April 1; deadline: May 1. In 2003-2004, 99% of undergraduates applied for financial aid. Of those, 91% were determined to have financial need; Average financial aid package (proportion receiving): $6,920 (91%). Average amount of gift aid, such as scholarships or grants (proportion receiving): $3,620 (85%). Average amount of self-help aid, such as work study or loans (proportion receiving): $4,000 (91%). Average need-based loan (excluding PLUS or other private loans): $3,800. Among students who received need-based aid, the average percentage of need met: 75%. Among students who received aid based on merit, the average award (and the proportion receiving): $1,400 (6%). The average athletic scholarship (and the proportion receiving): $8,500 (4%). Average amount of debt of borrowers graduating in 2003: $18,000. Proportion who borrowed: 62%. **Student employment:** During the 2003-2004 academic year, 46% of undergraduates worked on campus. Average per-year earnings: $1,120. **Cooperative education programs:** agriculture, business, computer science, education, engineering, natural science, social/behavioral science, technologies. **Reserve Officers Training Corps (ROTC):** Army ROTC: Offered on campus; Navy ROTC: Offered on campus.

Rice University

PO Box 1892
Houston, TX 77251-1892
Private; www.rice.edu
Financial aid office: (713) 348-4958

■ **2004-2005 TUITION AND FEES:** $18,826
■ **ROOM AND BOARD:** $8,380

SAT I Score (25th/75th percentile): 1330-1530
2005 U.S. News College Ranking:
National Universities, 17
Acceptance Rate: 24%

....

Other expenses: Estimated books and supplies: $800. Personal expenses: $1,550. Financial aid: Priority filing date for institution's financial aid form: March 1. In 2003-2004, 77% of undergraduates applied for financial aid. Of those, 37% were determined to have financial need; 100% had their need fully met. Average financial aid package (proportion receiving): $12,903 (37%). Average amount of gift aid, such as scholarships or grants (proportion receiving): $10,461 (36%). Average amount of self-help aid, such as work study or loans (proportion receiving): $3,848 (27%). Average need-based loan (excluding PLUS or other private loans): $3,103. Among students who received need-based aid, the average percentage of need met: 100%. Among students who received aid based on merit, the average award (and the proportion receiving): $3,101 (19%). The average athletic scholarship (and the proportion receiving): $20,761 (10%). Average amount of debt of borrowers graduating in 2003: $12,942. Proportion who borrowed: 40%. Reserve Officers Training Corps (ROTC): Army ROTC: Offered at cooperating institution (University of Houston); Navy ROTC: Offered on campus.

Sam Houston State University

1803 Avenue I
Huntsville, TX 77341
Public; www.shsu.edu
Financial aid office: (936) 294-1724

■ 2004-2005 TUITION AND FEES:
    In state: $4,260; Out of state: $12,000
■ ROOM AND BOARD: $4,336

SAT I Score (25th/75th percentile): 910-1110
2005 U.S. News College Ranking:
Universities–Master's (West), third tier
Acceptance Rate: 76%

....

Financial aid: Priority filing date for institution's financial aid form: March 31; deadline: May 31. In 2003-2004, 60% of undergraduates applied for financial aid. Of those, 43% were determined to have financial need; Average financial aid package (proportion receiving): $5,637 (43%). Average amount of gift aid, such as scholarships or grants (proportion receiving): $3,507 (31%). Average amount of self-help aid, such as work study or loans (proportion receiving): $3,450 (33%). Average need-based loan

(excluding PLUS or other private loans): $3,467. Among students who received aid based on merit, the average award (and the proportion receiving): $1,626 (7%). The average athletic scholarship (and the proportion receiving): $4,979 (3%). Average amount of debt of borrowers graduating in 2003: $14,047. Proportion who borrowed: 53%. Student employment: During the 2003-2004 academic year, 8% of undergraduates worked on campus. Reserve Officers Training Corps (ROTC): Army ROTC: Offered on campus.

Schreiner University

2100 Memorial Boulevard
Kerrville, TX 78028
Private; www.schreiner.edu
Financial aid office: (830) 792-7217

■ 2004-2005 TUITION AND FEES: $14,440
■ ROOM AND BOARD: $6,480

SAT I Score (25th/75th percentile): 850-1110
2005 U.S. News College Ranking:
Liberal Arts Colleges, fourth tier
Acceptance Rate: 63%

....

Other expenses: Estimated books and supplies: $1,000. Transportation: $500. Personal expenses: $900. Financial aid: Priority filing date for institution's financial aid form: April 1; deadline: August 1. In 2003-2004, 77% of undergraduates applied for financial aid. Of those, 68% were determined to have financial need; 20% had their need fully met. Average financial aid package (proportion receiving): $13,219 (68%). Average amount of gift aid, such as scholarships or grants (proportion receiving): $10,434 (67%). Average amount of self-help aid, such as work study or loans (proportion receiving): $3,470 (57%). Average need-based loan (excluding PLUS or other private loans): $3,198. Among students who received need-based aid, the average percentage of need met: 71%. Among students who received aid based on merit, the average award (and the proportion receiving): $11,858 (15%). The average athletic scholarship (and the proportion receiving): $0 (0%). Average amount of debt of borrowers graduating in 2003: $15,758. Proportion who borrowed: 56%. Student employment: During the 2003-2004 academic year, 0% of undergraduates worked on campus. Average per-year earnings: $1,500.

Southern Methodist University

PO Box 750181
Dallas, TX 75275-0181
Private; www.smu.edu
Financial aid office: (214) 768-3016

■ 2004-2005 TUITION AND FEES: $25,358
■ ROOM AND BOARD: $8,852

SAT I Score (25th/75th percentile): 1110-1300
2005 U.S. News College Ranking:
National Universities, 71
Acceptance Rate: 65%

....

Other expenses: Estimated books and supplies: $600. Transportation: $300. Personal expenses: $1,100. Financial aid: Priority filing date for institution's financial aid form: February 1. In 2003-2004, 46% of undergraduates applied for financial aid. Of those, 39% were determined to have financial need; 45% had their need fully met. Average financial aid package (proportion receiving): $22,255 (39%). Average amount of gift aid, such as scholarships or grants (proportion receiving): $13,355 (34%). Average amount of self-help aid, such as work study or loans (proportion receiving): $5,320 (32%). Average need-based loan (excluding PLUS or other private loans): $3,511. Among students who received need-based aid, the average percentage of need met: 92%. Among students who received aid based on merit, the average award (and the proportion receiving): $5,485 (30%). The average athletic scholarship (and the proportion receiving): $25,455 (5%). Average amount of debt of borrowers graduating in 2003: $20,079. Proportion who borrowed: 54%. Cooperative education programs: business, engineering. Reserve Officers Training Corps (ROTC): Army ROTC: Offered at cooperating institution (Univ of Texas at Arlington); Air Force ROTC: Offered at cooperating institution (University of North Texas).

Southwestern Adventist University

PO Box 567
Keene, TX 76059
Private; www.swau.edu
Financial aid office: (817) 645-3921

■ 2004-2005 TUITION AND FEES: $11,858
■ ROOM AND BOARD: $5,534

2005 U.S. News College Ranking:
Comp. Colleges–Bachelor's (West), third tier

....

Southwestern University

PO Box 770
Georgetown, TX 78627-0770
Private; www.southwestern.edu
Financial aid office: (512) 863-1259

■ **2004-2005 TUITION AND FEES:** $20,220
■ **ROOM AND BOARD:** $6,870

SAT I Score (25th/75th percentile): 1150-1340
2005 U.S. News College Ranking:
Liberal Arts Colleges, 62
Acceptance Rate: 63%

Other expenses: Estimated books and supplies: $700. Transportation: $210. Personal expenses: $980. **Financial aid:** In 2003-2004, 65% of undergraduates applied for financial aid. Of those, 55% were determined to have financial need; 97% had their need fully met. Average financial aid package (proportion receiving): $17,781 (55%). Average amount of gift aid, such as scholarships or grants (proportion receiving): $10,653 (55%). Average amount of self-help aid, such as work study or loans (proportion receiving): $5,438 (47%). Average need-based loan (excluding PLUS or other private loans): $4,679. Among students who received need-based aid, the average percentage of need met: 97%. Among students who received aid based on merit, the average award (and the proportion receiving): $6,259 (23%). The average athletic scholarship (and the proportion receiving): $0 (0%). Average amount of debt of borrowers graduating in 2003: $16,301. Proportion who borrowed: 42%. **Student employment:** During the 2003-2004 academic year, 24% of undergraduates worked on campus. Average per-year earnings: $1,200. **Cooperative education programs:** engineering.

St. Edward's University

3001 S. Congress Avenue
Austin, TX 78704
Private; www.stedwards.edu
Financial aid office: (512) 448-8520

■ **2004-2005 TUITION AND FEES:** $15,960
■ **ROOM AND BOARD:** $6,268

SAT I Score (25th/75th percentile): 990-1200
2005 U.S. News College Ranking:
Universities–Master's (West), 25
Acceptance Rate: 70%

Other expenses: Estimated books and supplies: $870. Transportation: $832. Personal expenses: $2,370. **Financial aid:** In 2003-2004, 74% of undergraduates applied for financial aid. Of those, 60% were determined to have financial need; 14% had their need fully met. Average financial aid package (proportion receiving): $11,577 (60%). Average amount of gift aid, such as scholarships or grants (proportion receiving): $7,793 (53%). Average amount of self-help aid, such as work study or loans (proportion receiving): $4,447 (48%). Average need-based loan (excluding PLUS or other private loans): $4,221. Among students who received need-based aid, the average percentage of need met: 69%. Among students who received aid based on merit, the average award (and the proportion receiving): $4,770 (3%). The average athletic scholarship (and the proportion receiving): $8,717 (6%). Average amount of debt of borrowers graduating in 2003: $22,331. Proportion who borrowed: 64%. **Student employment:** During the 2003-2004 academic year, 20% of undergraduates worked on campus. Average per-year earnings: $2,000. **Cooperative education programs:** business. **Reserve Officers Training Corps (ROTC):** Army ROTC: Offered at cooperating institution (University of Texas–Austin); Air Force ROTC: Offered at cooperating institution (University of Texas–Austin).

Stephen F. Austin State University

SFA Station 13051
Nacogdoches, TX 75962
Public; www.sfasu.edu
Financial aid office: (936) 468-2403

■ **2004-2005 TUITION AND FEES:**
In state: $5,145; Out of state: $12,885
■ **ROOM AND BOARD:** $5,283

SAT I Score (25th/75th percentile): 940-1120
2005 U.S. News College Ranking:
Universities–Master's (West), third tier
Acceptance Rate: 73%

Other expenses: Estimated books and supplies: $905. Transportation: $1,874. Personal expenses: $1,557. **Financial aid:** Priority filing date for institution's financial aid form: April 1. In 2003-2004, 70% of undergraduates applied for financial aid. Of those, 53% were determined to have financial need; 28% had their need fully met. Average financial aid package (proportion receiving): $4,544 (52%). Average amount of gift aid, such as scholarships or grants (proportion receiving): $1,561 (43%). Average amount of self-help

aid, such as work study or loans (proportion receiving): $2,384 (43%). Average need-based loan (excluding PLUS or other private loans): $2,041. Among students who received need-based aid, the average percentage of need met: 60%. Among students who received aid based on merit, the average award (and the proportion receiving): $1,960 (4%). The average athletic scholarship (and the proportion receiving): $5,714 (3%). Average amount of debt of borrowers graduating in 2003: $11,070. Proportion who borrowed: 59%. Average per-year earnings: $4,100. **Reserve Officers Training Corps (ROTC):** Army ROTC: Offered on campus.

St. Mary's University of San Antonio

1 Camino Santa Maria
San Antonio, TX 78228
Private; www.stmarytx.edu
Financial aid office: (210) 436-3141

■ **2004-2005 TUITION AND FEES:** $17,756
■ **ROOM AND BOARD:** $6,498

SAT I Score (25th/75th percentile): 970-1160
2005 U.S. News College Ranking:
Universities–Master's (West), 14
Acceptance Rate: 81%

Other expenses: Estimated books and supplies: $1,000. Transportation: $600. Personal expenses: $1,177. **Financial aid:** Priority filing date for institution's financial aid form: February 15. In 2003-2004, 79% of undergraduates applied for financial aid. Of those, 72% were determined to have financial need; 23% had their need fully met. Average financial aid package (proportion receiving): $13,454 (72%). Average amount of gift aid, such as scholarships or grants (proportion receiving): $7,492 (64%). Average amount of self-help aid, such as work study or loans (proportion receiving): $5,207 (61%). Average need-based loan (excluding PLUS or other private loans): $4,488. Among students who received need-based aid, the average percentage of need met: 69%. Among students who received aid based on merit, the average award (and the proportion receiving): $8,897 (7%). The average athletic scholarship (and the proportion receiving): $9,576 (7%). Average amount of debt of borrowers graduating in 2003: $23,406. Proportion who borrowed: 81%. **Student employment:** During the 2003-2004 academic year, 11% of undergraduates worked on campus. Average per-year earnings: $4,500. **Reserve Officers Training Corps (ROTC):** Army ROTC: Offered on campus.

Sul Ross State University

E. Highway 90
Alpine, TX 79832
Public; www.sulross.edu
Financial aid office: (432) 837-8059

■ **2003-2004 TUITION AND FEES:**
In state: $3,402; Out of state: $10,482
■ **ROOM AND BOARD:** $3,950

ACT Score (25th/75th percentile): 15-19
2005 U.S. News College Ranking:
Universities–Master's (West), fourth tier
Acceptance Rate: 73%

Other expenses: Estimated books and supplies:
$692. Transportation: $691. Personal expenses:
$1,610. **Student employment:** During the 2003-
2004 academic year, 9% of undergraduates
worked on campus. Average per-year earnings:
$4,944.

Tarleton State University

Box T 0001, Tarleton Station
Stephenville, TX 76402
Public; www.tarleton.edu
Financial aid office: (254) 968-9070

■ **2004-2005 TUITION AND FEES:**
In state: $6,229; Out of state: $13,969
■ **ROOM AND BOARD:** $5,200

SAT I Score (25th/75th percentile): 860-1050
2005 U.S. News College Ranking:
Universities–Master's (West), fourth tier
Acceptance Rate: 90%

Other expenses: Estimated books and supplies:
$792. Transportation: $601. Personal expenses:
$1,919. **Financial aid:** Priority filing date for
institution's financial aid form: April 1; deadline: October 15. In 2003-2004, 71% of undergraduates applied for financial aid. Of those,
69% were determined to have financial need;
54% had their need fully met. Average financial
aid package (proportion receiving): $7,733
(56%). Average amount of gift aid, such as
scholarships or grants (proportion receiving):
$3,296 (41%). Average amount of self-help aid,
such as work study or loans (proportion receiving): $4,599 (40%). Average need-based loan
(excluding PLUS or other private loans): $3,336.
Among students who received need-based aid,
the average percentage of need met: 60%.
Among students who received aid based on
merit, the average award (and the proportion

receiving): $3,903 (17%). The average athletic
scholarship (and the proportion receiving):
$3,069 (3%). Average amount of debt of bor-
rowers graduating in 2003: $16,921. Proportion
who borrowed: 61%. **Student employment:**
During the 2003-2004 academic year, 8% of
undergraduates worked on campus. Average
per-year earnings: $2,500. **Reserve Officers
Training Corps (ROTC):** Army ROTC: Offered
on campus.

Texas A&M International University

5201 University Boulevard
Laredo, TX 78041-1900
Public; www.tamiu.edu
Financial aid office: (956) 326-2225

■ **2004-2005 TUITION AND FEES:**
In state: $3,833; Out of state: $11,573
■ **ROOM AND BOARD:** $6,166

SAT I Score (25th/75th percentile): 770-990
2005 U.S. News College Ranking:
Universities–Master's (West), third tier
Acceptance Rate: 65%

Other expenses: Estimated books and supplies:
$1,300. Transportation: $842. Personal expenses: $2,098. **Financial aid:** Priority filing date for
institution's financial aid form: March 15. In
2003-2004, 78% of undergraduates applied for
financial aid. Of those, 72% were determined to
have financial need; 27% had their need fully
met. Average financial aid package (proportion
receiving): $8,319 (70%). Average amount of
gift aid, such as scholarships or grants (proportion receiving): $5,743 (67%). Average amount
of self-help aid, such as work study or loans
(proportion receiving): $3,458 (28%). Average
need-based loan (excluding PLUS or other private loans): $3,484. Among students who
received need-based aid, the average percentage
of need met: 84%. Among students who
received aid based on merit, the average award
(and the proportion receiving): $3,582 (3%).
Average amount of debt of borrowers graduating in 2003: $12,100. Proportion who bor-
rowed: 54%. **Student employment:** During the
2003-2004 academic year, 5% of undergraduates worked on campus. Average per-year earnings: $4,800. **Reserve Officers Training Corps
(ROTC):** Army ROTC: Offered on campus.

Texas A&M University– College Station

College Station, TX 77843
Public; www.tamu.edu
Financial aid office: (979) 845-3236

■ **2004-2005 TUITION AND FEES:**
In state: $5,964; Out of state: $13,704
■ **ROOM AND BOARD:** $6,887

SAT I Score (25th/75th percentile): 1070-1300
2005 U.S. News College Ranking:
National Universities, 62
Acceptance Rate: 67%

Other expenses: Estimated books and supplies:
$1,186. Transportation: $692. Personal expenses: $1,618. **Financial aid:** Priority filing date for
institution's financial aid form: April 1. In
2003-2004, 51% of undergraduates applied for
financial aid. Of those, 28% were determined
to have financial need; 23% had their need fully
met. Average financial aid package (proportion
receiving): $8,115 (27%). Average amount of gift
aid, such as scholarships or grants (proportion
receiving): $4,644 (27%). Average amount of
self-help aid, such as work study or loans (proportion receiving): $2,312 (22%). Average need-
based loan (excluding PLUS or other private
loans): $3,342. Among students who received
need-based aid, the average percentage of need
met: 83%. Among students who received aid
based on merit, the average award (and the proportion receiving): $4,079 (6%). The average
athletic scholarship (and the proportion receiving): $8,709 (1%). Average amount of debt of
borrowers graduating in 2003: $16,500.
Proportion who borrowed: 34%. **Student
employment:** During the 2003-2004 academic
year, 27% of undergraduates worked on campus. Average per-year earnings: $2,275.
Cooperative education programs: agriculture,
business, computer science, engineering,
health professions, humanities, natural science,
social/behavioral science, technologies. **Reserve
Officers Training Corps (ROTC):** Army ROTC:
Offered on campus; Navy ROTC: Offered on
campus; Air Force ROTC: Offered on campus.

Texas A&M University–Commerce

PO Box 3011
Commerce, TX 75429
Public; www.tamu-commerce.edu
Financial aid office: (903) 886-5096

■ **2004-2005 TUITION AND FEES:**
 In state: $3,830; Out of state: $11,570
■ **ROOM AND BOARD:** $5,740

ACT Score (25th/75th percentile): 19-22
2005 U.S. News College Ranking:
National Universities, fourth tier
Acceptance Rate: 53%

Other expenses: Estimated books and supplies: $990. Transportation: $1,230. Personal expenses: $1,550. **Financial aid:** Priority filing date for institution's financial aid form: May 1. In 2003-2004, 75% of undergraduates applied for financial aid. Of those, 64% were determined to have financial need; 20% had their need fully met. Average financial aid package (proportion receiving): $6,993 (62%). Average amount of gift aid, such as scholarships or grants (proportion receiving): $4,751 (56%). Average amount of self-help aid, such as work study or loans (proportion receiving): $3,488 (49%). Average need-based loan (excluding PLUS or other private loans): $3,348. Among students who received need-based aid, the average percentage of need met: 70%. Among students who received aid based on merit, the average award (and the proportion receiving): $1,753 (14%). The average athletic scholarship (and the proportion receiving): $3,043 (1%). Average amount of debt of borrowers graduating in 2003: $16,892. Proportion who borrowed: 60%. **Cooperative education programs:** agriculture, art, business, computer science, education, engineering, humanities, natural science, social/behavioral science, technologies.

Texas A&M University–Corpus Christi

6300 Ocean Drive
Corpus Christi, TX 78412-5503
Public; www.tamucc.edu
Financial aid office: (361) 825-2338

■ **2004-2005 TUITION AND FEES:**
 In state: $4,272; Out of state: $12,012
■ **ROOM AND BOARD:** $7,755

SAT I Score (25th/75th percentile): 808-1058
2005 U.S. News College Ranking:
Universities–Master's (West), 58
Acceptance Rate: 84%

Other expenses: Estimated books and supplies: $840. Transportation: $1,372. Personal expenses: $1,245. **Financial aid:** Priority filing date for institution's financial aid form: April 1; deadline: April 1. In 2003-2004, 67% of undergraduates applied for financial aid. Of those, 64% were determined to have financial need; 5% had their need fully met. Average financial aid package (proportion receiving): $5,676 (61%). Average amount of gift aid, such as scholarships or grants (proportion receiving): $3,753 (44%). Average amount of self-help aid, such as work study or loans (proportion receiving): $3,769 (37%). Average need-based loan (excluding PLUS or other private loans): $3,656. Among students who received need-based aid, the average percentage of need met: 60%. Among students who received aid based on merit, the average award (and the proportion receiving): $4,153 (3%). The average athletic scholarship (and the proportion receiving): $7,872 (0%). Average amount of debt of borrowers graduating in 2003: $16,886. Proportion who borrowed: 59%. **Cooperative education programs:** education, health professions.

Texas A&M University–Galveston

PO Box 1675
Galveston, TX 77553-1675
Public; www.tamug.edu
Financial aid office: (409) 740-4500

■ **2004-2005 TUITION AND FEES:**
 In state: $4,098; Out of state: $11,178
■ **ROOM AND BOARD:** $4,870

SAT I Score (25th/75th percentile): 981-1261
2005 U.S. News College Ranking:
Liberal Arts Colleges, fourth tier
Acceptance Rate: 95%

Other expenses: Estimated books and supplies: $926. Transportation: $874. Personal expenses: $1,056. **Financial aid:** In 2003-2004, 55% of undergraduates applied for financial aid. Of those, 48% were determined to have financial need; 36% had their need fully met. Average financial aid package (proportion receiving): $9,281 (47%). Average amount of gift aid, such as scholarships or grants (proportion receiving): $4,201 (26%). Average amount of self-help aid, such as work study or loans (proportion receiving): $2,629 (1%). Average need-based loan (excluding PLUS or other private loans): $2,656. Among students who received need-based aid, the average percentage of need met: 37%. Among students who received aid based on merit, the average award (and the proportion receiving): $4,969 (6%). Average amount of debt of borrowers graduating in 2003: $9,870. Proportion who borrowed: 64%. **Student employment:** During the 2003-2004 academic year, 12% of undergraduates worked on campus. Average per-year earnings: $4,944. **Cooperative education programs:** other. **Reserve Officers Training Corps (ROTC):** Navy ROTC: Offered on campus.

Texas A&M University–Kingsville

MSC 105
Kingsville, TX 78363
Public; www.tamuk.edu
Financial aid office: (361) 593-3911

■ **2004-2005 TUITION AND FEES:**
 In state: $4,958; Out of state: $11,150
■ **ROOM AND BOARD:** $4,057

ACT Score (25th/75th percentile): 16-21
2005 U.S. News College Ranking:
National Universities, fourth tier
Acceptance Rate: 89%

Other expenses: Estimated books and supplies: $1,000. Transportation: $1,560. Personal expenses: $2,226. **Financial aid:** Priority filing date for institution's financial aid form: April 15. In 2003-2004, 91% of undergraduates applied for financial aid. Of those, 91% were determined to have financial need; 70% had their need fully met. Average financial aid package (proportion receiving): $6,500 (91%). Average amount of gift aid, such as scholarships or grants (proportion receiving): $5,850 (89%). Average amount of self-help aid, such as work study or loans (proportion receiving): $6,475 (73%). Average need-based loan (excluding PLUS or other private loans): $3,875. Among students who received need-based aid, the average percentage of need met: 89%. **Student employment:** During the 2003-2004 academic year, 18% of undergraduates worked on campus. Average per-year earnings: $1,752. **Cooperative education programs:** agriculture, education, home economics. **Reserve Officers Training Corps (ROTC):** Army ROTC: Offered on campus.

Texas Christian University

2800 S. University Drive
Fort Worth, TX 76129
Private; www.tcu.edu
Financial aid office: (817) 257-7858

■ **2004-2005 TUITION AND FEES:** $19,740
■ **ROOM AND BOARD:** $5,880

SAT I Score (25th/75th percentile): 1060-1260
2005 U.S. News College Ranking:
National Universities, 98
Acceptance Rate: 65%

Other expenses: Estimated books and supplies:
$780. Transportation: $324. Personal expenses:
$2,870. **Financial aid:** Priority filing date for
institution's financial aid form: May 1; deadline:
May 1. In 2003-2004, 55% of undergraduates
applied for financial aid. Of those, 43% were
determined to have financial need; 41% had
their need fully met. Average financial aid package (proportion receiving): $12,614 (43%).
Average amount of gift aid, such as scholarships or grants (proportion receiving): $8,877
(37%). Average amount of self-help aid, such as
work study or loans (proportion receiving):
$6,219 (34%). Average need-based loan (exclud-
ing PLUS or other private loans): $4,970.
Among students who received need-based aid,
the average percentage of need met: 94%.
Among students who received aid based on
merit, the average award (and the proportion
receiving): $7,979 (20%). The average athletic
scholarship (and the proportion receiving):
$15,604 (4%). **Reserve Officers Training Corps**
(ROTC): Army ROTC: Offered on campus; Air
Force ROTC: Offered on campus.

Texas College

2404 N. Grand Avenue, Box 4500
Tyler, TX 75712
Private; www.texascollege.edu
Financial aid office: (903) 593-8311

■ **2004-2005 TUITION AND FEES:** $7,700
■ **ROOM AND BOARD:** $4,730

2005 U.S. News College Ranking:
Comp. Colleges–Bachelor's (West), fourth tier
Acceptance Rate: 98%

Other expenses: Estimated books and supplies:
$800. Transportation: $650. Personal expenses:
$1,740. **Financial aid:** Priority filing date for insti-
tution's financial aid form: April 15; deadline:

April 15. In 2003-2004, 99% of undergraduates
applied for financial aid. Of those, 83% were
determined to have financial need; 64% had their
need fully met. Average financial aid package
(proportion receiving): $6,675 (83%). Average
amount of gift aid, such as scholarships or grants
(proportion receiving): $2,800 (83%). Average
amount of self-help aid, such as work study or
loans (proportion receiving): $0 (83%). Average
need-based loan (excluding PLUS or other private
loans): $2,000. Among students who received
need-based aid, the average percentage of need
met: 65%. Among students who received aid
based on merit, the average award (and the proportion receiving): $0 (0%). The average athletic
scholarship (and the proportion receiving):
$3,469 (14%). **Student employment:** During the
2003-2004 academic year, 0% of undergraduates
worked on campus.

Texas Lutheran University

1000 W. Court
Seguin, TX 78155-5999
Private; www.tlu.edu
Financial aid office: (830) 372-8075

■ **2004-2005 TUITION AND FEES:** $16,600
■ **ROOM AND BOARD:** $5,030

SAT I Score (25th/75th percentile): 930-1160
2005 U.S. News College Ranking:
Comp. Colleges–Bachelor's (West), 3
Acceptance Rate: 78%

Other expenses: Estimated books and supplies:
$740. Transportation: $800. Personal expenses:
$1,100. **Financial aid:** Priority filing date for
institution's financial aid form: April 1. In
2003-2004, 98% of undergraduates applied for
financial aid. Of those, 73% were determined to
have financial need; 80% had their need fully
met. Average financial aid package (proportion
receiving): $12,271 (73%). Average amount of
gift aid, such as scholarships or grants (proportion receiving): $10,993 (58%). Average amount
of self-help aid, such as work study or loans
(proportion receiving): $4,705 (56%). Average
need-based loan (excluding PLUS or other private loans): $4,126. Among students who
received need-based aid, the average percentage
of need met: 80%. Among students who
received aid based on merit, the average award
(and the proportion receiving): $9,491 (24%).
The average athletic scholarship (and the proportion receiving): $0 (0%). Average amount of
debt of borrowers graduating in 2003: $21,500.
Proportion who borrowed: 62%. **Student**
employment: During the 2003-2004 academic

year, 10% of undergraduates worked on cam-
pus. Average per-year earnings: $1,050. **Reserve**
Officers Training Corps (ROTC): Army ROTC:
Offered at cooperating institution (Texas State
University); Air Force ROTC: Offered at cooper-
ating institution (Texas State University).

Texas Southern University

3100 Cleburne
Houston, TX 77004
Public; www.tsu.edu
Financial aid office: (713) 313-7071

■ **2004-2005 TUITION AND FEES:**
 In state: $4,416; Out of state: $13,476
■ **ROOM AND BOARD:** $6,056

2005 U.S. News College Ranking:
National Universities, fourth tier

Other expenses: Estimated books and supplies:
$819. Transportation: $824. Personal expenses:
$1,909.

Texas State University–
San Marcos

601 University Drive
San Marcos, TX 78666
Public; www.txstate.edu
Financial aid office: (512) 245-2315

■ **2004-2005 TUITION AND FEES:**
 In state: $4,680; Out of state: $12,420
■ **ROOM AND BOARD:** $5,456

SAT I Score (25th/75th percentile): 970-1150
2005 U.S. News College Ranking:
Universities–Master's (West), 52
Acceptance Rate: 56%

Other expenses: Estimated books and supplies:
$950. Transportation: $840. Personal expenses:
$2,370. **Financial aid:** Priority filing date for insti-
tution's financial aid form: April 1. In 2003-
2004, 61% of undergraduates applied for financial aid. Of those, 52% were determined to have
financial need; 16% had their need fully met.
Average financial aid package (proportion receiving): $8,169 (50%). Average amount of gift aid,
such as scholarships or grants (proportion receiving): $3,651 (32%). Average amount of self-help
aid, such as work study or loans (proportion
receiving): $3,808 (34%). Average need-based
loan (excluding PLUS or other private loans):
$3,664. Among students who received need-
based aid, the average percentage of need met:

69%. Among students who received aid based on merit, the average award (and the proportion receiving): $6,804 (13%). The average athletic scholarship (and the proportion receiving): $6,424 (2%). Average amount of debt of borrowers graduating in 2003: $15,084. Proportion who borrowed: 55%. **Student employment:** During the 2003-2004 academic year, 5% of undergraduates worked on campus. Average per-year earnings: $3,795. **Cooperative education programs:** agriculture, home economics, technologies, vocational arts. **Reserve Officers Training Corps (ROTC):** Army ROTC: Offered on campus; Air Force ROTC: Offered on campus.

Texas Tech University

Box 42013
Lubbock, TX 79409
Public; www.ttu.edu
Financial aid office: (806) 742-3681

■ **2004-2005 TUITION AND FEES:**
In state: $5,848; Out of state: $13,588
■ **ROOM AND BOARD:** $6,360

SAT I Score (25th/75th percentile): 1020-1220
2005 U.S. News College Ranking:
National Universities, third tier
Acceptance Rate: 67%

Other expenses: Estimated books and supplies: $900. Transportation: $1,400. Personal expenses: $1,800. **Financial aid:** Priority filing date for institution's financial aid form: May 1. In 2003-2004, 62% of undergraduates applied for financial aid. Of those, 41% were determined to have financial need; 17% had their need fully met. Average financial aid package (proportion receiving): $6,318 (41%). Average amount of gift aid, such as scholarships or grants (proportion receiving): $3,248 (26%). Average amount of self-help aid, such as work study or loans (proportion receiving): $3,646 (32%). Average need-based loan (excluding PLUS or other private loans): $3,582. Among students who received need-based aid, the average percentage of need met: 68%. Among students who received aid based on merit, the average award (and the proportion receiving): $2,187 (26%). The average athletic scholarship (and the proportion receiving): $8,046 (1%). Average amount of debt of borrowers graduating in 2003: $15,780. Proportion who borrowed: 56%. **Student employment:** During the 2003-2004 academic year, 20% of undergraduates worked on campus. Average per-year earnings: $4,330. **Cooperative education programs:** agriculture, art, business, computer science, education, engineering, health professions, home economics, humanities, natural science, social/behavioral science, technologies, other. **Reserve Officers Training Corps (ROTC):** Army ROTC: Offered on campus; Air Force ROTC: Offered on campus.

Texas Wesleyan University

1201 Wesleyan
Fort Worth, TX 76105-1536
Private; www.txwesleyan.edu
Financial aid office: (817) 531-4420

■ **2004-2005 TUITION AND FEES:** $12,920
■ **ROOM AND BOARD:** $3,386

ACT Score (25th/75th percentile): 20
2005 U.S. News College Ranking:
Universities–Master's (West), 44
Acceptance Rate: 43%

Other expenses: Estimated books and supplies: $750. Transportation: $865. Personal expenses: $1,875. **Financial aid:** In 2003-2004, 79% of undergraduates applied for financial aid. Of those, 61% were determined to have financial need; 65% had their need fully met. Average financial aid package (proportion receiving): N/A (61%). Average amount of self-help aid, such as work study or loans (proportion receiving): $4,100 (58%). Average need-based loan (excluding PLUS or other private loans): $4,100. Among students who received aid based on merit, the average award (and the proportion receiving): N/A (23%). The average athletic scholarship (and the proportion receiving): $5,572 (8%). **Student employment:** During the 2003-2004 academic year, 1% of undergraduates worked on campus. Average per-year earnings: $2,500. **Reserve Officers Training Corps (ROTC):** Army ROTC: Offered at cooperating institution (Texas Christian University); Air Force ROTC: Offered at cooperating institution (Texas Christian University).

Texas Woman's University

Box 425619
Denton, TX 76204-5587
Public; www.twu.edu
Financial aid office: (940) 898-3051

■ **2004-2005 TUITION AND FEES:**
In state: $4,380; Out of state: $12,120
■ **ROOM AND BOARD:** $5,094

SAT I Score (25th/75th percentile): 820-1060
2005 U.S. News College Ranking:
National Universities, fourth tier
Acceptance Rate: 72%

Other expenses: Estimated books and supplies: $720. Transportation: $742. Personal expenses: $1,744. **Financial aid:** Priority filing date for institution's financial aid form: March 1. In 2003-2004, 73% of undergraduates applied for financial aid. Of those, 59% were determined to have financial need; 80% had their need fully met. Average financial aid package (proportion receiving): $10,412 (58%). Average amount of gift aid, such as scholarships or grants (proportion receiving): $3,934 (43%). Average amount of self-help aid, such as work study or loans (proportion receiving): $1,771 (48%). Average need-based loan (excluding PLUS or other private loans): $3,720. Among students who received need-based aid, the average percentage of need met: 98%. Among students who received aid based on merit, the average award (and the proportion receiving): $2,100 (5%). The average athletic scholarship (and the proportion receiving): $3,733 (2%). Average amount of debt of borrowers graduating in 2003: $14,173. Proportion who borrowed: 16%. **Student employment:** During the 2003-2004 academic year, 13% of undergraduates worked on campus. Average per-year earnings: $4,430. **Cooperative education programs:** art, business, computer science, health professions, home economics, humanities, natural science, social/behavioral science. **Reserve Officers Training Corps (ROTC):** Army ROTC: Offered at cooperating institution (University of Texas–Arlington); Air Force ROTC: Offered at cooperating institution (University of North Texas).

Trinity University

1 Trinity Place
San Antonio, TX 78212-7200
Private; www.trinity.edu
Financial aid office: (210) 999-8315

■ **2004-2005 TUITION AND FEES:** $20,635
■ **ROOM AND BOARD:** $7,580

SAT I Score (25th/75th percentile): 1220-1380
2005 U.S. News College Ranking:
Universities–Master's (West), 1
Acceptance Rate: 64%

Other expenses: Estimated books and supplies: $625. Transportation: $510. Personal expenses: $950. **Financial aid:** Priority filing date for institution's financial aid form: February 1; deadline: April 1. In 2003-2004, 54% of undergraduates applied for financial aid. Of those, 42% were determined to have financial need; 62% had their need fully met. Average financial aid package (proportion receiving): $15,486 (41%). Average amount of gift aid, such as scholarships or grants (proportion receiving): $10,905 (39%). Average amount of self-help aid, such as work study or loans (proportion receiving): $5,162 (33%). Average need-based loan (excluding PLUS or other private loans): $4,215. Among students who received need-based aid, the average percentage of need met: 86%. Among students who received aid based on merit, the average award (and the proportion receiving): $6,358 (37%). The average athletic scholarship (and the proportion receiving): $0 (0%). Proportion who borrowed: 31%. **Student employment:** During the 2003-2004 academic year, 35% of undergraduates worked on campus. Average per-year earnings: $1,650. **Reserve Officers Training Corps (ROTC):** Air Force ROTC: Offered at cooperating institution (University of Texas at San Antonio).

University of Dallas

1845 E. Northgate Drive
Irving, TX 75062-4736
Private; www.udallas.edu
Financial aid office: (972) 721-5266

- **2004-2005 TUITION AND FEES:** $19,162
- **ROOM AND BOARD:** $6,736

SAT I Score (25th/75th percentile): 1060-1320
2005 U.S. News College Ranking:
Liberal Arts Colleges, third tier
Acceptance Rate: 89%

Other expenses: Estimated books and supplies: $1,000. Transportation: $1,800. Personal expenses: $1,100. **Financial aid:** Priority filing date for institution's financial aid form: March 1. In 2003-2004, 80% of undergraduates applied for financial aid. Of those, 63% were determined to have financial need; 21% had their need fully met. Average financial aid package (proportion receiving): $14,036 (63%). Average amount of gift aid, such as scholarships or grants (proportion receiving): $9,935 (61%). Average amount of self-help aid, such as work study or loans (proportion receiving): $5,091 (51%). Average need-based loan (excluding PLUS or other private loans): $4,320. Among students who received need-based aid, the average percentage of need met: 76%. Among students who received aid based on merit, the average award (and the proportion receiving): $9,960 (31%). The average

athletic scholarship (and the proportion receiving): $0 (0%). Average amount of debt of borrowers graduating in 2003: $20,836. Proportion who borrowed: 65%. **Reserve Officers Training Corps (ROTC):** Army ROTC: Offered at cooperating institution (University of Texas at Arlington); Air Force ROTC: Offered at cooperating institution (University of North Texas).

University of Houston

212 E. Cullen Building
Houston, TX 77204
Public; www.uh.edu
Financial aid office: (713) 743-9090

- **2004-2005 TUITION AND FEES:** In state: $4,973; Out of state: $12,713
- **ROOM AND BOARD:** $6,030

SAT I Score (25th/75th percentile): 940-1170
2005 U.S. News College Ranking:
National Universities, fourth tier
Acceptance Rate: 78%

Other expenses: Estimated books and supplies: $1,150. Transportation: $2,350. Personal expenses: $2,900. **Financial aid:** Priority filing date for institution's financial aid form: April 1; deadline: April 1. In 2003-2004, 90% of undergraduates applied for financial aid. Of those, 77% were determined to have financial need; 31% had their need fully met. Average financial aid package (proportion receiving): $12,000 (58%). Average amount of gift aid, such as scholarships or grants (proportion receiving): $7,800 (44%). Average amount of self-help aid, such as work study or loans (proportion receiving): $4,500 (48%). Average need-based loan (excluding PLUS or other private loans): $4,200. Among students who received need-based aid, the average percentage of need met: 81%. Among students who received aid based on merit, the average award (and the proportion receiving): $2,800 (19%). The average athletic scholarship (and the proportion receiving): $8,331 (1%). Average amount of debt of borrowers graduating in 2003: $13,961. Proportion who borrowed: 30%. **Student employment:** During the 2003-2004 academic year, 75% of undergraduates worked on campus. Average per-year earnings: $5,900. **Cooperative education programs:** business, computer science, education, engineering, natural science, technologies, other. **Reserve Officers Training Corps (ROTC):** Army ROTC: Offered on campus; Navy ROTC: Offered at cooperating institution (Rice University); Air Force ROTC: Offered on campus.

University of Houston–Downtown

1 Main Street
Houston, TX 77002
Public; www.uhd.edu
Financial aid office: (713) 221-8041

- **2004-2005 TUITION AND FEES:** In state: $3,314; Out of state: $10,394

2005 U.S. News College Ranking:
Comp. Colleges–Bachelor's (West), fourth tier
Acceptance Rate: 100%

Reserve Officers Training Corps (ROTC): Army ROTC: Offered at cooperating institution (University of Houston Central Campus).

University of Mary Hardin-Baylor

900 College Street, UMHB Box 8425
Belton, TX 76513
Private; www.umhb.edu
Financial aid office: (254) 295-4517

- **2004-2005 TUITION AND FEES:** $12,380
- **ROOM AND BOARD:** $4,000

SAT I Score (25th/75th percentile): 930-1140
2005 U.S. News College Ranking:
Universities–Master's (West), 47
Acceptance Rate: 76%

Other expenses: Estimated books and supplies: $900. Transportation: $1,123. Personal expenses: $1,869. **Financial aid:** Priority filing date for institution's financial aid form: February 15. In 2003-2004, 86% of undergraduates applied for financial aid. Of those, 69% were determined to have financial need; 12% had their need fully met. Average financial aid package (proportion receiving): $11,228 (69%). Average amount of gift aid, such as scholarships or grants (proportion receiving): $4,922 (59%). Average amount of self-help aid, such as work study or loans (proportion receiving): $5,057 (54%). Average need-based loan (excluding PLUS or other private loans): $4,516. Among students who received need-based aid, the average percentage of need met: 75%. Among students who received aid based on merit, the average award (and the proportion receiving): $3,141 (21%). The average athletic scholarship (and the proportion receiving): $0 (0%). Average amount of debt of borrowers graduating in 2003: $13,437. Proportion who borrowed: 72%. **Student employment:** During the 2003-2004 academic year, 1% of undergraduates worked on campus. Average per-year earnings: $2,300. **Reserve Officers Training Corps (ROTC):** Air Force ROTC: Offered at cooperating institution (Baylor University).

University of North Texas

PO Box 311277
Denton, TX 76203
Public; www.unt.edu
Financial aid office: (940) 565-2302

■ **2004-2005 TUITION AND FEES:**
 In state: $5,850; Out of state: $13,590
■ **ROOM AND BOARD:** $5,100

SAT I Score (25th/75th percentile): 980-1220
2005 U.S. News College Ranking:
National Universities, fourth tier
Acceptance Rate: 68%

Other expenses: Estimated books and supplies: $1,030. Transportation: $1,130. Personal expenses: $1,080. **Financial aid:** Priority filing date for institution's financial aid form: June 1. In 2003-2004, 60% of undergraduates applied for financial aid. Of those, 43% were determined to have financial need; 18% had their need fully met. Average financial aid package (proportion receiving): $6,179 (41%). Average amount of gift aid, such as scholarships or grants (proportion receiving): $3,626 (31%). Average amount of self-help aid, such as work study or loans (proportion receiving): $3,915 (36%). Average need-based loan (excluding PLUS or other private loans): $3,433. Among students who received need-based aid, the average percentage of need met: 66%. Among students who received aid based on merit, the average award (and the proportion receiving): $2,555 (11%). The average athletic scholarship (and the proportion receiving): $3,131 (1%). Average amount of debt of borrowers graduating in 2003: $15,466. Proportion who borrowed: 43%. **Student employment:** During the 2003-2004 academic year, 14% of undergraduates worked on campus. Average per-year earnings: $5,000. **Cooperative education programs:** art, business, computer science, education, engineering, health professions, humanities, natural science, social/behavioral science, technologies. **Reserve Officers Training Corps (ROTC):** Army ROTC: Offered at cooperating institution (UT Arlington); Air Force ROTC: Offered on campus.

University of St. Thomas

3800 Montrose Boulevard
Houston, TX 77006-4696
Private; www.stthom.edu
Financial aid office: (713) 942-3465

■ **2004-2005 TUITION AND FEES:** $16,312
■ **ROOM AND BOARD:** $7,300

SAT I Score (25th/75th percentile): 1040-1240
2005 U.S. News College Ranking:
Universities–Master's (West), 26
Acceptance Rate: 89%

Other expenses: Estimated books and supplies: $800. Transportation: $1,628. Personal expenses: $1,696. **Financial aid:** Priority filing date for institution's financial aid form: March 1. In 2003-2004, 65% of undergraduates applied for financial aid. Of those, 58% were determined to have financial need; 16% had their need fully met. Average financial aid package (proportion receiving): $10,983 (57%). Average amount of gift aid, such as scholarships or grants (proportion receiving): $7,775 (54%). Average amount of self-help aid, such as work study or loans (proportion receiving): $3,846 (36%). Average need-based loan (excluding PLUS or other private loans): $3,712. Among students who received need-based aid, the average percentage of need met: 68%. Among students who received aid based on merit, the average award (and the proportion receiving): $6,795 (19%). The average athletic scholarship (and the proportion receiving): $0 (0%). Average amount of debt of borrowers graduating in 2003: $20,393. Proportion who borrowed: 49%. **Reserve Officers Training Corps (ROTC):** Army ROTC: Offered at cooperating institution (University of Houston).

University of Texas–Arlington

701 S. Nedderman Drive
Arlington, TX 76019
Public; www.uta.edu
Financial aid office: (817) 272-3568

■ **2004-2005 TUITION AND FEES:**
 In state: $5,300; Out of state: $14,360
■ **ROOM AND BOARD:** $4,829

SAT I Score (25th/75th percentile): 960-1180
2005 U.S. News College Ranking:
National Universities, fourth tier
Acceptance Rate: 77%

Financial aid: Priority filing date for institution's financial aid form: May 15. In 2003-2004, 61% of undergraduates applied for financial aid. Of those, 47% were determined to have financial need; 19% had their need fully met. Average financial aid package (proportion receiving): $8,014 (47%). Average amount of gift aid, such as scholarships or grants (proportion receiving): $4,381 (35%). Average amount of self-help aid, such as work study or loans (proportion receiving): $5,213 (38%). Average need-based loan (excluding PLUS or other private loans): $4,975. Among students who received need-based aid, the average percentage of need met: 80%. Among students who received aid based on merit, the average award (and the proportion receiving): $2,114 (12%). The average athletic scholarship (and the proportion receiving): $6,432 (1%). Average amount of debt of borrowers graduating in 2003: $12,934. Proportion who borrowed: 47%. **Cooperative education programs:** business, engineering, other. **Reserve Officers Training Corps (ROTC):** Army ROTC: Offered on campus; Air Force ROTC: Offered at cooperating institution (Texas Christian University).

University of Texas–Austin

Main Building, Room 7
Austin, TX 78712-1111
Public; www.utexas.edu
Financial aid office: (512) 475-6203

■ **2004-2005 TUITION AND FEES:**
 In state: $5,735; Out of state: $14,435
■ **ROOM AND BOARD:** $6,184

SAT I Score (25th/75th percentile): 1110-1350
2005 U.S. News College Ranking:
National Universities, 46
Acceptance Rate: 47%

Other expenses: Estimated books and supplies: $762. Transportation: $788. Personal expenses: $2,064. **Financial aid:** Priority filing date for institution's financial aid form: April 1. In 2003-2004, 66% of undergraduates applied for financial aid. Of those, 51% were determined to have financial need; 86% had their need fully met. Average financial aid package (proportion receiving): $8,750 (49%). Average amount of gift aid, such as scholarships or grants (proportion receiving): $5,450 (33%). Average amount of self-help aid, such as work study or loans (proportion receiving): $4,650 (44%). Average need-based loan (excluding PLUS or other private loans): $4,530. Among students who received need-based aid, the average percentage of need met: 94%. Among students who received aid based on merit, the average award (and the proportion receiving): $4,560 (26%). Average amount of debt of borrowers graduating in 2003: $16,500. Proportion who borrowed: 37%. **Cooperative education programs:** engineering. **Reserve Officers Training Corps (ROTC):** Army ROTC: Offered on campus; Navy ROTC: Offered on campus; Air Force ROTC: Offered on campus.

University of Texas–Brownsville

80 Fort Brown
Brownsville, TX 78520
Public; www.utb.edu
Financial aid office: (956) 544-8265

■ **2004-2005 TUITION AND FEES:**
   In state: $3,054; Out of state: $11,093
■ **ROOM AND BOARD:** $4,869

2005 U.S. News College Ranking:
Universities–Master's (West), fourth tier
Acceptance Rate: 100%

Other expenses: Estimated books and supplies: $544. Transportation: $1,395. Personal expenses: $2,232. **Financial aid:** Priority filing date for institution's financial aid form: April 1; deadline: January 1. In 2003-2004, 84% of undergraduates applied for financial aid. Of those, 79% were determined to have financial need; Average financial aid package (proportion receiving): $3,048 (78%). Average amount of gift aid, such as scholarships or grants (proportion receiving): $2,269 (74%). Average amount of self-help aid, such as work study or loans (proportion receiving): $1,916 (36%). Average need-based loan (excluding PLUS or other private loans): $1,769. Among students who received need-based aid, the average percentage of need met: 38%. Among students who received aid based on merit, the average award (and the proportion receiving): $2,085 (2%). The average athletic scholarship (and the proportion receiving): $1,428 (1%). **Cooperative education programs:** business, computer science, engineering, health professions, social/behavioral science, technologies, vocational arts.

University of Texas–Dallas

PO Box 830688
Richardson, TX 75083-0688
Public; www.utdallas.edu
Financial aid office: (972) 883-2941

■ **2004-2005 TUITION AND FEES:**
   In state: $6,243; Out of state: $13,983

SAT I Score (25th/75th percentile): 1110-1340
2005 U.S. News College Ranking:
National Universities, third tier
Acceptance Rate: 50%

Other expenses: Estimated books and supplies: $1,000. Transportation: $1,990. Personal expenses: $1,765. **Financial aid:** Priority filing date for institution's financial aid form: April 12; deadline: April 12. In 2003-2004, 56% of undergraduates applied for financial aid. Of those, 44% were determined to have financial need; 7% had their need fully met. Average financial aid package (proportion receiving): $7,910 (43%). Average amount of gift aid, such as scholarships or grants (proportion receiving): $3,134 (35%). Average amount of self-help aid, such as work study or loans (proportion receiving): $4,474 (33%). Average need-based loan (excluding PLUS or other private loans): $3,926. Among students who received need-based aid, the average percentage of need met: 67%. Among students who received aid based on merit, the average award (and the proportion receiving): $4,250 (4%). The average athletic scholarship (and the proportion receiving): $0 (0%). Average amount of debt of borrowers graduating in 2003: $12,605. Proportion who borrowed: 49%. **Student employment:** During the 2003-2004 academic year, 6% of undergraduates worked on campus. Average per-year earnings: $5,167. **Cooperative education programs:** other. **Reserve Officers Training Corps (ROTC):** Army ROTC: Offered at cooperating institution (University of Texas at Arlington); Air Force ROTC: Offered at cooperating institution (University of North Texas).

University of Texas–El Paso

500 W. University Avenue
El Paso, TX 79968
Public; www.utep.edu
Financial aid office: (915) 747-5204

■ **2004-2005 TUITION AND FEES:**
   In state: $3,848; Out of state: $10,928

SAT I Score (25th/75th percentile): 810-1030
2005 U.S. News College Ranking:
National Universities, fourth tier
Acceptance Rate: 98%

Other expenses: Estimated books and supplies: $648. Personal expenses: $1,349. **Financial aid:** Priority filing date for institution's financial aid form: March 15. In 2003-2004, 69% of undergraduates applied for financial aid. Of those, 54% were determined to have financial need;

28% had their need fully met. Average financial aid package (proportion receiving): $9,044 (53%). Average amount of gift aid, such as scholarships or grants (proportion receiving): $4,516 (46%). Average amount of self-help aid, such as work study or loans (proportion receiving): $5,205 (49%). Average need-based loan (excluding PLUS or other private loans): $4,964. Among students who received need-based aid, the average percentage of need met: 78%. Among students who received aid based on merit, the average award (and the proportion receiving): $1,874 (6%). The average athletic scholarship (and the proportion receiving): $7,550 (1%). Average amount of debt of borrowers graduating in 2003: $7,704. Proportion who borrowed: 40%. **Student employment:** During the 2003-2004 academic year, 10% of undergraduates worked on campus. Average per-year earnings: $6,000. **Cooperative education programs:** health professions, other. **Reserve Officers Training Corps (ROTC):** Army ROTC: Offered on campus; Air Force ROTC: Offered on campus.

University of Texas of the Permian Basin

4901 E. University Boulevard
Odessa, TX 79762-0001
Public; www.utpb.edu
Financial aid office: (432) 552-2620

■ **2004-2005 TUITION AND FEES:**
   In state: $3,877; Out of state: $11,617
■ **ROOM AND BOARD:** $4,058

SAT I Score (25th/75th percentile): 870-1090
2005 U.S. News College Ranking:
Universities–Master's (West), fourth tier
Acceptance Rate: 90%

Other expenses: Estimated books and supplies: $850. Transportation: $1,539. Personal expenses: $1,848. **Financial aid:** Priority filing date for institution's financial aid form: May 1. **Student employment:** During the 2003-2004 academic year, 11% of undergraduates worked on campus. Average per-year earnings: $1,180.

University of Texas–
Pan American

1201 W. University Drive
Edinburg, TX 78539-2999
Public; www.panam.edu
Financial aid office: (956) 381-2501

■ **2004-2005 TUITION AND FEES:**
In state: $3,152; Out of state: $10,820
■ **ROOM AND BOARD:** $4,333

ACT Score (25th/75th percentile): 15-21
2005 U.S. News College Ranking:
Universities–Master's (West), fourth tier
Acceptance Rate: 64%

Other expenses: Estimated books and supplies:
$600. Transportation: $582. Personal expenses:
$2,826. **Financial aid:** Priority filing date for
institution's financial aid form: February 28.
Average amount of debt of borrowers graduating in 2003: $12,175. Proportion who borrowed:
84%. Average per-year earnings: $5,602.
Cooperative education programs: health professions. **Reserve Officers Training Corps (ROTC):**
Army ROTC: Offered on campus; Air Force
ROTC: Offered on campus.

University of Texas–
San Antonio

6900 N. Loop 1604 W
San Antonio, TX 78249
Public; www.utsa.edu
Financial aid office: (210) 458-4154

■ **2004-2005 TUITION AND FEES:**
In state: $5,588; Out of state: $12,608
■ **ROOM AND BOARD:** $7,277

SAT I Score (25th/75th percentile): 860-1080
2005 U.S. News College Ranking:
Universities–Master's (West), third tier
Acceptance Rate: 99%

Other expenses: Estimated books and supplies:
$1,000. Transportation: $880. Personal expenses: $2,162. **Financial aid:** Priority filing date for
institution's financial aid form: March 1. In
2003-2004, 99% of undergraduates applied for
financial aid. Of those, 58% were determined to
have financial need; 14% had their need fully
met. Average financial aid package (proportion
receiving): $6,027 (55%). Average amount of
gift aid, such as scholarships or grants (proportion receiving): $3,455 (45%). Average amount
of self-help aid, such as work study or loans

(proportion receiving): $3,679 (43%). Average
need-based loan (excluding PLUS or other private loans): $3,586. Among students who
received need-based aid, the average percentage
of need met: 64%. Among students who
received aid based on merit, the average award
(and the proportion receiving): $1,579 (3%). The
average athletic scholarship (and the proportion
receiving): $6,569 (1%). Average amount of
debt of borrowers graduating in 2003: $18,000.
Proportion who borrowed: 55%. **Reserve
Officers Training Corps (ROTC):** Army ROTC:
Offered on campus; Air Force ROTC: Offered
on campus.

University of Texas–Tyler

3900 University Boulevard
Tyler, TX 75799
Public; www.uttyler.edu/mainsite/
admissions.html
Financial aid office: (903) 566-7180

■ **2004-2005 TUITION AND FEES:**
In state: $4,042; Out of state: $11,782
■ **ROOM AND BOARD:** $5,384

SAT I Score (25th/75th percentile): 930-1160
2005 U.S. News College Ranking:
Universities–Master's (West), third tier
Acceptance Rate: 82%

Financial aid: Priority filing date for institution's financial aid form: April 1. In 2003-2004,
65% of undergraduates applied for financial
aid. Of those, 53% were determined to have
financial need; 32% had their need fully met.
Average financial aid package (proportion
receiving): $6,714 (53%). Average amount of
gift aid, such as scholarships or grants (proportion receiving): $3,456 (39%). Average amount
of self-help aid, such as work study or loans
(proportion receiving): $3,464 (45%). Average
need-based loan (excluding PLUS or other private loans): $3,494. Among students who
received need-based aid, the average percentage
of need met: 80%. Among students who
received aid based on merit, the average award
(and the proportion receiving): $1,699 (25%).
The average athletic scholarship (and the proportion receiving): $0 (0%). Average amount of
debt of borrowers graduating in 2003: $13,937.
Proportion who borrowed: 49%. Average per-year earnings: $3,500.

University of the Incarnate
Word

4301 Broadway
San Antonio, TX 78209-6397
Private; www.uiw.edu
Financial aid office: (210) 829-6008

■ **2004-2005 TUITION AND FEES:** $16,082
■ **ROOM AND BOARD:** $5,746

SAT I Score (25th/75th percentile): 860-1100
2005 U.S. News College Ranking:
Universities–Master's (West), 58
Acceptance Rate: 87%

Other expenses: Estimated books and supplies:
$1,000. Transportation: $860. Personal expenses:
$1,460. **Financial aid:** Priority filing date for institution's financial aid form: April 1. In 2003-2004,
86% of undergraduates applied for financial aid.
Of those, 68% were determined to have financial
need; 66% had their need fully met. Average
financial aid package (proportion receiving):
$12,667 (68%). Average amount of gift aid, such
as scholarships or grants (proportion receiving):
$6,718 (65%). Average amount of self-help aid,
such as work study or loans (proportion receiving): $5,129 (57%). Average need-based loan
(excluding PLUS or other private loans): $4,878.
Among students who received need-based aid,
the average percentage of need met: 66%.
Among students who received aid based on
merit, the average award (and the proportion
receiving): $4,099 (18%). The average athletic
scholarship (and the proportion receiving):
$14,004 (4%). Average amount of debt of borrowers graduating in 2003: $24,998. Proportion
who borrowed: 67%. **Reserve Officers Training
Corps (ROTC):** Army ROTC: Offered on campus;
Air Force ROTC: Offered at cooperating institution (University of Texas at San Antonio).

Wayland Baptist University

1900 W. Seventh Street
Plainview, TX 79072
Private; www.wbu.edu
Financial aid office: (806) 291-3520

■ **2004-2005 TUITION AND FEES:** $9,250
■ **ROOM AND BOARD:** $3,420

ACT Score (25th/75th percentile): 16-24
2005 U.S. News College Ranking:
Universities–Master's (West), third tier
Acceptance Rate: 98%

Other expenses: Estimated books and supplies: $800. Transportation: $800. Personal expenses: $1,684. **Financial aid:** Priority filing date for institution's financial aid form: May 1. In 2003-2004, 79% of undergraduates applied for financial aid. Of those, 70% were determined to have financial need; 23% had their need fully met. Average financial aid package (proportion receiving): $8,436 (70%). Average amount of gift aid, such as scholarships or grants (proportion receiving): $6,213 (68%). Average amount of self-help aid, such as work study or loans (proportion receiving): $3,210 (54%). Average need-based loan (excluding PLUS or other private loans): $2,772. Among students who received need-based aid, the average percentage of need met: 76%. Among students who received aid based on merit, the average award (and the proportion receiving): $8,315 (15%). The average athletic scholarship (and the proportion receiving): $8,705 (4%). **Cooperative education programs:** computer science, engineering. **Reserve Officers Training Corps (ROTC):** Army ROTC: Offered at cooperating institution (Texas Tech University); Air Force ROTC: Offered at cooperating institution (Texas Tech University).

West Texas A&M University

2501 Fourth Avenue
Canyon, TX 79016-0001
Public; www.wtamu.edu
Financial aid office: (806) 651-2055

- **2004-2005 TUITION AND FEES:**
  In state: $2,908; Out of state: $9,100
- **ROOM AND BOARD:** $4,460

ACT Score (25th/75th percentile): 18-23
2005 U.S. News College Ranking:
Universities–Master's (West), third tier
Acceptance Rate: 77%

....

Financial aid: Priority filing date for institution's financial aid form: May 1. In 2003-2004, 58% of undergraduates applied for financial aid. Of those, 48% were determined to have financial need; 48% had their need fully met. Average financial aid package (proportion receiving): $2,615 (47%). Average amount of gift aid, such as scholarships or grants (proportion receiving): $2,312 (36%). Average amount of self-help aid, such as work study or loans (proportion receiving): $1,610 (21%). Average

need-based loan (excluding PLUS or other private loans): $3,346. Among students who received need-based aid, the average percentage of need met: 81%. Among students who received aid based on merit, the average award (and the proportion receiving): $847 (4%). The average athletic scholarship (and the proportion receiving): $2,392 (5%). **Student employment:** During the 2003-2004 academic year, 1% of undergraduates worked on campus. Average per-year earnings: $6,882. **Cooperative education programs:** agriculture, business, computer science, engineering, health professions, home economics, humanities, natural science, social/behavioral science, technologies.

Wiley College

711 Wiley Avenue
Marshall, TX 75670
Private; www.wileyc.edu
Financial aid office: (903) 927-3210

- **2004-2005 TUITION AND FEES:** $6,782
- **ROOM AND BOARD:** $4,214

ACT Score (25th/75th percentile): 13-18
2005 U.S. News College Ranking:
Comp. Colleges–Bachelor's (West), fourth tier
Acceptance Rate: 27%

....

Other expenses: Estimated books and supplies: $1,302. Transportation: $550. Personal expenses: $3,134. **Financial aid:** Priority filing date for institution's financial aid form: April 15. In 2003-2004, 76% of undergraduates applied for financial aid. Of those, 76% were determined to have financial need; 15% had their need fully met. Average financial aid package (proportion receiving): $6,061 (76%). Average amount of gift aid, such as scholarships or grants (proportion receiving): $4,453 (N/A). Average amount of self-help aid, such as work study or loans (proportion receiving): $3,227 (46%). Average need-based loan (excluding PLUS or other private loans): $2,945. Among students who received need-based aid, the average percentage of need met: 52%. Among students who received aid based on merit, the average award (and the proportion receiving): $6,638 (13%). Average amount of debt of borrowers graduating in 2003: $11,231. Proportion who borrowed: 16%. **Student employment:** During the 2003-2004 academic year, 34% of undergraduates worked on campus. Average per-year earnings: $1,500.

Utah

Brigham Young University–Provo

A-209 ASB
Provo, UT 84602
Private; www.byu.edu
Financial aid office: (801) 422-4104

- **2004-2005 TUITION AND FEES:** $3,280
- **ROOM AND BOARD:** $5,570

ACT Score (25th/75th percentile): 24-29
2005 U.S. News College Ranking:
National Universities, 74
Acceptance Rate: 78%

Other expenses: Estimated books and supplies: $1,240. Transportation: $1,470. Personal expenses: $1,680. **Financial aid:** Priority filing date for institution's financial aid form: April 15. In 2003-2004, 79% of undergraduates applied for financial aid. Of those, 40% were determined to have financial need; Average financial aid package (proportion receiving): $4,215 (37%). Average amount of gift aid, such as scholarships or grants (proportion receiving): $2,437 (29%). Average amount of self-help aid, such as work study or loans (proportion receiving): $1,779 (16%). Average need-based loan (excluding PLUS or other private loans): $1,779. Among students who received need-based aid, the average percentage of need met: 42%. Among students who received aid based on merit, the average award (and the proportion receiving): $2,991 (28%). The average athletic scholarship (and the proportion receiving): $5,894 (1%). Average amount of debt of borrowers graduating in 2003: $11,301. Proportion who borrowed: 39%. **Student employment:** During the 2003-2004 academic year, 39% of undergraduates worked on campus. Average per-year earnings: $4,800. **Cooperative education programs:** agriculture, business, education, engineering, health professions, natural science, social/behavioral science, technologies. **Reserve Officers Training Corps (ROTC):** Army ROTC: Offered on campus; Air Force ROTC: Offered on campus.

Southern Utah University

351 W. Center Street
Cedar City, UT 84720
Public; www.suu.edu
Financial aid office: (435) 586-7735

- **2004-2005 TUITION AND FEES:**
  In state: $3,054; Out of state: $9,008
- **ROOM AND BOARD:** $5,400

ACT Score (25th/75th percentile): 18-23
2005 U.S. News College Ranking:
Universities–Master's (West), third tier
Acceptance Rate: 78%

Reserve Officers Training Corps (ROTC): Army ROTC: Offered on campus.

University of Utah

200 S. University Street
Salt Lake City, UT 84112
Public; www.utah.edu
Financial aid office: (801) 581-8788

- **2004-2005 TUITION AND FEES:**
  In state: $4,000; Out of state: $12,410
- **ROOM AND BOARD:** $5,726

ACT Score (25th/75th percentile): 22-26
2005 U.S. News College Ranking:
National Universities, 111
Acceptance Rate: 86%

Other expenses: Estimated books and supplies: $1,086. Transportation: $954. Personal expenses: $2,358. **Financial aid:** Priority filing date for institution's financial aid form: March 15. In 2003-2004, 57% of undergraduates applied for financial aid. Of those, 40% were determined to have financial need; 14% had their need fully met. Average financial aid package (proportion receiving): $7,286 (36%). Average amount of gift aid, such as scholarships or grants (proportion receiving): $4,075 (29%). Average amount of self-help aid, such as work study or loans (proportion receiving): $5,195 (25%). Average need-based loan (excluding PLUS or other private loans): $4,759. Among students who received need-based aid, the average percentage of need met: 59%. Among students who received aid based on merit, the average award (and the proportion receiving): $3,127 (2%). The

average athletic scholarship (and the proportion receiving): $9,107 (0%). Average amount of debt of borrowers graduating in 2003: $12,400. Proportion who borrowed: 42%. **Student employment:** During the 2003-2004 academic year, 17% of undergraduates worked on campus. Average per-year earnings: $3,800. **Cooperative education programs:** agriculture, art, business, computer science, education, engineering, health professions, home economics, humanities, natural science, social/behavioral science, technologies. **Reserve Officers Training Corps (ROTC):** Army ROTC: Offered on campus; Navy ROTC: Offered on campus; Air Force ROTC: Offered on campus.

Utah State University

Old Main Hill
Logan, UT 84322
Public; www.usu.edu
Financial aid office: (435) 797-0173

- **2004-2005 TUITION AND FEES:**
  In state: $3,248; Out of state: $9,534
- **ROOM AND BOARD:** $4,230

ACT Score (25th/75th percentile): 21-26
2005 U.S. News College Ranking:
National Universities, third tier
Acceptance Rate: 94%

Other expenses: Estimated books and supplies: $1,000. Transportation: $1,260. Personal expenses: $1,820. **Financial aid:** In 2003-2004, 60% of undergraduates applied for financial aid. Of those, 55% were determined to have financial need; 13% had their need fully met. Average financial aid package (proportion receiving): $4,980 (54%). Average amount of gift aid, such as scholarships or grants (proportion receiving): $3,093 (42%). Average amount of self-help aid, such as work study or loans (proportion receiving): $4,140 (33%). Average need-based loan (excluding PLUS or other private loans): $3,861. Among students who received need-based aid, the average percentage of need met: 59%. Among students who received aid based on merit, the average award (and the proportion receiving): $3,033 (11%). The average athletic scholarship (and the proportion receiving): $6,246 (3%). Average amount of debt of borrowers graduating in 2003: $11,500. Proportion who borrowed: 47%.

Student employment: During the 2003-2004 academic year, 29% of undergraduates worked on campus. Average per-year earnings: $7,000. **Cooperative education programs:** agriculture, business, education, engineering, home economics, humanities, natural science, social/behavioral science. **Reserve Officers Training Corps (ROTC):** Army ROTC: Offered on campus; Air Force ROTC: Offered on campus.

Utah Valley State College

800 W. University Parkway
Orem, UT 84058-5999
Public; www.uvsc.edu
Financial aid office: (801) 863-8442

■ **2004-2005 TUITION AND FEES:**
In state: $3,166; Out of state: $9,096

ACT Score (25th/75th percentile): 17-22
2005 U.S. News College Ranking:
Comp. Colleges–Bachelor's (West), third tier
Acceptance Rate: 100%

Other expenses: Estimated books and supplies: $1,402. Transportation: $1,238. **Financial aid:** Priority filing date for institution's financial aid form: May 1. In 2003-2004, 56% of undergraduates applied for financial aid. Of those, 50% were determined to have financial need; 18% had their need fully met. Average financial aid package (proportion receiving): $6,120 (50%). Average amount of gift aid, such as scholarships or grants (proportion receiving): $2,371 (34%). Average amount of self-help aid, such as work study or loans (proportion receiving): $2,349 (31%). Average need-based loan (excluding PLUS or other private loans): $1,995. Among students who received need-based aid, the average percentage of need met: 64%. Among students who received aid based on merit, the average award (and the proportion receiving): $1,377 (5%). The average athletic scholarship (and the proportion receiving): $494 (1%). Average amount of debt of borrowers graduating in 2003: $5,575. Proportion who borrowed: 28%. **Student employment:** During the 2003-2004 academic year, 3% of undergraduates worked on campus. Average per-year

earnings: $7. **Cooperative education programs:** art, business, computer science, education, engineering, health professions, humanities, natural science, social/behavioral science, technologies, vocational arts. **Reserve Officers Training Corps (ROTC):** Army ROTC: Offered on campus; Air Force ROTC: Offered at cooperating institution (Brigham Young University).

Weber State University

1103 University Circle
Ogden, UT 84408-1103
Public; weber.edu
Financial aid office: (801) 626-7569

■ **2004-2005 TUITION AND FEES:**
In state: $2,876; Out of state: $8,736
■ **ROOM AND BOARD:** $6,400

ACT Score (25th/75th percentile): 18-24
2005 U.S. News College Ranking:
Universities–Master's (West), 47
Acceptance Rate: 100%

Financial aid: Priority filing date for institution's financial aid form: March 1. In 2003-2004, 80% of undergraduates applied for financial aid. Of those, 70% were determined to have financial need; 74% had their need fully met. Average financial aid package (proportion receiving): $5,450 (63%). Average amount of gift aid, such as scholarships or grants (proportion receiving): $3,750 (55%). Average amount of self-help aid, such as work study or loans (proportion receiving): $4,925 (63%). Average need-based loan (excluding PLUS or other private loans): $2,663. Among students who received need-based aid, the average percentage of need met: 89%. Average amount of debt of borrowers graduating in 2003: $10,500. Proportion who borrowed: 65%. **Student employment:** During the 2003-2004 academic year, 5% of undergraduates worked on campus. Average per-year earnings: $6,000. **Cooperative education programs:** health professions, social/behavioral science, technologies. **Reserve Officers Training Corps (ROTC):** Army ROTC: Offered on campus; Navy ROTC: Offered on campus; Air Force ROTC: Offered on campus.

Westminster College

1840 S. 1300 E
Salt Lake City, UT 84105-3697
Private; www.westminstercollege.edu
Financial aid office: (801) 832-2500

■ **2004-2005 TUITION AND FEES:** $18,422
■ **ROOM AND BOARD:** $5,636

ACT Score (25th/75th percentile): 24-26
2005 U.S. News College Ranking:
Universities–Master's (West), 22
Acceptance Rate: 84%

Financial aid: Priority filing date for institution's financial aid form: April 15. In 2003-2004, 79% of undergraduates applied for financial aid. Of those, 70% were determined to have financial need; 46% had their need fully met. Average financial aid package (proportion receiving): $14,130 (70%). Average amount of gift aid, such as scholarships or grants (proportion receiving): $9,761 (70%). Average amount of self-help aid, such as work study or loans (proportion receiving): $4,390 (68%). Average need-based loan (excluding PLUS or other private loans): $3,921. Among students who received need-based aid, the average percentage of need met: 89%. Among students who received aid based on merit, the average award (and the proportion receiving): $7,385 (25%). The average athletic scholarship (and the proportion receiving): $0 (0%). Average amount of debt of borrowers graduating in 2003: $15,600. Proportion who borrowed: 67%. **Student employment:** During the 2003-2004 academic year, 22% of undergraduates worked on campus. Average per-year earnings: $2,200. **Cooperative education programs:** art, business, computer science, education, health professions, humanities, natural science, social/behavioral science, other. **Reserve Officers Training Corps (ROTC):** Army ROTC: Offered at cooperating institution (University of Utah); Navy ROTC: Offered at cooperating institution (University of Utah); Air Force ROTC: Offered at cooperating institution (University of Utah).

Vermont

Bennington College

1 College Drive
Bennington, VT 05201
Private; www.bennington.edu
Financial aid office: (802) 440-4325

- **2004-2005 TUITION AND FEES:** $31,070
- **ROOM AND BOARD:** $7,710

SAT I Score (25th/75th percentile): 1140-1350
2005 U.S. College Ranking:
Liberal Arts Colleges, 96
Acceptance Rate: 68%

Other expenses: Estimated books and supplies: $800. Transportation: $400. Personal expenses: $1,800. **Financial aid:** Priority filing date for institution's financial aid form: March 1. In 2003-2004, 72% of undergraduates applied for financial aid. Of those, 65% were determined to have financial need; 6% had their need fully met. Average financial aid package (proportion receiving): $21,821 (65%). Average amount of gift aid, such as scholarships or grants (proportion receiving): $17,520 (65%). Average amount of self-help aid, such as work study or loans (proportion receiving): $4,772 (62%). Average need-based loan (excluding PLUS or other private loans): $3,780. Among students who received need-based aid, the average percentage of need met: 75%. Among students who received aid based on merit, the average award (and the proportion receiving): $4,589 (14%). The average athletic scholarship (and the proportion receiving): $0 (0%). Average amount of debt of borrowers graduating in 2003: $17,558. Proportion who borrowed: 77%. **Student employment:** During the 2003-2004 academic year, 22% of undergraduates worked on campus. Average per-year earnings: $1,865. **Cooperative education programs:** other.

Burlington College

95 North Avenue
Burlington, VT 05401
Private; www.burlingtoncollege.edu
Financial aid office: (802) 862-9616

- **2004-2005 TUITION AND FEES:** $14,170

2005 U.S. News College Ranking:
Liberal Arts Colleges, fourth tier
Acceptance Rate: 72%

Castleton State College

Castleton, VT 05735
Public; www.castleton.edu
Financial aid office: (802) 468-1286

- **2004-2005 TUITION AND FEES:**
  In state: $6,146; Out of state: $13,086
- **ROOM AND BOARD:** $6,454

SAT I Score (25th/75th percentile): 860-1070
2005 U.S. News College Ranking:
Universities–Master's (North), third tier
Acceptance Rate: 79%

Other expenses: Estimated books and supplies: $800. Transportation: $300. Personal expenses: $600. **Financial aid:** Priority filing date for institution's financial aid form: March 15. **Reserve Officers Training Corps (ROTC):** Army ROTC: Offered at cooperating institution (University of Vermont).

Champlain College

163 S. Willard Street
Burlington, VT 05401
Private; www.champlain.edu
Financial aid office: (800) 570-5858

- **2004-2005 TUITION AND FEES:** $13,850
- **ROOM AND BOARD:** $9,315

SAT I Score (25th/75th percentile): 1000-1130
2005 U.S. News College Ranking:
Comp. Colleges–Bachelor's (North), 16
Acceptance Rate: 63%

Other expenses: Estimated books and supplies: $600. **Financial aid:** Priority filing date for institution's financial aid form: May 1. In 2003-2004, 72% of undergraduates applied for financial aid. Of those, 60% were determined to have financial need; 16% had their need fully met. Average financial aid package (proportion receiving): $8,931 (60%). Average amount of gift aid, such as scholarships or grants (proportion receiving): $5,361 (49%). Average amount

of self-help aid, such as work study or loans (proportion receiving): $4,846 (57%). Average need-based loan (excluding PLUS or other private loans): $4,378. Among students who received need-based aid, the average percentage of need met: 65%. Among students who received aid based on merit, the average award (and the proportion receiving): $11,491 (14%). The average athletic scholarship (and the proportion receiving): $0 (0%). **Student employment:** During the 2003-2004 academic year, 7% of undergraduates worked on campus. Average per-year earnings: $2,100. **Reserve Officers Training Corps (ROTC):** Army ROTC: Offered at cooperating institution (University of Vermont).

College of St. Joseph

71 Clement Road
Rutland, VT 05701
Private; www.csj.edu
Financial aid office: (802) 773-5900

- **2004-2005 TUITION AND FEES:** $13,200
- **ROOM AND BOARD:** $6,600

SAT I Score (25th/75th percentile): 750-1010
2005 U.S. News College Ranking:
Universities–Master's (North), fourth tier
Acceptance Rate: 94%

Other expenses: Estimated books and supplies: $750. Transportation: $600. Personal expenses: $950. **Financial aid:** In 2003-2004, 83% of undergraduates applied for financial aid. Of those, 78% were determined to have financial need; 21% had their need fully met. Average financial aid package (proportion receiving): $10,432 (78%). Average amount of gift aid, such as scholarships or grants (proportion receiving): $6,430 (68%). Average amount of self-help aid, such as work study or loans (proportion receiving): $5,162 (74%). Average need-based loan (excluding PLUS or other private loans): $4,515. Among students who received need-based aid, the average percentage of need met: 74%. Among students who received aid based on merit, the average award (and the proportion receiving): $3,160 (4%). The average athletic scholarship (and the proportion receiving): $6,000 (0%). Average amount of debt of borrowers graduating in 2003: $19,567. Proportion who borrowed: 69%. **Student**

employment: During the 2003-2004 academic year, 0% of undergraduates worked on campus. Average per-year earnings: $0.

Goddard College

123 Pitkin Road
Plainfield, VT 05667
Private; www.goddard.edu
Financial aid office: (800) 468-4888

■ **2004-2005 TUITION AND FEES:** $9,080

2005 U.S. News College Ranking:
Universities–Master's (North), fourth tier

Financial aid: In 2003-2004, 47% of undergraduates applied for financial aid. Of those, 45% were determined to have financial need; 4% had their need fully met. Average financial aid package (proportion receiving): $6,302 (45%). Average amount of gift aid, such as scholarships or grants (proportion receiving): $2,997 (34%). Average amount of self-help aid, such as work study or loans (proportion receiving): $4,101 (44%). Average need-based loan (excluding PLUS or other private loans): $4,101. Among students who received need-based aid, the average percentage of need met: 40%. Among students who received aid based on merit, the average award (and the proportion receiving): $5,244 (3%). The average athletic scholarship (and the proportion receiving): $0 (0%). Average amount of debt of borrowers graduating in 2003: $15,921. Proportion who borrowed: 85%.

Green Mountain College

1 College Circle
Poultney, VT 05764-1199
Private; www.greenmtn.edu
Financial aid office: (802) 287-8210

■ **2004-2005 TUITION AND FEES:** $21,134
■ **ROOM AND BOARD:** $6,990

SAT I Score (25th/75th percentile): 890-1140
2005 U.S. News College Ranking:
Comp. Colleges–Bachelor's (North), third tier
Acceptance Rate: 60%

Other expenses: Estimated books and supplies: $800. Transportation: $800. Personal expenses: $250. **Financial aid:** Priority filing date for institution's financial aid form: March 1. In 2003-2004, 81% of undergraduates applied for financial aid. Of those, 62% were determined

to have financial need; 19% had their need fully met. Average financial aid package (proportion receiving): $11,780 (62%). Average amount of gift aid, such as scholarships or grants (proportion receiving): $7,930 (61%). Average amount of self-help aid, such as work study or loans (proportion receiving): $4,281 (62%). Average need-based loan (excluding PLUS or other private loans): $3,850. Among students who received need-based aid, the average percentage of need met: 68%. Among students who received aid based on merit, the average award (and the proportion receiving): $9,268 (8%). The average athletic scholarship (and the proportion receiving): $6,000 (1%). Average amount of debt of borrowers graduating in 2003: $19,638. Proportion who borrowed: 82%.

Johnson State College

337 College Hill
Johnson, VT 05656-9405
Public; www.johnsonstatecollege.com
Financial aid office: (802) 635-1380

■ **2004-2005 TUITION AND FEES:**
  In state: $5,980; Out of state: $12,920
■ **ROOM AND BOARD:** $6,454

SAT I Score (25th/75th percentile): 861
2005 U.S. News College Ranking:
Universities–Master's (North), fourth tier
Acceptance Rate: 38%

Other expenses: Estimated books and supplies: $800. **Student employment:** During the 2003-2004 academic year, 76% of undergraduates worked on campus. Average per-year earnings: $2,000. **Reserve Officers Training Corps (ROTC):** Army ROTC: Offered at cooperating institution (University of Vermont).

Lyndon State College

PO Box 919
Lyndonville, VT 05851
Public; www.lyndonstate.edu
Financial aid office: (802) 626-6218

■ **2004-2005 TUITION AND FEES:**
  In state: $7,056; Out of state: $13,996
■ **ROOM AND BOARD:** $6,454

SAT I Score (25th/75th percentile): 800-950
2005 U.S. News College Ranking:
Comp. Colleges–Bachelor's (North), third tier
Acceptance Rate: 94%

Other expenses: Estimated books and supplies: $700. Transportation: $200. Personal expenses: $650. **Student employment:** During the 2003-2004 academic year, 3% of undergraduates worked on campus. Average per-year earnings: $1,000. **Cooperative education programs:** business, computer science, education, natural science, social/behavioral science. **Reserve Officers Training Corps (ROTC):** Air Force ROTC: Offered at cooperating institution (Norwich University).

Marlboro College

PO Box A
Marlboro, VT 05344-0300
Private; www.marlboro.edu
Financial aid office: (802) 258-9237

■ **2004-2005 TUITION AND FEES:** $25,740
■ **ROOM AND BOARD:** $7,800

SAT I Score (25th/75th percentile): 1100-1340
2005 U.S. News College Ranking:
Liberal Arts Colleges, third tier
Acceptance Rate: 82%

Other expenses: Estimated books and supplies: $600. Transportation: $0. Personal expenses: $150. **Financial aid:** Priority filing date for institution's financial aid form: February 15; deadline: February 15. In 2003-2004, 91% of undergraduates applied for financial aid. Of those, 82% were determined to have financial need; 13% had their need fully met. Average financial aid package (proportion receiving): $16,791 (82%). Average amount of gift aid, such as scholarships or grants (proportion receiving): $13,036 (76%). Average amount of self-help aid, such as work study or loans (proportion receiving): $4,897 (78%). Average need-based loan (excluding PLUS or other private loans): $3,828. Among students who received need-based aid, the average percentage of need met: 82%. Among students who received aid based on merit, the average award (and the proportion receiving): $10,539 (16%). The average athletic scholarship (and the proportion receiving): $0 (0%). Average amount of debt of borrowers graduating in 2003: $16,505. Proportion who borrowed: 76%. **Student employment:** During the 2003-2004 academic year, 60% of undergraduates worked on campus. Average per-year earnings: $1,930.

Middlebury College

Middlebury, VT 05753
Private; www.middlebury.edu
Financial aid office: (802) 443-5158

■ **2004-2005 TUITION/FEES/ROOM AND BOARD:** $40,400

SAT I Score (25th/75th percentile): 1370-1490
2005 U.S. News College Ranking:
Liberal Arts Colleges, 11
Acceptance Rate: 23%

....

Financial aid: Priority filing date for institution's financial aid form: November 15; deadline: December 31. In 2003-2004, 47% of undergraduates applied for financial aid. Of those, 40% were determined to have financial need; 100% had their need fully met. Average financial aid package (proportion receiving): $25,899 (40%). Average amount of gift aid, such as scholarships or grants (proportion receiving): $22,160 (40%). Average amount of self-help aid, such as work study or loans (proportion receiving): $4,123 (36%). Average need-based loan (excluding PLUS or other private loans): $2,922. Among students who received need-based aid, the average percentage of need met: 100%. Among students who received aid based on merit, the average award (and the proportion receiving): $0 (0%). The average athletic scholarship (and the proportion receiving): $0 (0%). **Student employment:** During the 2003-2004 academic year, 30% of undergraduates worked on campus. Average per-year earnings: $2,600. **Reserve Officers Training Corps (ROTC):** Army ROTC: Offered at cooperating institution (University of Vermont).

Norwich University

158 Harmon Drive
Northfield, VT 05663
Private; www.norwich.edu
Financial aid office: (802) 485-2015

■ **2004-2005 TUITION AND FEES:** $19,650
■ **ROOM AND BOARD:** $7,090

SAT I Score (25th/75th percentile): 930-1170
2005 U.S. News College Ranking:
Universities–Master's (North), 56
Acceptance Rate: 71%

....

Other expenses: Estimated books and supplies: $500. Personal expenses: $1,080. **Financial aid:**

Priority filing date for institution's financial aid form: March 1. Average amount of debt of borrowers graduating in 2003: $25,505. Proportion who borrowed: 95%. **Reserve Officers Training Corps (ROTC):** Army ROTC: Offered on campus; Navy ROTC: Offered on campus; Air Force ROTC: Offered on campus.

Southern Vermont College

982 Mansion Drive
Bennington, VT 05201
Private; www.svc.edu
Financial aid office: (877) 563-6076

■ **2004-2005 TUITION AND FEES:** $12,498
■ **ROOM AND BOARD:** $6,432

SAT I Score (25th/75th percentile): 810-1000
2005 U.S. News College Ranking:
Comp. Colleges–Bachelor's (North), fourth tier
Acceptance Rate: 71%

....

St. Michael's College

1 Winooski Park
Colchester, VT 05439
Private; www.smcvt.edu
Financial aid office: (802) 654-3243

■ **2004-2005 TUITION AND FEES:** $25,535
■ **ROOM AND BOARD:** $6,250

SAT I Score (25th/75th percentile): 1020-1210
2005 U.S. News College Ranking:
Universities–Master's (North), 11
Acceptance Rate: 67%

....

Other expenses: Estimated books and supplies: $1,200. Transportation: $450. Personal expenses: $310. **Financial aid:** Priority filing date for institution's financial aid form: March 15. In 2003-2004, 75% of undergraduates applied for financial aid. Of those, 65% were determined to have financial need; 25% had their need fully met. Average financial aid package (proportion receiving): $17,529 (65%). Average amount of gift aid, such as scholarships or grants (proportion receiving): $12,743 (63%). Average amount of self-help aid, such as work study or loans (proportion receiving): $5,706 (59%). Average need-based loan (excluding PLUS or other private loans): $4,805. Among students who received need-based aid, the average percentage of need met: 86%. Among students who received aid based on merit, the average award (and the proportion receiving): $6,784 (15%).

The average athletic scholarship (and the proportion receiving): $30,100 (1%). Average amount of debt of borrowers graduating in 2003: $20,233. Proportion who borrowed: 80%. **Student employment:** During the 2003-2004 academic year, 6% of undergraduates worked on campus. Average per-year earnings: $1,275. **Reserve Officers Training Corps (ROTC):** Army ROTC: Offered at cooperating institution (University of Vermont).

University of Vermont

South Prospect Street
Burlington, VT 05405-0160
Public; www.uvm.edu
Financial aid office: (802) 656-3156

■ **2004-2005 TUITION AND FEES:**
   In state: $10,226; Out of state: $23,866
■ **ROOM AND BOARD:** $7,016

SAT I Score (25th/75th percentile): 1060-1250
2005 U.S. News College Ranking:
National Universities, 90
Acceptance Rate: 75%

....

Other expenses: Estimated books and supplies: $832. Personal expenses: $975. **Financial aid:** Priority filing date for institution's financial aid form: February 10. In 2003-2004, 66% of undergraduates applied for financial aid. Of those, 56% were determined to have financial need; 46% had their need fully met. Average financial aid package (proportion receiving): $14,960 (56%). Average amount of gift aid, such as scholarships or grants (proportion receiving): $10,079 (50%). Average amount of self-help aid, such as work study or loans (proportion receiving): $6,504 (47%). Average need-based loan (excluding PLUS or other private loans): $5,980. Among students who received need-based aid, the average percentage of need met: 82%. Among students who received aid based on merit, the average award (and the proportion receiving): $2,132 (12%). The average athletic scholarship (and the proportion receiving): $17,311 (1%). Average amount of debt of borrowers graduating in 2003: $23,114. Proportion who borrowed: 51%. **Student employment:** During the 2003-2004 academic year, 18% of undergraduates worked on campus. Average per-year earnings: $1,250. **Cooperative education programs:** agriculture, business, computer science, education, engineering, natural science. **Reserve Officers Training Corps (ROTC):** Army ROTC: Offered on campus.

Vermont Technical College

Randolph Center, VT 05061
Public; www.vtc.edu
Financial aid office: (800) 965-8790

■ **2004-2005 TUITION AND FEES:**
 In state: $11,096; Out of state: $13,986
■ **ROOM AND BOARD:** $6,454

SAT I Score (25th/75th percentile): 890-1130
2005 U.S. News College Ranking:
Unranked Specialty School–Engineering
Acceptance Rate: 61%

....

Other expenses: Estimated books and supplies: $1,500. Transportation: $100. Personal expenses: $500. **Financial aid:** Priority filing date for institution's financial aid form: March 1. In 2003-2004, 85% of undergraduates applied for financial aid. Of those, 74% were determined to have financial need; 19% had their need fully met. Average financial aid package (proportion receiving): $7,031 (70%). Average amount of gift aid, such as scholarships or grants (proportion receiving): $4,654 (58%). Average amount of self-help aid, such as work study or loans (proportion receiving): $2,918 (64%). Average need-based loan (excluding PLUS or other private loans): $2,681. Among students who received need-based aid, the average percentage of need met: 73%. Among students who received aid based on merit, the average award (and the proportion receiving): $2,300 (4%). Average amount of debt of borrowers graduating in 2003: $11,000. Proportion who borrowed: 60%. **Student employment:** During the 2003-2004 academic year, 20% of undergraduates worked on campus. Average per-year earnings: $850. **Cooperative education programs:** health professions.

Virginia

Averett University

420 W. Main Street
Danville, VA 24541
Private; www.averett.edu
Financial aid office: (434) 791-5646

■ **2004-2005 TUITION AND FEES:** $18,430
■ **ROOM AND BOARD:** $6,320

SAT I Score (25th/75th percentile): 860-1045
2005 U.S. News College Ranking:
Universities–Master's (South), third tier
Acceptance Rate: 89%

Other expenses: Estimated books and supplies:
$900. Transportation: $350. Personal expenses:
$1,400. **Financial aid:** In 2003-2004, 91% of
undergraduates applied for financial aid. Of
those, 84% were determined to have financial
need; 15% had their need fully met. Average
financial aid package (proportion receiving):
$10,980 (84%). Average amount of gift aid,
such as scholarships or grants (proportion
receiving): $8,292 (75%). Average amount of
self-help aid, such as work study or loans (proportion receiving): $4,099 (74%). Average
need-based loan (excluding PLUS or other private loans): $3,914. Among students who
received need-based aid, the average percentage
of need met: 66%. Among students who
received aid based on merit, the average award
(and the proportion receiving): $9,712 (15%).
The average athletic scholarship (and the proportion receiving): $0 (0%). Average amount of
debt of borrowers graduating in 2003: $18,507.
Proportion who borrowed: 38%. **Student
employment:** During the 2003-2004 academic
year, 7% of undergraduates worked on campus.
Average per-year earnings: $735. **Cooperative
education programs:** business, computer science, education, health professions, humanities, natural science, social/behavioral science,
other.

Bluefield College

3000 College Drive
Bluefield, VA 24605
Private; www.bluefield.edu
Financial aid office: (276) 326-4215

■ **2004-2005 TUITION AND FEES:** $10,615
■ **ROOM AND BOARD:** $5,570

SAT I Score (25th/75th percentile): 820-1030
2005 U.S. News College Ranking:
Comp. Colleges–Bachelor's (South), 45
Acceptance Rate: 67%

Other expenses: Estimated books and supplies:
$900. Transportation: $1,050. Personal expenses: $915. **Financial aid:** Priority filing date for
institution's financial aid form: March 10. In
2003-2004, 82% of undergraduates applied for
financial aid. Of those, 73% were determined to
have financial need; 24% had their need fully
met. Average financial aid package (proportion
receiving): $8,957 (73%). Average amount of
gift aid, such as scholarships or grants (proportion receiving): $5,403 (70%). Average amount
of self-help aid, such as work study or loans
(proportion receiving): $4,642 (60%). Average
need-based loan (excluding PLUS or other private loans): $4,430. Among students who
received need-based aid, the average percentage
of need met: 68%. Among students who
received aid based on merit, the average award
(and the proportion receiving): $6,464 (18%).
The average athletic scholarship (and the proportion receiving): $0 (0%). Average amount of
debt of borrowers graduating in 2003: $12,177.
Proportion who borrowed: 80%. **Student
employment:** During the 2003-2004 academic
year, 2% of undergraduates worked on campus.
Average per-year earnings: $1,300.

Bridgewater College

402 E. College Street
Bridgewater, VA 22812-1599
Private; www.bridgewater.edu
Financial aid office: (540) 828-5376

■ **2004-2005 TUITION AND FEES:** $17,990
■ **ROOM AND BOARD:** $8,480

SAT I Score (25th/75th percentile): 910-1120
2005 U.S. News College Ranking:
Liberal Arts Colleges, fourth tier
Acceptance Rate: 88%

Other expenses: Estimated books and supplies:
$895. Transportation: $450. Personal expenses:
$990. **Financial aid:** Priority filing date for
institution's financial aid form: March 1; deadline: August 1. In 2003-2004, 82% of undergraduates applied for financial aid. Of those,
72% were determined to have financial need;

28% had their need fully met. Average financial
aid package (proportion receiving): $16,169
(72%). Average amount of gift aid, such as
scholarships or grants (proportion receiving):
$12,092 (72%). Average amount of self-help
aid, such as work study or loans (proportion
receiving): $5,038 (58%). Average need-based
loan (excluding PLUS or other private loans):
$4,628. Among students who received need-
based aid, the average percentage of need met:
83%. Among students who received aid based
on merit, the average award (and the proportion receiving): $7,633 (24%). The average ath-
letic scholarship (and the proportion receiving):
$0 (0%). Average amount of debt of borrowers
graduating in 2003: $20,099. Proportion who
borrowed: 80%. **Student employment:** During
the 2003-2004 academic year, 7% of undergraduates worked on campus. Average per-year
earnings: $678.

Christendom College

134 Christendom Drive
Front Royal, VA 22630
Private; www.christendom.edu
Financial aid office: (540) 636-2900

■ **2004-2005 TUITION AND FEES:** $14,420
■ **ROOM AND BOARD:** $5,250

SAT I Score (25th/75th percentile): 1130-1330
2005 U.S. News College Ranking:
Liberal Arts Colleges, fourth tier
Acceptance Rate: 80%

Financial aid: Priority filing date for institution's financial aid form: March 15. In 2003-
2004, 68% of undergraduates applied for
financial aid. Of those, 54% were determined to
have financial need; 100% had their need fully
met. Average financial aid package (proportion
receiving): $9,730 (54%). Average amount of
gift aid, such as scholarships or grants (proportion receiving): $4,180 (50%). Average amount
of self-help aid, such as work study or loans
(proportion receiving): $5,080 (51%). Average
need-based loan (excluding PLUS or other private loans): $3,855. Among students who
received need-based aid, the average percentage
of need met: 90%. Among students who
received aid based on merit, the average award
(and the proportion receiving): $3,800 (14%).
The average athletic scholarship (and the pro-

portion receiving): $0 (0%). Average amount of debt of borrowers graduating in 2003: $10,050. Proportion who borrowed: 52%. **Student employment:** During the 2003-2004 academic year, 5% of undergraduates worked on campus. Average per-year earnings: $2,000.

Christopher Newport University

1 University Place
Newport News, VA 23606
Public; www.cnu.edu
Financial aid office: (757) 594-7170

■ **2004-2005 TUITION AND FEES:**
   In state: $5,314; Out of state: $12,626
■ **ROOM AND BOARD:** $7,200

SAT I Score (25th/75th percentile): 1040-1220
2005 U.S. News College Ranking:
Liberal Arts Colleges, fourth tier
Acceptance Rate: 58%

Other expenses: Estimated books and supplies: $801. Transportation: $763. Personal expenses: $1,674. **Financial aid:** Priority filing date for institution's financial aid form: March 1. In 2003-2004, 70% of undergraduates applied for financial aid. Of those, 48% were determined to have financial need; 5% had their need fully met. Average financial aid package (proportion receiving): $3,951 (43%). Average amount of gift aid, such as scholarships or grants (proportion receiving): $2,770 (31%). Average amount of self-help aid, such as work study or loans (proportion receiving): $2,986 (43%). Average need-based loan (excluding PLUS or other private loans): $2,823. Among students who received need-based aid, the average percentage of need met: 52%. Among students who received aid based on merit, the average award (and the proportion receiving): $1,451 (9%). The average athletic scholarship (and the proportion receiving): $0 (0%). Average amount of debt of borrowers graduating in 2003: $8,035. Proportion who borrowed: 71%. **Student employment:** During the 2003-2004 academic year, 20% of undergraduates worked on campus. Average per-year earnings: $1,500. **Cooperative education programs:** other. **Reserve Officers Training Corps (ROTC):** Army ROTC: Offered on campus.

College of William and Mary

PO Box 8795
Williamsburg, VA 23187-8795
Public; www.wm.edu
Financial aid office: (757) 221-2420

■ **2004-2005 TUITION AND FEES:**
   In state: $7,096; Out of state: $21,796
■ **ROOM AND BOARD:** $6,066

SAT I Score (25th/75th percentile): 1260-1440
2005 U.S. News College Ranking:
National Universities, 31
Acceptance Rate: 34%

Other expenses: Estimated books and supplies: $825. Transportation: $150. Personal expenses: $1,000. **Financial aid:** Priority filing date for institution's financial aid form: February 15; deadline: March 15. In 2003-2004, 41% of undergraduates applied for financial aid. Of those, 26% were determined to have financial need; 19% had their need fully met. Average financial aid package (proportion receiving): $8,664 (26%). Average amount of gift aid, such as scholarships or grants (proportion receiving): $6,963 (23%). Average amount of self-help aid, such as work study or loans (proportion receiving): $3,218 (21%). Average need-based loan (excluding PLUS or other private loans): $3,197. Among students who received need-based aid, the average percentage of need met: 80%. Among students who received aid based on merit, the average award (and the proportion receiving): $7,173 (17%). The average athletic scholarship (and the proportion receiving): $12,898 (5%). Average amount of debt of borrowers graduating in 2003: $20,355. Proportion who borrowed: 27%. **Student employment:** During the 2003-2004 academic year, 22% of undergraduates worked on campus. Average per-year earnings: $1,200. **Cooperative education programs:** art, business, computer science, education, engineering, health professions, humanities, natural science, social/behavioral science. **Reserve Officers Training Corps (ROTC):** Army ROTC: Offered on campus.

Eastern Mennonite University

1200 Park Road
Harrisonburg, VA 22802-2462
Private; www.emu.edu
Financial aid office: (540) 432-4139

■ **2004-2005 TUITION AND FEES:** $18,220
■ **ROOM AND BOARD:** $5,740

SAT I Score (25th/75th percentile): 930-1235
2005 U.S. News College Ranking:
Liberal Arts Colleges, third tier
Acceptance Rate: 82%

Other expenses: Estimated books and supplies: $790. Transportation: $500. Personal expenses: $750. **Financial aid:** Priority filing date for institution's financial aid form: April 15. In 2003-2004, 79% of undergraduates applied for financial aid. Of those, 70% were determined to have financial need; 69% had their need fully met. Average financial aid package (proportion receiving): $13,250 (70%). Average amount of gift aid, such as scholarships or grants (proportion receiving): $7,750 (64%). Average amount of self-help aid, such as work study or loans (proportion receiving): $6,500 (57%). Average need-based loan (excluding PLUS or other private loans): $5,700. Among students who received need-based aid, the average percentage of need met: 87%. Among students who received aid based on merit, the average award (and the proportion receiving): $6,310 (25%). The average athletic scholarship (and the proportion receiving): $0 (0%). Average amount of debt of borrowers graduating in 2003: $21,900. Proportion who borrowed: 93%. **Student employment:** During the 2003-2004 academic year, 5% of undergraduates worked on campus. Average per-year earnings: $1,800.

Emory and Henry College

PO Box 947
Emory, VA 24327
Private; www.ehc.edu
Financial aid office: (276) 944-6229

■ **2004-2005 TUITION AND FEES:** $16,690
■ **ROOM AND BOARD:** $6,250

SAT I Score (25th/75th percentile): 922-1135
2005 U.S. News College Ranking:
Liberal Arts Colleges, third tier
Acceptance Rate: 81%

Other expenses: Estimated books and supplies: $700. Transportation: $600. Personal expenses: $1,000. **Financial aid:** Priority filing date for institution's financial aid form: April 1; deadline: August 1. In 2003-2004, 89% of undergraduates applied for financial aid. Of those, 74% were determined to have financial need; 28% had their need fully met. Average financial aid package (proportion receiving): $12,706 (74%). Average amount of gift aid, such as scholarships or grants (proportion receiving):

$9,830 (71%). Average amount of self-help aid, such as work study or loans (proportion receiving): $3,886 (60%). Average need-based loan (excluding PLUS or other private loans): $3,564. Among students who received need-based aid, the average percentage of need met: 83%. Among students who received aid based on merit, the average award (and the proportion receiving): $6,601 (25%). The average athletic scholarship (and the proportion receiving): $0 (0%). Average amount of debt of borrowers graduating in 2003: $14,466. Proportion who borrowed: 67%.

Ferrum College

PO Box 1000
Ferrum, VA 24088
Private; www.ferrum.edu
Financial aid office: (540) 365-4282

■ **2004-2005 TUITION AND FEES:** $16,870
■ **ROOM AND BOARD:** $5,700

SAT I Score (25th/75th percentile): 780-970
2005 U.S. News College Ranking:
Comp. Colleges–Bachelor's (South), 38
Acceptance Rate: 74%

Other expenses: Estimated books and supplies: $800. Transportation: $430. **Financial aid:** Priority filing date for institution's financial aid form: March 1. In 2003-2004, 99% of undergraduates applied for financial aid. Of those, 87% were determined to have financial need; Average financial aid package (proportion receiving): $11,370 (87%). Average amount of gift aid, such as scholarships or grants (proportion receiving): $9,035 (87%). Average amount of self-help aid, such as work study or loans (proportion receiving): $5,281 (66%). Average need-based loan (excluding PLUS or other private loans): $2,931. Among students who received need-based aid, the average percentage of need met: 53%. Among students who received aid based on merit, the average award (and the proportion receiving): $2,589 (11%). The average athletic scholarship (and the proportion receiving): $0 (0%). Average amount of debt of borrowers graduating in 2003: $15,900. Proportion who borrowed: 78%. **Student employment:** During the 2003-2004 academic year, 25% of undergraduates worked on campus. Average per-year earnings: $1,500.

George Mason University

4400 University Drive
Fairfax, VA 22030
Public; www.gmu.edu
Financial aid office: (703) 993-2353

■ **2004-2005 TUITION AND FEES:**
In state: $5,580; Out of state: $16,680
■ **ROOM AND BOARD:** $5,900

SAT I Score (25th/75th percentile): 1000-1210
2005 U.S. News College Ranking:
National Universities, third tier
Acceptance Rate: 66%

Other expenses: Estimated books and supplies: $810. Transportation: $1,215. Personal expenses: $1,336. **Financial aid:** Priority filing date for institution's financial aid form: March 1. In 2003-2004, 72% of undergraduates applied for financial aid. Of those, 50% were determined to have financial need; 45% had their need fully met. Average financial aid package (proportion receiving): $6,917 (44%). Average amount of gift aid, such as scholarships or grants (proportion receiving): $4,266 (31%). Average amount of self-help aid, such as work study or loans (proportion receiving): $2,328 (36%). Average need-based loan (excluding PLUS or other private loans): $3,628. Among students who received need-based aid, the average percentage of need met: 63%. Among students who received aid based on merit, the average award (and the proportion receiving): $6,815 (14%). The average athletic scholarship (and the proportion receiving): $11,093 (2%). Average amount of debt of borrowers graduating in 2003: $14,215. Proportion who borrowed: 42%. **Cooperative education programs:** art, business, computer science, education, engineering, humanities, natural science, social/behavioral science, technologies. **Reserve Officers Training Corps (ROTC):** Army ROTC: Offered on campus; Navy ROTC: Offered at cooperating institution (George Washington); Air Force ROTC: Offered at cooperating institution (University of Maryland–College Park).

Hampden-Sydney College

PO Box 667
Hampden-Sydney, VA 23943
Private; www.hsc.edu
Financial aid office: (434) 223-6119

■ **2004-2005 TUITION AND FEES:** $22,946
■ **ROOM AND BOARD:** $7,370

SAT I Score (25th/75th percentile): 1030-1240
2005 U.S. News College Ranking:
Liberal Arts Colleges, third tier
Acceptance Rate: 71%

Other expenses: Estimated books and supplies: $900. Transportation: $800. Personal expenses: $800. **Financial aid:** Priority filing date for institution's financial aid form: March 1; deadline: May 1. In 2003-2004, 92% of undergraduates applied for financial aid. Of those, 52% were determined to have financial need; 32% had their need fully met. Average financial aid package (proportion receiving): $15,761 (52%). Average amount of gift aid, such as scholarships or grants (proportion receiving): $12,389 (51%). Average amount of self-help aid, such as work study or loans (proportion receiving): $4,608 (39%). Average need-based loan (excluding PLUS or other private loans): $3,801. Among students who received need-based aid, the average percentage of need met: 84%. Among students who received aid based on merit, the average award (and the proportion receiving): $14,307 (42%). The average athletic scholarship (and the proportion receiving): $0 (0%). Average amount of debt of borrowers graduating in 2003: $15,571. Proportion who borrowed: 52%. **Student employment:** During the 2003-2004 academic year, 25% of undergraduates worked on campus. Average per-year earnings: $1,200. **Reserve Officers Training Corps (ROTC):** Army ROTC: Offered at cooperating institution (Longwood University).

Hampton University

Tyler Street
Hampton, VA 23668
Private; www.hamptonu.edu
Financial aid office: (800) 624-3341

■ **2004-2005 TUITION AND FEES:** $13,506
■ **ROOM AND BOARD:** $6,424

SAT I Score (25th/75th percentile): 930-1110
2005 U.S. News College Ranking:
Universities–Master's (South), 29
Acceptance Rate: 60%

Other expenses: Estimated books and supplies: $843. Transportation: $1,575. Personal expenses: $1,183. **Financial aid:** Priority filing date for institution's financial aid form: March 1. In 2003-2004, 61% of undergraduates applied for financial aid. Of those, 61% were determined to have financial need; 2% had their need fully met. Average financial aid package (proportion receiving): $2,660 (60%). Average amount of gift aid, such as scholarships or grants (proportion receiving): $1,852 (31%). Average amount of self-help aid, such as work study or loans (proportion receiving): $2,284 (24%). Average need-based loan (excluding PLUS or other private loans): $2,445. Among students who received need-based aid, the average percentage of need met: 27%. Among students who received aid based on merit, the average award (and the proportion receiving): $5,195 (20%). The average athletic scholarship (and the proportion receiving): $14,805 (1%). Average amount of debt of borrowers graduating in 2003: $6,230. Proportion who borrowed: 84%. **Student employment:** During the 2003-2004 academic year, 1% of undergraduates worked on campus. Average per-year earnings: $1,500. **Cooperative education programs:** art, business, computer science, education, engineering, health professions, humanities, natural science, social/behavioral science, technologies, other. **Reserve Officers Training Corps (ROTC):** Army ROTC: Offered on campus; Navy ROTC: Offered on campus.

Hollins University

PO Box 9688
Roanoke, VA 24020
Private; www.hollins.edu
Financial aid office: (540) 362-6332

■ **2004-2005 TUITION AND FEES:** $21,675
■ **ROOM AND BOARD:** $7,700

SAT I Score (25th/75th percentile): 1040-1260
2005 U.S. News College Ranking:
Liberal Arts Colleges, 87
Acceptance Rate: 86%

Other expenses: Estimated books and supplies: $800. Transportation: $800. Personal expenses: $850. **Financial aid:** Priority filing date for institution's financial aid form: February 15; deadline: March 15. In 2003-2004, 97% of undergraduates applied for financial aid. Of those, 66% were determined to have financial need; 21% had their need fully met. Average financial aid package (proportion receiving): $17,513 (66%). Average amount of gift aid, such as scholarships or grants (proportion receiving): $12,402 (66%). Average amount of self-help aid, such as work study or loans (proportion receiving): $5,770 (56%). Average need-based loan (excluding PLUS or other private loans): $4,630. Among students who received need-based aid, the average percentage of need met: 79%. Among students who received aid based on merit, the average award (and the propor-

tion receiving): $7,558 (31%). The average athletic scholarship (and the proportion receiving): $0 (0%). Average amount of debt of borrowers graduating in 2003: $18,167. Proportion who borrowed: 69%. **Student employment:** During the 2003-2004 academic year, 8% of undergraduates worked on campus. Average per-year earnings: $1,548.

James Madison University

800 S. Main Street
Harrisonburg, VA 22807
Public; www.jmu.edu
Financial aid office: (540) 568-7820

■ **2004-2005 TUITION AND FEES:**
  In state: $5,476; Out of state: $14,420
■ **ROOM AND BOARD:** $6,116

SAT I Score (25th/75th percentile): 1080-1250
2005 U.S. News College Ranking:
Universities–Master's (South), 3
Acceptance Rate: 62%

Other expenses: Estimated books and supplies: $764. Transportation: $1,614. Personal expenses: $1,462. **Financial aid:** Priority filing date for institution's financial aid form: March 1. In 2003-2004, 76% of undergraduates applied for financial aid. Of those, 47% were determined to have financial need; 32% had their need fully met. Average financial aid package (proportion receiving): $6,102 (29%). Average amount of gift aid, such as scholarships or grants (proportion receiving): $4,380 (12%). Average amount of self-help aid, such as work study or loans (proportion receiving): $3,761 (23%). Average need-based loan (excluding PLUS or other private loans): $3,676. Among students who received need-based aid, the average percentage of need met: 52%. Among students who received aid based on merit, the average award (and the proportion receiving): $1,602 (2%). The average athletic scholarship (and the proportion receiving): $8,764 (2%). Average amount of debt of borrowers graduating in 2003: $11,639. Proportion who borrowed: 50%. **Student employment:** During the 2003-2004 academic year, 19% of undergraduates worked on campus. Average per-year earnings: $1,920. **Cooperative education programs:** other. **Reserve Officers Training Corps (ROTC):** Army ROTC: Offered on campus; Air Force ROTC: Offered at cooperating institution (U. of Virginia).

Liberty University

1971 University Boulevard
Lynchburg, VA 24502-2269
Private; www.liberty.edu
Financial aid office: (434) 582-2270

■ **2004-2005 TUITION AND FEES:** $13,150
■ **ROOM AND BOARD:** $5,400

SAT I Score (25th/75th percentile): 870-1120
2005 U.S. News College Ranking:
Universities–Master's (South), fourth tier
Acceptance Rate: 96%

Other expenses: Estimated books and supplies: $1,000. Transportation: $2,000. Personal expenses: $1,000. **Financial aid:** Priority filing date for institution's financial aid form: March 1. In 2003-2004, 97% of undergraduates applied for financial aid. Of those, 77% were determined to have financial need; 12% had their need fully met. Average financial aid package (proportion receiving): $9,689 (76%). Average amount of gift aid, such as scholarships or grants (proportion receiving): $4,736 (43%). Average amount of self-help aid, such as work study or loans (proportion receiving): $1,708 (18%). Average need-based loan (excluding PLUS or other private loans): $3,267. Among students who received need-based aid, the average percentage of need met: 66%. Among students who received aid based on merit, the average award (and the proportion receiving): $5,199 (14%). The average athletic scholarship (and the proportion receiving): $9,124 (1%). Average amount of debt of borrowers graduating in 2003: $15,085. Proportion who borrowed: 65%. **Student employment:** During the 2003-2004 academic year, 100% of undergraduates worked on campus. Average per-year earnings: $2,000. **Reserve Officers Training Corps (ROTC):** Army ROTC: Offered on campus; Air Force ROTC: Offered at cooperating institution (University of Virginia).

Longwood University

201 High Street
Farmville, VA 23909
Public; www.longwood.edu
Financial aid office: (434) 395-2077

■ **2004-2005 TUITION AND FEES:**
  In state: $6,441; Out of state: $12,901
■ **ROOM AND BOARD:** $5,424

SAT I Score (25th/75th percentile): 1010-1140
2005 U.S. News College Ranking:
Universities–Master's (South), 37
Acceptance Rate: 70%

....

Other expenses: Estimated books and supplies: $700. **Financial aid:** Priority filing date for institution's financial aid form: March 1. In 2003-2004, 65% of undergraduates applied for financial aid. Of those, 43% were determined to have financial need; 33% had their need fully met. Average financial aid package (proportion receiving): $7,258 (43%). Average amount of gift aid, such as scholarships or grants (proportion receiving): $3,855 (39%). Average amount of self-help aid, such as work study or loans (proportion receiving): $4,624 (36%). Average need-based loan (excluding PLUS or other private loans): $4,046. Among students who received need-based aid, the average percentage of need met: 79%. Among students who received aid based on merit, the average award (and the proportion receiving): $4,881 (21%). The average athletic scholarship (and the proportion receiving): $4,167 (3%). Average amount of debt of borrowers graduating in 2003: $14,574. Proportion who borrowed: 84%. **Student employment:** During the 2003-2004 academic year, 20% of undergraduates worked on campus. Average per-year earnings: $2,000. **Reserve Officers Training Corps (ROTC):** Army ROTC: Offered on campus.

Lynchburg College

1501 Lakeside Drive
Lynchburg, VA 24501
Private; www.lynchburg.edu
Financial aid office: (434) 544-8228

■ **2004-2005 TUITION AND FEES:** $23,065
■ **ROOM AND BOARD:** $5,600

SAT I Score (25th/75th percentile): 920-1130
2005 U.S. News College Ranking:
Universities–Master's (South), 37
Acceptance Rate: 76%

....

Other expenses: Estimated books and supplies: $600. Transportation: $400. Personal expenses: $500. **Financial aid:** Priority filing date for institution's financial aid form: March 1. In 2003-2004, 75% of undergraduates applied for financial aid. Of those, 64% were determined to have financial need; 34% had their need fully met. Average financial aid package (proportion receiving): $15,969 (64%). Average amount of gift aid, such as scholarships or grants (proportion receiving): $11,958 (64%). Average amount

of self-help aid, such as work study or loans (proportion receiving): $4,281 (49%). Average need-based loan (excluding PLUS or other private loans): $4,441. Among students who received need-based aid, the average percentage of need met: 84%. Among students who received aid based on merit, the average award (and the proportion receiving): $7,856 (36%). The average athletic scholarship (and the proportion receiving): $0 (0%). Average amount of debt of borrowers graduating in 2003: $17,727. Proportion who borrowed: 86%. **Student employment:** During the 2003-2004 academic year, 33% of undergraduates worked on campus. Average per-year earnings: $1,313.

Mary Baldwin College

New and Frederick Streets
Staunton, VA 24401
Private; www.mbc.edu
Financial aid office: (540) 887-7022

■ **2004-2005 TUITION AND FEES:** $19,991
■ **ROOM AND BOARD:** $5,689

SAT I Score (25th/75th percentile): 940-1190
2005 U.S. News College Ranking:
Universities–Master's (South), 22
Acceptance Rate: 78%

....

Other expenses: Estimated books and supplies: $700. **Financial aid:** Priority filing date for institution's financial aid form: May 15. In 2003-2004, 87% of undergraduates applied for financial aid. Of those, 78% were determined to have financial need; 46% had their need fully met. Average financial aid package (proportion receiving): $19,276 (78%). Average amount of gift aid, such as scholarships or grants (proportion receiving): $9,786 (77%). Average amount of self-help aid, such as work study or loans (proportion receiving): $5,364 (69%). Average need-based loan (excluding PLUS or other private loans): $3,196. Among students who received need-based aid, the average percentage of need met: 89%. Among students who received aid based on merit, the average award (and the proportion receiving): $12,432 (19%). The average athletic scholarship (and the proportion receiving): $0 (0%). Average amount of debt of borrowers graduating in 2003: $19,694. Proportion who borrowed: 73%. **Student employment:** During the 2003-2004 academic year, 32% of undergraduates worked on campus. Average per-year earnings: $1,700. **Cooperative education programs:** computer science, engineering, other. **Reserve Officers Training Corps (ROTC):** Army ROTC: Offered

on campus; Navy ROTC: Offered at cooperating institution (Virginia Military Institute); Air Force ROTC: Offered on campus.

Marymount University

2807 N. Glebe Road
Arlington, VA 22207
Private; www.marymount.edu
Financial aid office: (703) 284-1530

■ **2004-2005 TUITION AND FEES:** $17,090
■ **ROOM AND BOARD:** $7,520

SAT I Score (25th/75th percentile): 890-1100
2005 U.S. News College Ranking:
Universities–Master's (South), 48
Acceptance Rate: 81%

....

Other expenses: Estimated books and supplies: $800. Transportation: $470. Personal expenses: $900. **Financial aid:** Priority filing date for institution's financial aid form: March 1. In 2003-2004, 71% of undergraduates applied for financial aid. Of those, 58% were determined to have financial need; 21% had their need fully met. Average financial aid package (proportion receiving): $13,276 (57%). Average amount of gift aid, such as scholarships or grants (proportion receiving): $6,436 (44%). Average amount of self-help aid, such as work study or loans (proportion receiving): $4,460 (48%). Average need-based loan (excluding PLUS or other private loans): $3,942. Among students who received need-based aid, the average percentage of need met: 75%. Among students who received aid based on merit, the average award (and the proportion receiving): $6,870 (17%). Average amount of debt of borrowers graduating in 2003: $21,366. Proportion who borrowed: 71%. **Student employment:** During the 2003-2004 academic year, 11% of undergraduates worked on campus. Average per-year earnings: $1,800. **Reserve Officers Training Corps (ROTC):** Army ROTC: Offered at cooperating institution (Georgetown University).

Norfolk State University

700 Park Avenue
Norfolk, VA 23504
Public; www.nsu.edu
Financial aid office: (757) 823-8381

■ **2004-2005 TUITION AND FEES:**
  In state: $4,295; Out of state: $14,255
■ **ROOM AND BOARD:** $6,236

SAT I Score (25th/75th percentile): 810-970
2005 U.S. News College Ranking:
Universities–Master's (South), fourth tier
Acceptance Rate: 71%

....

Other expenses: Estimated books and supplies: $1,000. Personal expenses: $2,700. **Financial aid:** Priority filing date for institution's financial aid form: April 15. In 2003-2004, 90% of undergraduates applied for financial aid. Of those, 79% were determined to have financial need; 10% had their need fully met. Average financial aid package (proportion receiving): $8,146 (78%). Average amount of gift aid, such as scholarships or grants (proportion receiving): $5,086 (69%). Average amount of self-help aid, such as work study or loans (proportion receiving): $3,526 (67%). Average need-based loan (excluding PLUS or other private loans): $3,295. Among students who received need-based aid, the average percentage of need met: 87%. Among students who received aid based on merit, the average award (and the proportion receiving): $4,984 (9%). Average amount of debt of borrowers graduating in 2003: $15,467. Proportion who borrowed: 60%. **Student employment:** During the 2003-2004 academic year, 11% of undergraduates worked on campus. Average per-year earnings: $1,713. **Cooperative education programs:** technologies. **Reserve Officers Training Corps (ROTC):** Army ROTC: Offered on campus; Navy ROTC: Offered on campus.

Old Dominion University

5215 Hampton Boulevard
Norfolk, VA 23529
Public; www.odu.edu
Financial aid office: (757) 683-3683

■ **2004-2005 TUITION AND FEES:**
In state: $4,928; Out of state: $14,078
■ **ROOM AND BOARD:** $5,513

SAT I Score (25th/75th percentile): 930-1140
2005 U.S. News College Ranking:
National Universities, fourth tier
Acceptance Rate: 82%

....

Other expenses: Estimated books and supplies: $800. Transportation: $1,000. Personal expenses: $1,875. **Financial aid:** Priority filing date for institution's financial aid form: February 15; deadline: March 15. In 2003-2004, 82% of undergraduates applied for financial aid. Of those, 60% were determined to have financial need; 36% had their need fully met. Average financial aid package (proportion receiving):

$7,191 (58%). Average amount of gift aid, such as scholarships or grants (proportion receiving): $4,169 (41%). Average amount of self-help aid, such as work study or loans (proportion receiving): $4,285 (46%). Average need-based loan (excluding PLUS or other private loans): $3,928. Among students who received need-based aid, the average percentage of need met: 65%. Among students who received aid based on merit, the average award (and the proportion receiving): $2,936 (6%). The average athletic scholarship (and the proportion receiving): $8,258 (2%). Average amount of debt of borrowers graduating in 2003: $16,750. Proportion who borrowed: 80%. **Student employment:** During the 2003-2004 academic year, 7% of undergraduates worked on campus. Average per-year earnings: $1,854. **Cooperative education programs:** art, business, computer science, education, engineering, health professions, humanities, natural science, social/behavioral science, technologies, vocational arts. **Reserve Officers Training Corps (ROTC):** Army ROTC: Offered on campus; Navy ROTC: Offered on campus.

Radford University

PO Box 6890, RU Station
Radford, VA 24142
Public; www.radford.edu
Financial aid office: (540) 831-5408

■ **2004-2005 TUITION AND FEES:**
In state: $4,762; Out of state: $11,762
■ **ROOM AND BOARD:** $5,886

SAT I Score (25th/75th percentile): 910-1100
2005 U.S. News College Ranking:
Universities–Master's (South), 51
Acceptance Rate: 74%

....

Financial aid: Priority filing date for institution's financial aid form: March 1. In 2003-2004, 62% of undergraduates applied for financial aid. Of those, 42% were determined to have financial need; 73% had their need fully met. Average financial aid package (proportion receiving): $7,759 (40%). Average amount of gift aid, such as scholarships or grants (proportion receiving): $3,715 (27%). Average amount of self-help aid, such as work study or loans (proportion receiving): $3,272 (35%). Average need-based loan (excluding PLUS or other private loans): $3,259. Among students who received need-based aid, the average percentage of need met: 77%. Among students who received aid based on merit, the average award (and the proportion receiving): $5,600 (23%).

The average athletic scholarship (and the proportion receiving): $5,852 (3%). Average amount of debt of borrowers graduating in 2003: $14,906. Proportion who borrowed: 62%. **Student employment:** During the 2003-2004 academic year, 10% of undergraduates worked on campus. Average per-year earnings: $1,127. **Reserve Officers Training Corps (ROTC):** Army ROTC: Offered on campus.

Randolph-Macon College

PO Box 5005
Ashland, VA 23005-5505
Private; www.rmc.edu
Financial aid office: (804) 752-7259

■ **2004-2005 TUITION AND FEES:** $22,625
■ **ROOM AND BOARD:** $6,510

SAT I Score (25th/75th percentile): 1000-1200
2005 U.S. News College Ranking:
Liberal Arts Colleges, 105
Acceptance Rate: 77%

....

Other expenses: Estimated books and supplies: $1,000. Transportation: $780. Personal expenses: $720. **Financial aid:** Priority filing date for institution's financial aid form: February 1; deadline: March 1. In 2003-2004, 68% of undergraduates applied for financial aid. Of those, 57% were determined to have financial need; 22% had their need fully met. Average financial aid package (proportion receiving): $15,701 (57%). Average amount of gift aid, such as scholarships or grants (proportion receiving): $11,040 (57%). Average amount of self-help aid, such as work study or loans (proportion receiving): $5,580 (49%). Average need-based loan (excluding PLUS or other private loans): $4,902. Among students who received need-based aid, the average percentage of need met: 84%. Among students who received aid based on merit, the average award (and the proportion receiving): $11,012 (37%). Average amount of debt of borrowers graduating in 2003: $17,066. Proportion who borrowed: 63%. **Student employment:** During the 2003-2004 academic year, 39% of undergraduates worked on campus. Average per-year earnings: $1,200. **Reserve Officers Training Corps (ROTC):** Army ROTC: Offered at cooperating institution (University of Richmond).

Randolph-Macon Woman's College

2500 Rivermont Avenue
Lynchburg, VA 24503-1526
Private; www.rmwc.edu
Financial aid office: (434) 947-8128

■ **2004-2005 TUITION AND FEES:** $21,740
■ **ROOM AND BOARD:** $8,230

SAT I Score (25th/75th percentile): 1050-1260
2005 U.S. News College Ranking:
Liberal Arts Colleges, 83
Acceptance Rate: 86%

Other expenses: Estimated books and supplies: $800. Transportation: $500. Personal expenses: $1,000. **Financial aid:** Priority filing date for institution's financial aid form: March 1. In 2003-2004, 73% of undergraduates applied for financial aid. Of those, 66% were determined to have financial need; 38% had their need fully met. Average financial aid package (proportion receiving): $19,958 (66%). Average amount of gift aid, such as scholarships or grants (proportion receiving): $14,203 (66%). Average amount of self-help aid, such as work study or loans (proportion receiving): $5,803 (56%). Average need-based loan (excluding PLUS or other private loans): $4,281. Among students who received need-based aid, the average percentage of need met: 89%. Among students who received aid based on merit, the average award (and the proportion receiving): $15,351 (33%). The average athletic scholarship (and the proportion receiving): $0 (0%). Average amount of debt of borrowers graduating in 2003: $21,992. Proportion who borrowed: 68%. **Student employment:** During the 2003-2004 academic year, 65% of undergraduates worked on campus. Average per-year earnings: $1,860.

Regent University

1000 Regent University Drive
Virginia Beach, VA 23464-5037
Private; www.regent.edu
Financial aid office: (757) 226-4140

■ **2004-2005 TUITION AND FEES:** $8,946

2005 U.S. News College Ranking:
Universities–Master's (South), unranked

Other expenses: Estimated books and supplies: $334. Transportation: $2,043. Personal expenses: $4,918. **Financial aid:** Priority filing date for institution's financial aid form: March 15. In 2003-2004, 63% of undergraduates applied for financial aid. Of those, 61% were determined to have financial need; 2% had their need fully met. Average financial aid package (proportion receiving): $8,334 (61%). Average amount of gift aid, such as scholarships or grants (proportion receiving): $2,694 (27%). Average amount of self-help aid, such as work study or loans (proportion receiving): $5,202 (48%). Average need-based loan (excluding PLUS or other private loans): $5,202. Among students who received need-based aid, the average percentage of need met: 44%. Among students who received aid based on merit, the average award (and the proportion receiving): $3,163 (18%). The average athletic scholarship (and the proportion receiving): $3,556 (46%). Average amount of debt of borrowers graduating in 2003: $21,294. Proportion who borrowed: 55%.

Roanoke College

221 College Lane
Salem, VA 24153-3794
Private; www.roanoke.edu
Financial aid office: (540) 375-2235

■ **2004-2005 TUITION AND FEES:** $22,109
■ **ROOM AND BOARD:** $6,912

SAT I Score (25th/75th percentile): 1020-1210
2005 U.S. News College Ranking:
Liberal Arts Colleges, third tier
Acceptance Rate: 77%

Other expenses: Estimated books and supplies: $850. Transportation: $1,000. Personal expenses: $750. **Financial aid:** Priority filing date for institution's financial aid form: March 1. In 2003-2004, 70% of undergraduates applied for financial aid. Of those, 70% were determined to have financial need; 30% had their need fully met. Average financial aid package (proportion receiving): $17,852 (70%). Average amount of gift aid, such as scholarships or grants (proportion receiving): $13,649 (63%). Average amount of self-help aid, such as work study or loans (proportion receiving): $5,344 (50%). Average need-based loan (excluding PLUS or other private loans): $4,464. Among students who received need-based aid, the average percentage of need met: 91%. Among students who received aid based on merit, the average award (and the proportion receiving): $9,396 (25%). The average athletic scholarship (and the proportion receiving): $0 (0%). Average amount of debt of borrowers graduating in 2003: $17,679. Proportion who borrowed: 71%. **Student**

employment: During the 2003-2004 academic year, 30% of undergraduates worked on campus. Average per-year earnings: $1,500.

Shenandoah University

1460 University Drive
Winchester, VA 22601
Private; www.su.edu
Financial aid office: (540) 665-4538

■ **2004-2005 TUITION AND FEES:** $19,240
■ **ROOM AND BOARD:** $7,090

SAT I Score (25th/75th percentile): 880-1130
2005 U.S. News College Ranking:
Universities–Master's (South), 48
Acceptance Rate: 73%

Other expenses: Estimated books and supplies: $1,000. Transportation: $600. Personal expenses: $1,500. **Financial aid:** Priority filing date for institution's financial aid form: March 2; deadline: March 2. In 2003-2004, 66% of undergraduates applied for financial aid. Of those, 66% were determined to have financial need; 30% had their need fully met. Average financial aid package (proportion receiving): $12,712 (66%). Average amount of gift aid, such as scholarships or grants (proportion receiving): $6,655 (49%). Average amount of self-help aid, such as work study or loans (proportion receiving): $5,131 (66%). Average need-based loan (excluding PLUS or other private loans): $4,671. Among students who received need-based aid, the average percentage of need met: 84%. Among students who received aid based on merit, the average award (and the proportion receiving): $3,589 (11%). The average athletic scholarship (and the proportion receiving): $0 (0%). Average amount of debt of borrowers graduating in 2003: $18,588. Proportion who borrowed: 65%. **Student employment:** During the 2003-2004 academic year, 2% of undergraduates worked on campus. Average per-year earnings: $2,500.

St. Paul's College

115 College Drive
Lawrenceville, VA 23868
Private; www.saintpauls.edu
Financial aid office: (434) 848-6497

■ **2004-2005 TUITION AND FEES:** $9,816
■ **ROOM AND BOARD:** $5,290

SAT I Score (25th/75th percentile): 620-820
2005 U.S. News College Ranking:
Comp. Colleges–Bachelor's (South), fourth tier
Acceptance Rate: 81%

Other expenses: Estimated books and supplies: $1,400. Transportation: $1,400. Personal expenses: $1,760. **Financial aid:** In 2003-2004, 99% of undergraduates applied for financial aid. Of those, 99% were determined to have financial need; 2% had their need fully met. Average financial aid package (proportion receiving): $6,819 (99%). Average amount of gift aid, such as scholarships or grants (proportion receiving): $4,580 (99%). Average amount of self-help aid, such as work study or loans (proportion receiving): $1,239 (99%). Average need-based loan (excluding PLUS or other private loans): $3,542. Among students who received need-based aid, the average percentage of need met: 87%. Among students who received aid based on merit, the average award (and the proportion receiving): $0 (0%). The average athletic scholarship (and the proportion receiving): $0 (0%). Average amount of debt of borrowers graduating in 2003: $10,315. Proportion who borrowed: 80%. **Student employment:** During the 2003-2004 academic year, 2% of undergraduates worked on campus. Average per-year earnings: $3,200. **Reserve Officers Training Corps (ROTC):** Army ROTC: Offered at cooperating institution (Virginia State).

Sweet Briar College

134 Chapel Road
Sweet Briar, VA 24595
Private; www.sbc.edu
Financial aid office: (434) 381-6156

■ **2004-2005 TUITION AND FEES:** $21,080
■ **ROOM AND BOARD:** $8,520

SAT I Score (25th/75th percentile): 990-1190
2005 U.S. News College Ranking:
Liberal Arts Colleges, 68
Acceptance Rate: 88%

Other expenses: Estimated books and supplies: $600. Transportation: $600. Personal expenses: $750. **Financial aid:** Priority filing date for institution's financial aid form: March 1. In 2003-2004, 67% of undergraduates applied for financial aid. Of those, 67% were determined to have financial need; 90% had their need fully met. Average financial aid package (proportion receiving): $14,878 (67%). Average amount of gift aid, such as scholarships or grants (proportion receiving): $13,088 (54%).

Average amount of self-help aid, such as work study or loans (proportion receiving): $5,344 (49%). Average need-based loan (excluding PLUS or other private loans): $4,961. Among students who received need-based aid, the average percentage of need met: 92%. Among students who received aid based on merit, the average award (and the proportion receiving): $10,040 (41%). The average athletic scholarship (and the proportion receiving): $0 (0%). Average amount of debt of borrowers graduating in 2003: $17,250. Proportion who borrowed: 54%. **Student employment:** During the 2003-2004 academic year, 58% of undergraduates worked on campus. Average per-year earnings: $1,000.

University of Mary Washington

1301 College Avenue
Fredericksburg, VA 22401
Public; www.mwc.edu/admissions
Financial aid office: (540) 654-2468

■ **2004-2005 TUITION AND FEES:**
   In state: $4,670; Out of state: $12,800
■ **ROOM AND BOARD:** $5,760

SAT I Score (25th/75th percentile): 1130-1300
2005 U.S. News College Ranking:
Universities–Master's (South), 8
Acceptance Rate: 60%

Other expenses: Estimated books and supplies: $950. Transportation: $850. Personal expenses: $1,500. **Financial aid:** Priority filing date for institution's financial aid form: March 1. In 2003-2004, 86% of undergraduates applied for financial aid. Of those, 61% were determined to have financial need; 4% had their need fully met. Average financial aid package (proportion receiving): $3,660 (60%). Average amount of gift aid, such as scholarships or grants (proportion receiving): $3,050 (38%). Average amount of self-help aid, such as work study or loans (proportion receiving): $2,950 (42%). Average need-based loan (excluding PLUS or other private loans): $2,910. Among students who received need-based aid, the average percentage of need met: 57%. Among students who received aid based on merit, the average award (and the proportion receiving): $3,190 (12%). The average athletic scholarship (and the proportion receiving): $0 (0%). Average amount of debt of borrowers graduating in 2003: $12,665. Proportion who borrowed: 59%. **Student employment:** During the 2003-2004 academic

year, 50% of undergraduates worked on campus. Average per-year earnings: $1,500.

University of Richmond

28 Westhampton Way
Univ. of Richmond, VA 23173
Private; www.richmond.edu
Financial aid office: (804) 289-8438

■ **2004-2005 TUITION AND FEES:** $26,520
■ **ROOM AND BOARD:** $5,390

SAT I Score (25th/75th percentile): 1240-1390
2005 U.S. News College Ranking:
Universities–Master's (South), 1
Acceptance Rate: 42%

Other expenses: Estimated books and supplies: $1,050. Personal expenses: $990. **Financial aid:** In 2003-2004, 47% of undergraduates applied for financial aid. Of those, 32% were determined to have financial need; 40% had their need fully met. Average financial aid package (proportion receiving): $19,189 (32%). Average amount of gift aid, such as scholarships or grants (proportion receiving): $15,742 (31%). Average amount of self-help aid, such as work study or loans (proportion receiving): $3,805 (25%). Average need-based loan (excluding PLUS or other private loans): $3,432. Among students who received need-based aid, the average percentage of need met: 97%. Among students who received aid based on merit, the average award (and the proportion receiving): $11,596 (14%). The average athletic scholarship (and the proportion receiving): $18,516 (7%). Average amount of debt of borrowers graduating in 2003: $16,370. Proportion who borrowed: 39%. **Student employment:** During the 2003-2004 academic year, 24% of undergraduates worked on campus. Average per-year earnings: $1,450. **Reserve Officers Training Corps (ROTC):** Army ROTC: Offered on campus.

University of Virginia

Office of Admission, PO Box 400160
Charlottesville, VA 22904-4160
Public; www.virginia.edu
Financial aid office: (434) 982-6000

■ **2004-2005 TUITION AND FEES:**
   In state: $6,600; Out of state: $22,700
■ **ROOM AND BOARD:** $5,960

SAT I Score (25th/75th percentile): 1230-1430
2005 U.S. News College Ranking:
National Universities, 22
Acceptance Rate: 39%

....

Other expenses: Estimated books and supplies: $1,000. Personal expenses: $1,600. **Financial aid:** Priority filing date for institution's financial aid form: March 1. In 2003-2004, 38% of undergraduates applied for financial aid. Of those, 24% were determined to have financial need; 55% had their need fully met. Average financial aid package (proportion receiving): $12,408 (23%). Average amount of gift aid, such as scholarships or grants (proportion receiving): $9,564 (19%). Average amount of self-help aid, such as work study or loans (proportion receiving): $4,640 (17%). Average need-based loan (excluding PLUS or other private loans): $4,368. Among students who received need-based aid, the average percentage of need met: 92%. Among students who received aid based on merit, the average award (and the proportion receiving): $5,667 (18%). The average athletic scholarship (and the proportion receiving): $15,688 (3%). Average amount of debt of borrowers graduating in 2003: $13,522. Proportion who borrowed: 31%. Average per-year earnings: $1,400. **Cooperative education programs:** engineering. **Reserve Officers Training Corps (ROTC):** Army ROTC: Offered on campus; Navy ROTC: Offered on campus; Air Force ROTC: Offered on campus.

University of Virginia–Wise

1 College Avenue
Wise, VA 24293
Public; www.uvawise.edu
Financial aid office: (276) 328-0103

■ **2004-2005 TUITION AND FEES:**
 In state: $4,782; Out of state: $14,152
■ **ROOM AND BOARD:** $5,826

SAT I Score (25th/75th percentile): 870-1100
2005 U.S. News College Ranking:
Liberal Arts Colleges, fourth tier
Acceptance Rate: 78%

....

Other expenses: Estimated books and supplies: $675. Transportation: $300. Personal expenses: $1,200. **Financial aid:** Priority filing date for institution's financial aid form: April 1; deadline: April 1. In 2003-2004, 91% of undergraduates applied for financial aid. Of those, 70% were determined to have financial need; 95% had their need fully met. Average financial aid package (proportion receiving): $5,798 (70%).

Average amount of gift aid, such as scholarships or grants (proportion receiving): $3,556 (61%). Average amount of self-help aid, such as work study or loans (proportion receiving): $2,901 (50%). Average need-based loan (excluding PLUS or other private loans): $2,870. Among students who received need-based aid, the average percentage of need met: 95%. Among students who received aid based on merit, the average award (and the proportion receiving): $1,515 (18%). The average athletic scholarship (and the proportion receiving): $1,601 (9%). Average amount of debt of borrowers graduating in 2003: $7,414. Proportion who borrowed: 67%. **Cooperative education programs:** other.

Virginia Commonwealth University

Box 842527
Richmond, VA 23284
Public; www.vcu.edu
Financial aid office: (804) 828-6669

■ **2004-2005 TUITION AND FEES:**
 In state: $5,138; Out of state: $17,262
■ **ROOM AND BOARD:** $6,920

SAT I Score (25th/75th percentile): 950-1170
2005 U.S. News College Ranking:
National Universities, third tier
Acceptance Rate: 74%

....

Other expenses: Estimated books and supplies: $890. Transportation: $2,660. Personal expenses: $2,500. **Financial aid:** Priority filing date for institution's financial aid form: March 1. In 2003-2004, 70% of undergraduates applied for financial aid. Of those, 50% were determined to have financial need; 9% had their need fully met. Average financial aid package (proportion receiving): $7,000 (49%). Average amount of gift aid, such as scholarships or grants (proportion receiving): $3,400 (39%). Average amount of self-help aid, such as work study or loans (proportion receiving): $4,000 (42%). Average need-based loan (excluding PLUS or other private loans): $3,800. Among students who received need-based aid, the average percentage of need met: 54%. Among students who received aid based on merit, the average award (and the proportion receiving): $4,000 (4%). The average athletic scholarship (and the proportion receiving): $11,000 (1%). Average amount of debt of borrowers graduating in 2003: $19,370. Proportion who borrowed: 63%. **Cooperative education programs:** engineering. **Reserve Officers Training Corps (ROTC):** Army ROTC: Offered on campus.

Virginia Intermont College

1013 Moore Street
Bristol, VA 24201
Private; www.vic.edu
Financial aid office: (276) 466-7873

■ **2004-2005 TUITION AND FEES:** $15,200
■ **ROOM AND BOARD:** $5,650

SAT I Score (25th/75th percentile): 820-1091
2005 U.S. News College Ranking:
Comp. Colleges–Bachelor's (South), third tier
Acceptance Rate: 67%

....

Other expenses: Estimated books and supplies: $900. Transportation: $3,000. Personal expenses: $2,700. **Financial aid:** In 2003-2004, 83% of undergraduates applied for financial aid. Of those, 78% were determined to have financial need; 10% had their need fully met. Average financial aid package (proportion receiving): $10,935 (78%). Average amount of gift aid, such as scholarships or grants (proportion receiving): $3,014 (43%). Average amount of self-help aid, such as work study or loans (proportion receiving): $4,650 (69%). Average need-based loan (excluding PLUS or other private loans): $4,172. Among students who received need-based aid, the average percentage of need met: 10%. Among students who received aid based on merit, the average award (and the proportion receiving): $4,699 (9%). The average athletic scholarship (and the proportion receiving): $8,975 (18%). Average amount of debt of borrowers graduating in 2003: $12,131. Proportion who borrowed: 77%. **Student employment:** During the 2003-2004 academic year, 25% of undergraduates worked on campus. Average per-year earnings: $1,500.

Virginia Military Institute

VMI Parade
Lexington, VA 24450-0304
Public; www.vmi.edu
Financial aid office: (540) 464-7208

■ **2004-2005 TUITION AND FEES:**
 In state: $8,054; Out of state: $21,516
■ **ROOM AND BOARD:** $5,474

SAT I Score (25th/75th percentile): 1050-1230
2005 U.S. News College Ranking:
Liberal Arts Colleges, 77
Acceptance Rate: 51%

....

Other expenses: Estimated books and supplies: $650. Transportation: $300. Personal expenses: $1,350. **Financial aid:** Priority filing date for institution's financial aid form: March 1; deadline: March 1. In 2003-2004, 52% of undergraduates applied for financial aid. Of those, 43% were determined to have financial need; 63% had their need fully met. Average financial aid package (proportion receiving): $12,502 (42%). Average amount of gift aid, such as scholarships or grants (proportion receiving): $7,661 (40%). Average amount of self-help aid, such as work study or loans (proportion receiving): $3,870 (26%). Average need-based loan (excluding PLUS or other private loans): $3,619. Among students who received need-based aid, the average percentage of need met: 93%. Among students who received aid based on merit, the average award (and the proportion receiving): $6,421 (18%). The average athletic scholarship (and the proportion receiving): $11,592 (8%). Average amount of debt of borrowers graduating in 2003: $14,500. Proportion who borrowed: 32%. **Reserve Officers Training Corps (ROTC):** Army ROTC: Offered on campus; Navy ROTC: Offered on campus; Air Force ROTC: Offered on campus.

Virginia State University

1 Hayden Street
Petersburg, VA 23806
Public; www.vsu.edu
Financial aid office: (804) 524-5992

- **2004-2005 TUITION AND FEES:**
  In state: $4,412; Out of state: $11,272
- **ROOM AND BOARD:** $6,260

SAT I Score (25th/75th percentile): 710-890
2005 U.S. News College Ranking:
Universities–Master's (South), fourth tier
Acceptance Rate: 66%

Other expenses: Estimated books and supplies: $790. Transportation: $640. Personal expenses: $532. **Financial aid:** Priority filing date for institution's financial aid form: March 31; deadline: May 1. In 2003-2004, 96% of undergraduates applied for financial aid. Of those, 88% were determined to have financial need; Average financial aid package (proportion receiving): $7,975 (88%). Average amount of gift aid, such as scholarships or grants (proportion receiving): $3,926 (57%). Average amount of self-help aid, such as work study or loans (proportion receiving): $5,024 (70%). Average need-based loan (excluding PLUS or other private loans): $4,705. Among students who received need-

based aid, the average percentage of need met: 75%. Among students who received aid based on merit, the average award (and the proportion receiving): $4,376 (8%). The average athletic scholarship (and the proportion receiving): $3,025 (4%). Average amount of debt of borrowers graduating in 2003: $19,300.
Cooperative education programs: agriculture, art, business, computer science, education, engineering, home economics, humanities, natural science, social/behavioral science, technologies, vocational arts. **Reserve Officers Training Corps (ROTC):** Army ROTC: Offered on campus.

Virginia Tech

Office of Undergraduate Admissions
201 Burruss Hall
Blacksburg, VA 24061
Public; www.vt.edu
Financial aid office: (540) 231-5179

- **2004-2005 TUITION AND FEES:**
  In state: $5,838; Out of state: $16,531
- **ROOM AND BOARD:** $5,787

SAT I Score (25th/75th percentile): 1120-1280
2005 U.S. News College Ranking:
National Universities, 74
Acceptance Rate: 69%

Other expenses: Estimated books and supplies: $1,573. Transportation: $787. Personal expenses: $1,868. **Financial aid:** Priority filing date for institution's financial aid form: March 11; deadline: March 11. In 2003-2004, 63% of undergraduates applied for financial aid. Of those, 41% were determined to have financial need; 2% had their need fully met. Average financial aid package (proportion receiving): $7,175 (37%). Average amount of gift aid, such as scholarships or grants (proportion receiving): $4,115 (28%). Average amount of self-help aid, such as work study or loans (proportion receiving): $3,904 (33%). Average need-based loan (excluding PLUS or other private loans): $3,707. Among students who received need-based aid, the average percentage of need met: 77%. Among students who received aid based on merit, the average award (and the proportion receiving): $1,500 (6%). The average athletic scholarship (and the proportion receiving): $2,759 (0%). Average amount of debt of borrowers graduating in 2003: $25,611. Proportion who borrowed: 37%. **Cooperative education programs:** agriculture, business, computer science, education, engineering, natural science. **Reserve Officers Training Corps (ROTC):** Army

ROTC: Offered on campus; Navy ROTC: Offered on campus; Air Force ROTC: Offered on campus.

Virginia Union University

1500 N. Lombardy Street
Richmond, VA 23220
Private; www.vuu.edu
Financial aid office: (804) 257-5882

- **2004-2005 TUITION AND FEES:** $12,260
- **ROOM AND BOARD:** $10,836

SAT I Score (25th/75th percentile): 590-830
2005 U.S. News College Ranking:
Liberal Arts Colleges, fourth tier
Acceptance Rate: 77%

Other expenses: Estimated books and supplies: $600. **Student employment:** During the 2003-2004 academic year, 30% of undergraduates worked on campus. Average per-year earnings: $1,800.

Virginia Wesleyan College

1584 Wesleyan Drive
Norfolk, VA 23502-5599
Private; www.vwc.edu
Financial aid office: (757) 455-3345

- **2004-2005 TUITION AND FEES:** $20,448
- **ROOM AND BOARD:** $6,600

SAT I Score (25th/75th percentile): 880-1080
2005 U.S. News College Ranking:
Liberal Arts Colleges, fourth tier
Acceptance Rate: 79%

Other expenses: Estimated books and supplies: $800. Transportation: $1,300. Personal expenses: $1,800. **Financial aid:** Priority filing date for institution's financial aid form: March 1. In 2003-2004, 97% of undergraduates applied for financial aid. Of those, 85% were determined to have financial need; 11% had their need fully met. Average financial aid package (proportion receiving): $13,105 (77%). Average amount of gift aid, such as scholarships or grants (proportion receiving): $3,404 (30%). Average amount of self-help aid, such as work study or loans (proportion receiving): $4,531 (65%). Average need-based loan (excluding PLUS or other private loans): $4,206. Among students who received need-based aid, the average percentage of need met: 70%. Among students who received aid based on merit, the average award (and the proportion receiving): $4,766 (12%). Average amount of debt of borrowers graduating in 2003: $15,408. Proportion who borrowed: 70%. **Student employment:** During the 2003-2004 academic year, 13% of undergraduates worked on campus. Average per-year earnings: $1,700. **Reserve Officers Training Corps (ROTC):** Army ROTC: Offered at cooperating institution (Old Dominion University).

Washington and Lee University

Lexington, VA 24450-0303
Private; www.wlu.edu
Financial aid office: (540) 458-8717

■ **2004-2005 TUITION AND FEES:** $25,760
■ **ROOM AND BOARD:** $6,790

SAT I Score (25th/75th percentile): 1300-1440
2005 U.S. News College Ranking:
Liberal Arts Colleges, 13
Acceptance Rate: 31%

Other expenses: Estimated books and supplies: $1,500. Personal expenses: $1,590. **Financial aid:** Priority filing date for institution's financial aid form: February 1. In 2003-2004, 35% of undergraduates applied for financial aid. Of those, 29% were determined to have financial need; 95% had their need fully met. Average financial aid package (proportion receiving): $20,923 (29%). Average amount of gift aid, such as scholarships or grants (proportion receiving): $17,829 (22%). Average amount of self-help aid, such as work study or loans (proportion receiving): $4,993 (13%). Average need-based loan (excluding PLUS or other private loans): $4,307. Among students who received need-based aid, the average percentage of need met: 99%. Among students who received aid based on merit, the average award (and the proportion receiving): $8,663 (22%). Average amount of debt of borrowers graduating in 2003: $14,592. Proportion who borrowed: 38%. **Student employment:** During the 2003-2004 academic year, 13% of undergraduates worked on campus. Average per-year earnings: $1,950. **Reserve Officers Training Corps (ROTC):** Army ROTC: Offered at cooperating institution (Virginia Military Institute).

Washington

Central Washington University

400 E. University Way
Ellensburg, WA 98926-7501
Public; www.cwu.edu
Financial aid office: (509) 963-1611

■ **2004-2005 TUITION AND FEES:**
In state: $4,278; Out of state: $11,826
■ **ROOM AND BOARD:** $5,861

SAT I Score (25th/75th percentile): 880-1100
2005 U.S. News College Ranking:
Universities–Master's (West), 50
Acceptance Rate: 84%

Financial aid: Priority filing date for institution's financial aid form: March 1. In 2003-2004, 71% of undergraduates applied for financial aid. Of those, 50% were determined to have financial need; 19% had their need fully met. Average financial aid package (proportion receiving): $4,956 (49%). Average amount of gift aid, such as scholarships or grants (proportion receiving): $4,460 (42%). Average amount of self-help aid, such as work study or loans (proportion receiving): $4,530 (41%). Average need-based loan (excluding PLUS or other private loans): $4,339. Among students who received need-based aid, the average percentage of need met: 82%. Among students who received aid based on merit, the average award (and the proportion receiving): $4,543 (32%). The average athletic scholarship (and the proportion receiving): $1,990 (1%). Average amount of debt of borrowers graduating in 2003: $16,382. Proportion who borrowed: 63%. **Student employment:** During the 2003-2004 academic year, 24% of undergraduates worked on campus. Average per-year earnings: $3,000. **Cooperative education programs:** art, business, computer science, education, health professions, home economics, humanities, natural science, social/behavioral science, technologies, vocational arts, other. **Reserve Officers Training Corps (ROTC):** Army ROTC: Offered on campus; Air Force ROTC: Offered on campus.

City University

11900 N.E. First Street
Bellevue, WA 98005
Private; www.cityu.edu
Financial aid office: (800) 426-5596

■ **2003-2004 TUITION AND FEES:** $7,960

2005 U.S. News College Ranking:
Universities–Master's (West), unranked
Acceptance Rate: 100%

Cornish College of the Arts

710 E. Roy Street
Seattle, WA 98102
Private; www.cornish.edu
Financial aid office: (206) 726-5014

■ **2004-2005 TUITION AND FEES:** $19,900

2005 U.S. News College Ranking:
Unranked Specialty School–Fine Arts
Acceptance Rate: 81%

Financial aid: Priority filing date for institution's financial aid form: April 2; deadline: April 2.

Eastern Washington University

526 Fifth Street
Cheney, WA 99004
Public; www.ewu.edu
Financial aid office: (509) 359-2314

■ **2004-2005 TUITION AND FEES:**
In state: $4,062; Out of state: $13,539
■ **ROOM AND BOARD:** $5,460

SAT I Score (25th/75th percentile): 880-1120
2005 U.S. News College Ranking:
Universities–Master's (West), 52
Acceptance Rate: 81%

Other expenses: Estimated books and supplies: $822. Transportation: $1,434. Personal expenses: $2,094. **Financial aid:** Priority filing date for institution's financial aid form: April 1. In 2003-2004, 74% of undergraduates applied for financial aid. Of those, 62% were determined to have financial need; 14% had their need fully met. Average financial aid package (proportion receiving): $16,216 (61%). Average amount of gift aid, such as scholarships or grants (proportion receiving): $4,910 (45%). Average amount of self-help aid, such as work study or loans (proportion receiving): $4,090 (49%). Average need-based loan (excluding PLUS or other private loans): $3,837. Among students who received need-based aid, the average percentage of need met: 40%. Among students who received aid based on merit, the average award (and the proportion receiving): $3,474 (2%). The average athletic scholarship (and the proportion receiving): $5,714 (1%). Average amount of debt of borrowers graduating in 2003: $18,225. Proportion who borrowed: 67%. **Student employment:** During the 2003-2004 academic year, 42% of undergraduates worked on campus. Average per-year earnings: $2,074. **Reserve Officers Training Corps (ROTC):** Army ROTC: Offered on campus.

Evergreen State College

2700 Evergreen Parkway NW
Olympia, WA 98505
Public; www.evergreen.edu
Financial aid office: (360) 867-6205

■ **2004-2005 TUITION AND FEES:**
In state: $4,087; Out of state: $14,712
■ **ROOM AND BOARD:** $5,784

SAT I Score (25th/75th percentile): 1030-1270
2005 U.S. News College Ranking:
Liberal Arts Colleges, fourth tier
Acceptance Rate: 93%

Other expenses: Estimated books and supplies: $780. Transportation: $1,434. Personal expenses: $2,094. **Financial aid:** Priority filing date for institution's financial aid form: March 15. In 2003-2004, 76% of undergraduates applied for financial aid. Of those, 58% were determined to have financial need; 32% had their need fully met. Average financial aid package (proportion receiving): $10,006 (55%). Average amount of gift aid, such as scholarships or grants (proportion receiving): $5,406 (42%). Average amount of self-help aid, such as work study or loans (proportion receiving): $4,233 (45%). Average need-based loan (excluding PLUS or other private loans): $3,984. Among students who received need-based aid, the average percentage of need met: 79%. Among students who received aid based on merit, the average award (and the proportion receiving): $3,862 (1%). The average athletic scholarship (and the proportion receiving): $2,802 (4%). Average amount of debt of borrowers graduating in 2003: $13,000. Proportion who borrowed: 51%. **Student employment:** During the 2003-2004 academic year, 25% of undergraduates worked on campus. Average per-year earnings: $4,000.

Gonzaga University

502 E. Boone Avenue
Spokane, WA 99258-0001
Private; www.gonzaga.edu
Financial aid office: (509) 323-4049

■ **2004-2005 TUITION AND FEES:** $22,065
■ **ROOM AND BOARD:** $6,430

SAT I Score (25th/75th percentile): 1080-1280
2005 U.S. News College Ranking:
Universities–Master's (West), 4
Acceptance Rate: 77%

Other expenses: Estimated books and supplies: $800. Transportation: $1,200. Personal expenses: $1,700. **Financial aid:** Priority filing date for institution's financial aid form: February 1. In 2003-2004, 75% of undergraduates applied for financial aid. Of those, 64% were determined to have financial need; 31% had their need fully met. Average financial aid package (proportion receiving): $17,077 (62%). Average amount of gift aid, such as scholarships or grants (proportion receiving): $11,113 (51%). Average amount of self-help aid, such as work study or loans (proportion receiving): $6,650 (49%). Average need-based loan (excluding PLUS or other private loans): $5,407. Among students who received need-based aid, the average percentage of need met: 84%. Among students who received aid based on merit, the average award (and the proportion receiving): $6,618 (30%). The average athletic scholarship (and the proportion receiving): $12,206 (4%). Average amount of debt of borrowers graduating in 2003: $21,591. Proportion who borrowed: 73%. **Student employment:** During the 2003-2004 academic year, 22% of undergraduates worked on campus. Average per-year earnings: $2,800. **Reserve Officers Training Corps (ROTC):** Army ROTC: Offered on campus.

Henry Cogswell College

3002 Colby Avenue
Everett, WA 98201
Private; www.henrycogswell.edu
Financial aid office: (425) 258-3351

■ **2004-2005 TUITION AND FEES:** $15,840

SAT I Score (25th/75th percentile): 1020-1200
2005 U.S. News College Ranking:
Unranked Specialty School–Engineering
Acceptance Rate: 83%

Other expenses: Estimated books and supplies: $689. Transportation: $1,190. Personal expenses: $1,788. **Financial aid:** Priority filing date for institution's financial aid form: March 1. In 2003-2004, 84% of undergraduates applied for financial aid. Of those, 66% were determined to have financial need; Average financial aid package (proportion receiving): $5,584 (57%). Average amount of gift aid, such as scholarships or grants (proportion receiving): $4,690 (25%). Average amount of self-help aid, such as work study or loans (proportion receiving): $2,249 (52%). Average need-based loan (excluding PLUS or other private loans): $3,642. Among students who received aid based on merit, the average award (and the proportion receiving): $3,053 (N/A). Average amount of debt of borrowers graduating in 2003: $23,658. Proportion who borrowed: 41%. **Student employment:** During the 2003-2004 academic year, 1% of undergraduates worked on campus. Average per-year earnings: $2,400.

Heritage College

3240 Fort Road
Toppenish, WA 98948
Private; www.heritage.edu
Financial aid office: (509) 865-8502

■ **2004-2005 TUITION AND FEES:** $8,890

2005 U.S. News College Ranking:
Universities–Master's (West), fourth tier
Acceptance Rate: 66%

Other expenses: Estimated books and supplies: $750. Transportation: $1,984. Personal expenses: $2,094. **Financial aid:** Priority filing date for institution's financial aid form: February 10. In 2003-2004, 90% of undergraduates applied for financial aid. Of those, 87% were determined to have financial need; 6% had their need fully met. Average financial aid package (proportion

receiving): $10,161 (87%). Average amount of gift aid, such as scholarships or grants (proportion receiving): $7,643 (87%). Average amount of self-help aid, such as work study or loans (proportion receiving): $3,957 (64%). Average need-based loan (excluding PLUS or other private loans): $3,344. Among students who received need-based aid, the average percentage of need met: 67%. Among students who received aid based on merit, the average award (and the proportion receiving): $5,387 (3%). The average athletic scholarship (and the proportion receiving): $0 (0%). Average amount of debt of borrowers graduating in 2003: $14,172. Proportion who borrowed: 87%. **Student employment:** During the 2003-2004 academic year, 11% of undergraduates worked on campus. Average per-year earnings: $4,000.

Northwest College

PO Box 579
Kirkland, WA 98083
Private; www.nwcollege.edu
Financial aid office: (425) 889-5336

■ **2004-2005 TUITION AND FEES:** $14,900
■ **ROOM AND BOARD:** $6,450

SAT I Score (25th/75th percentile): 1050
2005 U.S. News College Ranking:
Comp. Colleges–Bachelor's (West), 18
Acceptance Rate: 90%

Other expenses: Estimated books and supplies: $850. Transportation: $400. Personal expenses: $1,600. **Financial aid:** Priority filing date for institution's financial aid form: March 1. In 2003-2004, 89% of undergraduates applied for financial aid. Of those, 78% were determined to have financial need; 22% had their need fully met. Average financial aid package (proportion receiving): $10,592 (78%). Average amount of gift aid, such as scholarships or grants (proportion receiving): $6,853 (74%). Average amount of self-help aid, such as work study or loans (proportion receiving): $4,723 (68%). Average need-based loan (excluding PLUS or other private loans): $3,798. Among students who received need-based aid, the average percentage of need met: 57%. Among students who received aid based on merit, the average award (and the proportion receiving): $9,059 (17%). The average athletic scholarship (and the proportion receiving): $6,612 (4%). Average amount of debt of borrowers graduating in 2003: $20,015. Proportion who borrowed: 91%. **Student employment:** During the 2003-2004 academic year, 17% of undergraduates worked

on campus. Average per-year earnings: $4,350.
Reserve Officers Training Corps (ROTC): Army
ROTC: Offered at cooperating institution
(University of Washington).

Pacific Lutheran University

Tacoma, WA 98447
Private; www.plu.edu
Financial aid office: (253) 535-7134

■ **2004-2005 TUITION AND FEES:** $20,790
■ **ROOM AND BOARD:** $6,410

SAT I Score (25th/75th percentile): 1000-1240
2005 U.S. News College Ranking:
Universities–Master's (West), 9
Acceptance Rate: 80%

Other expenses: Estimated books and supplies:
$750. Transportation: $100. Personal expenses:
$2,094. **Financial aid:** Priority filing date for
institution's financial aid form: January 31. In
2003-2004, 84% of undergraduates applied for
financial aid. Of those, 72% were determined to
have financial need; 28% had their need fully
met. Average financial aid package (proportion
receiving): $17,229 (71%). Average amount of
gift aid, such as scholarships or grants (proportion receiving): $7,135 (55%). Average amount
of self-help aid, such as work study or loans
(proportion receiving): $8,328 (66%). Average
need-based loan (excluding PLUS or other private loans): $6,802. Among students who
received need-based aid, the average percentage
of need met: 88%. Among students who
received aid based on merit, the average award
(and the proportion receiving): $6,135 (17%).
Average amount of debt of borrowers graduating in 2003: $22,190. Proportion who bor-
rowed: 60%. **Student employment:** During the
2003-2004 academic year, 40% of undergraduates worked on campus. Average per-year earnings: $3,000. **Reserve Officers Training Corps
(ROTC):** Army ROTC: Offered on campus.

Seattle Pacific University

3307 Third Avenue W
Seattle, WA 98119-1997
Private; www.spu.edu
Financial aid office: (206) 281-2061

■ **2004-2005 TUITION AND FEES:** $19,143
■ **ROOM AND BOARD:** $7,017

SAT I Score (25th/75th percentile): 1050-1290
2005 U.S. News College Ranking:
Universities–Master's (West), 13
Acceptance Rate: 92%

Other expenses: Estimated books and supplies:
$768. Transportation: $849. Personal expenses:
$1,548. **Financial aid:** Priority filing date for
institution's financial aid form: January 31. In
2003-2004, 75% of undergraduates applied for
financial aid. Of those, 63% were determined to
have financial need; 19% had their need fully
met. Average financial aid package (proportion
receiving): $16,249 (63%). Average amount of
gift aid, such as scholarships or grants (proportion receiving): $12,206 (62%). Average
amount of self-help aid, such as work study or
loans (proportion receiving): $7,049 (59%).
Average need-based loan (excluding PLUS or
other private loans): $5,566. Among students
who received need-based aid, the average percentage of need met: 80%. Among students
who received aid based on merit, the average
award (and the proportion receiving): $8,832
(28%). The average athletic scholarship (and
the proportion receiving): $12,333 (1%). Average
amount of debt of borrowers graduating in
2003: $19,714. Proportion who borrowed: 65%.
Reserve Officers Training Corps (ROTC): Army
ROTC: Offered at cooperating institution
(University of Washington); Navy ROTC:
Offered at cooperating institution (University of
Washington); Air Force ROTC: Offered at cooperating institution (University of Washington).

Seattle University

901 12th Avenue
Seattle, WA 98122-4340
Private; www.seattleu.edu
Financial aid office: (206) 296-2000

■ **2004-2005 TUITION AND FEES:** $21,285
■ **ROOM AND BOARD:** $7,038

SAT I Score (25th/75th percentile): 1020-1240
2005 U.S. News College Ranking:
Universities–Master's (West), 9
Acceptance Rate: 78%

Other expenses: Estimated books and supplies:
$1,170. Transportation: $1,347. Personal expenses: $1,890. **Financial aid:** Priority filing date for
institution's financial aid form: February 1. In
2003-2004, 78% of undergraduates applied for
financial aid. Of those, 66% were determined
to have financial need; 57% had their need fully
met. Average financial aid package (proportion
receiving): $19,380 (66%). Average amount of

gift aid, such as scholarships or grants (proportion receiving): $9,058 (58%). Average amount
of self-help aid, such as work study or loans
(proportion receiving): $7,322 (55%). Average
need-based loan (excluding PLUS or other private loans): $4,590. Among students who
received need-based aid, the average percentage
of need met: 86%. Among students who
received aid based on merit, the average award
(and the proportion receiving): $1,282 (7%).
The average athletic scholarship (and the proportion receiving): $8,206 (4%). Average
amount of debt of borrowers graduating in
2003: $26,096. Proportion who borrowed:
79%. **Student employment:** During the 2003-
2004 academic year, 11% of undergraduates
worked on campus. Average per-year earnings:
$4,474. **Reserve Officers Training Corps (ROTC):**
Army ROTC: Offered on campus; Navy ROTC:
Offered at cooperating institution (University of
Washington); Air Force ROTC: Offered at cooperating institution (University of Washington).

St. Martin's College

5300 Pacific Avenue SE
Lacey, WA 98503
Private; www.stmartin.edu
Financial aid office: (360) 438-4397

■ **2004-2005 TUITION AND FEES:** $18,950
■ **ROOM AND BOARD:** $5,720

SAT I Score (25th/75th percentile): 840-1130
2005 U.S. News College Ranking:
Universities–Master's (West), 44
Acceptance Rate: 75%

Other expenses: Estimated books and supplies:
$738. Transportation: $1,290. Personal expenses: $1,976. **Financial aid:** Priority filing date for
institution's financial aid form: March 1. In
2003-2004, 94% of undergraduates applied for
financial aid. Of those, 83% were determined to
have financial need; 35% had their need fully
met. Average financial aid package (proportion
receiving): $14,451 (83%). Average amount of
gift aid, such as scholarships or grants (proportion receiving): $9,895 (82%). Average amount
of self-help aid, such as work study or loans
(proportion receiving): $5,620 (72%). Average
need-based loan (excluding PLUS or other private loans): $4,160. Among students who
received need-based aid, the average percentage
of need met: 80%. Among students who
received aid based on merit, the average award
(and the proportion receiving): $10,336 (14%).
The average athletic scholarship (and the proportion receiving): $4,737 (6%). Average

amount of debt of borrowers graduating in 2003: $18,898. Proportion who borrowed: 56%. **Student employment:** During the 2003-2004 academic year, 5% of undergraduates worked on campus. Average per-year earnings: $1,500. **Reserve Officers Training Corps (ROTC):** Army ROTC: Offered at cooperating institution (Pacific Lutheran University).

University of Puget Sound

1500 N. Warner Street
Tacoma, WA 98416
Private; www.ups.edu
Financial aid office: (800) 396-7192

■ **2004-2005 TUITION AND FEES:** $26,880
■ **ROOM AND BOARD:** $6,730

SAT I Score (25th/75th percentile): 1145-1345
2005 U.S. News College Ranking:
Liberal Arts Colleges, 77
Acceptance Rate: 71%

Other expenses: Estimated books and supplies: $900. Transportation: $500. Personal expenses: $1,800. **Financial aid:** Priority filing date for institution's financial aid form: February 1. In 2003-2004, 67% of undergraduates applied for financial aid. Of those, 59% were determined to have financial need; 23% had their need fully met. Average financial aid package (proportion receiving): $19,217 (59%). Average amount of gift aid, such as scholarships or grants (proportion receiving): $13,011 (58%). Average amount of self-help aid, such as work study or loans (proportion receiving): $7,763 (51%). Average need-based loan (excluding PLUS or other private loans): $5,825. Among students who received need-based aid, the average percentage of need met: 83%. Among students who received aid based on merit, the average award (and the proportion receiving): $6,766 (26%). The average athletic scholarship (and the proportion receiving): $0 (0%). Average amount of debt of borrowers graduating in 2003: $23,782. Proportion who borrowed: 63%. **Student employment:** During the 2003-2004 academic year, 23% of undergraduates worked on campus. Average per-year earnings: $1,250. **Cooperative education programs:** agriculture, art, business, computer science, education, engineering, health professions, humanities, natural science, social/behavioral science. **Reserve Officers Training Corps (ROTC):** Army ROTC: Offered at cooperating institution (Seattle University @ Pacific Lutheran University).

University of Washington

Seattle, WA 98195
Public; www.washington.edu
Financial aid office: (206) 543-6101

■ **2004-2005 TUITION AND FEES:**
  In state: $5,380; Out of state: $18,010
■ **ROOM AND BOARD:** $8,214

SAT I Score (25th/75th percentile): 1070-1310
2005 U.S. News College Ranking:
National Universities, 46
Acceptance Rate: 71%

Other expenses: Estimated books and supplies: $900. Transportation: $396. Personal expenses: $2,253. **Financial aid:** Priority filing date for institution's financial aid form: February 28. In 2003-2004, 80% of undergraduates applied for financial aid. Of those, 56% were determined to have financial need; 43% had their need fully met. Average financial aid package (proportion receiving): $9,430 (48%). Average amount of gift aid, such as scholarships or grants (proportion receiving): $6,300 (36%). Average amount of self-help aid, such as work study or loans (proportion receiving): $4,800 (39%). Average need-based loan (excluding PLUS or other private loans): $4,600. Among students who received need-based aid, the average percentage of need met: 88%. Among students who received aid based on merit, the average award (and the proportion receiving): $3,260 (2%). The average athletic scholarship (and the proportion receiving): $14,100 (2%). Average amount of debt of borrowers graduating in 2003: $14,760. Proportion who borrowed: 50%. Average per-year earnings: $3,600. **Cooperative education programs:** business, engineering. **Reserve Officers Training Corps (ROTC):** Army ROTC: Offered on campus; Navy ROTC: Offered on campus; Air Force ROTC: Offered on campus.

Walla Walla College

204 S. College Avenue
College Place, WA 99324-1198
Private; www.wwc.edu
Financial aid office: (800) 656-2815

■ **2004-2005 TUITION AND FEES:** $17,829
■ **ROOM AND BOARD:** $4,725

ACT Score (25th/75th percentile): 20-26
2005 U.S. News College Ranking:
Universities–Master's (West), 32
Acceptance Rate: 55%

Other expenses: Estimated books and supplies: $825. Transportation: $1,500. Personal expenses: $2,160. **Financial aid:** In 2003-2004, 91% of undergraduates applied for financial aid. Of those, 74% were determined to have financial need; 24% had their need fully met. Average financial aid package (proportion receiving): $15,012 (74%). Average amount of gift aid, such as scholarships or grants (proportion receiving): $6,456 (56%). Average amount of self-help aid, such as work study or loans (proportion receiving): $6,849 (62%). Average need-based loan (excluding PLUS or other private loans): $4,953. Among students who received need-based aid, the average percentage of need met: 83%. Among students who received aid based on merit, the average award (and the proportion receiving): $4,173 (4%). Average amount of debt of borrowers graduating in 2003: $21,273. Proportion who borrowed: 75%. **Student employment:** During the 2003-2004 academic year, 71% of undergraduates worked on campus. Average per-year earnings: $3,000.

Washington State University

French Administration Building
Pullman, WA 99164
Public; www.wsu.edu
Financial aid office: (509) 335-9711

■ **2004-2005 TUITION AND FEES:**
  In state: $5,598; Out of state: $14,016
■ **ROOM AND BOARD:** $6,346

SAT I Score (25th/75th percentile): 950-1170
2005 U.S. News College Ranking:
National Universities, 120
Acceptance Rate: 78%

Other expenses: Estimated books and supplies: $912. Transportation: $1,316. Personal expenses: $2,104. **Financial aid:** Priority filing date for institution's financial aid form: March 1. In 2003-2004, 67% of undergraduates applied for financial aid. Of those, 53% were determined to have financial need; 26% had their need fully met. Average financial aid package (proportion receiving): $9,705 (52%). Average amount of gift aid, such as scholarships or grants (proportion receiving): $5,504 (35%). Average amount of self-help aid, such as work study or loans (proportion receiving): $5,249 (46%). Average need-based loan (excluding PLUS or other private loans): $4,640. Among students who received need-based aid, the average percentage of need met: 95%. Among students who received aid based on merit, the average award (and the proportion receiving): $3,245 (5%). The average athletic scholarship (and the proportion receiving): $11,504 (2%). Average amount of debt of borrowers graduating in 2003: $19,788. Proportion who borrowed: 52%. **Student employment:** During the 2003-2004 academic year, 39% of undergraduates worked on campus. Average per-year earnings: $2,500. **Cooperative education programs:** agriculture, art, business, computer science, education, engineering, health professions, home economics, humanities, natural science, social/behavioral science. **Reserve Officers Training Corps (ROTC):** Army ROTC: Offered on campus; Navy ROTC: Offered on campus; Air Force ROTC: Offered on campus.

Western Washington University

516 High Street
Bellingham, WA 98225
Public; www.wwu.edu
Financial aid office: (360) 650-3470

■ **2004-2005 TUITION AND FEES:**
In state: $4,446; Out of state: $13,833
■ **ROOM AND BOARD:** $6,273

SAT I Score (25th/75th percentile): 1020-1220
2005 U.S. News College Ranking:
Universities–Master's (West), 18
Acceptance Rate: 76%

Other expenses: Estimated books and supplies: $780. Transportation: $1,335. Personal expenses: $2,175. **Financial aid:** Priority filing date for institution's financial aid form: February 15. In 2003-2004, 60% of undergraduates applied for financial aid. Of those, 43% were determined to have financial need; 31% had their need fully met. Average financial aid package (proportion receiving): $8,258 (41%). Average amount of gift aid, such as scholarships or grants (proportion receiving): $5,027 (31%). Average amount of self-help aid, such as work study or loans (proportion receiving): $4,338 (35%). Average

need-based loan (excluding PLUS or other private loans): $4,052. Among students who received need-based aid, the average percentage of need met: 86%. Among students who received aid based on merit, the average award (and the proportion receiving): $3,359 (2%). The average athletic scholarship (and the proportion receiving): $5,472 (1%). Average amount of debt of borrowers graduating in 2003: $14,616. Proportion who borrowed: 55%. **Student employment:** During the 2003-2004 academic year, 10% of undergraduates worked on campus. Average per-year earnings: $1,783.

Whitman College

345 Boyer Avenue
Walla Walla, WA 99362-2083
Private; www.whitman.edu
Financial aid office: (509) 527-5178

■ **2004-2005 TUITION AND FEES:** $27,106
■ **ROOM AND BOARD:** $7,180

SAT I Score (25th/75th percentile): 1230-1430
2005 U.S. News College Ranking:
Liberal Arts Colleges, 35
Acceptance Rate: 51%

Other expenses: Estimated books and supplies: $1,350. **Financial aid:** Priority filing date for institution's financial aid form: January 5; deadline: February 11. In 2003-2004, 51% of undergraduates applied for financial aid. Of those, 42% were determined to have financial need; 55% had their need fully met. Average financial aid package (proportion receiving): $17,750 (42%). Average amount of gift aid, such as scholarships or grants (proportion receiving): $12,775 (42%). Average amount of self-help aid, such as work study or loans (proportion receiving): $5,160 (37%). Average need-based loan (excluding PLUS or other private loans): $3,625. Among students who received need-based aid, the average percentage of need met: 90%. Among students who received aid based on merit, the average award (and the proportion receiving): $7,450 (7%). The average athletic scholarship (and the proportion receiving): $0 (0%). Average amount of debt of borrowers graduating in 2003: $15,075. Proportion who borrowed: 52%. **Student employ-**

ment: During the 2003-2004 academic year, 40% of undergraduates worked on campus. Average per-year earnings: $1,372. **Cooperative education programs:** computer science, education, engineering, other.

Whitworth College

300 W. Hawthorne
Spokane, WA 99251
Private; www.whitworth.edu
Financial aid office: (800) 533-4668

■ **2004-2005 TUITION AND FEES:** $21,252
■ **ROOM AND BOARD:** $6,500

SAT I Score (25th/75th percentile): 1040-1270
2005 U.S. News College Ranking:
Universities–Master's (West), 5
Acceptance Rate: 75%

Other expenses: Estimated books and supplies: $744. Transportation: $1,440. Personal expenses: $2,237. **Financial aid:** Priority filing date for institution's financial aid form: March 1. In 2003-2004, 96% of undergraduates applied for financial aid. Of those, 73% were determined to have financial need; 19% had their need fully met. Average financial aid package (proportion receiving): $17,443 (73%). Average amount of gift aid, such as scholarships or grants (proportion receiving): $11,552 (70%). Average amount of self-help aid, such as work study or loans (proportion receiving): $5,671 (63%). Average need-based loan (excluding PLUS or other private loans): $4,559. Among students who received need-based aid, the average percentage of need met: 84%. Among students who received aid based on merit, the average award (and the proportion receiving): $6,947 (20%). The average athletic scholarship (and the proportion receiving): $0 (0%). Average amount of debt of borrowers graduating in 2003: $17,000. Proportion who borrowed: 69%. **Student employment:** During the 2003-2004 academic year, 51% of undergraduates worked on campus. Average per-year earnings: $3,000. **Cooperative education programs:** business. **Reserve Officers Training Corps (ROTC):** Army ROTC: Offered at cooperating institution (Gonzaga University).

West Virginia

Alderson-Broaddus College

College Hill
Philippi, WV 26416
Private; www.ab.edu
Financial aid office: (304) 457-6354

- **2004-2005 TUITION AND FEES:** $17,116
- **ROOM AND BOARD:** $5,534

ACT Score (25th/75th percentile): 18-23
2005 U.S. News College Ranking:
Comp. Colleges–Bachelor's (South), 28
Acceptance Rate: 64%

Other expenses: Estimated books and supplies: $800. Transportation: $820. Personal expenses: $1,500. **Financial aid:** Priority filing date for institution's financial aid form: March 1. In 2003-2004, 99% of undergraduates applied for financial aid. Of those, 96% were determined to have financial need; 44% had their need fully met. Average financial aid package (proportion receiving): $18,231 (96%). Average amount of gift aid, such as scholarships or grants (proportion receiving): $10,663 (96%). Average amount of self-help aid, such as work study or loans (proportion receiving): $6,106 (83%). Average need-based loan (excluding PLUS or other private loans): $5,406. Among students who received need-based aid, the average percentage of need met: 88%. Among students who received aid based on merit, the average award (and the proportion receiving): $7,265 (2%). The average athletic scholarship (and the proportion receiving): $7,563 (14%). Average amount of debt of borrowers graduating in 2003: $21,334. Proportion who borrowed: 80%.

Bethany College

Bethany, WV 26032
Private; www.bethanywv.edu
Financial aid office: (304) 829-7141

- **2004-2005 TUITION AND FEES:** $14,022
- **ROOM AND BOARD:** $6,668

SAT I Score (25th/75th percentile): 910-1150
2005 U.S. News College Ranking:
Liberal Arts Colleges, fourth tier
Acceptance Rate: 69%

Other expenses: Estimated books and supplies: $600. Transportation: $700. Personal expenses: $1,000. **Financial aid:** Priority filing date for institution's financial aid form: March 1; deadline: May 1. In 2003-2004, 95% of undergraduates applied for financial aid. Of those, 89% were determined to have financial need; 28% had their need fully met. Average financial aid package (proportion receiving): $16,500 (89%). Average amount of gift aid, such as scholarships or grants (proportion receiving): N/A (80%). Average amount of self-help aid, such as work study or loans (proportion receiving): $4,800 (89%). Average need-based loan (excluding PLUS or other private loans): $4,100. Among students who received need-based aid, the average percentage of need met: 88%. Among students who received aid based on merit, the average award (and the proportion receiving): N/A (8%). Average amount of debt of borrowers graduating in 2003: $18,000. Proportion who borrowed: 90%. **Student employment:** During the 2003-2004 academic year, 85% of undergraduates worked on campus. Average per-year earnings: $1,000.

Bluefield State College

219 Rock Street
Bluefield, WV 24701
Public; www.bluefieldstate.edu
Financial aid office: (304) 327-4020

- **2004-2005 TUITION AND FEES:**
  In state: $3,114; Out of state: $6,894

ACT Score (25th/75th percentile): 18
2005 U.S. News College Ranking:
Comp. Colleges–Bachelor's (South), fourth tier
Acceptance Rate: 97%

Financial aid: Priority filing date for institution's financial aid form: March 1. In 2003-2004, 67% of undergraduates applied for financial aid. Of those, 38% were determined to have financial need; 18% had their need fully met. Average financial aid package (proportion receiving): $5,000 (38%). Average amount of gift aid, such as scholarships or grants (proportion receiving): $3,000 (38%). Average amount of self-help aid, such as work study or loans (proportion receiving): $4,300 (29%). Average need-based loan (excluding PLUS or other private loans): $3,000. Among students who received need-based aid, the average percentage of need met: 70%. Among students who received aid based on merit, the average award (and the proportion receiving): $1,400 (13%). The average athletic scholarship (and the proportion receiving): $1,900 (5%). **Student employment:** During the 2003-2004 academic year, 2% of undergraduates worked on campus. Average per-year earnings: $3,000.

Concord College

PO Box 1000
Athens, WV 24712
Public; www.concord.edu
Financial aid office: (304) 384-6069

- **2004-2005 TUITION AND FEES:**
  In state: $3,548; Out of state: $7,968
- **ROOM AND BOARD:** $5,600

ACT Score (25th/75th percentile): 18-23
2005 U.S. News College Ranking:
Comp. Colleges–Bachelor's (South), 48
Acceptance Rate: 99%

Other expenses: Estimated books and supplies: $1,000. Transportation: $601. Personal expenses: $561. **Financial aid:** Priority filing date for institution's financial aid form: April 15. **Student employment:** During the 2003-2004 academic year, 21% of undergraduates worked on campus. Average per-year earnings: $1,248.

Davis and Elkins College

100 Campus Drive
Elkins, WV 26241
Private; www.davisandelkins.edu
Financial aid office: (304) 637-1373

- **2004-2005 TUITION AND FEES:** $15,665
- **ROOM AND BOARD:** $5,985

ACT Score (25th/75th percentile): 17-22
2005 U.S. News College Ranking:
Comp. Colleges–Bachelor's (South), 27
Acceptance Rate: 65%

Other expenses: Estimated books and supplies: $700. Transportation: $0. Personal expenses: $150. **Financial aid:** In 2003-2004, 84% of undergraduates applied for financial aid. Of those, 77% were determined to have financial need; 58% had their need fully met. Average financial aid package (proportion receiving): $15,769 (77%). Average amount of gift aid, such as scholarships or grants (proportion receiving): $2,999 (62%). Average amount of self-help aid, such as work study or loans (proportion receiving): $3,684 (64%). Average need-based loan (excluding PLUS or other private loans): $3,692. Among students who received need-based aid, the average percentage of need met: 89%. Among students who received aid based on merit, the average award (and the proportion receiving): $13,136 (7%). The average athletic scholarship (and the proportion receiving): $13,136 (7%). Average amount of debt of borrowers graduating in 2003: $8,902. Proportion who borrowed: 95%. **Student employment:** During the 2003-2004 academic year, 6% of undergraduates worked on campus. Average per-year earnings: $1,000. **Cooperative education programs:** other.

Fairmont State University

1201 Locust Avenue
Fairmont, WV 26554
Public; www.fscwv.edu
Financial aid office: (304) 367-4213

■ **2004-2005 TUITION AND FEES:**
  In state: $3,514; Out of state: $6,944
■ **ROOM AND BOARD:** $5,904

ACT Score (25th/75th percentile): 17-22
2005 U.S. News College Ranking:
Comp. Colleges–Bachelor's (South), third tier
Acceptance Rate: 75%

Other expenses: Estimated books and supplies: $1,200. Transportation: $1,900. Personal expenses: $1,200. **Financial aid:** Priority filing date for institution's financial aid form: March 1; deadline: March 1. In 2003-2004, 84% of undergraduates applied for financial aid. Of those, 70% were determined to have financial need; 13% had their need fully met. Average financial aid package (proportion receiving): $5,121 (70%). Average amount of gift aid, such as scholarships or grants (proportion receiving): $3,672 (60%). Average amount of self-help aid, such as work study or loans (proportion receiving): N/A (50%). Among students who received need-based aid, the average percentage of need met: 70%. Average amount of debt of borrowers graduating in 2003: $10,930. Proportion who borrowed: 87%. **Student employment:** During the 2003-2004 academic year, 0% of undergraduates worked on campus. Average per-year earnings: $2,500. **Cooperative**

education programs: education, health professions. **Reserve Officers Training Corps (ROTC):** Army ROTC: Offered at cooperating institution (West Virginia University).

Glenville State College

200 High Street
Glenville, WV 26351
Public; www.glenville.edu
Financial aid office: (304) 462-4103

■ **2004-2005 TUITION AND FEES:**
  In state: $3,276; Out of state: $7,854
■ **ROOM AND BOARD:** $5,060

ACT Score (25th/75th percentile): 17-21
2005 U.S. News College Ranking:
Comp. Colleges–Bachelor's (South), fourth tier
Acceptance Rate: 100%

Other expenses: Estimated books and supplies: $800. Transportation: $1,800. Personal expenses: $1,424. **Financial aid:** Priority filing date for institution's financial aid form: February 1. In 2003-2004, 87% of undergraduates applied for financial aid. Of those, 77% were determined to have financial need; 27% had their need fully met. Average financial aid package (proportion receiving): $7,554 (76%). Average amount of gift aid, such as scholarships or grants (proportion receiving): $4,026 (60%). Average amount of self-help aid, such as work study or loans (proportion receiving): $3,534 (56%). Average need-based loan (excluding PLUS or other private loans): $3,493. Among students who received need-based aid, the average percentage of need met: 81%. Among students who received aid based on merit, the average award (and the proportion receiving): $2,845 (8%). The average athletic scholarship (and the proportion receiving): $3,084 (3%). Average amount of debt of borrowers graduating in 2003: $14,835. Proportion who borrowed: 71%. **Student employment:** During the 2003-2004 academic year, 20% of undergraduates worked on campus. Average per-year earnings: $825. **Cooperative education programs:** health professions.

Marshall University

1 John Marshall Drive
Huntington, WV 25755
Public; www.marshall.edu
Financial aid office: (304) 696-3162

■ **2004-2005 TUITION AND FEES:**
  In state: $3,774; Out of state: $9,458
■ **ROOM AND BOARD:** $5,856

ACT Score (25th/75th percentile): 19-24
2005 U.S. News College Ranking:
Universities–Master's (South), 43
Acceptance Rate: 88%

Financial aid: Priority filing date for institution's financial aid form: March 1. In 2003-2004, 64% of undergraduates applied for financial aid. Of those, 49% were determined to have financial need; 39% had their need fully met. Average financial aid package (proportion receiving): $6,376 (48%). Average amount of gift aid, such as scholarships or grants (proportion receiving): $3,867 (33%). Average amount of self-help aid, such as work study or loans (proportion receiving): $4,525 (36%). Average need-based loan (excluding PLUS or other private loans): $4,454. Among students who received need-based aid, the average percentage of need met: 67%. Among students who received aid based on merit, the average award (and the proportion receiving): $3,611 (14%). The average athletic scholarship (and the proportion receiving): $8,369 (4%). Average amount of debt of borrowers graduating in 2003: $15,484. Proportion who borrowed: 53%. **Cooperative education programs:** education, other. **Reserve Officers Training Corps (ROTC):** Army ROTC: Offered on campus.

Mountain State University

PO Box 9003
Beckley, WV 25802
Private; www.mountainstate.edu
Financial aid office: (304) 253-7351

■ **2004-2005 TUITION AND FEES:** $6,750
■ **ROOM AND BOARD:** $5,440

ACT Score (25th/75th percentile): 16-20
2005 U.S. News College Ranking:
Comp. Colleges–Bachelor's (South), fourth tier
Acceptance Rate: 96%

Other expenses: Estimated books and supplies: $1,740. Transportation: $1,449. Personal expenses: $1,755. **Financial aid:** Priority filing date for institution's financial aid form: March 1. In 2003-2004, 90% of undergraduates applied for financial aid. Of those, 85% were determined to have financial need; Average financial aid package (proportion receiving): $5,853 (85%). Average amount of gift aid, such as scholarships or grants (proportion receiving): $3,877 (59%). Average amount of self-help aid, such as work study or loans (proportion receiving): $3,384 (69%). Average need-based loan (excluding PLUS or other private loans): $3,318.

Among students who received aid based on merit, the average award (and the proportion receiving): $2,742 (2%). The average athletic scholarship (and the proportion receiving): $7,432 (1%). Average amount of debt of borrowers graduating in 2003: $21,168. Proportion who borrowed: 61%. **Student employment:** During the 2003-2004 academic year, 12% of undergraduates worked on campus. Average per-year earnings: $1,751. **Cooperative education programs:** business, computer science, engineering, health professions, natural science, social/behavioral science, technologies.

Ohio Valley College

1 Campus View Drive
Vienna, WV 26105-8000
Private; www.ovc.edu
Financial aid office: (304) 865-6075

■ **2004-2005 TUITION AND FEES:** $12,012
■ **ROOM AND BOARD:** $5,380

ACT Score (25th/75th percentile): 17-22
2005 U.S. News College Ranking:
Comp. Colleges–Bachelor's (South), third tier
Acceptance Rate: 90%

Other expenses: Estimated books and supplies: $1,000. Transportation: $750. Personal expenses: $1,000. **Financial aid:** Priority filing date for institution's financial aid form: March 1. In 2003-2004, 80% of undergraduates applied for financial aid. Of those, 72% were determined to have financial need; 31% had their need fully met. Average financial aid package (proportion receiving): $9,223 (70%). Average amount of gift aid, such as scholarships or grants (proportion receiving): $3,616 (41%). Average amount of self-help aid, such as work study or loans (proportion receiving): $3,953 (64%). Average need-based loan (excluding PLUS or other private loans): $3,644. Among students who received need-based aid, the average percentage of need met: 89%. Among students who received aid based on merit, the average award (and the proportion receiving): $2,895 (15%). Average amount of debt of borrowers graduating in 2003: $16,717. Proportion who borrowed: 81%.

Salem International University

223 W. Main Street
Salem, WV 26426
Private; www.salemiu.edu
Financial aid office: (304) 782-5303

■ **2004-2005 TUITION AND FEES:** $9,500
■ **ROOM AND BOARD:** $4,540

ACT Score (25th/75th percentile): 18-23
2005 U.S. News College Ranking:
Universities–Master's (South), third tier
Acceptance Rate: 49%

Financial aid: Priority filing date for institution's financial aid form: April 15. **Student employment:** During the 2003-2004 academic year, 3% of undergraduates worked on campus. Average per-year earnings: $3,090.

Shepherd University

PO Box 3210
Shepherdstown, WV 25443-3210
Public; www.shepherd.edu
Financial aid office: (304) 876-5470

■ **2004-2005 TUITION AND FEES:**
  In state: $3,654; Out of state: $9,234
■ **ROOM AND BOARD:** $5,574

ACT Score (25th/75th percentile): 18-23
2005 U.S. News College Ranking:
Comp. Colleges–Bachelor's (South), 45
Acceptance Rate: 89%

Financial aid: Priority filing date for institution's financial aid form: March 1. In 2003-2004, 80% of undergraduates applied for financial aid. Of those, 51% were determined to have financial need; 23% had their need fully met. Average financial aid package (proportion receiving): $7,442 (48%). Average amount of gift aid, such as scholarships or grants (proportion receiving): $3,411 (27%). Average amount of self-help aid, such as work study or loans (proportion receiving): $3,563 (37%). Average need-based loan (excluding PLUS or other private loans): $3,424. Among students who received need-based aid, the average percentage of need met: 76%. Among students who received aid based on merit, the average award (and the proportion receiving): $3,119 (13%). The average athletic scholarship (and the proportion receiving): $3,681 (4%). Average amount of debt of borrowers graduating in 2003: $13,981. Proportion who borrowed: 67%. **Student employment:** During the

2003-2004 academic year, 10% of undergraduates worked on campus. Average per-year earnings: $2,346. **Cooperative education programs:** business, computer science, education, home economics, humanities, natural science, social/behavioral science. **Reserve Officers Training Corps (ROTC):** Air Force ROTC: Offered at cooperating institution (University of Maryland, College Park).

University of Charleston

2300 MacCorkle Avenue SE
Charleston, WV 25304
Private; www.ucwv.edu
Financial aid office: (304) 357-4760

■ **2004-2005 TUITION AND FEES:** $19,800
■ **ROOM AND BOARD:** $7,200

ACT Score (25th/75th percentile): 19-23
2005 U.S. News College Ranking:
Comp. Colleges–Bachelor's (South), 22
Acceptance Rate: 63%

Financial aid: Priority filing date for institution's financial aid form: March 1; deadline: August 15. **Student employment:** During the 2003-2004 academic year, 19% of undergraduates worked on campus. Average per-year earnings: $500. **Reserve Officers Training Corps (ROTC):** Army ROTC: Offered at cooperating institution (West Virginia State College).

West Liberty State College

Route 88, PO Box 295
West Liberty, WV 26074-0295
Public; www.wlsc.edu
Financial aid office: (304) 336-8016

■ **2004-2005 TUITION AND FEES:**
  In state: $3,340; Out of state: $8,314
■ **ROOM AND BOARD:** $5,006

ACT Score (25th/75th percentile): 17-21
2005 U.S. News College Ranking:
Comp. Colleges–Bachelor's (South), third tier
Acceptance Rate: 86%

Other expenses: Estimated books and supplies: $1,000. **Financial aid:** Priority filing date for institution's financial aid form: March 1. In 2003-2004, 81% of undergraduates applied for financial aid. Of those, 60% were determined to have financial need; 36% had their need fully met. Average financial aid package (proportion receiving): $5,025 (57%). Average amount of gift aid, such as scholarships or grants (proportion receiving): $3,649 (41%). Average amount of self-help aid, such as work study or loans (proportion receiving): $4,051 (52%). Average need-based loan (excluding PLUS or other private loans): $3,940. Among students who received need-based aid, the average percentage of need met: 77%. Among students who received aid based on merit, the average award (and the proportion receiving): $2,464 (11%). The average athletic scholarship (and the proportion receiving): $2,486 (7%). Average amount of debt of borrowers graduating in 2003: $13,800. Proportion who borrowed: 62%.

West Virginia State University

PO Box 1000
Institute, WV 25112
Public; www.wvsc.edu
Financial aid office: (304) 766-3131

■ 2004-2005 TUITION AND FEES:
In state: $3,232; Out of state: $7,410
■ ROOM AND BOARD: $4,800

2005 U.S. News College Ranking:
Comp. Colleges–Bachelor's (South), fourth tier

Other expenses: Estimated books and supplies: $918.

West Virginia University

PO Box 6201, President's Office
Morgantown, WV 26506-6201
Public; www.wvu.edu
Financial aid office: (800) 344-9881

■ 2004-2005 TUITION AND FEES:
In state: $3,938; Out of state: $12,060
■ ROOM AND BOARD: $6,084

ACT Score (25th/75th percentile): 20-25
2005 U.S. News College Ranking:
National Universities, third tier
Acceptance Rate: 92%

Other expenses: Estimated books and supplies: $800. Transportation: $1,090. Personal expenses: $1,274. Financial aid: Priority filing date for institution's financial aid form: February 15; deadline: March 1. In 2003-2004, 71% of undergraduates applied for financial aid. Of those, 50% were determined to have financial need; 25% had their need fully met. Average financial aid package (proportion receiving): $8,015 (47%). Average amount of gift aid, such

as scholarships or grants (proportion receiving): $3,327 (34%). Average amount of self-help aid, such as work study or loans (proportion receiving): $4,243 (39%). Average need-based loan (excluding PLUS or other private loans): $4,106. Among students who received need-based aid, the average percentage of need met: 88%. Among students who received aid based on merit, the average award (and the proportion receiving): $3,324 (36%). The average athletic scholarship (and the proportion receiving): $9,910 (2%). Average amount of debt of borrowers graduating in 2003: $20,145. Proportion who borrowed: 67%. Student employment: During the 2003-2004 academic year, 12% of undergraduates worked on campus. Cooperative education programs: engineering. Reserve Officers Training Corps (ROTC): Army ROTC: Offered on campus; Air Force ROTC: Offered on campus.

West Virginia University Institute of Technology

405 Fayette Pike
Montgomery, WV 25136
Public; www.wvutech.edu
Financial aid office: (304) 442-3228

■ 2004-2005 TUITION AND FEES:
In state: $6,637; Out of state: $9,486
■ ROOM AND BOARD: $4,730

ACT Score (25th/75th percentile): 17-22
2005 U.S. News College Ranking:
Comp. Colleges–Bachelor's (South), third tier
Acceptance Rate: 74%

Financial aid: Priority filing date for institution's financial aid form: February 1; deadline: April 1. In 2003-2004, 81% of undergraduates applied for financial aid. Of those, 57% were determined to have financial need; 13% had their need fully met. Average financial aid package (proportion receiving): $6,544 (56%). Average amount of gift aid, such as scholarships or grants (proportion receiving): $3,893 (45%). Average amount of self-help aid, such as work study or loans (proportion receiving): $3,353 (39%). Average need-based loan (excluding PLUS or other private loans): $3,234. Among students who received aid based on merit, the average award (and the proportion receiving): $775 (10%). The average athletic scholarship (and the proportion receiving): $2,911 (6%). Average amount of debt of borrowers graduating in 2003: $14,269. Proportion who borrowed: 48%. Student employment: During the 2003-2004 academic

year, 23% of undergraduates worked on campus. Average per-year earnings: $6. Reserve Officers Training Corps (ROTC): Army ROTC: Offered on campus.

West Virginia University– Parkersburg

300 Campus Drive
Parkersburg, WV 26101-9577
Public; www.wvup.edu
Financial aid office: (304) 424-8210

■ 2004-2005 TUITION AND FEES:
In state: $2,232; Out of state: $5,904

ACT Score (25th/75th percentile): 16-22
2005 U.S. News College Ranking:
Comp. Colleges–Bachelor's (South), fourth tier
Acceptance Rate: 100%

Financial aid: Priority filing date for institution's financial aid form: July 3. Cooperative education programs: business, computer science, engineering, health professions, natural science, social/behavioral science, technologies.

West Virginia Wesleyan College

59 College Avenue
Buckhannon, WV 26201
Private; www.wvwc.edu
Financial aid office: (304) 473-8080

■ 2004-2005 TUITION AND FEES: $20,450
■ ROOM AND BOARD: $5,200

SAT I Score (25th/75th percentile): 930-1140
2005 U.S. News College Ranking:
Liberal Arts Colleges, fourth tier
Acceptance Rate: 79%

Other expenses: Estimated books and supplies: $600. Transportation: $750. Personal expenses: $1,500. Financial aid: Priority filing date for institution's financial aid form: February 15. In 2003-2004, 83% of undergraduates applied for financial aid. Of those, 75% were determined to have financial need; 44% had their need fully met. Average financial aid package (proportion receiving): $18,927 (75%). Average amount of gift aid, such as scholarships or grants (proportion receiving): $15,165 (74%). Average amount of self-help aid, such as work study or loans (proportion receiving): $3,842 (73%). Average need-based loan (excluding PLUS or other private loans): $2,959. Among students who received need-based aid, the average percentage of need met: 91%. Among students who received aid based on merit, the average award (and the proportion receiving): $9,631 (21%). The average athletic scholarship (and the proportion receiving): $7,061 (9%). **Student employment:** During the 2003-2004 academic year, 70% of undergraduates worked on campus. Average per-year earnings: $1,000.

Wheeling Jesuit University

316 Washington Avenue
Wheeling, WV 26003
Private; www.wju.edu
Financial aid office: (304) 243-2304

■ **2004-2005 TUITION AND FEES:** $20,310
■ **ROOM AND BOARD:** $6,300

ACT Score (25th/75th percentile): 19-25
2005 U.S. News College Ranking:
Universities–Master's (South), 15
Acceptance Rate: 77%

Other expenses: Estimated books and supplies: $600. Transportation: $500. Personal expenses: $600. **Financial aid:** Priority filing date for institution's financial aid form: March 1. In 2003-2004, 91% of undergraduates applied for financial aid. Of those, 79% were determined to have financial need; 42% had their need fully met. Average financial aid package (proportion receiving): $16,062 (79%). Average amount of gift aid, such as scholarships or grants (proportion receiving): $4,852 (57%). Average amount of self-help aid, such as work study or loans (proportion receiving): $5,076 (67%). Average need-based loan (excluding PLUS or other private loans): $4,361. Among students who received need-based aid, the average percentage of need met: 91%. Among students who received aid based on merit, the average award (and the proportion receiving): $5,252 (21%). The average athletic scholarship (and the proportion receiving): $5,313 (13%). Average amount of debt of borrowers graduating in 2003: $11,440. Proportion who borrowed: 70%. **Student employment:** During the 2003-2004 academic year, 22% of undergraduates worked on campus. Average per-year earnings: $1,550.

Wisconsin

Alverno College

3400 S. 43rd Street, PO Box 343922
Milwaukee, WI 53234-3922
Private; www.alverno.edu
Financial aid office: (414) 382-6046

■ **2004-2005 TUITION AND FEES:** $14,410
■ **ROOM AND BOARD:** $5,400

ACT Score (25th/75th percentile): 17-21
2005 U.S. News College Ranking:
Comp. Colleges–Bachelor's (Midwest), 31
Acceptance Rate: 56%

Other expenses: Estimated books and supplies:
$700. Transportation: $500. Personal expenses:
$1,700. **Financial aid:** Priority filing date for
institution's financial aid form: April 15.
Average amount of debt of borrowers graduating in 2003: $30,000. Proportion who bor-
rowed: 97%. **Student employment:** During the
2003-2004 academic year, 0% of undergraduates worked on campus. Average per-year earnings: $0. **Reserve Officers Training Corps
(ROTC):** Army ROTC: Offered at cooperating
institution (Marquette University); Air Force
ROTC: Offered at cooperating institution
(Marquette University).

Beloit College

700 College Avenue
Beloit, WI 53511
Private; www.beloit.edu
Financial aid office: (608) 363-2663

■ **2004-2005 TUITION AND FEES:** $25,736
■ **ROOM AND BOARD:** $5,696

ACT Score (25th/75th percentile): 25-30
2005 U.S. News College Ranking:
Liberal Arts Colleges, 53
Acceptance Rate: 69%

Other expenses: Estimated books and supplies:
$500. Transportation: $300. Personal expenses:
$950. **Financial aid:** Priority filing date for insti-
tution's financial aid form: February 1; deadline:
March 1. In 2003-2004, 80% of undergraduates
applied for financial aid. Of those, 73% were
determined to have financial need; 100% had
their need fully met. Average financial aid package (proportion receiving): $18,635 (73%).

Average amount of gift aid, such as scholarships
or grants (proportion receiving): $14,026 (73%).
Average amount of self-help aid, such as work
study or loans (proportion receiving): $4,609
(73%). Average need-based loan (excluding PLUS
or other private loans): $3,344. Among students
who received need-based aid, the average percentage of need met: 100%. Among students
who received aid based on merit, the average
award (and the proportion receiving): $8,372
(15%). Average amount of debt of borrowers
graduating in 2003: $18,783. Proportion who
borrowed: 59%. **Student employment:** During
the 2003-2004 academic year, 49% of undergraduates worked on campus. Average per-year
earnings: $1,500. **Cooperative education pro-
grams:** engineering, health professions, other.

Cardinal Stritch University

6801 N. Yates Road
Milwaukee, WI 53217
Private; www.stritch.edu
Financial aid office: (414) 410-4048

■ **2004-2005 TUITION AND FEES:** $15,510
■ **ROOM AND BOARD:** $5,380

2005 U.S. News College Ranking:
Universities–Master's (Midwest), fourth tier
Acceptance Rate: 50%

Carroll College

100 N. East Avenue
Waukesha, WI 53186
Private; www.cc.edu
Financial aid office: (262) 524-7296

■ **2004-2005 TUITION AND FEES:** $18,170
■ **ROOM AND BOARD:** $5,600

ACT Score (25th/75th percentile): 21-24
2005 U.S. News College Ranking:
Comp. Colleges–Bachelor's (Midwest), 25
Acceptance Rate: 78%

Other expenses: Estimated books and supplies:
$814. Transportation: $995. Personal expenses:
$1,243. **Financial aid:** In 2003-2004, 99% of
undergraduates applied for financial aid. Of
those, 82% were determined to have financial

need; 80% had their need fully met. Average
financial aid package (proportion receiving):
$14,718 (82%). Average amount of gift aid,
such as scholarships or grants (proportion
receiving): $10,220 (82%). Average amount of
self-help aid, such as work study or loans (proportion receiving): $5,055 (70%). Average need-
based loan (excluding PLUS or other private
loans): $3,980. Among students who received
need-based aid, the average percentage of need
met: 100%. Among students who received aid
based on merit, the average award (and the proportion receiving): $7,084 (18%). The average
athletic scholarship (and the proportion receiving): $0 (0%). Average amount of debt of bor-
rowers graduating in 2003: $15,195. Proportion
who borrowed: 57%. **Student employment:**
During the 2003-2004 academic year, 64% of
undergraduates worked on campus. Average
per-year earnings: $1,500. **Reserve Officers
Training Corps (ROTC):** Army ROTC: Offered at
cooperating institution (Marquette University);
Air Force ROTC: Offered at cooperating institution (Marquette University).

Carthage College

2001 Alford Park Drive
Kenosha, WI 53140
Private; www.carthage.edu
Financial aid office: (262) 551-6001

■ **2004-2005 TUITION AND FEES:** $21,250
■ **ROOM AND BOARD:** $6,250

ACT Score (25th/75th percentile): 19-27
2005 U.S. News College Ranking:
Universities–Master's (Midwest), 31
Acceptance Rate: 73%

Other expenses: Estimated books and supplies:
$750. Transportation: $1,000. Personal expenses: $1,500. **Financial aid:** Priority filing date for
institution's financial aid form: February 15. In
2003-2004, 87% of undergraduates applied for
financial aid. Of those, 76% were determined
to have financial need; 5% had their need fully
met. Average financial aid package (proportion
receiving): $8,222 (75%). Average amount of
gift aid, such as scholarships or grants (proportion receiving): $4,262 (75%). Average amount
of self-help aid, such as work study or loans
(proportion receiving): $4,190 (61%). Average
need-based loan (excluding PLUS or other pri-

vate loans): $4,043. Among students who received need-based aid, the average percentage of need met: 39%. Among students who received aid based on merit, the average award (and the proportion receiving): $7,185 (11%). The average athletic scholarship (and the proportion receiving): $0 (0%). Average amount of debt of borrowers graduating in 2003: $17,100. Proportion who borrowed: 78%. **Student employment:** During the 2003-2004 academic year, 20% of undergraduates worked on campus. Average per-year earnings: $1,200. **Reserve Officers Training Corps (ROTC):** Army ROTC: Offered at cooperating institution (Marquette University); Air Force ROTC: Offered at cooperating institution (Marquette University).

Concordia University Wisconsin

12800 N. Lake Shore Drive
Mequon, WI 53097
Private; www.cuw.edu
Financial aid office: (262) 243-4569

■ **2004-2005 TUITION AND FEES:** $16,460
■ **ROOM AND BOARD:** $6,230

ACT Score (25th/75th percentile): 19-25
2005 U.S. News College Ranking:
Universities–Master's (Midwest), 63
Acceptance Rate: 80%

Other expenses: Estimated books and supplies: $1,000. Transportation: $210. Personal expenses: $1,400. **Financial aid:** Priority filing date for institution's financial aid form: May 1; deadline: May 1. In 2003-2004, 98% of undergraduates applied for financial aid. Of those, 98% were determined to have financial need; 30% had their need fully met. Average financial aid package (proportion receiving): $14,124 (98%). Average amount of gift aid, such as scholarships or grants (proportion receiving): $11,000 (89%). Average amount of self-help aid, such as work study or loans (proportion receiving): $3,800 (54%). Average need-based loan (excluding PLUS or other private loans): $3,500. Among students who received need-based aid, the average percentage of need met: 80%. Among students who received aid based on merit, the average award (and the proportion receiving): $5,200 (10%). The average athletic scholarship (and the proportion receiving): $0 (0%). Average amount of debt of borrowers graduating in 2003: $17,600. Proportion who borrowed: 60%. **Student employment:** During the 2003-2004 academic year, 38% of undergraduates worked on campus. Average per-year

earnings: $2,500. **Cooperative education programs:** other.

Edgewood College

1000 Edgewood College Drive
Madison, WI 53711-1997
Private; www.edgewood.edu
Financial aid office: (608) 663-2305

■ **2004-2005 TUITION AND FEES:** $16,050

ACT Score (25th/75th percentile): 19-24
2005 U.S. News College Ranking:
Universities–Master's (Midwest), third tier
Acceptance Rate: 80%

Other expenses: Estimated books and supplies: $750. Transportation: $577. Personal expenses: $1,875. **Financial aid:** Priority filing date for institution's financial aid form: March 15. In 2003-2004, 75% of undergraduates applied for financial aid. Of those, 65% were determined to have financial need; 14% had their need fully met. Average financial aid package (proportion receiving): $10,888 (65%). Average amount of gift aid, such as scholarships or grants (proportion receiving): $6,533 (59%). Average amount of self-help aid, such as work study or loans (proportion receiving): $5,264 (61%). Average need-based loan (excluding PLUS or other private loans): $4,067. Among students who received need-based aid, the average percentage of need met: 75%. Among students who received aid based on merit, the average award (and the proportion receiving): $8,015 (17%). The average athletic scholarship (and the proportion receiving): $0 (0%). Average amount of debt of borrowers graduating in 2003: $19,551. Proportion who borrowed: 65%. Average per-year earnings: $1,800.

Lakeland College

PO Box 359
Sheboygan, WI 53082
Private; www.lakeland.edu
Financial aid office: (920) 565-1214

■ **2004-2005 TUITION AND FEES:** $14,900
■ **ROOM AND BOARD:** $5,655

ACT Score (25th/75th percentile): 17-22
2005 U.S. News College Ranking:
Comp. Colleges–Bachelor's (Midwest), third tier
Acceptance Rate: 68%

Other expenses: Estimated books and supplies: $600. Transportation: $700. Personal expenses: $873. **Financial aid:** Priority filing date for institution's financial aid form: May 1. In 2003-2004, 83% of undergraduates applied for financial aid. Of those, 73% were determined to have financial need; 30% had their need fully met. Average financial aid package (proportion receiving): $9,563 (73%). Average amount of gift aid, such as scholarships or grants (proportion receiving): $7,025 (67%). Average amount of self-help aid, such as work study or loans (proportion receiving): $3,642 (63%). Average need-based loan (excluding PLUS or other private loans): $3,438. Among students who received need-based aid, the average percentage of need met: 82%. Among students who received aid based on merit, the average award (and the proportion receiving): $6,342 (24%). The average athletic scholarship (and the proportion receiving): $0 (0%). Average amount of debt of borrowers graduating in 2003: $16,561. Proportion who borrowed: 85%. **Student employment:** During the 2003-2004 academic year, 25% of undergraduates worked on campus. Average per-year earnings: $4,600.

Lawrence University

PO Box 599
Appleton, WI 54912
Private; www.lawrence.edu
Financial aid office: (920) 832-6583

■ **2004-2005 TUITION AND FEES:** $23,343
■ **ROOM AND BOARD:** $5,559

ACT Score (25th/75th percentile): 25-30
2005 U.S. News College Ranking:
Liberal Arts Colleges, 53
Acceptance Rate: 58%

Other expenses: Estimated books and supplies: $600. Transportation: $200. Personal expenses: $1,005. **Financial aid:** Priority filing date for institution's financial aid form: March 15. In 2003-2004, 70% of undergraduates applied for financial aid. Of those, 60% were determined to have financial need; 100% had their need fully met. Average financial aid package (proportion receiving): $21,596 (60%). Average amount of gift aid, such as scholarships or grants (proportion receiving): $15,380 (60%). Average amount of self-help aid, such as work study or loans (proportion receiving): $6,500 (57%). Average need-based loan (excluding PLUS or other private loans): $4,888. Among students who received need-based aid, the average percentage of need met: 100%. Among students who received aid based on merit, the average award (and the proportion receiving): $9,662 (31%). The average athletic scholarship (and the proportion receiving): $0 (0%). **Student employment:** During the 2003-2004 academic year, 52% of undergraduates worked on campus. Average per-year earnings: $2,000. **Cooperative education programs:** engineering, health professions, other.

Marian College of Fond du Lac

45 S. National Avenue
Fond du Lac, WI 54935
Private; www.mariancollege.edu
Financial aid office: (920) 923-7614

- **2004-2005 TUITION AND FEES:** $15,800
- **ROOM AND BOARD:** $4,740

ACT Score (25th/75th percentile): 18-22
2005 U.S. News College Ranking: Universities–Master's (Midwest), fourth tier
Acceptance Rate: 77%

Financial aid: Priority filing date for institution's financial aid form: March 1. In 2003-2004, 92% of undergraduates applied for financial aid. Of those, 79% were determined to have financial need; 36% had their need fully met. Average financial aid package (proportion receiving): $13,560 (79%). Average amount of gift aid, such as scholarships or grants (proportion receiving): $5,220 (68%). Average amount of self-help aid, such as work study or loans (proportion receiving): $5,128 (71%). Average need-based loan (excluding PLUS or other private loans): $4,115. Among students who received need-based aid, the average percentage of need met: 91%. Among students who received aid based on merit, the average award (and the proportion receiving): $4,299 (12%). The average athletic scholarship (and the proportion receiving): $0 (0%). Average amount of debt of borrowers graduating in 2003: $20,000. **Student employment:** During the 2003-2004 academic year, 21% of undergraduates worked on campus. Average per-year earnings: $1,300. **Cooperative education programs:** business, computer science, social/behavioral science, other. **Reserve Officers Training Corps (ROTC):** Army ROTC: Offered on campus.

Marquette University

PO Box 1881
Milwaukee, WI 53201-1881
Private; www.marquette.edu
Financial aid office: (414) 288-0200

- **2004-2005 TUITION AND FEES:** $21,932
- **ROOM AND BOARD:** $7,160

ACT Score (25th/75th percentile): 23-28
2005 U.S. News College Ranking: National Universities, 90
Acceptance Rate: 83%

Other expenses: Estimated books and supplies: $900. Transportation: $300. Personal expenses: $1,350. **Financial aid:** Priority filing date for institution's financial aid form: March 1. In 2003-2004, 72% of undergraduates applied for financial aid. Of those, 60% were determined to have financial need; 48% had their need fully met. Average financial aid package (proportion receiving): $16,853 (60%). Average amount of gift aid, such as scholarships or grants (proportion receiving): $10,774 (54%). Average amount of self-help aid, such as work study or loans (proportion receiving): $7,152 (49%). Average need-based loan (excluding PLUS or other private loans): $5,591. Among students who received need-based aid, the average percentage of need met: 86%. Among students who received aid based on merit, the average award (and the proportion receiving): $6,674 (21%). The average athletic scholarship (and the proportion receiving): $17,691 (1%). Average amount of debt of borrowers graduating in 2003: $22,924. Proportion who borrowed: 52%. **Student employment:** During the 2003-2004 academic year, 34% of undergraduates worked on campus. Average per-year earnings: $2,000. **Cooperative education programs:** business, engineering. **Reserve Officers Training Corps (ROTC):** Army ROTC: Offered on campus; Navy ROTC: Offered on campus; Air Force ROTC: Offered on campus.

Milwaukee Institute of Art and Design

273 E. Erie Street
Milwaukee, WI 53202
Private; www.miad.edu
Financial aid office: (414) 291-3272

- **2004-2005 TUITION AND FEES:** $22,030
- **ROOM AND BOARD:** $6,796

2005 U.S. News College Ranking: Unranked Specialty School–Fine Arts
Acceptance Rate: 83%

Other expenses: Estimated books and supplies: $1,650. Transportation: $1,624. Personal expenses: $1,624. **Financial aid:** Priority filing date for institution's financial aid form: March 1. Average amount of debt of borrowers graduating in 2003: $19,328. Proportion who borrowed: 82%. **Student employment:** During the 2003-2004 academic year, 30% of undergraduates worked on campus. Average per-year earnings: $1,000.

Milwaukee School of Engineering

1025 N. Broadway
Milwaukee, WI 53202-3109
Private; www.msoe.edu
Financial aid office: (414) 277-7511

- **2004-2005 TUITION AND FEES:** $24,174
- **ROOM AND BOARD:** $5,610

ACT Score (25th/75th percentile): 24-28
2005 U.S. News College Ranking: Unranked Specialty School–Engineering
Acceptance Rate: 65%

Other expenses: Estimated books and supplies: $1,300. Transportation: $1,300. Personal expenses: $1,800. **Financial aid:** Priority filing date for institution's financial aid form: March 15. In 2003-2004, 88% of undergraduates applied for financial aid. Of those, 83% were determined to have financial need; 14% had their need fully met. Average financial aid package (proportion receiving): $15,106 (83%). Average amount of gift aid, such as scholarships or grants (proportion receiving): $11,726 (83%). Average amount of self-help aid, such as work study or loans (proportion receiving): $3,811 (75%). Average need-based loan (excluding PLUS or other private loans): $3,530. Among students who received need-based aid, the average percentage of need met: 64%. Among students who received aid based on merit, the average award (and the proportion receiving): $11,795 (13%). The average athletic scholarship (and the proportion receiving): $0 (0%). Average amount of debt of borrowers graduating in 2003: $32,567. Proportion who borrowed: 75%. **Student employment:** During the 2003-2004 academic year, 10% of undergraduates worked on campus. Average per-year earnings: $4,000. **Reserve Officers Training Corps (ROTC):** Army ROTC: Offered at cooperating institution (Marquette University); Navy ROTC: Offered at cooperating institution (Marquette University); Air Force ROTC: Offered at cooperating institution (Marquette University).

Mount Mary College

2900 N. Menomonee River Parkway
Milwaukee, WI 53222
Private; www.mtmary.edu
Financial aid office: (414) 256-1258

■ **2004-2005 TUITION AND FEES:** $16,155
■ **ROOM AND BOARD:** $5,350

ACT Score (25th/75th percentile): 17-23
2005 U.S. News College Ranking:
Universities–Master's (Midwest), 68
Acceptance Rate: 65%

Other expenses: Estimated books and supplies: $900. Transportation: $970. Personal expenses: $1,362. **Financial aid:** Priority filing date for institution's financial aid form: March 1. In 2003-2004, 68% of undergraduates applied for financial aid. Of those, 62% were determined to have financial need; 20% had their need fully met. Average financial aid package (proportion receiving): $11,347 (62%). Average amount of gift aid, such as scholarships or grants (proportion receiving): $6,983 (60%). Average amount of self-help aid, such as work study or loans (proportion receiving): $4,925 (58%). Average need-based loan (excluding PLUS or other private loans): $4,194. Among students who received need-based aid, the average percentage of need met: 71%. Among students who received aid based on merit, the average award (and the proportion receiving): $6,037 (19%). The average athletic scholarship (and the proportion receiving): $0 (0%). Average amount of debt of borrowers graduating in 2003: $20,715. Proportion who borrowed: 65%.

Northland College

1411 Ellis Avenue
Ashland, WI 54806
Private; www.northland.edu
Financial aid office: (715) 682-1255

■ **2004-2005 TUITION AND FEES:** $18,715
■ **ROOM AND BOARD:** $5,390

ACT Score (25th/75th percentile): 22-26
2005 U.S. News College Ranking:
Comp. Colleges–Bachelor's (Midwest), 25
Acceptance Rate: 93%

Other expenses: Estimated books and supplies: $800. Transportation: $700. Personal expenses: $1,500. **Financial aid:** Priority filing date for institution's financial aid form: April 15. In 2003-2004, 90% of undergraduates applied for financial aid. Of those, 83% were determined to have financial need; 17% had their need fully met. Average financial aid package (proportion receiving): $14,321 (83%). Average amount of gift aid, such as scholarships or grants (proportion receiving): $8,937 (83%). Average amount of self-help aid, such as work study or loans (proportion receiving): $5,175 (76%). Average need-based loan (excluding PLUS or other private loans): $3,708. Among students who received need-based aid, the average percentage of need met: 79%. Among students who received aid based on merit, the average award (and the proportion receiving): $7,832 (7%). The average athletic scholarship (and the proportion receiving): $0 (0%). Average amount of debt of borrowers graduating in 2003: $18,622. Proportion who borrowed: 88%. **Student employment:** During the 2003-2004 academic year, 60% of undergraduates worked on campus. Average per-year earnings: $1,200. **Cooperative education programs:** engineering, natural science.

Ripon College

PO Box 248
Ripon, WI 54971-0248
Private; www.ripon.edu
Financial aid office: (920) 748-8101

■ **2004-2005 TUITION AND FEES:** $20,730
■ **ROOM AND BOARD:** $5,360

ACT Score (25th/75th percentile): 22-27
2005 U.S. News College Ranking:
Liberal Arts Colleges, third tier
Acceptance Rate: 84%

Financial aid: Priority filing date for institution's financial aid form: March 1. **Student employment:** During the 2003-2004 academic year, 21% of undergraduates worked on campus. Average per-year earnings: $794. **Reserve Officers Training Corps (ROTC):** Army ROTC: Offered on campus.

Silver Lake College

2406 S. Alverno Road
Manitowoc, WI 54220
Private; www.sl.edu
Financial aid office: (920) 686-6127

■ **2004-2005 TUITION AND FEES:** $15,500
■ **ROOM AND BOARD:** $6,170

ACT Score (25th/75th percentile): 17-21
2005 U.S. News College Ranking:
Universities–Master's (Midwest), fourth tier
Acceptance Rate: 77%

Other expenses: Estimated books and supplies: $800. Transportation: $1,000. Personal expenses: $1,125. **Financial aid:** Priority filing date for institution's financial aid form: April 15. **Student employment:** During the 2003-2004 academic year, 30% of undergraduates worked on campus.

St. Norbert College

100 Grant Street
De Pere, WI 54115-2099
Private; www.snc.edu
Financial aid office: (920) 403-3071

■ **2004-2005 TUITION AND FEES:** $21,510
■ **ROOM AND BOARD:** $5,980

ACT Score (25th/75th percentile): 22-27
2005 U.S. News College Ranking:
Comp. Colleges–Bachelor's (Midwest), 4
Acceptance Rate: 86%

Other expenses: Estimated books and supplies: $500. Transportation: $350. Personal expenses: $750. **Financial aid:** Priority filing date for institution's financial aid form: March 1. In 2003-2004, 75% of undergraduates applied for financial aid. Of those, 66% were determined to have financial need; 36% had their need fully met. Average financial aid package (proportion receiving): $15,507 (66%). Average amount of gift aid, such as scholarships or grants (proportion receiving): $10,899 (65%). Average amount of self-help aid, such as work study or loans (proportion receiving): $5,361 (58%). Average need-based loan (excluding PLUS or other private loans): $4,562. Among students who received need-based aid, the average percentage of need met: 89%. Among students who received aid based on merit, the average award (and the proportion receiving): $9,259 (30%). The average athletic scholarship (and the proportion receiving): $0 (0%). Average amount of debt of borrowers graduating in 2003: $16,854. Proportion who borrowed: 67%. **Student employment:** During the 2003-2004 academic year, 54% of undergraduates worked on campus. Average per-year earnings: $1,930. **Reserve Officers Training Corps (ROTC):** Army ROTC: Offered on campus.

University of Wisconsin–Eau Claire

105 Garfield Avenue
Eau Claire, WI 54701
Public; www.uwec.edu
Financial aid office: (715) 836-3373

■ **2004-2005 TUITION AND FEES:**
In state: $4,864; Out of state: $14,911
■ **ROOM AND BOARD:** $4,130

ACT Score (25th/75th percentile): 23-26
2005 U.S. News College Ranking:
Universities–Master's (Midwest), 20
Acceptance Rate: 60%

Financial aid: Priority filing date for institution's financial aid form: April 15. In 2003-2004, 64% of undergraduates applied for financial aid. Of those, 43% were determined to have financial need; 81% had their need fully met. Average financial aid package (proportion receiving): $6,577 (43%). Average amount of gift aid, such as scholarships or grants (proportion receiving): $4,102 (23%). Average amount of self-help aid, such as work study or loans (proportion receiving): $4,550 (40%). Average need-based loan (excluding PLUS or other private loans): $3,802. Among students who received need-based aid, the average percentage of need met: 96%. Among students who received aid based on merit, the average award (and the proportion receiving): $1,747 (9%). Average amount of debt of borrowers graduating in 2003: $15,061. Proportion who borrowed: 63%. **Student employment:** During the 2003-2004 academic year, 17% of undergraduates worked on campus. Average per-year earnings: $1,800. **Cooperative education programs:** computer science, health professions, humanities, natural science, social/behavioral science.

University of Wisconsin–Green Bay

2420 Nicolet Drive
Green Bay, WI 54311
Public; www.uwgb.edu
Financial aid office: (920) 465-2075

■ **2004-2005 TUITION AND FEES:**
In state: $6,154; Out of state: $15,201
■ **ROOM AND BOARD:** $4,856

ACT Score (25th/75th percentile): 20-25
2005 U.S. News College Ranking:
Universities–Master's (Midwest), 58
Acceptance Rate: 78%

Other expenses: Estimated books and supplies: $775. **Financial aid:** Priority filing date for institution's financial aid form: April 15. In 2003-2004, 76% of undergraduates applied for financial aid. Of those, 57% were determined to have financial need; 45% had their need fully met. Average financial aid package (proportion receiving): $6,831 (55%). Average amount of gift aid, such as scholarships or grants (proportion receiving): $3,970 (32%). Average amount of self-help aid, such as work study or loans (proportion receiving): $3,686 (39%). Average need-based loan (excluding PLUS or other private loans): $3,544. Among students who received need-based aid, the average percentage of need met: 80%. Among students who received aid based on merit, the average award (and the proportion receiving): $2,103 (1%). The average athletic scholarship (and the proportion receiving): $8,689 (2%). Average amount of debt of borrowers graduating in 2003: $13,000. Proportion who borrowed: 86%. **Student employment:** During the 2003-2004 academic year, 20% of undergraduates worked on campus. Average per-year earnings: $1,000. **Reserve Officers Training Corps (ROTC):** Army ROTC: Offered on campus.

University of Wisconsin–La Crosse

1725 State Street
La Crosse, WI 54601
Public; www.uwlax.edu
Financial aid office: (608) 785-8604

■ **2004-2005 TUITION AND FEES:**
In state: $4,958; Out of state: $14,934
■ **ROOM AND BOARD:** $4,570

ACT Score (25th/75th percentile): 23-26
2005 U.S. News College Ranking:
Universities–Master's (Midwest), 20
Acceptance Rate: 53%

Other expenses: Estimated books and supplies: $300. Transportation: $202. Personal expenses: $2,000. **Financial aid:** Priority filing date for institution's financial aid form: March 15. In 2003-2004, 72% of undergraduates applied for financial aid. Of those, 58% were determined to have financial need; 87% had their need fully met. Average financial aid package (proportion receiving): $4,099 (56%). Average amount of gift aid, such as scholarships or grants (proportion receiving): $3,624 (27%). Average amount of self-help aid, such as work study or loans (proportion receiving): $3,891 (49%). Average need-based loan (excluding PLUS or other private loans): $3,704. Among students who received need-based aid, the average percentage of need met: 89%. Among students who received aid based on merit, the average award (and the proportion receiving): $3,914 (12%). **Student employment:** During the 2003-2004 academic year, 22% of undergraduates worked on campus. **Reserve Officers Training Corps (ROTC):** Army ROTC: Offered on campus.

University of Wisconsin–Madison

500 Lincoln Drive
Madison, WI 53706
Public; www.wisc.edu
Financial aid office: (608) 262-3060

■ **2004-2005 TUITION AND FEES:**
In state: $5,860; Out of state: $19,860
■ **ROOM AND BOARD:** $6,250

ACT Score (25th/75th percentile): 26-30
2005 U.S. News College Ranking:
National Universities, 32
Acceptance Rate: 65%

Other expenses: Estimated books and supplies: $830. Transportation: $410. Personal expenses: $1,900. **Financial aid:** In 2003-2004, 54% of undergraduates applied for financial aid. Of those, 34% were determined to have financial need; 33% had their need fully met. Average financial aid package (proportion receiving): $10,302 (32%). Average amount of gift aid, such as scholarships or grants (proportion receiving): $5,655 (15%). Average amount of self-help aid, such as work study or loans (proportion receiving): $5,321 (28%). Average need-based loan (excluding PLUS or other private loans): $4,248. Among students who received aid based on merit, the average award (and the proportion receiving): $2,773 (15%). The average athletic scholarship (and the proportion receiving): $14,996 (1%). Average amount of debt of borrowers graduating in 2003: $16,395. Proportion who borrowed: 43%. **Student employment:** During the 2003-2004 academic year, 40% of undergraduates worked on campus. Average per-year earnings: $5,000. **Cooperative education programs:** agriculture, engineering. **Reserve Officers Training Corps (ROTC):** Army ROTC: Offered on campus; Navy ROTC: Offered on campus; Air Force ROTC: Offered on campus.

University of Wisconsin– Milwaukee

PO Box 413
Milwaukee, WI 53201
Public; www.uwm.edu
Financial aid office: (414) 229-6300

■ **2004-2005 TUITION AND FEES:**
   In state: $5,806; Out of state: $18,560
■ **ROOM AND BOARD:** $5,730

ACT Score (25th/75th percentile): 20-24
2005 U.S. News College Ranking:
National Universities, fourth tier
Acceptance Rate: 79%

Other expenses: Estimated books and supplies: $800. Transportation: $1,560. Personal expenses: $1,600. **Financial aid:** Priority filing date for institution's financial aid form: March 1. In 2003-2004, 74% of undergraduates applied for financial aid. Of those, 57% were determined to have financial need; 38% had their need fully met. Average financial aid package (proportion receiving): $7,750 (49%). Average amount of gift aid, such as scholarships or grants (proportion receiving): $1,781 (23%). Average amount of self-help aid, such as work study or loans (proportion receiving): $3,021 (42%). Average need-based loan (excluding PLUS or other private loans): $3,069. Among students who received need-based aid, the average percentage of need met: 68%. Among students who received aid based on merit, the average award (and the proportion receiving): $4,269 (2%). The average athletic scholarship (and the proportion receiving): $1,139 (0%). Average amount of debt of borrowers graduating in 2003: $20,925. **Cooperative education programs:** computer science, engineering. **Reserve Officers Training Corps (ROTC):** Army ROTC: Offered at cooperating institution (Marquette

University); Navy ROTC: Offered at cooperating institution (Marquette University); Air Force ROTC: Offered at cooperating institution (Marquette University).

University of Wisconsin– Oshkosh

800 Algoma Boulevard
Oshkosh, WI 54901
Public; www.uwosh.edu
Financial aid office: (920) 424-3377

■ **2004-2005 TUITION AND FEES:**
   In state: $4,650; Out of state: $14,670
■ **ROOM AND BOARD:** $4,315

ACT Score (25th/75th percentile): 19-26
2005 U.S. News College Ranking:
Universities–Master's (Midwest), 62
Acceptance Rate: 47%

Other expenses: Estimated books and supplies: $800. Transportation: $472. Personal expenses: $2,150. **Financial aid:** Priority filing date for institution's financial aid form: March 15. In 2003-2004, 68% of undergraduates applied for financial aid. Of those, 48% were determined to have financial need; 20% had their need fully met. Average financial aid package (proportion receiving): $2,500 (48%). Average amount of gift aid, such as scholarships or grants (proportion receiving): $1,200 (5%). Average amount of self-help aid, such as work study or loans (proportion receiving): $6,125 (32%). Average need-based loan (excluding PLUS or other private loans): $3,750. Among students who received need-based aid, the average percentage of need met: 30%. Among students who received aid based on merit, the average award (and the proportion receiving): $0 (0%). The average athletic scholarship (and the proportion receiving): $0 (0%). Average amount of debt of borrowers graduating in 2003: $15,000. Proportion who borrowed: 65%. **Student employment:** During the 2003-2004 academic year, 16% of undergraduates worked on campus. Average per-year earnings: $4,350. **Reserve Officers Training Corps (ROTC):** Army ROTC: Offered on campus.

University of Wisconsin– Parkside

900 Wood Road, PO Box 2000
Kenosha, WI 53141-2000
Public; www.uwp.edu
Financial aid office: (262) 595-2004

■ **2004-2005 TUITION AND FEES:**
   In state: $3,619; Out of state: $13,665
■ **ROOM AND BOARD:** $5,056

ACT Score (25th/75th percentile): 17-22
2005 U.S. News College Ranking:
Universities–Master's (Midwest), fourth tier
Acceptance Rate: 60%

Other expenses: Estimated books and supplies: $770. Personal expenses: $2,601. **Financial aid:** Priority filing date for institution's financial aid form: March 15. In 2003-2004, 73% of undergraduates applied for financial aid. Of those, 48% were determined to have financial need; 39% had their need fully met. Average financial aid package (proportion receiving): $5,953 (46%). Average amount of gift aid, such as scholarships or grants (proportion receiving): $4,098 (26%). Average amount of self-help aid, such as work study or loans (proportion receiving): $2,795 (34%). Average need-based loan (excluding PLUS or other private loans): $3,405. Among students who received need-based aid, the average percentage of need met: 78%. Among students who received aid based on merit, the average award (and the proportion receiving): $2,105 (4%). The average athletic scholarship (and the proportion receiving): $3,372 (1%). Average amount of debt of borrowers graduating in 2003: $12,500. **Student employment:** During the 2003-2004 academic year, 12% of undergraduates worked on campus. Average per-year earnings: $3,000. **Reserve Officers Training Corps (ROTC):** Army ROTC: Offered at cooperating institution (Marquette University).

University of Wisconsin– Platteville

1 University Plaza
Platteville, WI 53818
Public; www.uwplatt.edu
Financial aid office: (608) 342-1836

■ **2004-2005 TUITION AND FEES:**
   In state: $4,253; Out of state: $14,299
■ **ROOM AND BOARD:** $4,196

ACT Score (25th/75th percentile): 18-26
2005 U.S. News College Ranking:
Universities–Master's (Midwest), 63
Acceptance Rate: 80%

Other expenses: Estimated books and supplies: $300. Transportation: $410. Personal expenses: $1,170. Financial aid: Priority filing date for institution's financial aid form: March 15. Cooperative education programs: agriculture, art, business, computer science, education, engineering, health professions, home economics, humanities, natural science, social/behavioral science, technologies, vocational arts, other.

University of Wisconsin–River Falls

410 S. Third Street
River Falls, WI 54022
Public; www.uwrf.edu
Financial aid office: (715) 425-3141

■ **2004-2005 TUITION AND FEES:**
In state: $4,747; Out of state: $14,794
■ **ROOM AND BOARD:** $4,174

ACT Score (25th/75th percentile): 20-24
2005 U.S. News College Ranking:
Universities–Master's (Midwest), 52
Acceptance Rate: 74%

Financial aid: Priority filing date for institution's financial aid form: March 15. Student employment: During the 2003-2004 academic year, 25% of undergraduates worked on campus. Average per-year earnings: $1,500. Cooperative education programs: agriculture.

University of Wisconsin–Stevens Point

2100 Main Street
Stevens Point, WI 54481
Public; www.uwsp.edu
Financial aid office: (715) 346-4771

■ **2004-2005 TUITION AND FEES:**
In state: $4,729; Out of state: $14,775
■ **ROOM AND BOARD:** $4,220

ACT Score (25th/75th percentile): 21-25
2005 U.S. News College Ranking:
Universities–Master's (Midwest), 38
Acceptance Rate: 75%

Other expenses: Estimated books and supplies: $450. Transportation: $274. Personal expenses: $1,555. Financial aid: In 2003-2004, 83% of undergraduates applied for financial aid. Of those, 49% were determined to have financial need; 51% had their need fully met. Average financial aid package (proportion receiving): $6,308 (47%). Average amount of gift aid, such as scholarships or grants (proportion receiving): $4,311 (25%). Average amount of self-help aid, such as work study or loans (proportion receiving): $4,330 (43%). Average need-based loan (excluding PLUS or other private loans): $3,863. Among students who received need-based aid, the average percentage of need met: 88%. Among students who received aid based on merit, the average award (and the proportion receiving): $1,694 (5%). The average athletic scholarship (and the proportion receiving): $0 (0%). Average amount of debt of borrowers graduating in 2003: $14,013. Proportion who borrowed: 64%. Student employment: During the 2003-2004 academic year, 17% of undergraduates worked on campus. Average per-year earnings: $2,040. Reserve Officers Training Corps (ROTC): Army ROTC: Offered on campus.

University of Wisconsin–Stout

1 Clock Tower Plaza
Menomonie, WI 54751
Public; www.uwstout.edu
Financial aid office: (715) 232-1363

■ **2004-2005 TUITION AND FEES:**
In state: $6,263; Out of state: $16,588
■ **ROOM AND BOARD:** $4,224

ACT Score (25th/75th percentile): 19-23
2005 U.S. News College Ranking:
Universities–Master's (Midwest), 58
Acceptance Rate: 66%

Financial aid: Priority filing date for institution's financial aid form: April 1. In 2003-2004, 72% of undergraduates applied for financial aid. Of those, 50% were determined to have financial need; 62% had their need fully met. Average financial aid package (proportion receiving): $6,746 (50%). Average amount of gift aid, such as scholarships or grants (proportion receiving): $4,204 (25%). Average amount of self-help aid, such as work study or loans (proportion receiving): $4,592 (49%). Average need-based loan (excluding PLUS or other private loans): $3,978. Among students who received need-based aid, the average percentage of need met: 91%. Among students who

received aid based on merit, the average award (and the proportion receiving): $1,749 (6%). The average athletic scholarship (and the proportion receiving): $0 (0%). Average amount of debt of borrowers graduating in 2003: $16,746. Proportion who borrowed: 72%. Student employment: During the 2003-2004 academic year, 24% of undergraduates worked on campus. Average per-year earnings: $1,351. Cooperative education programs: art, business, computer science, education, engineering, home economics, humanities, natural science, social/behavioral science, technologies, vocational arts.

University of Wisconsin–Superior

Belknap and Catlin, PO Box 2000
Superior, WI 54880-4500
Public; www.uwsuper.edu
Financial aid office: (715) 394-8200

■ **2004-2005 TUITION AND FEES:**
In state: $4,276; Out of state: $14,322
■ **ROOM AND BOARD:** $4,246

ACT Score (25th/75th percentile): 20-24
2005 U.S. News College Ranking:
Universities–Master's (Midwest), third tier
Acceptance Rate: 77%

Other expenses: Estimated books and supplies: $730. Transportation: $730. Personal expenses: $1,430. Financial aid: Priority filing date for institution's financial aid form: April 15; deadline: May 15. In 2003-2004, 71% of undergraduates applied for financial aid. Of those, 57% were determined to have financial need; 58% had their need fully met. Average financial aid package (proportion receiving): $8,274 (55%). Average amount of gift aid, such as scholarships or grants (proportion receiving): $4,260 (32%). Average amount of self-help aid, such as work study or loans (proportion receiving): $4,222 (49%). Average need-based loan (excluding PLUS or other private loans): $3,966. Among students who received aid based on merit, the average award (and the proportion receiving): $1,263 (2%). Student employment: During the 2003-2004 academic year, 15% of undergraduates worked on campus. Average per-year earnings: $1,660. Cooperative education programs: engineering. Reserve Officers Training Corps (ROTC): Air Force ROTC: Offered at cooperating institution (University of Minnesota–Duluth).

University of Wisconsin–Whitewater

800 W. Main Street
Whitewater, WI 53190
Public; www.uww.edu
Financial aid office: (262) 472-1130

■ **2004-2005 TUITION AND FEES:**
In state: $4,494; Out of state: $15,044
■ **ROOM AND BOARD:** $3,120

ACT Score (25th/75th percentile): 22
2005 U.S. News College Ranking:
Universities–Master's (Midwest), 50
Acceptance Rate: 68%

Other expenses: Estimated books and supplies: $700. Transportation: $850. Personal expenses: $1,600. **Financial aid:** Priority filing date for institution's financial aid form: March 15. In 2003-2004, 61% of undergraduates applied for financial aid. Of those, 43% were determined to have financial need; 49% had their need fully met. Average financial aid package (proportion receiving): $5,970 (41%). Average amount of gift aid, such as scholarships or grants (proportion receiving): $3,790 (21%). Average amount of self-help aid, such as work study or loans (proportion receiving): $4,048 (37%). Average need-based loan (excluding PLUS or other private loans): $3,829. Among students who received need-based aid, the average percentage of need met: 75%. Among students who received aid based on merit, the average award (and the proportion receiving): $1,595 (10%). The average athletic scholarship (and the proportion receiving): $0 (0%). **Student employment:** During the 2003-2004 academic year, 20% of undergraduates worked on campus. Average per-year earnings: $1,750. **Reserve Officers Training Corps (ROTC):** Army ROTC: Offered on campus; Air Force ROTC: Offered on campus.

Viterbo University

900 Viterbo Drive
La Crosse, WI 54601
Private; www.viterbo.edu
Financial aid office: (608) 796-3900

■ **2004-2005 TUITION AND FEES:** $15,990
■ **ROOM AND BOARD:** $5,220

ACT Score (25th/75th percentile): 19-26
2005 U.S. News College Ranking:
Universities–Master's (Midwest), third tier
Acceptance Rate: 88%

Other expenses: Estimated books and supplies: $800. Transportation: $700. Personal expenses: $1,600. **Financial aid:** Priority filing date for institution's financial aid form: March 15. In 2003-2004, 88% of undergraduates applied for financial aid. Of those, 81% were determined to have financial need; 26% had their need fully met. Average financial aid package (proportion receiving): $13,534 (81%). Average amount of gift aid, such as scholarships or grants (proportion receiving): $8,859 (79%). Average amount of self-help aid, such as work study or loans (proportion receiving): $4,807 (76%). Average need-based loan (excluding PLUS or other private loans): $4,317. Among students who received need-based aid, the average percentage of need met: 70%. Among students who received aid based on merit, the average award (and the proportion receiving): $5,629 (15%). The average athletic scholarship (and the proportion receiving): $756 (1%). Average amount of debt of borrowers graduating in 2003: $15,703. Proportion who borrowed: 86%. **Student employment:** During the 2003-2004 academic year, 11% of undergraduates worked on campus. Average per-year earnings: $366. **Reserve Officers Training Corps (ROTC):** Army ROTC: Offered at cooperating institution (University of Wisconsin–La Crosse).

Wisconsin Lutheran College

8800 W. Bluemound Road
Milwaukee, WI 53226
Private; www.wlc.edu
Financial aid office: (414) 443-8856

■ **2004-2005 TUITION AND FEES:** $16,640
■ **ROOM AND BOARD:** $5,410

ACT Score (25th/75th percentile): 22-27
2005 U.S. News College Ranking:
Comp. Colleges–Bachelor's (Midwest), 23
Acceptance Rate: 84%

Other expenses: Estimated books and supplies: $700. Transportation: $300. Personal expenses: $1,470. **Financial aid:** Priority filing date for institution's financial aid form: March 1. In 2003-2004, 80% of undergraduates applied for financial aid. Of those, 75% were determined to have financial need; 30% had their need fully met. Average financial aid package (proportion receiving): $13,342 (75%). Average amount of gift aid, such as scholarships or grants (proportion receiving): $9,403 (75%). Average amount of self-help aid, such as work study or loans (proportion receiving): $4,435 (67%). Average need-based loan (excluding PLUS or other private loans): $3,447. Among students who received need-based aid, the average percentage of need met: 86%. Among students who received aid based on merit, the average award (and the proportion receiving): $9,161 (22%). The average athletic scholarship (and the proportion receiving): $0 (0%). Average amount of debt of borrowers graduating in 2003: $13,707. Proportion who borrowed: 71%. **Student employment:** During the 2003-2004 academic year, 50% of undergraduates worked on campus. Average per-year earnings: $1,620. **Reserve Officers Training Corps (ROTC):** Army ROTC: Offered at cooperating institution (Marquette University); Navy ROTC: Offered at cooperating institution (Marquette University); Air Force ROTC: Offered at cooperating institution (Marquette University).

Wyoming

University of Wyoming

1000 E. University Avenue
Laramie, WY 82071
Public; www.uwyo.edu
Financial aid office: (307) 766-2116

■ **2004-2005 TUITION AND FEES:**
  In state: $3,243; Out of state: $9,273
■ **ROOM AND BOARD:** $5,953

ACT Score (25th/75th percentile): 20-26
2005 U.S. News College Ranking:
National Universities, third tier
Acceptance Rate: 95%
....

Other expenses: Estimated books and supplies: $1,000. Transportation: $679. Personal expenses: $2,000. **Financial aid:** Priority filing date for institution's financial aid form: February 1. In 2003-2004, 66% of undergraduates applied for financial aid. Of those, 48% were determined to have financial need; 68% had their need fully met. Average financial aid package (proportion receiving): $8,944 (47%). Average amount of gift aid, such as scholarships or grants (proportion receiving): $4,030 (19%). Average amount of self-help aid, such as work study or loans (proportion receiving): $1,115 (42%). Average need-based loan (excluding PLUS or other private loans): $5,474. Among students who received need-based aid, the average percentage of need met: 75%. Among students who received aid based on merit, the average award (and the proportion receiving): $3,421 (39%). Average amount of debt of borrowers graduating in 2003: $15,250. Proportion who borrowed: 44%. **Student employment:** During the 2003-2004 academic year, 30% of undergraduates worked on campus. Average per-year earnings: $2,185. **Cooperative education programs:** agriculture, business, education, health professions, home economics, natural science, social/behavioral science, technologies, vocational arts. **Reserve Officers Training Corps (ROTC):** Army ROTC: Offered on campus; Air Force ROTC: Offered on campus.

Index of Schools

Abilene Christian University, 451
Adams State College, 175
Adelphi University, 341
Adrian College, 289
Agnes Scott College, 198
Alabama Agricultural and Mechanical University, 142
Alabama State University, 142
Alaska Pacific University, 149
Albany State University, 198
Albertson College, 210
Albertus Magnus College, 180
Albion College, 289
Albright College, 406
Alcorn State University, 307
Alderson-Broaddus College, 489
Alfred University, 341
Alice Lloyd College, 250
Allegheny College, 406
Allen University, 432
Alliant International University, 155
Alma College, 289
Alvernia College, 406
Alverno College, 494
American International College, 273
American University, 186
Amherst College, 273
Anderson College, 432
Anderson University, 225
Andrews University, 289
Angelo State University, 451
Anna Maria College, 273
Antioch College, 382
Appalachian State University, 368
Aquinas College, 290
Arcadia University, 406
Arizona State University West, 150
Arizona State University, 150

Arkansas Baptist College, 151
Arkansas State University, 151
Arkansas Tech University, 151
Armstrong Atlantic State University, 198
Art Academy of Cincinnati, 382
Art Center College of Design, 155
Art Institute of Boston, 273
Asbury College, 250
Ashland University, 382
Assumption College, 274
Atlanta College of Art, 198
Atlantic Union College, 274
Auburn University, 142
Auburn University–Montgomery, 142
Augsburg College, 299
Augusta State University, 198
Augustana College, 212
Augustana College, 439
Aurora University, 212
Austin College, 451
Austin Peay State University, 442
Averett University, 473
Avila University, 311
Azusa Pacific University, 155

Babson College, 274
Baker College of Flint, 290
Baker University, 244
Baldwin-Wallace College, 382
Ball State University, 225
Barber Scotia College, 368
Bard College, 341
Barnard College, 341
Barry University, 189
Barton College, 368
Bates College, 262
Bay Path College, 274

Baylor University, 451
Becker College, 275
Belhaven College, 307
Bellarmine University, 250
Bellevue University, 323
Belmont Abbey College, 368
Belmont University, 442
Beloit College, 494
Bemidji State University, 299
Benedict College, 432
Benedictine College, 244
Benedictine University, 212
Benjamin Franklin Institute of Technology, 275
Bennett College, 368
Bennington College, 469
Bentley College, 275
Berea College, 250
Berklee College of Music, 275
Berry College, 199
Bethany College, 155
Bethany College, 244
Bethany College, 489
Bethel College, 225
Bethel College, 244
Bethel College, 442
Bethel University, 299
Bethune-Cookman College, 189
Biola University, 156
Birmingham-Southern College, 142
Black Hills State University, 439
Blackburn College, 212
Bloomfield College, 331
Bloomsburg University of Pennsylvania, 406
Blue Mountain College, 307
Bluefield College, 473
Bluefield State College, 489

Bluffton University, 382
Boise State University, 210
Boricua College, 342
Boston Architectural Center, 275
Boston College, 276
Boston Conservatory, 276
Boston University, 276
Bowdoin College, 262
Bowie State University, 267
Bowling Green State University, 393
Bradley University, 213
Brandeis University, 276
Brenau University, 199
Brescia University, 251
Brevard College, 369
Brewton-Parker College, 199
Briar Cliff University, 236
Bridgewater College, 473
Bridgewater State College, 277
Brigham Young University–Hawaii, 208
Brigham Young University–Provo, 467
Brown University, 429
Bryan College, 442
Bryant College, 429
Bryn Athyn College, 407
Bryn Mawr College, 407
Bucknell University, 407
Buena Vista University, 236
Buffalo State College, 342
Burlington College, 469
Butler University, 225

Cabrini College, 407
Cal Poly–San Luis Obispo, 160
Caldwell College, 331
California Baptist University, 156
California College of the Arts, 155
California Institute of Technology, 156
California Institute of the Arts, 156
California Lutheran University, 157
California State Polytechnic University–Pomona, 157

California State University–Bakersfield, 157
California State University–Chico, 157
California State University–Dominguez Hills, 157
California State University–Fresno, 158
California State University–Fullerton, 158
California State University–Hayward, 158
California State University–Long Beach, 158
California State University–Los Angeles, 159
California State University–Monterey Bay, 159
California State University–Northridge, 159
California State University–Sacramento, 159
California State University–San Bernardino, 160
California State University–San Marcos, 160
California State University–Stanislaus, 160
California University of Pennsylvania, 408
Calumet College of St. Joseph, 226
Calvin College, 290
Cameron University, 396
Campbell University, 369
Campbellsville University, 251
Canisius College, 342
Capital University, 393
Capitol College, 267
Cardinal Stritch University, 494
Carleton College, 299
Carlow College, 408
Carnegie Mellon University, 408
Carroll College, 320
Carroll College, 494
Carson-Newman College, 443

Carthage College, 494
Case Western Reserve University, 393
Castleton State College, 469
Catawba College, 369
Catholic University of America, 186
Cazenovia College, 342
Cedar Crest College, 408
Cedarville University, 393
Centenary College of Louisiana, 257
Centenary College, 331
Central Christian College, 245
Central College, 236
Central Connecticut State University, 180
Central Methodist University, 311
Central Michigan University, 290
Central Missouri State University, 311
Central State University, 384
Central Washington University, 484
Centre College, 251
Chadron State College, 323
Chaminade University of Honolulu, 208
Champlain College, 469
Chapman University, 160
Charleston Southern University, 432
Chatham College, 409
Chestnut Hill College, 409
Cheyney University of Pennsylvania, 409
Chicago State University, 213
Chowan College, 369
Christendom College, 473
Christian Brothers University, 443
Christian Heritage College, 161
Christopher Newport University, 474
City University, 484
Claflin University, 433
Claremont McKenna College, 161
Clarion University of Pennsylvania, 409
Clark Atlanta University, 199
Clark University, 277
Clarke College, 236

Duke University, 370
Duquesne University, 411

Earlham College, 226
East Carolina University, 370
East Central University, 396
East Stroudsburg University of
    Pennsylvania, 411
East Tennessee State University, 444
East Texas Baptist University, 452
Eastern Connecticut State University,
    180
Eastern Illinois University, 214
Eastern Kentucky University, 252
Eastern Mennonite University, 474
Eastern Michigan University, 291
Eastern Nazarene College, 278
Eastern New Mexico University, 338
Eastern Oregon University, 401
Eastern University, 411
Eastern Washington University, 484
East-West University, 214
Eckerd College, 189
Edgewood College, 495
Edinboro University of Pennsylvania,
    411
Edward Waters College, 190
Elizabeth City State University, 370
Elizabethtown College, 412
Elmhurst College, 214
Elmira College, 347
Elms College (College of Our Lady of
    the Elms), 278
Elon University, 371
Embry Riddle Aeronautical University,
    190
Emerson College, 278
Emmanuel College, 200
Emmanuel College, 278
Emory and Henry College, 474
Emory University, 201
Emporia State University, 245
Endicott College, 278
Erskine College, 435

Eureka College, 214
Evangel University, 312
Evergreen State College, 484
Excelsior College, 348

Fairfield University, 181
Fairleigh Dickinson University, 332
Fairmont State University, 490
Faulkner University, 143
Fayetteville State University, 371
Felician College, 332
Ferris State University, 292
Ferrum College, 475
Fisk University, 444
Fitchburg State College, 279
Flagler College, 190
Florida A&M University, 190
Florida Atlantic University, 190
Florida Gulf Coast University, 191
Florida Institute of Technology, 191
Florida International University, 191
Florida Memorial College, 191
Florida Southern College, 192
Florida State University, 192
Fontbonne University, 312
Fordham University, 348
Fort Hays State University, 245
Fort Lewis College, 176
Fort Valley State University, 201
Framingham State College, 279
Francis Marion University, 435
Franciscan University of Steubenville,
    386
Franklin and Marshall College, 412
Franklin College, 226
Franklin Pierce College, 328
Franklin University, 386
Freed-Hardeman University, 444
Fresno Pacific University, 162
Friends University, 245
Frostburg State University, 268
Furman University, 435
Gallaudet University, 186
Gannon University, 412

Gardner-Webb University, 371
Geneva College, 412
George Fox University, 401
George Mason University, 475
George Washington University, 187
Georgetown College, 252
Georgetown University, 187
Georgia College and State University,
    201
Georgia Institute of Technology, 201
Georgia Southern University, 202
Georgia Southwestern State
    University, 202
Georgia State University, 202
Georgian Court University, 333
Gettysburg College, 413
Glenville State College, 490
Goddard College, 470
Golden Gate University, 162
Goldey Beacom College, 184
Gonzaga University, 485
Gordon College, 279
Goshen College, 227
Goucher College, 268
Grace College and Seminary, 227
Grace University, 324
Graceland University, 238
Grambling State University, 257
Grand Canyon University, 150
Grand Valley State University, 292
Grand View College, 238
Gratz College, 413
Green Mountain College, 470
Greensboro College, 371
Greenville College, 215
Grinnell College, 238
Grove City College, 413
Guilford College, 372
Gustavus Adolphus College, 301
Gwynedd-Mercy College, 413

Hamilton College, 348
Hamline University, 302
Hampden-Sydney College, 475

Suffolk University, 285

Sul Ross State University, 458

SUNY College Environmental Science and Forestry, 360

SUNY College of A&T–Cobleskill, 361

SUNY College of Arts and Sciences–Geneseo, 361

SUNY College of Arts and Sciences–New Paltz, 361

SUNY College–Brockport, 360

SUNY College–Cortland, 360

SUNY College–Old Westbury, 361

SUNY College–Oneonta, 362

SUNY College–Potsdam, 362

SUNY–Albany, 359

SUNY–Binghamton, 360

SUNY–Empire State College, 362

SUNY–Farmingdale, 362

SUNY–Fredonia, 362

SUNY–Oswego, 363

SUNY–Plattsburgh, 363

SUNY–Purchase College, 363

SUNY–Stony Brook, 363

Susquehanna University, 423

Swarthmore College, 423

Sweet Briar College, 480

Syracuse University, 364

Tabor College, 247

Talladega College, 145

Tarleton State University, 458

Taylor University, 233

Teikyo Post University, 182

Temple University, 423

Tennessee State University, 448

Tennessee Technological University, 448

Tennessee Wesleyan College, 448

Texas A&M International University, 458

Texas A&M University–College Station, 458

Texas A&M University–Commerce, 459

Texas A&M University–Corpus Christi, 459

Texas A&M University–Galveston, 459

Texas A&M University–Kingsville, 459

Texas Christian University, 460

Texas College, 460

Texas Lutheran University, 460

Texas Southern University, 460

Texas State University–San Marcos, 460

Texas Tech University, 461

Texas Wesleyan University, 461

Texas Woman's University, 461

The Citadel, 433

The Franciscan University, 238

Thiel College, 424

Thomas Aquinas College, 169

Thomas College, 263

Thomas Edison State College, 337

Thomas More College, 255

Thomas University, 205

Tiffin University, 392

Toccoa Falls College, 206

Tougaloo College, 309

Touro College, 364

Towson University, 271

Transylvania University, 255

Trevecca Nazarene University, 449

Trinity Christian College, 222

Trinity College, 182

Trinity College, 188

Trinity University, 461

Tri-State University, 233

Troy State University–Dothan, 145

Troy State University–Montgomery, 145

Troy State University–Troy, 145

Truman State University, 317

Tufts University, 285

Tulane University, 260

Tusculum College, 449

Tuskegee University, 146

Union College, 325

Union College, 364

Union Institute and University, 392

Union University, 449

United States Air Force Academy, 177

United States Coast Guard Academy, 182

United States Merchant Marine Academy, 364

United States Military Academy, 365

United States Naval Academy, 271

Unity College, 264

University at Buffalo–SUNY, 365

University of Akron, 392

University of Alabama, 146

University of Alabama–Birmingham, 146

University of Alabama–Huntsville, 146

University of Alaska–Anchorage, 149

University of Alaska–Fairbanks, 149

University of Alaska–Southeast, 149

University of Arizona, 150

University of Arkansas, 153

University of Arkansas–Little Rock, 153

University of Arkansas–Monticello, 153

University of Arkansas–Pine Bluff, 153

University of Bridgeport, 183

University of California–Berkeley, 170

University of California–Davis, 170

University of California–Irvine, 170

University of California–Los Angeles, 170

University of California–Riverside, 171

University of California–San Diego, 171

University of California–Santa Barbara, 171

University of California–Santa Cruz, 172

University of Central Arkansas, 153

University of Central Florida, 195

University of Central Oklahoma, 399

University of Charleston, 491
University of Chicago, 223
University of Cincinnati, 392
University of Colorado–Boulder, 177
University of Colorado–Colorado
    Springs, 177
University of Colorado–Denver, 178
University of Connecticut, 183
University of Dallas, 462
University of Dayton, 392
University of Delaware, 185
University of Denver, 178
University of Detroit Mercy, 296
University of Dubuque, 241
University of Evansville, 233
University of Findlay, 393
University of Florida, 195
University of Georgia, 206
University of Great Falls, 321
University of Hartford, 183
University of Hawaii–Hilo, 209
University of Hawaii–Manoa, 209
University of Houston, 462
University of Houston–Downtown,
    462
University of Idaho, 211
University of Illinois–Chicago, 223
University of Illinois–Springfield, 223
University of Illinois–Urbana-
    Champaign, 223
University of Indianapolis, 233
University of Iowa, 241
University of Judaism, 172
University of Kansas, 248
University of Kentucky, 255
University of La Verne, 172
University of Louisiana–Lafayette, 260
University of Louisiana–Monroe, 261
University of Louisville, 255
University of Maine–Augusta, 264
University of Maine–Farmington, 264
University of Maine–Fort Kent, 264
University of Maine–Machias, 264
University of Maine–Orono, 265

University of Maine–Presque Isle, 265
University of Mary Hardin-Baylor, 462
University of Mary Washington, 480
University of Mary, 381
University of Maryland–Baltimore
    County, 271
University of Maryland–College Park,
    271
University of Maryland–Eastern
    Shore, 272
University of Maryland–University
    College, 272
University of Massachusetts–Amherst,
    285
University of Massachusetts–Boston,
    286
University of
    Massachusetts–Dartmouth, 286
University of Massachusetts–Lowell,
    286
University of Memphis, 449
University of Miami, 195
University of Michigan–Ann Arbor,
    296
University of Michigan–Dearborn,
    297
University of Michigan–Flint, 297
University of Minnesota–Crookston,
    305
University of Minnesota–Duluth, 305
University of Minnesota–Morris, 305
University of Minnesota–Twin Cities,
    305
University of Mississippi, 309
University of Missouri–Columbia, 317
University of Missouri–Kansas City,
    317
University of Missouri–Rolla, 317
University of Missouri–St. Louis, 318
University of Mobile, 147
University of Montana, 322
University of Montana–Western, 322
University of Montevallo, 147
University of Nebraska–Kearney, 325

University of Nebraska–Lincoln, 326
University of Nebraska–Omaha, 326
University of Nevada–Las Vegas, 327
University of Nevada–Reno, 327
University of New England, 265
University of New Hampshire, 330
University of New Haven, 183
University of New Mexico, 339
University of New Orleans, 261
University of North Alabama, 147
University of North
    Carolina–Asheville, 377
University of North Carolina–Chapel
    Hill, 377
University of North
    Carolina–Charlotte, 377
University of North
    Carolina–Greensboro, 378
University of North
    Carolina–Pembroke, 378
University of North
    Carolina–Wilmington, 378
University of North Dakota, 381
University of North Florida, 195
University of North Texas, 463
University of Northern Colorado, 178
University of Northern Iowa, 242
University of Notre Dame, 234
University of Oklahoma, 399
University of Oregon, 404
University of Pennsylvania, 424
University of Pittsburgh, 424
University of Pittsburgh–Bradford,
    424
University of Pittsburgh–Greensburg,
    425
University of Pittsburgh–Johnstown,
    425
University of Portland, 404
University of Puget Sound, 487
University of Redlands, 172
University of Rhode Island, 430
University of Richmond, 480
University of Rio Grande, 393

About the Authors & Editors

Founded in 1933, Washington, D.C.–based *U.S.News & World Report* delivers a unique brand of weekly magazine journalism to its 12.2 million readers. In 1983, *U.S. News* began its exclusive annual rankings of American colleges and universities. The *U.S. News* education franchise is second to none; its annual college and graduate school rankings are among the most eagerly anticipated magazine issues in the country.

Margaret Mannix, editor, is an assistant managing editor at *U.S.News & World Report*, where she helps direct the magazine's money and business coverage. She also coordinates the magazine's Paying for College features and was the co-editor of the *U.S. News* book *Paying for College*.

Robert Morse is the director of data research at *U.S.News & World Report*. He is in charge of the research, data collection, methodologies, and survey design for the annual "America's Best Colleges" rankings and the "America's Best Graduate Schools" rankings.

Jodie T. Allen is managing editor of *U.S.News & World Report* for money and business and writes the biweekly Funny Money column for the magazine. She was formerly Washington editor for *Slate* magazine and editor of the *Washington Post*'s Sunday Outlook section and an editorial writer and business columnist for the *Post*.

Brian Kelly is the executive editor of *U.S.News & World Report*. As the magazine's No. 2 editor, he oversees the weekly magazine, the website, and a series of newsstand books. He is a former editor at the *Washington Post* and the author of three books.

Acknowledgments

The editors would like to thank the many people whose hard work and expertise are reflected in this book. First of all, we'd like to thank *U.S. News* writers **Megan Barnett**, **Kim Clark**, **Caroline Hsu**, **Justin Ewers**, **Vicky Hallett**, **Paul J. Lim**, **Angie C. Marek**, and **Nisha Ramachandran**, who contributed chapters or passages to the book. We'd also like to thank freelance writers **Michelle Andrews**, **Kristin Davis**, **Mary Kathleen Flynn**, **Christine Larson**, **Jill Rachlin Marbaix**, and **Leonard Wiener** for their contributions.

Samuel Flanigan, *U.S. News* deputy director of data research, produced the College Cost and Financial Aid Directory and the *U.S. News* Insider's Index.

The editors are also grateful to the *U.S. News* fact checking team, which helped make sure our facts, figures, and advice was on target.

Thanks also to **David Griffin**, creative director at the magazine for his work in designing the book.

We'd also like to thank several college financial aid experts who reviewed portions of the manuscript and provided feedback: **Scott Friedhoff**, vice president for enrollment, Allegheny College; **Robert S. Lay**, dean for enrollment management, and **Bernard Pekala**, director of financial strategies, Boston College; **Geordie Crossan**, president, NBS Financial Services; **Julia Benz**, director of student financial services, and **Bonnie Rogers**, associate director of student financial services, Rice University.